DATE DUE

THE INQUISITION
OF THE MIDDLE AGES

THE INQUISITION
OF THE MIDDLE AGES

THE MACMILLAN COMPANY
NEW YORK • CHICAGO
DALLAS • ATLANTA • SAN FRANCISCO
LONDON • MANILA

IN CANADA
BRETT-MACMILLAN LTD.
GALT, ONTARIO

THE INQUISITION
OF THE MIDDLE AGES

BY HENRY CHARLES LEA

An abridgment by Margaret Nicholson

NEW YORK   THE MACMILLAN COMPANY   1961

EDITOR'S FOREWORD

HENRY CHARLES LEA, born in Philadelphia in 1825, was the first American historian to write on European subjects using as his authorities only the original sources. For A *History of the Inquisition of the Middle Ages*, he said he had "had the archives of Europe ransacked for unprinted material"—town records, books of sentences of the inquisitors, papal records, and letters, diaries, and reports that had long been forgotten. As a result, the Middle Ages about which he wrote suddenly became alive. Henry Howard Furness felt this keenly: "The sources whence he drew his statements cannot be impugned. They are the very words of the speakers, the very acts of the governments, the very decrees of the church. . . . Here are your facts. Lament, deplore, extenuate as you will, but deny you cannot." The *History* was published in 1887–1888, and within a dozen years had been translated into French, German, and Italian, and had become the acknowledged authority in the field. The Macmillan Company, which became Lea's publisher in 1905, reissued the English edition in 1908 and again in 1921.

Lea believed that the subject was one that the general public, as well as historians and scholars, would be interested in, and he consciously strove to write in clear, direct, and untechnical language. But the work was too long, and consequently too expensive, for the average reader. In France the problem was solved by issuing selected chapters separately in pamphlet form for a few centimes each; in Italy a one-volume condensation was published, with Lea's blessing, in 1914. The original edition in English, however, remained chiefly the treasure of scholars, and reached the general reader only through quotations—and often misquotations, because quoted out of context —in textbooks, histories, and encyclopedias.

This abridgment has been made in the hope of bringing to the general reader what is conceded to be the one indispensable work on the subject. In trying to preserve the comprehensive scope of the original edition, I have made most of the deletions from the multiplicity of Lea's examples; from his wealth of heresies and heretics I have retained only a few of the leading exponents of each type. But

I have tried to keep the essence of the tapestry as Lea wove it, with no tampering with fact or conclusion. I have also kept Lea's spelling of names and places—the contemporary forms he found in his sources—which may at first seem strange to twentieth-century eyes, but which to me contribute to the conviction of authenticity.

Reluctantly I have omitted the documentation, both for economy of space and because most of the citations are of untranslated and unavailable sources in at least seven different languages. The quality and validity of these references may be judged by a statement of James Bryce: "He verified every reference, he neglected no out-of-the-way authority from which information could be obtained." Lea described his practice in an article in *The Nation* in 1869, in reference to an earlier work on sacerdotal celibacy: "At an early period in my historical studies I found the danger of trusting to second-hand authorities. For years, therefore, my effort has been to accumulate around me all the authorities requisite for independent work. . . . I have made it a rule never to trust a citation or reference where I had the means of consulting the original authority, so that I could myself judge the spirit as well as the letter of the matter referred to."

A History of the Inquisition of the Middle Ages covers the period from the twelfth to the middle of the sixteenth century. The Spanish Inquisition, which was taking shape when the earlier Inquisition was dying out in Europe, is covered in four later volumes. At Lea's death in 1909 he was at work on a history of witchcraft.

Lord Bryce also said of Lea, "His books were never written with any purpose or bias save that of eliciting the facts." To Lea, Bryce went on to say, the three cardinal sins were cruelty, perfidy, and rapacity, and were hateful wherever they were found, not to be excused by differences of time or country. The withholding of evidence, the crime of suspicion, guilt by association, condemnation for refusal to name associates—these reflect the methods used by medieval Church and State to compel uniformity of belief and to suppress independent thought and action. The reader cannot fail to find lessons applicable to our own time.

I am grateful to the University of Pennsylvania, to which Lea's literary properties were bequeathed, and to The Macmillan Company for permitting me to make this abridgment.

M. N.

New York, May 1961

AUTHOR'S PREFACE

THE HISTORY of the Inquisition naturally divides itself into two portions, each of which may be considered as a whole. The Reformation is the boundary-line between them, except in Spain, where the New Inquisition was founded by Ferdinand and Isabella. In the present work I have sought to present an impartial account of the institution as it existed during the earlier period. . . .

The Inquisition was not an organization arbitrarily devised and imposed upon the judicial system of Christendom by the ambition or fanaticism of the Church. It was rather a natural—one may almost say an inevitable—evolution of the forces at work in the thirteenth century, and no one can rightly appreciate the process of its development and the results of its activity without a somewhat minute consideration of the factors controlling the minds and souls of men during the ages that laid the foundation of modern civilization. To accomplish this it has been necessary to pass in review nearly all the spiritual and intellectual movements of the Middle Ages, and to glance at the condition of society in certain of its phases.

At the commencement of my historical studies I speedily became convinced that the surest basis of investigation for a given period lay in an examination of its jurisprudence, which presents without disguise its aspirations and the means regarded as best adapted for their realization. I have accordingly devoted much space to the origin and development of the inquisitorial process, feeling convinced that in this manner only can we understand the operations of the Holy Office and the influence which it exercised on successive generations. By the application of the results thus obtained it has seemed to me that many points which have been misunderstood or imperfectly appreciated can be elucidated. If in this I have occasionally been led to conclusions differing from those currently accepted, I beg the reader to believe that the views presented have not been hastily formed, but that they are the outcome of a conscientious survey of all the original sources accessible to me.

No serious historical work is worth the writing or the reading unless it conveys a moral, but to be useful the moral must develop itself in the mind of the reader without being obtruded upon him. Especially is this the case in a history treating of a subject which has called forth the fiercest passions of man, arousing alternately his highest and his basest impulses. I have not paused to moralize, but I have missed my aim if the events narrated are not so presented as to teach their appropriate lesson. . . .

Philadelphia, August 1887   [H. C. L.]

NOTE ON PROPER NAMES

IN THE source material with which Mr. Lea worked, proper names varied not only in form, according to the native language of the reporter, but also in the individual spelling of the scribe. Thus we find *Peter, Pedro, Pietro, Piero, Pierre* all referring to the same person, or *Bartholomew, Bartolomeo, Bartolommeo.* For the most part, Mr. Lea kept the spelling of each scribe, but for some well-known people he used the Anglicized form—*Joan of Arc, Peter Cantor, John Huss.* This should be kept in mind in reading the text and using the index. In the latter, most listings are under the given name, e.g., *Étienne de St. Thibéry,* not *St. Thibéry, Étienne. Luke Wadding,* however, would appear under *Wadding.*

In the list of popes I have tried to use the spelling of the native country, but as so many variations appear, only one, or possibly one alternative, is given. Occasionally when I have been unable to discover the original spelling I have used the Anglicized version.

[Ed.]

POPES AND ANTIPOPES

1073–85   GREGORY VII   (St., Hildebrand)
1130–43   INNOCENT II   (Gregorio Papareschi)
1145–53   EUGENIUS III   (Bernardo Paganelli)
1154–9   ADRIAN IV   (Nicholas Breakspear)
1159–81   ALEXANDER II   (Rolando Orlando Bandinelli)
1181–5   LUCIUS III   (Ubaldo Allucingoli)
1185–7   URBAN III   (Uberto Crivelli)
1191–8   CELESTIN(E) III   (Giacinto Bobo [Orsini])
1198–1216   INNOCENT III   (Lotario de' Conti di Segni)
1216–27   HONORIUS III   (Cencio Savelli)
1227–41   GREGORY IX   (Ugolino Conti de Segni)
1241   CELESTIN(E) IV   (Goffredo Castiglione)
1243–54   INNOCENT IV   (Sinibaldo de' Fieschi)
1254–61   ALEXANDER IV   (Rinaldo [Conti de Segni])
1261–4   URBAN IV   (Jacques Pantaléon)
1265–8   CLEMENT IV   (Gui Foucaux [Gui Foulques])
1271–6   GREGORY X   (Tebaldo Visconti)
1276   INNOCENT V   (Pierre de Tarentaise)
1276   ADRIAN V   (Ottobuono de' Fieschi)
1276–7   JOHN XXI   (XX)   (Pedro Giuliano-Rebulo)
1277–80   NICHOLAS III   (Giovanni Gaetano Orsini)
1281–5   MARTIN IV   (Simon Mompitié de Brion)
1285–7   HONORIUS IV   (Giacomo Savelli)
1288–92   NICHOLAS IV   (Girolamo Masci)
1294   CELESTIN(E) V   (St., Pietro Morrone)
1294–1303   BONIFACE VIII   (Benedetto Gaetano)
1303–4   BENEDICT XI   (Niccolo Boccasini)
1305–14   CLEMENT V   (Bertrand de Goth [Gouth])
1316–34   JOHN XXII   (XXI)   (Jacques d'Ozo [Duèse])

1328–30	NICHOLAS V (antipope) (Pier di Corbario)
1334–42	BENEDICT XII (Jacques Fournier)
1342–52	CLEMENT VI (Pierre Roger)
1352–62	INNOCENT VI (Étienne Aubert)
1362–70	URBAN V (Guillaume Grimoard)
1370–78	GREGORY XI (Pierre Roger de Beaufort)
1378–89	URBAN VI (Bartolommeo Prignano)
1378–94	CLEMENT VII (antipope) (Robert of Geneva)
1389–1404	BONIFACE IX (Piero Tomacelli)
1394–1417	BENEDICT XIII (antipope) (Pedro de Luna)
1404–6	INNOCENT VII (Cosimo de' Migliorati)
1406–15	GREGORY XII (Angelo Coriaro [Correr])
1409–10	ALEXANDER V (antipope) (Pietro Philarghi)
1410–15	JOHN XXIII (XXII) (antipope) (Baldassare Cossa)
1417–31	MARTIN V (Otto Colonna)
1425–9	CLEMENT VIII (antipope)
1431–47	EUGENIUS IV (Gabriel Condulmieri)
1439–49	FELIX V (antipope) (Amadeus of Savoy)
1447–55	NICHOLAS V (Tomaso Parentucelli)
1455–8	CALIXTUS III (Alphonso de Borgia)
1458–64	PIUS II (Æneas Silvius [Eneo Silvio de Piccolomini])
1464–71	PAUL II (Pietro Barbo)
1471–84	SIXTUS IV (Francesco della Rovere)
1484–92	INNOCENT VIII (Giovanni Battista Cibo)
1492–1503	ALEXANDER VI (Rodrigo Borgia)
1503	PIUS III (Francesco Nanni-Todeschini-Piccolomini)
1503–13	JULIUS II (Giuliano della Rovere)
1513–21	LEO X (Giovanni de' Medici)
1522–3	ADRIAN VI (Adrian Dedel)

CONTENTS

BOOK I
ORIGIN AND ORGANIZATION
OF THE INQUISITION

CHAPTER I
THE CHURCH

AS THE twelfth century drew to a close, the Church was approaching a crisis in its career. History records no such triumph of intellect over brute strength as that which, in an age of turmoil and battle, was wrested from the fierce warriors of the time by priests who had no material force at their command and whose power was based alone on the souls and consciences of men. Step by step the supremacy of the Roman See had been asserted and enforced, until it enjoyed the universal jurisdiction which enabled it to bend to its wishes every prelate, under the naked alternative of submission or expulsion. The papal mandate, just or unjust, reasonable or unreasonable, was to be received and implicitly obeyed, for there was no appeal from the representative of St. Peter.

Thus entrusted with responsibility for the fate of mankind, it was necessary that the Church should possess the powers and the machinery requisite for the due discharge of a trust so unspeakably important. Besides supervision over matters of faith and discipline, of marriage, of inheritance, and of usury, which belonged to it by general consent, there were comparatively few questions between man and man which could not be made to include some case of conscience involving the interpellation of spiritual interference, especially when agreements were customarily confirmed with the sanction of the oath; the cure of souls implied a perpetual inquest over the aberrations of every member of the flock.

Not only did the humblest priest wield a supernatural power which marked him as one elevated above the common level of humanity, but his person and possessions were alike inviolable. No matter what crimes he might commit, secular justice could not take cognizance of them, and secular officials could not arrest him. He was amenable only to the tribunals of his own Order, from whose decisions an appeal to the supreme jurisdiction of distant Rome conferred too often virtual immunity.

The line of separation between the laity and the clergy was widened and deepened by the enforcement of the canon requiring

3

celibacy on the part of all concerned in the ministry of the altar. Revived about the middle of the eleventh century, the compulsory celibacy of the priesthood divided them from the people, preserved intact the vast acquisitions of the Church, and furnished it with an innumerable army whose aspirations and ambitions were necessarily restricted within its circle. The man who entered the service of the Church was no longer a citizen. He owed no allegiance superior to that assumed in his ordination. He was released from the distraction of family cares and the seduction of family ties. The Church was his country and his home, and its interests were his own.

The Church, moreover, offered the only career open to men of all ranks and stations. In the sharply defined class distinctions of the feudal system, advancement was almost impossible to one not born within the charmed circle of gentle blood. In the Church, however much rank and family connections might assist in securing promotion to high place, yet talent and energy could always make themselves felt despite lowliness of birth. Urban II and Adrian IV sprang from the humblest origin; Urban IV was the son of a cobbler, Pius II of a farmer, and Sixtus V of a shepherd; in fact, the annals of the hierarchy are full of those who rose from the lowest ranks of society to the most commanding positions. The Church thus constantly recruited its ranks with fresh blood. Free from the curse of hereditary descent, through which crowns and coronets frequently lapsed into weak and incapable hands, it called into its service an indefinite amount of restless vigor for which there was no other sphere of action. The character of the priest was indelible; the vows taken at ordination could not be thrown aside; the monk, when once admitted to the cloister, could not abandon his Order unless it were to enter another of more rigorous observance. The Church Militant was thus an army encamped on the soil of Christendom, with its outposts everywhere, subject to the most efficient discipline, and animated with a common purpose, every soldier panoplied with inviolability. There was little that could not be dared or done by the commander of such a force, whose orders were listened to as oracles of God.

"Princes," says John of Salisbury, "derive their power from the Church, and are servants of the priesthood."

"The least of the priestly order is worthier than any king," exclaims Honorius of Autun; "prince and people are subjected to the clergy, which shines superior as the sun to the moon."

Innocent III used a more spiritual metaphor when he declared that the priestly power was as superior to the secular as the soul of man was to his body; and he summed up his estimate of his own position by pronouncing himself to be the Vicar of Christ, the Christ of the Lord, the God of Pharaoh, placed midway between God and man, this side of God but beyond man, less than God but greater than man, who judges all, and is judged by none. That he was supreme over all the earth—over pagans and infidels as well as over Christians—was legally proved and universally taught by the mediæval doctors. Though the power thus vaingloriously asserted was fraught with evil in many ways, yet was it none the less a service to humanity that, in those rude ages, there existed a moral force superior to high descent and martial prowess, which could remind king and noble that they must obey the law of God even when uttered by a peasant's son.

Yet, in achieving this supremacy, much had been of necessity sacrificed. The Christian virtues of humility and charity and self-abnegation had virtually disappeared in the contest which left the spiritual power dominant over the temporal. The affection of the populations was no longer attracted by the graces and loveliness of Christianity; submission was purchased by the promise of salvation, to be acquired by faith and obedience, or was extorted by the threat of perdition or by the sharper terrors of earthly persecution. Practically, the whole body of Christians no longer constituted the Church; that body was divided into two essentially distinct classes, the shepherds and the sheep; and the lambs were often apt to think, not unreasonably, that they were tended only to be shorn. The worldly prizes offered by an ecclesiastical career drew into the ranks of the Church able men, it is true, but men whose object was worldly ambition rather than spiritual development.

This was inevitable in the state of society which existed in the early Middle Ages. While angels would have been required to exercise becomingly the tremendous powers claimed and acquired by the Church, the methods by which clerical preferment and promotion were secured were such as to favor the unscrupulous rather

than the deserving. To understand fully the causes which drove
so many thousands into schism and heresy, leading to wars and
persecutions and the establishment of the Inquisition, it is necessary to cast a glance at the character of the men who represented
the Church, and at the use they made, for good or for evil, of the
absolute spiritual despotism which had become established.

As regards the methods of election to the episcopate there cannot be said at this period to have been any settled and invariable
rule. The ancient form of election by the clergy, with the acquiescence of the people of the diocese, was still preserved in theory,
but in practice the electoral body consisted of the cathedral canons; while the confirmation required of the king, or semi-inde-
pendent feudal noble, and of the pope frequently rendered the
election an empty form, in which the royal or papal power might
prevail, according to the tendencies of time and place. The constantly
increasing appeals to Rome, as to the tribunal of last resort, gave
to the Holy See a rapidly growing influence, which, in many cases,
amounted almost to the power of appointment; and Innocent II, at
the Lateran Council of 1139, applied the feudal system to the
Church by declaring that all ecclesiastical dignities were received and
held of the popes like fiefs. Whatever rules, however, might be
laid down, they could not operate in rendering the elect better
than the electors. The oath which cardinals were obliged to take on
entering a conclave—"I call God to witness that I choose him whom
I judge according to God ought to be chosen"—was notoriously
inefficacious in securing the election of pontiffs fitted to serve as the
vicegerents of God; and so, from the humblest parish priest to the
loftiest prelate, all grades of the hierarchy were likely to be filled by
worldly, ambitious, self-seeking, and licentious men.

Under these circumstances simony, with its attendant evils, was
almost universal. It was related as a supreme instance of the virtue of
Peter, Cardinal of St. Chrysogono, formerly Bishop of Meaux, that
he had, in a single election, refused the dazzling bribe of 500 marks of
silver. Temporal princes were more ready to turn the power of confirmation to profitable account, and few imitated the example of
Philip Augustus, who, when the abbacy of St. Denis became vacant,
and the provost, the treasurer, and the cellarer of the abbey each
sought him secretly and gave him 500 livres for the succession, quietly

went to the abbey, picked out a simple monk standing in a corner, conferred the dignity on him, and handed him the 1,500 livres. Even where the consideration paid for preferment was not actually money, the effect was equally deplorable. Peter Cantor assures us that if those who were promoted for relationship were required to resign, it would cause general destruction throughout the Church; and worse motives were constantly at work. About the year 1100 the Archbishop of Tours, having gratified Philip I by disregarding the excommunication under which he lay, claimed his reward by demanding that the vacant see of Orleans should be given to a youth whom he loved not wisely but too well, and who was so notorious for the facility with which he granted his favors that he was popularly known as Flora, in allusion to a noted courtesan of the day, and ribald love songs addressed to him were openly sung in the streets. Such of the Orleans clergy as threatened trouble were put out of the way by false accusations and exiled, and the remainder not only submitted, but even made a jest of the fact that the election took place on the Feast of the Innocents.

Under such influences it was in vain that the better class of men who occasionally appeared in the ranks of the hierarchy, such as Lanfranc, Anselm, St. Bruno, St. Bernard, St. Norbert, and others, struggled to enforce respect for religion and morality. In those days of violence, the meek and humble had little chance, and the prizes were for those who could intrigue and chaffer, or whose martial tendencies offered promise that they would make the rights of their churches and vassals respected. The wealthy abbeys and powerful bishoprics came to be largely regarded as appropriate means to provide for younger sons of noble houses, or to increase the influence of leading families. By such methods they passed into the hands of those whose training had been military rather than religious. Worldly and turbulent, there was little to differentiate the prelate from the baron, and the latter had no more scruple in making reprisals on Church property than on secular possessions. The people, on whom fell the crushing weight of these conflicts, could only look upon the baron and priest as enemies both. This was especially the case in Germany, where the prelates were princes as well as priests, and where a great religious house like the Abbey of St. Gall was the temporal ruler of the Cantons of St. Gall and Appenzel, until the

latter threw off the yoke after a long and devastating war. The
historian of the abbey chronicles with pride the martial virtues of
successive abbots, and in speaking of Ulric III, who died in 1117, he
remarks that, worn out with many battles, he at last passed away in
peace.

In fact, the records of the time bear ample testimony to the
rapine and violence, the flagrant crimes and defiant immorality of
these princes of the Church. The only tribunal to which they were
amenable was that of Rome. It required the courage of desperation
to cause complaints to be made there against them, and when such
complaints were made, the difficulty of proving charges, the length
to which proceedings were drawn out, and the notorious venality of
the Roman curia, afforded virtual immunity. When a resolute and
incorruptible pontiff like Innocent III occupied the papal chair, there
was some chance for sufferers to make themselves heard, and the
number of such trials alluded to in his epistles show how widespread
and deep-rooted was the evil. Yet, even under him, the protraction of
the proceedings and the evident shrinking from final condemnation
show how little encouragement there was for prosecutions likely to
react so dangerously on the prosecutor. In 1198, Gérard de Rouge-
mont, Archbishop of Besançon, was accused by his chapter of perjury,
simony, and incest. When summoned to Rome the accusers did
not dare to prosecute the charges, though they did not withdraw
them, and Innocent, charitably quoting the woman taken in adultery,
sent Gérard back to purge himself and be absolved. Then followed
a long course of undisturbed scandals, through which religion in his
diocese became a mockery. He continued to live in incest with his
relative, the Abbess of Remiremont, and other concubines, one of
whom was a nun and another the daughter of a priest; no church
could be consecrated or preferment conferred without payment;
by his exactions and oppressions his clergy were reduced to live
like peasants and were exposed to the contempt of their parishioners; and monks and nuns who could bribe him were allowed
to abandon their convents and marry. At last another attempt
was made, in 1211, to remove him, which, after more than a year,
resulted in a sentence that he should undergo canonical purgation,
i.e. find two bishops and three abbots to join him in an oath of
disculpation, when negotiations about the character of the oath

ensued, lasting until 1214. Finally the citizens rose and drove him out; he retired to the Abbey of Bellevaux, where he died in 1225.

Even where the enormity of offenses did not call for papal intervention, the episcopal office was prostituted in a thousand ways of oppression and exaction which were sufficiently within the law to afford the sufferers no opportunity of redress. As St. Bernard says, boys were inducted into the episcopate at an age when they rejoiced rather at escaping from the ferule of their teachers than at acquiring rule; but, soon growing insolent, they learn to sell the altar and empty the pouches of their subjects. In thus exploiting their office the bishops only followed the example set them by the papacy, which, directly or through its agents, by its exactions, made itself the terror of the Christian churches. Arnold, who was Archbishop of Trèves from 1169 to 1183, won great credit for his astuteness in saving his people from spoliation by papal nuncios, for whenever he heard of their expected arrival he used to go to meet them, and by heavy bribes induce them to bend their steps elsewhere.

This was by no means the only mode in which the supreme jurisdiction of Rome worked inestimable evil throughout Christendom. While the feudal courts were strictly territorial and local, and the judicial functions of the bishops were limited to their own dioceses so that every man knew to whom he was responsible in a tolerably well-settled system of justice, the universal jurisdiction of Rome gave ample opportunity for abuses of the worst kind. The pope, as supreme judge, could delegate to anyone any portion of his authority, and the papal chancery was not too nice in its discrimination as to the character of the persons to whom it issued letters empowering them to exercise judicial functions and enforce them with the last dread sentence of excommunication—letters, indeed, which, if the papal chancery is not wronged, were freely sold to all able to pay for them. Europe thus was traversed by multitudes of men armed with these weapons, which they used without remorse for extortion and oppression. Bishops, too, were not backward in thus farming out their more limited jurisdictions, and in the confusion thus arising, it was not difficult for reckless adventurers to pretend to the possession of these delegated powers and use them for the basest purposes, no one daring to risk the possible consequences of resistance. An additional

complication which not unnaturally followed was the fabrication
and falsification of these letters. It was not easy to refer to Rome to
ascertain the genuineness of a papal brief confidently produced by its
bearer, and the impunity with which powers so tremendous could be
assumed was irresistibly attractive. When Innocent III ascended the
throne he found a factory of forged letters in full operation in Rome,
and although this was suppressed, the business was too profitable to
be broken up by even his vigilance. Nor was this industry confined
to Rome. About the same period Stephen, Bishop of Tournay, discovered in his episcopal city a similar nest of counterfeiters, who
had invented an ingenious instrument for the fabrication of the papal
seals.

Too many bishops used all their abundant opportunities for the
fleecing of their flocks. Peter Cantor, an unexceptionable witness,
describes them as fishers for money and not for souls, with a thousand frauds to empty the pockets of the poor. They have, he says,
three hooks with which to catch their prey in the depths—the confessor, to whom is committed the hearing of confessions and the cure
of souls; the dean, archdeacon, and other officials, who advance the
interest of the prelate by fair means or foul; and the rural provost,
who is chosen solely with regard to his skill in squeezing the pockets
of the poor and carrying the spoil to his master. These places were
frequently farmed out, and the right to despoil the people was sold
to the highest bidder. The detestation in which these gentry were
held is illustrated by the story of an ecclesiastic who, having by an
unlucky run of the dice lost all his money but 5 sols, exclaimed in
blasphemous madness that he would give them to anyone who would
teach him how most greatly to offend God, and a bystander was adjudged to have won the money when he said, "If you wish to offend
God beyond all other sinners, become an episcopal official or col-
lector."

From this burst of indignation we see that the main instrument
of exaction and oppression was the judicial functions of the episcopate. Considerable revenues, it is true, were derived from the sale of
benefices and the exaction of fees for all official acts, and many prelates did not blush to derive gain from the licentiousness universal
among a celibate clergy by exacting a tribute known as *cullagium*,
on payment of which the priest was allowed to keep his concubine

in peace, but the spiritual jurisdiction was the source of the greatest profit to the prelate and of the greatest misery to the people. Even in the temporal courts, the fines arising from litigation formed no mean portion of the income of the seigneurs; and in the Courts Christian, embracing the whole of spiritual jurisprudence and much of temporal, there was an ample harvest to be gathered. As Peter Cantor says, the most holy sacrament of matrimony, owing to the remote consanguinity coming within the prohibited degrees, was made a subject of derision to the laity by the venality with which marriages were made and unmade to fill the pouches of the episcopal officials. Excommunication was another fruitful source of extortion. If an unjust demand was resisted, the recalcitrant was excommunicated, and then had to pay for reconciliation in addition to the original sum. When a priest was inducted into a benefice, it was customary to exact of him an oath that he would not overlook any offenses committed by his parishioners, but would report them to the Ordinary that the offenders might be prosecuted and fined, and that he would not allow any quarrels to be settled amicably; and though Alexander III issued a decretal pronouncing all such oaths void, yet they continued to be required.

It was hardly to be expected that prelates such as filled most of the sees of Christendom should devote themselves to the real duties of their position. Foremost among these duties was that of preaching the word of God and instructing their flocks in faith and morals. The office of preacher, indeed, was especially an episcopal function; he was the only man in the diocese authorized to exercise it; it formed no part of the duty or training of the parish priest, who could not presume to deliver a sermon without a special license from his superior. It need not surprise us, therefore, to see this portion of Christian teaching and devotion utterly neglected, for the turbulent and martial prelates of the day were too wholly engrossed in worldly cares to bestow a thought upon a matter for which their unfitness was complete. In 1031 the Council of Limoges expressed a wish that preaching should be done not only at the episcopal seat, but in other churches, when the will of God inspires a competent doctor to the task; but the Church slumbered on until the spread of heresy aroused it to a sense of its unwisdom in neglecting so powerful a source of influence. The Troubadour Inquisitor Izarn does not hesitate to declare that heresy never could have spread had there been good preachers to oppose it, and that it never could have been subdued but for the Dominicans.

The character of the lower orders of ecclesiastics could not be reasonably expected to be better than that of their prelates. It is the universal complaint of the age that benefices were openly sold, or were bestowed through favor, without examination into the qualifications of the appointee or the slightest regard as to his fitness. Even the rigid virtue of St. Bernard did not prevent him, in 1151, from soliciting a provostship for a graceless youth, the nephew of his friend the Bishop of Auxerre, though repentance induced by cooler reflection led him to withdraw his application, which he could the more easily do on learning that his friend, in dying, had left no less than seven churches to his beloved nephew. In the same year he was more cautious in refusing Count Thibaut of Champagne some preferment which he had asked for his son, a child of tender years; but the mere request for it shows how benefices, when not sold, were wont to be distributed; and it is safe to say that there were few like Bernard, with courage and conviction to reject the solicitations of the powerful. It is true that the canon law was full of admirable precepts respecting the virtues and qualifications requisite for incumbents, but in practice they were a dead letter. Alexander III was moved to indignation when he learned that the Bishop of Coventry was in the habit of giving churches to boys under 10 years of age, but he could only order that the cures should be entrusted to competent vicars until the nominees reached a proper age, and this age he himself fixed at 14; while other popes charitably reduced to 7 the minimum age for holding simple benefices or prebends.

One of the most fruitful sources of quarrel and discontent was the tithe. This most harassing and oppressive form of taxation had long been the cause of incurable trouble, aggravated by the rapacity with which it was enforced, even to the pitiful collections of the gleaner. The resistance of the people to its exaction in some places was such that its nonpayment was stigmatized as heresy, and everywhere we see it the cause of altercation between pastor and flock, and between rival claimants, giving rise to a very intricate branch of canon law. Carlyle states that at the outbreak of the French Revolution there were no less than 60,000 cases arising from tithes then pending before the courts, and though the statement may be exaggerated, it is by no means improbable. Anciently the tithe had been divided into four parts, of which one went to the bishop, one to the parish priest, one to the fabric of the Church, and one to the poor, but in the prevailing acquisitiveness of the period, bishop and priest each seized and held all they could get, the Church received little, and the poor none at all.

The portion of the tithe which the priest could retain in this scramble was rarely sufficient for his wants, addicted as he frequently was to dissolute living, and exposed to the rapacity of his superiors. The form of simony which consists in selling his sacred ministrations therefore became general. Confession, which was now becoming obligatory, afforded a wide field for perverse ingenuity. Some confessors rated the sacrament of penitence so low that for a chicken or a pint of wine they would grant absolution for any sin, but others understood its productiveness far better. It is related by a contemporary of Einhardt, the priest of Soest, that he sharply reproved a parishioner who, in preparation for Easter, confessed incontinence during Lent, and demanded of him 18 deniers that he might say 18 masses for his soul. Another came who said that during Lent he had abstained from his wife, and he was fined the same amount for masses because he had lost the chance of begetting a child, as was his duty. Both men had to sell their harvests prematurely to raise money to pay the fine, and, happening to meet upon the market-place, compared notes, when they complained to the Dean and Chapter of St. Patroclus, and the story came out, but Einhardt was permitted to continue his speculative career. Marriage and funeral ceremonies were refused until the fees demanded were paid in advance, and the Eucharist was withheld from the communicant unless he offered an oblation. To the believer in transubstantiation nothing could be more inexpressibly shocking, and Peter Cantor well describes the priests of his day as worse than Judas Iscariot, who sold the body of the Lord for 30 pieces of silver, while they do it daily for a denier.

If the faithful Christian thus was mulcted throughout life at every turn, the pursuit of gain was continued to his deathbed, and even his body had a speculative value which was turned to account by the ghouls who quarrelled over it. The necessity of the final sacraments for salvation gave rise to an occasional abuse by which they were

refused unless an illegal fee or perquisite was paid, but this we may
well believe was not usual. More profitable was the custom by which
the fears of approaching judgment were exploited and legacies for
pious uses were suggested as an appropriate atonement for a life of
wickedness or cruelty. So general was the custom of leaving considerable sums for the pious ministrations by which the Church lightened
the torments of purgatory, and so usual was the bestowal of oblations at the funeral, that the custody of the corpse became a source
of gain not to be despised, and the parish in which the sinner had
lived and died claimed to have a reversionary right in the ashes which
were thus so profitable. In some places the parish church asserted a
right by custom to certain payments on the death of a parishioner,
and the Council of Worcester, in 1240, decided that when this claim
would reduce the widow and orphans to beggary, the Church should
mercifully content itself with one-third of the estate and relinquish
the other two-thirds to the family of the defunct; while in Lisbon
the last consolations of religion were denied to anyone who refused
to leave a portion, usually a third, of his property to the Church.

On no point were the relations between the clergy and the people
more delicate than on that of sexual purity. At the period under
consideration the enforced celibacy of the priesthood had become
generally recognized in most of the countries owing obedience to
the Latin Church. It had not been accompanied, however, by the
gift of chastity so confidently promised by its promoters. Deprived
as was the priesthood of the gratification afforded by marriage to
the natural instincts of man, the wife at best was succeeded by the
concubine; at worst by a succession of paramours, for which the
functions of priest and confessor gave peculiar opportunity. So
thoroughly was this recognized that a man confessing an illicit amour
was forbidden to name the partner of his guilt for fear it might lead
the confessor into the temptation of abusing his knowledge of her
frailty. The age was not particularly sensitive on the subject of female
virtue, but yet the spectacle of a priesthood professing ascetic purity
as an essential prerequisite to its functions, and practicing a dissolute-
ness more cynical that that of the average laymen, was not adapted
to raise it in popular esteem; while the individual cases in which
the peace and honor of families were sacrificed to the lusts of the
pastor necessarily tended to rouse the deepest antagonism. As for
darker and more deplorable crimes, they were sufficiently frequent,

not alone in monasteries from which women were rigorously excluded; and moreover, they were committed with virtual immunity. So long as the priest did not defy the canons by marrying, everything could be forgiven. Alexander II, who labored so strenuously to restore the rule of celibacy, in 1064 decided that a priest of Orange who had committed adultery with the wife of his father was not to be deprived of communion for fear of driving him to desperation; and, in view of the fragility of the flesh, he was to be allowed to remain in holy Orders, though in the lower grades. Two years later the same pope charitably diminished the penance imposed on a priest of Padua who had committed incest with his mother, and left it to his bishop whether he should be retained in the priesthood.

Yet perhaps the most efficient cause of demoralization in the clergy, and of hostility between them and the laity, was the personal inviolability and the immunity from secular jurisdiction which they succeeded in establishing as a recognized principle of public law. While this was doubtless necessary for the independence, and even for the safety, of a presumably peaceful class in an age of violence, it worked unhappily in a double sense. The readiness with which acquittal was obtainable in ecclesiastical procedure by canonical purgation, or the "wager of law," and the comparative mildness of the penalties in case of conviction, relieved the ecclesiastic in great measure from the terrors of the law, and removed from him the necessity of restraining his evil propensities. At the same time it attracted to the Church vast numbers of worthless men, who, without abandoning their worldly pursuits, entered the lower grades and enjoyed the irresponsibility of their position, to the injury of its character and the detriment of all who came in contact with them. How, in maintaining it privileges, the Church habitually threw its ægis over those least deserving of sympathy is well illustrated by the intervention of Innocent III in favor of Waldemar, Bishop of Sleswick. He was the natural son of Cnut V of Denmark, and had headed an armed insurrection against Waldemar II, the reigning king, on the suppression of which he was cast into prison. Innocent demanded his liberation, as his incarceration was a violation of the immunities of the Church. Waldemar II naturally hesitated thus to expose his kingdom to the repetition of revolt, and Innocent at first modified his command in so far as to order the offender conveyed to Hungary and liberated there, promising that he should not be permitted again

to disturb the realm; but Bishop Waldemar subsequently evoked the
case to Rome, where, in spite of his being the offspring of a double
adultery and thus ineligible to holy orders, and in spite of the representations of the Danish envoys that he had been guilty of perjury,
adultery, apostasy, and dilapidation, Innocent, in behalf of the
liberties of the Church, restored him to his bishopric and patrimony,
with the special privilege of administering it by deputy if he feared
that residence would endanger his personal safety.

The monastic Orders formed too large and important a class not
to share fully in the responsibility of the Church for good or for
evil. Great as were their unquestioned services to religion and culture,
they were peculiarly exposed to the degrading tendencies of the age,
and their virtues suffered proportionally. In too many cases the
abbeys became centers of corruption and disturbance, the nunneries
scarce better than houses of prostitution, and the monasteries feudal
castles where the monks lived riotously and waged war upon their
neighbors as ferociously as the turbulent barons, with the added disadvantage that, as there was no hereditary succession, the death of
an abbot was apt to be followed by a disputed election producing
internal broils and outside interference. It is true that all establishments were not lost to the duties for which they had received so
abundantly of the benefactions of the faithful. In the famine of 1197,
though the monastery of Heisterbach was still young and poor, the
Abbot Gebhardt distributed alms so lavishly that sometimes he fed
1,500 people a day, while the mother-house of Hemmenrode was
even more liberal, and supported all the poor of its district till harvest
time. At the same time a Cistercian abbey in Westphalia slaughtered
all its flocks and herds and pledged its books and sacred vessels to
feed the starving. Such instances go far to redeem the institution of
monachism, but for the most part the abbeys were sources of evil
rather than of good.

This is scarce to be wondered at if we consider the material from
which their inmates were drawn. It is the severest reproach upon
their discipline to find so enthusiastic an admirer of the strict
Cistercian Rule as Cæsarius of Heisterbach asserting as an admitted
fact that boys bred in monasteries made bad monks and frequently
became apostates. As for those who took the vows in advanced life,
he enumerates their motives as sickness, poverty, captivity, infamy,

mortal danger, dread of hell or desire of heaven, among which the predominance of selfish impulses was not likely to secure a desirable class of devotees. In fact, he assures us that criminals frequently escaped punishment by agreeing to enter monasteries, which thus in some sort became penal settlements, and he illustrates this with the case of a robber baron in 1209, condemned to death for his crimes by the Count Palatine Henry, who was rescued by Daniel, Abbot of Schonau, on condition of his entering the Cistercian Order.

It was not that earnest efforts were lacking to restore the neglected monastic discipline. Ingenuity was taxed to frame new and severer Rules, such as the Premonstratensian, the Carthusian, the Cistercian, which should repel all but the most ardent souls in search of ascetic self-mortification, but as each Order grew in repute for holiness, the liberality of the faithful showered wealth upon it, and with wealth came corruption. Few communities had the cautious wisdom of the early denizens in the celebrated Priory of Grammont, before it became the head of a powerful Order. When its founder and first prior, St. Stephen of Thiern, after his death in 1124, commenced to show his sanctity by curing a paralytic knight and restoring sight to a blind man, his single-minded followers took alarm at the prospect of wealth and notoriety thus about to be forced upon them. His successor, Prior Peter of Limoges, accordingly repaired to his tomb and reproachfully addressed him:

O servant of God, thou hast shown us the path of poverty and hast earnestly striven to teach us to walk therein. Now thou wishest to lead us from the straight and narrow way of salvation to the broad road of eternal death. Thou hast preached the solitude, and now thou seekest to convert the solitude into a market-place and a fair. We already believe sufficiently in thy saintliness. Then work no more miracles to prove it and at the same time to destroy our humility. Be not so solicitous for thy own fame as to neglect our salvation; this we enjoin on thee, this we ask of thy charity. If thou dost otherwise, we declare, by the obedience which we have vowed to thee, that we will dig up thy bones and cast them into the river.[1]

[1] Prior Peter's fear that the convent would be converted into a market-place and a fair is illustrated by the complaint of the Council of Béziers in 1233, that many religious houses were in the habit of retailing their wine within the sacred enclosure, and attracting consumers by having jugglers, actors, gamblers, and strumpets there.

This mingled supplication and threat proved sufficient, and until St. Stephen was formally canonized he ceased to perform the miracles so dangerous to the souls of his followers.

The theory of justification by works, to which the Church owed so much of its power and wealth, had, in its development, to a great extent deprived religion of all spiritual vitality, replacing its essentials with a dry and meaningless formalism. It was not that men were becoming indifferent to the destiny of their souls, for never, perhaps, have the terrors of perdition, the bliss of salvation, and the never-ending efforts of the arch-fiend possessed a more burning reality for man, but religion had become in many respects a fetichism.

That sin, confessed and repented, could be absolved through penance was a doctrine dating back to primitive times. That penance could be redeemed by sacrifices made for the Church was a corollary of later origin, but yet well established at this period. Now the Church was the depository of the treasure of salvation, and the pope, as the Vicar of God, had the unlimited dispensation of that treasure. It was for him to prescribe the methods by which the faithful could partake of it, and no theologian before Wickliff was hardy enough to question his decisions. According to the modern theory of indulgences they shorten, by specified times, the duration of torment in purgatory, after the soul has escaped condemnation to hell by confession and absolution. In the Middle Ages the distinction was not so nice, and the rewards promised were more direct. At first they consisted in a remission for specified times of the penance imposed for absolution, in return for pious works, pilgrimages to shrines, contributions towards the building of churches, bridges, etc.—for a spiritual punishment could be commuted to a corporal or to a pecuniary one. Abuses, of course, crept in, denounced by Abelard, who vents his indignation at the covetousness which habitually made a traffic of salvation. Alexander III, about 1175, expressed his disapproval of these corruptions, and the Great Council of Lateran, in 1215, sought to check the destruction of discipline and the contempt felt for the Church by limiting to one year the amount of penance released by any one indulgence. Great opposition was excited when St. Francis of Assisi procured, in 1223, from Honorius III the celebrated "Portiuncula" indulgence, whereby all who visited the Church of Santa Maria de Portiuncula, at Assisi, from the vespers of August

1st to the vespers of August 2d, obtained complete and entire remission of all sins committed since baptism. Boniface VIII, when he
conceived the fruitful idea of the jubilee, carried this out still further
by promising to all who should perform certain devotions in the
basilicas of St. Peter and St. Paul, during the year 1300, not only
plena venia, but *plenissima*, of all their sins.

When the Church sought to arouse Europe to supreme exertion
for the redemption of the Holy Sepulcher some infinite reward was
requisite to excite the enthusiasm requisite for the crusades. If
Mahomet could stimulate his followers to court death by the promise
of immediate and eternal bliss to him who fell fighting for the
Crescent, the vicegerent of the true God must not be behindhand in
his promises to the martyrs of the Cross. Accordingly when Urban
II held the Council of Clermont, which resolved on the first crusade,
the device of plenary indulgence was introduced, and the military
pilgrims were exhorted to have full faith that those who fell repentant would gain the completest fruit of eternal mercy. The device was so successful that it became an established rule in all the
holy wars in which the Church engaged. As the novelty of crusading
wore off, however, still greater promises were necessary. In 1291,
Nicholas IV promised full remission of sins to everyone who would
send a crusader or go at another's expense; while he who went at
his own expense was vaguely told that in addition he would have
an increase of salvation—a term which the Decretalists perhaps could
not find it easy to explain. Finally, forgotten sins were included in
the pardon, as well as those confessed and repented.

Still further rewards were offered when personal ambition and
vindictiveness were to be gratified in the crusade preached by Innocent IV against the Emperor Conrad IV, after the death of Frederic
II, when he granted a larger remission of sins than for the voyage
to the Holy Land, and included the father and mother of the crusader
as beneficiaries in the assurance of heaven. A profitable device had
also been introduced by which crusaders, unwilling or unable to perform their vow, were absolved from it on a money payment propor-
tioned to their ability, and very large sums were raised in this manner,
which were expended, nominally at least, for the furtherance of the
holy cause.

The sale of indulgences illustrates effectively the sacerdotalism

which formed the distinguishing feature of mediæval religion. The
supernatural powers claimed for the priest interposed him as the
mediator between God and man. The implements he wielded—
the Eucharist, the relics, the holy water, the chrism, the exorcism, the
prayer—became in some sort fetiches which had a power of their
own entirely irrespective of the moral or spiritual condition of him
who employed them or of him for whom they were employed. How
sedulously this fetichism was inculcated by those who profited from
the control of the fetiches is shown by a thousand stories and incidents of the time. A twelfth-century chronicler piously narrates
that when, in 887, the relics of St. Martin of Tours were brought
home from Auxerre, whither they had been carried to escape the
Danish incursions, two cripples of Touraine, who earned an easy
livelihood by beggary, on hearing of the approach of the saintly bones,
counselled together to escape from the territory as quickly as possible,
lest the returning saint should cure them and thus deprive them of
claims on the alms of the charitable. Their fears were well founded,
but their means of locomotion were insufficient, for the relics arrived in Touraine before they could get beyond the bounds of the
province, and they were cured in spite of themselves.

The Eucharist was particularly efficacious as a fetich. The consecrated wafer was popularly believed to possess a magic efficacy of
incomparable power, and stories are numerous of the punishment
inflicted on those who sacrilegiously sought thus to use it. A priest
who retained it in his mouth for the purpose of using it to overcome
the virtue of a woman of whom he was enamored was afflicted with
the hallucination that he had swelled to the point that he could not
pass through a doorway; and on burying the sacred object in his
garden it was changed into a small crucifix bearing a man of flesh
and freshly bleeding. So when a woman kept the wafer and placed it
in her beehive to stop an epidemic among the bees, the pious insects
built around it a complete chapel, with walls, windows, roof, and
bell-tower, and inside an altar on which they reverently placed it.

The power of these magic formulas was wholly disconnected with
any devotional feeling on the part of those who employed them. The
efficacy of St. Thomas of Canterbury was illustrated by a story of a
matron whose veneration for him led her to invoke him on all occasions, and even to teach her pet bird to repeat the formula *"Sancte*

Thoma adjuva me!" Once a hawk seized the bird and flew away with it, but on the bird's uttering the accustomed phrase, the hawk fell dead and the bird returned unhurt to its mistress.

The picture I have drawn of the Church in its relations with the people is perhaps too unrelieved in its blackness. All popes were not like Innocent IV and John XXII; all bishops were not cruel and licentious; all priests were not intent solely on impoverishing men and dishonoring women. In many sees and abbeys, and in thousands of parishes, doubtless there were prelates and pastors earnestly seeking to do God's work. Yet the evil was more apparent than the good; the humble workers passed away unobtrusively, while pride and cruelty and lust and avarice were demonstrative and far-reaching in their influence. No more unexceptionable witness as to the Church of the twelfth century can be had than St. Bernard, and he is never weary of denouncing the pride, the wickedness, the ambition, and the lust that reigned everywhere. The Church is left poor and bare and miserable, neglected and bloodless. Her children seek not to bedeck, but to spoil her; not to guard her, but to destroy her; not to defend, but to expose; not to institute, but to prostitute; not to feed the flock, but to slay and devour it. They exact the price of sins and give no thought to sinners. "Whom can you show me among the prelates who does not seek rather to empty the pockets of his flock than to subdue their vices?" St. Bernard's contemporary, Potho of Pruhm, in 1152, voices the same complaints. The Church is rushing to ruin, and not a hand is raised to stay its downward progress; there is not a single priest fitted to rise up as a mediator between God and man and approach the divine throne with an appeal for mercy.

Gilbert of Gemblours tells the same tale. The prelates for the most part enter the Church not by election but by the use of money and the favor of princes; they enter not to feed, but to be fed; not to minister, but to be ministered to; not to sow, but to reap; not to labor, but to rest; not to guard the sheep from the wolves, but, fiercer than wolves, themselves to tear the sheep. St. Hildegarde, in her prophecies, espouses the cause of the people against the clergy:

The prelates are ravishers of the churches; their avarice consumes all that it can acquire. With their oppressions they make us paupers and contaminate us and themselves . . . God did not command that one son should have both coat and cloak and that the other should go naked, but ordered the cloak to be given to one and the coat to the other. Let the laity then have the cloak on account of the cares of the world, and let the clergy have the coat that they may not lack that which is necessary.

One of the main objects in convoking the Great Council of Lateran was the correction of the prevailing vices of the clergy, and it adopted numerous canons looking to the suppression of the chief abuses, but in vain. Those abuses were too deeply rooted, and four years later Honorius III, in an encyclical addressed to all the prelates of Christendom, says that he finds the evils of the Church increasing rather than diminishing. The ministers of the altar, worse than beasts wallowing in their dung, glory in their sins, as in Sodom. They are a snare and a destruction to the people. "Thus it is that heresies flourish. Let each of you gird his sword to his thigh and spare not his brother and his nearest kindred."

What was accomplished by this earnest exhortation may be estimated from the description which Robert Grosseteste, Bishop of Lincoln, gave of the Church in the presence of Innocent IV and his cardinals in 1250. The details can well be spared, but they are summed up in his assertion that the clergy were a source of pollution to the whole earth; they were Antichrists and devils masquerading as angels of light, who made the house of prayer a den of robbers. When the earnest Inquisitor of Passau, about 1260, undertook to explain the stubbornness of the heresy which he was vainly endeavoring to suppress, he did so by drawing up a list of the crimes prevalent among the clergy, which is awful in the completeness of its details. A church such as he describes was an unmitigated curse, politically, socially, and morally.

This is all ecclesiastical testimony. How the clergy were regarded by the laity is illustrated in a remark by William of Puy-Laurens, that it was a common phrase "I had rather be a priest than do that." It was inevitable that such a religion should breed dissidence and such a priesthood provoke revolt.

C HAPTER II
HERESY

JUST as the Church's triumph over king and kaiser was complete a new enemy arose in the awakened consciousness of man. The dense ignorance of the tenth century had begun in the eleventh to yield to the first faint pulsations of intellectual movement. Early in the twelfth century that movement shows in its gathering force the promise of the development which was to render Europe the home of art and science, of learning, culture, and civilization. The stagnation of the human mind could not be thus broken without leading to inquiry and to doubt. When men began to reason and to ask questions, to criticize and to speculate on forbidden topics, it was not possible for them to avoid seeing how woeful was the contrast between the teaching and the practice of the Church, and how little correspondence existed between religion and ritual, between the lives of monk and priest and the profession of their vows. Such a book as Abelard's *Sic et Non*, in which the contradictions of tradition and decretal were pitilessly set forth, was not only an indication of mental disquiet ripening to rebellion, but a fruitful source of future trouble in sowing the seeds of further investigation and irreverence. Vainly, at the command of the Roman curia, might Gratian seek to show, in his famous *Concordantia Discordantium Canonum*, that the contradictions might be reconciled, and that the canon law was not merely a mass of clashing rules called forth by special exigencies, but a harmonious body of spiritual law. The fatal word had been spoken, and the efforts of the Glossators, of Masters of Sentences, of Angelic Doctors, and of the innumerable crowd of scholastic theologians and canon lawyers, with all their skillful dialectics, could never restore to the minds of men the placid and unbroken trust in the divine inspiration of the Church Militant.

Even more menacing to the Church was the revival of the civil law. The ardor with which it came, by the middle of the twelfth century, to be studied in all the great centers of learning is incontestable, and men found, to their surprise, that there was a system of

23

jurisprudence of wonderful symmetry and subtle adjustment of right, immeasurably superior to the clumsy and confused canon law and the barbarous feudal customs, while drawing its authority from immutable justice as represented by the sovereign, and not from canon or decretal, from pope or council, or even from Holy Writ. The clear-sightedness of St. Bernard was not in fault when, as early as 1149, he recognized the danger to the Church, and complained that the courts rang with the laws of Justinian rather than with those of God.

To understand fully the effect of this intellectual movement upon the popular mind and heart, we must picture to ourselves a state of society in many respects wholly unlike our own. It is not only that in civilized lands settled institutions have rendered men more submissive to law and custom, but the diffusion of intelligence and the training of generations have brought them more under the control of reason and rendered them less susceptible to impulse and emotion. Even in modern times we have seen the possibilities of popular frenzy when reason is dethroned by passion. Yet the madness of the Reign of Terror is no unapt illustration of the violent emotions to which mediæval populations were subject, for good or for evil, giving occasion to the startling contrasts which render the period so picturesque, with splendid exhibitions of the loftiest enthusiasm or with hideous deeds of brutality. Unaccustomed to restraint, vigorous manhood asserted itself in all its greatness and its littleness, whether in wreaking vengeance upon the defenseless or in offering itself joyfully as a sacrifice to humanity. In the deplorable condition of society, torn with unceasing and savage neighborhood war and ground under the iron heel of feudalism, the common man might indeed well imagine that the reign of Antichrist was ever imminent, or might welcome any change which possibly might benefit, and scarce could injure, his condition. The invisible world, moreover, with its mysterious attraction and horrible fascination, was ever present and real to everyone. Demons were always around him, to smite him with sickness, to ruin his pitiful little cornfield or vineyard, or to lure his soul to perdition; while angels and saints were similarly ready to help him, to listen to his invocations, and to intercede for him at the throne of mercy, which he dared not to address directly. It was among a population thus impressionable, emotional, and superstitious, slowly awakening in the intellectual dawn, that orthodoxy and heterodoxy—the forces of conservatism and progress—were to fight the battle in which neither could win permanent victory.

It is a noteworthy fact, presaging the new form which modern civilization and enlightenment were to assume, that the heresies which were to shake the Church to its foundations were no longer, as of old, mere speculative subtleties propounded by learned theologians and prelates in the gradual evolution of Christian doctrine. Nor have we, for the most part, to deal with the governing classes, for the alliance between Church and State to keep the people in subjection had been handed down from the Roman Empire, and however much monarchs like John of England or Frederic II had to complain of ecclesiastical pretensions, they never dared to loosen the foundations on which rested their own prerogatives. As a rule, heresy had to be thoroughly disseminated among the people before those of gentle blood would meddle with it, as we shall see in Languedoc and Lombardy. The real danger to the hierarchy came from obscure men, laboring among the poor and oppressed, who, in their misery and degradation, felt that the Church had failed in its mission, whether through the worldliness of its ministers or through defects in its doctrine. On the one hand we have sectaries holding fast to all the essentals of Christianity, with antisacerdotalism as their mainspring, and on the other hand we have Manichæans.

In briefly reviewing these and their vicissitudes, it must be borne in mind that, with scarce an exception, the authorities are exclusively their antagonists and persecutors. Saving a few Waldensian tracts and a single Catharan ritual, their literature has wholly perished. We are left, for the most part, to gather their doctrines from those who wrote to confute them or to excite popular odium against them, and we can only learn their struggles and their fate from their ruthless exterminators. I shall say no word in their praise that is not based upon the admissions or accusations of their enemies; and if I reject some of the abuse lavished upon them, it is because that abuse is so manifestly conscious or unconscious exaggeration that it is deprived of all historical value.

The antisacerdotal heresies were directed against the abuses in doctrine and practice which priestcraft had invented to enslave the souls of men. One feature common to them all was a revival of the

Donatist tenet that the sacraments are polluted in polluted hands, so that a priest living in mortal sin is incapable of administering them. In 1059 the Synod of Rome, under the impulsion of Nicholas II, had adopted a canon forbidding anyone to be present at the mass of a priest known to keep a concubine or wife. This was inviting the flock to sit in judgment on the pastor; and though it remained virtually a dead letter for fifteen years, when it was revived and effectually put in force by Gregory VII, in 1074, it produced immense confusion, for continent priests were rare exceptions. Although Urban II endeavored to point out that it was merely a matter of discipline, and that the virtue of the sacraments remained unaltered in the hands of the worst of men, still it was difficult for the popular mind to recognize so subtle a distinction. The question continued to plague the Church until, about 1230, Gregory IX abandoned the position of his predecessors, and undertook to settle it by an authoritative decision that every priest in mortal sin is suspended, as far as concerns himself, until he repents and is absolved, yet his offices are not to be avoided, because he is not suspended as regards others, unless the sin is notorious by judicial confession or sentence, or by evidence so clear that no tergiversation is possible. To the Church it was, of course, impossible to admit that the virtue of the sacrament depended upon the virtue of the ministrant, but these finedrawn distinctions show how the question troubled the minds of the faithful, and how readily the heresy could suggest itself that transubstantiation might fail in the hands of the wicked.

One or two of the earlier antisacerdotal heresies may be mentioned which were local and temporary in their character, but which have interest as showing how ready were the lower ranks of the people to rise in revolt against the Church, and how contagious was the enthusiasm excited by any leader bold enough to voice the general feeling of unrest and discontent. In the south of France, the condition of society was especially favorable for their propagation. There the population and civilization were wholly different from those of the north. The first wave of the Aryan invasion of Europe had driven to the Mediterranean littoral the ancient Ligurian inhabitants, who had left abundant traces of their race in the swarthy skins and black hair of their descendants. Greek and Phœnician colonies had still further crossed the blood. Gothic domination had been long continued, and the Merovingian conquest had scarce given to the Frank a foothold in the soil. Even Saracenic elements were not wanting to make up the strange admixture of races which rendered the citizen of Narbonne or Marseilles so different a being from the inhabitant of Paris—quite as different as the *langue d'Oc* from the *langue d'Oyl*. The contrast of civilization was as marked as that of race. Nowhere in Europe had culture and luxury made such progress as in the south of France. Chivalry and poetry were assiduously cultivated by the nobles; and even in the cities, which had acquired for themselves a large measure of freedom and which were enriched by trade and commerce, the citizens boasted a degree of education and enlightenment unknown elsewhere. Nowhere in Europe, moreover, were the clergy more negligent of their duties or more despised by the people. There was little earnestness of religious conviction among either prelates or nobles to stimulate persecution, so that there was considerable freedom of belief. In no other Christian land did the Jew enjoy such privileges. His right to hold land in *franc-alleu* was similar to that of the Christian; he was admitted to public office, and his administrative ability rendered him a favorite in such capacity with both prelate and noble; his synagogues were undisturbed; and the Hebrew school of Narbonne was renowned in Israel as the home of the Kimchis. Under such influences, those who really possessed religious convictions were but little deterred by prejudice or the fear of persecution from criticizing the shortcomings of the Church, or from seeking what might more nearly respond to their aspirations.

It was in such a population as this that the first antisacerdotal heresy was preached in Vallonise about 1106 by Pierre de Bruys, a native of the diocese of Embrun. The prelates of Embrun, Gap, and Die endeavored in vain to stay his progress until they procured assistance from the king, when he was driven out and took refuge in Gascony. For twenty years he continued his mission, and the openness and success with which he taught is shown by the story that in one place, to show his contempt for the objects of sacerdotal veneration, he caused a great pile of consecrated crosses to be accumulated, and then, setting fire to them, deliberately roasted meat at the flames. Persecution at length became more active, and about the year 1126 he was seized and burned at St. Gilles.

His teaching was simply antisacerdotal. Pædo-baptism was useless,

for the faith of another cannot help him who cannot use his own—
a far-reaching proposition, fraught with immeasurable consequences.
For the same reason offerings, alms, masses, prayers and other good
works for the dead are useless and each will be judged on his own
merits. Churches are unnecessary and should be destroyed, since God
listens to those who deserve it, whether invoked in church or tavern,
in temple or market-place, before the altar or before the stable; and
the Church of God does not consist of a multitude of stones piled
together, but in the united congregation of the faithful. As for the
cross, as a senseless thing it is not to be invoked with foolish prayers,
but is rather to be destroyed as the instrument on which Christ was
tortured to death. His only recorded utterance is his vigorous rejection of the sacrament:

O people, believe not the bishops, the priests, and the clerks, who, as
in much else, seek to deceive you as to the office of the altar, where they
lyingly pretend to make the body of Christ and give it to you for the
salvation of your souls. They plainly lie, for the body of Christ was but
once made by Christ in the supper before the Passion, and but once given
to the disciples. Since then it has never been made and never given.

There was evidently nothing to do with such a man but to burn
him, but even this did not suffice to suppress his heresy. The Pe-
trobrusians continued to diffuse his doctrines, secretly or openly, and,
some five or six years after his death, Peter the Venerable of Cluny
considered them still so formidable as to require his controversial
tract, to which we are indebted for almost all we know about the
sect. This is dedicated to the Bishops of Embrun, Arles, Die, and
Gap, and urges them to renewed efforts for the suppression of the
heresy by preaching and by the arms of the laity.

All their efforts might well be needed, for Pierre de Bruys was
succeeded by a yet more formidable heresiarch. Little is known of
the earlier life of Henry, the Monk of Lausanne, except that he left
his convent there under circumstances for which St. Bernard afterwards reproached him. We hear of him at Le Mans, perhaps as early
as 1116, but the dates are uncertain. Here his austerities gained him
the veneration of the people, which he turned with disastrous effect
upon the clergy. We know little of his doctrines at this time, except
that he rejected the invocation of saints, but we are told that his

eloquence was so persuasive that under its influence women abandoned their jewels and sumptuous apparel, and young men married
courtesans to reclaim them. While thus teaching asceticism and charity, he so lashed the vices of the Church that the clergy throughout
the diocese would have been destroyed but for the active protection
of the nobles. Henry had taken advantage of the absence in Rome
of the bishop, the celebrated Hildebert of Le Mans, who, on his return, overcame the heretic in disputation and forced him to abandon
the field. We have glimpses of his activity in Poitiers and Bordeaux,
and then lose sight of him till we find him a prisoner of the Archbishop of Arles, who took him to the presence of Innocent II at the
Council of Pisa, in 1134. Here he was convicted of heresy and condemned to imprisonment, but was subsequently released and sent
back to his convent, whence he departed with the intention of
entering the strict Cistercian Order at Clairvaux. What led to his
resuming his heretical mission we do not know, but we meet him
again, bolder than before, adopting substantially the Petrobrusian
tenets, rejecting the Eucharist, refusing all reverence for the priesthood, all tithes, oblations, and other sources of ecclesiastical revenue,
and all attendance at church.

The scene of this activity was southern France, where the embers
of Petrobrusianism were ready to be kindled into flame. His success
was immense. In 1147 St. Bernard despairingly describes the condition
of religion in the extensive territories of the Count of Toulouse:

The churches are without people, the people without priests, the
priests without the reverence due them, and Christians without Christ.
. . . Men die in their sins, and their souls are hurried to the dread
tribunal, neither reconciled by penance nor fortified by the holy communion. The little ones of Christ are debarred from life since baptism is
denied them. The voice of a single heretic silences all those apostolic and
prophetic voices which have united in calling all the nations into the
Church of Christ.

The prelates of southern France were powerless to arrest the progress
of the bold heresiarch, and imploringly appealed for assistance. The
nobles would not aid them, for, like the people, they hated the clergy
and were glad of the excuses which Henry's doctrines gave them for
spoiling and oppressing the Church. The papal legate, Alberic, was

summoned, and he prevailed upon St. Bernard to accompany him with Geoffrey, Bishop of Chartres, and other men of mark. Though St. Bernard was sick, the perilous condition of the tottering establishment aroused all his zeal, and he unflinchingly undertook the mission.

If we may believe the accounts of his disciples, the success of Bernard was immense. His reputation had preceded him, and it was heightened by the stories of miracles which he daily performed, no less than by his burning eloquence and skill in disputation. Crowds flocked to hear him preach, and were converted. At Albi, the cathedral was scarcely able to hold the multitude which assembled to listen to him. On the conclusion of his discourse he adjured them: "Repent, then, all ye who have been contaminated. Return to the Church; and that we may know who repents, let each penitent raise his right hand"—and every hand was raised. Scarce less effective was his rejoinder when, after preaching to an immense assemblage, he mounted his horse to depart and a hardened heretic, thinking to confuse him, said, "My lord abbot, our heretic, of whom you think so ill, has not a horse so fat and spirited as yours." "Friend," replied the saint, "I deny it not. The horse eats and grows fat for itself, for it is but a brute and by nature given to its appetites, whereby it offends not God. But before the judgment seat of God I and your master will not be judged by horse's necks, but each by his own neck. Now, then, look at my neck and see if it is fatter than your master's, and if you can justly reprehend me." Then he threw down his cowl and displayed his neck, long and thin and wasted by maceration and austerities, to the confusion of the misbelievers.

St. Bernard challenged Henry to a disputation, which the prudent heretic declined, whether through fear of his antagonist's eloquence or a reasonable regard for the safety of his own person. It mattered little which, for his refusal discredited him in the eyes of many of the nobles who had hitherto protected him, and thenceforth he was obliged to lie in hiding. Orthodoxy took heart and was soon on his track: he was captured the next year and brought in chains before his bishop. His end is not known, but he is presumed to have died in prison.

Arnald of Brescia's heresy was much more limited in its scope. A pupil of Abelard, he was accused of sharing his master's errors, and incorrect notions respecting pædo-baptism and the Eucharist were attributed to him. Whatever may have been his theological aberrations, his real offense was the energetic way in which he lashed the vices of the clergy and stimulated the laity to repossess the ample wealth and extended privileges which the Church had acquired. Profoundly convinced that the evils of Christendom arose from the worldliness of the ecclesiastical body, he taught that the Church should hold neither temporal possessions nor jurisdiction, and should confine itself rigidly to its spiritual functions. Of austere and commanding virtue, irreproachable in his self-denying life, trained in all the learning of the schools, and gifted with rare persuasive eloquence, he became the terror of the hierarchy, and found the laity ready enough to listen and to act upon doctrines which satisfied their worldly aspirations as well as their spiritual longings. The Second Lateran Council, in 1139, endeavored to suppress the revolt which he excited in the Lombard cities by condemning and imposing silence on him; he refused obedience, and the next year Innocent II included him in the condemnation of Abelard, and ordered both to be imprisoned and their writings burned. Arnald had fled from Italy to France, and now he was driven to Germany, where we find his restless activity at work in Constance and then in Torgau, pursued by the sleepless watchfulness of St. Bernard. According to the latter, his conquests over souls in Switzerland were rapid, for his teeth were arms and arrows, and his tongue was a sharp sword. After the death of Innocent II he returned to Rome in 1145 or 1146. The new pope, Eugenius III, speedily wearied with the turbulence of the city which had exhausted his predecessors, abandoned it and finally sought refuge in France. Arnald was not idle in these movements, and was generally held responsible for them. Eugenius, on his return to Italy, in 1148, issued from Brescia a condemnation of Arnald, but the citizens stood firm, and the pope was only allowed to return to his city on condition of allowing Arnald to remain there. After the death of Conrad III, in 1152, Eugenius hastened to win the support of the new King of the Romans, Frederic Barbarossa, by intimating that Arnald and his partisans were conspiring to elect another emperor and make the empire Roman in fact as well as in name. Blindly overlooking the irreconcilable antagonism between the temporal and spiritual swords, Frederic cast his fortunes with the pope, swore to subdue for him the rebellious city and regain for him the territory of which he had been deprived; while Eugenius, on his side, promised to crown him when he should invade Italy, and to use freely the artillery of excommunication for the abasement of his enemies. The domination of the Roman populace had not been wholly moderate and peaceful, and at length, in 1154, in some popular uprising, the Cardinal of Santa Pudenziana was slain. Adrian IV, who had recently ascended the papal throne, took advantage of the opportunity and set the novel example of laying an interdict on the capital of Christianity until Arnald should be expelled from the city; the fickle populace, dismayed at the deprivation of the sacrament, indispensable to all Christians at the approaching Easter solemnities, were withdrawn from Arnald's support, and he retired to the castle of a friendly baron of the Campagna. The next year Frederic reached Rome, after entering into engagements with Adrian which included the sacrifice of Arnald, and he lost no time in performing his share of the bargain. Arnald's protectors were summoned to surrender him, and were obliged to obey. For the cruel ending the Church sought to shirk the responsibility, but there would seem to be no reasonable doubt that he was regularly condemned by a spiritual tribunal as a heretic, for he was in holy Orders and could be tried only by the Church, after which he was handed over to the secular arm for punishment. He was offered pardon if he would recant his erroneous doctrines, but he persistently refused, and passed his last moments in silent prayer. Whether or not he was mercifully hanged before being reduced to ashes is perhaps doubtful, but those ashes were cast into the Tiber to prevent the people of Rome from preserving them as relics and honoring him as a martyr. Yet, though Arnald failed in his attempt to revolutionize society, this sacrifice was not wholly in vain. His teachings left a deep impress in the minds of the population, and his followers in secret cherished his memory and his principles for centuries. Secret associations of Arnaldistas were formed who called themselves "Poor Men," and adopted the tenet that the sacraments could only be administered by virtuous men. In 1184 we find them condemned by Lucius III at the so-called Council of Verona, and even until the sixteenth century their name occurs in the lists of heresies proscribed in successive bulls and edicts.

Far greater in importance and more durable in results was the antisacerdotal movement unconsciously set on foot by Peter Waldo

of Lyons, in the second half of the twelth century. He was a rich
merchant, unlearned, but eager to acquire the truths of Scripture, to
which end he caused the translation into Romance of the New Testament and a collection of extracts from the Fathers, known as *Sentences*. Diligently studying these, he learned them by heart, and arrived at the conviction that nowhere was the apostolic life observed
as commanded by Christ. Striving for evangelical perfection, he gave
his wife the choice between his real estate and his movables. On her
selecting the former, he sold the latter; portioned his two daughters
and placed them in the Abbey of Fontevraud, and distributed the
rest of the proceeds among the poor then suffering from a famine.
As he devoted himself to preaching the Gospel through the streets
and by the wayside, admiring imitators of both sexes sprang up
around him, whom he dispatched as missionaries to the neighboring
towns. They entered houses, announcing the Gospel to the inmates;
they preached in the churches, they discoursed in the public places,
and everywhere they found eager listeners, for, as we have seen, the
negligence of the clergy had rendered the function of preaching
almost a forgotten duty. According to the fashion of the time, they
speedily adopted a peculiar form of dress, including, in imitation of
the apostles, a sandal with a kind of plate upon it, whence they acquired the name of the "Shoed," *Insabbatati*, or *Zaptati*—though the
appellation which they bestowed upon themselves was that of *Li
Poure de Lyod*, or Poor Men of Lyons.

It was not possible that ignorant zeal could thus undertake the
office of religious instruction without committing errors which acute
theologians could detect. Complaint speedily arose of the scandals
which the new evangelists disseminated, and the Archbishop of
Lyons summoned them before him and prohibited them from further preaching. They disobeyed and were excommunicated. Peter
Waldo then appealed to the pope (probably Alexander III), who approved his vow of poverty and authorized him to preach when permitted by the priests—a restriction which was observed for a time
and then disregarded. The obstinate Poor Men gradually put forward
one dangerous tenet after another, while their attacks upon the
clergy became sharper and sharper; yet as late as the year 1179 they
came before the Council of Lateran, submitted their version of the
Scriptures, and asked for license to preach. Walter Mapes, who was

present, ridicules their ignorant simplicity, yet he bears emphatic testimony to their zeal in imitating the apostles and following Christ. Again they applied to Rome for authority to found an order of preachers, but Lucius III objected to their sandals, to their monkish copes, and to the companionship of men and women in their wandering life. Finding them obstinate, he finally anathematized them at the Council of Verona in 1184, but they still refused to abandon their mission, or even to consider themselves separated from the Church. Though again condemned in a council held at Narbonne, they agreed, about 1190, to take the chances of a disputation held in the Cathedral of Narbonne with Raymond of Daventry, a religious and God-fearing Catholic, as judge. Of course the decision went against them, and of course they were as little inclined as before to submit, but the colloquy has an interest as showing what progress at that period they had made in dissidence from Rome. The six points on which the argument was held were:

(1) That they refused obedience to the authority of pope and prelate;
(2) That all, even laymen, can preach;
(3) That, according to the apostles, God is to be obeyed rather than man;
(4) That women may preach;
(5) That masses, prayers, and alms for the dead are of no avail, with the addition that some of them denied the existence of purgatory; and
(6) That prayer in bed, or in a chamber, or in a stable, is as efficacious as in a church.

All this was rebellion against sacerdotalism rather than actual heresy; but we learn, about the same period, from the "Universal Doctor," Alain de l'Isle, who, at the request of Lucius III, wrote a tract for their refutation, that they were prepared to carry these principles to their legitimate but dangerous conclusions, and that they added various other doctrines at variance with the teachings of the Church.

Good prelates, they held, who led apostolic lives, were to be obeyed, and to them alone was granted the power to bind and loose —which was striking a mortal blow at the whole organization of the Church. Merit, and not ordination, conferred the power to consecrate and bless; everyone, therefore, who led an apostolic life had this power, and as they assumed that they all led such a life, it followed that they, although laymen, could execute all the functions of the priesthood. It likewise followed that the ministrations of sinful priests were invalid, though at first the French Waldenses were not willing to admit this, while the Italians boldly affirmed it. A further error was that confession to a layman was as efficacious as to a priest, which was a serious attack upon the sacrament of penitence; though, as yet, the Fourth Council of Lateran had not made priestly confession indispensable, and Alain is willing to admit that in the absence of a priest, confession to a layman is sufficient. The system of indulgences was another of the sacerdotal devices they rejected; and they added three specific rules of morality which became distinctive characteristics of the sect. Every lie is a mortal sin; every oath, even in a court of justice, is unlawful; and homicide is under no circumstances to be permitted, whether in war or in execution of judicial sentences. This necessarily involved nonresistance, rendering the Waldenses dangerous only from such moral influence as they could acquire. Even as late as 1217, a well-informed contemporary assures us that the four chief errors of the Waldenses were their wearing sandals after the fashion of the apostles, their prohibition of oaths and of homicide, and their assertion that any member of the sect, if he wore sandals, could in case of necessity consecrate the Eucharist.

These principles, if universally adopted, would have reduced the Church to a condition of apostolic poverty, and would have swept away much of the distinction between priest and layman. Besides, the sectaries were inspired with the true missionary spirit; their proselyting zeal knew no bounds; they wandered from land to land promulgating their doctrines, and finding everywhere a cordial response, especially among the lower classes. We are told that one of their chief apostles carried with him various disguises, appearing now as a cobbler, then as a barber, and again as a peasant, and though this may have been, as alleged, for the purpose of eluding capture, it shows the social stratum to which their missions were addressed. The Poor Men of Lyons multiplied with incredible rapidity throughout Europe; the Church became seriously alarmed, and not without reason, for an ancient document of the sectaries shows a tradition among them that under Waldo, or immediately afterwards, their councils had an average attendance of about 700 members present.[1]

[1] The time and place of Peter Waldo's death are not known.

Not long after the Colloquy of Narbonne in 1194, the note of persecution was sounded by Alonso II of Aragon, in an edict which is worthy of note as the first secular legislation, with the exception of the Assizes of Clarendon, in the modern world against heresy. The Waldenses and all other heretics anathematized by the Church are ordered, as public enemies, to quit his dominions by the day after All-Saints'. Anyone who receives them, listens to their preaching, or gives them food shall incur the penalties of treason, with confiscation of all his goods and possessions. Any heretic remaining after three days' notice of the law can be despoiled by anyone, and any injury inflicted on him, short of death or mutilation, so far from being an offense, shall be regarded as meriting the royal favor. The ferocious atrocity of these provisions, which rendered the heretic an outlaw and exposed him without a trial to the cupidity or malice of every man, was exceeded three years later by Alonso's son, Pedro II. In a national council in Girona, in 1197, he renewed his father's legislation, adding the penalty of the stake for the heretic. If any noble failed to eject these enemies to the Church, the officials and people of the diocese were ordered to proceed to his castle and seize them without responsibility for any damages committed, and anyone failing to join in the foray was subjected to the heavy fine of 20 pieces of gold to the royal fisc. Harmless as the Waldenses might seem to be, they were recognized as most dangerous enemies, to be mercilessly persecuted.

In a sect so widely scattered, it was inevitable that differences of organization and doctrine should arise, and that there should be variations in the rapidity of independent development. The early Waldenses were not Protestants in our modern sense, and, in spite of persecution, many of them long continued to regard themselves as members of the Church of Rome. In the crucial test of belief in transubstantiation, for instance, as early as the thirteenth century, an experienced inquisitor, in drawing up instructions for the examination of Waldenses, assumes disbelief in the existence of the body and blood in the Eucharist as one of the points whereby to detect them, and in 1332 we hear of such a denial among the Waldenses of Savoy. Yet about this latter date Bernard Gui assures us that they believed in it, and M. Montet has shown from their successive writings how their views on the subject changed. The inquisitor who burned the Waldenses of Cologne in 1392 tells us that they denied transubstantiation, but they added, that if it occurred it could not be wrought in the hands of a sinful priest. The anti-sacerdotalism in which the sect took its rise naturally tended to do away with all that interposed mediators between God and man, although this progress was by no means uniform. The Waldenses burned in Strassburg in 1212 rejected all distinction between the laity and the priesthood. In Lombardy, about the same time, the community elected ministers either temporary or for life. Bernard Gui speaks of three orders among them—deacons, priests, and bishops; and when the *Unitas Fratrum* of Bohemia was organized in 1467, it had recourse, as we shall see hereafter, to the Waldensian Bishop Stephen to consecrate its first bishops. Yet the antisacerdotal tendencies were so strong that the difference between the laity and priesthood was greatly diminished, and the power of the keys was wholly rejected. About 1400, the *Nobla Leyczon* declares that all the popes, cardinals, bishops, and abbots since the days of Silvester could not pardon a single mortal sin, for God alone has the power of pardon. As the soul thus dealt directly with God, the whole machinery of indulgences and so-called pious works was thrown aside. It is true that faith without works was idle—*"la fe es ociosa sensa las obras"*—but good works were piety, repentance, charity, justice, not pilgrimages and formal exercises, the founding of churches and the honoring of saints.

The Waldensian system thus created a simple church organization with a tendency ever to grow simpler. In some places it was the custom for each head of a family on Holy Thursday to administer communion in a simple fashion, consecrating the elements and distributing them himself. Yet of necessity there was a recognized priesthood, known as the Perfected, or *Majorales*, who taught the faithful and converted the unbeliever, who renounced all property and separated themselves from their wives, or who had observed strict chastity from youth, who wandered around hearing confessions and making converts, and were supported by the voluntary contributions of those who labored for their bread. One marked distinction between them and the laity was that, when on trial before the Inquisition, the prohibition of swearing was relaxed in favor of the latter, who might take an oath under compulsion, while the Perfects would die rather than violate the precept. The inquisitors, while complaining of the ingenuity with which the heretics evaded their examination, admitted that all were much more solicitous to save their friends and kindred than themselves.

With this tendency towards a restoration of evangelical simplicity, it followed that the special religious teaching of the Waldenses was to a great extent ethical. The reply of an unfortunate before the Inquisition of Toulouse, when asked what his instructors had taught him, was "that he should neither speak nor do evil, that he should do nothing to others that he would not have done to himself, and that he should not lie or swear"—a simple enough formula, but one which practically leaves little to be desired. In fact, the unanimous testimony of their persecutors is that their external virtues were worthy of all praise, and the contrast between the purity of their lives and the depravity which pervaded the clergy of the Church is more than once deplored by their antagonists as a most effective factor in the dissemination of heresy. An inquisitor who knew them well describes them:

Heretics are recognizable by their customs and speech, for they are modest and well regulated. They take no pride in their garments, which are neither costly nor vile. They do not engage in trade, to avoid lies and oaths and frauds, but live by their labor as mechanics—their teachers are cobblers. They do not accumulate wealth, but are content with necessaries. They are chaste and temperate in meat and drink. They do not frequent taverns or dances or other vanities. They restrain themselves from anger. They are always at work; they teach and learn and consequently pray but little. They are to be known by their modesty and precision of speech, avoiding scurrility and detraction and light words and lies and oaths. They do not even say *vere* or *certe*, regarding them as oaths.

Such is the general testimony, and the tales of the sexual abominations customary among them may safely be set down as devices to excite popular detestation, grounded possibly on extravagances of asceticism, such as were common among the early Christians, for the Waldenses held that connubial intercourse was only lawful for the procurement of offspring. An inquisitor admits his disbelief of these stories, for which he had never found a basis worthy of credence, nor does anything of the kind make its appearance in the exami-

nations of the sectaries under the skillful handling of their persecutors, until in the fourteenth and fifteenth centuries the Inquisitors
of Piedmont and Provence found it expedient to extract such confessions from their victims.

There was also objected to them the hypocrisy which led them
to conceal their belief under assiduous attendance at mass and
confession; but this, like the ingenious evasions under examination,
which so irritated their inquisitorial critics, may readily be pardoned
to those with whom it was the necessity of self-preservation, and
who, at least during the earlier period, had often no other means of
enjoying the sacraments they deemed essential to salvation. But
their crowning offense was their love and reverence for Scripture and
their burning zeal in making converts. The Inquisitor of Passau
informs us that they had translations of the whole Bible in the vulgar
tongue, which the Church vainly sought to suppress, and which they
studied with incredible assiduity. He knew a peasant who could
recite the Book of Job word for word; many of them had the whole
of the New Testament by heart, and, simple as they were, were
dangerous disputants. As for the missionary spirit, he tells of one
who, on a winter night, swam the river Ips in order to gain a chance
of converting a Catholic; and all, men and women, old and young,
were ceaseless in learning and teaching. After a hard day's labor
they would devote the night to instruction; they sought the lazar-
houses to carry salvation to the leper; a disciple of ten days' standing would seek out another whom he could instruct, and when the
dull and untrained brain would fain abandon the task in despair
they would speak words of encouragement: "Learn a single word
a day, in a year you will know three hundred, and thus you will gain
in the end." Surely if ever there was a God-fearing people it was these
unfortunates under the ban of Church and State, whose secret pass-
words were, "Ce dit sainct Pol, Ne mentir," "Ce dit sainct Jacques,
Ne jurer," "Ce dit sainct Pierre, Ne rendre mal pour mal, mais biens
contraires."

The sincerity with which the Waldenses adhered to their beliefs
is shown by the thousands who cheerfully endured the horrors of
the prison, the torture chamber, and the stake, rather than return
to a faith they believed to be corrupt. I have met with a case in 1320,
in which a poor old woman at Pamiers submitted to the dreadful

sentence for heresy simply because she would not take an oath. She answered all interrogations on points of faith in orthodox fashion, but though offered her life if she would swear on the Gospels, she refused to burden her soul with the sin, and for this she was condemned as a heretic.

CHAPTER III
THE CATHARI

OF ALL the heresies with which the early Church had to contend, none had excited such mingled fear and loathing as Manichæism. Manes had so skillfully compounded Mazdean Dualism with Christianity and with Gnostic and Buddhist elements, that his doctrine found favor both with the subtle intellects of the schools and with the toiling masses. Instinctively recognizing it as the most dangerous of rivals, the Church, as soon as it could command the resources of the State, persecuted it relentlessly. Persecution attained its end, after prolonged struggle, in suppressing all outward manifestations of Manichæism within the confines of the imperial power, though it long afterwards maintained a secret existence, even in the West. In the East it withdrew ostensibly to the boundaries of the empire, still keeping up hidden relations with its sectaries scattered throughout the provinces, and even in Constantinople itself. It abandoned its reverence for Manes as the paraclete and transferred its allegiance to two others of its leaders, Paul and John of Samosata, from the first of whom it acquired the name of Paulicianism.

In all essentials the doctrine of the Paulicians was identical with that of the Cathari. In the Paulician faith we find two coequal principles, God and Satan, of whom the former created the invisible, spiritual, and eternal universe, the latter the material and temporal, which he governs. Satan is the Jehovah of the Old Testament; the prophets and patriarchs are robbers, and, consequently, all Scripture anterior to the Gospels is to be rejected. The New Testament, however, is Holy Writ, but Christ was not a man, but a phantasm—the Son of God who appeared to be born of the Virgin Mary and came from Heaven to overthrow the worship of Satan. Transmigration provides for the future reward or punishment of deeds done in life. The sacraments are rejected, and the priests and elders of the Church are only teachers without authority over the faithful. Such are the outlines of Paulicianism as they have reached us, and their identity with the belief of the Cathari is too marked for us to

41

accept the theory which assigns to the latter an origin among the
dreamers of the Bulgarian convents. A further irrefragable evidence
of the derivation of Catharism from Manichæism is furnished by
the sacred thread and garment which were worn by all the Perfect
among the Cathari. This custom is too peculiar to have had an
independent origin, and is manifestly the Mazdean *kosti* and
saddarah, the sacred thread and shirt, the wearing of which was
essential to all believers, and the use of which by both Zends and
Brahmans shows that its origin is to be traced to the prehistoric
period anterior to the separation of those branches of the Aryan
family. Among the Cathari the wearer of the thread and vestment
was what was known among the inquisitors as the *hæreticus indutus*
or *vestitus*, initiated into all the mysteries of the heresy.

Catharism thus was a thoroughly antisacerdotal form of belief.
It cast aside all the machinery of the Church. Consequently the
sacraments, the sacrifices of the altar, the suffrages and interposition
of the Virgin and saints, purgatory, relics, images, crosses, holy
water, indulgences, and the other devices by which the priest procured salvation for the faithful were rejected, as well as the tithes
and oblations which rendered the procuring of salvation so profitable.
Yet the Catharan Church, as the Church of Christ, inherited the
power to bind and to loose bestowed by Christ on his disciples; the
Consolamentum, or Baptism of the Spirit, wiped out all sin, but no
prayers were of use for the sinner who persisted in wrongdoing.
Curiously enough, though Catharism translated the Scripture, it
retained the Latin language in its prayers, which were thus unin-
telligible to most of the disciples, and it had its consecrated class who
conducted its simple services. Some regular form of organization
was necessary for the government of its rapidly increasing communities and for the missionary work which was so zealously carried
forward. Thus there came to be four orders selected from among the
"Perfected," who were distinguished from the mass of believers, or
simple "Christians"—the Bishop, the Filius Major, the Filius Minor,
and the Deacon. The Filius Major was elected by the congregation,
and promotions were made to the episcopate as vacancies occurred.
Ordination was conferred by the imposition of hands or *Consolamentum*, administered to all who were admitted to the Church.
The belief that sacraments were vitiated in sinful hands gave rise

to considerable anxiety, and to guard against it the *Consolamentum* was generally repeated a second and a third time. It was generally, though not universally, held that the lower in grade could not consecrate the higher, and therefore in many cities there were habitually two bishops, so that in the case of death consecration should not be sought at the hands of a Filius Major.

The Catharan ritual was severe in its simplicity. The Catholic Eucharist was replaced by the benediction of bread, which was performed daily at table. He who was senior by profession or position took the bread and wine, while all stood up and recited the Lord's Prayer. The senior then saying, "The grace of our Lord Jesus Christ be with us," broke the bread, and distributed it to all present. This blessed bread was regarded with special reverence by the great mass of the Cathari, who were, as a rule, merely *crezentz, credentes,* or believers, and not fully received or "perfected" in the Church. These would sometimes procure a piece of this bread and keep it for years, occasionally taking a morsel. Every act of eating or drinking was preceded by prayer; when a perfected minister was at table, the first drink and every new dish that was tasted was accompanied by the guests with *"Benedicite,"* to which he responded *"Diaus vos benesiga."* There was a monthly ceremony of confession, which, however, was general in its character and was performed by the assembled faithful. The great ceremony was the *Cossolament, Consolamentum,* or Baptism of the Holy Ghost, which reunited the soul to the Holy Spirit, and which, like the Christian baptism, worked absolution of all sin. It required two ministrants, and could be performed by anyone of the Perfected not in mortal sin—even by a woman. This was the process of "heretication," as the inquisitors termed the admission into the Church, and except in the case of those who proposed to become ministers was, as a rule, postponed until the deathbed, probably for fear of persecution; but the *credens* frequently entered into an agreement, known as *la covenansa,* binding himself to undergo it at the last moment, and this engagement authorized its performance even though he had lost the power of speech and was unable to make the responses. In form it was exceedingly simple, though it was generally preceded by preparation, including a prolonged fast. The ministrant addressed the postulant, "Brother, dost thou wish to give thyself to our faith?" The neophyte, after several genuflexions and blessings, said, "Ask God for this sinner, that he may lead me to a good end and make me a good Christian," to which the ministrant rejoined, "Let God be asked to make thee a good Christian and to bring thee to a good end. Dost thou give thyself to God and to the Gospel?" and after an affirmative response, "Dost thou promise that in future thou wilt eat no meat, nor eggs, nor cheese, nor any victual except from water and wood; that thou wilt not lie or swear or do any lust with thy body, or go alone when thou canst have a comrade, or abandon the faith for fear of water or fire or any other form of death?" These promises being duly made, the bystanders knelt, while the minister placed on the head of the postulant the Gospel of St. John and recited the text: "In the beginning was the Word," etc., and invested him with the sacred thread. Then the kiss of peace went round, the women receiving it by a touch of the elbow.

The ceremony was held to symbolize the abandonment of the Evil Spirit, and the return of the soul to God, with the resolve to lead henceforth a pure and sinless life. With the married, the assent of the spouse was of course a condition precedent. When this heretication occurred on the deathbed, it was commonly followed by the *Endura* or "privation." The ministrant asked the neophyte whether he desired to be a confessor or a martyr; if the latter, a pillow or a towel (known among the German Cathari as *Untertuch*) was placed over his mouth while certain prayers were recited; if he chose the former he remained without food or drink, except a little water, for three days; and in either case, if he survived, he became one of the Perfected. This *Endura* was also sometimes used as a mode of suicide, which was frequent in the sect. Torture at the end of life relieved them of torment in the next world, and suicide by voluntary starvation, by swallowing pounded glass or poisonous potions, or opening the veins in a bath, was not uncommon—and, failing this, it was a kind office for the next of kin to extinguish life when death was near. The ceremony known to the sectaries as *Melioramentum*, and described by the inquisitors as "veneration," was important as affording to them a proof of heresy. When a *credens* approached or took leave of a minister of the sect, he bent the knee thrice, saying "*Benedicite*," to which the minister replied, "*Diaus vos benesiga*." It was a mark of respect to the Holy Ghost assumed to dwell in the minister, and in the records of trials we find it eagerly inquired into, as it served to convict those who performed it.

These customs and the precepts embodied in the formula of heretication illustrate the strong ascetic tendency of the faith. As all matter was the handiwork of Satan, it was in its nature evil; the spirit was engaged in a perpetual conflict with it, and the Catharan's earnest prayer to God was not to spare the flesh sprung from corruption, but to have mercy on the imprisoned spirit—*"no aias merce de la carn nada de corruptio, mais aias merce de l'esperit pausat en carcer."* Consequently, whatever tended to the reproduction of animal life was to be shunned. To mortify the flesh the Catharan fasted on bread and water three days in each week, except when travelling, and in addition there were in the year three fasts of forty days each. Marriage was forbidden except among a few, who permitted it between virgins provided they separated as soon as a child was born, and the mitigated Dualists, who confined the prohibition to the Perfect and permitted marriage to the believers. Among the rigid, carnal matrimony was replaced by the spiritual union between the soul and God effected by the rite of *Consolamentum*. In a confession before the Inquisition of Toulouse in 1310, it is said of one heretic teacher that he would not touch a woman for the whole world; in another case a woman relates of her father that after he was hereticated he told her she must never touch him again, and she obeyed the command even when he was on the deathbed. So far was this carried that the use of meat, of eggs, of milk, of everything, in short, which was the result of animal propagation, was inhibited, except fish, which by a strange inconsistency seems to have been regarded as having some different origin. The condemnation of marriage and the rejection of meat constituted, with the prohibition of oaths, the chief external characteristics of Catharism, by which the sectaries were marked and known.

There was nothing in such a faith to attract the sensual and carnal-minded. Although the asceticism which it inculcated was beyond the reach of average humanity, its ethical teachings were admirable. As a rule they were reasonably obeyed, and the orthodox admitted with regret the contrast between the heretics and the faithful. It is true that the exaggerated condemnation of marriage expressed in the formula that relations with a wife were as sinful as incest with mother or sister was naturally enough perverted into the statement that such incest was permissible and was practiced. Wild stories, moreover, were told of the nightly orgies in which the lights were extinguished and promiscuous intercourse took place; and the stubbornness of heresy was explained by telling how, when a child was born of these foul excesses, it was tossed from hand to hand through a fire until it expired; and that from its body was made an infernal eucharist of such power that whoever partook of it was thereafter incapable of abandoning the sect. There is ample store of such tales, but however useful they might be in exciting popular detestation of heresy, the candid and intelligent inquisitors who had the best means of knowing the truth admit that they have no foundation in fact; and in the many hundreds of examinations and sentences I have read there is no allusion to anything of the kind, except in some proceedings of Frà Antonio Secco among the Alpine valleys in 1387. As St. Bernard says, "If you interrogate them, nothing can be more Christian; as to their conversation, nothing can be less reprehensible, and what they speak they prove by deeds. As for the morals of the heretic, he cheats no one, he oppresses no one, he strikes no one; his cheeks are pale with fasting, he eats not the bread of idleness, his hands labor for his livelihood." The theologians who combated them ridiculed them as ignorant churls, and in France they were popularly known by the name of Texerant (*Tisserands*), on account of the prevalence of the heresy among the weavers, whose monotonous occupation doubtless gave ample opportunity for thought. Rude and ignorant they might be for the most part, but they had skilled theologians for teachers, and an extensive popular literature. Their familiarity with Scripture is vouched for by the warning of Lucas, Bishop of Tuy, that the Christian should dread their conversation as he would a tempest, unless he is deeply skilled in the law of God, so that he can overcome them in argument.

Their proselyting zeal was especially dreaded. No labor was too severe, no risks too great, to deter them from spreading the faith which they deemed essential to salvation. Missionaries wandered over Europe to carry the glad tidings to benighted populations, regardless of hardship and undeterred by the fate of their brethren whom they saw expiate at the stake the hardihood of their revolt. Externally they professed to be Catholics, and were exemplary in the performance of their religious duties till they had won the confidence of their new neighbors and could venture on the attempt of secret conversion whenever they saw opportunity. They scattered by the wayside writings in which the poison of their doctrine was skillfully conveyed without being obtrusive, and sometimes they had no scruple in calling to their aid the superstitions of orthodoxy, as when such writings would promise indulgences to those who would read them carefully and circulate them among their neighbors, or when they purported to come from Jesus Christ and be conveyed by angels. It does not say much for the intelligence of the clergy when we are told that many priests were corrupted by such papers, picked up by shepherds and carried to them to be deciphered.

The zeal for the faith which prompted these eccentric missionary efforts manifested itself in a resolute adherence to the precepts enjoined on the neophyte when admitted into the circle of the Perfects. As in the case of the Waldenses, while the Inquisition complained bitterly of the difficulty of obtaining an avowal from the simple *credens*, whose rustic astuteness eluded the practiced skill of the interrogator, it was the general testimony that the perfected heretic refused to lie or to take an oath; and one member of the Holy Office warns his brethren not to begin by asking "Are you truly a Catharan?" for the answer will simply be "Yes," and then nothing more can be extracted; but if the Perfect is exhorted by the God in whom he believes to tell all about his life, he will faithfully detail it without falsehood.

Such was the faith whose rapid spread throughout the south of Europe filled the Church with well-grounded dismay; and, however much we may deprecate the means used for its suppression, we cannot but admit that the cause of orthodoxy was in this case the cause of progress and civilization. Had Catharism become dominant, its influence could not have failed to prove disastrous. Its asceticism with regard to commerce between the sexes, if strictly enforced, could only have led to the extinction of the race, and as this involves a contradiction of nature, it would have probably resulted in lawless concubinage and the destruction of the institution of the family, rather than in the disappearance of the human race and the return of exiled souls to their Creator, which was the *sum-*

mum bonum of the true Catharan. Its condemnation of the visible universe and of matter in general as the work of Satan rendered sinful all striving after material improvement, and the conscientious belief in such a creed could only lead man back, in time, to his original condition of savagism.

It was about 970 that John Zimiski transplanted the Paulicians to Thrace, whence they spread with great rapidity through the Balkan Peninsula. Our materials for an intimate acquaintance with that age are very scanty, but when we see that Gerbert of Aurillac, on his election to the archiepiscopate of Reims in 991, was obliged to utter a profession of faith in which he declared his belief that Satan was wicked of free will, that the Old and New Testaments were of equal authority, and that marriage and the use of meat were allowable, it shows that Paulician opinions were already well understood and dreaded as far north as Champagne. There seems, indeed, to have been a center of Catharism there, for in 1100 a peasant named Leutard, at Vertus, was convicted of teaching antisacerdotal doctrines which were evidently of Manichæan origin, and he is discreetly said to have drowned himself in a well when overcome in argument by Bishop Liburnius.

Shortly after this Cathari were discovered in Aquitaine, where they made many converts, and their heresy spread secretly throughout southern France in spite of the free use of the fagot. Even as far north as Orleans it was discovered in 1017, under circumstances which aroused general attention. A female missionary from Italy had carried the infection there, and a number of the most prominent clergy of the city fell victims to it. In their proselyting zeal they sent out emissaries and were discovered. On hearing of it, King Robert the Pious hastened to Orleans with Queen Constance, and summoned a council of bishops to determine what should be done to meet the novel and threatening danger. The heretics, on being questioned, made no secret of their faith and boldly declared themselves ready to die rather than to abandon it. They were taken beyond the walls and again, in the presence of the blazing pyre, were entreated to recant, but they preferred death.

About the same time we hear of others in Lombardy, in the Castle of Monforte near Asti, who were the objects of active persecution by the neighboring nobles and bishops, and who were burned whenever they could be captured. At length, about 1040, Eriberto, Archbishop of Milan, in visiting his province, came to Asti, and, hearing of these heretics, sent for them. They came willingly enough, including their teacher, Gherardo, and the Countess of Monforte; all boldly professed their faith, and were carried by Eriberto back to Milan, where he hoped to convert them. In place of this, they labored to spread their heresy among those who crowded to see them in prison, until the enraged people, against the will of the archbishop, forcibly dragged them out and gave them the choice between the cross and the stake. A few of them yielded, but the most part, covering their faces with their hands, boldly leaped into the flames. In 1045 we find them in Chalons, when Bishop Roger applied to Bishop Wazo of Liége, asking what he should do with them, and whether the secular arm should be called in to prevent the leaven from corrupting the whole people, to which the good Wazo replied that they should be left to God, "for those whom the world now regards as tares may be garnered by him as wheat when comes the harvest-time. Those whom we deem the adversaries of God he may make superior to us in heaven." By the year 1052 the heresy had extended to Germany, where the pious emperor, Henry the Black, caused a number to be hanged at Goslar. During the rest of the century we hear little more of them, though traces of them occur at Toulouse in 1056 and Béziers in 1062, and about the year 1200 they are described as infecting the whole diocese of Agen.

In the twelfth century the evil continued unabated in northern France. Count John of Soissons was noted as a protector of heretics, but, in spite of his favor, Lisiard, the bishop, captured several, and gave the first example of what subsequently became common enough—the use of the ordeal to determine heretical guilt. One, at least, of the accused floated when thrown into exorcised water, and the bishop, not knowing what to do with them, held them in prison while he went to the Council of Beauvais, in 1114, to consult his episcopal brethren. The populace, however, felt no doubts on the subject, and, fearing that they would be deprived of their prey, broke open the jail and burned them during the bishop's absence.

As the century wore on the manifestations of heresy became more numerous. In 1144 at Liége again; in 1153 again in Artois; in 1157 at Reims; about 1170 at Besançon; and in 1180 at Reims again.

This latter case has picturesque features recited for us by one of the actors in the drama, Gervais of Tilbury, at that time a young man and a canon of Reims. Riding out one afternoon as part of the retinue of his archbishop, William, his fancy was caught by a pretty girl laboring alone in a vineyard. He lost no time in pressing his suit, but was repulsed with the assertion that if she listened to his addresses she would be irretrievably damned. Virtue so severe as this was a manifest sign of heresy, and the archbishop, coming up, ordered her at once into custody, for he recognized her as necessarily belonging to the Cathari, whom Philip of Flanders had for some time been mercilessly persecuting. Under examination, she gave the name of her instructress, who was forthwith arrested, and who manifested such thorough familiarity with Scripture and such consummate dexterity in defending her faith, that no doubt was felt of her being inspired by Satan. The defeated theologians respited the pair till the next day, when they obstinately refused to yield to threats or promises and were unanimously condemned to the stake. At this the elder woman laughed, saying, "Foolish and unjust judges, think you to burn me in your fire? I fear not your sentence, and dread not your stake." With that she pulled from her bosom a ball of thread and tossed it out of the window, retaining one end, and calling out, "Take it!" The ball arose in the air, and the old woman followed it through the window, and was seen no more. The girl was left, and as she was insensible alike to offers of wealth and threats of punishment, she was duly burned, suffering her torment cheerfully and without a groan.

The Teutonic peoples were comparatively free from the infection, although the propinquity of the Rhinelands to France led to occasional visitations. About 1110 we hear of some heretics at Trèves, who seem to have escaped without punishment, though two among them were priests, and in 1200 eight more were found there and burned. In 1145 a number were discovered in Cologne, some of whom were tried; but, during the examination, the impatient populace, fearing to be balked of their spectacle, broke in, carried off the culprits, and burned them out of hand. In 1163 fugitives from the Flemish persecution were found at Cologne—eight men and three women, who had taken refuge in a barn. As they associated with no one, and did not frequent the churches, the Christian neighbors recognized them as heretics, seized them, and took them before the bishop; they boldly avowed their faith, and suffered burning with the resolute gladness which distinguished the sect. We hear of others, about the same time, burned at Bonn, but this scanty catalogue exhausts the list of German heresies in the twelfth century.

England was likewise little troubled with heresy. It was shortly after the persecutions in Flanders that in 1166 there were discovered 30 rustics—men and women—German in race and speech, probably Flemings, fleeing from the pious zeal of Henry of Reims, who had come and were endeavoring to propagate their errors. They made but one convert, a woman, who deserted them in the hour of trial. The rest stood firm when Henry II, then engaged in his quarrel with Becket and anxious to prove his fidelity to the Church, called a council of bishops at Oxford to determine their faith. They openly avowed it and were condemned to be scourged, branded in the face with a key, and driven forth. The importance which Henry attached to the matter is shown by his devoting, soon after, in the Assizes of Clarendon, an article to the subject, forbidding anyone to receive them under penalty of having his house torn down, and requiring all sheriffs to swear to the observance of the law, and to make all stewards of the barons and all knights and franc-tenants swear likewise—the first secular law on the subject in any statute book since the fall of Rome. England was not hospitable to heresy and we hear little more of it there. Towards the close of the century some heretics were found in the province of York, and early in the next century a few were discovered in London, and one was burned; but practically the orthodoxy of England was unsullied until the rise of Wickliff.

Italy, as the channel through which the Bulgarian heresy passed to the West, was naturally deeply infected. Milan had the reputation of being its center, whence missionaries were dispatched to other lands, whither pilgrims resorted from the western kingdoms, and where originated the sinister term of Patarins, by which the Cathari became generally known to the people of Europe.[1] Yet the popes,

---

[1] The nomenclature of the heresy is quite extensive. The sectaries called themselves *Cathari*, or the pure. The origin of the term *Patarin* has been the subject of considerable dispute, but there would seem to be no doubt that it arose in

involved in a death-struggle with the empire and frequently wanderers abroad, paid little attention to them during the first half of the twelfth century, and the indications which have reached us of their existence are scanty, though sufficient to show that they were numerous and aggressive in the consciousness of growing strength. At Orvieto, in 1125, they actually obtained the mastery for a while, but after a bloody struggle were subdued by the Catholics. In 1150 the effort was resumed by Diotesalvi of Florence and Gherardo of Massano; but the bishop succeeded in expelling them, when they were replaced by two women missionaries—Milita of Monte-Meano, and Giulitta of Florence—whose piety and charity won the esteem of the clergy and sympathy of the people, until the heresy was discovered in 1163, when many heretics were burned and hanged, and the rest exiled. Soon afterwards Peter the Lombard undertook to propagate it again, and formed a numerous community, embracing many nobles, and towards the close of the century San Pietro di Parenzo earned his canonization by his severe measures of repression, in retaliation for which the heretics took his life in 1199.

All the northern half of the peninsula, from the Alps to the

Milan about the middle of the eleventh century. In the Romance dialects *pates* signifies old linen; rag-pickers in Lombardy were called *Patari*, and the quarter inhabited by them in Milan was known, even up to the last century, as *Pattaria*, or *Contrada de' Pattari*. In the eleventh-century quarrels, the papalists held secret meetings in the Pattaria, and were contemptuously designated by their antagonists as *Patarins*—a name which was finally recognized and accepted by them. As the papal condemnation of clerical marriage was stigmatized as Manichæan, and as the papalists were supported by the secret heretics, followers of Gherardo di Monforte, the name was not unnaturally transferred to the Cathari in Lombardy, and it spread from there throughout Europe. In Italy the word *Cathari*, vulgarized into *Gazzari*, was also commonly used, and came gradually to designate all heretics; The Cathari, from their Bulgarian origin, were also known as *Bulgari, Bugari, Bulgri, Bugres*—a word which has been retained with an infamous signification in the English, French, and Italian vernaculars. From the number of weavers among them they were also known in France as *Texerant*, or *Textores*. The term *Speronistæ* was derived from Robert de Sperone, bishop of the French Cathari in Italy. More local designations were *Piphili, Telonarii*, and *Boni Homines*, or *Bonshommes*. The term *Albigenses*, from the district of Albi, where they were numerous, was first employed by Geoffroy of Vigeois in 1181, and became generally used during the crusades against Raymond of Toulouse.

In the official language of the Inquisition of the thirteenth century, "heretic" always means Catharan, while the Vaudois (Waldenses, from Waldo, pronounced Valdoo) are specifically designated as such.

Patrimony of St. Peter, was honeycombed with Catharism, and even as far south as Calabria it was to be found. When Innocent III in 1198 ascended the papal throne he at once commenced active proceedings for its extermination, and the obstinacy of the heretics may be estimated by the struggle in Viterbo, a city subject to the temporal as well as spiritual jurisdiction of the papacy. In March 1199, Innocent, stimulated by the increase of heresy and the audacity of its public display, wrote to the Viterbians, renewing and sharpening the penalties against all who received or favored heretics. Yet, in spite of this, in 1205 the heretics carried the municipal election and elected as chamberlain a heretic under excommunication. Innocent's indignation was boundless. If the elements, he told the citizens, should conspire to destroy them, leaving their memory an eternal shame, the punishment would be inadequate. He ordered obedience to be refused to the newly elected municipality, which was to be deposed; that the bishop, who had been ejected, should be received back, that the laws against heresy should be enforced, and that if all this was not done within fifteen days the people of the surrounding towns and castles were commanded to take up arms and make active war upon the rebellious city. Even this was insufficient. Two years later, in February 1207, there were fresh troubles, and it was not until June of that year, when Innocent himself came to Viterbo, and all the Patarins fled at his approach, that he was able to purify the town by tearng down all the houses of the heretics and confiscating all their property.

It was in southern France, however, that the struggle was deadliest and the battle was fought to its bitter end. There the soil, as we have seen, was the most favorable, and the growth of heresy the rankest. Early in the century we find open resistance at Albi, when Bishop Sicard, aided by the Abbot of Castres, endeavored to imprison obstinate heretics and was baffled by the people, leading to a dangerous quarrel between the civil and ecclesiastical jurisdictions. In 1119 Calixtus II presided over a council at Toulouse which condemned the heresy, but was forced to content itself with sentencing the heretics to expulsion from the Church. It is perhaps remarkable that when Innocent II, driven from Rome by the antipope Pier-Leone, was wandering through France and held a great council at Reims in 1131, no measures were taken for the repression of heresy; but when restored to Rome he seems to have awakened to the necessity of action, and in the Second Lateran Council in 1139 he issued a decisive decree which is interesting as the earliest example of the interpellation of the secular arm. Not only were the Cathari condemned and expelled from the Church, but the temporal authorities were ordered to coerce them and all those who favored or defended them. This policy was followed up in 1148 by the Council of Reims, which forbade anyone to receive or maintain on his lands the heretics dwelling in Gascony, Provence, and elsewhere, and not to afford them shelter in passing or give them a refuge, under pain of excommunication and interdict.

When Alexander III was exiled from Rome by Frederic Barbarossa and his antipope Victor, and came to France, he called in 1163 a great council at Tours. It was an imposing assemblage, comprising 17 cardinals, 124 bishops (including Thomas Becket) and hundreds of abbots, besides hosts of other ecclesiastics and a vast number of laymen. This august body, after performing its first duty of anathematizing the rival pope, proceeded to deplore the heresy which had spread like a cancer throughout Gascony. The prelates were ordered to be vigilant in suppressing it by anathematizing all who should permit heretics to dwell on their lands or should hold intercourse with them, in buying or selling, so that, being cut off from human society, they might be compelled to abandon their errors. All secular princes were commanded to imprison them and to confiscate their property. By this time it is evident that heresy was no longer concealed but displayed itself openly and defiantly; and the futility of the papal commands was shown two years later at the council, or rather colloquy, of Lombers near Albi. This was a public disputation between representatives of orthodoxy and the *bos-homes*, *bos Crestias*, or "good men," as they styled themselves, before judges agreed upon by both sides, in the presence of Pons, Archbishop of Narbonne, and sundry bishops, besides the most powerful nobles of the region—Constance, sister of King Louis VII and wife of Raymond of Toulouse, Trencavel of Béziers, Sicard of Lautrec, and others. Nearly all of the population of Lombers and Albi assembled, and the proceedings were evidently regarded as of the greatest public interest and importance. A full report of the discussion, including the decision against the Cathari, has reached us from several orthodox

sources, but the only interest which the affair has is in showing that
heresy had outgrown all the means of repression at command of the
local churches, that reason had to be appealed to in place of force,
that heretics had no scruple in manifesting and declaring themselves,
and that the Catholic disputants had to submit to their demands in
citing only the New Testament as an authority. The powerlessness
of the Church was still further exhibited in the fact that the council,
after its argumentative triumph, was obliged to content itself with
simply ordering the nobles of Lombers no longer to protect the
heretics.

Evidently the Church was powerless. When it could condemn
the doctrines and not the persons of heretics it confessed to the
world that it possessed no machinery capable of dealing with opposition on a scale of such magnitude. The Cathari saw this plainly,
and in 1167 they dared to hold a council of their own at St. Félix
de Caraman near Toulouse. Their highest dignitary, Bishop Nicetas,
came from Constantinople to preside; bishops were elected for the
vacant sees of Toulouse, Val d'Aran, Carcassonne, Albi, and France
north of the Loire; commissioners were named to settle a disputed
boundary between the sees of Toulouse and Carcassonne; in short,
the business was that of an established and independent Church,
which looked upon itself as destined to supersede the Church of
Rome.

Its progress during the next ten years was such as to justify its
most enthusiastic hopes. Raymond V of Toulouse, whose power was
virtually that of an independent sovereign, adhered to Frederic
Barbarossa, acknowledged the antipope Victor and his successors,
and cared nothing for Alexander III, who was received by the rest of
France; and the Church, distracted by the Schism, could offer little
opposition to the development of heresy. By 1177, however, Alexander triumphed and received the submission of Frederic. Raymond
necessarily followed his suzerain and suddenly awoke to the necessity
of arresting the progress of heresy. Powerful as he was, he felt himself unequal to the task. The burgesses of his cities, independent
and intractable, were for the most part Cathari. A large portion of
his knights and gentlemen were secretly or avowedly protectors of
heresy; the common people throughout his dominions despised the
clergy and honored the heretics. In a state of chronic war with

powerful vassals and more powerful neighbors, it was impossible for Raymond to undertake the extermination of a half or more of his subjects. Whether he was sincere in his desire to suppress heresy is doubtful, but in any case his situation is interesting as an illustration of the difficulties which surrounded his son and grandson, and led to the crusades and the extinction of his house. Whatever his motives, Raymond craftily placed himself on the right side. He called upon the king, Louis VII, to come to his assistance, and applied to Bernard's successor, Henry of Clairvaux, head of the great Cistercian Order, to support his appeal. He described the condition of religion in his dominions as desperate. If the king would come, Raymond promised personally to conduct him through the land and point out the heretics to be chastised, and with their united efforts success could hardly fail to crown the good work.

Henry II of England, who as Duke of Aquitaine was nearly concerned in the matter, had just concluded a peace with Louis of France, and, free from the preoccupation of mutual war, the monarchs conferred together with the intention of proceeding in person with a heavy force in response to Raymond's appeal. The Abbot of Clairvaux also wrote to Alexander III, with more earnestness than courtesy, stimulating him to do his duty and put down heresy as he had quelled Schism; the least the pope could do was to instruct his legate, Cardinal Peter of St. Chrysogono, to remain longer in France and to attack the heretics. During these preliminaries the zeal of the monarchs cooled, and in place of marching at the head of armies they contented themselves with sending a mission consisting of the cardinal legate, the Archbishops of Narbonne and Bourges, Henry of Clairvaux and other prelates, at the same time urging the Count of Toulouse, the Viscount of Turenne, and other nobles to aid them.

If Raymond was sincere, this was not the assistance he required. The kings had resolved to depend upon the spiritual sword, and he was too shrewd to exhaust his strength in an unaided struggle with his subjects, especially as a menacing league was then forming against him by Alonso II of Aragon with the nobles of Narbonne, Nîmes, Montpellier, and Carcassonne. While, therefore, he protected the missionary prelates, he made no pretense of drawing the carnal sword. When they entered Toulouse the heretics crowded around them, peering and calling them hypocrites, apostates, and other opprobrious names; and Henry of Clairvaux consoles himself for the insignificant results of the mission with the reflection that if it had been postponed three years, they would not have found a Catholic in the city. Lists of heretics, interminable in length, were made out for them, at the head of which stood Pierre Mauran, an old man of great wealth and influence, and so universally respected by his co-religionists that he was popularly known as John the Evangelist. He was selected to be made an example. After many tergiversations he was convicted of heresy, when, to save his confiscated property, he agreed to recant and undergo such penance as might be assigned to him. Stripped to the waist, with the Bishop of Toulouse and the Abbot of St. Sernin busily scourging him on either side, he was led through an immense crowd to the high altar of the Cathedral of St. Stephen, where, for the good of his soul, he was ordered to undertake a three years' pilgrimage to the Holy Land, to be daily scourged through the streets of Toulouse until his departure, to make restitution of all Church lands occupied by him and of all moneys acquired by usury, and to pay to the count 500 pounds of silver in redemption of his forfeited property. This resolute beginning produced the desired effect, and multitudes of Cathari hastened to make their peace with the Church; but how little real result it had is shown by the fact that when Mauran returned from Palestine his fellow-citizens thrice honored him with election to the office of *capitoul*, and his family remained bitterly anti-Catholic.

In September 1178 Alexander III published the call for the assembling of the Third Council of Lateran, and an ominous allusion in it to the tares which choke the wheat and must be pulled up by the roots shows that he recognized the futility of all measures heretofore adopted to check the daily growing power of heresy. Accordingly, when the council met, in 1179, it bemoaned the damnable perversity of the Patarins, who publicly seduced the faithful throughout Gascony, the Albigeois, and the Toulousain; it commended the employment of force by the secular power to compel men to their own salvation; and it anathematized, as usual, the heretics and those who sheltered and protected them. It then proceeded to take a step of much significance in proclaiming a crusade against all these enemies of the Church—the first experiment of a resort to this weapon against Christians, which afterwards became so common and gave the Church in its private quarrels the services of a warlike militia in every land, ever ready to be mobilized. Two years' indulgence was promised to all who should take up arms in the holy cause; they were received under the protection of the Church, and those who should fall were assured of eternal salvation.

Immediately on his return from the council Pons, Archbishop of Narbonne, made haste to publish this decree, with all its anathemas and interdicts, and Henry of Clairvaux was sent as papal legate to preach and lead the crusade. His eloquence enabled him to raise a considerable force of horse and foot, with which, in 1187, he fell upon the territories of the Viscount of Béziers and laid siege to the stronghold of Lavaur, where the Viscountess Adelaide, daughter of Raymond of Toulouse, and the leading Patarins had taken refuge. We are told that Lavaur was captured through a miracle, and that in various parts of France consecrated wafers dropping blood announced the success of the Christian arms. Roger of Béziers hastened to make his submission and swear no longer to protect heresy. Raymond de Baimiac and Bernard Raymond, the Catharan bishops who were taken prisoners, renounced their heresy and were rewarded with prebends in two churches of Toulouse. Many other heretics gave in their submission but returned to the false faith as soon as the danger was past. The short term for which the crusaders had enlisted expired; the army disbanded, and the next year the cardinal-legate went back to Rome, having accomplished virtually nothing except to increase the mutual exasperation by the devastation of the country through which his troops had passed.

For a quarter of a century Catharism was allowed to develop in comparative toleration throughout the territories of Gascony, Languedoc, and Provence. There have been few crises in the history of the Church more dangerous than that which Lothario Conti, when he assumed the triple crown as Innocent III at the early age of 38, was called upon to meet. In his consecration sermon he announced that one of his principal duties would be the destruction of heresy, and of this he never lost sight to the end, amid his endless conflicts with emperors and princes. It is fortunate for civilization that he possessed the qualifications which enabled him to guide the shattered bark of St. Peter through the tempest and among the rocks —if not always wisely, yet with a resolute spirit, an unswerving purpose, and an unfailing trust that accomplished his mission in the end.

CHAPTER IV
THE ALBIGENSIAN CRUSADES

IN HIS opening address to the Great Lateran Council, Innocent III had no scruple in declaring to the assembled fathers: "The corruption of the people has its chief source in the clergy. From this arise the evils of Christendom: faith perishes, religion is defaced, liberty is restricted, justice is trodden under foot, the heretics multiply, the schismatics are emboldened, the faithless grow strong." Yet when in 1204 the legates Innocent sent to oppose the Albigenses appealed to him for aid against prelates whom they had failed to coerce, Innocent curtly bade them attend to the object of their mission and not allow themselves to be diverted by less important matters. The reply fairly indicates the policy of the Church. Thoroughly to cleanse the Augean stable was a task from which even Innocent's fearless spirit might well shrink.

It was the stronghold of heresy in southern France which gave rise to chief concern in Rome, and to this Innocent resolutely bent his energies. Raymond VI of Toulouse, in the full vigor of mature manhood, at the age of 38, had, in January 1195, succeeded his father in the possession of territories which rendered him the most powerful feudatory of the monarchy and almost an independent sovereign. Besides the county of Toulouse, the duchy of Narbonne conferred on him the dignity of first lay peer of France. He was likewise suzerain, with more or less direct authority, of the Marquisate of Provence, the Comtat Venaissin and the counties of St. Gilles, Foix, Comminges, and Rodez, and of the Albigeois, Vivarais, Gévaudan, Velai, Rouergue, Querci, and Agenois. So far as matrimonial alliances can have weight, Raymond was strengthened with them on every side, for he was of close kindred to the royal houses of Castile, Aragon, Navarre, France, and England. His fourth wife was Joan of England, whom he married in 1196 in pursuance of a favorable treaty with her brother Richard, thus relieving him of the enmity of that redoubtable warrior, who, as Duke of Aquitaine, had pressed his father hard. Almost at the same time he was liberated

from another formidable hereditary foe by the death of Alonso II of
Aragon, whose large possessions and still larger pretensions in
southern France had at times almost threatened the extinction of the
house of Toulouse. With his successor, Pedro II, Raymond's relations
were most friendly, cemented in 1200 by his marriage with Pedro's
sister Eleanor, and in 1205 by the engagement of his young son, Raymond VII, with Pedro's infant daughter. Though the distant sovereignty of France troubled him but little, yet the friendliness
manifested to him on his accession by Philip Augustus was a not unimportant element in the prosperity which on every side seemed to
give him assurance of a peaceful and fortunate reign. Thus secured
against external aggression and confident of the future, he recked
little of an excommunication which had been fulminated against him
in 1195 by Celestin III on account of the invasion of the rights of
the Abbey of St. Gilles—an excommunication which Innocent III
removed shortly after his accession, but not without words of reproof
and warning, which Raymond defiantly disregarded, thus laying the
foundation of a quarrel destined to result disastrously. Though not
a heretic, his indifference on religious questions led him to tolerate
the heresy of his subjects. Most of his barons were either heretics or
favorably inclined to a faith which, by denying the pretensions of
the Church, justified its spoliation, or, at least, liberated them from
its domination. Raymond himself was doubtless influenced by the
same motive, and when in 1195 the Council of Montpellier anathematized all princes who neglected to enforce the Lateran canons
against heretics and mercenaries, he paid no attention to its utterances. Toleration had endured for nearly a generation; the land was
blessed with peace after almost interminable war, and all the dictates
of worldly prudence counselled him to follow in his father's footsteps. Surrounded by one of the gayest and most cultured courts in
Christendom, fond of women, a patron of poets, somewhat irresolute
of purpose, and enjoying the love of his subjects, nothing could have
appeared to him more objectless than a persecution such as Rome
held to be the most indispensable of his duties.

   The condition of the Church in his dominions might well excite the indignation of a pontiff like Innocent III. A chronicler assures
us that among many thousands of the people there were but few
Catholics to be found; and although this is doubtless an exaggeration,

we have seen in the preceding chapter what rapid strides heresy had made. The evil was constantly increasing, and unless checked it seemed only a question of time when the Church would disappear throughout all the Mediterranean provinces of France. Yet it must be said for the credit of the heretics that there was no manifestation of a persecuting spirit on their part. The rapacity of the barons, it is true, was rapidly depriving the ecclesiastics of their revenues and possessions; as they neglected their duties, and as the law of the strongest was all-prevailing, the invader of Church property had small scruple in despoiling lazy monks and worldly priests; but the Cathari, however much they may have deemed themselves the Church of the future, seem never to have thought of extending their faith by force. They reasoned and argued and disputed when they found a Catholic zealous enough to contend with them, and they preached to the people; but, content with peaceable conversions and missionary work, they dwelt in perfect amity with their orthodox neighbors. To the Church this state of affairs was unbearable. By the very law of its being it can brook no rivalry in its domination over the human soul; and, in the present case, as toleration was slowly but surely leading to its destruction, it was bound by its sense of duty no less than of self-preservation to put an end to a situation so abhorrent.

Innocent was consecrated February 22, 1198, and by April 1st we find him writing to the Archbishop of Ausch, deploring the spread of heresy and the danger of its becoming universal. The prelate and his brethren are ordered to extirpate it by the utmost rigor of ecclesiastical censures, and if necessary by bringing the secular arm to bear though the assistance of princes and people. Not only are heretics themselves to be punished, but all who have any dealings with them. or who are suspect by reason of undue familiarity with them. By April 21st he had two commissioners ready to represent the Holy See on the spot—Rainier and Gui—whom he sent armed with letters to all the prelates, princes, nobles, and people of southern France, empowering them to enforce whatever regulations they might see fit to employ to avert the imminent peril to the Church arising from the countless increase of Cathari and Waldenses. Those heretics who will not return to the true faith are to be banished and their property confiscated; these provisions are to be enforced by the secular authorities under penalty of interdict for refusal or negligence, and with the reward for obedience of the same indulgences as those granted for a pilgrimage to Rome or Compostella; and all who consort or deal with heretics or show them favor or protection are to share their punishment. Rainier's powers evidently proved insufficient, and in July 1199 they were enlarged, both as a reformer and a persecutor, and he was appointed legate, to be received and obeyed with as much reverence as the pope himself.

For a time at least, these efforts at reform only rendered matters worse. Angered and humiliated by the powers conferred on the representatives of Rome, and alarmed at the attempts to punish their evil lives, the local prelates were in no mood to second the exertions put forth for the eradication of heresy, and at one time it would even seem as though they might be driven to make common cause with the heretics in order to protect themselves and their clergy. Rainier fell sick in the summer of 1202 and was replaced by Pierre de Castelnau and Raoul, two Cistercian monks of Fontfroide, who succeeded, after infinite trouble, by threats of the royal vengeance, in persuading the magistracy of Toulouse to swear to abjure heresy and expel heretics, in return for an oath pledging immunity and the preservation of the liberties of the city. Encouraged by this apparent success, they undertook the task of obtaining a similar oath from Count Raymond. When they summoned the Archbishop of Narbonne to accompany them to the count, however, he not only refused, but declined to aid them in any way, and it was only after long entreaty that he would even furnish them a horse for the journey. With the Bishop of Béziers their success was no better. He also declined to go with them to Raymond, and when they asked his co-operation in summoning the consuls of Béziers to abjure heresy and defend the Church against heretics, he not only withheld it, but impeded their efforts. Though he finally promised to excommunicate the magistrates for contumacy, he never did so, in spite of the fact that heresy so predominated in the town that the viscount was obliged to authorize the cathedral canons to fortify the Church of St. Peter for fear that the heretics would seize it.

Enough time had been lost in half-measures while the evil was daily increasing in magnitude, and Innocent proceeded to put forth the whole strength of the Church. To the monks of Fontfroide he adjoined as chief legate the "Abbot of abbots," Arnaud of Citeaux, head of the great Cistercian Order, a stern, resolute, and implacable man, full of zeal for the cause and gifted with rare persistency. Since the time of St. Bernard the abbots of Citeaux had seemed to feel a personal responsibility for the suppression of heresy in Languedoc, and Arnaud was better fitted for the work before him than any of his predecessors. To the legation thus constituted, at the end of May 1204 Innocent issued a fresh commission of extraordinary powers. The prelates of the infected provinces were ordered to obey humbly whatever the legates might see fit to command, and the vengeance of the Holy See was threatened for slackness or contumacy. Wherever heresy existed, the legates were armed with authority "to destroy, throw down, or pluck up whatever is to be destroyed, thrown down, or plucked up, and to plant and build whatever is to be built or planted." With one blow the independence of the local churches was destroyed and an absolute dictatorship was created. Not only were the legates directed to deliver all impenitent heretics to the secular arm for perpetual proscription and confiscation of property, but they were empowered to offer complete remission of sins, the same as for a crusade to the Holy Land, to Philip Augustus and his son, Louis Cœur-de-Lion, and to all nobles who should aid in the suppression of heresy. The dangerous classes were also stimulated by the prospect of pardon and plunder through a special clause authorizing the legates to absolve all under excommunication for crimes of violence who would join in persecuting heretics—an offer which subsequent correspondence shows was not unfruitful. To Philip Augustus, also, Innocent wrote at the same time, earnestly exhorting him to draw the sword and slay the wolves who had thus far found no one to withstand their ravages in the fold of the Lord. If he could not proceed in person, let him send his son, or some experienced leader, and exercise the power conferred on him for the purpose by Heaven. Not only was remission of sins promised him, as for a voyage to Palestine, but he was empowered to seize and add to his dominions the territories of all nobles who might not join in persecution and expel the hated heretic.

Innocent might well feel disheartened at the failure of this vigorous move. The prelates of the infected provinces, indignant at the usurpation of their rights, were less disposed than ever to second the efforts of the legates. Philip Augustus was unmoved by the dazzling bribes, spiritual and temporal, offered to him. He had already had the benefit of an indulgence for a crusade to the Holy Land, and had probably not found his spiritual estate much benefited thereby; while his recent acquisitions in Normandy, Anjou, Poitou, and Aquitaine, at the expense of John of England, required his whole attention, and might be endangered by creating fresh enmities in too sudden a renewal of conquest. He took no steps, therefore, in response to the impassioned arguments of Innocent, and the legates found the heretics more obdurate than ever.

The case seemed desperate, when a new light fell as though from heaven upon those groping blindly in the darkness. About midsummer in 1206 the three legates met at Montpellier, and the result of their conference was a determination to withdraw from the thankless labor. By chance, a Spanish prelate, Diego de Azevedo, Bishop of Osma, arrived there on his return from Rome, where he had vainly supplicated Innocent to permit his resignation of his bishopric in order that he might devote his life to missionary work among the infidel. On learning the decision of the legates, he earnestly dissuaded them, and suggested their dismissing their splendid retinues and worldly pomp and going among the people, barefooted and poor like the apostles, to preach the Word of God. The idea was so novel that the legates hesitated, but finally assented, if an example were set them by one in authority. Diego offered himself for the purpose and was accepted, whereupon he sent his servitors home, retaining only his sub-prior, Domingo [Dominic] de Guzman, who had already, on the voyage towards Rome, converted a heretic in Toulouse. Arnaud returned to Citeaux to hold a General Chapter of the Order and to obtain recruits for the missionary work, while the other two legates with Diego and Dominic commenced their experiment at Caraman, where for eight days they disputed with the heresiarchs Baldwin and Thierry. We are told that they converted all the simple folk, but that the lord of the castle would not allow the two disputants to be expelled.

With the opening of spring in 1207, Arnaud had held his chapter and obtained numerous volunteers for the pious work, among them no less than twelve abbots. Taking boats, they descended the Saone to the Rhone and proceeded to their field of labor, where they separated into twos and threes, wandering barefoot among the towns and villages. For three months they labored diligently, finding thousands of heretics and few orthodox, but the harvest was scanty and conversions rarely rewarded their pains—in fact, the only practical result was to excite the heretics to renewed missionary zeal. It speaks well for the tolerant temper of the Cathari that men who had been invoking the most powerful sovereigns of Christendom to exterminate them should have incurred no real danger in a task apparently so full of risk. The missionaries had to complain of occasional insult, but never were even threatened with injury, except perhaps, at Béziers, Pierre de Castelnau, who seems to have attracted to himself the special dislike of the sectaries. It shows, moreover, the zealous care with which the Church restricted the office of preaching that the legates, in spite of the extraordinary powers with which they were clothed, felt obliged to apply to Innocent for special authority to confer the license to teach in public on those whom they deemed worthy. The favorable answer of the pope was in reality one of the important events of the century, for it gave the impulsion out of which eventually grew the great Dominican Order.

Pierre de Castelnau left his colleagues and visited Provence to make peace among the nobles, in the hope of uniting them for the expulsion of heretics. Raymond of Toulouse refused to lay down his arms until the intrepid monk excommunicated him and laid his dominions under interdict, reproaching him bitterly to his face for his perjuries and other misdeeds. Raymond submitted in patience to this reproof, while Pierre applied to Innocent for confirmation of the sentence. By this time Raymond had acquired the special hatred of the papalists, through his neglect to persecute his heretical subjects, in spite of his readiness to take what oaths were required of him. They accused him of being at heart a heretic, and stories were circulated that he always carried with him perfected heretics, disguised in ordinary vestments, together with a New Testament, that he might be hereticated in case of sudden death; that he knew that he would in the end be disinherited for the sake of the "Good Men," but that he was ready to suffer even beheading for them. All this and much more, including exaggerated gossip about his undoubted frailties, was diligently published in order to render him odious, but there is no proof that his religious indifference ever led him to deviate from the faith, and no accusation that he had ever interfered with the legates in their mission. They were free to make what converts they could by persuasion or argument, but he committed the unpardonable crime of refusing to plunge his dominions in blood.

Innocent promptly confirmed the sentence of his legate, May 29, 1207, in an epistle to Raymond which was an unreserved expression of the passions accumulated through long years of zealous effort frustrated in its results. In the harshest vituperation of ecclesiastical rhetoric, Raymond was threatened with the vengeance of God here and hereafter. The excommunication and interdict were to be strictly observed until due satisfaction and obedience were rendered; and he was warned that these must be speedy, or he would be deprived of certain territories which he held of the Church, and if this did not suffice, the princes of Christendom would be summoned to seize and partition his dominions. Yet in the recital of misdeeds which were held to justify this rigorous sentence there was nothing that had not been for two generations so universal in Languedoc that it might almost be regarded as a part of the public law of the land. He had continued to wage war when desired by the legates to make peace, and had refused to suspend operations on feast-days or holidays; he had violated his oaths to purge his land of heresy, and had shown such favor to heretics as to render his own faith vehemently suspected; in derision of the Christian religion he had bestowed public office on Jews; he had despoiled the Church and ill-treated certain bishops; he had continued to employ bands of mercenaries and had increased the tolls. Such is the summary of crime alleged against him, which we may reasonably assume to cover everything possibly susceptible of proof.

Innocent waited awhile to prove the effect of this threat and the results of the missionary effort so auspiciously started by Bishop Azevedo. Both were null. Raymond, indeed, made peace with the Provençal nobles, and was released from excommunication, but he showed no signs of awakening from his exasperating indifference on the religious question, while the Cistercian abbots, disheartened by the obstinacy of the heretics, dropped off one by one, and retired to their monasteries. Legate Raoul died, and Arnaud of Citeaux was called elsewhere by important affairs. Bishop Azevedo went to Spain to set his diocese in order and return to devote his life to the work; but he, too, died when on the point of setting out. He had left

behind him the saintly Dominic, who was quietly bringing together
a few ardent souls, the germs of the great Order of Preachers, and
Pierre de Castelnau remained as the sole representative of Rome until
Raoul was replaced by the Bishop of Conserans. Everything had been
tried and had failed, except the appeal to the sword, and to this Innocent again recurred with all the energy of despair. A milder tone
towards Philip Augustus with regard to his matrimonial complications between Ingeburga of Denmark and Agnes of Meran might
predispose him to vindicate the wrongs of the Church; but, while
condescending to this, Innocent now addressed not only the king
but all the faithful throughout France, and the leading magnates
were honored with special missives. November 16, 1207, the letters
were sent out, representing the incessant and alarming growth of
heresy and the failure of all endeavors to bring the heretics to reason.
Nothing was left but an appeal to arms; and to all who would
embark in this good work the same indulgences were offered as for
a crusade to Palestine. The lands of all engaged in it were taken
under the special protection of the Church, and those of the heretics
were abandoned to the spoiler. All creditors of crusaders were
obliged to postpone their claims without interest, and clerks taking
part were empowered to pledge their revenues in advance for two
years.

Earnest and impassioned as was this appeal, it fell, like the
previous one, upon deaf ears. Philip Augustus coolly responded that
his relations with England did not allow him to let the forces of his
kingdom be divided, but that, if he could be assured of a two years'
truce, then, if the barons and knights of France wanted to undertake
a crusade, he would permit them, and aid it with 50 livres a day for
a year. Apparently the present effort was destined to prove as inefficient as the former one had been, when a startling incident suddenly
changed the whole aspect of affairs. The murder of Pierre de Castelnau sent a thrill of horror throughout Christendom like that caused
by the assassination of Becket thirty-eight years before. Of its details
the accounts are so contradictory that it is impossible to speak of it
with precision. This much we know, that Pierre had greatly angered
Raymond by the bitterness of his personal reproaches; that the count,
aroused by the sense of impending danger in the fresh call for a
crusade, had invited the legates to an interview at St. Gilles, promis-

ing to show himself in all things an obedient son of the Church; that difficulties arose in the conference, the demands of the legates being greater than Raymond was willing to concede. The Romance version of the catastrophe is that, during the conference, Pierre became entangled in an angry religious dispute with one of the gentlemen of the court, who drew his dagger and slew him; that the count was greatly concerned at an event so deplorable, and would have taken summary vengeance on the murderer but for his escape and hiding with friends at Beaucaire. The story carried to Rome by the Bishops of Conserans and Toulouse, who hastened thither to inflame Innocent against Raymond, was that, wearied with the count's tergiversations, the legates announced their intentions to withdraw, when Raymond was heard to threaten them with death, saying that he would track them by land and water. That the Abbot of St. Gilles and the citizens, unable to appease his wrath, furnished the legates with an escort, and they reached the Rhone in safety, where they passed the night. While preparing to cross the river in the morning (January 16, 1208), two strangers who had joined the party approached the legates, and one of them suddenly thrust his lance through Pierre, who, turning on his murderer, said, "May God forgive thee, for I forgive thee!" and speedily breathed his last; and that Raymond, so far from punishing the crime, protected and rewarded the perpetrator, even honoring him with a seat at his own table. It may well be that a proud and powerful prince, exasperated by continued objurgation and menace, may have uttered some angry expression, which an overzealous servitor hastened to translate into action, and Raymond, certainly, never was able to clear himself of suspicion of complicity; but there are not wanting indications to show that Innocent eventually regarded his exculpation as satisfactory.

The crime gave the Church an enormous advantage, of which Innocent hastened to make the most. On March 10 he issued letters to all the prelates in the infected provinces commanding that, in all churches, on every Sunday and feast-day, the murderers and their abettors, including Raymond, be excommunicated with bell, book, and candle, and every place cursed with their presence was declared under interdict. As no faith was to be kept with him who kept not faith with God, all of Raymond's vassals were released from their oaths of allegiance, and his lands were declared the prey of any Catholic who might assail them, while, if he applied for pardon, his first sign of repentance must be the extermination of heresy throughout his dominions. These letters were also sent to Philip Augustus and his chief barons, with eloquent adjurations to assume the cross and rescue the imperilled Church from the assaults of the emboldened heretics; commissioners were sent to negotiate and enforce a truce for two years between France and England, that nothing might interfere with the projected crusade, and every effort was made to transmute into warlike zeal the horror which the sacrilegious murder was so well fitted to arouse. Arnaud of Citeaux hastened to call a General Chapter of his Order, where it was unanimously resolved to devote all its energies to preaching the crusade, and soon multitudes of monks were inflaming the passions of the people and offering redemption in every church and on every market-place in Europe.

Other special motives contributed in this case to render the crusade attractive. There was antagonism of race, jealousy of the wealth and more advanced civilization of the south, and a natural desire to complete the Frankish conquest so often begun and never yet accomplished. More than all, the pardon to be gained was the same as that for the prolonged, dangerous, and costly expedition to Palestine, while here the distance was short and the term of service limited to forty days. Whether Philip Augustus contributed in men or money is more than doubtful, but he made no opposition to the service of his barons, and endeavored to turn his acquiescence to account in the affair of his divorce, while he declined personal participation on the ground of the threatening aspect of his relations with King John and the Emperor Otho. He significantly warned the pope, however, that Raymond's territories could not be exposed to seizure until he had been condemned for heresy, which had not yet been done, and that when such condemnation should be pronounced it would be for the suzerain, and not for the Holy See, to proclaim the penalty. This was strictly in accordance with existing law, for the principle had not yet been introduced into European jurisprudence that suspicion of heresy annulled all rights—a principle which the case of Raymond went far to establish, for the Church without a trial stripped him of his possessions and then decided that he had forfeited them, after which the king could only acquiesce in the decision.

Scruples of this kind, however, did not dampen the zeal of those whom the Church summoned to defend the faith. Recruits were drawn from distant Bremen on the one hand, and Lombardy on the other, and we even hear of Slavonian barons leaving the original home of Catharism to combat it in its seat of latest development. It was during the preaching of this crusade that villages and towns in Germany were filled with women who, unable to expend their religious ardor in taking the cross, stripped themselves naked and ran silently through the roads and streets.

All this was necessarily a work of time, and Raymond sought in the interval to conjure the coming storm. Roused at last from his dream of security, he recognized the fatal position in which the murder of the legate had placed him. He hastened to his uncle, Philip Augustus, who received him kindly and counselled submission, but forbade an appeal to his enemy, the Emperor Otho. Raymond, however, in his despair, sought the emperor, whose vassal he was for his territories beyond the Rhone, obtaining no help, and incurring the ill-will of Philip, which was of much greater moment. On his return, learning that Arnaud was about to hold a council at Aubinas, Raymond hurried thither with his nephew, the young Raymond Roger, Viscount of Béziers, and endeavored to prove his innocence and make his peace, but was coldly refused a hearing, and was referred to Rome. Returning much disconcerted, he took counsel with his nephew, who advised resisting the invasion to the death; but Raymond's courage was unequal to the manly part. They quarrelled, whereupon the hotheaded youth commenced to make war on his uncle, while the latter sent envoys to Rome for terms of submission, and asked for new and impartial legates to replace those who were irrevocably prejudiced against him. Innocent demanded that, as security for his good faith, Raymond should place in the hands of the Church his seven most important strongholds, after which he should be heard and, if he could prove his innocence, be absolved. Raymond gladly ratified the conditions, and earnestly welcomed Milo and Theodisius, the new representatives of the Church, who treated him with such apparent friendliness that, when Milo subsequently died at Arles, Raymond mourned greatly, believing that he had lost a protector who would have saved him from his misfortunes. He did not know that the legates had secret instructions from Innocent to amuse him with fair promises, to detach him from the heretics, and when they should be disposed of by the crusaders, to deal with him as they should see fit.

The seven castles were duly delivered to Master Theodisius, thus fatally crippling Raymond for resistance; the consuls of Avignon, Nîmes, and St. Gilles were sworn to renounce their allegiance to him if he did not obey implicitly the future commands of the pope, and he was reconciled to the Church by the most humiliating of cere-monies. The new legate, Milo, with some twenty archbishops and bishops, went to St. Gilles, and there, June 18, 1209, arrayed them-selves before the portal of the Church of St. Gilles. Stripped to the waist, Raymond was brought before them as a penitent, and swore on the relics of St. Gilles to obey the Church in all matters whereof he was accused. Then the legate placed a stole around his neck, in the fashion of a halter, and led him into the church, while he was industriously scourged on his naked back and shoulders up to the altar, where he was absolved. The curious crowd assembled to witness the degradation of their lord was so great that return through the entrance was impossible, and Raymond was carried down to the crypt where the martyred Pierre de Castelnau lay buried. Besides the extirpation of heresy, he was to dismiss all Jews from office and all his mercenary bands from his service; he was to restore all prop-erty of which the churches had been despoiled, to keep the roads safe, to abolish all arbitrary tolls, and to observe strictly the Truce of God.

All that Raymond had gained by these sacrifices was the privi-lege of joining the crusade and assisting in the subjugation of his country. It is true that in July, Innocent wrote to Raymond benig-nantly congratulating him on his purgation and submission, and promising him that it should redound to his worldly as well as spiritual benefit; but the same courier carried a letter to Milo urging him to continue as he had begun; and Milo, on whom Raymond was basing his hopes, soon after, hearing a report that the count had gone to Rome, warned his master, with superabundant caution, not to spoil the game.

"As for the Count of Toulouse," writes the legate, "that enemy of truth and justice, if he has sought your presence to recover the castles in my hands, as he boasts that he can easily do, be not moved by his tongue, skillful only in his slanders, but let him, as he deserves, feel the hand of the Church heavier day by day. After I had received security for his oath on at least fifteen heads, he has perjured himself on them all. Thus he has manifestly forfeited his rights on Melgueil as well as the seven castles which I hold. They are so strong by nature and art that, with the assistance of the barons and people who are devoted to the Church, it will be easy to drive him from the land which he has polluted with his vileness."

The absolution which had cost so much was withdrawn, and Raymond was again excommunicated and his dominions laid under a fresh interdict, because he had not, within 60 days, during which he was with the crusaders, performed the impossible task of expelling all heretics, and the city of Toulouse lay under a special anathema because it had not delivered to the crusaders all the heretics among its citizens. Subsequently a delay until All-Saints' (Nov. 1) was mercifully granted to Raymond to perform all the duties imposed on him; but he was evidently prejudged and nothing but his destruction would satisfy the implacable legates.

Meanwhile the crusaders had assembled in numbers such as never before, according to the delighted Abbot of Citeaux, had been gathered together in Christendom. The legates had been empowered to levy what sums they saw fit from all the ecclesiastics in the kingdom, and to enforce the payment by excommunication. As for the laity, their revenues were likewise subjected to the legatine discretion, with the proviso that they were not to be coerced into payment without the consent of their seigneurs. With all the wealth of the realm thus under contribution, it was not difficult to provide for the motley host whose campaign opened under a spirit-stirring adjuration of the vicegerent of God.

Under this inspiration the crusaders assembled at Lyons about St. John's day (June 24, 1209), and Raymond hastened from the scene of his humiliation at St. Gilles to complete his infamy by leading them against his countrymen, offering them his son as a hostage in pledge of his good faith. He was welcomed by them at Valence, and, under the supreme command of Legate Arnaud, guided them against his nephew of Béziers. The latter, after a vain attempt at composition with the legate, had hurriedly placed his strongholds in condition of defense and levied what forces he could to resist the onset.

The war, despite its religious origin, was already assuming a national character. The position taken by Raymond and the rejected submission of the Viscount of Béziers, deprived the Church of all colorable excuse for further action; but the men of the north were eager to complete the conquest commenced seven centuries before by Clovis, and the men of the south, Catholics as well as heretics, were virtually unanimous in resisting the invasion. We hear nothing of religious dissensions among them, and comparatively little of assistance rendered to the invaders by the orthodox, who might be presumed to welcome the crusaders as liberators from the domination of a hated antagonistic faith. Toleration had become habitual and race instinct was too strong for religious feeling, presenting almost the solitary example of the kind during the Middle Ages, when nationality had not yet been developed out of feudalism and religious interests were universally regarded as dominant. This explains the remarkable fact that the pusillanimous course of Raymond was distasteful to his own subjects, who were constantly urging him to resistance, and who clung to him and his son with a fidelity that no misfortune or selfishness could shake, until the extinction of the House of Toulouse left them without a leader.

Raymond Roger had fortified and garrisoned his capital, and then, to the great discouragement of his people, had withdrawn to the safer stronghold of Carcassonne. Reginald, Bishop of Béziers, was with the crusading forces, and when they arrived before Béziers, humanely desiring to save it from destruction, he obtained from the legate authority to offer it full exemption if the heretics, of whom he had a list, were delivered up or expelled. Nothing could be more moderate from the crusading standpoint, but when he entered the town and called the chief inhabitants together the offer was unanimously spurned. Catholic and Catharan were too firmly united in the bonds of common citizenship for one to betray the other. They would, as they declared, although abandoned by their lord, rather defend themselves to such extremity that they should be reduced to eat their children. This unexpected answer stirred the legate to such wrath that he swore to destroy the place with fire and sword—to spare neither age nor sex, and not to leave one stone upon another.

While the chiefs of the army were debating as to the next step, suddenly the camp followers, a vile and unarmed folk, as the legates reported inspired by God, made a rush for the walls and carried them, without orders from the leaders and without their knowledge. The army followed, and the legate's oath was fulfilled by a massacre almost without parallel in European history. From infancy in arms to tottering age, not one was spared—7,000, it is said, were slaughtered in the Church of Mary Magdalen to which they had fled for asylum —and the total number of slain is set down by the legates at nearly 20,000, which is more probable than the 60,000 or 100,000 reported by less trustworthy chroniclers. A fervent Cistercian contemporary informs us that when Arnaud was asked whether the Catholics should be spared, he fiercely replied, "Kill them all, for God knows his own!" In the mad carnage the town was set on fire, and the sun of that awful July day closed on a mass of smoldering ruins and blackened corpses.

Similar good-fortune had attended the smaller crusading armies on their way to join the main body. One, under the Viscount of Turenne and Gui d'Auvergne, had captured the almost impregnable castle of Chasseneuil after a short siege. The garrison obtained terms and were allowed to depart, but the inhabitants were left to the discretion of the conquerors. The choice between conversion and the stake was offered them, and, proving obstinate in their errors, they were pitilessly burned. Such terror pervaded the land that when a fugitive came to the Castle of Villemur falsely reporting that the crusaders were coming and would treat it like the rest, the inhabitants abandoned it under cover of the night and themselves set it on fire. Innumerable strongholds, in fact, were surrendered without a blow, or were found vacant, though amply provisioned and strengthened for a siege, and a mountainous region bristling with castles, which would have cost years to conquer if obstinately defended, was occupied in a campaign of a month or two. The populous and mutinous town of Narbonne, to save itself, adopted the severest laws against heresy, raised a large subvention in aid of the crusade, and surrendered sundry castles as security.

Without dallying over the ruins of Béziers, the crusaders, till under the guidance of Raymond, moved swiftly to Carcassonne, a place regarded as impregnable, where Raymond Roger had elected to make his final stand. On August 1st, only nine days after the sack of Béziers, a regular siege was commenced. The outer suburb, which was scarce defensible, was carried and burned after a desperate resistance. The second suburb, strongly fortified, cost a prolonged effort, in which all the resources of the military art of the day were brought into play on both sides, and when it was no longer tenable the besieged evacuated and burned it. There remained the city itself, the capture of which seemed hopeless. Terms were offered to the viscount; he was free to depart with eleven of his own choosing, if the city and its people were abandoned to the discretion of the crusaders, but he rejected the proposal with indignation. Still, the situation was becoming insupportable; the town was crowded with refugees from the surrounding country; the summer had been cursed with drought, and the water supply had given out, causing a pestilence under which the wretched people were daily dying by scores. In his anxiety for peace the young viscount allowed himself to be decoyed into the besieging camp, where he was treacherously detained as a prisoner—dying shortly after, it was said of dysentery, but not without well-grounded suspicions of foul play. Deprived of their chief, the people lost heart; but to avoid the destruction of the city, they were allowed to depart, carrying with them nothing but their sins— the men in their breeches and the women in their chemises—and the place was occupied without further struggle. Curiously enough, we hear nothing of any investigation into their faith, or any burning of heretics.

The siege of Carcassonne brings before us two men, with whom we shall have much to do hereafter, representing so typically the opposing elements in the contest that we may well pause for a moment to give them consideration. These are Pedro II of Aragon and Simon de Montfort.

Pedro was the suzerain of Béziers, and the young viscount was bound to him with ties of close friendship. Though when appealed to in advance for aid he had declined, yet when he heard of the sack of Béziers he hurried to Carcassonne to mediate if possible for his vassal, though his efforts were fruitless. He was everywhere regarded as a model for the chivalry of the South. Heroic in stature and trained in every knightly accomplishment, he was ever in the front of battle; and on the tremendous day of *Las Navas de Tolosa*, which broke the Moorish power in Spain, it was he, by common consent, among all the kings and nobles present, who won the loftiest renown. In the bower he was no less dangerous than in the field. His gallantries were countless, and his licentiousness notorious, even in that age of easy morals. He was munificent to prodigality, fond of magnificent display, courteous to all comers, and magnanimous to all enemies. Like his father, Alonso II, moreover, he was a troubadour, and his songs won applause, none the less hearty, perhaps, that he was a liberal patron of rival poets. With all this his religious zeal was ardent, and he gloried in the title of el *Católico*. This he manifested not only in the savage edict against the Waldenses, referred to in a previous chapter, but by an extraordinary act of devotion to the Holy See. In 1095 his ancestor, Pedro I, had placed the kingdom of Aragon under the special protection of the popes, from whom his successors were to receive it on their accession and to pay an annual tribute of 500 mancuses. In 1204 Pedro II resolved to perform this act of fealty in person. With a splendid retinue he sailed for Rome, where he took an oath of allegiance to Innocent, including a pledge to persecute heresy. He was crowned with a crown of unleavened bread, and received from the pope the scepter, mantle, and other royal insignia, which he reverently laid upon the altar of St. Peter, to whom he offered his kingdom, taking in lieu his sword from Innocent, subjecting his realm to an annual tribute, and renouncing all rights of patronage over churches and benefices. As an equivalent for all this he was satisfied with the title of First Alferez or Standard-Bearer of the Church and the privilege for his successors of being crowned by the Archbishop of Tarragona in his cathedral church. Impulsive and generous, Pedro's career reads like a romance of chivalry, and, with such a character, it was impossible for him to avoid participating in the Albigensian wars, in which he had a direct interest, owing to his claims upon Provence, Montpellier, Béarn, Roussillon, Gascony, Comminges, and Béziers.

In marked contrast with this splendid knight-errantry was the solid and earnest character of de Montfort, who had distinguished himself, as was his wont, at the siege of Carcassonne. He was the first to lead in the assault on the outer suburb; and when an attack upon the second had been repulsed and a crusader was left writhing in the ditch with a broken thigh, de Montfort with a single squire leaped

back into it, under a shower of missiles, and bore him off in safety.
The younger son of the Count of Evreux, a descendant of Rollo the
Norman, he was Earl of Leicester by right of his mother the heiress,
and had won a distinguished name for prowess in the field and
wisdom and eloquence in the council. Religious to bigotry, he never
passed a day without hearing mass; and the true-hearted affection
which his wife, Alice of Montmorency, bore him, shows that his
reputation for chastity—a rare virtue in those days—was probably not
undeserved. In 1201 he had joined the crusade of Baldwin of
Flanders; and when, during the long detention in Venice, the crusaders sold their services to the Venetians for the destruction of
Zara, de Montfort alone refused, saying that he had come to fight
the infidel and not to make war on Christians. He left the host in
consequence, made his way to Apulia, and with a few friends took
ship to Palestine, where he served the cross with honor. When the
Albigensian crusade was preached, one of the Cistercian abbots who
devoted himself most earnestly to the work was Gui of Vaux-Cernay,
who had been a crusader with de Montfort at Venice. It was owing
to Gui's persuasion that the Duke of Burgundy took the cross on the
present occasion, and he was the bearer of letters from the duke to
de Montfort making him splendid offers if he would also take up
arms. At de Montfort's castle of Rochefort, Gui found the pious
count in his oratory, and set forth the object of his mission. De
Montfort hesitated, and then, taking up a psalter, opened it at
random and placed his finger on a verse which he asked the abbot
to translate for him. It read:

For he shall give his angels charge over thee, to keep thee in all thy
ways. They shall bear thee in their hands, that thou hurt not thy foot
against a stone (Ps. xci. 11, 12).

The divine encouragement was manifest. De Montfort took the
cross, which was to be his life's work, and the brilliant valor of the
Catalan knight proved no match for the deep earnestness of the
Norman, who felt himself an instrument in the hand of God.

With the capture of Carcassonne, the brief service of forty days
which sufficed to earn pardon was rendered, and the crusaders were
eager to return home. The legate naturally held that the conquered

territory was to be so occupied and organized that heresy should have no further foothold there, and it was offered first to the Duke of Burgundy and then successively to the Counts of Nevers and St. Pol, but all were too wary to be tempted, and alleged in refusal that the Viscount of Béziers had already been sufficiently punished. Then two bishops and four knights, with Arnaud at their head, were appointed to select the one on whom the confiscated land should be bestowed; and these seven unanimously selected de Montfort. We may well believe, from his reputation for sagacity, that his unwillingness to accept the offer was unfeigned, and that after prayers had proved unavailing, he yielded only to the absolute commands of the legate, speaking with all the authority of the Holy See. He made it a condition, however, that the continued and efficient support which he foresaw would be requisite should be given him. This was duly promised, with little intention of fulfillment. The Count of Nevers, between whom and the Duke of Burgundy a mortal quarrel had arisen, withdrew almost immediately after the capture of Carcassonne, and with him the great body of the crusaders. The duke remained for a short time, when he likewise turned his face homewards, and de Montfort was left with but about 4,500 men, mostly Burgundians and Germans, for whose services he was obliged to offer double pay.

De Montfort's position was perilous in the extreme. It mattered little that in August, during the full flush of success, the legates had held a council in Avignon which ordered all bishops to swear every knight, noble, and magistrate in their dioceses to exterminate heresy. Such oaths were but an empty form, and the homage which de Montfort received from his new vassals was equally hollow. It is true that he regulated his boundaries with Raymond, who promised to marry his son with du Montfort's daughter, and he styled himself Viscount of Béziers and Carcassonne, but Pedro of Aragon refused to receive his homage, and secretly comforted the castellans who still held out with promises of early assistance, while others who had submitted revolted, and castles which had been occupied were recaptured. The country was recovering from its terror. An annoying partisan warfare sprang up; small parties of his men were cut off, and his rule extended no farther than the reach of his lance. Yet with all this he succeeded in subduing additional strongholds, and extended his dominion over the Albigeois and into the territory of the Count of Foix. He hastened, moreover, to acquire the good graces of Innocent, whose confirmation of his new dignity was requisite, and whose influence for further succor he earnestly implored. All tithes and first fruits were to be rigorously paid to the churches; anyone remaining under excommunication for forty days was to be heavily fined according to his station; Rome was to receive from the devastated land an annual tax of 3 deniers on every hearth, while a yearly tribute from the count himself was vaguely promised. To this, in November, Innocent replied, full of joy at the wonderful success which had wrested 500 cities and castles from the grasp of heretics. He graciously accepted the offered tribute, and confirmed de Montfort's title to both Béziers and Albi, with an adjuration to be sleepless in the extirpation of heresy; but he could scarce have appreciated the crusader's perilous position, for he excused himself from efficient aid on the score of complaints which reached him from Palestine that the succor sorely needed there had been diverted to subdue heretics nearer home. He therefore only called upon the Emperor Otho, the Kings of Aragon and Castile, and sundry cities and nobles from whom no real aid could be expected. The archbishops of the whole infected region were directed to persuade their clergy to contribute to him a portion of their revenues, and his troops were exhorted to be patient and to ask no pay until the following Easter.

After losing most of his conquests, de Montfort's position became more hopeful towards the spring of 1210, as his forces were swelled by the arrival of successive bands of "pilgrims"—as these peaceful folk were accustomed to style themselves—and his ambitious views expanded. The short term for which the cross was assumed rendered it necessary to turn the newcomers to immediate account, and de Montfort was unceasingly active in recovering his ground and in reducing the castles which still held out. It is not worth our while to follow in detail these exploits of military religious ardor, which, when successful, were usually crowned by putting the garrison to the sword and offering the noncombatants the choice between obedience to Rome and the stake. The spirit of the respective parties was well exhibited at the capitulation of Minerve, where Robert Mauvoisin, de Montfort's most faithful follower, objected to the clause which spared the heretics who should recant, and was told by Legate

Arnaud that he need not fear the conversion of many, as ample experience had shown their prevailing obstinacy. Arnaud was right; for, with the exception of three women, they unanimously refused to secure safety by apostasy, and saved their captors the trouble of casting them on the blazing pyre by leaping exultingly into the flames.

If Raymond had fancied that he had skillfully saved himself at the expense of his nephew of Béziers, he had at last discovered his mistake. Arnaud of Citeaux had fully resolved upon his ruin, and de Montfort was eager to extend his lordship and the purity of the faith. Already, in the autumn of 1209, the citizens of Toulouse had been startled by a demand from the legate to surrender all whom his envoys might select as heretics, under pain of excommunication and interdict. They protested that there were no heretics among them; that all who were named were ready to purge themselves of heresy; that Raymond V had, at their instance, passed laws against heretics, under which they had burned many and were burning all who could be found. Therefore they appealed to the pope, naming January 29, 1210, as the day for the hearing. At the same time de Montfort had notified Raymond that unless the legate's demands were conceded he would assail him and enforce obedience. Raymond replied that he would settle the matter with the pope, and lost no time in appealing in person to Philip Augustus and the Emperor Otho, from whom he received only fair words. On reaching Rome he was apparently more fortunate. He had a strong case. He had never been convicted, or even tried, for the crimes whereof he was accused; he had always professed obedience to the Church and readiness to prove his innocence, according to the legal methods of the age, by the canonical purgation; he had undergone cruel penance as though convicted, and had been absolved as though forgiven, since when he had rendered faithful and valuable service against his friends and had made what reparation he could to the churches he had despoiled. He boldly asserted his innocence, demanded a trial, and claimed the restoration of his castles. Innocent seems at first to have been touched by the wrongs inflicted on him. The citizens of Toulouse he pronounced to have justified themselves, and ordered their excommunication removed. As regards Raymond, he instructed the Archbishops of Narbonne and Arles to assemble a council of prelates and nobles for the trial which Raymond so earnestly demanded. If there an accuser should assert his heresy and responsibility for the murder of Pierre de Castelnau, both sides should be heard and judgment be rendered and sent to Rome for final decision; if no formal accuser appeared, then fitting purgation should be assigned to him, on performance of which he should be declared a good Catholic and his castles be restored. All this was fair seeming enough, yet in an accompanying letter to the legate Arnaud, Innocent praises him warmly for what had been done and explains that the conduct of the matter has been ostensibly entrusted to the new commissioner, Master Theodisius, merely as a lure for Raymond; or, to use the pope's own words, that the legate was to be the hook of which Theodisius was the bait. To lull Raymond to a more complete sense of security, on his final audience Innocent presented him with a rich mantle and with a ring which he drew from his own finger.

Joy reigned in Toulouse when the count returned, bringing with him the removal of the interdict and the promise of a speedy settlement of the troubles. Legate Arnaud entered fully into the spirit of his instructions and suddenly became friendly. We even hear of a visit paid by him and de Montfort to Raymond in Toulouse, where they were magnificently received; and Raymond, it is said, was persuaded to give the citadel of the town, known as the Château Narbonnois, as a residence to the legate, from whose hands it passed into those of de Montfort, costing eventually the lives of a thousand men for its recapture. Arnaud, moreover, exacted a promise of 1,000 livres toulousains from the citizens before he would give effect to the papal letters removing the interdict; when one half was paid, he gave them his benediction, but a delay in raising the other half caused him to renew the interdict, which cost them much trouble to remove.

Master Theodisius joined the legate at Toulouse, as we are told by a fiercely orthodox eyewitness, for the purpose of consulting with him as to the most plausible excuse for eluding Innocent's promise to Raymond of an opportunity of purgation, for they foresaw that he would purge himself and that the destruction of the faith would follow. The readiest method of obtaining this object lay in Raymond's failure to perform the impossible task assigned him of clearing his lands of heresy; but in order to avoid the appearance of premeditated unfairness, the solemn mockery was arranged of assigning him a day three months distant, to appear at St. Gilles and offer his purgation as to heresy and the murder of the legate—a warning being added about his slackness in persecution. At the appointed time, in September 1210, a number of prelates and nobles were assembled at St. Gilles, and Raymond presented himself with his compurgators in the full confidence of a final reconciliation with the Church. He was coolly informed that his purgation would not be received; that he was manifestly a perjurer in not having executed the promises to which he had repeatedly sworn, and his oath being worthless in minor matters, it could not be accepted in charges so weighty as those of heresy and legate-murder, nor were those of his accomplices any better. A man of stronger character would have been roused to indignation at this contemptuous revelation of the deception practiced on him; but Raymond, overwhelmed with the sudden destruction of his illusions, simply burst into tears—which was duly recorded by his judges as an additional proof of his innate depravity, and he was promptly again placed under the excommunication. For form's sake, however, he was told that when he should clear the land of heresy and otherwise show himself worthy of mercy, the papal commands in his favor would be fulfilled. Innocent's approbation of this cruel comedy is seen in a letter addressed by him to Raymond, in December 1210, expressing his grief that the count had not yet performed his promises to exterminate heretics, and warning him that if he did not do so his lands would be delivered to the crusaders. Raymond at length began to see that his ruin was the deliberate purpose of the legates. The restoration of his castles was hopeless, and it was time for him to prepare himself as best he could for the inevitable war. With this object, to unite his subjects, he circulated a list of conditions which he said had been proposed to him at a conference in Arles, in February 1211—conditions which were onerous and degrading to the last degree to the people as well as to himself—which would have placed the whole territory and its population under the control of the legates and of de Montfort, would have branded every inhabitant, Catholic as well as heretic with the mark of servitude, and would have banished Raymond to the Holy Land virtually for life. Whether such demands were really made or not, their effect was great upon the people, who rallied around their sovereign and were ready for any self-sacrifice.[1]

That the list of conditions was supposititious is rendered probable by other negotiations in which Raymond desperately strove to avert the inevitable rupture. In December 1210 we find him at Narbonne in conference with the legates, de Montfort, and Pedro of Aragon, where impracticable terms were offered him, and where Pedro finally consented to receive de Montfort's homage for Béziers. Shortly afterwards another meeting was held at Montpellier, equally fruitless, except for de Montfort, who made a treaty with Pedro and received from him his infant son Jayme to be held as a hostage. In the spring of 1211 Raymond again visited de Montfort at the siege of Lavaur and allowed provisions to be supplied for a while to the crusaders from Toulouse, although he had fruitlessly endeavored to prevent the marching of a contingent which the Toulousains furnished to the besiegers. Almost as soon as Lavaur was taken, May 3, 1211, de Montfort fell upon his territories and captured some of his castles, apparently without defiance or declaration of war, when Raymond made a last miserable effort of submission by offering his whole possessions, except the city of Toulouse, to be held by the legate and de Montfort as security for the performance of what might be demanded of him, reserving only his life and his son's right of inheritance. Even these terms were contemptuously rejected. The Count of Bar was speedily expected with a large force of crusaders, whose forty days' term was to be utilized to the utmost, and the siege of Toulouse was resolved on.

As soon as the citizens heard of this design they sent an embassy to the crusaders to deprecate it. They had been reconciled to the Church, and had assisted at the siege of Lavaur, but they were sternly told that they would not be spared unless they would eject Raymond from the city and renounce their allegiance to him. This they refused unanimously. All the old civic quarrels were forgotten, and as one man they prepared for resistance. It is a noteworthy illustration of the strength of the republican institution of the civic

---

[1] The sole authority for this extraordinary document is Guillem de Tudela, followed by the Historien du Comte de Toulouse (Vaissette, III. Pr. 30). Though generally accepted by historians, I cannot regard it as genuine, and its only explanation seems to be that it was manufactured by Raymond to arouse the indignation of his people.

commune, that the siege of Toulouse was the first considerable check received by the crusaders. The town was well fortified and garrisoned; the Counts of Foix and Comminges had come at the summons of their suzerain, and the citizens were earnest in defense. They not only kept their gates open, but made breaches in the walls to facilitate the furious sallies which cost the besiegers heavily. The latter retired, June 29th, under cover of the night, so hastily that they abandoned their sick and wounded, having accomplished nothing except the complete devastation of the land—dwellings, vineyards, orchards, women and children were alike indiscriminately destroyed in their wrath—and de Montfort turned from the scene of his defeat to carry the same ravage into Foix. This final effort of self-defense was naturally construed as fautorship of heresy and drew from Innocent a fresh excommunication of Raymond and of the city for "persecuting" de Montfort and the crusaders.

Encouraged by his escape, Raymond now took the offensive, but with little result. The siege of Castelnaudary was a failure, and a good deal of desultory fighting occurred, mostly to the advantage of de Montfort, whose military skill was exhibited to the best advantage in his difficult position. The crusade was still industriously preached throughout Christendom, and his forces were irregularly renewed with fresh swarms of "pilgrims" for forty days' service, so that he would frequently find himself at the head of a considerable army, which again would soon melt away to a handful. To utilize this varying stream of strangers of all nationalities in a country which was bitterly hostile required capacity of a high order, and de Montfort proved himself thoroughly equal to it. His opponents, though frequently greatly superior in numbers, never ventured on a pitched battle, and the war was one of sieges and devastations, conducted on both sides with savage ferocity. Prisoners were frequently hanged, or less mercifully blinded or mutilated, and mutual hate grew stronger and fiercer as de Montfort gradually extended his boundaries and Raymond's territories grew less and less.

Early in 1212 the Abbot of Vaux-Cernay received in the bishopric of Carcassonne the reward of his zeal in furthering the crusade, and Legate Arnaud obtained the great archbishopric of Narbonne. Not content with the ecclesiastical dignity, Arnaud claimed to be likewise duke, giving rise to a vigorous quarrel with de Montfort, who, notwithstanding his devotion to the Church, had no intention of surrendering to it his temporal possessions. Possibly it was the commencement of coolness between them that induced Arnaud to favor the crusade preached at the request of Alonso IX of Castile, at that time threatened by a desperate effort of the Moors to regain their Spanish possessions. Much as de Montfort needed every man, the new Archbishop of Narbonne marched into Spain at the head of a large force of crusaders to swell the army with which the Kings of Aragon, Castile, and Navarre advanced against the Saracen.

The spring and summer of 1212 saw an almost unbroken series of successes for de Montfort, until Raymond's territories were reduced to Montauban and Toulouse, and the latter city, crowded with refugees from the neighboring districts, was virtually beleaguered, as the crusaders from their surrounding strongholds made forays up to the very gates. De Montfort desired the papal confirmation of his new acquisitions, and for this application was made to Rome by the legates. Innocent assumed a tone of grave surprise. It is true, he said, that the count had been found guilty of many offenses against the Church, for which he had been excommunicated and his lands exposed to the first comer; but the loss of most of them had served as a punishment, and it must be remembered that, although suspected of heresy and of the murder of the legate, he had never been convicted, nor did the pope know why his commands to afford him an opportunity of purging himself had never been carried out. In the absence of a formal trial and conviction his lands could not be adjudged to another. The proper forms must be observed, or the Church might be deemed guilty of fraud in continuing to hold the castles made over to it in pledge. He wound up by ordering them to report to him the full and simple truth. Another letter, to Master Theodisius and the Bishop of Riez cautioned them not to be remiss in their duty, as they were said to have thus far been, which undoubtedly refers to their withholding from Raymond the opportunity of justification.

To this Theodisius and the Bishop of Riez replied that they had not been remiss, but had repeatedly summoned Raymond to justify himself, and that Raymond had neglected to make reparation to certain prelates and churches, which was quite likely, seeing that de Montfort had been giving him ample occupation. They proceeded, however, to make a bustling show of activity in compliance with

Innocent's present commands, and they called a council at Avignon to give a colorable pretext for pushing Raymond to the wall. Avignon, however, was fortunately unhealthy, so that many prelates refused to attend, and Theodisius had a timely sickness, rendering a postponement necessary. Another council was therefore summoned to convene at Lavaur, a castle not far from Toulouse, in the hands of de Montfort, who, at the request of Pedro of Aragon, graciously granted an eight days' suspension of hostilities for the purpose.

The matter, in fact, had assumed a shape which could no longer be eluded. Pedro of Aragon, fresh from the triumph of Las Nevas, was a champion of the faith who was not to be treated with contempt, and he had finally come forward as the protector of Raymond and of his own vassals. As overlord he could not passively see the latter stripped of their lands, and his interests in the whole region were too great for him to view with indifference the establishment of so overmastering a power as de Montfort was rapidly consolidating. The conquered fiefs were being filled with Frenchmen; a parliament had just been held at Pamiers to organize the institutions of the country on a French basis, and everything looked to an overturning of the old order. It was full time for him to act. He had already sent a mission to Innocent to complain of the proceedings of the legates as arbitrary, unjust, and subversive of the true interests of religion, and he came to Toulouse for the avowed purpose of interceding for his ruined brother-in-law.

Pedro's envoys drew from Innocent a command to de Montfort to give up all lands seized from those who were not heretics, and instructions to Arnaud not to interfere with the crusade against the Saracens by using indulgences to prolong the war in the Toulousain. This action of Innocent, coupled with the powerful intercession of Pedro, created a profound impression, and all the ecclesiastical organization of Languedoc was summoned to meet the crisis. When the council assembled at Lavaur, in January 1213, a petition was presented by King Pedro, humbly asking mercy rather than justice for the despoiled nobles. He produced a formal cession executed by Raymond and his son and confirmed by the city of Toulouse, together with similar cessions made by the Counts of Foix and Comminges and by Gaston of Béarn, of all their lands, rights, and jurisdictions to him, to do with as he might see fit in compelling them to obey the commands of the pope in case they should prove recalcitrant. He asked restitution of the lands conquered from them, on their rendering due satisfaction to the Church for all misdeeds; and if Raymond could not be heard, the proposal was made that he should retire in favor of his young son—the father serving with his knights against the infidel in Spain or Palestine, and the youth being retained in careful guardianship until he should show himself worthy the confidence of the Church.

No submission could be more complete. There was no pretense of shielding heretics, who could, under such a settlement, be securely exterminated; but the prelates assembled at Lavaur were under the domination of passions and ambitions and hatreds which rendered them deaf to everything that might interfere with the predetermined purpose. The ruin of the house of Toulouse was essential to their comfort—they might well believe even to their personal safety—and it was pressed unswervingly. As legates, Master Theodisius and the Bishop of Riez presided, while the assembled prelates of the land were led by the intractable Arnaud of Narbonne. All forms were duly observed. The legates, as judges, asked the opinion of the prelates as assessors, whether Raymond should be admitted to purgation. A written answer was returned in the negative, not only for the reason that he was too notorious a perjurer to be listened to, but also because of fresh offenses committed during the war, the slaying of crusaders who were attacking him being seriously included among his sins. As a further subterfuge it was agreed that the excommunication under which he lay could only be removed by the pope. Shielding themselves behind this answer, the legates notified Raymond that they could proceed no further without special license from the pope—a repetition of the eternal shifting of responsibility, like a shuttlecock from one player in the game to another—and when Raymond implored for mercy and begged an interview, he was coldly told that it would be useless trouble and expense for both parties. There remained the appeal of King Pedro to be disposed of, and this was treated with the same disingenuous evasion. The prelates undertook to answer this without the legates, so as to be able to say that Raymond's affairs were out of their hands, as he had himself committed them to the legates; and, besides, his excesses had rendered him unworthy of all mercy or kindness. As for the other three nobles, their crimes were recited, especially their self-defense against the crusaders, and it was added, that if they would satisfy the Church and obtain absolution,their complaints would be listened to; but no method was indicated by which absolution could be obtained, and no notice was deigned to the guarantees offered in Pedro's petition. Indeed, Arnaud of Narbonne, in his capacity of legate, wrote to him in violent terms, threatening him with excommunication for consorting with excommunicants and accused heretics, and his request for a truce until Pentecost was refused on the ground that it would interfere with the success of the crusade, which was still preached in France with a vigor justifying doubts of the sincerity of Innocent's orders to the contrary.

The whole proceedings were so defiant a mockery of justice that there was a very manifest alarm lest Innocent should repudiate them and yield to the powerful intercession of King Pedro. Master Theodisius and several bishops were dispatched to Rome with the documents so as to bring personal influence to bear. Raymond was painted in the blackest colors. The effort he had made to obtain succor from the Emperor Otho, and the assistance at one time rendered him by Savary de Mauleon, lieutenant of King John in Aquitaine, were skillfully used to excite odium, as both these monarchs were hostile to Rome; and he was even accused of having implored help from the Emperor of Morocco, to the subversion of Christianity itself. Fearing that this might be insufficient, letters were showered on Innocent by bishops from every part of the troubled region, assuring him that peace and prosperity had followed on the footsteps of the crusaders, that the land which had been ravaged by heretics and bandits was restored to religion and safety, that if but one more supreme effort were made and the city of Toulouse were wiped out, with its villainous brood, the faithful could enjoy the Land of Promise; but that if Raymond were allowed to raise his head, chaos would come again, and it would be better for the Church to take refuge among the barbarians. In all this nothing was said to the pope of the guarantees offered through King Pedro, who was obliged, in March 1213, to transmit to Rome copies of the cessions executed by the inculpated nobles, duly authenticated by the Archbishop of Tarragona and his suffragans.

Master Theodisius and his colleagues found the task harder than they had anticipated. Innocent had solemnly declared that Raymond should have the opportunity of vindication, and that condemnation should only follow trial. He was now required to eat his words, while the persistent refusal to allow a trial must have shown him that the charges so industriously made were destitute of proof. The struggle was hard for a proud man, but he finally yielded to the pressure, though the delay of the decision until May 21, 1213, shows what effort it cost. When the decree came, however, its decisiveness proved that pride and consistency had been overcome. Innocent's letters to his legates have not reached us, but to Pedro he wrote sternly, commanding him to abandon the protection of heretics unless he was ready to be included in the objects of the new crusade which was threatened if further resistance was attempted. The orders Pedro had obtained for the restoration of nonheretical lands were withdrawn as granted through misrepresentation, and the lords of Foix, Comminges, and Navarre were remitted to the discretion of Arnaud of Narbonne. The city of Toulouse could obtain reconciliation by banishment and confiscation inflicted on all whom Foulques, its fanatic bishop, might point out, and no peace or truce or other engagement entered into with heretics was to be observed. As to Raymond, the complete silence with respect to him was more significant than could have been the severest animadversions. He was simply ignored, as though no further account was to be taken of him.

Meanwhile both parties had proceeded without waiting the event in Rome. In France the crusade had been vigorously preached; Louis Cœur-de-Lion, son of Philip Augustus, had taken the cross with many barons, and great hopes were entertained of the overwhelming force which would put an end to further resistance, when Philip's preparations for the invasion of England caused him to intervene and stop the movement which threatened seriously to interfere with his designs. On the other hand, King Pedro entered into still closer alliance with Raymond and the excommunicated nobles, and received an oath of fidelity from the magistracy of Toulouse. When the papal mandate was received, he made a pretense of obeying it, but continued his preparations for the war, among which the one which best illustrates the man and the age was his procuring from Innocent the renewal of Urban's bull of 1095, placing his kingdom under the special protection of the Holy See, with the privilege that it should not be subjected to interdict except by the pope himself.

The rupture came with a formal declaration of war from Pedro, accepted by de Montfort, though he had but few troops and the hoped-for reinforcements from France were not forthcoming; indeed, a legate sent by Innocent to preach the crusade for the Holy Land had turned in that direction all the effort which Philip would permit to be made. Pedro had left in Toulouse his representatives and had gone to his own dominions to raise forces, with which he recrossed the Pyrenees and was received enthusiastically by all those who had submitted to de Montfort. He advanced to the castle of Muret, within ten miles of Toulouse, where de Montfort had left a slender garrison, and was joined by the Counts of Toulouse, Foix, and Comminges, their united forces amounting to a considerable army, though far from the 100,000 men represented by the eulogists of de Montfort.

The siege of Muret commenced September 10, 1213. Word was immediately carried to de Montfort, who lay about 25 miles distant at Fanjeaux, with a small force, including seven bishops and three abbots sent by Arnaud of Narbonne to treat with Pedro. Notwithstanding the disparity of numbers, he did not hesitate a moment to advance and succor his people. Sending back the Countess Alice to Carcassonne, he set forth at once, hastily collecting such troops as were within reach. At Bolbonne, near Saverdun, where he halted to hear mass, Maurin, the sacristan, afterwards Abbot of Pamiers, expressed wonder at his risking with a mere handful of men an encounter with a warrior so renowned as the King of Aragon. De Montfort in reply drew from his pouch an intercepted letter to a lady in Toulouse, in which Pedro assured her that he was coming out of love for her to drive the Frenchman from her land, and when Maurin asked him what he meant by it, he exclaimed, "What do I mean? God help me as much as I little fear him who comes for the sake of a woman to undo the work of God!"

The next day de Montfort entered Muret, which was besieged only on one side, the enemy interposing no obstacle, as they hoped to capture the chief of the crusaders. The bishops sought to negotiate with Pedro, but no terms could be reached, and the following morning, Thursday, September 13, the crusaders, numbering perhaps a thousand cavaliers, sallied forth for the attack. As de Montfort drew away in the opposite direction, the besiegers at first thought that he was abandoning the town, and they were only undeceived when he wheeled and they saw he had made a circuit to obtain a level field for the attack. Count Raymond counselled awaiting the onset behind the rampart of wagons and exhausting the crusaders with missiles, but the fiery Catalan rejected the advice as pusillanimous. Armor was donned in hot haste, and the horsemen rushed forth in a confused mass, leaving the footmen to continue the labors of the siege. Emulous rather of the fame of a good knight than of a general, Pedro was immediately behind the vanguard, as two squadrons of the crusaders came on in solid order, and was readily found by two renowned French knights, Alain de Roucy and Florent de Ville, who had concerted to set upon him. He was speedily thrown from his horse and slain. The confusion into which his followers were thrown was converted into a panic as de Montfort, at the head of a third squadron, charged them in flank. They turned and fled, followed by the Frenchmen, who slew them without mercy, and then, returning from the pursuit, fell upon the camp where the infantry had remained unconscious of the evil fortune of the field. Here the slaughter was tremendous, until the flying wretches succeeded in crossing the Garonne, in which many were drowned. The loss of the crusaders was less than 20, that of the allies from 15,000 to 20,000, and no one was hardy enough to doubt that the hand of God was visible in a triumph so miraculous. Yet King Jayme tells us that his father's death, and the consequent loss of the battle, arose from his prevailing vice. The Albigensian nobles, to ingratiate themselves with him, had placed their wives and daughters at his disposal, and he was so exhausted by his excesses that on the morning of the battle he could not stand at the celebration of the mass.[2]

With the few men at his command de Montfort was unable to follow up his advantage, and the immediate effect of the miraculous victory was scarcely perceptible. The citizens of Toulouse professed a desire for reconciliation, but when Bishop Foulques demanded 200 hostages as security, they refused to give more than 60, and when the bishop assented to this, they withdrew the offer. De Montfort made a foray into Foix, carrying desolation in his track, and showed himself before Toulouse, but was soon put on the defensive. When

[2] Don Jayme himself, then a child in his sixth year, was still in the hands of de Montfort as a hostage, and if the Catalan chroniclers speak truth, it was with difficulty that the young king was recovered, even after Innocent III had ordered his release.

he came peaceably to the city of Narbonne, of which he claimed the overlordship, he was refused entrance; the same thing happened to him at Montpellier, and he was obliged to digest these affronts in silence. His condition, indeed, was almost desperate in the winter of 1214, when affairs suddenly took a different turn. The prohibition to preach the crusade in France was removed, and news came that an army of 100,000 fresh pilgrims might be expected after Easter. Besides this, a new legate, Cardinal Peter of Benevento, arrived with full powers from the pope, and at Narbonne received the unqualified submission of the Counts of Toulouse, Foix, and Comminges, of Aimeric, Viscount of Narbonne, and of the city of Toulouse. All these agreed to expel heretics and to comply explicitly with all demands of the Church, furnishing whatever security might be demanded. Raymond, moreover, placed his dominions in the hands of the legate, at whose command he engaged to absent himself, either at the English court or elsewhere, until he could go to Rome; and in effect, on his return to Toulouse he and his son lived as private citizens with their wives, in the house of David de Roaix. Rome having thus obtained everything that she had ever demanded, the legate absolved all the penitents and reconciled them to the Church.

If the land expected peace with submission it was cruelly deceived. The legate had merely desired to tide de Montfort over the time during which in his weakness he might have been overwhelmed, and to amuse the threatened provinces until the arrival of the fresh swarm of pilgrims. The trick was perfectly successful, and the monkish chronicler is delighted with the fraud so astutely conceived and so dexterously managed. His admiring ejaculation, "O pious fraud of the legate! O fraudulent piety!" is the key which unlocks to us the secrets of Italian diplomacy with the Albigenses.

In spite of King Philip's war with John of England and the Emperor Otho, the expected hordes of crusaders poured down upon the unhappy southern provinces. Their initial exploit was the capture of Maurillac, notable to us as conveying the first distinct reference to the Waldenses in the history of the war. Of these sectaries, seven were found among the captives; they boldly affirmed their faith before the legate, and were burned, as we are told, with immense rejoicings by the soldiers of Christ. With his wonted ability de Montfort made use of his reinforcements to extend his authority

over the Agenois, Quercy, Limousin, Rouergue, and Périgord. Resistance being now at an end, the legate, in January 1215, assembled
a council of prelates at Montpellier. The council fulfilled its functions by deposing Raymond and electing de Montfort as lord over
the whole land; and, as the confirmation of Innocent was required, an
embassy was sent to Rome, which obtained his assent. He declared
that Raymond, who had never yet had the trial so often demanded,
was deposed on account of heresy; his wife was to have her dower,
and 150 marks were assigned to her, secured by the Castle of Beaucaire. The final disposition of the territory was postponed for the
decision of the General Council of Lateran, called for the ensuing
November; and meanwhile it was confided to the custody of de
Montfort, whom the bishops were exhorted to assist and the inhabitants to obey, while from its revenues some provision was
contemptuously ordered to be made for the support of Raymond.
Bishop Foulques returned to his city of Toulouse, of which he was
virtually master, under the legate who continued to hold it and
Narbonne to keep them out of the hands of Louis Cœur-de-Lion,
who was shortly expected in fulfillment of his crusader's vow; and the
faidits, as the dispossessed knights and gentlemen were called, were
graciously permitted to seek a livelihood throughout the country,
provided they never entered castles or walled towns, and travelled on
ponies with but one spur, and without arms.

Louis came with a noble and gallant company, who earned the
pardon of their sins by a peaceful pilgrimage of forty days. He
showed no disposition to demand for the crown the acquisitions made
by previous crusades, and advantage was taken of his presence to
obtain temporary investiture for de Montfort and to order the
dismantling of the two chief centers of discontent—Toulouse and
Narbonne. Meanwhile the two Raymonds had withdrawn—possibly
to the English court, where King John is said to have given them
10,000 marks in return for the rendering of a worthless homage.
Foreign humiliations and domestic revolt, however, rendered John
useless as an ally, and Raymond awaited, with what patience he
might, the assembling of the Great Council to which the final
decision of his fate had been referred.

In April 1213 had gone forth the call for the Parliament of
Christendom, the Twelfth General Council, where the assembled

wisdom and piety of the Church were to deliberate on the recovery of the Holy Land, the reformation of the Church, the correction of excesses, the rehabilitation of morals, the extirpation of heresy, the strenghtening of faith, and the quieting of discord. By the appointed day, November 1, 1215, the prelates had gathered together, and Innocent's pardonable ambition was gratified in opening and presiding over the most august assemblage that Latin Christianity had ever seen. The Frankish occupation of Constantinople gave opportunity for the reunion, nominal at least, of the Eastern and the Western Churches, and Patriarchs of Constantinople and Jerusalem were there in humble obedience to St. Peter. All that was foremost in Church and State had come, in person or by representative. Every monarch had his ambassador there, to see that his interests suffered no detriment from a body which, acting under the direct inspiration of the Holy Ghost, and under the principle that temporal concerns were wholly subordinate to spiritual, might have little respect for the rights of sovereigns. The most learned theologians and doctors were at hand to give counsel on points of faith and intricate questions of canon law. The princes of the Church were present in numbers wholly unprecedented. Two centuries were to pass away before Europe was again to show its collective strength in a body such as now crowded the ample dimensions of the Basilica of Constantine; and it is a weighty illustration of the service which the Church has rendered in counteracting the centrifugal tendencies of the nations, that such a federative council of Christendom, attainable in no other way, was brought together at the summons of the Roman pontiff.

The Counts of Toulouse, Foix, and Comminges had reached Rome in advance, where they were joined by the younger Raymond, coming through France from England disguised as the servitor of a merchant, to escape the emissaries of de Montfort. In repeated interviews with Innocent they pleaded their cause, and produced no little impression on him. Arnaud of Narbonne, embittered by his quarrel with de Montfort, is said to have aided them, but the other prelates, to whom it was almost a question of life or death, were so violent in their denunciations of Raymond, and drew so fearful a picture of the destruction impending over religion, that Innocent, after a short period of irresolution, was deterred from action. De Montfort had sent his brother Gui to represent him, and when the council met both parties pressed their claims before it. Its decision was prompt, and, as might be expected, was in favor of the champion of the Church. The verdict, as promulgated by Innocent, December 15, 1215, recited the labors of the Church to free the province of Narbonne from heresy, and the peace and tranquillity with which its success had been crowned. It assumed that Raymond had been found guilty of heresy and spoliation, and therefore deprived him of the dominion which he had abused, and sentenced him to dwell elsewhere in penance for his sins, promising him 400 marks a year so long as he proved obedient. His wife was to retain the lands of her dower, or to receive a competent equivalent for them. All the territories won by the crusaders, together with Toulouse, the center of heresy, and Montauban, were granted to de Montfort, who was extolled as the chief instrument in the triumph of the faith. The other possessions of Raymond, not as yet conquered, were to be held by the Church for the benefit of the younger Raymond, to be delivered to him when he should reach the proper age, in whole or in part, as might be found expedient, provided he should manifest himself worthy. So far as Count Raymond was concerned, the verdict was final; thereafter the Church always spoke of him as "the former count," *quondam comes.*

The highest tribunal of the Church Universal had spoken, and in no uncertain tone; and we may see a significant illustration of the forfeiture of its hold on popular veneration in the fact that this, in place of meeting with acquiescence, was the signal of revolt. Apparently the decision had been awaited in the confidence that it would repair the long course of wrong and injustice perpetrated in the name of religion; and, with the frustration of that hope, there was no hesitation in resorting to resistance, with the national spirit inflamed to the highest pitch of enthusiasm. If de Montfort thought that his conquests were secured by the voice of the Lateran fathers, and by King Philip's reception of the homage which he lost no time in rendering, he only showed how little he had learned of the temper of the race with which he had to deal.

The younger Raymond, at this time a youth of 18, hardened by years of adversity, was winning in manner, and is said to have made a most favorable impression on Innocent, who dismissed him with a benediction and good advice; not to take what belonged to another, but to defend his own—"*res de l'autrui non pregas; lo teu, se degun lo te vol hostar, deffendas*"—and he made haste to follow the counsel, according to his own interpretation. The part of his inheritance which had been reserved for him under custody of the Church lay to the east of the Rhone, and thither, on their return from Italy early in 1216, father and son took their way, to find a basis of operations. The outlook was encouraging, and after a short stay the elder Raymond proceeded to Spain to raise what troops he could. Marseilles, Avignon, Tarascon—the whole country, in fact—rose as one man to welcome their lord, and demanded to be led against the Frenchmen, reckless of the fulminations of the Church, and placing life and property at his disposal. The part which the cities and the people play in the conflict becomes henceforth even more noticeable than heretofore—the semi-republican communes fighting for life against the rigid feudalism of the north.

De Montfort met this unexpected turn of fortune with his wonted activity, but his hour of prosperity was past, and one might almost say, with the Church historians, that he was weighed down by the excommunication launched at him by the implacable Arnaud of Narbonne, whom he had treated harshly in their quarrel over the dukedom—an excommunication which he wholly disregarded, not even intermitting his attendance at mass. Obliged, after hard fighting, to leave Beaucaire to its fate, he marched in angry mood to Toulouse, which was preparing to recall its old lord. He set fire to the town in several places, but the citizens barricaded the streets, and resisted his troops step by step, till accommodation was made, and he agreed to spare the city for the immense sum of 30,000 marks; but he destroyed what was left of the fortifications, rendered the place as defenseless as possible, and disarmed the inhabitants. Despite his excommunication, he still had the earnest support of the Church. Innocent died July 20, 1216, but his successor, Honorius III, inherited his policy, and a new legate, Cardinal Bertrand of St. John and St. Paul, was, if possible, more bitter than his predecessors in the determination to suppress the revolt against Rome. The preaching of the crusade had been resumed, and in the beginning of 1217, with fresh reinforcements of crusaders and a small contingent furnished by Philip Augustus, de Montfort crossed the Rhone and made rapid progress in subduing the territories left to young Raymond.

He was suddenly recalled by the news that Toulouse was in rebellion; that Raymond VI had been received there with rejoicing, bringing with him auxiliaries from Spain; that Foix and Comminges, and all the nobles of the land, had flocked thither to welcome their lord, and that the Countess of Montfort was in peril in the Château Narbonnais, the citadel outside of the town. Abandoning his conquests, he hastened back, and in September 1217 commenced the second siege of the heroic city. In spite of the defenseless condition of the town, which men and women unitedly worked night and day to repair; in spite of the threatening and beseeching letters which Honorius wrote to the Kings of Aragon and France, to the younger Raymond, the Count of Foix, the citizens of Toulouse, Avignon, Marseilles, and all whom he thought to deter or excite; in spite of heavy reinforcements brought by a vigorous renewal of preaching the crusade, for nine weary months the siege dragged on, in furious assaults and yet more furious sallies, with intervals of suspended operations as the crusading army swelled or decreased. De Montfort's brother Gui and his eldest son Amauri were seriously wounded. The baffled chieftain's troubles were rendered sorer by the legate, who taunted him with his ill-success, and accused him of ignorance or slackness in his work. Sick at heart, and praying for death as a welcome release, on the morrow of St. John's day, 1218, de Montfort was superintending the reconstruction of his machines, after repelling a sally, when a stone from a mangonel, worked, as Toulousain tradition says, by women, went straight to the right spot—"E venc tot dret la peira lai on era mestiers"—it crushed in his helmet, and he never more spoke word.

If proof were lacking of de Montfort's preeminent capacity it would be furnished by the rapid undoing of all that he had accomplished, in the hands of his son and successor Amauri. His death was regarded as the signal of liberation, and wherever the French garrisons were not too strong, the people arose, massacred the invaders, and gave themselves back to their ancient lords. Vainly did Honorius recognize Amauri as the successor to his father's lordships, put the two Raymonds to the ban, and grant Philip Augustus a twentieth of ecclesiastical revenues as an incentive to another crusade, while plenary indulgence was offered to all who would serve. Vainly did Louis Cœur-de-Lion, with his father's sanction, and accompanied by the Cardinal-Legate Bertrand, lead an army of pilgrims which numbered in its ranks no less than 33 counts and 20 bishops. They penetrated, indeed, to Toulouse, but the third siege of the unyielding city was no more successful than its predecessors, and Louis was obliged to withdraw ingloriously, having accomplished nothing but the massacre of Marmande, where 5,000 souls were put to the sword. Indeed, the pitiless cruelty and brutal licentiousness habitual among the crusaders, who spared no man in their wrath and no woman in their lust, aided no little in inflaming the resistance to foreign domination. One by one the strongholds still held by the French were wrested from their grasp, and but very few of the invaders founded families who kept their place among the gentry of the land.

Early in 1222, Amauri, reduced to desperation, offered to Philip Augustus all his possessions and claims, urging Honorius to support the proposal. The pope welcomed it as the only feasible mode of accomplishing the result for which years of effort had been fruitlessly spent, and he wrote to the king, May 14, representing that in this way alone could the Church be saved. The Church had made itself the national enemy, and we can easily believe the description which Honorius gives of the lamentable condition of orthodoxy in Languedoc. Heresy was openly practiced and taught; the heretic bishops set themselves up defiantly against the Catholic prelates, and there was danger that the pestilence would spread throughout the land. In spite of all this, however, and of an offer of a twentieth of the church revenues and unlimited indulgences for a crusade, Philip turned a deaf ear to the entreaty; and when Amauri's offer was transferred to Thibaut of Champagne, and the latter applied to the king for encouragement, he was coldly told that if, after due consideration, he resolved on the undertaking, the king wished him all success, but could render him no aid nor release him from his obligations of service in view of the threatening relations with England. Possibly encouraged by this, the younger Raymond in June appealed to Philip as his lord, and, if he dared so to call him, as his kinsman, imploring his pity, and begging in the humblest terms his intervention to procure his reconciliation to the Church, and thus remove the incapacity of inheritance to which he was subjected.

This must have been suggested by the expectation of the death of Raymond VI, which occurred shortly after, in August 1222. It made no change in the political or religious situation, but is not without interest in view or the charge of heresy so persistently made and used as an excuse for his destruction. In 1218 he had executed his will, in which he left legacies to the Templars and Hospitallers of Toulouse, declared his intention of entering the latter order, and desired to be buried with them. On the morning of his sudden death he had twice visited for prayer the church of la Daurade, but his agony was short and he was speechless when the Abbot of St. Sernin, who had been hurriedly sent for, reached his bedside, to administer to him the consolations of religion. A Hospitaller who was present cast over him his cloak with the cross, to secure the burial of the body for his house; but a zealous parishioner of St. Sernin pulled it off, and a disgraceful squabble arose over the dying man, for the abbot claimed the sepulture, as the death chanced to take place in his parish, and he summoned the people not to allow the corpse to be removed beyond its precincts. This ghastly struggle over the remains has its ludicrous aspect, from the fact that the Church would never permit the inhumation of its enemy, and the body remained unburied in spite of the reiterated efforts of Raymond VII, after his reconciliation, to secure the repose of his father's soul. It was in vain that the inquest ordered by Innocent IV, in 1247, gathered evidence from 120 witnesses to prove that Raymond VI had been the most pious and charitable of men and most obedient to the Church. His remains lay for a century and a half the sport of rats in the house of the Hospitallers, and when they disappeared piecemeal, the skull was still kept as an object of curiosity, at least until the end of the seventeenth century.

After his father's death Raymond VII pursued his advantage, and in December Amauri was reduced to offering again his claims to Philip Augustus, only to be exposed to another refusal. In May 1223 there seem to have been hopes that Philip would undertake a crusade, and the Legate Conrad of Porto, with the Bishops of Nîmes, Agde, and Lodève, wrote to him urgently from Béziers describing the deplorable state of the land in which the cities and castles were daily opening their gates to the heretics. Negotiations with Raymond followed, and matters went so far that we find Honorius writing to his legate to look after the interest of the Bishop of Viviers in the expected settlement. There was fresh urgency felt for the pacification in the absence of any hope of assistance from the king, since the progress of the Catharan heresy was ever more alarming. Additional energy had been infused into it by the activity of its Bulgarian antipope. Heretics from Languedoc were resorting to him in increasing numbers and returning with freshened zeal; and his representative, Bartholomew, Bishop of Carcassonne, who styled himself, in imitation of the popes, Servant of the servants of the Holy Faith, was making successful efforts to spread the belief. Truces between Amauri and Raymond were therefore made and conferences held, and finally the legate called a council to assemble at Sens, July 6, 1223, where a final pacification was expected. It was transferred to Paris, because Philip Augustus desired to be present, and its importance in his eyes must have been great, since he set out on his journey thither in spite of a raging fever, to which he succumbed on the road, at Meudon, July 14. Raymond's well-grounded hopes were shattered on the eve of realization, for Philip's death rendered the council useless and changed in a moment the whole face of affairs. Louis, on the very day of his coronation, promised the legate that he would undertake the matter; Honorius urged it with vehemence, and in February 1224 Louis accepted a conditional cession from Amauri of all his rights over Languedoc. Raymond thus found himself confronted by the King of France as his adversary.

The situation was full of new and unexpected peril. But a month before, Amauri, in utter penury, had been obliged to surrender what few strongholds he yet retained, and had quitted forever the land which he and his father had cursed. The triumph, so long hoped for and won by so many years of persistent struggle, was a Dead-Sea apple, full of ashes and bitterness. The discomfited adversary was now replaced by one who was rash and enterprising, who wielded all the power gained by Philip's long and fortunate reign, and whose pride was enlisted in avenging the check which he had received five years before under the walls of Toulouse. Already in February he wrote to the citizens of Narbonne, praising their loyalty and promising to lead a crusade three weeks after Easter, which should restore to the crown all the lands forfeited by the house of Toulouse. Zealous as he was, however, he felt that the eagerness of the Church warranted him in driving the best bargain he could for his services to the faith, and he demanded as conditions of taking up arms that peace abroad and at home should be assured to him, that a crusade should be preached with the same indulgences as for the Holy Land, that all his vassals not joining in it should be excommunicated, that the Archbishop of Bourges should be legate in place of the Cardinal of Porto, that all the lands of Raymond, of his allies, and of all who resisted the crusade should be his prize, that he should have a subsidy of 60,000 livres parisis a year from the Church, and that he should be free to return as soon or remain as long as he might see fit.

Louis asserted that these conditions were accepted, and went on with his preparations, while Raymond made desperate efforts to conjure the coming storm. Henry III of England used his good offices with Honorius, and Raymond was encouraged to make offers of obedience through envoys to Rome, whose liberalities among the officials of the curia are said to have produced a most favorable impression. Honorius replied in a most gracious letter, promising to send Romano, Cardinal of Sant' Angelo, as legate to arrange a settlement, and he followed this by informing Louis that the offers of Frederic II to recover the Holy Land were so favorable that everything else must be postponed to that great object, and all indulgences must be used solely for that purpose; but that if he will continue to threaten Raymond, that prince will be forced to submit. Instructions were at the same time sent to Arnaud of Narbonne to act with other prelates in leading Raymond to offer acceptable terms. Louis, justly indignant at being thus played with, made public protestation that he washed his hands of the whole business, and told the pope that the curia might come to what terms it pleased with Raymond, that he had nothing to do with points of faith, but that his rights must be respected and no new tributes be imposed. At a parliament held in Paris, May 5, 1224, the legate withdrew the indulgences granted against the Albigenses and approved of Raymond as a good Catholic, while Louis made a statement of the whole transaction in terms which showed how completely he felt himself to be duped. He turned his military preparations to account, however.

by wrenching from Henry III a considerable portion of the remaining English possessions in France.

Nothing remained but to settle the terms, and Raymond's escape had been too narrow for him to raise difficulties on this score. At Pentecost (June 2) with his chief vassals, he met Arnaud and the bishops at Montpellier, where he agreed to observe and maintain the Catholic faith throughout his dominions, and expel all heretics pointed out by the Church, to maintain peace and dismiss the bandit mercenaries, to restore all rights and privileges to the churches, to pay 20,000 marks for reparation of ecclesiastical losses and for Amauri's compensation, on condition that the pope would cause Amauri to renounce his claims and deliver up all documents attesting them. If this would not suffice, he would submit himself entirely to the Church, saving his allegiance to the king. As an evidence of good faith he reinstated his father's old enemy, Theodisius, in the bishopric of Agde. These conditions were transmitted to Rome for approbation with notice that a council would be held August 20 for their ratification, and Honorius returned an equivocal answer which might be construed as accepting them. On the appointed day the council met at Montpellier. Amauri sent a protest begging for bishops desperately not to throw away the fruits of victory within their grasp. The King of France, he said, was on the point of making the cause his own, and to abandon it now would be a scandal and a humiliation to the Church Universal. Nothwithstanding this, the bishops received the oaths of Raymond and his vassals to the conditions previously agreed, with the addition that the decision of the pope should be followed as to the composition with Amauri, and that any further commands of the Church should be obeyed, saving the supremacy of the king and the emperor, for all of which satisfactory security was offered.

What more the Church could ask it is hard to see. Raymond had triumphed over it and all the crusaders whom it could muster, and yet he offered submission as complete as could reasonably have been exacted of his father in the hour of his deepest abasement. At this very time, moreover, a public disputation held at Castel-Sarrasin between some Catholic priests and Catharan ministers shows the growing confidence of heresy and the necessity of an accommodation if its progress was to be checked. Yet the vicissitudes and surprises in this business were not yet exhausted. In October, when Raymond's envoys reached Rome to obtain the papal confirmation of the settlement, they were opposed by Gui de Montfort, sent by Louis to prevent it. There were not wanting Languedocian bishops who feared that with peace they would be forced to restore possessions usurped during the troubles, and who consequently busied themselves with proving that Raymond was at heart a heretic. Honorius shuffled with the negotiation until the commencement of 1225, when he sent Cardinal Romano again to France with full powers as legate, and with instructions to threaten Raymond and to bring about a truce between France and England so as to free Louis's hands. He wrote to Louis in the same sense, while to Amauri he sent money and words of encouragement.

After several conferences with Louis and the leading bishops and nobles, the legate convened a national council at Bourges in November 1225 for the final settlement of the question. Raymond appeared before it, humbly seeking absolution and reconciliation; he offered his purgation and whatever amends might be required by the churches, promising to render his lands peaceful and secure and obedient to Rome. As for heresy, he not only engaged to suppress it, but urged the legate to visit every city in his dominions and make inquisition into the faith of the people, pledging himself to punish rigorously all delinquents and to coerce any town offering opposition. On the other hand, Amauri exhibited the decrees of Innocent condemning Raymond VI and bestowing his lands on Simon de Montfort, and Philip's recognition of the latter. There was much wrangling in the council until the legate ordered each archbishop to deliberate separately with his suffragans and deliver to him the result in writing, to be submitted to the king and pope, under the seal of secrecy, enforced by excommunication.

What were really the conclusions reached in the Albigensian matter by the archiepiscopal caucuses no one might reveal, but with pope and king resolved on intervention there could be little doubt as to the practical result. It was announced that no peace honorable to the Church could be reached with Raymond, and that a tithe of ecclesiastical revenues for five years was offered to Louis if he would undertake the holy war. Reckless as was Louis, however, and eager to clutch at the tempting prize, he shrank from the encounter with the obstinate patriotism of the south while involved in hostilities with England. He demanded therefore that Honorius should prohibit Henry III from disturbing the French territories during the crusade. When Henry received the papal letters he was eagerly preparing an expedition to relieve his brother, Richard of Cornwall, but his counsellors urged him not to prevent Louis from entangling himself in so difficult and costly an enterprise. In the nick of time, news arrived from Richard giving good accounts of his success; Henry's anxieties were calmed, and he gave the required assurances, in spite of an alliance into which he had shortly before entered with Raymond. As a further precaution to ensure the success of the crusade, all private wars were forbidden during its continuance.

The question of religion had practically disappeared by this time, except as an excuse for indulgences and ecclesiastical subsidies and as a cloak for dynastic expansion. If Raymond had not yet actively persecuted his heretic subjects it was merely because of the impolicy, under constant threats of foreign aggression, of alienating so large a portion of the population on which he relied for support. He had shown himself quite ready to do so in exchange for reconciliation to the Church, and he had urged the legate to establish an organized inquisition throughout his dominions. The coming struggle thus, even more than its predecessors, was to be a war of races, with the whole power of the north, led by the king and the Church, against the exhausted provinces which clung to Raymond as their suzerain. We cannot wonder that he was willing to submit to any terms to avert it, for he was left to breast the tempest alone. His greatest vassal, the Count of Foix, it is true, stood by him, but the next in importance, the Count of Comminges, made his peace, and is found acting for the king; the Count of Provence entered into the alliance against him, while, at a warning from Louis, Jayme of Aragon and Nuñez Sancho of Roussillon forbade their subjects from lending aid to the heretic.

Meanwhile the crusade was organized on the largest scale. At a great parliament held in Paris, January 28, 1226, the nobles presented an address urging the king to undertake it and pledging their assistance to the end. He assumed the cross under condition that he should lay it aside when he pleased, and his example was followed by nearly all the bishops and barons, though we are told that many did so unwillingly, holding it an abuse to assail a faithful Christian who, at the Council of Bourges, had offered all possible satisfaction. Amauri and his uncle Gui executed a renunciation of all their claims in favor of the crown; the cross was diligently preached throughout the kingdom, with the customary offer of indulgences, and the legate guaranteed that the ecclesiastical tithe granted for five years should amount to at least 100,000 livres per annum. The only cloud to mar the prospect was the discovery that Honorius had sent letters and legates to the barons of Poitou and Aquitaine, ordering them within a month to return to their allegiance to England in spite of any oaths taken to the contrary. This curious piece of treachery can only be explained by persuasive bribes from Raymond or from Henry III, and Louis promptly met it with liberal payments to the pope, by which he procured the suspension of the letters. This being got out of the way, another council was held March 29, where Louis commanded his lieges to assemble on May 17, at Bourges, fully equipped and prepared to remain with him as long as he should stay in the south. The forty days' service which had so repeatedly snatched from de Montfort the fruits of his victories was no longer to arrest the tide of a permanent conquest.

On the appointed day the chivalry of the kingdom gathered around their monarch at Bourges, but before setting forth there was much to be done. The legate was busy dismissing the boys, women, old men, paupers, and cripples who had assumed the cross. These he forced to swear as to the amount of money which they possessed; of this he took the major part and let them go after granting them absolution from the vow. Louis drove a thriving trade of the same kind from a higher class of crusaders by accepting heavy payments from those who owed him service and were not ambitious of the glory or the perils of the expedition. He also forced the Count of La Marche to send back to Raymond his young daughter Jeanne, betrothed to La Marche's son, and reserved, as we shall see, for loftier nuptials. To Bourges likewise flocked many of the nobles of Narbonne, eager to show their loyalty by doing homage to the king and to advise him not to advance through their district, which was devastated by war, but to march by way of the Rhone to Avignon— disinterested counsel which he adopted.

Louis set forth from Lyons with a magnificent army consisting, it is said, of 50,000 horse and innumerable foot. The terror of his coming preceded him; many of Raymond's vassals and cities made haste to offer their submission. When the host reached Avignon, however, and Louis proposed to march through the city, the inhabitants, with sudden fear, shut their gates in his face, and though they offered him unmolested passage around it, he resolved on a siege, in spite of its being a fief of the empire. It had lain for ten years under excommunication, and was noted as a nest of Waldenses, so the Cardinal-Legate Romano ordered the crusaders to purge it of heresy by force of arms. The task proved no easy one. From June 10 till about September 10 the citizens resisted desperately, inflicting heavy loss upon the besiegers. Raymond had devastated the surrounding country and was ever on the watch to cut off foraging parties, so that supplies were scanty. An epidemic set in, and a plague of flies carried infection from the dead to the living. Disaffection in the camp aggravated the trouble. Pierre Mauclerc of Britanny was offended with Louis for traversing his plot of marriage with Jeanne of Flanders, whose divorce from her husband he had procured from the pope, and he entered into a league with Thibaut of Champagne and the Count of La Marche, who were all suspected of entertaining secret relations with the enemy. Thibaut even left the army without leave, after forty days of service, returned home and commenced strengthening his castles. The crusade, so brilliantly begun, was on the point of abandoning its first serious enterprise, when the Avignonese, reduced to the utmost straits, unexpectedly offered to capitulate. Considering the customs of the age, the terms were not hard. They agreed to satisfy the king and Church, they paid a considerable ransom, their walls were thrown down and 300 fortified houses in the town were dismantled, and they received as bishop, at the hands of the legate, Nicholas de Corbie, who instituted laws for the suppression of heresy.

From Avignon Louis marched westward, everywhere receiving the submission of nobles and cities until within a few leagues of Toulouse. The reduction of that obstinate focus of heresy was apparently all that remained to complete the ruin of Raymond and the success of the crusade, when Louis suddenly turned his face homeward. No explanation of this unlooked-for termination of the campaign is furnished by any of the chroniclers, but it is probably to be sought in the sickness which pursued the crusaders, and possibly in the commencement of the disease which terminated the march and the life of the king at Montpensier on November 8, not without suspicion of poisoning by Thibaut of Champagne. Throughout Europe, however, the retreat was regarded as the result of serious military reverses. Louis had designed to return the following year, and had left garrisons in the places which had submitted to him, with Humbert de Beaujeu, a renowned captain, in supreme command, and Gui de Montfort under him, but their feats of arms were few.

Saved as by a miracle from the ruin which had seemed inevitable, Raymond lost no time in recovering a portion of his dominions. The death of Louis worked a complete revolution in the situation, and, for a time at least, he had little to fear. It is true that Louis IX, a child of 13, was crowned without delay at Reims, and the regency was confided to his mother, Blanche of Castile, but the great barons were restive, and the conspiracy hatched before the walls of Avignon was yet in existence. Britanny, Champagne, and La Marche ostentatiously kept away from the coronation, delayed offering their homage, and intrigued with England. Gregory IX, who mounted the papal throne March 19, 1227, took the regent and the boy-king under the papal protection, on the ground of their being engaged in war against heresy; but the succors which they sent from time to time to Humbert de Beaujeu were probably only enough to give color to a continuance of the ecclesiastical tithe, which the four great provinces of Reims, Rouen, Sens, and Tours resisted till the legate authorized the regent to seize Church property and compel the payment.

The war dragged on through 1227 with varying result. De Beaujeu, assisted by Pierre Amiel of Narbonne and Foulques of Toulouse, captured, after a desperate siege, the castle of Bécède, when the garrison was slaughtered and the heretic deacon Géraud de Motte and his comrades were burned. Raymond recovered Castel-Sarrasin, but could not prevent the crusaders from devastating the land up to the walls of Toulouse. The following year found both parties inclined for peace. The regent Blanche had ample motives to come to terms. With all her firmness and capacity the task before her was no easy one. The nobles of Aquitaine were corresponding with Henry III, who always cherished the hope of reconquering the territories wrenched from the English crown by Philip Augustus. The great barons, despising the rule of a woman, were quarrelling between themselves and involving a large portion of the kingdom in war. The hope of completing the conquest of the south could scarce repay the constant drain on the royal resources, while chronic warfare there was highly dangerous in the explosive condition of the realm. Every motive of policy would therefore incline Queen Blanche to listen to the humble prayers for reconciliation which Raymond and his father had never ceased to utter, and a way of securing for the royal line the rich inheritance of the house of Toulouse seemed to offer itself in the fact that Raymond had but one child, Jeanne, still unmarried. A union between her and one of the younger brothers of Louis, with a reversion of the territories to them and to their heirs, would attain peaceably all the political advantages of the crusade, while, as to its religious objects, Raymond had left no doubts of his willingness to secure them.

Gregory was quite content thus to close the war which Innocent had commenced twenty years before. In March 1228 he wrote to Louis IX, urging him to make peace according to the judgment of the legate, Cardinal Romano, who had full powers in the premises, and it was in the name of the legate that the first overtures were made to Raymond through the Abbot of Grandselve. That the marriage was the pivot up on which the negotiations turned is shown by another letter of June 25, authorizing Romano to dispense with the impediment of consanguinity if the union between Jeanne and one of the king's brothers would lead to peace. Another epistle of October 21, announcing to all the prelates of France that he had renewed the indulgences for a crusade against the Albigenses, would seem to show that the terms offered to Raymond were hard of acceptance, and that renewed pressure on him was necessary. This was enforced by extensive devastations in his territories, and in December 1228 he gave the abbot full power to assent to whatever might be agreed upon by Thibaut of Champagne, who acted as mediator for him. Finally, on Holy Thursday, April 12, 1229, the long war came to an end. Before the portal of Notre Dame de Paris Raymond humbly approached the legate and begged for

reconciliation to the Church; barefooted and in his shirt he was conducted to the altar as a penitent, received absolution in the presence
of the dignitaries of Church and State, and his followers were relieved from excommunication. After this he constituted himself a
prisoner in the Louvre until his daughter and five of his castles should
be in the hands of the king, and 500 toises of the walls of Toulouse
should be demolished.

The terms to which he had agreed were hard and humiliating.
He swore to persecute heresy with his whole strength, including
heretics and believers, their protectors and receivers, and not sparing
his nearest kindred, friends, and vassals. On all these, speedy punishment was to be inflicted, and an inquisition for their detection was
to be instituted in such form as the legate might dictate, while in its
aid Raymond agreed to offer the large reward of 2 marks per head
for every perfected heretic captured during two years, and 1 mark
forever thereafter. He was to defend the Church and all its members
and privileges; to enforce its censures by seizing the property of all
who should remain for a year under excommunication; to restore
all church lands and lands of ecclesiastics occupied since the commencement of the troubles, and to pay as damages for personal
property taken the sum of 10,000 silver marks; to enforce for the
future the payment of tithes, and, as a special fine, to pay 5,000
marks to five religious houses named, besides 6,000 marks to be
expended in fortifying certain strongholds to be held by the king
as security for the Church, and between 3,000 and 4,000 marks to
support for ten years at Toulouse two masters in theology, two
decretalists, and six masters in grammar and the liberal arts. Moreover, as penance, he agreed to assume the cross immediately on
receiving absolution, and to proceed within two years to Palestine,
to serve there for five years—a penance which he never performed,
though repeatedly summoned to do so, until in 1247 he made preparations for a departure which was arrested by death.

The interests of the Church and of religion being thus provided
for, the marriage of Jeanne with one of the king's brothers was
treated as a favor bestowed on Raymond. It was tacitly assumed
that all his dominions had been forfeited, and the king graciously
granted him all the lands comprised within the ancient bishopric
of Toulouse, subject to their reversion after his death to his

daughter and her husband, in such wise that whether there was issue of the marriage or not, or whether she survived her husband or not, they passed irrevocably to the royal family. Agen, Rouergue, Quercy, except Cahors, and part of Albi were likewise granted to Raymond, with reversion to his daughter in default of lawful heirs; but the king retained the extensive territories comprised within the duchy of Narbonne and the counties of Velay, Gévaudan, Viviers, and Lodève. The marquisate of Provence, beyond the Rhone, a dependency of the empire, was given to the Church. Raymond thus lost two-thirds of his vast dominions.

The king's assumed right to the territories thus disposed of arose partly from the conquests of his father, and partly from Amauri, who a few days later executed a third cession of all his claims without reserve or consideration, other than what the king in his bounty might see fit to grant. The reward he obtained was the reversion of the dignity of Constable of France, which fell in the next year on the death of Matthieu de Montmorency. In 1237 he foolishly revived his claims, again styled himself Duke of Narbonne, made an unsuccessful effort to seize Dauphiné in right of his wife, and invaded the county of Melgueil, thereby incurring the wrath of Gregory IX, who ordered him as a penance to join the crusade then preparing to start for the Holy Land. In effect he did so, and Gregory generously granted him, to be paid after he was beyond seas, the large sum of 3,000 marks out of the fund arising from the redemption of their vows by crusaders staying at home. In 1238 he sailed, and his customary ill-luck pursued him, for in 1241 we hear of him as a prisoner of the Saracens, and Gregory again came to his aid by contributing to his ransom 4,000 marks from the same redemptive fund. His death occurred the same year at Otranto, on his return from Palestine, thus closing a life of strange vicissitudes and almost uninterrupted misfortune.

The house of Toulouse was thus reduced from the position of the most powerful feudatory, with possessions greater than those of the crown, to a condition in which it was to be no longer dreaded, though Gregory IX and Frederic II, in 1234, at the reiterated request of Louis IX, restored to it the marquisate of Provence, probably as a reward for increased zeal in persecution. Raymond no longer, as Duke of Narbonne, held the first rank among the six lay peers of France, but was relegated to the fourth place. The treaty resulted as its framers intended. In 1229 Jeanne of Toulouse and her destined husband Alphonse, brother of Louis, were children in their ninth year. Their marriage was deferred until 1237, and when Raymond, in 1249, closed his unquiet career, they succeeded to his territories. They both died without issue in 1271, and Philip III took possession not only of the county of Toulouse, as provided for in the settlement, but also of the other possessions which Jeanne had vainly attempted to dispose of by will, thus rendering the crown supreme throughout southern France.

The battle of toleration against persecution had been fought and lost; nor, with such a warning as the fate of the two Raymonds, was there risk that other potentates would disregard the public opinion of Christendom by ill-advised mercy to the heretic. Calling upon the State for its assured support, the Church made haste to reap the fruits of victory, and the Inquisition was soon at work among those who had so long bidden her defiance.

CHAPTER V
THE MENDICANT ORDERS

DESPITE the persecuting edicts of Alonso and Pedro, the Waldensian heresy had taken deep root in Aragon. Durán de Huesca, the Catalan, was one of its leaders, and took part in the disputation held at Pamiers about 1207 between the Waldenses and the Bishops of Osma, Toulouse, and Conserans. It is probable that Dominic also took part in it, and as the two men had so much in common, one is tempted to believe that to Dominic's eloquence was due the conversion of Durán, which was the only substantial result of the colloquy. Durán was too earnest a man to remain satisfied with assuring his own salvation, and sought thenceforth to win over other erring souls. He conceived the idea of founding an order which should serve as a model of poverty and self-abnegation, and be devoted to preaching and missionary work, thus fighting the heretics with the very weapons they had found so efficacious in obtaining converts from the wealthy and worldly Church. Filled with this inspiration, he labored among his brethren and brought many of them over to his way of thinking, from Spain to Italy. In Milan a hundred of them agreed to return to the Church if a building erected by them for a school, which the archbishop had torn down, were restored to them. Durán, with three companions, presented himself before Innocent, who was satisfied with his profession of faith and approved of his plan. Most of the associates were clerks, who had already given away all their possessions in charity. Renouncing the world, they proposed to live in the strictest chastity, praying seven times a day and observing specified fasts in addition to those prescribed by the Church. Absolute poverty was to be enforced; all gifts of gold and silver were to be refused, and only the necessaries of food and clothing were to be accepted. A habit of white or gray was adopted, with sandals to distinguish them from the Waldenses. Those of them who were learned and fit for the work were to devote themselves to preaching to the faithful and converting the heretic. Laymen unable to serve in this capacity were to live in houses and labor with their hands, giving due tithes, oblations, and first fruits to the Church. The care of the poor, moreover, was to be a special duty, and a rich layman in the diocese of Elne proposed to build for them a hospital with fifty beds, to erect a church, and to distribute garments to the naked. They were to elect their own superior, but were to be in nowise exempt from the regular juris-diction of the prelates.

In this institution of the *Pauperes Catholici*, or Poor Catholics —as they called themselves in contradistinction to the *Pauperes de Lugduno* or Waldenses—there lay the possibilities of all that Dominic and Francis afterwards conceived and executed. It was the origin, or at least the precursor, of the great Mendicant Orders, the germ of the great fructifying idea which accomplished results so marvellous; and while it is not likely that Francis in Italy bor-rowed his conception from Durán, it is more than probable that Dominic in France, where he must have been familiar with the movement, was led by the plan of the Poor Catholics to that of the Preaching Friars, which was so closely modelled on it. Yet though at the start Durán had apparently far better prospects of success than either Dominic or Francis, his project was foredoomed from the beginning. Already in 1209 he had communities planted in Aragon, Narbonne, Béziers, Usez, Carcassonne, and Nîmes, but the prelates of Languedoc were universally suspicious of the project and secretly or actively hostile. Cavils were raised at the reconcilia-tion of converted heretics; complaints were made that the conversions were feigned and that the converts were lacking in respect for the Church and its observances. In vain Durán appealed to Innocent. In vain Innocent, who viewed the project with the intuition of a Christian statesman, assured him of the papal protection, and wrote again and again to the prelates commanding them to favor the Poor Catholics, reminding them that wandering sheep were to be wel-comed back to the fold, and that souls were to be won by gentleness and mercy. The passions and the prejudices which he had unchained in Languedoc had grown beyond his control, and the Poor Catholics disappeared in the tumult. After 1212 we hear little more of them. It was left to other hands to develop the enormous possibilities of the scheme which Durán had devised.

Far different were the results achieved by Domingo de Guzman, whom the Latin Church reverences as St. Dominic, the greatest and most successful of its champions. Born at Calaruega, in Old Castile, in 1170, of a stock which his brethren love to connect with the royal house, his saintliness was so penetrating that it reflected back upon his mother, who is reverenced as St. Juana de Aga, and at one time there was danger that even his father might be drawn into the saintly circle. Ten years of training in the University of Palencia made of Dominic an accomplished theologian and equipped him thoroughly for the missionary work to which his life was devoted. Entering the Chapter of Osma, he was speedily made subprior, and in this capacity we have seen him accompany his bishop, who from 1203 onward for some years was employed on missions that carried him through Languedoc. Dominic's biographers relate that his career was determined by an incident in this first voyage, when he chanced to lodge in the house of a heretic of Toulouse and spent the night in converting him. This success, and the sight of the wide extent of heresy, led him to devote his life to its extirpation. When in 1206 Bishop Diego dismissed his retinue and remained to evangelize the land, Dominic alone was retained; when Diego returned to Spain to die, Dominic remained behind and continued to make Languedoc the scene of his activity.

The legend which has grown around Dominic represents him as one of the chief causes of the overthrow of the Albigensian heresies. Doubtless he did all that an earnest and single-hearted man could do in a cause to which he had surrendered himself, but historically his influence was imperceptible. The monk of Vaux-Cernay alludes to him but once, as a follower of Bishop Diego. That he was one of the preachers licensed by the legates under the authority granted by Innocent III in 1207 is shown by an absolution issued by him which has chanced to be preserved, in which he styles himself canon of Osma and *prædicator minimus*; but his subordinate position is indicated by the absolution being subject to the pleasure of Legate Arnaud, from whom his authority was derived. This and a dispensation to a burgher of Toulouse to lodge a heretic in his house are the only extant evidences of his activity as a missionary. Yet already his talent for organization had been shown by his founding the Monastery of Prouille. One of the most efficient means by which the heretics propagated their belief was by establishments in which poor girls of gentle blood could obtain gratuitous education. To meet them on their own ground, Dominic, about 1206, conceived the idea of a similar foundation for Catholics, and with the aid of Bishop Foulques of Toulouse he carried it out. Prouille became a large and wealthy convent, which boasted of being the germ of the great Dominican Order.

For the next eight years the life of Dominic is a blank. He emerges again to view after the battle of Muret had destroyed the hopes of Count Raymond, when the cause of orthodoxy seemed triumphant and the field was unobstructed for conversions. In 1214 he was in his forty-fifth year, in the full strength of mature manhood, yet having thus far accomplished nothing that gave promise of what was to follow. Divested of their supernatural adornments, the accounts which we have of him show him to us as a man of earnest, resolute purpose, deep and unalterable convictions, full of zeal for the propagation of the faith, yet kindly in heart, cheerful in temper, and winning in manner. It is significant of the impression produced on his contemporaries that with scarce an exception the miracles related of him are beneficent ones—raising the dead, healing the sick and converting heretics, not by punishment, but by showing that he spoke by command of the Almighty. His endless scourgings, his tireless vigils, and, when exhausted nature could bear them no longer, his short repose on a board, or in the corner of a church where he had passed the night, his almost uninterrupted prayer, his superhuman fasts, are probably only harmless exaggerations of the truth. So, too, may be the legends which tell of his boundless charity and his love for his fellows; how, when a student, in a time of dearth he sold all his books to relieve the distress around him, and would, unless divinely prevented, have sold himself to redeem from the Moors a captive whose sister he saw overwhelmed with grief. Whether these stories be true or not, they at least show us the ideal which his immediate disciples thought to realize in him.

The brief remaining years of Dominic's life witnessed the rapid garnering of the harvest sowed in the period of humble but zeal-ous obscurity. In 1214 Pierre Cella, a rich citizen of Toulouse, moved by his earnestness, resolved to join him in his mission work, and gave for the purpose a stately house near the Château Narbon-nais, which for more than a hundred years remained the home of the Inquisition. A few other zealous souls gathered around him, and the little fraternity commenced to live like monks. Bishop Foulques assigned to them a sixth of the tithes, to provide them with books and other necessaries, that they might not lack the means of training themselves and others for the work of preaching, which was the main object of the community. It is noteworthy that in the inception of the plan there was no thought of employing force. The heretics of Languedoc lay defenseless at the feet of de Montfort, an easy prey to the spoiler, but Dominic's project only looked to their peaceful conversion and to performing the duties of instruction and exhortation of which the Church had been so wholly neglectful.

All eyes were now bent on the Lateran Council, which was to decide the fate of the land. Foulques of Toulouse on his voyage thither took with him Dominic to obtain from the pope his approval of the new community. Tradition relates that Innocent hesitated; his experience with Durán de Huesca had not taught him to expect much from the irregular action of enthusiasts; the council had forbidden the formation of new orders of monkhood, and had commanded that zeal for the future should satisfy itself with those already established. Yet Innocent's doubts were removed by a dream in which he saw the Lateran Basilica tottering and ready to fall, and a man in whom he recognized the humble Dominic supporting it on his shoulders. Thus divinely warned that the crumbling church edifice was to be restored by the man whose zeal he had despised, he approved the project on condition that Dominic and his brethren should adopt the Rule of some established Order.

Dominic returned and assembled his brethren at Prouille. They were by this time 16 in number, and it is a curious illustration of the denationalizing influence of the Church to observe in this little gathering of earnest men in that remote spot that Castile, Navarre, Normandy, France, Languedoc, England, and Germany were represented. This self-devoted band adopted the Rule of the Canons Regular of St. Augustin, which was Dominic's own, and elected Matthieu le Gaulois as their abbot. He was the first and last who bore this title, for as the Order grew its organization was modified to secure greater unity and at the same time greater freedom of action. It was divided into provinces, the head of each being a provincial prior. Supreme over all was the General Master. These offices were filled by election, with tenure during good behavior, and provisions were made for stated assemblies, or chapters, both provincial and general. Each brother, or friar, was held to implicit obedience. Like a soldier on duty, he was liable at any moment to be dispatched on any mission that the interest of religion or of the Order might demand. They deemed themselves, in fact, soldiers of Christ, not devoted, like the monks, to a life of contemplation, but trained to mix with the world, exercised in all the arts of persuasion, skilled in theology and rhetoric, and ready to dare and suffer all things in the interest of the Church Militant. The name "Preaching Friars," which acquired such worldwide significance, was the result of accident. During the Lateran Council, while Dominic was in Rome, Innocent had occasion to address a note to him and ordered his secretary to begin, "To brother Dominic and his companions"; then, correcting himself, he said, "To brother Dominic and the preachers with him," and finally, considering further, "to Master Dominic and the brethren preachers." This greatly pleased them, and they at once commenced calling themselves Friar Preachers.

Curiously enough, poverty formed no part of the original design. The impulse to found the Order was given by Cella's donation of his property and the share of the tithes offered by Bishop Foulques; and, as soon as it was organized, Dominic had no scruple in accepting three churches from Foulques—one in Toulouse, one in Pamiers, and one in Puylaurens. It was not until the success of the Franciscans had shown the attractive power of poverty that it was adopted by the Dominicans in the General Chapter of 1220. It was finally embodied in the constitution adopted by the Chapter of 1228, which prohibited that lands or revenues should be acquired, ordered Preachers not to solicit money, and classed among the graver offenses the retention by a brother of any of the things forbidden to be received. The Order speedily outgrew these restrictions, but Dominic himself set an example of the utmost rigidity in this respect, and when he died in Bologna, in 1221, it was in the bed of Friar Moneta, as he had none of his own, and in Moneta's gown, for his own was worn out and he had not another to replace it; and when the Rule was adopted in 1220 such property as was not essential for the needs of the Order was made over to the Convent of Prouille.

All that now was lacking was the papal confirmation of the Order and its statutes. Before Dominic could reach Rome on the errand to obtain this, Innocent had died, but his successor, Honorius III, entered fully into his views, and the sanction of the Holy See was given on December 21, 1216. Returning to Toulouse in 1217, Dominic lost no time in dispersing his followers. The little band seemed absurdly inadequate for the task, but Dominic never hesitated. Some were sent to Spain, others to Paris, others again to Bologna, while Dominic himself went to Rome, where, under the favor of the papal court, his enthusiasm was rewarded with an abundance of disciples. Those who went to Paris were warmly received and were granted the house of St. Jacques, where they founded the famous convent of the Jacobins, which endured until the Order was swept away in the Revolution.

It is not worth while to follow further in detail the marvellous growth of the Order in all the lands of Europe. In 1221, when Dominic as General Master held the second General Chapter in Bologna, the Order already had 60 convents and was organized into 8 provinces—Spain, Provence, France, England, Germany, Hungary, Lombardy, and Romagnola. The same year witnessed the death of Dominic, but his work was done and his removal from the scene made no change in the mighty machine he had built and set in motion. Everywhere the strongest intellects of the age were donning the Dominican scapular, and everywhere they were earning the respect and veneration of the people. Their services to the papacy were fully recognized, and they are speedily found filling important offices in the curia. In 1243 the learned Hugh of Vienne became the first Dominican cardinal, and in 1276 the Dominicans rejoiced to see Brother Peter of Tarentaise raised to the chair of St. Peter as Innocent V. Yet the delay in Dominic's canonization would seem to show that personally he made less impression on his contemporaries than his followers would have us believe. Although he died in 1221, the bull enrolling him in the calendar of saints only bears date July 3, 1234. Francis, who died in 1226, was canonized within two years; the young Franciscan, Antony of Padua, who died in 1231, was recognized as a saint in 1233. That thirteen years should have elapsed in the case of Dominic shows that his merits were recognized but slowly.

If the Franciscans were in the end closely assimilated to the Dominicans, it was through the overmastering demands of the work to be accomplished by both, for in their origin the Orders were destined to objects as diverse as the characters of their founders. If St. Dominic was the type of the active practical missionary, St. Francis was the ideal of the contemplative ascetic, modified by boundless love and charity for his fellows.

Born in 1182, Giovanni Bernardone was the son of a prosperous trader of Assisi, who trained him in his business. Accompanying his father on a voyage to France, he came back with the accomplishment of speaking French, which gained for him among his companions the nickname of Francesco, a name which he adopted as his own. A dissipated youth was brought to a sudden close in his twentieth year by a dangerous illness which resulted in his conversion, and thereafter he devoted himself to works of mercy and charity, earning for himself with no little verisimilitude the reputation of insanity. In order to restore the dilapidated church of St. Damiani he stole a quantity of his father's cloths, which he sold at Foligno, together with the horse that carried them. Finding him irrevocably bent on following his own devices, the exasperated parent took him before the bishop to make him renounce all claim on his inheritance, which Francis willingly did, and to render the renunciation more complete stripped off all his clothes, save a hair shirt worn to mortify the flesh, when the bishop, to cover his nakedness, gave him the wornout cloak of a peasant serving-man.

Francis was now fairly embarked on a life of wandering beggary, which he used to so good an account that he was able to restore four churches which were sinking to ruin. He had no thought other than to work out his own salvation in poverty and acts of loving charity, but the fame of his holiness spread, and the Blessed Bernard of Quintavalle asked to be associated with him. The solitary ascetic at first was indisposed to companionship, but to learn the will of God he thrice opened the Gospels at random, and his finger lit on the three texts on which the great Franciscan Order was founded:

And Jesus said unto him, If thou wilt be perfect, go and sell that thou hast and give to the poor, and thou shalt have treasure in heaven: and come and follow me (Matt. xix. 21).

Be not ye therefore like unto them, for your Father knoweth what things ye have need of before ye ask him (Matt. VI. 8).

Then said Jesus unto his disciples, If any man will come after me, let him deny himself, and take up his cross and follow me (Matt. XVI. 24).

The command was obeyed and the recruit accepted. Others joined from time to time, till the little band numbered eight. Then Francis announced that the time had come for them to evangelize the world, and dispersed them in pairs to the four points of the compass. On their reuniting, four more volunteers were added, when Francis drew up a Rule for their governance, and the twelve proceeded to Rome, according to the Franciscan legend, at the time of the Lateran Council, to procure the papal confirmation. When Francis presented himself to the pope in the aspect of a beggar the pontiff indignantly ordered him away, but tradition relates that a vision that night induced him to send for the mendicant. There was much hesitation among the papal advisers, but the earnestness and eloquence of Francis won the day, and finally the Rule was approved and the brethren were authorized to preach the Word of God.[1]

Even yet they were undecided whether to abandon themselves to the contemplative life of anchorites or to undertake the great work of evangelization which lay before them in its immensity. They withdrew to Spoleto and counselled earnestly together without being able to reach a conclusion, until a revelation from God, which we can readily believe as actual to a mind such as that of Francis, turned the scale, and the Franciscan Order, in place of dying out in a few scattered hermitages, became one of the most powerful organizations of Christendom, though the abandoned hovel to which they restored on their return to Assisi gave little promise of future splendor. The rapidity of the growth of the Order may be measured by the fact that when Francis called together his first General Chapter in 1221, it was attended by brethren variously reported as from 3,000 to 5,000, including a cardinal and several

---

[1] This account is doubtless colored by the result and adapted unconsciously to the successive stages of a formal religious organization. At first, however, the brethren were not expected to abandon their ordinary pursuits. They were required to follow their regular handicraft, earning their livelihood, and not living on alms except in case of necessity. See the First Rule, as reconstructed by Prof. Kard Müller, *Die Anfänge des Minoritenordens*, Freiburg, i. B., 1885, p. 186.

bishops; and when, in the General Chapter of 1260, under Bonaventura, the Order was redistributed to accord with its growth, it was
partitioned into 33 provinces and 3 vicariates, comprehending in all
182 guardianships. The Order then extended into every corner of what
was regarded as the civilized world and its contiguous regions.

The Minorites, as in humility they called themselves, were so
different in their inception from any existing organization of the
Church that when, in 1219, St. Francis made the first dispersion
and sent his disciples to evangelize Europe, those who went to
Germany and Hungary were regarded as heretics, and were roughly
handled and expelled. In France they were taken for Cathari, to
whose wandering perfected missionaries their austerity doubtless
gave them close resemblance, and it was only after the authorities had
consulted Honorius III that they were relieved from suspicion.
In Spain five of them endured martyrdom. Innocent had only given
a verbal approbation of the Rule; he was dead, and something
more formal was requisite to protect the brethren from persecution. Francis accordingly drew up a second Rule, more concise
and less rigid than the first, which he submitted to Honorius.
The pope approved it, though not without objecting to some of
the clauses; but Francis refused to modify them, saying that it
was not his but Christ's, and that he could not change the words
of Christ. From this his followers assumed that the Rule had been
divinely revealed to him. This belief passed into the traditions of
the Order, and the Rule has been maintained unaltered in letter,
though, as we shall see, its spirit has been more than once explained
away by ingenious papal casuists.

It is simple enough, amounting hardly to more than a gloss on
the entrance oath required of each friar: to live according to the
Gospel, in obedience, chastity, and without possessing property.
The applicant for admission was required to sell all he had and
give it to the poor, and if this were impossible the will so to do
sufficed. Each one was permitted to have two gowns, but they
must be vile in texture, and were to be patched and repaired as
long as they could be made to hang together. Shoes were allowed
to those who found it impossible to forego them. All were to go
on foot, except in case of sickness or necessity. No one was to receive
money, either directly or through a third party, except that the

ministers (as the provincial superiors were called) could do so for the care of the sick and for provision of clothing, especially in rigorous climates. Labor was strenuously enjoined on all those able to perform it, but wages were not to be in money, but in necessaries for themselves and their brethren. The clause requiring absolute poverty caused, as we shall see, a schism in the order, and therefore is worth giving textually:

The brethren shall appropriate to themselves nothing, neither house, nor place, nor other thing, but shall live in the world as strangers and pilgrims, and shall go confidently after alms. In this they shall feel no shame, since the Lord for our sake made himself poor in the world. It is this perfection of poverty which has made you, dearest brethren, heirs and kings of the kingdom of heaven. Having this, you should wish to have naught else under heaven.

The head of the Order, or General Minister, was chosen by the provincial ministers, who could at any time depose him when the general good required it. Faculties for preaching were to be issued by the General, but no brother was to preach in any diocese without the assent of the bishop.

This is all; and there is nothing in it to give promise of the immense results achieved under it. What gave it an enduring hold on the affections of the world was the spirit which the founder infused in it and in his brethren. No human creature since Christ has more fully incarnated the ideal of Christianity than Francis. Amid the extravagance of his asceticism, there shines forth the Christian love and humility with which he devoted himself to the wretched and neglected—the outcasts for whom, in that rude time, there were few indeed to care. Of all the miseries of that age of misery, the hardest lot was that of the leper, who was cut off from all intercourse with fellow men, and who, when he wandered abroad for alms from the lazar-house in which he was herded, was obliged, by clattering sticks, to give notice of his approach. It was to these, the most helpless and hopeless and abhorred of mankind, that the boundless charity and love of Francis was especially directed. The example he set in his own person he required to be followed by his brethren; when noble or simple applied for admission to the Order he was told that prominent among the obligations which he assumed was that of humbly serving the lepers in their hospitals. Francis did not hesitate to sleep in the lazar-houses, to handle the dangerous sores of the afflicted, to apply medicaments, and to minister to the sufferings of the body as well as of the soul. The Franciscans were ever foremost in the cure of the sick; they tended the hospitals in the midst of pestilence, and to their intelligent devotion is due whatever progress the science of healing made in the dark ages. We are told, moreover, that the tender love of Francis lavished itself on the brute creation as well as on man—on insects, birds, and beasts, whom he was wont to call his brethren and sisters, and for whom he was never weary in caring. All the stories related of him and his immediate disciples, in fact, are instinct with love and self-sacrifice, with humility and patience and long-suffering, with the control of the passions, and with endless striving to subdue all that renders human nature imperfect and to realize the standard that Christ had erected for the guidance of man.

To the pride and cruelty of the age he opposed patience and humility. "The perfection of gladness," he says, "consists not in working miracles, in curing the sick, expelling devils, or raising the dead; nor in learning and knowledge of all things; nor in eloquence to convert the world, but in bearing all ills and injuries and injustice and despiteful treatment with patience and humility." So far from valuing himself on his virtues, he humbly confesses that he had himself not lived up to the Rule, and apologizes for it through his infirmity and ignorance. With all this there was too much kindliness in his nature for gloom, and cheerfulness was a virtue which he constantly inculcated. Sadness he held to be one of the most deadly weapons of Satan, while cheerfulness was the Christian's thankful acknowledgment of the blessings bestowed by God upon his creatures. This was consequently a distinguishing characteristic of the friars in the early days of the Order. In Eccleston's simple and quiet narration of their advent to England in 1224, when nine of them crossed to Dover without knowing what their fate might be from day to day, there is something singularly beautiful in the picture of their trustfulness, their patience, their unfailing cheerfulness under privation and disappointment, and in their tireless activity in ministerng to the spiritual and corporeal wants of the neglected children of the Church.

The Mendicants came upon Christendom like a revelation—men who had abandoned all that was enticing in life to imitate the apostles, to convert the sinner and unbeliever, to instruct the ignorant, to offer salvation to all; in short, to do what the Church was paid so enormously in wealth and privileges and power for neglecting. Wandering on foot over the face of Europe, rejecting alms in money but receiving thankfully whatever coarse food might be set before the wayfarer, taking no thought for the morrow, but busied eternally in the work of lifting men up from the sordid cares of daily life, of ministering to their infirmities and of bringing to their darkened souls a glimpse of heavenly light—such was the aspect in which the earliest Dominicans and Franciscans presented themselves to the eyes of men who had been accustomed to see in the ecclesiastic only the sensual worldling intent solely upon the indulgence of his appetites. It is no wonder that such an apparition accomplished much in restoring to the populations the faith in Christianity which had begun to be so sorely shaken, or that it spread through Christendom the hope of an approaching regeneration in the Church which greatly lessened popular impatience under its exactions. It is no wonder, moreover, that the love and veneration of the people followed the Mendicants; that the charitable showered their gifts upon them, to the destruction of the primal obligation of poverty; that the men of earnest convictions pressed forward to join their ranks. Raymond of Pennaforte, Alexander Hales, Albertus Magnus, Thomas Aquinas, Bonaventura, Roger Bacon, Duns Scotus are names which show how irresistibly the men of highest gifts were led to seek among the Dominicans or Franciscans their ideal of life.

There was another instrumentality of vast importance, in utilizing which both Francis and Dominic manifested their organizing ability—the Tertiary Orders through which laymen, without abandoning the world, were assimilated to the respective brotherhoods, aided in their labors, shared in their glory, and added to their influence, thus stimulating and utilizing the zeal of the community at large. Francis, though unlearned in scholastic theology and untrained in rhetoric, possessed a simple eloquence that carried the hearts of his hearers. On one occasion he produced by his preaching so profound an impression that all the inhabitants of the town, men, women, and children, begged admission to his Order. This was manifestly impossible, and he bethought him of framing a Rule by which persons of both sexes, while remaining in the world, could be subjected to wholesome discipline and be connected with the fraternity, which in turn promised them its protection. Of the restrictions placed on them perhaps the most significant was that they should carry no weapons of offense except for the defense of the Roman Church, the Christian faith, and their own lands. The project and the Rule were approved by the pope in 1221, and the official name of the organization was "The Brothers and Sisters of Penitence," though it became popularly known as the Tertiary Order of Minorites, or Franciscans. Under the more aggressive name of *Militia Jesu Christi*, or Soldier of Christ, Dominic founded a similar association of laymen connected with his Order. The idea proved a most fruitful one. It reorganized to some degree the Church by removing a portion of the barrier which separated the layman from the ecclesiastic. It brought immense support to the Mendicant Orders by enlisting with them multitudes of the earnest and zealous, as well as those who from less worthy motives sought to share their protection and enjoy the benefit of their influence. Types of both classes may be found in the royal house of France, for both St. Louis and Catherine de Médicis were Tertiaries of St. Francis.

To comprehend fully the magnitude and influence of these movements we must bear in mind the impressionable character of the populations and their readiness to yield to contagious emotion. The most formidable and significant manifestation of this universal restlessness and gregarious enthusiasm is seen in the uprising of the peasantry—the first of the wandering bands known as Pastoureaux. Suddenly, about Easter, 1251, there appeared a mysterious preacher, known as the Hungarian, advanced in years, and clothed with the attributes which most excite popular awe and veneration. In his clenched hand he carried a paper given to him by the Virgin Mary herself, which was his mandate and commission. Tall and pale, gifted with eloquence to win the hearts of the multitude, speaking like a native in French and German and Latin, he set forth, preaching from town to town the supineness of the rich and powerful who allowed the Holy Land to remain in the grasp of the Infidel and the good King Louis to languish in his Egyptian dungeon. God had tired of the selfishness and ambition of the nobles, and he called the poor and humble, without arms and captains, to rescue the Holy Places and the Good King. All this found ready response, but even greater applause followed his attacks upon the clergy. The Mendicant Orders were vagrants and hypocrites; the Cistercians were greedy of money and lands; the Benedictines proud and gluttonous; the canons wholly given to secular aims and the lusts of the flesh; the bishops and their officials were money-seekers, who shrank from no trickery to accomplish their aims. As for Rome, no terms of objurgation were too strong for the papal court. The people listened to this rhetoric with delight, and eagerly joined a movement which promised a reform in some unseen way.

There were not lacking those high in station who, carried away with the general enthusiasm, imagined that God was about to work miracles with the poor and helpless after the great ones of the earth had failed. Even Queen Blanche, eager for any means that promised to liberate her son, looked upon the movement for a while with favor, and lent it her countenance. It swelled and grew till the wandering multitudes amounted to more than 100,000 men, bearing 50 banners as an emblem of victory. It was impossible, of course, to confine such an uprising to the peaceful and humble. No sooner did it assume proportions promising immunity than it inevitably drew to itself all the disorderly elements inseparable from the society of the time—the *ruptarii* and *ribaldi*, who figure so largely in the Albigensian troubles. These flocked to it from all sides, bringing knife and dagger, sword and ax, and giving to the immense procession a still more menacing aspect.

On June 11, 1251, they entered Orleans, against the commands of the bishop but welcomed by the people, though the richer citizens prudently locked their doors. All might have passed peaceably there as elsewhere but for a hotheaded student of the flourishing university of the city, who interrupted the preaching of the Hungarian to denounce him as a liar, and was promptly brained by a zealous follower. A tumult followed, in which the Pastoureaux made short work of the Orleans clergy, breaking into their houses, burning their books, and slaying many, or tossing them into the Loire; and, what is most significant, the people are described as looking on approvingly.

On hearing this the Regent Blanche said, "God knows I thought they would recover the Holy Land in simplicity and holiness. But

since they are deceivers, let them be excommunicated and destroyed."
Accordingly they were excommunicated, but before the anathema
could be published they had reached Bourges, where, in a tumult, the
Hungarian was slain, and they broke up into bands. The authorities,
recovering from their stupor, pursued the luckless wretches everywhere, who were slain like mad dogs. Some emissaries who penetrated
to England, and succeeded in raising a revolt of some 500 peasants,
met the same fate.

Even more remarkable as a manifestation of popular emotion was
the first apparition of the Flagellants. Suddenly, in 1259, in Perugia,
no one knew why, the population was seized with a fury of devotional
penitence, without incitement by friar or priest. The contagion
spread, and soon the whole of upper Italy was filled with tens of
thousands of penitents. Nobles and peasants, old and young, even
to children five years of age, walked solemnly in procession, two by
two, naked except a loin-cloth, weeping and praying God for mercy,
and scourging themselves with leather thongs to the drawing of
blood. The women decently inflicted the penance on themselves in
their chambers, but the men marched through the cities by day and
night, in the sharpest winter, preceded by priests with crosses and
banners, to the churches, where they prostrated themselves before the
altars. Usurers and robbers restored their ill-gotten gain; criminals
confessed their sins and renounced their vices; the prison doors were
thrown open, and the captives walked forth; homicides offered themselves on their knees, with drawn swords, to the kindred of their
victims, and were embraced with tears; old enmities were forgiven,
and exiles were permitted to return to their homes. The movement
even spread to the Rhinelands and throughout Germany and Bohemia; but whatever hopes were aroused of the regeneration of man
vanished with the subsidence of the excitement, which disappeared
as rapidly as it came, and was even denounced as a heresy.

It was in a population subject to such tempests of emotion that
the Mendicant Orders came to gather to themselves the potential
religious exaltation of the time. Everything favored them. The papal
court early recognized in them an instrument more efficient than
had yet been devised to bring the power of the Holy See to bear
directly upon the Church and the people in every corner of Christendom; to break down the independence of the local prelates; to com-

bat the temporal enemies of the papacy, and to lead the people into direct relations with the successor of St. Peter. Privileges and exemptions of all kinds were showered upon them, until, by a series of bulls issued between 1240 and 1244 by Gregory IX and Innocent IV, they were rendered completely independent of the regular ecclesiastical organization. A time-honored rule of the Church required that any excommunication or anathema could only be removed by him who had pronounced it, but this was revolutionized in their favor. Not only were the bishops required to give absolution to any Dominican or Franciscan who should apply for it, except in cases of such enormity that the Holy See alone could act, but the Mendicant priors and ministers were authorized to absolve their friars from any censures inflicted on them. These extraordinary measures removed them entirely from the regular jurisdiction of the establishment; the members of each Order became responsible only to their own superiors, and in their all-pervading activity throughout Europe they could secretly undermine the power and influence of the local hierarchy and replace it with that of Rome, which they so directly represented.

The Holy See was thus provided with a militia, recruited and sustained at the expense of the faithful, panoplied in invulnerability, and devoted to its exclusive service. Human ingenuity could have devised no more efficient army, for not only were they full of zeal and inspired with profound convictions, but the reputation for superior sanctity which they everywhere acquired secured for them popular sympathy and support, and gave them an enormous advantage in any contest with local churches.

It is easy to imagine that such functions as these produced antagonism between the new Orders and the old organization which they were undermining and supplanting. Yet this was perhaps the least of the causes of bitterness between them. A far more fruitful source of discord was the intrusion of the Mendicants in the office of preaching and hearing confessions. We have seen how jealously the former had always been reserved by the bishops and how utterly it had been neglected until the primary object of St. Dominic had been to supply the deficiency. The Church was scarce better prepared to discharge the duty of the confessional, which the Lateran Council had rendered obligatory and had confined to the priesthood. In the populous town of Montpellier there was only one church in which the sacrament of penitence could be administered, and as late as 1247, Ypres, with 200,000 inhabitants, had but four parish churches. If the Church Militant was to perform its duty, and if it was to regain the veneration of the people, these deficiencies must be supplied.

The first efforts of Dominic had been based on the power granted to the legates of Languedoc to issue licenses for preaching, and these were, of course, at the time independent of episcopal permission, but in the Rule of 1228 it was especially provided that no friar should preach in a diocese without first obtaining permission of the bishop, and in no case was he to declaim against the vices of the secular priesthood. The intrusion of the Mendicants on the functions of the parish priests was gradual, and was commenced with the privilege granted them of celebrating mass on portable altars. Some resistance was made to this, but it was broken down; and when Gregory IX in 1227 signalized his accession by empowering both Orders to preach, hear confessions, and grant absolution everywhere, the wandering friars, in spite of the prohibitions of the Rules, gradually invaded every parish and performed all the duties of the cure of souls. Complaints were loud and reiterated, and were sometimes listened to, but were more frequently answered by an emphatic confirmation of the innovation.

The matter was made worse by the fact that everywhere the laity welcomed the intruders and preferred them to their own curates. Training and experience rendered them far more skillful directors of conscience than the indolent incumbents, and there arose a natural popular feeling that the penance which they imposed was more holy and their absolution more efficacious. A friar would come and set up his portable altar, as he said, for a day. His preaching was attractive; penitents aroused to a sense of their sins would hasten to confess; his stay was prolonged and he became a fixture. If the place was populous, he would be joined by others. The gifts of the charitable would flow in. A modest chapel and cloisters would be provided, which grew till it overshadowed the parish church and was filled at its expense. Worse than all, the dying sinner would assume the robe of the Mendicant on his deathbed, bequeath his body to the friars, and make them the recipient of his legacies, leading to a prolonged and embittered renewal of the old ghoul-like quarrels over corpses.

Whenever an open conflict arose, the decision would be almost certainly in favor of the friars, and the clergy saw with dismay that the upstarts were supplanting them in all their functions, in the veneration of the people, and in the profitable results of that veneration.

The University of Paris was the center of scholastic theology. Cosmopolitan in its character, a long line of great teachers had lectured to immense masses of students from every land, until its reputation was European and it was looked upon as the bulwark of orthodoxy. In every episcopate it could count its graduates and the holders of its degrees, who looked back upon it with filial affection as to their *alma mater*. It had welcomed Dominic's first missionaries when they came to Paris to found a house of the Order, and it had admitted Dominicans to its corps of teachers. Suddenly there arose a quarrel, the insignificance of its cause showing the tension which existed and the eagerness of all classes of the clergy to repress the growing influence of the Mendicants. The University had always been jealous of its privileges, among which not the least was the jurisdiction which it enjoyed over its students. One of these was slain and several were wounded by the Paris watch in a disturbance, and the reparation tendered for the offense was deemed insufficient. The University closed its doors, but the Dominican teachers Bonushomo and Elias continued their lectures. To punish this contumacy they were ordered to be silent, and students were forbidden to listen to them. They appealed to the pope, but their appeal was disregarded; and when the University resumed its functions, they were required to take an oath to observe its statutes, provided there was nothing therein to conflict with the Rule of the Order. This they refused unless they were allowed two teachers of theology, and after a delay of a fortnight they were expelled. The provincials of both Orders at Paris took up the quarrel and appealed to Rome, and Innocent IV demanded the repeal of the obnoxious rules.

The gage of battle was thrown and the University was resolved on no half-measures. It would reduce the Mendicants to the condition of the other religious Orders and earn the gratitude of all the prelates and clergy by stripping them of the privileges which rendered them so dangerous. For this purpose it was necessary to win the favor of Rome, and the students enthusiastically assessed themselves, economizing in their expenses that they might contribute to the fund. The leader of the faculty in the quarrel was William of St. Amour, noted both as a preacher and a teacher, learned, eloquent, and inflexible of purpose. He was sent to the Holy See, where he found Innocent IV in a frame of mind adapted to listen to his arguments that the Mendicant Rules were fitted only to lead souls to perdition. The pope had been the friend of the Orders, and had confirmed and enlarged their privileges, but just now was out of humor. The Dominicans asserted that this arose from their having secretly received into the Order one of his cousins whom he loved greatly and intended to advance in the world; and also from the malevolence of another cousin, who proposed to build at Genoa a fortress-palace to dominate the city, and had been prevented by the Dominicans' refusing to sell a piece of ground essential to his purpose. Innocent's mind must indeed have been receptive of William of St. Amour's arguments. In July and August 1254, he had issued repeated briefs in favor of the Mendicants and against the University. On November 21 he promulgated the bull *Etsi Animarum*, known among the Mendicants as the "terrible" bull, by which the members of all religious Orders were forbidden to receive in their churches on Sundays and feast-days the parishioners of others; they were not to hear confessions without the special license of the parish priests, they were not to preach in their own churches before mass, so that parishioners should not be drawn away from their parish churches, nor were they to preach in the parish churches, nor when bishops preached or caused preaching to be done.

The bull was in reality a terrible one, for it shattered at a blow the edifice erected with such infinite labor and self-sacrifice. To meet it, the Dominicans not only summoned their greatest and wisest members, but appealed to Heaven. Every friar was ordered daily after matins to recite seven psalms and the litanies of the Virgin and St. Dominic. A brother, during this exercise, was encouraged with a vision of the Virgin pleading with the Son and saying, "Listen to them, my Son, listen to them!" He did listen to them, for though we may doubt the Dominican story that Innocent was stricken with paralysis the very day that he signed the "*crudelissimum edictum*," he certainly did die on December 7, within sixteen days after it, and a pious Roman had a vision of his soul being handed over to the two wrathful saints, Dominic and Francis. Moreover the Cardinal of Albano, whose hostility to the Orders had led him to take an active part in advising Innocent to the measure, was imprudent enough to boast that he had caused the subjugation of the Mendicants to the bishops and would place them under the feet of the lowest priests. The same day a beam in his house gave way; he fell and broke his neck. It would perhaps be unjust to accuse the Dominicans of having assisted nature in these catastrophes; but, strange as it seems to hear them boast of having prayed a pope to death, they certainly do relate with pride that "Beware of the Dominican litanies, for they work miracles," became a common phrase.

The death of Innocent saved the Mendicant Orders. The new pope, Alexander IV, was especially favorable to the Mendicants. When John of Parma, the Franciscan General, came to him with the customary request that he would appoint a cardinal as "Protector" of the Order, he refused, saying that so long as he lived it should need no other protector than himself. On December 31, ten days after his elevation, he addressed letters to both Orders asking their suffrages and intercession with God, and the same day he issued an encyclical, revoking the "terrible" bull of Innocent and pronouncing it void.

Before such a judge the case of the University was lost. On April 14, 1255, appeared the bull *Quasi lignum vitæ*, deciding the quarrel in favor of the Dominicans. Yet William of St. Amour returned to Paris resolved to carry on the war. In the pulpit he and his friends thundered forth against the Mendicants. They were not specifically named, but there was no mistaking the ingenious application to them of the signs foretold by the prophets of those who should usher in the days of Antichrist, nor the description of the Pharisees and Publicans made to fit them. Another weapon which lay to St. Amour's hand was eagerly grasped. In 1254 there appeared a work under the title *Introduction to the Everlasting Gospel*, of which the authorship was ascribed to John of Parma. We shall have occasion to recur to this, and need only say here that a section of the Franciscans were strongly inclined to the mysticism which now began to show itself, and that the writings of Abbot Joachim of Flora, now revived and hardily developed, predicted the downfall, in 1260, of the existing order of things in Church and State, the

substitution of a new evangel for that of Christ, and the replacement
of the hierarchy by mendicant monachism. The *Introduction to the
Everlasting Gospel* attracted universal attention and offered too
tempting an opening for attack to be neglected.

The University sullenly held out, while Alexander fulminated bull
after bull against the recalcitrants, threatening them with varied
penalties, and finally calling in the assistance of the secular arm by
an appeal to St. Louis. The clergy of Paris, delighted with the opportunity afforded by the temporary unpopularity of the Mendicants,
reviled them from the pulpit and even attacked them personally
with blows and threats of worse treatment, till they scarce ventured
to appear in the streets and beg their daily bread. The controversy
raged wilder as the indomitable St. Amour, undeterred by Alexander's
request to the king to throw him into jail, issued a tract entitled
De Periculis novissimorum Temporum, in which he boldly set forth
all the arguments of his discourses against the Mendicants. He proved
that the pope had no right to contravene the commands of the
prophets and apostles, and that popes were convicted of error when
they upturned the established order of the Church in permitting
these wandering hypocrites and false prophets to preach and hear
confessions. Whoever asserts that Christ was a beggar denies that
he was the Messiah, and thus is a heresiarch who destroys the foundation of all Christian faith. An able-bodied man commits sacrilege if
he receives the alms of the poor for his own use, and if the Church
has permitted this for the monks it has been in error and should be
corrected. This was answered by Aquinas and Bonaventura. The
former, in his tract *Contra Impugnantes Religionem*, proved in the
most finished style of scholastic logic that the friars have a right to
teach, to preach and hear confessions, and to live without labor.
Bonaventura also replied in several treatises—*De Paupertate Christi*,
in which he earnestly pleaded the example of Christ as an argument
for poverty and mendicancy; *Libellus Apologeticus* and *Tractatus
quia Fratres Minores prædicent*, in which he carried the war into
the enemy's territory with a vigorous and plain-spoken onslaught on
the shortcomings and defects and sins and corruption and vileness
of the clergy.

Yet this wordy war was mere surplusage. On the appearance of
St. Amour's book, St. Louis had hastened to send copies to Alex-

ander for judgment. The University likewise sent St. Amour at the head of a delegation to demand the condemnation of *The Everlasting Gospel.* Albertus Magnus and Bonaventura came to defend their Orders, and a hot disputation was held before the consistory. *The Everlasting Gospel* and its Introduction were condemned with decent reserve by a special commission assembled at Anagni, in July 1255, but St. Amour's book was declared by the bull *Romanus Pontifex,* October 5, 1256, to be lying, scandalous, deceptive, wicked, and execrable. It was ordered to be burned before the curia and the University; every copy was to be surrendered within eight days to be burned, and anyone presuming to defend it was pronounced a rebel. The envoys of St. Louis and the University were obliged to subscribe to a declaration assenting to this and to the right of the Mendicants to preach and hear confessions and to live on alms without labor.

The victory was won for the Mendicants. The University submitted ungraciously to the power of the papacy, and the unconquerable William of St. Amour alone held out. He had sworn to abide by the mandates of the Church, but he refused to recant like his comrades. When about to return, in August 1257, Alexander forbade him to go to France and perpetually interdicted him from teaching, and so great was the dread which he inspired that the pope wrote to St. Louis asking him to prevent the inflexible theologian from entering his kingdom. Yet from abroad St. Amour maintained an active correspondence with his old colleagues, and the University continued in a state of disquiet. Though the Mendicants were allowed to teach, they were ridiculed in indecent rhymes and lampoons, which were eagerly circulated; and, on Palm Sunday of 1259 the beadle of the University, Guillot of Picardy, interrupted the preaching of Thomas Aquinas by publishing a scandalous and libellous book against the Mendicants. The final act of the quarrel is seen in an epistle of Alexander's, December 3, 1260, authorizing the Bishop of Paris to absolve those who had incurred excommunication by keeping copies of St. Amour's book, on their surrendering them to be burned. Still St. Amour remained steadfast in exile. He was allowed to return to Paris by Clement IV, who ascended the papal throne in 1264, and in 1266 St. Amour sent to the pontiff another book on the same theme. Clement had hastened, in 1265, to proclaim his good will to the Mendicant Orders by a bull in which he confirmed in the amplest manner their independence of the bishops, and, as was inevitable, he rejected St. Amour's new book as filled with the old virus. William died in 1272, obstinate and unrepentant, and was honorably buried in his native village of St. Amour, though he is reputed as a heretic by all good Dominicans and Franciscans.

Spasmodic resistance, however hopeless, still continued. About 1284 the interpretation put on some fresh concessions by Martin IV aroused the antagonism anew. The whole Gallican Church uprose. In 1287 the Archbishop of Reims called a provincial council to consider the subject. He pathetically described the unbearable encroachments of the friars, the intolerable injuries inflicted on both clergy and laity, and the necessity of an appeal to Rome. The expenses of such an appeal were known to be heavy, and all the bishops agreed to contribute 5 per cent of their revenues, while a levy of 1 per cent was made on all abbots, priors, deans, chapters, and parochial churches of the province. The pious Franciscan Salimbene informs us that 100,000 livres tournois were raised and Honorius IV was won over. On Good Friday of 1287 he was to issue a bull depriving the Mendicants of the right to preach and hear confessions. They were in despair, but this time it was the prayers of the Franciscan that prevailed. The hand of God fell upon Honorius in the night of Wednesday, he died on Thursday, and the Orders were saved.

In 1351 the clergy again took heart for another attack. Possibly the devotion shown by the Mendicants during the Black Death, when 25 million human beings were swept away, when the priests abandoned their posts, and the friars alone were found to tend the sick and console the dying, may have led to fresh progress by them and have enkindled antagonism anew.[2] Be this as it may, a vast deputation, embracing cardinals, bishops, and minor clergy, waited on Clement VI and petitioned for the abolition of the Orders, or at least the prohibition of their preaching and hearing confessions, and enjoying the burial profits, by which they were enormously enriched at the expense of the parish priests. The Mendicants deigned no

---

[2] During the Black Death, of 140 Dominicans at Montpellier, but 7 survived; in Marseilles, of 160, not one. The mortality in the Franciscan Order was reckoned at 124,434 members, which is a manifest exaggeration.

reply, but Clement spoke for them, denying the allegation of the petition that they were useless to the Church, and asserting that, on the contrary, they were most valuable: .

And if their preaching be stopped, about what can you preach to the people? If on humility, you yourselves are the proudest of the world, arrogant and given to pomp. If on poverty, you are the most grasping and most covetous, so that all the benefices in the world will not satisfy you. If on chastity—but we will be silent on this, for God knoweth what each man does and how many of you satisfy your lusts. You hate the Mendicants and shut your doors on them lest they should see your mode of life, while you waste your temporal wealth on pimps and swindlers. You should not complain if the Mendicants receive some temporal possessions from the dying to whom they minister when you have fled, nor that they spend it in buildings where everything is ordered for the honor of God and the Church, in place of wasting it in pleasure and licentiousness. And because you do not likewise, you accuse the Mendicants, for most of you give yourselves up to vain and worldly lives.

Under this fierce rebuke, even though uttered by a pope whom St. Birgitta denounced as himself a follower of the lusts of the flesh, there was evidently nothing practicable but submission.

At the Lateran Council of 1515, a determined effort was made by the bishops to obtain the revocation of the special privileges of the Mendicants. By refusing to vote for any measures, they obtained a promise of this, but skillful delay enabled Leo X to elude performance till the following year, when a compromise was effected, which merely shows by what it forbade to the Mendicants how contemptuous had been their defiance of episcopal authority. In 1519 Erasmus complains in a letter to Albert, Cardinal-Archbishop of Mainz: "The world is overburdened with the tyranny of the Mendicants, who, though they are the satellites of the Roman See, are yet so numerous and powerful that they are formidable to the pope himself and even to kings. To them, when the pope aids them, he is more than God, when he displeases them he is worthless as a dream."

It must be confessed that both Dominicans and Franciscans had greatly fallen away from the virtues of their founders. Scarce had the Orders commenced to spread when false brethren were found who, contrary to their vow of poverty, made use of their faculty of preach-

ing for purposes of gain; as early as 1233 we find Gregory IX sharply
reminding the Dominican Chapter-General that the poverty professed by the Order should be genuine and not fictitious. The wide
employment of the friars by the popes as political emissaries necessarily diverted them from their spiritual functions, attracted ambitious and restless men into their ranks, and gave the institutions a
worldly character thoroughly in opposition to their original design.
Their members, moreover, were peculiarly subject to temptation.
Wanderers by profession, they were relieved from supervision, and
were subject only to the jurisdiction of their own superiors and to the
laws of their own Orders, thus intensifying and rendering peculiarly
dangerous the immunity common to all ecclesiastics.

The "Seraphic Religion" of the Franciscans was especially subject to the reaction of human imperfection. This was manifest even
in the lifetime of St. Francis, who resigned the generalate on account
of the abuses which were creeping in, and offered to resume it if the
brethren would walk according to his will. It was inevitable that
trouble should come between those who conscientiously adhered to
the Rule in all its strictness and the worldlings who saw in the Order
the instrument of their ambition; and it did not need the prophetic
spirit to lead Francis to predict on his deathbed future scandals and
divisions and the persecution of those who would not consent to
error—a forecast which we will see abundantly verified, as well as
that in which he foretold that the Order would become so defamed
that it would be ashamed to be seen in public.

In 1257 St. Bonaventura, who had just succeeded John of Parma
as General of the Order, varied his controversy with William of St.
Amour by an encyclical to his provincials in which he bewailed the
contempt and dislike felt universally for the Order, caused by its
greedy seeking after money; the idleness of so many of its members,
leading them into all manners of vices; the entrusting of preaching
and confession to those wholly unfit; the greedy grasping after legacies
and burial fees; and in general the extravagance which would inevitably cause the chilling of charity. Evidently the assaults of St.
Amour and the complaints of the clergy were not without foundation; but this vigorous rebuke was ineffective, and ten years later
Bonaventura was obliged to repeat it in even stronger terms. This
time he expressed his special horror at the shameless audacity of

those brethren who, in their sermons to the laity, attacked the vices of the clergy, and gave rise to scandals, quarrels, and hatreds; and he wound up by declaring, "It is a foul and profane lie to assert one's self the voluntary professor of absolute poverty and then refuse to submit to the lack of anything; to beg abroad like a pauper and to roll in wealth at home." Bonaventura's declamations were in vain, and the struggle in the Order continued, until it ejected its stricter members as heretics, as we shall see when we come to consider the Spiritual Franciscans and the Fraticelli. In the succeeding century both Orders gave free rein to their worldly propensities. St. Birgitta, in her *Revelations,* which were sanctioned by the Church as inspired, declares that "although founded upon vows of poverty they have amassed riches, place their whole aim in increasing their wealth, dress as richly as bishops, and many of them are more extravagant in their jewelry and ornaments than laymen who are reputed wealthy."

The activity of the Mendicants was too great to be confined to the defense of the Holy See and to the religious revival by which for a time they reacquired for Rome the veneration of the people. One of the collateral objects to which they devoted a portion of their energies was missionary work, and in this they set a worthy example to their successors, the Jesuits of the sixteenth and seventeenth centuries. No distance and no danger deterred them from the task of winning souls to Christianity, and in these arduous labors there was a noble emulation between the two Orders.

Their special field of activity, however, which more particularly concerns us, was that of the conversion and persecution of heretics —of the Inquisition, which they made their own. It was inevitable that this should fall into their hands as soon as the inadequacy of the ancient episcopal courts required the organization of a new system. The discovery and conviction of the heretic was no easy task. It required special training, and that training was exactly what the Orders sought to give their neophytes to fit them for the work of preaching and conversion. With no ties of locality, soldiers of the cross ready to march to any point at the word of command, they could be dispatched at a moment's notice whenever their services were required. Moreover, their peculiar devotion to the Holy See rendered them especially useful in organizing the papal Inquisition, which was to supersede by degrees the episcopal jurisdiction and prove so efficient an instrument in reducing the local churches to subjection.

That Dominic was the founder of the Inquisition and the first Inquisitor-General has become a part of Roman tradition. It is affirmed by all the historians of the Order, and it is confirmed by quoting a bull of Innocent III appointing him Inquisitor-General. Yet it is safe to say that no tradition of the Church rests on a slenderer basis. That Dominic devoted the best years of his life to combating heresy there is no doubt, and as little that, when a heretic was deaf to argument or persuasion, he would cheerfully stand by the pyre and see him burned, like any other zealous missionary of the time; but in this he was no more prominent than hundreds of others, and of organized work in this direction he was utterly guiltless. Indeed, from the year 1215, when he laid the foundation of his Order, he was engrossed in it to the exclusion of all other objects, and was obliged to forego his cherished design of ending his days as a missionary to Persia. We shall see that it was not until more than ten years after his death that such an institution as the papal Inquisition can be said to have existed.

A similar legendary halo exaggerates the exclusive glory, claimed by the Order, of organizing and perfecting the Inquisition. The bulls of Gregory IX alleged in support of the assertion are simply special orders to individual Dominican provincials to depute brethren fitted for the purpose to the duty of preaching against heresy and examining heretics and prosecuting their defenders. The fact simply is that there was no formal confiding of the Inquisition to the Dominicans any more than there was any formal founding of the Inquisition itself. As the institution gradually assumed shape and organization in the effort to find some effectual means to ferret out concealed heretics, the Dominicans were the readiest instrument at hand, especially as they professed the function of preaching and converting as their primary business. As conversion became less the object, and persecution the main business of the Inquisition, the Franciscans were equally useful, and the honors of the organization were divided between them.

Yet the earliest inquisitors, properly so called, were unquestionably Dominicans. When, after the settlement between Raymond of

Toulouse and St. Louis, the extirpation of heresy in the Albigensian territories was seriously undertaken, it was Dominicans who were sent thither to work under the direction of the bishops. In northern France the business gradually fell almost exclusively into the hands of Dominicans. In Aragon, as early as 1232, they are recommended to the Archbishop of Tarragona as fitting instruments, and in 1249 the institution was confided to them. Eventually southern France was divided between them and the Franciscans, the western portion being given to the Dominicans, while the Comtat Venaissin, Provence, Forcalquier, and the states of the empire in the provinces of Arles, Aix, and Embrun were under charge of the Franciscans. As for Italy, it was in 1254 formally divided between them by Innocent IV, the Dominicans being assigned to Lombardy, Romagnola, Tarvesina, and Genoa, while the central portion of the peninsula fell to the Franciscans. This division, however, was not always strictly observed, for at times we find Franciscan inquisitors in Milan, Romagnola, and Tarvesina. In Germany and Austria the Inquisition, as we shall see, never took deep root, but, in so far as it was organized there, it was in Dominican hands, while Bohemia and Dalmatia were under the care of Franciscans.

Sometimes the two Orders were conjoined. In 1237 the Franciscan Étienne de Saint Thibéry was associated with the Dominican Guillem Arnaud in Toulouse, in hopes that the reputation of his Order for greater mildness might diminish the popular aversion for the new institution. In April 1238, Gregory IX appointed the provincials of the two Orders in Aragon as inquisitors for that kingdom, and in the same year the same policy was pursued in Navarre.

It was found the wisest course, however, to define sharply the boundaries of their respective jurisdictions, for the active and incessant jealousy between the two bodies rendered any concurrence or competition between them an explosive mine liable to be started by a spark. Their mutual hatreds began early, and the unscrupulous means by which they were gratified were a perpetual scandal and danger to the Church. So ineradicable was the hostility between the two Orders that Clement IV established the rule that there should be a distance of at least 3,000 feet between their respective possessions —a regulation which only led to new and more intricate disputes.

In the busy world of the thirteenth century there was thus no

agency more active than that of the Mendicant Orders, for good
and for evil. On the whole perhaps the good preponderated, for
they undoubtedly aided in postponing a revolution for which the
world was not yet ready. Though the self-abnegation of their earlier
days was a quality too rare and perishable to be long preserved, and
though they soon sank to the level of the social order around them,
yet had their work not been altogether lost. They had brought
afresh to men's minds some of the forgotten truths of the Gospel,
and had taught them to view their duties to their fellows from a
higher plane. How well they recognized and appreciated their own
services is shown by the story, common to the legend of both Orders,
which tells that while Dominic and Francis were waiting the approval of Innocent III a holy man had a vision in which he saw
Christ brandishing three darts with which to destroy the world, and
the Virgin inquiring his purpose. Then said Christ, "The world is
full of pride, avarice, and lust; I have borne with it too long, and
with these darts will I consume it." The Virgin fell on her knees
and interceded for man, but in vain, until she revealed to him that
she had two faithful servants who would reduce it to his dominion.
Then Christ desired to see the champions; she showed him Dominic
and Francis, and he was content. The pious author of the story
could hardly have foreseen that in 1627 Urban VIII would be obliged
to deprive the Mendicant Friars of Cordova of their dearly prized
immunity, and to subject them to episcopal jurisdiction, in the hope
of restraining them from seducing their spiritual daughters in the
confessional.

CHAPTER VI
THE INQUISITION FOUNDED

WHEN the existence of hidden crime is suspected there are three stages in the process of its suppression—the discovery of the criminal, the proof of his guilt, and finally his punishment. Of all others the crime of heresy was the most difficult to discover and to prove, and when its progress became threatening the ecclesiastics on whom fell the responsibility of its eradication were equally at a loss in each of the three steps to be taken.

It was not that the Church was devoid of the machinery for discharging its admitted function of suppressing heresy. Charlemagne's civilizing policy made efficient use of all instrumentalities capable of maintaining order and security in his empire, and the bishops assumed an important position in his system. During the troubles which followed the division of the empire, as the feudal system arose on the ruins of the monarchy, gradually the bishops not only threw off dependence on the crown, but acquired extensive rights and powers in the administration of the canon law, which now no longer depended on the civil or municipal law, but assumed to be its superior. Thus came to be founded the spiritual courts which were attached to every episcopate and which exercised exclusive jurisdiction over a constantly widening field of jurisprudence. Of course all errors of faith necessarily came within their purview.

The organization and functions of these courts received a powerful impetus through the study of the Roman law after the middle of the twelfth century. Ecclesiastics monopolized to such an extent the educated intelligence of the age that at first there were few besides themselves to penetrate into the mysteries of the Code and Digest. Even in the second half of the thirteenth century Roger Bacon complains that a civil lawyer, even if wholly untrained in canon law and theology, had a much better chance of high preferment than a theologian, and he exclaims in bitterness that the Church is governed by lawyers to the great injury of all Christian folk. Thus the old archdeacon gave way, not without vituperation, before the formal episcopal judge, known as the Official or Ordinary, who was usually a doctor of both laws—an LL.D. in fact. These episcopal courts, moreover, were soon surrounded by a crowd of clerkly advocates, whose zeal for their clients often outran their discretion, furnishing the first mediæval representatives of the legal profession.

Following in the traces of the civil law, there were three forms of action in criminal cases—*accusatio, denunciatio,* and *inquisitio.* In *accusatio* there was an accuser who formally inscribed himself as responsible and was subject to the *talio* in case of failure. *Denunciatio* was the official act of the public officer, such as the *testis synodalis* or archdeacon, who summoned the court to take action against offenders coming within his official knowledge. In *inquisitio* the Ordinary cited the suspected criminal, imprisoning him if necessary; the indictment, or *capitula inquisitionis,* was communicated to him, and he was interrogated thereupon, with the proviso that nothing extraneous to the indictment could be subsequently brought into the case to aggravate it. If the defendant could not be made to confess, the Ordinary proceeded to take testimony, and though the examination of witnesses was not conducted in the defendant's presence, their names and evidence were communicated to him, he could summon witnesses in rebuttal, and his advocate had full opportunity to defend him by argument, exception, and appeal. The Ordinary finally gave the verdict; if uncertain of guilt, he prescribed the *purgatio canonica,* or oath of denial shared by a given number of peers of the accused, more or less, according to the nature of the charge and degree of suspicion. In all cases of conviction by the inquisitorial process, the penalty inflicted was lighter than in accusation or denunciation. The danger was recognized of a procedure in which the judge was also the accuser; a man must be popularly reputed as guilty before the Ordinary could commence inquisition against him, and this not by merely a few men or by his enemies, or those unworthy of belief. There must be ample ground for esteeming him guilty before this extraordinary power vested in the judge could be exercised. It is important to bear in mind the equitable provisions of all this episcopal jurisdiction when we come to consider the methods the Inquisition erected on these foundations.

Theoretically there also existed a thorough system of general inquisition or inquest for the detection of all offenses, including heresy;

and as it was only an application of this which gave rise to the Inquisition, it is worth our brief attention. The idea of a systematic investigation into infractions of the law was familiar to secular as well as to ecclesiastical jurisprudence. In the Roman law, although there was no public prosecutor, it was part of the duty of the ruler or proconsul to make perquisition after all criminals with a view to their detection and punishment. The *Missi Dominici* of Charlemagne were officials commissioned to traverse the empire, making inquisition into all cases of disorder, crime, and injustice, with jurisdiction over clerk and layman alike. They held their assizes four times a year, listened to all complaints and accusations, and were empowered to redress all wrongs and to punish all offenders of whatever rank. The same device is seen in the itinerant justiciaries of England, at least as early as the Assizes of Clarendon in 1166, when, utilizing the Anglo-Saxon organization, they made an inquest in every hundred and tithing by the lawful men of the vicinage to try and punish all who were publicly suspected of crime, giving rise to the time-honored system of the grand jury—in itself a prototype of the incipient papal Inquisition.

At the commencement of the tenth century we find in use a method which was subsequently imitated by the Inquisition. As the bishop reached each parish in his visitation, the whole body of the people was assembled in a local synod. From among these he selected seven men of mature age and approved integrity, who were then sworn on relics to reveal without fear or favor whatever they might know or hear, then or subsequently, of any offense requiring investigation. These *testes synodales,* or synodal witnesses, became an institution established, theoretically at least, in the Church, and long lists of interrogatories were drawn up to guide the bishops in examining them so that no possible sin or immorality might escape.

The Church thus possessed an organization well adapted for the discovery and investigation of heretics. All that it lacked were the men who should put that organization to use; and the progress of heresy up to the date of the Albigensian crusades manifests how utterly neglectful were the prelates of the day. Successive popes made fruitless efforts to induce them to use the means at their disposal for a systematic and vigorous onslaught on the sectaries. From the assembly of prelates who attended, in 1184, the meeting at Verona between Lucius III and Frederic Barbarossa, the pope issued a decretal at the instance of the emperor and with the assent of the bishops, which if strictly and energetically obeyed might have established an episcopal instead of a papal Inquisition. In addition to the oath prescribed to every ruler, to assist the Church in persecuting heresy, all archbishops and bishops were ordered, either personally or by their archdeacons or other fitting persons, once or twice a year to visit every parish where there was suspicion of heresy, and compel two or three men of good character, or the whole vicinage if necessary, to swear to reveal any reputed heretic, or any person holding secret conventicles, or in any way differing in mode of life from the faithful in general. The prelate was to summon to his presence those designated, who, unless they could purge themselves at his discretion, or in accordance with local custom, were to be punished as the bishop might see fit. Similarly, any who refused to swear were to be condemned and punished as heretics *ipso facto*.

This effort failed to arouse the hierarchy from their sloth. The weapons rusted in the careless hands of the bishops, and the heretics became ever more numerous and more enterprising. An occasional earnest fanatic was found, like Foulques of Toulouse or Henry of Strassburg, who labored vigorously in the suppression of heresy, but for the most part the prelates were as negligent as ever.

The popes endeavored to overcome this episcopal indifference by a sort of irregular and spasmodic legatine Inquisition. As the direct representatives and plenipotentiaries of the vicegerent of God the legates carried and exercised the supreme authority of the Holy See into the remotest corners of Christendom. That they should be employed in stimulating languid persecution was inevitable. In the absence of any systematic method of procedure they were even used in special cases to supplement the ignorance of local prelates. In Toulouse, after the Treaty of Paris in 1229, we find the most noteworthy case of the concurrence of legatine and episcopal action. After Count Raymond had been reconciled to the Church, he returned in July to his dominions, followed by the Cardinal-Legate Romano, to see to the execution of the treaty and to turn back the armed "pilgrims" who were swarming to fight for the cross, and who revenged themselves for their disappointment by wantonly destroying the harvests and creating a famine in the land. In September a council was assembled at Toulouse, consisting of all the prelates of Languedoc and most of the leading barons. This adopted a canon ordering anew all archbishops, bishops, and exempted abbots to put in force the device of the synodal witnesses, but there is no trace of any obedience to this command or of any results arising from it. Under the impulsion of the legate and of Foulques of Toulouse, however, the council itself was turned into an inquisition. A converted perfected Catharan, named Guillem de Solier, was found and was restored to his legal rights in order to enable him to give evidence against his former brethren, while Bishop Foulques industriously hunted up other witnesses. Each bishop present took his share in examining these, sending to Foulques the evidence reduced to writing, and thus, we are told, a vast amount of business was accomplished in a short time. It was found that the heretics had mostly pledged each other to secrecy, and that it was virtually impossible to extract anything from them, but a few of the more timid came forward voluntarily and confessed, and of course each one of these, under the rules in force, was obliged to tell all he knew about others. A vast amount of evidence was thus collected, which was taken by the legate for the purpose of deciding the fate of the accused, and with it he left Toulouse for Montpellier. A few of the more hardy offenders endeavored to defend themselves judicially, and demanded to see the names of the witnesses, even following the legate to Montpellier for that purpose; but he, under the pretext that this demand was for the purpose of slaying those who had testified against them, adroitly eluded it by exhibiting a combined list of all the witnesses, so that the culprits were forced to submit without defense. He then held another council at Orange, and sent to Foulques the sentences, which were duly communicated to the accused assembled for the purpose in the church of St. Jacques. All the papers of the inquisition were carried to Rome by the legate for fear that if they should fall into the hands of the evil-minded they would be the cause of many murders—and, in fact, a number of the witnesses were slain on simple suspicion.

All this shows how crude and cumbrous an implement was the episcopal and legatine Inquisition even in the most energetic hands, and how formless and tentative was its procedure. Trained experts were needed whose sole business it should be to unearth the offenders.

and extort a confession of their guilt. As this necessity became more and more apparent two new factors contributed to the solution of the long-vexed problem.

The first of these was the organization of the Mendicant Orders, whose peculiar fitness for the work might well make their establishment seem a providential interposition to supply the Church of Christ with what it most sorely needed. As the necessity grew apparent of special and permanent tribunals devoted exclusively to the widespread sin of heresy, there was every reason why they should be wholly free from the local jealousies and enmities which might tend to the prejudice of the innocent, or the local favoritism which might connive at the escape of the guilty. If, in addition, the examiners and judges were men specially trained to the detection and conversion of the heretic; if, also, they had by irrevocable vows renounced the world; if they could acquire no wealth and were dead to the enticements of pleasure, every guarantee seemed to be afforded that their momentous duties would be fulfilled with the strictest justice—that while the purity of the faith would be protected, there would be no unnecessary oppression or cruelty or persecution dictated by private interests and personal revenge. Their unlimited popularity was also a warrant that they would receive far more efficient assistance in their arduous labors than could be expected by the bishops, whose position was generally that of antagonism to their flocks and to the petty seigneurs and powerful barons whose aid was indispensable. Thus to the public of the thirteenth century the organization of the Inquisition and its commitment to the children of St. Dominic and St. Francis appeared a perfectly natural or rather inevitable development arising from the admitted necessities of the time and the instrumentalities at hand.

The other factor which promised success to the Church in an organized effort to discharge the duty of persecution was the secular legislation against heresy which at this period took form and shape. We have seen the spasmodic edicts of England and Aragon in the twelfth century, which have interest as showing the absence of anterior penal laws. To put in action any comprehensive system of persecution, it was requisite to overcome the centrifugal tendency of mediæval legislation, which finds its ultimate expression in free Navarre, where every town of importance had its special *fuero*, and almost every house its individual custom. Innocent III endeavored at the Lateran Council of 1215 to secure uniformity by a series of regulations defining the attitude of the Church to heretics, and the duties which the secular power owed to exterminate them under pain of forfeiture, and this became a recognized part of canon law; but in the absence of active secular co-operation its provisions for a while remained practically a dead letter. It was reserved for the arch-enemy of the Church, Frederic II, to break down, throughout the greater part of Europe, the particularism of local statutes and place the population at the mercy of such emissaries as the popes might send to represent them. It was requisite for him to acquire the favor of Honorius III to secure his coronation in 1220; and when the inevitable rupture took place, it was still necessary for him to meet the charge of heresy so freely brought against him by manifesting special zeal in the persecution of heretics, though doubtless, if left to himself, philosophic indifference would have led him to tolerate any form of belief that did not threaten disobedience to the ruler.

In a series of edicts dating from 1220 to 1239 he thus enacted a complete and pitiless code of persecution, based upon the Lateran canons. Those who were merely suspected of heresy were required to purge themselves at command of the Church, under penalty of being deprived of civil rights and placed under the imperial ban; while, if they remained in this condition for a year, they were to be condemned as heretics. Heretics of all sects were outlawed; and when condemned as such by the Church they were to be delivered to the secular arm to be burned. If, through fear of death, they recanted, they were to be thrust in prison for life, there to perform penance. If they relapsed into error, thus showing that their conversion had been fictitious, they were to be put to death. All the property of the heretic was confiscated and his heirs disinherited. His children, to the second generation, were declared ineligible to any positions of emolument or dignity, unless they should win mercy by betraying their father or some other heretic. All *credentes*, fautors, defenders, receivers, or advocates of heretics were banished forever, their property confiscated, and their descendants subjected to the same disabilities as those of heretics. Those who defended the errors of heretics were to be treated as heretics unless, on admonition, they mended their ways. The houses of heretics and their receivers were to be destroyd, never to be rebuilt. Although the evidence of a heretic was not receivable in court, yet an exception was made in favor of the faith, and it was to be held good against another heretic. All rulers and magistrates, present or future, were required to swear to exterminate with their utmost ability all whom the Church might designate as heretics, under pain of forfeiture of office. The lands of any temporal lord who neglected, for a year after summons by the Church, to clear them of heresy, were exposed to the occupancy of any Catholics who, after extirpating the heretics, were to possess them in peace without prejudice to the rights of the suzerain, provided he had offered no opposition. When the papal Inquisition was commenced, Frederic hastened, in 1232, to place the whole machinery of the State at the command of the inquisitors, who were authorized to call upon any official to capture whomsoever they might designate as a heretic, and hold him in prison until the Church should condemn him, when he was to be put to death.

This fiendish legislation was hailed by the Church with acclamation, and was not allowed to remain, like its predecessors, a dead letter. The coronation edict of 1220 was sent by Honorius to the University of Bologna to be read and taught as a part of practical law.[1] It was consequently embodied in the authoritative compilation of the feudal customs, and its most stringent enactments were incorporated in the Civil Code. The whole series of edicts was subsequently promulgated by successive popes in repeated bulls, commanding all states and cities to inscribe these laws irrevocably in their local statute books. It became the duty of the inquisitors to swear all magistrates and officials to enforce them, and to compel their obedience by the free use of excommunication. In 1222, when the magistrates of Rieti adopted laws conflicting with them, Honorius

---

[1] The coronation edict, which formed the basis of all subsequent legislation against heresy, was drawn up by the papal curia, and sent, a fortnight before the ceremony, to the Legate Bishop of Tusculum, with orders to procure the imperial signature and return it, so that it could be published under the emperor's name in the church of St. Peter. Nothing could seem a plainer duty to an ecclesiastic of the time than that the Church should stimulate the temporal ruler to the sharpest persecution of heresy. It was doubtless the outlawry of heretics pronounced by the edicts of Frederic which enabled the Inquisition to establish the settled principle that the heretic could be captured and despoiled at any time and by any person, and that the spoiler could retain his goods—provided always that he was not an official of the Holy Office.

at once ordered the offenders removed from office; in 1253, when
some of the Lombard cities demurred, Innocent IV promptly
ordered the inquisitors to subdue them; and in the recension of the
laws of Florence made as late as 1355, they still appear as an integral
part. Finally, they were incorporated in the latest additions to the
Corpus Juris as part of the canon law itself, and, technically speaking, they may be regarded as in force to the present day.

This virtually provided for a very large portion of Europe, extending from Sicily to the North Sea. The western regions made haste
to follow the pious example. Coincident with the Treaty of Paris, in
1229, was an *Ordonnance* issued in the name of the boy-king, Louis
IX, giving efficient assistance by the royal officials to the Church in
its efforts to purge the land of heresy. In the territories which remained to Count Raymond his vacillating course gave rise to much
dissatisfaction, until, in 1234, he was compelled to enact, with the
consent of his prelates and barons, a statute drawn up by Raymond
du Fauga of Toulouse, which embodied all the practical points of
Frederic's legislation, and decreed confiscation against everyone who
failed, when called upon, to aid the Church in the capture and detention of heretics. In the compilations and law books of the latter
half of the century we see the system thoroughly established as the
law of the whole land, and in 1315 Louis le Hutin formally adopted
the edicts of Frederic and made them valid throughout France.

Meanwhile zeal or jealousy led, in the confusion and uncertainty
of this transition period, to the experiment, in several parts of Italy,
of a secular Inquisition. In Rome, in 1231, Gregory IX drew up a
series of regulations which was issued by the Senator Annibaldo in
the name of the Roman people. Under this the senator was bound
to capture all who were designated to him as heretics, whether by
inquisitors appointed by the Church or other good Catholics, and
to punish them within eight days after condemnation. Of their confiscated property one-third went to the detector, one-third to the
senator, and one-third to repairing the city walls. Any house in which
a heretic was received was to be destroyed and converted forever into
a receptacle of filth. *Credentes* were treated as heretics, while fautors,
receivers, etc., forfeited one-third of their possessions, applicable to
the city walls. A fine of 20 lire was imposed on anyone cognizant
of heresy and not denouncing it; while the senator who neglected

to enforce the law was subject to a mulct of 200 marks and perpetual disability to office. Not satisfied with the local enforcement of these regulations, Gregory sent them to the archbishops and princes throughout Europe, with orders to put them in execution in their respective territories, and for some time they formed the basis of inquisitorial proceedings. In Rome the perquisition was successful, and the faithful were rewarded with the spectacle of a considerable number of burnings; while Gregory, encouraged by success, proceeded to issue a decretal, forming the basis of all subsequent inquisitorial legislation, by which condemned heretics were to be abandoned to the secular arm for exemplary punishment, those who returned to the Church were to be perpetually imprisoned, and everyone cognizant of heresy was bound to denounce it to the ecclesiastical authorities under pain of excommunication.

In 1226 an effort was made to check the rapid spread of Catharism in Florence by the arrest of the heretic bishop Filippo Paternon, whose diocese extended from Pisa to Arezzo. He was tried, in accordance with the existing Florentine statutes, by the bishop and *podestà* conjointly, when he cut short the proceedings by abjuration, and was released; but he speedily relapsed, and became more odious than ever to the orthodox. In 1227 a converted heretic complained of this backsliding to Gregory IX, and the pontiff, who had just ascended the papal throne, made haste to remedy the evil by issuing a commission, which may be regarded as the foundation of the papal Inquisition. Yet it was exceedingly unobtrusive, though the church of Florence was so directly under papal control. Bearing date June 20, 1227, it simply authorizes Giovanni di Salerno, prior of the Dominican house of Santa Maria Novella, with one of his *frati* and Canon Bernardo, to proceed judicially against Paternon and his followers and force them to abjuration; acting, in case of obstinacy, under the canons of the Lateran Council, and, if necessary, calling upon the clerks and laymen of the sees of Florence and Fiesole for aid. Thus, while there was no scruple in invading the jurisdiction of the Bishop of Florence, there was no legislation other than the Lateran canons to guide the proceedings. The commissioners succeeded in capturing Bishop Paternon and cast him in prison, but he was forcibly rescued by his friends and disappeared, leaving his episcopate to his successor, Torsello.

Frà Giovanni retained his commission until his death in 1230, when a successor was appointed in the person of another Dominican, Aldobrandino Cavalcanti. Still, their jurisdiction was as yet wholly undetermined, for in June 1229, we hear of the Abbot of San Miniato carrying to Gregory IX, in Perugia, two leading heretics, Andrea and Pietro, who were forced to a public abjuration in presence of the papal court; and in several cases in 1234 we find Gregory IX intervening, taking bail of the accused and sending special instructions to the inquisitor in charge. Yet the Inquisition was gradually taking shape, for shortly afterwards there were numerous heretics discovered, some of whom were burned, their trials being still preserved in the archives of Santa Maria Novella. How little thought there could have been of founding a permanent institution is shown, in 1233, by the persecuting statutes drawn up by Bishop Ardingho, approved by Gregory, and ordered by him to be irrevocably inscribed in the statute book of Florence. In these the bishop is still the persecuting representative of the Church, and there is no allusion to inquisitors. The *podestà* is bound to arrest anyone pointed out to him by the bishop, and to punish him within eight days after the episcopal condemnation, with other provisions borrowed from the edicts of Frederic II. Frà Aldobrandino seems to have relied rather on preaching than on persecution; in fact he nowhere in the documents signed by him qualifies himself as inquisitor, and neither his efforts nor those of Bishop Ardingho were able to prevent the rapid growth of heresy. In 1235, when the project of an organized Inquisition throughout Europe was taking shape, Gregory appointed the Dominican Provincial of Rome inquisitor throughout his extensive province, which embraced both Sicily and Tuscany; but this seems to have proved too large a district, and about 1240 we find the city of Florence under the charge of Frà Ruggieri Calcagni. He was of a temper well fitted to extend the prerogatives of his office and to render it effective; but it was not until 1243 that he qualified himself as "*Inquisitor Domini Papæ in Tuscia,*" and in a sentence rendered in 1245 he is careful to call himself inquisitor of Bishop Ardingho as well as of the pope, and recites the episcopal commission given him as authority to act. In the proceedings of this period the rudimentary character of the Inquisition is evident. One confession in 1244 bears only the names of two *frati*, the inquisitor not being even present. In 1245 there are sentences signed by Ruggieri alone, while other proceedings show him to be acting conjointly with Ardingho. He may be said, indeed, to have given the Inquisition in Florence form and shape when, about 1243, he opened for the first time his independent tribunal in Santa Maria Novella, taking as assessors two or three prominent friars of the convent and employing public notaries to make record of his proceedings.

The Inquisition has sometimes been said to have been founded April 20, 1233, the day on which Gregory issued two bulls making the persecution of heresy the special function of the Dominicans; but the apologetic tone in which he addresses the prelates shows how uncertain he felt about their enduring this invasion of their jurisdiction, while the character of his instructions proves that he had no conception of what the innovation was to lead to. His immediate object seems rather the punishment of priests and other ecclesiastics, concerning whom there was a standing complaint that they favored heretics by instructing them how to evade examination by concealing their beliefs and feigning orthodoxy. After reciting the necessity of subduing heresy and the raising up by God of the preaching friars, Gregory proceeds to tell the bishops:

We, seeing you engrossed in the whirlwind of cares and scarce able to breathe in the pressure of overwhelming anxieties, think it well to divide your burdens that they may be more easily borne. We have therefore determined to send preaching friars against the heretics of France and the adjoining provinces, and we beg, warn, and exhort you, ordering you as you reverence the Holy See, to receive them kindly and treat them well, giving them in this, as in all else, favor, counsel, and aid, th   they may fulfill their office.

The other bull is addressed "to the Priors and Friàrs of the Order of Preachers, Inquisitors," and after alluding to the sons of perdition who defend heresy, it proceeds:

Therefore you, or any of you, wherever you may happen to preach, are empowered, unless they desist from such defense [of heretics] on moni- tion, to deprive clerks of their benefices forever, and to proceed against them and all others, without appeal, calling in the aid of the secular arm, if necessary, and coercing opposition, if requisite, with the censures of the Church, without appeal.

This experiment of investing all the Dominican preachers with legatine authority to condemn without appeal was inconsiderate. It could only lead to exasperation, as we shall see hereafter in Germany, and Gregory soon adopted a more practical expedient. Shortly after the issue of these bulls we find him ordering the Provincial Prior of Toulouse to select some learned friars who should be commissioned to preach the cross in the diocese, and to proceed against heretics in accordance with the recent statutes. Though here there is still some incongruous mingling of duties, yet Gregory had finally hit upon the device which remained the permanent basis of the Inquisition—the selection by the provincial of certain fitting brethren, who exercised within their province the delegated authority of the Holy See. Under this bull the provincial appointed Friars Pierre Cella and Guillem Arnaud, whose labors will be detailed in a subsequent chapter. Thus the Inquisition, as an organized system, may be considered as fairly commenced, though it is noteworthy that these early inquisitors in their official papers qualify themselves as acting under legatine and not under papal authority. How little idea there was as yet of creating a general and permanent institution is seen when the Archbishop of Sens complained of the intrusion of inquisitors in his province, and Gregory, by a brief of February 4, 1234, apologetically revoked all commissions issued for it, adding a suggestion that the archbishop should call in the assistance of the Dominicans if he thought that their superior skill in confuting heretics was likely to prove useful.

As yet there was no idea of superseding the episcopal functions. About this time we find Gregory writing to the bishops of the province of Narbonne, threatening them if they shall not inflict due chastisement on heretics, and making no allusion to the new expedient; and as late as October 1, 1234, Pierre Amiel, Archbishop of Narbonne, exacted an oath from his people to denounce all heretics to him or to his officials, apparently in ignorance of the existence of special inquisitors. Even where the latter were commissioned, their powers and responsibilities were wholly undefined. As they were regarded simply in the light of assistants to the bishops in the exercise of episcopal jurisdiction over heresy, it was naturally to the bishops that were referred the questions which immediately arose. Many points on the treatment of heretics had been settled, not only by Gregory's Roman statutes of 1231, but by the Council of Toulouse in 1229 and those of Béziers and Arles in 1234, yet matters of detail constantly suggested themselves in practice, and a new code of some kind was evidently required to render persecution effective. The suspension of the Inquisition for some years at the request of Count Raymond postponed this, but when the Holy Office resumed its functions in 1241 the necessity became pressing. Accordingly a great council of the three provinces of Narbonne, Arles, and Aix was assembled at Narbonne in 1243 or 1244, where an elaborate series of canons were framed, which remained the basis of inquisitorial action. These were addressed to "Our cherished and faithful children in Christ the Preaching Friars Inquisitors"; and though the bishops discreetly say,

We write this to you, not that we wish to bind you down by our counsels, as it would not be fitting to limit the liberty accorded to your discretion by other forms and rules than those of the Holy See, to the prejudice of the business; but we wish to help your devotion as we are commanded to do by the Holy See, since you, who bear our burdens, ought to be, through mutual charity, assisted with help and advice in our own business,

yet the tone of the whole is that of absolute command, both in the definition of jurisdiction and the instructions as to dealing with heretics. It is highly significant that, in surrendering control over the bodies of their flocks, these good shepherds strictly reserved to themselves the profits to be expected from persecution, for they straitly enjoined upon the new officials, "You are to abstain from these pecuniary penances and exactions, both for the sake of the honor of your Order, and because you will have fully enough other work to attend to." While thus carefully preserving their financial interests, they abandoned what was vastly more important, the right of passing judgment and imposing sentence. Sentences of this period are rendered in the name of the inquisitors, though if the bishop took part, as was frequently the case, he is mentioned as an assessor.

This invasion of the bishop's jurisdiction was evidently too great an innovation to be permanent; indeed, almost immediately we find the Cardinal Legate of Albano instructing the Archbishop of Narbonne to order the inquisitors not to condemn heretics or impose penances without the concurrence of the bishops. This order had to be repeated and rendered more absolute; and the question was settled in this sense by the Council of Bézie s in 1246, where the bishops, on the other hand, surrendered the fines to be used for the expenses of the Inquisition, and drew up another elaborate series of instructions for the inquisitors, "willingly yielding to your devout requests which you have humbly made to us." For a while the popes continued to treat the bishops as responsible for the suppression of heresy in their respective dioceses, and consequently as the real source of jurisdiction. Still, in spite of this, the sentences of Bernard de Caux, from 1246 to 1248, bear no trace of episcopal concurrence. There evidently was jealousy and antagonism. In 1248 the Council of Valence was obliged to coerce the bishops into publishing and observing the sentences of the inquisitors, by interdicting the entry into their own churches to those who refused to do so, showing that the bishops were not consulted about the sentences and were indisposed to enforce them. In 1249 we find the Archbishop of Narbonne complaining to the pope that the Inquisitor Pierre Durant and his colleagues had, without his knowledge, absolved the Chevalier Pierre de Cugunham, who had been convicted of heresy, whereupon Innocent forthwith annulled their proceedings. In fact the pardoning power seems to have been considered as specially vested in the Holy See, and about this period we find several instances in which it is conferred by Innocent on bishops, sometimes with and sometimes without injunctions to confer with the inquisitors. Finally this question of practice was settled by adopting the habit of reserving in every sentence the right to modify, increase, diminish, or abrogate it.

Inasmuch as the inquisitors in 1246 still expected the bishops to defray their expenses, they recognized themselves, at least in theory, as merely an adjunct to the episcopal tribunals. The bishops, moreover, were expected to build the prisons for the confinement of converts, and though they eluded this and the king was obliged to do it, the Council of Albi, held in 1254 by the papal legate, Zoen of Avignon, assumes that the prisons are under episcopal control. The same council drew up an elaborate series of instructions for the treatment of heretics, which marks the termination of episcopal control of such matters, for all subsequent regulations were issued by the Holy See. Even so experienced a persecutor as Bernard de Caux, notwithstanding his neglect of episcopal jurisdiction in his sentences, admitted in 1248 his subordination to the episcopate by applying for advice to Guillem of Narbonne, and the archbishop replied, not only with directions as to special cases, but with general instructions.

There is an effort to retain vanishing authority in the offer made in 1252 by the Bishops of Toulouse, Albi, Agen, and Carpentras to give full authority as inquisitors to any Dominicans who might be selected by the commissioners of Alphonse of Poitiers, only stipulating that their assent must be asked to all sentences, and promising to observe in all cases the rules established by the Inquisition. Yet Alexander IV, after some vacillation, in 1257 rendered the Inquisition independent by releasing it from the necessity of consulting with the bishops even in cases of obstinate and confessed heretics, and this he repeated in 1260. In 1273 Gregory X, after alluding to the action of Alexander IV, proceeds to direct that inquisitors in deciding upon sentences shall proceed in accordance with the counsel of the bishops or their delegates, so that the episcopal authority may share in decisions of such moment. Up to this period the Inquisition seems to have been regarded as merely a temporary expedient to meet a special exigency, and every pope on his accession had issued a series of bulls renewing its provisions. Henceforth it was considered a permanent part of the machinery of the Church, and its rules were definitely settled. Gregory's decision in favor of concurrent episcopal and inquisitorial action in all cases of condemnation consequently remained unaltered.

If there was this not unnatural vacillation in regulating the delicate relations of these competing jurisdictions, there was none whatever in regard to those between the Inquisition and society at large. Even in its early years of tentative existence it developed such abundant promise of usefulness in bringing the secular laws to bear upon heresy that means were sought to give it a fixed organization which should render it still more efficient in its functions both of detection and punishment. The death of Frederic II, in 1250, in removing the principal antagonist of the papacy, offered the opportunity of giving practical enforcement to his edicts, and accordingly, May 15, 1252, Innocent IV issued to all the potentates and rulers of

Italy his famous bull, *Ad extirpanda,* a carefully considered and elaborate law which should establish machinery for systematic persecution as an integral part of the social edifice in every city and every state. All rulers were ordered in public assembly to put heretics to the ban, as though they were sorcerers. Anyone finding a heretic could seize him, and take possession of his goods. Each chief magistrate, within three days after assuming office, was to appoint, on the nomination of his bishop and of two friars of each of the Mendicant Orders, twelve good Catholics with two notaries and two or more servitors whose sole business was to arrest heretics, seize their goods, and deliver them to the bishop or his vicars. Their wages and expenses were to be defrayed by the State, their evidence was receivable without oaths, and no testimony was good against the concurrent statement of any three of them. They held office for six months, to be reappointed or replaced then, or at any time, on demand of the bishop and friars; they were entitled to one-third of the proceeds of all fines and confiscations inflicted on heretics; they were exempt from all public duties and services incompatible with their functions, and no statutes were to be passed interfering with their actions. The ruler was bound when required to send his assessor or a knight to aid them, and every inhabitant when called upon was obliged to assist them, under a heavy penalty. When the inquisitors visited any portion of the jurisdiction they were accompanied by a deputy of the ruler elected by themselves or by the bishop. In each place visited, this official was to summon under oath three men of good repute, or even the whole vicinage, to reveal any heretics within their knowledge, or the property of such, or of any persons holding secret conventicles or differing in life or manners from the ordinary faithful. The State was bound to arrest all accused, to hold them in prison, to deliver them to the bishop or inquisitor under safe escort, and to execute within fifteen days all judgments pronounced against them. The ruler was further required, when called upon, to inflict torture on those who would not confess and betray all the heretics of their acquaintance. If resistance was made to an arrest, the community where it occurred was liable to an enormous fine unless it delivered up to justice within three days all who were implicated. The ruler was required to have four lists made out of all who were defamed or banned for heresy; this was to be read in public thrice a year and a copy given to the bishop, one to the Dominicans and one to the Franciscans; he was likewise to execute the destruction of houses within ten days of sentence, and the exaction of fines within three months, throwing in prison those who could not pay and keeping them until they should pay. The proceeds of fines, commutations, and confiscations were divisible into three parts, one enuring to the city, one to those concerned in the business, and the remainder to the bishop and inquisitors to be expended in persecuting heresy.

The enforcement of this stupendous measure was provided for with equally careful elaboration. It was to be inscribed ineffaceably in all the local statute books, together with all subsequent laws which the popes might issue, under penalty of excommunication for recalcitrant officials, and interdict upon the city. At the same time Innocent issued instructions to the inquisitors to enforce by excommunication the embodiment of this and of the edicts of Frederic in the statutes of all cities and states, and he soon after conferred on them the dangerous power of interpreting, in conjunction with the bishops, all doubtful points in local laws on the subject of heresy.

These provisions are not the wild imaginings of a nightmare, but sober matter-of-fact legislation shrewdly and carefully devised to accomplish a settled policy, and it affords us a valuable insight into the public opinion of the day to find that there was no effective resistance to its acceptance. Before the death of Innocent IV, in 1254, he made one or two slight modifications suggested by experience in its working. In 1255, 1256, and 1257 Alexander IV revised the bull, explaining some doubts which had arisen, and in 1259 he reissued the bull as a whole. In 1265 Clement IV again went over it carefully, making some changes, principally in adding the words "inquisitors" in passages where Innocent had only designated the bishops and friars, thus showing that the Inquisition had during the interval established itself as the recognized instrumentality in the persecution of heresy; and the next year he repeated Innocent's emphatic order to the inquisitors to enforce the insertion of his legislation and that of his predecessors upon the statute books everywhere, with the free use of excommunication and interdict.

In Italy this furnished the Inquisition with a completely organized personnel paid and sustained by the State, rendering it a substantive institution armed with all the means and appliances necessary for the thorough performance of its work. Whether the popes ever endeavored to render the bulls operative elsewhere does not appear, but if they did so they failed, for the measure was not recognized as in force beyond the Alps. Yet this was scarce necessary so long as public law and the conservative spirit of the ruling class everywhere rendered it the highest duty of the citizen of every degree to aid in every way the business of the inquisitor, and pious monarchs hastened to enforce the obligation of their subjects. By the terms of the Treaty of Paris all public officials were obliged to aid in the inquisition and capture of heretics, and all inhabitants, males over 14 years of age and females over 12, were to be sworn to reveal all offenders to the bishops. The Council of Narbonne in 1229 put these provisions in force; that of Albi in 1254 included inquisitors among those to whom the heretic was to be denounced, and it freely threatened with the censures of the Church all temporal seigneurs who neglected the duty of aiding the Inquisition and of executing its sentences of death or confiscation.

The right to abrogate any laws that impeded the freest exercise of the powers of the Inquisition was likewise arrogated on both sides of the Alps. When, in 1257, Alexander IV heard with indignant emotion that Mantua had adopted certain damnable statutes interfering with the absolutism of the Inquisition, he straightway ordered the Bishop of Mantua to investigate the matter and to annul anything which should impede or delay its operations, enforcing his action by excommunicating the authorities and laying an interdict on the city. This was simply in furtherance of the bull *Ad extirpanda,* but in 1265 Clement IV repeated the order and made it universally applicable, and it was carried into the canon law as the expression of the undoubted rights of the Church. This rendered the Inquisition virtually supreme in all lands, and it became an accepted maxim of law that all statutes interfering with the free action of the Inquisition were void, and those who enacted them were to be punished; where such laws existed the inquisitor was instructed to have them submitted to him, and if he found them objectionable the authorities were obliged to repeal or modify them. It was not the fault of the Church if a bold monarch like Philippe le Bel occasionally ventured to incur divine vengeance by protecting his subjects.

Beyond the Alps there was no legal responsibility admitted, as in Italy, to defray the expenses of the Inquisition by the State, but royal generosity was amply sufficient to keep the organization in effective condition. Its necessary expenses were exceedingly small. The Dominican convents furnished buildings in which to hold its tribunals. The public officials were bound under royal order and the tremendous penalties involved in suspicion of heresy to render service whenever called upon. If the bishops had neglected the duty of establishing and maintaining prisons, the royal zeal stepped in, built them and kept them up. Besides this, the inquisitors, whenever they needed aid and counsel, were empowered to summon experts to attend them and to enforce obedience to the summons. All the learning and wisdom of the land were made subservient to the supreme duty of suppressing heresy and were placed gratuitously at the service of the Inquisition; and any prelate who hesitated to render assistance of any kind when called upon was threatened in no gentle terms with the full force of the papal vengeance.

That the powers thus conferred on the inquisitors were real and not merely theoretical we see in 1260 in the case of Capello di Chia, a powerful noble of the Roman province, who incurred the suspicion of heresy, was condemned, proscribed, and his lands confiscated. When he refused to submit, Frà Andrea, the inquisitor, called for assistance on the citizens of the neighboring town of Viterbo, and they obeyed him by raising an army with which he marched to besiege Capello in his castle of Cole-Casale. Capello had craftily conveyed his lands to a Roman noble named Pietro Giacomo Surdi, and the pious enterprise of the Viterbians was arrested by a command from the senator of Rome forbidding violence to the property of a good Catholic Roman citizen. Then Alexander IV intervened, ordering Surdi to withdraw from the quarrel, as his claim to the castle was null and void. He likewise commanded the senator to abandon his indefensible position, and warmly thanked the Viterbians for the zeal and alacrity with which they had obeyed the summons of Frà Andrea.

In the exercise of this almost limitless authority, inquisitors were practically relieved from all supervision and responsibility. Even a papal legate was not to interfere with them or inquire into heresy within their inquisitorial districts. They were not liable to excommunication while in discharge of their duties, nor could they be suspended by any delegate of the Holy See. Moreover, they were released from all obedience to their provincials and generals, whom they were even forbidden to obey in anything relating to the business of their office, and they were secured from any attempt to undermine them with the curia by the enormous privilege of being able to go to Rome at any time and to stay there as long as they might see fit. At first their commissions were thought to expire with the death of the pope who issued them, but in 1267 they were declared to be continuously valid.

The question of the removability of inquisitors was one which bore directly upon their subordination or independence, and was the subject of much conflicting legislation. When the power of appointment was first conferred upon the provincials it carried with it authority to remove and replace them after consultation with discreet brethren; and in 1244 Innocent IV declared that the provincials and generals of the Mendicant Orders had full power to remove, revoke, supersede, and transfer all members of their Orders serving as inquisitors, even when commissioned by the pope. Later popes issued conflicting orders, until at length Boniface VIII decided in favor of the removing power; but the inquisitors claimed that it could only be exercised for cause and after due trial, which practically reduced it to a nullity. It is true that in the reformatory effort of Clement V *ipso facto* excommunication, removable only by the pope, was provided for three crimes of inquisitors—falsely prosecuting or neglecting to prosecute for favor, enmity, or profit; extorting money; and confiscating church property for the offense of a clerk—but these provisions, although they called forth the earnest protest of Bernard Gui, only amounted to a declaration of what was desirable, and were of no practical effect.

It is not to be imagined that this gigantic structure which over-shadowed Christendom was allowed to establish itself wholly without opposition, despite the favor of popes and kings. When we come to consider the details of its history we shall find numerous cases of popular resistance, desperate and isolated struggles, crushed remorselessly before revolt could so extend as to become dangerous. It required, indeed, courage to foolhardiness for anyone to raise hand or voice against an inquisitor, no matter how cruel or nefarious were his actions. Under the canon law, anyone, from the meanest to the highest, who opposed or impeded in any way the functions of an inquisitor, or gave aid or counsel to those who did so, became at once excommunicate. After the lapse of a year in this condition he was legally a heretic to be handed over without further ceremony to the secular arm for burning. The awful authority which thus shrouded the inquisitor was rendered yet more terrible by the elasticity of definition given to the crime of impeding the Holy Office and the tireless tenacity with which those guilty of it were pursued. If friendly death came to shield them, the Inquisition attacked their memories, and visited their offenses upon their children and grandchildren.

The northern nations were too far removed from the focus of heresy to be exposed to aberrations from the faith at the time when papal supremacy found its most useful instruments in the Mendicant inquisitors. Consequently the papal Inquisition cannot be said to have had an existence in the British Islands, Denmark, or Scandinavia. The edicts of Frederic II had no currency there; and when, in 1277, Robert Kilwarby, Archbishop of Canterbury, and the masters of Oxford denounced certain errors springing from the Averrhoist doctrines, and when, in 1368, Archbishop Langham denounced as heretical 30 articles of scholastic speculation, even had there been martyrs ready, there were no laws under which to punish them, although lawyers had sought to introduce the penalty of the stake, and it had once been inflicted by a council of Oxford, in 1222, on a clerk who had apostatized to Judaism.

When Wickliff came and was followed by Lollardry, the English conceptions of the relations between Church and State had already become such that there was no thought of applying to Rome for a special tribunal with which to meet the threatened danger. The statute of May 25, 1382, directs the king to issue to his sheriffs commissions to arrest Wickliff's travelling preachers, and aiders and abettors of heresy, and to hold them till they justify themselves "selonc reson et la ley de seinte esglise"; and, in the following July, royal letters ordered the authorities of Oxford to make inquisition for heresy throughout the University. The weakness of Richard II allowed the Lollards to become a powerful political as well as religious party, but their chances disappeared with the revolution which placed Henry IV on the throne. The support of the Church was a necessity to the new dynasty, which lost no time in earning its gratitude. After the burning of Sawtré by a royal warrant confirmed by Parliament in 1400, the statute *de hæretico comburendo* for the first time inflicted in England the death penalty as a settled punishment for heresy. For obstinate heresy or relapse, involving under the canon law abandonment to the secular arm, the bishops and their commissioners were the sole judges, and, on their delivery of such convicts, the sheriff of the county or the mayor and bailiffs of the nearest town were obliged to burn them before the people on an eminence. One of the earliest measures of the reign of Edward VI was the repeal of this law, but with the reaction under Philip and Mary came a revival of the sharp laws against heresy. Scarce had the Spanish marriage been concluded when an obedient Parliament re-enacted the legislation, which afforded ample machinery for the numerous burnings which followed. The earliest act of the first Parliament of Elizabeth was the repeal of the legislation of Philip and Mary and of the old statutes which it had revived; but the writ *de hæretico comburendo* had become an integral part of English law and survived until the desire of Charles II for Catholic toleration caused him, in 1676, to procure its abrogation and the restraint of the ecclesiastical courts "in cases of atheism, blasphemy, heresy, and schism and other damnable doctrines and opinions" to the ecclesiastical remedies of "excommunication, deprivation, degradation, and other ecclesiastical censures not extending to death." Scotland was more tardy than England in humanitarian development, but the last execution for heresy in the British Islands was that of a youth of 18, a medical student named Aikenhead, who was hanged in Edinburgh in 1696.

In Ireland the fiery temper of the Franciscan, Richard Ledrede, Bishop of Ossory, led him into a prolonged struggle with presumed heretics—the Lady Alice Kyteler, accused of sorcery, and her accomplices. So little was known in Ireland of the laws concerning heresy that at first the secular officials refused contemptuously to take the oath prescribed by the canons to aid inquisitors in their persecuting duties, but Ledred finally obliged them to do so and had the satisfaction of burning some of the accused in 1325. He incurred, however, the enmity of the chief personages of the island, leading to a countercharge of heresy against himself. For years he was obliged to live in exile, and it was not till 1354 that he was able to reside quietly in his diocese. Even Alexander, Archbishop of Dublin, in 1347, was declared to have been a fautor of heresy because he interfered with Ledrede's violent proceedings; and, in 1351, his successor, Archbishop John, was directed to take active measures to punish those who had escaped from Ossory and had taken refuge in his see.

When the Hussite troubles became alarming and there was danger that the disaffection might spread to the north, Martin V in 1421 authorized the Bishop of Sleswick to appoint a Franciscan, Friar Nicholas John, as Inquisitor for Denmark, Norway, and Sweden, but there is no trace of his activity in those regions, and the Inquisition may be considered as nonexistent there.

As the mediæval missions for the conversion of schismatics and heathen were exclusively Dominican and Franciscan, the churches which they built up, however slender in membership, were nevertheless completely equipped with apparatus for preserving the orthodoxy of converts, and thus we read of Inquisitions in Africa and Asia. Friar Raymond Martius is honored as the founder of the Inquisition in Tunis and Morocco. About 1370 Gregory XI appointed the Dominican Friar John Gallus as Inquisitor in the East, who in conjunction with Friar Elias Petit planted the institution, as we are told, in Armenia, Russia, Georgia, and Wallachia, while Upper Armenia was similarly provided by Friar Bartolomeo Ponco. On the death of Friar Gallus, Urban VI, about 1378, applied to the Dominican General to select three brethren to serve as inquisitors, one in Armenia and Georgia, one in Greece and Tartary, and one in Russia and the two Wallachias; and in 1389 one of these, Friar Andreas of Caffa, obtained the privilege of appointing an associate in his extensive province of Greece and Tartary. In the fourteenth century an inquisitor seems to have been regarded as a necessary portion of the missionary outfit. Even in the fabled Ethiopian empire of Prester John we hear of an Inquisition founded in Abyssinia by the Dominican Friar, St. Pantaleone, and another in Nubia by Friar Bartolomeo de Tybuli, who was also honored as a saint in those regions.

Properly to govern and direct an engine of such infinite power, dealing with the life and happiness of countless thousands, would require more than human wisdom and virtue; and it may be worth a moment's attention to see what was the ideal of those to whom the practical working of the Holy Office was confided. Bernard Gui, the most experienced inquisitor of his day, concludes his elaborate instructions on procedure with some general directions on conduct and character. The inquisitor, he tells us, should be diligent and fervent in his zeal for the truth of religion, for the salvation of souls, and for the extirpation of heresy. Amid troubles and opposing accidents he should grow earnest, without allowing himself to be inflamed with the fury of wrath and indignation. He must not be sluggish of body, for sloth destroys the vigor of action. He must be intrepid, persisting through danger to death, laboring for religious truth, neither precipitating peril by audacity nor shrinking from it through timidity. He must be unmoved by the prayers and blandishments of those who seek to influence him, yet not be, through hardness of heart, so obstinate that he will yield nothing to entreaty, whether in granting delays or in mitigating punishment, according to place and circumstance, for this implies stubbornness; nor must he be weak and yielding through too great a desire to please, for this will destroy the vigor and value of his work. In doubtful matters he must be circumspect and not readily yield credence to what seems probable, for such is not always true; nor should he obstinately reject the opposite, for that which seems improbable often turns out to be fact. He must listen, discuss, and examine with all zeal, that the truth may be reached at the end. Like a just judge, let him so bear himself in passing sentence of corporal punishment that his face may show compassion, while his inward purpose remains unshaken, and thus will he avoid the appearance of wrath leading to the charge of cruelty. In imposing pecuniary penalties, let his face preserve the severity of justice as though he were compelled by necessity and not allured by cupidity. Let truth and mercy, which should never leave the heart of a judge, shine forth from his countenance, that his decisions may be free from all suspicion of covetousness or cruelty.

CHAPTER VII
THE INQUISITION AT WORK

1. ORGANIZATION

The organization of the Inquisition was simple, yet effective. To the secular prelacy it left the gorgeous vestments and the imposing splendors of worship, the picturesque processions and the showy retinues of retainers. The inquisitor wore the simple habits of his Order. When he appeared abroad he was at most accompanied by a few armed familiars, partly as a guard, partly to execute his orders. Every detail in the Inquisition was intended for work and not for show. It was built up by resolute, earnest men of one idea who knew what they wanted, who rendered everything subservient to the one object, and who sternly rejected all that might embarrass with superfluities the unerring and ruthless justice which it was their mission to enforce.

The previous chapter has shown us the simplicity which marked the beginnings of the institution, consisting virtually of the individual friars selected to hunt up heretics and determine their guilt. Their districts were naturally coterminous with the provinces of the Mendicant Orders, and these provinces each comprised many bishoprics. Though the chief town of each province came to be regarded as the seat of the Inquisition, yet it was the duty of the inquisitor to go in pursuit of the heretics, to visit all places where heresy might be suspected to exist, and to summon the people to assemble, exactly as the bishops formerly did in their visitations, with the added inducement of an indulgence of 20 or 40 days for all who attended.

Nothing could well be devised more effective than these visitations and during the busy times of the Inquisition they must have formed an important portion of its functions. A few days in advance of his visit to a city, the inquisitor would send notice to the ecclesiastical authorities requiring them to summon the people to assemble at a specified time. To the populace thus brought together he preached on the faith, urging them to its defense with such eloquence as he could command, summoning everyone within a certain radius to come forward within 6 or 12 days and reveal to him whatever they may have known or heard of anyone leading to the belief or suspicion that he might be a heretic, or defamed for heresy, or that he had spoken against any article of faith, or that he differed in life and morals from the common conversation of the faithful. Neglect to comply with this command incurred *ipso facto* excommunication, removable only by the inquisitor himself; compliance with it was rewarded with an indulgence of three years. At the same time he proclaimed a "time of grace," varying from 15 to 30 days, during which any heretic coming forward spontaneously, confessing his guilt, abjuring, and giving full information about his fellow sectaries, was promised mercy. This mercy varied at different times from complete immunity to exemption from the severer penalties of death, imprisonment, exile, or confiscation. After the expiration of the term they were told that no mercy would be shown; while it lasted, the inquisitor was instructed to keep himself housed, so as to be ready at any moment to receive denunciations and confessions; and long series of interrogatories, most searching and suggestive, were drawn up to prompt him in the examination of those who should present themselves.

It is easy to imagine the terror into which a community would be thrown when an inquisitor suddenly descended upon it and made his proclamation. No one could know what stories might be circulating about him which zealous fanaticism or personal enmity might exaggerate and carry to the inquisition, and in this the orthodox and the heretic would suffer alike. All scandals passing from mouth to mouth would be brought to light. All confidence between man and man would disappear. Old grudges would be gratified in safety. To him who had been heretically inclined the suspense would grow day by day more insupportable, with the thought that some careless word might have been treasured up to be now revealed by those who ought to be nearest and dearest to him, until at last he would yield and betray others rather than be betrayed himself. We may well believe Bernard Gui when he says that each revelation led to others, until the invisible net extended far and wide, and that not the least of the benefits arising were the confiscations which were sure to follow.

These preliminary proceedings were commonly held in the convent of the Order to which the inquisitor belonged, if such there were, or in the episcopal palace if it were a cathedral town. In other cases the church or municipal buildings would afford the necessary accommodation. Each inquisitor, however, necessarily had his headquarters to which he would return after these forays, carrying with him the depositions of accusers and confessions of accused, and such prisoners as he deemed it important to secure, the secular authorities being bound to furnish him the necessary transportation and guards. Others he would cite to appear before him at a specified time, taking sufficient bail to secure their punctuality. In the earlier period, the seat of his tribunal was the Mendicant convent, while the episcopal or public prison was at his disposal for the detention of his captives; but in time special buildings were provided, amply furnished with the necessary appliances and dungeons—cells built along the walls and thence known as *murus*, in contradistinction to the *carcer* or prison—where the unfortunates awaiting sentence were under the immediate supervision of their judge. It was here, for the most part, that the judicial proceedings were carried on, though we occasionally hear of the episcopal palace being used, especially when the bishop was zealous and co-operated with the Inquisition.

During the earlier period there was no limitation on the age of the inquisitor; the provincial who held the appointing power could select any member of his Order. That this frequently led to the nomination of young and inexperienced men is presumable from the language in which Clement V, when reforming the Holy Office, prescribed 40 years as the minimium age in future. Bernard Gui remonstrated against this, not only because younger men were often thoroughly capable of the duties, but also because bishops and their ordinaries who exercised inquisitorial power were not required to be so old. The rule, however, held good. In 1422 the Provincial of Toulouse appointed an Inquisitor of Carcassonne, Friar Raymond du Tille, who was only 32 years of age. Though he was confirmed by the general of the Order, it was held that the office was vacant until an appeal was made to Martin V, who ordered the Official of Alet to investigate his fitness, and, if found worthy, the Clementine canon might be suspended in his favor.

The trials were usually conducted by a single inquisitor, though sometimes two would work together. One, however, sufficed, but he generally had subordinate assistants, who prepared the cases for him, and took the preliminary examinations. He had a right to call upon the provincial to assign to him as many of these assistants as he deemed necessary, but he could not select them for himself. Sometimes, when the bishop was eager for persecution and careless of the episcopal dignity, he would accept the position; and it was frequently filled by the Dominican prior of the local convent.

These assistants represented the inquisitor during his absence and thus were closely assimilated to the commissioners who came to be a permanent feature of the Holy Office. Even in the twelfth century it was determined that a judicial delegate of the Holy See could delegate his powers; and in 1246 the Council of Béziers authorized the inquisitor to appoint a deputy whenever he wished to have an inquest made in any place to which he could not himself proceed. Yet the formal authority to appoint commissioners with full powers does not seem to have been granted to inquisitors until 1262 by Urban IV, and this had to be confirmed by Boniface VIII towards the close of the century. These commissioners, or vicars, differed from the assistants, inasmuch as they were appointed and discharged at the discretion of the inquisitor. They became a permanent feature of the institution and conducted its business in places remote from the main tribunal; or, in case of the absence or incapacity of the inquisitor, one of them might be summoned to replace him temporarily, or the inquisitor could appoint a vicar-general. Like their principal, they had, after the Clementine reforms in 1317, to be at least 40 years of age, and they wielded full inquisitorial powers, in the citation, arrest, and examination of witnesses and prisoners, even to the infliction of torture and condemnation to imprisonment. Whether they could proceed to final sentence in capital cases was a disputed question, and Eymerich recommends that such authority should always be reserved to the inquisitor himself; but, as we shall see, the cases of Joan of Arc and of the Vaudois of Arras show that this reservation was rarely observed.

In the later period there seems to have been occasionally another official with the title of "counsellor." In a document of 1423 the person filling this position is not a Dominican, but is qualified as a licentiate in law; and doubtless such a functionary was a useful and usual member of the tribunal, though with no precise official status. Eymerich recommends that a commissioner should always associate with himself some discreet lawyer to save him from mistakes which may redound to the disadvantage of the Inquisition, call for papal interposition, and perhaps cost him his place.

As absolute secrecy became a main feature of all the proceedings of the Inquisition after its earlier tentative period, it was a universal rule that testimony, whether of witnesses or of accused, should only be taken in the presence of two impartial men, not connected with the institution, but sworn to silence. The inquisitor was empowered to compel the attendance of anyone whom he might summon to perform this duty. These representatives of the public were preferably clerics, and usually Dominicans, "discreet and religious men," who were expected to sign with the notary the written report of the testimony in attestation of its fidelity. Though not alluded to in the instructions of the Council of Béziers in 1246, a deposition taken in 1244 shows that already the practice had become customary; and the frequent repetitions of the rule by successive popes and its embodiment in the canon law show what importance was attached to it as a means of preventing injustice and giving at least a color of impartiality to the proceedings.

The personnel of the tribunal was completed by the notary—an official of considerable standing and dignity in the Middle Ages. All the proceedings of the Inquisition were taken down in writing—every question and every answer—each witness and each defendant being obliged to confirm his testimony when read over to him at the close of the interrogatory, and judgment was finally rendered on an inspection of the evidence thus recorded. The function of the notary was no light one, and occasionally scriveners were called in to his assistance, but he formally attested every document. Not only was there the fearful multiplication of papers accumulating in the current business of the tribunal, and their careful transcription for preservation, but the several Inquisitions were continually furnishing each other with copies of their records, so that a considerable force must have been employed. As in everything else, the inquisitor was empowered to call for gratuitous service on the part of anyone whom he might summon, but the continuous business of the office required undivided attention, and its proper dispatch rendered desirable the peculiar training acquired by experience. In the earlier periods, the authorization to impress any notary to serve, and the advice to select if possible Dominicans who had been notaries, shows that the itinerant tribunals depended for the most part on this chance conscription; but in the permanent seats of the Inquisition the notary was a regular official, in receipt of a salary. In the attempted reform of Clement V it was provided that he should take his official oath before the bishop as well as before the inquisitor, and to this Bernard Gui objected on the ground that the exigencies of business sometimes required the force to be suddenly increased to two or three or four, and that in places where no public notaries were to be had, other competent persons were necessarily employed on the spur of the moment, as it often happens that the guilty will confess when in the mood, and if their confession is not promptly taken they draw back. Curiously enough, the power to appoint notaries was regarded with so much jealousy that it was denied to the inquisitor. He may if he choose, says Eymerich, send three or four names to the pope, who will appoint them for him, but this leads to such bad feeling on the part of the local authorities that he had better content himself with the notaries of the bishops or of the secular rulers.

The enormous mass of documents produced by these innumerable busy hands was the object of well-deserved solicitude. At the very inception of the work its value was recognized. In 1235 we hear of the confessions of penitents being sedulously recorded in books kept for the purpose. This speedily became the universal custom, and the inquisitors were instructed to preserve careful records of all their proceedings, from the first summons to the final sentence in every case, together with lists of all who took the oath enforced on everyone to defend the faith and persecute. With what elaborate care they were rendered practically useful is shown by the *Book of Sentences of the Inquisition of Toulouse*, from 1308 to 1323, printed by Limborch, where at the end there is an index of the 636 culprits sentenced, grouped under their places of residence alphabetically arranged, with reference to the pages on which their names occur and brief mention of the several punishments inflicted on each, and of any subsequent modifications of the penalty, thus enabling the official who wished information about the people of any hamlet to see at a glance who among them had been suspected and what had been done.

The temptation to falsify the records when an enemy was to be struck down was exceedingly strong, and the opponents of the Inquisition had no hesitation in declaring that it was freely yielded to. Friar Bernard Délicieux, speaking for the whole Franciscan Order of Languedoc, in a formal document of the year 1300, not only declared that the records were unworthy of trust, but that they were generally believed to be so. We shall see hereafter facts which fully justified this assertion, and the popular mistrust was intensified by the jealous secrecy which rendered it an offense punishable with excommunication for anyone to possess any papers relating to the proceedings of the Inquisition or to prosecutions against heretics. On the other hand, the temptation on the part of those who were endangered to destroy the archives was equally strong, and the attempts to effect this show the importance attached to their possession. As early as 1235 we find the citizens of Narbonne, in an insurrection against the Inquisition, carefully destroying all the books and records. About 1285, at Carcassonne, a plot was entered into by the consuls of the town and several of its leading ecclesiastics to destroy the inquisitorial records. They bribed one of the familiars, Bernard Garric, to burn them, but the conspiracy was discovered and its authors punished. One of these, a lawyer named Guillem Garric, languished in prison for about 30 years before his final sentence in 1321.

Not the least important among the functionaries of the Inquisition were the lowest class—the apparitors, messengers, spies, and bravos, known generally as "familiars," which came to have so ill-omened a significance in the popular ear. The service was not without risk, and it had few attractions for the honest and peaceable, but it was full of promise for the reckless and evil-minded. Not only did they enjoy the immunity from secular jurisdiction attaching to all in the service of the Church, but the special authority granted by Innocent IV, in 1245, to the inquisitors to absolve their familiars for acts of violence rendered them independent even of the ecclesiastical tribunals. Besides, as any molestation of the servants of the Inquisition was qualified as impeding its operations and thus savoring of heresy, anyone who dared to resist aggression rendered himself liable to prosecution before the tribunal of the aggressor. All that was needed to render this social scourge complete was devised when the familiars were authorized to carry arms. The murders at Avignonet in 1242, and other similar events, seemed to justify the inquisitors in desiring an armed guard; and the service of tracking and capturing heretics was frequently one of peril, yet the privilege was a dangerous one to bestow on such men as could be got for the work, while releasing them from the restraints of law. In the turbulence of the age the carrying of weapons was rigidly repressed in all peace-loving communities. As early as the eleventh century we find it prohibited in the city of Pistoja, and in 1228 in Verona. In Bologna knights and doctors only were allowed to bear arms, and to have one armed servant. Such regulations were of inestimable value in the progress of civilization, but they amounted to little when the inquisitor could arm anyone he pleased, and invest him with the privileges and immunities of the Holy Office.

As early as 1249 the scandals and abuses arising from the unlimited employment of scriveners and familiars called forth the indignant rebuke of Innocent IV, who commanded that their numbers should be reduced to correspond with the bare exigencies of duty. In those countries in which the Inquisition was supported by the State there was not much opportunity for the development of overgrown abuses of this nature. In Naples, Charles of Anjou, in permitting the carrying of arms, specifies three as the number of familiars for each inquisitor. Eymerich assures us that all such interference is unlawful, and that any secular ruler who endeavors to prevent the familiars of the Holy Office from bearing arms is impeding the Inquisition and is a fautor of heresy, while Bernard Gui characterizes in similar terms any limitation of the number of officials below what the inquisitor may deem requisite, all of which, according to Zanghino, is punishable at the discretion of the inquisitor.

I have already alluded to the duty of every secular official to lend aid whenever called upon. This duty was recognized and enforced so that the organization of the Inquisition may be said to have embraced that of the State, whose whole resources were placed at its disposition. The oath of obedience which the inquisitor was empowered to exact of all holding official station was no mere form. Refusal to take it was visited with excommunication, leading to prosecution for heresy in case of obduracy, and humiliating penance on submission. At times it was neglected by careless inquisitors, but the earnest ones made a point of it. Bernard Gui, at all his *autos de fé*, solemnly administered it to all the royal officials and local magistrates, and when, in May 1309, Jean de Maucochin, the royal Seneschal of the Tolosain and Albigeois, declined to take it, he was speedily brought to see his error, and submitted within a month. Any hesitation on the part of public officials to grant assistance when summoned was promptly punished. In 1303, when Bonrico di Busca, vicar of the Podestà of Mandrisio, refused to furnish men to the representatives of the Milanese Inquisition, he was condemned to a fine of 100 imperial solidi, to be paid within five days. Even the condition of an excommunicate, which rendered an official incapable of performing any other function, did not relieve him from this duty; he could be called upon to execute the commands of the inquisitor, but he was warned that he must not imagine himself competent therefore to do anything else.

In addition to this the Inquisition had, to a greater or less extent, at its service the whole orthodox population, and especially the clergy. It was the duty of every man to give information about all cases of heresy with which he might become acquainted, under pain of incurring the guilt of fautorship. It was further his duty to arrest all heretics, as Bernard de St. Genais found in 1242, when he was tried by the Inquisition of Toulouse for the offense of not capturing certain heretics when it was in his power to do so. The parish priests were required, whenever called upon, to cite their parishioners for appearance, either publicly from the pulpit or secretly as the case might require, and to publish all sentences of excommunication. They were also held to the duty of surveillance over penitents to see that penances were duly performed, and to report any cases of neglect.

An important feature in the organization of the Inquisition was the assembly in which the fate of the accused was finally determined. The inquisitor had technically no power to pass sentence by himself. We have seen how, after various fluctuations of policy, the co-operation of the bishops was established as indispensable. As in everything else, the inquisitors contemptuously neglected this limitation on their powers, and when Clement V endeavored to reform abuses he pronounced null and void any sentences rendered independently, yet to avert delays he permitted consent to be expressed in writing if after eight days a meeting could not be arranged. If we may judge from some specimens of these written consultations which have reached us, they were perfunctory to the last degree and placed no real check upon the discretion of the inquisitor. Still, Bernard Gui complained bitterly even of this restriction, in terms which show how little respect had previously been paid to the rule, and he adds, in justification, that one bishop kept the trials of some persons of his diocese from being finished for two years and more, while another delayed the celebration of an *auto de fé* for six months. He himself observed the regulation scrupulously, both before and after the publication of the Clementines, and in the reports of the *autos* held by him in Toulouse the participation of the bishops of the prisoners, or of episcopal delegates, is always carefully specified. Yet how easy was the evasion of this, as of all other regulations for the protection of the accused, is seen when even Bernard Gui accepted commissions from three bishops—those of Cahors, St. Papoul, and Montauban—to act for them in the *auto* of September 30, 1319. This device became frequent, and inquisitors constantly rendered sentence on their individual responsibility under power granted them by the bishops, as in the persecutions of the Waldenses of Piedmont in 1387, and that of the witches of Canavese in 1474.

This episcopal concurrence in the sentence was reached in consultation with the assembly of experts. As the inquisitors from the beginning were chosen rather with regard to zeal than learning, it was soon found requisite to associate with them in the rendering of sentences men versed in the civil and canon law, which had by this time become an intricate study requiring the devotion of a lifetime. Accordingly they were empowered to call in experts to deliberate with them over the evidence and advise with them on the sentence to be rendered, and those who were thus summoned could not refuse to serve gratuitously, though it is intimated that the inquisitor can pay them if he feels so inclined. At first it would seem as though notables were assembled at the condemnation of prominent heretics rather to give solemnity to the occasion than for actual consultation, as when, in 1237, at the sentence passed on Alaman de Roaix in Toulouse, the presence is recorded of the Bishop of Toulouse, the Abbot of Moissac, the Dominican and Franciscan provincials, and a number of other notables. The amount of work, in fact, performed by the Inquisition of Languedoc in the early years of its existence would seem to preclude the idea of any serious deliberation by counsellors thus called in, who would have to consider the interminable reports of examinations and interrogations; especially as, at a comparatively early date, the practice was adopted of allowing a number of culprits to accumulate whose fate was determined and announced in a solemn *Sermo* or *auto de fé*. Still, the form was kept up, and in 1247 a sentence rendered by Bernard de Caux and Jean de St. Pierre on seven relapsed heretics is specified as being "with the counsel of many prelates and other good men." In the final shape which the assembly of counsellors assumed, we find it summoned to meet on Fridays, the *Sermo* always taking place on Sundays. The assessors were always to be jurists and Mendicant friars, selected by the inquisitor in such numbers as he saw fit. They were severally sworn on the Gospels to secrecy, and to give good and wise counsel, each according to his conscience and the knowledge vouchsafed him by God. The inquisitor then read over to them his summary of each case, sometimes withholding the name of the accused, and they voted the sentence—"Penance at the discretion of the inquisitor"—"That person is to be imprisoned, or abandoned to the secular arm," while the Gospels lay on the table in their midst, "so that our judgment may come from the face of God and our eyes may see justice."

As a rule it is safe to assume that these proceedings were scarcely more than formal. Not only was the inquisitor at liberty to present each case in such aspect as he saw fit, but it became the custom to call in such numbers of experts that in the press of business deliberation was scarce possible. Thus the Inquisitor of Carcassonne, Henri de Chamay, assembled at Narbonne, December 10, 1328, besides himself and the episcopal Ordinary, 42 counsellors, consisting of canons, jurisconsults, and lay experts. In the two days allotted to them this unwieldy assemblage despatched 34 cases, which would show that little consideration could have been given to each. In only two cases, indeed, was there any difference of opinion expressed, and these were of no special importance. On September 8, 1329, he held another assembly at Carcassonne, attended by 47 experts, which in its two days' session acted upon 40 cases. Yet these assemblies were not always so expeditious and self-effacing. From Narbonne Henri de Chamay passed to Pamiers, where, January 7, 1329, he called together 35 experts besides the Bishop of Toulouse. On the first day several cases were postponed for greater deliberation, and of these some were acted upon and others were not. Considerable debate took place, each individual expressing his opinion, and the result was apparently settled by the majority vote. They evidently felt the responsibility of the decision; and yet the impossibility of deliberate action by so cumbrous a body is seen in their bunching together all the cases of "believing" heretics, condemning them *en masse* to prison, and leaving it with the inquisitor to determine the character of the imprisonment for each individual.

Yet, while the forms were thus preserved, the inquisitors, with their customary arbitrary disregard of all that limited their discretion, paid attention or not to the decisions of the experts, as best suited them. In the sentences which follow the reports of these assemblies it is by no means unusual to find names which had never been laid before them. After the assembly of Pamiers, for instance, which showed so much disposition to act for itself, there is a sentence condemning five defuncts, only two of whom are named in the proceedings. On the same occasion, another culprit, Ermessende, daughter of Raymond Monier, was condemned by the assembly for false-witness to the *murus largus*, or simple prison, and was sentenced by the inquisitor to *murus strictus*, or imprisonment in chains, which was a very different penalty. It fact, it was a disputed point whether the inquisitor was bound to obey the counsel of the assembly, and though Eymerich decides in the affirmative, Bernardo di Como positively asserts the negative.

From the necessity of these consultations with bishops and experts it is easy to understand the origin of the *Sermo generalis*, or *auto de fé*. It was evidently impossible to bring all parties together to consult over each individual case, and not only was convenience served by allowing the cases to accumulate, but opportunity was also afforded of arranging an impressive solemnity which should strike terror on the heretic and comfort the hearts of the faithful. In the rudimentary Inquisition of Florence in 1245, where the Inquisitor Ruggieri Calcagni and Bishop Ardingho were zealously cooperating and no assembly of experts was required, we find the heretics sentenced and executed day by day, singly or in twos or threes, but the form was already adopted of assembling the people in the cathedral and reading the sentence to them. In Toulouse the fragment of the Register of Sentences of Bernard de Caux and Jean de Saint-Pierre, from March 1246 to June 1248, shows a similar disregard of form. The *autos* or *Sermones* are sometimes held every few days—there are five in May 1246—and often there are only one or two heretics to be sentenced, rendering it exceedingly probable that the co-operation of the bishop was not asked for, especially as he is never mentioned as joining in the condemnation. There are always present, however, a certain number of local magistrates, civil and ecclesiastical, and the ceremony is usually performed in the cloister of the church of St. Sernin, though other places are sometimes mentioned, and among them the Hôtel-de-Ville twice, showing that divine service as yet formed no part of the solemnity.

With time the ceremony grew in stateliness and impressiveness. Sunday became prescribed for it, and as no other sermons were allowed on that day in the city, it was forbidden to be held on Quadragesima or Advent Sunday, or any other of the principal feast-days. Notice was given in advance from all the pulpits summoning all the people to be present and obtain the indulgence of forty days. A staging was erected in the center of the church, on which the "penitents" were placed, surrounded by the secular and clerical officials. The sermon was delivered by the inquisitor, after which the oath of obedience was administered to the representatives of the civil power, and a solemn decree of excommunication was fulminated against all who should in any manner impede the operations of the Holy Office. Then the notary commenced reading the confessions one by one in the vulgar tongue, and as each was finished the culprit was asked if he acknowledged it to be true— care being taken, however, only to do this when he was known to be truly penitent and not likely to create scandal by a denial. On his replying in the affirmative he was asked whether he would repent, or lose body and soul by persevering in heresy; and on his expressing a desire to abjure, the form of abjuration was read and he repeated it, sentence by sentence. Then the inquisitor absolved him from the *ipso facto* excommunication which he had incurred by heresy, and promised him mercy if he behaved well under the sentence about to be imposed. The sentence followed, and thus the penitents were brought forward successively, commencing with the least guilty and proceeding with those incurring severer penalties. Those who were to be "relaxed," or abandoned to the secular arm, were reserved to the last, and for them the ceremony was adjourned to the public square, where a platform had been constructed for the purpose, in order that the holy precincts of the church might not be polluted by a sentence leading to blood. For the same reason it was not to be performed on a holy day. The execution, however, was not to take place on the same day, but on the following, so as to afford the convicts time for conversion, that their souls might not pass from temporal to eternal flame, and care was enjoined not to permit them to address the people, lest sympathy should be aroused by their assertions of innocence.

We can readily picture to ourselves the effect produced on the popular mind by these awful celebrations, when, at the bidding of the Inquisition, all that was great and powerful in the land was called together humbly to take the oath of obedience and witness its exercise of the highest expression of human authority, regulating the destinies of fellow creatures here and hereafter. In the great *auto de fé* held by Bernard Gui at Toulouse, in April 1310, the solemnities lasted from Sunday the 5th until Thursday the 9th. After the preliminary work of mitigating the penances of some deserving penitents, 20 persons were condemned to wear crosses and perform pilgrimages, 65 were consigned to perpetual imprisonment, three of them in chains, and 18 were delivered to the secular justice and were duly burned. In that of April 1312, 51 were sentenced to crosses, 86 to imprisonment, 10 defunct persons were pronounced worthy of prison and their estates confiscated, the bones of 36 were ordered to be exhumed and burned, 5 living ones were handed over to the secular court to be burned, and 5 more condemned for contumacy in absenting themselves. Sometimes, however, a godless heretic would interfere with the prescribed order of solemnities, as when, in October 1309, Amiel de Perles, a noted Catharan teacher, who defiantly avowed his heterodoxy, immediately on his capture commenced the *endura* and refused all food and drink. Unwilling thus to be robbed of his victim, Bernard hastened the usual dilatory proceedings, and gave to Amiel the honor of a special *auto* in which he was the only victim.

The effectiveness of the organization was unhampered by any

limits of jurisdiction, so that there was no resting-place, no harbor
of refuge for the heretic in any land where the Inquisition existed.
Vainly might he change his abode, it was ever on his track. A suspicious stranger would be observed and arrested; his birthplace
would be ascertained, and as soon as swift messengers could traverse
the intervening distance, full official documents on his antecedents
would be received from the Holy Office of his former home. It was
a mere matter of convenience whether he should be tried where he
was caught or sent back, for every tribunal had full jurisdiction over
all offenses committed within its district, and over all such offenders
wherever they should stray. When Jacopo della Chiusa, one of the
assassins of St. Peter Martyr, discreetly absented himself, notices
commanding his capture were sent as far as the Inquisition of Carcassonne. How the same tireless and unforgiving zeal was habitually
brought to bear upon the humblest objects is seen in the case of
Arnaud Ysarn, who, when a youth of 15, was condemned at Toulouse
in 1309, after an imprisonment of two years, to wear crosses and
perform certain pilgrimages, his sole offense being that he had once
"adored" a heretic at the command of his father. He wore the insignia of his shame for more than a year, when, finding that they
prevented him from earning a livelihood, he threw them off and
obtained employment as a boatman on the Garonne between Moissac
and Bordeaux. In his obscurity he might well fancy himself safe;
but the inquisitorial police was too well organized, and he was
discovered. Cited in 1312 to appear, he was afraid to do so, though
urged by his father to take the chance of mercy. In 1315 he was
excommunicated for contumacy, and, remaining under the censure
for a year, he was finally declared a heretic, and was condemned
as such in the *auto de fé* of 1319. In June 1321, by command of
Bernard Gui, he was captured at Moissac, but escaped on the road
to be recaptured and taken to Toulouse. He had been guilty of no
act of heresy during the interval, but his contumacious rejection of
the chastisement of the Inquisition was an offense worthy of death,
and he was mercifully treated in being condemned, in 1322, to
imprisonment for life on bread and water.

To render it an instrumentality perfect for the work assigned
to it, all that was wanting to the Inquisition was its subjection to
a chief who should command the implicit obedience of its mem-

bers and weld the organization into an organic whole. This function the pope could perform but imperfectly amid the overwhelming diversity of his cares, and he needed a minister who, as Inquisitor-General, could devote his undivided attention to the innumerable questions arising from the conflict between orthodoxy
and heresy, and between papal supremacy and local episcopal independence. The importance of such a measure seems to have made
itself felt at a comparatively early period, and in 1262 Urban IV
created a virtual Inquisitor-General when he ordered all inquisitors
to report, either in person or by letter, to Caietano Orsini, Cardinal
of S. Niccolò in carcere Tulliano, all impediments to the due
performance of their functions, and to obey the instructions he might
give. Cardinal Orsini speaks of himself as Inquisitor-General, and he
labored to bring the several tribunals into the closest relations with
each other and subjection to himself. May 19, 1273, we find him
ordering the Italian inquisitors to furnish to the inquisitors of France
facilities for the transcription of all the depositions of witnesses
already on record in their archives, as well as of all future ones. The
perpetual migration of Catharans and Waldenses between France
and Italy rendered this information most valuable, and the French
inquisitors had requested it of him, but the excessive diffuseness of
the inquisitorial documents made the task appalling in magnitude
and cost, and the terms of the cardinal's missive show that it was
not expected to be welcome. Another letter of his, dated May 24,
1273, to the inquisitors of France, indicates that for a time at least
the general instructions to the functionaries of the Holy Office were
issued through him.

We have no further evidence of his activity, but his elevation
to the papacy in 1277, as Nicholas III, may possibly indicate that
the position was one which afforded abundant opportunities of influence, perhaps rendering its possessor disagreeably, if not dangerously powerful, and when Nicholas appointed his nephew, Cardinal Latino Malebranca, as his successor in the office, he may have
felt it necessary to secure himself by keeping the position in his
family. Malebranca was Dean of the Sacred College, and his influence was shown when, in 1294, he ended the weary conflict of the
conclave by procuring the election of Celestin V. He did not survive
the short pontificate of Celestin, and the proud and vigorous Boni-

face VIII regarded it as impolitic or unnecessary to continue the office. It remained in abeyance under the Avignonese popes, until Clement VI revived it for William, Cardinal of S. Stefano in Monte Celio, who signalized his zeal by burning several heretics, and in other ways. After his death the post remained vacant.

2. THE INQUISITORIAL PROCESS

If we would rightly appreciate the methods of the Inquisition we must understand the relations which the inquisitor conceived to exist between himself and the offenders brought before his tribunal. As a judge, he was vindicating the faith and avenging God for the wrongs inflicted on him by misbelief. He was more than a judge, however; he was a father-confessor striving for the salvation of the wretched souls perversely bent on perdition.

His duty, moreover, was distinguished from that of the ordinary judge by the fact that the task assigned to him was the impossible one of ascertaining the secret thoughts and opinions of the prisoner. The crime he sought to suppress was purely a mental one—acts, however criminal, were beyond his jurisdiction. The accused might be regular in his attendance at mass; he might be liberal in his oblations, punctual in confession and communion, and yet be a heretic at heart. When brought before the tribunal he might profess the most unbounded submission to the decisions of the Holy See, the strictest adherence to orthodox doctrine, the freest readiness to subscribe to whatever was demanded of him, and yet be secretly a Catharan or a Vaudois, fit only for the stake. To the conscientious judge, eager to destroy the foxes which ravaged the vineyard of the Lord, the task of exploring the secret heart of man was no easy one. We cannot wonder that he speedily emancipated himself from the trammels of recognized judicial procedure, which would have rendered his labors futile. Resolved to accomplish a predetermined end, he inevitably reached the practical conclusion that the sacrifice of a hundred innocent men were better than the escape of one guilty.

Thus of the three forms of criminal actions—accusation, denunciation, and inquisition—the third necessarily became, in place of an exception, the invariable rule, and at the same time it was stripped of the safeguards by which its dangerous tendencies had been in some degree neutralized. If a formal accuser presented himself, the inquisitor was instructed to discourage him by pointing out the danger of the *talio* to which he was exposed by inscribing himself; and by general consent this form of action was rejected in consequence of its being "litigious"—that is, because it afforded the accused some opportunities of defense. That there was danger to the accuser, and that the Inquisition practically discouraged the process, was shown in 1304, when the Inquisitor Frà Landulfo imposed a fine of 150 ounces of gold on the town of Theate because it had officially accused a man of heresy and had failed in the proof. The action by denunciation was less objectionable, because in it the inquisitor acted *ex officio*; but it was unusual, and the inquisitorial process at an early period became substantially the only one followed.

About 1278 an experienced inquisitor lays down the rule as one generally received, that in places much suspected of heresy every inhabitant must be cited to appear, must be forced to abjure heresy and to tell the truth, and be subjected to a detailed interrogatory about himself and others, in which any lack of frankness will subject him hereafter to the dreadful penalties of relapse. That this was not a mere theoretical proposition appears from the great inquests held by Bernard de Caux and Jean de Saint-Pierre in 1245 and 1246, when there are recorded 230 interrogatories of inhabitants of the little town of Avignonet, 100 of those of Fanjeaux, and 420 of Mas-Saintes-Puelles.

From this responsibility there was no escape for anyone who had reached the age at which the Church held him able to answer for his own acts. What this age was, however, was a subject of dispute. The Councils of Toulouse, Béziers, and Albi assumed it to be 14 for males and 12 for females, when they prescribed the oath of abjuration to be taken by the whole population, and this rule was adopted by some authorities. Others contented themselves with the definition that the child must be old enough to understand the purport of an oath, while there were not wanting high authorities who reduced the age of responsibility to 7 years, and those who more charitably fixed it at 9½ for girls and 10½ for boys. It is true

that in Latin countries, where minority did not cease until the age
of 25, no one beneath that age had a standing in court, but this was
readily evaded by appointing for him a "curator," under whose
shadow he could be tortured and condemned; and when we are
told that no one below the age of 14 should be tortured, we are left
to conjecture the minimum age of responsibility for heresy.

Nor could the offender escape by absenting himself. Absence
was contumacy and only increased his guilt by adding a fresh and
unpardonable offense, besides being technically tantamount to confession. Accordingly, when a party failed to appear, after due citation published in his parish church and proper delay, there was no
hesitation in proceeding against him to conviction *in absentia*—
the absence of the culprit being piously supplied by "the presence of
God and the Gospels" when the sentence was rendered. Contumacious absence, in fact, was in itself enough. Frederic II in his earliest
edict, in 1220, following the Lateran Council of 1215, had declared
that the suspect who did not clear himself within twelve months was
to be condemned as a heretic, and this was applied to the absent, who
were ordered to be sentenced after a year's excommunication, whether
anything was proved against them or not. Enduring excommunication for a year without seeking its removal was evidence of heresy
as to the sacraments and the power of the keys, if nothing else, and
some authorities were so rigid with regard to this that the Council of
Béziers denounced the punishment of heresy for all who remained
excommunicate for forty days.

As little was there any escape by death. It mattered not that
the sinner had been called to the judgment seat of God, the faith
must be vindicated by his condemnation and the faithful be edified
by his punishment. If he had incurred only imprisonment or the
lighter penalties, his bones were simply dug up and cast out. If
his heresy had deserved the stake, they were solemnly burned. A
simulacrum of defense was allowed to heirs and descendants. on
whom were visited the heavy penalties of confiscation and personal disabilities. How unflagging was the zeal with which these
mortuary prosecutions were sometimes carried on is visible in the
case of Armanno Pongilupo of Ferrara, over whose remains war was
waged between the Bishop and the Inquisitor of Ferrara for 32 years

after his death, in 1269, ending with the triumph of the Inquisition in 1301.

At best the inquisitorial process was a dangerous one in its conjunction of prosecutor with judge, and when it was first introduced in ecclesiastical jurisprudence careful limitations to prevent abuse were felt to be absolutely essential. The danger was doubled when the prosecuting judge was an earnest zealot bent on upholding the faith and predetermined on seeing in every prisoner before him a heretic to be convicted at any cost. All the safeguards which human experience had shown to be necessary in judicial proceedings of the most trivial character were deliberately cast aside in these cases, where life and reputation and property through three generations were involved. Every doubtful point was decided "in favor of the faith." The inquisitor, with endless iteration, was empowered and instructed to proceed summarily, to disregard forms, to permit no impediments arising from judicial rules or the wrangling of advocates, to shorten the proceedings as much as possible by depriving the accused of the ordinary facilities of defense, and by rejecting all appeals and dilatory exceptions. The validity of the result was not to be vitiated by the omission at any stage of the trial of the forms which had been devised to prevent injustice and subject the judge to responsibility.

Had the proceedings been public, there might have been some check upon this hideous system, but the Inquisition shrouded itself in the awful mystery of secrecy until after sentence had been awarded and it was ready to impress the multitude with the fearful solemnities of the *auto de fé*. Unless proclamation were to be made for an absentee, the citation of a suspected heretic was made in secret. All knowledge of what took place after he presented himself was confined to the few discreet men selected by his judge, who were sworn to inviolable silence, and even the experts assembled to consult over his fate were subjected to similar oaths. The secrets of that dismal tribunal were guarded with the same caution, and we are told by Bernard Gui that extracts from the records were to be furnished rarely and only with the most careful discretion. Paramo, in the quaint pedantry with which he ingeniously proves that God was the first inquisitor and the condemnation of Adam and Eve the first model of the inquisitorial process, triumphantly points out that he judged them in secret, thus setting the example which the Inquisition is bound to follow, and avoiding the subtleties which the criminals would have raised in their defense, especially at the suggestion of the crafty serpent. That he called no witnesses is explained by the confession of the accused, and ample legal authority is cited to show that these confessions were sufficient to justify the conviction and punishment. This blasphemous absurdity has its melancholy side, for it reveals to us the view which the inquisitors themselves took of their functions, assimilating themselves to God and wielding an irresponsible power which nothing short of divine wisdom could prevent from being turned into an engine of the most deadly injustice.

The ordinary course of a trial by the Inquisition was this. A man would be reported to the inquisitor as of ill-repute for heresy, or his name would occur in the confessions of other prisoners. A secret inquisition would be made and all accessible evidence against him would be collected. He would then be secretly cited to appear at a given time, and bail taken to secure his obedience, or if he were suspected of flight, he would be suddenly arrested and confined until the tribunal was ready to give him a hearing. Legally there required to be three citations, but this was eluded by making the summons "one for three"; when the prosecution was based on common report the witnesses were called apparently at random, making a sort of dragnet, and when the mass of surmises and gossip, exaggerated and distorted by the natural fear of the witnesses, eager to save themselves from suspicion of favoring heretics, grew sufficient for action, the blow would fall. The accused was thus prejudged. He was assumed to be guilty, or he would not have been put on trial, and virtually his only mode of escape was by confessing the charges made against him, abjuring heresy, and accepting whatever punishment might be imposed on him in the shape of penance. Persistent denial of guilt and assertion of orthodoxy, when there was evidence against him, rendered him an impenitent, obstinate heretic, to be abandoned to the secular arm. The process thus was an exceedingly simple one and is aptly summarized by an inquisitor of the fifteenth century in an argument against admitting the accused to bail. If one is caught in heresy, by his own confession, and is impenitent, he is to be delivered to the secular arm to be put to death; if penitent, he is to be thrust in prison for life, and therefore is not to be let loose on bail. If he denies, and is legitimately convicted by witnesses, he is, as an impenitent, to be delivered to the secular court to be executed.

Yet many reasons led the inquisitor earnestly to desire to secure confession. In numerous cases—indeed, no doubt in a majority—the evidence, while possibly justifying suspicion, was of too loose and undefined a character to justify condemnation, for every idle rumor was taken up, and any flimsy pretext which led to prosecution assumed importance when the inquisitor found himself bound to show that he had not acted unadvisedly, or when he had in prospect confiscation for the benefit of the faith. Even when the evidence was sufficient, there were motives equally strong to induce the inquisitor to labor with his prisoner in the hope of leading him to withdraw his denial and throw himself upon the mercy of the tribunal.

Bernard Gui, copying an earlier inquisitor, tells us eloquently that when the external evidence was insufficient for conviction, the mind of the inquisitor was torn with anxious cares. On the one side, his conscience pained him if he punished one who was neither confessed nor convicted; but he suffered still more, knowing by constant experience the falsity and cunning of these men, if he allowed them to escape through their vulpine astuteness, to the damage of the faith. In such case they were strengthened and multiplied, and rendered keener than ever, while the laity were scandalized at seeing the inefficiency of the Inquisition, baffled in its undertakings, and its most learned men played with and defied by rude and illiterate persons, for they believed the inquisitors to have all the proofs and arguments of the faith so ready at hand that no heretic could elude them or prevent their converting him. In another passage he points out how greatly profitable to the faith was the conversion of such persons, because not only were they obliged to betray their fellows and the hiding-places and conventicles of darkness, but those whom they had influenced were more ready to acknowledge their errors and seek in turn to be converted. As early as 1246 the Council of Béziers had pointed out the utility of such conversions, and had instructed the inquisitors to spare no pains in procuring them, and all subsequent authorities evidently regarded this as the first of their duties. They all agree, moreover, in holding delation [denouncement] of accomplices as the indispensable evidence of true conversion. How useful this was is seen in the case of Saurine Rigaud, whose confession is recorded at Toulouse in 1254, where it is followed by a list of 169 persons incriminated by her, their names being carefully tabulated with their places of residence for immediate action. Delation was so indispensable to the Inquisition that it was to be secured by rewards as well as by punishments. Bernard Gui tells us that those who voluntarily come forward and prove their zeal by confession and by betraying all their associates are not only to be pardoned, but their livelihood must be secured at the hands of princes and prelates; while betraying a single perfected heretic ensured immunity and perhaps additional reward. Confession thus became a matter of vital importance, and no effort was deemed too great, no means too repulsive, to secure it. This became the center of the inquisitorial process, and it is deserving of detailed consideration, not only because it formed the basis of procedure in the Holy Office, but also because of the vast and deplorable influence which it exercised for five centuries on the whole judicial system of continental Europe.

The first and readiest means was, of course, the examination of the accused. For this the inquisitor prepared himself by collecting and studying all the adverse evidence that could be procured, while the prisoner was kept in sedulous ignorance of the charges against him. Skill in interrogation was the one pre-eminent requisite of the inquisitor, and manuals prepared by experienced brethren for the benefit of the younger officials are full of details with regard to it and of carefully prepared forms of interrogations suited for every heretical sect. Constant training developed a class of acute and subtle minds, skilled to lay pitfalls for the incautious, versed in every art to confuse, prompt to detect ambiguities and to take advantage of hesitation or contradiction. Even in the infancy of the institution the consuls of Narbonne complained to those of Nîmes that the inquisitors, in their efforts to entrap the unwary, did not hesitate to make use of dialectics as sophistical as those with which students encountered each other in scholastic diversion. Nothing more ludicrous can well be imagined than the complaints of these veteran examiners, restricted by no rules, of the shrewd duplicity of their victims, who struggled, occasionally with success, to avoid criminating themselves, and they sought to explain it by asserting that wicked priests instructed them how to equivocate on points of faith.

An experienced inquisitor drew up for the guidance of his successors a specimen examination of a heretic, to show them the tergiversations for which they must be prepared when dealing with those who shrank from boldly denying their faith. Its fidelity is attested by Bernard Gui's reproducing it fifty years later in his *Practica*, and it is too characteristic an illustration of the encounter between the trained intellect of the inquisitor and the untutored shrewdness of the peasant struggling to save his life, to be omitted.

When a heretic is first brought up for examination, he assumes a confident air, as though secure in his innocence. I ask him why he has been brought before me. He replies, smiling and courteous, "Sir, I would be glad to learn the cause from you."

I. You are accused as a heretic, and that you believe and teach otherwise than Holy Church believes.

A. (Raising his eyes to heaven, with an air of the greatest faith) Lord, thou knowest that I am innocent of this, and that I never held any faith other than that of true Christianity.

I. You call your faith Christian, for you consider ours as false and heretical. But I ask whether you have ever believed as true another faith than that which the Roman Church holds to be true?

A. I believe the true faith which the Roman Church believes, and which you openly preach to us.

I. Perhaps you have some of your sect at Rome whom you call the Roman Church. I, when I preach, say many things, some of which are common to us both, as that God liveth, and you believe some of what I preach. Nevertheless you may be a heretic in not believing other matters which are to be believed.

A. I believe all things that a Christian should believe.

I. I know your tricks. What the members of your sect believe you hold to be that which a Christian should believe. But we waste time in this fencing. Say simply, Do you believe in one God the Father, and the Son, and the Holy Ghost?

A. I believe.

I. Do you believe in Christ born of the Virgin, suffered, risen, and ascended to heaven?

A. (Briskly) I believe.

I. Do you believe the bread and wine in the mass performed by the priests to be changed into the body and blood of Christ by divine virtue?

A. Ought I not to believe this?

I. I don't ask if you ought to believe, but if you do believe.

A. I believe whatever you and other good doctors order me to believe.

I. Those good doctors are the masters of your sect; if I accord with them you believe with me; if not, not.

A. I willingly believe with you if you teach what is good to me.

I. You consider it good to you if I teach what your other masters teach. Say, then, do you believe the body of our Lord Jesus Christ to be in the altar?

A. (Promptly) I believe.

I. You know that a body is there, and that all bodies are of our Lord. I ask whether the body there is of the Lord who was born of the Virgin, hung on the cross, arose from the dead, ascended, etc.?

A. And you, sir, do you not believe it?

I. I believe it wholly.

A. I believe likewise.

I. You believe that I believe it, which is not what I ask, but whether you believe it.

A. If you wish to interpret all that I say otherwise than simply and plainly, then I don't know what to say. I am a simple and ignorant man. Pray don't catch me in my words.

I. If you are simple, answer simply, without evasions.

A. Willingly.

I. Will you then swear that you have never learned anything contrary to the faith which we hold to be true?

A. (Growing pale) If I ought to swear, I will willingly swear.

I. I don't ask whether you ought, but whether you will swear.

A. If you order me to swear, I will swear.

I. I don't force you to swear, because as you believe oaths to be unlawful, you will transfer the sin to me who forced you; but if you will swear, I will hear it.

A. Why should I swear if you do not order me to?

I. So that you may remove the suspicion of being a heretic.

A. Sir, I do not know how unless you teach me.

I. If I had to swear, I would raise my hand and spread my fingers and say, "So help me God, I have never learned heresy or believed what is contrary to the true faith."

Then trembling as if he cannot repeat the form, he will stumble along as though speaking for himself or for another, so that there is not an absolute form of oath and yet he may be thought to have sworn. If the words are there, they are so turned around that he does not swear and yet appears to have sworn. Or he converts the oath into a form of prayer, as "God help me that I am not a heretic or the like"; and when asked whether he had sworn, he will say: "Did you not hear me swear?" And when further hard pressed he will appeal, saying, "Sir, if I have done amiss in aught, I will willingly bear the penance, only help me to avoid the infamy of which I am accused through malice and without fault of mine." But a vigorous inquisitor must not allow himself to be worked upon in this way, but proceed firmly till he makes these people confess their error, or at least publicly abjure heresy, so that if they are subsequently found to have sworn falsely, he can, without further hearing, abandon them to the secular arm. If one consents to swear that he is not a heretic, I say to him, "If you wish to swear so as to escape the stake, one oath will not suffice for me, nor ten, nor a hundred, nor a thousand, because you dispense each other for a certain number of oaths taken under necessity, but I will require a countless number. Moreover, if I have, as I presume, adverse witnesses against you, your oaths will not save you from being burned. You will only stain your conscience without escaping death. But if you will simply confess your error, you may find mercy." Under this anxiety, I have seen some confess.

The resources for procuring unwilling confession may be roughly divided into two classes—deceit and torture, the latter comprehending both mental and physical pain, however administered. Both classes were resorted to freely and without scruple, and there was ample variety to suit the idiosyncrasies of all judges and prisoners.

Perhaps the mildest form of the devices to entrap an unwary prisoner was the recommendation that the examiner should always assume the fact of which he was in quest and ask about the details, as, for instance, "How often have you confessed as a heretic?" "In what chamber of yours did they lie?" Going a step further, the inquisitor is advised during the examination to turn over the pages of evidence as though referring to it, and then boldly inform the prisoner that he is not telling the truth, for it is thus and thus; or to pick up a paper and pretend to read from it whatever is necessary to deceive him; or he can be told circumstantially that some of the masters of the sect have incriminated him in their revelations. To render these devices more effective, the jailer was instructed to worm himself into the confidence of the prisoners, with feigned interest and compassion, and urge them to confess at once, because the inquisitor is a merciful man who will take pity on them. Then the inquisitor was to pretend that he had conclusive evidence, and that if the accused would con-

fess and point out those who had led him astray, he should be allowed
to go home forthwith, with any other blandishments likely to prove
effective. A more elaborate trap was that of treating the prisoner with
kindness in place of rigor; sending trusty agents to his cell to gain
his confidence, and then urge him to confess, with promises of mercy
and that they would intercede for him. When everything was ripe,
the inquisitor himself would appear and confirm these promises,
with the mental reservation that all which is done for the conversion
of heretics is merciful, that penances are spiritual remedies, so that
when the unlucky wretch was prevailed upon to ask for mercy in
return for his revelations, he was to be led on with the general expression that more would be done for him than he asked.

That spies should play a prominent part in such a system was inevitable. The trusty agents who were admitted to the prisoner's
cell were instructed to lead him gradually on from one confession
to another until they should gain sufficient evidence to incriminate
him, without his realizing it. Converted heretics, we are told, were very
useful in this business. One would be sent to visit him and say that
he had only pretended conversion through fear, and after repeated
visits overstay his time and be locked up. Confidential talk would
follow in the darkness, while witnesses with a notary were crouching
within earshot to take down all that might fall from the lips of the
unconscious victim. Fellow prisoners were utilized whenever possible,
and were duly rewarded for treachery. In the sentence of a Carmelite
monk, January 17, 1329, guilty of the most infamous sorceries, it is
recorded in extenuation of his black catalogue of guilt, that while in
prison with sundry heretics he had aided greatly in making them
confess and had revealed many important matters which they had
confided to him, from which the Inquisition had derived great advantage and hoped to gain more.

These artifices were diversified with appeals to force. The heretic,
whether acknowledged or suspected, was at the mercy of the Church,
and if through tribulation of the flesh he could be led to see the error
of his ways, there was no hesitation in employing whatever means
were readiest to save his soul and advance the faith. Among the
miracles for which St. Francis was canonized it is related that a
certain Pietro of Assisi was captured in Rome on an accusation of
heresy and was confided for conversion to the Bishop of Todi, who

loaded him with chains and fed him on measured quantities of bread and water in a dark dungeon. Thus brought through suffering to repentance, on the vigil of St. Francis he invoked the saint for help with passionate tears. Moved by his zeal, St. Francis appeared to him and ordered him forth. His chains fell off and the doors flew open, but the poor wretch was so crazed by the sudden answer to his prayer that he clung to the doorpost with cries which brought the jailers running to him. The pious bishop hastened to the prison, and reverently acknowledging the power of God, sent the shivered fetters to the pope in token of the miracle. Even more illustrative and better authenticated is a case related by Nider as occurring when he was teaching in the University of Vienna. A heretic priest, thrown into prison by his bishop, proved obstinate, and the most eminent theologians who labored for his conversion found him their match in disputation. Believing that vexation brings understanding, they at length ordered him to be bound tightly to a pillar. The cords eating into the swelling flesh caused such torture that when they visited him the next day he begged piteously to be taken out and burned. Coldly refusing, they left him for another 24 hours, by which time physical pain and exhaustion had broken his spirit. He humbly recanted, retired to a Paulite monastery, and lived an exemplary life.

There was scant hesitation in employing any methods likely to crush the obduracy of the prisoner who refused the confession and recantation demanded of him. If he were likely to be reached through the affections, his wife and children were admitted to his cell in hopes that their tears and pleadings might work on his feelings and overcome his convictions. Alternate threats and blandishments were tried; he would be removed from his foul dungeon to commodious quarters, with liberal diet and a show of kindness, to see if his resolution would be weakened by alternations of hope and despair. The prisoner who refused to confess, or whose confession was deemed imperfect, was remanded to his cell and left to ponder in solitude and darkness. Except in rare cases, time was no object with the Inquisition and it could afford to wait. Perhaps in a few weeks his resolution might break down, and he might ask to be heard. If not, six months might elapse before he was again called up for hearing. If still obstinate he would be again sent back. Months would lengthen into years, perhaps years into decades, and find him still unconvicted and still a prisoner, hopeless and despairing. Should friendly death not intervene, the terrible patience of the Inquisition was nearly certain to triumph in the end, and the authorities all agree upon the effectiveness of delay. Three, five, or ten years are common as intervals between the first audience of a prisoner and his final conviction, nor are instances wanting of even greater delays. In the *auto de fé* of 1319, at Toulouse, Guillem Salavert was sentenced, who had made an unsatisfactory confession in 1299 and another in 1316; to the latter he had unwaveringly adhered, and at last Bernard Gui, overcome by his obstinacy, let him off with the penance of wearing crosses, in consideration of his twenty years' imprisonment without conviction.

When it was desired to hasten this slow torture, the object was easily accomplished by rendering the imprisonment unendurably harsh. As we shall see hereafter, the dungeons of the Inquisition at best were abodes of fearful misery, but when there was reason for increasing their terrors there was no difficulty. The *durus carcer et arcta vita*—chains and starvation in a stifling hole—was a favorite device for extracting confession from unwilling lips. Starvation, in fact, was reckoned as one of the regular and most efficient methods to subdue unwilling witnesses and defendants. In 1306 Clement V declared, after an official investigation, that at Carcassonne prisoners were habitually constrained to confession by the harshness of the prison, the lack of beds, and the deficiency of food, as well as by torture.

With all these resources at their command, it might seem superfluous for inquisitors to have recourse to the vulgar and ruder implements of the torture chamber. The rack and *strappado*, in fact, were in such violent antagonism, not only with the principles of Christianity, but with the practices of the Church, that their use by the Inquisition as a means of furthering the faith is one of the saddest anomalies of that dismal period. It was not until the study of the revived Roman law, and the prohibition of Ordeals by the Lateran Council of 1215, which was gradually enforced during the first half of the thirteenth century, that jurists began to feel the need of torture and accustom themselves to the idea of its introduction. The earliest instances with which I have met occur in the Veronese Code of 1228 and the Sicilian Constitutions of Frederic II in 1231, and in both of these the references to it show how sparingly and hesitatingly it was employed. Even Frederic, in his ruthless edicts from 1220 to 1239, makes no allusion to it, but, in accordance with the Verona decree of Lucius III, prescribes the recognized form of canonical purgation for the trial of all suspected heretics. Yet it rapidly won its way in Italy, and when Innocent IV, in 1252, published his bull *Ad extirpanda*, he adopted it, and authorized its use for the discovery of heresy. A decent respect for the old-time prejudices of the Church, however, forbade him to allow its administration by the inquisitors themselves or their servitors. It was the secular authorities who were ordered to force all captured heretics to confess and accuse their accomplices, by torture which should not imperil life or injure limb, "just as thieves and robbers are forced to confess their crimes and accuse their accomplices." The unrepealed canons of the Church, in fact, prohibited all ecclesiastics from being concerned in such acts, and even from being present where torture was administered, so that the inquisitor whose zeal should lead him to take part in it was thereby rendered "irregular" and unfit for sacred functions until he could be "dispensed" or purified. This did not suit the policy of the institution. Possibly outside Italy, where torture was as yet virtually unknown, it found difficulty in securing the co-operation of the public officials; everywhere it complained that this cumbrous mode of administration interfered with the profound secrecy which was an essential characteristic of its operations. But four years after the bull of Innocent IV, Alexander IV in 1256 removed the difficulty with characteristic indirection by authorizing inquisitors and their associates to absolve each other and mutually grant dispensations for irregularities—a permission which was repeatedly reiterated, and which was held to remove all impediment to the use of torture under the direct supervision of the inquisitor and his ministers. In Naples, Frà Tommaso d'Aversa is seen, in 1305, personally inflicting the most brutal tortures on the Spiritual Franciscans; and when he found it impossible in this manner to make them convict themselves, he employed the ingenious expedient of starving for a few days one of the younger brethren, and then giving him strong wine to drink; when the poor wretch was fuddled there was no difficulty in getting him to admit that he and his twoscore comrades were all heretics.

Torture saved the trouble and expense of prolonged imprisonment; it was a speedy and effective method of obtaining what revelations might be desired, and it grew rapidly in favor with the Inquisition, while its extension throughout secular jurisprudence was remarkably slow. In 1260 the charter granted by Alphonse of Poitiers to the town of Auzon specially exempts the accused from torture, no matter what the crime involved. When the despairing cry of the population induced Clement V to order an investigation into the iniquities of the Inquisition of Carcassonne, the commission issued to the cardinals sent thither in 1306 recites that confessions were extorted by torture so severe that the unfortunates subjected to it had only the alternative of death; and in the proceedings before the commissioners the use of torture is so frequently alluded to as to leave no doubt of its habitual employment. It is a noteworthy fact, however, that in the fragmentary documents of inquisitorial proceedings which have reached us the references to torture are singularly few. Apparently it was felt that to record its use would in some sort invalidate the force of the testimony. Thus, in the cases of Isarn Colli and Guillem Calverie it happens to be stated that they retracted their confessions made under torture, but in the confessions themselves there is nothing to indicate that it had been used. In the 636 sentences borne upon the register of Toulouse from 1309 to 1323 the only allusion to torture is in the recital of the case of Calverie, but Bernard Gui, who conducted the Inquisition of Toulouse during this period, has too emphatically expressed his sense of the utility of torture on both principals and witnesses for us to doubt his readiness in its employment.

The result of Clement's investigation in 1306 led to an effort at reform which was agreed to in the Council of Vienne in 1311. Among the abuses he sought to limit was that of torture, and to this end he ordered that it should not be administered without the concurrent action of bishop and inquisitor if this could be had within the space of eight days. Bernard Gui emphatically remonstrated against this as seriously crippling the efficiency of the Inquisition, and he proposed to substitute for it the meaningless phrase that torture should only be used with mature and careful deliberation, but his suggestion was unheeded, and the Clementine regulation remained the law of the Church.

The inquisitors, however, were too little accustomed to restraint in any form to submit long to this infringement on their privileges. It is true that disobedience rendered the proceedings void, and the unhappy wretch who was unlawfully tortured without episcopal consultation could appeal to the pope, but this did not undo the work; Rome was distant, and the victims of the Inquisition for the most part were too friendless and too helpless to protect themselves in such illusory fashion. In Bernard Gui's *Practica*, written probably about 1328 or 1330, he speaks only of consultation with experts, making no allusions to bishops; cunning casuists, moreover, discovered that Clement had only spoken of torture in general and had not specifically alluded to witnesses, whence they concluded that one of the most shocking abuses of the system, the torture of witnesses, was left to the sole discretion of the inquisitor, and this became the accepted rule. It required only an additional step to show that after the accused had been convicted by evidence or had confessed, he became a witness to the guilt of his friends and thus could be arbitrarily tortured to betray them.

While witnesses who were supposed to be concealing the truth could be tortured as a matter of course, there was some discussion among jurists as to the amount of adverse evidence that would justify placing the accused on the rack. Eymerich tells us that when there are two incriminating witnesses, a man of good reputation can be tortured to ascertain the truth, while if he is of evil repute he can be condemned without it or can be tortured on the evidence of a single witness. Zanghino, on the other hand, asserts that the evidence of a single witness of good character is sufficient for the authorization of torture, without distinction of persons, while Bernardo di Como says that common report is enough. In time elaborate instructions were drawn up for the guidance of inquisitors in this matter, but their uselessness was confessed in the admission that, after all, the decision was to be left to the discretion of the judge. How little sufficed to justify the exercise of this discretion is seen when jurists held it to be sufficient if the accused, on examination, was frightened and stammered and varied in his answers, without any external evidence against him.

In the administration of torture the rules adopted by the Inquisition became those of the secular courts of Christendom at large, and therefore are worth brief attention. Eymerich, whose instructions on the subject are the fullest we have, admits the grave difficulties which surrounded the question, and the notorious uncertainty of the result. Torture should be moderate, and effusion of blood be scrupulously avoided, but then, what was moderation? Some prisoners were so weak that at the first turn of the pulleys they would concede anything asked them; others so obstinate that they would endure all things rather than confess the truth. Those who had previously undergone the experience might be either the stronger or the weaker for it, for with some the arms were hardened, while with others they were permanently weakened. In short, the discretion of the judge was the only rule.

Both bishop and inquisitor ought rightfully to be present. The prisoner was shown the implements of torment and urged to confess. On his refusal he was stripped and bound by the executioners and again entreated to speak, with promises of mercy in all cases in which mercy could be shown. This frequently produced the desired result, and we may be assured that the efficacy of torture lay not so much in what was extracted by its use as in the innumerable cases in which its dread, near or remote, paralyzed the resolution with agonizing expectations. If this proved ineffectual, the torture was applied with gradually increased severity. In the case of continued obstinacy additional implements of torment were exhibited and the sufferer was told that he would be subjected to them all in turn. If still undaunted, he was unbound, and the next or third day was appointed for renewal of the infliction. According to rule, torture could be applied but once, but this, like all other rules for the protection of the accused, was easily eluded. It was only necessary to order, not a repetition, but a "continuance" of the torture, and no matter how long the interval, the holy casuists were able to continue it indefinitely.

During the interval fresh solicitations were made to elicit confession, and these being unavailing, the accused was again subjected to torment either of the same kind as before or to others likely to prove more efficacious. If he remained silent after torture deemed sufficient by his judges, some authorities say that he should be discharged and that a declaration was to be given him that nothing had been proved against him; others, however, order that he should be remanded to prison and be kept there. The trial of Bernard Délicieux, in 1319, reveals another device to elude the prohibition of repeated torture, for the examiners could at any moment order the torture to satisfy their curiosity about a single point, and thus could go on indefinitely with others.

Any confession made under torture required to be confirmed after removal from the torture chamber. Usually the procedure appears to be that the torture was continued until the accused signified his readiness to confess, when he was unbound and carried into another room where his confession was made. If, however, the confession was extracted during the torture, it was read over subsequently to the prisoner and he was asked if it were true: there was, indeed, a rule that there should be an interval of 24 hours between the torture and the confession, or its confirmation, but this was commonly disregarded. Silence indicated assent, and the length of silence to be allowed for was, as usual, left to the discretion of the judge, with warning to consider the condition of the prisoner, whether young or old, male or female, simple or learned. In any case the record was carefully made that the confession was free and spontaneous, without the pressure of force or fear. If the confession was retracted, the accused could be taken back for a "continuance" of the torture—provided always that he had not been "sufficiently" tortured before.

The question as to the retraction of confession was one which exercised to no small degree the inquisitorial jurists, and practice was not wholly uniform. Some authorities draw a distinction between confessions made "spontaneously" and those extorted by torture or its threat, but in practice the difference was disregarded. The most merciful view taken of revocation is that of Eymerich, who says that if the torture had been sufficient, the accused who persistently revokes is entitled to a discharge. In this Eymerich is alone. Some authorities recommend that the accused be forced to withdraw his revocation by repetition of torture. Others content themselves with regarding it as impeding the Inquisition, and as such including it in the excommunication regularly published by parish priests and at the opening of every *auto de fé*, and this excommunication included notaries who might wickedly aid in drawing up such revocations. The general presumption of law, however, was that the confession was true and the retraction a perjury, and the view taken of such cases was that the retraction proved the accused to be an impenitent heretic, who had relapsed after confession and asking for penance. As such there was nothing to be done with him but to hand him over to the secular arm for punishment without a hearing. How strictly the rule was construed which regarded revocation as relapse is seen in the remark of Zanghino, that if a man had confessed and abjured and been set free under penance, and if he subsequently remarked in public that he had confessed under fear of expense or to avoid heavier punishment, he was to be regarded as an impenitent heretic, liable to be burned as a relapsed.

There was an additional question of some nicety which arose when the retracted confession incriminated others besides the accused; in this case the most merciful view taken was that, if it was not to be held good against them, the one who confessed was liable to punishment for false-witness. As no confession was sufficient which did not reveal the names of partners in guilt, those inquisitors who did not regard revocation as relapse could at least imprison the accused for life as a false witness.

The inquisitorial process as thus perfected was sure of its victim. No one whom a judge wished to condemn could escape. The form in which it became naturalized in secular jurisprudence was less arbitrary and effective, yet Sir John Fortescue, the chancellor of Henry VI, who in his exile had ample opportunity to observe its working, declares that it placed every man's life or limb at the mercy of any enemy who could suborn two unknown witnesses to swear against him.

CHAPTER VIII
MODUS OPERANDI

1. EVIDENCE

FROM almost the inception of the Holy Office there was an effort to lay down rules on what constituted evidence of heresy; the Council of Narbonne, in 1244, winds up an enumeration of the various indications by saying that it is sufficient if the accused can be shown to have manifested by any word or sign that he had faith or belief in heretics or considered them to be "good men" (*bos homes*). In the voluminous examinations and depositions that have reached us from the archives of the Inquisition we find the witnesses allowed and encouraged to say everything that may occur to them. Great weight was attached to popular report or belief, and to ascertain this the opinion of the witness was freely received, whether based on knowledge or prejudice, hearsay evidence, vague rumors, general impressions, or idle gossip.

Naturally the conscientious inquisitor recognized the vicious circle in which he moved and sought to satisfy himself that he could designate infallible signs which would justify the conclusion of heresy. For the Cathari it sufficed to show that the accused had venerated one of the perfected, had asked a blessing, had eaten of the blessed bread, had been voluntarily present at an heretication, had entered into the *covenansa* to be hereticated on the deathbed, etc. For the Waldenses such indications were considered to be the confessing of sins to and accepting penance from those known not to be regularly ordained by an orthodox bishop, praying with them according to their rites by bending the knees with them on a bench or other inclined object, being present with them when they pretended to make the Host, receiving "peace" from them, or blessed bread. All this was easily catalogued, but beyond it lay a region of doubt concerning which authorities differed. Bernard Gui mentions that some inquisitors held that visiting heretics, giving them alms, guiding them in their journeys, and the like was sufficient for condemnation, but he agrees with Gui Foucoix in not so considering it, as all this might be done through carnal affection or for hire.

How insignificant were the tokens on which a man's fate might depend may be understood by a single instance. In 1234 Accursio Aldobrandini, a Florentine merchant in Paris, made the acquaintance of some strangers with whom he conversed several times, giving their servant on one occasion 10 sols, and bowing to them when they met, out of politeness. This latter act was equivalent to the "veneration" which was the crucial test of heresy, and when he chanced to learn that his new acquaintances were heretics he felt himself lost. Hastening to Rome, he laid the matter before Gregory IX, who exacted bail of him and sent a commission to the Bishop of Florence to investigate the antecedents of Accursio. The report was examined by the cardinals of Ostia and Preneste and found to be emphatic in commending his orthodoxy, so he escaped with a penance prescribed by Raymond of Pennaforte, the papal penitentiary, and Gregory wrote to the Inquisitors of Paris not to molest him. Under such a system the most devout Catholic could never feel safe for a moment.

In spite of all efforts to define the indefinable, absolute certitude could not, in a vast range of cases, be reached except through confession. In order, therefore, to avert the misfortune of acquitting those who could not be brought to confess, it became necessary to invent a new crime—that known as "suspicion of heresy." This opened a wide field for the endless subtleties and refinements in which the jurists of the schools delighted, rendering their so-called science of law a worthy rival of scholastic theology. Suspicion thus was primarily divided into three grades, designated as "light," "vehement," and "violent," and the glossators revel in defining the amount and quality of evidence which renders the accused guilty of any of these, with the usual result that practically the matter was left to the discretion of the tribunal. That a man against whom nothing substantial was proved should be punished merely because he was suspected of guilt may seem to modern eyes a scant measure of justice; but to the inquisitor it appeared a wrong to God and man that anyone should escape against whose orthodoxy there rested a shadow of a doubt. Like much else taught by the Inquisition, this found its way into general criminal law, which it perverted for centuries.

Two witnesses were usually assumed to be necessary for the condemnation of a man of good repute, though some authorities demanded more. Yet when a case threatened to fail for lack of
testimony, it was agreed that if two witnesses to the same fact could
not be had, single witnesses to two separate facts of the same general
character would suffice. When there was only one witness in all, the
accused was still put on his purgation. With the same determination to remove all obstacles in the way of conviction, if a witness
revoked his testimony it was held that if his evidence had been favorable to the accused, the revocation annulled it; if adverse, the revocation was null.[1]

The same disposition to construe everything in favor of the faith
governed the admissibility of witnesses of evil character. The Roman
law rejected the evidence of accomplices, and the Church had
adopted the rule. In the False Decretals it had ordered that no one
should be admitted as an accuser who was a heretic or suspected of
heresy, was excommunicate, a homicide, a thief, a sorcerer, a diviner,
a ravisher, an adulterer, a bearer of false witness, or a consulter of
diviners and soothsayers. Yet when it came to prosecuting heresy
all these prohibitions were thrown to the winds. As early as the time
of Gratian, infamous and heretical witnesses were receivable against
heretics. The edicts of Frederic II rendered heretics incapable of
giving testimony, but this disability was removed when they testified
against heretics. That there was some hesitation on this point we see
in the legatine Inquisition held in Toulouse in 1229, where it is recorded that Guillem Solier, a converted heretic, was restored in
fame in order to enable him to bear witness against his former associates, and even as late as 1260 Alexander IV was obliged to re-
assure the French inquisitors that they could safely use the evidence
of heretics; but the principle became a settled one, adopted in the
canon law, and constantly enforced in practice. It was the same with
excommunicates, perjurers, infamous persons, usurers, harlots, and all
those who, in the ordinary criminal jurisprudence of the age, were
regarded as incapable of bearing witness, yet whose evidence was

---

[1] In the lay courts, if a witness swore to the innocence of the accused and
subsequently changed his testimony, the first statement was held good and the
second was rejected, but in cases of heresy the incriminating evidence was always
received.

receivable against heretics. All legal exceptions were declared inoperative except that of mortal enmity.[2]

In the ordinary criminal law of Italy no evidence was received from a witness under 20, but in cases of heresy such testimony was taken, and, though not legal, it sufficed to justify torture. In France the distinction seems to have been less rigidly defined, and the matter probably was left, like so much else, to the discretion of the inquisitors. In the records of the Inquisition the age of the witness is rarely stated, but I have met with one case, in 1244, after the capture of the pestilent nest of heretics at Montségur, where the Inquisition gathered so goodly a harvest, when the age of a witness, Arnaud Olivier, happens to be mentioned as 10 years. He admitted having been a Catharan "believer" since he had reached the age of discretion, and thus was responsible for himself and others. His evidence is gravely recorded against his father, his sister, and nearly 70 others; and in it he is made to give the names of 65 persons who were present about a year before at the sermon of a Catharan bishop. The wonderful exercise of so young a memory does not seem to have excited any doubts of the validity of his testimony, which must have been held conclusive against the unfortunates enumerated, as he stated that they all "venerated" their prelate.

Wives and children and servants were not admitted to give evidence in favor of the accused, but their testimony if adverse to him was welcomed, and was considered peculiarly strong. In short, the only exception which could be taken to an accusing witness was malignity. If he was a mortal enemy of the prisoner it was presumed that his testimony was rather the prompting of hate than zeal for the faith, and it was required to be thrown out. In the case of the dead, the evidence of a priest that he had shriven the defunct and administered the *viaticum* went for nothing; but if he testified that the departed had confessed to being a heretic, had recanted, and had received absolution, then his bones were not exhumed and burned, but the heirs had to endure such penance of fine or confiscation as would have been inflicted on him if alive.

Of course no witness could refuse to give evidence. No privilege or vow or oath released him from the duty. If he was unwilling and

[2] Under the contemporary English law, criminals and accomplices were rejected as accusers, even in high treason.

paltered or prevaricated and equivocated, there was the gentle persuasion of the torture chamber. Even the secrecy of the confessional
was not respected in the frenzied effort to obtain all possible information against heretics. All priests were enjoined to make strict inquiries of their penitents as to their knowledge of heretics and fautors
of heresy. When the confessor succeeded in learning anything he
was told to write it down and then endeavor to induce his penitent
to reveal it to the proper authorities. Failing in this, he was, without
mentioning names, to consult God-fearing experts as to what he
ought to do—with what effect can readily be conjectured, since the
very fact of consulting as to his duty shows that the obligation of
secrecy was not to be deemed absolute.[3]

After this glimpse at the inquisitorial system of evidence, we hardly
need the assurance of the legists that less was required for conviction
in heresy than in any other crime, and inquisitors were instructed
that slender testimony was sufficient to prove it—*probatur quis
hœreticus ex levi causa.* Yet evil as was all this, the crowning infamy
of the Inquisition in its treatment of testimony was withholding
from the accused all knowledge of the names of the witnesses against
him. In the ordinary courts, even in the inquisitorial process, their
names were communicated to him along with the evidence they had
given, and it will be remembered that when the Legate Romano held
his inquest at Toulouse, in 1229, the accused followed him to Montpellier with demands to see the names of those who had testified
against them, when the cardinal recognized their right to this, but
eluded it by showing merely a list of all the witnesses who had appeared during the whole inquest, giving as an excuse the danger to
which they were exposed from the malevolence of those who had
suffered by their evidence. In 1244 and 1246 the Councils of Narbonne and Béziers ordered the inquisitors not to indicate in any
manner the names of the witnesses, alleging as a reason the "prudent
wish" of the Holy See, although in the instructions of the Cardinal
of Albano the saving clause of "risk" is expressed. When Innocent

[3] Heresy was a "reserved" case for which the ordinary confessor could not give
absolution. Thus a man of Realmont in Albigeois who repented of having been
present at a Catharan conventicle went to a Franciscan and confessed, accepting
the penance imposed of the minor pilgrimages and some other penitential acts.
On his return from their performance, however, he was seized by the Inquisition,
tried and imprisoned.

IV and his successors regulated the inquisitorial procedure, the same limitation to cases in which divulging the names would expose the witnesses to danger was sometimes omitted and sometimes repeated, and when Boniface VIII embodied in the canon law the rule of withholding the names he expressly cautioned bishops and inquisitors to act with pure intentions, not to withhold the names when there was no peril in communicating them, and if the peril ceased they were to be revealed. Although in the inquisitorial manuals the limitation of risk is usually mentioned, the instructions with regard to the conduct of the trials always assume that the prisoner is kept in ignorance of the names of the witnesses against him. As early as the time of Gui Foucoix, that jurist treats it as the universal practice; in the later periods we are coolly informed by both Eymerich and Bernardo di Como that cases were rare in which risk did not exist; that it was great when the accused was rich and powerful, but greater still when he was poor and had friends who had nothing to lose. Eymerich evidently considers it much more decent to refuse the names than to adopt the expedient of some inquisitors who furnished, like Cardinal Romano, the names written on a different piece of paper and so arranged that their identification with their evidence was impossible, or who mixed up other names with those of the witnesses.

From this withholding of names it was but a step to withholding the evidence altogether, and that step was sometimes taken. In truth the whole process was so completely at the arbitrary discretion of the inquisitor, and the accused was so wholly without rights, that whatever seemed good in the eyes of the former was allowable in the interest of the faith. We are told that if a witness retracted his evidence, the fact should not be made known to the defendant lest it should encourage him in his defense, but the judge is recommended to bear it in mind when rendering judgment. The tender care for the safety of witnesses even went so far that it was left to the conscience of the inquisitor whether or not to give the accused a copy of the evidence itself if there appeared to be danger to be apprehended from doing so.

Among the many evils springing from this concealment, which released witnesses and accusers from all responsibility, not the least was the stimulus which it afforded to delation and the temptation created to gratify malice by reckless perjury. Even without any special desire to do mischief, an unfortunate whose resolution had been broken down by suffering and torture, when brought at last to confess, might readily be led to make his story as satisfactory as possible to his tormentors by mentioning all names that might occur to him as being present at conventicles and heretications. There can be no question that the business of the Inquisition was greatly increased by the protection which it thus afforded to informers and enemies, and that it was made the instrument of an immense amount of false-witness. The inquisitors felt this danger and frequently took such precautions as they could without trouble, by warning a witness of the penalties incurred by perjury, making him obligate himself in advance to endure them, and rigidly questioning him whether he had been suborned. Occasionally, also, we find a conscientious judge like Bernard Gui carefully sifting evidence, comparing the testimony of different witnesses, and tracing out incompatibilities which proved that one at least was false. He accomplished this twice, once in 1312 and again in 1316, the earlier case presenting some peculiar features. A man named Pons Arnaud came forward spontaneously and accused his son Pierre of having endeavored to have him hereticated when under apparently mortal sickness. The son denied it. Bernard, on investigation, found that Pons had not been sick at the date specified, and that there had been no heretics at the place named. Armed with this information he speedily forced the accuser to confess that he had fabricated the story to injure his son. Creditable as is this case to the inquisitor, it is hideously suggestive of the pitfalls which lay around the feet of every man; and no less so is an instance in which Henri de Chamay, Inquisitor of Carcassonne, in 1329, resolutely traced out a conspiracy to ruin an innocent man, and had the satisfaction of forcing five false witnesses to confess their guilt. Rare instances such as these, however, offered but a feeble palliation for the inherent vices of the system, and in spite of the severe punishment meted out to those who were discovered, the crime was of very frequent occurrence. The security with which it could be committed renders it safe to assume that detection occurred in a very small proportion of the cases; so when among the scanty documents that have reached us we see 6 false witnesses (of whom two were priests and one a clerk), sentenced at an *auto de fé* held at Pamiers in 1323; 4 at Narbonne in December 1328; 1, a few weeks after, at Pamiers; 4 more at Pamiers in January 1329, and 7 (one of whom was a notary) at Carcassonne in September 1329, we may conclude that if the full records of the Inquisition were accessible, the list would be a frightful one, and would suggest an incalculable amount of injustice which remained undiscovered. We do not need the admission of Eymerich that witnesses are found frequently to conspire together to ruin an innocent man, and we may well doubt his assurance that persistent scrutiny by the inquisitor will detect the wrong.

A false witness, when detected, was treated with as little mercy as a heretic. As a symbol of his crime two pieces of red cloth in the shape of tongues were affixed to his breast and two to his back, to be worn through life. As the degree of criminality varied, so there were differences in the severity of punishment. Those condemned in Pamiers in 1323 were let off without incarceration. The four at Narbonne, in 1328, were regarded as peculiarly culpable, having been suborned by enemies of the accused, and they were accordingly condemned to the severest form of imprisonment, on bread and water, with chains on hands and feet. The assembly of experts held at Pamiers for the *auto* of January 1329 decided that, in addition to imprisonment, either lenient or harsh, according to the gravity of the offense, the offenders should make good any damage accruing to the accused. Zanghino tells us that in his time there was no defined legal penalty, and that the false witness was to be punished at the discretion of the inquisitor—another instance of the tendency which pervades the whole inquisitorial jurisprudence, to fetter the tribunals with as few rules as possible, to clothe them with arbitrary power, and trust to God, in whose name and for whose glory they professed to act, to inspire them with the wisdom necessary for the discharge of their irresponsible trust.

2. THE DEFENSE

FROM the preceding sketch it may readily be inferred that scant opportunities for defense were allowed by the Holy Office. The suspected heretic was prejudged. The effort of the inquisitor was to force him to admit his guilt and seek reconciliation with the Church. To accomplish this effectually the facilities for defense were systematically reduced to a minimum.

It is true that in 1246 the Council of Béziers lays down the rule that the accused shall have proper opportunities for defense, including necessary delays and the admission of exceptions and legitimate replies; but if this were intended as a check on the arbitrary operations which already characterized the Inquisition, it was wholly disregarded. In the first place, the secrecy of the tribunal enabled the judge to do as he might think best. In the second place, the only possible remaining check to arbitrary action was removed by denying to the accused the advantage of counsel. Then, as now, the intricacy of legal forms rendered the trained advocate a necessity to every man on trial; the layman, ignorant of his rights and of the method of enforcing them, was utterly helpless. So thoroughly was this understood that in the ecclesiastical courts it was frequently a custom to furnish advocates gratuitously to poor men unable to employ them, and in the charter granted by Simon de Montfort in 1212 to his newly acquired territories, it was provided that justice should always be gratuitous, and that counsel should be provided by the court for pleaders too poor to retain them. When this right thus was recognized in the most trifling cases, to refuse it to those who were battling for their lives before a tribunal in which the judge was also prosecutor was more than the Church at first dared openly to do, but it practically reached the result by indirection. Innocent III, in a decretal embodied in the canon law, had ordered advocates and scriveners to lend no aid or counsel to heretics and their defenders, or to undertake their causes in litigation. This, which was presumably intended as one of the disabilities inflicted on defiant and acknowledged heretics, was readily applied to suspects who were not yet convicted, for their guilt was always assumed in advance. The Councils of Valence and Albi, in 1248 and 1254, while ordering inquisitors not to embarrass themselves with the vain jangling of lawyers in the conduct of the prosecution, significantly make reference to this provision of the canon law as applicable to counsel who might be so hardy as to aid the defense. That this became a recognized principle is shown by Bernard Gui's assertion that advocates who excuse and defend heretics are to be held guilty of fautorship of heresy—a crime which became heresy itself if satisfaction at the discretion of the inquisitor was not rendered within a twelvemonth. When to this we add the perpetually reiterated commands to the inquisitors to proceed without regard to legal forms or the wrangling of advocates, and the notice to notaries that he who drew up the revocation of a confession was excommunicated as an impeder of the Inquisition, it will readily be seen that there was no need for formally refusing counsel to the accused, and that there was no practical benefit permitted from the admission of the barren generality that one who believed a heretic to be innocent and endeavored to prove him so was not on that account liable to punishment. Eymerich is careful to specify that the accused has the right to employ counsel, and that a denial of this justifies an appeal, but then he also states that the inquisitor can prosecute any advocate or notary who undertakes the cause of heretics; and a century earlier a manuscript manual for inquisitors directs them to prosecute as defenders of heresy any advocates who take such cases.

In reality no advocate could be of material service to the accused, save in the most exceptional cases. Enmity was the only source of disability in a witness, and this had to be mortal—there must have been bloodshed between the parties, or other cause sufficient to induce one to seek the life of the other. As this was the only possible mode of escape, the cruelty of withholding from the prisoner the names of the adverse witnesses becomes doubly conspicuous. He was forced to grope in the dark and blindly name such persons as he imagined might have a hand in his misfortunes. If he failed to hit upon any who appeared in the case, the evidence against him was conclusive, as far as it went. If he chanced to name some of the witnesses, he was interrogated about the causes of enmity; the inquisitor examined into the facts of the alleged quarrel, and decided as he saw fit on the retention or the rejection of their testimony. Conscientious jurists like Gui Foucoix and inquisitors like Eymerich warned their brethren that as the accused had so slender a chance of guessing the sources of evidence, the judge ought to investigate for himself and discard any that seemed to be the product of malice; but there were others who sought rather to deprive the poor wretch of every straw that might postpone his sinking. One device was to ask him, as though casually, at the end of his examination, whether he had any enemies who would so disregard the fear of God as to accuse him falsely, and if, thus taken unawares, he replied in the negative, he debarred himself from any subsequent defense; or the most damaging witness would be selected and the prisoner be asked if he knew him, when a denial would estop him from claiming enmity.

The enviable simplicity which the inquisitorial process thus assumed in the absence of counsel and of all practical opportunities for defense can perhaps best be illustrated by one or two cases. In the Inquisition of Carcassonne, June 19, 1252, P. Morret is called up and asked if he wishes to defend himself against the matters found in the indictment against him. He has nothing to allege except that he has enemies, of whom he names five. Apparently he did not happen to guess any of the witnesses, for the case proceeded by reading the evidence to him, after which he is again asked thrice if he has anything further to say. To this he replies in the negative, and the case ends by assigning January 29 for the rendering of sentence. Two years later at Carcassonne, a certain Bernard Pons was more lucky, for he happened to guess aright in naming his wife as an inimical witness, and we have the proceedings of the inquest held to determine whether the enmity was mortal. Three witnesses are examined, all of whom swear that she is a woman of loose character; one deposes that she had been taken in adultery by her husband; another that he had beaten her for it, and the third that he had recently heard her say that she wished her husband dead that she might marry a certain Pug Oler, and that she would willingly become a leper if that would bring it about. This would certainly seem sufficient, but Pons appears nevertheless not to have escaped. So thoroughly hopeless, indeed, was the prospect of any effort at defense that it frequently was not even attempted, and the accused, like Arnaud Fabri at Carcassonne, August 26, 1252, when asked if he wished a copy of the evidence against him, would despairingly decline it. It was a customary formula in a sentence to state that the convict had been offered opportunity for defense and had not availed himself of it, showing how frequently this was the case.[4]

In the case of prosecution of the dead, the children or the heirs

[4] In the register of the Inquisition of Carcassonne from 1249 to 1258 M. Molinier has found two cases in which the accused was allowed to introduce evidence in his favor. In one of these G. Vilanière called two witnesses to prove an alibi; in the other Guillem Nègre brought forward a letter of reconciliation and penitence. In neither case was the defendant successful.

were scrupulously cited to appear and defend his memory, as they were necessarily parties to the case through the disabilities and confiscation following upon condemnation. Proclamation was also made publicly in the churches inviting anyone else who chose to appear or who had any interest in the matter by reason of holding property of the deceased; and then a third public notice was given that if no one came forward on the day named, definitive sentence would be rendered. In a case occurring in 1327, Jean Duprat, Inquisitor of Carcassonne, orders the priests of all the churches in the dioceses of Carcassonne, Narbonne, and Alet to publish the notice during divine service on every Sunday and feast-day till the day of hearing, and to send him a notarial attestation of their action. The sentences in these cases are careful to recite these notices so sedulously served on all concerned; but notwithstanding this display of a desire to do exact justice, the proceedings were quite as hollow a mockery as those against the living. That it was so recognized is seen at the *auto* of 1309 at Toulouse, where there were four dead persons sentenced, and it is stated that in one case no one appeared, and in the other three the heirs obeyed the citation but renounced all defense. Sometimes, when deathbed heretications had occurred, the children put in the plea of *non compos*, which was admitted to be good, but as none of the family was allowed to testify, and only disinterested witnesses of approved orthodoxy were received, instances of success must have been rare indeed.

That plain-spoken friar, Bernard Délicieux, declared, in the presence of Philippe le Bel and all his court, that if St. Peter and St. Paul were accused of "adoring" heretics and were prosecuted after the fashion of the Inquisition, there would be no defense open for them. Questioned as to their faith, they would answer like masters in theology and doctors of the Church, but when told that they had adored heretics, and they asked what heretics, some names, common in those parts, would be mentioned, but no particulars would be given. When they would ask for statements as to time and place, no facts would be furnished, and when they would demand the names of the witnesses these would be withheld. How, then, asked Bernard, could the holy apostles defend themselves, especially when anyone who wished to aid them would himself be attacked as a fautor of heresy?

Theoretically an appeal lay to the pope from the Holy Office, and

to the metropolitan from the bishop, for denial of justice or irregularity of procedure, but it had to be made before sentence was
rendered, as condemnation was final. Possibly this may have held
out some prospect of benefit in the case of bishops exercising their
inquisitorial jurisdiction. In that of inquisitors, when *Apostoli*, or
letters remanding the case to the Holy See, were demanded, it rested
with them to grant affirmative ("reverential") ones, or negative ones.
The former admitted the transfer of the case; the latter kept it in
the inquisitor's hands unless it was formally taken from him by the
pope. This, it is safe to say, could rarely happen, and, as the proceeding was an intricate one, it could only be resorted to by experts.
A man like Master Eckart, supported by the whole Dominican Order,
could undertake it, even though in the end he fared no better at
the hands of John XXII than he would have done at those of the
Archbishop of Cologne. When in 1323 the Sire de Partenay, one
of the most powerful nobles of Poitou, was cited for heresy by Friar
Maurice, the Inquisitor of Paris, and was thrown into the Temple
by Charles le Bel, he appealed from Maurice as a judge prejudiced by
personal hatred. Charles sent him under guard to John XXII at
Avignon, who at first refused to entertain the appeal, but at length,
by the influential intercession of Partenay's friends, was induced to
appoint several bishops as assessors to the inquisitor, and after long-
protracted proceedings the interest of Partenay was sufficient to obtain his liberation. Cases like these, however, are exceptional and
have no bearing upon the thousands of humble folk and *petite
noblesse* who filled the prisons of the Inquisition and figured in its
autos de fé.

There was another class of cases, however, in which the interference
of the pope occasionally gave relief, for the Holy See could set aside
all rules. The curia was always greedy for money, and, outside Italy,
had no share in the confiscations. It can therefore readily be imagined
that men of wealth whose whole property was at stake might well
consent to divide it with the papal court, whose all-powerful intervention would thereby be secured. As early as 1245 the Bishops of
Languedoc are found complaining to Innocent IV of the number of
heretics who thus obtain exemption. Not only those undergoing trial,
but those fearing to be cited, those excommunicated for contumacy,
or legitimately sentenced, escape the jurisdiction of the Inquisition

and enjoy immunity on the strength of letters granted by the papal penitentiaries. I have met with a number of special cases of this interference of the Holy See with the Holy Office, one at least of which indicates the means of persuasion employed. In letters of December 28, 1248, the papal penitentiary Algisius orders the release, without confiscation, of six prisoners of the Inquisition who had confessed to heresy, one of the reasons assigned being the liberal contributions which they had made to the cause of the Holy Land.

This kind of papal intervention, however, was in contravention of the law and not in its fulfillment, and need not be weighed in considering the result of the inquisitorial process. That result was condemnation in some form or other so uniformly that it may be regarded as inevitable. In the Register of Carcassonne from 1249 to 1258, comprising about 200 cases, there does not occur a single instance of a prisoner discharged as innocent. It is true that the interrogatory of Alizaïs Debax, March 27, 1249, is followed by the note "she was not heard a second time because she was considered innocent," but this apparent exception is nullified by a second memorandum, *"crucesignata est"*—she was condemned to the public infamy of wearing crosses, probably to confirm the popular impression that the Inquisition never missed its mark. On this side of the Alps it was a recognized rule that no one should be acquitted. The utmost stretch of justice, when the accusation failed entirely, was a sentence of not proven. The charges were simply declared not to be substantiated, and the inquisitors were carefully warned never to pronounce a man innocent, so that there might be no bar to subsequent proceedings in case of further evidence. Possibly in Italy, in the fourteenth century, this rule may have been neglected, for Zanghino gives a formula of acquittal, based, significantly enough, on the evidence being proved to be malicious.

Clement V recognized the injustice wrought under this system when he embodied in the canon law a declaration that inquisitors abused to the injury of the faithful the wise provisions made for the defense of the faith; when he forbade them to convict anyone or act either for or against the accused through love, hate, or the hopes of gain, under penalty of excommunication, removable only by the Holy See. Bernard Gui hotly denied these assertions, which he declared to be precisely those with which the heretics defamed the Holy Office to its great damage. To impute heresy to the innocent, he said, is worthy of damnation, but none the less so is it to slander the Inquisition. In spite, he adds, of the refutation of the accusations brought against it, this canon assumes their truth and the heretics exult over its disgrace. If the heretics exulted, their rejoicings were premature. The Inquisition went its way in the accustomed paths, and Clement's well-meant effort at reform proved wholly unavailing.

The erection of suspicion into a crime gave ample opportunity for the habitual avoidance of acquittal. This took its origin in the customs of mediæval codes, which required the accused, against whom a probable case was made out, to demonstrate his innocence either by the Ordeal, or by the form of purgation known in England as the Wager of Law, in which he produced a prescribed number of his friends to share with him the oath of denial. In the coronation edict of Frederic II, those who were suspected of heresy were required to purge themselves in this manner. Suspicion might arise from many causes, the chief of which was popular rumor and belief. Omission to take the oath abjuring heresy imposed on all the inhabitants of Languedoc, within the term prescribed, was sufficient, or neglect to reveal heretics, or the possession of heretical books. The intricate questions to which this extension of criminality gave rise are fairly illustrated in the discussion of an inquisitor whether those who listened to the instructions of the Waldenses, "Do not lie, nor swear, nor commit fornication, but give to every man his due; go to church, pay your tithes, and the perquisites of the priests," and, knowing this to be good advice, conclude the utterers to be good men —whether such are to be considered suspect of heresy; and he tells us that after diligent consideration he must decide in the affirmative, and order them to purgation. Chancellor Gerson admits that due allowance should be made for variations of habits and manners in different places and times, but the ordinary inquisitor was troubled with few such scruples. It was easier to treat the suspect as criminals; to classify suspicion into its three grades of light, vehement, and violent; to prescribe punishment for it, and to inflict the disabilities of heresy on the suspect and their descendants. Nothing more condemnatory of the whole system can well be imagined than the explanation of Eymerich that suspects are not heretics; that they are

not to be condemned for heresy, and that therefore their punishment should be lighter, except in the case of violent suspicion.
Against violent suspicion there was no defense possible, and no evidence to be admitted. The culprit might not be a heretic or entertain any error of belief, but if he would not abjure (and abjuration
included confession), he was to be handed over to the secular arm;
if he confessed and sought reconciliation, he was to be imprisoned for
life.

For light and vehement suspicion the accused was ordered to
furnish compurgators in his oath of denial. These were to be men of
his own rank in life, who knew him personally and who swore to
their belief in his orthodoxy and in the truth of his exculpatory
oath. Their number varied, at the discretion of the inquisitor, with
the degree of suspicion to be purged away, from 3 to 20 or 30, and
even more. In the case of strangers, however, who had no acquaintances, the inquisitor was advised to be moderate. If the suspect
was unable to procure the required number of compurgators, or
neglected to do so within a year, the law of Frederic II was enforced,
and he was usually condemned as a heretic to burning alive; although some inquisitors argued that this was only presumptive, not
absolute proof, and that he could escape the stake by confessing and
abjuring—of course being subject to the penance of perpetual prison.
If he succeeded and duly performed his purgation, he was by no
means acquitted. If the suspicion against him was vehement he
could still be punished; even if it was light the fact that he had
been suspected was an ineradicable blot. With the curious logical
inconsequence characteristic of inquisitorial procedure, in addition
to the purgation, he was obliged to abjure the heresy of which he
had cleared himself; this abjuration remained of record against
him, and in case of a second accusation his escape from the previous
one was not reckoned as having proved his innocence, but as an
evidence of guilt. If the purgation had been for light suspicion, his
punishment now was increased; and if it had been for vehement
suspicion, he was now regarded as a relapsed, to whom no mercy
could be shown, but who was handed over to the secular arm without
a hearing. Practically, however, this injustice is important chiefly
as a manifestation of the spirit of the Inquisition; its methods were
too thorough to render frequent a recourse to purgation, and

Zanghino, when he treats of it, feels obliged to explain it as a custom little known. One case, however, is on record at Angermünde, where the Inquisitor Friar Jordan, in 1336, tried by this method a number of persons accused of the mysterious Luciferan heresy, when 14 men and women who were unable to procure the requisite number of compurgators were duly burned.

An indispensable formality in all cases in which the culprit was admitted to reconciliation with the Church was abjuration of heresy. Of this there were various forms adapted to the different occasions of its use—whether for suspicion, light, vehement, or violent, or after confession and repentance. It was performed in public, at the *autos de fé*, except in rare cases, such as those of ecclesiastics likely to cause scandal, and it frequently embodied a pecuniary penalty for infraction of its promises and security for their performance. The principal point to be observed in all was to see that the penitent abjured heresy in general as well as the special heresy with which he had been charged. If this were duly attended to, he could always be handed over to the secular arm in case of relapse, except when the abjuration had been for light suspicion. If it were neglected, and he had, for instance, abjured Catharism only, he might subsequently indulge in some other form of heresy, such as Waldensianism or usury, and have the benefit of another chance. The importance attached to the abjuration is illustrated by a case in the Inquisition of Toulouse in 1310. Sibylla, wife of Bernard Borell, had been forced to confession and abjuration in 1305. Continuing her heretical practices, she was arrested in 1309 and again obliged to confess. As a relapsed heretic she was doomed irrevocably to the stake, but, luckily for her, the abjuration could not be found among the papers of the Holy Office, and though the rest of the record seems to have been accessible, she could only be prosecuted as though for a first offense, and she escaped with imprisonment for life.

In the case of suspects of heresy who cleared themselves by compurgation, abjuration, of course, did not include confession. In accusations of heresy supported by evidence, however, no one could be admitted to abjuration who did not confess that of which he was accused. In ordinary cases, where torture was freely used, confession was almost a matter of course. There were extraordinary cases, however, like that of Huss at Constance, where torture was spared and where the accused denied the doctrines attributed to him. In such cases the necessity of confession prior to abjuration must be borne in mind if we are to understand the inevitable consequences.

3. THE SENTENCE

Technically, the list of penalties available to the inquisitor was limited. He never condemned to death, but merely withdrew the protection of the Church from the hardened and impenitent sinner who afforded no hope of conversion, or from him who showed by relapse that there was no trust to be placed in his pretended repentance. Except in Italy, he never confiscated the heretic's property; he merely declared the existence of a crime which, under the secular law, rendered the culprit incapable of possession. At most he could impose a fine, as a penance, to be expended in good works. His tribunal was a spiritual one, and dealt only with the sins and remedies of the spirit. Such, at least, was the theory of the Church, and this must be borne in mind if we would understand what may occasionally seem to be inconsistencies and incongruities—especially in view of the arbitrary discretion which left to the individual inquisitor such opportunity to display his personal characteristics in dealing with the penitents before him.

This sometimes led to a lenity which would be otherwise inexplicable, as in the case of the murderers of St. Peter Martyr. Pietro Balsamo, known as Carino, one of the hired assassins, was caught red-handed, and his escape by bribery from prison created a popular excitement leading to a revolution in Milan. Yet, when recaptured, he repented, was forgiven, and allowed to enter the Dominican Order, in which he peacefully died, with the repute of a *beato*; and though the Church never formally recognized his right to the public worship paid to him in some places, still, in one of the stalls of the martyr's own great church of Sant' Eustorgio, he appears with the title of the blessed Acerinus in a chiaroscuro of 1505, among the Dominican saints. Not one, indeed, of those concerned in the assassination appears to have been put to death, and the leading instigator of the crime, Stefano Confaloniere of Aliate, a notorious heretic and fautor of heretics, after repeated abjurations, releases, and relapses, was not imprisoned until 1295, forty-three years after the murder. It was the same when, soon afterwards, the Franciscan Inquisitor Pier da Bracciano was assassinated, and Manfredo di Sesto, who had hired the assassins, was brought before Rainerio Saccone, the Inquisitor of Milan. He confessed the crime and other offenses in aid of heresy, but was only ordered to present himself to the pope and receive penance. When he contumaciously neglected to do this, Innocent IV merely ordered the magistrates of Italy to arrest and detain him if he should be found.

The penances customarily imposed by the Inquisition were comparatively few in number. They consisted, first, of pious observances —recitation of prayers, frequenting of churches, the discipline, fasting, pilgrimages, and fines nominally for pious uses, such as a confessor might impose on his ordinary penitents. These were for offenses of trifling import. Next in grade are the *pœnœ confusibiles*—the humiliating and degrading penances, of which the most important was the wearing of yellow crosses sewed upon the garments, and, finally, the severest punishment among those strictly within the competence of the Holy Office, the *murus*, or prison. Confiscation, as I have said, was an incident, and the stake, like it, was the affair of the secular power; and though both were really controlled by the inquisitor, they will be more conveniently considered separately. The Councils of Narbonne and Béziers, in addition, prescribe a purely temporal punishment—banishment, either temporary or perpetual—but this would appear to have been rarely employed, although in the earlier period it occasionally occurs in sentences, or is found among the penances to which repentant heretics pledged themselves to submit.

Before the Inquisition was founded, about 1208, St. Dominic, while acting under the authority of the Legate Arnaud, converted a Catharan named Pons Roger, and prescribed for him a penance which has chanced to be preserved. It will give us an insight into what were considered reasonable terms of readmission to the Church, at a time when it was straining every nerve to win the heretics back, and before it had fairly resorted to the use of force. On three Sundays the penitent is to be stripped to the waist and scourged by the priest from the entrance of the town of Tréville to the church door. He is to abstain forever from meat and eggs and cheese, except on Easter, Pentecost, and Christmas, when he is to eat of them in sign of his abnegation of his Manichæan errors. For twoscore days, twice a year, he is to forego the use of fish, and for three days in each week that of fish, wine, and oil, fasting, if his health and labors will permit. He is to wear monastic vestments, with a small cross sewed on each breast. If possible, he is to hear mass daily, and on feast-days to attend church at vespers. Seven times a day he is to recite the canonical hours, and, in addition, the *Paternoster* ten times each day and twenty times each night. He is to observe the strictest chastity. Every month he is to show this paper to the priest, who is to watch its observance closely, and this mode of life is to be maintained until the legate shall see fit to alter it, while for infraction of the penance he is to be held as a perjurer and a heretic, and be segregated from the society of the faithful.

This shows how the various forms of penance were mingled together at the discretion of the ghostly father. The same is seen in an exceedingly lenient sentence imposed in 1258 by the Inquisitors of Carcassonne on Raymond Maria, who had confessed to various acts of heresy committed 20 or 30 years before, and who, for other reasons, had strong claims for merciful treatment. Raymond is ordered to fast from the Friday after Michaelmas until Easter, and to eat no meat on Saturdays, but he can redeem the fast by giving a denier to a poor man. Every day he is to recite seven times the *Paternoster* and *Ave Maria*. Within three years he is to visit the shrines of St. Mary of Roche-amour, St. Rufus of Aliscamp, St. Gilles of Vauverte, St. William of the Desert, and Santiago de Compostella, bringing home testimonial letters from the rector of each church; and in lieu of other penances he is to give 6 livres Tournois to the Bishop of Albi to aid in building a chapel. He is to hear mass at least every Sunday and feast-day, and to abstain from all work on those days.

In these cases there is no mention of flagellation, but that was so general a feature of penance that it is frequently taken for granted in prescribing pilgrimages and attendance at church. We have seen Raymond of Toulouse submitting to it, and however abhorrent it may be to our modern ideas, it did not carry with it that sense of humiliation which to us appears inseparable from it. Stripped as much as decency and the inclemency of the weather would permit, the penitent presented himself every Sunday, between the Epistle and the Gospel, with a rod in his hand, to the priest engaged in celebrating mass, who soundly scourged him in the presence of the congregation. On the first Sunday in every month, after mass, he was to visit, similarly equipped, every house in which he had seen heretics, and receive the same infliction; and on the occasion of every solemn procession he was to accompany it in the same guise, to be beaten at every station and at the end. Apparently it lasted as long as the wretched life of the penitent, or at least until it pleased the inquisitor to remember him and liberate him.

The pilgrimages, which were regarded as among the lightest of penances, were mercies only by comparison. Performed on foot, the number commonly enjoined might well consume several years of a man's life, during which his family might perish. These pilgrimages were not without peril and hardship, although the hospitality exercised by the numerous convents on the road enabled the poorest pilgrim to sustain life. The penitential pilgrimages were divided into two classes—the greater and the less. In Languedoc the greater pilgrimages were customarily 4—to Rome, Compostella, St. Thomas of Canterbury, and the Three Kings of Cologne. The smaller were 19 in number, extending from shrines of local celebrity to Paris and Boulogne-sur-mer. The cases in which they were employed may be estimated by the sentence passed by Bernard Gui in 1322 on three culprits whose only offense was that, some 15 or 20 years before, they had seen Waldensian teachers in their fathers' houses without knowing what they were. Commencing within three months, the penitents were required to perform 17 of the minor pilgrimages, reaching from Bordeaux to Vienne, bringing back, as usual, from each shrine testimonial letters of the visit. In one case, occurring in 1308, a culprit was excused from pilgrimages on account of his age and weakness, and was only required to make two visitations a year in the city of Toulouse. Considerate humanity such as this is not sufficiently common in the annals of the Inquisition for an example of it to be passed in silence.

At the inception of the Inquisition the pilgrimage universally ordered for men was that to Palestine, as a crusader. Indeed, the Legate Cardinal Romano commanded this for all who were suspect of heresy. In the wholesale persecutions in Languedoc the numbers of these unwilling crusaders were so great that alarm was excited lest they should pervert the faith in the land of its origin, and about 1242 or 1243 a papal prohibition was issued, forbidding it for the future. The Council of Béziers, in 1246, commits to the discretion of the inquisitors whether penitents shall serve beyond seas, or send a man-at-arms to represent them, or fight the battles of the faith nearer home, against heretics or Saracens. The term of service was also left to the inquisitors, but was usually for two or three years, though sometimes for seven or eight, and those who went to Palestine, if they were so fortunate as to return, were obliged to bring back testimonial letters from the Patriarch of Jerusalem or Acre. As late as 1321 we find Guillem Garric condemned to go beyond seas with the next convoy and remain until recalled by the inquisitor; if legitimately impeded (which was likely, as he was an old man who had rotted in a dungeon for thirty years) he could replace himself with a competent fighting man, and if he neglected to do so, he was condemned to perpetual prison. This sentence affords one of the rare instances of banishment, for Guillem, besides furnishing a substitute, is ordered to expatriate himself to such place as shall be designated, during the pleasure of the inquisitor.

These penances did not interfere with the social position and self-respect of the penitent. Far heavier was the apparently simple penalty of wearing the crosses, which was known as a *pœna confusibilis*, or humiliating punishment. The two little crosses of St. Dominic grew to conspicuous pieces of saffron-colored cloth, of which the arms were 2½ fingers in breath, 2½ palms in height, and 2 palms in width, one sewed on the breast and the other on the back, though occasionally one on the breast sufficed. If the convert during his trial had committed perjury, a second transverse arm was added at the top; and if he had been a perfected heretic, a third cross was placed upon the cap. Another form was that of a hammer, worn by prisoners temporarily liberated on bail; while other emblematical forms were prescribed as the fancy of the inquisitor might dictate.[5] They were never to be laid aside, in doors or out, and when worn out the penitent was obliged to renew them. During the latter half of the thirteenth century those who went beyond seas might abandon

---

[5] At an early period there is a single allusion to another *pœna confusibilis* in the shape of a wooden collar or yoke worn by the penitent. This occurs at La Charité, in 1233, and I have not met with it elsewhere.

their crosses during their crusade, but were obliged to reassume them on returning.

Though this penance was regarded as merciful in comparison with imprisonment, it was not easily endurable, and we can readily understand the sharp penalties required to enforce obedience. In the sentences of Pierre Cella it is only prescribed in aggravated cases, and then merely for from one to five years, though subsequently it grew to be universal, and without a limit of time. The unfortunate penitent was exposed to the ridicule and derision of all whom he met, and was heavily handicapped in every effort to earn a livelihood. Even in the earlier time, when a majority of the population of Languedoc were heretics, and the cross-wearers were so numerous that their presence in Palestine was dreaded, the Council of Béziers, in 1246, feels obliged to warn the people that penitents should be welcomed and their cheerful endurance of penance should be a subject of gratulation for all the faithful, and therefore it strictly forbids ridicule of those who wear crosses, or refusal to transact business with them.

The Inquisition recognized the hardships to which its penitents were exposed, and sometimes in mercy mitigated them. Thus, in 1250, at Carcassonne, Pierre Pelha receives permission to lay aside the crosses temporarily during a voyage which he is obliged to make to France. Bernard Gui assures us that young women were frequently excused from wearing them, because with them they would be unable to find husbands; and among the formulas of his *Practica* one which exempts the penitent from crosses enumerates the various reasons usually assigned, such as the age or infirmity of the wearer (presumably rendering him a safe object of insult) or on account of his children, whom he may not otherwise be able to support, or for the sake of his daughters, whom he cannot marry.

It will be remembered that at the outset there was some discussion whether it should be competent for the inquisitors to inflict the pecuniary penance of fines. The voluntary poverty and renunciation of money of the Mendicants had not yet become so obsolete that the incongruity could be overlooked of their using their almost limitless discretion in levying fines and handling the money thence accruing. That they commenced it early is shown by a sentence of 1237, in which Pons Grimoardi, a voluntary convert, is required to pay to the order of the inquisitor 10 livres Morlaas, while in 1245, in Florence, one rendered by the indefatigable Inquisitor Ruggieri Calcagni shows that already fines were habitual there. It was not without cause, therefore, that the Council of Narbonne, in 1244, in its instructions to inquisitors, ordered them to abstain from pecuniary penances both for the sake of the honor of their Order and because they would have ample other work to do. The Order itself felt this to be the case and, as inquisitors were not yet, at least in theory, emancipated from the control of their superiors, in 1242 the Provincial Chapter of Montpellier had endeavored to enforce the rules of the Order by strictly prohibiting them from inflicting pecuniary penances for the future, or from collecting those which had already been imposed. How little respect was shown to these injunctions is visible from a bull of Innocent IV, in 1245, in which, to preserve the reputation of the inquisitors, he orders all fines paid over to two persons selected by the bishop and inquisitor, to be expended in building prisons and in supporting prisoners, in compliance with which the Council of Béziers, in 1246, abandoned the position taken by the Council of Narbonne, and agreed that the fines should be employed on the prisons, and in defraying the necessary expenses of the Inquisition. In an inquisitorial manual of the period this is specified as the destination of the fines, but the power was speedily abused, and in 1249 Innocent IV sternly rebuked the inquisitors in general for the heavy exactions which they wrung from their converts. This apparently had no effect, and in 1251 he prohibited them wholly from levying fines if any other form of penance could be employed. Yet the inquisitors finally triumphed and won the right to inflict pecuniary penances at discretion. These were understood to be for pious uses, in which term were included the expenses of the Inquisition; and as they were payable to the inquisitors themselves, they doubtless were so expended—it is to be hoped in accordance with the caution of Eymerich, "decently and without scandal to the laity." Pierre Cella, the first Inquisitor of Toulouse, frequently added to the pilgrimages or other penances imposed the obligation of maintaining a priest or a poor man for a term of years or for life.

Scarcely separable from the practice of fines was that of commuting penances for money. In 1255, the Inquisitors of Toulouse allowed twelve of the principal citizens of Lavaur to commute their penances into money to be contributed to building the church which was afterwards the Cathedral of Lavaur; and in 1258 they assisted the church of Najac in the same way by allowing a number of the inhabitants to redeem their penalties for its benefit. The public utility of bridges caused them to be included in the somewhat elastic term of pious uses. Thus, in 1310, at Toulouse, Matthieu Aychard is released from wearing crosses and performing certain pilgrimages on condition of contributing 40 livres Tournois to a new bridge then under construction at Tonneins; and in a formula for such transactions given by Bernard Gui, absolution and dispensation from pilgrimages and other penances are said to be granted in consideration of the payment of 50 livres for the building of a certain bridge, or of a certain church, or "to be spent in pious uses at our discretion." This last clause shows that commutations were by no means always thus liberally disposed of, and in fact they often inured to the benefit of those imposing them. We have a specimen of this in letters of the Inquisitor of Narbonne in 1264, granting absolution to Guillem du Puy in consideration of his giving 150 livres Tournois to the Inquisition.

Penitents who died before fulfilling their penance afforded a specially favorable opportunity for such transactions as these. There might be a distinction drawn in practice between those who were taken off while humbly performing the penance assigned to them, and those who had wilfully neglected its commencement; but legally the nonfulfillment of penance entailed condemnation for heresy whether in the dead or living. In 1329, for instance, the Inquisition of Carcassonne ordered the exhumation and cremation of the bones of seven persons declared to have died in heresy for not having fulfilled the penance enjoined on them, which of course carried with it the confiscation of their property and the subjection of their descendants to the usual disabilities. The Councils of Narbonne and Albi directed the inquisitors to exact satisfaction at discretion from the heirs of those who had died before judgment, if they would have been condemned to wear crosses, as well as those who had confessed and been sentenced, and who had not lived to complete their penance. Gui Foucoix expresses his belief that in these cases the penitent is admitted to purgatory, and he decides that nothing should be demanded from his heirs; but even his authority did not overcome the more palatable doctrine of the councils, and a contemporary manual directs the inquisitor to exact a "congruous satisfaction." The Inquisitor of Carcassonne had prescribed five years' pilgrimage to the Holy Land for Jean Vidal, who died before performing it. March 21, 1252, his heirs, under citation, swore that his whole estate was worth 20 livres, and gave security to obey the decision of the inquisitor, which was announced the following August, and proved to be a demand for 20 livres. In another case, Raymonde Barbaira had died before accomplishing some pilgrimages with crosses to which she had been sentenced. An inventory of her property showed it to consist of some bedding, clothing, a chest, a few cattle, and 4 sous in money, which had been divided up among her kindred, and from this pitiful inheritance the inquisitor, on March 7, 1256, demanded 40 sous, for the payment of which by Easter the heirs had to give security. Even in the case of fautors who were not heretics, the heirs were obliged to perform any pecuniary penance which had been inflicted upon them.

A more legitimate source of income, but yet one which opened the door to grave abuses, was the custom of taking bail, which of course was liable to forfeiture, serving, in such cases, as an irregular form of commutation. The convert who was absolved on abjuring was also required to give security that he would not relapse. Thus, in 1234, we see Lantelmo, a Milanese noble, ordered to give bail in 2,000 lire, and two Florentine merchants bailed by their friends in 2,000 silver marks. Forfeited bail was payable to the inquisitor, sometimes directly, and sometimes through the hands of the bishops, and was to be used for the expenses of the Inquisition. The usual form of bond pledged all the property of the principal and that of two sureties, jointly and severally; and as a general rule bail may be said to have been universal, except in cases where the offense was regarded as too serious to admit of it, or when the offender could not procure it.

It was impossible that these methods of converting sentences into current coin could flourish without introducing widespread corruption. Admission to bail might be the result of favoritism or degenerate into covert bribery. That these fruitful sources of gain were not abundantly worked would be incredible even in the absence of proof, but proof sufficient exists. In 1302 Boniface VIII

wrote to the Dominican Provincial of Lombardy that the papal ears
had been lacerated with complaints of the Franciscan Inquisitors
of Padua and Vicenza, whose malicious cupidity had wronged many
men and women by exacting from them immense sums and inflicting
on them all manner of injuries. He had sent Gui, Bishop of Saintes,
to investigate these complaints, who reported them well founded,
and he orders the provincial to replace the delinquents with Dominicans. The change brought little relief, for the very next year
Mascate de' Mosceri, a jurist of Padua, appealed to Benedict from
the new Dominican inquisitor, Frà Benigno, who was vexing him
with prosecutions in order to extort money from him; and in 1304
Benedict was obliged to address to the Inquisitors of Padua and
Vicenza a grave warning as to the official complaints which still
arose about their fraudulent prosecution of good Catholics by means
of false witnesses. The investigation set on foot by Clement V convinced him of the truth of such facts, and at the Council of Vienne,
in 1311, he caused the adoption of canons, embodied in the Corpus
Juris, which placed on record conspicuously his conviction that the
inquisitorial office was frequently abused by the extortion of money
from the innocent and the escape of the guilty through bribery.
The remedy he devised, of *ipso facto* excommunication in such cases,
was complained of by Bernard Gui on the ground that it would
invalidate the rightful acts, as well as the evil ones, of the wrong-
doer.

In 1346 the whole republic of Florence rose against their inquisitor,
Piero di Aquila, for various abuses, among which figured extortion.
A single witness swore to 66 cases of extortion, and in a partial
list of them which has been preserved the sums exacted vary from 25
to 1,700 gold florins. Villani tells us that in two years he had thus
amassed more than 7,000 florins, an enormous sum in those days; that
there were no heretics in Florence at the time, and that the offenses
which thus proved so lucrative to him consisted of usury and thoughtless blasphemy. As for usury, Alvaro Pelayo tells us that at that time
the Bishops of Tuscany set the example by habitually so employing the
church funds, but the inquisitors did not meddle with the prelates.
As for blasphemy, the subtle refinements which converted simple
blasphemous expressions into heresy, as set forth by Eymerich, show
how readily a skillful inquisitor could speculate on idle oaths.

Boccaccio doubtless had Frà Piero in memory when he described
the Inquisitor of Florence who, like all his brethren, had an eye as
keen to discover a rich man as a heretic, and who extracted a heavy
douceur from a citizen for boasting in his cups that he had wine so
good that Christ would drink it.

I have dwelt at some length upon this feature of the Inquisition
because it is one which has rarely received attention, although
it inflicted misery and wrong to an almost unlimited extent. While
the horrors of the crowded dungeon can scarce be exaggerated, yet
more widely exasperating was the sleepless watchfulness which was
ever on the alert to plunder the rich and to wrench from the poor
the hard-earned gains on which a family depended for support. It
was only in rare cases that the victims dared to raise a cry, and rarer
still were those in which that cry was heard; but sufficient instances
have reached us to prove what a scourge was the institution, in this
aspect alone, on all the populations cursed by its presence. At a very
early period the wealthy recognized that well-timed liberality was
advisable towards those who held such power in the hollow of their
hands. In 1244 the Dominican Chapter of Cahors lifted a warning
voice and ordered inquisitors not to allow their brethren to receive
presents which would expose the whole Order to disrepute; but this
scrupulousness wore off, and even a man of high character like
Eymerich could argue that inquisitors may properly be the recipients
of gifts, though he dubiously adds that they ought to be refused from
those under trial, except in special circumstances.

There was one purely temporal penalty which came within the
competence of the Inquisition—the designation of the houses which
were to be destroyed in consequence of the contamination of heresy.
The origin of this curious practice is not readily traced. Under the
Roman law, buildings in which heretics held their conventicles
with the owner's consent were not torn down, but were forfeited to
the Church. Yet as soon as heresy began to be formidable we find
their destruction commanded by secular rulers with singular unanimity. The earliest provision I have met with occurs in the Assizes
of Clarendon in 1166, which order the razing of all houses in which
heretics were received. The example was followed by the Emperor
Henry VI in the edict of Prato in 1194, by Otho IV in 1210, and
by Frederic II in the edict of Ravenna in 1232, as an addition to his

coronation edict of 1220, from which it had been omitted. In France the Council of Toulouse in 1229 decreed that any house in which a heretic was found was to be destroyed, and this was given the force of secular law by Count Raymond in 1234. Castile seems to be the only land in which the regulation was not observed, owing doubtless to the direct derivation of its legislation from the Roman law, for, in the *Partidas*, houses in which heretics were sheltered are ordered to be given to the Church. Elsewhere such dwellings were razed to the ground, and the site, as accursed, was to remain forever a receptacle for filth and unfit for human habitation; yet the materials could be employed for pious uses unless they were ordered to be burned by the inquisitor who rendered the sentence.

In France the royal officials in charge of the confiscations came at length to object to this destruction of property, which was sometimes considerable, as the castle of the seigneur was as liable to it as the cabin of the peasant. In 1329 it forms one of the points for which Inquisitor Henri de Chamay asked and obtained the confirmation of Philippe de Valois, and the same year he had the satisfaction, in an *auto* held in September, to order the destruction of four houses and a farm, whose owners had been hereticated in them on their deathbeds. Some fifty years later, however, a quarrel on the subject between the king's representatives and the Inquisitors of Dauphiné resulted differently. Charles le Sage, after consulting with the pope, issued letters of October 19, 1378, ordering that the penalty should no longer be enforced. The independent spirit of northern Germany manifested itself in the same manner, and in the *Sachsenspiegel* there is a peremptory command that no houses shall be destroyed except for rape committed within them. In Italy the custom continued, as there the confiscations did not inure to the sovereign, but it was held that if the owner had no guilty knowledge of the use made of his house he was entitled to keep it. Lawyers disputed, however, as to the perpetuity of the prohibition to build on the spot, some holding that possession by a Catholic for forty years conferred a right to erect a new house, which others denied, arguing that a perpetual and imprescriptible servitude had been created. The inquisitors, in process of time, arrogated to themselves the power to issue licenses to build anew on these sites.

Another temporal penalty may be alluded to as illustrating the unlimited discretion enjoyed by the inquisitors. When, in 1321, the town of Cordes made humble submission for its long-continued insubordination to its bishop and inquisitor, the penance assigned to the community by Bernard Gui and Jean de Beaune was the construction of a chapel of such size as might be ordered, in honor of St. Peter Martyr, St. Cecilia, St. Louis, and St. Dominic, with the statues of those saints in wood or stone above the altar; and, to complete the humiliation of the community, the portal was to be adorned with statues of the bishop and of the two inquisitors, the whole to be finished within two years. Doubtless the people of Cordes built the chapel without delay, but they hesitated at this glorifying of their oppressors, for, 27 years afterwards, in 1348, we find the municipal authorities summoned before the Inquisition of Toulouse and compelled to give pledges that the portal shall forthwith be completed and the inquisitorial effigies be erected.

The severest penance the inquisitor could impose was incarceration. It was, according to the theory of the inquisitors, not a punishment, but a means by which the penitent could obtain, on the bread of tribulation and water of affliction, pardon from God for his sins, while at the same time he was closely supervised to see that he persevered in the right path and was segregated from the rest of the flock, thus removing all danger of infection. Of course it was only used for converts. The defiant heretic who persisted in disobedience, or who pertinaciously refused to confess his heresy and asserted his innocence, could not be admitted to penance, and was handed over to the secular arm.

In the bull *Excommunicamus* of Gregory IX, in 1229, all who after arrest were converted to the faith through fear of death were ordered to be incarcerated for life, thus to perform appropriate penance. The Council of Toulouse almost simultaneously made the same regulation, and manifested its sense of the real value of the involuntary conversions by adding the caution that they be prevented from corrupting others. The Ravenna decree of Frederic II, in 1332, adopted the same rule and made it settled legal practice. The Inquisition at its inception thus found the rule established, and enforced it with the relentless vigor which it manifested in all its functions. It was represented as a special mercy shown to those who had forfeited all claims on human compassion. The

Council of Narbonne, in 1244, specifically declared that, except when special indulgence could be procured from the Holy See, no husband was to be spared on account of his wife, or wife on account of her husband, or parent in consideration of helpless children; neither sickness nor old age should claim mitigation. In a fragment which has been preserved of the Register of Sentences in the Inquisition of Toulouse from 1246 to 1248, comprising 192 cases, with the exception of 43 contumacious absentees, the sentence is invariably imprisonment. Of these, 127 are perpetual, 6 are for ten years, and 16 for an indefinite period, as may seem expedient to the Church. It apparently was not till a later period that the order of the Council of Narbonne was obeyed, and the sentence always was for life. In the later periods this proportion will not hold good, for all inquisitors were not like the fierce Bernard de Caux, who then ruled the Holy Office in Toulouse; but perpetual imprisonment remained to the last the principal penance inflicted on penitents, although the decrees of Frederic and the canons of the Councils of Toulouse and Narbonne were not held to apply to those who abjured heartily after arrest.

In the later sentences which have reached us it is often not easy to guess why one prisoner is incarcerated and another let off with crosses, when the offenses enumerated of each would seem to be indistinguishable. All alike were converts, but he whose conversion appeared to be hearty and spontaneous was considered to be entitled to the easier penance, while the harsher one was inflicted when the conversion seemed to be enforced and the result of fear. Yet how relentlessly a man like Bernard Gui could enforce the strict measure of the law is seen in the case of Pierre Raymond Dominique, who had been cited to appear in 1309, had fled and incurred excommunication, had consequently, in 1315, been condemned as a contumacious heretic, and in 1321 had voluntarily come forward and surrendered himself on a promise that his life should be spared. His acts of heresy had not been flagrant, and he pleaded as an excuse for his contumacy his wife and seven children, who would have starved had they been deprived of his labor, but in spite of this he was incarcerated for life. Even the stern Bernard de Caux was not always so merciless. In 1246, we find him, in sentencing Bernard Sabbatier, a relapsed heretic, to perpetual imprisonment, adding that as the culprit's father is a good Catholic and old and sick, the son may remain with him and support him as long as he lives, meanwhile wearing the crosses.

There were two kinds of imprisonment, the milder, or *murus largus*, and the harsher, known as *murus strictus* or *durus* or *arctus*. All were on bread and water, and the confinement, according to rule, was solitary, each penitent in a separate cell, with no access allowed to him, to prevent his being corrupted or corrupting others; but this could not be strictly enforced, and about 1306 Geoffroi d'Ablis stigmatizes as an abuse the visits of clergy, and laity of both sexes, permitted to prisoners. Husband and wife, however, were allowed access to each other if either or both were imprisoned; and late in the fourteenth century Eymerich agrees that zealous Catholics may be admitted to visit prisoners, but not women and simple folk who might be perverted, for converted prisoners, he adds, are very liable to relapse, and to infect others, and usually end with the stake.

In the milder form, or *murus largus*, the prisoners apparently were, if well behaved, allowed to take exercise in the corridors, where sometimes they had opportunities of converse with each other and with the outside world. In the harsher confinement, or *murus strictus*, the prisoner was thrust into the smallest, darkest, and most noisome of cells, with chains on his feet—in some cases chained to the wall. This penance was inflicted on those whose offenses had been conspicuous, or who had perjured themselves by making incomplete confessions, the matter being wholly at the discretion of the inquisitor. I have met with one case, in 1328, of aggravated falsewitness, condemned to *murus strictissimus*, with chains on both hands and feet. When the culprits were members of a religious order, to avoid scandal the proceedings were usually held in private, and the imprisonment would be ordered to take place in a convent of their own Order. As these buildings, however, usually were provided with cells for the punishment of offenders, this was probably of no great advantage to the victim. In the case of Jeanne, widow of B. de la Tour, a nun of Lespenasse, in 1246, who had committed acts of both Catharan and Waldensian heresy, and had prevaricated in her confession, the sentence was confinement in a separate cell in her own convent, where no one was to enter or see her, her food being pushed in through an opening left for the purpose—in fact, the living tomb known as the *in pace*.[6]

While the penance prescribed was a diet of bread and water, the Inquisition, with unwonted kindness, did not object to its prisoners receiving from their friends contributions of food, wine, money, and garments, and among its documents are such frequent allusions to this that it may be regarded as an established custom. Collections were made among those secretly inclined to heresy to alleviate the condition of their incarcerated brethren, and it argues much in favor of the disinterested zeal of the persecuted that they were willing to incur the risk attendant on this benevolence, for any interest shown towards these poor wretches exposed them to accusation to fautorship.

The prisons were naturally built with a view to economy of construction and space rather than to the health and comfort of the captives. The papal orders were that they should be constructed of small, dark cells for solitary confinement, only taking care that the *enormis rigor* of the incarceration should not extinguish life. M. Molinier's description of the Tour de l'Inquisition at Carcassonne, which was used as the inquisitorial prison, shows how literally these instructions were obeyed. It was a horrible place, consisting of small cells, deprived of all light and ventilation, where through long years the miserable inmates endured a living death far worse than the short agony of the stake. In these abodes of despair they were completely at the mercy of the jailers and their servants. If a prisoner alleged violence or ill-treatment his oath was contemptuously refused, while that of the prison officials was received. A glimpse into the discipline of these establishments is afforded by the instructions given in 1282 by Frère Jean Galande, Inquisitor of Carcassonne, to the jailer Raoul and his wife Bertrande. Under pain of irrevocable dismissal he is

---

[6] The cruelty of the monastic system of imprisonment known as *in pace*, or *vade in pacem*, was such that those subjected to it speedily died in all the agonies of despair. In 1350 the Archbishop of Toulouse appealed to King John to interfere for its mitigation, and he issued an *Ordonnance* that the superior of the convent should twice a month visit and console the prisoner, who, moreover, should have the right twice a month to ask for the company of one of the monks. Even this slender innovation provoked the bitterest resistance of the Dominicans and Franciscans, who appealed to Pope Clement VI, but in vain. The hideous abuse of keeping a prisoner in chains was forbidden by the contemporary English law.

prohibited in future from keeping scriveners or horses in the prison; from borrowing money or accepting gifts from the prisoners; from retaining the money or effects of those who die; from releasing prisoners or allowing them to go beyond the first door, or to eat with him; from employing the servants on any other work or sending them anywhere, or gambling with them, or permitting them to gamble with each other.

With such jailers it is probably rather to their corruption than to any lack of strength in the buildings that we may attribute the occasional escape of the inmates, which appears to have been by no means an infrequent occurrence. Even those who were confined in chains sometimes effected their liberation. More sufficient, however, as a means of release from the horrors of these foul dungeons was the excessive mortality caused by their filthy and unventilated squalor. Occasionally, as we have seen, the unfortunate were unlucky enough to live through protracted confinement, and there is one case in which a woman was graciously discharged, with crosses, in view of her having been for 33 years in the prison of Toulouse. As a rule, however, we may conclude that the expectation of life was very short.

In Bernard Gui's Register of Sentences, comprising his operations between 1308 and 1322, there are 636 condemnations recorded, which may be thus classified:

Delivered to the secular court and burned	40
Bones exhumed and burned	67
Imprisoned	300
Bones exhumed of those who would have been imprisoned	21
Condemned to wear crosses	138
Condemned to perform pilgrimages	16
Banished to Holy Land	1
Fugitives	36
Condemnation of the Talmud	1
Houses to be destroyed	16
	636

This may presumably be taken as a fair measure of the comparative frequency of the several punishments in use.

One peculiarity of the inquisitorial sentence remains to be noted. It always ended with a reservation of power to modify, to mitigate, to increase, and to reimpose at discretion. As early as 1244 the Council of Narbonne instructed the inquisitors always to reserve this power, and it became established as an invariable custom. Even without its formal expression, Innocent IV, in 1245, conferred on the inquisitors, acting with the advice and consent of the bishop of the penitent, authority to modify the penance imposed. The bishop, in fact, usually concurred in these alterations of sentences, but Zanghino informs us that though his assent should be asked, it was not essential, except in the case of clerks. The inquisitor, however, had no power to grant absolute pardons, which was reserved exclusively to the pope.

This power to mitigate sentences was frequently exercised. It served as a stimulus to the penitents to give evidence by their deportment of the sincerity of their conversion, and, perhaps, also, it was occasionally of benefit as a means of depleting overcrowded jails. Thus in Bernard Gui's Register of Sentences there occur 119 cases of release from prison, with the obligation to wear the crosses, and of these 51 were subsequently relieved from the crosses. In 1328, in a single sentence, 23 persons were released from the prison of Carcassonne, their penance being commuted to crosses, pilgrimages, and other observances. What the measure of mercy was in such cases may be guessed from another sentence of commutation at Carcassonne in 1329, liberating 10 penitents, among them the Baroness of Montréal. They were required to wear the yellow crosses for life and to perform 21 pilgrimages, embracing shrines as distant as Rome, Compostella, Canterbury, and Cologne. They were to hear mass every Sunday and feast-day during life, and present themselves with rods to the officiating priest and receive the discipline in the face of the congregation; and also to accompany all processions and be similarly disciplined at the final station. These mitigatory sentences, moreover, like the original ones, strictly reserved the power of alteration and reimposition, with or without cause. Just as no verdict of acquittal ever was issued, so the Council of Béziers, in 1246, and Innocent IV, in 1247, told the inquisitors that when they liberated a prisoner he was to be warned that the slightest cause of suspicion would lead him to be punished without mercy, and that they must retain the right to incarcerate him again without the formality of a fresh trial or sentence if the interest of the faith required. If Bernard Gui in his *Formulary* gives a draft of pardon for person and property and disabilities of heirs, he adds a caution that it is never, or most rarely, to be used. When some great object was to be attained, such as the capture of a prominent heretic teacher, the inquisitors might stretch their authority and hold out promises of this kind to his disciples to induce them to betray him— promises which, it is pleasant to say, were almost universally spurned. If special penances had been imposed, on their fulfillment the inquisitor, if he saw fit, might declare the penitent to be a man of good character, but this did not alter the reservation in the original sentence.

The fate of the dead was harder than that of the living. If he had died after confession and repentance, his punishment was only that which he would have received if alive, the digging up replacing imprisonment, and his heirs being forced to perform or compound for any lighter penance; but if he had not confessed and there was evidence of heresy he was classed with the impenitent heretics, his remains were delivered to the secular arm, and his property hopelessly confiscated. The same spirit pursued the descendants. In the Roman law the crime of treason was pursued with merciless vindictiveness, and its provisions are constantly quoted by the canon lawyers as precedents for the punishment of the heresy. It was natural, therefore, that Frederic II should apply the Roman practice to heresy, and should extend its provision to grandchildren. This, like the rest of his legislation, was eagerly adopted and enforced by the Church. Alexander IV, however, in a bull of 1257, repeatedly reissued by his successors, explained that this did not apply in cases where the culprit had made amends and performed penance, and this was still further lightened by Boniface VIII, who removed the incapacity from grandchildren by the female line of those who had died in heresy. In this form it remained permanently in the canon law.

The Inquisition depended so much upon secular officials for assistance that there was some justification in its seeking to prevent those who might be suspected of sympathizing with heresy from holding office in which they could thwart its plans and aid the offender. Yet as there was no prescription of time for proceedings against the dead, so was there none in invoking disabilities against their descendants. No one could feel sure that evidence might not at any moment be discovered or manufactured against some long-deceased parent or grandparent, which would ruin his career, and that some industrious searcher into the archives might not find some blot on his genealogical tree. In 1288 Phillipe le Bel writes to the Seneschal of Carcassonne that Raymond Vitalis of Avignon is exercising the office of notary in Carcassonne, though his maternal grandfather, Roger Isarn, is said to have been burned for heresy. If this is the fact, the seneschal is ordered to deprive him of the position. In 1292 Guiraud d'Auterive, a sergeant-at-arms of the king, was proceeded against on the same grounds, and we find Guillem de S. Seine, the Inquisitor of Carcassonne, furnishing to the royal procureur evidence that, in 1256, Guiraud's father and mother had confessed to acts of heresy, and that, in 1276, his uncle, Raymond Carbonnel, had been burned as a perfected heretic. In these cases we see the royal power invoked for the dismissal of the official, but in the perfected theory of the Inquisition the inquisitor had the power to deprive of office anyone whose father or grandfather had been a heretic or defender of heretics. In order to avoid questions like these, when a penitent had fulfilled his penance, prudent children would take out letters declaratory of the fact, so as to have evidence of capacity to hold office. In special cases the inquisitor had power to relieve descendants of these disabilities, and this was occasionally done; but, like the remission of penance, this relief was only a suspension, liable at any moment to forfeiture on the slightest manifestation of heretical tendencies.

Underlying all these sentences was another on which they, and, indeed, the whole power of the inquisition, were based in last resort —the sentence of excommunication. Theoretically the censures of the Inquisition might be the same as those of any other ecclesiastics authorized to cut men off from salvation, but the latter had so habitually abused their functions that the anathema in the mouth of priests who were neither feared nor respected lost, at times at least, its awe-inspiring authority. The secular authorities, moreover, were bound to put to the ban and confiscate the property of anyone whom the inquisitor might excommunicate for heresy or fautorship. As the inquisitors were fond of boasting, their curse was stronger in four ways than that of the secular clergy: they could coerce the temporal government to outlaw the excommunicate; they could force it to confiscate his property; they could condemn anyone remaining under excommunication for a year; and they could inflict the major excommunication upon anyone communicating with their excommunicates. Of all excommunications that of the inquisitor worked the speediest vengeance and inspired the sharpest terror, and the boldest shrank from provoking it.

CHAPTER IX
THE SECULAR ARM

1. CONFISCATION

ALTHOUGH, for the most part, confiscation was technically not the work of the Inquisition, the distinction was rather nominal than real. Even when the inquisitor did not pronounce the sentence of confiscation, it was the accompaniment of the sentence that he did pronounce. It was therefore one of the most serious of the penalties at his disposal.

For the source of this, as of so much else, we must look to the Roman law. It is true that, cruel as were the imperial edicts against heresy, they did not go to the length of thus indirectly punishing the innocent. Even when the detested Manichæans were mercilessly condemned to death, their property was confiscated only when their heirs were also heretics. It was otherwise with crime. Any conviction involving deportation or the mines carried with it confiscation, though the wife could reclaim her dower and any gifts made to her before the commission of the offense, and so could children emancipated from the *patria potestas*. In *majestas*, or treason, the offender was liable to condemnation after death, involving the confiscation of his estate, which was held to have lapsed to the fisc at the time when he first conceived the crime. These provisions furnished the armory whence pope and king drew the weapons which rendered the pursuit of heresy attractive and profitable.

King Roger, who occupied the throne of the Two Sicilies during the first half of the twelfth century, seems to have been the first to apply the Roman practice by decreeing confiscation for all who apostatized from the Catholic faith, yet the Church cannot escape the responsibility of naturalizing this penalty in European law. The Council of Tours, held by Alexander III in 1163, commanded all secular princes to imprison heretics and confiscate their property. Lucius III, in his Verona decretal of 1184, sought to obtain for the Church the benefit of the confiscation which he again declared to be incurred by heresy. One of the earliest acts of Innocent III, in his double capacity of temporal prince and head of Christianity, was to address a decretal to his subjects of Viterbo, in which he says:

In the lands subject to our temporal jurisdiction we order the property of heretics to be confiscated; in other lands we command this to be done by the temporal princes and powers, who, if they show themselves negligent therein, shall be compelled to do it by ecclesiastical censures. Nor shall the property of heretics who withdraw from heresy revert to them, unless some one pleases to take pity on them. For as, according to the legal sanctions, in addition to capital punishment, the property of those guilty of *majestas* is confiscated, and life simply is allowed to their children through mercy alone, so much the more should those who wander from the faith and offend the Son of God be cut off from Christ and be despoiled of their temporal goods, since it is a far greater crime to assail spiritual than temporal majesty.[1]

This decretal, which was adopted into the canon law, embodies the whole theory of the subject. In imitation of the Roman law of *majestas*, the property of the heretic was forfeited from the moment he became a heretic or committed an act of heresy. When the ecclesiastical tribunals declared him to be, or to have been, a heretic, confiscation operated itself; the act of seizing the property was a matter for the secular power to whom it inured, and the mercy which might spare it could only be shown by that power.

The relation of the Inquisition to confiscation varied essentially with time and place. In France the principle was generally recognized that the title to property devolved to the fisc as soon as the crime had been committed. Gui Foucoix treats the subject as one

[1] Confiscation was an ordinary resource of mediæval law. In England, from the time of Alfred, property as well as life was forfeited for treason (Alfred's Dooms 4), a penalty which remained until 1870. In France murder, false-witness, treachery, homicide, and rape were all punished with death and confiscation. By the German feudal law the fief might be forfeited for a vast number of offenses, but the distinction was drawn that, if the offense was against the lord, the fief reverted to him; if simply a crime, it descended to the heirs. In Navarre, confiscation formed part of the penalties of suicide, murder, treason, and even of blows or wounds inflicted where the queen or royal children were dwelling. There is a case in which confiscation was enforced on a man because he struck another at Olite, which was within a league of Tafalla, where the queen chanced to be staying at the time.

wholly outside the functions of the inquisitor, who at most can only advise the secular ruler or intercede for mercy; while he holds that those only are legally exempt from forfeiture who come forward spontaneously and confess before any evidence has been taken against them. In accordance with this, there is, as a rule, no allusion to confiscation in the sentences of the French Inquisition, though in one or two instances chance has preserved for us, in the accounts of the *procureurs des encours*, or royal stewards of the confiscations, evidence that estates were sold and covered into the fisc in cases in which the forfeiture is not specified in the sentence. In condemnations of absentees and of the dead, confiscation is occasionally declared, as though in these the State might need some guidance, but even here the practice is not uniform. In the Register of Bernard de Caux (1246–1248), in 32 cases of contumacious absentees confiscation is included in the sentence, and in 9 similar ones it is omitted, as well as in 159 condemnations to prison in which it was undoubtedly operative. Strictly speaking, it was recognized that the inquisitor had no power to remit confiscations without permission from the fisc, and the custom of extending mercy to those who came forward voluntarily and confessed was founded upon a special concession to that effect granted by Raymond of Toulouse to the Inquisition in 1235. As soon as a suspected heretic was cited or arrested the secular officials sequestrated his property and notified his debtors by proclamation. In 1328, in a record of an assembly of experts held at Pamiers, the presence is specified of Arnaud Assalit, royal *procureur des encours* of Carcassonne, so that probably by this time it had become customary for that official to attend these deliberations and thus obtain early notice of the sentences to be passed.

It Italy it was long before any settled practice was established. In 1252 a bull of Innocent IV directs the rulers of Lombardy, Tarvisina, and Romagna to confiscate without fail the property of all who were excommunicated as heretics, or as receivers, defenders, or fautors of heretics, thus recognizing confiscation as a matter belonging to the secular power. Yet soon the papal authority succeeded in obtaining a share of the spoils, even beyond the limits of the States of the Church, as is seen in the bulls *Ad extirpanda* of Innocent IV and Alexander IV, and the matter thus became one in which the Inquisition had a direct interest. Zanghino tells us that formerly confiscations were decreed in the States of the Church by the ecclesiastical judges and elsewhere by the secular power, but that in his time (circa 1320) they were everywhere (in Italy) included in the jurisdiction of the episcopal and inquisitorial courts, and the secular authorities had nothing to do with them; but he adds that confiscation is prescribed by law for heresy, and that the inquisitor has no discretion to remit it, except in the case of voluntary converts with the assent of the bishop. Yet though the forfeiture occurs *ipso facto* by the commission of the crime, it requires a declaratory sentence of confiscation. This consequently was expressed in the most formal manner in the condemnation of the accused by the Italian Inquisition, and the secular authorities were told not to interfere unless called upon.

At a very early period in some places the Italian inquisitors seem to have undertaken not only to decree but to control the confiscations. About 1245 we find the Florentine Inquisitor Ruggieri Calcagni sentencing a Catharan named Diotaiuti for relapse, with a fine of 100 lire. Ruggieri acknowledges the receipt of this, to be applied to the pope or to the furtherance of the faith, and formally concedes the rest of the heretic's estate to his wife Jacoba, thus exercising ownership over the whole. Yet this was not maintained, for in 1283 there is a sentence of the Podestà of Florence, reciting that the Inquisitor Frà Salomone da Lucca had notified him that the widow Ruvinosa, lately deceased, had died a heretic, and that her property was to be confiscated; whereupon he orders it to be seized and sold, and the proceeds divided according to the papal constitutions. At length, however, the inquisitors assumed and exercised full control over the handling of the confiscations. In the conveyance of a confiscated house by the municipal authorities of Florence, in 1327, to the Dominicans, the deed is careful to assert that it is made with the assent of the inquisitor.

In Germany the Diet of Worms in 1231 indicates the confusion existing in the feudal mind between heresy and treason by allowing the allodial lands and personal property of the condemned to descend to the heirs, while fiefs were confiscated to the suzerain. If he was a serf, his goods inured to his master; but from all personal property was deducted the cost of burning its owner and the *droits de justice* of the seigneur-justicier. Two years later the Council of

Mainz protested against the injustice, which quickly showed itself in Germany as elsewhere, of assuming guilt as soon as a man was accused, and treating his property as though he were convicted. It directed that the estates of those on trial should remain untouched until sentence was rendered, and anyone who should plunder or partition them should be excommunicated until he made restitution. Finally, however, when the Emperor Charles IV endeavored to introduce the Inquisition into Germany in 1369, he adopted the Italian custom and ordered one-third of the confiscations to be made over to the inquisitors.

The exact degree of criminality which entailed confiscation is not capable of very rigid definition. We have seen that Innocent III commanded it for all heretics, but what constituted technical heresy was not so easily determined. The Council of Béziers, in 1233, demanded it for all reconciled converts not condemned to wear crosses, and those of Béziers in 1246, and Albi in 1254, prescribed it for all whom the inquisitors should penance with imprisonment. Still, in a sentence of February 19, 1237, in which the Inquisitors of Toulouse condemn some 20 or 30 penitents to perpetual imprisonment, confiscation is only threatened as an additional punishment in case they do not perform the penance. Imprisonment finally was admitted by legists as the invariable test; although St. Louis, when in 1259 he mitigated his *Ordonnance* of 1229, ordered confiscation not only for those who were condemned to prison, but for those who contumaciously refused obedience to citations and those in whose houses heretics were found, his officials being instructed to ascertain from the inquisitors in all cases, while pending, whether the accused deserved imprisonment, and if so, retain the sequestrated property. When he further provided, as a special grace, that the heirs should be restored to possession in cases where the heretic had offered himself for conversion before citation, had entered a religious order, and had worthily died there, he shows how universal confiscation had previously been and how ruthlessly the principle had been enforced that a single act of heresy forfeited all ownership.

According to the most lenient construction of the law, therefore, the imprisonment of a reconciled convert carried with it the confiscation of his property, and as imprisonment was the ordinary penance, confiscation was general. In the early zeal of persecution everything was swept away in wholesale seizure, but in 1237 Gregory IX assumed that the dowers of Catholic wives ought to be exempt in certain cases, and in 1247 Innocent IV erected it into a rule that such dowers should be restored to the wives and should not be included in future forfeitures, although heresy would not justify divorce, and in 1258 St. Louis accepted this rule. It was subject to serious limitations, however, since under the canon law the wife could not claim it if she had been cognizant of the husband's heresy when she married, and, according to some authorities, if she had lived with him after ascertaining it, or even if she had failed to inform against him within forty days after discovering it. As the children were incapable of inheritance, she only held the dower for life, after which it fell into the fisc.

Although in principle confiscation was an affair of the State, the division of the spoils did not follow any invariable rule. Before the organization of the Inquisition, when the Waldenses of Strassburg were burned, it is mentioned that their forfeited property was equally divided between the Church and the secular authorities, but Lucius III endeavored to turn all forfeitures to the benefit of the Church. In the papal territory there could be little question as to this, and Innocent IV, in his bull *Ad extirpanda*, showed disinterestedness in devoting the whole proceeds to the stimulation of persecution. One-third was given to the local authorities, one-third to the officials of the Inquisition, and one-third to the bishop and inquisitor, to be expended in the assault on heresy—provisions which were retained in the recensions of the bull by Alexander IV and Clement IV, while forfeited bail went exclusively to the inquisitor. Yet this was held to refer only to the independent states of Italy, for in 1260 we find Alexander IV ordering the Inquisitors of Rome and Spoleto to sell the confiscated estates of heretics and pay over the proceeds to the pope himself; and a transaction of 1261 shows Urban IV collecting 320 lire from some confiscations at Spoleto. At length, both in the Roman province and elsewhere throughout Italy, the custom settled down to a tripartite division between the local community, the Inquisition, and the papal camera, the reason for the latter, as given by Benedict XI, being that the bishops appropriated to themselves the share entrusted to them for the persecution of heresy.

Nothing could exceed the minute thoroughness with which every fragment of a confiscated estate was followed up and seized. The account of the collections of confiscated property from 1302 to 1313 by the *procureurs des encours* of Carcassonne is extant in MS., and shows how carefully the debts due to the condemned were looked after, even to a few pence for a measure of corn. As the collectors never credit themselves with amounts paid in discharge of debts due by these estates, it is evident that the rule that a heretic could give no valid obligations was strictly construed and that creditors were shamelessly cheated.

The cruelty of the process of confiscation was enhanced by the pitiless methods employed. As soon as a man was arrested for suspicion of heresy his property was sequestrated and seized by the officials, to be returned to him in the rare cases in which his guilt might be declared not proven. This rule was enforced in the most rigorous manner, every article of his household gear and provisions being inventoried, as well as his real estate. Whether innocent or guilty, his family was turned out-of-doors to starve or to depend upon the precarious charity of others—a charity chilled by the fact that any manifestation of sympathy was dangerous. In addition to the misery inflicted by these wholesale confiscations on the thousands of innocent and helpless women and children thus stripped of everything, it would be almost impossible to exaggerate the evil which they entailed upon all classes in the business of daily life. All safeguards were withdrawn from every transaction. No creditor or purchaser could be sure of the orthodoxy of him with whom he was dealing; and, even more than the principle that ownership was forfeited as soon as heresy had been committed by the living, the practice of proceeding against the memory of the dead after an interval virtually unlimited, rendered it impossible for any man to feel secure in the possession of property, whether it had descended in his family for generations, or had been acquired within an ordinary lifetime.

Prosecution of the dead, as we have seen, was a mockery in which virtually defense was impossible and confiscation inevitable. How unexpectedly the blow might fall is seen in the case of Gherardo of Florence. He was rich and powerful, a member of one of the noblest

and oldest houses, and was consul of the city in 1218. Secretly a
heretic, he was hereticated on his deathbed between 1246 and 1250,
but the matter lay dormant until 1313, when Frà Grimaldo, the Inquisitor of Florence, brought a successful prosecution against his
memory. In the condemnation were included his children Ugolino,
Cante, Nerlo, and Bertuccio, and his grandchildren, Goccia, Coppo,
Frà Giovanni, Gherardo prior of S. Quirico, Goccino, Baldino, and
Marco—not that they were heretics, but that they were disinherited
and subjected to the disabilities of descendants of heretics.

Not only were all alienations made by heretics set aside and the
property wrested from the purchasers, but all debts contracted by
them, and all hypothecations and liens given to secure loans, were
void. Thus doubt was cast upon every obligation that a man could
enter into. Even when St. Louis softened the rigor of confiscation
in Languedoc, the utmost concession he would make was that
creditors should be paid for debts contracted by culprits before they
became heretics, while all claims arising subsequently to an act of
heresy were rejected. As no man could be certain of the orthodoxy
of another, it will be evident how much distrust must have been
thrown upon even the commonest transactions of life. The blighting
influence of this upon the development of commerce and industry
can readily be perceived, coming as it did at a time when the commercial and industrial movement of Europe was beginning to usher
in the dawn of modern culture. It was this, among other incidents of
persecution, which arrested the promising civilization of the south
of France and transferred to England and the Netherlands, where
the Inquisition was comparatively unknown, the predominance in
commerce and industry which brought freedom and wealth and
power and progress in its train.

Persecution, as a steady and continuous policy, rested, after all,
upon confiscation. It was this which supplied the fuel to keep up
the fires of zeal, and when it was lacking the business of defending
the faith languished lamentably. When Catharism disappeared under the brilliant aggressiveness of Bernard Gui, the culminating point
of the Inquisition was passed, and thenceforth it steadily declined,
although still there were occasional confiscated estates over which
king, prelate, and noble quarrelled for some years to come. The
Spirituals, Dulcinists, and Fraticelli were Mendicants, who held prop-

erty to be an abomination; the Waldenses were poor folk; the only prizes were an occasional sorcerer or usurer. Still, as late as 1337 the office of bailli of the confiscations for heresy in Toulouse was sufficiently lucrative to be worth purchasing under the prevailing custom of selling all such positions, and the collections for the preceding fiscal year amounted to 640 livres 6 sols.

The intimate connection between the activity of persecuting zeal and the material results to be derived from it is well illustrated in the failure of the first attempt to extend the Inquisition into Franche Comté. John, Count of Burgundy, in 1248 represented to Innocent IV the alarming spread of Waldensianism throughout the province of Besançon and begged for its repression. Apparently the zeal of Count John did not lead him to pay for the purgation of his dominions, and the plunder to be gained was inconsiderable, for in 1255 Alexander IV granted the petition of the friars to be relieved from the duty, in which they averred that they had exhausted themselves fruitlessly for lack of money.

In 1375 Gregory XI persuaded King Frederic of Sicily to allow the confiscations to inure to the benefit of the Inquisition, so that funds might not be lacking for the prosecution of the good work. At the same time he made a vigorous effort to exterminate the Waldenses who were multiplying in Dauphiné. There were prisons to be built and crowds of prisoners to be supported, and he directed that the expenses should be defrayed by the prelates whose negligence had given opportunity for the growth of heresy. Although he ordered this to be enforced by excommunication, it would seem that the constipated purses of the bishops could not be relaxed, for soon after we find the inquisitor laying claim to a share in the confiscations, on the reasonable ground of his having no other source whence to defray the necessary expenses of his tribunal. The royal officials insisted on keeping the whole, and a lively contest arose, which was referred to King Charles le Sage. The monarch dutifully conferred with the Holy See and, in 1378, issued an *Ordonnance* retaining the whole of the confiscations and assigning to the inquisitor a yearly stipend—the same as that paid to the tribunals of Toulouse and Carcassonne—of 190 livres Tournois, out of which all the expenses of the Inquisition were to be met; with a proviso that if the allowance was not regularly paid then the inquisitor should be at liberty to de-

tain a portion of the forfeitures. No doubt this agreement was observed for a time, but it lapsed in the terrible disorders which ensued
on the insanity of Charles VI. In 1409 Alexander V left to his legate
to decide whether the Inquisitor of Dauphiné should receive 300
gold florins a year, to be levied on the Jews of Avignon, or 10 florins
a year from each of the bishops of his extensive district, or whether
the bishops should be compelled to support him and his officials in
his journeys through the country. These precarious resources disappeared in the confusion of the civil wars and invasion which so
nearly wrecked the monarchy. In 1432, when Frère Pierre Fabri,
Inquisitor of Embrun, was summoned to attend the Council of
Basle, he excused himself on account of his preoccupation with the
stubborn Waldenses and also on the ground of his indescribable
poverty, "for never have I had a penny from the Church of God, nor
have I a stipend from any other source."

2. THE STAKE

Like confiscation, the death penalty was a matter with which the
Inquisition had theoretically no concern. In the earlier periods the
sentence is simply a condemnation as a heretic, accompanied by excommunication, or it merely states that the offender is no longer
considered as subject to the jurisdiction of the Church. Sometimes
there is the addition that he is abandoned to secular judgment—
"relaxed," according to the terrible euphemism which assumed that
he was simply discharged from custody. When the formulas had
become more perfected there is frequently the explanatory remark
that the Church has nothing left to do to him for his demerits; and
the relinquishment to the secular arm is accompanied with the
addition *"debita animadversione puniendum"*—that he is to be duly
punished by it. The adjuration that this punishment, in accordance
with the canonical sanctions, shall not imperil life or limb, or shall
not cause death or effusion of blood, does not appear in the earlier
sentences, and was not universal even at a later period.

That this appeal for mercy was the merest form is admitted by
Pegna, who explains that it was used only that the inquisitors might
seem not to consent to the effusion of blood, and thus avoid incur-

ring "irregularity." The Church took good care that the nature of the request should not be misapprehended. It taught that in such cases all mercy was misplaced unless the heretic became a convert and proved his sincerity by denouncing all his fellows. The remorseless logic of St. Thomas Aquinas rendered it self-evident that the secular power could not escape the duty of putting the heretic to death, and that it was only the kindness of the Church that led it to give the criminal two warnings before handing him over to meet his fate. The inquisitors themselves had no scruples on the subject and condescended to no subterfuges respecting it, but always held that their condemnation of a heretic was a sentence of death. They showed this in averting the pollution of a church by not uttering these sentences within the sacred precincts, this portion of the ceremony of an *auto de fé* being performed in the public square. One of their teachers in the thirteenth century, copied by Bernard Gui in the fourteenth, argues: "The object of the Inquisition is the destruction of heresy. Heresy cannot be destroyed unless heretics are destroyed: heretics cannot be destroyed unless their defenders and fautors are destroyed, and this is effected in two ways, viz., when they are converted to the true Catholic faith, or when, on being abandoned to the secular arm, they are corporally burned."

In a commission issued by Philippe le Bon of Burgundy, November 9, 1431, ordering his officials to render obedience to Friar Kaleyser, recently appointed Inquisitor of Lille and Cambrai, among the duties enumerated is that of inflicting due punishment on heretics "as he shall decree, and as is customary." In the accounts of the royal *procureurs des encours*, the costs of these executions in Languedoc were charged against the proceeds of the confiscations as part of the expenses of the Inquisition, thus showing that they were not regarded as ordinary incidents of criminal justice, to be defrayed out of the ordinary revenues, but as peculiarly connected with and dependent upon the operations of the Inquisition, of which the royal officials only acted as ministers. How modern is the pretension that the Church was not responsible for the atrocity is apparent when, as late as the seventeenth century, the learned Cardinal Albizio, in controverting Frà Paolo as to the control of the Inquisition by the State in Venice, had no scruple in asserting that "the inquisitors in conducting the trials, regularly came to the sentence, and if it

was one of death it was immediately and necessarily put into execution by the doge and the senate." Boniface VIII only recorded the
current practice when he embodied in the canon law the provision
whereby the secular authorities were commanded to punish duly
and promptly all who were handed over to them by the inquisitors,
and the inquisitors were rigidly instructed to proceed against all
magistrates who proved recalcitrant, while they were at the same time
cautioned only to speak of executing the laws without specifically
mentioning the penalty, in order to avoid falling into "irregularity,"
though the only punishment recognized by the Church as sufficient
for heresy was burning alive.

We are not to imagine, however, from these reduplicated commands that the secular power, as a rule, showed itself in the slightest
degree disinclined to perform the duty. Raymond VII of Toulouse
himself, in the fit of piety which preceded his death in 1249, caused
80 believers in heresy to be burned at Berlaiges, near Agen, after they
had confessed in his presence, apparently without giving them the
opportunity of recanting. From the contemporary sentences of Bernard de Caux, it is probable that, had these unfortunates been tried
before that ardent champion of the faith, not one of them would
have been condemned to the stake. Quite as significant was the suit
brought by the Maréchal de Mirepoix against the Seneschal of Carcassonne, because the latter had invaded his right to burn for himself all his subjects condemned as heretics by the Inquisition. In
1269 the Parlement of Paris decided the case in his favor, after which,
on March 18, 1270, the seneschal acceded to his demand that the
bones of seven men and three women of his territories, recently
burned at Carcassonne, should be solemnly surrendered to him in
recognition of his right; or, if they could not be found and identified,
then, as substitutes, ten canvas bags filled with straw—a ghastly
symbolic ceremony which was actually performed two days later,
and a formal notarial act executed in attestation of it.

If, however, from any cause, the secular authorities were reluctant
to execute the death sentence, the Church had little ceremony in
putting forth its powers to coerce obedience. When, for instance,
the first resistance in Toulouse had been broken down and the Holy
Office had been reinstated there, the inquisitors in 1237 condemned
six men and women as heretics; but the *viguier* and consuls refused

to receive the convicts, to confiscate their property, and "to do with them what was customary to be done with heretics"—that is, to burn them alive. Thereupon the inquisitors, after counselling with the bishop, the Abbot du Mas, the Provost of St. Étienne, and the Prior of La Daurade, proceeded to excommunicate solemnly the recalcitrant officials in the Cathedral of St. Étienne.

In view of this unvarying policy of the Church during the three centuries under consideration, and for a century and a half later, there is a typical instance of the manner in which history is written to order, in the quiet assertion of a modern Catholic historian of the Inquisition:

The Church took no part in the corporal punishment of heretics. Those who perished miserably were only chastised for their crimes, sentenced by judges invested with the royal jurisdiction. The record of the excesses committed by the heretics of Bulgaria, by the Gnostics and Manichæans, is historical, and capital punishment was only inflicted on criminals confessing to robbery, assassination, and violence. The Albigenses were treated with equal benignity; . . . the Catholic Church deplored all acts of vengeance, however great was the provocation given by the ferocity of those factious masses.[2]

So completely, in truth, was the Church convinced of its duty to see that all heretics were burned that, at the Council of Constance, the eighteenth article of heresy charged against John Huss was that, in his treatise de Ecclesia, he had taught that no heretic ought to be abandoned to secular judgment to be punished with death. In his defense even Huss admitted that a heretic who could not be mildly led from error ought to suffer bodily punishment; and when a passage was read from his book in which those who deliver an unconvicted heretic to the secular arm are compared to the Scribes and Pharisees who delivered Christ to Pilate, the assembly broke out into a storm of objurgation, during which even the sturdy reformer, Cardinal Pierre d'Ailly, was heard to exclaim, "Verily those who drew up the articles [against Huss] were most moderate, for his writings are much more atrocious."

The obstinate heretic who preferred martyrdom to apostasy was

[2] Rodrigo, *Historia Verdadera de la Inquisition*, Madrid, 1876, I. 176-77.

by no means the sole victim doomed to the stake. The secular law-giver had provided this punishment for heresy, but had left to the Church its definition, and the definition was enlarged to serve as a gentle persuasive that should supplement all deficiencies in the inquisitorial process. Where testimony deemed sufficient existed, persistent denial only aggravated guilt, and the profession of orthodoxy was of no avail. If two witnesses swore to having seen a man "adore" a perfected heretic it was enough, and no declaration of readiness to subscribe to all the tenets of Rome availed him, without confession, abjuration, recantation, and acceptance of penance. Such a one was a heretic, to be pitilessly burned. It was the same with the contumacious who did not obey the summons to stand trial. Persistent refusal of the oath was likewise technical heresy, condemning the recalcitrant to the stake. Even when there was no proof, in violent suspicion, refusal to abjure worked the same result in a twelvemonth. A retracted confession was similarly regarded. In short, the stake supplied all defects. It was the *ultima ratio*, and although not many cases have reached us in which executions actually occurred on these grounds, there is no doubt that such provisions were of the utmost utility in practice, and that the terror which they inspired extorted many a confession, true or false, from unwilling lips.

As early as 1184 the Verona decree of Lucius III provides that those who, after abjuration, relapse into the abjured heresy shall be delivered to the secular courts, without even the opportunity of being heard. The Ravenna edict of Frederic II, in 1232, prescribed death for all who, by relapse, showed that their conversion had been a pretext to escape the penalty of heresy. In 1244 the Council of Narbonne alludes to the great multitude of such cases, and, following Lucius III, orders them to be relaxed without a hearing. Yet these stern mandates were not enforced. In 1233 we find Gregory IX contenting himself with prescribing perpetual imprisonment for such cases, which he speaks of as being already numerous. In a single sentence of February 19, 1237, the Inquisitors of Toulouse condemn 17 relapsed heretics to perpetual imprisonment. Raymond de Pennaforte, at the Council of Tarragona, in 1242, alludes to the diversity of opinion on the subject, and pronounces in favor of imprisonment; and, in 1246, the Council of Béziers, in giving similar instructions, speaks of them as being in accordance with the apostolic mandates.

Even this degree of severity was not always inflicted. In 1242 Pierre Cella prescribes only pilgrimages and crosses for such offenders, and, in a case occurring in Florence in 1245, Frá Ruggieri Calcagni lets off the culprit with a not extravagant fine.

What to do with these multitudes of false converts was evidently a question which perplexed the Church no little, and, as usual, a solution, at least for the time, was found in leaving the matter to the discretion of the inquisitors. In answer to the inquiries of the Lombard Holy Office, the Cardinal of Albano, about 1245, tells the officials to make use of such penalties as they shall deem appropriate. In 1248 Bernard de Caux asked the same question of the Archbishop of Narbonne, and was told that, according to the "apostolic mandates," those who returned to the Church a second time, humbly and obediently, might be let off with perpetual imprisonment, while those who were disobedient should be abandoned to the secular arm. Under these instructions the practice varied, though it is pleasant to be able to say that, in the vast majority of cases, the inquisitors leaned to the side of mercy. Even the ardent zeal of Bernard de Caux allowed him to use his discretion gently. In his Register of Sentences, from 1246 to 1248, there are 60 cases of relapse, none of which is punished more severely than by imprisonment, and in some of them the confinement is not perpetual. The same lenity is observable in various sentences rendered during the next ten years, both by him and by other inquisitors. Yet, with one exception, the codes of instruction which date about this period assume that relapse is always to be visited with relaxation, and that the offender is to have no hearing in his defense. In the exceptional instance the compiler illustrates the uncertainty which existed by sometimes treating relapse as punishable with imprisonment and sometimes as entailing the stake. In Languedoc, under the Treaty of Paris, an oath of abjuration was administered every two years to all males over 14 and all females over 12, and any subsequent act of heresy was technically a relapse. This, perhaps, explains the indecision of the Inquisitors of Toulouse. It was impossible to burn all such cases.

Whatever be the cause, there evidently was considerable doubt in the minds of inquisitors about the penalty of relapse, and it must be recorded to their credit that in this they were more merciful than the current public opinion of the age. Jean de Saint-Pierre, the col-

league of Bernard de Caux, followed his example in always condemning the relapsed to imprisonment, and when, after Bernard's
death, in 1252, Frère Renaud de Chartres was adjoined to him, the
same rule continued to be observed. Frère Renaud found, however,
to his horror, that the secular judges disregarded the sentence and
mercilessly burned the unhappy victims, and that this had been going
on under his predecessors. The civil authorities defended their course
by arguing that in no other way could the land be purged of heresy,
which was acquiring new force under the mistaken lenity of the inquisitors. Frère Renaud felt that he could not overlook this cruelty in
silence as his predecessors had done. He therefore reported the facts to
Alphonse of Poitiers, and informed him that he proposed to refer
the matter to the pope, pending whose answer he would keep his
prisoners secure from the brutal violence of the secular officials.

What was the papal response we can only conjecture, but it
doubtless leaned rather to the rigorous zeal of Alphonse's officials
than to the milder methods of Frère Renaud, for it was about this
time that Rome definitely decided for the unconditional relaxation
of all who were guilty of relapsing into heresy which had once been
abjured. The precise date of this I have not been able to determine.
In 1254 Innocent IV contents himself, in a very aggravated case of
double relapse occurring in Milan, with ordering destruction of houses
and public penance, but in 1258 relaxation for relapse is alluded to
by Alexander IV as a matter previously irrevocably settled—possibly
by the very appeal of Frère Renaud. It seems to have taken the inquisitors somewhat by surprise, and for several years they continued
to trouble the Holy See with the question how such a rule was to be
reconciled with the universally received maxim that the Church
never closes her bosom to her wayward children seeking to return.
To this the explanation was given that the Church was not closed to
them, for if they showed signs of penitence they might receive the
Eucharist, even at the stake, but without escaping death. In this
shape the decision was embodied in the canon law, and made a part
of orthodox doctrine in the *Summa* of St. Thomas Aquinas. The
promise of the Eucharist frequently formed part of the sentence, and
the victim was always accompanied to execution by holy men striving
to save his soul until the last—though it is shrewdly advised that the
inquisitor himself had better not exhibit his zeal in this way, as his

appearance will be more likely to excite hardening than softening of the heart.

Although inquisitors continued to assume discretion in these cases and did not by any means invariably send the relapsed to the stake, still relapse became the main cause of capital punishment. This gave a fresh importance to the question of what legally constituted relapse, and led to endless definitions and subtleties. It became necessary to determine with some precision, when the offender was refused a hearing, the exact amount of criminality in both the first and second offenses which would justify condemnation for impenitent heresy. There were cases in which a first trial had only developed suspicion without proof, and it seemed hard to condemn a man to death for an assumed second offense when he had not been proved guilty of the first. Hesitating to do so, the inquisitors applied to Alexander IV to resolve their doubts and he answered in the most positive manner. When the suspicion had been "violent" he said, it was "by a sort of legal fiction" to be held as legal proof of guilt, and the accused was to be condemned. When it was "light" he was to be punished more heavily than for a first offense, but not with the full penalty of relapse. This decision was repeated by Alexander and his successors with a frequency which shows how puzzling were the points which came up for discussion, but the rule of condemnation was finally carried into the canon law and became the unalterable policy of the Church. The authorities, except Zanghino, agree that in such cases there was no room for mercy.

Besides these enigmas there were others respecting forms of guilt which might reasonably be regarded as less deserving of the last resort. Thus relapse into fautorship gave rise to considerable divergence of views. The Council of Narbonne, in 1244, was of opinion that those guilty of this offense should be sent to the pope for absolution and the imposition of penance—a cumbrous procedure, not likely to find favor. During the middle period of the Inquisition, the authorities, including Bernard Gui, while not prescribing relaxation to the secular arm, suggest that penance be sufficiently severe to inspire wholesome fear in others; while, towards the end of the fourteenth century, Eymerich holds that a relapsed fautor is to be abandoned to secular justice without a hearing. Even those defamed for heresy, if after due purgation they again incur defamation, are strictly liable to the same fate, though this was so hard a measure that Eymerich proposes that such cases should be referred to the pope.

There was another class of offenders who gave the inquisitors endless trouble, and for whom it was difficult to frame rigid and invariable rules—those who escaped from prison or omitted to fulfill the penances assigned to them. According to theory, all penitents were converts to the true faith who acceped penance as their hope of salvation. To reject it subsequently was therefore an evidence that the conversion had been feigned. From the beginning, therefore, these culprits were classed with the relapsed. In 1248 the Council of Valence ordered them to have the benefit of a warning, after which further persistence in disobedience rendered them liable to the full penalty of obstinate heresy; and this was sometimes provided for in the sentence itself, by a clause which warned them that any disregard of the observances enjoined would expose them to the fate of perjured and impenitent heretics. Yet as late as 1260 Alexander IV seems at a loss what rule to prescribe in such cases, and merely talks vaguely of excommunication and reimposition of the penalties, with the assistance, if necessary, of the secular authorities. About the same period Gui Foucoix pronounced in favor of the death penalty for these offenders, but Bernard Gui held this to be too severe, and advised leaving them to the discretion of the inquisitor—a discretion which he himself had no hesitation in exercising. The two most frequent varieties of the offense were laying aside the yellow crosses and prison-breaking. The former was never, so far as I have seen, punished with death, though visited with penalties sufficiently sharp to serve as a deterrent. The latter, according to the later inquisitors, was capital—the escaped prisoner was a relapsed heretic, to be burned without a hearing. Some jurists argued that a failure fully to betray all heretics of whom the convert had knowledge—a pledge to do so forming a necessary part of the oath of abjuration—constituted relapse, but Bernard Gui regards this as unduly harsh. Absolute refusal to perform the penance enjoined was, of course, evidence of obstinate heresy, leading inevitably to the stake. Such cases were naturally rare, for penance was only prescribed for those who had confessed and had asked for reconciliation; but there is one on record of a woman, in the latter half of the fifteenth century, before the

Inquisition of Cartagena, who was duly abandoned to the secular arm.

Notwithstanding these extensions of the death penalty, I am convinced that the numbers of victims who actually perished at the stake is considerably less than has ordinarily been imagined. Frequent as recourse to the stake undoubtedly was, it formed but a comparatively small part of the instrumentalities of repression. The records of those evil days have mostly disappeared, and there is now no possibility of reconstructing their statistics, but if this could be done I have no doubt that the actual executions by fire would excite surprise by falling far short of the popular estimate. No one can suspect the learned Dom Brial of prejudice or of ordinary lack of accuracy, and yet in his Preface to Volume XXI of the *Recueil des Historiens des Gaules* he quotes as trustworthy an assertion that Bernard Gui, during his service as Inquisitor of Toulouse from 1308 to 1323, put to death no less than 637 heretics. Now that, as we have seen,[3] was the total number of sentences uttered by the tribunal during those years, and of these sentences only 40 were capital—in addition to 67 dead heretics condemned to be exhumed and burned, for the most part because they were not alive to recant. Again, no inquisitor left behind him a more enviable record for zeal and activity in the relentless persecution of heresy than Bernard de Caux, who labored in the earlier period when the land was yet full of heresy, and heretics had not yet been cowed into submissiveness. Bernard Gui characterizes him as "a persecutor and hammer of heretics, a holy man and full of God, . . . wonderful in his life, wonderful in doctrine, wonderful in extirpating heresy." Such a man is not to be accused of undue tenderness towards heretics, and yet, in his Register of Sentences from 1246 to 1248, there is not a single case of abandonment to the secular arm, unless we may reckon as such the condemnations of contumacious absentees, who were necessarily declared to be heretics. These, indeed, were liable to be burned by the secular justice, but in fact they could always save themselves by submission, and this very register affords a very striking instance in point. There was no more obnoxious heretic in Toulouse than Alaman de Roaix. He belonged to one of the noblest families in the city, and one which furnished many members to the heretic church,

[3] See page 236.

of which he himself was suspected of being a bishop. In 1229 the Legate Romano had condemned him and had imposed on him the penance of a crusade to the Holy Land, which he had sworn to perform and never fulfilled. In 1237 the earliest inquisitors, Guillem Arnaud and Étienne de Saint-Thibéry, again took up his case, finding him unremittingly active in protecting heretics and disseminating heresy, spoiling, ransoming, wounding, and slaying priests and clerks, and this time they condemned him *in absentia*. He became a *faidit*, or proscribed man, living sword in hand and plundering the orthodox to support himself and his friends. No more aggravated case of obstinate heresy and persistent contumacy can well be imagined, and yet when he acknowledged his errors, January 16, 1248, professed conversion, and asked for penance, a score of years after his first conversion, he was only condemned to imprisonment.

In fact, as we have already seen, the endeavors of the inquisitors were directed much more to obtaining conversions with confiscations and betrayal of friends than to provoking martyrdoms. An occasional burning only was required to maintain a wholesome terror in the minds of the population. With his 40 cases of concremation in 15 years, Bernard Gui managed to crush the last convulsive struggle of Catharism, to keep the Waldenses in check, and repress the zealous ardor of the Spiritual Franciscans. The really effective weapons of the Holy Office, the real curses with which it afflicted the people, can be looked for in its dungeons and confiscations, in the humiliating penances of the saffron crosses, and in the invisible police with which it benumbed the heart and soul of every man who had once fallen into its hands.[4]

A few words will suffice as to the repulsive subject of the execution itself. When the populace was called together to view the last agonies of the martyrs of heresy, its pious zeal was not mocked by any ill-advised devices of mercy. The culprit was tied living to a post set high enough over a pile of combustibles to enable the faith-

---

[4] These conclusions are almost invariably quoted by writers on the Inquisition. Perhaps Mr. Lea was thinking only of the orderly Inquisition as first organized in Languedoc. As we shall see in the following chapters, all inquisitors had not the restraint of Bernard Gui and Bernard de Caux. In Picenza "28 wagonloads" of heretics were burned; at Sermione Frà Filippo burned 70; 36 Waldenses were burned in Bingen in 1392 and 100 at Steyer in 1297. "Paramo boasts" that in a century and a half the Holy Office burned 30,000 witches; and so on. [Ed.]

ful to watch every act of the tragedy to its awful end. Holy men accompanied him to the last, to snatch his soul if possible from Satan; and, if he were not a relapsed, he could, as we have seen, save also his body at the last moment. Yet even in these final ministrations we see a fresh illustration of the curious inconsistency with which the Church imagined that it could shirk the responsibility of putting a human creature to death, for the friars who accompanied the victim were strictly warned not to exhort him to meet death promptly or to ascend firmly the ladder leading to the stake, or to submit cheerfully to the manipulations of the executioner, for if they did so they would be hastening his end and thus fall into "irregularity"—a tender scruple, it must be confessed, and one singularly out of place in those who had accomplished the judicial murder.

As for minor details, we happen to have them preserved in an account by an eyewitness of the execution of John Huss at Constance, in 1415. He was made to stand upon a couple of fagots and tightly bound to a thick post with ropes, around the ankles, below the knee, above the knee, at the groin, the waist, and under the arms. A chain was also secured around the neck. Then it was observed that he faced the east, which was not fitting for a heretic, and he was shifted to the west; fagots mixed with straw were piled around him to the chin. Then the Count Palatine Louis, who superintended the execution, approached with the Marshal of Constance, and asked him for the last time to recant. On his refusal they withdrew and clapped their hands, which was the signal for the executioners to light the pile. After it had burned away there followed the revolting process requisite to utterly destroy the half-burned body—separating it in pieces, breaking up the bones and throwing the fragments and the viscera on a fresh fire of logs. When, as in the cases of Arnaldo of Brescia, some of the Spiritual Franciscans, Huss, Savonarola, and others, it was feared that relics of the martyr would be preserved, especial care was taken, after the fire was extinguished, to gather up the ashes and cast them in a running stream.

There is something grotesquely horrible in the contrast between this crowning exhibition of human perversity and the cool business calculation of the cost of thus sending a human soul to its Creator. In the accounts of Arnaud Assalit we have a statement of the ex-

penses of burning four heretics at Carcassonne, April 24, 1323. It
runs thus:

For large wood	55 sols 6 deniers.
For vine-branches	21 sols 3 deniers.
For straw	2 sols 6 deniers.
For four stakes	10 sols 9 deniers.
For ropes to tie the convicts	4 sols 7 deniers.
For the executioners, each 20 sols	80 sols.
In all	8 livres 14 sols 7 deniers

or, a little more than 2 livres apiece.

When the heretic had eluded his tormentors by death and his
body or skeleton was dug up and burned, the ceremony was necessarily less impressive, but nevertheless the most was made of it. As
early as 1237 Guillem Pelisson, a contemporary, describes how at
Toulouse a number of nobles and others were exhumed, when "their
bones and stinking corpses" were dragged through the streets, preceded by a trumpeter proclaiming *"Qui aytal fara, aytal perira"*—
Who does so shall perish so—and at length were duly burned "in
honor of God and of the blessed Mary his mother, and the blessed
Dominic his servant." This formula was preserved to the end, and
it was not economical from a pecuniary point of view. In Assalit's
accounts we find that in 1323 it cost 5 livres 19 sols and 6 deniers,
for labor to dig up the bones of three dead heretics, a sack and cord
in which to stow them, and two horses to drag them to the Grève,
where they were burned the next day.

The agency of fire was also invoked by the Inquisition to rid the
land of pestilent and heretical writings, a matter not without interest
as signalizing the commencement of its activity in what subsequently
became the censorship of the press. The burning of books displeasing
to the authorities was a custom respectable by its antiquity. Constantine demanded the surrender of all Arian works under penalty
of death. In 435 Theodosius II and Valentinian III ordered all
Nestorian books to be burned, and another law threatens punishment
on all who will not deliver up Manichæan writings for the same fate.
During the ages of barbarism which followed there was little to call
forth this method of repressing the human mind, but with the

revival of speculation the ancient measures were speedily again called into use. When, in 1210, the University of Paris was agitated with the heresy of Amauri, the writings of his colleague, David de Dinant, together with the *Physics* and *Metaphysics* of Aristotle, to which it was attributed, were ordered to be burned. Allusion has already been made to the burning of Romance versions of the Scriptures by Jayme I of Aragon and to the commands of the Council of Narbonne, in 1229, against the possession of any portion of Holy Writ by laymen, as well as to the burning of William of St. Amour's book, *De periculis*. Jewish books were the objects of special detestation, in the suppression of which the Church was unwearying. It was started by a converted Jew named Nicholas de Rupella, who, about 1236, called the attention of Gregory IX to the blasphemies with which the Hebrew books were filled, and especially the Talmud. In June 1239, Gregory issued letters to the Kings of England, France, Navarre, Aragon, Castile, and Portugal, and to the prelates in those kingdoms, ordering that on a Sabbath in the following Lent, when the Jews would be in their synagogues, all their books should be seized and delivered to the Mendicant Friars.

Like the *luz* or *os coccygis*, which the Rabbis held to be indestructible, the Talmud could not be wiped out of existence, and, in 1255, St. Louis, in his instructions to his seneschals in the Narbonnais, again orders all copies to be burned, together with all other books containing blasphemies; while in 1267 Clement IV instructed the Archbishop of Tarragona to coerce by excommunication the King of Aragon and his nobles to force the Jews to deliver up their Talmuds and other books to the inquisitors for examination, when, if they contain no blasphemies, they may be returned, but if otherwise they are to be sealed up and securely kept. Alonso the Wise of Castile was wiser, if, as reported, he caused the Talmud to be translated, in order that its errors might be exposed to the public. How fruitless were all these efforts is seen in a formal sentence recited by Bernard Gui in the *auto de fé* of 1319. Under the impulsion of the Inquisition the royal officials had again made diligent perquisition and had collected all the copies of the Talmud on which they could lay their hands. Experts in the Hebrew tongue had then been employed to examine them carefully, and after mature counsel between the inquisitors and the jurists called in to assist, the books were condemned to be carried in two carts through the streets of Toulouse, while the royal officers proclaimed in loud voice that their fate was due to their blasphemies against the Lord Jesus Christ and his mother the most holy Virgin and the Christian name, after which they were to be solemnly burned. Even as late as 1554 Julius III repeated the command to the Inquisition to burn it without mercy, and all Jews were ordered, under pain of death, to surrender all books blaspheming Christ—a provision which was embodied in the canon law and remains there to this day. The censorship of the Inquisition was not confined to Jewish errors, but its activity in this direction will be more conveniently considered hereafter.

BOOK II
THE INQUISITION IN THE SEVERAL LANDS OF CHRISTENDOM

CHAPTER X
LANGUEDOC

THE men who laid the foundations of the Inquisition in Languedoc had before them an apparently hopeless task. Practical toleration had existed for so many generations, and so many families had heretic members, that the population at large was yet to be educated in the holy horror of doctrinal aberrations. National feeling, moreover, and the memory of the twenty years during which Catholic and Catharan had stood side by side in defense of the fatherland, had created the strongest bonds of sympathy between the different sects.

To undertake, in such an environment, the apparently hopeless task of suppressing heresy required men of exceptional character, and they were not wanting. Such men as Pierre Cella, Guillem Arnaud, Arnaud Catala, Pons de Saint-Gilles, and Bernard de Caux bearded prince and prelate, were as ready to endure as merciless to inflict, and yet were kind to the miserable and overflowing with tears in their prayers and discourses. They were the culminating development of the influences which produced the Church Militant of the Middle Ages, and in their hands the Inquisition was the most effective instrument whereby it maintained its supremacy. A secondary result was the complete subjugation of the south to the King of Paris and its unification with the rest of France.

If the faithful had imagined that the Treaty of Paris of 1229 had ended the contest with heresy they were quickly undeceived. The blood money for the capture of heretics, promised by Count Raymond, was indeed paid when earned, for the Inquisition undertook to see that this was done, but the earning of it was dangerous. Nobles and burghers alike protected and defended the proscribed classes, and those who hunted them were slain without mercy when occasion offered.

Urgent as was evidently the need of some organized body devoted exclusively to persecution, the appointment of the first inquisitors, in 1233, seems not to have been regarded as possessing any special significance. It was merely an experiment, from which no great results were anticipated. Frère Guillem Pelisson, who shared in the labors and perils of the nascent Inquisition, and who enthusiastically chronicled them, evidently does not consider it as an innovation worthy of particular attention; he passes over its founding as an incident of less moment than the succession to the Priory of Toulouse:

> Frère Pons de Saint-Gilles was made Prior of Toulouse, who bore himself manfully and effectively for the faith against the heretics, together with Frère Pierre Cella of Toulouse and Frère Guillem Arnaud of Montpellier, whom the lord pope made inquisitors against the heretics in the dioceses of Toulouse and Cahors. Also, the Legate Archbishop of Vienne made Frère Arnaud Catala, who was then of the Convent of Toulouse, inquisitor against the heretics.

Thus colorless is the only contemporary account of the establishment of the Holy Office.

How little the functions of these new officials were at first understood is manifested by an occurrence, which is also suggestive of the tension of public feeling. In a quarrel between two citizens, one of them, Bernard Peitevin, called the other, Bernard de Solier, a heretic. This was a dangerous reputation to have, and the offended man summoned his antagonist before the consuls. The heretical party, we are told, had obtained the upper hand in Toulouse, and the magistrates were all either sympathizers with or believers in heresy. Bernard Peitevin was condemned to exile for a term of years, to pay a fine both to the complainant and to the city, and to swear publicly in the town hall that he had lied and that de Solier was a good Catholic. The sentence was a trifle vindictive, and Peitevin sought counsel of the Dominicans, who recommended him to appeal to the bishop. The inquisitors Pierre Cella and Guillem Arnaud appeared as advocates of the appellant in the bishop's court and so clearly proved de Solier's heresy that the miserable wretch fled to Lombardy.

Pierre and Guillem then began to make an inquest through the city, and cited numerous suspects, all of whom found defenders among the chief citizens. One of the accused, named Jean Teisseire, asserted himself to be a good Catholic because he had no scruples in maintaining marital relations with his wife, in eating flesh, and in lying and swearing, and he warned the crowd that they were liable to the same charge and that it would be wiser for them to make common cause than to abandon him. When he was condemned, and the *viguier*, the official representative of the count, was about to conduct him to the stake, so threatening a clamor arose that the prisoner was hurried to the bishop's prison, still proclaiming his orthodoxy. Intense excitement pervaded the city, and menaces were freely uttered to destroy the Dominican convent and to stone all the friars, who were accused of persecuting the innocent. While in prison Teisseire pretended to fall mortally sick and asked for the sacraments; but when the bailli of Lavaur brought to Toulouse some perfected heretics and delivered them to the bishop, Teisseire allowed himself to be hereticated by them in prison and grew so ardent in the faith under their exhortations that when they were taken out for examination he accompanied them, declaring that he would share their fate. They were all condemned, including Teisseire, who obstinately refused to recant, and no further opposition was offered when they were all duly burned.

Here we see the inquisitorial jurisdiction completely subordinate to that of the bishop, but when the inquisitors soon afterwards left Toulouse to hold inquests elsewhere they acted with full independence. At Moissac they condemned Jean du Gard, who fled to Montségur, and they cited a certain Folquet, who, in terror, entered the convent of Belleperche as a Cistercian monk, and, finding that this was of no avail, finally fled to Lombardy. Meanwhile Frère Arnaud Catala and our chronicler, Guillem Pelisson, descended upon Albi, where they penanced a dozen citizens by ordering them to Palestine, and in conjunction with another inquisitor, Guillem de Lombers, burned two heretics, Pierre de Puechperdut and Pierre Bomassipio.

The terror which Pelisson boasts that these proceedings spread through the land was probably owing not only to the evidence they afforded of an organized system of persecution, but also to their introduction of a much more effective method of prosecution than had heretofore been known. The "heretic," so called, was the perfected teacher who disdained to deny his faith, and his burning was accepted by all as a matter of course, as also was that of the *credens* or believer, who was defiantly contumacious and persisted in admitting and adhering to his creed. Hitherto, however, the believer who professed orthodoxy seems generally to have escaped, in the imperfection of the judicial means of proving his guilt. The friars were especially fitted for the detection of this particularly dangerous secret misbelief, and their persistence in worrying their victims to the death was well calculated to spread alarm, not only among the guilty, but among the innocent.

As the holy work assumed shape and its prospects of results grew more encouraging, the zeal of the hunters of men increased, while the fear and hatred of the hunted became more threatening. On both sides passion was fanned into flame. At Albi June 14, 1234, Arnaud Catala ordered the episcopal bailli to dig up the bones of a heretic woman named Beissera whom he had condemned. The bailli sent back word that he dared not do it. Arnaud left the episcopal synod in which he was sitting, coolly went to the cemetery, himself gave the first strokes of the mattock, and then, ordering the officials to proceed with the work, returned to the synod. The officials quickly rushed after him, saying that they had been ejected from the burial ground by a mob. Arnaud returned and found it occupied by a crowd of howling sons of Belial, who quickly closed in on him, striking him in the face and pummelling him on all sides, with shouts of "Kill him! he has no right to live!" Some endeavored to drag him into the shops to slay him, but he was rescued and taken back to the synod, followed by a mass of men fiercely shouting for his death. The whole city, indeed, seemed to be of one mind, and many of the principal burghers were leaders of the tumult. It is satisfactory to learn that, although Arnaud mercifully withdrew the excommunication which he launched at the rebellious city, his successor, Frère Ferrer, wrought the judgment of God upon the guilty, imprisoning many of them and burning others.

In Toulouse, the center both of heresy and persecution, in spite of mutterings and menaces, open opposition to the Inquisition was postponed longer than elsewhere. Although Raymond VII is constantly represented by the Church party as the chief opponent of the Holy Office, it was probably his influence that succeeded in staving off so long the inevitable rupture. Hard experience from childhood could scarce have rendered him a fervent Catholic, yet that experience had shown him that the favor and protection of the Church were indispensable if he would retain the remnant of territory and power that had been left to him. His heart was bent on obtaining from Rome a restoration of the Marquisate of Provence, and in this he was strongly backed by King Louis. Towards the close of the year 1234 he sought an interview with Gregory and succeeded in effecting it. His reconciliation with the papacy appeared to be complete. His military reputation stood high, and Gregory made use of his visit to confide to him the leadership of the papal troops in a campaign against the rebellious citizens of Rome, who had expelled the head of the Church from their city. Though he did not succeed in restoring the pope, they parted on the best of terms, and he returned to Toulouse as a favored son of the Church, ready on all points to obey her behests.

There he found matters rapidly approaching a crisis which tested to the utmost his skill in temporizing. At Easter, 1235, the promise of grace for voluntary confession brought forward such crowds of penitent heretics that the Dominicans were insufficient to take their testimony, and were obliged to call in the aid of the Franciscans and all the parish priests of the city. Encouraged by this, the prior, Pons de Saint-Gilles, commenced to seize those who had not come forward spontaneously. Among these was a certain Arnaud Dominique, who, to save his life, promised to betray eleven heretics residing in a house at Cassers. This he fulfilled, though four of them escaped through the aid of the neighboring peasants, and he was set at liberty. The long-suffering of the heretics, however, was at last exhausted, and shortly afterwards he was murdered in his bed at Aigrefeuille by the friends of those whom he had thus sacrificed. The situation was becoming unbearable, and soon the ceremony of dragging through the streets and burning the bodies of some dead heretics aroused an agitation so menacing that Count Raymond was sent for in hopes that his interposition might avert the most deplorable consequences. He came to Toulouse and begged the inquisitors to suspend for a time the vigor of their operations, but he was not listened to. Then he turned to the papal legate, Jean, Archbishop of Vienne, complaining especially of Pierre Cella, whom he considered to be inspired with personal enmity to himself and whom he regarded as the chief author of the troubles. His request that Cella's operations should be confined to Querci was granted. That inquisitor was sent to Cahors,

where, with the assistance of Pons Delmont and Guillem Pelisson
he vigorously traversed the land and forced multitudes to confess
their guilt.

Guillem Arnaud was in no way abashed by the banishment of
his colleague. Returning from a brief absence at Carcassonne, of
which more anon, he summoned for trial as believers twelve of the
leading citizens of Toulouse, one of them a consul. They refused
to appear, and threatened him with violence unless he should
desist. On his persisting, word was sent him, with the assent of
Count Raymond, that he must either leave the city or abandon
his functions as inquisitor. He took council with his Dominican
brethren and it was unanimously agreed that he should proceed
in his duty. The consuls then ejected him by force; he was accompanied to the bridge over the Garonne by all the friars, and as
he departed the consuls recorded a protest to the effect that if he
would desist from the inquisition he could remain; otherwise, in
the name of the count and in their own, they ordered him to leave
the city. He went to Carcassonne, whence he ordered the Prior
of Saint-Étienne and the parish priests to repeat the citations to the
parties already summoned. When this order was bravely obeyed
in spite of threats, the consuls sent for the prior and priests, and
after keeping them in the town hall part of a night, expelled them
from the town and publicly proclaimed that anyone daring to repeat
the citations should be put to death, and that anyone obeying the
summons of an inquisitor should answer for it in body and goods.
Another proclamation followed, in which the name of Count Raymond was used, prohibiting anyone to give or sell anything to the
bishop, the Dominicans, or the canons of Saint-Étienne. This forced
the bishop to leave the city, as we are told that no one dared even
to bake a loaf of bread for him, and the populace, moreover, invaded his house, beat his clerks, and stole his horses. The Dominicans
fared better, for they had friends hardy enough to supply them with
necessaries; when the consuls posted guards around their house, bread
and cheese and other food was thrown over their walls in spite of the
arrest of some of those engaged in it. Matters became more serious
when the indomitable Guillem Arnaud sent from Carcassonne a
letter to the prior saying, that as no one dared to cite the contumacious citizens, he was forced to order two of the friars to sum-

mon them to appear before him personally in Carcassonne to answer for their faith, and that two others must accompany them as witnesses. Tolling the convent bell, the prior assembled the brethren, and said to them with a joyful countenance: "Brethren, rejoice, for I must send four of you through martyrdom to the throne of the Most High. Such are the commands of our brother, Guillem the inquisitor, and whoever obeys them will be slain on the spot, as threatened by the consuls. Let those who are ready to die for Christ ask pardon." With a common impulse the whole body cast themselves on the ground, which was the Dominican form of asking pardon, and the prior selected four, Raymond de Foix, Jean de Saint-Michel, Gui de Navarre, and Guillem Pelisson. These intrepidly performed their duty, even penetrating when necessary into the bedchambers of the accused. Only in one house were they ill-treated, and even there, when the sons of the person cited drew knives upon them, the bystanders interfered.

There was evidently nothing to be done with men who thus courted martyrdom. To gratify them would be suicidal, and the consuls decided to expel them. On being informed of this the prior distributed among trusty friends the books and sacred vessels and vestments of the convent. The next day (November 5 or 6, 1235) the friars, after mass, sat down to their simple meal, during which the consuls came with a great crowd and threatened to break in the door. The friars marched in procession to their church, where they took their seats, and when the consuls entered and commanded them to depart they refused. Then each was seized and violently led forth, two of them who threw themselves on the ground near the door being picked up by the hands and feet and carried out. They were not otherwise maltreated, and they turned the affair into a procession, marching two by two and singing *Te Deum* and *Salve Regina*. At first they went to a farm belonging to the church of Saint-Étienne, but the consuls posted guards to see that nothing was furnished to them, and the next day the prior distributed them among the convents of the province.

It is significant of the position which Guillem Arnaud's steadfastness had already won for his office that to him was conceded the vindication of this series of outrages on the immunity of the Church. Bishop Raymond had joined him in Carcassonne without anathe-

matizing the authors of his exile, but now the the anathema promptly
went forth, November 10, 1235, uttered by the inquisitor with the
names of the Bishops of Toulouse and Carcassonne appended as
assenting witnesses. It was confined to the consuls, but Count Raymond was not allowed to escape the responsibility. The excommunication was sent to the Franciscans of Toulouse for publication, and
when they obeyed they too were expelled, in no gentle fashion, and
the rebellious city was virtually left without ecclesiastics. Further
excommunications followed, now including the count, and Prior
Pons de Saint-Gilles hastened to Italy to pour the story of his woes
into the sympathizing ears of the pope and the sacred college.
Gregory assailed the count as the chief offender. A minatory brief
of April 28, 1236, addressed to him is couched in the severest
language. He is held responsible for the audacious acts of the consuls; he is significantly reminded of the unperformed vow of the
crusade; he is a manifest fautor and protector of heretics; his lands
are a place of refuge for those flying from persecution elsewhere,
while zealous churchmen seeking to restrain them are slain and
abused with impunity. All this he is peremptorily ordered to correct
and to sail with his knights to the Holy Land in the "general
passage" of the following March. It scarcely needed the reminder,
which the pope did not spare him, of the labors which the Church
and its crusaders had undergone to purge his lands of heresy. Raymond had gone as far as he dared in the effort to protect his subjects,
and it would be manifest folly to draw upon his head and theirs
another inroad of the marauders whom the pope with a word could
let loose upon him to earn salvation with the sword.

The epistle to Raymond was accompanied with one to the legate,
instructing him to compel the count to make amends and perform
the crusade. King Louis was also appealed to and was urged to
hasten the marriage between his brother Alphonse and Raymond's
daughter Jeanne. With the specter of all Europe in arms looming up
before him Raymond could do nothing but yield. When the legate
summoned him to meet the inquisitors at Carcassonne he meekly
went there and promised to return the bishop and friars and clergy
to Toulouse, and this promise he kept. That Guillem Arnaud returned with them is a matter of course.

Pierre Cella was still restricted to his diocese of Querci, and as

Guillem required a colleague, a concession was made to popular feeling by appointing a Franciscan, it being imagined that the comparative mildness of that Order might serve to modify the hatred felt towards the Dominicans. The post was conferred on the provincial minister, Jean de Notoyra, but his other duties were too engrossing, and he substituted Frère Étienne de Saint-Thibéry, who had the reputation of being a modest and courteous man.

Guillem Arnaud's activity was untiring. During his exile in Carcassonne he had occupied himself with the trial of the Seigneur de Niort, whom he sentenced in February or March, 1236. In the early months of 1237 we hear of him in Querci, co-operating with Pierre Cella in harrying the heretics of Montauban. During his absence there occurred a crowning mercy in Toulouse, which threw the heretics into a spasm of terror and contributed greatly to their destruction. Raymond Gros, who had been a perfected heretic for more than twenty years, was suddenly converted. Tradition relates that a quarter of a century before he had been seized and consigned to the stake, when the prophetic spirit of St. Dominic, foreseeing that he would return to the Church and perform shining service in the cause of God, rescued him from the flames. On April 2, without heralding, he presented himself at the Dominican convent, humbly begged to be received into the Church, and promised to do whatever should be required of him. With the eagerness of an impassioned convert he proceeded to reveal all that lifelong intercourse with the Cathari had brought to his knowledge. Several days were required to write down all the names and facts that crowded to his lips. The lists embraced prominent nobles and citizens, confirming suspicion in many cases and revealing heresy in other quarters where it was wholly unlooked for.

Guillem Arnaud hurried back from Montauban to take full advantage of this act of Providence. The heretics were stunned. Many fled, some of whose names reappear in the massacre of Avignonet and the final catastrophe of Montségur. Many recanted and furnished further revelations. It is difficult to exaggerate the severity of the blow thus received by heresy. Toulouse was its headquarters. Here were the nobles and knights, the consuls and rich burghers who had thus far defied scrutiny and had protected their less fortunate comrades. A single sentence of February 19, 1238, in which more than 20 penitents were consigned *en masse* to perpetual imprisonment, shows the extent of the harvest and the haste of the harvesters.

The progress of the Inquisition, however, was not destined to be uninterrupted. Count Raymond, apparently reckless of the numerous excommunications under which he lay, so far from sailing for Palestine in March, had seized Marseilles, which was in rebellion against its suzerain, the Count of Provence. This aroused anew the indignation of Gregory. He peremptorily ordered Raymond to desist from his enterprise on Marseilles and to perform his crusader's vow. An appeal was made to King Louis and Queen Blanche, whose intervention procured for Raymond not only a postponment of the crusade for another year, but an order to the legate empowering him to grant the count's request to take the Inquisition entirely out of the hands of the Dominicans, if, on investigation, he should find justification for Raymond's assertion that they were actuated by hatred towards himself. Fresh troubles had arisen at Toulouse. July 24, 1237, the inquisitors had again excommunicated the *viguier* and consuls, because they had not arrested and burned Alaman de Roaix and some other heretics, condemned *in absentia*, and Raymond was resolved, if possible, to relieve himself and his subjects from the cruel oppression to which they were exposed.

In this his efforts were crowned with most unlooked-for success. May 13, 1238, he obtained a suspension for three months of all inquisitorial proceedings, during which time his envoys sent to Gregory were to be heard. They seem to have used most persuasive arguments, for Gregory wrote to the Bishop of Toulouse to continue the suspension until the new legate, the Cardinal-Bishop of Palestrina, should examine the complaints against the Dominicans and consider the advisability of granting Raymond's request that the business of persecution should be confined, as formerly, to the bishops. Raymond's crusade was also reduced to three years, to be performed voluntarily, provided he would give to King Louis sufficient security that he would sail the following year.

Suddenly, in 1240, an insurrection occurred, headed by Trencavel, son of that Viscount of Béziers whom we have seen entrapped by Simon de Montfort and dying opportunely in his hands. He brought with him from Catalonia troops of proscribed knights and gentlemen, and was greeted enthusiastically by the vassals and subjects of his house. Count Raymond, his cousin, held aloof; but his ambiguous conduct showed plainly that he was prepared to act on either side as success or defeat might render advisable. At first the rising seemed to prosper. Trencavel laid siege to his ancestral town of Carcassonne and the spirit of his followers was shown when, on the surrender of the suburb, they slaughtered in cold blood 30 ecclesiastics who had received solemn assurance of free egress to Narbonne. It required but a small force of royal troops under Jean de Beaumont to crush the insurrection as quickly as it had arisen, and to inflict a vengeance which virtually annihilated the *petite noblesse* of the region; but, nevertheless, the lesson it taught was not to be neglected. Church and State both could see now, if not before, that the Inquisition was a necessary factor in securing to both the advantages gained in the crusades.

The case of the Seigneurs de Niort, powerful nobles of Fenouillèdes, who had taken part in Trencavel's insurrection, is interesting from the light it throws upon the connection between the religion and the politics of the time, the difficulties which the Inquisition experienced in dealing with stubborn heresy and patriotism, and the damage inflicted on the heretic cause by the abortive revolt. The three brothers—Guillem Guiraud, Bernard Otho, and Guiraud Bernard—with their mother, Esclarmonde, had long been a quarry which both the inquisitors and the royal Seneschal of Carcassonne had been eager to capture. Guillem had earned the reputation of a valiant knight in the wars of the crusades, and the brothers had managed to hold their castles and their power through all the vicissitudes of the time. In 1233 we hear of their having, not long before, laid waste with fire and sword the territories of Pierre Amiel, Archbishop of Narbonne, and they had assailed and wounded him while on his way to the Holy See, an exploit which led Gregory IX to order the archbishop, in conjunction with the Bishop of Toulouse, to proceed against them energetically, while at the same time he invoked the secular arm by a pressing command to Count Raymond. The evidence was conflicting. The archbishop swore at great length to the misdeeds of his enemies. They were all heretics. On the other hand, there were not wanting witnesses who boldly defended them. A priest swore to having seen Bernard Otho assist in capturing heretics, and an archdeacon declared that he would not have remained in the land but for the army which Bernard raised after the death of the late king, adding that he believed the prosecution arose rather from hate than from charity. Nothing came of this attempt, but when the Inquisition was established it was promptly brought to bear on the nobles who persisted in maintaining their feudal independence in spite of the fact that their immediate suzerain was now the king. In 1235 the Inquisitor Guillem Arnaud, while in Carcassonne, with the Archdeacon of Carcassonne as assistant, cited the three brothers and their mother to answer before him. Bernard Otho and Guillem obeyed the summons, but would confess nothing. Then the seneschal seized them; under compulsion Guillem made confession ample to warrant the inquisitor in sentencing him to perpetual prison, while Bernard, remaining obdurate, was condemned as a contumacious heretic and the seneschal made preparations to burn him. Guiraud and his mother, Esclarmonde, were further condemned for contumacious absence. Guiraud, however, who had wisely kept at large, began to fortify his castles and make warlike demonstrations so formidable that the Frenchmen scattered through the land took alarm. The Maréchal de la Foi, Levis of Mirepoix, stood firm, but the rest so worked upon the seneschal that the brothers were released, and the inquisitors had only the barren satisfaction of condemning the whole family on paper. Equally vain was an effort made two years later by the inquisitors to compel Count Raymond to carry out their sentence by confiscating the lands of the contumacious nobles, but the failure of Trencavel's revolt forced them to sue for peace. Bernard Otho was again brought before the Inquisition, and Guillem de Niort made submission for himself and brothers, surrendering their castles to the king on condition that he would procure their reconciliation with the Church, and that of their mother, nephews, and allies, and, failing to accomplish this by the next Pentecost, that he would restore their castles and grant them a month of truce to put themselves in defense. King Louis ratified the treaty in January 1241, but refused, when the time came, to restore the castles, only agreeing to pay over the revenues on consideration that the brothers should reside outside of Fenouillèdes. When Guillem died in 1256, Louis kept both castles and revenues, under pretext that the treaty had been a personal one with Guillem. The new order of things by this time had become so firmly established that no further resistance was to be dreaded. The extinction of this powerful family is a typical example of the manner in which the independence of the local seigneurie was gradually broken down by means of the Inquisition, and the authority of crown and Church was extended over the land.

Montségur for years had been the Mount Tabor of the Cathari —the place of refuge in which, as its name implies, they could feel secure when safety could be hoped for nowhere else. It had been destroyed, but early in the century Raymond de Péreille had rebuilt it, and for forty years he held it as an asylum for heretics, whom he defended to the utmost of his ability. In 1232 the Catharan bishops Tento of Agen and Guillabert de Castres of Toulouse, with a number of ministers, forseeing, in the increasing pressure of persecution, the necessity of some stronghold which should serve as an asylum, arranged with Raymond de Péreille that he should receive and shelter all fugitives of the sect and guard the common treasure to be deposited there. His castle, situated in the territories of the Maréchaux de Mirepoix, had never opened its gates to the Frenchmen. Its almost inaccessible peak had been sedulously strengthened with all that military experience could suggest or earnest devotion could execute. Ever since the persecutions of the Inquisition commenced we hear of those who fled to Montségur when they found the inquisitor's hand descending upon them. Dispossessed knights, *faidits* of all kinds, brought their swords to its defense; Catharan bishops and ministers sought it when hard pressed, or made it a resting-place in their arduous and dangerous mission work. Such a stronghold in the hands of desperate men was a menace to the stability of the new order in the State; to the Church it was an accursed spot whence heresy might at any moment burst forth to overspread the land again. Its destruction had long been the desire of all good Catholics, and Count Raymond's pledge to King Louis to capture it had been one of the conditions on which his suspicious relations with Trencavel had been condoned.

On Ascension night, 1242, while Pierre Cella was tranquilly winding up his work at Montauban, the world was startled with the news that a holocaust of the terrible inquisitors had been made at Avignonet, a little town about 12 leagues from Toulouse. The stern Guillem Arnaud and the courteous Étienne de Saint-Thibéry were making, like their colleague Pierre Cella, a circuit through the district subjected to their mercy, and in the spring of 1242 they came to Avignonet. Raymond d'Alfaro was its bailli for the count, who was his uncle through his mother, Guillemetta, a natural daughter of Raymond VI. When he heard that the inquisitors and their assistants were coming he lost no time in preparing for their destruction. A swift messenger was dispatched to the heretics of Montségur, and in answer to his summons Pierre Roger of Mirepoix, with a number of knights and their retainers, started at once. They halted in the forest of Gaiac, near Avignonet, where food was brought them, and they were joined by about 30 armed men of the vicinage, who waited with them till after nightfall.

The victims came unsuspectingly to the trap. There were eleven in all. The two inquisitors, with two Dominican friars, and one Franciscan; the Benedictine Prior of Avignonet; Raymond de Costiran, Archdeacon of Lezat, a former troubadour, of whose verses only a single obscene song remains; a clerk of the archdeacon, a notary, and two apparitors—in all a court fully furnished for the dispatch of business. They were hospitably received and housed in the castle of the count, where on the morrow they were to open their tribunal. When darkness came a selected band of twelve, armed with axes, left the forest and stole cautiously to a postern of the castle, where they were met by Golairan, a comrade of d'Alfaro, who assured himself that all was right, and returned to see what the inquisitors were doing. Coming back, he reported that they were drinking; but a second visit, after an interval, brought the welcome news that they were going to bed. As though apprehensive of danger, they had remained together in the great hall, and had barricaded the door. The gate was opened, the men of Montségur were admitted and were joined by d'Alfaro, armed with a mace, and 25 men of Avignonet, and the fact that an esquire in the service of the inquisitors was with him indicates that there was treachery at work. The hall door was quickly broken down, the assassins rushed in, and, after dispatching their victims, there was a fierce chorus of gratified vengeance, each man boasting of his share in the bloody deed. The plunder of the victims was eagerly shared between the assassins— their horses, books, garments—even to their scapulars.

Like the murder of the Legate Pierre de Castelnau in 1208, the massacre of Avignonet was a fatal error. Its violation of the traditional sanctity of the ecclesiastic sent a thrill of horror even among those who had small sympathy with the cruelty of the Inquisition, while the deliberateness of its planning and its unsparing ferocity gave color to the belief that heresy was only to be extirpated by force. Frère Ferrer, the Inquisitor of Carcassonne, made due inquest into the affair, and after the capture of Montségur in 1244, some of the participants confessed all the details, but the real culprits escaped. Count Raymond, it is true, when he had leisure from pressing business, hanged a few of the underlings, but we find Raymond d'Alfaro, in 1247, promoted to be Viguier of Toulouse and representing his master in the proceedings with regard to the burial of the old count, and, finally, he was one of the nine witnesses to Raymond's last will. Another ringleader, Guillem du Mas-Saintes-Puelles, is recorded as taking the oath of allegiance to Count Alphonse, in 1249, after the death of Raymond. Guillem's participation in the murders has special interest as showing the antagonism created by the violence of the Inquisition, for in 1233, as Bailli of Lavaur, he had dutifully seized a number of heretics and carried them to Toulouse, where they were promptly burned.

The massacre of Avignonet came at a time peculiarly unfortunate for Count Raymond, who was nursing comprehensive and far-reaching plans for the rehabilitation of his house and the independence of his land. He had been busy in effecting a widespread alliance which should wring from the House of Capet its conquests of the last quarter of a century. He had been joined by the Kings of England, Castile, and Aragon, and the Count de la Marche, and everything bid fair for his reconquest of his old domains. The massacre of Avignonet was a most untoward precursor of the revolt which burst forth immediately afterwards. The rising, for a while, had promised success, and Raymond even reassumed his old title of Duke of Narbonne. King Louis, however, was equal to the occasion, and allowed the allies no time to concentrate their forces. His victories over the English and Gascons at Taillebourg and Saintes, July 19 and 23, deprived Raymond of all hope of assistance from that quarter. Without help from his allies and deserted by many of his vassals, he was obliged to lay down his arms, December 22. When suing for peace he pledged himself to extirpate heresy and to punish the assassins of Avignonet with an effusiveness which shows the importance attached to these conditions. The sagacity and moderation of King Louis granted him easy terms, but one of the stipulations of settlement was that every male inhabitant over the age of 15 should take an oath to assist the Church against heresy, and the king against Raymond, in case of another revolt. Thus the purity of the faith and the supremacy of the foreign domination were once again recognized as inseparably allied.

The triumph of both had been secured. This ended the last serious effort of the south to recover its independence. Henceforth it was to pass irrevocably into the hands of the stranger, and the Inquisition was to have unrestricted opportunity to enforce conformity in religion. It was in vain that Raymond, at the Council of Béziers, April 20, 1243, summoned the bishops of his dominions, urging them personally or through proper deputies, whether Cistercians, Dominicans, or Franciscans, to make diligent inquisition after heresy, and pledged the assistance of the secular arm for its extirpation. It was equally in vain that, immediately on the accession of Innocent IV in June, a deputation of Dominicans, frightened by the warning of Avignonet, earnestly alleged many reasons why the dangerous burden should be lifted from their shoulders. The pope peremptorily refused, and ordered them to continue their holy labors, even at the risk of martyrdom.

The peril, indeed, was apparent rather than real—it had passed away in the revulsion which followed the useless bloodshed of Avignonet and the failure of Raymond's rebellion. There was a rising tide in favor of orthodoxy. A confraternity organized in October 1243 by Durand, Bishop of Albi, is probably only the expression of what was going on in many places. Organized under the protection of St. Cecilia, the members of the association pledged themselves not only to mutual protection, but to aid the bishop to execute justice on heretics, Vaudois, and their fautors, and to defend inquisitors as they would their own bodies. A new legate, Zoen, Bishop-Elect of Avignon, was dispatched to Languedoc, with instructions to act vigorously.

Still more menacing to the heretic cause was the reconciliation at last effected between Raymond and the papacy. In September 1243 the count visited Italy, where he had an interview with Frederic

II in Apulia, and with Innocent in Rome. There seems to have been little difficulty in reaching an understanding, to which the good offices of Louis IX powerfully contributed. December 2, Raymond was released from his various excommunications; January 1, 1244, the absolution was announced to King Louis and the prelates of the kingdom, who were ordered to publish it in all the churches, and January 7 the Legate Zoen was instructed to treat him with fatherly affection and not permit him to be molested. In all this absolution had only been given *ad cautelam*, or provisionally, for a special excommunication had been decreed against him as a fautor of heretics, after the massacre of Avignonet, by the Inquisitors Ferrer and Guillem Raymond. Against this he had made a special appeal to the Holy See in April 1243, and a special bull of May 16, 1244, was required for its abrogation. Raymond was fairly won over. He had evidently resolved to accommodate himself to the necessities of the time, and the heretic had nothing further to hope or the inquisitor to fear from him.

Yet so long as heresy retained the stronghold of Montségur as a refuge and rallying point, its secret and powerful organization could not be broken. The capture of that den of outlaws was a necessity of the first order, and as soon as the confusion of the rebellion of 1242 had subsided it was undertaken as a crusade, not by Raymond, but by the Archbishop of Narbonne, the Bishop of Albi, the Seneschal of Carcassonne, and some nobles. The heretics, on their side, were not idle. Some baillis of Count Raymond sent them Bertrand de la Bacalairia, a skillful maker of military engines, to aid them in the defense, who made no scruple in affirming that he came with the assent of the count, and from every side money, provisions, arms, and munitions of war were poured into the stronghold. In the spring of 1243 the siege began, prosecuted with indefatigable ardor by the besiegers and resisted with desperate resolution by the besieged. It is significant of the public temper that sympathizers in the besiegers' camp permitted tolerably free communication between the besieged and their friends and gave them warning of the plans of attack. Even the treasure which had been stored up in Montségur was conveyed away safely through the investing lines, about Christmas 1243, to Pons Arnaud de Châteauverdun in the Savartès. Secret relations were maintained with Count Raymond, and the besieged were buoyed up with promises that if they would hold out until Easter 1244, he would march to their relief with forces supplied by the Emperor Frederic II. It was all in vain. The siege dragged on its weary length for nearly a year, till, on the night of March 1, 1244, guided by some shepherds who betrayed their fellow-countrymen, by almost inaccessible paths among the cliffs, the crusaders surprised and carried one of the outworks. The castle was no longer tenable. A brief parley ensued, and the garrison agreed to surrender at dawn, delivering up to the archbishop all the perfected heretics among them, on condition that the lives of the rest should be spared. Although a few were let down from the walls with ropes and thus escaped, the capitulation was carried out, and the archbishop's shrift was short. At the foot of the mountain peak an enclosure of stakes was formed, piled high with wood, and set on fire. The Perfect were asked to renounce their faith, and on their refusal were cast into the flames. Thus perished 205 men and women. The conquerors might well write exultingly to the pope, "We have crushed the head of the dragon!"

Although the lives of the rest of the captives were guaranteed, they were utilized to the utmost. For months the Inquisitors Ferrer and P. Durant devoted themselves to the examinations to secure evidence against heretics far and near, dead and alive. From the aged Raymond de Péreille to a child ten years of age, they were forced, under repeated interrogatories, to recall every case of adoration and heretication that they could remember, and page after page was covered with interminable lists of names of those present at sermons and *consolamenta* through a period extending back to thirty or forty years before, and embracing the whole land as far as Catalonia. We can only guess at the means by which this information was extracted from the prisoners. Torture had not yet been introduced; life had been promised, and perpetual imprisonment was inevitable for such pronounced heretics; and when we see Raymond de Péreille himself, who had endured unflinchingly the vicissitudes of the crusades and had bravely held out to the last, ransacking his memory to betray all whom he had ever seen adore a minister, we can imagine the horrors of the two months' preliminary captivity which had so broken his spirit as to bring him to this depth of degradation.

For the next few years the life of the inquisitors was a busy one. The stunned populations grew used to the despair of the penitents sentenced to perpetual prison, the dragging of decomposed corpses through the streets, and the horror of the Tophets where the victims passed through temporal to eternal flame. Still there is a slight indication that the service was not wholly without danger from the goadings of vengeance or the courage of despair, when the Council of Béziers, in 1246, ordering travelling inquests, makes exception in the cases when it may not be safe for the inquisitors to visit the places personally where the inquisition should be held; and Innocent IV, in 1247, authorizes the inquisitors to cite the accused to come to them, in view of the perils arising from the ambushes of heretics.

The fearless and indefatigable men who now performed the functions of Inquisitor in Languedoc can rarely have taken advantage of this concession to weakness. Bernard de Caux, who so well earned the title of the Hammer of Heretics, was at this time the leading spirit of the Inquisition of Toulouse and he had for colleague a kindred spirit in Jean de Saint-Pierre. Together they made a thorough inquest over the whole province, passing the population through a sieve with a completeness which must have left few guilty consciences unexamined. There is extant a fragmentary record of this inquest, covering the years 1245 and 1246, during which no less than 600 places were investigated, embracing about one half of Languedoc. In all this Count Raymond, now thoroughly fitted in the Catholic groove, was an earnest participant. As his stormy life drew to its close, harmony with the Church was too great an element of comfort and prosperity for him to hesitate in purchasing it with the blood of a few of his subjects, whom, indeed, he could scarce have saved had he so willed.

When St. Louis undertook his disastrous crusade to Damietta he was unwilling to leave behind him so dangerous a vassal as Raymond. The vow of service to Palestine had long since been remitted by Innocent IV, but the count was open to persuasion, and the bribes offered show at once the importance attached to his presence with the host and to his absence from home. The king promised him some 20,000 livres for his expenses and the restitution of the duchy of Narbonne on his return. The pope agreed to pay him 2,000 marks on his arrival beyond seas, and that he should have during his absence all the proceeds of the redemption of vows and all legacies bequeathed to the crusade. Stimulated by these dazzling rewards, he assumed the cross in earnest, and his ardor for the purity of the faith grew stronger.

Death spared Raymond the misfortunes of the ill-starred Egyptian crusade. When his preparations were almost complete he was seized with mortal illness and died, September 27, 1249, with his latest breath ordering his heirs to restore the sums which he had received for the expedition, and to send 50 knights to serve in Palestine for a year. That his death was generally regretted by his subjects we can readily believe. Not only was it the extinction of the great house which had bravely held its own from Carlovingian times, but the people felt that the last barrier between them and the hated Frenchmen was removed. The heiress Jeanne had been educated at the royal court, and was French in all but birth. Moreover, she seems to have been a nonentity whose influence is imperceptible, and the scepter of the south passed into the hands of Alphonse of Poitiers, an avaricious and politic prince, whose zeal for orthodoxy was greatly stimulated by the profitable confiscations resulting from persecution. When the rich heritage fell in, he and his wife were with his brother, King Louis, in Egypt, but the vigilant regent, Queen Blanche, promptly took possession in their name, and on their return, in 1251, they personally received the homage of their subjects. By a legal subtlety Alphonse evaded the payment of the pious legacies of Raymond's will, and compounded for it by leaving, on his departure for the north, a large sum to provide for the expenses of the Inquisition, and to furnish wood for the execution of its sentences.

The fate of Languedoc was now irrevocably sealed. Hitherto there had been hopes that perhaps Raymond's inconstancy might lead him to retrace the steps of the last few years. Moreover, his subjects had shared in the desire, manifested in his repeated marriage projects, that he should have an heir to inherit the lands not pledged in succession to his daughter. He was but in his fifty-first year, and the expectation was not unreasonable that his line might be perpetuated and the southern nationality be preserved. All this was now seen to be a delusion, and the most sanguine Catharan could look forward to nothing but a life of concealment ending in

prison or fire. Many fled to Lombardy, where, even after the death of
Frederic II, the civic troubles and the policy of local despots afforded
some shelter from the Inquisition. Yet many remained and pursued
their wandering missions among the faithful, perpetually tracked
by inquisitorial spies, but rarely betrayed. Rainerio Saccone, the
converted Catharan, who had the best means of ascertaining the facts,
computes, about this time, that there were in Lombardy 150 perfected refugees from France, while the churches of Toulouse, Carcassonne, and Albi, including that of Agen, then nearly destroyed,
numbered 200 more. The proscribed heretics, thus nursing their faith
in secret, gave the inquisitors ample occupation. As their ranks
were thinned by persecution and flight, and as their skill in concealment increased with experience, there could no longer be the immense harvests of penitents reaped by Pierre Cella and Bernard de
Caux, but there were enough to reward the energies of the friars
and to tax the adroitness of their spies. The organization of the Inquisition, moreover, was gradually perfected. In 1254 the Council of
Albi carefully revised the regulations concerning it. Fixed tribunals
were established, and the limitations of the inquisitorial districts
were strictly defined. For Provence and the territories east of the
Rhone, Marseilles was the headquarters, eventually confided to the
Franciscans. The rest of the infected regions were left to the Dominicans, with tribunals at Toulouse, Carcassonne, and Narbonne; and,
from such fragmentary documents as have reached us, at this time
the Inquisition at Carcassonne rivalled that of Toulouse in energy
and effectiveness. For a while safety was sought by heretics in
northern France, but the increasing vigor of the Inquisition estab-
ished there drove the unfortunate refugees back, and in 1255 a bull
of Alexander IV authorized the Provincial of Paris and his inquisitors to pursue the fugitives in the territories of the Count of
Toulouse. To this period is also to be ascribed the complete subjection of all secular officials to the behests of the inquisitors. The
piety of St. Louis and the greed of Alphonse of Poitiers and Charles
of Anjou rivalled each other in placing all the powers of the State
at the disposal of the Holy Office and in providing for its expenses.

The last shadow of open resistance was dissipated in the year
1255. After the fall of Montségur the proscribed and disinherited
knights, the *faidits*, and the heretics had sought to establish among

the mountains some stronghold where they could feel safe for a moment. Driven from one retreat after another, they finally took possession of the castle of Quéribus, in the Pyrenees of Fenouillèdes. In the early spring of 1255 this last refuge was besieged by Pierre d'Auteuil, the royal Seneschal of Carcassonne. The defense was stubborn, but by August the place was in his hands, and nothing remained for the outlaws but the forest and the caverns.

With the land at its feet, the Inquisition had no hesitation in attacking the loftiest nobles, for all men were on a level in the eyes of the Most High, and the Holy Office was the avenger of God. The most powerful vassal of the houses of Toulouse and Aragon was the Count of Foix, whose extensive territories on both sides of the Pyrenees rendered him almost independent in his mountain fastnesses. Count Roger Bernard II, known as the Great, had been one of the bravest and most obstinate defenders of the land, and, after the pacification of 1229, Raymond had been obliged to threaten him with war to force him to submit. His memory was proudly treasured in the land as *"Rogier Bernat lo pros et sens dengun reproche."* His family was deeply tinctured with heresy. His wife and one of his sisters were Waldenses, another sister was a Catharan, and the monk of Vaux-Cernay describes him as an enemy of God and a cruel persecutor of the Church. Yet, when he yielded in 1229, although he does not seem to have energetically fulfilled his oath to persecute heresy in his domains, he was in other respects a loyal subject and faithful son of the Church. In 1237 he counselled his son, then Vizconde de Castelbo in Aragon, to allow the Inquisition in his lands, which resulted in the condemnation of many heretics, although Ponce, Bishop of Urgel, his personal enemy, had refused to relieve him of excommunication as a fautor of heresy until 1240, when he submitted to the conditions imposed, abjured heresy, and was reconciled. At his death, in 1241, he left liberal bequests to the Church, and especially to his ancestral Cistercian Abbey of Bolbonne, in which he died in monkish habit, after duly receiving the sacraments. His son, Roger IV, gave the *coup de grâce* to the rising of 1242 by placing himself under the immediate sovereignty of the crown, and defeating Raymond after the victories of St. Louis had driven back the English and Gascons. He had some troubles with the Inquisition, but a bull of Innocent IV in 1248 eulogizes his devotion to the Holy See and rewards him with the power to release from the saffron crosses six penitents of his choice; and in 1261 he issued an edict commanding the enforcement of the rule that no office within his domains should be held by anyone condemned to wear crosses, anyone suspected of heresy, or the son of anyone similarly defamed.

All this would seem to give ample guarantee of the orthodoxy and loyalty of the House of Foix, but the Inquisition could not condone its ancient patriotism and tolerance. Besides, if Roger Bernard the Great could be convicted of heresy, the confiscation of the broad inheritance would effect a great political object and afford ample spoils for all concerned. Twenty-two years after his death, therefore, in 1263, proceedings were commenced against his memory. A faithful servitor of the old count still survived, Raymond Bernard de Flascan, bailli of Mazères, who had attended his lord day and night during his last sickness. If he could be brought to swear that he had seen heretication performed on the deathbed, the desirable object would be attained. Frère Pons, the Inquisitor of Carcassonne, came to Mazères, found the old man an unsatisfactory witness, and threw him into a dungeon. Suffering under a severe strangury, he was starved and tormented with all the cruel ingenuity of the Inquisition without his resolution giving way. This was continued for 32 days, when Pons resolved to carry him back to Carcassonne, where possibly the appliances for bringing refractory witnesses to terms were more efficacious. Before the journey, which he expected to be his last, the faithful bailli was given a day's respite at the Abbey of Bolbonne, which he utilized by executing a notarial instrument, November 26, 1263, attested by two abbots and a number of monks, in which he recited the trials already endured, solemnly declared that he had never seen the old count do anything contrary to the faith of Rome, but that he had died a good Catholic, and that if, under the severe torture to which he expected to be subjected, human weakness should lead him to assert anything else, he would be a liar and a traitor, and no credence should be given to his words.

What became of the poor wretch does not appear. Doubtless he perished in the terrible Mur of Carcassonne under the combination of disease, torture, and starvation. His judicial murder, however,

was gratuitous, for the old count's memory remained uncondemned.
Yet Roger Bernard III, despite the papal favor and the proofs he
had given of adhesion to the new order of things, was a perpetual
target for inquisitorial malice. When lying in mortal illness at
Mazères, in December 1264, he received from Étienne de Gâtine,
then Inquisitor of Narbonne, an imperious order, with threats of
prosecution in case of failure, to capture and deliver up his bailli
of Foix, Pierre André, who was suspect of heresy and had fled on
being cited to appear. The count dared only in reply to express
surprise that no notice had been given him that his bailli was
wanted, adding that he had issued orders for his arrest, and would
have personally joined in the pursuit had not sickness rendered him
incapable. At the same time he requested *Apostoli*, and appealed to
the pope, to whom he retailed his grievances. The inquisitors, he said,
had never ceased persecuting him; at the head of armed forces they
were in the habit of devastating his lands under pretext of searching
for heretics, and they would bring under their protection his special
enemies, until his territories were nearly ruined and his jurisdiction
set at naught. He therefore placed himself and his dominions under
the protection of the Holy See. He probably escaped further personal troubles, for he died two months later, in February 1265, like
his father, in the Cistercian habit and in the Abbey of Bolbonne;
but in 1292 his memory was assailed before Bertrand de Clermont,
Inquisitor of Carcassonne. The effort was fruitless, for in 1297 Bertrand gave to his son, Roger Bernard IV, a declaration that the accusation had been disproved, and that neither he nor his father
should suffer in person or property in consequence of it.

In 1271 Alphonse and Jeanne, who had accompanied St. Louis
in his unlucky crusade to Tunis, died without issue, during the homeward journey. The line of Raymond was thus extinct, and the
land passed irrevocably to the crown. Philippe le Hardi took possession even of the territories which Jeanne had endeavored, as was
her right, to alienate by will, and though he surrendered the Agenois to Henry III, he succeeded in retaining Querci. When, October
8, 1271, Guillaume de Cobardon, royal Seneschal of Carcassonne,
issued his orders regulating the new régime, one of the first things
thought of was the confiscations. All castles and villages which had
been forfeited for heresy were taken into the king's hand, without

prejudice to the right of those to whom they might belong, thus throwing the burden of proof upon all claimants, and cutting out assigns under alienations. In 1272 Philippe paid a visit to his new territories; it was designed to be peaceful, but some violences committed by Roger Bernard IV of Foix caused him to come at the head of an army, with which he easily overcame the resistance of the count, occupied his lands, and threw him into a dungeon. Released in 1273, the count in 1276 rendered such assistance in the invasion of Navarre that Philippe took him into favor and restored his castles, on his renouncing all allegiance to Aragon. Thus the last show of independence in the south was broken down, and the monarchy was securely planted on its ruins.

This consolidation of the south of France under the kings of Paris was not without compensating advantages. The study of the Roman law was beginning to bear fruit in the State as well as in the Church, and the imperial theories of absolutism as inherent in kingship were gradually altering all the old relations. The king's court was expanding into the Parlement, and was training a school of civil lawyers who lost no opportunity of extending the royal jurisdiction and of legislating for the whole land in the guise of rendering judgments. In the appeals which came ever more thickly crowding into the Parlement from every quarter, the mailed baron found himself hopelessly entangled in the legal intricacies which were robbing him of his seignorial rights almost without his knowledge; and the *Ordonnances*, or general laws, which emanated from the throne, were constantly encroaching on old privileges, weakening local jurisdictions, and giving to the whole country a body of jurisprudence in which the crown combined both the legislative and the executive functions.

It was to the royal power, thus rising to supremacy, that the people instinctively turned for relief from the inquisitorial tyranny which was becoming insupportable. Dangerous as was any manifestation of discontent, the people of Albi and Carcassonne, reduced to despair by the cruelty of the Inquisitors Jean Galande and Jean Vigoureux, mustered courage, and in 1280 presented their complaints to Philippe le Hardi. It was difficult to sustain their charges with specific proofs, and after a brief investigation their reiterated requests for relief were dismissed as frivolous. In the agitation against the

Inquisition thus commenced, it must be borne in mind that heretics had little to do. By this time they were completely cowed and were quite satisfied if they could enjoy their faith in secret. The opposition arose from good Catholics, the magistrates of cities and substantial burghers, who saw the prosperity of the land withering under the deadly grasp of the Holy Office, and who felt that no man was safe whose wealth might arouse cupidity or whose independence might provoke revenge. The provisions which brought confiscation on the descendants of heretics, moreover, were peculiarly hard to endure, for ruin impended over everyone against whom the inquisitor might see fit to produce from his records evidence of ancestral heresy. It was against these records that the next attempt was directed. Foiled in their appeal to the throne, the consuls of Carcassonne and some of its prominent ecclesiastics, in 1283 or 1284, formed a conspiracy to destroy the books of the Inquisition containing the confessions and depositions. How far this was organized it would be difficult now to say. The statements of the witnesses conflict so hopelessly on material points, even as to dates, that there is little dependence to be placed on them. They were evidently extracted under torture, and if they are credible the consuls of the city and the archdeacon, Sanche Morlana, the episcopal Ordinary, Guillem Brunet, other episcopal officials and many of the secular clergy were not only implicated in the plot, but were heretics in full affiliation with the Cathari. According to the evidence Bernard Garric, who had been a perfected heretic and a *filius major*, but had been converted and was now a familiar of the Inquisition, was selected as the instrument. He was approached, and after some bargaining he agreed to deliver the books for 200 livres Tournois, for the payment of which the consuls went security. How the attempt failed and how it was discovered does not appear, but probably Bernard at the first overtures confided the plot to his superiors and led on the conspirators to their ruin.

The whole community was now at the mercy of the Inquisition, and it was not disposed to be lenient in its triumph. While the trials were yet going on, the citizens made a fresh appeal to Pierre Chalus, the royal chancellor, who was passing through Toulouse on a mission to Aragon. This was easily disposed of, for on September 13, 1285, the inquisitors triumphantly brought before him Bernard Garric to repeat the confession made a week previous. He had thoroughly learned his lesson, and the only conclusion which the royal representative could reach was that Carcassonne was a hopeless nest of heretics, deserving the severest measures of repression. As a last resort recourse was had to Honorius IV, but the only result was a brief from him to the inquisitors expressing his grief that the people of Carcassonne should be impeding the Inquisition and ordering the punishment of the recalcitrants irrespective of their station, order, or condition, an expression which shows that the opposition had not arisen from heretics.

The secretly guilty were sufficiently influential, and the innocent sufficiently apprehensive, to keep up the agitation which had been commenced, and at last it began to bear fruit. A new Inquisitor of Carcassonne, Nicholas d'Abbeville, was quite as cruel and arbitrary as his predecessors, and when the people prepared an appeal to the king he promptly threw into jail the notary who drew up the paper. In their desperation they disregarded this warning; a deputation was sent to the court, and this time they were listened to. May 13, 1291, Philippe le Bel addressed a letter to his Seneschal of Carcassonne reciting the injuries inflicted by the Inquisition on the innocent through the newly invented system of torture, by means of which the living and the dead were fraudulently convicted and the whole land rendered desolate. The royal officials were therefore ordered no longer to obey the commands of the inquisitors in making arrests, unless the accused be a confessed heretic or persons worthy of faith vouch for his being publicly defamed for heresy. A month later he announced his intention of sending deputies to Languedoc armed with full authority to make permanent provision in the matter. It is impossible to exaggerate the importance of these manifestoes as marking a new era in the relations between the temporal and spiritual authorities. For far less than this all the chivalry and scum of Europe had been promised salvation if they would drive Raymond of Toulouse from his inheritance.

In September 1293, Philippe went a step further and threw his ægis over the unfortunate Jew. Although Jews as a class were not liable to persecution by the Inquisition, still, if after being once converted they reverted to Judaism, or if they proselyted among Christians to obtain converts, or if they were themselves converts from Christianity, they were heretics in the eyes of the Church, they fell under inquisitorial jurisdiction and were liable to be abandoned to the secular arm. The bull *Turbato corde*, ordering the inquisitors to be active and vigilant in prosecuting all who were guilty of these offenses, issued in 1268 by Clement IV, was reissued by successive popes with a pertinacity showing the importance attached to it, and when we see Frère Bertrand de la Roche, in 1274, officially described as Inquisitor in Provence against heretics and wicked Christians who embrace Judaism, and Frère Guillaume d'Auxerre in 1285 qualified as "Inquisitor of Heretics and Apostate Jews in France," it is evident that these cases formed a large portion of inquisitorial business. As the Jews were peculiarly defenseless, this jurisdiction gave wide opportunity for abuse and extortion, which was doubtless turned fully to account. Philippe owed them protection, for in 1291 he had deprived them of their own judges and ordered them to plead in the royal courts, and now he proceeded to protect them in the most emphatic manner. To Simon Brisetête, Seneschal of Carcassonne, he sent a copy of the bull *Turbato corde*, with instructions that while this was to be implicitly obeyed, no Jew was to be arrested for any cause not specified therein, and, if there was any doubt, the matter was to be referred to the royal council. He further enclosed an *Ordonnance* directing that no Jew in France was to be arrested on the requisition of any person or friar of any Order, no matter what his office might be, without notifying the seneschal or bailli, who was to decide whether the case was sufficiently clear to be acted upon without reference to the royal council.

Philippe had thus intervened in the most decided manner and the oppressed populations of Languedoc might reasonably hope for permanent relief, but his subsequent policy belied their hopes. It vacillated in a manner which is only partially explicable by the shifting political exigencies of the times so far as we can penetrate them. Towards the end of 1295 there was issued an *Ordonnance* applicable to the whole kingdom, forbidding the arrest of anyone on the demand of a friar of any Order, no matter what his position might be, unless the seneschal or bailli of the jurisdiction was satisfied that the arrest should be made, and the person asking it showed a commission from the pope. Moreover, if any persons were then in durance contrary to the provisions of the *Ordonnance,* they were to be set at liberty. Even this did not effect its object sufficiently, and a few months later, in 1296, Philippe complained to his Seneschal of Carcassonne of the numbers who were arrested by the royal officers, and confined in the royal prisons on insufficient grounds. To prevent this, arrests were forbidden except in cases of such violent presumption of heresy that they could not be postponed, and the officials were instructed, when called upon by the inquisitors, to make such excuses as they could.

No previous sovereign had ventured thus to trammel the Inquisition. These regulations, in fact, rendered it virtually powerless; even its prisons were the king's and might be withdrawn at any time. Phillipe's quarrel with Boniface VIII was now beginning. Between January 1296 and February 1297 appeared the celebrated bulls *Clericis laicos, Ineffabilis amoris, Excitat nos,* and *Exiit a te,* whose encroachments on the secular powers aroused Philippe to resistance, and this doubtless gave a sharper zest to his desire to diminish in his dominions the authority of so purely papal an institution as the Inquisition. So shrewd a prince could readily see its effectiveness as an instrument of papal aggression, for the Church could make what definition it pleased of heresy; and Boniface did not hesitate to give him fair warning, when, in October 1297, he ordered the Inquisitor of Carcassonne to proceed against certain officials of Béziers who had rendered themselves in the papal eyes suspect of heresy because they remained under excommunication, incurred for imposing taxes on the clergy, boasting that food had not lost its savor to them nor sleep its sweetness, and who, moreover, dared with polluted lips to revile the Holy See itself. Under such an extension of jurisdiction Philippe himself might not be safe, and it is no wonder that tentative efforts made in 1296 and 1297 to find some method of reconciling the recent royal *Ordonnances* with the time-honored absolutism of the Inquisition proved failures.

Meanwhile, the exigencies of Italian politics caused Boniface suddenly to retrace his steps. His quarrel with the Cardinals Giacomo and Pietro Colonna rendered it advisable to propitiate Philippe. In May 1297, he assented to a tithe conceded to the king by his bishops, and in the bull *Noveritis* (July 1297) he exempted France from the operation of the *Clericis laicos,* while in *Licet per speciales* (July

1298) he withdrew his pretension imperatively to prolong the arm-
istice between France and England. A truce was thus patched up
with Philippe, who hastened to manifest his good will to the Holy
See by abandoning his subjects again to the inquisitors. In *Liber
Sextus* of the Decretals, published by Boniface March 3, 1298, the
pope included, with customary imperiousness, a canon commanding
the absolute obedience of all secular officials to the orders of inquisitors under penalty of excommunication, which if endured for a
year carried with it condemnation for heresy. This was his answer to
the French monarch's insubordinate legislation, and Philippe at the
moment was not inclined to contest the matter. In September he
meekly enclosed the canon to his officials with instructions to obey
it in every point, arresting and imprisoning all whom inquisitors or
bishops might designate, and punishing all whom they might condemn.

Under this varying policy the fate of the people of Languedoc
was hard. Nicholas d'Abbeville, the Inquisitor of Carcassonne, was
a man of inflexible severity, bent on pushing his prerogatives to the
utmost. He had an assistant worthy of him in Foulques de Saint-
Georges, the Prior of the Convent of Albi, which was under his
jurisdiction. He had virtually another assistant in the bishop, Bernard de Castanet, who delighted to act as inquisitor, impelled alike
by fanaticism and by greed. Prior to his elevation in 1276 Bernard
had been auditor of the papal camera, which shows him to have
been an accomplished legist, and he was also a patron of art and
literature, but he was ever in trouble with his people. In 1277, he
had succeeded in so exasperating them that his palace was swept by
a howling mob and he barely escaped with his life. In 1282 he commenced the erection of the cathedral of St. Cecilia, a gigantic building, half-church, half-fortress, which swallowed enormous sums and
stimulated his hatred of heresy by supplying a pious use for the
estates of heretics.

To such men the protection granted to his subjects by Philippe
was most distasteful, and not without reason. More demonstrative,
if not more earnest, was the feeling which the royal policy aroused
in Carcassonne. The *Ordonnances* had not only crippled the Inquisition, but had shown the disfavor with which it was regarded
by the king, and in 1295 some of the leading citizens, who had been

compromised in the trials of 1285, found no difficulty in arousing the people to open resistance. For a while they controlled the city, and inflicted no little injury on the Dominicans and on all who ventured to support them. Nicholas d'Abbeville was driven from the pulpit when preaching, pelted with stones and pursued with drawn swords, and the judges of the royal court on one occasion were glad to escape with their lives, while the friars were beaten and insulted when they appeared in public and were practically segregated as excommunicates. Bernard Gui, an eyewitness, naturally attributes this to the influence of heresy, but it is impossible for us now to conjecture how much may have been due to religious antagonism, and how much to the natural reaction among the orthodox against the intolerable oppression of the inquisitorial methods.

For some years the Inquisition of Carcassonne was suspended. As soon as secular support was withdrawn public opinion was too strong, and it succumbed. This lasted until the truce between king and pope again placed the royal power at the disposal of the inquisitors. In their despair the citizens then sent envoys to Boniface VIII, with Aimeric Castel at their head, supported by a number of Franciscans. Boniface listened to their complaints and proposed to depute the Bishop of Vicenza as commissioner to examine and report, but the papal referendary, afterwards Cardinal of S. Sabina, required a bribe of 10,000 florins as a preliminary. It was promised him, but Aimeric, having secured the good offices of Pierre Flotte and the Duke of Burgundy, thought he could obtain his purpose for less, and refused to pay it. When Boniface heard of the refusal he angrily exclaimed, "We know in whom they trust, but by God all the kings in Christendom shall not save the people of Carcassonne from being burned, and specially the father of that Aimeric Castel!" The negotiation fell through, and Nicholas d'Abbeville had his triumph. A large portion of the citizens were wearied with the disturbances, and were impatient under the excommunication which rested on the community. The prosperity of the town was declining, and there were not wanting those who predicted its ruin. The hopelessness of further resistance was apparent, and matters being thus ripe for a settlement, a solemn assembly was held, April 27, 1299, when the civic magistrates met the inquisitor in the presence of the Bishops of Albi and Béziers, Bertrand de Clermont, Inquisitor of Toulouse, the royal officials,

sundry abbots and other notables. Nicholas dictated his own terms
for the absolution asked at his hands. Those who were manifest
heretics, or specially defamed, or convicted by legal proof must take
their chance. The rest were to be penanced as the bishops and the
Abbot of Fontfroide might advise, excluding confiscation and personal or humiliating penalties. All this was reasonable enough from
an ecclesiastical point of view, but so deep-seated was the distrust,
or so strong the heretical influence, that the people asked 24 hours
for consideration, and on reassembling the next day refused the
terms. Six months passed, their helplessness and isolation each day
becoming more apparent, until, October 8, they reassembled, and
the consuls asked for absolution in the name of the community.
Nicholas was not severe. The penance imposed on the town was the
building of a chapel in honor of St. Louis, which was accomplished
in the year 1300 at the cost of 90 livres Tournois. The consuls, in
the name of the community, secretly abjured heresy. Twelve of the
most guilty citizens were reserved for special penances, viz., four of
the old consuls, four councillors, two advocates, and two notaries.
(Of these the fate was doubtless deplorable. Chance has preserved
to us the sentence passed on one of the authors of the troubles,
Guillem Garric, by which we find that he rotted in the horrible
dungeon of Carcassonne for 22 years before he was brought forward
for judgment in 1321, when in consideration of his long confinement
he was given the choice between the crusade and exile, and the
crushed old man fell on his knees and gave thanks to Jesus Christ
and to the inquisitors for the mercy vouchsafed him.) Some years
later intense excitement was created when Frère Bernard Délicieux
obtained sight of the agreement, and discovered that the consuls had
been represented in it as confessing that the whole community had
given aid to manifest heretics, that they had abjured in the name of
all, and thus that all citizens were incapacitated for office and were
exposed to the penalties of relapse in case of further trouble. This
excited the people to such a point that the Inquisitor Geoffroi
d'Ablis was obliged to issue a solemn declaration, August 10, 1303,
disclaiming any intention of thus taking advantage of the settlement;
and notwithstanding this, when King Philippe came to Carcassonne
in 1305 the agreement was pronounced fraudulent, the Seneschal
Gui Caprier was dismissed for having affixed his seal to it, and con--

fessed that he had been bribed to do so by Nicholas d'Abbeville with 1,000 livres Tournois.

Encouraged by the crippling and suspension of the Inquisition, the Catharan propaganda had been at work with renewed vigor. In 1299 the Council of Béziers sounded the alarm by announcing that perfected heretics had made their appearance in the land, and ordering close search made after them. At Albi, Bishop Bernard was, as usual, at variance with his flock, who were pleading against him in the royal court to preserve their jurisdiction. The occasion was opportune. He called to his assistance the Inquisitors Nicholas d'Abbeville and Bertrand de Clermont, and towards the close of the year 1299 the town was startled by the arrest of 25 of the wealthiest and most respected citizens, whose regular attendance at mass and observance of all religious duties had rendered them above suspicion. The trials were pushed with unusual celerity, and, from the manner in which those who at first denied were speedily brought to confession and to revealing the names of their associates, there was doubtless good ground for the popular belief that torture was ruthlessly and unsparingly used; in fact, allusions to it in the final sentence of Guillem Calverie, one of the victims, leave no doubt on the subject. Abjuration saved them from the stake, but the sentence of perpetual imprisonment in chains was a doubtful mercy for those who were sentenced, while a number were kept interminably in jail awaiting judgment.

When Boniface VIII swore that he would cause the burning of Aimeric Castel's father, he uttered no idle threat. Nicholas d'Abbeville, a fitting instrument, was at hand, and to him he privately gave the necessary verbal instructions. Castel Fabri, the father, had been a citizen of Carcassonne distinguished for piety and benevolence no less than for wealth. A friend of the Franciscan Order, he had died, in 1278, in the hands of its friars, six of whom kept watch in the sick room until his death, and he had been buried in the Franciscan cemetery. Suddenly, in 1300, the people of Carcassonne were startled by a notice, read in all the parish churches, summoning those wishing to defend the memory of Castel Fabri to appear before the Inquisition on a day named, as the deceased was proved to have been hereticated on his deathbed. The moment was well chosen, as Aimeric Castel, the son, was absent. The Franciscans, for whom the accused had doubtless provided liberally in his will, felt themselves called upon to assume his defense. Hastily consulting, they determined to send their lector, Bernard de Licgossi, or Délicieux, to the General Chapter then assembling at Marseilles, for instructions. The wife of Aimeric Castel provided for the expenses of the journey, and Bernard returned with instructions from the provincial to defend the memory of the deceased, while Eléazar de Clermont, the syndic of the convent, was deputed by the Guardian of Narbonne to cooperate with him. Meanwhile Nicholas had proceeded to condemnation, and when, July 4, 1300, Bernard and Eléazar presented themselves to offer the testimony of the friars who had watched the dying man, Nicholas received them standing, refused to listen to them, and on their urging their evidence left the room in the most contemptuous manner. In the afternoon they returned to ask for a certificate of their offer and its refusal, but found the door of the Inquisition closed, and could not effect an entrance.

The next step was to take an appeal to the Holy See and ask for *Apostoli*, but this was no easy matter. So general was the terror inspired by Nicholas that the doctor of decretals, Jean de Penne, to whom they applied to draw the paper, refused unless his name should be kept inviolably secret, and 19 years afterwards Bernard when on trial refused to reveal it until compelled to do so. To obtain a notary to authenticate the appeal was still harder. All those in Carcassonne absolutely refused, and it was found necessary to bring one from a distance, so that it was not until July 16 that the document was ready for service. How seriously, indeed, all parties regarded what should have been a very simple business is shown by the winding-up of the appeal, which places, until the case is decided, not only the body of Castel Fabri, but the appellants and the whole Franciscan convent, under the protection of the Holy See. When they went to serve the instrument on Nicholas the doors, as before, were found closed and entrance could not be effected. It was therefore read in the street and left tacked on the door, to be taken down and treasured and brought forward in evidence against Bernard in 1319. We have no further records of the case, but that the appeal was ineffectual is visible in the fact that in 1322–3 the accounts of Arnaud Assalit show that the royal treasury was still receiving an income from the confiscated estates of Castel Fabri; while in 1329 the still unsatisfied vengeance of the Inquisition ordered the bones of his wife Rixende to be exhumed.

The case of Castel Fabri might have passed unnoticed had it not chanced to bring into collision with the Inquisition the lector of the convent of Carcassonne. Bernard Délicieux was no ordinary man; in fact a contemporary assures us that in the whole Franciscan Order there were few who were his equals. Entering the Order about 1284, his position of lector or teacher shows the esteem felt for his learning, and we find him in relations with the leading minds of the age, such as Raymond Lully and Arnaldo de Vilanova. His eloquence made him much in request as preacher; his persuasiveness enabled him to control those with whom he came in contact, while his enthusiastic ardor prompted him to make any sacrifices necessary to a cause which had once enlisted his sympathies. He was no admirer of toleration, for he devoutly wished the extermination of heresy, but experience and observation had convinced him that in Dominican hands the Inquisition was merely an instrument of oppression and extortion, and he imagined that by transferring it to the Franciscans its usefulness would be preserved while its evils would be removed. Boniface VIII about this time replaced the Franciscan Inquisitors of Padua and Vicenza with Dominicans for the purpose of repressing similar evils, and the converse operation might seem worth attempting in Languedoc. In the hope of alleviating the sufferings of the people, Bernard devoted himself to the cause for years, incurring obloquy, persecution, and ingratitude. Yet in the struggle he had the sympathies of his own Order, which everywhere throughout Languedoc manifested itself the enemy of the Dominican Inquisition. Vainly the inquisitors complained to the Franciscan prelates of Bernard as an impeder of the Holy Office. The Dominicans asserted that Franciscan zeal was solely caused by jealousy; the Franciscans retorted that their friends were the special objects of inquisitorial persecution. King Philippe's confessor was a Dominican, Queen Joanna's a Franciscan, and the two courtly friars took part, for and against the Inquisition, with a zeal which rendered them important factors in the struggle.

The *coup-de-main* executed on the so-called heretics of Albi in December 1299 and the early months of 1300 had excited consternation too general for the matter to be passed over. King Philippe's quarrel with Boniface was breaking out afresh, and he might not be averse to making his subjects feel that they had a protector in the throne. With the advice of his council an investigation was ordered and confided to the Bishops of Béziers and Maguelonne, but the inquisitors arrogantly refused to allow the secrets of their office to be invaded. This was not calculated to remove popular disquiet, and in 1301 Philippe sent to Languedoc two officials armed with supreme powers, under the name of Reformers. One of them, Jean de Pequigny, Vidame of Amiens, was a man of high character for probity and sagacity; the other was Richard Nepveu, Archdeacon of Lisieux, of whom we hear little in the following years, except that he quietly slipped into the vacant episcopate of Béziers.

The Reformers established themselves at Toulouse, where Foulques de Saint-Georges had been inquisitor since Michaelmas 1300, and speedily gathered much damaging testimony against him, for he was accused not only of unduly torturing persons for purposes of extortion, but of gratifying his lusts by arresting women whose virtue he failed otherwise to overcome. Thither flocked representatives of Albi, with the wives and children of the prisoners, beseeching and imploring the representatives of the king for justice, and promising revelations if they would issue letters of safety to those who would give information. The Bishop of Albi came also to justify himself, and on his return to his episcopal seat he was welcomed with a manifestation of the feeling entertained for him by his flock, whom the coming of the Reformers encouraged in the expression of their sentiments. When his approach was announced a crowd of men and women rushed forth from the gates to meet him with shouts of "Death, death, death to the traitor!" It may perhaps be doubted whether, as reported, he bore the threats and insults with patience akin to that of Christ, ordering his followers to keep their weapons down; certain it is that he was roughly handled and had difficulty in safely reaching his palace. Even more menacing was the action of a number of the chief citizens, who bound themselves by a notarial instrument to prosecute him and Nicholas d'Abbeville in the king's court. As a consequence, the bishop's temporalities were sequestrated, and eventually the enormous fine of 20,000 livres stripped him of a portion of his ill-gotten gains for the benefit of the king.

The Reformers, meanwhile, had sent for Bernard Délicieux, who was then quietly performing his duties as lector in the convent of Narbonne. He must already have made himself conspicuous in the affair of Castel Fabri and was evidently regarded as a desirable ally in the impending struggle. According to his own story he advised Pequigny to let the Inquisition alone, as experience had shown that effort was useless; but on being called again to Toulouse on some business connected with the Priory it was arranged, at Pequigny's suggestion, that he should accompany a deputation which the citizens of Albi were sending to the king to invoke his active intervention. The court was at Senlis, and there appeared Pequigny to justify himself, and Frère Foulques with several Dominicans, eager to establish the innocence of the Inquisition.

The battle was fought out before the king. Bernard urged the suspension of the inquisitors during an investigation, or that the Dominicans should be permanently declared ineligible while awaiting final action by the Holy See. Supported by Frère Guillaume, the king's Dominican confessor, Foulques preferred charges against Pequigny, but could furnish no proofs. Pequigny retorted with accusations against Foulques, and a commission, consisting of the Archbishop of Narbonne and the Constable of France, was appointed to hear both sides. After due deliberation, it reported in favor of Pequigny, and the king took the unheard-of step of removing the inquisitor. He at first requested this of the Dominican Provincial of Paris, who possessed the power to do so, but that official called together a chapter, which contented itself with appointing an adjunct, and ordering Foulques to retain office till the middle of the following Lent, in order to complete the trials which he had already commenced. This gave Philippe great offense, which he expressed in the most outspoken terms in letters to his chaplain and to the Bishop of Toulouse. Simultaneously, December 8, 1301, he wrote to the bishop, the Inquisitor of Toulouse, and the Seneschals of Toulouse and Albi, stating that the imploring cries of his subjects, including prelates and ecclesiastics, counts, barons, and other distinguished men, convinced him that Foulques was guilty of the charges preferred against him, including crimes abhorrent to the human mind. His detestable excesses had created such general terror that a rising of the people was to be apprehended unless some speedy remedy was had. Some further unavailing opposition was made to Foulques's removal, but not much was gained by the appointment of his successor, Guillaume de Morières, who had previously succeeded him in the Priory of Albi. Foulques was gratified with the important Priory of Avignon, and when he subsequently died in poverty at Lyons he was regarded by his Order almost in the light of a martyr.

Philippe had not contented himself with getting rid of Foulques, but had endeavored to introduce reforms which are interesting not only as a manifestation of the royal supremacy which he assumed, but also as the model of all subsequent endeavors to curb the abuses of the Inquisition. First, the prison which the crown had built on its own land in Toulouse for the use of the Inquisition was to be placed under the charge of someone selected by both bishop and inquisitor, and in case of their disagreement by the royal seneschal. The inquisitor was deprived of the power of arbitrary arrest. He was obliged to consult the bishop, and when they could not agree the question was to be decided by a majority vote in an assemblage consisting of certain officials of the cathedral and of the Franciscan and Dominican convents. Arrests were only to be made by the seneschal, after these preliminaries had been observed, except in case of foreign heretics who might escape. In no case was either bishop or inquisitor entitled to obedience when acting individually, for, as the king declared, "We cannot endure that the life and death of our subjects shall be abandoned to the discretion of a single individual, who, even if not actuated by cupidity, may be insufficiently informed." At the same time Philippe was careful to manifest due solicitude for the suppression of heresy, for he published anew the severe edict of St. Louis; and on the appointment of Guillaume de Morières to the Inquisition of Toulouse he wrote to the seneschal instructing him to place the royal prisons at the inquisitor's disposal, to pay him the customary stipend, and to aid him in every way until further orders.

While the new regulations may have promised relief elsewhere, they gave little comfort at Albi, the inquisitorial proceedings of whose bishop had given rise to the whole disturbance. Its citizens were still languishing in the prison of the Inquisition of Carcassonne, and a numerous deputation of both sexes was sent to the king, accompanied by two Franciscans, Jean Hector and Bertrand de Villedelle. Again Bernard Délicieux was present, having this time been

opportunely chosen to represent the Order on a summons from
Philippe for consultation on the subject of his quarrel with Pope
Boniface. They all followed the king to Pierrefonds and then to
Compiègne. He gave them fair words, promised a speedy visit to
Languedoc, and consoled them with a donation of 1,000 livres,
which he could well afford to do, for the confiscated estates of the
prisoners were in his hands, and were never released.

All this, of course, gave little satisfaction; nor were the people
placated by the removal of Nicholas d'Abbeville, for he was succeeded in the Inquisition of Carcassonne by Geoffroi d'Ablis, who
was as energetic and unsparing as his predecessor, and who brought
royal letters, dated January 1, 1303, ordering all officials to render
him the customary obedience. As Albi had no local inquisitors of its
own, being within the jurisdiction of the tribunal of Carcassonne,
the discontent vented itself on the Dominicans, who were regarded
as the representatives of the hated tribunal. On the first Sunday in
Advent, December 2, 1302, when the friars went as usual to preach
in the churches they were violently ejected and assailed with cries
of "Death to the traitors!" and were fortunate in being able to
regain their convent. This state of things continued for several years,
during which they scarce dared to show themselves in the streets,
and were never secure from insult. All alms and burial fees were
withdrawn, and the people refused even to attend mass in their
church.

The prisoners of Albi were still as far as ever from liberation, and
Bernard Délicieux urged Pequigny to come to Carcassonne and
consider their case on the spot. In the summer of 1303 he did so,
and was met by a large number of the people of Albi, men and
women, praying him to liberate them. To violate the prisons of the
Inquisition was so serious a matter that Pequigny seems to have
wished the backing of an enraged populace before he would venture
on the step; he anticipated resistance so confidently that with his
privity Bernard assembled fourscore men, with skilled mechanics,
in the Franciscan convent, ready to break open the jails in case
of necessity. Their services were not needed. Geoffroi d'Ablis yielded,
and in August 1303 Pequigny removed the prisoners of Albi. He did
not discharge them, however, but merely transferred them to the
royal prisons, and refused to carry them to the king as Bernard

advised. Possibly their treatment for a while may have been gentler, but they derived no permanent advantage from the movement. The Inquisition obtained possession of them again, and we shall see that it held them to the last.

Meanwhile advantage was taken of the access obtained to them to procure from them statements of the tortures which they had endured, and lists were made of the names of those whom they had been forced to accuse as heretics. These were circulated throughout the land and excited general alarm, the Franciscans being especially active in giving them publicity. On the other hand, the Inquisitor Geoffroi d'Ablis was equal to the emergency. He cited Pequigny to stand trial for impeding the Inquisition, and on his refusal excommunicated him, September 29; and as soon as word could be carried to Paris he was published as excommunicate by the Dominicans there. This audacious act brought all parties to a sense of the nature of the conflict which had sprung up between Church and State. The consuls and people of Albi addressed to the queen an earnest petition beseeching her to prevail upon the king not to abandon them by withdrawing the Reformers, who had already done so much good and on whom depended their last hope. A fruitless effort also was made to prevent the publication of the excommunication. At Castres, October 13, Jean Ricoles, stipendiary priest of the church of St. Mary, published it from the pulpit, as he was bound to do, and was promptly arrested by the deputy of the royal Viguier of Albi and carried to the Franciscan convent, where he was threatened and maltreated, and the friars used every effort to persuade him to withdraw it. This in itself was a grave violation of clerical immunity, and it was soon recognized that such proceedings were worse than useless. Pequigny's authority was paralyzed until the excommunication should be removed, and this could only be done by the man who had uttered it, or by the pope himself.

The prospect of relief was darkened by the election, October 21, of Benedict XI, himself a Dominican and necessarily predisposed in favor of the Inquisition. Special exertions evidently were required unless all that had been gained was to be lost, and, at best, litigation in the Roman court was a costly business. Pequigny had appealed to the pope, and, October 29, he wrote from Paris to the cities of Languedoc asking for their aid in the persecution which he had brought upon himself in their cause. Bernard Délicieux promptly busied himself to obtain the required assistance. By his exertions the three cities of Carcassonne, Albi, and Cordes entered into an alliance and pledged themselves to furnish the sum of 3,000 livres, one half by Carcassonne and the rest by the other two, and to continue in the same proportions as long as the affair should last. After Pequigny's death they renewed their obligation to his oldest son Renaud; but as the matter was much protracted, they grew tired, and Bernard, who had raised some of the money on his own responsibility, was left with heavy obligations, of which he vainly sought restitution at the hands of the ungrateful cities.

The quarrel was thus for a time transferred to Rome. Pequigny went to Italy with envoys from the king and from Carcassonne and Albi to plead his cause, and was opposed by Guillaume de Morières, the Inquisitor of Toulouse, sent thither to manage the case against him. Benedict was not slow in showing on which side his sympathies lay. At Perugia, while the pope was conducting the solemnities of Pentecost, May 17, 1304, Pequigny ventured to enter the church. Benedict saw him, and, pointing to him, said to his marshal, P. de Brayda, "Turn out that Patarin!"—an order which the marshal zealously obeyed. The significance of the incident was not small, and after the death of both Benedict and Pequigny, Geoffroi d'Ablis caused a notarial instrument recounting it to be drawn up and duly authenticated as one of the documents of the process.

The climate of Italy was very unhealthy for Transmontanes. Morières died at Perugia, and Pequigny followed him at Abruzzo, September 29, 1304, the anniversary of his excommunication. Having remained for a year under the ban for impeding the Inquisition, he was legally a heretic, and his burial in consecrated ground is only to be explained by the death of Benedict a short time before. Geoffroi d'Ablis demanded that his bones be exhumed and burned, while Pequigny's sons carried on the appeal for the rehabilitation of his memory. The matter dragged on till Clement V referred it to a commission of three cardinals. These gave a patient hearing to both sides, who argued the matter exhaustively, and submitted all the necessary documents and papers. At last, July 23, 1308, they rendered their decision to the effect that the sentence of excommunication had been unjust and iniquitous, and that its revocation should be published in all places where it had been announced.

Meanwhile Philippe le Bel had at last fulfilled his promise to visit in person his southern provinces and rectify on the spot the wrongs of which his subjects had so long complained. He was expecting a favorable termination to his negotiation with Benedict for the removal of the excommunications launched by Boniface VIII against himself and his subjects and chief agents. When, therefore, he reached Toulouse on Christmas Day 1303, he was not disposed to excite unnecessarily Benedict's prejudices. From Albi and Carcassonne multitudes flocked to him with cries for redress and protection, and Pequigny spoke eloquently in their behalf. The inquisitors were represented by Guillem Pierre, the Dominican provincial, while Bernard Délicieux was foremost in the debate. It was on this occasion that he made his celebrated assertion that St. Peter and St. Paul would be convicted of heresy if tried with inquisitorial methods.

Philippe patiently heard both sides, and recorded his conclusions in an edict of January 13, 1304, which was in the nature of a compromise. It recited that the king had come to Languedoc for the purpose of pacifying the country excited by the action of the Inquisition, and had had prolonged consultation on the subject with all who were entitled to express an opinion. The result thus reached was that the prisoners of the Inquisition should be visited by royal deputies in company with inquisitors; the prisons were to be safe, but not punitive. In the case of prisoners not yet sentenced, the trials were to be carried to conclusion under the conjoined supervision of the bishops and inquisitors, and this co-operation was to be observed in the future, except at Albi, where the bishop, being suspected, was to be replaced by Arnaud Novelli, the Cistercian Abbot of Fontfroide. The royal officials were strictly ordered to aid in every way the inquisitors and episcopal Ordinaries when called upon, and to protect from injury and violence the Dominicans, their churches and houses.

At Albi the change had the wished-for effect. No more heretics were found and no further prosecutions were required. Yet the refusal of the king to entertain any project of reform other than his previous one of curbing the Inquisition with an illusory episcopal supervision was a grievous disappointment. So many hopes had been built upon the royal presence in the land that the result caused universal dismay, which was not relieved by Philippe's subsequent action. When he visited Carcassonne he was urged to see the unfortunate captives whose persecution had been the cause of the troubles, but he refused, and sent his brother Louis to look at them. Worse than all, the citizens had designed to propitiate him and demonstrate their loyalty by offering him some elaborate silver vessels. These were yet in the hands of the goldsmiths of Montpellier when the royal party came to Carcassonne, so they were sent after him to Béziers, where the presentation was made, a portion to him and the rest to the queen. She accepted the offering, but he not only rejected it, but, when he learned what the queen had done, forced her to return the present. This threw the consuls of Carcassonne into despair. Offerings of this kind from municipalities to the sovereign were so customary and their gracious acceptance so much a matter of course, that refusal in this instance seemed to argue some most unfavorable intentions on the part of the king, which was not unlikely, seeing that Elias Patrice, the leading citizen of Carcassonne, had plainly told him when there that if he did not render them speedy justice against the Inquisition they would be forced to seek another lord, and when Philippe ordered him from his presence the citizens obeyed Patrice's command to remove the decorations from the streets. Imagining that Philippe had been won over by the Dominicans and that his protection would be withdrawn, the prospect of being abandoned to the mercy of the Inquisition seemed so terrible that they wildly declared that if they could not find another lord to protect them they would burn the town and with the inhabitants seek some place of refuge. In consultation with Frère Bernard it was hastily determined to offer their allegiance to Ferrand, son of the King of Majorca.

The younger branch of the House of Aragon, which drew its title from the Balearic Isles, held the remnants of the old French possessions of the Catalans, including Montpellier and Perpignan. It had old claims to much of the land, and its rule might well be hailed by the people as much more welcome than the foreign domination to which they had been unwillingly subjected. Had the whole region agreed to transfer its allegiance, its reduction might have cost Philippe a doubtful struggle, embarrassed as he was with the chronic disaffection of the Flemings. When, however, the project was broached to the men of Albi, they refused peremptorily to embark in it, and there can be no stronger proof of the desperation of the Carcassais than their resolution to persist in it single-handed. Ferrand and his father were at Montpellier entertaining the French court, which they accompanied to Nîmes. He eagerly listened to the overtures, and asked Frère Bernard to come to him at Perpignan. Bernard went thither with a letter of credence from the consuls, which he prudently destroyed on the road. The King of Majorca, when he heard of the offer, chastened his son's ambition by boxing his ears and pulling him around by the hair, and he ingratiated himself with his powerful neighbor by communicating the plot to Philippe.

Although there could have been no real danger from so crazy a project, the relation of the southern provinces to the crown were too strained for the king not to exact a vengeance which should prove a warning. A court was assembled at Carcassonne which sat through the summer of 1305 and made free use of torture in its investigations. Albi, which had taken no part in the plot, escaped an investigation by a bribe of 1,000 livres to the Seneschal Jean d'Alnet, but the damage inflicted on the Franciscan convent shows that the Dominicans were keen to make reprisals for what they had suffered. The town of Limoux had been concerned in the affair; it was fined and disfranchised, and 40 of its citizens were hanged. As for Carcassonne, all of its eight consuls, with Elias Patrice at their head, and seven other citizens were hanged in their official robes, and the city was deprived of self-government and subjected to the enormous fine of 60,000 livres, a sentence from which it vainly appealed to the Parlement. As Bernard Gui observes with savage exultation, those who had croaked like ravens against the Dominicans were exposed to the ravens.[1] Aimeric Castel, who had sought in this way to obtain redress for the wrong done to his father's memory and estate, escaped by flight, but was captured and long lay a prisoner, finally making his peace with a heavy ransom, and a harvest of fines was gathered into the royal exchequer from all who could be accused of privity. As for Frère Bernard, he received early intelligence from Frère

---

[1] Bernard Gui's allusion refers to the insults offered to the Dominicans during the troubles of Carcassonne, when those who ventured into the streets were followed with cries of "Coac, Coac!" "ad modum corvi."

Durand, the queen's confessor, of the discovery of the plot, and headed a delegation of citizens of Albi who went to Paris to protest their innocence. There Durand informed them that Albi was not implicated, and they returned, leaving Bernard. At the request of the king, Clement V had him arrested and carried to Lyons, whence he was taken by the papal court to Bordeaux; and when it went to Poitiers he was confined in the convent of St. Junian of Limoges. In May 1307, at the instance of Clement, Philippe issued letters of amnesty to all concerned, and remitted to Carcassonne the portion of its fine not yet paid, and in Lent, 1308, Bernard was allowed to come to Poitiers. He boldly complained to the king of his arrest and of the punishment which had involved the innocent with the guilty. As he still had no license to leave the papal court, he accompanied it to Avignon, and was at length discharged with the royal assent—the heavy bribes paid to three cardinals by his friends of Albi having perhaps something to do with his immunity. He returned to Toulouse, and we hear of no further activity on his part. His narrow escape probably sobered his restless enthusiasm, and as the reform of the Inquisition seemed to have been taken resolutely in hand by Clement V he might well persuade himself that there was no further call for self-sacrifice.

The death of Benedict XI, in July 1304, had given fresh hopes to the sufferers from the Inquisition. There was an interregnum of nearly a year before the election of his successor, Clement V, June 5, 1305. Bertrand de Goth, Cardinal-Archbishop of Bordeaux, was a Gascon by birth, and, though an English subject, was doubtless more familiar than the Italians with the miseries and needs of Languedoc. His transfer of the papacy to French soil was also a good augury. Hardly had the news of his election reached Albi, when Frère Bernard was busy in organizing a mission to represent to him in the name of the city the necessity of relief, and when he visited Toulouse the wives of the prisoners still languishing in confinement were taken thither to make their woes emphatically known. Hardly had Clement been consecrated at Lyons when these complaints poured in and were substantiated by two Dominicans, Bertrand Blanc and François Aimeric, who were as emphatic as the representatives of Albi in their denunciations of inquisitorial methods and abuses. Geoffroi d'Ablis hurried there from Carcassonne to defend himself in such haste that he left no one to take his place, and was obliged to send from Lyons, September 29, 1305, a commission to Jean de Faugoux and Gerald de Blumac to act in his stead. His efforts to justify the Inquisition were unavailing, more especially, perhaps, because the people of Albi bribed Cardinal Raymond de Goth, the pope's nephew, with 2,000 livres Tournois, the Cardinal of Santa Croce with as much, and the Cardinal Pier Colonna with 500. March 13, 1306, Clement commissioned two cardinals, Pierre of San Vitale (afterwards of Palestrina) and Berenger of SS. Nereo and Achille (afterwards of Frascati), who were about to pass through Languedoc on a mission, to investigate and make such temporary changes as they should find necessary.

On April 16, 1306, the cardinals held a public session at Carcassonne in presence of all the notables of the place. The consuls of Carcassonne and the delegates of Albi preferred their complaints and were supported by the two Dominicans, Blanc and Aimeric, who had appeared before the pope. On the other hand, Geoffroi d'Ablis and the deputy of the Bishop of Albi defended themselves and complained of the popular riots and the ill-treatment to which they had been exposed. After hearing both sides the cardinals adjourned further proceedings until January 25, at Bordeaux, where Carcassonne, Albi, and Cordes were each to send four procurators to conduct the matter. As this office was a most dangerous one, the cardinals gave security to them against the Inquisition during the performance of their duty. This was no idle precaution, and Aimeric Castel, one of the representatives of Carcassonne, found himself in such danger that in September 1308 he was obliged to procure from Clement a special bull forbidding the inquisitors to assail him until the termination of the affair. Even greater danger impended over any witnesses called upon to prove the falsification of records, as they were bound to silence under oaths which exposed them to the stake as relapsed heretics in case they revealed their evidence, and the cardinals were asked to absolve them from these oaths.

If there were any further formal proceedings in this matter, which thus assumed the shape of a litigation between the people and the Inquisition, they have not reached us. Yet the cardinals, before continuing their journey, took some steps which showed that they were convinced of the truth of the accusations. They visited the prison of Carcassonne, and caused the prisoners, 40 in number, of whom three were women, to be brought before them. Some were sick, others worn with age, and all tearfully complaining of the horrors of their lot, the insufficiency of food and bedding, and the cruelty of their keepers. The cardinals dismissed all the jailers and attendants except the chief, and put the prison under the control of the Bishop of Carcassonne. One of the cardinals visited the prison of the Bishop of Albi, where he found the jailers well spoken of, but was shocked with the condition of the prisoners. Many of them were in chains and all in narrow, dark cells, where some of them had been confined for five years or more without being yet condemned. He ordered all chains removed, that light should be introduced in the cells, and that new and less inhuman ones should be built within a month. As regards general amelioration in inquisitorial proceedings, the only regulation which they issued was a confirmation of Philippe's expedient, requiring the co-operation of the diocesan with the inquisitor, and this was withdrawn by Clement, August 12, 1308, in an apologetic bull declaring that the cardinals had exceeded his intentions. Even with regard to the inexcusable detention of prisoners for long years without conviction or sentence, Clement found himself powerless to effect reform in the most flagrant cases. The inquisitors had in their archives a bull of Innocent IV authorizing them to defer indefinitely passing sentence when they deemed that delay was in the interest of the faith, and of this they took full advantage. Of the captives seized by the Bishop of Albi in 1299, many were still unsentenced when the Cardinal of San Vitale examined his prisons. Five years afterwards, in 1310, Clement wrote to the Bishop of Albi and Geoffroi d'Ablis that the citizens of Albi had repeatedly appealed to him to have their trials completed either to condemnation or absolution. He therefore orders the trials proceeded with at once and the results submitted for confirmation to the Cardinals of Palestrina and Frascati, his former commissioners. The Bishop and Geoffroi d'Ablis contemptuously disregarded this command; some of the prisoners named in it had died before its date, whence they argued that the papal letter had been surreptitiously obtained. When this contumacy reached the ears of Clement, some year or two later, he wrote to Geraud, then Bishop of Albi, and Geoffroi, peremptorily reiterating his commands and ordering them to try both living and dead. In spite of this, Geoffroi maintained his sullen contumacy. We have no means of knowing the fate of most of these unfortunates, who probably rotted to death in their dungeons without their trials being concluded. After Clement and his cardinals had passed away, and no further interference was to be dreaded, in 1319 two surviving ones, Guillem Salavert and Isarn Colli, were brought out for further examination, when the former confirmed his confession and the latter retracted it as extorted under torture. Six months later, Guillem Calverie of Cordes, who had been imprisoned in 1301, was abandoned to the secular arm for retracting his confession (probably before Clement's cardinals), and Guillem Salavert was allowed to escape with wearing crosses, in consideration of his 19 years' imprisonment without conviction. Even as late as 1328 attested copies made by order of the royal judge of Carcassonne of inventories of personal property of Raymond Calverie and Jean Baudier, two of the prisoners of 1299–1300, show that their cases were still the subject of litigation. Even more remarkable is the case of Guillem Garric, held in prison for complicity in the attempt to destroy the records at Carcassonne in 1284. Royal letters of 1312 recite that his merits and piety had caused Clement V to grant him full pardon, wherefore the king restores to him and his descendants his confiscated castle of Monteirat. Yet the Inquisition did not relax its grip, but waited until 1321, when he was brought forth from prison, and in consideration of his contrition Bernard Gui mercifully sentenced the old man to perpetual banishment from France within thirty days.

The outcome of all this struggle and investigation is to be found in the measures of reform adopted in 1312 by the Council of Vienne at Clement's instance. The five books of canon law known as the "Clementines," which were enacted by the council, were retained for revision by Clement, who was on the point of publishing them when he died, April 20, 1314. They were held in suspense during the long interregnum which followed, and were not authoritatively given to the world until October 25, 1317, by John XXII. The canons relating to the Inquisition have been alluded to above, and it will be remembered that they only restricted the power of the inquisitor by requiring episcopal concurrence in the use of torture, or of harsh confinement equivalent to torture, and in the custody of prisons.

Clement died at Carpentras and was followed in about seven months (November 29) by Philippe le Bel. The cardinals on whom devolved the choice of a successor to St. Peter were torn with dissensions. Two years passed away without the election of a visible head of the Church, and the faithful might well fear that they had seen the last of the popes. The French court, however, had found itself so well abetted by a French pope that its policy required the chair of St. Peter to be filled, and in 1316 Louis le Hutin sent his brother, Philippe le Long, then Count of Poitiers, to Lyons with orders to get the cardinals together. For six months the business lagged without prospect of result, when Philippe received the news of the sudden death of his brother, and that the widowed queen claimed to be pregnant. The prospect of a vacant throne, or at least of a regency, awaiting him in Paris rendered further dallying in Lyons insupportable, nor could he well depart without bringing his errand to a successful issue. Consequently he invited the reverend fathers to a colloquy in the Dominican convent, and when they were thus safely hived he sternly told them that they should not depart till they had chosen a pope. His guards blocked every entrance, and he hastened off to Paris, leaving them to deliberate in captivity. Thus entrapped they made a merit of necessity, though forty days were still required before they proclaimed Jacques d'Ozo, Cardinal of Porto, as the Vicar of Christ.

With the election of John XXII the troubles of the Inquisition of Languedoc were over. Though he published the Clementines, he soon let it be seen that the inquisitors had nothing to fear from him, and they made haste to pay off the accumulated scores of vengeance. The first victim was Bernard Délicieux. During the pontificate of Clement and the interregnum he had lived in peace and might well imagine that his enthusiasm for the people of Languedoc had been forgotten. His earnest nature had led him to join the section of his order known as the Spirituals, and he had been prominent in the movements by which, during the vacancy of the Holy See, they had gained possession of the convents of Béziers and Narbonne. One of the first cares of John XXII was to heal this schism in the Order, and he promptly summoned before him the friars of Béziers and Narbonne. Bernard had not hesitated in signing an appeal to the pope, and he now boldly came before him at the head of his brethren. When he undertook to argue their cause he was accused of having impeded the Inquisition and was promptly arrested. Besides the charge of impeding the Inquisition, others of encompassing by magic arts the death of Benedict XI, and of treason in the affair of Carcassonne were brought against him. A papal commission was formed to investigate these matters, and for more than two years he was held in close prison while the examination went slowly on. At length it was ready for trial, and September 3, 1319, a court was convened at Castelnaudari consisting of the Archbishop of Toulouse and the Bishops of Pamiers and St. Papoul, when the archbishop excused himself and left the matter in the hands of his associates, who transferred the court to Carcassonne, September 12. The importance attached to the trial is shown by the fact that at it the Inquisition was represented by the Inquisitor Jean de Beaune, and the king by his Seneschal of Carcassonne and Toulouse and his "Reformers," Raoul, Bishop of Laon, and Jean, Count of Forez.

The official report of the trial has been preserved in all its immense prolixity, and there are few documents of that age more instructive as to what was then regarded as justice. Some of Bernard's old accomplices, such as Arnaud Garsia, Guillem Fransa, Pierre Probi, and others, who had already been seized by the Inquisition, were brought forward to be tried with him and were used as witnesses to save their own lives by swearing his away. The old man, worn with two years of imprisonment and constant examination, was subjected for two months to the sharpest cross-questioning on occurrences dating from 12 to 18 years previous, the subjects of the multiform charges being ingeniously intermingled in the most confusing manner. Under pretext of seeking the salvation of his soul he was solemnly and repeatedly admonished that he was legally a heretic for remaining for more than a year under the *ipso facto* excommunication incurred by impeding the Inquisition, and that nothing could save him from the stake but absolute submission and full confession. Twice he was tortured, the first time October 3, on the charge of treason, and the second, November 20, on that of necromancy; and though the torture was ordered to be "moderate," the notaries who assisted at it report that the shrieks of the victim attested its sufficiency. In neither case was anything extracted from him, but the efficacy of the combined pressure thus brought to bear on a man weakened by age and suffering is shown by the manner in which he was brought day by day to contradict and criminate himself, until at last he threw himself on the mercy of the court and humbly begged for absolution.

In the sentence, rendered December 8, he was acquitted of attempting the life of Benedict XI, while on the other charges his guilt was aggravated by no less than 70 perjuries committed under examination. After abjuration, he was duly absolved and condemned to degradation from holy orders and imprisonment for life, in chains and on bread and water, in the inquisitorial prison of Carcassonne. Considering the amnesty proclaimed in 1307 by Philippe le Bel, and the discharge of Frère Bernard in 1308, it seems strange that now the representatives of Philippe le Long at once protested against the sentence as too mild, and appealed to the pope. The judges themselves did not think so, for in delivering the prisoner to Jean de Beaune they humanely ordered that in view of his age and debility, and especially the weakness of his hands (doubtless crippled in the torture chamber), the penance of chains and bread and water should be omitted. Jean de Beaune may be pardoned if he felt a fierce exultation when the ancient enemy of his office was thus placed in his hands to expiate the offense which had so harassed his predecessors; and that exultation was perhaps increased when, February 26, 1320, the relentless pope, possibly to gratify the king, countermanded the pitying order of the bishops, and required the sentence to be executed in all its terrible rigor. Under these hardships the frail body which had been animated by so dauntless a spirit soon gave way, and in a few months merciful death released the only man who had dared to carry on a systematic warfare with the Inquisition.

The progress of reaction had been rapid. With the election of John XXII, the Inquisition recognized that its hour of triumph had come and took in hand the survivors of those who had been conspicuous in the disturbances of fifteen years before. The unconvicted prisoners of 1299 and 1300, whom it had held in defiance of the reiterated orders of Clement—at least those who had not rotted to death in its dungeons—were brought forth and disposed of. A still more emphatic assertion of its renewed mastery was the subjection

and "reconciliation" of the rebellious towns. Of what took place at
Carcassonne we have no record, but it probably was the same as the
ceremonies performed at Albi. There, March 11, 1319, the consuls
and councillors and a great crowd of citizens were assembled in
the cathedral cemetery, before Bishop Bernard and the Inquisitor
Jean de Beaune. There, with uplifted hands, they all professed repentance in the most humiliating terms and swore to accept whatever penance might be imposed upon them, and thereafter to obey
implicitly the bishop and inquisitor. Then those present, together
with the dead who had shown signs of penitence, were relieved
from excommunication, the rest of the population being required
to apply for absolution within a month. The town was to make good
all expenses and losses accruing to the episcopate and Inquisition by
reason of the troubles; it was to build and complete within two years
a chapel to the cathedral and a portal to the Dominican church; to
give 50 livres to the Carmelites to be expended on their church, and,
finally, to construct marble tombs for Nicholas d'Abbeville and
Foulques de Saint-Georges at Lyons and Carcassonne, where those
inquisitors had died in poverty and exile by reason of the rebellion
of the inhabitants. Ten pilgrimages were designated for the survivors
of those who in 1301 had bound themselves to prosecute Bishop
Bertrand and Nicholas d'Abbeville in the royal court, as well as for
those who had served as consuls and councillors from 1302 to 1304.
Thus the Inquisition celebrated its triumph in the long struggle.
It had won the victory, and its opponents could only save themselves
by unconditional surrender.

Catharism by this time had been forced back to the humbler
class among whom it had found its first disciples. The nobles and
gentlemen who had so long upheld it had perished or been impoverished by the remorseless confiscations of three-quarters of a
century. The rich burghers of the cities—merchants and professional
men—had learned the temptations held out by their wealth and the
impossibility of avoiding detection. Yet the old beliefs were still
rooted among the simple folk of country hamlets and especially
in the wild valleys among the foothills of the eastern Pyrenees.
The active intercourse with Lombardy, and even with Sicily, was
still kept up, and there were not wanting earnest ministers who
braved every danger to administer to believers the consolations of

their religion and to spread the faith in the fastnesses which were
its last refuge. Chief among these was Pierre Autier, formerly a
notary of Ax (Pamiers). His early life had not been pure, for we
hear of his *druda*, or mistress, and his natural children, but with
advancing years he embraced all the asceticism of the sect, to
which he devoted his life. Driven to Lombardy in 1295, he returned in 1298 to remain on his native soil to the end, and to endure a war to the knife from the Inquisition. His property was
confiscated and his family dispersed and ruined. The region to
which he belonged lay at the foot of the Pyrenees, rugged, with
few roads and many caves and hiding-places, whence escape across
the frontier to Aragon was comparatively facile; it was full of his
kindred, who were devoted to him, and here for eleven years he
maintained himself, lurking in disguise and wandering from place to
place with the emissaries of the Holy Office ever on his track. Already,
in 1300, he was so conspicuous that every effort was made for his
apprehension. A certain Guillem Jean offered the Dominicans of
Pamiers to betray him, but the treachery became known among the
faithful, two of whom, Pierre d'Aére and Philippe de Larnat, enticed
Guillem to the bridge at Alliat by night, seized him, gagged him, carried him off to the mountains, and, after extorting a confession, cast
him over a precipice. Worthy lieutenants of Pierre Autier were his
brother Guillem and his son Jacques, Amiel de Perles, Pierre Sanche,
and Sanche Mercadier, whose names occur everywhere throughout
the confessions as active missionaries.

The work of Geoffroi d'Ablis in Carcassonne seems to be principally directed to determining the protectors and refuges of Pierre
Autier. At Toulouse Bernard Gui was energetically employed in the
same direction. The heretic was driven from place to place, but the
fidelity of his disciples seemed to render all efforts vain, and finally
Bernard was driven to the expedient of issuing, August 10, 1309, a
special proclamation as an incitement for his capture:

Friar Bernard Gui, Dominican, Inquisitor of Toulouse, to all worshippers of Christ, the reward and crown of eternal life. Gird yourselves,
Sons of God; arise with me, Soldiers of Christ, against the enemies of
his Cross, those corrupters of the truth and purity of Catholic faith,
Pierre Autier, the heresiarch, and his coheretics and accomplices, Pierre

Sanche and Sanche Mercadier. Hiding in concealment and walking in darkness, I order them by the virtue of God, to be tracked and seized wherever they may be found, promising eternal reward from God, and also a fitting temporal payment to those who will capture and produce them. Watch, therefore, O pastors, lest the wolves snatch away the sheep of your flock! Act manfully, faithful zealots, lest the adversaries of the faith fly and escape!

This stirring exhortation was superfluous, for the prey was captured before it could have been published. The arrest of nearly all his family and friends, in 1308–9, had driven Pierre Autier from his accustomed haunts. About St. John's Day (June 24) 1309, he found' refuge with Perrin Maurel of Belpech, near Castelnaudari, where he lay for five weeks or more. Thither came his daughter Guillelma, who remained with him a short time, and the two departed together. The next day he was captured. Perrin Maurel was also seized, and with customary fidelity stoutly denied everything until Pierre Autier, in prison, advised him in December to confess.

This triumph was followed in October by the capture of Amiel de Perles, who forthwith placed himself in *endura*, refusing to eat or drink, and, as he was fast sinking, to prevent the stake from being robbed of its prey, a special *auto de fé* was hurriedly arranged for his burning, October 23. While yet his strength lasted, however, Bernard Gui enjoyed the ghastly amusement of making the two heresiarchs in his presence perform the act of heretical "adoration."

Pierre Autier was not burned until the great *auto de fé* of April 1310, when Geoffroi d'Ablis came from Carcassonne to share in the triumph. The heresiarch had not sought to conceal his faith, but boldly declared his obnoxious tenets and had pronounced the Church of Rome the synagogue of Satan. That he was subjected to the extremity of torture, however, there can be no reasonable doubt—not to extract a confession, but to force him to betray his disciples and those who had given him refuge. His intimate acquaintance with all the heretics of the land was a source of information too important for Bernard Gui to shrink from any means of acquiring it; and the copious details obtained are alluded to in too many subsequent sentences for us to hesitate as to the methods by which the heresiarch was brought to place his friends and associates at the mercy of his tormentors.

This may be said to close the bloody drama of Catharism in Languedoc. Armed with the revelations thus obtained, Bernard Gui and Geoffroi d'Ablis required but a few years more to convert or burn the remnant of Pierre Autier's disciples who could be caught, and to drive into exile those who eluded their spies.

Thus the Inquisition triumphed, as force will generally do when it is sufficiently strong, skillfully applied, and systematically continued without interruption. In the twelfth century the south of France had been the most civilized land of Europe. There commerce, industry, art, science, had been far in advance of the age. The cities had won virtual self-government, were proud of their wealth and strength, jealous of their liberties, and self-sacrificing in their patriotism. The crusaders came, and their unfinished work was taken up and executed to the end by the Inquisition. It left a ruined and impoverished country, with shattered industry and failing commerce. The native nobles were broken by confiscation and replaced by strangers who occupied the soil, introducing the harsh customs of northern feudalism, or the despotic principles of the Roman law, in the extensive domains acquired by the crown. The precocious civilization which had promised to lead Europe in the path of culture was gone, and to Italy was transferred the honor of the Renaissance. In return for this was unity of faith and a Church which had been hardened and vitiated and secularized in the strife.

Yet in the very triumph of the Inquisition was the assurance of its decline. Supported by the State, it had earned and repaid the royal favor by the endless stream of confiscations which it poured into the royal coffers. Perhaps nothing contributed more to the consolidation of the royal supremacy than the change of ownership which threw into new hands so large a portion of the lands of the south. In the territories of the great vassals the right to the confiscations for heresy became recognized as an important portion of the *droits seigneuriaux*. In the domains of the crown they were granted to favorites or sold at moderate prices to those who thus became interested in the new order of things. The royal officials grasped everything on which they could lay their hands, whether on the excuse of treason or of heresy, with little regard to any rights; and although the integrity of Louis IX caused an inquest to be held in 1262, which restored a vast amount of property illegally held, this was but a small fraction of the whole. With the disappearance of Catharism, Languedoc became as much a part of the monarchy as l'Isle de France, and the career of its Inquisition merges into that of the rest of the kingdom.

CHAPTER XI
FRANCE

ALTHOUGH Catharism never obtained in the north sufficient foothold to render it threatening to the Church, guardians of the faith were requisite in lands where heretics were few and hidden as well as in those where they were numerous and enjoyed protection from noble and city. Under the pious king St. Louis, who declared that the only argument a layman could use with a heretic was to thrust a sword into him up to the hilt, they were sure of ample support from the secular power.

Accordingly when in 1233 the experiment was tried of appointing Pierre Cella and Guillem Arnaud as inquisitors in Toulouse, a similar tentative effort was made in the northern part of the kindgom. Here also it was the Dominican Order which was called upon to furnish the necessary zealots, and in western Burgundy the Church was fortunate in finding a proper instrument. Like Rainerio Saccone, Frère Robert, known as *le Bugre*, had been a Patarin. The peculiar fitness thence derived for detecting the hidden heretic was rendered still more effective by the special gift which he is said to have claimed, of being able to recognize them by their speech and carriage. In addition, he was fitted for the work by the ardent fanaticism of the convert, by his learning, his fiery eloquence, and his mercilessness. When, early in 1233, instructions to persecute heresy were sent to the Prior of Besançon, Robert was nominated to represent him and act as his substitute, and, eager to manifest his zeal, he lost no time in making a descent upon La Charité. This was the place that was notorious as a center of heresy in the twelfth century, and repeated efforts had been made to purify it.

We have no means of knowing what measures Robert adopted, but there can be no doubt that he was active and unsparing. It was not long before the Archbishop of Sens, in whose province La Charité lày, expostulated with Gregory upon this interference with his jurisdiction, and in this he was joined by other prelates. They assured the pope that there was no heresy in their provinces and no neces-

sity for these extraordinary measures. Gregory thereupon revoked all
commissions early in February 1234. Had Robert been an ordinary
man this might have postponed for some time the extension of the
Inquisition in France, but he was too ardent to be repressed. In
June 1234 we find St. Louis paying for the maintenance of heretics
in prison at St. Pierre-le-Moutier, near Nevers, which would seem
as though Frère Robert had succeeded in getting to work again on
his old field of operations. Meanwhile he had not been idle elsewhere.
At Peronne he burned 5 victims; at Elincourt, 4, besides a pregnant
woman who was spared for a time at the intercession of the queen.
His methods were speedy, for before Lent was out we find him at
Cambrai, where, with the assistance of the Archbishop of Reims
and three bishops, he burned about 20 and condemned others to
crosses and prison. Thence he hastened to Douai, where in May
he had the satisfaction of burning 10 more and condemning numerous others to crosses and prison. All this was sufficient to convince
Gregory that he had been misinformed about the absence of heresy,
and we find him in August 1235 excitedly announcing to the Dominican provincial that God had revealed to him that the whole of
France was boiling with the venom of heretical reptiles, and that the
business of the Inquisition must be resumed with loosened rein. Frère
Robert was to be commissioned again, with fitting colleagues to scour
the whole kingdom. The Archbishop of Sens was strictly ordered to
lend efficient help to him, and Robert himself was honored with a
special papal commission empowering him to act throughout the
whole of France.

This was pouring oil upon the flames. Robert's untempered
fanaticism had required no stimulus, and now it raged beyond all
bounds. The kingdom, by Gregory's thoughtless zeal, was delivered
up to one who was little better than a madman. Supported by the
piety of St. Louis, the prelates were obliged to aid him and carry out
his behests, and for several years he traversed the provinces of
Flanders, Champagne, Burgundy, and France with none to curb or
oppose him. Those whom he designated as heretics had the alternative of abjuration, with perpetual imprisonment, or of the stake—
varied occasionally with burial alive. In one term of two or three
months he is said to have thus dispatched about 50 unfortunates of
either sex. The terror spread by his arbitrary and pitiless proceedings

rendered him formidable to high and low alike, until at length the evident confounding of the innocent with the guilty raised a clamor to which even Gregory IX was forced to listen. An investigation was held in 1238 which exposed his misdeeds, though not before he had time, in 1239, to burn a number of heretics at Montmorillon in Vienne, and 27, or, according to other accounts, 183, at Mont-Wimer, where, at this holocaust pleasing to God, there were present the King of Navarre with a crowd of prelates and nobles and a multitude widely estimated at 700,000 souls. Robert's commission was withdrawn, and he expiated his insane cruelties in perpetual prison.

The unlucky termination of Robert's career did not affect his colleagues, and thenceforth the Inquisition was permanently established throughout France in Dominican hands. Yet scarce a trace of their strenuous labors has been left to us. Heretics throughout the north were comparatively few and scattered; the chroniclers of the period take no note of their discovery and punishment, nor even of the establishment of the Inquisition itself. We know, however, that King Louis welcomed them in his old hereditary dominions, as he did in the newly acquired territories of Languedoc, and stimulated their zeal by defraying their expenses. In the accounts of the royal baillis for 1248 we find entries of sums disbursed for them in Paris, Orleans, Issoudun, Senlis, Amiens, Tours, Yèvre-le-Chatel, Beaumont, St. Quentin, Laon, and Macon, showing that his liberality furnished them with means to do their work, not only in the domains of the crown, but in those of the great vassals.

In Provence, where Pons de l'Esparre, the Dominican prior, had at first carried on a kind of volunteer chase after heretics, we see an inquisitor officially acting in 1245. This district, comprising the whole southeastern portion of modern France, with Savoy, was confided to the Franciscans. In 1266, when they were engaged in Marseilles in mortal strife with the Dominicans, the business of persecution would seem to have been neglected, for we find Clement IV ordering the Benedictines of St. Victor to make provision for extirpating the numerous heretics of the valley of Rousset, where they had a dependency. The Inquisition of Provence was extended in 1288 over Avignon and the Comtat Venaissin, whose governor was ordered to defray from the confiscations the expenses of the Inquisitors Bertrand de Cigotier and Guillem de Saint-Marcel. In 1292 Dauphiné was likewise included, thus completing the organization in the territories east of the Rhone.

Little remains to us of the organization thus perfected over the wide territory stretching from the Bay of Biscay to the Rhine. The laborers were vigorous, and labored according to the light which was in them, but the men and their acts are buried beneath the dust of the forgotten past. We hear constantly of refugees from Toulouse and Carcassonne flying for safety to Lombardy and even to Sicily, but never to Touraine or Champagne, nor do we ever meet with cases in which the earnest missionaries of Catharism sought converts beyond the Cévennes. This may fairly be ascribed to the vigilance of the inquisitors.

In 1308 we hear of a certain Étienne de Verberie of Soissons, accused before the inquisitor of blasphemous expressions concerning the body of Christ. He alleged drunkenness in excuse, and was mercifully treated. Shortly afterwards occurred the first formal *auto de fé* of which we have cognizance at Paris, on May 31, 1310. A renegade Jew was burned, but the principal victim was Marguerite de Hainault, or la Porete. She is described as a *"béguine clergesse,"* the first apostle in France of the German sect of Brethren of the Free Spirit, whom we shall consider more fully hereafter. Her chief error was the doctrine that the soul, absorbed in Divine love, could yield without sin to all the demands of the flesh, and she regarded with insufficient veneration the sacrifice of the altar. She had written a book to propagate these doctrines which had, before the year 1305, been condemned as heretical and burned by Gui II, Bishop of Cambrai. He had mercifully spared her, while forbidding her under pain of the stake from circulating it in future or disseminating its doctrines. In spite of this she had again been brought before Gui's successor, Philippe de Marigny, and the Inquisitor of Lorraine, for spreading it among the simple folk called Beghards, and she had again escaped. Unwearied in her missionary work, she had even ventured to present the forbidden volume to Jean, Bishop of Chalons, without suffering the penalty due to her obstinacy. In 1308 she extended her propaganda to Paris and fell into the hands of Frère Guillaume de Paris, the inquisitor, before whom she persistently refused to take the preliminary oath requisite to her examination. He was probably too preoccupied with the affair of the Templars to give her prompt justice, and for 18 months she lay in the inquisitorial dungeons under the consequent excommunication. This alone would have sufficed for her conviction as an impenitent heretic, but her previous career rendered her a relapsed heretic. Instead of calling an assembly of experts, as was customary in Languedoc, the inquisitor laid a written statement of the case before the canonists of the University, who unanimously decided, May 30, that if the facts as stated were true, she was a relapsed heretic, to be relaxed to the secular arm. Accordingly, on May 31, she was handed over, with the customary adjuration for mercy, to the prévôt of Paris, who duly burned her the next day, when her noble manifestation of devotion moved the people to tears of compassion. Another actor in the tragedy was a disciple of Marguerite, a clerk of the diocese of Beauvais named Guion de Cressonessart. He had endeavored to save Marguerite from the clutches of the Inquisition, and on being seized had, like her, refused to take the oath. His brain seems to have turned during his detention, for at length he astonished the inquisitor by proclaiming himself the Angel of Philadelphia and an envoy of God, who alone could save mankind. The inquisitor in vain pointed out that this was a function reserved solely for the pope, and as Guion would not withdraw his claims he was convicted as a heretic. For some reason, however, not specified in the sentence, he was only condemned to degradation from orders and to perpetual imprisonment.

The next case of which we hear is that of the Sieur de Partenay, in 1323, to which allusion has already been made.[1] Its importance to us lies in its revealing the enormous and almost irresponsible authority wielded by the Inquisition at this period. When such a man could be so handled at the mere word of an angry friar, meaner victims stood little chance. This case in the north and the close of Bernard Gui's career in Toulouse, about the same time, mark the apogee of the Inquisition in France. Thenceforth we have to follow its decline.

Yet for some years longer there was a show of activity at Carcassonne, where Henri de Chamay was a worthy representative of the older inquisitors. January 16, 1329, in conjunction with Pierre Bruni he celebrated an *auto de fé* at Pamiers, where 35 persons were

[1] See page 215.

permitted to lay aside crosses, and 12 were released from prison with crosses, 6 were pardoned, 7 were condemned to perpetual imprisonment, together with 4 false witnesses, 8 had arbitrary penances assigned them, 4 dead persons were sentenced, and a friar and a priest were degraded. As the see of Pamiers, to which this *auto* was confined, was a small one, the number of sentences uttered indicates active work. December 12 of the same year, Henri de Chamay held another at Narbonne, where the fate of some 40 delinquents was decided. Then, January 7, 1329, he held another at Pamiers; May 19, one at Béziers; September 8, one at Carcassonne, where 6 unfortunates were burned and 21 condemned to perpetual prison. Shortly afterwards he burned 3 at Albi, and towards the end of the year he held another *auto* at a place not named, where 8 persons were sentenced to prison, 3 to prison in chains, and 2 were burned.

Activity continued for some little time longer, but the records have perished which would supply the details. We happen to have the accounts of the Sénéchaussée of Toulouse, for 1337, which show that Pierre Bruni, the inquisitor, was by no means idle. The receiver of confiscations enumerates the estates of 30 heretics from which collections are in hand; there was an *auto de fé* celebrated and paid for; the number of prisoners in the inquisitorial jail is stated at 82. The terrible vicissitudes of the English war doubtless soon afterwards slackened the energy of the inquisitors, but we know that there were *autos de fé* celebrated at Carcassonne in 1346, 1357, and 1383, and one at Toulouse in 1374.

With the return of peace under Charles le Sage the Inquisition had freer scope. The Beghards, or Brethren of the Free Spirit, undeterred by the martyrdom of Marguerite la Porete, had continued to exist in secret. In September 1365, Urban V notified the prelates and inquisitors throughout France that they were actively at work propagating their doctrines, and he sent detailed information of their tenets and the places where they were to be found to the Bishop of Paris, with orders to communicate it to his fellow prelates and the Inquisition. If any immediate response to this was made, the result has not reached us, but in 1372 we find Frère Jacques de More, *inquisiteur des Bougres*, busy in eradicating them. They called themselves the Company of Poverty, and were popularly known by the name of Turelupins; as in

Germany, they were distinguished by their peculiar vestments, and they propagated their doctrines largely by their devotional writings in the vernacular. Charles V rewarded the labors of the inquisitor with a donation of 50 francs, and received the thanks of Gregory XI for his zeal. The outcome of the affair was the burning of the books and garments of the heretics in the swine market beyond the Porte Saint-Honoré, together with the female leader of the sect, Jeanne Daubenton. Her male colleague escaped by death in prison, but his body was preserved in quicklime for fifteen days, in order that he might accompany his partner in guilt in the flames.

The sect was a stubborn one, however, especially in Germany, as we shall see hereafter, and in the early part of the next century Chancellor Gerson still considers it of sufficient importance to combat its errors repeatedly. In May 1421, twenty-five of these sectaries were condemned at Douai by the Bishop of Arras. Twenty of them recanted and were penanced with crosses and banishment or imprisonment, but five were stubborn and sealed their faith with martyrdom in the flames.

In 1381 Frère Jacques de More had a more illustrious victim in Hugues Aubriot. A Burgundian by birth, Aubriot's energy and ability had won for him the confidence of King Charles, who had made him Prévôt of Paris. To him the city owed the first system of sewerage that had been attempted, as well as the Bastille, which he built as a bulwark against the English, and he imposed some limitation on the flourishing industry of the *filles de vie*. His good government gained him the respect and affection of the people, but he made a mortal enemy of the University by disregarding the immunities on the preservation of which, in the previous century, it had staked its existence. In mockery of its wrath, when building the Petit-Châtelet, he named two foul dungeons after two of the principal quarters of the University, *le Clos Bruneau* and *la Rue du Foing*, saying that they were intended for the students. Under the strong rule of Charles V the University had to digest its wrongs as best it could, but after his death, in 1380, it eagerly watched its opportunity. This was not long in coming, nor, in the rivalry between the Dukes of Berri and Burgundy, was it difficult to enlist the former against Aubriot as a Burgundian. The rule of the princes, at once feeble and despotic, invited disorder, and when the people, November 25, 1380, rose against the Jews, pillaged their houses, and forcibly baptized their children, Aubriot incurred the implacable enmity of the Church by forcing a restoration of the infants to their parents. The combination against him thus became too strong for the court to resist. It yielded, and on January 21, 1381, he was cited to appear before the bishop and inquisitor. He disdained to obey the summons, and his excommunication for contumacy was published in all the churches of Paris. This compelled obedience, and when he came before the inquisitor, on February 1, he was at once thrown into the episcopal prison while his trial proceeded. The charges were most frivolous, except the affair of the Jewish children and his having released from the Châtelet a prisoner accused of heresy, placed there by the inquisitor. It was alleged that on one occasion one of his sergeants had excused himself for delay by saying that he had waited at church to see God (the elevation of the Host), when Aubriot angrily rejoined, "Sirrah, know ye not that I have more power to harm you than God to help"; and again that when someone had told him that they would see God in a mass celebrated by Silvestre de la Cervelle, Bishop of Coutances, he replied that God would not permit himself to be handled by such a man as the bishop. On the strength of this flimsy gossip he was actually condemned to be burned without the privilege allowed to all heretics of saving himself by abjuration; but the princes intervened and succeeded in obtaining this for him. On May 17 a solemn *auto de fé* was held. On a scaffold erected in front of Nôtre Dame, Aubriot humbly confessed and recanted the heresies of which he had been convicted, and received the sentence of perpetual imprisonment, which of course carried with it the confiscation of his wealth, while the rejoicing scholars of the University lampooned him in halting verses. He was thence conveyed to a dungeon, where he lay until 1382, when the insurrection of the Maillotins occurred. The first thought of the people was of their old prévôt. They broke open the prison, drew him forth and placed him at their head. He accepted the post, but the same night he quietly withdrew and escaped to his native Burgundy, where his adventurous life ended in peaceful obscurity.

After this we hear little more of the Inquisition of Paris, although it continued to exist. When, in 1388, the eloquence of Thomas of Apulia drew wondering crowds to listen with veneration to his teaching that the law of the Gospel was simply love, with the deduction that the sacraments, the invocation of saints, and all the inventions of the current theology were useless; when he wrote a book inveighing against the sins of prelate and pope, and asserting, with *The Everlasting Gospel*, that the reign of the Holy Ghost had supplanted that of the Father and the Son, and when he boldly announced himself as the envoy of the Holy Ghost sent to reform the world, the Inquisition was not called upon to silence even this revolutionary heretic. It was the Prévôt of Paris who ordered him to desist from preaching, and, when he refused, it was the bishop and University who tried him, ordered his book to be burned on the Place de Grève, and would have burned him had not the medical alienists of the day testified to his insanity and procured for him a commutation of his punishment to perpetual imprisonment.

Various causes had long been contributing to deprive the Inquisition in France of the importance which it had once enjoyed. Not only had it become superfluous as an instrument for the throne, but the throne which it had aided to establish had become supreme and had reduced it to subjection. Even in the plenitude of inquisitorial power the tendency to regard the royal court as possessing a jurisdiction higher than that of the Holy Office is shown in the case of Amiel de Lautrec, Abbot of S. Sernin. In 1322 the Viguier of Toulouse accused him to the Inquisition for having preached the doctrine that the soul is mortal in essence and only immortal through grace. The Inquisition examined the matter and decided that this was not heresy. The royal *procureur-général*, dissatisfied with this, appealed from the decision, not to the pope but to the Parlement. No question more purely spiritual can well be conceived, and yet the Parlement gravely entertained the appeal and asserted its jurisdiction by confirming the decree of the Inquisition.

This was ominous of the future, although the indefatigable Henri de Chamay, apparently alarmed at the efforts successfully made by Philippe de Valois to control and limit spiritual jurisdictions, procured from that monarch, in November 1329, a *Mandement* confirming the privileges of the Inquisition, placing all temporal nobles and officials afresh at its disposal, and annulling all letters emanating from the royal court, whether past or future, which should in any way impede inquisitors from performing their functions in accordance with their commissions from the Holy See. The evolution of the monarchy was proceeding too rapidly to be checked. Henri de Chamay himself, in 1328, had officially qualified himself as inquisitor, deputed not by the pope, as had always been the formula proudly employed, but by the king, and a judicial decision to this effect followed soon after. It was Philippe's policy to enforce and extend the jurisdiction of the crown, and in pursuance of this he sent Guillaume de Villars to Toulouse to reform the encroachments of the ecclesiastical tribunals over the royal courts. In 1330 de Villars, in the performance of his duty, caused the registers of the ecclesiastical courts to be submitted to him, after which he demanded those of the Inquisition. When we remember how arrogantly Nicholas d'Abbeville had refused a sight of them to the bishops sent by Phillipe le Bel, and how long Jean de Pequigny hesitated before he interfered with Geoffroi d'Ablis, we can measure the extent of the silent revolution which had occurred during the interval in the relations between Church and State, by the fact that de Villars, on being refused, coolly proceeded to break open the door of the chamber in which the registers were kept. The inquisitor appealed, and again it was not to the pope, but to the Parlement, and that body, in condemning de Villars to pay the costs and damages, did so on the ground that the Inquisition was a royal and not an ecclesiastical court. This was a Pyrrhic victory; the State had absorbed the Inquisition.

The Great Schism, followed by the Councils of Constance and Basle, did much to shake the power on which the Inquisition was founded. The position of Charles VII towards Rome was consistently insubordinate, and the Pragmatic Sanction which he published in 1438 secured the independence of the Gallican Church and strengthened the jurisdiction of the Parlement. When Louis XI abrogated it in 1461, the remonstrances of his Parlement form a singularly free-spoken indictment of papal vices, and that body continued to treat the instrument as practically in force, while Louis himself, by successive measures, gradually re-established its principles. Had not the Concordat of Francis I, in 1516, swept it away, when he conspired with Leo X to divide the spoils of the Church, it would eventually have rendered France independent of Rome. Francis knew so well the opposition it would excite that he hesitated for a year to submit the measure to his Parlement for registration, and the Parlement deferred the registration for another year, till at last the negotiator of the concordat, Cardinal Duprat, brought to bear sufficient pressure to accomplish the object. During the discussion the University had the boldness to protest publicly against it, and to lodge with the Parlement an appeal to the next general council.

During this period of antagonism to Rome the University of Paris had contributed no little to the abasement of the Inquisition by supplanting it as an investigator of doctrine and judge of heresy. Its ancient renown, fully maintained by an uninterrupted succession of ardent and learned teachers, gave it great authority. It was a national institution of which clergy and laity alike might well be proud, and at one time it appeared as though it might rival the Parlement in growing into one of the recognized powers of the State. In the fearful anarchy which accompanied the insanity of Charles VI it boldly assumed a right to speak on public affairs, and its interference was welcomed. In 1411 the king, who chanced at the time to be in the hands of the Burgundians, appealed to it to excommunicate the Armagnacs, and the University zealously did so. In 1412 it presented a remonstrance to the king on the subject of the financial disorders of the time and demanded a reform. Supported by the Parisians, at its dictate the financiers and thieves of the government, with the exception of the chancellor, were dismissed in 1413, greatly to the discontent of the courtiers.

To what an extent the University in time replaced the Inquisition in its neglected and forgotten functions is shown in 1498, in the case of the Observantine Franciscan, Jean Vitrier. In the restlessness and insubordination which heralded the Reformation, this obscure friar anticipated Luther even more than did John of Wesel, although in the strictness of his asceticism he taught that a wife might better break her marriage vow than her fasts. In his preaching at Tournay he counselled the people to drag the concubines and their priests from their houses with shame and derision; he affirmed that it was a mortal sin to listen to the masses of concubinary priests. Pardons and indulgences were the offspring of hell: the faithful ought not to purchase them, for they were not intended for the maintenance of brothels. These were old heresies for which any inquisitor would promptly offer the utterer the alternative of abjuration or the stake; but the prelates and magistrates of Tournay referred the matter to the University, which laboriously extracted from Vitrier's sermons 16 propositions for condemnation.

It is not to be supposed, however, that the Inquisition, though fallen from its former dignity, had ceased to exist or to perform its functions after a fashion. It was to the interest of the popes to maintain it, and the position of inquisitor, though humble in comparison with that which his predecessors enjoyed, was yet a source of influence, and possibly of profit, which led to its being eagerly sought. In 1414 we find two contestants for the post at Toulouse, and in 1424 an unseemly quarrel between two rivals at Carcassonne, yet the position thus eagerly sought had no legitimate means of support. In the terrible disorders of the times the royal stipends had been withdrawn. Alexander V, in 1409, instructed his legate, the Cardinal of S. Susanna, that some method must be devised of meeting the expenses of the inquisitor, his associate, his notary, and his servant, and in 1418 Martin V wrote to the Archbishop of Narbonne that he must find some means of supplying the necessary expenses of the Inquisition. Under such circumstances the attraction of the office may, perhaps, be discerned from a petition, in this same year 1418, from the citizens of Avignon in favor of the Jews. The protection afforded by the Avignonese popes to this proscribed class had rendered the city a Jewish center, and they were found of much utility; but they were constantly molested by the inquisitors, who instituted frivolous prosecutions against them, doubtless not without profit. Martin listened kindly to the appeal, and it proves the degradation of the Inquisition that he gave the Jews a right to appoint an assessor who should sit with the inquisitor in all cases in which they were concerned.

I shall have occasion hereafter to speak of the part played by the Inquisition in the tragedy of Joan of Arc, and need here only allude to the appointment in 1431, by Eugenius IV, of Frère Jean Graveran to be Inquisitor of Rouen, where he was already exercising the functions of the office, and where he was succeeded in 1433 by Frère Sébastien l'Abbé, who had been papal penitentiary and chaplain— another evidence of the partition of France during the disastrous English war.

With the pacification of France and the final expulsion of the

English, Nicholas V seems to have thought the occasion opportune
for reviving and establishing the Inquisition on a firmer and broader
basis. A bull of August 1, 1451, to Hugues le Noir, Inquisitor of
France, defines his jurisdiction as extending not only over the
Kingdom of France, but also over the Duchy of Aquitaine and all
Gascony and Languedoc. Thus, with the exception of the eastern
provinces, the whole was consolidated into one district, with its
principal seat probably in Toulouse. The jurisdiction of the inquisitor
was likewise extended over all offenses that had hitherto been considered doubtful—blasphemy, sacrilege, divination, even when not
savoring of heresy, and unnatural crimes. He was further released
from the necessity of episcopal co-operation, and was empowered to
carry on all proceedings and render judgment without calling the
bishops into consultation. Two centuries earlier these enormous
powers would have rendered Hugues almost omnipotent, but now
it was too late. In 1458 the Franciscan Minister of Burgundy represented to Pius II the deplorable condition of the institution in the
extensive territories confided to his Order, comprising the great
archiepiscopates of Lyons, Vienne, Arles, Aix, Embrun, and
Tarantaise, and covering both sides of the Rhone and a considerable
portion of Savoy. In the thirteenth century Clement IV had placed
this region under the control of the Burgundian Minister, but with
the lapse of time his supervision had become nominal. Ambitious
friars had obtained directly from the popes commissions to act as
inquisitors in special districts, and therefore acknowledged no authority but their own. Others had assumed the office without appointment from anyone. Scandals were numerous, the people were oppressed, and the Order exposed to opprobrium. Pius hastened to put
an end to these abuses by renewing the obsolete authority of the
minister, with full power of removal, even of those who enjoyed
papal commissions. Yet only three years later, we find Pius renewing
the old abuses by a special appointment of Brother Bartholomäus of
Eger as Inquisitor of Grenoble. That such commissions were sold,
or conferred as a matter of favor, there can be no reasonable doubt.
Only this can explain a form of appointment which became common:
"Inquisitor in the Kingdom of France," "without prejudice to other
inquisitors authorized by us or by others"—a sort of letter-of-marque
to cruise at large and make what the appointees could from the faith-

ful. Similarly significant is the appointment of Frère Pierre Cordrat, confessor of Jean, Duke of Bourbon, in 1478, to be Inquisitor of Bourges, thus wholly disregarding the consolidation of the kingdom by Nicholas V.

Several cases occurring about this period are interesting as illustrations of the spread of the spirit of inquiry and independence, and of the subordinate position to which the Inquisition had sunk. In 1459, at Lille, there was burned a heretic known as Alphonse of Portugal, who led an austere life as an anchorite and frequented the churches assiduously, but who declared that since Gregory the Great there had been no true pope, and consequently no valid administration of the sacraments. Still more significant is the case, in 1484, of Jean Laillier, a priest in Paris, a theological licentiate, and an applicant for the doctorate in theology. In his sermons he had been singularly free-spoken. He denied the validity of the rule of celibacy; he quoted Wickliff as a great doctor; he rejected the supremacy of Rome and the binding force of tradition and decretal; so far from St. Francis's occupying the vacant throne of Lucifer in heaven, he was rather with Lucifer in hell; since the time of Silvester the Holy See had been the church of avarice and of imperial power, where canonization could be obtained for money. So weak had become the traditional hold of the Church on the consciences of men that this revolutionary preaching seems to have aroused no opposition, even on the part of the Inquisition; but Laillier, not content with simple toleration, applied to the University for the doctorate, and was refused admission to the preliminary disputations unless he should purge himself, undergo penance, and obtain the assent of the Holy See. Laillier thereupon boldly applied to the Parlement, asking it to compel the University to admit him. The Parlement entertained no doubts as to its own competence, but decided the case in a manner not looked for by the hardy priest. It ordered Louis, Bishop of Paris, in conjunction with the inquisitor and four doctors selected by the University, to prosecute Laillier to due punishment. The bishop and inquisitor agreed to proceed separately and communicate their processes to each other; but Laillier must have had powerful backers, for Bishop Louis, without conferring with his colleague or the experts, allowed Laillier to make a partial recantation and a public abjuration couched in the most free and easy terms, absolved him, June 23, 1486, pronounced him free from suspicion of heresy, restored him to his functions, and declared him capable of promotion to all grades and honors. Frère Jean Cossart, the inquisitor, who had been diligently collecting evidence of many scandalous doctrines of Laillier's and vainly communicating them to the bishop, was forced to swallow this affront in silence, but the University felt its honor engaged and was not inclined to submit. November 6, 1486, it issued a formal protest against the action of the bishop, appealed to the pope, and demanded *Apostoli*. Innocent VIII promptly came to the rescue. He annulled the decision of the bishop and ordered the inquisitor, in conjunction with the Archbishop of Sens and the Bishop of Meaux, to throw Laillier into prison, while they should investigate the unrecanted heresies and send the papers to Rome for decision. It is not a little singular that the Bishop of Meaux, who was selected to sit in judgment on Laillier, was at this very time under censure by the University for reviving the Donatist heresy of the insufficiency of the sacraments in polluted hands—the Eucharist of a fornicating priest was of no more account, he said, than the barking of a dog. Many an unfortunate Waldensian had been burned for less than this, but the inquisitor had not dared to hold him to account.

The career of the Waldenses forms so interesting and well-defined an episode in the history of persecution that I have hitherto omitted reference to that sect, in order to present a brief, continuous outline of its relations with the Inquisition, which found in it, after the disappearance of the Cathari, the only really important field of labor in France. Although by no means as numerous or as powerful in Languedoc as the Cathari, the Waldenses formed an important heretical element. In the sentences of Pierre Cella, rendered in Querci in 1241 and 1242, we have abundant testimony to their numbers and activity. Thus, references occur to them:

At Gourdon in	55	cases	out of	219
At Montcucq in	44	"	" "	84
At Sauveterre in	1	case	" "	5
At Belcayre in	3	cases	" "	7
At Montauban in	175	"	" "	252
At Moissac in	1	case	" "	94
At Montpezat in	no	"	" "	22
At Montaut in	no	"	" "	23
At Castelnau in	1	"	" "	11

and although many of these are mere allusions to having seen them or had dealings with them, the comparative frequency of the reference indicates the places where their heresy was most flourishing.

They had a regular organization—schools for the young; cemeteries where their dead were buried; missionaries who traversed the land to spread the faith, and who customarily refused all alms save hospitality. A certain Pierre des Vaux is frequently referred to as one of the most active and most beloved of these, regarded, according to one of his disciples, as an angel of light. Public preaching in the streets was constant, and numerous allusions are made to disputations held between the Waldensian ministers and the Catharan perfects. Still, the utmost good feeling existed between the two persecuted sects. Men were found who confessed to believing in the Waldenses and to performing acts of adoration to the Cathari—in the common enmity to Rome any faith which was not orthodox was regarded as good. The reputation of the Waldenses as skillful leeches was a powerful aid in their missionary labors. They were constantly consulted in cases of disease or injury, and almost without exception they refused payment for their ministrations, save food. One woman confessed to giving 40 sols to a Catharan for medical services, while to Waldenses she gave only wine and bread. We learn also that they heard confessions and imposed penance; that they celebrated a sacramental supper in which bread and fish were blessed and partaken of, and that bread which they consecrated with the sign of the cross was regarded as holy by their disciples. Notwithstanding the strength and organization of the sect, the Waldenses were evidently looked upon by Pierre Cella with a less unfavorable eye than the Cathari, and the penances imposed on them were habitually lighter.

From Lyons the Waldensian belief had spread to the north and east, as well as to the south and west. It is a curious fact that while the Cathari never succeeded in establishing themselves to any extent beyond the Romance territories, the Waldenses were already, in 1192, so numerous in Lorraine that Eudes, Bishop of Toul, in ordering them to be captured, not only promises remission of sins as a reward, but feels obliged to add that if, for rendering this service, the faithful are driven away from their homes, he will find them in food and clothing. In Franche Comté, John, Count of Burgundy,

bears emphatic testimony to their numbers in 1248, when he solicited
of Innocent IV the introduction of the Inquisition in his dominions,
and its discontinuance in 1257 doubtless left them to multiply in
peace. It was, however, in the mountains of Auvergne and the Alpine
and sub-Alpine regions stretching between Geneva and the Mediterranean that they found the surest refuge.

In 1251, when Alphonse and Jeanne guaranteed at Beaucaire the
liberties of Avignon and the Comtat Venaissin, the Bishop-Legate
Zoen earnestly urged them to destroy the Waldenses there. There
were amply laws on the municipal statute books of Avignon and
Arles for the extermination of "heretics and Waldenses," but the
local magistracy was slack in their enforcement and was obliged to
swear to extirpate the sectaries. The Waldenses were mostly simple
mountain folk, with possessions that offered no temptation for confiscation, and persecuting energy was more profitable and more use-
fully directed against the richer Cathari. We hear that from 1271 to
1274 the zeal of Guillaume de Cobardon, Seneschal of Carcassonne,
urged the inquisitors to active work against the Waldenses, resulting
in numerous convictions, but among the far more populous communities near the Rhone the Inquisition was not introduced into
the Comtat Venaissin until 1288, nor into Dauphiné until 1292,
and in both cases we are told that it was caused by the alarming
spread of heresy. In 1288 the same increase is alluded to in the
provinces of Arles, Aix, and Embrun, when Nicholas IV sent to the
nobles and magistrates there the laws of Frederic II, with orders
for their enforcement, and to the inquisitors a code of instructions
for procedure.

The Inquisition was crippled for a while by its contest with
Philippe le Bel and Clement V, and when it resumed unrestricted
operations, Pierre Autier and his Catharan disciples absorbed its
energies. Although the sentences of Bernard Gui at Toulouse commence in 1308, it is not until the *auto de fé* of 1316 that any
Waldenses appear among its victims, when one was condemned to
perpetual imprisonment and one was burned as an unrepentant
heretic. The *auto* of 1319 appears to have been a jail delivery, for
poor wretches appear in it whose confessions date back to 1309,
1311, 1312, and 1315. On this occasion 18 Waldenses were condemned to pilgrimages with or without crosses, 26 to perpetual

prison, and 3 were burned. In the *auto* of 1321 a man and his wife who obstinately refused to abjure were burned. In that of 1322 eight were sentenced to pilgrimages, of whom 5 had crosses, 2 to prison, 6 dead bodies were exhumed and burned, and there is an allusion to the brother of one of the prisoners who had been burned at Avignon.

In his *Practica* Bernard Gui gives a clear and detailed statement of the Waldensian belief as it existed at this time, the chief points of which may be worth enumerating as affording us a definite view of the development of the faith in its original seat after a century and a half of persecution. There was no longer any self-deceit as to connection with the Roman Church. Persecution had done its work, and the Waldenses were permanently severed. They had a complete organization, consisting of bishops, priests, and deacons, and they held in some large city one or two general chapters every year, in which orders were conferred and measures for mission work were perfected. Although they still believed in transubstantiation, the making of the body and blood of Christ depended on the purity of the ministrant; a sinner was impotent to effect it, while it could be done by any righteous man or woman. It was the same with absolution: they held the power of the keys direct from Christ, and heard confessions and imposed penance. Their antisacerdotalism was strongly expressed in the simplification of their faith. There was no purgatory, and consequently masses for the dead or the invocation of the saints were of no avail; the saints, in fact, neither heard nor helped man, and the miracles performed in their name in the churches were fictitious. The fasts and feasts prescribed in the calendar were not to be observed, and the indulgences so lavishly sold were useless. As of old, oaths and homicide were forbidden. Yet enough of the traditional ascetic tendencies were preserved to lead to the existence of a monastic fraternity whose members divested themselves of all individual property, and promised chastity, with obedience to a superior. Bernard Gui refers, with a brevity which shows how little importance he attached to them, to stories about sexual abominations performed in nocturnal assemblies, and he indicates the growth of popular superstition by a brief allusion to a dog which appears in these gatherings and sprinkles the sectaries with his tail.

The nonresistance doctrines of the Waldenses rendered them, as a rule, a comparatively easy prey, but human nature sometimes asserted itself, and a sharp persecution carried on at this period by Frère Jacques Bernard, Inquisitor of Provence, provoked a bloody reprisal. In 1321 he sent two deputies—Frères Catalan Fabri and Pierre Paschal—to the diocese of Valence to make inquisition there. Former raids had left the people in an angry mood. Multitudes had been subjected to the humiliation of crosses, and these and their friends vowed revenge on the appearance of the new persecutors. A plot was rapidly formed to assassinate the inquisitors at a village where they were to pass the night. For some reason, however, they changed their plans, and passed on to the Priory of Montoison. The conspirators followed them, broke down the doors, and slew them. Strangely enough, the Prior of Montoison was accused of complicity in the murder and was arrested when the murderers were seized.

A few Waldenses appear in the prosecutions of Henri de Chamay of Carcassonne in 1328 and 1329, and, from the occasional notices which have reached us in the succeeding years, we may conclude that persecution, more or less fitful, never wholly ceased; while, in spite of this, the heresy kept constantly growing. After the disappearance of Catharism, indeed, it was the only refuge for ordinary humanity when dissatisfied with Rome. The Beghards were mystics whose speculations were attractive only to a certain order of minds. The Spirituals and Fraticelli were Franciscan ascetics. The Waldenses sought only to restore Christianity to its simplicity; their doctrines could be understood by the poor and illiterate, and they found constantly wider acceptance among the people, in spite of all the efforts put forth by the waning power of the Inquisition. Benedict XII, in 1335, summoned Humbert II, Dauphin of Viennois, and Adhémar of Poitou to assist the inquisitors. Humbert obeyed, and from 1336 to 1346 there were expeditions sent against them which drove them from their homes and captured some of them. Of these a portion abjured and the rest were burned; their possessions were confiscated and the bones of the dead exhumed. The secular and ecclesiastical officials of Embrun joined in these efforts, but they had no permanent result. In Languedoc Frère Jean Dumoulin, Inquisitor of Toulouse, in 1344 attacked them vigorously, but only succeeded in scattering them throughout Béarn, Foix, and Aragon. In 1348

Clement VI again urged Humbert, who responded with strict orders to his officers to aid the ecclesiastical authorities with what force might be necessary, and this time we hear of 12 Waldenses brought to Embrun and burned on the square in front of the cathedral. When Dauphiné became a possession of the crown the royal officials were equally ready to assist. Letters of October 20, 1351, from the governor, order the authorities of Briançon to give the inquisitor armed support in his operations against the heretics of the Briançonnais, but this seems to have been ineffective; and the next year Clement VI appealed to the Dauphin Charles, and to Louis and Joanna of Naples, to aid Frère Pierre Dumont, the Inquisitor of Provence, and summoned prelates and magistrates to co-operate in the good work. The only recorded result of this was the penancing of 7 Waldenses by Dumont in 1353. More successful were the labors of Guillaume de Bordes, Archbishop of Embrun from 1352 to 1363, surnamed the Apostle of the Waldenses, who tried the unusual expedient of kindness and persuasion. He personally visited the mountain valleys and had the satisfaction of winning over a number of the heretics. With his death his methods were abandoned, and Urban V, from 1363 to 1365, was earnest in calling upon the civil power and in stimulating the zeal of the Provençal Inquisitors Frères Hugues Cardilion and Jean Richard. The celebrated Inquisitor François Borel now appears upon the scene. Armed expeditions were sent into the mountains, which had considerable success. Many of the heretics were obstinate and were burned, while others saved their lives by abjuration. Their pitiful little properties were confiscated; one had a cow, another two cows and clothes of white cloth. In the purse of another, more wealthy, were found 2 florins—a booty which scarce proved profitable, for the wood to burn him and a comrade cost 62 sols and 6 deniers. One woman named Juven who was burned possessed a vineyard. The vintage was gathered and the must stored in her cabin, when the wrathful neighbors fired it at night and destroyed the product.

When Gregory XI ascended the pontifical throne in 1370, his attention was early directed to the deplorable condition of the Church in Provence, Dauphiné, and the Lyonnais. The whole region was full of Waldenses, and many nobles were now beginning to embrace the heresy. He set to work vigorously, appointing inquisitors and stimulating their zeal, but the whole system by this time was so discredited that his labors were ineffectual. The royal officials, so far from aiding the inquisitors, had no scruple in impeding them. Unsafe places were assigned to them in which to conduct their operations; they were forced to permit secular judges to act as assessors with them; their proceedings were submitted for revision to the secular courts, and even their prisoners were set at liberty without consulting them. The secular officials refused to take oaths to purge the land of heresy and openly protected heretics, especially nobles, when prosecutions were commenced against them.

Gregory duly complained of this to Charles le Sage in 1373, but to little purpose, and in 1375 he returned to the charge still more vigorously. Not only was the king requested to send a special deputy to the infected district, but the pope wrote directly to the royal lieutenant, Charles de Banville, reproaching him for his protection of heretics and threatening him if he did not mend his ways. Certain nobles who had become conspicuous as favorers of heresy were significantly reminded of the fate of Raymond of Toulouse; Amedeo of Savoy was summoned to assist, and the Tarantaise was added to the district of Provence that nothing might interfere with the projected campaign. As the spread of heresy was attributable to the lack of preachers and to the neglect of prelates and clergy in instructing their flocks, the inquisitor was empowered to call in the services of Dominicans, Franciscans, Carmelites, and Augustinians, to spread over the land and teach the people the truths of religion. These multiplied efforts at length began to tell. Charles issued orders to enforce the laws against heresy, and when Gregory sent a special Apostolic Internuncio, Antonio, Bishop of Massa, to direct operations, persecution began in earnest. Frère François Borel, the Inquisitor of Provence, had long been struggling against the indifference of the prelates and the hostility of the secular power. Now that he was sure of efficient seconding he was like a hound slipped from the leash. His forays against the miserable populations of Freyssinières, l'Argentière, and Val-Pute (or Val-Louise) have conferred on him a sinister reputation, unredeemed by the efficient aid he contributed to regaining the liberties of his native town of Gap.

The immediate success which rewarded these efforts was so overwhelming as to bring new cause for solicitude. The Bishop of Massa's mission commenced early in May 1375, and by June 17, Gregory is concerned about the housing and support of the crowds of wretches who had been captured. In spite of numerous burnings of those who proved obstinate, the prisons of the land were insufficient for the detention of the captives, and Gregory at once ordered new and strong ones to be built in Embrun, Avignon, and Vienne. To solve the financial complications which immediately arose, the bishops, whose negligence was accountable for the growth of heresy, were summoned within three months to furnish 4,000 gold florins to build the prisons, and 800 florins per annum for five years for the support of the prisoners. This they were allowed to take from the legacies for pious uses, and the restitutions of wrongly acquired funds, with a threat, if they should demur, that they should be deprived of these sources of income and be excommunicated besides. The bishops, however, were no more amenable to such arguments than those of Languedoc had been in 1245, and, after the three months had passed, Gregory answers, October 5, the anxious inquiry of the Bishop of Massa as to how he shall feed his prisoners, by telling him that it is the business of every bishop to support those of his diocese, and that anyone who refuses to do so is to be coerced with excommunication and the secular arm. This was a mere *brutum fulmen*, and in 1376 he endeavored to secure a share in the confiscations, but King Charles refused to divide them, though in 1378 he at last agreed to give the inquisitors a yearly stipend for their own support, similar to that paid to their brethren at Toulouse.

All other devices being exhausted, Gregory at last had recourse to the unfailing resource of the curia—an indulgence. There is something so appallingly grotesque in tearing honest, industrious folk from their homes by the thousand, in thrusting them into dungeons to rot and starve, and then evading the cost of feeding them by presenting them to the faithful as objects of charity, that the proclamation which Gregory issued August 15, 1376, is perhaps the most shameless monument of a shameless age:

To all the faithful in Christ: As the help of prisoners is counted among pious works, it befits the piety of the faithful to mercifully assist the incarcerated of all kinds who suffer from poverty. As we learn that our beloved son, the Inquisitor François Borelli, has imprisoned for safe-keeping or punishment many heretics and those defamed for heresy, who in consequence of their poverty cannot be sustained in prison unless the pious liberality of the faithful shall assist them as a work of charity; and as we wish that these prisoners shall not starve, but shall have time for repentance in the said prisons; now, in order that the faithful in Christ may through devotion lend a helping hand, we admonish, ask, and exhort you all, enjoining it on you in remission of your sins, that from the goods which God has given you, you bestow pious alms and grateful charity for the food of these prisoners, so that they may be sustained by your help, and you, through this and other good works inspired by God, may attain eternal blessedness!

What effect on the future of the Waldenses a continuance of Gregory's remorseless energy would have wrought can only be matter of conjecture. He died March 27, 1378, and the Great Schism which speedily followed gave the heretics some relief, during which they continued to increase, although in 1380 Clement VII renewed the commission of Borel, whose activity was unabated until 1393, and his victims were numbered by the hundred. A good many conversions rewarded his labors, and the converts were allowed to retain their property on payment of a certain sum of money. In 1393 he is said to have burned 150 at Grenoble in a single day. San Vicente Ferrer was a missionary of a different stamp, and his self-devoted labors for several years in the Waldensian valleys won over numerous converts. His memory is still cherished there, and the village of Puy-Saint-Vincent, with a chapel dedicated to him, shows that his kindly ministrations were not altogether lost.

After the Church had reorganized itself at the Council of Constance it had leisure to look after the interests of the faith, although its energies were mostly monopolized by the Hussite troubles. In 1417 we hear of Catharine Sauve, an anchorite, burned at Montpellier for Waldensian doctrines by the Deputy-Inquisitor Frère Raymond Cabasse, assisted by the Bishop of Maguelonne. In 1432 the Council of Bourges complained that the Waldenses of Dauphiné had taxed themselves to send money to the Hussites, whom they recognized as brethren. On August 23 of this year, we have a letter from Frère Pierre Fabri to the Council of Basle, excusing himself for not obeying a summons to attend it.[2] He describes the Waldenses

[2] See page 250.

as flourishing as numerously as ever in the valleys of Freyssinières, Argentière, and Pute, which had been almost depopulated by the ferocious raids of François Borel. He now has in his dungeons of Embrun and Briançon six relapsed heretics, who have revealed to him the names of more than 500 others whom he is about to seize, and whose trials will be a work of time, but as soon as he can absent himself without prejudice to the faith his first duty will be to attend the council.

It is not until 1475 that we find the inquisitors again at work in their old hunting ground among the valleys around the headwaters of the Durance. The Waldenses had quietly multiplied again. They held their conventicles undisturbed, they dared openly to preach their abhorred faith, and their missionary zeal was rewarded with abundant conversions. Worse than all, when the bishops and inquisitors sought to repress them, they appealed to the royal court, which was so untrue to its duty that it granted them letters of protection. In vain Sixtus IV sent special commissions armed with full powers to put an end to this disgraceful state of things. Men at this time in France recked little of papal authority, and the commissioners found themselves scorned. Sixtus, therefore, July 1, 1475, addressed an earnest remonstrance to Louis XI. The king was surely ignorant of the acts of his representatives; he would hasten to disavow them and lend the whole power of the State, as of old, to the support of the Inquisition.

The correspondence which ensued would be interesting reading if it were accessible. Its purport, however, can readily be discerned in the *Ordonnance* of May 18, 1478, which marks in the most emphatic manner the supremacy which the State had obtained over the Church. The king assumed that his subjects of Dauphiné were all good Catholics. In a tone of contemptuous insolence he alludes to the old Mendicants (*vieux mendiens*) styling themselves inquisitors, who vex the faithful with accusations of heresy and harass them with prosecutions in the royal and ecclesiastical courts for purposes of extortion or to secure the confiscation of their property. He therefore forbids his officers to aid in making such confiscations, decrees that the heirs shall be reinstated in all cases that have occurred, and in order to put a stop to the abuses of the inquisitors he strictly enjoins that for the future they shall not be permitted to prosecute the inhabitants in any manner.

This put an end for a time to the labors of the Inquisition against the Waldenses of Dauphiné, but the troubles of the latter were by no means over. The death of Louis, in 1483, deprived them of their protector, and the Italian policy of Charles VIII rendered him less indifferent to the wishes of the Holy See. At the request of the Archbishop of Embrun, Innocent VIII ordered the persecutions renewed. The Franciscan Inquisitor Jean Veyleti, whose excesses had caused the appeal to the throne in 1475, was soon again at work, and had the satisfaction of burning both consuls of Freyssinières. Though the Waldenses had represented themselves to Louis XI as faithful Catholics, the ancient errors were readily brought to light by the efficient means of torture. Wearied with their stubbornness, the archbishop, in June and July 1486, summoned them either to leave the country or to come forward and submit, and as they did neither he excommunicated them. This was equally ineffective, and he appealed again to Innocent VIII, who resolved to end the heresy with a decisive blow. Accordingly, in 1488, a crusade on a large scale was organized in both Dauphiné and Savoy. The papal commissioner, Alberto de' Capitanei, obtained the assistance of the Parlement of Grenoble, and a force was raised under the command of Hugues de La Palu, Comte de Vanax, to attack them on every side.

In March 1489, the crusaders advanced. The valley of Pragelato was the first assailed, and, after a few days, was reduced to the alternative of death or abjuration, when 15 obstinate heretics were burned. In Val Cluson and Freyssinières the resistance was more stubborn and there was considerable carnage, which so frightened the inhabitants of Argentière that they submitted peaceably. In Val Louise the people took refuge in the cavern of Aigue Fraide, which they imagined inaccessible, but La Palu succeeded in reaching it, and built fires in the mouth, suffocating the unhappy refugees. This, and the confiscations which followed, divided between Charles VIII and the Archbishop of Embrun, gave a fatal blow to Waldensianism in the valleys. To prevent its resuscitation the legate left behind him François Ploireri as Inquisitor of Provence, who continued to harass the people with citations and condemnations for contumacy, burning an occasional *barbe* and confiscating the property of relapsed heretics.

With a new king, in the person of Louis XII, there came a new

phase in the affairs of the Waldenses. A conference was held in
Paris before the royal chancellor, where envoys from Freyssinières
met Rostain, the new Archbishop of Embrun, and deputies of the
Parlement of Grenoble. It was resolved to send to the spot papal
and royal commissioners, with power to determine the status of the
so-called heretics. They went to Freyssinières and examined witnesses, who satisfied them that the population were good Catholics,
in spite of the urgent assertions of the archbishop that they were
notorious heretics. All the excommunications were removed, which
put an end to the prosecutions. On October 12, 1502, Louis XII
confirmed the decision, and Alexander VI, to whose son, Cæsar
Borgia, Louis had given the Duchy of Valentinois, embracing the
territory in question, was not disposed to run counter to the royal
wishes. The Waldenses were, however, unable to loosen the grip of
the Archbishop of Embrun on the property which he had confiscated,
in spite of positive orders for its restoration from the king, but at
least they were allowed, under the guise of Catholicism, to worship
God after their own fashion, until the crowding pressure of the
Reformation forced them to a merger with the Calvinists. In the
Briançonnais, in spite of occasional burnings, heresy continued to
spread until, in 1514, Antoine d'Estaing, Bishop of Angoulême, was
sent thither, when the measures he adopted, vigorously enforced by
the secular authorities, put an end to it in a few years.

CHAPTER XII
THE SPANISH PENINSULA

THE kingdom of Aragon, stretching across both sides of the Pyrenees, with a population kindred in blood and speech to that of Mediterranean France, was particularly liable to inroads of heresy from the latter. It is somewhat remarkable, therefore, that we hear nothing specifically of the Cathari in Aragon proper. Matthew Paris, indeed, tells a wild tale of how, in 1234, they were so numerous in the parts of Spain that they decreed the abrogation of Christianity and raised a large army with which they burned churches and spared neither age nor sex, until Gregory IX ordered a crusade against them throughout western Europe, when in a stricken field they were all cut off to a man; but this may safely be set down to the imagination of some pilgrim returning from Compostella and desiring to repay a night's hospitality at St. Alban's. That many Cathari existed in Aragon there can be no doubt, but they are never described as such, and the only heretics of whom we hear by name are *los encabats*— the Insabbatati or Waldenses. It was against these that the savage edicts of Alonso II and Pedro II were directed, towards the close of the twelfth century.

During the minority of Jayme I, the Aragonese probably awaited the results of the Albigensian war with feelings enlisted in favor of their race rather than of orthodoxy. As it drew to a close, however, Don Jayme, in 1226, issued an edict prohibiting all heretics from entering his kingdom, doubtless moved thereunto by the numbers who sought escape from the crusade of Louis VIII, and he followed this, in 1228, with another, depriving heretics, with their receivers, fautors, and defenders, of the public peace. The next step, we are told by the chroniclers of the Inquisition, was taken in consequence of the urgency of Raymond of Pennaforte, the Dominican confessor of the young king, who prevailed on him to obtain from Gregory IX inquisitors to purge his land. This is based on the bull *Declinante*, addressed, May 26, 1232, to Esparrago, Archbishop of Tarragona, and his suffragans, instructing them to make inquest in their dioceses after heretics, either personally or by Dominicans or other fitting persons, and to punish such as might be found. In the following year, Don Jayme issued from Tarragona a statute on the subject, showing that the matter was regarded as pertaining to the State rather than to the Church. Seigneurs who protected heretics in their lands forfeited them to the lord, or, if allodial, to the king. Houses of heretics, if allodial, were to be torn down; if held in fief, forfeited to the lord. All defamed or suspected of heresy were declared ineligible to office. That the innocent might not suffer with the guilty, no one was to be punished as a heretic or believer except by his bishop or such ecclesiastic as had authority to determine his guilt. Bishops were ordered, when it might seem expedient to them in places suspected of heresy, to appoint a priest or clerk, while the king or his bailli would appoint two or three laymen, whose duty it should be to investigate heretics, and, taking precautions against their escape, to report them to the bishop or to the royal officials, or to the lord of the place. In this incongruous mixture of clerical and lay elements there may be the germ of an Inquisition, but one of a character very different from that which was at this time taking shape at Toulouse.

To what extent this crude expedient was put in practice we have no means of knowing. Esparrago died soon afterwards and was succeeded in the archiepiscopal seat of Tarragona by Guillen Mongriu, whose vigorous and martial temperament was illustrated by his conquest of the island of Iviza. Mongriu speedily found that the domestic Inquisition would not work, and applied for the solution to Gregory, who sent him, April 30, 1235, a code of instructions drawn up by Raymond of Pennaforte. About this time we find the first record of active work in persecution, which illustrates the absence of all formal inquisitorial procedure. Robert, Count of Rosellon, was one of the great feudatories of the crown of Aragon. He seems to have been involved, as most nobles were, in some disputes over fiefs and tithes with the Bishop of Elne, whose diocese was in his territories. The bishop accused him of being the chief of the heretics of the region and of using his castles as a refuge for them. All this was very likely true—at least the bishop had no difficulty in finding witnesses to prove it, and Robert obediently abjured, but subsequently relapsed. Don Jayme accordingly had him arrested and imprisoned, but Robert managed to escape and shut himself in one of his in-accessible mountain strongholds. His position, however, was desperate, and his lands liable to confiscation; he therefore expressed to Gregory IX his desire to return to the bosom of the Church, and offered to serve with his followers against the Saracen as long as the pope might designate. Gregory therefore wrote, February 8, 1237, to Raymond of Pennaforte, that if the count would for three years with his subjects assist in the conquest of Valencia, and give sufficient security that in case of relapse his territories should be forfeited to the crown, he could be absolved. On hearing this the good bishop hastened to the papal court and declared that if Robert was absolved he and his witnesses would be exposed to the imminent peril of death, and that heresy would triumph in his diocese; but, on receiving assurances that his fiefs and tithes would be taken care of, he quieted down and offered no further opposition.

Under the impulsion of Gregory and of Raymond of Pennaforte, Dominican inquisitors had at last been resorted to, and in this year, 1237, we first become cognizant of them. In right of his wife Ermessende, Roger Bernard the Great of Foix was Vizconde of Castelbo, a fief held of the Bishop of Urgel, with whom he had had a bitter war.[1] He gave Castelbo to his son Roger, who, by the advice of his father in 1237 allowed the Inquisition free scope there, placing the castle in the hands of Ramon Fulco, Vizconde of Cardona, in the name of the Archbishop of Tarragona and the bishops assembled at the Council of Lerida. That council thereupon appointed a number of inquisitors, including Dominicans and Franciscans, who made a descent on Castelbo. It had long been noted as a nest of Catharans and the inquisitors had no difficulty in finding victims. They ordered two houses to be destroyed, exhumed and burned the bones of 18 persons, condemned as heretics and carried off as prisoners some 45 men and women, condemned 15 who fled, and were undecided about sundry others. Still, the Bishop of Urgel was not satisfied, and he gratified his rancor by condemning and excommunicating Roger Bernard as a defender of heretics, and it was not until 1240 that the latter, through the intervention of the Archbishop of Tarragona, procured from the bishop absolution and a certificate that he recognized him *"per bon et per leyal e per Catholich."*

[1] See page 288.

In 1238 the Inquisition of Aragon may be said to be founded. In April of that year Gregory IX wrote to the Franciscan Minister and Dominican Prior of Aragon, deploring the spread of heresy through the kingdom, and placed in the hands of the Mendicants the sword of the Word of God, which was not to be restrained from blood. At the same time he made a similar provision for Navarre, which was likewise said to be swarming with heretics. As an independent institution, however, the Inquisition of Navarre seems never to have advanced beyond an embryonic condition, and it was subsequently incorporated into the Inquisition of Aragon.

In Aragon the institution gradually took shape. Berenger de Palau, Bishop of Barcelona, was busily engaged in organizing it throughout his diocese at the time of his death in 1241, and the vicar who replaced him while the see was vacant completed it. In 1242 Pedro Arbalate, who had succeeded Guillen Mongriu as archbishop, with the assistance of Raymond of Pennaforte held the Council of Tarragona to settle the details of procedure. Under the guidance of so eminent a canonist, the code drawn up by the council showed a thorough knowledge of the principles guiding the Church in its dealings with heretics, and long continued to be referred to as an authority not only in Spain, but in France. At the same time its careful definitions, which render it especially interesting to us, indicate that it was prepared for the instruction of a Church which as yet practically knew nothing of the principles of persecution firmly established elsewhere. It was probably under the impulse derived from these movements that active persecution was resumed at Castelbo, which does not seem to have been purified by the raid of 1237. This time the heretics were not as patient as before, and resorted to poison, with which they succeeded in taking off Fray Ponce de Blanes, or de Espira, the inquisitor, who had made himself peculiarly obnoxious by his vigorous pursuit of heresy for several years. This aroused all the martial instincts of the retired Archbishop Guillen Mongriu, who assembled some troops, besieged and took the castle, burned many of the heretics, and imprisoned the rest for life. An organized effort was made to extend the Inquisition throughout the kingdom, and the parish priests were individually summoned to lend it all the aid in their power.

Still, the progress of organization seems to have been exceedingly slow. King Jayme grew dissatisfied and in 1254 urgently demanded a fresh effort of Innocent IV. This time the pope concluded, at Jayme's suggestion, to place the matter entirely in Dominican hands; but so little had been done in the way of general organization that he confided the choice of inquisitors to the priors of Barcelona, Lerida, Perpignan, and Elne, each one to act within his own diocese, unless, indeed, there were inquisitors already in function under papal commissions—a clause which shows the confusion existing at the time. At that time the whole peninsula constituted but one Dominican province, and in 1262 Urban IV again adopted the plan, in general use elsewhere, of empowering the provincial to appoint the inquisitors—now limited to two. This long remained the basis of organization; but after the division of the province into two, by the General Chapter of Cologne in 1301, the Aragonese chafed under their subordination to the Provincial of Spain, whose territories consisted only of Castile, León, and Portugal. The struggle was protracted, but the Inquisition of Aragon at last achieved independence in 1351, when Fray Nicholas Roselli, the Provincial of Aragon, obtained from Clement VI the power of appointing and removing the inquisitors of the kingdom.

Meanwhile the inquisitors had not been inactive. Fray Pedro de Cadreyta rendered himself especially conspicuous. In conjunction with his colleague, Fray Pedro de Tonenes, and Arnaldo, Bishop of Barcelona, he rendered final judgment, January 11, 1257, against the memory of Ramon, Count of Urgel, as a relapsed heretic who had abjured before the Bishop of Urgel, and whose bones were to be exhumed; but, with unusual lenity, the widow, Timborosa, and the son, Guillen, were admitted to reconciliation and not deprived of their estates. Twelve years later, in 1269, we find Cadreyta, together with another colleague, Fray Guillen de Colonico, and Abril, Bishop of Urgel, condemning the memory of Arnaldo, Vizconde of Castelbo, and of his daughter Ermessende, whom we know as the heretic wife of Roger Bernard the Great of Foix. They had both been dead more than thirty years, and her grandson, Roger Bernard III of Foix, who had inherited the Vizcondado of Castelbo, was duly cited to defend his ancestors; but if he made the attempt, it was vain, and their bones were ordered to be exhumed. It is not likely that these sturdy champions of the faith confined their attention to the dead, though the only execution we happen to hear of at this period is that of Berenguer de Amoros, burned in 1263. That the living, indeed, were objects of fierce persecution is rendered more than probable by the martyrdom of Cadreyta, who was stoned to death by the exasperated populace of Urgel, and who thus furnished another saint for local cult.

During the remainder of the century we hear little more of the Inquisition of Aragon, but with the opening of the fourteenth century there would appear to be an increase of vigor. In 1302 Fray Bernardo celebrated several *autos de fé*, in which a number of heretics were abandoned to the secular arm. In 1304 Fray Domingo Peregrino had an *auto* in which we are told that those who were not burned were banished, with the assent of King Jayme II. In 1314 Fray Bernardo Puigcercos was so fortunate as to discover a number of heretics, of whom he burned some and exiled others. To Juan de Longerio, in 1317, belongs the doubtful honor of condemning the works of Arnaldo de Vilanova. The names of Arnaldo Burguete, Guillen de Costa, and Bernardo de Puycerda have also reached us as successful inquisitors, but their recorded labors were principally directed against the Spiritual Franciscans, and will be more particularly noted hereafter. The Aragonese seem not to have relished the methods of the Inquisition, for in 1325 the Cortes, with the assent of King Jayme II, prohibited for the future the use of the inquisitorial process and of torture. Whether or not this was intended to apply to the ecclesiastical as well as to the secular courts it is impossible now to tell, but, if it were, it had no permanent result.

In 1356 the Inquisitor Nicholas Roselli was created Cardinal of S. Sisto, and was succeeded after a short interval by Nicolas Eymerich, the most noteworthy man of whom the Aragonese Inquisition can boast. Trained in varied learning, and incessant in industry, of his numerous works but one has had the honors of print—his *Directorium Inquisitorum*, in which, for the first time, he systematized the procedure of his beloved institution, giving the principles and details which should guide the inquisitor in all his acts. The book remained an authority to the last, and formed the basis of almost all subsequent compilations. Eymerich's conception of the model inquisitor was lofty. At a time when the Inquisition was declining and falling into contempt, he boldly insisted on its most extreme prerogatives as an imprescriptible privilege. If he assumed that the heretic had but one right—that of choosing between submission and the stake—he was in this but the conscientious exponent of his age, and his writings are instinct with the conviction that the work of the inquisitor is the salvation of souls.

From Eymerich's lament over the difficulty of providing for the expenses of an institution so necessary to the Church, it is evident that the Kings of Aragon had not felt it their duty to support the Holy Office, while the bishops, he tells us, were as firm as their brethren in other lands in evading the responsibility which by right was incumbent on them. The confiscations, he adds, amounted to little or nothing, for heretics were poor folk—Waldenses, Fraticelli, and the like. In fact, so far as we can gather, the sum of Eymerich's activity during his long career is so small that it shows how little was left of heresy by this time. Occasional Fraticelli and Waldenses and renegade Jews or Saracens were all that rewarded the inquisitor, with every now and then some harmless lunatic whose extravagance unfortunately took a religious turn, or some oversubtle speculator on the intricacies of dogmatic theology. We shall see hereafter how Eymerich fared in seeking the condemnation of Raymond Lully's writings, and need only say here that the result was his suspension from office, to be succeeded by his capital enemy Bernardo Ermengaudi, in 1386, and that after the succession to the throne in 1387 of Juan I, who was bitterly hostile to him, he was twice proscribed and exiled, and was denounced by the king as an obstinate fool, an enemy of the faith inspired by Satan, together with other unflattering qualifications.

The next inquisitor, Bernardo Puig, is said to have been earnest and successful, punishing many heretics and confuting many heresies. In Valencia, about 1390, there was a case in which Pedro de Ceplanes, priest of Cella, read in his church a formal declaration that there were three natures in Christ—divine, spiritual, and human. A merchant of the town loudly contradicted it, and a tumult arose. The Inquisitor of Valencia promptly arrested the too-ingenious theologian, who only escaped the stake by public recantation and condemnation to perpetual imprisonment; but he broke jail and fled to the Balearic Isles, interjecting an appeal to the Holy See.

A case occurring in 1423 would seem to indicate that the Inquisition had lost much of the terror which had rendered it formidable. Fray Pedro Salazo, Inquisitor of Rosellon and Cerdaña, threw in prison on charges of heresy a hermit named Pedro Freserii, who enjoyed great reputation for sanctity among the people. The accused declared that the witnesses were personal enemies, and his friends lodged an appeal with Martin V. The pope referred the matter to Bernardo, Abbot of the Benedictine Monastery of Arles, in the diocese of Elne. Bernardo deputed the case to a canon of the church of Elne, who acquitted the accused without awaiting the result of another appeal to the pope interjected by the inquisitor; and Martin finally sent the matter to the Ordinary of Narbonne, with power to summon all parties before him and decide the case definitely. The whole transaction shows a singular want of respect for the functions of the Inquisition.

Ferdinand the Catholic succeeded to the throne of Aragon in 1479, as he had already done, in 1474, to that of Castile by right of his wife Isabella. Even before the organizing of the new Inquisition in Aragon in 1483, it is probable that the influence of Ferdinand had done much to restore the power of the institution. In 1482, on the eve of the change, we find the Inquisition of Aragon acting with renewed vigor and boldness, under the Dominican, Juan de Epila. As a preparatory step to placing the dominions of the crown of Aragon under Torquemada as inquisitor-general, it was requisite to get rid of Cristobal Gualvez, who had been Inquisitor of Valencia since 1452, and who had disgraced his office by his crimes. Sixtus IV had a special enmity to him, and, in ordering his deposition, stigmatized him as an impudent and impious man, whose unexampled excesses were worthy of severe chastisement; and when Sixtus, in 1483, extended Torquemada's authority over the whole of Spain, with power to nominate deputies, he excepted "that son of iniquity, Cristobal Gualvez," who had been interdicted from the office in consequence of his demerits, and whom he even deprived of the function of preaching.

The great kingdom of Castile and Léon, embracing the major portion of the Spanish Peninsula, never enjoyed the blessing of the mediæval Inquisition. It was more independent of Rome than any other monarchy of the period. Lordly prelates, turbulent nobles, and cities jealous of their liberties allowed scant opportunity for the centralization of power in the crown. The people were rude and uncultured, and not much given to theological speculation. Their superfluous energy, moreover, found ample occupation in the task of winning back the land from the Saracen. The large population of Jews and of conquered Moors gave them peculiar problems to deal with which would have been complicated rather than solved by the methods of the Inquisition, until the union of Aragon and Castile under Ferdinand and Isabella, followed by the conquest of Granada, enabled those monarchs to undertake seriously the business, attractive both to statecraft and to fanaticism, of compelling uniformity of faith.

It is true that the Dominican legend relates how Dominic returned from Rome to Spain as inquisitor-general, on the errand of establishing the Inquisition for the purpose of punishing the renegade converted Jews and Moors; how he was warmly seconded by San Fernando III; how he organized the Inquisition throughout the land, celebrating himself the first *auto de fé* at Burgos, where 300 apostates were burned, and the second *auto* in the presence of the saintly king, who himself carried on his shoulders fagots for the burning of his subjects; how, after this, he established the Inquisition in Aragon, whence he journeyed to Paris and organized it throughout France. All this can rank in historical value with the veracious statement of an old chronicler—a compatriot of the Pied Piper of Hamelin—that St. Boniface was an inquisitor, and that, with the support of Pepin le Bref, he burned many heretics. Detailed lists are given of the successive inquisitors-general of the Peninsula, but these are simply the Dominican provincials of Spain, who were empowered by the popes to appoint inquisitors, and whose exercise of that power did not extend beyond Aragon. Even Paramo, although he tries to prove that there were inquisitors nominally in Castile, is forced to admit that practically there was no Inquisition there.

We reach firmer ground with the codes known as *El Fuero Real* and *Las Siete Partidas*, the first issued by Alonso the Wise, in 1255, and the second about ten years later. By this time the Inquisition was at its height. It was thoroughly organized and wherever it existed the business of suppressing heresy was exclusively in its hands. Yet not only does Alonso take no count of it, but in his regulation by secular law of the relations between the heretic and the Church he shows how completely, up to this period, Spain had remained outside the great movements of the twelfth and thirteenth centuries. Heresy, it is true, is one of the matters pertaining to the ecclesiastical tribunals, and anyone can accuse a heretic before his bishop or vicar. If the accused is found not to believe as the Church teaches, effort is to be made to convert him, and if he returns to the faith he is to be pardoned. If he proves obstinate, he is to be handed over to the secular judge. Then, however, his fate is decided without reference to the laws the Church had endeavored to introduce throughout Christendom. If the culprit had received the *consolamentum*, or is a believer observing the rites, he is to be burned; but if a believer not observing the rites, he is to be banished or imprisoned until he returns to the faith. Anyone learning heresy, but not yet a believer, is fined 10 pounds of gold to the fisc, or, if unable to pay, to receive 50 lashes in public. In the case of those who die in heresy or are executed, their estates pass to Catholic descendants, or, in default of these, to the next of kin; if without such kindred, the property of laymen goes to the fisc, of ecclesiastics, to the Church. No one, after condemnation for heresy, can hold office, inherit property, make a will, execute a sale, or give testimony. The house where a wandering heretic missionary is sheltered is forfeited to the Church, if inhabited by the owner; if rented, the offending tenant is fined 10 pounds of gold or publicly scourged. A *rico home* or noble sheltering heretics in his lands or castles, and persisting after a year's excommunication, forfeits the land or castle to the king; and if a non-noble his body and property are at the king's pleasure. Prosecutions of the dead are humanely limited to five years after decease. All this shows that Alonso and his counsellors recognized the duty of the State to preserve the purity of the faith, but that they considered it wholly an affair of the State, in which the Church had no voice beyond ascertaining the guilt of the accused.

In 1401 Boniface IX made a demonstration by appointing the provincial, Vicente de Lisboa, Inquisitor over all Spain, directing that his expenses should be paid by the bishops, and that no superior of his Order could remove him. The only heresy specifically alluded to in the bull is the idolatrous worship of plants, trees, stones, and altars—apparently superstitious relics of paganism which indicate the condition of religion and culture in the Peninsula. Boniface's action could hardly have been taken with any expectation of result, as Spain rendered obedience to Benedict XIII, the antipope of Avignon, and it was probably only a move in the political game of the Great Schism. Whatever the motive, however, the effort was fruitless, for Fray Vicente was already dead in the odor of sanctity at the date of the bull. On learning this, Boniface returned to the charge, February 1, 1402, by empowering forever thereafter the Dominican Provincial of Spain to appoint and remove inquisitors, or to act as such himself, with all the privileges and powers accorded to the office by the canons. Inoperative as this remained, it at least had the advantage of supplying to the Spanish historians an unbroken line of inquisitors-general to be catalogued.

This, perhaps, technically justifies Alonso Tostado, Bishop of Avila, who soon afterwards alludes to inquisitors in Spain investigating those defamed for heresy, and it explains the remarks of Sixtus IV when, in January 1482, he confirmed the two inquisitors appointed at Seville by Ferdinand and Isabella at the commencement of their reforms, and forbade their naming more, for the reason that the appointees of the Dominican provincial were sufficient. In spite of all this, the Spanish Inquisition was simply potential, not existent. When Alonso de Almarzo, Abbot of the great Benedictine foundation of Anteallares of Compostella, with his accomplices, was tried for selling throughout Spain and Portugal indulgences warranted to release the souls of the damned from hell, for counterfeiting the papal *Agnus Dei*, for forging and altering papal letters, and for persuading Jewish converts to apostatize, had there been an Inquisition it would promptly have taken cognizance of the culprits; but in place of this the case was referred to Nicholas V, who instructed the Bishop of Tarazona to proceed against them. Alonso de Spina, about 1460, sorrowfully admits the absence of all persecution of heresy. "No one investigates the errors of heretics. The ravening wolves, O Lord, have gained admittance to thy flock, for the shepherds are few. There are many hirelings, and because they are hirelings they care only for shearing, not for feeding the sheep!" and he draws a deplorable picture of the Spanish Church, distracted with heretics, Jews, and Saracens.

Evidently some more efficient and less cumbrous method was

requisite if the population of reunited Spain was to enjoy the blessing of uniformity in faith. It did not take long for the piety of Isabella and the policy of Ferdinand to discover appropriate means.

In Portugal, Affonso II, at the commencement of his reign in 1211, had manifested his zeal by inducing his Cortes to adopt severe laws for the repression of heresy; but when Sueiro Gomes, the first Dominican Provincial of Spain, endeavored to introduce in his kingdom inquisitors of the Order, Affonso refused to admit them, and successfully insisted that heretics should be tried as heretofore by the ordinary episcopal courts. This rebuff sufficed for nearly a century and a half, and there must have been considerable freedom of thought, for, about 1325, Alvaro Pelayo gives a long list of the errors publicly defended in the schools of Lisbon by Thomas Scotus, a renegade friar. Their nature may be appreciated from his repetition of the Averrhoistic assertion that there had been three deceivers— Moses who deceived the Jews, Christ the Christians, and Mahomet the Saracens. He seems to have enjoyed immunity until he declared that St. Antony of Padua kept concubines, when the Franciscan prior had him incarcerated, and his trial followed. At last, by a bull dated January 17, 1376, Gregory XI authorized Agapito Colonna, Bishop of Lisbon, to appoint, for this time only, a Franciscan inquisitor, as heresies were known to be spreading, and there were no inquisitors in the kingdom. Under this authority Agapito appointed the first Portuguese inquisitor, Martino Vasquez. From what we have seen elsewhere we may reasonably doubt his success in collecting his stipend; but, small as his receipts may have been, they were the equivalent of his service, for no trace of any labors performed by him remains.

The Great Schism commenced in 1378, and as Portugal acknowledged Urban VI while Spain adhered to the antipope Clement VII, the Dominican province of Spain divided itself, the Portuguese choosing a vicar-general, and finally a provincial, Gonçalo, in 1418, when Martin V legalized the separation. This perhaps explains why Martino Vasquez was succeeded by another Franciscan. In 1394 Rodrigo de Cintra, calling himself Inquisitor of Portugal and Algarve, applied to Boniface IX for confirmation, which was graciously accorded to him. Rodrigo was preacher to King João I and his career, like that of his predecessor, is a blank. He was followed by a Dominican, Vicente de Lisboa, who had been Provincial of Spain at the time of the disruption, when he returned to Portugal and became confessor of Dom João. No trace of his inquisitorial activity exists. The next appointment of which we hear is that of another confessor of Dom João, in 1413, this time a Franciscan, Affonso de Alprão, of whose doings no record has been preserved. When, in 1418, the kingdom was reorganized as an independent Dominican province, the earnest annalists of the Inquisition assume that under the bull of Boniface IX in 1402, each successive provincial was likewise an inquisitor-general, and the lists of these worthies are laboriously paraded as such, until the founding of the New Inquisition in 1531.

The New Inquisition of Spain was a model which the smaller kingdom would naturally be expected to adopt, and to ardent Catholics there might well seem to be a necessity for such an institution in view of the problems arising from the large influx of New Christians flying from Spanish persecution. Dom Manoel, indeed, at one time entertained so seriously the idea of establishing the Spanish Inquisition in his dominions that, in 1515, he ordered his ambassador at Rome, D. Miguel da Silva, to obtain from Leo X the same privileges as those which had been conceded to Castile, but from some cause the project was abandoned. His son, Dom João III, who succeeded him in 1521, was a weak-minded fanatic, and it is only singular that the introduction of the Inquisition on the Spanish model was delayed for still ten years. The struggle which took place over the measure belongs, however, to a period beyond our present limits.

CHAPTER XIII
ITALY

FOR centuries the normal condition of Italy was not far removed from anarchy. Spasmodic attempts of the empire to make good its claim to overlordship were met by the steady policy of the papacy to extend its temporal power over the peninsula. During the century occupied by the reigns of the Hohenstaufens (1152–1254), the popes sought to erect a rampart by stimulating the cities to establish their independence and form self-governing republics, and it thus created for itself a party in all of them. North of the Patrimony of St. Peter the soil of Italy thus became fractioned into petty states under institutions more or less democratic. For the most part they were torn with savage internal feuds between factions which, as Guelf or Ghibelline, hoisted the banner of pope or of kaiser as an excuse for tearing each other to pieces. Occasionally some overmastering necessity might bring about a temporary union, as when the Lombard League, in 1177, broke the Barbarossa's power on the field of Legnano, but, in general, the chronicles of the period are a confused mass of murderous strife inside and outside the gates of every town.

When every town was divided against itself, heresy could bargain for toleration by holding the balance of power, and was frequently able, by throwing its weight on one side or the other, to obtain a share in the government. When the formulas of persecution became defined under Honorius III, Gregory IX, and Frederic II, and fautorship was made equivalent to heresy, the factions and the nobles who tolerated or protected heretics became involved in the common anathema, and whole communities were stigmatized as given over to false idols. Yet although Ghibelline and heretic were frequently held by the popes to be almost convertible terms, there was in reality no test capable of universal application. Traditional hostility to the empire rendered Milan an intensely Guelf community, and yet it was everywhere recognized as the greatest center of heresy.

Although Stephen of Bourbon relates that a converted heretic informed him that in Milan there were no less than 17 heterodox sects

362

which bitterly disputed with each other, yet they can, as in France, be reduced to two main classes—Cathari, or Patarins, and Waldenses. About the middle of the thirteenth century Rainerio Saccone estimates the total number of Catharan churches from Constantinople to the Pyrenees at 4,000, with a countless congregation of believers, and nearly two-thirds of the whole number were concentrated in northern Italy, chiefly in Lombardy, and constituted a notable portion of the population.

Lombardy, in fact, was the center whence Catharism was propagated throughout Europe. For more than half a century it served as a refuge to the persecuted saints of Languedoc and as a source whence to draw missionaries and teachers. About 1240 a certain Yvo of Narbonne was falsely accused of heresy and fled to Italy, where he was received as a martyr, and had full opportunity of penetrating into the secrets of the sectaries. In a letter to Géraud, Archbishop of Bordeaux, he describes their organization throughout Italy, with ramifications extending into all the neighboring lands. From all the cities of Lombardy and Tuscany their youth were sent to Paris to perfect themselves in logic and theology. Catharan merchants frequented fairs and obtained entrance into houses where they lost no opportunity of scattering the seed of false doctrine. Milan was the headquarters whither every year delegates were sent from the churches throughout Christendom, bringing contributions for the support of the central organization, and receiving instructions as to the symbol, changed every twelvemonth, whereby the wandering Patarin could recognize the houses of his brethren and safely claim hospitality.

It was in the valleys of the Cottian Alps, to which they spread from Dauphiné, that the Waldenses settled themselves most firmly. In those inhospitable regions, till then almost uninhabited, their marvellous and self-denying industry occupied every spot where incessant labor could support life. There they rapidly increased and filled the valleys of Luserna, Angrogna, San Martino, and Perosa.

When Honorius III in 1220 obtained from Frederic II the ferocious coronation edict against heresy, he may well have imagined that the way was open for its immediate suppression. If so, he was not long in discovering his mistake. Whatever professions Frederic might make, or whatever rigor he might exercise in his Sicilian dominions, it was no part of his policy to estrange the Ghibelline leaders, or to strengthen the Guelfic factions in the turbulent little republics he sought to reduce to subjection. His whole reign was an internecine conflict, open or concealed, with Rome, and he was too much of a free-thinker to have any scruples about the sources whence he could draw strength for himself or annoyance for his enemy. In central and upper Italy, therefore, his laws were for the most part virtually a dead letter.

Something more than imperial edicts was plainly necessary, and Honorius, in casting around for methods to check the spread of heresy, appointed in 1224 the Bishops of Brescia and Modena as commissioners with special powers to exterminate the heretics of Lombardy—as inquisitors, in fact, this being one of the steps which gradually led to the establishment of the Inquisition, the usefulness of the Dominicans in this respect not having yet been divined. The Bishop of Modena, however, undertook a mission to convert the pagans of Prussia, and the Bishop of Rimini was substituted in his place. The prelates commenced with Brescia itself, and ordered the tearing down of certain houses where heretical preachers had been accustomed to hold forth. At once an armed insurrection broke out. Several churches were burned, and the heretics parodied from them the anathema by casting lighted torches from the windows, and solemnly excommunicating all members of the Church of Rome. It was not until after a severe and prolonged conflict that the Catholics obtained the upper hand, and then the terms prescribed by Honorius were so mild as to indicate that it was not deemed politic to drive the defeated party to despair.

Gregory IX was a man of sterner temper than Honorius, and, despite his octogenary age, his advent to the pontificate in 1227 was the signal for unrelenting war on heresy. Within three weeks of his accession peace was signed, under the auspices of the papacy, between Frederic II and the Lombard League, with provisions for the suppression of heresy. Gregory immediately summoned the Lombards to perform their duty. Hitherto, he told them, all their pretended efforts had been fraudulent. Heretics had been permitted to preach their doctrines publicly, while ecclesiastics had been outlawed and imprisoned. All this must cease, the provisions of the treaty of peace must be enforced, and, if they continued in their evil courses, the Holy See would find means to coerce them in their perversity.

These were brave words, though the political condition of Lombardy rendered them ineffective. Nearer home, however, Gregory had fairer opportunity of enforcing his will, and we have already seen how promptly he recognized the utility of the Order of Dominic and laid the foundations of the Inquisition by his tentative action in Florence. While this was taking shape his zeal was stimulated by the discovery in 1231 that in Rome itself heresy had become so bold that it ventured to assert itself openly, and that many priests and other ecclesiastics had been converted. Probably the first *auto de fé* on record was that held by the Senator Annibaldo at the portal of Santa Maria Maggiore, when these unfortunates were burned or condemned to perpetual prison, and Gregory took advantage of the occasion to issue the decretal which became the basis of inquisitorial procedure, and to procure the enactment of severe secular laws in the name of the senator. The details I have already given[1] and they need not be repeated here; but Gregory did not content himself with what he thus accomplished in Rome. His aid just then was desirable to Frederic II in his Lombard complications, and to Gregory's urgency may doubtless be attributed the severe legislation of the Sicilian Constitutions, issued about this time, and the Ravenna decrees of 1232. Shortly afterwards, indeed, we find Frederic writing to him that they are like father and son; that they should sharpen the spiritual and temporal swords respectively committed to them against heretics and rebels, without wasting effort on sophistry. It is not probable that Gregory counted much on the zeal of the emperor, but he sent the edict of Annibaldo to Milan, with instructions that it be adopted and enforced there.

It was now that Gregory hit upon the final and successful experiment of confiding to the Dominicans the suppression of heresy as part of their regular duties. A fresh impulse was felt all along the line. The Church suddenly found that it could count upon an unexpected reserve of enthusiasm, despising danger and reckless of consequences, which in the end could hardly fail to triumph. A new class of men now appears upon the scene—San Piero Martire, Giovannni da Vicenza, Rolando da Cremona, Rainerio Saccone—worthy to rank

[1] See page 151.

with their brethren in Languedoc, who devoted themselves to what they held to be their duty with a singleness of purpose which must command respect, however repulsive their labors may seem to us. On the one hand these men had an easier task than their western colleagues, for they had not to contend with the jealousy, or submit to the control, of the bishops. The independence of the Italian episcopate had been broken down in the eleventh century. Besides, the bishops naturally belonged to the Guelfic faction and welcomed any allies who promised to aid them in crushing the antagonistic party in their turbulent cities. On the other hand, the political dissensions which raged everywhere increased enormously the difficulties and dangers of the task.

In Italy, as in France, the organization of the Inquisition was gradual. As the tribunal by degrees assumed shape, a definite code of procedure was established which was virtually the same everywhere, except with regard to the power of confiscation, the application of the profits of persecution, and the acquittal of the innocent. The problems which the founders of the Inquisition had to meet in Italy, and the methods in which these were met, can best be illustrated by a rapid glance at what remains to us of the careers of some of the men who undertook the apparently hopeless task.

The earliest name I have met with bearing the title of Inquisitor of Lombardy is that of a Frà Alberico in 1232. The Cardinal Legate Goffredo undertook to quiet civil strife in Bergamo, with the consent of all factions, by appointing as *podestà* Pier Torriani of Milan; and at the same time he seized the opportunity to make a raid on heretics, a number of whom he cast into prison. No sooner was his back turned than the citizens refused to receive his *podestà*, elected in his place a certain R. di Madello, and, what was worse, set at liberty the captive heretics. Thereupon the legate placed the city under interdict, which brought the people to their senses, and they agreed to stand to the mandate of the Church. Gregory accordingly, November 3, 1232, instructed Alberico, as Inquisitor of Lombardy, to reconcile the city on condition that the people refund to Pier Torriani all his expenses and give sufficient security to exterminate heresy.

Frà Rolando de Cremona, noted as the first Dominican licentiate of the University of Paris, had been tracking heretics in Toulouse with unbending zeal. Hardly had he quitted Languedoc when we find him, in 1233, actively at work in the congenial duty of suppressing heresy at Piacenza. The 25 years which had elapsed since the Piacenzans had shown themselves so indifferent to their spiritual privileges had not greatly increased their respect for orthodoxy. Rolando assembled them, preached to them, and then ordered the *podestà* to expel the heretics. The result did not correspond to his expectations. With the connivance of the *podestà*, the heretics and their friends arose and made a general onslaught on the clergy, including the bishop and the friars, in which a monk of San Sabino was slain and Rolando and some of his comrades were wounded. The Dominicans carried Rolando, half dead, from the city, which was placed under interdict by the bishop. Then a revulsion of feeling occurred; Rolando was asked to return, and full satisfaction was promised. He prudently kept away, but ordered the imprisonment of the *podestà* and 24 others till the pleasure of the pope should be known. Gregory took advantage of the opportunity by sending thither the Archdeacon of Novara, with instructions to place the city under control of the orthodox party, taking ample security that the heretics should be suppressed; but this arrangement did not please the citizens, who rose again and liberated the prisoners. Sharp as was this experience, it did not dull the edge of Rolando's zeal, for the next year we find him at work in the Milanese, where he received rough treatment at the hands of Lantelmo, a noble who sheltered heretics in his castle near Lodi. For this Lantelmo was condemned to be led through the streets, stripped and with a halter around his neck, to Rolando's presence, and there to accept such penance as the friar, at command of the pope, might enjoin on him.

During this transition period, while the Inquisition was slowly taking shape, one of the most notable of the Dominicans engaged in the work of persecution was Giovanni Schio da Vicenza. Known as the Apostle of Peace, his eloquence at Bologna in 1233 had induced the opposing parties to lay down their arms and swear to mutual forgiveness. After this success, Gregory urged him to undertake a similar mission to Florence, where constant civic war was accompanied by recrudescence of heresy. Gregory assumed that Giovanni acted under the direct inspiration of the Holy Ghost and did not venture to send him orders, but only requests. The Bolognese were so loath to part with him that they used gentle violence to retain him, and only let him go after Gregory had ordered their city laid under interdict and had threatened to deprive of its episcopal dignity any place which should detain him against his will. After completely succeeding in his mission to Florence he was dispatched on a similar one to Lombardy. The League, which had been so efficient an instrument in curbing the imperial power, was breaking up. Fears were entertained that Frederic would soon return from Germany with an army, and a portion of the Lombard cities and nobles were disposed to invite him. Some countervailing influence was required, and nothing more effective than Giovanni's eloquence could be resorted to. At Padua, Treviso, Conigliano, Ceneda, Oderzo, Belluno, and Feltre he preached on the text "Blessed are the feet of the bearers of peace" with such effect that even the terrible Ezzelin da Romano is said to have twice burst into tears. The whole land was pacified, save the ancestral quarrel between Ezzelin and the counts of Campo San Piero, which unpardonable wrongs had rendered implacable. After a visit to Mantua, the Apostle of Peace went to Verona, then besieged by an army of Mantuans, Bolognese, Brescians, and Faenzans, where he persuaded the assailants to withdraw, and the Veronese, in gratitude, proclaimed him *podestà*, by acclamation. He promptly made use of the position to burn in the market-place some 60 heretics of both sexes, belonging to the noblest families of the city. Then he summoned to a great assembly, in a plain hard by, all the confederate cities and nobles.

The multitude obedient to his call was diversely estimated at from 40,000 to 50,000 souls, who were wrought by his eloquence to mutual forgiveness. After denouncing as rebels and enemies of the Church all who adhered to Frederic or invited him to Italy, Giovanni induced his auditors to swear to accept such settlement of their quarrels as he should dictate, and when he announced the terms they unanimously signed the treaty.

Meanwhile he had visited his native place, Vicenza, on invitation of the bishop, and had so impressed the people that they gave him their statutes to revise at his pleasure, and proclaimed him duke, marquis, and count of the city—titles which belonged to the bishop, who also offered to make over the episcopate to him.[2] During his

[2] So great became his reputation that Gregory IX was seriously disturbed at a report that Giovanni contemplated making himself pope. A consistory was

absence at Verona, Uguccione Pileo, an enemy of the Schia family, induced the people to revolt, when Giovanni hastened back and suppressed the rebellion, putting to death, with torture, a number of citizens, who are charitably supposed to have been heretics. Uguccione brought up reinforcements; a fierce battle was fought in the streets, and Giovanni was worsted and taken prisoner. A letter of condolence, addressed to him in prison by Gregory, September 22, 1233, serves to fix the date of this, and to show how powerless was the papacy to protect its agents in the fierce dissensions of the period. Giovanni was obliged to ransom himself and return to Verona, and thence to Bologna. The peace he had effected was of short duration. The chronic wars broke out afresh, and Giovanni, at the instance of Gregory, came again to pacify them. In this he succeeded, but no sooner was his back turned than hostilities were renewed. Gregory made a third attempt, through the Bishops of Reggio and Treviso, who induced the warring factions to lay down their arms for a while; but the main object of presenting a united front and keeping Frederic out of Italy was lost. Ezzelin and a number of the cities urged his coming, and the decisive victory of Cortenuova, in November 1237, dissolved the Lombard League which had so long held the empire in check, and made him master of Lombardy.

For some years Giovanni Schio led a comparatively quiet existence in Bologna, but in 1247, by which time the Inquisition was fairly taking shape, Innocent IV appointed him perpetual Inquisitor throughout Lombardy, arming him with full powers and releasing him from all subjection or accountability to the Dominican general or provincial. In the existing condition of the north of Italy the commission was virtually inoperative, and we hear nothing further of his activity, even after the death of Frederic in 1250, until in 1256 the long-delayed crusade was undertaken against Ezzelin da Romano. By his fiery eloquence he raised in Bologna a considerable force of

---

assembled to consider the advisability of excommunicating him, and that step would have been taken had not the Bishop of Modena sworn upon a missal that he had once seen an angel descend from heaven while Giovanni was speaking, and place a golden cross upon his brow. A confidential mission was sent to Bologna to investigate his career there, which returned with authentic accounts of numberless miracles performed by him, among them no less than ten resuscitations of the dead. So holy a man could not well be thrust from the pale of the Church, and the project was abandoned.

crusaders, at whose head he marched against the tyrant of the Trevisan, but, disgusted with the quarrels of the leaders, he returned to Bologna before the final catastrophe, and he is supposed to have perished in 1265, in the crusade against Manfred, when there was a contingent of 10,000 Bolognese in the army of Charles of Anjou.

The most noteworthy in all respects of the dauntless zealots who fought the battle against heresy was Piero da Verona, better known as St. Peter Martyr. Born at Verona in 1203 or 1206, of a heretic family, his legend relates that he was divinely led to recognize their errors. When a schoolboy of only seven years of age his uncle chanced to ask him what he learned, and he repeated the orthodox creed. His uncle thereupon told him he must not say that God created the heaven and the earth, for he was not the creator of the visible universe; but the child, filled with the Holy Ghost, overcame his elder in argument, who thereupon urged the parents to remove him from school, but the father, who hoped to see him become a leader of the sect, allowed him to complete his education. His orthodox zeal grew with his growth, and in 1221 he entered the Dominican Order. His confessor testified that he never committed a mortal sin, and the bull of his canonization bears emphatic evidence to his humility, his meek obedience, his sweet benignity, his exhaustless compassion, his unfailing patience, his wonderful charity, his passionate supplications to God for martyrdom, and the innumerable miracles which illustrated his life.

Before the Dominicans were armed with the power of persecution Piero earnestly devoted himself to the original function of the Order, that of controverting heresy and preaching against heretics. In this the success of the young apostle was marvelously aided by his thaumaturgic development. At Ravenna, Mantua, Venice, Milan, and other places, numerous wonders are related of his performance. At Cesena, the success of his efforts at conversion irritated the heretics, who, on one occasion, interrupted his preaching in the public square by volleys of filth and stones discharged from a house near by. He several times mildly entreated them to desist, but in vain, when, inspired by divine wrath, he launched a terrible imprecation against them. Instantly the house crumbled in ruin, burying the sacrilegious wretches, nor could it be rebuilt until long afterwards.

When the Dominicans were charged with the duty of persecution, his zeal naturally caused him to be selected as one of the earliest laborers. In 1233 he was sent to Milan, where thus far all efforts had proved ineffectual to rouse the authorities and the citizens to undertake the holy work. Not only did he cause Gregory's legislation of 1231 to be adopted in the municipal law, but he stimulated the *podestà*, Oldrado da Tresseno, and the archbishop, Enrico da Settala, to work in earnest. A number of heretics were burned, who were probably the first victims of fanaticism which Milan had seen since the time of the Cathari of Monforte. So strong was the impression made by these executions that they earned for Oldrado the honor of an equestrian portrait in bas-relief, with the inscription, "*Qui solium struxit, Catharos ut debuit uxit,*" which is still to be seen adorning the wall of the Sala del Consiglio, now the *Archivio pubblico*. It fared worse with the archbishop, who was rendered so unpopular that he was banished, for which the magistracy was duly excommunicated; but he, too, had posthumous reward, for his tomb bore the legend "*instituto inquisitore jugulavit hœreses.*" Piero also founded in Milan a company, or association, for the suppression of heresy, which was taken under immediate papal protection—the model of that which ten years later did such bloody work in Florence. We may safely assume that his fiery activity continued unabated, though we hear nothing of him until 1242, when we again find him in Milan so vigorously at work that he is said to have caused a sedition which nearly ruined the city.

Two years later we meet him fighting heresy in Florence. That city, it will be remembered, was the subject of the earliest inquisitorial experiments, Frà Giovanni di Salerno, Prior of Santa Maria Novella, having been commissioned to prosecute heretics in 1228, and being succeeded after his death, in 1230, by Frà Aldobrandini Cavalcante, and about 1241 by Frà Ruggieri Calcagni. The first two of these accomplished little, being, in fact, rather preachers than inquisitors. The heretics were protected by the Ghibelline faction and the partisans of Frederic II, and heresy, far from decreasing, spread rapidly in spite of occasional burnings. Many of the most powerful families were heretics or open defenders of heresy—the Baroni, Pulci, Cipriani, Cavalcanti, Saraceni, and Malpresa. The Baroni built a stronghold at San Gaggio, beyond the walls, which served as a refuge for the Perfected, and there were plenty of houses in the town where they could hold their conventicles in safety. The Cipriani had two palaces, one at Mugnone and the other in Florence, where troops of Cathari assembled under the leadership of a heresiarch named Marchisiano, and there were great schools at Poggibonsi, Pian di Cascia, and Ponte a Sieve. Under the energetic management of Ruggieri Calcagni, however, the Florentine Inquisition rapidly took shape and executions became frequent, while in the confessions of the accused allusions are made to heretics burned elsewhere, showing that persecution was becoming active wherever political conditions rendered it possible. Each trial revealed fresh names, and as the circle spread the prosecutions became more numerous and terrible. The Signoria was coerced by papal letters to enforce the citations of the inquisitor, and as the prisoners multiplied and their depositions were taken, fully a third of the citizens, including many nobles, were found to be involved. Excited by the magnitude of the developments, Ruggieri determined to strike at the chiefs, and, invoking the aid of the Priors of the Arts, he seized a number of them and condemned to the stake those who proved contumacious. The time had evidently come when they must choose between open resistance and destruction. The Baroni assembled their followers, broke open the jails, and carried off the prisoners, who were distributed through various strongholds in the Florentine territory, where they continued to preach and spread their doctrines.

Matters were rapidly approaching a crisis. On the one hand it was impossible for so large a body as the heretics to permit themselves to be slaughtered with impunity; on the other hand, the persecutors were maddened with excitement at the prospect of at last triumphing over the adversaries who had so long defied them. Innocent IV wrote pressingly to the Signoria commanding energetic support for the inquisitor, and he summoned from Lombardy Piero da Verona to lend his aid in the approaching struggle. Towards the end of 1244 Piero hastened to the conflict, and his eloquence drew such crowds that the Piazza di Santa Maria Novella had to be enlarged to accommodate the multitude. He utilized the enthusiasm by enrolling the orthodox nobles in a guard to protect the Dominicans, and formed a military order under the name of the *Società de' Capitani di Santa Maria*, uniformed in a white doublet with a red cross, and these led the organization known as the *Compagnia della Fede*, sworn to defend the Inquisition at all hazards, under privileges granted by the Holy See. Thus encouraged and supported, Ruggieri pushed forward the trials, and numbers of victims were burned. This was a challenge the heretics could only decline under pain of annihilation. They likewise organized under the lead of the Baroni, and it was not difficult to persuade the *podestà*, Ser Pace di Pesannola of Bergamo, recently appointed by Frederic II, that the interest of his master required him to protect them. Thus the perennial quarrel between the Church and the empire filled the streets of Florence with bloodshed under the banners of orthodoxy and heterodoxy.

Ruggieri provoked the conflict without flinching. He cited the Baroni before him, and when they contemptuously refused to appear he procured a special mandate from Innocent IV. This they obeyed with the utmost docility, about August 1, 1245, swearing to stand to the mandates of the Church, and depositing 1,000 lire as security; but when they understood that he was about to render sentence against them, they appealed to the *podestà*. Ser Pace thereupon sent his officers, August 12, to Ruggieri, ordering him to annul the proceedings as contrary to the mandate of the emperor, to return the money taken as bail, and, in case of contumacy, to appear the next day before the *podestà* under penalty of 1,000 marks. Ruggieri's only notice of this was a summons the next day to Ser Pace to appear before the Inquisition as suspect of heresy and fautorship. The fervid rhetoric of Frà Piero poured oil upon the flames, and the city found itself divided into two factions, not unequally matched and eager to fly at each other. Taking advantage of the assembling of the faithful in the churches on a feast-day, the *podestà* sounded the tocsin, and many unarmed Catholics are said to have been slaughtered before the altars. Then on St. Bartholomew's day (August 24) Ruggieri and Bishop Ardingho, in the Piazza di S. Maria Novella, publicly read a sentence condemning the Baroni, confiscating their possessions, and ordering their castles and palaces to be destroyed, which naturally led to a bloody collision between the factions. Piero then placed himself at the head of the *Compagnia della Fede*, carrying a standard like the other captains, among whom the de' Rossi were the most conspicuous. Under his leadership two murderous battles were fought, one at the Croce al Trebbio and the other in the Piazza di S. Felicità, in both of which the heretics were utterly routed. Mon-

uments still mark the scene of these victories; and until recent times
the banner which San Piero gave to the de' Rossi was still carried by
the *Compagnia de San Piero Martire* on the celebration of his birth-
day, April 29, while the one which he bore himself is preserved
among the relics of Santa Maria Novella and is publicly displayed on
his feast-day.

Thus was destroyed in Florence the power of the heretics and of
the Ghibellines. Ruggieri, for his steadfast courage, was rewarded,
before the close of 1245, with the bishopric of Castro, and was succeeded as inquisitor by San Piero himself, whose indefatigable zeal
allowed the heretics no rest. Many of them, recognizing the futility
of further resistance, abandoned their errors; others fled, and when
Piero left Florence he could boast that heresy was conquered and the
Inquisition established on an impregnable basis.

While Ruggieri, in the summer of 1245, was precipitating the conflict in Florence, Innocent IV, in the Council of Lyons, was passing
sentence of dethronement on Frederic II and trying to find some
aspirant hardy enough to accept the imperial crown. Frederic
laughed the sentence to scorn and easily disposed of his would-be
competitors, but he was obliged to struggle hard to maintain his
Italian possessions, and his death, December 13, 1250, relieved the
papacy from the most formidable antagonist which its ambitious
designs had ever encountered. Skilled equally in the arts of war and
peace, intellectually far in advance of his age, and encumbered with
few scruples, Frederic's brilliant abilities and indomitable courage
had been the one obstacle in the papal path towards domination over
Italy and the foundation on that basis of a universal theocratic
monarchy. His son, Conrad IV, a youth of 21, was scarce to be
dreaded in comparison, though Innocent cautiously waited for a
while in Lyons before venturing into Italy. After reaching Genoa,
June 8, 1251, he addressed to Piero da Verona and Viviano da
Bergamo a brief which shows that the intervening six months had
not sufficed to dull his rejoicing at the death of his great opponent.
A dithyrambic burst of exultation is followed by the declaration that
thanks to God for this inestimable mercy are to be rendered not so
much in words as in deeds, and of these the most acceptable is the
purification of the faith. Inquisitors are to be sent into all parts
of Lombardy; Piero and Viviano are ordered to proceed forthwith to

Cremona, armed with all necessary powers; rulers who do not zealously assist them will be coerced with the spiritual sword, and, if this proves insufficient, Christendom will be aroused to destroy them in a crusade. This bull was followed by a rapid succession of others addressed to the Dominican provincials and to potentates, ordering strenuous co-operation—bulls issued in such haste that, June 13, 1252, the pope was obliged to explain that the blunders and omissions arising from the hurried work of the scribes are not to invalidate them. The whole was crowned, May 15, 1252, by the issue of the bull *Ad extirpanda*, of which I have given an abstract in a former chapter.

We have no details of what Piero accomplished as inquisitor at Cremona, or at Milan to which he was afterwards transferred. Within nine months after he had been summoned to action, however, he had become such an object of terror that in despair a plot was laid for his assassination. The matter was entrusted to Stefano Confaloniero, a noble of Aliate, and the hire of the assassins, 25 lire, was furnished by Guidotto Sachella. The week before Easter, 1252, Stefano proposed the murder to Manfredo Clitoro of Giussano, who agreed to do it, and associated with him Carino da Balsamo. At the same time Giacopo della Chiusa undertook to go to Pavia to slay Rainerio Saccone, and made the journey, but failed to accomplish his mission. The other conspirators were more successful. Frà Piero at that time was Prior of Como, and went thither to pass his Easter. He was obliged to return to Milan on Low Sunday, April 7, as on that day expired the term of 15 days which he had assigned to a contumacious heretic. During Easter week Stefano, with Manfredo and Carino, went to Como and awaited Piero's departure. It shows the austerity of the man that he set out on foot, April 7, though weakened with a quartan fever, and accompanied only by a single friar, Domenico. Manfredo and Carino followed them as far as Barlassina, and set upon them in a lonely spot. Carino acted as executioner, laying open Piero's head with a single blow, mortally wounding Domenico, and then, finding that Piero still breathed, plunging a dagger in his breast. Some passing travellers carried the body of the martyr to the convent of San Sempliciano, while Domenico was conveyed to Meda, where he died five days afterwards. As for the conspirators, I have already alluded to the strange delay which postponed for 43 years the final sentence of Stefano Confaloniero, and to the repentance and beatification of Carino, who became St. Acerinus.[3] Giacopo della Chiusa seems to have escaped, and Manfredo and a certain Tommaso were captured and confessed.[4] Manfredo admitted that he had been concerned in the murder of two other inquisitors, Frà Pier di Bracciano and Frà Catalano, both Franciscans, at Ombraida in Lombardy. He was simply ordered to present himself to the pope for judgment, but in place of obeying he very naturally fled, and there is no record of his subsequent fate.

The Church made much shrewder use of the martyrdom than the exaction of vulgar vengeance. Its whole machinery was set to work at once to impress the populations with the sanctity of the martyr. When the General Chapter of the Order assembled at Bologna in May, Innocent wrote to them in terms of the most extravagant hyperbole respecting him, and urged them to fresh exertions in the cause of Christ. By August 31, he ordered the commencement of proceedings of canonization, and before a year had elapsed, March 25, 1253, the bull of canonization was issued—I believe the most speedy creation of a saint on record. Before the century was out, Giacopo di Voragine compared his martyrdom with that of Christ, and he assures us that the disappearance of heresy in the Milanese was owing to the merits of the saint. In 1373, Gregory XI granted permission to erect a small oratory on the spot of the murder, which grew to be a magnificent church with a splendid convent, through the offerings of the pilgrims who flocked thither. The authenticity of the martyr's sanctity was proved when, in 1340, 87 years after death, the body was translated to a tomb of marvellous workmanship, and was found in a perfect state of preservation; and when the sepulchre was opened in 1736 it was still found uncorrupted, with wounds corresponding exactly to those described in the annals.

Hardly were the splendid obsequies of San Piero completed when his place was occupied by Guido da Sesto and Rainerio Saccone da Vicenza. The latter had been high in the Catharan Church, when he was converted, and he could render invaluable aid in persecuting

[3] See page 220.

[4] Frà Tommaso's disgrace was not perpetual. We shall meet him hereafter as inquisitor, alternately protecting and persecuting the Spiritual Franciscans. If the accounts of the latter be true, his death in 1306 was a visitation of God for the frightful cruelties inflicted upon them.

his old associates, whom he pursued with all the ruthless bigotry of an apostate. The fact that he was singled out with San Piero by the conspirators to be slain shows how thoroughly he had earned the hate of the persecuted. Rainerio was at once transferred to Milan as the man best fitted to replace the martyr, and he justified the selection by the unbending firmness with which he vindicated the authority of his office.

Heretics were more numerous than ever in Lombardy, for the active work carried on in Languedoc by Bernard de Caux and his colleagues had caused a wholesale emigration. All of Rainerio's resolution and energy were required for the work before him. In the March of Treviso, Ezzelin da Romano, whose influence extended far to the west, continued openly to protect heresy, and even in Lombardy the hopes excited by Frederic's death threatened to prove fallacious. In 1253, when Conrad IV passed through Treviso to recover possession of his Sicilian kingdom, he appointed as his Lombard vicar-general Uberto Pallavicino, who soon became as obnoxious to the Church as Ezzelin himself; and, though Conrad died in 1254, and Innocent IV seized Naples as a forfeited fief of the Church, Pallavicino's power continued to increase, and he soon established relations with Manfred, Frederic's illegitimate son, who wrested Naples from the papacy and became the chief of the Ghibelline faction.

One of Rainerio's first enterprises, in 1253, was summoning Egidio, Count of Cortenuova, before his tribunal, as a fautor and defender of heresy. The castle of Cortenuova, near Bergamo, had been razed as a nest of heretics, and its reconstruction prohibited, but the count had seized the castle of Mongano, which was claimed by the Bishop of Cremona, and had converted it into a den of heretics, who enjoyed immunity under his protection. He disdained to obey the citation and was duly excommunicated. He paid no attention to this, and on March 23, 1254, Innocent IV ordered the authorities of Milan, under pain of ecclesiastical censures, to take the castle by force and deliver its inmates to the inquisitors for trial. The count, however, was in close alliance with Pallavicino, "that enemy of God and the Church," and the Milanese appear to have had no appetite for the enterprise at the time. Mongano continued to be a place of refuge for the persecuted until 1269, when the Milanese were at last stimulated to undertake the siege, and on capturing it handed it over to the Dominicans.

Better success awaited Rainerio's efforts with Roberto Patta da Giussano, a Milanese noble who for 20 years had been one of the most conspicuous defenders of heresy in Lombardy. At his castle of Gatta he publicly maintained heretic bishops, allowing them to build houses, and establish schools whence they spread their pernicious doctrines through the land. Roberto had been cited by the archbishop and had abjured heresy, but the heretics of Gatta had continued to enjoy his protection. It was otherwise when, in 1254, Rainerio and Guido summoned him again. On his failing to appear they summarily condemned him as a heretic, declared his property confiscated and his descendants subject to the usual disabilities. Roberto saw that the new officials were not to be trifled with. He hastened to make his peace, binding himself to submit to any terms which the pope might dictate; and Innocent doubtless deemed himself merciful when, August 19, 1254, he ordered the castle of Gatta and all the heretic houses to be destroyed by fire, the bones in the cemetery to be dug up and burned, and the count to perform such salutary penance as Rainerio might prescribe.

The papal power was now at its height. Conrad IV had died May 20, 1254, not without suspicion of poison; Innocent IV had seized his Sicilian kingdoms, and for a brief space he might well imagine himself on the eve of becoming the undisputed temporal as well as spiritual head of Italy. Every effort was made to perfect the Inquisition and to render it efficient both as a political instrument and as a means of bringing about the long-desired uniformity of belief. On March 8 Innocent had taken an important step in its organization by ordering the Franciscan Minister of Rome to appoint friars of his Order as inquisitors in all the provinces south of Lombardy. On the 29th he proceeded to reorganize the Lombard Inquisition by instructing the provincial to appoint four inquisitors whose power should extend from Bologna and Ferrara to Genoa. Under this impulsion and the restless energy of Rainerio no time was lost in extending the institution in every direction save where Ghibelline potentates such as Ezzelin and Uberto prevented its introduction. We chance to have an illustration of the process in the records of the little republic of Asti, on the confines of Savoy. In 1254 two inquisitors, Frà Giovanni da Torino and Frà Paulo da Milano, with their associates, appeared before the council of the republic and announced to them that the pope enjoined them to admit the Inquisition within their territories. The Astigiani answered that they were ready to obey the pontiff, but they had no laws providing for persecution and it would be necessary to frame one. Accordingly an *Ordenamento* was drawn up prescribing obedience to the constitutions of Innocent IV and Frederic II, and it was forthwith added to the local statutes.

The death of Innocent IV, December 7, 1254, made no difference in the energy with which the progress of the Inquisition was pushed. The accession of Alexander IV was signalized by a succession of bulls repeating and enforcing the regulations of his predecessor, and urging prelates and inquisitors to increased activity. To overcome the resistance of such cities as were slack in the duty of capturing all who were designated for arrest by the inquisitors, the latter were empowered to punish such delinquency with the heavy fine of 200 silver marks. Under this impulsion Rainerio assembled the people of Milan, August 1, 1255, in the Piazza del Duomo, read to them his commission, and gave them notice that, although he had hitherto acted with great mildness, the time had passed for trifling. He therefore gave three formal warnings, attested by a notarial instrument duly witnessed, that all who should in any way impede the Inquisition were excommunicate as fautors of heresy, and would be prosecuted to such penalties as their audacity deserved. By January 1257, Rainerio had risen to the position of Supreme Inquisitor over the whole of Lombardy and the Marchcs of Genoa and Treviso, with power to appoint deputies, and it would be difficult to set limits to the power thus concentrated in the hands of the ex-Catharan.

Territorially, however, his authority was circumscribed by the possessions of Uberto and Ezzelin, within which no inquisitor dared venture. In this very year, 1257, Piacenza, which had fallen under control of Uberto, was placed in such complete hostility to the Church that it was deprived of its episcopate, and its bishop, Alberto, was transferred to Ferrara. In Vicenza, which was ruled by Ezzelin, matters were even worse. There the heretics had a recognized chief named Piero Gallo, of the Borgo di San Piero, whose name was adopted by them as a rallying cry, to which the Catholics responded with *"viva Volpe!"*—a member of the family of Volpe being the leader of their faction; and so thoroughly did this become encrusted in the habits of the people that we are told in the seventeenth century that the cry of the citizens of the Borgo (than corruptly called Porsampiero) was still *"viva Gallo!"* while that of the dwellers in the Piazza and Porta Nuova was *"viva Volpe!"* Ezzelin would permit no persecution, and when the blessed Bortolamio di Breganze, one of the immediate disciples of St. Dominic, was made Bishop of Vicenza in 1256, he was reduced to seeking conversions by persuasion. After preaching for a while with little effect he had a public discussion with Piero Gallo, and so impressed him by argument that the heretic was converted. We may reasonably doubt the assertion that Ezzelin's displeasure at this feat was the cause of Bortolamio's banishment from his see, but, whatever was the motive, the bishop was consoled by Alexander IV, who sent him as nuncio to England. During his absence, in 1258, his archdeacon, Bernardo Nicelli, was bolder, and made a capture of importance in the person of the Catharan bishop, Viviano Bogolo. He endeavored to convert his prisoner, but his powers of persuasion were insufficient, and Ezzelin set the heretic at liberty.

So long as these Ghibelline chiefs retained power it was evident that the hopes based on the death of Frederic II were not destined to fruition. Every motive had long conspired to render the Church eager for the destruction of Ezzelin, and every expedient had been tried to reduce him to subjection. As far back as 1221 Gregory IX, then legate in Lombardy, had extorted from him assurances of his hatred of heresy. In 1231 his sons, Ezzelin and Alberico, were at the papal court expressing horror at his crimes and promising to deliver him up for trial as a heretic if he would not reform, in order to escape the disinheritance which they would otherwise incur under Frederic's laws. Ezzelin's courage never wavered, and his adventurous career was pursued with scarce a check. When Frederic II overcame the resistance of Lombardy, he gave, in 1238, his natural daughter Selvaggia to Ezzelin in marriage and created him imperial vicar. The unanimous testimony of the ecclesiastical chroniclers represents him as a monster whose crimes almost transcend the capacity for evil of human nature, but the unrelieved blackness of the picture defeats the object of the painter. Possibly he may have been among the worst of the Italian despots of the time, when faithlessness and contempt for human suffering were the rule, but the long, unbroken success which attended him shows that he must have had qualities which attached men to him, and the report that he was twice moved to tears by the eloquence of Frà Giovanni Schio indicates a degree of sensibility impossible in one utterly depraved. The anecdote related by Benvenuto da Imola, that he carried on his back his sister's lover Sordello to and from the place of assignation, and then gave the frightened troubadour a friendly warning, presupposes a character at variance with that currently attributed to him.

While Frederic was at peace with the Church, Ezzelin appears to have been let alone; and when the quarrel broke out afresh, after the emperor's subjugation of Lombardy, Ezzelin was again attacked. Frederic's excommunication of April 7, 1239, was followed, November 20, by that of Ezzelin. This time there is no mention of fautorship of heresy, but only of his encroachments on the church of Treviso and of his remaining under excommunication for more than three years. Nothing came of this, and in 1244 Innocent IV resolved to see whether the Inquisition could not be used to better effect. Frà Rolando da Cremona was commissioned to make inquest on him as one publicly defamed for heresy by reason of his association with heretics; and as the accused was "terrible and powerful," the inquisitor was empowered to publish the legal citations in any place where he could do so in safety. The result of this trial *in absentia* was conclusive. It was found that he was the son of a heretic, that his kinsmen were heretics, that under his protection heresy had spread throughout the March of Treviso, and it was decided that he did not believe in the faith of Christ. In March 1248, Innocent pronounced his condemnation as a manifest heretic, but promised him that he would learn the abundant clemency of the Church if he would present himself in person by the next Ascension day (May 28). The wary old chief did not allow his curiosity about the extent of papal clemency to overcome his caution, and abstained from placing his person in Innocent's power. He sent envoys, however, who offered to purge him of the suspicion of heresy by swearing to his orthodoxy; but Innocent held that he must appear in person and offered him a safe-conduct in coming and going. There was no security promised in staying, however, and Ezzelin was cautious. The term allowed him passed away, and he was duly excommunicated. After two years more he was notified that unless he appeared by August

1, 1250, he would be subjected to the statutes against heresy. The obdurate sinner was equally unmoved by this, and in June 1251 the Bishop of Treviso and the Dominican Prior of Mantua were ordered to summon him personally again to appear by a given time, offering him ample security for his safety: if he disobeyed, his subjects of Treviso were commanded to coerce him, and if this failed a crusade was to be preached against him.

The Neapolitan conquest and the death of Innocent IV postponed the organization of the crusade, but at length, in June 1256, it set out from Venice under the leadship of the Legate Filippo, Archbishop-Elect of Ravenna. The capture by assault of Padua, Ezzelin's most important city, was an encouraging commencement of the campaign, but the seven-days' sack to which the unfortunate town was abandoned showed that the soldiers of the cross were determined to make the most of the indulgences which they had earned. Under its incompetent captain the crusade dragged on without further result until, in 1258, the legate was utterly routed near Brescia and captured, together with his astrologer, the Dominican Everard. Brescia fell into Ezzelin's hands, who, more powerful than ever, entertained designs upon Milan, where he had relations with the Ghibelline faction. When all danger seemed to him past, however, there was a sudden revulsion of fortune. The Ghibelline chiefs of Lombardy, Uberto Pallavicino and Buoso di Dovara, lords of Cremona, had been in alliance with him; they had aided in the capture of Brescia, with the understanding that they were to share in its possession, but he had monopolized the conquest, and they were resolved on revenge. June 11, 1259, they signed a treaty against Ezzelin with the Milanese and with Azzo d'Este, the head of the Lombard Guelfs. Ezzelin took the field with a heavy force, hoping to gain possession of Milan through the intelligences which he had within the walls, but on the march he was attacked by Uberto, Buoso, and Azzo, who by skillful strategy dispersed his troops and captured him, grievously wounded. His savage pride would not brook this degradation: he tore the bandages from his wound, refused all aid, and died in a few days.[5]

---

[5] The ferocity of the age is seen in the treatment bestowed on Ezzelin's brother Alberico, when captured with his family. He was gagged and tied to a tree, his wife and daughters were burned alive before his eyes, his sons were slain and their limbs thrown in his face, and then he was deliberately hacked in pieces. Alberico was a man of culture, a troubadour, and a patron of the *gai science*.

No greater service could have been rendered to the Church than that performed by Uberto, who had been in field and council the soul of the alliance that destroyed the dreaded Ezzelin and threw open, after 30 years of fruitless effort, the March of Treviso to the Inquisition. Some show of favor in return for such services would have been wise, as it might have won over the powerful Ghibelline chief. In the treaty of June 11, however, the allies had alluded to Manfred as King of Sicily, and had pledged themselves to labor for his reconciliation with the pope. No service, especially after it had become irrevocable, could overbalance this recognition of the hated son of Frederic. Uberto, Buoso, and the Cremonese had been absolved from excommunication when they entered the alliance, but Alexander IV wrote, December 13, 1259, to his legate in Lombardy that the absolution was worthless because it had not been administered by a Dominican or a Franciscan, who alone were empowered to grant it; if, however, the allies would repudiate Manfred and give sufficient security to obey the mandates of the Church and to restore all Church property, they might still be absolved.

Apparently Alexander's head had been turned by the triumph over Ezzelin, but he knew little of the man whom he thus treated with such ingratitude. By intrigues with the Torriani and other powerful nobles of Milan, Uberto created for himself a party in that city, and in 1260 he procured his election as *podestà* for five years. Rainerio Saccone vainly endeavored to prevent a consummation so deplorable. He assembled the citizens, denounced Uberto as vehemently suspected of heresy and as a manifest defender of heretics, and threatened that if it was persisted in he would ring all the church bells and summon the people and clergy and *Crocesegnati* to oppose it by force. Unfortunately the citizens did not take in good part this somewhat insolent interference of a stranger with their internal affairs; or, as Alexander IV describes it, "this wholesome counsel given in the spirit of humility and kindness." In wrath they assembled and rushed to the Dominican convent, where they gave Rainerio the alternative of leaving the city or faring worse. He chose the wiser alternative and departed.

It was in vain that Alexander, in the bull detailing these griefs, ordered Rainerio and the other inquisitors to prosecute the guilty parties. It was in vain also that he approved, October 14, 1260, the statutes of an association of Defenders of the Faith recently formed in Milan in honor of Jesus Christ, the Blessed Virgin, St. John the Baptist, and St. Peter Martyr, whose members pledged themselves to give assistance, armed or otherwise, to the Inquisition. Uberto was now the most powerful man in Lombardy, and wherever his influence extended he prohibited inquisitors from performing their functions. Heretics were safe under his rule, and they flocked to his territories from other parts of Lombardy and from Languedoc and Provence. He cared as little as Ezzelin for the impotent papal thunder, and quietly went on strengthening his position and adding city after city to his dominions. Between his success in the north and the daily extending influence of Manfred's wise and vigorous rule in the south, it looked for a while as though the ambitious designs of the papacy were permanently crushed, and that the Italian Inquisition might come to an untimely end.

There have been few revolutions more pregnant with results than that which occurred when the popes, renouncing the hope of acquiring for themselves the kingdom of Sicily, succeeded in arousing the ambition of Charles of Anjou, and caused a crusade to be preached everywhere in his behalf. The papacy fully recognized the supreme importance of the issue and staked everything upon it. The treasures of salvation were poured forth with unstinted hand, and plenary indulgences were given to all who would contribute a fourth of their income or a tenth of their property. The temporal treasury of the Church was drawn upon with equal liberality. Three years' tithe of all ecclesiastical revenues in France and Flanders were granted to Charles, and when all this proved insufficient, Clement IV sacrificed the property of the Roman churches without hesitation. An effort to raise 100,000 livres by pledging it brought in only 30,000, and then he pawned for 50,000 more the plate and jewels of the Holy See.

Vainly Uberto sought to prevent the passage of the crusaders through Lombardy. The fate of Italy—one may almost say of the papacy—was decided, February 26, 1266, on the plain of Benevento, where Guelf and Ghibelline from all portions of the Peninsula faced each other. Had Charles been defeated it would have fared ill with the Holy See. In the previous August, Clement had despairingly answered Charles's demands for money by declaring that he had none and could get none—that England was hostile, that Germany was almost openly in revolt, that France groaned and complained, that Spain scarce sufficed for her internal necessities, and that Italy did not furnish her own share of expenses. After the battle, however, he could exultingly write, in May, to Cardinal Ottoboni of San Adriano, his legate in England, that "Charles of Anjou holds in peace the whole kingdom of that pestilent man, obtaining his putrid body, his wife, his children, and his treasure," adding that already the Mark of Ancona had returned to obedience, that Florence, Siena, Pistoja, and Pisa had submitted, that envoys had come from Uberto and Piacenza, and that others were expected from Cremona and Genoa; and on June 1 he announced the submission of Uberto and of Piacenza and Cremona.

Although one by one Uberto's cities revolted from him in the general terror, his submission was only to gain time, and in 1267 he risked another cast of the die by joining in the invitation to Italy of the young Conradin, but the defeat and capture of that prince at Tagliacozza, in August 1268, followed by his barbarous execution in October, extinguished the house of Suabia and the hopes of the Ghibellines. Charles of Anjou was master of Italy; he was created Imperial Vicar in Tuscany; even in the north we find him this year appointing Adalberto de' Gamberti as *podestà* in Piacenza. Before the close of 1268 Uberto Pallavicino died, broken with age and in utter misery, while besieged in his castle of Gusaliggio by the Piacenzans and Parmesans. For a presumed heretic he made a good end, surrounded by Dominicans and Franciscans, confessing his sins and receiving the viaticum, so that, as a pious chronicler observes, we may humbly believe that his soul was saved.

Under these circumstances, the long interregnum of nearly three years, which occurred after the death of Clement IV in 1268, made little difference. The Inquisition could be organized everywhere, and could perform its functions unhampered. By this time, too, its powers, its duties, and its mode of procedure had become thoroughly defined and universally recognized, and neither prelate nor potentate dared to call them in question.

No time had been lost in enforcing unity of belief in the territories redeemed from Ghibelline control. As early as February 1259, the Franciscan Minister of Bologna was ordered to appoint two friars as inquisitors in Romagnola. At Vicenza, no sooner was quiet restored after the death of Ezzelin than Frà Giovanni Schio was sent thither to remove the excommunication incurred by the people in consequence of their subjection to Ezzelin. The exiled Bishop Bortolamio, on his return from England, had tarried with St. Louis, whose confessor he had been in Palestine, where he had served as papal legate during the saintly king's crusade. As soon as he heard of the death of Ezzelin he hastened homeward, bearing with him the priceless treasures of a thorn of the crown and a piece of the cross, which St. Louis had bestowed upon him in parting. At once he commenced to build the great Dominican church and convent of the Santa Corona. We are told that the presence of the relics worked the miracle of relieving the city of its three leading sins— avarice, heresy, and discord. As for heresy, the miracle lay in the unlooked-for conversion of the chief heretic of the district, Gieremia, known as the Archbishop of the Mark, who, with his son Alticlero, made public recantation. The heretic bishop, Viviano Bogolo, fled to Pavia, where he was recognized and burned. His two deacons, Olderico da Marola and Tolomeo, with eight others, probably Per- fects, were obstinate, and were promptly burned. These examples were sufficient. The *credentes* furnished no further martyrs, and heresy, at least in its outward manifestation, was extinguished.

In some places, unblessed with such wonder-working relics, the Inquisition had greater trouble in establishing orthodoxy. In Piacenza it is said to have found the burning of 28 wagonloads of heretics necessary. At Sermione for 16 years the inhabitants defiantly refused to allow persecution. Though Catholic themselves, they continued to afford protection to heretics, who naturally flocked thither as one refuge after another was rendered unsafe by the zeal of the inquisi- tors. It was in vain that Frà Timedeo, the inquisitor, obtained evi- dence by sending there a female spy, named Costanza da Bergamo, who pretended to be a heretic, received the *consolamentum*, and was then unreservedly admitted to their secrets. At last the scandal of such ungodly toleration became unendurable, and the Bishop of Verona prevailed upon Mastino and Alberto della Scala of Ve- rona, and Pinamonte de' Bonacolsi of Mantua, to reduce Sermione to obedience. It was obliged to submit in 1276, delivering up no less than 174 perfected heretics, and humbly asking to be restored to Catholic unity. Frà Filippo Bonaccorso, the Inquisitor of Treviso,

applied to John XXI for instructions as to the treatment of the penitent community. The pope was a humane and cultured man who
cared more for poetry than theology, and he was disposed to be
lenient with repentant sinners. He instructed Frà Filippo to remove
the interdict if the town would appoint a syndic to abjure heresy in
its name, and to swear in future to seize all heretics and deliver them
to the Inquisition, any infraction of the oath to work a renewal,
ipso facto, of the interdict. Every inhabitant was then to appear
personally before the inquisitor and make full confession of everything relating to heresy, to abjure, and to accept such penance as
might be assigned—all infamous penalties, disabilities, imprisonment, and confiscation being mercifully excluded. Obstinate heretics
were to be dealt with according to the canons, and of these there
were found 70, whom Frà Filippo duly condemned, and had the satisfaction of seeing burned. To ensure the future purity of the faith,
in 1278 a Franciscan convent was built at Sermione with the proceeds
of a fine of 4,000 lire levied upon Verona as one of the conditions
of removing the interdict, and in 1289 Ezzelin's castle of Illasio was
given to some of the nobles who had been conspicuous in the reduction of Sermione, as a reward for their service.

Thus heresy, deprived of all protection, was gradually stamped
out, and the Inquisition established its power in every corner of
the land. In the territories that once had been Ghibelline the mere
fact of having adhered of necessity to Ezzelin during the period of
his unquestioned domination long continued sufficient to justify
prosecution for heresy, entailing the desirable result of confiscation.
When Ezzelin's generation passed away, the memory of the dead
was assailed and the descendants were disinherited. In all this there
was no pretense of errors of faith, but the men to whom the Church
entrusted the awful powers of the Inquisition seemed implacably
determined to erase from the land every trace of those who had once
dared to resist its authority. At last, in 1304, the authorities of
Vicenza appealed to Benedict XI no longer to allow the few survivors of Ezzelin's party and their descendants to be thus wronged,
and the pope graciously granted their petition. By this time the
empire was but a shadow; Ghibellinism represented no living force
that the papacy could reasonably dread, and its persecution had
long been merely the gratification of greed or malice.

The triumph of the Inquisition had not been effected wholly

without resistance. In 1277 Frà Corrado Pagano undertook a raid against the heretics of the Valtelline. It was doubtless organized on an extended scale, for he took with him two associates and two notaries. The heretics were numerous, and did not lack protectors, for Corrado da Venosta, one of the most powerful nobles of the region, cut short the enterprise by slaughtering the whole party, on St. Stephen's Day, December 26. Nicholas III made every effort to avenge the murder, even invoking the assistance of Rodolf of Hapsburg, and his joy was extreme when, in November 1279, the *podestà* and people of Bergamo succeeded in capturing Corrado de Venosta and his accomplices. Nicholas at once ordered their delivery, under safe escort, to the Inquisitors Anselmo da Alessandria, Daniele da Giussano, and Guidone da Coconate, who were instructed to inflict a punishment sufficient to intimidate others from imitating their wickedness.

The same year a popular ebullition in Parma shows how slender was the hold which the Inquisition possessed on the people. Frà Florio had been diligent in the exercise of his functions, and we are told that he had burned innumerable heretics, when he chanced at Parma to have before him a woman guilty of relapse. It was a matter of course to condemn her to relaxation, and she was duly burned. In place of being piously impressed by the spectacle the Parmesans were inspired by Satan to indignation, which expressed itself by sacking the Dominican convent, destroying the records of the Inquisition, and maltreating the friars so that one of them died within a few days. The Dominicans thereupon abandoned the ungrateful city, marching out in solemn procession. The magistrates showed singular indifference to punishing this misdeed, and when summoned by the Cardinal Legate of Ostia, the representatives who presented themselves lacked the necessary authority, so that, after vainly waiting for satisfaction, he laid an interdict upon the city. This was not removed till 1282, and even then the guilty were not punished. In 1285 we find Honorius IV taking up the matter afresh and summoning the Parmesans to send delegates to him within a month to receive sentence; what that sentence was does not appear, but in 1287 the humbled citizens petitioned the Dominicans to return, received them with great honor, and voted them 1,000 lire, in annual installments of 200 lire, wherewith to build a church.

Earnest and unsparing as were the labors of the inquisitors, it seemed impossible to eradicate heresy. Its open manifestations were readily suppressed, but in secret it still flourished and maintained its organization. How difficult, indeed, was the task of detecting it under the mask of orthodoxy is illustrated by the case of Armanno Pongilupo. In Ferrara heretics were numerous. Armanno's parents were both Cathari; he was a *consolatus* and his wife a *consolata*. In 1254 he was detected and imprisoned; he confessed and abjured, and was released. From his Catharan bishop he received absolution for his oath of abjuration, and was received back into the sect. From this time until his death, in 1269, he was unceasingly engaged in propagating Catharan doctrines and in ministering to the wants of his less fortunate brethren in the clutches of the Inquisition. Meanwhile he preserved an exterior of the strictest Catholicism; he was regular in attendance at the confessional, and wholly devoted to piety and good works. He died in the odor of sanctity, was buried in the cathedral, and immediately he began to work miracles. A magnificent tomb arose over his remains, an altar was erected, and, as the miraculous manifestations of his sanctity multiplied, his chapel became filled with images, to the no little profit of the church fortunate enough to possess him. Adored as a saint in the popular cult, there came a general demand for his canonization, in which the pride of the city was warmly enlisted, but which was steadfastly opposed by the Inquisition. In the confessions of heretics before it the name of Armanno constantly recurred as that of one of the most active members of the sect, and ample evidence accumulated as to his unrepentant heresy. Then arose a curious conflict, waged on both sides with unremitting vigor for 32 years. Hardly had the remains been committed to honorable sepulture in the cathedral when Frà Aldobrandini, the inquisitor who had tried him in 1254, ordered the archpriest and chapter to exhume and burn the corpse, and on their refusal excommunicated them and placed the cathedral under interdict. From this they appealed to Gregory X and set to work to gather the evidence for canonization. At different times five several inquests were held and superabundant testimony was forthcoming as to the success with which his suffrage was invoked, how the sick were healed, the blind made to see, and the halt to walk, while numerous priests bore emphatic witness to his pre-eminent piety

during life. Gregory and Aldobrandini passed away leaving the matter
unsettled. Frà Florio, the next inquisitor, sent to Rome expressly to
urge Honorius IV to come to a decision, but Honorius died without
concluding the matter. On the accession of Boniface VIII in 1294,
Frà Guido da Vicenza, then inquisitor, again visited Rome to procure a termination of the affair. Still the contending forces were
too evenly balanced for either to win. At length the Lord of Ferrara, Azzo X, interposed, for the contest between the inquisitor
and the secular clergy seriously threatened the peace of the city.
In 1300 Boniface appointed a commission to make a thorough investigation, with power to decide finally, and in 1301 sentence was
rendered to the effect that Armanno had died a relapsed heretic;
that his bones should be exhumed and burned, the sarcophagus containing them and the altar erected before it be destroyed; that all
statues, images, and other offerings set up in his honor in the
cathedral and in other Ferrarese churches should be removed within
ten days; and that all his property, real and personal, was confiscated
to the Inquisition, any sales or conveyances made of them during
the years which had elapsed since his death being void. Frà Guido's
triumph was complete, and on the death of the Bishop of Ferrara,
in 1303, he was rewarded with the episcopate.

The Inquisition was thus thoroughly established and at work
in northern and central Italy, and heresy was gradually disappearing
before its remorseless and incessant energy. There were two regions,
however, Venice and the Two Sicilies, which thus far we have not
considered, as they were in some sort independent of the movement
which we have traced in the rest of the peninsula.

Naples, like the other portions of southern Europe, had been
exposed to the infection of heresy. The allusions of the Abbot
Joachim of Flora to the Cathari indicate that their existence and
doctrines were familiar facts in Calabria, though as Rainerio makes
no allusion to any Catharan church in Italy south of Florence it is
presumable that the sectaries were widely scattered and unorganized.
Cathari driven from Languedoc, who perhaps found even Lombardy insecure, were tolerably sure of refuge in the wild and se-
cluded valleys of Calabria and the Abruzzi, lying aside from the
great routes of travel. The domination in Naples of Innocent IV
was too brief for the organization of any systematized persecution,

and when Manfred reconquered the kingdom, although he seems
to have felt his position too precarious to risk open toleration, and,
under pressure from Jayme of Aragon, he ordered Bishop Vivian
and his disciples, who had settled in Apulia, to leave his dominions,
yet he went no further in active measures of repression.

Charles of Anjou came as a crusader and as the champion of
the Church. Scarce was his domination assured by the execution of
Conradin, October 29, 1268, than we see him zealously employed
in establishing the Inquisition throughout the kingdom. There was
one inquisitor for Bari and the Capitanata, one for Otranto, and one
for the Terra di Lavoro and the Abruzzi; and in 1271 one was added
for Calabria and one for Sicily. Most of them were Dominicans,
but we meet with at least one Franciscan, Frà Benvenuto.

Few details have been preserved to us of the activity of the
Inquisition in Naples. We know that heretics continued to exist
there, but the wild and mountainous character of much of the
country doubtless afforded them abundant opportunities of safe
asylum. In August 1269, a letter of Charles ordering the seizure
of 68 heretics designated by Frà Benvenuto shows that the work
was being energetically prosecuted, and in another letter of March 14,
1270, there is an allusion to three others whom Frà Matteo di
Castellamare had recently caused to be burned in Benevento. The
Inquisitors of Languedoc, moreover, made haste, as early as 1269, to
send agents to Naples to hunt the refugees whom their severity had
driven there, and Charles ordered every assistance to be rendered to
them. But the Neapolitan Inquisition, even under the Angevines,
seems never to have attained the compact and effective organization
of which we have seen the results elsewhere, though Charles II was
an eager persecutor who stimulated the zeal of his inquisitors, and his
son Robert earned the name of the Pious.

When, as the result of the Sicilian Vespers in 1282, the Island
of Sicily passed into the hands of Pedro III of Aragon, it was placed
in the bitterest antagonism towards the Holy See, and no active
persecution is to be looked for. It was not till 1302 that Boniface VIII
was brought to accept the accomplished fact, and to acknowledge
Frederic of Aragon as King of Trinacria. The Inquisition soon followed. In 1304 we find Benedict XI ordering Frederic to receive and
give all due assistance to Frà Tommaso di Aversa the inquisitor, and

all other inquisitors who may be sent thither. Yet the introduction of the Inquisition in the island was nominal rather than real except, as we shall see, with regard to the Templars, and Sicily long remained a safe refuge for the persecuted Fraticelli. Doubtless Arnaldo de Vilanova contributed to this by the picture which he presented to Frederic of the inquisitors of the day. They were a diabolical pest, trafficking in their offices, abandoned to hatred, greed, and lust, with no one to condemn them or to repress their fury.

The Republic of Venice was always a law unto itself. Though forming part of the March of Treviso, its predominant interests in the thirteenth century lay to the east of the Adriatic, and it did not become a formidable power on the mainland until the acquisition of Treviso in 1339. That of Padua, in 1405, followed by Verona, Vicenza, Feltre, Belluno, and Brescia, greatly increased its strength, and in 1448 it wrenched Bergamo from the dukes of Milan. Thus its policy with regard to the Inquisition eventually controlled the whole of the March of Treviso, and a considerable portion of Lombardy.

That policy held at bay in all things the pretensions of the Holy See, and looked with extreme suspicion on whatever might give the popes an excuse for interference with either the domestic policy or the foreign enterprises of the Signoria. Fairly orthodox, though not bigoted, Venice held aloof from the strife between Guelf and Ghibelline, and was not involved in the anathemas lavished upon Ezzelin da Romano. Venice, in fact, was the basis of operations in the crusade against him, and it was a Venetian who led the expedition up the Brenta which captured Padua. Yet the republic made no haste to join in the movement for the extermination of heresy so energetically pushed by Gregory IX and his successors. The constitutions of Frederic II were never inscribed in its statute books. In 1229 the official oath of the Doge Giacopo Tiepoli, which, as is customary, contains the criminal code of the day, embodies no allusion to heresy or its suppression, and the same is true of the criminal statute of 1232 by the same doge. Yet the duty to punish heresy was at length recognized, though the civil authorities would abate no jot of their right to control the administration of justice in spiritual as well as in temporal matters. The ancient jurisdiction of the episcopal courts was alone recognized, but the judgment of the bishops was subject to revision by the council before the death penalty could be inflicted.

This could by no means be satisfactory to the papacy, and when the death of Frederic II led to an immediate effort to extend the Inquisition through the territories hitherto closed to it, Venice was not forgotten. By a bull of June 11, 1251, Innocent IV ordered the Frati Vicenzo of Milan and Giovanni of Vercelli to proceed to Venice and persecute heretics there with the same powers as those exercised by inquisitors elsewhere in Lombardy. Whether the good friars made the attempt to exercise these powers is questionable; if they did so, their ill-success is unquestionable. There is a document of 1256 which contains an oath to pursue heretics and to denounce them, not to the ecclesiastical tribunals, but to the doge or to the magistrates— an oath presumably administered to the secular inquisitors established in 1249.

As the pressure of the Inquisition extended throughout Lombardy and the Marches, the persecuted heretics naturally sought a refuge in Venetian territory, where supervision was so much more negligent. It was in vain that about 1286 Frà Filippo of Mantua, the Inquisitor of Treviso, was sent by Honorius IV with a summons to the republic to inscribe in its laws the constitutions against heresy of Frederic and of the popes. In 1288, Nicholas IV lost patience with this persistent contumacy. He peremptorily ordered the Signoria to adopt the imperial and papal laws, and commanded that the doge should swear not only not to impede the Inquisitor of Treviso in his duties, but to assist him. In default of obedience he threatened to proceed against the city both spiritually and temporally.

The position of the republic was already indefensible under the public law of the period. It was so administering its own laws as to afford an asylum to a class universally proscribed, and it was refusing to allow the Church to apply the only remedy deemed appropriate to this crying evil. It therefore yielded to the inevitable, but in a manner to preserve its own autonomy and independence. It absolutely refused to incorporate in its own statutes the papal and imperial laws, but, August 4, 1289, it empowered the doge, Giovanni Dandolo, to give assistance to the inquisitor when called upon, without referring each case to the Senate. A further wise provision decreed that all fines and confiscations should inure to the State, which in turn undertook to defray the expenses of the Holy Office. For this purpose the proceeds of the corn-tax were set aside, and the money was deposited with the Provveditore delle Viare, who disbursed it on the requisition of the inquisitor. This compromise was accepted by Nicholas IV, August 28, 1288, and was duly embodied in the official oath of the next doge, Piero Gradenigo. Thus, while the inquisitor had full opportunity of suppressing heresy, the temptation to abuse his office for purposes of extortion was reduced to a minimum, and the State, by retaining in its hands all the financial portion of the business, was able at any time to exercise control.

The Inquisition soon chafed under these limitations. In 1292, Nicholas IV complained to Piero Gradenigo that the terms of the agreement were not carried out. The Inquisitors Bonagiunta of Mantua and Giuliano of Padua reported that the papal and imperial laws against heresy were not enforced, and that under the arrangement for expenditures they were unable to employ a force of familiars sufficient to detect and seize the heretics. The Signoria, apparently, had not seen fit to abolish the office of secular inquisitors provided by the legislation of 1249. These were three in number, and were known as the *tre Savi dell' eresia*, or *assistenti*. It was hardly possible that a duplicate organization such as this could work without clashing. The situation became intolerable, and in 1301 Frà Antonio, the Inquisitor of Treviso, resolved to put an end to it. He notified the three *Savi*, Tommaso Viaro, Marino Zorzi, and Lorenzo Segico, to recognize no superior save himself. Their submission not being forthcoming, he proceeded to Venice, and addressed to the Doge Gradenigo a monition ordering him, under pain of excommunication, to swear to obey all the papal constitutions on heresy. Gradenigo refused, alleging that this would be a violation of his oath of office. The three *Savi* continued their functions and perhaps even enlarged them; it had become customary for them to be selected from among the senators, and they acted in conjunction with the inquisitor in all cases coming within his jurisdiction. As Venice extended her conquests on the mainland, in all cities under her domination the *rettori* or governors performed this function, and their participation was required in all prosecutions for heresy, not only by the inquisitor, but by the bishops.

In Italy, as in France, the history of the Inquisition during the fourteenth and fifteenth centuries is one of decadence. It is true that in Italy it had not to contend with the consolidation of power in the hands of a monarch, but the Captivity of Avignon and the debasement of the papacy under the influence of the French court, co-operating with the rise of the cities in wealth and culture, conduced to the same result; while the Great Schism, followed by the Councils of Constance and Basle, tended to emancipate the minds of men and foster independence. During the fourteenth century much of the inquisitorial activity was devoted to the new heresy of the Fraticelli, which will be referred to hereafter.

As regards the Cathari, unceasing and unsparing repression gradually annihilated the sect which, during the first half of the thirteenth century, seemed almost able to dispute with Rome the possession of Italy on equal terms. Yet in Italy the Cathari lasted long after they had disappeared from France. Driven from the plains of Lombardy and central Italy, they took refuge in places less accessible. In 1340 we hear of them in Corsica, when Gerald, the Franciscan general, sent his friars thither, who succeeded in exterminating them for a time. In 1369 we again find Franciscans, under Frà Mondino da Bologna, zealously at work there, and earnestly supported by Gregory XI. In 1372 and 1373 Gregory wrote to the Bishops of Marrana and Ajaccio, and to Frà Gabriele da Montalcino, urging renewed activity, and, with singular lenity, authorizing them to remit the death penalty in cases of single relapse. These hunted refugees were mostly in the forests and mountains, and to subdue them a chain of spiritual forts was established, in the shape of Franciscan houses.

On the mainland, in spite of the vigilance of the Inquisition, Cathari continued to exist in Piedmont. In 1388 Frà Antonio Secco of Savigliano had the good fortune to lay hands on one of the active members of the sect, Giacomo Bech of Chieri, near Turin. In 1370 Bech had fallen into the hands of the inquisitor, Frà Tommaso da Casacho, had been forced to confess, and had been released after abjuration in reward for his betraying his fellow disciples. The report of his examination before Frà Antonio and the Bishop of Turin, which has been printed by Sig. Girolamo Amati, gives full details of the condition of the sect. After his tongue had been loosened by repeated applications of torture, his confession shows that it was numerous in the vicinage, and that it comprised members of many noble families—the Patrizi, Bertoni, Petiti, Narro, and ancestors of Balbi and Cavour.

Frà Antonio's labors had been already rewarded by the discovery of another sect of Cathari in the valleys to the west and northwest of Turin. Their heresiarch was Martino del Prete, and the community of Chieri had vainly endeavored to win them over to unity. In Pignerol, Frà Antonio had, in November 1387, arrested a suspected heretic named Antonio Galosna, who passed for a Franciscan Tertiary. The Inquisition in those parts was greatly dependent upon the secular authorities, and the Count of Savoy, Amadeo VII, was not disposed to second it with zeal. When Galosna at first denied, Antonio succeeded in having him tortured till he promised to tell everything if released from torture, and accordingly the next day he made confession; but Giovanni di Brayda, the chamberlain of Amadeo, and Antonio da Valencia, the Judge of Pignerol, promised him that if he would retract they would effect his deliverance. The Castellan of Pignerol, in whose charge he was, also offered to liberate him on receiving 5 florins for himself and 70 more for necessary expenses; but, although Galosna pledged all his property to raise the sum, this device seems to have failed. On December 29 he was brought before the count himself, after being warned by di Brayda that if he confirmed his confession he should be hanged. He accordingly retracted it, but was not liberated, and a month later, in the presence of the count and the inquisitor, he repeated that his confession had been extorted by violence. Apparently he was made the subject of a prolonged debate between State and Church, in which the latter triumphed, for on May 29 we find him in the possession of the Bishop of Turin and of the inquisitor, undergoing examination in the castle of Dross, near Turin.

He proved a mine of information well worth the repeated interrogatories which extended from May 29 to July 10, for he had been a member of the sect for 25 years and a wandering missionary for 15, and was familiar with all the congregations, which appear to have been numerous, some in the neighborhood of Turin, but mostly in the lower Alpine valleys between Pignerol and Susa. Though he repeatedly alludes to the sectaries as "Vaudois," they had no affinity with the Waldenses, and it is observable that he makes no reference to their existence in any of the distinctive

Waldensian valleys. They were mostly poor folk—peasants, servants, muleteers, innkeepers, and artisans—and the chiefs of their "synagogues" were generally of this class, although occasionally a clerk, a canon, a notary, or other educated person is enumerated among the members. What were their precise distinctive tenets it is not easy to define with accuracy. Galosna's rough handling had evidently rendered him eager to satisfy the credulity of his examiners, and the imaginative character of some of his revelations casts a doubt on the truthfulness of them all. The applicant for initiation had to drink a beverage, foul of aspect, made with the excrement of a toad kept for the purpose, and its power was such that whoso once partook of it could never thereafter abandon the sect. Martino del Prete, the chief heresiarch, had a black cat as large as a lamb, which he declared to be the best friend he had on earth. We may safely set down the accounts of the sexual abominations which succeeded religious services in the conventicles, when the lights were extinguished, as worthy of equal credence. Contradictions in the repeated statements of the doctrines taught show that Galosna's imagination served him better than his memory in his prolonged examinations. He was told that in joining the sect he would secure salvation in glory with God the Father, and yet he declares that the sect rejected immortality, and held that the soul died with the body —and again, that there was no purgatory, but only heaven and hell hereafter. They believed, moreover, in God the Father who created the heavens, but they worshipped the Great Dragon, the creator of the world, who fought God and the angels, and was more powerful than he on earth. Christ was not the Son of God, but of Joseph, and was worthy of no special reverence. Altogether the account is hopelessly confused, but we can discern the dualism of a bastard Catharism, and allusions are made to the *consolamentum* and the sacrament of bread. Like Jacopo Bech, Galosna had already abjured in the hands of Frà Tommaso da Casacho. Both were therefore relapsed; there was no mercy for them, and on September 5, 1388, they were abandoned to the secular arm in Turin and burned. Unfortunately the record ends here, and we have no details as to the rich harvest which Frà Antonio must have reaped from the ample information obtained from his victims as to the scattered members of the sects.

Italian Waldensianism continued to flourish in the mountain

fastnesses of Piedmont, where the endless struggle with parsimonious nature fostered the hardier virtues. The kindlier climate and less aggressive Inquisition of Naples finally rendered the southern colonies the headquarters of the sect, with which constant intercommunication was kept up. In 1387 we are told that the chief pontiff resided in Apulia and that the Waldensian community at Barge in Piedmont was presided over by two Apulians. A century later the mother communities in the Cottian Alps still looked to southern Italy as the center of their Church.

In 1292 we hear of persecutions in the Val Perosa, and again in 1312 there were burnings of obstinate heretics in the valleys, but these efforts effected little, for in 1332 a brief of John XXII describes the Waldensian church of the diocese of Turin as being in a most flourishing condition. When Frà Giovanni Alberto, the Inquisitor of Turin, had recently made an effort to repress them, they boldly rose in arms. On the public square of Angrogna they slew the parish priest Guillelmo, whom they suspected of furnishing information, and Alberto himself they besieged in a castle where he had taken refuge, so that he was glad to escape with his life.

Gregory XI was especially zealous in the warfare with heresy, and we have already seen how earnest were his efforts to suppress the Waldenses of Provence and Dauphiné. Those of Piedmont had rendered themselves peculiarly obnoxious. Frà Antonio Pavo had recently gone to "Bricarax," a place deeply infected with heresy, to preach against them—his sermon, of course, including a summons before his tribunal—when in place of humbly submitting, a dozen of them, incited by the Evil One, had set upon him as he left the church and had slain him. Another inquisitor, probably Pietro di Ruffia, had met the same fate in the Dominican cloister at Susa. Such misdeeds demanded exemplary chastisement, and Gregory's exhortations to Charles V of France were accompanied with the strongest urgency on Amadeo VI of Savoy to clear his land of brambles. We have seen how successful were the labors of the Nuncio, Antonio Bishop of Massa, and the Inquisitor of Provence, François Borel. They did not confine their energies to the French valleys. The Waldenses of the Val di Susa were exposed to the most pitiless persecution; on a Christmas night Borel with an armed force attacked Pragelato, putting to the sword all whom he could reach.

A succession of inquisitors—Piero di Castelmonte, Ruffino di Terdona, Tommaso da Casacho, and Michele Grassi—undaunted by the fate of their predecessors, wasted their energies on the Piedmontese Waldenses without reducing them to subjection. The pitiless forays of Borel drove the poor wretches from their native valleys, and they poured over into Piedmont. Amadeo VII, who succeeded his father in 1383, seems to have given the Inquisition but slender support, and it had little encouragement in its efforts to subdue the stubborn mountaineers. The fragmentary records of Frà Antonio Secco, who undertook the work in the spring of 1387, show how fruitless was the endeavor to co-operate with the ruthless proselytism of Borel. One of his first cases had been a certain Lorenzo Bandoria, who had abjured before Antonio Pavo, and who under torture confessed to continued heresy. Here was a clear case of relapse, and accordingly, on March 31, he was abandoned to the secular arm and all his property declared confiscated to the Inquisition. This proved a mere *brutum fulmen*, for on May 6 Frà Antonio was obliged to issue a mandate to Ugonetto Bruno, Lord of Ozasco, ordering him, under pain of 100 marks, to capture Lorenzo and present him before the tribunal the next day, while the treasurer of Ozasco was required, under threat of excommunication, to appear at the same time with an inventory of all the convict's property. As Lorenzo had been handed over to the Castellan of Pignerol for execution, it is evident that the officials refused to carry out the sentences of the inquisitor, nor does this new effort appear to have had any better result. Many of his citations were disregarded, and when, on May 19, he ordered the lords of Ozasco to arrest three heretics under penalty of 100 marks, no attention seems to have been paid to the command. This insubordination increased, and as the season advanced we observe that when an accused refuses to confess, the dread entry "the lord inquisitor is not content" is not followed by the customary torture, but that the culprit is mercifully dismissed under bail. One case gave Frà Antonio infinite disgust. On June 27 he cited Giacomo Do and Sanzio Margarit of Sangano; they did not appear, but on August 6 he found them in Turin and seized them. For 15 days he kept them in chains, when they broke jail, but by the help of God he caught them again and carried them to the castle of Avegliana, where they remained 10 days. He had been unable to get them tortured, and they would not confess without it; the magistrates of Avegliana appealed to Count Amadeo, who ordered them released, and Frà Antonio records the unwillingness with which he obeyed the command.

The final blow came when in December he issued a summons to all the officials of Val Perosa, reciting that their land was full of heretics and that they must appear before him in Pignerol to purge themselves and their communities of this infamy. They did not obey, but through the intervention of the Piedmontese chancellor, Giovanni di Brayda, and other courtiers, they agreed to pay Count Amadeo 500 florins a year, for which he was to prevent the inquisitor from visiting Val Perosa, and they were to be exempted from obeying his citations. This was too much to endure, and Frà Antonio shook the dust of Pignerol from his feet for the more promising chase of the Cathari near Turin, first denouncing the officials of Val Perosa as having incurred excommunication and the penalties of contumacy, the only result of which was to draw upon his head the wrath of Count Amadeo.

During the Great Schism persecution slackened, but in 1416 fresh decrees were issued against the Waldenses. Our knowledge of details is but fragmentary at best, and it is impossible to construct a complete history of the conflict between them and the Inquisition, but we may fairly infer that the latter was at least spasmodically active. A petition addressed to the Duke of Savoy by the lords of Luserna recites that the inhabitants of the valley were in full rebellion, owing to repeated persecution. Again, we know that between 1440 and 1450 Frà Bertrando Piero, vicar of the inquisitor, in one raid burned at Coni 22 relapsed heretics, and confiscated their property.

In 1475 a more serious war of extermination was commenced against them under the Duchess Yolande, Regent of Savoy, in conjunction with the simultaneous action of the Inquisition in Dauphiné. Louis XI, who stopped the persecution so unceremoniously in his own dominions, felt interest enough in the matter to extend protection over the unfortunates in his sister's territories, and his word had power sufficient to dampen the zeal of the duchess, who was wholly dependent on him after the misfortunes of Charles the Bold. The death of Louis, in 1483, deprived the Waldenses of their protector, and persecution recommenced. An order of Duke Carlo I, in 1484, to inquire into the violences committed by the people of Angrogna, Villaro, and Bobbio because their lords endeavored to suppress their heresies, shows how soon and how bitterly the struggle broke out afresh. The heretics scattered through the towns of Piedmont were mercilessly dealt with by the inquisitors, but those who inhabited the mountain valleys were safe, except from assault by overwhelming forces. In April 1487, Innocent VIII recites how the Inquisitor-General Frà Blasio di Monreale had gone to the infected district, and had vainly sought by earnest exhortations to induce the heretics to abandon their errors; how they had contemptuously defied his censures, had attacked his house, slain his familiar, and pillaged his goods. More strenuous efforts were evidently requisite, and Innocent appointed Alberto de' Capitanei, Archdeacon of Cremona, as papal nuncio and commissioner to Piedmont and Dauphiné, with instructions to coerce the people to receive Frà Blasio and permit the free exercise of his office. From February to May 1488, Alberto duly issued his citations to the heretics, and as they were contumacious, he condemned them accordingly and abandoned them in mass to the secular arm. Meanwhile a force estimated at 18,000 crusaders had been raised in France and Piedmont, which advanced in four columns so as to block every avenue of escape. The slaughter in Val Louise has already been alluded to.[6] The Val d'Angrogna was more fortunate, and in the attack upon it the crusading army was virtually annihilated. This victory earned for the Waldenses a respite, and in 1490 Carlo I invited them to a conference at Pignerol, where he granted them peace and confirmed their privileges. In 1498 they were visited by Lucas of Prague and Thomas Germanus, envoys of the *Unitas Fratrum* of Bohemia. Through these they addressed a letter to the Bohemian King Ladislas and his nobles, boasting that they did not frequent the Catholic churches, fiercely denouncing the vices of the priesthood, and arguing that the benediction of such men was rather a malediction.

Soon after, their spirit was put to the test in the Valley of the Po, where whole villages were found to consist of Waldenses. Marguerite de Foix, Marchioness of Saluces, put troops at the command of the Inquisitor Angelo Ricciardino, who had found his ordinary machinery

[6] See page 347.

baffled. The villages of Pravillelm, Beitoneto, and Oncino were raided; most of the inhabitants succeeded in escaping to Luserna, but some were captured, and five were sentenced to be burned, March 24, 1510. A heavy snowstorm delayed the execution, and during the ensuing night the prisoners broke jail and joined their comrades. The inquisitor, however, was not to be balked of his exhibition, and replaced the fugitives with three prisoners to whom he had promised pardon in consideration of the fullness of their confessions, and who were duly burned. The deserted villages were confiscated and made over to good Catholics, but the refugees at intervals descended on them, slaying and spoiling without mercy, till no one dared to dwell there. Finally the marchioness yielded, and for a round sum of money, in 1512, permitted the exiles to return and dwell in peace. The triumph of toleration thus won by the sword was but local and temporary. In Savoy, the statutes published in 1513 contain all the time-honored provisions for the suppression of heresy, with instructions to all public officials to aid in every way the Inquisition, whose expenses are to be defrayed out of the confiscations. Continued persecution was thus provided for, nor was it averted when, in 1530, the Waldenses opened negotiations with the Protestants of Switzerland, resulting in their final incorporation with the Calvinists.

It only remains for us to note cursorily such indications as have reached us of the activity and condition of the Inquisition in the several provinces of Italy during the fourteenth and fifteenth centuries. We have a somewhat vague description of its vigilance in 1318, in pursuing certain heretics who are described as Lollards—whether Beghards or Waldenses does not appear, but probably the latter, as we are told that when concealment became impossible the men escaped to Bohemia, leaving some women with children at the breast, whereupon the women were burned, and the children given to good Catholics to be brought up in the faith. In 1344 we hear of a great popular excitement, caused by the belief that a number of victims of the Inquisition had suffered unjustly. It was possibly the feeling thus aroused which led, in 1346, to the murder in the Milanese of a Franciscan inquisitor conspicuous for his persecuting zeal. How the political passions of the time hindered the functions of the Holy Office is seen in the case of Frà Ubertino di Carleone, a bustling Franciscan, subsequently Bishop of Lipari, who, about 1360, was accused of heresy by the Inquisitor of Piacenza. He at once proclaimed that his Ghibellinism was the motive of the prosecution, and aroused the factions of the city to a tumult, under cover of which he escaped.

Inquisitors continued to be regularly appointed, and to perform such of their functions as they could, but the decline in their usefulness is shown by one of the earliest acts of Martin V, in 1417, before leaving Constance, in commissioning the Observantine Franciscan, Giovanni da Capistrano, as a special inquisitor against the heretics of Mantua. From this time, in fact, when an effective effort against heresy was called for, the regular machinery of the Inquisition was no longer relied upon.

In Tuscany the growing insubordination felt towards the Inquisition was manifested at Siena, in 1340, by the enactment of laws checking some of its abuses. Frà Simone Filippi, the inquisitor, complained to Benedict XII, who at once pronounced them null and void, and ordered them erased from the statute book. The relations between the Holy Office and the people at this period, however, are more significantly displayed in a series of events occurring at Florence, of which the details chance to have been preserved. In Tuscany the triumph of orthodoxy had been complete. A sermon of Frà Giordano da Rivalto, in 1304, asserts that heresy was virtually exterminated. This is confirmed by Villani, who tells us that, by the middle of the century, there were no heretics in Florence. This is doubtless too absolute an assertion, but the existence of a few scattered Waldenses and Fraticelli offered scant excuse for such an establishment as the inquisitor was accustomed to maintain. In 1337 the papal nuncio, Bertrand, Archbishop of Embrun, took the incumbent of the office severely to task for the abuse of appointing an excessive number of assistants, and ordered him in future to restrict himself to four counsellors and assessors, two notaries, two jailers, and twelve ministers or familiars. This was by no means a small or inexpensive body of officials; the Inquisition's share of confiscations from the few poverty-stricken heretics who could occasionally be picked up evidently was insufficient to maintain such a corps, and means, either fair or foul, must be found to render the income of the office adequate to the wants of those who depended upon it for their fortunes. This was done, on the one hand by cheating the papal camera, and on the other by extorting money on false charges of heresy and by selling to bravoes licenses to carry arms. The former device was one which, when detected, was difficult to condone, and its discovery caused, in the commencement of 1344, a sudden vacancy in the Florentine Inquisition. The republic was in the habit of suggesting names to the Franciscan General for appointment, and sometimes its requests were respected. In the present case it asked, February 26, that the Tuscan inquisitor, Frà Giovanni da Casale, be permitted to exercise his functions within the city, but the suggestion was unheeded, and in March the post was given to Frà Piero di Aquila. Frà Piero was a distinguished member of the Franciscan Order. But two months earlier he had been appointed chaplain to Queen Joanna of Naples, and his *Commentaries on the Sentences of Peter Lombard* were highly esteemed, receiving, in 1480, the honor of an edition printed at Speier. A man so gifted was warmly welcomed, and the republic thanked the Franciscan General for the selection.

The Cardinal of Santa Sabina, while visiting various courts in the capacity of papal legate, had had occasion to collect large sums. In charity to him we may assume, what doubtless was the truth, that the money belonged to the pope, although it stood in the cardinal's name on the books of his bankers, the great Florentine company of Acciajuoli. In receiving it the members of the company bound themselves for its repayment and agreed to subject themselves to the Court of Auditors of the Apostolic Chamber. In 1343 a commercial and financial crisis paralyzed the commerce and industry of the city, and there was owing the cardinal some 12,000 florins, which the Acciajuoli were unable to pay. Not only the Acciajuoli, but the Bardi, the Peruzzi, and other great banking houses had closed their doors, and ruin stared the Florentines in the face. There was at least one creditor, however, who was resolved to get his money.

On October 9, 1343, Clement VI wrote to the republic, stating the claim of the cardinal and ordering the Signoria to compel the Acciajuoli to pay it. Under the circumstances this was clearly impossible, but judgment against the debtors had been rendered by the auditors of the papal camera. This was enough to bring the affair within the sphere of spiritual jurisdiction, and authority was sent to the Inquisitor Frà Piero to execute the sentence, calling in the aid of the secular arm, and, if necessary, laying an interdict on the city. The matter dragged on until, November 23, 1345, Frà Piero appeared before the Gonfalonieri and the Priors of the Arts, and summoned them to imprison the debtors until payment, under pain of excommunication and interdict. Still the money was not forthcoming, and although such assets of the Acciajuoli as could be seized were delivered to Frà Piero, and security was given for the balance, he held the whole community responsible for the debt. The discussion became angry, and when the inquisitor, in violation of a law of the republic, committed the indiscretion of arresting Salvestro Baroncelli, a member of the bankrupt company, as he was leaving the palace of the Priors of the Arts, his three familiars who had committed the offense were, in compliance with a savage statute, punished with banishment and the loss of the right hand.

All this did not extract the money from the bankrupts, and Frà Piero laid the city under interdict. Inside the walls the Florentines might disregard the censures of the Church, but a commercial community could not afford to be cut off from intercourse with the world. Her citizens and their goods were scattered in every trade center in Christendom, and were virtually outlawed by the interdict. The priors, therefore, on June 14, 1346, humbled their pride and sent commissioners to Clement authorized to bind the republic to pay the debt of the Acciajuoli to the cardinal, not exceeding 7,000 florins, in eight months. Their submission was graciously received, and, February 28, 1347, the pope ordered the interdict removed, providing, however, for its *ipso facto* renewal in case the obligation for 6,600 florins was not met at maturity.

Meanwhile another scene of the comedy was developing itself. In its contest with Frà Piero the republic had not stood solely on the defensive. The papal nuncio at Lucca, who had in charge the prosecutions against the inquisitors for embezzling the sums due to the camera, had appointed as his deputy in Florence Niccolò, Abbot of Santa Maria, who proceeded against Frà Piero on that charge, to which the Signoria added the accusation, sustained by abundant testimony, of extorting from citizens large sums of money by fraudulent prosecutions for heresy. By March 16, 1346, the Signoria was asking the appointment of Frà Michele di Lapo as his successor. Frà Piero was a fugitive, and refused to return and stand his trial. After due delay, in 1347, the Abate Niccolò, being armed with papal authority, declared him in default and contumacious, and then proceeded to excommunicate him. The excommunication was published in all the churches of Florence, and Frà Piero was thus cut off from the faithful and abandoned to Satan. He could afford to regard all this with calm philosophy. His success in collecting the cardinal's money entitled him to reward, and the booty of 7,000 florins, which he had personally carried off from Florence as the result of his two years' inquisitorial career, could doubtless be used to advantage. While Niccolò was vainly citing him, he was promoted, February 12, 1347, to the episcopate of Sant-Angeli de' Lombardi, and his excommunication was answered, June 29, 1348, by his translation to the presumably preferable see of Trivento. All that the Florentines could do was to petition repeatedly that in future inquisitors should be selected from among their own citizens, who would be less likely than strangers to be guilty of extortions and scandals.

The Signoria also made a more promising effort at self-protection by passing various laws imitated from those adopted not long before at Perugia. It was decreed that no citizen could be arrested without the participation of the *podestà*, who was required to seize all persons designated to him by the bishop—the inquisitor not being alluded to—which would seem to leave small opportunity for independent action by the latter, especially as he was deprived of his private jail and was ordered to send all prisoners to the public prison. He was further prohibited from inflicting pecuniary punishments, and all whom he condemned as heretics were to be burned. This was revolutionary in a high degree, and did not tend to harmonize the relations between the republic and the papacy. The desperate quarrel between them which arose in 1375 was caused by political questions, but it was embittered by troubles arising from the Inquisition, especially as a demand made by Innocent VI, in 1355, for a revision of their statutes remained unheeded.

In 1373 Frà Piero di Ser Lippo, who had already served as Tuscan inquisitor in 1371, was again appointed to replace a certain Frà Andrea di Ricco. With some intervals Frà Piero served until at least 1384, and he proved no more disposed than his predecessors to yield to the resistance which the methods of the Inquisition inevitably provoked in the free Italian cities. Pistoia had followed the example of Florence in endeavoring to protect its citizens by municipal statutes, and in 1375 it was duly placed under interdict and its citizens were excommunicated. At the same time Frà Piero complained of Florence as impeding the free action of the Inquisition, and Gregory at once ordered the Signoria to abrogate the obnoxious statutes. No attention was paid to these commands by Florence, and when the rupture came the Florentine mob expressed its feelings by destroying the inquisitorial prison and driving the inquisitor from the city. It was also alleged that in the disturbances a monk named Niccolò was tortured and buried alive. These misdeeds, although denied by the Signoria, were alleged as a justification of the bull of March 31, 1376, fulminated against Florence by Gregory. In this he not only excommunicated and interdicted the city, but specially outlawed the citizens, exposing their property wherever found to seizure, and their persons to slavery. Everywhere throughout Christendom the goods of Florentines were seized and the merchants were glad to beg their way home, stripped of all they possessed. Not all were so fortunate, as some pious monarchs, like Edward III, in addition reduced them to servitude. No commercial community could long endure a contest waged after this fashion, and, as before, Florence was compelled to submit. In the peace signed July 28, 1378, the republic agreed to annul all laws restricting the Inquisition and interfering with the liberties of the Church, and it authorized a papal commissioner to expunge them from the statute book. The Great Schism, however, weakened for a time the aggressive energy of the papacy, and much of the obnoxious legislation reappears in the revised code of 1415.

In the Two Sicilies the Inquisition dragged on a moribund existence. Letters of King Robert in 1334 and 1335 and of Joanna I in 1342 and 1343 show that inquisitors continued to be appointed, but they were limited to making 50 arrests each, and record of these was required to be entered in the royal courts; they had no jails, and the royal officials received their prisoners and tortured them when called upon. When efforts were to be made against the Fraticelli,

Urban V, in 1368, deemed it necessary to send a special inquisitor, Frà Simone del Pozzo, to Naples.

In 1451, the Inquisition obtained fresh vitality in Sicily, however, by means of an ingenious device. Frà Enrico Lugardi, Inquisitor of Palermo, produced a most impudent forgery in the shape of a long and elaborate privilege purporting to have been issued by the Emperor Frederic II in 1224, ordering all his Sicilian subjects to give aid and comfort to the "inquisitors of heretical pravity," and stating that, as it was unfitting that all confiscations should inure to the royal fisc without rewarding the inquisitors for their toils and perils, the confiscations henceforth should be divided equally between the fisc, the Inquisition, and the Holy See; moreover, all Jews and infidels were required once a year to supply inquisitors and their attendants, when in prosecution of their duty, with all necessaries for man and beast. Though the fraudulent character of this document was conspicuous on its face, to say nothing of a blunder in the regnal year of its date, the age was not a critical one; Frà Enrico seems to have had no trouble in inducing King Alonso to confirm it, and it was subsequently confirmed again in 1477 by Ferdinand and Isabella.

Ferdinand the Catholic, in founding the New Spanish Inquisition, obtained for his grand inquisitor the power of nominating deputies in all the dependencies of Castile and Aragon. About 1487 Fray Antonio de la Peña was sent to Sicily in that capacity, who speedily organized the Holy Office on its new basis throughout the island; and in 1492 an edict of banishment was issued against the Jews, who, as of old, were the chief objects of persecution. On the mainland there was more trouble. When, in 1503, Ferdinand acquired the kingdom of Naples, the Great Captain, Gonsalvo of Cordova, finding the people excited with the fear that the Spanish Inquisition might be introduced, made a solemn compact that no inquisitors should be sent thither. The old rules were kept in force; no one was allowed to be arrested without a special royal warrant, and no inquisitor could exercise any functions without the confirmation of his commission by the royal representative. Under the excuse that the Jews and New Christians expelled from Spain found refuge in Naples, in 1510 Andres Palacio was sent there as inquisitor, but the populace rose in arms and made demonstrations so threatening that even Ferdinand's fanaticism was forced to give way. The movements of the French in the north of Italy were disquieting, the loyalty of the Neapolitans was not to be relied upon, and the inquisitor was withdrawn with a promise that no further effort would be made to force upon the people the dreaded tribunal. Even Julius II recognized the necessity of this and assented to the understanding. The Calabrian and Apulian Waldenses thus had a respite until the progress of the Reformation in Italy aroused the Church to renewed efforts and to a complete reorganization of its machinery of persecution.

CHAPTER XIV
GERMANY

IN 1209 Henry of Veringen, Bishop of Strassburg, accompanied Otho IV on his coronation expedition to Rome. He is said to have carried home with him some theologians eager to punish aberrations from the faith, and a little investigation showed to his horror that his land was full of misbelievers. A searching inquest was organized, and he soon had 500 prisoners representing all classes of society. He was a humane man, as the times went, and he sincerely sought their conversion, but his clergy were no match for the sectaries in knowledge of Scripture, and the faith gained little by the attempt. Recourse to stronger measures was evidently requisite, and he announced that all who were obstinate should be burned. This brought most of them to their senses; heretic books and writings were eagerly surrendered, and the converts abjured. About a hundred of them, however, under the persuasion of their leader, a priest of Strassburg named John, were obdurate, including 12 priests, 23 women, and a number of nobles. Some form of trial seems to have been thought necessary, and resort was had to the old expedient of the red-hot-iron ordeal. The heretics protested against it as a manifest tempting of God, but their objections were unavailing; those who denied their heresy were subjected to it, and naturally but few escaped. One of them, named Reinhold, appealed to Innocent III against this form of trial, and the pope promptly responded by forbidding its further use in such matters. In 1212 at Strassburg there were 80 obstinate ones, whose heresy was proved by the Ordeal. They were all burned the same day in a ditch beyond the walls, and in the sixteenth century the hollow was still known to the citizens as the *Ketzergrube*. The property of the condemned was duly confiscated and was divided between the magistrates and those who had labored so successfully in vindicating the faith.

The Cathari appear to have virtually disappeared from Germany, where their foothold, at best, had been precarious. On the other hand, Waldenses were numerous and nearly all the heretics burned

410

at Strassburg belonged to this sect. From their writings and confessions a list of 300 errors was compiled, afterwards condensed into 17, and these were read before them to the people while they were on their way to the place of execution. Priest John, their leader, admitted the correctness of all save one alleging promiscuous sexual intercourse, which he indignantly denied. Those which he admitted show how rapidly their doctrines were developing to their logical conclusions, and how impassable was the gulf which already separated them from the Church. All the holy orders were rejected, and this led to the abolition of sacerdotal celibacy; disbelief in purgatory was definitely adopted, with its consequences as to prayers and masses for the dead, and there had already been invented the dogma that Christ and his disciples held no property.

The Ortlibenses or Ordibarii, who were also represented among the victims of Strassburg, demand a somewhat more detailed consideration than their immediate importance would seem to justify, because, although comparatively few in numbers, they present the earliest indication of a peculiar tendency in German free thought which we shall find reproduce itself in many forms and constitute, with almost unconquerable stubbornness, the principal enemy with which the Inquisition had to deal.

Early in the century Maître David de Dinant, a schoolman of Paris, whose subtlety of argumentation rendered him a favorite with Innocent III, had indulged in dangerous speculations derived from the Aristotelian philosophy, as transmitted through the Arab commentators, adulterated with neo-Platonic elements, which transmuted the theism of the Greek into a kind of mystic pantheism. These speculations were carried still further by his fellow schoolman, Amauri de Bène, a favorite of the heir-apparent, Prince Louis. His views were condemned by the University in 1204; he appealed to the Holy See, but was compelled to abjure in 1207, when he is said to have died of mortification. He had disciples, however, who propagated his doctrines in secret. They were mostly men of education and intelligence, theologians of the University and priests, except a certain goldsmith named Guillaume, who was esteemed as a prophet of the little sect. Amauri had taught that God was the essence of all creatures, and, as light could not be seen of itself, but only in the air, so God was invisible except in his creatures. The inevitable deduction from this was that after death all beings would return to God, and in Him be unified in eternal rest. This swept away the doctrines of future retribution, purgatory, and hell, and, as the Amaurians did not fail to point out, the innumerable observances through which the Church controlled the consciences and the wealth of man through its power over the keys and the treasury of salvation. As this was destructive to the ecclesiastical system, so was the doctrine equally subversive of morality, which taught that such was the virtue of love and charity that whatever was done in their behalf could be no sin, and, further, that anyone filled with the Holy Ghost was impeccable, no matter what crime he might commit, because that Spirit which is God cannot sin, nor can man, who is nothing of himself, so long as the Spirit of God is in him.

In his proselyting zeal, Guillaume the goldsmith, in 1210, approached a certain Maître Raoul de Nemours, who feigned readiness of conviction, and reported the matter to Pierre, Bishop of Paris, and Maître Robert de Curzon, the papal supervisor of preaching in France. By their advice he pretended conversion and accompanied the Amaurians on a missionary tour which lasted for three months and extended as far as Langres. When fully informed of all details, he communicated with the authorities, and arrests were made. A council of bishops was convened in Paris, which found no difficulty in condemning all concerned; those who were in orders were degraded, and they were all handed over to the secular authorities. Four of the leaders were imprisoned for life and 10 were burned. The remains of Amauri were exhumed and exposed to the dogs, after which his bones were scattered in the fields; the writings of the enthusiasts were forbidden to be read; the study of natural science in the University was suspended for three years, and the works of Aristotle, which had given rise to the heresy, were publicly burned.

The doctrine of impeccability was likely to give loosened rein to human passion in those whose spiritual exaltation did not lift them above the weakness of the flesh, and there may be truth in the accusations current against the Amaurians, that the disciples of both sexes abandoned themselves to scandalous license, under the pretext of yielding to the demands of Christian love. Yet they at least preserved an exterior of sanctity and devotion, and they prudently abstained from putting into practice their theories of the uselessness of the sacraments and of all external cult.

The heresy was thus crushed in its birthplace, where we hear no more of it except that there were teachers of it in Dauphiné, where they were confounded with the Waldenses. The seed, however, was widely scattered, to bear fruit in foreign soil. The University of Paris drew together eager searchers after knowledge from every country in Europe, and it could not be difficult for the Amaurians to find among those from abroad converts who would prove useful missionaries. In 1215, Robert de Curzon includes the works of a certain Maurice the Spaniard in his condemnation of those of David de Dinant and Amauri. Another disciple is said to have been Ortlieb, the teacher of the sectaries known by his name, whose fate we have seen at Strassburg. That the heresy was known not to be extinguished is shown by the fact that in 1215 the Great Council of Lateran still deemed it necessary to utter a formal condemnation of the doctrines of Amauri, which it stigmatized as crazy rather than heretical.

We know little of the faith originally professed by the Brethren of the Free Spirit, as the followers of Ortlieb called themselves. The principal account we have of their doctrines in the thirteenth century concerns itself much more with the results in denying the efficacy of sacerdotal observances than with the principles which led to those results; but there are indications of pantheism in the assertion of the eternity of the uncreated universe, in the promise of eternal life to all, while denying the resurrection of the flesh, and in the mystic representation of the Trinity by three members of the sect. No immorality is attributed to them; the severest continence was prescribed by them, even in marriage; the only generation of children permitted was spiritual, through conversion, while homicide, lying, and oaths were strictly forbidden.

It was not long before another consequence, especially shocking to the faithful, was drawn from the fruitful premises of pantheism. If God was the essence of all creatures, Satan himself could not be excepted; if all were to be eventually reunited in God, Satan and his angels could not be condemned to eternal perdition. So infinite were the conclusions which flowed from the bold assumptions of the Amaurians, that those who accepted their views inevitably diverged in the applications, as they attributed greater or less importance to one series of propositions or another. There were some who took special interest in this theory as to Satan, and as their utterances were peculiarly exasperating to the orthodox, they were designated as a separate sect under the name of Luciferans. Of these we hear much but see little. Their doctrines were exaggerated into devil worship, and they were included in the list of heretics to be periodically anathematized with a zeal which attributed to them vastly greater importance than their scanty numbers deserved. The most extravagant and repulsive stories were circulated about their hideous rites, which gradually took shape under the current superstitions as to witchcraft. At the period under consideration they formed the basis of the wildest and most ferocious epidemic of persecution that the world had yet seen.

The first indication we have of this tendency occurs in the case of Henry Minneke, Provost of the Cistercian nunnery of Neuwerke in Goslar. In 1222 Minneke was accused before his bishop, Conrad von Reisenberg of Hildesheim, of certain heretical opinions. An assembly of prelates was held, which took testimony of his nuns, and found him guilty. He was simply ordered to teach his doctrines no longer. When he disobeyed he was summoned before Bishop Conrad, who sentenced him to return to his Premonstratensian monastery and ordered the nuns to elect another provost. To this, again, he paid no attention, and the bishop seems to have had no recourse but to implore the intervention of Honorius III. When the pope ordered the sentence executed, the nuns interjected an appeal back to him and to the emperor. Both appeals were rejected; Minneke was declared a diseased member of the Church, and the nuns were told that they should rejoice in being liberated from his influence. Still he remained firm, and the bishop was obliged to consult the cardinal-legate, Cinthio of Porto, before he ventured to throw the indomitable heretic into prison. From his jail, Minneke himself appealed to the pope, asserting that he had been condemned unheard and offering to submit to incarceration for life if he should refuse to recant any erroneous opinions of which he might be convicted. Honorius thereupon, in May 1224, ordered Bishop Conrad to bring his prisoner before the legate and an assembly of prelates for a final hearing and judgment. About October 1, at Bardewick, Cinthio met an assembly of the bishops of North Germany, where it was decided that Minneke was convicted of having encouraged the nuns to regard him as greater than any other born of woman; he had on many points relaxed the severe Cistercian discipline; in his sermons he had so exalted the state of virginity as to represent marriage as a sin; in a vision he had seen Satan praying to be forgiven, and he had asserted that in heaven there was a woman greater than the Virgin, whose name was Wisdom. The culprit was handed over to the secular authorities, and was duly burned in 1225.

This case has a further interest for us, inasmuch as one of the participators in the final judgment was a man who filled all Germany with his fame, and who was the most perfect embodiment of the pure fanaticism of his time—Conrad of Marburg. Though a secular priest and holding himself aloof from both Mendicant Orders, Conrad steeped himself in the severest poverty and gained his bread by beggary. Though he could have aspired to any dignity in the Church, which reverenced him as its greatest apostle, and though for years all the benefices of Thuringia were placed by the Landgrave Louis at his absolute disposal, he never accepted a single preferment. Devoted solely to the work of the Lord, his fiery soul and unrelaxing energies were directed with absolute singleness of purpose to advancing the kingdom of heaven upon earth, according to the light which was in him.

What were his conceptions of the duty of man to his Creator can best be judged by his course as spiritual director of St. Elizabeth of Thuringia. The daughter of Andreas of Hungary, born in 1207, married in 1221, at the age of 13, to Louis of Thuringia, a mother at 14, a widow at 20, and dying of self-inflicted austerities in her twenty-fourth year, Elizabeth was the rarest type of womanly gentleness and self-abnegation, of all Christian virtues and spiritual aspirations. When but eighteen years of age she placed herself under Conrad's direction. Such implicit obedience did he exact that on one occasion when he had sent for her to hear him preach, and she was unable to do so on account of an unexpected visit from her sister-in-law, the Margravine of Misnia, he angrily declared that he would leave her. She went to him the next day and entreated for pardon; on his continuing obdurate, she and her maidens, whom he blamed for the matter, cast themselves at his feet, when he caused them all to be stripped to their shifts and scourged. It is no wonder that he inspired her with such terror that she was wont to say "If I so much dread a mortal man, how is God to be rightly dreaded?"

After the death of Louis, whom she tenderly loved, and when his brother Henry despoiled her and drove her out penniless, with her children, she submitted with patient resignation and earned her living by beggary; and when he was forced to compound for her dower-rights with money, she made haste to distribute it in charity. Under the influence of the diseased pietism inculcated by Conrad, she abandoned her children to God and devoted herself to succoring casual outcasts and lepers; and the depth of her humility was shown when scandal made busy with her fame in consequence of her relations with Conrad. On being warned of this and counselled to greater prudence, she brought forth the bloody scourge which she used, and said, "This is the love the holy man bears to me. I thank God, who has deigned to accept this final oblation from me. I have sacrificed everything—station, wealth, beauty—and have made myself a beggar, intending only to preserve the adornment of womanly modesty; if God chooses to take this also, I hold it to be a special grace." It was this spirit that Conrad's brutal fanaticism sought to break, contradicting her in all things, and demanding of her every possible sacrifice. Merely to add to her afflictions he drove away, one by one, the faithful serving-women who idolized her, finally expelling Guda, who had been her companion since infancy in Hungary. When she disobeyed his orders he used to beat her, which she endured with pleasure, in memory of the blows inflicted on Christ. Once he sent for her to come to him at Oldenburg to determine whether he would put her into an extremely rigid convent there. The nuns asked him to let her visit them, and he gave her permission, expecting that she would decline in view of the excommunication hanging over all intruders on the sacred precincts. Supposing, however, that she had leave, she went, while her woman Irmengard stood outside, received the key, and opened the door. For this Conrad made them both lie down, and ordered his faithful comrade, Friar Gerhard, to beat them with a heavy rod, so that they bore the marks of the flogging for weeks.

Conrad had long been a man of mark, and his qualities were well known to those who made use of him. His burning eloquence was adapted to move the passions of the people, and as early as 1214 he had been honored with a commission to preach in Germany the crusade which was one of the objects for which the Great Council of Lateran was assembled. His mission as preacher brought him into direct relations with Rome, and his success in inducing thousands to take the cross gave him high repute with the curia, doubtless enhanced by the disinterestedness which asked for no reward. In 1220 he was entrusted with the duty of compelling the Emperor Frederic to fulfill his long-delayed vow of leading an expedition to the Holy Land, and he was further made chief of the business of preaching in its behalf, by being empowered to commission assistants throughout Germany. In these letters he is addressed as *Scholasticus* or head of the church schools in Mainz, showing that he then held that dignity. In 1227 still greater evidence was given of the confidence reposed in him. In March Gregory IX had mounted the papal throne with full resolve to crush the rising powers of heresy. On June 12, he wrote to Conrad, commending highly the diligence with which he was tracking and pursuing heretics. In order that his labors might be more efficacious, Conrad was directed to nominate whomsoever he might see fit as his assistants, and with them to inquire energetically after all who were infected with heresy, so that the extirpation of the tares from the fields of the Lord might proceed with due authority. Though the Inquisition was scarce as yet even a prospective conception, this was in effect an informal commission as Inquisitor-General for Germany.

Eight days later, on June 20, another commission was sent to Conrad, which increased enormously his power and influence. The German Church was as corrupt and depraved as its neighbors, and all efforts to purify it had thus far proved failures. Gregory, whose residence beyond the Alps as legate had rendered him familiar with its condition, describes its priesthood as abandoned to lasciviousness, gluttony, and all manner of filthy living, corrupting the people by their evil example, and causing the name of the Lord to be blasphemed. To remedy these evils, he now commissioned Conrad as reformer, with full powers to enforce the regulations of the cardinal-legate, and the monasteries were especially designated as objects for his regenerating hand.

Armed with almost illimitable powers, Conrad was now the foremost German ecclesiastic of the time, yet at this time his ill-balanced impulsiveness was concentrating his energies on the torturing of St. Elizabeth. There is no trace of his exercising his inquisitorial functions, and the only record of his activity as a reformer is his re-organizing the nunnery of Nordhausen by the simple expedient of expelling the nuns, who all led ungodly lives. Yet his services as a persecutor never were more needed. The excommunication of the Emperor Frederic, on September 29 of the same year, for temporarily abandoning his crusade, had set Church and State fairly by the ears, and had inspired the heretics with fresh hopes. Everywhere their missionary activity redoubled, and the land was said to be full of them. In each diocese they had a bishop to whom they gave the name of the regular incumbent, and they pretended to have a pope whom they called Gregory, so that, under examination, they could swear that they held the faith of the bishop and of Pope Gregory. In 1229 the Waldenses were again discovered in Strassburg, and for several years persecution continued there, resulting in burning many obstinate heretics and penancing those who yielded.

Local measures such as these were manifestly insufficient, and thus far all efforts at a comprehensive system of persecution had failed. In 1231 Gregory was busily occupied in organizing some more efficient method, and Germany was not forgotten. The Roman statutes of Annibaldo and the papal edicts of that year were sent to the Teutonic prelates, June 20, with letters blaming them for their lenity, and ordering them to put vigorously into force the new edicts. Under this earnest impulsion the sluggishness of the bishops was somewhat stimulated. The Archbishop of Trèves made a perquisition through his city, and found three schools of heretics in full activity. He called a synod for the trial of those who were captured, and had the satisfaction of burning three men, and a woman named Leu-chardis, who had borne the reputation of exceeding holiness, but who was found, upon examination, to belong to the dreaded sect of Luciferans.

Still the results did not correspond to Gregory's desires. In October of the same year he sought to spur Conrad on to a discharge of his duty by praising in the most exalted terms his activity and success in exterminating heretics, and by exhorting him to redoubled energy. The need of earnest work was more pressing than ever. Conrad was therefore given full discretionary powers; he was not even required to hear the cases, but only to pronounce judgment, which was to be final and without appeal—justice to those suspect of heresy being, apparently, of no moment. He was authorized to command the aid of the secular arm, to excommunicate protectors of heresy, and to lay interdict on whole districts. The recent decrees of the Holy See were referred to as his guide, and heretics who would abjure were to have the benefit of absolution, care being taken that they should have no further opportunity of mischief—a delicate expression for condemning them to lifelong incarceration. When Conrad received these extensive powers he was so dangerously ill that his life was despaired of, and before he had fairly recovered St. Elizabeth died, November 29, 1231. Harsh as was his nature, her loss affected him severely, and for a considerable time his energies were concentrated on fruitless efforts for her canonization. In intervals of leisure, however, he exercised his powers on such heretics as were unlucky enough to be within easy reach. In Marburg itself many suspects were seized, including knights, priests, and persons of condition, of whom some recanted and the rest were burned.

Results so far below what might reasonably have been expected could not but be disappointing to Gregory. One expedient remained —to try whether among the Dominicans there might not be found men able and willing to devote themselves fearlessly and exclusively to the holy work. Between the end of 1231 and that of 1232, therefore, commissions were sent to various Dominican establishments empowering their officials to undertake the work. The Treaty of Ceperano, in 1230, had restored peace between the empire and the papacy, and Frederic's aid was invoked to give the imperial sanction to the new experiment. From Ravenna, in March 1232, he issued a constitution addressed to all the prelates and potentates of the empire, ordering their efficient co-operation in the extirpation of heresy. The secular authorities were commanded to arrest all who should be designated to them by the inquisitors, to hold them safely until condemnation, and to put to a dreadful death those convicted of heresy or fautorship, or to imprison for life such as should recant and abjure. Relapse was punishable with death, and descendants to the second generation were declared incapable of holding fiefs or public office.

Suddenly there appeared on the scene a Dominican named Conrad Tors, said to be a convert from heresy, who, without special commission, commenced to clear the land of error. He carried with him a layman named John, one-eyed and one-handed, of thoroughly disreputable character, who boasted that he could recognize a heretic at sight. Apparently with little more evidence than this, Conrad Tors raided from town to town, condemning his victims wholesale, and those whom he delivered to the magistrates they were compelled by popular excitement to burn. Soon, however, a revulsion of feeling took place, and then the Dominican shrewdly enlisted the support of the nobles by directing his attacks against the more wealthy and holding out the prospect of extensive confiscations to be divided. When remonstrated with he is said to have replied, "I would burn a hundred innocent if there was one guilty among them." Stimulated by this shining example, many Dominicans and Franciscans joined him, and became his eager assistants in the work.

Whether, as reported, Conrad Tors, to strengthen himself, sought out Conrad of Marburg and persuaded him to take part in the good work, or whether the latter, scenting the battle from afar, was aroused from his torpor and rushed to the fray, cannot positively be determined. This much is certain, that at length he came forward, and not only lent the weight of his great name to the proceedings, but urged them to a crueller and wider development with all his vehemence of character and implacable severity.

The heresy of which the miserable victims of this onslaught were accused was not Waldensian, but Luciferan. Its hideous rites were described in full detail by Master Conrad to Pope Gregory, and are worth repeating as illustrating the superstitions concerning witchcraft which, for centuries, worked such cruel wrong in every corner of Europe. That Conrad obtained these wild fictions in endless duplication from those who stood before his judgment seat there need be no reasonable doubt. The reports of witch trials in later times are too numerous and authentic for us to question the readiness of self-accusation of those who saw no other means of escape, or their eagerness to propitiate their judge by responding to every incriminating suggestion, and telling him what they found him desirous of hearing. Crude as were Conrad's methods, the inquisitorial process proved its universal effectiveness by their producing confessions as surely as the more elaborate refinements invented by his successors, although he had not the advantage of the use of torture.

According to these revelations, when a novice is received into the sect and first attends the assembly, there appears to him a toad, which he kisses either on the posteriors or on the mouth. Occasionally it is a goose or a duck, and sometimes it is as large as an oven. Then there comes to him a man of wonderful paleness, with the blackest of eyes, and so thin that he is but skin and bone. Him the novice likewise kisses, finding him ice-cold, and with that kiss all remembrance of the Catholic faith vanishes from his heart. Then all sit down to a feast, after which, from a statue which is always present, there descends a black cat, as large as a dog, with the tail bent back. She comes down backwards and her posteriors are kissed, first by the novice, then by the master of the assembly, and finally by all who are worthy and perfect, while those who are imperfect receive peace from the master. Then each resumes his place, songs are sung, and the master says to his next neighbor, "What does this teach?" The answer is, "The highest peace," and another adds, "And that we must obey." All lights are then extinguished and indiscriminate intercourse takes place, after which the candles are relighted, each one takes his seat, and from a dark corner appears a man shining like the sun in his upper half, while from the hips down he is black like the cat. He illuminates the whole place, and the master, taking a fragment of the novice's garment, hands it to him, saying, "Master, I give this to thee which has been given to me." To this the shining man replies, "Thou hast served me well, thou wilt serve me more and better. I leave to thy care what thou hast given me," and then he disappears. Each year at Easter they receive the host, carry it home in their mouths, and spit it out into a cesspool to show their contempt for the Redeemer. They hold that God unjustly and treacherously cast Satan into hell; the latter is the Creator, who in the end will overcome God, when they expect eternal bliss with him.

This transparent tissue of inventions was apparently doubted by no one, and it excited almost to insanity the credulous old man who filled the papal chair. He replies that he is drunk with wormwood: "If against such men the earth should rise up, and the stars of heaven reveal their iniquity, so that not only men, but the elements, should unite in their destruction, wiping them from the face of the earth without sparing sex or age, and rendering them an eternal opprobrium for the nations, it would not be a sufficient and worthy punishment of their crimes." If they cannot be converted, the strongest remedies must be used. Conrad was instructed forthwith to preach a crusade against them, and the bishop of the province, the emperor, and his son, King Henry, were ordered to exert all their powers for the extirpation of the wretches.

The means Master Conrad took to obtain these avowals from his victims were simple in the extreme. As officially reported, after the bursting of the bubble, to Gregory by his own penitentiary, the Dominican Bernard, and the Archbishop of Mainz, the accused was allowed simply the option of confessing what was demanded of him and receiving penance, or of being burned for denial—which, in fact, was the essence of the inquisitorial process, reduced to its simplest terms. Conrad had no prisons at his disposal, and the infliction of wearing crosses seems to have been unknown to him, so he devised the penance of shaving the head as a mark of humiliation for his converts, who were, of course, obliged to give the names of all whom they had seen in the hideous assemblies.

At the outset he had fallen into the hands of a designing woman, a vagrant about 20 years old who had quarrelled with her relations, and who, coming by chance to Bingen, and observing what was going on, saw her opportunity of revenge. She pretended to be of the sect, that her husband had been burned, that she wished to perish likewise, but added that if the Master would believe her she would reveal the names of the guilty. Conrad eagerly swallowed the bait, and sent her with his assistants to Clavelt, where she caused the burning of her kindred. Creatures of this kind were sure not to be lacking, and it was even said that cunning heretics caused themselves to be accused, and accepted penance, for the purpose of incriminating Catholics. As no one had the slightest opportunity of defense, some steadfast men preferred to be burned and thus earn salvation, rather than to confess to lies and falsely accuse others. The weaker ones who saved their lives, when pressed to name their accomplices, would often say, "I know not whom to accuse: tell me the names of those you suspect"; or, when interrogated about individuals, would evasively reply, "They were as I was; they were in the assemblies as I was," which was apparently sufficient. "Thus," proceeds the official report to the pope, "brother accused brother, the wife the husband, and the master the servant. Others gave money to the shaven penitents in order to learn from them methods of evasion and escape, and there arose a confusion unknown for ages. I, the archbishop, first by my- self and afterwards with the two archbishops of Trèves and Cologne, warned Master Conrad to proceed in so great a matter with more moderation and discretion, but he refused."

From this last fact we gather that the prelates of the land, while not interfering effectively to protect their people, had at least taken no part in the insane persecution. Conrad had found plenty of assistants among the Dominicans and Franciscans, but the secular hierarchy had held aloof. The German prelates were great secular princes, combining civil and spiritual authority. The three electoral archbishops—Mainz, Trèves, and Cologne—stood on a level as tem- poral lords with the most powerful princes of the empire, and the wide extent of many of the dioceses rendered the bishops scarcely less formidable. Frederic II, by his Constitutions of 1232, had in- creased their secular authority by rendering them absolute masters of the episcopal cities, whose municipal rights and liberties he abolished, but at the same time he had given the imperial sanction to the papal Inquisition and had rendered it everywhere supreme. It is no wonder that they felt alarmed, that they withheld their co- operation as far as they safely could, and that well-grounded jealousy would lead them to seize the first opportunity of crushing the in- truding upstarts.

Fortunately for the German people, Conrad's blind recklessness was not long in affording them the desired chance. Beginning with the lowly and helpless, his operations had rapidly advanced to the higher classes. In his eyes the meanest peasant and the loftiest noble were on an equality, but his witnesses at first had not dared to accuse the high-born and powerful. It is quite possible, indeed, that, as the persecution became more dreadful, some of them may have felt that the surest mode of bringing on a crisis was to involve the magnates of the land. Rumors were spread impugning the faith of the Counts of Aneberg, Lotz, and Sayn. Conrad eagerly directed his interrogatories to obtaining evidence against them, and summoned them to appear before him. Count Sayn was an especially notable prey, as he was one of the most powerful nobles of the diocese, whose extensive possessions were guarded by castles renowned for strength, and whose reputation was that of a stern and cruel man.

The crime of which he was accused was that of riding on a crab, and open defiance was expected from him. Sigfried, the Archbishop of Mainz, to make a show of obedience to the papal commands, had called a provincial council to assemble March 13, 1233. When it met, it deplored the prevalence of heresy, it prayed the prelates to labor zealously for the suppression of the evil and commanded them to enforce in their respective dioceses the recent decrees of the pope and of the emperor; it deprecated the practice of seizing the property of suspects before their guilt was determined; it ordered the bishops to provide prisons for coiners and incorrigible clerks, without alluding to the imprisonment of heretics; it endeavored to maintain episcopal jurisdiction by enacting that inquisitors must obtain letters from the bishop before exercising their powers in any diocese; finally, it anticipated the resistance of Count Sayn and the other inculpated nobles by directing that if any magnate, relying upon the strength of his castles and the support of his subjects, should refuse to appear after three citations, his bishop should preach a crusade against him with indulgences, and he should be manfully assailed.

Thus, while ostensibly obeying the commands of the pope and emperor, the action of the bishops was practically directed to limiting the powers of the inquisitors. As for the threat of a crusade, its significance is seen in the steps actually taken in the case of Count Sayn. That shrewd noble saw that he could rely upon episcopal protection if he could promise the bishops efficient support, and he had sufficient interest with King Henry to induce him to join with Sigfried of Mainz in calling a council for July 25, to consider his case. The king and his princes attended the assembly as well as the prelates, so that it was rather an imperial diet than an ecclesiastical council. The count asserted his innocence and offered to prove it by conjurators. Conrad, who was present, found his position suddenly changed. The assembly was, in reality, a national protest against the supremacy of the papal Inquisition, and the inquisitor, in place of being a judge armed with absolute jurisdiction, was merely a prosecutor. He presented his witnesses, but in that august presence the hearts of some of them failed, and they withdrew; others felt emboldened to declare that they had been forced to accuse the count in order to save their own lives, and those who persisted were easily shown to be personal enemies of the accused. The whole assemblage seemed inspired with a common desire to put an end to Conrad's arbitrary proceedings, and the prosecution broke down totally. King Henry alone, perhaps already meditating his rebellion against his father and anxious not to offend either the nobles or the papacy, desired to postpone the matter for further consideration. The count pressed earnestly for immediate judgment, but the Archbishop of Trèves interposed: "My lord, the king wishes the case postponed"; then turning to the people, "I announce to you that Count Sayn departs from here unconvicted, and as a good Catholic." Master Conrad sullenly muttered, "If he had been convicted it would have been different," and withdrew. The count finally agreed to allow the matter to be referred to Rome, and ecclesiastics of distinction were appointed to lay the proceedings before the Holy See for final decision.

Maddened by his defeat, Conrad at once proceeded to preach in the streets of Mainz a crusade against some nobles who had been summoned and who had not appeared. To this both the archbishop and the king objected, and he was forced to desist. With his usual impulsiveness he then abruptly determined to quit an ungrateful world, and to live henceforth in retirement at Marburg. The king and archbishop offered him an armed escort, but he would accept nothing save letters of surety, and with these he departed to meet his fate. Those against whom his crusade had been preached lay in wait for him near Marburg and dispatched him, July 31, regardless of his entreaties for mercy. His faithful follower, Friar Gerhard, refused the opportunity offered him to escape, threw himself on the body of his master, and perished with him. The scene of the murder is supposed to be Kappeln on the Lahnsberg, where a chapel was erected to commemorate it. The body was carried to Marburg and buried by the side of St. Elizabeth, and when the latter was translated to the magnificent Elizabethskirche, his bones were also carried thither.

With Conrad's withdrawal from the Council of Mainz the proceedings of which he had been the mainspring came to an end. "Thus," says a contemporary ecclesiastic, "ceased this storm, the most dangerous persecution of the faithful since the days of Constantius the Heretic and Julian the Apostate. People once more began to breathe. Count Sayn was a wall for the mansion of the Lord, lest this madness should rage further, enveloping guilty and innocent alike, bishops and princes, religious and Catholics, like peasants and heretics." The murderers evidently felt that they had nothing to dread from public opinion, for they voluntarily came forward and offered to submit themselves to the judgment of the Church as regards the heresy whereof Conrad had accused them, and to the secular tribunals as regards the homicide, agreeing to present themselves for examination at a diet of the empire which was ordered for February 1234 at Frankfort.

Gregory, who in June had been ordering a crusade preached against the heretics, and had been stimulating prince and prelate to a yet more ferocious persecution, was moved to regret when the envoy of the assembly of Mainz, Conrad, the *Scholasticus* of Speier, presented letters from the king and bishops describing the arbitrary methods of his inquisitor. He ordered letters drawn up prescribing a more regular form of trial for heretics; but before the envoy had permission to depart, there arrived the originator of the trouble, Conrad Tors, with the pitiful tale of the Master's martyrdom. At this news the emotional pope could not contain his wrath. The letters just written were recalled and torn up, and the unlucky envoy was threatened with the deprivation of all his benefices. Under the remonstrances of the Sacred College, however, Gregory's ire subsided sufficiently to allow him to renew the letters and to enable the envoy to depart unscathed. The pope solaced himself, however, with pouring out his grief at full length in letters to the German prelates. The death of Conrad was a thunderclap which had shaken the walls of the Christian sanctuary. No words were strong enough to describe the transcendant merits and services of the martyr, and no punishment could be invented too severe for the murderers. The Dominican provincial, Conrad, was commanded, in conjunction with the bishops, to carry on the Inquisition vigorously, and to preach a crusade against the heretics.

In spite of this furious wrath, the German prelates maintained a most provoking calmness. The fanatic Conrad, Bishop of Hildesheim, it is true, preached a crusade as ordered by the pope, and under his impulsion the Landgrave, Conrad of Thuringia, zealously purged his land of heretics, while his brother, Henry Raspe, and Hartmann, Count of Kiburg (Zurich), took the cross under the same auspices, and received, in consequence, papal protection for their dominions.

Even this measure of activity, however, was regarded unfavorably in Germany, and there was no response to the cry for vengeance. The Diet of Frankfort duly assembled February 2, 1234, and the first business recorded was an accusation brought by King Henry himself against the Bishop of Hildesheim for having preached the crusade; it was treated as an offense, and though he was pardoned by unanimous request, the recalcitrance against the papal tendencies was none the less significant. Then the memory of the martyred Conrad was arraigned, and this, as a matter of faith, was discussed by the ecclesiastics separately. There were twenty-five archbishops and bishops present, who were almost unanimous in condemning him, while the Bishop of Hildesheim and a Dominican named Otto strenuously defended him. One of the prelates exclaimed that Master Conrad ought to be dug up and burned as a heretic; but no conclusion seems to have been reached, for the proceedings were interrupted by a procession of those whom he had shaved in penance the preceding year, who marched in with a cross at their head, and complained of his cruelty with dolorous cries, when a tumult arose from which his defenders were glad to escape with their lives. On the following Monday the solemn purgation of Count Sayn took place in the field of judgment beyond the walls. Eight bishops, twelve Cistercian and three Benedictine abbots, twelve Franciscan and three Dominican friars, who, with many other clerks and numerous nobles, took part in his oath of denial, show how emphatically the German hierarchy desired to disclaim all sympathy with Conrad's acts. Count Solms, whom Conrad had forced to confession, went through the same ceremony, declaring with tears in his eyes that the fear of death alone had compelled him to admit himself guilty. The diet then proceeded to legislate for the future. It simply commanded that all who exercised judicial functions should use every effort to purge the land of heresy, but at the same time it cautioned them to prefer justice to unjust persecution.

Two months later, April 2, 1234, a council was held at Mainz for final action. Count Sayn and others who had been accused were subjected to a form of examination, were declared innocent, and were restored to reputation and to their possessions. Conrad's unlucky witnesses who had been forced to commit perjury were ordered to undergo a penance of seven years; those who had accused the innocent were maliciously sent to the pope for the imposition of penance, and he was, in the same spirit, asked what should be done about those whom Conrad had unjustly burned. As for the murderers, they were simply excommunicated.

All this was a direct challenge to the Holy See, but Gregory prudently delayed action. He sent his penitentiary, Bernard, who made an investigation on the spot, and, in conjunction with Archbishop Sigfried, furnished him with a report to which we are indebted for most of our knowledge of the affair. On receiving this, Gregory expressed his regret that he had entrusted to Master Conrad the enormous powers which had led to a result so lamentable. Still his decision was delayed. Towards the end of the year 1234 he appealed earnestly to the German bishops for aid in his quarrel with the Romans, which continued until he made peace with them in April 1235. His hands were now free, but it was not until July that he trusted himself to express his indignation. Then he scolded most vehemently the Council of Mainz for daring, in the absence of any defenders of the faith, to absolve those whom Conrad had prosecuted, and for sending to him for absolution the murderers, without having first exacted of them full satisfaction for their detestable crime. His sentence upon them is that they shall join the crusade to Palestine when it sets sail the following March, giving good security to insure their obedience, and meanwhile they shall visit all the greater churches in the region of the crime, barefooted and naked, except drawers, with a halter around the neck, and a rod in the hand, and, when the affluence of people is the greatest, cause themselves to be scourged by all the priests, while they chant the penitential psalms, and publicly confess their guilt. After this they may be absolved.

The immediate author of the troubles met with the fate which he deserved. Conrad Tors, on his return from Rome, endeavored to resume his interrupted labors, but the temper of the people had changed, and the victims were no longer unresisting. At Strassburg he summoned the Junker Heinz von Müllenheim, who unceremoniously settled the accusation by slaying him. His assistant, the one-eyed John, met an even more ignominious fate, for he was recognized at Freiburg and hanged.

Thus ended this terrible drama, which left an impression of horror

on the souls of the German people not easily effaced. One good result there undoubtedly was. The universal detestation excited by
Conrad's fanaticism rendered it comparatively easy for the bishops
to maintain the jurisdiction which they had assumed, and to keep
the Inquisition confined within narrow limits. For a time this was
doubtless facilitated by the open quarrels between Frederic II and
the papacy, but even after his death, during the Great Interregnum
and the reigns of emperors who were more or less dependent upon
the Holy See, more than a century was to pass away before the
popes, who were so zealously organizing and strengthening it elsewhere, made a serious effort to establish the Inquisition in Germany.

In the codes which embody the customs current in mediæval
Germany there is no recognition whatever of the existence of such
a body as the Inquisition. The *Sachsenspiegel*, which contains the
municipal law of the northern provinces, provides, it is true, the
punishment of burning for those convicted of unbelief, poisoning,
or sorcery, but says nothing as to the manner of trial; and the rule
enunciated that no houses shall be destroyed except when rape is
committed in them or a violated woman is carried into them, shows
that the demolition of the residences and refuges of heretics was
unknown within its jurisdiction. The code throughout is singularly
disregardful of ecclesiastical pretensions, and richly earned the papal
anathema bestowed upon it when its practical working happened to
attract the attention of the Roman curia.

The *Schwabenspiegel*, or code in force in southern Germany, is
much more complaisant to the Church, but it knows of no jurisdiction over heretics save that of the bishops. It admits that an
emperor rendering himself suspect in the faith can be put under
ban by the pope. It provides death by fire for the heretic. It directs
that when heretics are known to exist, the ecclesiastical courts shall
proceed against them. If a secular prince does not punish heresy he
is to be excommunicated by the episcopal court; if he remains under
the censure for a year the bishop is to report him to the pope, who
shall deprive him of his rank and honors, and the emperor is bound
to execute his sentence by stripping him of all his possessions, feudal
and allodial. All this shows ample readiness to accept the received
ecclesiastical law of the period on heresy, but utter ignorance of the
inquisitorial process is revealed in the provision which inflicts the

talio on whoever accuses another of certain crimes, including heresy, without being able to convict him. When the accuser had to accept the chances of the stake, prosecutions were not apt to be common.

Towards the close of the thirteenth century and the opening of the fourteenth, attention was aroused to the dangerous tendencies of certain forms of belief lurking among some semi-religious bodies which had long enjoyed the favor of the pious and the protection of the Church, known by the names of Beguines, Beghards, Lollards, Cellites, etc. Infinite learned trifling has been wasted in imagining derivations for these appellations. The Beguines and Beghards themselves assert their descent from St. Begga, mother of Pepin of Landen, who built a Benedictine nunnery at Andennes. Another root has been sought in Lambert-le-Bègue, or the Stammerer, a priest of St. Christopher at Liège, about 1180, who became prominent by denouncing the simony of the canons of the cathedral. His connection with the Beguines arose from his affording them shelter in his house at St. Christopher, which has remained until modern times the largest and richest Beguinage of the province. The soundest opinion, however, would seem to be that both Beghard and Beguine are derived from the old German word *beggan*, signifying either to beg or to pray, while Lollard is traced to *lullen*, to mutter prayers.[1]

The motives were numerous which impelled multitudes to desire a religious life without assuming the awful and irrevocable vows that cut them off absolutely from the world. This was especially the case

---

[1] In popular use the words *Lollard* and *Beghard* were virtually convertible, and yet there is a difference between them. The associations of Lollards were founded during a pestilence at Antwerp about the year 1300. They were laymen who devoted themselves to the care of the sick and insane, and specially to the burial of the dead, supplying the funds partly by labor and partly by begging. The name was derived from the low and soft singing of the funeral chants, but they called themselves *Alexians*, from their patron, St. Alexis, and *Cellites* from dwelling in cells. The word *Lollard* gradually grew to have the significance of external sanctity covering secret license, and was promiscuously applied to all the mendicants outside the regular Orders. The Cellite associations spread from the Netherlands through the Rhinelands and all over Germany. Constantly the subject of persecution, along with the Beghards, their value was recognized by the magistrates of the cities who endeavored to protect them. In 1472 Charles the Bold obtained from Sixtus IV a bull receiving them into the recognized religious Orders, thus withdrawing them from episcopal jurisdiction; and in 1506 Julius II granted them special privileges. The associations of Alexian Brothers still exist, devoted to the care of the sick, and have flourishing hospitals in the United States, as well as in Europe.

among women who chanced to be deprived of their natural guardians and who sought in those wild ages the protection which the Church alone could confer. Thus associations were formed, originally of women, who simply promised chastity and obedience while they lived in common, who assisted either by labor or beggary in providing for the common support, who were assiduous in their religious observances, and who performed such duties of hospitality and of caring for the sick as their opportunities would allow. The Netherlands was the native seat of this fruitful idea, and as early as 1065 there is a charter extant given by a convent of Beguines at Vilvorde, near Brussels. The drain of the crusades on the male population increased enormously the number of women deprived of support and protection, and gave a corresponding stimulus to the growth of the Beguinages. In time men came to form similar associations, and soon Germany, France, and Italy became filled with them. To earn a livelihood by beggary was in itself an approach to sanctity, as we have seen in the case of Conrad of Marburg and St. Elizabeth. About 1230 a certain Willem Cornelis, of Antwerp, gave up a prebend and devoted himself to teaching the pre-eminent virtue of poverty. He carried the received doctrine on the subject, however, to lengths too extravagant, for he held that poverty consumed all sin, as fire ate up rust, and that a harlot, if poor, was better than a just and continent rich man; and though he was honorably buried in the church of the Virgin Mary, yet when, four years later, these opinions came to be known, Bishop Nicholas of Cambrai caused his bones to be exhumed and burned.

Extremes such as this show us the prevailing tendencies of the age, and it is necessary to appreciate these tendencies in order to understand how Europe came to tolerate the hordes of holy beggars, either wandering or living in communities, who covered the face of the land, and drained the people of their substance. Of the two classes the wanderers were the most dangerous, but in both there was the germ of future trouble.

The rapid growth of these communities in the thirteenth century is easily explicable. Not only did they respond to the spiritual demands of the age, but they enjoyed the most exalted patronage. In Flanders the counts seem never wearied of assisting them. Gregory IX and his successors took their institution under the special pro-

tection of the Holy See. St. Louis provided them with houses in
Paris and other cities, and left them abundant legacies in his will,
in which he was imitated by his sons. Under such encouragement
their numbers increased enormously. In Paris there were multitudes.
About 1240 they were estimated at 2,000 in Cologne and its vicinity,
and there were as many in the single Beguinage of Nivelle, in
Brabant. The great Beguinage of Ghent, founded in 1234 by the
Countesses of Flanders, Jeanne and Marguerite, is described in the
seventeenth century as resembling a small town, surrounded with
wall and fosse, containing open squares, conventual houses, dwellings,
infirmary, church, and cemetery, inhabited by 800 or 1,000 women,
the younger living in the convents, the older in separate houses.
They were tied by no permanent vows and were free to depart and
marry at any time, but so long as they were inmates they were bound
to obey the Grand Mistress. Those who thus lived in communities
could be subjected to wholesome supervision and established rules,
but it was otherwise with those who maintained an independent
existence, either in one spot or wandering from place to place. Their
customary persistent cry through the streets—"Brod durch Gott"—
became a shibboleth unpleasantly familiar to the inhabitants of the
German cities.

The Church was not long in recognizing the danger inherent in
these practices when withdrawn from close supervision. In 1259, a
council of Mainz strongly reproved the pestiferous sect of Beghards
and Beguttæ (Beguines), who wandered through the streets crying
"Brod durch Gott," preaching in caverns and other secret places,
and given to various practices disapproved by the Church. In 1267
the Council of Trèves forbade their preaching in the streets on
account of the heresies which they disseminated. In 1287 a council
of Liège deprived all who did not live in the Beguinages of the right
to wear the peculiar habit and enjoy the privileges of Beguines.

All this points to the adoption, by the followers of Ortlieb who
called themselves Brethren of the Free Spirit, of the habit and appellation of the Beghards and Beguines, and the gradual invasion
among the latter of the doctrines derived from Amauri. Comparatively few of the Lollards, Beghards, or Beguines were contaminated
with these heresies, but they all had to share the responsibility, and
the communities of both sexes, who led the most regular lives and

were inspired with the purest orthodoxy, were exposed to unnumbered tribulations for lack of a distinctive appellation. It became even worse when John XXII plunged into a quarrel with the Spiritual Franciscans, drove them into open rebellion, and persecuted the new heresy which he had thus created. In France the Tertiary Franciscans were popularly known as Beguines, and this became the appellation customarily bestowed on these Spiritual heretics, and adopted by the Avignonese popes to designate them. Not only has this led to much confusion on the part of heresiologists, but its effect, for a time, on the fortunes of the virtuous and orthodox Beguines of both sexes was most disastrous. The heretic Beghards, it is true, adopted for themselves the title of Brethren of the Free Spirit; the rebellious Franciscans insisted that they were the only legitimate representatives of the Order, and, at most, assumed the term of Spirituals to distinguish themselves from their carnal-minded conventual brethren; but the authorities were long in admitting these distinctions, and, in the eyes of the Church at large, the condemnation of Beghards and Beguines covered all alike.

We have here to do only with the Brethren of the Free Spirit, whose doctrines, as we have seen, were derived from the speculations of the Amaurians carried to Germany by Ortlieb of Strassburg. Descriptions of their errors have reached us from so many sources, covering so long a period, with so general a consensus in fundamentals, that there can be little doubt as to the main principles of their faith. Many of the peculiarly repulsive extravagances attributed to them, however, may safely be ascribed to keen-witted schoolmen engaged in trying individual heretics, and forcing them to admit consequences logically but unexpectedly deduced from their admitted premises. There was no little intellectual activity in the sect, and their tracts and books of devotion, written in the vernacular, were widely distributed and largely relied upon as means of missionary effort. These, of course, have wholly disappeared, and we are left to gather their doctrines from the condemnations passed upon them.

The foundation of their creed was pantheism. God is everything that is. There is as much of the divinity in a louse as in a man or in any other creature. All emanates from Him and returns to Him. As the soul thus reverts to God after death, there is neither purgatory nor hell, and all external cult is useless. Man, being thus God by

nature, has in him all that is divine, and each one may say that
he himself created the universe. One of the accusations brought
against Master Eckart was that he had declared that his little finger
created the world. Man can so unite himself with God that he can
do whatever God does; he thus needs no God; he is impeccable, and
whatever he does is without sin. In this state of perfection he grieves
at nothing, he rejoices at nothing, he is free from all virtue and all
virtuous actions. No one is bound to labor for his bread; as all things
are in common, each one may take what his necessities or desires
may prompt.

The practical deductions from these doctrines were not only
destructive to the Church, but dangerous to the moral and social
order. The lofty mysticism of the teachers might preserve them from
the evil results which flowed from the presumption of impeccability. In their austere stoicism they condemned all sexual indulgence
save that of which the sole object was the procurement of offspring.
They taught that a woman in marrying should deeply deplore the
loss of her virginity, and that no one was perfect in whom promiscuous nakedness could awaken either shame or passion. That tests
of this kind were not infrequent, the history of ill-regulated enthusiasm, from the time of the early Christians, will not permit us
to doubt, and the Beghards succeeded so well in subduing the senses
that a hostile controversialist can only suggest Satanic influence,
well known to demonologists for its refrigerating power, as an
explanation of their wonderful self-control under such temptation.
Yet this rare exaltation of austerity was not possible to all natures.
Such a doctrine was attractive to those who desired excuse and
opportunity for license, and the evidence is too abundant and confirmatory for us to doubt that, at least in some cases, the sectaries
abandoned themselves to the grossest sensuality. It is noteworthy
that, in order to describe the divine internal light which they enjoyed, they invented for themselves the term Illuminism, which
for more than three centuries continued to be of most serious import.

As a branch of the sect may be reckoned the Luciferans, who
have been alluded to above. Pantheism, of course, included Satan
as an emanation from God, and it was not difficult to assume that
his fallen state was an injustice. In 1312 Luciferans were discovered

at Krems, in the diocese of Passau, whose bishop, Bernhard, together with Conrad, Archbishop of Salzburg, and Frederic, Duke of Austria, undertook their extirpation with the aid of the Dominican Inquisition, which seems to have maintained some foothold in those regions. The persecution lasted until 1315, but the sect was not exterminated, and reappeared repeatedly in after-years. It is reported to have been thoroughly organized, with twelve "apostles" who travelled annually throughout Germany, making converts and confirming the believers in the faith. All the ceremonies of external worship were rejected, but they did not enjoy the impeccability of Illuminism, for two of their ministers were held to enter paradise every year, where they received from Enoch and Elias the power of absolving their followers, and this power they communicated to others in each community. Those who were detected proved obdurate; they were deaf to all persuasion, and met their death in the flames with the utmost cheerfulness. One of the apostles who was burned at Vienna stated, under torture, that there were 8,000 of them scattered throughout Bohemia, Austria, and Thuringia, besides numbers elsewhere. Bohemia was especially infected with these errors, and Trithemius, in the opening years of the sixteenth century, states that there were still thousands of them in that kingdom. This is doubtless an exaggeration, if not a complete mistake, but they were again discovered in Austria in 1338 and 1395, and many of them were burned.

The tendency to mysticism which found its complete expression in the Brethren of the Free Spirit influenced greatly the development of German religious thought in channels which, although assumedly orthodox, trenched narrowly upon heresy. In Germany the mystic tendency of religious sentiment during the fourteenth century is the most marked spiritual phenomenon of the period. Few names in the first quarter of the century were more respected than that of Master Eckart, who stood high in the ranks of the great Dominican Order. If the 28 articles finally condemned by John XXII as heretical be correctly extracted from Eckart's teachings, there can be no doubt that he was deeply infected with the pantheistic speculations of the Brethren of the Free Spirit, that he admitted the common divinity of man and God, and shared in the dangerous deductions which proved that sin and virtue were the same in the eyes of God. To a hierarchy founded on sacerdotalism, moreover, nothing could be more revolutionary than the rejection of external cult, which was the necessary conclusion from the doctrine that there is no virtue in external acts, but that only the internal operations of the soul are of moment; that no man should regret the commission of sin, or ask anything of God.

The importance of Eckart's views lies not so much in his own immediate influence as in that of his disciples. He was the founder of the school of German mystics, through whom the speculations of Amauri of Bène, in various dilutions, made a deep impression on the religious development of the fourteenth and fifteenth centuries. All the leaders in the remarkable association known as the Friends of God, drew, directly or indirectly, their inspiration from Master Eckart, and all, to a greater or less extent, reveal their affinity to the Brethren of the Free Spirit, although they succeeded in keeping technically within the limits of orthodoxy.

John of Rysbroek, humane and gentle as he was, regarded the Brethren of the Free Spirit with such horror that he deemed them worthy of the stake. Yet, though he avoided their pantheism, he taught, like them, the supreme end of existence in the absorption of the individual into the infinite substance of God; moreover, the Perfect, inflamed by divine love, are dead to themselves and to the world, and are thus incapable of sin. It is no wonder that Gerson regarded as dangerous these doctrines, so nearly akin to those of the Beghards, and though Rysbroek might hesitate to draw from them the conclusions inevitable to hardier thinkers, they were sufficient to render unsuccessful the attempt made, in 1624, to canonize him, in spite of the incontestable miracles wrought at his tomb. His most distinguished disciple was Gerard Groot, who partially outgrew the metaphysical subtleties of his teacher and turned his energies to the more practical directions out of which sprang the Brethren of the Common Life. Groot was equally severe upon the corruption of the clergy and the errors of the heretics. When the introduction of the Inquisition into Germany drove the Brethren of the Free Spirit to find new places of refuge, some of them went to Holland, where the prevalence of pantheistic mysticism gave opportunity of spreading their doctrines. Groot's own views sufficiently resembled theirs to render their bolder speculations doubly offensive to him, and he sought to repress them with especial zeal. The convent of Augustinian Hermits at Dordrecht had the reputation of being tainted with the heresy, and Groot was eager to detect and punish it. Bartholomew, one of the Augustinians, was particularly suspected, and Groot proposed to follow him secretly with a notary and take down his words. In this, or some other way, evidence was obtained; there was no Inquisition in Holland, and Groot procured his citation before Florent, Bishop of Utrecht, about the year 1380. Bartholomew denied the expressions attributed to him and was let off with an injunction to repeat the denial publicly in Kampen and Zwolle, where he was said to have uttered his heresies. This unexpected lenity excited the indignation of Groot, who had sufficient influence to induce Bishop Florent to take up the case again and try it personally. Bartholomew endeavored to escape his persecutor by appearing a day in advance of the one set for his trial, but word was sent to Groot, who threw himself into a wagon, and by travelling all night reached Utrecht in time. On this occasion he was successful; Bartholomew was condemned as a heretic, abjured, and was sentenced to wear crosses in the form of scissors. The Augustinians did not lack friends, and they retaliated on those who had busied themselves in the matter. The magistrates of Kampen prosecuted some women who had served as witnesses and fined them, and they also banished for ten years Werner Keynkamp, a friend of Groot, who subsequently was thrice prior of houses of Brethren of the Common Life. Groot himself did not escape, for soon afterwards Bishop Florent, for the purpose of silencing him, issued an order withdrawing all commissions to preach. Groot then endeavored to procure from Urban VI papal commissions as preacher and inquisitor, and sent to Rome 10 florins to pay for the bulls. Fortunately for his fame, he died, in 1384, before the return of his messenger, and Holland was spared the effects of his inconsiderate zeal. In his gentler capacity he left his mantle to Florent Radewyns, under whom were developed the communities of the Common Life. These spread rapidly throughout the Netherlands and Germany, and though occasionally the subject of inquisitorial persecution, they were covered by the decision of Martin V, when Matthew Grabon, at the Council of Constance, endeavored to procure the condemnation of the Beguines. After this they flourished without opposition, supporting themselves by disseminating culture, as educators and copiers of manuscripts. After the Reformation the communities rapidly died out, although the house of Emmerich, near Düsseldorf, remained to be closed by Napoleon, in 1811, and the four brethren then ejected from it continued to observe the rules, till the last one, Gerard Mulder, died at Zevenaar, March 15, 1854. One branch of the brethren, however, adopted the Rule of the canons-regular of St. Augustin. Their convent of Windesheim became the model which was universally followed, and the order had the honor of training two such men as Thomas-à-Kempis and Erasmus. *The Imitation of Christ* is the final exquisite flower of the moderated mysticism of John of Rysbroek. Brought down to practical life, this mysticism contributed largely to the spiritual movement which culminated in the Reformation, for it taught the dependence of the individual on himself alone for salvation. In this the Brethren of the Common Life were active. To them dogma became less important than the interior discipline which should fit men to be really children of God. Preaching among the people and teaching in the schools, such brethren as Henry Harphius, John Brugman, Denis Van Leeuwen, Jon Van Goch, and John Wessel of Groningen, were unwittingly undermining the power of the hierarchy, although they virtually escaped all imputation of heresy.

Less lasting, though more noticeable at the time, was the association of Friends of God, which formed itself in the upper Rhinelands. The most prominent disciple of Master Eckart was John Tauler, who retained enough of his master's doctrines to render him amenable to the charge of heresy had there been in those days a German Inquisition in working order. In the heights of his illuminated quietism all the personality of the devotee was lost in the abyss of Divinity. The individual could bring his soul into relations with the Godhead so intimate that it was virtually lost in the Divine Essence, and he could become so thoroughly under the influence of the Holy Ghost that he was, so to speak, inspired, and his acts were the acts of the Third Person of the Trinity.

Great as was Tauler's renown as the foremost preacher of his day, he bowed as a little child before the mysterious layman known as the Friend of God in the Oberland. In the full strength of mature manhood, when at least fifty years of age and when all Strassburg was hanging on his words, a stranger sought his presence and probed to the bottom his secret weaknesses. He was a Pharisee, proud of his learning and his skill in scholastic theology; before he could be fit for the guidance of souls he must cast off all reliance on his own strength and become as an infant relying on God alone. Overcome by the mystic power of his visitor, Tauler subdued his pride, and in obedience to the command of the stranger, who never revealed his name, he for two years abstained from preaching and from hearing confessions. From this struggle with himself he emerged a new man, and formed one of the remarkable band of Friends of God whom the nameless stranger was engaged in selecting and uniting.

This association was not numerous, for only rare souls could rise to the altitude in which they would surely wish only what God wishes and dislike what God dislikes; but its adepts were scattered from the Netherlands to Genoa, and from the Rhinelands to Hungary. Terrible were the struggles and spiritual conflicts, the alternations of hope and despair, or ravishing ecstasies and hideous temptations, with which God tried the neophyte who sought to ascend into the serene atmosphere of mystic Illuminism—struggles and conflicts which form a strangely resembling prototype of those which for long years tested the steadfastness of John Bunyan.

In many of their tenets and practices there is a strange reverberation of Hinduism, all the stranger that there can be no possible connection between them, unless there may be some elements derived from mystic Arabic Aristotelianism, which so strongly influenced scholastic thought. As the old Brahmanic *tapas,* or austere meditation, enabled man to acquire a share of the divine nature, so the interior exercises of the Friends of God assimilated man to the Divinity, and the miraculous powers which they acquired find their prototypes in the Rishis and Rahats. The self-inflicted barbarities of the Yoga system were emulated in the efforts necessary to subdue the rebellious flesh; Rulman Merswin, for instance, used to scourge himself with wires and then rub salt into the wounds. The religious ecstasies of the Friends of God were the counterpart of the Samadhi or beatific insensibility of the Hindu; and the supreme good which they set before themselves was the same as that of the Sankhya school—the renunciation of the will and the freedom from all passions and desires, even that of salvation. Yet these resemblances were modified by the Christian sense of the omnipotence and omnipresence of God, and by the more practical character of the Western mind, which ordered its votaries, if laymen, to continue their wordly life; if rich, not to despoil themselves, but to employ their riches in good works, and to discharge their duties to man as well as to God. Rulman Merswin was a banker, and continued in active business while founding the community of the Grün Wöhrd and writing the treatises which were the support and the comfort of the faithful. Yet the chief of them all and his immediate disciples founded a hermitage in the wilderness, where they devoted themselves to propitiating the wrath of God. The unutterable wickedness of man called for divine vengeance. Earthquakes, pestilence, famine, had been disregarded warnings, and only the intercession of the Friends of God had obtained repeated reprieves. The Great Schism, in 1378, was a still greater calamity, and in 1379 an angel messenger informed them that the final punishment was postponed for a year, after which they must not ask for further delay. Still, in 1380, thirteen of them were mysteriously called to assemble in a "divine diet," to which an angel brought a letter informing them that, at the prayer of the Virgin, God had granted a respite of three years provided they would constitute themselves "prisoners of God," living the life of recluses in absolute silence, broken only two days in the week from noon to eve, and then only to ask for necessaries or to give spiritual counsel. To this they assented, and not long afterwards they disappear from view.

Not only are the Friends of God noteworthy as a significant development of the spiritual tendencies of the age, but they have a peculiar interest for us from their relations with the Church on the one hand and with the Brethren of the Free Spirit on the other. They were an outgrowth of the latter, though they avoided the deplorable moral extravagances of the parent sect. The "Ninth Rock," which was the supreme height of ascetic illuminism of the Beghards, reappears in the same sense in the most notable of Rulman Merswin's works, long attributed to Henry Suso. It is no wonder that Nider confounded the Friends of God with the Beghards, though Merswin's *Baner Buechelin* was written for the purpose of denouncing the errors of the latter. In much, as we have seen, they differed from the current doctrines of the Church, carrying their aberrations further than those which in the seventeenth century were so severely repressed in Molinos and the Illuminati. To these they added special errors of their own. Many Jews and Moslems, they said, were saved, for God abandons none who seek him, and though they cannot enjoy Christian baptism, God himself baptizes them spiritually in the sufferings of the death agony. They refused to denounce the heretic to human justice for fear of anticipating divine justice; they could tolerate him in the world as long as God saw fit to do so. Yet they had one saving principle which preserved them from the consequences of their errors. While denouncing in the strongest language the corruptions and worldliness of the establishment, they professed the most implicit obedience to Rome, and much could be pardoned so long as the supremacy of the Holy See was not called in question. When, in June 1377, the Friend of God in the Oberland was inspired to visit, with a comrade, Gregory XI, and warn him of the dangers which threatened Christendom, they spoke to him with the utmost freedom, and though he at first was angered, he finally recognized in them the envoys of the Holy Ghost and honored them greatly, urging them to resume their abandoned design of founding a great institution of their order. He did not even take offense when they threatened him with death within the twelvemonth if he did not reform the Church.[2] In effect he died March 28, 1378; but, if we may believe Gerson, his dying regrets were not that he had neglected these warnings, but that by too credulously listening to the visions of male and female prophets he had paved the way for the Great Schism, which he foresaw would break out when he was removed from the scene.

After this hasty review of the more orthodox developments of mysticism we may return to the history of the Brethren of the Free Spirit, who maintained the pantheistic doctrine in all its crudity, and did not shrink from its legitimate deductions. Towards the close of the thirteenth century the transcendent merits of beggary, so long acknowledged, began to be questioned. In 1274 the Council

[2] There is nothing improbable in the freedom of speech attributed to the Friends of God in their interview with Gregory. Apocalyptic inspiration was common at the period, and St. Birgitta of Sweden, and St. Catharine of Siena, were not particularly reticent in their language to the successors of St. Peter.

of Lyons endeavored to suppress the unauthorized mendicant associations. In 1286 Honorius IV condemned the Segarellists, and
some ten years later the persecution, by Boniface VIII, of the
Celestines and stricter Franciscans showed that poverty was no
longer to be regarded as the supreme virtue. About the same time
he issued a bull ordering the active persecution of some heretics,
whose teaching that perfection required men and women to go
naked and not to labor with the hands would seem to identify them
with the Brethren of the Free Spirit. The same feeling manifested
itself contemporaneously in Germany. The first instance of actual
persecution recorded is a curt notice that, in 1290, the Franciscan
lector at Colnar caused to be arrested two Beghards and two
Beguines, and several others at Basle whom he considered to be
heretics. Two years later the Provincial Council of Mainz, held at
Aschaffenburg, emphatically repeated the condemnation of the
Beghards and Beguines, while other canons regulating the recognized
communities of Beguines show that the distinction was clearly
drawn between those who led a settled life under supervision and
the wandering beggars who disseminated doctrines little understood,
but regarded with suspicion.

It was Henry von Virnenburg, Archbishop of Cologne, however,
who commenced the war against them which was to last so long.
Elected in 1306, he immediately assembled a provincial council, of
which the first two canons are devoted to them with an amplitude
proving how important they were becoming. They wore a long
tabard and tunics with cowls, distinguishing them from the people
at large; they had the hardihood to engage in public disputation
with the Franciscans and Dominicans, and the obstinacy to refuse
to be overcome in argument, and, what was worse, their persistent
beggary was so successful that it sensibly diminished the alms which
were the support of the authorized mendicant. The archbishop
pronounced them excommunicated heretics, to be suppressed by
the secular arm unless they recanted within fifteen days. Yet the
Beghards continued to assail the Mendicants with such ardor and
success that the Franciscans applied for succor to their General,
Gonsalvo. The necessity must have been pressing, for in 1308 he
sent to their assistance the greatest schoolman of the Order, Duns
Scotus. He was received with the enthusiasm which his eminence

merited, but, unfortunately, he died in November of the same year, and the Beghards were able to continue their proselytism without efficient opposition.

This missionary fervor seems to have attracted attention to the sect, leading to special condemnation under the authority of the General Council of Vienne, which was assembled in November 1311. The heresy had evidently been studied with some care, for the first tolerably complete account which we have of its doctrines is embodied in the canon proscribing it. Bishops and inquisitors were ordered to perform their office diligently in tracking all who entertained it, and seeing that they were duly punished unless they would freely abjure. Unfortunately, Clement's zeal was not satisfied with this. The pious women who lived in communities under the name of Beguines were not easily distinguishable from the heretical wanderers. In another canon, therefore, the Beguinages are described as infected with those who dispute about the Trinity and the Divine Essence and disseminate opinions contrary to the faith. These establishments are therefore abolished. At the same time there was evidently a feeling that this was inflicting a wrong, and the canon ends with the contradictory declaration that faithful women, either vowing chastity or not, may live together in houses and devote themselves to penitence and the service of God. There was a lamentable lack of clearness about this which left it for the local prelates to interpret their duty according to their wishes.

The Clementines, or book of canon law containing these provisions, were not issued during Clement's life, and it was not until November 1317 that John XXII, gave them legal force by their authoritative publication. During the interim we hear nothing of persecution, until August 1317, just before the issue of the Clementines, when John of Zurich, Bishop of Strassburg, suddenly took the matter up. He did not act under the canons of Vienne, but under those of 1310 adopted by the Council of Mainz, of which province he was a suffragan; but an allusion to the penalties decreed by the Holy See shows that the action at Vienne was known. He threatened with excommunication all who should not within three days lay aside the distinguishing garments of the sect, and forbade anyone to read or listen to or possess their hymns and writings, which were to be delivered up for burning within 15 days. The fact that among them were many clerks in holy orders, monks, married folks, and others, shows that their opinions were widely held among those who were not mere wandering beggars—the latter probably being merely the missionaries who made converts and administered to the spiritual needs of the faithful. John made a visitation of his diocese, in which he found many of the sectaries. He organized an Inquisition of learned theologians, by whom they were tried; those who recanted were sentenced to wear crosses—the first authentic record in Germany of the use of this penance—and those who were obstinate he handed over to the secular arm to be burned. Multitudes of Beghards fled from the diocese, and in June 1318 the bishop had the satisfaction of reporting his success to his fellow suffragans and urging them to follow his example.

Meanwhile the publication of the Clementines had produced results not corresponding exactly to the intentions of Clement. The canon directed against the heretics received little attention, and five years elapsed before we hear of any serious persecutions under it. The heretics were poor; there were no spoils to tempt episcopal officials to the thankless labor of tracking them and trying them, and few of the bishops had the zeal of John of Zurich. The Beguinages, however, were an easy prey; there was property to be confiscated in reward of intelligent activity. Besides, many of the establishments were under the supervision of the Mendicant Orders, and were virtually or absolutely Tertiary houses, the destruction of which gratified the inextinguishable jealousy between the secular clergy and the Orders. The bishops for the most part, therefore, neglected the saving clause of the canon respecting the Beguinages, and construed literally and pitilessly the orders for their abolition. So eager were they to gratify their vindictiveness against the Mendicants that, when these interfered to save their Tertiaries, they were excommunicated as fautors and defenders of heresy. Thus arose a persecution which, though bloodless, was most deplorable. All through France and Germany and Italy the poor creatures were turned adrift upon the world, without means of support. Those who could, found husbands; many were driven to a life of prostitution.

The Church had declared, in the Great Council of Lateran, that no congregations should be allowed to exist save under some approved Rule. The Beguines had gradually, almost unconsciously, grown up in practical contravention of this canon. The solution of their present difficulties lay in attaching themselves to some recognized Order, and John XXII, in 1319, recognizing the mischief wrought by the heedless legislation of Vienne, promised exemption from further persecution of those who would become Mendicant Tertiaries. Large numbers of them sought this refuge, though their adhesion was more nominal than real. They preserved their self-government, their habits of labor, and their ownership of individual property. In a bull of December 31, 1320, and others of later date, John drew the distinction between those who lived piously and obediently in their houses, and those who wandered around disputing on matters of faith. The former, he is told, amount to 200,-000 in Germany alone, and he bitterly reproached the bishops who were disturbing them on account of the comparatively small number whose misconduct had drawn forth the misinterpreted condemnation of Clement. They are in future to be left in peace. This, at least, put an end, in 1321, to the persecution of those of Strassburg.

The innocent Beguines thus obtained a breathing-space, and the gaps in their ranks were soon filled up. The obnoxious members, however, felt the effects of the Clementine canon as severely as the habitual sloth and indifference of the German prelates in such matters would permit. Archbishop Henry of Cologne was one of the few who manifested an active interest in the matter, and his exertions were rewarded with considerable success. The Lollards and Beghards no longer ventured to show themselves publicly, and in the absence of organized machinery it was not easy to detect them, but in 1322 the archbishop had the good-fortune to capture the most formidable heresiarch of the region. Walter, known as the Lollard, was a Hollander, and was the most active and successful of the Beghard missionaries. He was not an educated man, but he had a keen intelligence and ready eloquence, indefatigable enthusiasm and persuasiveness. His proselyting labors were facilitated by his numerous writings in the vernacular, which were eagerly circulated from hand to hand. He had been busy in Mainz, where he had numerous disciples, and came from there to Cologne, where he chanced to fall into the archbishop's hands. He made no secret of his belief, refused to abjure, and welcomed death in the service of his faith. The severest tortures were vainly employed to force him to reveal the names of his fellow believers; his constancy was unalterable, and he perished in the flames with cheerfulness.

Throughout Westphalia, Bishops Ludwig of Munster, Gottfrid of Osnabruck, Gottfrid of Minden, and Bernhard of Paderborn had been active in eradicating the heresy within their dioceses. In 1335 there were some victims burned in Metz. The Magdeburg Archbishop Otto was of more tolerant temper. In 1336 a number of "Brethren of the Lofty Spirit" were detected in his city, who did not hesitate, under examination, to admit their belief, which to pious ears sounded like the most horrible blasphemy; yet he liberated them after a few days' confinement on their simply recanting their errors verbally. In this same year, however, we have the first instance of a papal inquisitor at work in north Germany. Friar Jordan, an Augustinian eremite, held a commission as inquisitor in both sections of Saxony. He was not well versed in the inquisitorial process, for when at Angermünde in the Uckermark he came upon a nest of Luciferans, he offered them the opportunity of canonical purgation. Fourteen of them failed to procure the requisite number of conjurators, and were duly burned.

Since the disputed election of Louis of Bavaria, in 1314, the relations between the empire and the papacy had been strained. The victory of Mühldorf in 1322, which assured to Louis the sovereignty, had been followed in 1323 by an open rupture with John XXII, after which the strife had been internecine. Each declared his enemy a heretic who had forfeited all rights, and the interdicts which John showered over Germany had been met by Louis with cruel persecution of all ecclesiastics obeying them, wherever he could enforce his power. Such a state of affairs had not been favorable for the persecution of heresy; it may, partially at least, explain the immunity enjoyed in so many places by heretics, and the impossibility of introducing the Inquisition in any form of general organization. Though the papacy assumed that the imperial throne was vacant, and asserted that, during such vacancy, the government of the empire devolved upon the pope, these pretensions could not practically be made good. With the death of Louis in 1347 and the recognition of his rival, Charles IV—the "priest's emperor"—Rome might fairly hope that all obstacles would be removed; that the opposition of the episcopate to the Inquisition would be broken down, and that the field would be open for a persistent and systematic persecution, which would soon relieve Germany of the reproach of toleration. When Clement VI, in 1348, could paternally reprove the young emperor for lack of dignity in the fashion of his garments, which were too short and too tight for his imperial station, the youth could surely be relied upon to obey whatever instructions might be sent him with regard to the suppression of heresy. The same year saw the appointment of John Schandeland, doctor of the Dominican house at Strassburg, as papal Inquisitor for all Germany.

Scarcely, however, had the pope and emperor felt their positions assured, and preparations had been thus made to take advantage of the situation, when a catastrophe supervened which defied all human calculation. The weary fourteenth century was nearing the end of its first half when Europe was scourged with a calamity which might well seem to fulfill all that apocalyptic prophets had threatened of the vengeance of God on the sins of man. In 1347 the plague known as the Black Death invaded Europe from the East, making leisurely progress during 1348 and 1349 through France, Spain, Hungary, Germany, and England. No corner of Europe was spared, and on the high seas it is said that vessels with rich cargoes were found floating, of which the crews had perished to the last man. Boccaccio, as an eyewitness, tells us that the mortality within the walls of Florence from March to July 1348 amounted to 100,000 souls; that in the fields the harvests lay ungathered; that in the city palaces were tenantless and unguarded; that parents forsook children and children parents. In Avignon the mortality was estimated at 100,000; Clement VI shut himself up in his apartments in the sacred palace, where he built large fires to ward off the pestilence, and would allow none to approach him. In Paris 50,000 were said to have perished; in St. Denis 16,000; in Strassburg 16,000. That these figures, though vague, are not improbable, is shown by the case of Béziers, where, in 1348, Mascaro, who was chosen *escudier* to fill a vacancy, records in his diary that all the consuls were carried off, all their *escudiers* or assistants, and all the *clavars* or tax collectors, and that out of every 1,000 inhabitants only 100 escaped. As though Nature did not cause sufficient misery, man contributed his share by an uprising against the Jews. They were accused of causing the plague by poisoning the waters and the pastures, and the blind wrath of the population did not stop to consider that they drank from the same wells as the Christians, and suffered with them in the pestilence. From the Atlantic to Hungary they were tortured and slain with sword and fire. At Erfurt 3,000 are said to have perished, and in Bavaria the number was computed at 12,000.[3]

Such being the tendencies of the age, it is no wonder that the profound emotions caused by the fearful scourge of the Black Death found relief in a gregarious outburst of penitence. Germany had suffered less than the rest of Europe, only one fourth of the population being estimated as perishing, but the religious sensibilities of the people had been stirred by the interdicts against Louis of Bavaria, and the pestilence had been preceded by earthquakes, which were portents of horror. In this state of mental tension it needed but a touch to send an impulse through the whole population. Suddenly, in the spring of 1349, the land was covered with bands of Flagellants, like those whom we have seen nearly a century before, expiating their sins by public scourging. Some said that the example was set in Hungary; others attributed it to different places, but it spread so rapidly that it seemed to be the result of a universal consentaneous impulse. All the proceedings, at least at first, were conducted decently and in order. The Flagellants marched in bands of moderate size, each under a leader and two lieutenants. Beggary was strictly prohibited, and no one was admitted to fellowship who would not promise obedience to the captain, and who had not money to defray his own expenses, though the hospitality universally offered in

[3] Accusations such as were brought against the Jews were no new thing. In 1321 all the lepers throughout Languedoc were burned on the charge that they had been bribed by the Jews to poison the wells. Doubtless torture was employed to obtain the confessions, which were freely made. The story went that the King of Granada, finding himself hard pressed by the Christians, gave great sums to leading Jews to effect in this way the desolation of Christendom. The Jews, fearing that they would be suspected, employed the lepers. Four great councils of lepers were held in various parts of Europe, where every lazar-house was represented except two in England; there the attempt was resolved upon, and the poison was distributed. King Philippe le Long was in Poitou at the time; when the news was brought him he returned precipitately to Paris, whence he issued orders for the seizure of all the lepers of the kingdom. Numbers of them were burned, as well as Jews. At the royal castle of Chinon, near Tours, an immense trench was dug, and filled with blazing wood, where, in a single day, 160 Jews were burned. The royal treasury is said to have acquired 150,000 livres from the property of Jews burned and exiled.

the towns through which they passed was freely accepted to the extent of lodging and meals; but two nights were never to be spent in the same place. Monks and priests, nobles and peasants, women and children were marshalled together in common contrition to placate an offended God. They chanted rude hymns and scourged themselves at stated times, the men stripping to the waist and using a scourge knotted with four iron points, so lustily laid on that an eyewitness says that he had seen two jerks requisite to disengage the point from the flesh. They taught that this exercise, continued for 33½ days, washed from the soul all taint of sin, and rendered the penitent pure as at birth.

From Poland to the Rhine the processions of Flagellants met with little opposition, except in a few towns, such as Erfurt, where the magistrates prohibited their entrance, and in the province of Magdeburg, where Archbishop Otto suppressed them. They spread through Holland and Flanders, but when they invaded France, Philippe de Valois interfered, and they penetrated no farther than Troyes. When the Flagellants of Strassburg proposed to form a permanent confraternity, Charles IV, who was in that city, peremptorily forbade it. Already dangerous characters were attracted to the wandering bands; in many places their zeal had led to the merciless persecution of the Jews, and there were not lacking symptoms of a significant antagonism to the Church, manifesting itself in attacks upon ecclesiastics and clerical property. The Church, in fact, looked askance upon a religious manifestation not of her prescription, and her susceptibilities were not soothed by the daily reading, amid the flagellation, of a letter brought by an angel to the church of St. Peter, in Jerusalem, relating that God, incensed at the non-observance of Sundays and Fridays, had scourged Christendom, and would have destroyed the world but for the intercession of the angels and the Virgin. The Mendicants, who endeavored to discourage this independent popular penitence, incurred the bitterest hostility, which had no scruple in finding expression. On the borders of Misnia two Dominicans who endeavored to reason with a band of Flagellants were set upon with stones; one had sufficient agility to escape, but the other was lapidated to death.

When in Basle about a hundred of the principal citizens organized themselves into a confraternity, and made a flagellating pilgrimage to Avignon, they excited great admiration among the citizens, and most of the cardinals were disposed to think highly of the new penitential discipline. Clement VI penetrated deeper below the surface. The movement bore within it the germ of revolution, as threatening and as dangerous as that of the Poor Men of Lyons, or of any of the sects which had thus far been successfully combated, and self-preservation required its prompt suppression at any cost. From the standpoint of worldly wisdom this reasoning was unanswerable, but members of the Sacred College were obstinate. They prevailed upon Clement not to execute his first intention of casting the Flagellants into prison, and the discussion on the policy to be pursued must have been protracted, for it was not until October 20, 1349, that the papal bull of condemnation was issued. All prelates were ordered to suppress them forthwith; those who refused obedience were to be imprisoned until further orders, and the aid of the secular arm was to be called upon if necessary.

Clement was correct in his anticipation of the effects of the new discipline on the minds of the faithful. When the subject came up for discussion at the Council of Constance in 1417, and San Vicente Ferrer was inclined to regard it with favor, Gerson took him delicately to task and wrote a tract to show the evils resulting from the practice. Experience, he said, had shown that the members of the sect of Flagellants were led to look with contempt on sacramental confession and the sacrament of penitence, for they exalted their peculiar form of penance, not only over that prescribed by the Church, but even over martyrdom, because they shed their own blood, while the blood of martyrs was shed by others.

This shows that the practice had risen to the rank of a new heresy. When Clement's bull was received by the German prelates they fully comprehended the dangers which it sought to avert, and addressed themselves vigorously to its enforcement. The Flagellants were denounced from the pulpit as an impious sect, condemned by the Holy See. Those who would humbly return to the Church would be received to mercy, while the obdurate would be made to experience the full rigor of the canons. This thinned the ranks considerably, but there were enough persistent ones to furnish a new harvest of martyrs. Even ecclesiastics could not be prevented from adhering to the obnoxious sect. William of Gennep, Archbishop of Cologne, in a provincial council excommunicated all clerks who joined the Flagellants; yet this was so completely disregarded that in his vernal synod of 1353 he was obliged to order all deans and rectors of churches to make provision for the public excommunication by name of all the disobedient, to be followed within a fortnight by their suspension. It is not to be doubted that the Brethren of the Free Spirit took full advantage of the excitement prevailing in men's minds, and of the upturning which resulted, both spiritually and socially. When the bands of Flagellants first made their appearance they were joined in many places, we are told, by the heretics known as Lollards, Beghards, and Cellites. Involved in common persecution, they grew to have common interests, and they became too intimately associated together not to lend each other mutual support.

Thus far the faith had not gained the advantage which had naturally been expected to follow the undisputed domination of the pious Charles IV. At the end of 1352 Innocent VI ascended the papal throne and promptly repeated the attempt to introduce the papal Inquisition in Germany by renewing, in July 1353, the commission as inquisitor of Friar John Schandeland, and writing earnestly to the German prelates to lend him all assistance. That Innocent's attempt to introduce the Inquisition proved a failure may be gathered from the action of William of Gennep, in his vernal synod of Cologne in 1357. While deploring the increase of the pernicious sect of Beghards, which threatens to infect his whole city and diocese, he makes no allusion whatever to the papal Inquisition and the canons. All parish priests are directed to proceed against the heretics, and excommunication is pronounced against those who aid the Beghards with alms.

In 1367 Urban V returned to the work by commissioning two Inquisitors for Germany, the Dominicans Louis of Willenberg and Walter Kerlinger, with powers to appoint vicars. The Beghards were the only heretics alluded to as the object of their labors; prelates and magistrates were ordered to lend their assistance and to place all prisons at their disposal until the German Inquisition should have such places of its own. The choice of inquisitors was shrewd. Of Friar Louis we hear little, but Friar Walter (variously named Kerling, Kerlinger, Krelinger, and Keslinger) was a man of influence, a chaplain and favorite of the emperor, who had the temper of a per-

secutor and the ambition to magnify his office. In 1369 he became
Dominican Provincial of Saxony, and continued to perform the
duplicate functions until his death in 1373. He lost no time in getting to work, for in 1368 we hear of a Beghard burned in Erfurt, and
to his unwearied exertions is generally attributed the temporary
suppression of the sect.

Still there was at first no appearance of any hearty support
from either the spiritual or temporal potentates of Germany, and
without this the business of persecution could only languish. When,
however, the emperor made his Italian expedition, in 1368, the
opportunity was utilized to arouse him to a sense of his neglected
duties. It was rare indeed for an emperor to have the cordial support
of the papacy, and we may reasonably assume that Charles was
made to see that through their union the Inquisition might be
rendered serviceable to both in breaking down the independence
of the great prince-bishops. Thus when that institution was falling
into desuetude in the lands of its birth, it was for the first time
regularly organized in Germany and given a substantive existence.
From Lucca, on June 9 and 10, 1369, the emperor issued two edicts,
which excel all previous legislation in the unexampled support accorded to inquisitors. All prelates, princes, and magistrates are ordered to expel and treat as outlaws the sect of Beghards and Beguines,
commonly known as *Wilge Armen* or *Conventschwestern*, who beg
with the vainly prohibited formula, *"Brod durch Gott!"* At the
command of Walter Kerlinger and his vicars or other inquisitors,
all who give alms to the proscribed class shall be arrested and so
punished as to serve as a terror to others. Moreover, all inquisitors
are taken under the special imperial favor and protection. All the
powers, privileges, liberties, and immunities granted to them by
preceding emperors or by the rulers of any other land are conferred
upon them, and confirmed, notwithstanding any laws or customs to
the contrary. To enforce these privileges, two dukes (Saxony and
Brunswick), two counts (Schwartzenberg and Nassau), and two
knights (Hanstein and Witzeleyeven) are appointed conservators
and guardians, with instructions to act whenever complaint is made
to them by the inquisitors. They shall see that one-third of the confiscations are handed over to the Inquisition, and shall proceed
directly and fearlessly against anyone impeding or molesting it in

any manner, making examples of them, both in person and property. Besides this, anyone impeding or molesting any of the inquisitors or their agents, directly or indirectly, openly or secretly, is declared punishable with confiscation of all property for the benefit of the imperial treasury, and deprivation of all honors, dignities, privileges, and immunities.

These portentous edicts provided for the personnel of the Inquisition and the exercise of its powers, but to render it a permanent institution there were still lacking houses in which it could hold its tribunals, and prisons in which to keep its captives. The imperial resources were not adequate to this, and nothing was to be expected from the piety of princes and prelates. Somebody must be despoiled for its benefit—somebody too defenseless to resist, yet possessed of property sufficient to be tempting. These conditions were exactly filled by the orthodox Beghards and Beguines, who, since their temporary persecution after the publication of the Clementines, had continued to prosper and to enjoy the donations of the pious. A week after the issue of the edicts just described, another was published in which these poor creatures are described as cultivating a sacrilegious poverty, and their communities, if left undisturbed, will become seminaries of error. Moreover, the Inquisition has no house, domicile, or strong tower for the detention of the accused and for the perpetual incarceration of those who abjure, whereby many heretics remain unpunished. Therefore the houses of the Beghards are given to the Inquisition to be converted into prisons; those of the Beguines are ordered to be sold and the proceeds divided into thirds, one part being assigned to repairing roads and the walls of the towns, another to be given to inquisitors, to be expended on pious uses, among which is included the maintenance of prisoners. But three days' notice is given to the victims prior to expulsion from their homes.

If the Inquisition could have been permanently established in Germany this unscrupulous measure would have accomplished the object. Between the imperial favor and Kerlinger's energy it at last had a fair start. The last edict alludes to two additional inquisitors whom Kerlinger was authorized to appoint and to his successful labors, by which the heretic Brethren of the Free Spirit had been completely destroyed in the provinces of Magdeburg and Bremen, and in Thuringia, Hesse, Saxony, and elsewhere. Probably this is exaggerated, but we learn from other sources that Kerlinger was zealously active and that his labors were rewarded with success. In Magdeburg and Erfurt he burned a number of heretics and forced the rest to outward conformity or to flight. We hear of him at Nordhausen in 1369, where he captured 40 Beghards; of these 7 were obdurate and were burned, and the rest abjured and accepted penance. This is probably a fair example of his work, and we may believe Gregory XI when, in 1372, he says that the Inquisition had destroyed heresy and heretics in the central provinces and driven them to the outlying districts of Brabant, Holland, Stettin, Breslau, and Silesia, where they are gathered in such multitudes that they hope to be able to maintain themselves; wherefore he earnestly calls upon the prelates and nobles to bring the good work to an end by efficiently supporting the Holy Office in its final labors. Apparently Kerlinger had not been anxious to divide his authority by exercising his power to appoint two additional colleagues, and Gregory now intervened to relieve him of this duty and place the German Inquisition on a permanent footing by assimilating its organization to that of the institution elsewhere. He increased the number of inquisitors to five and placed their appointment and removal in the hands of the Dominican master and provincial, or either of them. Kerlinger and Louis, however, were to remain as two of the five, and no power, whether imperial or episcopal, should have authority to interfere with the free exercise of their functions.

A further extension of the power of the Inquisition granted by Charles IV was of no great importance at the time, but has the highest interest to us as the first indication of what was to come. A leading feature of the Beghard propaganda was the circulation among the laity of written tracts and devotional works. Composed in the vernacular, they reached a class which was not wholly illiterate and yet was unable to profit by the orthodox works of which Latin was the customary vehicle. For the suppression of this method of missionary work the Inquisition was entrusted with a censorship of literature, to which further reference will be made hereafter. Less interesting to us, but probably more important at the time, was the permission granted to the inquisitors to appoint notaries. This concession was looked upon as a special favor.

As regards the seizure of the Beguinages, it was ruthlessly carried out by Kerlinger. Those of Mühlhausen had been very flourishing, and on February 16, 1370, four of them were delivered by him to the magistrates to be converted to public uses—probably the city's share of the plunder. It would seem, however, that obstacles were thrown in his way. As these houses were benevolent gifts for pious uses the bishops could assert them to be under their jurisdiction and not subject to an imperial edict; nobles and citizens, moreover, had been trained to regard their inoffensive inmates with favor, and were not eager to share in the spoils. Whatever may have been their motives, Kerlinger could not have found the way open to the general confiscation that he desired. In 1371 he was obliged to petition Gregory XI, reciting the existence of heretics called Beghards and Beguines, and the imperial edict confiscating their conventicles, the confirmation of which he desired. There was nothing to lead Gregory to suppose that there was in this anything but the well-understood confiscation of heretical property, and he willingly gave the desired confirmation.

Although the Brethren of the Free Spirit were the chief objects of this inquisitorial activity, the Flagellants were not neglected. In 1369 we hear of an outbreak of women coming from Hungary, which was summarily suppressed in Saxony. In 1372 Flagellants reappeared in various parts of Germany, asserting the peculiar efficacy of their penance as replacing the sacraments of the Church, so that Gregory XI felt it necessary to direct the inquisitors to exterminate them. In 1373 and 1374 this irrepressible tendency took a new shape, known as the Dancing Mania, which broke out at the consecration of a church in Aix-la-Chapelle. Bands of both sexes, mostly consisting of poor and simple folk, poured into Flanders from the Rhinelands, dancing and singing as though possessed by the Furies. Under intense spiritual excitement the performer would leap and dance until he fell to earth with convulsions, when his comrades would revive him by jumping upon him, or a cloth which he wore, tied around the belly, would be tightly twisted with a stick. This was generally looked upon as a kind of demoniacal possession until a multitude of these dancers assembled at Herestal and consulted together as to the best plan for slaying all the priests, canons, and clergy of Liège, when the madness was recognized as no longer harmless. Though not in itself a heresy, it led in some places to heretical opinions on the sacraments, for it was popularly explained by attributing it to defective baptism, caused by the universal practice among priests of keeping concubines.

Scarce had the Inquisition been fairly organized and had settled to its work, when its arbitrary proceedings awakened active opposition. As the heretic Beghards and Beguines were the principal objects of its activity, and the orthodox ones of its cupidity, the sufferings of the latter speedily awoke compassion which found expression in terms so decided that Gregory XI could not refuse to listen. Accordingly, in April 1374, he wrote to the Archbishops of Mainz, Trèves, and Cologne, reciting these complaints and ordering a report about the life of the persons concerned, who should be protected and cherished if innocent, and be punished if guilty. At least from Cologne and Worms, probably from the other prelates, came answers that the persecuted communities were composed of faithful Catholics. In Cologne the magistrates intervened and complained energetically to the pope that a Dominican inquisitor was vexing the poor folk, and they asked that his proceedings be stopped. The victims, they said, were people of little culture, who were interrogated with questions so difficult that the most skillful theologians could scarce answer them, while their edifying lives had led the clergy to protect them against the threats of the Inquisition. Proceedings were thus checked, but still the peculiar garments which the devotees had always worn furnished an excuse for continued persecution, and another appeal was made to Gregory, to which he responded in December 1377 by ordering the prelates not to permit their molestation on this account so long as they were good Catholics and obedient to the ecclesiastical authorities. The German bishops were thus fully armed with papal authority to restrict the operations of the inquisitors, and those who, like Bishop Lambert of Strassburg, were themselves disposed to persecution, did not dare to proceed further. The regular communities of Beghards and Beguines were assured of toleration, and if the heretical Brethren of the Free Spirit managed to share in this immunity, it probably did not give the prelates much concern.

All this was discouraging to the zeal of inquisitors, whose institution had hardly yet taken root in the land, but worse was still to

follow. In 1378 both Gregory XI and Charles IV died. The election
of Urban VI gave rise to the Great Schism, and Wenceslas, the son
and successor of Charles, was notoriously indifferent to the interest of
religion as represented by the Church. Thus deprived of its two
indispensable supporters, the Inquisition could not make head against
episcopal jealousy. Still, it did not entirely pretermit its labors. In
1392 we hear of a papal inquisitor named Martin who travelled
through Suabia to Würzburg, finding in the latter place a number
of peasants belonging to the sect of Flagellants and Beghards. They
had not in them the stuff of martyrs, and accepted the penance imposed upon them of joining in a crusade then preaching against the
Turks—the first time for nearly a century that we meet with this
penalty. Then Martin went to Erfurt—always a heretical center—
where he came upon numerous heretics of the same kind. Some of
these were obstinate and were duly burned, others accepted penance,
and the rest sought safety in flight.

About this period, after a long interval, we again become cognizant of the existence of Waldenses. The Beghards had succeeded
in concentrating upon themselves the attention of the papal and
episcopal inquisitions, and the followers of Peter Waldo had remained unnoticed, doubtless owing their safety to outward conformity, though by absenting themselves from their parishes about
the Eastertide they sometimes managed to escape taking communion
for five or six years in succession. Thus laboring quietly and peacefully, preaching by night in cellars, mills, and other retired places,
they gained numerous converts among the peasants and artisans, who
saw in the sanctity of their lives, as sadly admitted by the so-called
Peter of Pilichdorf, the strongest contrast with the scandalous license
of the clergy. About 1390 they were discovered in Mainz, where for
a hundred years they had lurked undisturbed. The archbishop,
Conrad II, kept the matter in his own hands. In 1392 he issued
a commission, as espiscopal inquisitors, to Frederic, Bishop of Toul,
Nicholas of Saulheim, the Dean of St. Stephen, and John Wasmod,
of Homburg, a priest of the cathedral, to whom the papal inquisitor
could adjoin himself if he so chose. These inquisitors were armed
with full authority to arrest, try, torture, sentence, and abandon to
the secular arm all heretics, and were instructed to proceed in accordance with the practice of the Inquisition. A number of Waldenses

were already in the episcopal prison, and they made diligent perquisition after the rest. By free use of torture they obtained the necessary
avowals and evidence. Those who were obstinate were handed over
to the secular arm, and an *auto de fé* celebrated at Bingen in 1392,
where 36 wretches were burned, proved that the papal Inquisition
itself could not have been more effective.

When attention was once attracted to this secret heresy, it was
not long before Waldenses were discovered everywhere. In a short
list of them, dated 1391, Poland, Hungary, Bavaria, Suabia, and
Saxony are represented. The author of the tract which passes under
the name of Peter of Pilichdorf, who took an energetic part both
with the pen and in action in suppressing this suddenly discovered
heresy, informs us, in 1395, that the Netherlands, Westphalia,
Prussia, and Poland were not infected with it, while Thuringia,
Misnia, Bohemia, Moravia, Austria, and Hungary numbered their
heretics by thousands. Curiously enough, in this list he omits
Pomerania, where, along the Baltic regions, the Waldenses were
thickly scattered from Stettin to Königsberg. The heresy had been
deeply rooted there for at least a century, and the local priesthood seem to have borne no ill-will to the harmless sectaries, who
conformed outwardly to the orthodox observances. Even when in
confession intimations of the heresy escaped, as sometimes happened,
they were wisely and mercifully overlooked. They had long been
unmolested when one of their ministers, known as Brother Klaus,
who had visited them in 1391 and had heard many confessions, apparently became frightened at the movement against them. He
apostatized, and seems to have betrayed the names of his penitents.
The Church made haste to secure the fruits of his repentance.
Brother Peter, Provincial of the Celestinian Order, was appointed
papal inquisitor, and early in 1393 he came to Stettin armed with
full powers from the Archbishop of Prague and the Bishops of
Lebus and Camin to represent them. He issued citations, both general
ones from the pulpits of the infected region, and special summonses
to individuals. This naturally caused great excitement, and some
of the suspects fled. Friar Peter was lenient with those who spontaneously confessed and abjured; all took the oaths, including that
of persecuting heretics, with only an occasional manifestation of

hesitancy. Torture seems to have been unnecessary; there was no exhibition of obstinacy, and no burnings.

From Pomerania, Friar Peter hastened to the south, where he found Waldenses as numerous, and less inclined to submission. He has left a brief memorial of his labors, written in 1395, in which he expresses his fears that the heresy would become dominant, as the Waldenses were resorting to force, and were employing arson and homicide to intimidate the orthodox. His only evidence of this, however, is that on September 8, those of Steyer, to punish the parish priest for receiving the inquisitors in his house, burned his barn, and affixed to the town gates, by night, a warning in the shape of a half-burned brand and a bloody knife. This offense was cruelly avenged, for in 1397 at Steyer more than 100 Waldenses of either sex were burned. In this relentless persecution the case of a child of ten condemned to wear crosses shows how unsparing were the tribunals, while others in which the culprits were burned for relapse, having already abjured before the inquisitor, Henry of Olmütz, indicate that this was not the first effort made to exterminate the heresy.

There evidently was ample work for the Inquisition in Germany, but it seems to have been more anxious to repair its defeat in the contests with the Beghards than to operate against the Waldenses. To some extent the bishops and most of the inquisitors joined in this, but the suspects had friends among the prelates, who wrote, towards the close of 1393, to Boniface IX, eulogizing their piety, obedience, and good works, and asking protection for them. To this Boniface responded, January 7, 1394, in a brief addressed to the German prelates, ordering them to investigate whether these persons are contaminated with the errors condemned by Clement V and John XXII, and whether they follow any reproved religious Order; if not, they are to be efficiently protected. The Inquisition did not remain passive under this interference with its operations. It represented to Boniface that for a hundred years heresies had lurked under the outward fair-seeming of the Beghards and Beguines, in consequence of which, almost every year, obstinate heretics had been burned in the different cities of the empire, and that their suppression was impeded by certain papal constitutions which were urged in their protection. Boniface was easily moved to reversing his recent action, and by a bull of January 31, 1395, he restored to vigor the decrees of Urban V, Gregory XI, and Charles IV, under which he ordered the Inquisition to prosecute earnestly the Beghards, Lollards, and Zwestriones. This gave full power to molest the orthodox associations as well as the heretic Brethren of the Free Spirit, and a severe storm of persecution burst over them. Even some of the bishops joined in this, as appears from a synod held in Magdeburg about this time, which ordered the priests to excommunicate and expel them. Yet this again aroused their friends, and Boniface was induced to reissue his bull with an addition which, like the contradictory provisions of the Clementines, shows the perplexity caused by the admixture of orthodoxy and heresy among the Beguines. After repeating his commands for their suppression, he adds that there are pious organizations known as Beghards, Lollards, and Zwestriones, which shall be permitted to wear their vestments, to beg, and to continue their mode of life, excommunication being threatened against any inquisitor who shall molest them, unless they have been convicted by the Ordinaries of the diocese.

This left the matter very much to the discretion of the local authorities, but the Inquisition made haste to fortify its position. Under pretext that the bulls of Gregory XI were becoming worn by age and use, it procured their renewal from Boniface IX, in 1395, though the pope is careful to express that he grants no new privileges. In 1399 it succeeded in having the number of inquisitors increased to six for the Dominican province of Saxony alone, on the plea that its wide extent and populous cities rendered the existing force insufficient. A few weeks later Boniface issued another bull, ordering the prelates and secular rulers of Germany to give all aid and protection to Friar Eylard Schöneveld and other inquisitors, and especially to lend the use of their prisons, as the Inquisition in those parts is said to have none of its own, which shows that Kerlinger's scheme of obtaining them from the property of the Beghards had not proved a success.

With the year 1400 the comparative peace which the Beguines had enjoyed for some fifteen years came to an end. Their most dreaded enemy was the Dominican John of Mühlberg, whose purity of life and energy in battling with the moral and spiritual errors of his time won him a wide reputation throughout Germany, so that when he died in exile, driven from Basle by the clergy whom his attacks had embittered, he was long regarded by the people as a saint and a martyr. About 1400 he stirred up in Basle a struggle with the Beguines, which for ten years kept the city in an uproar. Primarily an episode in the hostility between the Dominicans and Franciscans, it extended to the clergy and magistrates, and finally to the citizens at large. In 1405 the Beguines were expelled, but the Franciscans obtained from the papacy bulls ordering them restoration, and the retraction of all that had been said against them. At last, in 1411, Bishop Humbert and the town council, excited by a fiery sermon of John Pastoris, abolished the associations, which were forced to abandon their living in common and their vestments, or to leave the place. The city of Berne followed this example, and the magistrates of Strassburg took the same course, when some of the Beguines adopted the former alternative and some the latter. Many of these took refuge secretly at Mainz. They were discovered, and the Archbishop John II, holding them to be heretics, ordered them to be prosecuted. The matter was entrusted to Master Henry von Stein, who set vigorously about it. The refugees from Strassburg, mostly women, were thrown into prison; we also hear of a nun who was incarcerated, and of a youth from Rotenburg, who was mounted on a hogshead in the public square, and in the presence of the populace was obliged to accept the penance of crosses.

Gerson's numerous allusions to the Turelupins and Beghards show that at this period the sect was regarded as seductively dangerous. With all his tendency to mysticism, Gerson could recognize the peril incurred by those whom he describes as deceived through too great a desire to reach the sweetness of God, and who mistake the delirium of their own hearts for divine promptings. He was especially averse to the spiritual intimacy between the sexes, where devotion screened the precipice on the brink of which they stood. Mary of Valenciennes, he says, was especially to be avoided on this account, for she applied what is set forth about the divine fruition to the passions seething in her own soul, and she argues that he who reaches the perfection of divine love is released from the observance of all precepts. Thus the Brethren of the Free Spirit were practically the same in the fifteenth century as in the times of Ortlieb and Amauri.

Giles Cantor, who founded in Brussels the sect which styled

itself Men of Intelligence, was probably a disciple of Mary of Valenciennes, and the name was adopted merely to cover its affiliation with the proscribed Brethren of the Free Spirit. Its doctrines were substantially the same in their mystic pantheism and Illuminism; and their practical application is seen in the story that on one occasion Giles was moved by the spirit to go naked for some miles when carrying provision to a poor person. So open a manifestation would have ensured his prosecution had there been any machinery for persecution in Brabant; but he was allowed to propagate his doctrines in peace untill he died. He was succeeded in the leadership of the sect by a Carmelite known as William of Hilderniss, and at length it attracted, in 1411, the attention of Cardinal Peter d'Ailly, Bishop of Cambrai. Fortunately for William, the bishop chose to direct the proceedings himself, and they show complete disregard of inquisitorial methods. He appointed special commissioners, who made an inquisition; both the names and the testimony of the witnesses were submitted to William, who made what defense he could. In rendering judgment d'Ailly called in the Dominican Prior of St. Quentin, who was inquisitor of the district of Cambrai, and the sentence was as irregular as the proceedings. William had no desire for martyrdom, and abjured the heresy; he was required to purge himself with six compurgators, after which he was to undergo the penance of three years' confinement in a castle of the bishop's, while if he failed in his purgation he was to be imprisoned in a convent of his Order during the archbishop's pleasure—a most curious and illogical medley. He succeeded in finding the requisite number of compurgators, but though he disappeared from the scene his sect was by no means extinguished, and we hear of the persecution of a heresiarch as late as 1428.

That Clement VI did not err when he foresaw the dangerous errors lurking under the devotion of the Flagellants was demonstrated in 1414. The sect still existed, and its crude theories on the efficacy of flagellation had gradually been developed into an antisacerdotal heresy of the most uncompromising character. A certain Conrad Schmidt was the constructive heresiarch who gave to its belief an organized completeness, and his death made no diminution of the zeal of his disciples, nor did the failure of his prophecy of the end of the world in 1369. The curious connection between the Flagellants and the Beghards is indicated by the fact that these Flagellant Brethren, or Brethren of the Cross, as they styled themselves, regarded Conrad as the incarnation of Enoch, and a certain Beghard who had been burned at Erfurt about 1364, as Elias—an angel having brought their souls from heaven and infused them into Schmidt and this Beghard while yet in the womb. Schmidt was to preside at the approaching Day of Judgment, which was constantly believed to be at hand, Antichrist being the pope and the priests, whose reign was drawing to an end.

Conrad Schmidt had promulgated his errors in Thuringia, where his sectaries were discovered in 1414 at Sangerhausen. Thither sped the Inquisitor Schöneveld—called Henry by the chroniclers, but probably the same as the Eylard. The princes of Thuringia and Misnia were ordered to assist him, and they were eager to share in the suppression of a heresy which threatened to revolutionize the social order. Before Schöneveld left the scene of action he had caused the burning of 91 at Sangerhausen, 44 in the neighboring town of Winkel, and many more in other villages. Yet such was the persistence of the heresy that even this wholesale slaughter did not suffice for its suppression. Two years later its remains were discovered, and again Schöneveld was sent for. To those who abjured he assigned penances, and handed over the obstinate to the secular arm. His assizes must have been hurried, for he did not stay to witness the execution of those whom he had condemned, and after his departure the princes gathered all together, both penitents and impenitents, some 300 in number, and burned the whole of them in one day. This terrible example produced the profound impression that was desired, and hereafter the sect of Flagellants may be regarded as unimportant.

From this time forward the attention of the Church was mainly directed to Hussitism, the most formidable enemy that it had encountered since the Catharism of the twelfth century. Yet the attention of the persecutors was not so exclusively directed to the Hussites as to allow the Brethren of the Free Spirit to escape, and in their zeal they continued to molest the orthodox Beguines in spite of the action of Martin V at Constance. In 1431 Eugenius IV found himself obliged to intervene for their protection. In a bull, addressed to the German prelates, he recites the favorable action of his predecessors and the troubles to which, in spite of this, they were exposed by the inquisitors. Those who wander around without fixed habitations he orders to be compelled to dwell in the houses of the confraternity, and those who reside quietly and piously are to be efficiently protected. The bishops are authorized to enforce its provisions by the censures of the Church, without appeal, even if those who interfere with the Beguines enjoy special immunities, thus subjecting the inquisitors to excommunication by the prelates. This stretch of papal power exasperated Doctor Felix Hemmerlin, Cantor of Zurich, who detested the Beguines. He wrote several bitter tracts against them, and explained the favor shown them by Eugenius by irreverently stating that the pope had himself been once a Beghard at Padua. In one of his numerous assaults upon them, written probably about 1436, he alludes to several recent cases within a limited region, which would indicate that in spite of the papal protection of the Beguines, the Brethren of the Free Spirit were actively persecuted, and that, if the statistics of the whole empire could be procured, the number of victims would be found not small. In Zurich a certain Burchard and his disciples were tried and penanced with crosses but they were subsequently found to be relapsed and were all burned. In Würtemberg there was a great heresiarch punished, whose conviction was only secured after infinite pains. Then from Bohemia there come Beghards every year who seduce a countless number to heresy in Berne and Soleure. This leads one to think that Hemmerlin, in his passion, may confound Hussites with Beghards, and this is confirmed by his assertion that there is in Upper Germany no heresy save that introduced by the foxes of this pernicious sect. Nider, writing immediately after the Council of Basle had effected a settlement with the Hussites, declares that heretics were few and powerless, skulking in concealment and not to be dreaded, although he had, in describing the errors of the Brethren of the Free Spirit, stated that they were still by no means uncommon in Suabia.

In 1446 the Council of Würzburg found it necessary to repeat the canon of that of Mainz in 1310, ordering the expulsion of all wandering Beghards using the old cry of *"Brod durch Gott"* and preaching in caverns and secret places, showing the maintenance of the traditional customs and also the absence of more active persecution. In 1453 Nicholas V formally adjoined them to the Mendicant Orders as Tertiaries. Some of them obeyed and formed a distinct class, known as Zepperenses, from their principal house at Zepper. They diminished greatly in number, however, and in 1650 Innocent X united them with the Tertiaries of Italy, under the General Master residing in Lombardy. The female portion of the associations, which became distinctively known as Beguines, were more fortunate. They were able to preserve their identity and their communities, which remain flourishing to the present day, especially in the Netherlands, where in 1857 the great Beguinage of Ghent contained 600 Beguines and 200 *locataires* or boarders.

It was impossible that Hussitism should triumph in Bohemia without awakening an echo throughout Germany, or that the Hussites should abstain from missionary and proselyting efforts. In 1423 the Council of Siena, under the presidency of papal legates, showed itself fully alive to the danger. It sharply reproved both inquisitors and episcopal Ordinaries for the supineness which alone could explain the threatening spread of heresy. The earnest tone of the council reflects the alarm that was everywhere felt, and it unquestionably led to renewed exertions, though only a few instances of successful activity chance to be recorded. In 1420, a priest, known as Henry Grünfeld, who had embraced Hussite doctrines, was burned at Ratisbon, where also in 1423 another priest named Henry Rathgeber met the same fate. Even after the Council of Basle had recognized the Hussites as orthodox, they were still persecuted as heretics elsewhere. About 1450 John Müller ventured to preach Hussite doctrines throughout Franconia, where he gained a numerous following, but he was forced to fly, and 130 of his disciples were seized and carried to Würzburg. There they were persuaded to recant by the Abbot John of Grumbach and Master Anthony, a preacher of the cathedral. More tragic was the fate of Frederic Reiser, a Suabian, educated in Waldensianism. Under the guise of a merchant he had served as a preacher among the Waldensian churches which maintained a secret existence throughout Germany. At Heilsbronn he was captured in a Hussite raid, when, carried to Mount Tabor, he recognized the practical identity of the faiths and received ordination at the hands of the Taborite Bishop Nicholas. He labored to bring about a union of the churches, and wandered as a missionary through Germany, Bohemia, and Switzerland. Finally he settled at Strassburg and gathered a community of disciples around him. He called himself "Frederic, by the grace of God bishop of the faithful in the Roman Church who spurn the Donation of Constantine." He was detected in 1458 and arrested with his followers. Under torture he confessed all that was required of him, only to withdraw it when removed from the torture chamber. The burgomaster, Hans Drachenfels, and the civic magistracy earnestly opposed his execution, but they were obliged to yield, and he was burned, together with his faithful servant, Anna Weiler, an old woman of Nürnberg.

Reiser had been especially successful with the descendants of the Pomeranian Waldenses who abjured before the Inquisitor Peter in 1393. They appear to have by no means abandoned their heresy, and were easily brought to the modifications which assimilated them to the Hussites—the adoption of bishops, priests, and deacons, the communion in both elements, and the honoring of Wickliff, Huss, and Jerome of Prague. In 1458, a tailor of Selchow, named Matthew Hagen, was arrested with three disciples and carried to Berlin for trial by order of the Elector Frederic II. He had been ordained as a priest in Bohemia by Reiser, and had returned to propagate the doctrines of the sect and administer its sacraments. His followers weakened and abjured, but he remained steadfast, and was abandoned to the secular arm.

There was, in fact, enough in common between the doctrines of the more radical Hussites and those of the Waldenses to bring the sects eventually together. The Waldenses had by no means been extirpated, and when, in 1467, the remnant of the Taborites known as the Bohemian Brethren opened communication with them, the envoys sent had no difficulty in finding them on the confines between Austria and Moravia, where they had existed for more than two centuries. They had a bishop named Stephen, who speedily called in another bishop to perform the rite of ordination for the Brethren, showing that the heretic communities were numerous and well organized. The negotiations unfortunately attracted attention, and the Church made short work of those on whom it could lay its hands. Bishop Stephen was burned at Vienna and the flock was scattered, many of them finding refuge in Moravia.

Others fled as far as Brandenburg, where already there were flourishing Waldensian communities. These were soon afterwards discovered, and steel, fire, and water were unsparingly used for their destruction, without blotting them out. A portion of those who escaped emigrated to Bohemia, where they were gladly received by the Bohemian Brethren and incorporated into their societies. The close association thus formed between the Brethren and the Waldenses resulted in a virtual coalescence which gave rise to a new word in the nomenclature of heresy. When, in 1479, Sixtus IV confirmed Friar Thomas Gognati as Inquisitor of Vienna, he urged him to put forth every exertion to suppress the Hussites and Nicolinistæ. These latter, who took their name from Nicholas of Silesia, were evidently Bohemian Brethren who adhered to the extreme doctrine common to both sects, that nothing could justify putting a human being to death.

Signs, indeed, were not wanting in the fifteenth century of the inevitable rupture of the sixteenth. Prominent among those who boldly defied the power of Rome was Gregory of Heimburg, whom Ullman designates as the citizen-Luther of the fifteenth century. He first comes into view at the Council of Basle, in the service of Æneas Sylvius (later Pius II), who was then one of the foremost advocates of the reforming party, and he remained steadfast to the principles which his patron bartered for the papacy. A forerunner of the Humanists, he labored to diffuse classical culture, and with his admiration for the ancients he had imbibed the imperial theory of the relations between Church and State. The power of the keys, he taught, had been granted to the apostles collectively; these were represented by general councils, and the monopoly in the hands of the pope was a usurpation. His free expression of opinion infallibly brought him into collision with his early patron, and the antagonism was sharpened when Pius II convoked the assembly of princes at Mantua to provide for a new crusade. Gregory, who was there as counsellor of the princes, boldly declared that this was only a scheme to augment the papal power and drain all Germany of money. When Nicholas of Cusa was appointed Bishop of Brixen and claimed property and rights regarded by Sigismund of Austria as belonging to himself, Sigismund, under Gregory's advice, arrested the bishop. Thereupon Pius, in June 1460, laid Sigismund's territories under interdict, and induced the Swiss to attack him. Gregory drew up an appeal to a general council, which Sigismund issued, although Pius had forbidden such appeals, and he further had the hardihood to prove by Scripture, the fathers, and history, that the Church was subject to the State. It was no wonder that Gregory shared his master's excommunication. In October 1460 he was declared a heretic, and all of the faithful were ordered to seize his property and punish him. To this he responded in vigorous appeals and replications, couched in the most insolent and contemptuous language towards both Pius and Nicholas. In October 1461, Pius sent Friar Martin of Rotenburg to preach the faith and preserve the faithful from the errors of Sigismund and his heresiarch Gregory, and he offered an indulgence of two years and eighty days to all who would render him assistance in his need. He also ordered the magistrates of Nürnburg to seize Gregory's property and expel him or deliver him up for punishment. We next find Gregory aiding Diether, Archbishop of Cologne, in his quarrel with Pius over the demand of the Holy See for annates; but Diether resigned, Sigismund made his peace, and Gregory was abandoned to his excommunication, even the city of Nürnburg withdrawing its protection. He then took refuge in Bohemia with George Podiebrad, whom he served efficiently as a controversialist, earning a special denunciation as a heretic of the worst type from Paul II, in 1469. Podiebrad died in 1471 and Gregory then went to Saxony, where Duke Albert protected him and effected his reconciliation with Sixtus IV. He was absolved at Easter, 1472, only to die in the following August, after spending a quarter of a century in ceaseless combat with the papacy.

If Gregory of Heimburg embodies the revolt of the ruling classes against Rome, Hans of Niklaushausen shows us the restless spirit of opposition to sacerdotalism which was spreading among the lower strata of society. Hans Böheim was a wandering drummer or fifer from Bohemia, who chanced to settle at Niklaushausen, near Würzburg. He began to have revelations from the Virgin which suited so exactly the popular wishes that crowds speedily assembled to listen to him. She instructed him to announce to her people that Christ could no longer endure the pride, the avarice, and the lust of the priesthood, and that the world would be destroyed in consequence of their wickedness unless they promptly showed signs of amendment. As the fame of these revelations spread, crowds flocked to hear the inspired teacher, from the Rhinelands, Bavaria, Thuringia, Saxony, and Misnia, so that at times he addressed an audience of 20,000 to 30,000 souls. They were peaceful and orderly; men and women slept in the neighboring fields and woods and caves without fear of robbery or violence; they had money to spend, moreover, for the offerings of gold and silver, jewels, garments, and wax were large—large enough, indeed, to tempt the greed of the potentates, for after the downfall of Hans the spoils were divided between the Count of Wertheim, suzerain of Niklaushausen, the Bishop of Würzburg, and his metropolitan, the Archbishop of Mainz.

Bishop Rudolph of Würzburg repeatedly forbade the pilgrimage to Niklaushausen, but in vain, and at length he was led to take more decided steps. The great festivity of the region was the feast of St. Kilian, the martyr of Würzburg, falling on July 8. On the Sunday previous, July 6, 1476, Hans significantly told his audience to return the following Saturday armed, but to leave their women and children at home. Matters were evidently approaching a crisis, and the bishop did not wait for the result, but sent a party of guards, who seized Hans and conveyed him to a neighboring stronghold. The next day about 6,000 of his deluded followers, including many women and children, set out for the castle, without arms, believing that its walls would fall at their demand. They refused to disperse when summoned, but were readily scattered by a sally of men-at-arms, supported by a discharge from the cannon of the castle, in which many were slain. Hans was easily forced by torture to confess the falsity of his revelations and the deceits by which he and his confederates had stimulated the excitement by false miracles; but his confession did not avail him, and he was condemned to be burned. He walked resolutely to the stake, singing a hymn, but his fortitude gave way and he shrieked in agony as the flames reached him. To prevent his ashes from being treasured as relics, they were carefully collected and cast into the river. The priest and Beghard who had served as his confederates sought safety in flight, but were caught and confessed, after which they were discharged; but two peasants—one who had suggested the advance upon the castle and one who had wounded the horse of one of the guards who captured Hans—were beheaded.

If Gregory of Heimburg and Hans of Niklaushausen represent the antagonism to Rome which pervaded the laity from the highest to the lowest, John von Ruchrath of Wesel indicates that even in the Church the same spirit was not wanting. One of the most eminent theologians and preachers of whom Germany could boast, celebrated in the schools as the "Light of the World" and the "Master of Contradictions," he was a hardy and somewhat violent disputant, who in his sermons had no scruple in presenting his opinions in the most offensive shape. Like Luther, of whom he was the true precursor, he commenced by an assault upon indulgences. Step by step he advanced to strip the Church of its powers, and was led to reject the authority of tradition and the Fathers, recurring to Scripture as the sole basis of authority. How little he recked of the feelings of those whose faith he assailed is seen in his remark that if fasting was instituted by St. Peter, it was probably to obtain a better market for his fish.

It shows how rusty had become the machinery of persecution and the latitude allowed to free speech that John of Wesel was permitted so long, without interference, to disseminate from the pulpit and professorial chair these opinions, as dangerous as any emitted by Waldenses, Wickliffites, or Hussites. In fact, but for the bitter quarrel between the Realists and Nominalists, it is probable that he would have been unmolested to the end and enabled to close his days in peace. He was a leader of the Nominalists, and the Dominican Thomists of Mainz were resolved to silence him. The Archbishop of Mainz was Diether of Isenburg, who had been forced to abandon his see in 1463, but had resumed it in 1475 on the death of his competitor, Adolph of Nassau; he did not wish another conflict with Rome, to which he was exposed in consequence of his public denunciations of the papal auctions of the archiepiscopal pallium; he was threatened with this unless he would surrender John of Wesel as a victim, and he yielded to the pressure in 1479.

In the great province of Mainz there was no inquisitor, and as there was a Dominican inquisitor at Cologne, in the person of Friar Gerhard von Elten, he was sent for. He came, accompanied by Friar Jacob Sprenger, not yet an inquisitor, but whom we shall see hereafter in that capacity busy in burning witches. With him came the theologians from the Universities of Heidelberg and Cologne, who were to sit as experts and assessors, and so carefully were they

selected that one of the Heidelberg doctors, to whom we are indebted for an account of the proceedings, tells us that among them
all there was but one Nominalist.

The proceedings are a curious travesty of the inquisitorial process.
There was no secrecy attempted; everything was conducted in an
assembly consisting of laymen as well as ecclesiastics, prominent
among whom we recognize the Count of Wertheim, fresh from the
plunder of Hans of Niklaushausen. After a preliminary meeting,
when the assembly convened for business, February 8, 1479, the Inquisitor von Elten opened the proceedings by suggesting that two
or three friends of the accused should warn him to repent of his
errors and beg for mercy, in which case he should have mercy, but
otherwise not. A deputation was thereupon dispatched, but their
mission was not speedily performed. A high official was sent to
hurry the matter, but at that moment John of Wesel entered, pallid,
bent with age, leaning on his staff, and supported by two Franciscans.
He was made to sit on the floor; von Elten repeated to him the
message, and when he attempted to defend himself he was cut
short, badgered and threatened, until he was brought to sue for
pardon. After this he was put through a long and exhausting examination, and was finally remanded until the next day. Then he was
again brought out and examined afresh, when he endeavored to defend his views. "If all men renounce Christ," he said, "I will still
worship him and be a Christian," to which von Elten retorted, "So
say all heretics, even when at the stake." Finally it was resolved that
three doctors should be deputed to exhort him to abandon his
errors.

On the 10th the deputies labored with him. "If Christ were here,"
he told them, "and were treated like me, you would condemn him
as a heretic—but he would get the better of you with his subtlety."
At length he was persuaded to acknowledge that his views were
erroneous, on the deputies agreeing to take the responsibility on
their own consciences. He had long been sick when the trial was
commenced; age,ˢ weakness, and the dark and filthy dungeon had
broken down his powers of resistance, and he submitted. He publicly
recanted and abjured, his books were burned before his face, and
he was sentenced to imprisonment for life in the Augustinian monastery of Mainz. He did not long survive his misery, for he died in

1481. The trial excited great interest among all the scholars of Germany, who were shocked at this treatment of a man so eminent and distinguished. Yet his writings survived him and proved greatly encouraging to the early Reformers. Melanchthon enumerates him among those who by their works kept up the continuity of the Church of Christ.

The persecution of John Reuchlin, like that of John of Wesel, sprang from scholastic antagonisms, but its development shows how completely, during the interval, the inquisitorial power had wasted away. Reuchlin was a pupil of John Wessel; as the leader of the Humanists, and the foremost representative in Germany of the new learning, he was involved in bitter controversy with the Dominicans, who, as traditional Thomists, were ready to do battle to the death for scholasticism. The ferocious jocularity with which Sebastian Brandt dilates, in his most finished Latinity, upon the torture and burning of four Dominicans at Berne in 1509, for frauds committed in the controversy over the Immaculate Conception, indicates the temper which animated the hostile parties, even as its lighter aspect is seen in the unsparing satire of Erasmus and of the *Epistolæ Obscurorum Virorum*. When, therefore, Reuchlin stood forward to protect Jews and Jewish literature against the assaults of the renegade Pfefferkorn, the opportunity to destroy him was eagerly seized. In 1513 a Dominican inquisitor, the Prior Jacob von Hochstraten, came from Cologne to Mainz on an errand precisely similar to that of his predecessor von Elten. Unlike John of Wesel, however, Reuchlin felt that he could safely appeal to Rome, where Leo X was himself a man of culture and a Humanist. Leo was well disposed, and commissioned the Bishop of Speier to decide the question, which was in itself a direct blow at the inquisitorial power. Reuchlin was declared free of all suspicion of heresy, the prosecution was pronounced frivolous, and the costs were put upon Hochstraten, with a threat of excommunication for disobedience. This was confirmed at Rome in 1415, where silence was imposed on Reuchlin's accusers under a penalty of 3,000 marks. The Humanists celebrated their victory with savage rejoicing. Eleutherius Bizenus printed a tract summoning, in rugged hexameters, all Germany to assist in the triumph of Reuchlin. The Dominicans are characterized as worse than Turks, and the author wonders what unjust pope and cowardly emperor had enabled them to impose their yoke on the land. These were brave words, but premature. The quarrel had attracted the attention of all Europe, the Dominican Order itself and all it represented were on trial, and it could not afford to submit to defeat. Hochstraten hastened to Rome; the Dominicans of the great University of Cologne did not hesitate to say that if the pope maintained the sentence they would appeal to the future council, they would refuse to abide by his decision, they would pronounce him to be no pope and organize a schism. Leo cowered before the storm he had provoked, and in 1416 he issued a mandate superseding the sentence, but the spirit of insubordination was growing strong in Germany, and Franz von Sickingen, the free-lance, compelled its observance. As the Lutheran revolt grew more threatening, however, the support of the Dominicans became more and more indispensable, and in 1420 Leo settled the matter by setting aside the decision of the Bishop of Speier, imposing silence on Reuchlin, and laying all the costs on him. Hochstraten, moreover, was restored to his office.

The reparation came too late to render the Inquisition of any service, now that its efficiency was more sorely needed than ever before. Had it existed in Germany in good working order, Luther's career would have been short. When, October 31, 1517, he nailed his propositions concerning indulgences on the church door of Wittenberg and publicly defended them, an inquisitor such as Bernard Gui would have speedily silenced him, either by forcing him to a public recantation, or handing him over to be burned if he proved obstinate. In Germany there was nothing to take the place of the Inquisition, and a latitude of speech had become customary. This perhaps explains why the significance of Luther's revolt was better appreciated at Rome than on the spot. After he had been formally declared a heretic by the Auditor-General of the Apostolic Chamber, the Legate Cardinal Caietano wrote that he could terminate the matter himself, and that it was rather a trifling affair to be brought before the pope. He did not fulfill his instructions to arrest Luther and tell him that if he would appear before the Holy See to excuse himself he would be treated with undeserved clemency. After the scandal had been growing for a twelvemonth, Leo again wrote to Caietano to summon Doctor Martin before him, and to condemn or absolve him as might prove requisite. Before these last instructions reached Caietano, Luther came in answer to a previous summons, but, though he professed himself in all things an obedient son of the Church, he practically manifested an ominous independence, and was conveyed away unharmed. The legate trusted to his powers as a disputant rather than to force; and had he attempted the latter, he had no machinery at hand to frustrate the instructions given by the Augsburg magistrates for Luther's protection. In the paralysis of persecution the inevitable revolution went forward.

CHAPTER XV
BOHEMIA

THERE is no historical foundation for the legend that Peter Waldo's missionary labors carried him into Bohemia, where he died, but there can be no question what the Waldensian heresy found a foothold among the Czechs at a comparatively early date. The Inquisitor of Passau, about the middle of the thirteenth century, describes the flourishing condition of the Waldensian churches in Austria, along the borders of Bohemia and Moravia, and the intense zeal of propagandism which animated their members. That the heresy should cross the boundary line was inevitable, and it ran little risk of persecution until it gained strength enough to declare itself openly. The alarm was first sounded by Innocent IV in 1245, who summoned the prelates of Hungary to intervene, as those of Bohemia apparently were not to be depended upon. Innocent describes the heresy as established so widely that it embraced not only the simple folk, but also princes and magnates. These are all declared excommunicate, their lands confiscated for the benefit of the first occupant, and any who shall relapse after recantation are to be abandoned to the secular arm without a hearing.

We have no means of knowing whether any action was taken in consequence of this decree, but if efforts were made they did not succeed in eradicating the heresy. In 1257 King Premysl Otokar II applied to Alexander IV for aid in its suppression, and two Franciscans, Lambert the German and Bartholomew, lector in Brunn, received the papal commission as inquisitors throughout Bohemia and Moravia. No traces of their activity have reached us, nor is there any evidence that their places were filled when they died or retired. When, after a long interval, we again hear of persecution, it is in a shape that shows that the Bishop of Prague was not disposed to invite papal encroachments on his jurisdiction. In 1301 a synod of Prague deplored the spread of heresy and ordered everyone cognizant of it to give information to the episcopal inquisitors, from which we may infer that the elaborate legislation elsewhere in force for the detection and punishment of heresy was virtually unknown in Bohemia.

In 1318 John of Drasic, the Bishop of Prague, was summoned to Avignon by John XXII to answer accusations brought against him by Frederic of Schönberg, Canon of Wyschehrad, as a fautor of heresy. The complaint set forth that heretics were so numerous that they had an archbishop and seven bishops, each of whom had 300 disciples. The description of their faith would seem to indicate that there were both Waldenses and Luciferans, and that their doctrines had been commingled. They are described as considering oaths unlawful; confession and absolution could be administered indifferently by layman or priest; the divine unity and the resurrection of the dead were denied; Jesus had only a phantasmic body; and Lucifer was expected finally to reign. There were also the customary accusations of sexual excesses committed in nocturnal assemblies held in caverns. The good bishop, it appears, only permitted these wretches to be arraigned by his inquisitors after repeated pressure from John of Luxembourg, the king. Fourteen of them were convicted and handed over to the secular arm, but the bishop interfered, to the great disgust of the king, and forcibly released them, except a physician named Richard, who was imprisoned; the bishop, moreover, discharged the inquisitors, who evidently were his own officials and not papal appointees. These were serious offenses on the part of a prelate, and he expiated his lenity by a confinement of several years in Avignon.

Papal attention being thus called to the existence of heresy in the east of Europe, steps were immediately taken for the introduction of the Inquisition. In 1318 John XXII commissioned the Dominican Peregrine of Oppolza and the Franciscan Nicholas of Cracow as Inquisitors in the diocese of Cracow and Breslau, while Bohemia and Poland were entrusted to the Dominican Colda and the Franciscan Hartmann. As usual, the secular and ecclesiastical powers were commanded to afford them assistance, whenever called upon, to stem the flood of heresy that was infecting the people.

Among these heretics there may have been Brethren of the Free Spirit, but they were probably for the most part Waldenses, who at this time had a thoroughly organized Church in Bohemia, whence emissaries were sent to Moravia, Saxony, Silesia, and Poland. No doubt active measures of repression were carried out with little inter-mission, though chance has only preserved an indication of in-quisitorial proceedings about the year 1330. In 1335 Benedict XII appointed the Franciscan Peter Naczeracz as Inquisitor in the diocese of Olmutz, and the Dominican Gall of Neuburg for that of Prague. All prelates were commanded to lend their aid, and King John was especially reminded that he held the temporal sword for the purpose of subduing the enemies of the faith. His son, the future Emperor Charles IV, at that time in charge of the kingdom, was similarly appealed to.

Bohemia and its subject provinces were thus thoroughly infected with heresy, mostly Waldensian, when several changes took place which increased the prominence of the kingdom and stimulated vastly its intellectual activity. In 1344 Prague was separated from its far-off metropolis of Mainz and was erected into an archbishopric, for which Charles, then Margrave of Bohemia, provided a zealous and enlightened prelate in the person of Arnest of Pardubitz. Two years later, in 1346, Charles was elected King of the Romans by the Electors of Trèves and Cologne in opposition to Louis of Bavaria, as the supporter of the papacy; and a month later he succeeded to the throne of Bohemia through the knightly death of the blind King John at Crécy. Still more influential and far-reaching in its results was the founding in 1347 of the University of Prague, to which the combined favor of pope and emperor gave immediate luster. Arch-bishop Arnest assumed its chancellorship, learned schoolmen filled its chairs; students flocked to it from every quarter, and it soon rivalled in numbers and reputation its elder sisters of Oxford, Paris, and Bologna.

During the latter half of the century, Bohemia, under these auspices, was one of the most flourishing kingdoms of Europe. Its mines of the precious metals gave it wealth; the freedom enjoyed by its peasantry raised them mentally and morally above the level of the serfs of other lands; culture and enlightenment were diffused from its University. It was renowned throughout the Continent for the splendor of its churches, which in size and number were no-where exceeded. At the monastery of Königsaal, where the Bohemian kings lay buried, around the walls of the garden the whole of the Scriptures, from Genesis to Revelations, was engraved, with letters enlarging in size with their distance from the ground, so that all could be easily read. In the bitter struggles of after generations the reign of King Charles was fondly looked back upon as the golden age of Bohemia. Wealth and culture, however, were accompanied with corruption. Concubinage was almost universal, and simony pervaded the Church in all its ranks, the sacraments were sold and penitence compounded for. All the abuses for which clerical immunity furnished opportunity flourished, and the land was overrun by vagrants whose tonsure gave them charter to rob and brawl, and dice and drink.

We hear nothing of papal inquisitors after those commissioned by Benedict XII in 1335; Archbishop Arnest, however, soon after his accession, set resolutely to work to purify the morals of his Church and to uproot heresy. He held synods frequently, he instituted a body of Correctors, whose duty it was to visit all portions of the province and punish all transgressions, and he organized an episcopal Inquisition for the purpose of tracking out and suppressing heresy. In the fragmentary remains of his synodal acts, the frequency with which this latter duty is insisted upon serves as a measure of its importance and of the numbers of those who had forsaken the Church. In the earliest synod whose proceedings have reached us the first place is given to this subject; the archdeacons were directed to make diligent perquisition in their respective districts, both personally and through the deans and parish priests, and all who were found guilty or suspect of heresy were to be forthwith denounced to the archbishop or the inquisitor. Similar instructions were issued in 1355; and after Arnest's death in 1364, his successor, John Ocko, was equally vigilant, as appears from the acts of his synods in 1366 and 1371. The neighborhood of Pisek was especially contaminated, and from the acts of the Consistory of 1381 it appears that a priest named Johl, of Pisek, could not be ordained because both his father and grandfather had been heretics. In this same year Archbishop John, as papal legate for his own province and for the dioceses of Ratisbon, Bamberg, and Misnia, held a council at Prague, in which he mournfully described the spread of the Waldenses and Sarabites —the latter probably Beghards. He sharply reproved the bishops who, through sloth or parsimony, had not appointed inquisitors, and threatened that if they did not do so forthwith, he would do it himself. When, ten years later, the Church took the alarm and acted vigorously, the Waldenses of Brandenburg who were prosecuted declared that their teachers came from Bohemia.

In all this activity for the suppression of heresy the episcopal Inquisition alone is referred to. The bull of Gregory XI, in 1372, ordering the appointment of five inquisitors for Germany, confines their jurisdiction to the provinces of Cologne, Mainz, Utrecht, Magdeburg, Salzburg, and Bremen, and pointedly omits that of Prague, although the zeal of Charles IV might have been expected to secure the blessings of the institution for his hereditary realm. This is the more curious, moreover, since the intellectual movement started by the University of Prague was producing a number of men distinguished not only for learning and piety, but for their bold attacks on the corruptions of the Church and their questioning of some of its most profitable dogmas. The appearance of these precursors of Huss is one of the most remarkable indications of the tendencies of the age in Bohemia, and shows how the Waldensian spirit of revolt had unconsciously spread among the population.

Conrad of Waldhausen, who died in 1369, is reckoned the earliest of these. He maintained strict orthodoxy, but his denunciation in his sermons of the vices of the clergy, and especially of the Mendicants, created a deep sensation. More prominent was Milicz of Kremsier, who in 1363 resigned the office of private secretary to the emperor, and several rich preferments, in order to devote himself exclusively to preaching. His sermons in Czech, German, and Latin were filled with audacious attacks on the sins of clergy and laity, and the evils of the time led him to prophesy the advent of Antichrist between 1365 and 1367. In the latter year he went to Rome in order to lay before Urban V his views on the present and future of the Church. While awaiting Urban's advent from Avignon, he affixed on the portal of St. Peter's an announcement of a sermon on the subject, which led the Inquisition to throw him into prison, but in October, on the arrival of the pope, he was released and treated with distinction. On his return to Prague he preached with greater violence than ever. To get rid of him the priesthood accused him to the emperor and archbishop, but in vain. Then they formulated 12 articles of accusation against him to the pope, and obtained in January 1374, from Gregory XI, bulls denouncing him as a persistent heresiarch who had filled all Bohemia, Poland, Silesia, and the neighboring lands with his errors. According to them, he not only taught that Antichrist had come, that the Church was extinct, that pope, cardinals, bishops and prelates showed no light of truth, but he permitted to his followers the unlimited gratification of their passions. Milicz undauntedly pursued his course until an inquisitorial prosecution was commenced against him, when he appealed to the pope. In Lent, 1374, he went to Avignon, where he readily proved his innocence, and on May 21 was admitted to preach before the cardinals, but he died June 29, before the decision of his case was published.

The spirit of indignation and disquiet did not confine itself to denunciations of clerical abuses. Men were growing bolder, and began to question some of the cherished dogmas which gave rise to those abuses. In the synod of 1384 one of the subjects discussed was whether the saints were cognizant of the prayers addressed to them, and whether the worshipper was benefited by their suffrages —the mere raising of such a question showing how dangerously bold had become the spirit of inquiry. The man who most fitly represented this tendency was Mathias of Janow, whom the Archbishop John of Jenzenstein utilized in his efforts to reform the disorders of the clergy. Mathias was led to trace the troubles to their causes, and to teach heresies from the consequences of which even the protection of the archbishop could not wholly defend him. In the synod of 1389 he was forced to make public recantation of his errors in holding that the images of Christ and the saints gave rise to idolatry; that relics were of no service, and the intercession of saints was useless; while his teaching that everyone should be urged to take communion daily foreshadowed the eucharistic troubles which play so large a part in the Hussite excitement. Yet he was allowed to escape with six months' suspension from preaching and hearing confessions outside his own parochial church, a mistaken lenity which he repaid by continuing to teach the same errors more audaciously than ever.

While Bohemia was thus the scene of an agitation the outcome of which no man could foretell, a similar movement was running a still more rapid course in England, which was destined to exercise a decisive influence on the result. The assaults of John Wickliff were the most serious danger encountered by the hierarchy since the Hildebrandine theocracy had been established. It was not the poor peasant or artisan who found the Scriptures in contradition to the teaching of the pulpit and with the practical examples set by the sacerdotal class; but it was a man who stood in learning and argumentative power on a level with the foremost schoolmen of the Middle Ages; who could quote not only Christ and the apostles, but the Fathers and doctors of the Church, the decretals and the canons, Aristotle and his commentators; who could weave all these into the dialectics so dear to students and masters of theology, and who could frame a system of philosophy suited to the intellectual wants of the age. It was the secret of Wickliff's influence that he had worked out his conclusions in single-hearted efforts to search for truth; he spared neither prince nor prelate; he labored to instruct the poor more zealously perhaps than to influence the great, and men of all ranks, from the peasant to the schoolman, recognized in him a leader who sought to make them better, stronger, more valiant in the struggle with Apollyon. It is no wonder that his fame as a heresiarch filled all the schools and became everywhere synonymous with rebellion against the sacerdotal system; that simple Waldenses in Spain and Germany became thereafter known as Wickliffites. Yet the endurance of his teachings was due to his Bohemian disciples; at home, after a brief period of rapid development, they were virtually crushed out by the combined power of Church and State.

As the heresy of Huss was in nearly all details copied from Wickliff, it is necessary, in order to understand the nature of the Hussite movement, to cast a brief glance at the views of the English reformer. In 1388 and 1389, about four years after his death, 25 articles of accusation were brought against his followers, whose reply gives, in the most vigorous English, a summary of his tenets. The document in question shows the Wickliffite belief to be that the popes of the period were Antichrist; all the hierarchy, from the pope down, were accursed by reason of their greed, their simony, their cruelty, their lust of power, and their evil lives. The pope was not to be obeyed, and his excommunication and that of his bishops were to be disregarded. The indulgences so freely proffered in return for money or for the services of crusaders in slaying Christians were fraudulent. Yet the power of the keys in pious hands was not denied—"Certes, as holy prestis of lyvynge and cunnynge of holy writte han keyes of heven and bene vicaris of Jesus Crist, so viciouse prestis, unkonnynge of holy writte, ful of pride and covetise, han keyes of helle and bene vicaris of Sathanas." Though auricular confession might be useful, it was not necessary, for men should trust in Christ. Image worship was unlawful, and representations of the Trinity were forbidden— "Hit semes that this offrynge ymages is a sotile cast of Antichriste and his clerkis for to drawe almes fro pore men. . . . Certis, these ymages of hemselfe may do nouther gode nor yvel to mennis soules, but thai myghtten warme a man's body in colde if thai were sette upon a fire." The invocation of saints was useless; the best of them could do nothing but what God ordained, and many of those customarily invoked were in hell, for in modern times sinners stood a better chance of canonization than holy men. It was the same with their feast-days; those of the apostles and early saints might be observed, but not the rest. Song was not to be used in divine service, and prayer was as efficient anywhere as in church, for the churches were not holy—"all suche chirches bene gretely poluted and cursud of God, nomely for sellynge of leccherie and fals swering upon bokus." Ecclesiastics must not live in luxury and pomp, but as poor men "gyvynge ensaumple of holynes by ther conversacion." The Church must be deprived of all its temporalities, and whatever was necessary for the support of its members must be held in common. Tithes and offerings were not to be given to sinful priests; it was simony for a priest to receive payment for his spiritual ministrations, though he might sell his labor in honest vocations, such as teaching and the binding of books, and though no one was forbidden to make an oblation at mass, provided he did not seek to obtain more than his share in the sacrifice. All priests and deacons were to preach zealously, for which no special license or commission was required.

All these tenets of which they were accused the Wickliffites admitted and defended in the most incisive fashion, but there were two articles which they denied. Wickliff's teaching so closely resembled that of the Waldenses that it was natural that the orthodox should attribute to him the two Waldensian errors which regarded all oaths as unlawful, and held that priests in mortal sin could not administer the sacraments. To the former, his followers replied that, though they rejected all unnecessary swearing, they admitted that

"If hit be nedeful for to swere for a spedful treuthe men mowe wele swere as God did in the olde lawe." As to the latter, they said that the sinful priest can give sacraments efficient to those who worthily receive them, though he receive damnation unto himself. The prominence of the Fraticelli also suggested the imputation that the Wickliffites believed the entire renunciation of property to be essential to salvation; but this they denied, saying that a man might make lawful gains and hold them, but that he must use them well.

All these antisacerdotal teachings flowed directly from the resoluteness with which Wickliff carried out to its logical conclusion the Augustinian doctrine of predestination, thus necessarily striking at the root of all human mediation, the suffrages of the saints, justification by works, and all the machinery of the Church for the purchase and sale of salvation. In this, as in the rest, Huss followed him, though the distinction between his principles and the orthodox ones of the Thomists and other schoolmen was too subtle to render this point one which the Church could easily condemn.

The one serious speculative error of Wickliff lay in his effort to reconcile the mystery of the Eucharist with the stubborn fact that after consecration the bread remained bread and the wine continued to be wine. He did not deny conversion into the body and blood of Christ; they were really present in the sacrifice, but his reason refused to acknowledge transubstantiation, and he invented a theory of the remanence of the substance coexisting with the divine elements. Into these dangerous subtleties Huss refused to follow his master. It was the one point on which he declined to accept the reasoning of the Englishman, and yet, as we shall see, it served as a principal excuse for hurrying him to the stake.

Wickliff's career as a heresiarch was unexampled, and its peculiarities serve to explain much that would otherwise be incomprehensible in the growth and tolerance of his doctrines in Bohemia, and in the simplicity with which Huss refused to believe that he could himself be regarded as a heretic. Although as early as 1377, the assistance which Wickliff rendered to Edward III in diminishing the papal revenues moved Gregory XI to command his immediate prosecution as a heretic, yet the political situation was such as to render ineffectual all efforts to carry out these instructions; he was never even excommunicated and was allowed to die peacefully in his rectory of Lutterworth on the last day of the year 1384. No further action was taken by Rome until the question of his heresy was raised in Prague. Although in 1409 Alexander V ordered Archbishop Zbinco not to permit Wickliff's errors to be taught or his books to be read, yet when in 1410 John XXIII referred his writing to a commission of four cardinals, who convoked an assembly of theologians for their examination, a majority decided that Archbishop Zbinko had not been justified in burning them. It was not until the Council of Rome, in 1413, that there was a formal and authoritative condemnation pronounced, and it was left for the Council of Constance, in 1415, to proclaim Wickliff a heresiarch, to order his bones exhumed, and to define his errors with the authority of the Church Universal. Huss might well, to the last, believe in the authenticity of the spurious letters of the University of Oxford, brought to Prague about 1403, in which Wickliff was declared perfectly orthodox, and might conscientiously assert that his books continued to be read and taught there.

The marriage of Anne of Luxembourg, sister of Wenceslas of Bohemia, to Richard II, in 1382, led to considerable intercourse between the kingdoms until her death in 1394. Many Bohemians visited England during the excitement caused by Wickliff's controversies, and his writings were carried to Prague, where they found great acceptance. Huss tells us that about 1390 they commenced to be read in the University of Prague, and that they continued thenceforth to be studied. A MS. in the Hofbibliothek of Vienna gives a catalogue of 90 of them which were known in Bohemia, and it is to those regions that we must look for the remains of his voluminous labors, the greater part of which were successfully suppressed at home.

John of Husinec, commonly known as Huss, who became the leading exponent and protomartyr of Wickliffitism in Bohemia, is supposed to have been born in 1369. In 1393 at the University of Prague he obtained the degree of bachelor of arts; in 1394 that of bachelor of theology; in 1396 that of master of arts; but the doctorate he never attained, though in 1398 he was already lecturing in the University; in 1401 he was dean of the philosophical faculty, and rector in 1402. Curiously enough, he embraced the Realist philosophy, and won great applause in his combats with the Nominalists. So little promise did his early years give of his career as a reformer that, in 1392, he spent his last 4 groschen for an indulgence, when he had only dry crusts for food. In 1400 he was ordained as priest, and two years later he was appointed preacher to the Bethlehem chapel, where his earnest eloquence soon rendered him the spiritual leader of the people. The study of Wickliff's writings, begun shortly after this, quickened his appreciation of the evils of a corrupted Church, and when Archbishop Zbinco of Hasenburg, shortly after his consecration in 1403, appointed him as preacher to the annual synods, Huss improved the opportunity to address to the assembled clergy a series of terrible invectives against their worldliness and filthiness of living, which excited general popular hatred and contempt for them. After one of peculiar vigor, in October 1407, the clamor among the ecclesiastics grew so strong that they presented a formal complaint against him to Archbishop Zbinco, and he was deprived of the position. By this time he was recognized as the leader in the effort to purify the Church, and to reduce it to its ancient simplicity, with such men as Stephen Palecz, Stanislas of Znaim, John of Jessinetz, Jerome of Prague, and many others eminent for learning and piety as his collaborators. To some of these he was inferior in intellectual gifts, but his fearless temper, his unbending rectitude, his blameless life, and his kindly nature won for him the affectionate veneration of the people and rendered him its idol.

Discussion grew hot and passions became embittered. Old jealousies and hatreds between the Teutonic and Czech races contributed to render the religious quarrel unappeasable. The fiery diatribes of the Bethlehem chapel were listened to eagerly, while the Wickliffite doctrines, which taught the baselessness of the whole sacerdotal system, were welcomed as a revelation, and spread rapidly through all classes. King Wenceslas was inclined to give them such support as his indolence and self-indulgence would permit, and his queen, Sophia, was even more favorably disposed. Yet the clergy and their friends could not submit quietly to the spoliation of their privileges and wealth, although the Great Schism, in weakening the influence of the Roman curia, rendered its support less efficient. Preachers who assailed their vices were thrown into prison as heretics and were exiled, and the writings of Wickliff, which formed the key of the position, were fiercely assaulted and desperately defended. The weak point in them was the substitution of remanence for tran-substantiation; and although this was discarded by Huss and his followers, it served as an unguarded point through which the whole position might be carried. The synod of 1405 asserted the doctrine of transubstantiation in its most absolute shape; anyone teaching otherwise was pronounced a heretic, and was ordered to be reported to the archbishop for punishment. In 1406 this was repeated in a still more threatening form, showing that the Wick-liffite views had obstinate defenders. Already, in 1403, a series of 45 articles extracted from Wickliff's works was formally condemned by the University. Around these the battle raged with fury; the condemnation was repeated in 1408, and in 1410 Archbishop Zbinco solemnly burned in the courtyard of his palace 200 of the forbidden books, while the populace revenged itself by singing through the streets rude rhymes, in which the prelate is said to have burned books which he could not read; for his ignorance was notorious, and he was reported to have first acquired the alphabet after his elevation.

In the strife between rival popes it suited the policy of King Wenceslas, in 1408, to maintain neutrality, and he induced the University to send envoys to the cardinals who had renounced allegiance to both Benedict XIII and Gregory XII. In this mission were included Stephen Palecz and Stanislas of Znaim, but the whole party fell, in Bologna, into the hands of Balthasar Cossa, the papal legate (afterwards antipope John XXIII), who threw them all in prison as suspect of heresy, and it required no little effort to secure their release. This adventure cooled the zeal of Stephen and Stanislas; they gradually changed sides, and from the warmest friends of Huss they became, as we shall see, his most dangerous and implacable enemies.

In this affair the University had not seconded the wishes of the king with the alacrity which he had expected, and Huss took advantage of the royal displeasure to effect a revolution in that institution, which had hitherto proved the chief obstacle in the progress of reform. It was divided, in the ordinary manner, into four "nations." As each of these nations had a vote, the Bohemians constantly found themselves outnumbered by the foreigners. It was now proposed to adopt the constitution of the University of Paris, where the French nation had three votes, and all the foreign nations collectively but one. The vacillation of Wenceslas delayed decision, but in January 1409 he signed the decree which ordered the change. The German students and professors bound themselves by a vow to procure the revocation of the decree or to leave the University. Failing in the former they abandoned the city in vast numbers, founding the University of Leipsic, and spreading throughout Europe the report that Bohemia was a nest of heretics. The dyke was broken, and the flood of Wickliffitism poured over the land with little to check its progress. In vain did Alexander V and John XXIII command Archbishop Zbinco to suppress the heresy, and in vain did the struggling prelate hold assemblies and issue comminatory decrees. The tide bore all before it, and Zbinco at last, in 1411, abandoned his ungrateful see to appeal to Wenceslas's brother Sigismund, then recently elected King of the Romans, but died on the journey.

This removed the last obstacle. The new archbishop, Albik of Unicow, previously physician to Wenceslas, was old and weak, and more given to accumulating money than to defending the faith. He was said to carry the key of his wine-cellar himself, to have only a wretched old crone for a cook, and to sell habitually all presents made to him. Thoroughly unfitted for the crisis, he resigned in 1413, and was succeeded by Conrad of Vechta, who, after some hesitation, cast his lot with the followers of Huss.

Everything thus conspired to accelerate the progress of the revolution. Huss, who had hitherto, for the most part, confined himself to assaults upon the local ecclesiastical establishment, began to direct his attacks at the papacy itself, and in the writings of Wickliff he found ample store of arguments, which he used with great effect. He also made use of another of Wickliff's methods by the employment of itinerant priests. This was peculiarly well adapted to accomplish the object in view, for the Bohemians were given to listening to sermons, and the unlicensed preaching for which the negligence of the established clergy gave opportunity had been a frequent source of complaint since the year 1371. The people flocked in crowds to hear them, in spite of priestly anathemas, and the great mass of the nation, from nobles to peasants, eagerly adopted the new doctrines, and were prepared to support them to the death.

Matters were rapidly tending to an open rupture with Rome. In 1410 John XXIII, soon after his accession, referred to Cardinal Otto Colonna the complaints which came to Rome against Huss. On September 20 Colonna summoned him to appear in person. Huss sent deputies, who appealed from the cardinal to the pope, but they were thrown into prison and severely handled; and while the appeal was pending, in February 1411, Colonna excommunicated him. On March 15 the excommunication was published in all the churches of Prague save two; the people stood by Huss, and an interdict was extended over the city, which was generally disregarded, and Huss continued to preach. While affairs were in this threatening position a new cause of trouble led to an explosion. Just as Wickliff had been stirred to fresh hostility against the papacy by the crusade which, under orders from Urban VI, the Bishop of Norwich had preached against France for its support of the rival pope Clement VII; just as Luther was to be aroused from his obscurity by the indulgence-selling of Tetzel when Leo X wanted money; so the Bohemians were stimulated to active opposition when John XXIII, towards the close of 1411, proclaimed a crusade with Holy Land indulgences against Ladislas of Naples, who upheld the claims of Gregory XII. Stephen Palecz, till then associated with Huss, was dean of the theological faculty. His experience of the Bolognese prison rendered him timorous about withstanding John XXIII, and he declared that there was no authority to prevent the publication of the indulgence. Huss was bolder, and a controversy arose between them which converted their former friendship into an enmity. June 16, 1412, Huss held in the Carolinum a disputation which was a powerful and eloquent attack upon the power of the keys, which lay at the foundation of the whole papal system. Absolution was dependent on the subjective condition of the penitent; as many popes who concede indulgences are damned, how can they defend their pardons before God? the sellers of indulgences are thieves; the pope and the whole Church Militant often err; and an unjust papal excommunication is to be disregarded.

A few days after the disputation a crowd led by Wok of Waldstein, a favorite of King Wenceslas, carried the papal bulls of indulgence to the pillory and publicly burned them. The well-known legend attributes to Jerome of Prague a leading part in this, and relates that the bulls were strung around the neck of a strumpet mounted on a cart, who solicited the favor of the mob with lascivious gestures. No punishment was inflicted on the participants, and Wok of Waldstein continued to enjoy the royal favor. The defiance of the pope was complete, and the temper of the people was shown on July 12, when in three several churches three young mechanics named Martin, John, and Stanislas, interrupted the preachers proclaiming the indulgences, and declared them to be a lie. They were arrested and beheaded in spite of Huss's intercession; many others were imprisoned, and some were exposed to torture. Then the people assumed a threatening aspect; the three who had been executed were reverenced as martyrs; tumults occurred, and the prisoners were released. Soon afterwards a Carmelite was begging at the doors of his church with an array of relics displayed upon a table, with the indulgences attached to them to excite the liberality of the pious. A disciple of Huss denounced the affair as a fraud and kicked over the table, and when he was seized by the friars a band of armed men broke into the house and released him, not without bloodshed.

John XXIII could not avoid taking up the gage of battle thus thrown down. The Bohemian clergy appealed to him piteously, representing the oppression to which they were subjected, and stating that many of them had been slain. He promptly responded. The major excommunication, to be published in all its awful solemnity in Prague, was pronounced against Huss; the Bethlehem chapel was ordered to be levelled with the earth; his followers were excommunicated, and all who would not within thirty days abjure heresy were summoned to answer in person before the Roman curia. In spite of this Huss continued to preach, and when an attempt was made to arrest him in the pulpit the threatening aspect of the congregation prevented its execution. He appealed to a general council, and then to God, in a protest which, in lofty terms, asserted the nullity of the sentence pronounced against him. Yet the clergy, for the most part gladly, obeyed the bull of excommunication, and Huss's presence in Prague led to a cessation of all church observances; divine service was suspended, the new-born were not baptized, and the dead lay unburied. At the request of the king, Huss left Prague and retired to Kosihradek, whence he directed the movements of his adherents in the city and busied himself in active controversial writing, the chief product of which was the *De Ecclesia*, an attack on the papacy in unmeasured language borrowed from Wickliff, which was publicly read in the Bethlehem chapel on July 8, 1413.

King Wenceslas had vainly tried to bring about a pacification of the troubles in which passions were daily growing wilder. It was no longer a question of reforming the morals of the clergy, on the necessity of which all were agreed. The controversy had drifted to the causes of clerical corruption, springing, as Wickliff and Huss and their disciples said, from the very principles on which the whole structure of Latin Christianity was based. Either the power of the keys was a truth vital to the salvation of mankind, or it was a lie boldly utilized to gratify the lust of power and the greed of avarice. Between these two antagonistic postulates dialectic subtlety was powerless to frame a reconciliation, and argument only hardened each side in its belief. Wearied at last with his unavailing efforts, Wenceslas finally cut the matter short by banishing the leaders of the conservatives, Stephen Palecz, Stanislas of Znaim, Peter of Znaim, and John Elias. Stanislas retired to Moravia, where, after incredible industry in controversial writing, he died on the road to the Council of Constance; Stephen survived him and revenged them both.

Huss and his adherents were now masters of the field; and though he abstained from returning to Prague, except an occasional visit incognito, until his departure for Constance, he could truly say, when he stood up in the council to meet his accusers, "I came hither of my own free will. Had I refused to come neither the king nor the emperor could have forced me, so numerous are the Bohemian lords who love me and who would have afforded me protection." And when the Cardinal Peter d'Ailly indignantly exclaimed, "See the impudence of the man," and a murmur ran around the whole assembly, John of Chlum calmly arose and said, "He speaks the truth, for though I have little power compared with others in Bohemia, I could easily defend him for a year against the whole strength of both monarchs. Judge, then, how much more could they whose forces are greater and whose castles are stronger than mine."

While thus in Bohemia the upholders of the old order of things were silenced and reformation in the morals of the clergy was enforced with no gentle hand, the news spread around Christendom that the long-desired General Council was to be convoked at last for the settlement of the Great Schism, the reformation of the Church from its head downwards, and the suppression of heresy. With the rival vicars of Christ each showering perdition upon the adherents of the others, the spiritual condition of the faithful was most anxious and a solution of the tremendous question was the most pressing necessity for all who believed what the Latin Church had assiduously taught for a thousand years. Second only in importance to this was the reform of the abuses and corruption of the clergy, which made themselves felt everywhere, from the courts of the pontiffs to the meanest hamlet. Heresy also was to be met and suppressed, for the aspect of matters in Bohemia was threatening, and Sigismund, the emperor-elect, as the heir of his childless brother Wenceslas, was deeply concerned in the pacification of the kingdom. In vain John XXIII endeavored to have the council held in Italy, where he could control it. The nations insisted on some place where the free parliament of Christendom could convene unshackled and debate unchecked. Sigismund selected the episcopal city of Constance; John, hard pressed by Ladislas of Naples and driven from Rome, was forced to yield, and, December 9, 1413, issued his bull convoking the assemblage for the first of the following November. Not only were all prelates and religious corporations ordered to be represented, but all princes and rulers were commanded to be there in person or by deputy. Imperial letters from Sigismund, which accompanied the bull, gave assurance that the powers of State and Church would be combined to reach the result desired by all.

No such assemblage had been seen in Christendom since Innocent III, two centuries before, in the plenitude of his power, had summoned the representatives of Latin Christianity to sit with him in the Lateran. The council might boast fewer mitred heads than the earlier, but it was a far more important body. From its decision there could be no appeal, and the questions to be submitted to it were far more weighty than those which had tasked the consciences of the Lateran fathers. From every part of Europe the Church sent its best and worthiest to take counsel together in this crisis of its fate— men like Chancellor Gerson and Cardinal Peter d'Ailly of Cambrai, as earnest for reform and as sensible of existing wrongs as Wickliff or Huss themselves. The universities poured forth their ablest doctors of theology and canon law. Princes and potentates were there in person or by their representatives, and crowds of every rank in life, from the noble to the juggler. One chronicler assures us that there were, besides members of the council, 60,500 persons present, of whom 16,000 were of gentle blood, from knights and squires up to princes. The same authority informs us that there were 450 public women, but an official census of the council, carefully taken, reports that the number was not less than 700, and even *succubi* were popularly said to have joined in the nefarious trade. Thus the strength and the weakness, the virtue and the vice of the fifteenth century were gathered together to find relief as best they might for the troubles which threatened to overwhelm the Church. After many doubts and much hesitation John XXIII fulfilled his promise to be present, relying upon his stores of gold to win a triumph over his adversaries and over the council itself.

It was inevitable that Huss should tempt his fate at Constance. To both Sigismund and Wenceslas it was of the utmost importance that some authoritative decision should put an end to the strife within the Bohemian Church. The reformers had always professed their desire to submit their demands to a free general council, and Huss himself had appealed to such a council from the papal sentence of excommunication. To hesitate now would be to admit that he dared not face the assembled piety and learning of the Church, and to confess himself a heretic. The host of adversaries in the Bohemian clergy whom his bitter invectives had inflamed and whose preferment had been forfeited through the agitation he had led would surely be there to blacken him and to misrepresent his cause, and all would be lost if he were not present to defend it in person. Besides, incredible as it may seem, he believed himself to be in full communion with the Church, that he would find the council in sympathy with his views, and that certain sermons he had prepared would, when delivered before the assembled prelates, be efficient in bringing about the reforms which he advocated. In his singleness of mind he could not comprehend that men who had thundered as vehemently as himself against current abuses and corruptions, but who had not dared to assail the principles from which those evils sprang, would shrink back aghast from his bolder doctrinal aberrations, and would regard him as a heretic.

When, therefore, the imperial and royal wishes for his presence at Constance were signified to him, with a promise of safe-conduct and full security, he willingly assented, and so anxious was he to be present at the opening of the council that he did not even wait for the promised safe-conduct. That some discussion took place among his friends as to the danger to be incurred there can be no doubt. Jerome of Prague, when on trial, asserted that he had persuaded Huss to go, and Huss in one of his letters from prison alludes to the warnings he had received. He himself was evidently not wholly without misgivings. A sealed letter left with his disciple, Master Martin, not to be opened till news should be received of his death, alludes to the persecution he had suffered for restraining the inordinate lives of the clergy, and his expectation that it would soon reach its consummation. He makes disposition of his slender effects —his gray gown, his white gown, and 60 grossi, which comprise the whole of his worldly gear—and expresses his remorse for the time wasted before his ordination, when he used to play chess to the loss of his own temper and that of others. A letter in the vernacular to his disciples also announces his fear that his enemies may seek in the council to take his life by false testimony. He asks the prayers of his friends that he may have eloquence to uphold the truth and constancy to endure to the last. Still, he did not wholly neglect precautions. Not only did he procure from the Inquisitor Nicholas, Bishop of Nazareth, a certificate of his orthodoxy, but he posted, August 26, throughout Prague a notice in Latin and Bohemian that he would appear before the archbishop, then holding a convocation of the Bohemian clergy, and challenged all who impugned his faith to come forward and accuse him either there or at Constance, asserting his readiness to submit to the punishment of heresy in case he was convicted, but that accusers who failed should be subjected to the *talio*. When John of Jessinetz, his representative, presented himself the next day at the door of the convocation, he was refused admission on the pretext that the body was deliberating on national affairs, and he was told to come back another time. In the assembly of nobles, however, Huss obtained an audience of the archbishop, who was also papal legate, and who declared that he knew of nothing to render Huss guilty except that he ought to purge himself of the excommunication. Of this a certified notarial instrument was sent to Sigismund by Huss with the statement that under the imperial safe-conduct he was ready to go to Constance to defend publicly the faith for which he was prepared, if necessary, to die.

Huss set out, October 11, 1414, under the escort and protection of John and Henry of Chlum and Wenceslas of Duba, all his friends, and delegated for the purpose by Sigismund. The cavalcade consisted of more than thirty horse and two carriages. It was preceded, a day in advance, by the Bishop of Lubec, who announced that Huss was being carried in chains to Constance, and warned the people not to look at him, as he could read men's minds. Already his name had filled all Germany, and this advertisement was an additional incentive for crowds to gather and gaze on him as he passed. His reception served to foster the fatal illusions which he nursed. Everywhere, he wrote to his friends, he was treated as an honored guest and not as an excommunicate; no interdict was proclaimed where he stopped to rest, and he held discussions with magistrates and ecclesiastics. In all cities he posted notices on the church doors that he was on his way to Constance to defend his faith, and that anyone who desired to assail it was invited to do so before the council. On reaching Nuremburg, October 19, in place of deflecting to seek King Sigismund and obtain the promised safe-conduct, he proceeded direct to Constance, while Wenceslas of Duba went to the court and brought the document to him there a few days after his arrival. It was dated October 18.

On November 2 Huss reached Constance, to be greeted by a crowd of 12,000 men assembled to look upon the dreaded reforming heretic. As yet no ambassadors from any of the kings had arrived, and though John XXIII was there with his cardinals, no representatives from his rivals, Gregory XII and Benedict XIII, had presented themselves. What to do with the Bohemian Wickliffite was a problem which puzzled pope and cardinal, and after much discussion it was determined to suspend his excommunication, and permit him to frequent the churches freely, at the same time requesting him not to be present at the solemnities of the Council, lest it might lead to disorder.

Huss himself was utterly blind to the position which he occupied. On November 4, the day before the council was opened, he wrote to his friends at home that overtures had been made to him to settle matters quietly, but that he expected to win a great victory after a great fight. On the 16th he mentioned that when the pope was celebrating mass everyone but himself had assigned to him some function in the ceremony, and he characterized the omission as neglect, evidently considering that his position entitled him to recognition and distinction.

He knew that his opponents had not been idle, but he did not fear them. He had been preceded in Constance by two of his bitterest enemies—Michael of Deutschbrod, known as de Causis, and Wenceslas Tiem, Dean of Passau—and these, in a few days, were reinforced by a more formidable antagonist, Stephen Palecz, fully equipped with most dangerous extracts from Huss's writings. Wenceslas Tiem had been the bearer to Prague of the bull offering indulgences for the crusade against Ladislas of Naples, and his profitable trade had been broken up by Huss. Michael de Causis had been priest of the church of St. Adalbert in the Neustadt of Prague; he had gained the confidence of King Wenceslas by pretending that he could render profitable some abandoned gold mines near Iglau, and the king had entrusted him with a considerable sum of money for the purpose. After working a few days at the mines he decamped to Rome with the funds, which enabled him to purchase a commission as papal procurator *de causis fidei*, whence his appellation. He had already, in 1412, sent to Rome charges against Huss, which the latter pronounced to be lies. The day after Huss's arrival in Constance, Michael posted on the church doors that he would accuse him to the council as an excommunicate and suspect of heresy, but Huss adopted the advice of his friends to take no notice of it until the arrival of Sigismund, who was not expected until Christmas.

Meanwhile Huss himself gave ample cause for adverse comment. Almost immediately on his arrival he began to celebrate mass in his lodgings. This attracted the people in crowds, and was necessarily a cause of scandal. Otto, Bishop of Constance, sent John Tenger, his vicar, and Conrad Helye, his official, to request Huss to cease, as he had long been under papal excommunication; but he refused, saying that he did not consider himself excommunicated, and that he would celebrate mass as often as he pleased. Although thus defied, the bishop, to avoid disturbance, contented himself with forbidding the people from attendance. Soon after this Huss placed himself, with some provisions, in a covered wagon which was to be sent for hay. When the knights who were responsible for him could not find him, Henry of Lastenbock (Chlum) rushed to the burgomaster and demanded that he be searched for. The city was in an uproar; the gates were closed, horse and foot were sent in every direction to find him, and the circumstance was easily magnified into an attempt to escape.

The sturdy Bohemian was evidently a troublesome subject to deal with. The path the pope and his cardinals had to tread in managing the council was likely to be thorny enough without this additional element of disturbance and turbulence. It was far safer to disarm him at once, to anticipate his attacks by treating him legally as one accused of heresy and awaiting trial. Stephen Palecz and Michael de Causis, and a crowd of other Bohemian doctors and priests whom Huss had roughly handled, had already furnished ample material for his indictment, and in the inquisitorial process the first step was to make sure that the accused should not escape. On November 28 the cardinals, in consistory with the pope, sent to Huss's lodgings the Bishops of Augsburg and Trent, with Henry of Ulm, the burgomaster of Constance, to summon him at once before them to defend his faith. The envoys greeted him kindly, and though both he and John of Chlum protested that the summons was a violation of the safe-conduct, he immediately consented to go, although he said he had come to Constance to appear openly in the council, and not secretly before the cardinals. John of Chlum and some friends accompanied him to the palace occupied by the pope. When the cardinals told him he was accused of disseminating many heresies, he replied that he would rather die than be convicted of a single one; he had come with alacrity to Constance, and if he was found in error he would willingly abjure. To this the cardinals said, "You have answered well." No further examination was had, but John XXIII, whose policy was to embroil the council with Sigismund, took occasion to ask John of Chlum whether Huss had an imperial safe-conduct, to which Chlum replied, "Holy father, you know that he has."

When the morning session was over, guards were placed over Huss and John of Chlum. The weary afternoon wore away in suspense, while the cardinals held another session in which Stephen Palecz and Michael de Causis were busy. The tedium of detention was broken only by a simple-looking Franciscan, who accosted Huss and asked for instruction on the subject of transubstantiation, and, on being satisfactorily answered, inquired about the union of humanity and divinity in Christ. Huss recognized that he was no simple inquirer, for he had asked the most difficult question in theology; he declined further colloquy, and on the retiring of the friar was informed by the guards that he was Master Didaco, renowned as the subtlest theologian of Lombardy. About nightfall John of Chlum was allowed to depart, while Huss was detained, and soon after Stephen and Michael came exultingly and told him that he was now in their power, and should not escape till he had paid the last penny. He was taken under guard to the house of the precentor of the cathedral, in charge of the Bishop of Lausanne, regent of the apostolic chamber, and after eight days was transferred to the Dominican convent on the Rhine. Here he was confined in a cell adjoining the latrines, where a fever soon caused his life to be despaired of.[1] His sudden death would have been a most untoward event, and the pope sent his own physicians to restore him. It was in vain that his friends in Prague procured from Archbishop Conrad a declaration affirming that he had never found Huss to vary from the faith in a single word. His fate had already been virtually decided.

John of Chlum's first thought on regaining his liberty was to hasten to the pope and to expostulate with him. When the safe-conduct had reached Constance, Chlum had at once exhibited it to John XXIII, who is reported to have declared, on reading it, that if his own brother had been slain by Huss the latter should be safe while in Constance so far as he was concerned. Now he disclaimed all responsibility and threw the blame on the cardinals. This question as to the safe-conduct and its violation has been the

---

[1] The special rigor of confinement near the latrines was well understood. In 1317, when John XXII delivered some Spiritual Franciscans to their brethren for safe-keeping, Friar François Sanche *"posuerunt fratres in quodam carcere juxta latrinas."*

subject of so warm a discussion, and it illustrates so completely a phase of the relations between the Church and heretics, that its brief consideration here is not out of place.

The imperial safe-conduct issued to Huss was in the ordinary form, without limitation or condition. It was addressed to all the princes and subjects of the empire, ecclesiastical and secular, and to all nobles and magistrates and officials, informing them that Huss was taken into the protection of the king and of the empire, and ordering that he be permitted to pass, remain, and return without impediment, and that all help which he might require should be extended to him. That it was intended as a safeguard during the council and the return home is shown by its issue, October 18, after Huss's departure from Prague, and its reaching him in Constance after his arrival there. That his imprisonment was at once looked upon as a gross violation of the imperial pledge is seen in the protests which John of Chlum affixed to the church doors on December 15, probably as soon as Sigismund could be heard from, and again on the 24th, when the king was near Constance and was to arrive the next day. This paper recited that Huss had come under the imperial protection and safe-conduct to answer in public audience all who might question his faith. That, in the absence of Sigismund, who would not have permitted it, and in contempt of his safe-conduct, Huss had been thrown into prison. That the imperial ambassadors had vainly demanded his release, and that when Sigismund comes he should plainly make known to all men his grief and indignation at this violation of the imperial pledge.

The suggestion that the safe-conduct was a mere passport designedly insufficient to protect Huss is a recent discovery which would not have been left to the ingenuity of modern times if it could have been alleged during the warm debate which raged over the question at Constance. That nobody thought of it then is sufficient proof that such an excuse is untenable. Such an assertion would have been all-sufficient when, May 13, 1415, the Bohemians in Constance presented a memorial to the council in which they referred to the treatment of Huss as a violation of the safe-conduct. Yet in its answer the council had no thought of making such an allegation. They had recourse only to a lie manufactured for the occasion, by asserting, in spite of the notorious existence of the safe-conduct in Constance at the time of Huss's arrest, that witnesses worthy of credit had proved that it had not been procured until fifteen days after that occurrence, and therefore that no public faith had been violated in the proceedings.

Sigismund at first fully justified the confidence reposed in him by Huss and John of Chlum. He made no attempt to say that his letters were not intended to protect Huss from prosecution, but treated them as having been wrongfully violated. As soon as he had heard of the arrest he had ordered Huss's release with a threat to break open the prisons in case of refusal. On his arrival at Constance, on Christmas Day, his indignation was boundless. He protested that he would leave Constance, and, in fact, made a show of doing so; he even threatened to withdraw the imperial protection from the council, but was plainly told by the cardinals that they would themselves break it up unless he yielded. The hopes of Christendom had been raised to too high a pitch for him to venture on such a risk. Naturally faithless, his insistence was a matter of pride, and self-interest easily won the day. It cost him little, therefore, when on January 1, 1415, the council formally asked him that free course of justice be allowed in the case of Huss, to issue a decree declaring the council free in all matters of faith and capable of proceeding against all who were defamed for heresy; moreover, he pledged himself to set at naught the threats which were freely uttered of defending Huss at all hazards. Yet the discussion still continued during January, and the pressure on him from Bohemia was so strong that for a while he still fluctuated irresolutely, but, April 8, he formally revoked all letters of safe-conduct.

He had finally taken his position, and he redeemed his hesitation with great show of zeal. When, on June 7, Huss had his second hearing before the council, Sigismund thanked the prelates for their consideration for him as shown in their leniency to Huss, whom he sternly advised to submit, for he could look for no human help; "We will never protect you in your errors and pertinacity. Rather, indeed, than do so we will prepare the fire for you with our own hands."

The trial of Huss has been the subject of much eloquence. It is the most conspicuous instance of an inquisitorial process on record, and to those unacquainted with the procedure which had grown up

in the development of the Holy Office, its practical denial of justice
has seemed a willful perversity on the part of the council, while the
pathetic figure of the sufferer has awakened the warmest sympathy.
Yet, in fact, the only deviations of the council from the ordinary
course of such affairs were special marks of lenity towards the accused. He was not subjected to the torture and, at the instance of
Sigismund, he was thrice permitted to appear before the whole
body and defend himself in public session. When, therefore, we
see how inevitable was his condemnation, how he could have saved
himself only with perjury, we can in some degree estimate the innumerable wrongs inflicted on countless thousands of obscure and
forgotten victims. In this aspect the trial is worthy of examination,
for though it presents no novel points of procedure, except the concessions made to Huss, it affords an instructive example of the manner
in which the inquisitorial process described in preceding chapters
was practically applied.

We have seen that Huss was arrested November 28, 1414. Michael
de Causis, Stephen Palecz, and others of his enemies had presented
formal articles of accusation against him. These, drawn up in the
name of Michael, accused him of maintaining the remanence of
the substance in the Eucharist after consecration, of asserting the
vitiation of the sacraments in the hands of sinful priests and denying
the power of the keys under the same conditions, of holding that the
Church should have no temporal possessions, of disregarding excommunication, of granting the cup to the laity, of defending the
45 condemned articles of Wickliff, of exciting the people against the
clergy, and of other errors and offenses. This was more than sufficient
to justify his trial, and the process was commenced without delay
by the appointment, December 1, of commissioners to examine him.
These commissioners were, in fact, inquisitors, and the council at
large served as the assembly of experts in which, as it will be remembered, final assent was given to the judgment. One of the commissioners at least, Bernardo, Bishop of Città di Castello, was
already familiar with the matter, for, only the year before, as papal
nuncio in Poland, he had assisted in driving away Jerome of Prague.
In addition to the articles of Michael de Causis there was a kind of
indictment against Huss presented to the commissioners by the
procurators and promoters of the council, reciting the troubles at

Prague, his excommunication, and his teaching of Wickliffite heresies.

At first the proceedings were pushed with a vigor which seemed to promise a speedy termination of the case. As soon as Huss recovered from his first sickness there was submitted to him a series of 42 errors extracted from his writings by Palecz. To these he replied *seriatim* in writing, explaining the false constructions which he asserted had been placed on some passages, defending some, and limiting and conditioning others. As he was denied the use of books, even of the treatises which were the source of the charges, these answers manifest a wonderful retentiveness of memory and quickness and clearness of intellect. Sometimes he was visited in his prison by the commissioners and personally interrogated. A Carthusian, writing from Constance, May 19, relates that the day before he had been present at such an examination and had never seen so bold and audacious a scoundrel or one who could so cautiously conceal the truth. We also have his own account of one of these interviews. The commissioners were accompanied by Michael and Stephen to prompt them. Each article was read to him and he was asked if such was his belief; he replied, explaining the sense in which he held it. Then he would be asked if he would defend it, and he would answer no, but that he would stand to the decision of the council. Nothing could seem more submissive or more orthodox, and under any other system of jurisprudence conviction might well appear impossible. Heresy, however, as we have seen, was a crime; once committed, even through ignorance, a simple return to the Church was not enough; belief in the errors must be admitted, and then abjured, before the criminal could be considered as penitent and entitled to the substitution of perpetual imprisonment for the death penalty.

Thousands of miserable wretches had been convicted on a tithe of the evidence now brought against Huss. Stephen Palecz, a man of the highest repute, swore before the commissioners that since the birth of Christ there had been no more dangerous heretics than Wickliff and Huss, and that all who customarily attended the sermons of the latter believed in the remanence of the substance of bread in the Eucharist. What Palecz testified there were scores of others to substantiate and amplify. Many of these errors he indignantly denied having entertained, but it was in vain. In vain he wrote out in prison, as early as March 5, 1415, his tract, *De Sacramento Corporis et Sanguinis*, in which he declared that full transubstantiation took place; that God worked the miracle irrespective of the merits of the celebrant; that the body and blood of Christ were both in the bread and in the wine, and that he had taught this doctrine since 1401, before he was a priest. In vain during his public audience of June 8 he disputed earnestly in favor of the same belief. The witnesses swore to the contrary. He had no right to call rebutting testimony, and could only appeal to God and his conscience. He was proved a heretic who must confess and abjure or be burned.

His only possible line of defense, as has been shown above, would have lain in disabling the witnesses for mortal enmity—for enmity such as would lead them to seek his life—and even this would not have been available against the errors the commissioners had extracted, falsely, as he asserted, from his writings. As regards the witnesses, the commissioners made an unusual concession to him when, during his sickness in December, some fifteen of them were taken to his cell that he might see them sworn. Some of them, it is said, declared that they knew nothing; others were bitterly hostile to him. To this extent he knew some of the names, and others he was acquainted with because they were attached to depositions taken in advance at Prague for Michael de Causis, which by some means had fallen into the hands of Huss before he started for Constance. Some of these names, probably on this account, were attached to the article on the subject of remanence presented in the hearing of June 7, but in the final sentence no names are mentioned; the witnesses to each article are designated simply by titles, such as a canon of Prague, a priest of Litomysl, a master of arts, a doctor of theology, etc., and when Huss asked the name of one of them it was refused. This was strictly in accordance with rule.

Yet the hostility of those who testified against him was notorious. The Bohemians in Constance, in their memorial of May 31, 1415, to the council, declared that the testimony against him was given by those who were his mortal enemies. At one time he or his friends thought of disabling them on this account, but when he asked the commissioners to permit him to employ an advocate who could take the necessary exceptions to the evidence, although they at first assented they finally refused, saying that it was against the law for anyone to defend a suspected heretic. This, as we have seen, was strictly true, and if the maintenance of the rule may seem harsh, we must remember on the other hand that the friends of Huss were allowed unexampled liberty in working in his behalf. If there had been any disposition to enforce the law they could have been reduced to instant silence and have been grieviously punished for fautorship. Huss was kept in the Dominican convent until March 24. Although his petition to be allowed to see his friends was refused, they were permitted to furnish him with writing materials, and he employed his enforced leisure in composing a number of tracts which, written without the aid of books, show his extensive and accurate acquaintance with Scripture and the Fathers. His sweet temper won the good will of all who were brought in contact with him, and he gratefully alludes to the kindness with which he was treated both by his guards and by the clerks of the papal chamber. Letters were conveyed back and forth clandestinely, sometimes carried in food, in spite of the vigilance of his enemies.

All this ceased when the quarrel between pope and council culminated. On March 20 John XXIII secretly fled from Constance, when the guards placed over Huss delivered the keys to Sigismund and followed their master. The council then handed Huss over to the custody of the Bishop of Constance, who carried him in chains by night to the castle of Gottlieben, some miles from the city across the Rhine. His friends had requested that he should have a more airy prison, and the request was more than granted, for he was now confined in a room at the top of a tower. Though his feet were fettered he was able to move about during the day, but at night his arm was chained to the wall. As escape was impossible, the confinement was evidently intended to be punitive. Here he was completely isolated from all intercourse with his fellow beings and left to his own dreary introspection. Disease added to the harshness of his prison. From the foul Dominican cell to the windy turret of Gottlieben, he was exposed to every variety of unwholesome conditions. Stone, an affection hitherto unknown to him, tormented him greatly. On one occasion a severe attack of fever, accompanied by excessive vomiting, so prostrated him that his guards carried him out of his cell thinking him about to die. Yet throughout all his letters from prison the beautiful patience of the man shines forth. For the enemies who were pursuing him to the death there is only forgiveness; for the trials with which God has seen fit to test his servant there is only submission. He overflows with gratitude for the steadfast affection of his friends, and sends touching requests of remembrance to them all; he teaches charity and gently points out the way to moral and spiritual improvement. There is neither the pride of martyrdom nor the desire for retribution; all is resignation and love and humility.

Hope seemed justified when the rupture occurred between the pope and the council. No sooner was Huss made aware of the flight of John XXIII than he begged his friends to see Sigismund instantly and procure his liberation. The answer was his transfer to the tower of Gottlieben. When the pope was brought back a prisoner to the same castle, and the council proceeded to try and condemn him as a simonist and dilapidator who was ruining the Church, while his personal vices and crimes, unfit for description, were a scandal to Christendom, such confirmation of all that the Wickliffites had urged might well seem to justify the expectation that Huss would be released with honor. John XXIII, however, with the wisdom of the children of the world, essayed no defense; he confessed all that was laid to his charge, submitted to the council, and was eventually, after a few years of imprisonment, rewarded by Martin V with the lofty post of Dean of the Sacred College. Huss, with the constancy of the children of light, refused to perjure himself by confession, and there could be no escape for him.

The council had been assembled to reform the Church, and was performing its duty in its own way, but nothing could be further from the thoughts of its most zealous members than the revolutionary reform of Wickliff and Huss, which would reduce the Church to apostolic poverty and deprive it of all temporal power. Besides the doctrinal errors, there was ample material in Huss's writings to prove him a most dangerous enemy of the whole ecclesiastical system. He had written his tract *De Ablatione Bonorum* in defense of one of the 45 condemned Wickliffite articles, which asserted that the temporal lord could at will deprive of their temporalities ecclesiastics who were habitual delinquents. His tract *De Decimis* defended another of the articles, contending that no one in mortal sin could be a temporal lord, a prelate, or a bishop. John Gerson, one of the leading members of the council, had, as Chancellor of the University of Paris, before coming to Constance, drawn up a series of 20 such dangerous errors, extracted from Huss's treatise *De Ecclesia*, and had urged Archbishop Conrad of Prague to extirpate the Wickliffite heresy by calling in the secular arm. Huss, in his deductions from the Wickliffite doctrines of predestination, had overthrown the very foundations of the hierarchical system. Among the cardinals in the council, Ottone Colonna had fulminated the papal excommunication which Huss had disregarded; Zabarella and Brancazio had been actively concerned in the proceedings against him before the curia —all of these and many others were thoroughly familiar with his revolutionary doctrines. Michael de Causis had intercepted a letter, written by Huss from prison, in which the ministers of the council were alluded to as the servants of Antichrist, and when this was brought to him by the commissioners he acknowledged its authenticity.

It thus was idle to suppose that the council, because it had deposed John XXIII, would set free so contumacious a heretic, whose very virtues only rendered him the more dangerous. The inquisitorial process must go on to the end. Even during the bitterest and most doubtful portion of the contest, before the pope had been brought back to Constance, the successive steps of the trial received due attention. On April 17 four new commissioners were appointed to replace the previous ones, whose commissions from the pope were held to have expired, and the new commission was expressly granted power to proceed to final sentence. The only doubt arising was whether the condemnation of Wickliff, with which the case of Huss was inextricably related, should be uttered in the name of the pope or in that of the council, and its publication, May 4, in the latter form, showed that the assembly had no hesitation as to its duty in stamping out the heresy of the master and of the disciple. Yet how little the friends of Huss understood the real position of affairs, and how false hopes had been excited by the rupture with the pope, is seen in their efforts at this juncture to press the trial to a conclusion. Under the procrastinating policy of the Inquisition it is quite possible that Huss would have been left to his solitary musings for a time indefinitely longer, in hopes that his resolution would at last give way, but for the efforts of his friends, who hoped to secure his release. On May 13 they presented a memorial complaining of his treatment, in violation of the safe-conduct and of the pledged faith of the empire. On May 16 the council replied to the effect that as far back as 1411 Huss had had a hearing before the Holy See and had been excommunicated, and had since then not only proved himself a heretic, but a heresiarch, by remaining under excommunication and preaching forbidden doctrines, even in Constance itself. As for the safe-conduct, we have seen how it was pretended to have been procured after the arrest. This elusive answer might have shown how the case was already prejudged by those who were to decide it; yet again, on May 18, the Bohemians presented a rejoinder urging promptitude. It was fully expected in Constance that a session would be held on the 22d, at which Huss would be condemned; but about this time attention was engrossed by the trial of John XXIII, who was at length deposed, May 29, and notified of his deposition on the 31st. Sigismund was now preparing for the voyage to Spain, which was expected to take place in June, and if anything was to be done with Huss before his departure further delay was inadmissible. Probably the Bohemians imagined that in some indefinable way he would yet save their leader. On May 31, therefore, they presented another memorial, reiterating their complaints about the safe-conduct and asking for a speedy public hearing. Sigismund entered during the discussion and strenuously urged the public audience, which was finally promised. Huss's friends further urged that he should be brought from his prison and be allowed a few days to recover from his incarceration, and a show was made of complying with the request. On the same day John of Chlum had the satisfaction of forwarding to Gottlieben an order for the transmission of Huss to Constance. The next day, June 1, a special deputation from the council followed and presented to him the 30 articles which had been proved against him. They reported that he submitted himself to the council, but he maintained that he only agreed to do so on such points as he could be proved to have taught erroneously. At last he was brought to Constance in chains and confined in the Franciscan convent.

In the routine of the inquisitorial process there was no necessity for further parley with the accused. The articles of heresy were

proved against him, and if he continued to deny them, delivery to
the secular arm was a matter of course. There had been no intention
of permitting such an innovation on the regular procedure as a public
audience, but Sigismund could see, if the council could not, that its
denial would have a most unfortunate influence on public opinion in
Bohemia, where, in the prevailing ignorance of the inquisitorial
rules, it would be claimed that the council was afraid to face their
champion and was forced to condemn him unheard. The audiences
which followed were thus wholly irregular, and may be briefly dismissed as in no sense entitled to the importance which has commonly
been ascribed to them.

On June 5 a congregation of the council was held in the Franciscan convent. At first the intention was to carry out the ordinary
inquisitorial procedure by considering, in the absence of Huss, the
articles proved against him, but Peter Mladenowic hastened to
John of Chlum and Wenceslas of Duba, who forthwith appealed
to Sigismund. The latter at once sent the Palsgrave Louis and
Frederic Burggrave of Nuremburg to the council, with orders that
nothing should be done until Huss was present and his books were
before them for verification. At length, therefore, he had the long-
desired opportunity of meeting his adversaries, and defending himself in public debate. The books from which his errors had been
extracted were laid before him, and he acknowledged them to be his.
The articles were taken up in succession. He was required to answer
to each a simple *yea* or *nay*, and when he desired to explain anything a scene of indescribable confusion arose. When he asked to
be taught wherein he had erred he was told that he must first recant
his heresies, which was strictly in accordance with the law. The day
wore away in the discussion, and it had to be renewed on the 7th,
and again on the 8th—Sigismund being present on these latter occasions. Huss defended himself with wonderful quickness of thought
and dialectical skill, but nothing could be more unlike the free
debate which he had deluded himself into anticipating when he left
Prague. Although the Cardinal of Ostia, who presided, endeavored
to show fairness, the assembly at times became a howling mob with
shouts of "Burn him! Burn him!" Interruptions were incessant, he
was baited on all sides with questions, and frequently his replies
were drowned in clamor. As a judicial act it was a mockery, but it

served the purpose desired by Sigismund, and the Church had shown itself not afraid of public discussion with the heresiarch. At the end of the third day of this tumultuous wrangling Huss was exhausted almost to fainting. The night before toothache had deprived him of sleep, an attack of fever supervened, and six months of harsh imprisonment had left him little physical endurance. The proceedings terminated with the cardinals' urging him to recant and promising him merciful treatment if he would throw himself upon the mercy of the council. He asked for another hearing, saying that he would submit if his arguments and authorities were insufficient. To this Cardinal Peter d'Ailly replied that the unanimous decision of the doctors was that he must confess his error in publishing the articles ascribed to him, he must swear never in future to believe or teach them, and must recant them publicly. Huss begged the council for the love of God not to force him to wrong his conscience, for abjuration meant the renunciation of an error previously entertained, and many of those brought against him he had never held. Sigismund asked him why he could not renounce errors which he said had been ascribed to him through perjury, and Huss had to explain to him the technical meaning of abjuration. One member of the council even objected to the accused being admitted to recantation, because he was not to be trusted, but this would have been wholly illegal. It was impossible, in such a crowd of eager persecutors, to maintain the legal forms in all strictness, and there followed a number of volunteer accusations by individuals. Finally, as Huss was withdrawn, John of Chlum succeeded in giving him a friendly grasp of the hand and a word of sympathy. That touch and voice were a solace which nerved him for the yet harder trials of the succeeding weeks.

His endurance was now to be tested to the uttermost. The wise policy of the Inquisition, which preferred a confessed penitent to a martyr, was especially applicable in this case, for though Sigismund and the council underestimated the Bohemian fervor and obstinacy, the dullest could see that Huss's confessing to having taught heresy and seeking reconciliation would dispirit his followers, while no one could guess the extent of the conflagration which might spread from his pyre. Accordingly efforts were redoubled to induce him to confess and recant. Sigismund had prepared the way by assuring him during the public audience that no mercy would be shown him and that persistent denial would bring him to the stake, while he was not notified that behind the bland promises of mercy for submission there lay a sentence, which, while expressing joy at his humbly seeking absolution, pronounced him to be pernicious, scandalous, and seditious, and condemned him to degradation from the priesthood and to perpetual imprisonment. The council could do no otherwise, for this, as we have seen, was the punishment provided by the canons for repentant heretics, and yet in estimating the firmness of Huss we must bear in mind that no intimation of it seems to have been made to him.

For a month the struggle continued. Huss asked for a confessor, and intimated that he would prefer Stephen Palecz, the enemy who had hounded him to the death. Palecz came and heard his confession, and then urged him to abjure, saying that he ought not to mind the humiliation. "The humiliation of condemnation and burning is greater," replied Huss, "how then can I fear humiliation? But advise me: what would you do if you knew for certain that you did not hold the errors imputed to you? Would you abjure?" Palecz burst into tears and could only stammer, "It is difficult." He wept again freely when Huss begged his pardon for harsh words used in the heat of strife, and especially for calling him a falsifier. Another confessor was sent to him, who listened to him kindly and gave him absolution without insisting on preliminary abjuration, which was a most irregular concession—indeed, almost incredible. Many others were allowed to visit him in the hope of persuading him to confess and recant. One learned doctor urged his submission, saying, "If the council told me I had but one eye, I would confess it to be so, though I know I have two," but Huss was impervious to such example. An Englishman adduced the precedent of the English doctors who had, without exception, abjured the heresies of Wickliff when required to do so; but when Huss offered to swear that he had never held or taught the heresies imputed to him, and that he would never hold or teach them, his baffled advisers withdrew.

The most formidable effort, however, was of an official character. At the final hearing of June 8, Cardinal Zabarella had promised him that a recantation in a form strictly limited would be submitted to him, and the promise was fulfilled in a paper skillfully drawn up, so as to satisfy his scruples. It represented him as protesting anew that much had been imputed to him which he had never believed, but that nevertheless he submitted himself in everything to the correction and orders of the council in abjuring, revoking, and retracting, and in accepting whatever merciful penance the council might prescribe for his salvation. Carefully as this was phrased to elude the difficulty, Huss rejected it without hesitation. In some matters, he said, he would be denying the truth, in others he would be perjuring himself. Then one of the fathers of the council—supposed to be the Cardinal of Ostia, the highest in rank of the Sacred College—addressed him as his "dearest and most cherished brother," with the most honeyed persuasiveness, begging him not to confide too absolutely in his own judgment. In making the abjuration it will not be he that condemns truth, but the council; as for perjury, if perjury there be, it will fall on the heads of those who exact it. Yet Huss was not to be enticed with such allurements; he could not quiet his conscience with casuistry such as this, and he deliberately chose death. In daily expectation of the dreadful sentence, he quietly put his simple affairs in order. Peter Mladenowic, the notary, had rendered him zealous service and should be paid out of his 60 grossi. His little debts were to be settled, and his books, apparently his only other property, were to be distributed. Kind remembrances were sent to his numerous friends, and they were told if they had learned any good of him to hold fast to it; if they had seen in him aught reprehensible to cast it aside. It was not that he was insensible, for he describes in moving terms the mental conflicts and agony which he endured in his hopeless prison, expecting each day to be led forth to an agonizing death. Solicitous to retain the good opinion of his disciples, he managed to transmit to them, on June 18, a copy of the articles proved against him, together with a report of what his defense had been. Of those drawn from his writings he retracted none, although many he declared to be false and garbled. Those alleged against him by witnesses he mostly asserted to be lies, and he concluded, "It only remains for me to abjure and revoke and undergo fearful penance or to burn. May the Father, Son, and Holy Ghost grant me the spirit of wisdom and fortitude to persevere to the end and to escape the snares of Satan!"

In hope of his weakening, the end was postponed until the

approaching departure of Sigismund rendered further delay impossible. Yet effort was not abandoned till the last. On July 1 a deputation of prelates endeavored to persuade him that he could reasonably recant, but he handed them a written confession calling God to witness that he had never taught many of the articles; as for the rest, if there were error in them he detested it, but he could not abjure any of them. Puzzled by his unexpected tenacity of purpose, and earnestly desirous of avoiding the catastrophe, a final and unprecedented concession was agreed upon. On July 5 Zabarella and Peter d'Ailly sent for him and offered to let him deny the heresies proved by witnesses if he would abjure those extracted from his books. This was, in fact, an abandonment of all inquisitorial precedent, but Huss had persistently declared that most of the latter were fraudulently drawn, so as to attribute to him errors which he had never held, and he was immovable. As a last resource, later in the same day, Sigismund sent his friends John of Chlum and Wenceslas of Duba, with four bishops, to ask him whether he would persevere or recant, but his answer was as firm as ever. To the friendly adjuration of John of Chlum he replied with tears that he would willingly revoke anything in which he could be proved to have erred. The bishops pronounced him obstinate in error and left him.

Thus the extraordinary efforts of the council to save itself and him were vain, and nothing remained but the inevitable final act of the tragedy. The next day, July 6, saw the most gorgeous *auto de fé* on record. The cathedral of Constance was crowded with Sigismund and his nobles, the great officers of the empire with their insignia, the prelates in their splendid robes. While mass was sung, Huss, as an excommunicate, was kept waiting at the door; when brought in he was placed on an elevated bench by a table on which stood a coffer containing priestly vestments. After some preliminaries, including a sermon by the Bishop of Lodi, in which he assured Sigismund that the events of that day would confer on him immortal glory, the articles of which Huss was convicted were recited. In vain he protested that he believed in transubstantiation and in the validity of the sacrament in polluted hands. He was ordered to hold his tongue, and on his persisting the beadles were told to silence him, but in spite of this he continued to utter protests. The sentence was then read in the name of the council, condemning him both for his written errors and those which had been proved by witnesses. He was declared a pertinacious and incorrigible heretic who did not desire to return to the Church; his books were ordered to be burned, and himself to be degraded from the priesthood and abandoned to the secular court. Seven bishops arrayed him in priestly garb and warned him to recant while yet there was time. He turned to the crowd, and with broken voice declared that he could not confess the errors which he had never entertained, lest he should lie to God, when the bishops interrupted him, crying that they had waited long enough. He was degraded in the usual manner, stripped of his sacerdotal vestments, his fingers scraped; but when the tonsure was to be disposed of an absurd quarrel arose among the bishops whether the head should be shaved with a razor or the tonsure be destroyed with scissors. Scissors won the day, and a cross was cut in his hair. Then on his head was placed a conical paper cap adorned with painted devils and the inscription, "This is the heresiarch." In accordance with the universal custom no proceedings by the secular authorities were regarded as necessary. As soon as the ecclesiastical court had pronounced him a heretic and handed him over, the laws against heresy operated of themselves. Sigismund, it is true, might have delayed the execution for six days, but this would have been so unusual as to have excited most unfavorable comment. He therefore briefly ordered the Palsgrave Louis to take charge of the culprit and to do to him as to a heretic. Louis called to Hans Hazen, the imperial vogt of Constance, "Vogt, take him as judged of both of us and burn him as a heretic." Then he was led forth, and the council calmly turned to other business, unconscious that it had performed the most momentous act of the century.

The place of execution was a meadow near the river, to which he was conducted by 2,000 armed men, with Palsgrave Louis at their head, and a vast crowd, including many nobles, prelates, and cardinals. The route followed was circuitous, in order that he might be carried past the episcopal palace, in front of which his books were burning, whereat he smiled, but when he came in sight of the stake he fell on his knees and prayed. He was asked if he wished to confess, and said that he would gladly do so if there were space. A wide circle was formed, and Ulrich Schorand, who, according to custom, had been providently empowered to take advantage of any final weakening, came forward, saying, "Dear sir and master, if you will recant your unbelief of heresy, for which you must suffer, I will willingly hear your confession; but if you will not, you know right well that, according to canon law, no one can administer the sacrament to a heretic." To this Huss answered, "It is not necessary: I am no mortal sinner." He desired to take leave of his keepers, and when they were brought to him he thanked them for their kindness, saying that they had been to him rather brothers than jailers. Then he commenced to address the crowd in German, telling them that he suffered for errors which he did not hold, sworn to by perjured witnesses; but this could not be permitted, and he was cut short. When bound to the stake and two cartloads of fagots and straw were piled up around him the palsgrave and vogt for the last time adjured him to abjure. He only repeated that he had been convicted by false witnesses of errors never entertained by him. They clapped their hands and then withdrew, and the executioners applied the fire. Twice Huss was heard to exclaim, "Christ Jesus, Son of the living God, have mercy upon me!" then a wind springing up and blowing the flames and smoke into his face checked further utterance. Palsgrave Louis, seeing Huss's mantle on the arm of one of the executioners, ordered it thrown into the flames lest it should be reverenced as a relic. With the same view the body was carefully reduced to ashes and thrown into the Rhine, and even the earth around the stake was dug up and carted off; yet the Bohemians long hovered around the spot and carried home fragments of the neighboring clay, which they reverenced as relics of their martyr. The next day thanks were returned to God, in a solemn procession in which figured Sigismund and his queen, the princes and nobles, 19 cardinals, 2 patriarchs, 77 bishops, and all the clergy of the council. A few days later Sigismund, who had delayed his departure for Spain to see the matter concluded, left Constance, feeling that his work was done.

Great was the disgust of the orthodox when they learned that their pious view of the matter was not entertained in Prague, and it required the most positive assurances of eyewitnesses to make them believe the incredible fact that, from king to peasant in Bo-

hemia, there was practical unanimity in the belief that he who
had been condemned and executed as a heretic was a martyr; that
he was inserted in the calendar of saints, with his feast on July 6,
the day of his execution. The good fathers, however, were not long
in finding that they had made a grave mistake as to the Bohemian
temper, and that they had only succeeded in inflaming the disease
which they had sought to eradicate. As soon as the defiance excited
in Bohemia could be learned in Constance, the council made haste
to write, July 26, to the authorities there, protesting that Huss and
Jerome of Prague had been treated with all tenderness, that the
persistent heresy of the former had forced his delivery to the secular
court for judgment, and that all similar heretics would be treated
in the same manner. The Bohemians were exhorted to justify, by
similar persecution, the good opinion of their orthodoxy which the
council had formed from the report of the Bishop of Litomysl. This
good opinion was not sustained when a protest was received from
the barons of Bohemia and Moravia, hastily drawn up as soon as
the news of the execution had reached them—a protest the council
promptly ordered to be burned. Its letter of July 26 led to the convocation of a national assembly, in which an address was framed
and received the signatures of nearly 500 barons, knights, and gentlemen. In this they asserted their belief in Huss's purity and orthodoxy;
that he had unjustly been put to death without confession or lawful
conviction; that Jerome they supposed had shared the same fate;
that the defamation of the kingdom for heresy was the work of
liars. and that anyone who asserted it, saving Sigismund, lied in his
throat, was the vilest of traitors and the worst of heretics, and as
such they would prosecute him before the future pope. A more
dangerous symptom of rebellion was a pledge signed by the magnates,
agreeing that all priests should be allowed to preach freely the truths
of Scripture, that no bishop should be permitted to interfere with
them unless they taught errors, and that no excommunications or
interdicts from abroad should be received or observed.

It was probably this stimulus of Bohemian disaffection which led
the council to act vigorously in the case of Jerome of Prague, whom
the Bohemian nobles had erroneously believed to have shared the
fate of Huss. Jerome of Prague stands before us as one of those
meteoric natures which would be dismissed as half-mythical, if the

substantial facts on record did not fix the details of his career with an exactness leaving no room for doubt. Born at Prague, his early training was received at a time when men's minds were beginning to waver in the confusion of the Great Schism and under the impulsion of the Wickliffite writings. About the year 1400 he was brought under the influence of Huss, and thereafter he continued to be his steadfast adherent and supporter. Already, at Paris, Cologne, Heidelberg, and Cracow—at all of which he had been decorated with the honors of the universities—he had disturbed the philosophic calm of the schools with his subtleties on the theory of universals; at Paris, indeed, the disturbance had gone so far that John Gerson, the Chancellor of the University, had driven him forth, perhaps retaining a grudge which explains his zeal in the prosecution of his old antagonist. His restless spirit left scarce a region of the known civilized world unvisited. At Oxford, attracted by the reputation of Wickliff, he had copied with his own hand the *Dialogus* and the *Trialogus*, and had carried those outpourings of revolt to Prague. On a second visit he had been seized as a heretic, and had escaped through the intervention of the University of Prague. In Palestine he had trodden in the footsteps of the Saviour and had bent in reverence at the Holy Sepulchre. In Lithuania he had sought to convert the heathen. In Russia he had endeavored to win over the schismatic Greek. In Poland and Hungary he had scattered the doctrines of Wickliff and Huss. Driven out of Hungary in 1410, he was arrested and thrown in prison in Vienna, by the papal Inquisitor and episcopal official, for teaching Hussitism and infecting with it the University of that city. His trial was commenced and a day was set for its hearing, prior to which he was allowed his liberty on his oath not to leave the city, under pain of excommunication. Claiming that an extorted oath was of no force, he escaped, and from Olmütz wrote a free-and-easy letter to the Bishop of Passau, suggesting that the prosecutors and witnesses may be sent to Prague, where the trial can be finished. The excommunication, indeed, followed him to Prague, but in the tumultuous condition of Bohemia it gave him no trouble. In 1413 he again visited Poland, where in a short time he succeeded in causing an unprecedented excitement, and was speedily sent back to Prague. His whole life had been spent in intellectual digladiation, from his youthful philosophic contests to the maturer struggles with the overwhelming forces of the hierarchy. A layman, not in holy orders, he had preached to admiring crowds of Majjars, Poles, and Czechs; nor was he wholly unskilled in the use of the arms of the flesh. On his trial he admitted that he had once been drawn into a quarrel with some monks in a monastery, when two of them attacked him with swords, and he defended himself successfully with a weapon hastily snatched from the hand of a bystander. His commanding presence, his glittering eyes, his sable hair and flowing beard, his deep and impressive voice, enabled him to throw his influence over all with whom he came in contact; while his miraculous store of learning, his unmatched readiness, and the subtlety of his intellect rendered him an enemy of the Church only one degree less dangerous than the steadfast and irreproachable Huss.

Jerome had watched from Prague the fate of his friend with daily increasing anxiety, and when the rupture between pope and council seemed to promise immunity for the opponents of hierarchical corruption he could not resist the temptation to aid in his rescue, and to assist in what appeared to be the approaching overthrow of the evils which he had so long combated. April 4, 1415, he came secretly to Constance, but speedily found how groundless were his hopes and how dangerous was the atmosphere of the place. Christann of Prachaticz, one of Huss's chief disciples, had recently ventured to visit Constance, had been arrested, and articles of accusation had been presented against him, when on the intervention of the Bohemian ambassadors he had been liberated under oath to present himself when summoned—an oath which he had forfeited by promptly escaping to Bohemia. Jerome contented himself with posting a notice on the walls affirming the orthodoxy of Huss; he withdrew at once to Ueberlingen and asked for a safe-conduct. The response was ambiguous, but, like a moth hovering around the fatal flame, he returned to Constance, where, April 7, he affixed another notice on the church doors addressed to Sigismund and the council. It stated that he had come of his own free will to answer all accusations of heresy, and if convicted he was ready to endure the penalty, but he asked a safe-conduct in coming and going, and if incarcerated or treated with violence during his stay the council would be committing injustice of which he could not suspect so many learned and wise men. This senseless bravado is only to be explained by his erratic temperament. He suddenly changed his mind, and on April 9, after obtaining from the Bohemians at Constance testimonial letters, he escaped from the city, none too soon, for the officials were in search of his lodgings, which they discovered a few days after at the Gutjar, in St. Paul Street, where in his haste he had left behind him the significant memento of a sword. This time he no longer trifled with fate, but travelled rapidly towards Bohemia. At Hirsau, however, his impetuous temper led him into a discussion in which he stigmatized the council as a synagogue of Satan. He was seized April 24, and the papers found upon him betrayed him. John of Bavaria threw him into the castle of Sulzbach, notified the council of his capture, and in obedience to its commands he was forthwith carried thither in chains.

Meanwhile the council had responded to his appeal by publishing, April 18, a formal inquisitorial citation summoning him, as a suspected and defamed heretic, to appear for trial within fifteen days, in default of which he would be proceeded against in contumacy. A safe-conduct was offered him, but it was expressly declared subject to the exigencies of the faith. Unaware of his capture, on May 2 a new citation was published and his trial as contumacious was ordered, and this was repeated on the 4th. On May 24 his captors brought him to the city loaded with chains, and took him to the Franciscan convent, where a tumultuous congregation of the council greeted his arrival. Here Gerson gratified his rancor against his old opponent, loudly berating him for having taught falsely at Paris, Heidelberg, and Cologne, and the rectors of the two latter universities corroborated the accusations. His replies were sharp and ready, but were drowned in the roar of fresh charges, mingled with shouts of "Burn him! Burn him!" Thence he was carried to a dungeon in the Cemetery of St. Paul, where he was chained hand and foot to a bench too high for him to sit on, and for two days he was fed on bread and water, until his friends ascertained his place of imprisonment and made interest with the jailer to give him better food. He soon fell dangerously sick and asked for a confessor, after which he was less rigorously fettered, but he never left the prison except for audience and execution.

Stephen Palecz, Michael de Causis, and the rest were ready with their accusations, nor could there be difficulty in accumulating a mass of testimony sufficient to convict twenty such men as Jerome. His trial proceeded according to the regular inquisitorial process, the commissioners finding him much more learned and skillful than Huss; but, brilliant as was his defense when under examination, his nervous temperament unfitted him to bear, like Huss, the long-protracted agony. Sometimes with dialectic subtlety he turned his examiners to ridicule, at others he vacillated between obduracy and submission. Finally he weakened under the strain, while the rebellious attitude of the Bohemians doubtless led the council to increase the pressure. On September 11 he was brought before the assembly, where he read a long and elaborate recantation. Huss's sweetness of temper, he said, had attracted him, and his earnest exposition of Scripture had led him to believe that such a man could not teach heresy. He could not believe that the 30 articles condemned by the council were really Huss's, until he had obtained a book in Huss's own handwriting, and on comparing them article by article he found them to be so. He therefore spontaneously and of free will condemned them, some of them as heretical, others as erroneous, others as scandalous. He also condemned the 45 articles of Wickliff; he submitted himself wholly to the council, he condemned whatever it condemned, and he asked for fitting penance to be assigned him. He did not even shrink from a deeper degradation. He wrote to Bohemia that Huss had been justly executed, that he had become convinced of his friend's errors and could not defend them.

This was not a strictly formal abjuration such as was customarily required of prisoners of the Inquisition, yet it might have sufficed. At the next general session, September 23, Jerome was placed in the pulpit, where he repeated his recantation, winding up by a solemn oath of abjuration in which he invoked an eternal anathema on all who wandered from the faith and on himself if he should do so. He had been told that he would not be allowed to return to Bohemia, but might select some Swabian monastery in which to reside, on condition that he should write home, over his hand and seal, that his teaching and that of Huss were false and not to be followed. This he promised to do, as, indeed, he had already done, but he was remanded to his prison, though his treatment was somewhat less harsh than before.

Had the council been wise, it would have treated him as leniently as possible. A dishonored apostate, his power of evil was gone, and generosity would have been policy. The canons, however, prescribed harsh prison for converted heretics, whose conversion was always regarded as doubtful, and the assembled fathers were too bigoted to be wise. John Gerson, whose hostility seems to have been insatiable, called the attention of the council, October 29, to the unsatisfactory character of Jerome's revocation. Some Carmelites, apparently arriving from Prague, furnished new accusations, and demands were made that he be required to answer additional articles. Accordingly, February 24, 1416, a new commission was appointed and the whole ground was gone over again in examining him, from the Wickliffite heresies to his exciting rebellion in Prague and contumaciously enduring the excommunication incurred in Vienna. April 27 the commissioners made their report, and the *Promotor Hæreticæ Pravitatis*, or prosecutor for heresy, accompanied it with a long indictment enumerating his offenses. Jerome, resolved on death, had recovered his audacity; he not only, in spite of his recantation, had denied that he was a heretic, but complained of unjust imprisonment and claimed to be indemnified for expenses and damages. His dialectical dexterity had evidently nonplussed the slower intellects of his examiners. The council was asked, in conclusion, to diminish the diet on which he was described as feasting gluttonously, and by judicious starvation to bring him to submission. Moreover, authority was asked to use torture and to force him to answer definitely yes or no to all questions as to his belief. If then he continues contumaciously to deny what has been or may be proved against him, he is to be handed over to the secular arm as a pertinacious and incorrigible heretic.

In this case, more than in that of Huss, the council seems to have taken upon itself the part of an inquisitorial tribunal, with its commissioners simply as examiners to take testimony. There is no evidence that it consented to the superfluous infamy of torturing, or even of starving its victim. The commissioners were left to their own devices to extract a confession, and May 9 they made another report of the whole case from beginning to end, for what object is not apparent, unless to demonstrate their helplessness. Having thus wearied them out, Jerome finally promised to answer categorically before the council. The concession was made to him, and at a general session held May 23 he was brought in and the oath was offered to him. He refused to take it, saying that he would do so if he would be allowed to speak freely, but if he was only to say yes or no he would not. As the articles were read over he remained silent as to a portion, while to the rest he answered affirmatively or negatively, occasionally making a distinction, and answering with admirable readiness the interruptions which assailed him from all sides. The day wore away in this, and the completion of the hearing was adjourned till the 26th. Again the same scene occurred till the series of articles was exhausted, when the chief of the commissioners, John, Patriarch of Constantinople, summed up, saying that Jerome was convicted of fourfold heresy; but as he had repeatedly asked to be heard he should be allowed to speak, in order to silence absurd reflections on the council; moreover, if he was prepared to confess and repent, he still would be received to mercy, but if obdurate, justice must take its course.

Of the scene which followed we have a vivid account in a letter to Leonardo Aretino from Poggio Bracciolini, who attended the council as apostolic secretary. Poggio had already been profoundly impressed with the quickness of a man who for 340 days had lain in the filth and squalor of a noisome dungeon, but now he breaks forth in unqualified admiration: "He stood fearless, undaunted, not merely despising death, but longing for it, like another Cato. O man worthy of eternal remembrance among men! If he held beliefs contrary to the rules of the Church I do not praise him, but I admire his learning, his knowledge of so many things, his eloquence, and the subtlety of his answers."

His address was a skillful vindication, gliding with seemingly careless negligence over the dangerous spots in his career and giving most plausible explanations of that which could not be suppressed, as though the Bohemian troubles had been solely due to political differences. As for his recantation, his judges had promised him kindly treatment if he would throw himself on the mercy of the council. He was but a man, with a human dread of a dreadful death by fire; he had weakly yielded to persuasion, he had abjured, he had written to Bohemia as required, he had condemned the teaching of John Huss. Here he rose to the full height of his eloquence. Huss was a just and holy man, to whom he would cleave to the last; no sin that he had ever committed so weighed upon his conscience as his cowardly abjuration, which now he solemnly revoked. Wickliff had written with a profounder truth than any man before him, and dread of the stake alone could have induced him to condemn such a master, saving only the doctrine on the sacrament, of which he could not approve. Then he burst forth into a ringing invective on the vices of the clergy, and especially of the Roman curia, which had stimulated Wickliff and Huss to their efforts for reform. The good fathers of the council might be stunned for a moment by the fierce self-sacrifice of the man who thus deliberately threw away his life, but they soon recovered themselves, and quietly assigned the following Saturday for his definite sentence. Although, as a self-confessed relapsed, he was entitled to no further consideration, they proposed, with unusual mercy, to give him four days to reconsider and repent.

On May 30 the final acts of the tragedy were hurried through; the council assembled early, and by ten o'clock Jerome was at the stake. After the mass, the Bishop of Lodi preached a sermon. The nobles present were called upon to mark how Huss and Jerome, two base-born men, plebeians of the lowest rank and unknown origin, had dared to trouble the noble kingdom of Bohemia, and what evils had sprung from the presumption of those two peasants. Then Jerome in a few dignified sentences replied, deploring his condemnation of Wickliff and Huss. His abjuration was read to him; he acknowledged it; he said it had been extorted by the dread of fire. Then the prosecutor asked for a definite sentence in writing against him, and the head commissioner, John of Constantinople, read a long one condemning him as a supporter of Wickliff and Huss, and ending with the declaration that he was a relapsed heretic and anathematized excommunicate. To this the council unanimously responded *"Placet."* There was no pretense of asking mercy for him. He was handed over to the secular power with a command that it should do its duty under the sentence rendered. Not being in orders, there was no ceremony of degradation to be performed, but a tall paper crown with painted devils was brought. He tossed his cap among the prelates and put on the crown, saying, "Our Lord Jesus Christ, when about to die for me, wore a crown of thorns. In place of that, I gladly bear this for his sake," and with this he was hurried off to execution on the same spot where Huss had suffered.

The details of the execution were much the same, except that Jerome was stripped and a cloth tied around his loins. He sang the Creed and a litany, and when his voice could no longer be heard in the flames his lips were still seen to move as though praying to himself; after his beard was burned off, a blister the size of an egg was seen to form itself, showing that he still was alive, and his agony was unusually prolonged, through his extraordinary strength and vitality. One eyewitness says that he shrieked awfully, but other unfriendly witnesses declare that he continued praying till his voice was checked by the fire, and Poggio, who was present, was much impressed with his cheerful courage to the last. When bound to the stake, the executioner offered to light the fire from behind, where he could not see it, but he refused: "Come forward," he said, "and light the fire where I can see it. Had I feared this, I would not have been here." After it was over, his bedding, shoes, cap, and all his personal effects were brought from his dungeon and thrown upon the pile, that no relic of him might be left, and the ashes were cast into the Rhine.

It only remained to secure the submission of John of Chlum, the courageous defender of Huss. He had remained in Constance and was in the power of the council. What means were adopted for his abasement do not appear, but, on July 1, he swore to maintain the faith, admitted that Huss and Jerome had suffered justly, and desired letters of his declaration to be made, that he might send them to Bohemia.

C HAPTER XVI
THE HUSSITES

ON AUGUST 31, 1415, the Council of Constance issued to John, Bishop of Litomysl, letters commissioning him with inquisitorial powers to suppress all heresy in Bohemia; if he could not perform his office in safety elsewhere he was authorized to summon all suspect to his episcopal seat at Litomysl. Wenceslas dutifully issued to him a safe-conduct, but the irate Bohemians were already ravaging his territories, and he consulted prudence in not venturing his person there. The canons evidently could not be enforced amid a people so exasperated; so, on September 23, after listening to the recantation of Jerome, the council tried a further expedient, by appointing John, Patriarch of Constantinople, and John, Bishop of Senlis, as commissioners (or, rather, inquisitors) to try all Hussite heretics. They were empowered to summon all heretics or suspects to appear before them in the Roman curia by public edict, to be posted in the places frequented by heretics, or in the neighboring territories if it were dangerous to attempt it at the residences of the accused. If the object had been to secure the legal condemnation *in absentia* of the mass of the Bohemian nation, it was well adapted for the purpose; but as the nation was seething in revolt, and was venerating Huss and Jerome with as much ardor as was shown in Rome to St. Peter and St. Paul, its only effect was to strengthen the hands of the extremists.

On December 30, an address was delivered to the council, signed by 450 Bohemian nobles, reiterating their complaints of the execution of Huss and withdrawing themselves from all obedience. This hardy challenge was accepted February 20, 1416, by citing all the signers and other supporters of Huss and Wickliff to appear before the council within 50 days and answer to the charge of heresy, in default of which they were to be proceeded against as contumacious. As it was not safe to serve this citation on them personally, or, indeed, anywhere in Bohemia, it was ordered to be affixed on the church doors at Constance, Ratisbon, Vienna, and Passau. On June 3 the offenders were declared to be in contumacy, and on September 4 the further prosecution of the matter was entrusted to John of Constantinople.

Here the affair seems to have dropped, for it had long been evident that the inquisitorial methods were of no avail when the accused constituted the great body of a nation. As early as March 27, 1416, the council had resolved to appeal to force, if yet there was sufficient zeal for orthodoxy in Bohemia to render such appeal successful. John of Litomysl was armed with legatine powers and dispatched with letters to the lords of Hazemburg, John of Michaelsburg, and other barons known as opponents of the popular cause. The council recited in moving terms its patience and tenderness in dealing with Huss, who had perished merely through his own hardness of heart. In spite of this, his followers had addressed to the council libellous and defamatory letters. The barons are therefore summoned, in conjunction with the legate, to banish and exterminate all these persecutors, regardless of friendship and kinship. Bishop John's mission was a failure, in spite of letters written by Sigismund, March 21 and 30, in which he thanked the Catholic nobles for their devotion, and warned the Hussite magnates that, if they persisted, Christendom would be banded against them in a crusade. The University of Prague responded, May 23, with a public declaration, certifying to the unblemished orthodoxy and supereminent merits of Huss. Jerome, whom the University supposed already executed, was similarly lauded for his learning and orthodoxy, and was declared to have in death triumphed gloriously over his enemies. In this the University represented with moderation the prevailing opinion in Bohemia. The more earnest disciples did not hesitate to declare that the Passion of Christ was the only martyrdom fit to be compared with that of Huss.

There was evidently no middle term which could reconcile conflicting opinions so firmly entertained; and, as the Catholic nobles of Bohemia could not be stimulated to undertake a civil war, the council naturally turned to Sigismund. In December 1416 a doleful epistle was addressed to him, complaining that the execution of Huss and Jerome, in place of repressing heresy, had rendered it more violent than ever. Sigismund is therefore requested to do his duty and reduce by force these rebellious heretics. Sigismund replied that he had forwarded the document to Wenceslas, and that if the latter had not power to suppress the heretics he would assist him with all his force. Sigismund was in no position to undertake the task, but after waiting for nine months he saw an opportunity of attacking his brother, who had been utterly powerless to control the storm. In a circular letter of September 3, 1417, addressed to the faithful in Bohemia, he drew a moving picture of the excesses committed on the Bohemian clergy, compelled by Neronian tortures to abjure their faith. His brother was suspected of favoring the heretics, as no one could conceive that such wickedness could be committed under so powerful a king without his connivance, and the council had decided to proceed against him, but had consented to delay at the instance of Sigismund, who for three years had been strenuously endeavoring to avert the prosecution.

Shortly after this, November 11, 1417, the weary Schism was closed by the election to the papacy of Martin V. Under the impulsion of a capable and resolute pontiff, who, as Cardinal Ottone Colonna, had, in 1411, condemned and excommunicated Huss, the reunited Church pressed eagerly forward to render the conflict inevitable. In February 1418 the council published a series of 24 articles as its ultimatum. King Wenceslas must swear to suppress the heresy of Wickliff and Huss. Priests and Catholics who had been driven out were to be reinstated and compensated; image and relic worship to be resumed and the rites of the Church observed. All infected with heresy were to abjure it, while their leading doctors, John Jessenitz, Jacobel of Mies, Simon of Rokyzana, and six others, were to betake themselves to Rome for trial. Communion in both elements was to be specially abjured, and all who held the doctrines of Wickliff and Huss, or regarded Huss and Jerome as holy men, were to be burned as relapsed heretics. Finally, everyone was required to lend assistance to the episcopal officials when called upon, under pain of punishment as fautors of heresy. Sigismund promised to visit the rebellious region with four bishops and an inquisitor, and to burn all who would not recant.

This was speedily followed, February 22, 1418, by a bull of Martin V, addressed to the prelates and inquisitors, not only of Bohemia and Moravia, but of the surrounding territories, Passau, Salzburg, Ratisbon, Bamberg, Misnia, Silesia, and Poland. The pope expressed his grief and surprise that the heretics had not been brought to repentance by the miserable deaths of Huss and Jerome. The prelates and inquisitors were ordered to track them out and deliver them to the secular arm; and such as proved themselves remiss in the work were to be removed, and replaced with more energetic successors. Secular potentates were commanded to seize and hold in chains all heretics, and to punish them duly when convicted. If this was intended to give countenance to Sigismund's promised expedition it proved useless, for the royal promise ended as Sigismund's were wont to do, and the next we hear of him is a letter of December 1418 to Wenceslas, threatening that unlucky monarch with a crusade if he shall not suppress heresy.

The glimpse into the condition of Bohemia afforded by these documents is perhaps somewhat highly colored, yet on the whole not incorrect. The kingdom was almost wholly withdrawn from obedience to the Church. The Wickliffite doctrines adopted by Huss were triumphant, and the pressure of central authority being removed, men were naturally using the unaccustomed liberty to develop further and further hostility to the sacerdotal system. Utraquism, or communion in both elements, had been received with a frenzy of welcome which seems almost inexplicable, which was only stimulated by the interdict pronounced on it by Archbishop Conrad, November 1, 1415, and repeated February 1, 1416. When, in 1417, the University of Prague issued a solemn declaration in its favor and pronounced void any human ordinance modifying the command of Christ and the custom of the early Church, it speedily became the distinguishing mark which separated the Hussite from the Catholic. Other innovations had already been introduced, and it was impossible that all should agree on the bounds to be set between conservatism and progress. Already there was forming the sect which, in carrying out the views of Wickliff, came to be known as Taborites. The more conservative element, which adopted the name of Calixtins, or Utraquists, satisfied with what had been acquired, endeavored to set bounds to the zeal which threatened to remove all the ancient landmarks.

In the spirit of unrest which was abroad, men and women of the more advanced views from all parts of the kingdom began assembling on a mountain near Bechin, to which they gave the name of Tabor, where they received the sacrament in both kinds. These assemblages were larger on feast-days, and on the day of Mary Magdalen, July 22, 1419, the multitude was computed at 40,000. Numbers gave courage, and there was even talk of deposing King Wenceslas and replacing him with Nicholas Lord of Hussinetz, whose popularity had been increased by his banishment for advocating their cause with the monarch. From this they were dissuaded by their chief spiritual leader, the priest Wenceslas Coranda, who pointed out that as the king was an indolent drunkard, permitting them to do what they liked, they would scarce benefit themselves by a change. The abandonment of this project, however, did not assure peace. On July 30 there was a tumult in the Neustadt of Prague; at command of the king, the authorities endeavored to prevent the progress of a procession bearing the sacrament; the people rose, and under the lead of John Ziska, whose zeal and audacity were rapidly bringing him to the front, they rushed into the town hall and cast out of the windows such of the magistrates as they found there, who were promptly slain by the mob below. The agitation and alarm caused by this affair brought on King Wenceslas an attack of paralysis, of which he died August 15.

With the death of the king the untamable passions burst forth. Two days afterwards the churches and convents were mobbed, the images and organs were broken, and those in which the cup had been refused to the laity were the objects of special vengeance. Priests and monks were taken prisoners, and within a few days the Dominican and Carthusian convents were burned. Queen Sophia endeavored, in vain, to maintain order with such of the barons as remained loyal; civil war broke forth, until, on November 13, the queen concluded with the cities of Prague a truce to last until April 23, 1420, the queen promising to maintain the law of God and communion in both elements, while the citizens pledged themselves to refrain from image-breaking and the destruction of convents. Mutual exasperation, however, was too great to be restrained. Ziska came to Prague and destroyed churches and monasteries in the city and neighborhood; Queen Sophia laid siege to Pilsen; a neighborhood war broke out in which shocking cruelties were perpetrated on both sides; German miners of Caurzim and Kuttenberg threw into abandoned mines all the Calixtins on whom they could lay their hands, and some Bavarians who were coming to the assistance of Rackzo of Ryzmberg tied to a tree and burned the priest Naakvasa, a zealous Calixtin.

Sigismund was now the lawful King of Bohemia and he came to claim his inheritance. As a preliminary step he sent envoys to Prague offering to leave the use of the cup as it had been under Wenceslas, to call a general assembly of the nation, and after consultation to refer any questions to the Holy See. A meeting of the barons and clergy was held, which agreed to accept the terms. On Christmas Day, 1419, he came to Brünn, and thither flocked the magnates and representatives of the cities to tender their allegiance. The envoys of Prague, it is true, persisted in using the cup, and there was an interdict in consequence placed on Brünn during their stay, but when he ordered them to remove the chains from the streets of Prague and destroy the fortifications which they had raised against the castle, there was no refusal, and on their return, January 3, 1420, his commands were obeyed. His natural faithlessness soon showed itself. He changed all the castellans and officials who were favorable to the Hussites; the Catholics who had fled or been expelled returned and commenced to triumph over their enemies; and a royal edict was issued, in obedience to the decrees of Constance, commanding all those in authority to exterminate the Wickliffites and Hussites and those who used the sacramental cup. Still, the kingdom made no sign of organized opposition to him, except that the provident Ziska and his followers, seeing the wrath to come, diligently set to work to fortify Mount Tabor. Strong by nature, it soon was made virtually impregnable, and for a generation it remained the stronghold of the extremists. Mostly peasant-folk, they showed to the chivalry of Europe what could be done by freemen, animated by religious zeal and race hatred; their rustic wagons made a rampart which the most valiant knights learned not to assail; armed sometimes only with iron-shod flails, the hardy zealots did not hesitate to throw themselves upon the best-appointed troops, and often bore them down with the sheer weight of the attack. Wild and undisciplined, they were often cruel, but their fanatic courage rendered them a terror to all Germany.

Nothing, probably, could have averted an eventual explosion but, for the moment, it seemed that Sigismund was about to enter on peaceable possession of his kingdom. Suddenly, however, an act of inconsiderate and gratuitous fanaticism set all Bohemia aflame. Some trouble in Silesia had called Sigismund to Breslau, where he was joined by a papal legate armed by Martin V with power to proclaim a crusade with Holy Land indulgences. John Krasa, a merchant of Prague, who chanced to be there, talked overboldly about the innocence of Huss; he was arrested, persisted in his faith, and was condemned by the legate and prelates who were with Sigismund to be dragged by the heels at a horse's tail to the place of execution and burned. While lying in prison he was joined by Nicholas of Bethlehem, a student of Prague, who had been sent by the city to Sigismund to offer to receive him if he would not interfere with the use of the cup to the laity. In place of listening to him he was tried as a heretic and thrown into prison to await the result. Krasa encouraged him to endure to the last, and both were brought forth on March 15, 1420, to undergo the punishment. As the feet of Nicholas were about to be attached to the horse, his courage gave way and he recanted. Krasa was undaunted; the legate followed him, as he was dragged to the place of execution, exhorting him to repent, but in vain; he was attached half-dead to the stake and duly burned. Two days later, March 17, the legate proclaimed the crusade. A new Albigensian war was inevitable.

There was wavering no longer in Bohemia. The events at Breslau united all, with the exception of a few barons and such Germans as were left, in resistance against Sigismund. By April 3 the citizens of Utraquist Prague had bound themselves by a solemn oath with the Taborites to defend themselves against him to the last, and were busy in preparations to sustain a siege. Sigismund's forces were wholly inadequate for the conquest of a virtually united kingdom. After an advance to Kuttenberg he was forced to withdraw and await the assembling of the crusade, which took long to organize, and did not burst in its fury over Bohemia until the following year, 1421. In its mass of 150,000 men all Europe was represented, from Russia to Spain and from Sicily to England. The reunited Church aroused all Christendom to stamp out the revolt, and the treasures of salvation were poured lavishly forth to exterminate those who dared to maintain the innocence of Huss and Jerome, and to take the Eucharist as all Christians had done until within two hundred years.

Five times during 1421 the crusaders invaded Bohemia, and five times they were beaten back disastrously. The gain to the faith was scarce perceptible, for Sigismund stripped the churches of all their precious ornaments, declaring that he was not impelled by lack of reverence, but by a prudent desire to prevent their falling into the hands of the Hussites. Both sides perpetrated cruelties happily unknown save in the ferocity of religious wars. During the siege of Prague all Bohemians captured were burned as heretics whether they used the cup or not; and on July 19 the besieged demanded of the magistrates 16 German prisoners, whom they took outside of the walls and burned in hogsheads in full sight of the invading army.

It is not our province to follow in detail this bloody struggle, in which for ten years the Hussites successfully defied all the forces that Martin and Sigismund could raise against them. When the crusaders came they presented a united front, but within the line of common defense they were torn with dissensions, bitter in proportion to their exaltation of religious feeling. The right of private judgment when once established was not easily restrained, nor could it be expected that those who were persecuted would learn from persecution the lesson of tolerance. In the wild tumult, intellectual, moral, and social, which convulsed Bohemia, no doctrines were too extravagant to lack believers.

The Calixtins virtually regarded the teachings of Huss and Jacobel of Mies as a finality. When, after the death of Wenceslas, the necessity of some definite declaration of principles was felt, the University of Prague, on August 1, 1420, adopted, with but one dissenting voice, four articles which became for more than a century the distinguishing platform of their sect. As concisely enunciated by the University they appeared simple enough:

 I. Free preaching of the Word of God;
 II. Communion in both elements for the laity;
 III. The clergy to be deprived of all dominion over temporal possessions, and to be reduced to the evangelical life of Christ and the apostles;
 IV. All offenses against divine law to be punished without exception of person or condition.

These four articles were speedily accepted by the strongly Calixtin community of Prague, and were proclaimed to the world in various forms which added to their completeness and rendered their purport definite. Anyone was declared a heretic who did not accept the Apostles', Athanasian, and Nicene creeds, the seven sacraments of the Church, and the existence of purgatory. Offenses against the law of God were declared to be worthy of death, and were defined to be, among the people, fornication, banqueting, theft, homicide, perjury, avarice, usury, etc.: among the clergy, simoniacal exactions, such as fees for administering the sacraments, for preaching, burying, bell-ringing, consecration of churches and altars, as well as the sale of preferment; also concubinage and fornication, quarrels, greedy exactions of tribute, etc.

Upon this basis the Calixtin Church proceeded to organize itself in a council held at Prague in 1421. Four leading doctors, John of Przibram, Procopius of Pilsen, Jacobel of Mies, and John of Neuberg, were made supreme governors of the clergy throughout the kingdom, with absolute power of punishment. No one was to teach any new doctrine without first submitting it to them or to a provincial synod. Transubstantiation was emphatically affirmed as well as the seven sacraments. The daily use of the Eucharist was recommended to all, including infants and the sick. The canon of the mass was simplified and restored to primitive usage. Auricular confession was prescribed, as well as the use of the chrism and of holy water in baptism. Clerks were to be distinguished by tonsure, vestments, and conduct. Every priest was to possess a copy of the Scriptures, or at least of the New Testament, and stringent regulations were adopted for the preservation of priestly morality, including the prohibition of their protection by any layman after conviction.

Thus the Calixtin Church kept as close as possible to the old lines. It accepted all Catholic dogmas, even the power of the keys in sacramental penance, and was only a revolt against the abuses which had grown out of the worldly aspirations of the clergy. It was a Puritan reform, and it founded a Puritan society. When in 1436, after the reconciliation effected at Basle, Sigismund held his court in Prague, the Bohemians speedily complained that the city was becoming a Sodom, with dicing, tavern-haunting, and public women. It must have sounded strange to them to be coolly told by the Bishop of Coutances, who was the legate of the council empowered to enforce the settlement, that it would be well if public sins could be eradicated, but that strumpets must be tolerated to prevent greater evils.

The Calixtins thus sought to keep themselves strictly within the pale of orthodoxy, and deemed themselves greatly injured and insulted by the appellation of heretic, but in the intellectual and spiritual excitement which stirred Bohemia to the depths, it was impossible that all earnest souls should thus pause on the threshold. Under the energetic leadership of Ziska, Coranda, Nicholas of Pilgram, and other resolute men, the progressive elements were rapidly moulded into a powerful party, which after sloughing off impracticable enthusiasts presented itself with a definite creed and purpose. When the Calixtins, in 1421, defined their position, the Taborites did the same. While they accepted the four articles of the Calixtins, they reduced the Church to a state of the utmost apostolic simplicity. All images were to be burned; there was no outward sign of distinction between layman and priest, the latter wearing beards, rejecting the tonsure, and using ordinary garments; all priests, moreover, were bishops, and could perform the rite of consecration; they baptized in running water, celebrated mass anywhere, reciting the simple words of consecration and the Paternoster in a loud voice and in the vernacular; all consecration of sacred vessels, oil, and water was forbidden; purgatory, which Huss had accepted, was denied, and to manifest their contempt for the suffrages of the saints they ate more than usual on fast-days and saints'-days; auricular confession was derided—for venial sins confession to God sufficed, for mortal ones, public confession before the brethren, when the priest would assign a penalty commensurate with the offense. At the same time the rude and uncultured vigor of the Taborites led them to regard all human learning as a snare. Those who studied the liberal arts were regarded as heathen and as sinning against the Gospel, and all writings of the doctors, save what were expressly contained in the Bible, were to be destroyed.

What were their views with respect to the Lord's Supper cannot be stated with precision. Laurence of Brezowa, a Calixtin bitterly hostile to them, says that they consecrated the elements in a loud voice and in the vulgar tongue, that the people might be assured that they were receiving the real body and the real blood, which infers belief in transubstantiation. On the other hand, the Taborite Bishop, Nicholas of Pilgram, strongly asserted that Christ was only present spiritually, that no veneration was due to the consecrated elements, and that there was less idolatry in those who of old adored moles and bats and snakes than in Christians who worshipped the host, for those things at least had life. During the negotiations in January 1433, the legates of the council presented a series of 28 articles attributed to the Bohemians, and asked for definite answers, yea or nay. One of these was a denial of transubstantiation, and the Bohemians could never be induced to make the desired reply. Peter Chelcicky reproached the Taborites with concealing their belief on the subject, but it is probable that there was no absolute accord among them.

It was impossible that harmony could be preserved between Taborite and Calixtin when there was so marked a divergence of religious conviction. They quarrelled and held conferences and persecuted each other, but they presented a united front to the levies of crusaders which Europe repeatedly sent against them, and Sigismund's hope of reconquering the throne of his fathers grew more and more remote. The death of Ziska, in 1424, made little difference, save that his immediate followers organized themselves into a separate party under the name of Orphans, but continued in all things to co-operate with the Taborites. He was succeeded in the leadership by the warrior-priest Procopius Rasa, or the Great, whose military skill continued to hold banded Europe at bay. Hussitism, moreover, was spreading into the neighboring lands, especially to the south and east, requiring the strenuous efforts of the Inquisition to eradicate it from Hungary and the Danubian provinces. In Poland its missionary efforts called forth an edict from King Ladislas V, April 6, 1424, ordering all his subjects to join in exterminating heretics; every Pole who returned from a sojourn in Bohemia was subjected to examination by the inquisitors or episcopal officials, and all who should not return by June 1 were declared heretics, their estates confiscated, and their children subjected to the customary disabilities. The Church was completely baffled. It had triumphed over a similar revolt in Languedoc, and had shown the world, in characters of blood and fire, how it utilized its triumphs. It now had a different problem to solve. Force having failed, it was obliged to discover some formula of reconciliation which should not too nearly peril its claim to infallibility.

Meanwhile the Church was perplexed with another yet more

vexatious question. Christendom never ceased to clamor for the reform of which it had been cheated at Constance. Skillful procrastination had wearied the reforming fathers, and they had consented, in 1418, to the dissolution of the council, hoping that the promises made in the election of Martin V would be fulfilled. They took the precaution, however, to provide for an endless series of councils, which might be expected to resume and complete their unfinished work. Another general council was ordered to be held in five years, then one in seven years thereafter, and finally a perpetual succession at intervals of ten years, with careful provisions to nullify the expected evasions of the popes.

As far as relates to Germany, Martin endeavored to perform the two duties for which he had been elected—the suppression of heresy and the reformation of the Church—by sending, in 1422, Cardinal Branda thither as legate. To accomplish the former object the legate was directed to preach another crusade, that of 1421 having ended so disastrously. As regards the latter, the papal commission and the decree issued in conformity with it by Branda describe the vices of the German clergy in terms quite as severe as those employed by Huss and his followers, and furnish a complete justification of the Bohemian revolt. But the constitution which Brand issued to cure these evils attacked only the symptoms and not the cause of the disease, and it consequently remained inoperative. When the Council of Siena assembled, in 1423, it remained to be seen whether the unfinished work of Constance would be completed. Under the presidency of four papal legates it was held that the attendance of prelates and princes was too small to permit the work of reformation to be undertaken, but was sufficient to justify the council in confirming the promises made by Martin of forgiveness of sins for all who were summoned to lend their aid in the good work without delay. All commerce of every kind with the heretics was forbidden, especially in victuals, cloth, arms, gunpowder, and lead; everyone trading with them, or any prince permitting communication with them over his lands, was pronounced subject to the punishments decreed against heresy. Bohemia was to be isolated and starved into submission by a material blockade enforced by spiritual censures.

As for reformation, all efforts seriously to consider it were skillfully blocked by the legates. The disappointment of the council at the baffling of its efforts was leading to a tension that grew dangerous. Finally, finding that under the control of the papacy no reformatory action was possible, the attempt was made to shorten to two or three years the seven years' interval that was to elapse before the next council. All the several nations had agreed to it, when its enactment was prevented by the legates' suddenly dissolving the council, March 8, 1424, in spite of a protest intimating very plainly that they had prevented all reformatory legislation. The seven years' interval was preserved, and the next council was indicated for Basle, in March 1431. The reformers consoled themselves by pointing out that, of the four papal representatives concerned in thus strangling the council, three died within a year, of terrible deaths, manifestly the divine vengeance on their wickedness.

The time fixed for the assembling of the Council of Basle, was rapidly drawing nigh without any action on the part of Martin looking to its convocation. At length, on November 8, 1430, there appeared on the doors of the papal palace, and in the most conspicuous places in Rome, an anonymous notice, purporting to be issued by two Christian kings, reciting the necessity of holding a council in obedience to the decrees of Constance, and appending some conclusions to the effect that if the pope and cardinals impede it, or even evade promoting it, they are to be held as fautors of heresy; that if the pope does not open the council himself or by his deputies, those who may be present will be compelled by divine law to withdraw obedience from him and that they will be forced to proceed summarily to his deposition and that of the cardinals as fautors of heresy. It was evident that Christendom was determined to have the council, with the pope or without him, and Martin, after holding out till the last moment, was compelled to yield. He had appointed, January 11, 1431, Cardinal Giuliano Cesarini as legate to preach another crusade with plenary indulgences against the Hussites, and to him he issued, February 1, a commission to open and preside at the council. One of those most earnest in bringing this about was the Cardinal of Siena. Had he been able to forecast the future he would have tempered his zeal. Within three weeks Martin was dead, and on March 3 the Cardinal of Siena was elected his successor, taking the name of Eugenius IV.

Cardinal Giuliano went on his double mission and preached the fifth crusade against the Hussites. Bohemian forays had stimulated Germany to an earnest effort to crush the troublesome rebels, and he found himself at the head of an army variously estimated at from 80,000 to 130,000 men. The Bohemians applied to the Emperor Sigismund for a safe-conduct to Basle, offering to submit the questions at issue to debate on the basis of Scripture. This was refused, and they were told that they must agree to stand to the decisions of the council without limitation. They preferred the arbitrament of arms, and issued a protest to the Christian world in which, with coarse good sense, they defined their position, attacked the temporal power of the papacy, and ridiculed the indulgences issued for their subjugation. This document was received by the council on August 10, very nearly on the day on which, at Taas, the crusaders fled without striking a blow, on hearing the battle hymn of the dreaded Hussite troops. As a military leader Cardinal Giuliano was evidently a failure, and it only remained for him to try peaceful measures. The German princes, alarmed and exhausted, showed evident signs of determination to come to terms with their unconquerable neighbors. It was a hard necessity, but there was no alternative, and on October 15 the council resolved to invite the Bohemians to a conference and to give them a safe-conduct, although the letters were not forwarded until November 26.

Meanwhile the inevitable quarrels between pope and council had broken out with bitterness. But three weeks after the invitation to the Bohemians had been dispatched, on December 18, Eugenius took the extreme step of dissolving the council and calling another to be held in eighteen months at Bologna, where he would preside in person. Sigismund remonstrated energetically, and the council, assured of his support, refused to obey. Cardinal Giuliano was won over and made himself its mouthpiece. It may safely be said that few popes have received from a subordinate so vigorous a reproof as that in which Giuliano gave his reasons for disobedience, and it contains so vivid a picture of the times that a brief abstract of it cannot well be spared.

Clerical wickedness, he says, in Germany is such that the laity are irritated to the last degree against the Church, wherefore it is greatly to be feared that if there is no reformation they will execute their public threats of rising, like the Hussites, against the clergy. . . . The

Bohemians have been invited to the council; they have replied and are expected to come. If the council is dissolved, what will the heretics say? Will not the Church confess herself defeated when she dares not await those whom she has invited? . . . . A host of warriors has fled before them, and now the Church Universal flies! . . . So many councils have been held in our days from which no reformation has come! From this one the nations have expected some fruit. If it be thus dissolved, and when there is no hope of our correction, the laity will justly assail us, like the Hussites. . . . The council was some restraint upon them, but when they lose all hope they will persecute us publicly, and the whole blame will be thrown upon the Roman curia, which breaks up the assembly convened to effect reform. Latterly the city of Magdeburg has expelled her archbishop and clergy; the citizens march with wagons like the Bohemians, and are said to have sent for a Hussite captain, and they have, moreover, a league with many other communities of those parts. . . . At Bamberg there is fierce discord between the citizens on the one side and the bishop and chapter on the other, which is especially dangerous by reason of the neighborhood of the heretics. If the council is dissolved these quarrels will increase, and many other communities will be drawn in.

Making due allowance for inevitable rhetorical exaggeration this picture is a true one. Hussite ideas were rapidly spreading through Germany. If the hopes built on the council were destroyed, the Church might well expect a general revolt. Sustained by the united support of Cismontane Christendom, the council resolutely went its way. Sigismund urged it to stand firm, and in November 1432 he issued an imperial declaration that he would sustain it against all assailants. Eugenius held out until February 1433, when he assented to its continuance, but in July he again dissolved it, and in September repeated the command. Then the council commenced active proceedings to arraign and try him, and in December he revoked these bulls. In the subsequent quarrel the council decreed his suspension in January 1439, and his deposition in June, while the election of Amedeo of Savoy as Felix V was confirmed in November of the same year.

Into the details of the interminable negotiations which followed between the council and the Hussites it is not worth while to enter.

The latter carried their point, and, in a conference held at Eger, May 18, 1432, it was agreed that the questions should be debated on the basis of the Scriptures and the writings of the early Fathers. The four articles, which were the common ground of Calixtins and Taborites, were put forward as their demands, and to these they steadily adhered through all the dreary discussions in Basle, Prague, Brünn, Stuhlweissenberg, to the final conference of Iglau in July 1436. The discussions were often hot and angry, and the good fathers of Basle were sometimes scandalized at the freedom of speech of the Bohemian delegates. When John of Ragusa alluded to the Hussites as heretics, John Rokyzana, one of the Calixtin delegates, indignantly denied it, and demanded that if anyone accused them of heresy he should offer the *talio* and prove it. Procopius, who represented the Taborites, joined in and declared that he would not have come to Basle had he known that he would be thus insulted. Time and skill were required to pacify the Bohemians, and John of Ragusa and the Archbishop of Lyons were forced to apologize formally. On another occasion the Inquisitor Henry of Coblentz, a Dominican doctor, complained that Ulric of Znaim, a deputy of the Orphans, had said that monks were introduced by the devil. Ulric denied it, and Procopius intervened, saying that he had remarked to the legate that if the bishops came from the apostles, and priests from the 72 disciples, the others could have had no other source but the devil. This sally raised a general laugh, which was increased when Rokyzana called to the inquisitor, "Doctor, make Dom Procopius provincial of your order." These trifles have their significance when compared with the shouts of "Burn him! Burn him!" which assailed Huss at Constance. In fact the Hussites were urged to incorporate themselves with the council, but they were too shrewd to fall into the snare.

By unbending firmness the Bohemians carried their point, and secured the recognition of the four articles, which became celebrated in history as the Compactata—Magna Charta of the Bohemian Church until swept away by the Counter-Reformation. This was agreed to in Prague, November 26, 1433, and confirmed by mutual clasp of hands between the legates of the council and the deputies of the three Bohemian sects, but matters were by no means settled. The four articles were brief and simple declarations which admitted of unlimited diversity of construction. The dialecticians of the council had no difficulty in explaining them away, until they practically amounted to nothing; the Hussites, on the other side, with equal facility, expanded them to cover all that they could possibly wish to claim. Hardly was the handclasping over when it was found that the Bohemians asserted that the permission of communion in both elements meant that they were to continue to administer it to infants, and to force it proscriptively on everyone—positions to which the council could by no means assent. So far, indeed, was the matter as yet from being settled, that, in April 1434, the council levied a half-tithe on Christendom for a crusade against the Hussites, which enabled it to stimulate with liberal payments the zeal of the Bohemian Catholic nobles.

It is not likely that any results would have been reached but for events which at first seemed to threaten the continuance of the negotiations. The Taborites could only have consented to treat on the basis, so inadequate to them, of the four articles, in the confidence that the practical application would cover a vastly wider sphere. After the preliminary agreement of November 26, the construction assumed by the legates of the council made them draw back. The affair was reaching a conclusion, and it was necessary to have a definite understanding of that to which they were binding themselves. After the departure of the legates from Prague, in January 1434, hot discussions arose between the Taborites and the Calixtins as to the continuance of the negotiations. There were political as well as religious differences between them. The Taborites were mostly peasants and poor folk; they wanted no nobles or gentlemen in their ranks and seem to have had republican tendencies, as they desired to add to the four articles two others, providing for the independence of Bohemia and for the retention of all confiscated property. Both parties became exasperated, and flew to arms for a contest decisive as to their respective mastery. The Taborites had for some time been besieging Pilsen, a city which held out for Sigismund. Learning that their friends in the Neustadt of Prague had been slaughtered without distinction of age or sex, to the number, it is said, of 22,000, they raised the siege, May 9, to take vengeance on the city, but after a demonstration before it, they withdrew towards Moravia. Meanwhile the Calixtins had formed an alliance with the Catholic barons,

who had been liberally subsidized by the council, and followed them
with a formidable force. The shock came at Lipan, on Sunday, May
30. All day and night the battle raged, and until the third hour of
Monday morning. When it was over, Procopius, Lupus, and 13,000
Taborites lay dead upon the field, and the murderous nature of the
strife is seen in the fact that but 700 prisoners were taken, though
we may question the claim of the victors that the battle cost them
but 200 men, and we may hope that there is exaggeration in
the boast that they burned several thousand of those whom they
subsequently captured. The power of the Taborites was broken. It
is true that they continued to hold Mount Tabor until finally crushed
by George Podiebrad, in 1452; but after Lipan they were only a
troublesome element of insubordination, and not a factor in the
political situation. The congratulatory letters sent by some of the
victors to Sigismund, and the effusive joy with which he communicated the news to the council, show that the victory was one for
the Catholics.

Even after the virtual elimination of the Taborites there were
ample subjects of dispute, and at one time the prospect seemed so
unpromising that preliminary arrangements were set on foot, in
August 1434, for organizing a new crusade on the proceeds of the
half-tithe levied shortly before. One source of endless trouble sprang
from the personal ambition of Rokyzana. Learned, able, a hardy
disputant, and a skilled man of affairs, he had determined to be
Archbishop of Prague, and this object he pursued with unalterable
constancy. At first he endeavored to have a clause inserted that the
people and the clergy should be empowered to elect an archbishop,
who should be acknowledged and confirmed by the emperor and the
pope. This being rejected, he procured of Sigismund a secret agreement that the election should be held, and that the emperor would
do all in his power to secure the confirmation by the pope. Although
this, when discovered, was protested against by the legates and
refused by the council itself, he proceeded, in 1435, to obtain an
election by the national assembly of Bohemia, to the great disgust
of the orthodox, who reasonably dreaded this example of a return
of the primitive methods of selecting prelates. Again Sigismund
secretly accepted this, while the legates declared it to be invalid, and
that, as an infraction of the Compactata, it must be annulled. On

this question the whole negotiation was nearly wrecked, and it was only settled by Sigismund and his son-in-law and heir, Albert of Austria, promising to issue letters recognizing Rokyzana as archbishop, and to compel obedience to him as such. After this it required but a fortnight more of quarrelling to bring the matter to a termination, and signatures to the Compactata were duly exchanged July 5, 1436, amid general rejoicings. Sigismund, restored to the throne of his fathers, made a show of complying with his promise, by writing to the council a letter asking Rokyzana's confirmation, at the same time explaining to the legates that he considered the council ought to refuse, but that he did not wish to break with his new subjects too suddenly. Of course the confirmation never came, and with all convenient speed Sigismund forgot the pledge to enforce obedience to him.

A peace in which all parties distrusted each other and placed radically different interpretations on its conditions was not likely to heal dissensions so profound. When Sigismund was fairly seated on the throne, there followed an endless series of bickerings, as the rites and ceremonies and usages of the Roman Church were restored, supplanting the simpler worship which had prevailed for twenty years. Consecrations, confirmations, images, relics, holy water, benedictions, were one by one introduced—even the hated religious Orders were surreptitiously smuggled in. On Corpus Christi day, May 30, 1437, a gorgeous procession swept through the streets of Prague bearing the host on high; the legate, the Archbishop of Kalocsa, and the Bishop of Segnia headed it, and were dutifully followed by the emperor and empress, the nobles and a mass of citizens. As a mute protest, Rokyzana met the splendid array, attended only by three priests, and bearing both host and cup. To the stern puritans who had struggled so long, the imposing ceremony must have seemed a bitter mockery, for the Empress Barbara, who occupied a conspicuous position in the ranks, was a woman notorious for shameless licentiousness, and, moreover, was an avowed atheist, who disbelieved in the immortality of the soul.

Within three weeks of this celebration, Rokyzana was a fugitive, seeking the protection of George Podiebrad at Hradecz, not without reason, if Æneas Sylvius is correct in saying that Sigismund was about to arrest him. Had Sigismund lived, he might have overcome all resistance, and reduced the land to obedience to Rome. His power was constantly growing. In March the surrender of the Taborite stronghold of Konigingrätz filled the Hussites with consternation. Not long after siege was laid to Zion, the fastness of John Rohacz, a powerful baron who had refused submission. He was finally captured in it, brought to Prague, and hanged in the presence of the emperor with 60 of his followers and a priest. Tradition relates that on that very day Sigismund was attacked with an ulcer which grew constantly worse and ended his days in December. Almost simultaneous with this was the decision by the Council of Basle on the question of communion in both elements, in which it skillfully evaded the inconsistency of the prohibition of the cup, and pronounced it to be the law of the Church, not to be modified without authority. As Albert of Austria, the son-in-law and successor of Sigismund, was a zealous Catholic prince, the council was emboldened in January 1438 to issue an edict reciting and ordering the strict enforcement of the implacable bull of February 22, 1418, by Martin V, directed against the errors of Wickliff, Huss, and Jerome. This evidence of what they were to expect as the outcome of the Compactata gave the Taborites and the disaffected parties in Bohemia new energy. After a fruitless appeal to the council an alliance was made with Poland, whose boy-king, Casimir, was elected as a competitor. Thus strengthened they offered effective resistance to Albert, who up to his sudden death, October 27, 1439, was unable to occupy the whole of his kingdom. Four months later, Ladislas, his posthumous son, was born, and a long minority, with its accompanying turbulence, enabled the Calixtins again to get the upper hand, over both the Taborites and the Catholics. Rokyzana returned from exile in 1440 and speedily became the most powerful man in Bohemia. In 1441 a council held at Kuttenberg organized the national Church on a Calixtin basis. Several conferences were held with the Taborites, and the points at issue were referred to the national diet held in January 1444. Its emphatic decision in favor of the Calixtin doctrine broke up the Taborite organization. The cities still held by them surrendered one by one, and the members were scattered, for the most part joining the Calixtins.

After the death of Albert what central authority there was in Bohemia was lodged in the hands of two governors, Ptacek representing the Calixtins, and Mainhard of Rosenberg, the victor of Lipan, the Catholics. In October 1443 we hear of the Emperor Frederic III as about starting for Bohemia where he expected to receive the regency, but his hopes were frustrated. Ptacek died in 1445, and the choice for his succession fell upon George Podiebrad, a powerful baron, who, though only 24, had acquired a high reputation for military ability and sagacity. He was largely under the influence of Rokyzana, to whom doubtless his election was due. After a long interval, Rome again appeared upon the scene. Nichols V, who ascended the papal throne in 1447, sent, in 1448, John, Cardinal of Sant' Angelo, to Prague as legate. The Bohemians earnestly urged him to ratify the Compactata and confirm Rokyzana as archbishop. He promised an answer, but finding the situation embarrassing, he secretly left Prague with Mainhard of Rosenberg. Popular indignation enabled George by a *coup d'état*, in which there was considerable bloodshed, to render himself master of Prague and to cast Mainhard into prison, where he died soon after. George thus became the undisputed master of Bohemia. When Ladislas, in 1452, was recognized as king, George secured the regency, and when the young monarch died towards the close of 1457, at the early age of eighteen, George's coronation as king soon followed. Under him, until just before his death in 1471, Rokyzana's influence was almost unbounded.

The situation of Bohemia, as a member of the Latin Church, was unprecedented. Rome had never proposed to recognize the compromise made by the council. While the latter was busy in endeavoring to win back the Hussites, Eugenius was laboring for their extermination by the usual methods, in such regions as he could reach. The relations between Bohemia and Hungary had long been close, and Hussitism had spread widely throughout the latter kingdom as well as in the Slavic territories to the south. As Sigismund was King of Hungary, the Compactata were supposed to cover the Hungarian Hussites, and were published in Hungarian as well as in Bohemian, German, and Latin. We have seen, however, how false he was to his Bohemian subjects, and those of Hungary he cheerfully abandoned to Rome. Six weeks after the signature of the Compactata at Iglau, on August 22, 1436, Eugenius commissioned the indefatigable persecutor, Frà Giacomo della Marca, as Inquisitor of

Hungary and Austria. Frà Giacomo lost no time. Before the close of the year he had traversed Hungary from end to end, with merciless severity. The Archbishop of Gran, the Chapter of Kalocsa, the Bishop of Waradein, were loud in his praises. Their dioceses, they said, had been infected with heretics so numerous that a rising was anticipated which would have exceeded in horror the Bohemian wars, but this holy man had exterminated them. The numbers whom he put to death are not enumerated, but they must have been considerable from the expressions employed, and from the terror inspired, for his associates declared that in this expedition he had received the submission of 55,000 converts. Earnestly the Bishops of Csanad and Transylvania appealed to him to visit their dioceses, which abounded in heretics; and as the latter prelate speaks of the Hussites having penetrated to his bishopric from Moldavia, it shows how widely the heresy had been diffused through southeastern Europe.

Suddenly, in 1437, Frà Giacomo's career was interrupted. He had crushed the Fraticelli of Italy, the wild Cathari of Bosnia, and the fiercer Hussites of Hungary, but when he attacked the orthodox concubinary priests of Fünfkirchen, and strove to force them to abandon the illicit partners who were universally kept, they proved too strong for even his iron will. They raised such a storm at this attempted invasion of their accustomed privileges that he was obliged to abandon his work and fly for his life. He appealed to Eugenius, and Eugenius to Sigismund. The latter wrote to Henry, the Bishop of Fünfkirchen, peremptorily ordering him to recall Giacomo and give him every aid, and also to Giacomo, assuring him of support. Thus assailed, Bishop Henry gave instructions that Giacomo should be supplied with all necessaries, but the attempt to enforce chastity on the priesthood seems to have been abandoned. He appears to have meddled no longer with the private lives of the orthodox clergy, but to have devoted his energies to the easier work of exterminating heretics.

Early in 1437 we hear of him south of the Danube, where the Bishop of Sreim praised his effective work; by putting to death all who could not be converted, he had saved the diocese from a rising of the Hussites, in which all the clergy would have been slain. Eugenius rewarded him by describing him as "a vigorous and most ruthless extirpator of heresy," and granting him the power of appointing subordinate inquisitors, thus rendering him an inquisitor-general in all the wide region confided to him. It was doubtless owing to his efforts that in Poland the barons and cities entered into a solemn league and covenant to suppress heresy, April 25, 1438—just before Poland intervened in Bohemia to protect the Hussites from the Emperor Albert. In 1439 Giacomo's zeal received a check on the more immediate fields of his labors. In Sreim he delivered to the secular arm, as convicted heretics, a priest and three associates; their friends assembled in force, broke open the prison and carried off the culprits, and, what is difficult to understand, unless the heresy was merely concubinage, the Archbishop of Kalocsa, when appealed to, protected the criminals. Giacomo had recourse to the Emperor Albert, who wrote sharply to the archbishop in June; and this proving ineffectual, again in August. What was the result of the affair is not known; Albert died in October, and in 1440 Giacomo left Hungary on account of ill-health.

If Rome was thus active in repressing Hussitism, and thus regardless of the Compactata while crippled by the quarrel with the fathers of Basle, it may readily be imagined that, after the abdication of Felix V and the restoration of unquestioned supremacy, Nicholas V was not disposed to respect the bargain made by the council or to regard the Calixtins in any light but that of heretics. It was in vain that the Bohemians proffered obedience if only the Compactata were confirmed, with a tacit condition that Rokyzana's claims to the archbishopric should be recognized. Ostensibly the sole difficulty in the way of reunion lay in the use of the cup by the laity and the communion of infants; save this there was by this time but little to distinguish the Calixtins from the rest of the Latin churches. The papacy had taken its position, however, and it would have plunged all Christendom into war rather than admit that the Council of Basle had been justified in purchasing peace by conceding communion in both elements. Behind this, however, was the question of Rokyzana's confirmation. Æneas Sylvius informs us that in 1451 he convinced George Podiebrad of the impossibility of effecting this, and secured a promise that the attempt should be abandoned, pledging himself that if George would present the names of several suitable persons the pope would select one, and peace would then be established. This treated the Compactata as of minor importance, and was doubtless wholly unauthorized. Neither George nor Rokyzana gave up their hopes; the effort was renewed again and again, now with the pope, now with the Emperor Frederic III, and now with the German Diet, but all to no purpose. Occasionally when there was an object to be gained hopes would be held out, only to be withdrawn. The papal emissaries represented Rokyzana to Rome as the most wicked and perfidious of heresiarchs, whose recognition would be the destruction of what remained of Catholicism in Bohemia, and there never was the slightest idea of confirming him.

When the overthrow of Mainhard of Rosenberg and the concentration of power in the hands of George Podiebrad showed that no further hopes were to be built on the Catholic party in Bohemia, Nicholas V fell back upon the old methods and resolved to try what could be done by a missionary inquisitor. He had at hand an instrument admirably fitted for the work. Giovanni da Capistrano, Vicar-General of the Observantine Franciscans, had commenced his career as an inquisitor in 1417; he was now in his sixty-sixth year, vigorous and implacable as ever. Small and insignificant in appearance, shrivelled by austerities until he seemed to consist only of skin and bone and nerves, he rarely tasted meat and allowed himself but four hours of sleep out of the twenty-four, the remainder being all too few for his restless and indefatigable activity. His saintly and self-denying life had gained him enviable powers as a thaumaturge, and his reputation as a preacher drew crowds to listen to his eloquence. In 1451 he was busy in exterminating the Fraticelli, but he suspended his bloody work at the call of Nicholas to undertake the conversion of the Hussites.

Nothing was omitted that could contribute to the dramatic effect of his mission. Everywhere on his road multitudes assembled to see and listen to the man of God, and everywhere his miraculous powers manifested the authenticity of his mission. At Brescia he addressed an assembly computed at 120,000 souls, and, though walls and trees were broken down by the masses of men gathered thickly upon them, not a human being was injured. At the crossing of the river Sile, near Treviso, the party, with true Observantine austerity, had no money to pay ferriage, and the surly ferryman refused free transportation; but Capistrano quietly took the habit of San Bernardino, which he carried with him, laid it upon the waters, and they shrank away till all had passed dry-shod, when they resumed their former volume. Thus heralded, his way through Venice and Vienna was a triumphal progress.

In vain the emperor asked permission for him to visit Prague. Podiebrad and Rokyzana refused it peremptorily, and Capistrano's zeal for martyrdom was not sufficient to prompt him to disregard their wishes. Furnished with imperial letters to the Catholic nobles and to their leader, Ulric Mainhard of Rosenberg, he turned in July to the safer region of Moravia, where presumably the influence of Podiebrad and Rokyzana was not so strong. Here his career indicates how little foundation there was for the persistent Catholic complaints of the proscriptive intolerance of the Calixtins. Though on Bohemian territory, Catholic and Hussite seem to have been dwelling together in mutual harmony; the Bishop of Olmütz was a Catholic, and no hindrance seems to have been experienced by Capistrano in his labors for the conversion of the so-called heretics. Beginning at Brünn, August 1, 1451, there is a register containing names and dates of more than 11,000 conversions made by him up to May 1452. Yet at the same time he was restricted to persuasion, and was not allowed to use inquisitorial methods. As his converts were voluntary, he smoothed the path of the repentant heretic, reconciling him to the Church with only the infliction of a salutary penance, and allowing him to retain all his possessions and dignities. Yet in 1453 he had no difficulty in exercising his inquisitorial office pitilessly when the victims were unfortunate Jews. A country priest was said to have sold them eight consecrated hosts for use in their infernal rites. Capistrano seized those implicated, tortured them to confession, and burned them, while a woman who was implicated was torn with red-hot pincers. An old Jewess embraced Christianity, and soon afterwards was slain. The Jews were accused of the murder, and also of that of a Christian boy. Capistrano made another onslaught on them, and this time burned no less than 41.

During all this the Calixtin leaders had not been wholly indifferent. At the commencement of Capistrano's mission Rokyzana wrote to him in a friendly tone, remonstrating with him for condemning as a heresy the communion in both elements, which the Council of Basle had permitted to the Bohemians. Some correspondence ensued, there were negotiations for a conference, and at one time hopes were entertained of an accommodation. Capistrano, however, skillfully eluded a disputation on various pretexts, but really, as we learn from his confidential letter to the Cardinal-Legate Nicholas of Cusa, because he knew that the Calixtins had on their side the weight of authority and tradition. Both parties gradually lost their temper and published against each other letters filled with scurrility. Having thus rendered amicable negotiations impossible, Capistrano could safely, in 1452, ask Podiebrad for a safe-conduct to Prague, and on its refusal summon him to render the aid and service due to him as apostolic commissioner and inquisitor.

During the remainder of the year 1452 we find Capistrano travelling through Germany; at Leipsic he paused long enough for his eloquence to win for his rigid Order sixty professors and students. His efforts to raise a crusade against Bohemia, however, were frustrated by the capture of Constantinople in May 1453. The immense impression which this produced throughout Christendom, the universal alarm at the progress of the Turk, and the necessity of defending Europe, speedily threw into the shade all minor questions. A new crusade was imperatively wanted, but it could not be wasted upon Bohemia and the Utraquists.

During the summer of 1453, as we have seen, Capistrano was tranquilly employing his enforced leisure in burning Jews at Breslau. Thence he went to Poland, where we find him at Cracow throwing into prison a physician, Master Paul, whom he suspected of being an emissary of Rokyzana. He applied again to Podiebrad for a safe-conduct to Prague, which was curtly refused on the ground that when it had been previously offered it had not been accepted, and that Ladislas did not want the peace of his kingdom disturbed.

A brief and clear-cut letter of Æneas Sylvius to Capistrano, dated July 26, 1454, tells him to give up the dream of getting to Prague and go to Frankfort, where he will be useful. An assembly of princes had been held in Ratisbon, where a crusade had been agreed upon, and Philip of Burgundy had consented to lead it. Final arrangements were to be made in Frankfort in October, and there Æneas Sylvius wanted the aid of Capistrano's tireless ardor. When they reached Frankfort, however, the zeal of the princes had cooled, and they declared the purpose of the pope and emperor was to steal their money and not to fight. They demanded that the business should be conducted by a general council which should at the same time repress the Holy See—in fact, both parties were selfishly endeavoring to turn the agony of Europe to account: the pope to raise money, and the princes to recover their independence. All that Æneas and Capistrano could obtain was a promise that at the Pentecost of 1455 they would meet the emperor and determine what could be done. In February and March 1455 they began to assemble at Neuberg, near Vienna, where Podiebrad again used every effort to procure Rokyzana's confirmation. As for the crusade, the energies of Christendom seemed paralyzed by the petty jealousies and ambitions of its rulers. At last, under the unflagging eloquence of Æneas and Capistrano, things appeared to be taking shape, when the news was received of the death of Nicholas V on March 22. Everything fell to pieces, and the princes departed, postponing action until the next year.

Calixtus III was elected April 8, with a speed which showed how dangerous a papal interregnum was considered. He at once sent legates to preach the crusade throughout Europe, and commenced to build warships on the Tiber. The Hungarians, who were justly excited at the impending invasion of Mahomet II, begged Capistrano to come to them and use his eloquence. Calixtus gave him permission, confirmed all the powers conferred on him by Nicholas, and he undertook the task which was to complete his life's work. Yet even these new duties did not wholly distract his attention from the hated Hussites. The juncture seemed favorable for a reconciliation, which every motive of policy dictated. Besides, Æneas Sylvius had just been promoted to the cardinalate, and that crafty diplomat had succeeded in making the Bohemians look upon him as their friend. They hoped to obtain not only the confirmation of the Compactata, but the cardinal's hat for Rokyzana. Hearing of this, Capistrano wrote, March 24, 1456, from Buda to Calixtus dissuading him in the most vigorous terms. The Hussites are the worst of mankind, fearing neither God nor man; the Compactata are their sole bulwark; if these are confirmed, the Hussites will rise and declare themselves. The warning was sufficient and the overtures were rejected.

Suddenly the news came that Mahomet II was advancing and

had laid siege to Belgrade. Ladislas, who was King of Hungary as well as of Bohemia, was at Buda-Pesth, and with his uncle, the Count of Cillei, on pretext of a hunting excursion, basely fled to Austria. John Hunyady, Count of Transylvania, who had been regent of the kingdom, organized the Hungarian forces, with some German crusaders who had come to his assistance, while Capistrano marched with him as papal commander of the crusade. With a flotilla of boats on the Danube, Hunyady, on July 14, 1456, cut his way into the town through the beleaguering forces. The attack and the defense were furious until the 22d, when a fierce assault by the Turks was repulsed, and the besieged followed the retreating enemy, burned one of their camps, spiking some of their cannon and carrying the rest back into the town, where they did good service during the rest of that memorable day. Mahomet gathered together his forces for a last desperate attempt, which was a failure, and during the night he fled, leaving 24,000 men upon the field, and 300 cannon. His army was utterly dispersed, and this disaster, aided by the heroic resistance of Scanderbeg in Albania, arrested the Turkish invasion and gave Europe a breathing spell. It cost, however, the lives of the two heroes to whom it was due. The stench of the dead bodies sickened the army of the victors, and John Hunyady fell a victim, August 11, to the epidemic, which prevented the following up of the advantage. Capistrano had thrown himself into the work with all his self-forgetful enthusiasm. He passed days without food, and nights without rest; for 17 days, it is said, before the victory, he slept but seven hours in all. He was in his 71st year, and when the strain was past exhausted nature paid the penalty. A slow fever set in, August 6, under which he wasted away, and died, October 23. He was perhaps the most perfect type which the age produced of the ideal son of the Church: a purely artificial creation, in which the weakness of humanity disappeared with some of its virtues, and the whole nature, with its rare powers, was concentrated in unselfish devotion to a mistaken purpose. Yet, as Æneas Sylvius shrewdly points out, there was one weak spot left in his nature. In the letters in which he and Hunyady described the victory of Belgrade neither chief gave credit to the other. As Æneas says, "Capistrano had despised the pomps of the world, he had fled from its delights, he had trampled down avarice, he had overcome lust, but he could not contemn glory."

No one could be found worthy to replace Capistrano but his friendly rival, Giacomo della Marca, who was accordingly despatched, in 1457, to the scene of his labors of 20 years previous, armed with the same powers, as inquisitor and crusader. The danger from the Turk was still too pressing for him to waste thought on the former function, and he devoted himself to stimulating and organizing the war against the Moslem until his health gave way, and he returned to Italy. He was replaced by his disciples, Giovanni da Tagliacozza and Michele da Tussicino, who were followed in 1461 by Frà Gabriele da Verona; but though Franciscans still continued for a generation to labor for the conversion of the Calixtins, they had little success in the absence of power to employ the customary inquisitorial methods, of which more hereafter.

In fact, the prospects of reducing Bohemia to obedience were steadily diminishing. The only hope of Rome lay in the approaching majority of the Catholic youth Ladislas; but when, on the eve of his marriage with the daughter of Charles VII of France, he suddenly died, towards the close of 1457, not without suspicions of foul play,[1] and George Podiebrad soon afterwards was elected and crowned, it might well seem that, short of Divine interposition, the peaceful return of Bohemia was not to be looked for. Yet at first it looked as though an accommodation might be reached. Podiebrad caused himself to be crowned according to the Roman rite; having no bishop of his own, he borrowed from his son-in-law, Matthias Corvinus of Hungary, those of Raab and Bacs, to perform his consecration; in his coronation oath he swore obedience to Calixtus and his successors, to restore the Catholic religion, and to persecute heretics; he wrote to Calixtus as a faithful son of the Church, and obtained from him letters recognizing him as King of Bohemia; he sent envoys to Rome, who held out promises that Rokyzana would follow, and settle on a lasting basis the submission of Bohemia.

Calixtus died but a few months later and was succeeded by Æneas Sylvius, who took the name of Pius II. The new pope had been occupied almost exclusively with German and Bohemian affairs, which he knew better than any living man; he had taken part in the

---

[1] Pius II did not hesitate to publish to Christendom a positive assertion that George poisoned Ladislas, and said that, though the facts were obscure, the Viennese physicians in attendance attributed his death to poison.

negotiations resulting in the Compactata; he was shrewd, clear-headed, and troubled with few scruples, and, sharing fully in the papal anxiety to unite Christendom against the Turks, he might be expected to recognize the vital importance of reconciliation with Bohemia. George made haste to send an embassy to renew his protestations of obedience, and to ask for the confirmation of the Compactata. Pius gave a dubious response; George could win his recognition as king by extirpating heresy, and he promised to send legates. They came, but the pope, although he addressed George as king and as his dearest son when soliciting his co-operation in the crusade, shortly afterwards took a step which, with his knowledge of Bohemia, he knew could not but provoke a rupture. Wenceslas, Dean of Prague, was a Catholic and a bitter enemy of Rokyzana, and this man Pius appointed as administrator of the archbishopric, thus ousting Rokyzana. All at once was in uproar. Wenceslas endeavored to assert himself, but the power remained in Rokyzana's hands. George threw into prison Fantinus, who had been his procurator in the curia, and who had been sent with a commission as papal orator, and detained him there for three months. Frederic III, whom George, by a stroke of happy audacity, had recently liberated from a siege by his rebellious subjects in the castle of Vienna, interposed, and delayed the explosion of the papal wrath; but to his earnest request that George should be acknowledged as king Pius returned an absolute refusal. George was a heretic, incapable of the crown, and his subjects' oaths of allegiance were void; only by returning to the Church could he hope to be fitted for the royal dignity. In June 1464 Pius, in full consistory, published a bull reciting all the griefs of the Church against Bohemia, pronouncing the Compactata void, as never having been confirmed by the Holy See, and summoning George before him to stand trial for heresy within three terms of 60 days each. In two months Pius was dead, but his successor, Paul II, carried forward the proceedings with the old inquisitorial weapons. Three cardinals were appointed in 1465 to try George as a relapsed heretic, and summoned him in August to appear before them within six months for judgment. Without waiting for the expiration of the term, early in December, Paul issued a bull absolving all George's subjects from their allegiance, alleging as a reason for haste that the sentence would grow more difficult by delay. In 1468 another summons was issued to him to appear before the cardinals for judgment; and in February 1469 his name was placed as that son of perdition, the Hussite George Podiebrad, together with those of Rokyzana and Gregory of Heimburg, in the curse of the *Cœna Domini*, to be anathematized thrice a year in all cathedrals, both in Latin and in the vernacular.

All this was not a mere *brutum fulmen*. It was not difficult to excite rebellion among turbulent subjects and attacks from ambitious neighbors. With all his vigor and capacity George found the maintenance of his position by no means easy. When, in 1468, the German princes had agreed upon a five years' truce in order to concentrate their energies against the Moslem, Paul II threw the empire into confusion by sending the Bishop of Ferrara to preach a crusade with plenary indulgences against Bohemia. The kingdom was bestowed upon Matthias Corvinus of Hungary, who took the cross, and with an army of crusaders occupied Moravia. A long war ensued, during which George died, in 1471, released from excommunication on his deathbed, and Ladislas II, son of Casimir of Poland, was elected as his successor. In 1475 the rivals came to terms; both were recognized as kings of Bohemia, while Matthias was to have for life Moravia, Silesia, and the greater part of Lusatia, and the survivor was to enjoy the whole kingdom. On the death of Matthias, in 1490, Ladislas recovered the three provinces, and shortly afterward added Hungary to his dominions.

Ladislas was a good Catholic, and Sixtus IV, who had aided in his election, hoped that the opportunity had at last arrived to break down the stubbornness of the Calixtins. The king made the attempt, but bloody tumults in Prague, which nearly cost him his life, showed that, slight as was the difference between Catholic and Utraquist, the old fanaticism for the cup survived. At length, in 1485, at the Diet of Kuttenberg, mutual toleration was agreed upon, and Ladislas, who was of easy disposition, ran no further risks. Thus the anomalous position of Bohemia as a member of Latin Christendom became more remarkable than ever. The great majority of the people were Calixtins and therefore heretics, but the Church had to abandon the attempt to coerce them to salvation. Missionary inquisitors were commissioned from time to time, but practically their efforts were limited to persuasion. As the invention of printing facilitated controversy, polemical zeal multiplied treatises to prove the iniquity of the Utraquist heresy, but the Utraquists were not to be converted. They maintained the Compacata as the charter of their religious independence. When, in 1526, King Louis fell in the disastrous day of Mohacz, and the House of Austria, in the person of Ferdinand I, obtained the Bohemian throne, good Catholic though Ferdinand was, he was obliged to pledge himself to preserve the Compactata.

It is not to be imagined that the teachings of Wickliff and Huss were wholly forgotten in Utraquist degeneracy. Their real inheritors were the Taborites, and although these, in their disorderly enthusiasm, vainly contended against the spirit of the age and disappeared from sight under the strong hand of Podiebrad, the seed which they had nurtured was not wholly lost. When such men as these were driven forth and scattered among the people they were much more likely to make converts than to be converted, and though lost to sight they were assuredly not false to their convictions. The reactionary course of Rokyzana and Podiebrad during the succeeding years could hardly fail to provoke discontent among the more earnest even of the Calixtins and to furnish fresh disciples and teachers. Materials existed for a sect representing the doctrines which, a generation earlier, had set Bohemia aflame; and although when that sect timidly appeared it prudently and sedulously disavowed all affiliation with the hated and dreaded Taborites, there can be no doubt that it was, to a great extent, composed of the same elements.

These new sectaries first present themselves in an organized form in 1457. Earnest, humble Christians, they differed from the Taborites in a yet closer approach to Waldensianism, due probably to the influence of Peter Chelcicky, who, without belonging to them, was yet to some extent their teacher. Like the Waldenses, they rejected the oath and the sword—nothing would justify the taking of human life, and consequently they were nonresistants. The sacraments were worthless in polluted hands. Priests might hear confessions and impose penances, but they could not absolve; they could only announce the forgiveness of God. As for the mystery of the Eucharist, they prudently adopted the formula of Peter Chelcicky, which eluded the difficulty by affirming that the believer receives.

the body and blood of Christ, without pretending to explain or daring to discuss the matter. On this basis was founded the brotherhood of love and charity which represents more nearly the Christian ideal than anything the world had seen for thirteen centuries. With extreme simplicity of life there was no exaggeration of asceticism. Heaven was not to be stormed by mortification of the flesh, but was to be won by the sedulous discharge of the duties imposed on man by his Creator. Such was the *Unitas Fratrum*—the Bohemian or Moravian Brotherhood—and that a society thus defenseless and unresisting should endure the savage vicissitudes of that transitional period, and maintain itself to the present time, shows that force is not necessarily the last word in human affairs.

At first the Brotherhood seems to have enjoyed the favor of Rokyzana, whose doctrines they claimed to follow, and whose nephew Gregory was one of their earliest leaders, along with Michael, priest of Zamberg. Rokyzana's fluctuating policy, as the archbishopric seemed to approach or recede, soon led him to hold aloof, and when they drew apart from the Calixtins and organized themselves as a separate body he had no objection to seeing them persecuted. In vain they declared that they were neither Waldenses nor Taborites. When, about 1461, Gregory, with a few companions, ventured secretly to Prague, they were betrayed as conspiring Taborites and put to the torture. It shows their state of religious exaltation that Gregory swooned on the rack and had a beatific vision. It may be put to the credit of Rokyzana that when he saw his nephew insensible from the torture he burst into tears, exclaiming, "O my Gregory, I would I were where thou art!" and that he soon afterwards obtained from Podiebrad permission for them to settle at Liticz. Here they prospered amid alternate peace and persecution, their numbers rapidly increasing.

In retaining all the sacraments they retained belief in the necessity of apostolical succession for that of ordination; but they became oppressed with misgivings as to the efficacy of the sacerdotal character of their priests, derived as it was through the Church of Rome. Some of them proposed sending to the legendary Christians of India, but they met with two men who had been in the East, and the accounts they received of the Oriental churches satisfied them that the succession there had been lost. Then they bethought them of the Greeks, but they met some Greeks in Prague from whom they learned that fees were required for ordination, thus rendering it void through simony. Finally they turned to the Waldenses, of whom there was a community on the Austrian border. These claimed to descend from the primitive Church; that their ancestors had separated from Rome when the papacy was secularized under Silvester by the donation of Constantine, and that they had preserved the apostolic succession untainted. It remained for the brethren to see whether it was the will of God that they should organize themselves by means of these Waldenses. At Lhotka, in 1467, an assembly of about 60 chosen deputies was held. After fasting and earnest prayer, recourse was had to the lot, to decide whether they should separate themselves from the Roman priesthood. The result was affirmative. Then they selected nine men, from among whom three or two or one should be drawn, or none, if God so willed it. Twelve cards were taken, on three of which was written "is," and on nine "is not." These were mingled together, and a youth was directed to distribute nine of them among the men selected. All three with "is" proved to have been distributed, and the assembly devoutly thanked God for showing them the path to follow. Michael of Zamberg was sent to the Waldensian Bishop Stephen, who investigated his faith and life, and thanked God, with tears, that it had been vouchsafed him before he died to see such pious men. After episcopal consecration Michael returned; careful inquiry was made as to the antecedents of one of the three elect, named Matthias, and he was duly consecrated as bishop by Michael, who thereupon laid down both his Waldensian episcopate and Catholic priesthood, and was again ordained anew by Matthias. Thus all connection with Rome was sundered, and intimate relations were established with the Waldenses. Although the official name remained the "Unity of the Brethren," gradually the despised term of Waldenses came to be recognized, and was freely used by the body to designate themselves, in their confessions of faith and apologetic tracts.

Gregory had moulded the Church of the Brethren on the strictest basis. Members on entering were not, it is true, obliged to contribute their property to the common fund, but this was frequently done. The closest watch was kept on the conduct of each, and any dereliction was visited with expulsion, not to be revoked without evidence of change of heart. No one was allowed to take an oath, even in court, to hold an office, to keep an inn, to follow any trade except in the necessaries of life. Any noble desiring to join was required to lay aside his rank and resign whatever offices he might hold. In 1479 two barons and several knights applied for admission, when the rules were strictly enforced, and some submitted while others withdrew. This rigor at last caused violent dissensions, and in 1490 the synod of Brandeis relaxed the rules. The puritan party recalcitrated and were strong enough to cause a revocation of this action in a subsequent synod. Much ill-feeling was generated, until, in 1495, at the synod of Reichenau, there was mutual forgiveness and a moderation of the rules. Yet two of the puritan leaders, Jacob of Wodnan and Amos of Stekna, refused to accept the compromise, and founded the sect known as Amosites, or the Little Party, which maintained a separate existence for 46 years.

During this period the Brethren had been subjected to repeated and severe persecution. Sometimes driven for refuge to the mountain and forest, whence they earned the name of *Jamnici*, or cave-dwellers, they counted their roll of martyrs who had testified in the dungeon or at the stake to the strength of their convictions. Yet the little band steadily grew. In the year 1500 it was deemed necessary to increase the number of bishops to four. In Bohemia and Moravia they counted between 300 and 400 churches with nearly 200,000 members. There were few villages and scarce any towns in which they were not to be found, and they had powerful protectors among the nobility, who, by the enslavement of the peasants in 1487, had become practically independent and able to shelter them during periods of persecution. The Brethren were active in education and in the use of the press. Every parish had its school, and there were higher institutions of learning, especially at Jung-bunzlau and Litomysl. Of the six Bohemian printing offices they possessed three, while the Catholics had but one and the Calixtins two. Of the 60 books issued in Bohemia between 1500 and 1510, 50 were printed by the Brethren.

From this period until the death of Ladislas, in 1516, they were subjected to intermittent persecution, especially in Bohemia. Ladislas, in his will, left instructions for their extermination "for the sake of his soul's salvation and of the true faith"; but the minority of his son Louis, only ten years old, the breaking-out of disturbances, and the feuds between Catholic and Calixtin brought them peace. The exiled pastors returned, the churches were reopened, and public service was resumed. With the rise of Lutheranism and the negotiations between the Bohemians and the German Protestants their history passes beyond our present horizon, except to allude to the fidelity with which they endured the shocks of the Counter-Reformation, and succeeded in transmitting to our own time the lessons which they had learned from Peter Waldo and John Wickliff. They brought across the Atlantic the union of fearless zeal with the gentler Christian virtues, and in the annals of Pennsylvania the name of Moravian came to represent all that serves as the firmest and surest foundation of social organization.

Book III
SPECIAL FIELDS OF INQUISITORIAL ACTIVITY

CHAPTER XVII
THE SPIRITUAL FRANCISCANS

WHILE the mission of both Mendicant Orders was to redeem the Church from the depth of degradation into which it had sunk, the Domincans were more especially trained to take part in the active business of life. They accommodated themselves to the world, like the Jesuits of later days, and the worldliness which necessarily came with success awakened little antagonism within the organization.

It was otherwise with the Franciscans. Though, as we have seen, the founders determined not to render the Order simply a contemplative one, the salvation of the individual through retreat from the world bore a much larger part in their motives than in those of Dominic and his followers. Absolute poverty and self-abnegation were its primal principles, and it inevitably drew to itself the intellects that sought a refuge from the temptations of life in self-absorbing contemplation. As the organization grew in wealth and power there were necessarily developed within it antagonisms in two directions. On the one hand, it nourished a spirit of mysticism, which sometimes found the trammels of orthodoxy oppressive. On the other, the men who continued to cherish the views of the founders on the supreme obligation of absolute poverty could not reconcile their consciences to the accumulation of wealth and its display in splendor, and they rejected the ingenious devices that sought to accommodate the possession of riches with the abnegation of all possession.

In fact, the three vows of poverty, obedience, and chastity were all equally impossible of absolute observance. The first was irreconcilable with human necessities, the others with human passions. As for poverty, we shall see to what inextricable complications it led, despite the efforts of successive popes, until the imperious will and resolute common sense of John XXII brought the Order from its seraphic heights down to the everyday necessities of human life— at the cost, it must be confessed, of a schism. The trouble was increased by the fact that St. Francis, foreseeing the efforts which would be made to evade the spirit of the Rule, had in his Testament strictly forbidden all alterations, glosses, and explanations.

The more serious trouble concerning poverty was not long in developing itself. Next to St. Francis himself in the Order stood Elias. When, through infirmity or inability to maintain discipline, Francis retired from the generalate, Elias was Vicar-General of the Order, to whom Francis submitted himself as humbly as the meanest brother, and on the death of the saint, in October 1226, it was Elias who notified the brethren throughout Europe of the event, and informed them of the Stigmata, which the humility of Francis had always concealed. Although in February 1227 Giovanni Parenti of Florence was elected general, Elias seems practically to have retained control. Elias was worldly and ambitious; he had the reputation of being one of the ablest men of affairs in Italy; he could foresee the power attaching to the command of the Order, and he had not much scruple as to the means of attaining it. He undertook the erection of a magnificent church at Assisi to receive the bones of the humble Francis, and he was unsparing in his demands for money to aid in its construction. The very handling of money was an abomination in the eyes of all true brethren, yet all the provinces were called upon to contribute, and a marble coffer was placed in front of the building to receive the gifts of the pious.

When the edifice was sufficiently advanced, a General Chapter was held in 1230 to solemnize the translation of the saintly corpse. Elias sought to utilize the occasion for his own election to the generalate by summoning to it only those brethren on whose support he could reckon, but Giovanni got wind of this and made the summons general. Elias then caused the translation to be effected before the brethren had assembled; his faction endeavored to forestall the action of the chapter by carrying him from his cell, breaking open the doors, and placing him in the general's seat. Giovanni appeared, and after tumultuous proceedings his friends obtained the upper hand; the disturbers were scattered among the provinces, and Elias retreated to a hermitage, where he allowed his hair and beard to grow, and through this show of sanctity obtained reconciliation to the Order. Finally, in the chapter of 1232, his ambition was rewarded. Giovanni was deposed and he was elected general.

These turbulent intrigues were not the only evidence of the

rapid degeneracy of the Order. Before Francis's Testament was five years old his commands against evasions of the Rule by cunning interpretations had been disregarded. The chapter of 1231 had applied to Gregory IX to know whether the Testament was binding upon them in this respect, and he replied in the negative, for Francis could not bind his successors. They also asked about the prohibition to hold money and property, and Gregory ingeniously suggested that this could be effected through third parties, who could hold money and pay debts for them, arguing that such persons should be regarded not as their agents, but as the agents of those who gave the money or of those to whom it was to be paid. These elusory glosses of the Rule were not accepted without an energetic opposition, nor was the bitterness diminished by the use Elias made of his position. His rule was arbitrary, and for seven years, in defiance of the regulations, he held no General Chapter. He levied exactions on all the provinces to complete the great structure at Assisi. Those who resisted him were relegated to distant places. Even while yet only vicar he had caused St. Anthony of Padua, who had come to Assisi to worship at the tomb of Francis, to be scourged to the blood, when Anthony only expostulated with, "May the blessed God forgive you, brethren!" Worse was the fate of Cæsarius of Speier, who had been appointed Provincial of Germany in 1221 by St. Francis himself, and had built up the Order to the north of the Alps. He was the leader of the puritan malcontents, who were known as Cæsarians, and he felt the full wrath of Elias. Thrown into prison, he lay there in chains for two years. At length the fetters were removed, and, early in 1239, his jailer having left the door of his cell open, he ventured forth to stretch his cramped limbs in the wintry sun. The jailer returned and thought that he was attempting to escape. Fearing the anger of Elias, he rushed after the prisoner and dealt him a mortal blow with a cudgel. Cæsarius was the first but by no means the last martyr who shed his blood for the strict observance of a Rule breathing nothing but love and charity.

In 1237 Elias had sent visitors to the different provinces, whose conduct caused general exasperation. The brethren of Saxony appealed to him and, finding this fruitless, they carried their complaint to Gregory. The pope at length was roused to intervene. A General

Chapter was convened in 1239, when, after a stormy scene, the pope finally announced to Elias that his resignation would be received. Elias was a skillful negotiator, and was looked upon with a friendly eye by Frederic II, who forthwith declared that the dismissal was done in his despite, for Elias was at the time engaged in an effort to heal the breach between the papacy and the empire. Elias at once took refuge with Frederic and became his intimate companion. Gregory made an effort to capture him by inviting him to a conference. Failing in this, a charge was brought against him of visiting poor women at Cortona without permission, and on refusing to obey a summons he was excommunicated.

Thus already in the Franciscan Order there were established two well-defined parties, which came to be known as the Spirituals and the Conventuals, the one adhering to the strict letter of the Rule, the other willing to find excuses for its relaxation in obedience to the wants of human nature and the demands of worldliness. After the fall of Elias the former had the supremacy during the brief generalates of Alberto of Pisa and Haymo of Feversham. In 1244 the Conventuals triumphed in the election of Crescenzio Grizzi da Jesi.

The Order was constantly growing, it was constantly acquiring property, and its needs were constantly increasing. A bull of Gregory IX in 1239, authorizing the Franciscans of Paris to acquire additional land with which to enlarge their monastery of Saint-Germain-des-Près, is an example of what was going on all over Europe. In 1244, at the chapter which elected Crescenzio, the Englishman John Kethene succeeded, against the opposition of nearly the whole body of the assembly, in obtaining the rejection of Gregory's definition, but the triumph of the Puritans was short-lived. Crescenzio sympathized with the laxer party and applied to Innocent IV for relief. In 1245 the pope responded with a declaration in which he not only repeated the device of Gregory IX by authorizing deposits of money with parties who were to be regarded as agents, but ingeniously assumed that houses and lands, the ownership of which was forbidden to the Order, should be regarded as belonging to the Holy See, which granted their use to the friars. Even papal authority could not render these transparent subterfuges satisfying to the consciences of the Spirituals, and the growing worldliness of the Order provoked continuous agitation. Under Simone da Assisi, Giacopo Manfredo, Matteo da Monte Rubiano, and Lucido, 72 earnest brethren, finding Crescenzio deaf to their remonstrances, prepared to appeal to Innocent. Crescenzio anticipated them, and obtained from the pope in advance a decision under which he scattered the recalcitrants in couples throughout the provinces for punishment. Fortunately his reign was short. Tempted by the bishopric of Jesi, he resigned, and in 1248 was succeeded by Giovanni Borelli, better known as John of Parma, who at the time was professor of theology in the University of Paris.

The election of John of Parma marked a reaction in favor of strict observance. The exiled Spirituals were recalled and allowed to select their own domiciles. During the first three years John visited on foot the whole Order, in the most humble guise, so that he was unrecognized and could remain in a convent for several days, observing its character, when he would reveal himself and reform its abuses. He suspended the declaration of Innocent IV until the pontiff, better informed, could be consulted. It was, however, impossible for him to control the tendencies to relaxation of the Rule, and his efforts only served to strengthen disaffection which finally grew to determined opposition. After consultation between some influential members of the Order it was resolved to bring before Alexander IV formal accusations against him and the friends who surrounded him.

To understand the position of the Spirituals at this time and subsequently, it is necessary to cast a glance at one of the most remarkable spiritual developments of the thirteenth century. Its opening years had witnessed the death of Joachim of Flora, a man who may be regarded as the founder of modern mysticism. Sprung from a rich and noble family, and trained for the life of a courtier under Roger, the Norman Duke of Apulia, a sudden desire to see the holy places took him, while yet a youth, to the East, with a retinue of servitors. A pestilence was raging when he reached Constantinople, which so impressed him with the miseries and vanities of life that he dismissed his suite and continued his voyage as a humble pilgrim with a single companion. His legend relates that he fell in the desert overcome with thirst, and had a vision of a man standing by a river of oil, and saying to him, "Drink of this stream," which he did to satiety, and when he awoke, although previously illiterate, he had a knowledge of all Scripture. The following Lent he passed in an old well on Mount Tabor; in the night of the Resurrection a great splendor appeared to him, he was filled with divine light to understand the concordance of the Old and New Laws, and every difficulty and every obscurity vanished. These tales, repeated until the seventeenth century, show the profound and lasting impression which he left upon the minds of men.

Thenceforth his life was dedicated to the service of God. Returning home, he entered the priesthood and the severe Cistercian Order. Even the Cistercian discipline did not satisfy his thirst for austerity, however, and he retired to a hermitage at Pietralata, where his reputation for sanctity drew disciples around him, and in spite of his yearning for solitude he found himself at the head of a new Order, of which the Rule, anticipating the Mendicants in its urgency of poverty, was approved by Celestin III in 1196. Already it had spread from the mother-house of San Giovanni in Fiore, and numbered several other monasteries.

Joachim considered himself inspired, and he had no hesitation in speaking of his works as divinely revealed. During his lifetime he enjoyed the reputation of a prophet. When Richard of England and Philip Augustus were at Messina, they sent for him to inquire about the outcome of their crusade, and he is said to have foretold that the hour had not yet come for the deliverance of Jerusalem. Others of his fulfilled prophecies are also related, and the mystical character of the apocalyptic speeculations which he left behind him served to increase, after his death, his reputation as a seer.

Joachim's immense and durable reputation as a prophet was due not so much to his genuine works, however, as to the spurious ones circulated under his name. These were numerous—Prophecies of Cyril, and of the Erythræan Sybil, Commentaries on Jeremiah, the *Vaticinia Pontificum*, the *De Oneribus Ecclesiæ* and *De Septem Temporibus Ecclesiæ*. In some of these, reference to Frederic II would seem to indicate a period of composition about the year 1250, when the strife between the papacy and empire was at the hottest. There can be little doubt that their authors were Franciscans of the Puritan party, and their fearless denunciations of existing evils show how impatient had grown the spirit of dissatisfaction. The apocalyptic prophecies were freely interpreted as referring to the carnal worldliness which pervaded all orders in the Church; all are reprobate, none are elect; Rome is the Whore of Babylon, and the papal curia the most venal and extortionate of all courts; the Roman Church is the barren fig-tree, accursed by Christ, which shall be abandoned to the nations to be stripped. It would be difficult to exaggerate the antagonism displayed in these writings, even to the point of recognizing the empire as the instrument of God which is to overthrow the pride of the Church.

Of Joachim's genuine writings the one which perhaps attracted the most attention in his own day was a tract on the nature of the Trinity, attacking the definition of Peter Lombard, and asserting that it attributed a Quaternity to God. The subtleties of theology were dangerous, and in place of proving the Master of Sentences a heretic, Joachim himself narrowly escaped. Thirteen years after his death, the Great Council of Lateran, in 1215, thought his speculation sufficiently important to condemn it as erroneous in an elaborate refutation, which was carried into the canon law. Fortunately Joachim, in 1200, had expressly submitted all his writings to the judgment of the Holy See and had declared that he held the same faith as that of Rome. The council, therefore, refrained from condemning him personally and expressed its approbation of his Order of Flora; but notwithstanding this the monks found themselves derided and insulted as the followers of a heretic, until, in 1220, they procured from Honorius III a bull expressly declaring that he was a good Catholic, and forbidding all detraction of his disciples.

His most important writings, however, were his expositions of Scripture composed at the request of Lucius III, Urban III, and Clement III. Of these there were three—the *Concordia*, the *Decachordon* or *Psalterium decem Cordarum*, and the *Expositio in Apocalypsin*. In these his system of exegesis is to find in every incident under the Old Law the prefiguration of a corresponding fact in chronological order under the New Dispensation, and by an arbitrary parallelism of dates to reach forward and ascertain what is yet to come. He thus determines that mankind is destined to live through three states—the first under the rule of the Father, which ended at the birth of Christ, the second under that of the Son, and the third under the Holy Ghost. The reign of the Son, or of the New

Testament, he ascertains by varied apocalyptic speculations is to last through 42 generations, or 1260 years. In the 42nd generation there will be a purgation which will separate the wheat from the chaff— such tribulations as man has never yet endured. After this, religion will be renewed; man will live in peace and justice and joy; all shall know God, from sea to sea, and the glory of the Holy Ghost shall be perfect. With endless amplitude he illustrates the progressive character of the relations between God and man in the successive eras. The first state, under God, was of the circumcision; the second, under Christ, is of the crucifixion; the third, under the Holy Ghost, will be of quietude and peace. Under the first was the order of the married; under the second, that of the priesthood; under the third will be that of monachism, which has already had its precursor in St. Benedict.

It is a curious fact that while Joachim's metaphysical subtleties respecting the Trinity were ostentatiously condemned as a dangerous heresy, no one seems at the time to have recognized the far more perilous conclusions to be drawn from these apocalyptic reveries. To us, for the moment, their chief significance lies in the proof which they afford that the most pious minds confessed that Christianity was practically a failure. Mankind had scarce grown better under the New Law. Vices and passions were as unchecked as they had been before the coming of the Redeemer. The Church, in place of elevating man, had been dragged down to his level. Joachim himself might seek to evade these deductions from his premises, yet others could not fail to make them, and nothing could be more subversive of the established spiritual and temporal order of the Church. Yet for a time his speculations attracted little attention and no animadversion. It is possible that the condemnation of his theory of the Trinity may have cast a shadow over his exegetical works and prevented their general dissemination, but they were treasured by kindred spirits, and copies of them were carried into various lands and carefully preserved.

Gradually the writings of Joachim obtained currency, and with the ascription to him of the false prophecies which appeared towards the middle of the century his name became more widely known and of greater authority. In Provence and Languedoc, especially, his teachings found eager reception. Harried successively by the crusades and the Inquisition, and scarce as yet fairly reunited with the Church, those regions furnished an ample harvest of earnest minds which might well seek in the hoped-for speedy realization of Joachim's dreams compensation for the miseries of the present. Nor did those dreams lack an apostle of unquestionable orthodoxy. Hugues de Digne, a hermit of Hyères, had a wide reputation for learning, eloquence, and sanctity. He had been Franciscan Provincial of Provence, but had laid down that dignity to gratify his passion for austerity. Hugues was intimate with the leading men of the Order; Alexander Hales, Adam de Marisco, and John of Parma are named as among his close friends. With the latter, especially, he had the common bond that both were earnest Joachites.

If the Joachitic Franciscans developed the ideas of their teacher with greater boldness and definiteness, their ardor had ample excuse. They had seen how the teachings of Francis and the New Revelation of which he had been the medium were perverted by worldly men to purposes of ambition and greed; how the Order, which should have been the germ of human redemption, was growing more and more carnal, and how its saints were martyred by their fellows. Unless the universe were a failure and the promises of God were lies, there must be a term to human wickedness; and as the Gospel of Christ and the Rule of Francis had not accomplished the salvation of mankind, a new gospel was indispensable. Besides, Joachim had predicted that there would arise a new religious Order which would rule the world and the Church in the halcyon age of the Holy Ghost. They could not doubt that this referred to the Franciscans as represented by the Spiritual group, which was striving to uphold in all its strictness the Rule of the venerated founder.

Prominent members of the Order had openly embraced the Joachitic doctrines, and his prophecies, genuine and spurious, were applied to all events as they occurred. In 1248 Salimbene, the chronicler, who was already a warm believer, met at the Franciscan convent of Provins (Champagne) two ardent condisciples, Gherardo da Borgo San Donnino and Bartolommeo Ghiscolo of Parma. St. Louis was just setting forth on his ill-starred Egyptian crusade. The Joachites foretold that the expedition would be a failure, that the king would be taken prisoner, and that pestilence would decimate the host. This was not calculated to render them popular; the peace of the good brethren was sadly broken by quarrels, and the Joachites found it advisable to depart. Salimbene went to Auxerre, Ghiscolo to Sens, and Gherardo to Paris, where his learning secured for him admission to the University as the representative of Sicily and he obtained a chair in theology. Here for four years he pursued his apocalyptic studies.

Suddenly, in 1254, Paris was startled with the appearance of a book under the title *The Everlasting Gospel*—a name derived from the Apocalypse—"And I saw another angel fly in the midst of heaven, having the everlasting gospel to preach unto them that dwell on the earth, and to every nation, and kindred, and tongue, and people" (Rev. xiv. 6). It consisted of Joachim's three undoubted works, with explanatory glosses, preceded by a long Introduction, in which the hardy author developed the ideas of the prophet audaciously and uncompromisingly. The daring venture had an immediate and immense popular success. The rhymes of Jean de Meung indicate that the demand for it came from the laity rather than the clergy, and that it was sought by women as well as by men:

> Ung livre de par le grant diable
> Dit l'Évangile pardurable . . .
> A Paris n'eust home ne feme
> Au parvis devant Nostre-Dame
> Qui lors avoir ne le péust
> A transcrire, s'il li pléust.

Nothing more revolutionary in spirit, more subversive of the established order of the Church, can be conceived than the assertions which thus aroused popular sympathy and applause. Joachim's computations were accepted, and it was assumed absolutely that in six years, in 1260, the reign of Christ would end and the reign of the Holy Ghost begin. Even as Joachim had dwelt on the ascending scale of the three Eras, so the author of the Introduction characterized the progressive methods of the three Scriptures. The Old Testament is the first heaven, the New Testament the second heaven, the Everlasting Gospel the third heaven. The preaching and dissemination of this supreme and eternal law of God is committed to the barefooted Order (the Franciscans). In the blessed coming reign of the Holy Ghost men will live under the law of love, as in the first Era they lived in fear, and in the second in grace. Joachim had argued against the continuance of the sacraments; the Introduction regarded them as symbols and enigmas, from which man would be liberated in the time to come, for love would replace all the observances founded upon the second Dispensation. This was destructive of the whole sacerdotal system, and scarce less revolutionary was the bold declaration that the Abomination of Desolation would be a pope tainted with simony, who, towards the end of the sixth age, now at hand, would obtain the papacy.

The authorship of this bold challenge to an infallible Church was long attributed to John of Parma himself, but there would seem little doubt that it was the work of Gherardo—the outcome of his studies during the four years spent in the University of Paris, although John of Parma possibly had a hand in it. Certainly, as Tocco points out, he at least sympathized with it, for he never punished the author, in spite of the scandal which it brought upon the Order, and Bernard Gui tells us that at the time it was commonly ascribed to him. I have already related with what joy William of Saint Amour seized upon it in the quarrel between the University and the Mendicants, and the advantage it momentarily gave the former. Under existing circumstances it could have no friends or defenders. The only thing to be done with it was to suppress it as quietly as possible. Consideration for the Franciscan Order demanded this, as well as the prudence which counselled that attention should not be unduly called to it, although hundreds of victims had been burned for heresies far less dangerous.

The Spiritual section of the Franciscans was fatally compromised, and the worldly party, which had impatiently borne the strict rule of John of Parma, saw its opportunity of gaining the ascendency. Led by Bernardo da Bessa, the companion of Bonaventura, formal articles of accusation were presented to Alexander IV against the General. He was accused of listening to no explanations of the Rule and Testament, holding that the privileges and declarations of the popes were of no moment in comparison. It was not hinted that he was implicated in *The Everlasting Gospel,* but it was alleged that he pretended to enjoy the spirit of prophecy and that he predicted a division of the Order between those who procured papal relaxations and those who adhered to the Rule, the latter of whom would flourish under the dew of heaven and the benediction of God. Moreover, he defended the errors of Joachim concerning the Trinity, and his immediate comrades had not hesitated, in sermons and tracts, to praise Joachim immoderately and to assail the leading men of the Order. In this, as in the rest of the proceedings, the studied silence preserved as to *The Everlasting Gospel* shows how dangerous was the subject, and how even the fierce passions of the strife shrank from compromising the Order by admitting that any of its members was responsible for that incendiary production.

Alexander was easily persuaded, and a General Chaper was held in the Araccœli, February 2, 1257, over which he personally presided. John of Parma was warned to resign, and did so, pleading age, weariness, and disability. After a decent show of resistance his resignation was accepted and he was asked to nominate a successor. His choice fell upon Bonaventura, then only 34 years of age, whose participation in the struggle with the University of Paris had marked him as the most promising man in the Order, while he was not identified with either faction. He was duly elected, and the leaders of the movement required him to proceed against John and his adherents. Bonaventura for a while hesitated, but at length consented. Gherardo refused to recant, and Bonaventura sent for him to come to Paris. Gherardo was learned, pure-minded, temperate, modest, amiable—in a word, an admirable and lovable character; but nothing could wean him from his Joachitic convictions, though in his trial discreet silence, as usual, was observed about *The Everlasting Gospel*, and he was condemned as an upholder of Joachim's Trinitarian speculations. Had he not been a Franciscan he would have been burned. It was a doubtful mercy which consigned him to a dungeon and fed him on bread and water for eighteen years, until his weary life came to an end. He never wavered to the last, and his remains were thrust into a corner of the garden of the convent where he died. The same fate awaited his comrade Leonardo, and also another friar named Piero de' Nubili, who refused to surrender a tract of John of Parma's.

Then John himself was tried by a special court, to preside over which Alexander appointed Cardinal Caietano, afterwards Nicholas III. The accused readily retracted his advocacy of Joachim, but his

bearing irritated the judges, and, with Bonaventura's consent, he
would have shared the fate of his associates but for the strenuous
intercession of Ottoboni, Cardinal of S. Adrian, afterwards Adrian V.
Bonaventura gave him the option of selecting a place of retreat, and
he chose a little convent near Rieti. There he is said to have lived
for thirty-two years the life of an angel, without abandoning his
Joachitic beliefs. John XXI, who greatly loved him, thought of
making him a cardinal in 1277, but was prevented by death. Nicholas
III offered him the cardinalate, so as to be able to enjoy his advice,
but he quietly answered, "I could give wholesome counsel if there
were anyone to listen to me, but in the Roman court there is little
discussed but wars and triumphs, and not the salvation of souls."
In 1289, however, notwithstanding his extreme age, he accepted from
Nicholas IV a mission to the Greek Church, but he died at Camerino
soon after setting out. Buried there, he speedily shone in miracles;
he became the object of a lasting cult, and in 1777 he was formally
beatified, in spite of the opposition arising from his alleged authorship of the introduction to *The Everlasting Gospel*.

The faith of the Joachites was by no means broken by these reverses. The south of France was the headquarters of the sect, and, as
we shall see hereafter, the leaven long remained in Languedoc and
Provence, and gave a decided impress to the Spiritual Franciscanism
of those regions.

It was inevitable that the strife within the Order between property
and poverty should grow increasingly bitter. Questions were constantly arising which showed the incompatibility of the vows as laid
down by St. Francis with the functions of an organization which
had grown to be one of the leading factors of a wealthy and worldly
Church. In 1255 we find the sisters of the monastery of St. Elizabeth
complaining to Alexander IV that when property was given or bequeathed to them the ecclesiastical authorities enforced on them the
observance of the Rule, by compelling them to part with it within a
year by sale or gift, and the pope graciously promised that no such
custom should be enforced in future. About the same time John of
Parma complained that when his friars were promoted to the episcopate they carried away with them books and other things of which
they had properly only the use, being unable to own anything under
peril of their souls. Such troubles must have been of almost daily

occurrence, and it was inevitable that the increasing friction should result in schism. When the blessed Gilio, the third disciple who joined St. Francis, was taken to Assisi to view the splendid buildings erected in honor of the humble Francis, and was carried through magnificent churches, connected with a vast refectory, a spacious dormitory, and other offices and cloisters, adorned with lofty arches and spacious portals, he kept silent until one of his guides pressed him for an expression of admiration. "Brethren," he then said, "there is nothing lacking except your wives." This seemed somewhat irrelevant, till he explained that the vows of poverty and chastity were equally binding, and now that one was set aside the other might as well follow.

The Conventuals had lost no time in securing the results of their victory over John of Parma. Scarce had his resignation been secured, and before Bonaventura could arrive from Paris, they obtained from Alexander, February 20, 1257, a repetition of the declaration of Innocent IV which enabled the Order to handle money and hold property through the transparent device of agents and the Holy See. The disgust of the Puritan party was great, and even the implicit reverence prescribed for the papacy could not prevent ominous mutterings of disobedience, which in time were to ripen into open rebellion.

Although the removal of John of Parma from the generalate had been the victory of the Conventuals, the choice of Bonaventura might well seem to give to the Spirituals assurance of continued supremacy. In his controversy with William of Saint Amour he had taken the most advanced ground in denying that Christ and the apostles held property of any kind, and in identifying poverty with perfection:

Deep poverty is laudable; this is true of itself: therefore deeper poverty is more laudable, and the deepest, the most laudable. But this is the poverty of him who neither in private nor in common keeps anything for himself. . . . To renounce all things, in private or in common, is Christian perfection, not only sufficient but abundant: it is the principal counsel of evangelical perfection, its fundamental principle and sublime foundation.

Bonaventura honestly sought to restrain the growing laxity of the Order. Before leaving Paris he addressed, April 23, 1257, an encyclical letter to the provincials, calling their attention to the prevalent vices of the brethren and the contempt to which they exposed the whole Order. Again, some ten years later, at the instance of Clement IV, he issued another similar epistle, in which he strongly expressed his horror at the neglect of the Rule shown in the shameless greed of so many members, the importunate striving for gain, the ceaseless litigation caused by their grasping after legacies and burials, and the splendor and luxury of their buildings. But however earnest Bonaventura may have been, he lacked the fiery energy which enabled John of Parma to give effect to his convictions.

The question of poverty evidently was one incapable of permanent and satisfactory settlement. In vain Gregory X, about 1275, was appealed to, and decided that the injunction of the Rule against the possession of property, individually or in common, was to be strictly observed. The worldly party continued to point out the incompatibility of this with the necessities of human nature; the quarrel continually grew more envenomed, and in 1279 Nicholas III undertook to settle it with a formal declaration which should forever close the mouths of all cavillers. For two months he secretly labored at it in consultation with the two Franciscan cardinals, Palestrina and Albano, the General Bonagrazia, and some of the provincials. Then it was submitted to a commission in which was Benedetto Caietano, afterwards Boniface VIII. Finally it was read and adopted in full consistory, and it was included, twenty years later, in the additions to the canon law compiled and published by order of Boniface. No utterance of the Holy See could have more careful consideration and more solemn authority than the bull known as *Exiit qui seminat,* which subsequently became the subject of such deadly controversy.

It declares the Franciscan Rule to be the inspiration of the Holy Ghost through St. Francis. The renunciation of property, not only individual but in common, is meritorious and holy. Such absolute renunciation of possession had been practiced by Christ and the apostles, and had been taught by them to their disciples; it is not only meritorious, but lawful and possible, for there is a distinction between use, which is permitted, and ownership, which is forbidden. Following the example of Innocent IV and Alexander IV, the proprietorship of all that the Franciscans use is declared to be vested, now and hereafter, in the Roman Church and pontiff, which concede to the friars the usufruct thereof. The prohibition to receive and handle money is to be enforced, and borrowing is especially deprecated; but, when necessity obliges, this may be effected through third parties, although the brethren must abstain from handling the money or administering or expending it. As for legacies, they must not be left directly to the friars, but only for their use; and minute regulations are drawn up for exchanging or selling books and utensils. The bull concludes with instructions that it is to be read and taught in the schools, but no one, under pain of excommunication, shall do anything but expound it literally—it is not to be glossed or commented upon, or discussed, or explained away. All doubts and questions shall be submitted directly to the Holy See, and anyone disputing or commenting on the Franciscan Rule or the definitions of the bull shall undergo excommunication, removable only by the pope.

Unluckily, human nature did not cease to be human nature on crossing the threshold of a Franciscan convent. Unluckily, moreover, there were consciences too sensitive to be satisfied with fine-drawn distinctions ingeniously devised to evade the truth. There was still a body of recalcitrants, not numerous, it is true, but eminent for the piety and virtue of its members, which could not be reconciled by these subterfuges. These recalcitrants gradually formed themselves into two distinct bodies, one in Italy, and the other in southern France. At first there is little to distinguish them apart, and for a long while they acted in unison, but there gradually arose a divergence between them, which in the end became decisively marked, owing to the greater influence exercised in Languedoc and Provence by the traditions of Joachim and *The Everlasting Gospel*.

When Gregory X summoned the General Council of Lyons in 1274, the Lateran canon prohibiting the formation of unauthorized Orders was renewed. Gregory proposed to suppress all the congregations of hermits, but, at the instance of Cardinal Richard, the Carmelites and Augustinians were allowed to exist on sufferance until further order, while the audacity of other associations, not as yet approved, was condemned, especially that of the mendicants, whose multitude was declared to exceed all bounds. Such mendicant Orders as had been confirmed since the Council of Lateran were permitted to continue, but they were instructed to admit no new members, to acquire no new houses, and not to sell what they possessed without special license from the Holy See.

Some vague and incorrect rumors of this legislation penetrating to Italy led to an explosion which started one of the most extraordinary series of persecutions the history of human perversity affords. It was reported that the Council of Lyons had decreed that the Mendicants could hold property. Most of the brethren acquiesced readily enough, but those who regarded the Rule as divine revelation, not to be tampered with by any earthly authority, declared that it would be apostasy and a thing not to be admitted under any circumstances. It shows how strained were the relations between the factions that proceedings for heresy were forthwith commenced against these zealots. The rumor proved false, the excitement died away, and the prosecutions were allowed to slumber for a few years, when they were revived through fear that these extreme opinions, if left unpunished, might win over the majority. Liberato da Macerata, Angelo da Cingoli (il Clareno), Traymondo, Tommaso da Tollentino, and one or two others whose names have not reached us were the objurate ones who would make no concessions, even in theory. Angelo, to whom we owe an account of the matter, declared that they were ready to render implicit obedience, that no offense was proved against them, but that nevertheless they were condemned, as schismatics and heretics, to perpetual imprisonment in chains. They were to be deprived of the sacraments, even upon the deathbed, during life no one was to speak with them, not even the jailer who brought the daily pittance of bread and water to their cells. As a warning, moreover, the sentence was ordered to be read weekly in all the chapters, and no one was to presume to criticize it as unjust. This was no idle threat, for when Friar Tommaso da Casteldemilio heard it read and said it was displeasing to God, he was cast into prison, where he rotted to death in a few months. The fierce spirits in control of the Order were evidently determined that at least the vow of obedience should be maintained.

The prisoners seem to have lain in jail until after the election to the generalate of Raymond Gaufridi, at Easter 1289. Visiting the Mark of Ancona, where they were incarcerated, he investigated the case, blamed severely the perpetrators of the injustice, and set the martyrs free in 1290. The Order had been growing more lax in its observance than ever, in spite of the bull *Exiit qui seminat*. Matteo d'Acquasparta, who was general from 1287 to 1289, was easy and kindly, well-intentioned but given to self-indulgence, and by no means inclined to the effort requisite to enforce the Rule. Coffers were placed in the churches to receive offerings; bargains were made as to the price of masses and for the absolution of sinners; boys were stationed at the church doors to sell wax tapers in honor of saints; the friars habitually begged money in the streets, accompanied by boys to receive and carry it; the sepulture of the rich was eagerly sought for, leading to disgraceful quarrels with the heirs and with the secular clergy. So utter was the general demoralization that Nicholas, the Provincial of France, even dared to write a tract calling in question the bull *Exiit qui seminat* and its exposition of the Rule. As this was in direct contravention of the bull itself, Acquasparta felt compelled to condemn the work and to punish its author and his supporters, but the evil continued to work. In the Mark of Ancona and in some other places the reaction against asceticism was so strong that the Testament of Francis was officially ordered to be burned. In one instance it was actually burned on the head of a friar, N. de Recanate, who presumably had made himself obnoxious by insisting on its authority.

Raymond Gaufridi was earnestly desirous of restoring discipline, but the relaxation of the Order had grown past curing. His release of the Spirituals at Ancona caused much murmuring; he was ridiculed as a patron of fantastic and superstitious men, and conspiracies were set on foot that never ceased till his removal was effected in 1295. It was perhaps to conjure these attempts that he sent Liberato, Angelo, Tommaso, and two kindred spirits named Marco and Piero to Armenia, where they induced King Haito II to enter the Franciscan Order, and won from him the warmest eulogies. Even in the East, however, the hatred of their fellow missionaries was so earnest and so demonstrative that they were forced to return in 1293. On their arrival in Italy the provincial, Monaldo, refused to receive them or to allow them to remain until they could communicate with Raymond, declaring that he would rather entertain fornicators.

The unreasoning wrath which insisted on these votaries of poverty violating their convictions received a check when, in 1294, the choice of the exhausted conclave fell by chance on the hermit Pier Morrone, who suddenly found his mountain burrow transformed into the papal palace. Celestin V preserved in St. Peter's chair the predilection for solitude and maceration which had led him to the life of the anchorite. To him Raymond referred the Spirituals, whom he seemed unable to protect. Celestin listened to them kindly and invited them to enter his special Order—the Celestinian Benedictines—but they explained to him the difference of their vows, and how their brethren detested the observance of the Rule. Then in public audience he ordered them to observe strictly the Rule and Testament of Francis; he released them from obedience to all except himself and to Liberato, whom he made their chief; Cardinal Napoleone Orsini was declared their protector, and the abbot of the Celestinians was ordered to provide them with hermitages. Thus they were fairly out of the Order; they were not even to call themselves Minorites or Franciscans, and it might be supposed that their brethren would be as glad to get rid of them and their assumption of superior sanctity as they were to escape from oppression.

Yet the hatred provoked by the quarrel was too deep and bitter to spare its victims, and the breathing-space they enjoyed was short. Celestin's pontificate came to an abrupt termination. Utterly unfitted for his position, speedily made the tool of designing men, and growing weary of the load which he felt himself unable to endure, after less than six months he was persuaded to abdicate, in December 1294, and was promptly thrown into prison by his successor, Boniface VIII, for fear that he might be led to reconsider an abdication the legality of which might be questioned. All of Celestin's acts and grants were forthwith annulled, and Boniface's contempt for the unworldly enthusiasm of asceticism did not lead him to make any exception in favor of the Spirituals. Though he placed in his Sixth Book of Decretals the bull *Exiit qui seminat*, his practical exposition of its provisions is seen in two bulls issued July 17, 1296, by one of which he assigns to the Franciscans of Paris 1,000 marks, to be taken from the legacies for pious uses, and by the other he converts to them a legacy of 300 livres bequeathed by Ada, lady of Pernes, for the benefit of the Holy Land. Before his first year was out, Boniface had determined upon the removal of the General Raymond. October 29, 1295, he offered the latter the bishopric of Pavia, and on his protesting that he had not strength for the burden, Boniface said that he could not be fit for the heavier load of the generalate, of which he relieved him on the spot.

To Boniface's worldly mind the hordes of wandering mendicants, subjected to no authority, were an intolerable nuisance, whether it arose from ill-regulated asceticism or idle vagabondage. The decree of the Council of Lyons had failed to suppress the evil, and, in 1296 and 1297, Boniface issued instructions to all bishops to compel such wanderers or hermits, popularly known as *Bizochi*, either to lay aside their fictitious religious habits and give up their mode of life, or to betake themselves to some authorized Order. One remarkable clause gives special authority to the inquisitors to prosecute such of these *Bizochi* as may be members of their own Orders, thus showing that there was no heresy involved, as otherwise the inquisitors would have required no additional powers.

The following year Boniface proceeded to more active measures. He ordered the Franciscan, Matteo da Chieti, Inquisitor of Assisi, to visit personally the mountains of the Abruzzi and Mark of Ancona and to drive from their lurking-places the apostates from various religious Orders and the *Bizochi* who infested those regions. His previous steps had probably been ineffective, and possibly also he may have been moved to more decisive action by the rebellious attitude of the Spirituals and proscribed mendicants. So far from being content with the bull *Exiit qui seminat,* they held that its author, Nicholas III, had been deprived by God of the papal functions, and consequently that he had had no legitimate successors. Thereafter there had been no true ordinations of priest and prelate, and the real Church consisted in themselves alone. To remedy this, Frère Matthieu de Bodici came from Provence, bringing with him the books of Pierre Jean Olivi, and in the Church of St. Peter in Rome he was elected pope by five Spirituals and thirteen women. Boniface promptly put the Inquisition on their track, but they fled to Sicily, which, as we shall see, subsequently became the head-quarters of the sect.[1]

Friar Jordan, to whom we are indebted for these details, assumes that Liberato and his associates were concerned in this movement. The dates and order of events are hopelessly confused, but it would

---

[1] So far was Pierre Jean Olivi from participating in these rebellious movements that he wrote a tract to prove the legality of Celestin's abdication and Boniface's succession.

rather seem that the section of the Spirituals represented by Liberato kept themselves aloof from all such revolutionary projects. Their sufferings were real and prolonged, but had they been guilty of participating in the election of an antipope they would have had but the choice between perpetual imprisonment and the stake. They were accused of holding that Boniface was not a lawful pope, that the authority of the Church was vested in themselves alone, and that the Greek Church was preferable to the Latin—in other words of Joachitism—but Angelo declares emphatically that all this was untrue, and his constancy of endurance during fifty years of persecution and suffering entitles his assertion to respect. He relates that after their authorization by Celestin V they lived as hermits in accordance with the papal concession, sojourning as paupers wherever they could find a place of retreat, and strictly abstaining from preaching and hearing confessions, except when ordered to do so by bishops to whom they owed obedience. Even before the resignation of Celestin, the Franciscan authorities, irritated at the escape of their victims, disregarded the papal authority and endeavored with an armed force to capture them. Celestin himself seems to have given them warning of this, and the zealots, recognizing that there was no peace for them in Italy, resolved to expatriate themselves and seek some remote spot where they could gratify their ascetic longings and worship God without interference. They crossed the Adriatic and settled on a desert island off the Achaian coast. Here, lost to view, they for two years enjoyed the only period of peace in their agitated lives; but at length news of their place of retreat reached home and letters were dispatched to the nobles and bishops of the mainland, accusing them of being Cathari, while Boniface was informed that they did not regard him as pope, but held themselves to be the only true Church. In 1299 he commissioned Peter, Patriarch of Constantinople, to try them, when they were condemned without a hearing, and he ordered Charles II of Naples, who was overlord of the Morea, to have them expelled, an order which Charles transmitted to Isabelle de Villehardouin, Princess of Achaia. Meanwhile the local authorities had recognized the falsity of the accusations, for the refugees celebrated mass daily and prayed for Boniface as pope, and were willing to eat meat, but this did not relieve them from surveillance and annoyance.

The pressure became too strong, and the little community gradually broke up. An intention to accompany Frà Giovanni da Monte on a mission to Tartary had to be abandoned on account of the excommunication consequent upon the sentence uttered by the Patriarch of Constantinople. Liberato sent two brethren to appeal to Boniface, and then two more, but they were all seized and prevented from reaching him. Then Liberato himself departed secretly and reached Perugia, but the sudden death of Boniface (October 11, 1303) frustrated his object. The rest returned at various times, Angelo being the last to reach Italy, in 1305. He found his brethren in evil plight. They had been cited by the Dominican Inquisitor Tommaso di Aversa and had obediently presented themselves. At first the result was favorable. After an examination lasting several days, Tommaso pronounced them orthodox, and dismissed them, saying publicly, "Frà Liberato, I swear by Him who created me that never the flesh of a poor man could be sold for such a price as I could get for yours. Your brethren would drink your blood if they could." He even conducted them in safety back to their hermitages, and when the rage of the Conventuals was found to be unappeasable he gave them the advice that they should leave the kingdom of Naples that night and travel by hidden ways to the pope; if they could bring letters from the latter, or from a cardinal, he would defend them as long as he held the office. The advice was taken; Liberato left Naples that night, but fell sick on the road and died after a lingering illness of two years. Meanwhile, as we shall see hereafter, the exploits of Dolcino in Lombardy were exciting general terror, which rendered all irregular fraternities the object of suspicion and dread. The Conventuals took advantage of this and incited Frà Tommaso to summon before him all who wore unauthorized religious habits. The Spirituals were cited again, to the number of 42, and this time they did not escape so easily. They were condemned as heretics, and when Andrea da Segna, under whose protection they had lived, interposed in their favor, Tommaso carried them to Trivento, where they were tortured for five days. This excited the compassion of the bishop and nobles of the town, so they were transferred to Castro Mainardo, a solitary spot, where for five months they were afflicted with the sharpest torments. Two of the younger brethren yielded and accused themselves and their comrades, but revoked when released. Some of them died, and finally the survivors were ordered to be scourged naked through the streets of Naples and were banished from the kingdom, although no specific heresy was alleged against them in the sentence. Through all this the resolution of the little band never faltered. Convinced that they alone were on the path of salvation, they would not be forced back into the Order. On the death of Liberato, Angelo was chosen as their leader, and amid persecution and obloquy they formed a congregation in the Mark of Ancona, known as the Clareni, from the surname of their chief, and under the protection of the Cardinal Napoleone Orsini.

This group had not been by any means alone in opposing the laxity of the Conventuals, although it was the only one which succeeded in throwing off the yoke of its opponents. The Spirituals were numerous in the Order, but the policy of Boniface VIII led him to support the efforts of the Conventuals to keep them in subjection. Jacopone da Todi, the author of the *Stabat Mater*, was perhaps the most prominent of these, and his savage verses directed against the pope did not tend to harmonize the troubles. After the capture of Palestrina, in 1298, Boniface threw him into a foul dungeon, where he solaced his captivity with canticles full of the mystic ardor of divine love. It is related that Boniface once, passing the grating of his cell, jeeringly called to him, "Jacopo, when will you get out?" and was promptly answered, "When you come in." In a sense the prophecy proved true, for one of the first acts of Benedict XI, in December 1303, was to release Jacopone from both prison and excommunication.[2]

Such men, filled with the profoundest conviction of their holy calling, were not to be controlled by either kindness or severity. It was in vain that the General Giovanni di Murro, at the chapter

---

[2] A specimen of Jacopone's attacks on Boniface will show the temper of the times:

Ponesti la tua lingua	O pessima avarizia
Contra religione	Sete induplicata,
A dir blasfemia	Bever tanta pecunia
Senza niun cagione	E non esser saziata!

There is doubtless foundation for the story, related by Savonarola in a sermon, that Jacopone was once brought into the consistory of cardinals and requested to preach, when he solemnly repeated thrice, "I wonder that in consequence of your sins the earth does not open and swallow you."—Villari, *Frà Savonarola*.

of 1302, held in Genoa, issued a precept deploring the abandonment by the Order of holy poverty. He ordered the sale of all property, and forbade the members of the Order from appearing in any court. Yet while he was rigid as to the ownership of property, he was lax as to its use, and condemned as pernicious the doctrine that the vow of poverty involved restriction in its enjoyment. He was, moreover, resolved on extinguishing the schism in the Order, and his influence with Boniface was one of the impelling causes of the continued persecution of the Spirituals. Before the year was out Giovanni was created Cardinal Bishop of Porto and was allowed to govern the Order through a vicar; the reforms were partially enforced in some provinces for a short time; then they fell into desuetude, and matters went on as before.

In France, where the influence of Joachim and *The Everlasting Gospel* was much more lasting and pronounced than in Italy, the career of the Spirituals revolves around one of the most remarkable personages of the period—Pierre Jean Olivi. Born in 1247, he was placed in the Franciscan Order at the age of twelve, and was trained in the University of Paris, where he obtained the baccalaureate. His grave demeanor, seasoned with a lively wit, his irreproachable morals, his fervid eloquence, and the extent of his learning won for him universal respect, while his piety, gentleness, humility, and zeal for holy poverty gained for him a reputation for sanctity which assigned to him the gift of prophecy. That such a man should attach himself to the Spirituals was a matter of course, and equally so was the enmity which he excited by unsparing reproof of the laxity into which the Order had declined. In his voluminous writings he taught that absolute poverty is the source of all the virtues and of a saintly life; that the Rule prohibited all proprietorship, whether individual or in common, and that the vow bound the members to the most sparing use of all necessaries, the meanest garments, the absence of shoes, etc., while the pope had no power to dispense or absolve, and much less to order anything contrary to the Rule. The convent of Béziers, to which he belonged, became the center of the Spiritual sect, and the devotion which he excited was shared by the population at large, as well as by his brethren. The temper of the man was shown when he underwent his first rebuke. In 1278 some writings of his in praise of the Virgin were considered to trench too closely on Mariolatry. The Order had not yet committed itself to this, and complaint was made to the general, Geronimo d'Ascoli, afterwards Nicholas IV, who read the tracts and condemned him to burn them with his own hands. Olivi at once obeyed without any sign of perturbation, and when his wondering brethren asked how he could endure such mortification so tranquilly, he replied that he had performed the sacrifice with a thoroughly placid mind; he had not felt more pleasure in writing the tracts than in burning them at the command of his superior, and the loss was nothing, for if necessary he could easily write them again in better shape. A man so imperturbable could not fail to impress his convictions on those who surrounded him.

What his convictions really were is a problem not easily solved at the present day. The fierce antagonisms which he excited by his fiery onslaughts on individuals, as well as on the general laxity of the Order at large, caused his later years to be passed in a series of investigations for heresy. At the General Chapter of Strassburg, in 1282, his writings were ordered to be examined. In 1283 Bonagrazia di S. Giovanni, the general, came to France, collected and placed them all in the hands of seven of the leading members of the Order, who found in them propositions which they variously characterized as false, heretical, presumptuous, and dangerous, and ordered the tracts containing them to be surrendered by all possessing them. Olivi subscribed to the judgment in 1284, although he complained that he had not been permitted to appear in person before his judges and explain the censured passages, to which distorted meanings had been applied. With some difficulty he procured copies of his inculpated writings and proceeded to justify himself. The circle of his disciples continued to increase; incapable of the self-restraint of their master, and secretly imbued with Joachitic doctrines, they were not content with the quiet propagation of their principles, but excited tumult and sedition. Olivi was held responsible. The chapter held at Milan in 1285 elected as General Minister Arlotto di Prato, one of the seven who had condemned him, and issued a decree ordering a strict perquisition and seizure of his writings. Matteo d'Acquasparta vouched for his orthodoxy in appointing him teacher in the general school of the Order at Florence. Raymond Gaufridi, who succeeded Matteo d'Aquasparta, was a friend and admirer of Olivi, but could not prevent fresh proceedings, though he appointed him teacher at Montpellier. Excitement in Languedoc had reached a point which led Nicholas IV in 1290 to order Raymond to suppress the disturbers of the peace. He commissioned Bertrand de Cigotier, Inquisitor of the Comtat Venaissin, to investigate and report, in order that the matter might be brought before the next General Chapter, to be held in Paris. In 1292, accordingly, Olivi appeared before the chapter, professed his acceptance of the bull *Exiit qui seminat*, asserted that he had never intentionally taught or written otherwise, and revoked and abjured anything that he might inadvertently have said in contradiction of it. He was dismissed, but 29 of his zealous and headstrong followers, whom Bertrand de Cigotier had found guilty, were duly punished. His few remaining years seem to have passed in comparative peace. Two letters written in 1295, one to Corrado da Offida and the other to the sons of Charles II of Naples, then held as hostages in Catalonia, who had asked him to visit them, show that he was held in high esteem, that he desired to curb the fanatic zeal of the more advanced Spirituals, and that he could not restrain himself from apocalyptic speculation. On his deathbed, in 1298, he uttered a confession of faith in which he professed absolute submission to the Roman Church and to Boniface as its head. He also submitted all his works to the Holy See, and made a declaration of principles on the matters in dispute within the Order, which contained nothing that Bonaventura would not have signed, or Nicholas III would have impugned as contrary to the bull *Exiit*, although it sharply rebuked the money-getting practices and relaxation of the Order.

He was honorably buried at Narbonne, and then the controversy over his memory became more lively than ever, rendering it almost impossible to determine his responsibility for the opinions which were ascribed to him by both friends and foes. Certain it is that the Council of Vienne, in 1312, treated his memory with great gentleness. While it condemned with merciless severity the mystic extravagances of the Brethren of the Free Spirit, it found only four errors to note in the voluminous writings of Olivi—errors of merely speculative interest, such as are frequent among the schoolmen of the period—and these it pointed out without attributing them to him or even mentioning his name. All other questions relating to his teachings the council referred to the Franciscans for settlement, showing that they were deemed of minor importance, after they had been exhaustively debated before it by Bonagrazia da Bergamo in attack and Ubertino da Casale in defense. Thus the council condemned neither his person nor his writings; that the result was held as vindicating his orthodoxy was seen when, in 1313, his feast-day was celebrated with unexampled enthusiasm at Narbonne and was attended by a concourse equal to that which assembled at the anniversary of the Portiuncula. Moreover, after the heat of the controversy had passed away, the subsequent condemnation of his writings by John XXII was removed by Sixtus IV, towards the end of the fifteenth century.

On the other hand he was unquestionably the heresiarch of the Spirituals, both of France and Italy, regarded by them as the direct successor of Joachim and Francis. The *Historia Tribulationum* finds in the pseudo-Joachitic prophecies a clear account of all the events in his career. Enthusiastic Spirituals who held the revolutionary doctrines of *The Everlasting Gospel* testified before the Inquisition that the third age of the Church had its beginning in Olivi, who thus supplanted St. Francis himself. He was inspired of heaven; his doctrine had been revealed to him in Paris, some said, while he was washing his hands; others that the illumination came to him from Christ while in church, at the third hour of the day. Thus his utterances were of equal authority with those of St. Paul, and were to be obeyed by the Church without the change of a letter. It is no wonder that he was held accountable for the extravagances of those who regarded him with such veneration and recognized him as their leader and teacher.

When Olivi died, his former prosecutor, Giovanni di Murro, was General of the Order, and, strong as were his own ascetic convictions, he lost no time in completing the work which he had previously failed to accomplish. Olivi's memory was condemned as that of a heretic, and an order was issued for the surrender of all his writings, which was enforced with unsparing rigor, and continued by his successor, Gonsalvo de Balboa. Pons Botugati, a friar eminent for piety and eloquence, refused to surrender for burning some of the prohibited tracts, and was chained closely to the wall in a fetid dungeon, where bread and water were sparingly flung to him, and where he soon rotted to death in filth, so that when his body was hastily thrust into an unconsecrated grave it was found that already the flesh was burrowed through by worms. A number of other recalcitrants were also imprisoned with almost equal harshness, and in the next General Chapter the reading of all of Olivi's works was formally prohibited. That much incendiary matter was in circulation, attributed directly or indirectly to him, is shown by a catalogue of Olivist tracts, treating of such dangerous questions as the power of the pope to dispense from vows, his right to claim implicit obedience in matters concerning faith and morals, and other similar mutterings of rebellion.

The work of Olivi that called forth the greatest discussion, and as to which the evidences are peculiarly irreconcilable, was his *Postil on the Apocalypse*. It was from this that the chief arguments were drawn for his condemnation. In an inquisitorial sentence of 1318 we learn that his writings were then again under examination by order of John XXII; that they were held to be the source of all the errors which the sectaries were then expiating at the stake, and that until the papal decision, no one was to hold him as a saint or a Catholic. No formal judgment was rendered, however, until February 8, 1326, when John XXII finally condemned the *Postil on the Apocalypse* and the General Chapter of the Order forbade anyone to read or possess it. One of the reports of the experts upon it has reached us. The extracts on which their conclusions are based are quite sufficient to show that the work was an echo of the most dangerous doctrines of *The Everlasting Gospel*. The fifth age is drawing to an end, and, under the figure of the mystical Antichrist, there are prophecies about the pseudo-pope, pseudo-Christs, and pseudo-prophets in terms which clearly allude to the existing hierarchy. The Church is the Great Whore of Babylon. In forty generations from the harvest of the apostles there will be a new harvest of the Jews and of the whole world, to be garnered by the Evangelical Order, to which all power and authority will be transferred. There are to be a sixth and seventh age, after which comes the Day of Judgment. The date of this latter cannot be computed, but at the end of the thirteenth century the sixth age is to open. The carnal Church will expire, and the triumph of the Spiritual Church will commence.

It has been customary for historians to assume that this resurrection of *The Everlasting Gospel* was Olivi's work, though it is evident from the closing years of his career that he could not have been guilty of uttering such inflammatory doctrines, and this is confirmed by the silence of the Council of Vienne concerning them, although it condemned his other trifling errors after a thorough debate by his enemies and friends. Bonagrazia, in the name of the Conventuals, adduced a long list of his errors, including cursorily certain false and fantastic prophecies in the *Postil on the Apocalypse* and his stigmatizing the Church as the Great Whore. Had passages such as these existed they would have been set forth at length and defense would have been impossible. Ubertino, in reply, boldly characterized the assertion as mendacious and impious; Olivi, he declared, had always spoken most reverently of the Church and Holy See; the *Postil* itself closed with a submission to the Roman Church as the universal mistress, and in the body of the work the Holy See was repeatedly alluded to as the seat of God and of Christ. It is impossible that Ubertino can have quoted these passages falsely, for Bonagrazia would have readily overwhelmed him with confusion, and the Council of Vienne would have rendered a far different judgment. We know from undoubted sources that the revolutionary doctrines commonly attributed to Olivi were entertained by those who considered themselves and were considered to be his disciples, and we can only assume that in their misguided zeal they interpolated his *Postil*, and gave to their own mystic dreams the authority of his great name.

After the death of Olivi the Franciscan officials seem to have felt themselves unable to suppress the sect which was spreading and organizing throughout Languedoc. For some reason not apparent, the aid of the Inquisition was not called in. The regular Church authorities, however, were appealed to, and in 1299 Gilles, Archbishop of Narbonne, held at Béziers a provincial synod, in which were condemned the Beguines of both sexes who under the lead of learned men of an honorable Order (the Franciscans) engaged in religious exercises not prescribed by the Church, wore vestments distinguishing them from other folk, performed novel penances and abstinences, administered vows of chastity, often not observed, held nocturnal conventicles, frequented heretics, and proclaimed that the end of the world was at hand, and that already the reign of Antichrist had begun. The bishops were therefore ordered to investigate these sectaries closely and to suppress them. We see from this that there was rapidly growing up a new heresy based upon *The Everlasting Gospel*, with the stricter Franciscans as a nucleus, but extending among the people.

One of the most energetic and impetuous missionaries of these beliefs was Arnaldo de Vilanova, in some respects perhaps the most remarkable man of his time. As a physician he stood unrivalled. Kings and popes disputed his services, and his voluminous writings on medicine and hygiene were reprinted in collective editions six times during the sixteenth century, besides numerous issues of special treatises. As a chemist he is more doubtfully said to have left his mark in several useful discoveries. As an alchemist he had the repute of producing ingots of gold in the court of Robert of Naples, a great patron of the science, and his treatises on the subject were included in collections of such works printed as late as the eighteenth century. A student of both Arabic and Hebrew, he translated from Costa ben Luca treatises on incantations, ligatures, and other magic devices. He wrote on astronomy and on oneiromancy, for he was an expert expounder of dreams, and also on surveying and wine-making. He draughted laws for Frederic of Trinacria, which that enlightened monarch promulgated and enforced, and his advice to Frederic and his brother Jayme II of Aragon on their duties as monarchs stamps him as a conscientious statesman. When Jayme applied to him for the explanation of a mysterious dream he not only satisfied the king with his exposition, but proceeded to warn him that his chief duty lay in administering justice, first to the poor, and then to the rich. To Jayme he was not only physician but counsellor, venerable and much beloved, and he was repeatedly employed on diplomatic missions by the kings of both Aragon and Sicily.

Multifarious as were these occupations, they consumed but a portion of his restless activity. In dedicating to Robert of Naples his treatise on surveying, he describes himself:

> Yeu, Arnaut de Vilanova . . .
> Doctor en leys et en decrets,
> Et en siensa de strolomia,
> Et en l'art de medicina,
> Et en la santa teulogia—

and, although a layman, married, and a father, his favorite field of labor was theology, which he had studied with the Dominicans of Montpellier. In 1292 he commenced a work on the Tetragrammaton, or ineffable name of Jehovah, in which he sought to explain by natural reasons the mystery of the Trinity. Embarked in such speculations he soon became a confirmed Joachite. To a man of his spiritual tendencies and compassion for his fellows, the wickedness and cruelty of mankind were appalling, and especially the crimes of the clergy, among whom he reckoned the Mendicants as the worst. Their vices he lashed unsparingly, and he naturally fell in with the speculations of the pseudo-Joachitic writings, anticipating the speedy advent of Antichrist and the Day of Judgment. In numberless works composed in both Latin and the vernacular he commented upon and popularized the Joachitic books. Such a man naturally sympathized with the persecuted Spirituals. He boldly undertook their defense in sundry tracts, and when, in 1309, Frederic of Trinacria applied to him to expound his dream, he seized the opportunity to invoke the monarch's commiseration for their sufferings, by explaining to him how, when they sought to appeal to the Holy See, their brethren persecuted and slew them, and how evangelical poverty was treated as the gravest of crimes. He used his influence similarly at the court of Naples, thus providing for them, as we shall see, a place of refuge in their necessity.

With his impulsive temperament it was impossible for him to hold aloof from the bitter strife then raging. Before the thirteenth century was out he addressed letters to the Dominicans and Franciscans of Paris and Montpellier, to the Kings of France and Aragon, and even to the Sacred College, announcing the approaching end of the world; the wicked Catholics, and especially the clergy, were the members of the coming Antichrist. This aroused an active controversy, in which neither party spared the other. After a war of tracts the Catalan Dominicans formally accused him before the Bishop of Girona, and he responded that they had no standing in court, as they were heretics and madmen, dogs and jugglers, and he cited them to appear before the pope by the following Lent. It could only have been the royal favor which preserved him from the fate at the stake of many a less audacious controversialist; and when in 1300 King Jayme sent him on a mission to Philippe le Bel, he boldly laid his work on the advent of Antichrist before the University of Paris. The theologians looked askance on it, and, in spite of his ambassadorial immunity, on the eve of his return he was arrested without warning by the episcopal Official. The Archbishop of Narbonne interposed in vain, and he was bailed out on security of 3,000 livres, furnished by the Viscount of Narbonne and other friends. Brought before the masters of theology, he was forced by threats of imprisonment to recant upon the spot, without being allowed to defend himself, and one can well believe his statement that one of his most eager judges was a Franciscan, whose zeal was doubtless inflamed by the portentous appearance of another Olivi from the prolific South.

A formal appeal to Boniface was followed by a personal visit to the papal court. Received at first with jeers, his obstinacy provoked repression. As a relapsed, he might have been burned, but he was only imprisoned and forced to a second recantation, in spite of which Philippe le Bel, at the assembly of the Louvre in 1303, in his charges of heresy against Boniface asserted that the pope had approved a book of Arnaldo's which had already been burned by himself and by the University of Paris. Boniface, in releasing him, imposed on him silence on theologic matters, though appreciating his medical skill and appointing him papal physician. For a while he kept his peace, but a call from heaven forced him to renewed activity, and he solemnly warned Boniface of the divine vengeance if he remained insensible to the duty of averting the wrath to come by a thorough reformation of the Church. With a fierce denunciation of clerical corruptions he repeated the warning to Benedict XI, who responded by imposing a penance on him and seizing all his apocalyptic tracts.

For some years we know nothing of his movements, although his fertile pen was busily employed with little intermission, and the Church vainly endeavored to suppress his writings. In 1305 Fray Guillermo, Inquisitor of Valencia, excommunicated Gambaldo de Pilis, a servant of King Jayme, for possessing and circulating them. The king applied to Guillermo for his reasons, and, on being refused, angrily wrote to Eymerich, the Dominican General. He declared that Arnaldo's writings were eagerly read by himself, his queen and his children, by archbishops and bishops, by the clergy and the laity. He demanded that the sentence be revoked as uncanonical, else he would punish Fray Guillermo severely and visit with his displeasure all the Dominicans of his dominions. It was probably this royal favor which saved Arnaldo when he came near being burned at Santa Christina, and escaped with no worse infliction than being stigmatized as a necromancer and enchanter, a heretic and a pope of the heretics.

When the persecution of the Spirituals of Provence was at its height, Arnaldo procured from Charles the Lame of Naples, who was also Count of Provence, a letter to the general, Gerald, which for a time put a stop to it. In 1309 we find him at Avignon, on a mission from Jayme II, well received by Clement V, who prized highly his skill as a physician. He used this position effectively by persuading the pope to send for the leaders of the Spirituals, in order to learn from them what they complained of and what reformation they desired in their Order. With regard to his own affairs he was not so fortunate. At a public hearing before the pope and cardinals, in October 1309, he predicted the end of the world within the century, and the advent of Antichrist within its first 40 years; he dwelt at much length on the depravity of clergy and laity, and complained bitterly of the persecution of those who desired to live in evangelical poverty. All this was to be expected of him, but he added the incredible indiscretion of reading a detailed account of the dreams of Jayme II and Frederic of Trinacria, their doubts and his explanations and exhortations—matters, all of them, as sacredly confidential as the confession of a penitent. Cardinal Napoleone Orsini, the protector of the Spirituals, wrote to Jayme congratulating him on his piety as revealed by that wise and illuminated man Master Arnaldo, but this effort to conjure the tempest was unavailing. The Cardinal of Porto and Ramon Ortiz, Dominican Provincial of Aragon, promptly reported to Jayme that he and his brother had been represented as wavering in the faith and as believers in dreams.

Jayme's pride was deeply wounded. It was in vain that Clement assured him that he had paid no attention to Arnaldo's discourse; the king wrote to the pope and cardinals and to his brother denying the story of his dream and treating Arnaldo as an impostor. Frederic was less susceptible: he wrote to Jayme that the story could do them no harm, and that the real infamy would lie in abandoning Arnaldo in his hour of peril. Arnaldo took refuge with him, and not long afterwards was sent by him again to Avignon on a mission, but perished during the voyage. The exact date of his death is unknown, but it was prior to February 1311.

The interposition of Arnaldo offered to the Spirituals an unexpected prospect of deliverance. From Languedoc to Venice and Florence they were enduring the bitterest persecution from their superiors, when Arnaldo persuaded Clement to make an energetic effort to heal the schism in the Order and to silence the accusations the Conventuals brought against their brethren. An occasion was found in an appeal from the citizens of Narbonne setting forth that the books of Olivi had been unjustly condemned, that the Rule of the Order was disregarded, and those who observed it were persecuted, and further praying that a special cult of Olivi's remains might be permitted. A commission of important personages was formed to investigate the faith of Angelo da Clarino and his disciples, who still dwelt in the neighborhood of Rome, and who were pronounced good Catholics. Such leading Spirituals as Raymond Gaufridi, the former general, Ubertino da Casale, the intellectual leader of the sect, Raymond de Giniac, former Provincial of Aragon, Gui de Mirepoix, Bartolommeo Sicardi, and others were summoned to Avignon, where they were ordered to draw up in writing the points which they deemed requisite for the reformation of the Order. To enable them to perform this duty in safety they were taken under papal protection by a bull which shows in its minute specifications how real were the perils incurred by those who sought to restore the Order to its primitive purity. Apparently stimulated by these warnings, the general, Gonsalvo, at the Chapter of Padua in 1310, caused the adoption of many regulations to diminish the luxury and remove the abuses which pervaded the Order, but the evil was too deep-seated. He was resolved, moreover, on reducing the Spirituals to obedience, and the hatred between the two parties grew bitterer than ever.

The articles of complaint, 35 in number, which the Spirituals laid before Clement V in obedience to his commands formed a terrible indictment of the laxity and corruption which had crept into the Order. It was answered but feebly by the Conventuals, partly by denying its allegations, partly by dialectical subtleties to prove that the Rule did not mean what it said, and partly by accusing the Spirituals of heresy. Clement appointed a commission of cardinals and theologians to hear both sides. For two years the contest raged with the utmost fury. During its continuance Raymond Gaufridi, Gui de Mirepoix, and Bartolommeo Sicardi died—poisoned by their adversaries, according to one account, worn out with ill-treatment according to another. Clement had temporarily released the delegates of the Spirituals from the jurisdiction of their enemies, who had the audacity, March 1, 1311, to enter a formal protest against his action, alleging that they were excommunicated heretics under trial, who could not be thus protected. In this prolonged discussion the opposing leaders were Ubertino da Casale and Bonagrazia (Boncortese) da Bergamo. The former, while absorbed in devotion on Mont' Alverno, the scene of St. Francis's transfiguration, had been anointed by Christ and raised to a lofty degree of spiritual insight. His reputation is illustrated by the story that while laboring with much success in Tuscany he had been summoned to Rome by Benedict XI to answer some accusations brought against him. Soon afterwards the people of Perugia sent an embassy to the pope with two requests—one that Ubertino be restored to them, the other that the pope and cardinals would reside in their city—whereat Benedict smiled and said, "I see you love us but a little, since you prefer Frà Ubertino to us." He was a Joachite, moreover, who did not hesitate to characterize the abdication of Celestin as a horrible innovation, and the accession of Boniface as a usurpation. Bonagrazia was perhaps superior to his opponent in learning and not his inferior in devotion to what he deemed the truth, though Ubertino characterized him as a lay novice, skilled in the cunning tricks of the law. The antagonism of two such men upon the points at issue between them is the most striking illustration of the impracticable nature of the question which raised so heated a strife and cost so much blood.

The Spirituals failed in their efforts to obtain a decree of separation which should enable them to live according to their interpretation of the Rule, but in other respects the decision of the commission was wholly in their favor, in spite of the persistent effort of the Conventuals to divert attention from the real questions at issue to the assumed errors of Olivi. Clement accepted the decision and, in full consistory, ordered them to live in mutual love and charity, to bury the past in oblivion, and not to insult each other for past differences. Ubertino replied, "Holy Father, they call us heretics and defenders of heresy; there are whole books full of this in your archives and those of the Order. They must either allege these things and let us defend ourselves, or they must recall them. Otherwise there can be no peace between us." To this Clement rejoined, "We declare as pope, that from what has been stated on both sides before us, no one ought to call you heretics and defenders of heresy. What exists to that effect in our archives or elsewhere we wholly erase and pronounce to be of no validity against you." The result was seen in the Council of Vienne (1311–12), which adopted the canon known as *Exivi de Paradiso*, designed to settle forever the controversy which had lasted so long. Angelo da Clarino declares that this was based wholly upon the propositions of Ubertino; that it was the crowning victory of the Spirituals, and his heart overflows with joy when he communicates the good news to his brethren. It determined, he says, 80 questions concerning the interpretation of the Rule; hereafter those who serve the Lord in hermitages and are obedient to their bishops are secured against molestation by any person. The inquisitors, he further stated, were placed under control of the bishops, which he evidently regarded as a matter of special importance, for in Provence and Tuscany the Inquisition was Franciscan, and thus in the hands of the Conventuals. We have seen that Clement delayed issuing the decrees of the council. He was on the point of doing so, after careful revision, when his death, in 1314, caused a further postponement. John XXII, too, desired time for revision, and it was not until November 1317, that the canons were finally issued. That they underwent change in this process is more than probable, and the canon *Exivi de Paradiso* was on a subject peculiarly provocative of alteration. As it has reached us it certainly does not justify Angelo's pæan of triumph. It is true that it insists on a more rigid compliance with the Rule. It forbids the placing of coffers in churches for the collection of money; it pronounces the friars incapable of enjoying inheritances; it deprecates the building of magnificent churches and convents; it prohibits the acquisition of extensive gardens and great vineyards, and even the storing up of granaries of corn and cellars of wine where the brethren can live from day to day by beggary; it declares that whatever is given to the Order belongs to the Church of Rome, and that the friars have only the use of it. In short, it fully justified the complaints of the Spirituals and interpreted the Rule in accordance with their views, but it did not, as Angelo claimed, allow them to live by themselves in peace, and it subjected them to their superiors. This was to remand them into slavery, as the great majority of the Order were Conventuals, jealous of the assumption of superior sanctity by the Spirituals, and irritated by their defeat and by the threatened enforcement of the Rule in all its rigidity. This spirit was still further inflamed by the action of the General Gonsalvo, who zealously set to work to carry out the reforms prescribed by the canon. He traversed the various provinces, pulling down costly buildings and compelling the return of gifts and legacies to donors and heirs. This excited great indignation among the laxer brethren, and his speedy death, in 1313, was attributed to foul play. The election of his successor, Alessandro da Alessandria, one of the most earnest of the Conventuals, showed that the Order at large was not disposed to submit quietly to pope and council.

It is possible that Clement might have found some means of dissolving the bonds between these irreconcilable parties, but for the insubordination of the Italian Spirituals. These grew impatient during the long conferences which preceded the Council of Vienne. Subjected to daily afflictions and despairing of rest within the Order, they eagerly listened to the advice of Canon Martin of Siena, who assured them that, however few their numbers, they had a right to secede and elect their own general. Under the lead of Giacopo di San Gemignano they did so, and effected an independent organization. This was rank rebellion and greatly prejudiced the case of the Spirituals at Avignon. Clement would not listen to anything that savored of concessions to those who thus threw off their pledged obedience. He promptly sent commissions for their trial, and they were duly excommunicated as schismatics and rebels and disseminators of false and pestiferous doctrines. Persecution against them raged more furiously than ever. In some places, supported by the laity, they ejected the Conventuals from their houses and defended themselves by force of arms, disregarding the censures of the Church. Others made the best of their way to Sicily, and others again, shortly before Clement's death, sent letters to him professing submission and obedience, but the friends of the Spirituals feared to compromise themselves by even presenting them. After the accession of John XXII they made another attempt to reach the pope, but by that time the Conventuals were in full control and threw the envoys into prison as excommunicated heretics. Such of them as were able to do so escaped to Sicily. King Frederic, mindful of the lessons taught him by Arnaldo de Vilanova, received the fugitives graciously and allowed them to establish themselves, in spite of repeated remonstrances of John XXII. There Henry da Ceva had already sought refuge from the persecution of Boniface VIII and had prepared the way for those who were to follow. In 1313 there are allusions to a pope named Celestin whom the "Poor Men" in Sicily had elected, with a college of cardinals, who constituted the only true Church and who were entitled to the obedience of the faithful. Insignificant as this movement may have seemed at the time, it subsequently aided the foundation of the sect known as Fraticelli, who so long braved the unsparing rigor of the Italian Inquisition.

Into these dangerous paths of rebellion the original leaders of the Italian Spirituals were not obliged to enter, as they were released from subjection to the Conventuals, and could afford to remain in obedience to Rome. Angelo da Clarino writes to his disciples that torment and death were preferable to separation from the Church and its head; the power of the keys is from Christ, and submission is due in spite of persecution. Yet, together with these appeals are others which show how impracticable was the position created by the belief in St. Francis. If kings or prelates command what is contrary to the faith, then obedience is due to God, and death is to be welcomed. With clear reference to John, he says that if a pope condemns evangelical truth as an error he is to be left to the judgment of Christ and the doctors; if he excommunicates as heresy the poverty of the Gospel, he is excommunicate of God and is a heretic before Christ. Yet, though his faith and obedience were thus sorely tried, Angelo and his followers never attempted a schism. He died in 1337, worn out with 60 years of tribulation and persecution—a man of the firmest spirit, of the most saintly aspirations, who had exhausted himself in the hopeless effort to reconcile the irreconcilable. Though John XXII had permitted him to assume the habit and Rule of the Celestins, he was obliged to live in hiding, with his abode known only to a few faithful friends and followers, of some of whom we hear as on trial before the Inquisition as Fraticelli, in 1334. It was in the desert hermitage of Santa Maria di

Aspro in the Basilicata; but three days before his death a rumor spread that a saint was dying there, and such multitudes assembled that it was necessary to place guards at the entrance of his retreat, and admit the people two by two to gaze on his dying agonies. He was finally beatified by the Church, which through the period of two generations had never ceased to trample on him, but his little congregation, though lost to sight in the more aggressive energy of the Fraticelli, continued to exist, even after the tradition of self-abnegation was taken up under more fortunate auspices by the Observantines, until it was finally absorbed into the latter in the reorganization of 1517 under Leo X.

In Provence, even before the death of Clement V, there were ardent spirits, nursing the reveries of *The Everlasting Gospel*, who were not satisfied with the victory won at the Council of Vienne. When, in 1311, the Conventuals assailed the memory of Olivi, one of their accusations was that he had given rise to sects who claimed that his doctrine was revealed by Christ, that it was of equal authority with the Gospel, that since Nicholas III the papal supremacy had been transferred to them, and they consequently had elected a pope of their own. We hear of a Frère Raymond Jean, who, in a public sermon at Montréal, prophesied that they would suffer persecution for the faith, and when he was asked what he meant, boldly replied in the presence of several persons, "The enemies of the faith are among ourselves. The Church which governs us is symbolled by the Great Whore of the Apocalypse, who persecutes the poor and the ministers of Christ. You see we do not dare to walk openly before our brethren." He added that the only true pope was Celestin, who had been elected in Sicily, and his organization was the only true Church.

Thus the Spirituals were by no means a united body. Yet, whether their doctrines were submissive like those of Angelo, or revolutionary like those of Raymond Jean, they were all guilty of the unpardonable crime of independence, of thinking for themselves where thought was forbidden, and of believing in a higher law than that of papal decretals. Their steadfastness was soon to be put to the test. In 1314 the general Alessandro died, and after an interval of twenty months Michele da Cesena was chosen as his successor. To the chapter of Naples which elected him, the Spirituals of Narbonne sent a long memorial reciting the wrongs and afflictions which they had endured since the death of Clement had deprived them of papal protection. The nomination of Michele might seem to be a victory over the Conventuals. He was a distinguished theologian, of resolute and unbending temper, and resolved on enforcing the strict observance of the Rule. Within three months of his election he issued a general precept enjoining rigid obedience to it. The Spirituals might hope that at last they had a general after their own heart, but Michele was resolved that the Order should be a unit, and that all wanderers should be driven back into the fold.

A fortnight before the issuing of this precept the long interregnum of the papacy had been closed by the election of John XXII. There have been few popes who have so completely embodied the ruling tendencies of their time, and few who have exerted so large an influence on the Church, for good or for evil. He was short in stature but robust in health, choleric and easily moved to wrath, while his enmity once excited was durable, and his rejoicing when his foes came to an evil end savored little of the Christian pastor. Persistent and inflexible, a purpose once undertaken was pursued to the end regardless of opposition from friend or enemy. After the fashion of the time he was pious, for he celebrated mass almost every day, and almost every night he arose to recite the Office or to study. His chief characteristics, however, were ambition and avarice. To gratify the former he waged endless wars with the Visconti of Milan, in which, as we are assured by a contemporary, the blood shed would have incarnadined the waters of Lake Constance. As for the latter, he it was who first reduced to a system the "Taxes of the Penitentiary," which offered absolution at fixed prices for every possible form of human wickedness, from homicide and incest to ordination below the canonical age. Before he had been two years in the papacy he arrogated to himself the presentation to all the collegiate benefices in Christendom, under the convenient pretext of repressing simony. Another still more remunerative device was the practice of not filling a vacant episcopate from the ranks, but establishing a system of promotion from a poorer see to a richer one, and thence to archbishoprics, so that each vacancy gave him the opportunity of making numerous changes and levying tribute on each. Though for the most part parsimonious, he spent immense sums in advancing the fortunes of his nephew—or son—the Cardinal-Legate Poyet, who was endeavoring to found a principality in the north of Italy. He lavished money in making Avignon a permanent residence for the papacy, though it was reserved for Benedict XII to purchase and enlarge the enormous palace-fortress of the popes.

The evil which he wrought by his shameless traffic in benefices and the reputation which he left behind him are visible in the complaints which were made at the Council of Siena, a century later, by the deputies of the Gallican nation. They refer to his pontificate as that in which the Holy See reserved all benefices to itself, when graces, expectatives, etc., were publicly sold to the highest bidder, without regard to qualification, so that in France many benefices were utterly ruined by reason of the insupportable burdens laid upon them. Such was the man to whom was committed the settlement of the delicate scruples which vexed the souls of the Spirituals.

John had been actively engaged in the proceedings of the Council of Vienne and was thoroughly familiar with all the details of the question. When, therefore, the General Michele, shortly after his accession, applied to him to restore unity in the distracted Order, his imperious temper led him to take speedy and vigorous action. King Frederic of Trinacria was ordered to seize the refugees in his dominions, and deliver them to their superiors to be disciplined. Bertrand de la Tour, the Provincial of Aquitaine, was instructed to reduce to obedience the rebels of the convents of Béziers, Narbonne, and Carcassonne. Bertrand at first tried persuasion. The outward sign of the Spirituals was the habit. They wore smaller hoods, and gowns shorter, narrower, and coarser than the Conventuals; and, holding this to be in accordance with the precedent set by Francis, it was as much an article of faith with them as the absence of granaries and wine-cellars and the refusal to handle money. When he urged them to abandon these vestments they therefore replied that this was one of the matters in which they could not render obedience. Then he assumed a tone of authority under the papal rescript, and they rejoined by an appeal to the pope better informed, signed by 45 friars of Narbonne, and 15 of Béziers. On receipt of the appeal, John peremptorily ordered, April 27, 1317, all the appellants to present themselves before him within ten days, under pain of excommunication. They set forth, 74 in number, with Bernard

Délicieux at their head, and on reaching Avignon did not venture to lodge in the Franciscan convent, but bivouacked for the night on the public place in front of the papal doors.

They were regarded as much more dangerous rebels than the Italian Spirituals. The latter had already had a hearing in which Ubertino da Casale confuted the charges brought against them, and he, Goffrido da Cornone, and Philippe de Caux, while expressing sympathy and readiness to defend Olivi and his disciples, had plainly let it be seen that they regarded themselves as not personally concerned with them. John drew the same distinction; and though Angelo da Clarino was for a while imprisoned on the strength of an old condemnation by Boniface VIII, he was soon released and permitted to adopt the Celestin habit and Rule. Ubertino was told that if he would return for a few days to the Franciscan convent proper provision would be made for his future. To this he significantly replied, "After staying with the friars for a single day I will not require any provision in this world from you or anyone else," and he was permitted to transfer himself to the Benedictine Order, as were likewise several other of his comrades.

The Olivists were not to escape so easily. The day after their arrival they were admitted to audience. Bernard Délicieux argued their case so ably that he could only be answered by accusing him of having impeded the Inquisition, and John ordered his arrest. Then François Sanche took up the argument, and was accused of having vilified the Order publicly, when John delivered him to the Conventuals, who promptly imprisoned him in a cell next to the latrines. Then Guillaume de Saint-Amand assumed the defense, but the friars accused him of dilapidation and of deserting the Convent of Narbonne, and John ordered his arrest. Then Geoffroi attempted it, but John interrupted him, saying, "We wonder greatly that you demand the strict observance of the Rule, and yet you wear five gowns." Geoffroi replied, "Holy Father, you are deceived, for, saving your reverence, it is not true that I wear five gowns." John answered hotly, "Then we lie," and ordered Geoffroi to be seized until it could be determined how many gowns he wore. The terrified brethren, seeing that their case was prejudged, fell on their knees, crying, "Holy Father, justice, justice!" and the pope ordered them all to go to the Franciscan convent, to be guarded till he should determine what to do with them. Bernard, Guillaume, and Geoffroi, and some of their comrades were subjected to imprisonment in chains. Bernard's fate we have already seen.[3] As to the others, an inquisition was held on them, when all but 25 submitted, and were rigorously penanced by the triumphant Conventuals.

The recalcitrants were handed over to the Inquisition of Marseilles, under whose jurisdiction they were arrested. The inquisitor was Frère Michel le Moine, one of those who had been degraded and imprisoned by Clement V on account of their zeal in persecuting the Spirituals. Now he was able to glut his revenge. He had ample warrant for whatever he might please to do, for John had not waited to hear the Spirituals before condemning them. As early as February 17, he had ordered the Inquisitors of Languedoc to denounce as heretics all who styled themselves Fraticelli or *Fratres de paupere vita*. Then, April 13, he had issued the constitution *Quorumdam*, in which he had definitely settled the two points which had become the burning questions of the dispute—the character of vestments to be worn, and the legality of laying up stores of provisions in granaries, and cellars of wine and oil. These questions he referred to the General of the Order with absolute power to determine them. Such decisions were to be implicitly followed without thinking or asserting that they derogated from the Rule. The bull wound up with the significant words, "Great is poverty, but greater is blamelessness, and perfect obedience is the greatest good." There was a hard common sense about this which may seem to us even commonplace, but it decided the case against the Spirituals, and gave them the naked alternative of submission or rebellion.

This bull was the basis of the inquisitorial process against the 25 recalcitrants. The case was perfectly clear under it, and in fact all the proceedings of the Spirituals after its issue had been flagrantly contumacious—their refusal to change their vestments, and their appeal to the pope better informed. Before being handed over to the Inquisition they had been brought before Michele da Cesena, and their statements to him when read before the consistory had been pronounced heretical and the authors subject to the penalty of heresy. Efforts of course had been made to secure their submission, but in vain, and it was not until November 6, 1317, that letters

[3] See page 315.

were issued by John and by Michele da Cesena to the Inquisitor Michel, directing him to proceed with the trial. Of the details of the process we have no knowledge; the proceedings were protracted for exactly six months, the sentence being rendered on May 7, 1318, and most of the culprits were brought to repentance and abjuration. Only four of them had the physical and mental endurance to persevere to the last—Jean Barrani, Deodat Michel, Guillem Sainton, and Pons Rocha—and these were handed over the same day to the secular authorities of Marseilles and duly burned. A fifth, Bernard Aspa, who had said in prison that he repented, but who refused to recant and abjure, was mercifully condemned to prison for life. The rest were forced to abjure publicly and to accept the penances imposed by the inquisitor, with the warning that if they failed to publish their abjuration wherever they had preached their errors they would be burned as relapsed.

Although in the sentence the heresy of the victims is said to have been drawn from the poisoned doctrine of Olivi, there is no allusion to any Joachite error. It was simply a question of disobedience to the bull *Quorumdam*. They affirmed that this was contrary to the Gospel of Christ, which forbade them to wear garments of other fashion than that which they had adopted, or to lay up stores of corn and wine. To this the pope had no authority to compel them. Frivolous as the questions at issue undoubtedly were, it was on the one hand a case of conscience from which reason had long since been banished by the bitterness of controversy, and on the other the necessity of authority compelling obedience. If private judgment were allowed to set aside the commands of a papal decretal, the moral power of the papacy was gone, and with it all temporal supremacy. Thus John, before his pontificate was a year old, had succeeded in creating a new heresy—that which held it unlawful for Franciscans to wear flowing gowns or to have granaries and cellars. In the multiform development of human perversity there has been perhaps none more deplorably ludicrous than this, that man should burn his fellows on such a question, or that men should be found dauntless enough to brave the flames for such a principle, and to feel that they were martyrs in a high and holy cause.

The bull *Quorumdam* had created no little stir. A defense of it, written by an Inquisitor of Carcassonne and Toulouse, probably

Jean de Beaune, shows that its novel positions had excited grave doubts in the minds of learned men, who were not convinced of its orthodoxy, though not prepared to risk open dissent. To silence discussion, John assembled a commission of thirteen prelates and doctors, including Michele da Cesena, who after due consideration solemnly condemned as heretical the propositions that the pope had no authority to issue the bull and that obedience was not due to prelates who commanded the laying aside of short and narrow vestments and the storing up of corn and wine. All this was rapidly creating a schism, and the bull *Sancta Romana*, December 30, 1317, and *Gloriosam ecclesiam*, January 23, 1318, were directed against those who under the names of Fraticelli, Beguines, *Bizochi*, and *Fratres de paupere vita*, in Sicily, Italy, and the south of France, were organizing an independent Order under the pretense of observing strictly the Rule of Francis, receiving multitudes into their sect, building or receiving houses in gift, begging in public, and electing superiors. All such are declared excommunicate *ipso facto*, and all prelates are commanded to see that the sect is speedily extirpated.

The burning of the four martyrs of Marseilles in 1318 was the signal for active inquisitorial work. Throughout all the infected region the Holy Office bent its energies to the suppression of the new heresy; and as previously there had been no necessity for concealing opinions, the suspects were readily laid hold of. There was thus an ample harvest, and the rigor of the inquisition set on foot is shown by the order issued in February 1322 by John XXII, that all Tertiaries in the suspected districts should be summoned to appear and be closely examined. This caused general terror. In the archives of Florence there are preserved numerous letters to the papal curia, written in February 1322 by the magistrates and prelates of the Tuscan cities, interceding for the Tertiaries, and begging that they shall not be confounded with the new sect of Beguines. The test was simple. It was whether the accused believed that the pope had power to dispense with vows, especially those of poverty and chastity. It was a commonplace of the schools, which Aquinas proved beyond cavil, that he had no such power, and even as recently as 1311 the Conventuals, in arguing before Clement V, had admitted that no Franciscan could hold property or take a wife under command from the pope; but things had changed in the interval, and now those who adhered to the established doctrine had the alternative of recantation or the stake. Of course but a small portion of the culprits had the steadfastness to endure to the end against the persuasive methods which the Inquisition knew so well how to employ, and the number of the victims who perished shows that the sect must have been large. Our information is scanty and fragmentary, but we know that at Narbonne, where the bishops at first endeavored to protect the unfortunates until frightened by the threats of the inquisitors, there were 3 burned in 1319, 17 in Lent 1321, and several in 1322.

At Lunel there were 17 burned; at Béziers, 2 at one time and 7 at another; at Pézénas, several, with Jean Formayron at their head; at Toulouse, 4 in 1322, and others at Cabestaing and Lodève. At Carcassonne there were burnings in 1319, 1320, and 1321, and Henri de Chamay was active there between 1325 and 1330. A portion of his trials are still extant, with very few cases of burning, but Mosheim had a list of 113 persons executed at Carcassonne as Spirituals from 1318 to about 1350. All these cases were under Dominican inquisitors, and the Franciscans were even more zealous, if we may believe Wadding's boast that in 1323 there were 114 burned by Franciscan inquisitors alone.

Ferocious persecution such as this only intensified the convictions of the sufferers and their antagonism to the Holy See. Men who willingly offered themselves to be burned because they asserted that the pope had no power to dispense from the observance of vows; who declared that if there were but one woman in the world, and if she had taken a vow of chastity, the pope could give her no valid dispensation, even if it were to prevent the human race from coming to an end; who held that although the pope might have power over other Orders he had none over that of St. Francis, because his Rule was divine revelation, and not a word in it could be altered or erased —such men could only defend themselves against the pope by denying the source of his authority. All the latent Joachitic notions which had been dormant were vivified and became the leading principles of the sect.

The new Church had some sort of organization. In the trial of Naprous Boneta at Cascassonne, there is an allusion to a Frère Guillem Giraud, who had been ordained by God as pope in place of John XXII, who had been deposed by the divine will. There were not lacking saints and martyrs, besides Francis and Olivi. Fragments of the bodies and bones of those who perished at the stake were treasured up as relics, and even pieces of the stakes at which they suffered. One poor wretch who was burned at Toulouse in 1322 had inserted in his litany the names of 70 Spirituals who had suffered; he invoked them among the other saints, attaching equal importance to their intervention; and this was doubtless a customary and recognized form of devotion. Yet this cult was simpler than that of the orthodox Church, for it was held that the saints needed no oblations, and if a man had vowed a candle to one of them or to the Virgin, or a pilgrimage to Compostella, it would be better to give to the poor the money that it would cost.

The Church composed of these enthusiastic fanatics broke off all relations with the Italian Spirituals, whose more regulated zeal seemed lukewarmness and backsliding. The prisoners who were tried by Bernard Gui in 1322 at Toulouse described the Franciscan Order as divided into three fragments—the Conventuals, who insisted on having granaries and cellars, the Fraticelli under Henry da Ceva in Sicily, and the Spirituals, or Beguines, then under persecution.

The heights of exaltation reached in their religious delirium are illustrated by the career of Naprous Boneta, who was reverenced in the sect as an inspired prophetess. As early as 1315 she had fallen into the hands of the Inquisition at Montpellier, and had been thrown into prison, to be subsequently released. She and her sister Alissette were warmly interested in the persecuted Spirituals, and gave refuge to many fugitives in their house. As persecution grew hotter, her exaltation increased. In 1320 she commenced to have visions and ecstasies, in which she was carried to heaven and had interviews with Christ. Finally, on Holy Thursday, 1321, Christ communicated to her the Divine Spirit as completely as it had been given to the Virgin, saying, "The Blessed Virgin Mary was the giver of the Son of God: thou shalt be the giver of the Holy Ghost." Thus the promises of *The Everlasting Gospel* were on the point of fulfillment, and the Third Age was about to dawn. Elijah, she said, was St. Francis, and Enoch was Olivi; the power granted to Christ lasted until God gave the Holy Spirit to Olivi, and invested him with as much glory as had been granted to the humanity of Christ. The papacy had ceased to exist, the sacraments of the altar and of confession are superseded, but that of matrimony remains. That of penitence, indeed, still exists, but it is purely internal, for heartfelt contrition works forgiveness of sins without sacerdotal intercession or the imposition of penance. One remark, which she casually made before her judges, is noteworthy as manifesting the love and charity of these poor souls. The Spirituals and lepers, she said, who had been burned were like the innocents massacred by Herod—it was Satan who procured the burning of the Spirituals and lepers. This alludes to the hideous cruelties which were perpetrated on the lepers in 1321 and 1322, when the whole of France went mad with terror over a rumored poisoning of the wells by these outcasts, and when, it seems, the Spirituals were wise and humane enough to sympathize with them and condemn their murder. Naprous, at length, was brought before Henri de Chamay, the Inquisitor of Carcassonne, in 1325. Sincere in the belief of her divine mission, she fearlessly related her history and stated her faith, and in her replies to her examiners she was remarkably quick and intelligent. When her confession was read over to her she confirmed it, and to all exhortations to retract she quietly answered that she would live and die in it as the truth. She was accordingly handed over to the secular arm and sealed her convictions with her blood.

Extravagances of belief such as this were not accompanied with extravagance of conduct. Even Bernard Gui has no fault to find with the heretics' mode of life. They all vowed poverty and led a life of self-denial, some of them laboring with their hands and others begging by the wayside. In the towns and villages they had little dwellings which they called Houses of Poverty, and where they dwelt together. On Sundays and feast-days their friends would assemble and all would listen to readings from the precepts and articles of faith, the lives of the saints, and their own religious books in the vulgar tongue—mostly the writings of Olivi, which they regarded as revelations from God, and the *Transitus Sancti Patris*, which was a legendary account of his death. The only external signs by which Bernard says they were to be recognized were that on meeting one another, or entering a house, they would say, "Blessed be Jesus Christ," or "Blessed be the name of the Lord Jesus Christ." When praying in church or elsewhere they sat with hooded heads and faces turned to the wall, not standing or kneeling, or striking their hands, as was customary with the orthodox. This was all inoffensive enough, but they had one peculiarity to which Bernard as an inquisitor took strong exception. When on trial they were ready enough to confess their own faith, but nothing would induce them to betray their associates. In their simplicity they held that this would be a violation of Christian charity to which they could not lawfully be compelled, and the inquisitor wasted infinite pains in the endeavor to show that it is charity to one's neighbor, and not an injury, to give him a chance of conversion.

A sect based upon the absolute abnegation of property as its chief principle could never become dangerous, though it might be disagreeable, from its mute—or perhaps vivacious—protest against the luxury and worldliness of the Church. Springing as it did in a region and at a period in which the Inquisition was thoroughly organized, it had no chance of survival, and it speedily succumbed under the ferocious energy of the proceedings brought to bear against it.

CHAPTER XVIII
SEGARELLI AND DOLCINO

ABOUT the year 1260, Parma witnessed the commencement of another abnormal development of the great Franciscan movement. The year 1260 was that in which, according to Abbot Joachim, the era of the Holy Ghost was to open. The spiritual excitement which pervaded the population was seen in the outbreak of the Flagellants, which filled northern Italy with processions of penitents scourging themselves, and in the mutual forgiveness of injuries, which brought an interval of peace to a distracted land. In such a condition of public feeling, gregarious enthusiasm is easily directed to whatever responds to the impulse of the moment, and the self-mortification of a youth of Parma, called Gherardo Segarelli, found abundant imitators. Of low extraction, uncultured and stupid, he had vainly applied for admission into the Franciscan Order. Denied this, he passed his days vacantly musing in the Franciscan church. He remarked in the scriptural pictures which adorned the walls the representations of the apostles in the habits which art has assigned to them, and the conception grew upon him that the apostolic life and vestment would form the ideal religious existence, superior even to that of the Franciscans, which had been denied to him. As a preliminary, he sold his little property; then, mounting the tribune in the Piazza, he scattered the proceeds among the idlers sunning themselves there, who forthwith gambled it away with ample floods of blasphemy. Imitating literally the career of Christ, he had himself circumcised; then, enveloped in swaddling clothes, he was rocked in a cradle and suckled by a woman. His apprenticeship thus completed, he embarked on the career of an apostle, letting hair and beard grow, enveloped in a white mantle, with the Franciscan cord around his waist, and sandals on his feet. Thus accoutred he wandered through the streets of Parma crying at intervals *"Penitenzagite,"* which was his ignorant rendering of *"Penitentiam agite!"*—the customary call to repentance. At length he was joined by a certain Robert, a servant of the Franciscans, who, as Salimbene informs us, was a liar and a thief, too lazy to work,

610

who flourished for a while in the sect as Frà Glutto, and who finally apostatized and married a female hermit. Gherardo and Glutto wandered through the streets of Parma in their white mantles and sandals, calling the people to repentance. They gathered associates, and the number rapidly grew to 300. They obtained a house in which to eat and sleep, and lacked for nothing, for alms came pouring in upon them more liberally than on the regular Mendicants. The self-styled Apostles gave nothing in return—they could not preach, or hear confessions, or celebrate mass, and did not even pray for their benefactors. They were mostly ignorant peasants, attracted by an idle life which was rewarded with ample food and popular veneration. When gathered together in their assemblies they would gaze vacantly on Segarelli and repeat at intervals in honor of him, "Father! Father! Father!"

When the Council of Lyons, in 1274, endeavored to control the pest of unauthorized mendicant associations, it contented itself with prohibiting the reception of future members, in the expectation that they would thus gradually become extinguished. This was easily eluded by the Apostles, who, when a neophyte desired to join them, would lay before him a habit and say, "We do not dare to receive you, as this is prohibited to us, but it is not prohibited to you; do as you think fit." Thus the Order increased and multiplied, as we are told, beyond computation. In 1284 we hear of 72 postulants in a body passing through Modena and Reggio to Parma to be adopted by Segarelli, and a few days afterwards 12 young girls came on the same errand, wrapped in their mantles and styling themselves Apostolesses. Imitating Dominic and Francis, Segarelli sent his followers throughout Europe and beyond seas to evangelize the world. They penetrated far, for in 1287 we find the Council of Würzburg stigmatizing the wandering Apostles as tramps, and forbidding anyone to give them food. Pedro de Lugo (Galicia), who abjured before the Inquisition of Toulouse in 1322, testified that he had been inducted in the sect twenty years previous by Richard, an Apostle from Alessandria in Lombardy, who was busily spreading the heresy beyond Compostella.

Notwithstanding the veneration felt by the brethren for Segarelli he steadily refused to assume the headship of the Order, saying that each must bear his own burden. He seems to have hesitated somewhat about the form the association should assume, and consulted Alberto of Parma, one of the seven notaries of the curia, whether they should select a superior. Alberto referred him to the Cistercian Abbot of Fontanaviva, who advised that they should not found houses, but should continue to wander over the land wrapped in their mantles, and they would not fail of shelter by the charitable. Segarelli was nothing loath to follow his counsel, but a more energetic spirit was found in Guidone Putagi, brother of the Podestà of Bologna, who entered the Order with his sister Tripia. Finding that Segarelli would not govern, he seized command and for many years conducted affairs, but he gave offense by abandoning the poverty which was the essence of the association. He lived splendidly, we are told, with many horses, lavishing money like a cardinal or papal legate, till the brethren grew tired and elected Matteo of Ancona as his successor. This led to a split. Guidone retained possession of the person of Segarelli, and carried him to Faenza. Matteo's followers came there and endeavored to seize Segarelli by force; the two parties came to blows and the Anconitans were defeated. Guidone, however, was so much alarmed for his safety that he left the Apostles and joined the Templars.

Bishop Opizo of Parma, a nephew of Innocent IV, had a liking for Segarelli, and for his sake protected the Apostles, which serves to account for their uninterrupted growth. In 1286, however, three of the brethren misbehaved flagrantly at Bologna, and were summarily hanged by the *podestà*. This seems to have drawn attention to the sectaries, for about the same time Honorius IV issued a bull especially directed against them. They were commanded to abandon their peculiar vestments and enter some recognized Order; prelates were required to enforce obedience by imprisonment, and the faithful at large were ordered not to give them alms or hospitality. The Order was thus formally proscribed. Bishop Opizo hastened to obey. He banished the brethren from his diocese and imprisoned Segarelli in chains, but subsequently relenting kept him in his palace as a jester, for when filled with wine the Apostle could be amusing.

For some years we hear little of Segarelli and his disciples. The best evidence that the bull of Honorius failed in its purpose is the fact that in 1291 Nicholas IV deemed its reissue necessary. They were now in open antagonism to the Holy See—rebels and schismatics, rapidly ripening into heretics, and fair subjects of persecution. Accordingly, in 1494, we hear of four of them—two men and two women—burned at Parma, and of Segarelli's condemnation to perpetual imprisonment by Bishop Opizo. There is also an allusion to an earnest missionary of the sect, named Stephen, dangerous on account of the eloquence of his preaching, who was burned by the Inquisition. Segarelli had saved his life by abjuration, possibly after a few years he may have been released, but he did not abandon his errors; the Inquisitor of Parma, Frà Manfredo, convicted him as a relapsed heretic, and he was burned in Parma in 1300. An active persecution followed of his disciples. Many were apprehended by the Inquisition and subjected to various punishments, until Parma congratulated itself that the heresy was fairly stamped out.

Persecution, as usual, had the immediate effect of scattering the heretics, of confirming them in the faith, and of developing the heresy into a more decided antagonism towards the Church. Segarelli's disciples were not all ignorant peasants. In Tuscany a Franciscan of high reputation for sanctity and learning was in secret an active missionary, and endeavored even to win over Ubertino da Casale. Ubertino led him on and then betrayed him, and when we are told that he was forced to reveal his followers, we may assume that he was subjected to the customary inquisitorial processes.

We know nothing of any peculiar tenets taught by Segarelli. To wear the habit of the association, to live in absolute poverty, without labor and depending on daily charity, to take no thought of the morrow, to wander without a home, calling upon the people to repent, to preserve the strictest chastity, was the sum of his teaching, so far as we know, and this remained to the last the exterior observance of the Apostles. It was rigidly enforced. Even the austerity of the Franciscans allowed the friar two gowns, as a concession to health and comfort, but the Apostle could have but one, and if he desired it washed he had to remain in bed until it was dried. Like the Waldenses and Cathari, the Apostles seem to have considered the use of the oath as unlawful. They were accused, as usual, of inculcating promiscuous intercourse, and this charge seemed substantiated by the mingling of the sexes in their wandering life, and by the crucial test of continence to which they habitually exposed themselves, in imitation of the early Christians, of lying together naked; but the statement of their errors drawn up by the inquisitors who knew them, for the instruction of their colleagues, shows that license formed no part of their creed.

An epistle written by Frà Dolcino, about a month after Segarelli's execution, shows that minds more powerful that that of the founder had been at work framing a body of principles. Joachim had promised that the era of the Holy Ghost should open with the year 1260. That prophecy had been fulfilled by the appearance of Segarelli, whose mission had then commenced. Tacitly accepting this coincidence, Dolcino proceeds to describe four successive states of the Church. The first extends from the Creation to the time of Christ; the second from Christ to Silvester and Constantine, during which the Church was holy and poor; the third from Silvester to Segarelli, during which the Church declined, in spite of the reforms introduced by Benedict, Dominic, and Francis, until it had wholly lost the charity of God. The fourth state was commenced by Segarelli, and will last till the Day of Judgment. The epistle concludes with a mass of Apocalyptical prophecies respecting the approaching advent of Antichrist, the triumph of the saints, and the reign of holy poverty and love, which is to follow under a saintly pope. Dolcino announces himself as the special envoy of God, sent to elucidate Scripture and the prophecies, while the clergy and the friars are the ministers of Satan, who persecute now, but who will shortly be consumed, when he and his followers will prevail till the end.

Segarelli had perished at the stake July 18, and already in August here was a man assuming with easy assurance the dangerous position of heresiarch, proclaiming himself the mouthpiece of God, and promising his followers speedy triumph in reward for what they might endure under his leadership. Whether he was a fanatic or a charlatan can never be absolutely determined, but the balance of probability lies in his truthfulness. Dante recognized the greatness of Dolcino when he represents him as the only living man to whom Mahomet from the depths of hell deigns to send a message, as to a kindred spirit.

The paternity of Dolcino is variously attributed to Giulio, a priest of Trontano in the Val d'Ossola, and to Giulio, a hermit of Prato in the Valsesia, near Novara. Brought as a child to Vercelli, he was bred in the church of St. Agnes by a priest named Agosto, who had him carefully trained. Gifted with a brilliant intellect, he soon became an execellent scholar, and, though small of stature, he was pleasant to look upon and won the affection of all. His connection with Vercelli came to a sudden end. The priest lost a sum of money and suspected his servant Patras. The man took the boy and by torturing him forced him to confess the theft—rightly or wrongly. The priest interfered to prevent the matter from becoming public, but shame and terror caused Dolcino to depart in secret, and we lose sight of him until we hear of him in Trent, at the head of a band of Apostles. He had joined the sect in 1291; he must early have taken a prominent position in it, for he admitted in his final confession that he had thrice been in the hands of the Inquisition, and had thrice abjured. This he could do without forfeiting his position, for it was one of the principles of the sect, which greatly angered the inquisitors, that deceit was lawful when before the Inquisition; that oaths could then be taken with the lips and not with the heart; but that if death could not be escaped, then it was to be endured cheerfully and patiently, without betraying accomplices.

For three years after his epistle of August 1300, we know nothing of Dolcino's movements, except that he is heard of in Milan, Brescia, Bergamo, and Como, but they were busy years of propagandism and organization. The time of promised liberation came and passed, and the Church was neither shattered nor amended. Yet the capture of Boniface VIII at Anagni, in September 1303, followed by his death, might well seem to be the beginning of the end, and the fulfillment of the prophecy. In December 1303, therefore, Dolcino issued a second epistle, in which he announced as a revelation from God that the first year of the tribulations of the Church had begun in the fall of Boniface. In 1304 Frederic of Trinacria would become emperor, and would destroy the cardinals, with the new evil pope whom they had just elected; in 1305 he would carry desolation through the ranks of all prelates and ecclesiastics, whose wickedness was daily increasing. Until that time the faithful must lie hid to escape persecution, but then they would come forth, they would be joined by the Spirituals of the other Orders, they would receive the grace of the Holy Ghost, and would form the new Church which would endure to the end. Meanwhile he announced himself as the ruler of the Apostolic Congregation, consisting of 4,000 souls, living without external obedience, but in the obedience of the Spirit. About a hundred of either sex were organized in control of the brethren, and he had four principal lieutenants, Longino Cattaneo da Bergamo, Federigo da Novara, Alberto da Otranto, and Valderigo da Brescia. Superior to these was his dearly loved sister in Christ, Margherita. Margherita di Trank is described to us as a woman of noble birth, considerable fortune, and surpassing beauty, who had been educated in the convent of St. Catharine at Trent. Dolcino had been the agent of the convent, and had thus made her acquaintance. Infatuated with him, she fled with him, and remained constant to the last. He always maintained that their relations were purely spiritual, but this was naturally doubted, and the churchmen asserted that she bore him a child whose birth was represented to the faithful as the operation of the Holy Ghost.

Although in this letter of December 1303 Dolcino recognizes the necessity of concealment, perhaps the expected approaching fruition of his hopes may have encouraged him to relax his precautions. Returning in 1304 to the home of his youth with a few sectaries clad in the white tunics and sandals of the Order, he commenced making converts in the neighborhood of Gattinara and Serravalle, two villages of the Valsesia, a few leagues above Vercelli. A short distance above Serravalle, on the left bank of the Sesia, a stream fed by the glaciers of Monte Rosa, lay Borgo di Sesia, in the diocese of Novara. Thither a rich husbandman, much esteemed by his neighbors, named Milano Sola, invited Dolcino, and for several months he remained there undisturbed, making converts and receiving his disciples. Preparations made to dislodge him, however, convinced him that safety was only to be found in the Alps, and under the guidance of Milano Sola the Apostles moved up towards the head-waters of the Sesia and established themselves on a mountain crest, difficult of access, where they built huts. Thus passed the year 1304. Their numbers were not inconsiderable—some 1,400 of both sexes—inflamed with religious zeal, regarding Dolcino as a prophet whose lightest word was law. Thus contumaciously assembled in defiance of the summons of the Inquisition, they were in open rebellion against the Church. The State also soon became their enemy, for as the year 1305 opened, their slender stock of provisions was exhausted and they replenished their stores by raids upon the lower valleys.

The Church could not afford to brook this open defiance, to say nothing of the complaints of rapine and sacrilege which filled the land, yet it shows the dread which Dolcino already inspired that recourse was had to the pope, under whose auspices a formal crusade was preached. Armed with papal commissions, Rainerio, Bishop of Vercelli, and the inquisitors raised a considerable force and advanced to the mountain refuge of the Apostles. Dolcino, seeing the futility of resistance, decamped by night and established his little community on an almost inaccessible mountain, and the crusaders, apparently thinking them dispersed, withdrew. Dolcino was now fairly at bay; the only hope of safety lay in resistance, and since the Church was resolved on war, he and his followers would at least sell their lives as dearly as they could. His new retreat was on the Parete Calvo—the Bare Wall—whose name describes its character, a mountain overlooking the village of Campertogno. On this stronghold the Apostles fortified themselves and constructed such habitations as they could, and from it they ravaged the neighboring valleys for subsistence. The Podestà of Varallo assembled the men of the Valsesia to dislodge them, but Dolcino laid an ambush, attacked with stones and such other weapons as the Apostles chanced to have, and took him prisoner with most of his men, obtaining ransoms which enabled the sectaries to support life for a while longer. Their depredations continued till all the land within striking distance was reduced to a desert and the inhabitants driven off.

The winter of 1305–6 put to the test the endurance of the heretics on their bare mountaintop. As Lent came on they were reduced to eating mice and other vermin, and hay cooked in grease. The position became untenable, and on the night of March 10, compelled by necessity to abandon their weaker companions, they left the Parete Calvo, and, building paths which seemed impossible over high mountains and through deep snows, they established themselves on Monte Rubello, overlooking the village of Triverio, in the diocese of Vercelli. By this time, through want and exhaustion, their numbers were reduced to about a thousand, and their sole provisions were a few scraps of meat. With such secrecy and expedition had the move been executed that the first intimation that the people of Triverio had of the neighborhood of the dreaded heretics was a foray by night, in which their town was ravaged. We do not hear that

any of the unresisting inhabitants were slain, but we are told that 34
of the Apostles were cut off in their retreat and put to death. The
whole region was now alarmed, and the Bishop of Vercelli raised a
second force of crusaders, who bravely advanced to Monte Rubello.
Dolcino was rapidly learning the art of war; he made a sally from his
stronghold, though again some of his combatants were armed only
with stones, and the bishop's troops were beaten back with the loss
of many prisoners who were exchanged for food.

The heretic encampment was now organized for permanent occupation. Fortifications were thrown up, houses built, and a well
dug. Thus rendered inexpugnable, the hunted Apostles were in
safety from external attack, and they calmly awaited the fulfillment
of Dolcino's prophecies. Their immediate danger was starvation. The
mountaintops furnished no food, and the remains of the episcopal
army stationed at Mosso maintained a strict blockade. To relieve
himself, early in May, Dolcino by a clever stratagem lured them to
an attack, set upon them from an ambush, and dispersed them,
capturing many prisoners, who, as before, were exchanged for provisions. The bishop's resources were exhausted. Again he appealed to
Clement V, who anathematized the heretics and offered plenary
indulgence to all who would serve in the army of the Lord for thirty
days against them, or pay a recruit for such service. The papal letters
were published far and wide, a large force was raised, neighboring
heights were seized and machines erected which threw stones into
the heretic encampment and demolished their huts. A desperate
struggle took place for the possession of one commanding eminence,
where mutual slaughter so deeply tinged the waters of the Riccio that
its name became changed to that of Rio Carnaschio.

This third crusade was as fruitless as its predecessors. The
assailants were repulsed and fell back to Mosso, Triverio, and
Crevacore, while Dolcino, profiting by experience, fortified and
garrisoned six of the neighboring heights, from which he harried
the surrounding country and kept his people supplied with food.
Mosso, Triverio, Cassato, Flecchia, and other towns were burned,
and the accounts of the wanton spoliation and desecration of the
churches show how thoroughly antisacerdotal the sect had become.
To deprive them of resources it was forbidden to exchange food with
them for prisoners, and their captives were mercilessly put to death.

According to the contemporary inquisitor to whom we are indebted for these details, since the days of Adam there had never been a sect so execrable, so abominable, or which in a time so short accomplished so much evil. The worst of it was that Dolcino infused into his followers his own unconquerable spirit. In male attire the women accompanied the men in their expeditions. The land was abandoned by the inhabitants, and in December, seized with a sudden panic, the crusaders evacuated one of the forts, and the garrison of the other, amounting to 700 men, was rescued with difficulty.

Dolcino's military skill had thus triumphed in the field, but the fatal weakness of his position lay in his inability to support his followers. This was clearly apprehended by the Bishop of Vercelli, who built five new forts around the heretic position; and when we are told that all the roads and passes were strictly guarded so that no help should reach them, we may infer that, in spite of the devastation to which they had been driven, they still had friends among the population. During the winter of 1306–7 the sufferings of the Apostles were frightful. Hunger and cold did their work. Many perished from exhaustion. Others barely maintained life on grass and leaves, when they were fortunate enough to find them. Cannibalism was resorted to; the bodies of their enemies who fell in successful sorties were devoured, and even those of their comrades who succumbed to starvation.

To this there could be but one ending, and even the fervid genius of Dolcino could not indefinitely postpone the inevitable. As the dreary Alpine winter drew to an end, towards the close of March, the bishop organized a fourth crusade. A large army was raised to deal with the gaunt and haggard survivors; hot fighting occurred during Passion Week, and on Holy Thursday (March 23, 1307) the last entrenchments were carried. The resistance had been stubborn, and again the Rio Carnaschio ran red with blood. No quarter was given. "On that day more than a thousand of the heretics perished in the flames, or in the river, or by the sword, in the cruellest of deaths. Thus they who made sport of God the Eternal Father and of the Catholic faith came, on the day of the Last Supper, through hunger, steel, fire, pestilence, and all wretchedness, to shame and disgraceful death, as they deserved."

Strict orders had been given by the bishop to capture alive Dolcino and his two chief subordinates, Margherita and Longino Cattaneo, and great were the rejoicings when they were brought to him on Saturday, at the castle of Biella.

No case could be clearer than theirs, and yet the bishop deemed it necessary to consult Clement—a perfectly superfluous ceremony, explicable perhaps, as Gallenga suggests, by the opportunity which it afforded of begging assistance for his ruined diocese and exhausted treasury. The pæan of triumph in which the pope hastened to announce the glad tidings to Philippe le Bel shows how deep was the anxiety caused by the audacious revolt of the handful of Dolcinists. The Bishops of Vercelli, Novara, and Pavia, and the Abbot of Lucedio were granted the first fruits of all benefices becoming vacant during the next three years in their respective territories, and the former, in addition, was exempted during life from the exactions of papal legates, with some other privileges. While awaiting this response the prisoners were kept, chained hand and foot and neck, in the dungeon of the Inquisition at Vercelli, with numerous guards posted to prevent a rescue. The customary efforts were made to procure confession and abjuration, but while the prisoners boldly affirmed their faith they were deaf to all offers of reconciliation.

About two months passed away before Clement's orders were received, that they should be tried and punished at the scene of their crimes. The customary assembly of experts was convened in Vercelli; there could be no doubt of their guilt, and they were abandoned to the secular arm. For the superfluous cruelty which followed the Church was not responsible; it was the expression of the terror of the secular authorities, leading them to repress by an awful example the ever-present danger of a peasant revolt. On June 1, 1307, the prisoners were brought forth. Margherita's beauty moved all hearts to compassion, and this, coupled with the reports of her wealth, led many nobles to offer her marriage and pardon if she would abjure, but, constant to her faith and to Dolcino, she preferred the stake. She was slowly burned to death before his eyes, and then commenced his more prolonged torture. Mounted on a cart, provided with braziers to keep the instrument of torment heated, he was slowly driven along the roads through that long summer day and torn gradually to pieces with red-hot pincers. The marvellous

constancy of the man was shown by his enduring it without rewarding his torturers with a single change of feature. Only when his nose
was wrenched off was observed a slight shiver in the shoulders,
and when a yet crueller pang was inflicted, a single sigh escaped
him. While he was thus dying in lingering torture, Longino Cattaneo, at Biella, was similarly utilized to afford a salutary warning
to the people.

Dolcino and his immediate band of followers were thus exterminated, but there remained the thousands of Apostles, scattered
throughout the land, who cherished their belief in secret. Like the
Olivists, the Apostles held that Christ had withdrawn His authority
from the Church of Rome on account of its wickedness; all spiritual
power was transferred to the Spiritual Congregation, or Order of
Apostles, as they styled themselves. As time passed on without the
fulfillment of the apocalyptic promises, they seem to have abandoned
these hopes, but they continued to cherish the belief that they
had attained spiritual perfection, releasing them from all obedience
to man, and that there was no salvation outside their community.
There seems to have been no organization in the Order. Reception
was performed by the simplest of ceremonies. The postulant stripped
himself of all his garments, in sign of renunciation of all property;
he uttered no vows, but in his heart he promised to live henceforth
in poverty. After this he was never to receive or carry money, but
was to live on alms spontaneously offered to him, and was never to
reserve anything for the morrow. He made no promise of obedience
to mortal man, but only to God, to whom alone he was subject, as
were the apostles to Christ. One error they shared with the Waldenses—the prohibition of oaths, even in a court of justice.

The description which Bernard Gui gives of the Apostles shows
how fully they carried into practice the precepts of their simple creed.
They wore a special habit, closely approaching a conventual garb
—probably the white mantle and cord adopted by Segarelli. As they
wandered along the roads and through the streets they sang hymns,
or uttered prayers and exhortations to repentance. Whatever was
spontaneously set before them they ate with thankfulness, and when
appetite was satisfied they left what might remain and carried
nothing with them. In their humble fashion they seem to have imitated the apostles as best they could, and to have carried poverty

to a pitch which Angelo da Clarino himself might have envied. Bernard Gui, in addition, deplores their intractable obstinacy, and adduces a case in which he had kept one of them in prison for two years, subjecting him to frequent examination, before he was brought to confession and repentance—by what gentle persuasives we may readily guess.

All this may seem to us the most harmless of heresies, and yet the impression produced by the exploits of Dolcino caused it to be regarded as one of the most formidable. When the Brethren of the Free Spirit were condemned in the Clementines, Bernard Gui wrote earnestly to John XXII, urging that a clause should be inserted including the Apostles, whom he described as growing like weeds and spreading from Italy to Languedoc and Spain. This is probably one of the exaggerations customary in such matters, but about this time a Dolcinist named Jacopo da Querio was discovered and burned in Avignon. In 1316 Bernard Gui found others within his own district, when his energetic proceedings soon drove the poor wretches across the Pyrenees, and he addressed urgent letters to all the prelates of Spain, describing them and calling for their prompt extermination. Possibly this may have driven some of them back to France for safety, for in the *auto* of September 1322, at Toulouse, there figures a culprit whose fate illustrates the horror and terror inspired by the doctrines of the Dolcinists. Guillem Ruffi had been previously forced to abjuration as a Beguine, and subsequently had betrayed two of his former associates, one of whom had been burned and the other imprisoned. This would seem proof of his zeal for orthodoxy, and yet, when he happened to state that in Italy there were Fraticelli who held that no one was perfect who could not endure the test of continence above alluded to, adding that he had tried the experiment himself with success, and had taught it to more than one woman, this was considered sufficient, and without anything further against him he was incontinently burned as a relapsed heretic.

In spite of Bernard Gui's exaggerated apprehensions, the sect, although it continued to exist for some time, gave no further serious trouble. The Council of Cologne in 1306 and that of Trèves in 1310 allude to the Apostles, showing that they were not unknown in Germany. Yet about 1335 so well-informed a writer as Alvar

Pelayo speaks of Dolcino as a Beghard, showing how soon the memory of the distinctive characteristics of the sect had faded away. At this very time, however, a certain Zoppio was secretly spreading the heresy at Rieti, where it seems to have found numerous converts, especially among the women. Attention being called to it, Frà Simone Filippi, Inquisitor of the Roman province, hastened thither, seized Zoppio, and after examining him delivered him to the authorities. When he desired to proceed with the trial the magistrates refused to surrender the prisoner, and abused the inquisitor. Benedict XII was appealed to, who scolded the recalcitrant officials for defending a heresy so horrible that decency forbids his describing it; he threatened them with exemplary punishment for continued contumacy, and promised that, if they were afraid of damage to the reputation of their women, the latter should be mildly treated and spared humiliating penance on giving information as to their associates.

After a long interval we hear of the Apostles again in Languedoc, where, in 1368, the Council of Lavaur calls attention to them as wandering through the land and disseminating errors under an appearance of external piety, wherefore they are ordered to be arrested and punished by the episcopal courts. In 1374 the Council of Narbonne deemed it necessary to repeat this injunction; and in 1402 and 1403 the zeal of the Inquisitor Eylard was rewarded in Lubec and Wismar by the capture and burning of two Apostles. This is the last authentic record of a sect which a hundred years before had for a brief space inspired so wide a terror.

CHAPTER XIX
THE FRATICELLI

IN 1321, when the persecution of the Spirituals was at its height, the Dominican Inquisitor Jean de Beaune, whom we have seen as the colleague of Bernard Gui and the jailer of Bernard Délicieux, was engaged at Narbonne in the trial of one of the proscribed sect. To pass judgment he summoned an assembly of experts, among whom was the Franciscan Berenger Talon, teacher in the convent of Narbonne. One of the errors which he represented the culprit as entertaining was that Christ and the apostles had held no possessions, individually or in common. As this was the universal Franciscan doctrine, we can only regard it as a challenge when he summoned Frère Berenger to give his opinion respecting it. Berenger replied that it was not heretical, having been defined as orthodox in the decretal *Exiit*, when the inquisitor hotly demanded that he should recant on the spot. The position was critical, and Berenger, to save himself from prosecution, interjected an appeal to the pope. He hastened to Avignon, but found that Jean de Beaune had been before him. He was arrested; the Dominicans everywhere took up the question, and John XXII allowed it to be clearly seen that his sympathies were with them. Yet the subject was a dangerous one, as the bull *Exiit* had anathematized all who should attempt to gloss or discuss its decisions; and, as a preliminary to reopening the question, John was obliged, March 26, 1322, to issue a special bull, *Quia nonnunquam*, wherein he suspended, during his pleasure, the censures pronounced in *Exiit qui seminat*. Having thus intimated that the Church had erred in its former definition, he proceeded to lay before his prelates and doctors the significant question whether the pertinacious assertion that Christ and the apostles possessed nothing individually or in common was a heresy.

It was inevitable that the replies to the question submitted by John should be adverse to the poverty of Christ and the apostles. The bishops were universally assumed to be the representatives of the latter, and could not be expected to relish the assertion that their prototypes had been commanded by Christ to own no prop-

624

erty. The Spirituals had made a point of this. Olivi had proved not only that Franciscans promoted to the episcopate were even more bound than their brethren to observe the Rule in all its strictures, but that bishops in general were under obligation to live in deeper poverty than the members of the most perfect Order. Now that there was a chance of justifying their worldliness and luxury, it was not likely to be lost. Yet John himself for a while held his own opinion suspended. In a debate before the consistory, Ubertino da Casale, the former leader of the orthodox Spirituals, was summoned to present the Franciscan view of the poverty of Christ, and we are told that John was greatly pleased with his argument. Unluckily, at the General Chapter held at Perugia, May 30, 1322, the Franciscans appealed to Christendom at large by a definition addressed to all the faithful, in which they proved that the absolute poverty of Christ was the accepted doctrine of the Church, as set forth in the bulls *Exiit* and *Exivi de Paradiso*, and that John himself had approved of these in his bull *Quorumdam*. With a disputant such as John this was an act of more zeal than discretion. His passions were aroused, and he proceeded to treat the Franciscans as antagonists. In December of the same year he dealt them a heavy blow in the bull *Ad conditorem*, wherein with remorseless logic he pointed out the fallacy of the device of Innocent IV for eluding the provisions of the Rule by vesting the ownership of property in the Holy See and its use in the Friars. It had not made them less eager in acquisitiveness, while it had led them to a senseless pride in their own asserted superiority of poverty. He showed that use and consumption were tantamount to ownership, and that it was absurd to speak of Rome as owning an egg or a piece of cheese given to a friar to be consumed on the spot. Moreover, it was humiliating to the Roman Church to appear in the countless litigations in which the Order was involved, and the procurators who thus appeared in its name were said to abuse their position to the injury of many who were defrauded of their rights. For these reasons he annulled the provisions of Nicholas III, and declared that henceforth no ownership in the possessions of the Order should inhere in the Roman Church and no procurator act in its name.[1]

[1] Curiously enough, in this John did exactly what his special antagonists, the Spirituals, had desired. Olivi had long before pointed out the scandal of an Order vowed to poverty litigating eagerly for property and using the transparent cover of papal procurators.

The blow was shrewdly dealt, for though the question of the poverty of Christ was not alluded to, the Order was deprived of its subterfuge, and was forced to admit practically that ownership of property was a necessary condition of its existence. Its members, however, had too long nursed the delusion to recognize its fallacy now, and in January 1323, Bonagrazia, as procurator specially commissioned for the purpose, presented to the pope a written protest against his action. If Bonagrazia had not arguments to adduce he had at least ample precedents to cite in the long line of popes since Gregory IX, including John himself. He wound up by audaciously appealing to the pope, to Holy Mother Church, and to the apostles, and though he concluded by submitting himself to the decisions of the Church, he could not escape the wrath which he had provoked. It was not many years since Clement V had confined him for resisting the extravagance of the Spirituals: he still consistently occupied the same position, and now John cast him into a dungeon because he had not moved with the world, while the only answer to his protest was taking down from the church doors the bull Ad conditorem and replacing it with a revised edition, more decided and argumentative than its predecessor.

John was now fairly enlisted against the Franciscans, and their enemies lost no opportunity of inflaming his passions. He would listen to no defense of the decision of the Chapter of Perugia. In consistory a Franciscan cardinal and some bishops timidly ventured to suggest that possibly there might be some truth in it, when he angrily silenced them—"You are talking heresy"—and forced them to recant on the spot. When he heard that the greatest Franciscan schoolman of the day, William of Ockham, had preached that it was heretical to affirm that Christ and the apostles owned property, he promptly wrote to the Bishops of Bologna and Ferrera to investigate the truth of the report, and if it was correct to cite Ockham to appear before him at Avignon within a month. Ockham obeyed, and we shall hereafter see what came of it.

The papal decision on the momentous question was at last put forth, November 12, 1323, in the bull Cum inter nonnullos. The assertion that Christ and the apostles possessed no property was flatly declared to be a perversion of Scripture; it was denounced for the future as erroneous and heretical, and its obstinate assertion by the Franciscan chapter was formally condemned. To the believers in the supereminent holiness of poverty, it was stunning to find themselves cast out as heretics for holding a doctrine which for generations had passed as an incontrovertible truth, and had repeatedly received the sanction of the Holy See. Yet there was no help for it, and unless they were prepared to shift their belief with the pope, they could only expect to be delivered in this world to the Inquisition and in the next to Satan.

Suddenly there appeared a new factor in the quarrel, which speedily gave it importance as a political question of the first magnitude. The antagonism between the papacy and the empire had been recently assuming a more virulent aspect than usual under John's imperious management. Henry VII had died in 1313, and in October 1314 there had been a disputed election. Louis of Bavaria and Frederic of Austria both claimed the kaisership. Since Leo III, in the year 800, had renewed the line of Roman emperors by crowning Charlemagne, the ministration of the pope in an imperial coronation had been held essential, and had gradually enabled the Holy See to put forward undefined claims of a right to confirm the vote of the German electors. For the enforcement of such claims a disputed election gave abundant opportunity, nor were there lacking other elements to complicate the position. The Angevine papalist King of Naples, Robert the Good, had dreams of founding a great Italian Guelf monarchy, to which John XXII lent a not unfavorable ear, especially as his quarrel with the Ghibelline Visconti of Lombardy was becoming unappeasable. The traditional enmity between France and Germany, moreover, rendered the former eager in everything that could cripple the empire, and French influence was necessarily dominant in Avignon. An alliance between Robert and Frederic, with the assent of the pope, seemed to give Frederic assurance of recognition, when the battle of Mühldorf, September 28, 1322, decided the question. Frederic was a prisoner in the hands of his rival, and there could be no further doubt which of them should reign in Germany. It did not follow, however, that John would consent to place the imperial crown on the head of Louis.

So far was he from contemplating any such action that he still insisted on deciding between the claims of the competitors. Louis contemptuously left his pretensions unanswered and proceeded to settle matters by concluding a treaty with his prisoner and setting him free. Moreover, he intervened effectually in the affairs of Lombardy, rescued the Visconti from the Guelf league which was about to overwhelm them, and ruined the plans of the Cardinal Legate Bertrand de Poyet, John's nephew or son, who was carving out a principality for himself. It would have required less than this to awaken the implacable hostility of such a man as John, whose only hope for the success of his Italian policy now lay in dethroning Louis and replacing him with the French king, Charles le Bel. October 8, 1323, in the presence of a vast multitude, a bull was read and affixed to the portal of the cathedral of Avignon, which declared not only that no one could act as King of the Romans until his person had been approved by the pope, but repeated a claim made in 1317, that until such approval the empire was vacant and its government during the interregnum belonged to the Holy See. All of Louis's acts were pronounced null and void; he was summoned within three months to lay down his power and submit his person to the pope for approval, under pain of the punishments which he had incurred by his rebellious pretense of being emperor; all oaths of allegiance taken to him were declared annulled; all prelates were threatened with suspension and all cities and states with excommunication and interdict if they should continue to obey him. Louis at first received this portentous missive with singular humility. November 12 he sent to Avignon envoys, who did not arrive until January 2, 1324, to ask whether the reports which he had heard of the papal action were true, and if so to request a delay of six months in which to prove his innocence. To this John, on January 7, gave answer extending the term only two months from that day. Meanwhile Louis had taken heart, possibly encouraged by the outbreak of the quarrel between John and the Franciscans. On December 18, he issued the Nuremberg Protest, a spirited vindication of the rights of the German nation and empire against the pretensions of the papacy; he demanded the assembling of a general council before which he would make good his claims; it was his duty, as the head of the empire, to maintain the purity of the faith against a pope who was a fautor of heretics. It shows how little he yet understood the questions at issue that to sustain this last charge he accused John of unduly protecting the Franciscans against universal complaints that they habitually violated the secrecy of the confessional, this being apparently his version of the papal condemnation of John of Poilly's thesis that confession to a Mendicant friar was insufficient.

If Louis at first thought to gain strength by thus utilizing the jealousy and dislike felt by the secular clergy towards the Mendicants, he soon realized that a surer source of support was to be found in espousing the side of the Franciscans in the quarrel forced upon them by John. The two months' delay granted by John expired March 7 without Louis's making an appearance, and on March 25 the pope promulgated against him a sentence of excommunication, with a threat that he should be deprived of all rights if he did not submit within three months. To this Louis speedily rejoined in a document known as the Protest of Sachsenhausen, which shows that since December he had put himself in communication with the disaffected Franciscans, had entered into alliance with them, and had recognized how great was the advantage of posing as the defender of the faith and assailing the pope with the charge of heresy. After paying due attention to John's assaults on the rights of the empire, the Protest takes up the question of his recent bulls respecting poverty. John had declared before Franciscans of high standing that for forty years he had regarded the Rule of Francis as fantastic and impossible. As the Rule was revealed by Christ, this alone proves him to be a heretic. Moreover, as the Church is infallible in its definitions of faith, and as it has repeatedly, through Honorius III, Innocent IV, Alexander IV, Innocent V, Nicholas III, and Nicholas IV, pronounced in favor of the poverty of Christ and the apostles, John's condemnation of this tenet abundantly shows him to be a heretic. His two constitutions, *Ad conditorem* and *Cum inter nonnullos*, therefore, have cut him off from the Church as a manifest heretic teaching a condemned heresy, and have disabled him from the papacy; all of which Louis swore to prove before a general council to be assembled in some place of safety.

John proceeded with his prosecution of Louis by a further declaration, issued July 11, in which, without deigning to notice the Protest of Sachsenhausen, he pronounced Louis to have forfeited by his contumacy all claim to the empire; further obstinacy would deprive him of his ancestral dukedom of Bavaria and other possessions, and he was summoned to appear October 1, to receive final sentence. Yet John could not leave unanswered the assault upon his doctrinal position, and on November 10 he issued the bull *Quia quorumdam*, in which he argued that he had exercised no undue power in contradicting the decisions of his predecessors: he declared it a heresy to assert that Christ and the apostles had only simple usufruct, without legal possession, in the things which Scripture declared them to have possessed, for if this were true it would follow that Christ was unjust, which is blasphemy.

Thus the poverty of Christ was fairly launched upon the world as a European question. It is a significant illustration of the intellectual condition of the fourteenth century that in the subsequent stages of the quarrel between the papacy and the empire, involving the most momentous principles of public law, those principles, in the manifestoes of either side, assume quite a subordinate position. The shrewd and able men who conducted the controversy evidently felt that public opinion was much more readily influenced by accusations of heresy, even upon a point so trivial and unsubstantial, than by appeals to reason upon the conflicting jurisdictions of Church and State. Yet, as the quarrel widened and deepened, and as the stronger intellects antagonistic to papal pretensions gathered around Louis, they were able, in unwonted liberty of thought and speech, to investigate the theory of government and the claims of the papacy with unheard-of boldness. Unquestionably they aided Louis in his struggle, but the spirit of the age was against them. Spiritual authority was still too awful for successful rebellion, and when Louis passed away affairs returned to the old routine, and the labors of the men who had waged his battle in the hope of elevating humanity disappeared, leaving but a trace upon the modes of thought of the time.

The most audacious of these champions was Marsiglio of Padua. Interpenetrated with the principles of the imperial jurisprudence, in which the State was supreme and the Church wholly subordinated, he had seen in France how the influence of the Roman law was emancipating the civil power from servitude. He framed a conception of a political organization which should reproduce that of Rome under the Christian emperors, with a recognition of the people as the ultimate source of all civil authority. Aided by Jean de Jandun he developed these ideas with great skill in his *Defensor*

Pacis, and in 1326, when the strife between John and Louis was at its hottest, the two authors left Paris to lay the result of their labors before the emperor.

John had no hesitation in condemning the daring authors as heretics, and the protection which Louis afforded them added another count to the indictment against him for heresy. Jean de Jandun died in 1328, and Marsiglio not later than 1343, thus mercifully spared the disappointment of the failure of their theories. In so far as purely intellectual conceptions had weight in the conflict they were powerful allies for Louis. In the *Defensor Pacis* the power of the keys is argued away in the clearest dialectics. God alone has power to judge, to absolve, to condemn. The pope is no more than any other priest, and a priestly sentence may be the result of hatred, favor, or injustice, of no weight with God. Excommunication, to be effective, must not proceed from the judgment of a single priest, but must be the sentence of the whole community, with full knowledge of all the facts. It is no wonder that when, in 1376, a French translation of the work appeared in Paris it created a profound sensation. A prolonged inquest was held, lasting from September to December, in which all the learned men in the city were made to swear before a notary as to their ignorance of the translator.

More vehement and more fluent as a controversialist was the great schoolman, William of Ockham. When the final breach came between the papacy and the rigid Franciscans he was already under inquisitorial trial for his utterances. Escaping from Avignon with his general, Michele, he found refuge, like the rest, with Louis, whose cause he strengthened by skillfully linking the question of Christ's poverty with that of German independence. Those who refused to accept a papal definition on a point of faith could only justify themselves by proving that popes were fallible and their power not unlimited. Thus the strife over the narrow Franciscan dogmatism on poverty broadened until it embraced the great questions which had disturbed the peace of Europe since the time of Hildebrand, nearly three centuries before. In 1324 Ockham boasted that he had set his face like flint against the errors of the pseudo-pope, and that so long as he possessed hand, paper, pens, and ink, no abuse or lies or persecution or persuasion would induce him to desist from attacking them. He kept his promise literally, and for twenty years he poured forth a series of controversial works in defense of the cause to which he had devoted his life. Without embracing the radical doctrines of Marsiglio on the popular foundation of political institutions, he practically reached the same outcome. While admitting the primacy of the pope, he argued that a pope can fall into heresy, and so, indeed, can a general council, and even all Christendom. The influence of the Holy Ghost did not deprive man of free will and prevent him from succumbing to error, no matter what might be his station. There was nothing sure but Scripture; the poorest peasant might adhere to Catholic truth revealed to him by God, while popes and councils erred. A pope refusing to entertain an appeal to a general council, declining to assemble it, or arrogating its authority to himself is a manifest heretic, whom it is the duty of the bishops to depose, or, if the bishops refuse, then that of the emperor. But it was not only by the enunciation of general principles that he carried on the war; merciless were his assaults on the errors and inconsistencies of John XXII, who was proved guilty of 70 specific heresies. One by one William's colleagues died or submitted, and he was left alone, but he continued to shower ridicule on the curia and its creatures in his matchless dialectics. Even the death of Louis and the defeat of his cause did not stop his fearless pen. Church historians claim that in 1349 he at last made his peace and was reconciled, but this is more than doubtful, for Giacomo della Marca classes him with Michele and Bonagrazia as the three unrepentant heretics who died under excommunication.

This rapid glance at the larger aspects of the strife has been necessary to enable us to follow intelligently the vicissitudes of the discussion over the poverty of Christ, which occupied in the struggle a position ludicrously disproportionate to its importance. For some time after the issue of the bulls *Cum inter nonnullos* and *Quia quorumdam* there was a sort of armed neutrality between John and the heads of the Franciscan Order. Each seemed to be afraid of taking a step which should precipitate a conflict, doubtless secretly felt by both sides to be inevitable. Still there was a little skirmishing for position. In 1325 Michele had summoned the General Chapter to assemble at Paris, but he feared that an effort would be made to annul the declarations of Perugia, and that John would exercise a pressure by means of King Charles le Bel, whose influence was great through the number of benefices at his disposal. Suddenly, therefore, he transferred the call to Lyons, where considerable trouble was experienced through the efforts of Gerard Odo, a creature of the pope, and subsequently the successor of Michele, to obtain relaxations of the Rule as regarded poverty. Still the brethren stood firm, and these attempts were defeated, while a constitution threatening with imprisonment all who should speak disrespectfully of John XXII and his decretals indicates the passions which were seething under the surface. Not long after this we hear of a prosecution suddenly commenced against Ubertino da Casale, in spite of his Benedictine habit and his quiet residence in Italy. He seems to have been suspected of having furnished the arguments on the subject of the poverty of Christ in the Protest of Sachsenhausen, and, September 16, 1325, an order was sent for his arrest, but he got wind of it and escaped to Germany—the first of the illustrious band of refugees who gathered around Louis of Bavaria, though he appears to have made his peace in 1330.

In 1326 Michele issued decrees subjecting to a strict censorship all writing by the brethren and enforcing the rule which prohibited the discussion of doubtful opinions, thus muzzling the Order in the hope of averting dissension; but it was not in John's nature to rest satisfied with silence which covered opposition, and in August 1327 he advanced to the attack. In the bull *Quia nonnunquam*, addressed to archbishops and inquisitors, he declared that many still believed in the poverty of Christ in spite of his having pronounced such belief a heresy, and that those who entertained it should be treated as heretics. He therefore now orders the prelates and inquisitors to prosecute them vigorously, and though the Franciscans are not especially named, the clause which deprives the accused of all papal privileges and subjects them to the ordinary jurisdictions sufficiently shows that they were the object of the assault. At this time we hear of the Spirituals of Sicily crossing back to Calabria, and of John writing to Niccolò da Reggio, the Minister of Calabria, savage instructions to destroy them utterly. Lists are to be made out and sent to him of all who show them favor, and King Robert is appealed to for aid in the good work. Robert, in spite of his close alliance with the pope, was sincerely on the side of the Franciscans. He seems never to have forgotten the teachings of Arnaldo de Vilanova, and as his father, Charles the Lame, had interfered to protect the Spirituals of Provence, so now both he and his queen did what they could with the angry pope to moderate his wrath, and at the same time he urged the Order to stand firm in defense of the Rule. In the protection which he afforded he did not discriminate closely between the organized resistance of the Order under its general, and the irregular mutiny of the Fraticelli. His dominions, as well as Sicily, served as a refuge for the latter. With the troubles provoked by John their numbers naturally grew. They ranged themselves under Henry da Ceva, who had fled to Sicily from persecution under Boniface VIII; they elected him their general minister and formed a complete independent organization, which, when John triumphed over the Order, gathered in its recalcitrant fragments and constituted a sect whose strange persistence under the fiercest persecution we shall have to follow for a century and a half.

On the persecution of these insubordinate brethren Michele da Cesena could afford to look with complacency, and he evidently desired to regard the bull of August 1327 as directed against them. In June the pope had summoned him from Rome to Avignon, and he had excused himself on the ground of sickness. His messengers with his apologies were graciously received, and it was not until December 2 that he presented himself before John. The pope subsequently declared that he had been summoned to answer for secretly encouraging rebels and heretics, and doubtless the object was to be assured of his person, but he was courteously welcomed, and the ostensible reason given for sending for him was certain troubles in the provinces of Assisi and Aragon, in which Michele obediently changed the ministers. Until April 1328, he remained in the papal court, apparently on the best of terms with John.

Meanwhile the quarrel between the empire and the papacy had been developing apace. In the spring of 1326 Louis suddenly and without due preparation undertook an expedition to Italy, at the invitation of the Ghibellines, for his imperial coronation. When he reached Milan in April to receive the iron crown John sternly forbade his further progress, and on this being disregarded, proceeded to excommunicate him afresh. Thus commenced another prolonged series of citations and sentences for heresy, including the preaching of a crusade with Holy Land indulgences against the impenitent sinner. Unmoved by this, Louis slowly made his way to Rome, which he entered January 7, 1327, and where he was crowned on the 17th, in contemptuous defiance of papal prerogative, by four syndics elected by the people, after which, according to usage, he exchanged the title of King of the Romans for that of Emperor. As the defender of the faith he proceeded to try the pope on the charge of heresy, based upon his denial of the poverty of Christ. April 14 he promulgated a law authorizing the prosecution and sentence *in absentia* of those notoriously defamed for treason or heresy, thus imitating the papal injustice of which he himself complained bitterly; and, on the 17th, sentence of deposition was solemnly read to the assembled people before the basilica of St. Peter. It recited that it was rendered at the request of the clergy and people of Rome; it recapitulated the crimes of the pope, whom it stigmatized as Antichrist; it pronounced him a heretic on account of his denying the poverty of Christ, deposed him from the papacy, and threatened confiscation on all who should render him support and assistance.

As a pope was necessary to the Church, and as the college of cardinals were under excommunication as fautors of heresy, recourse was had to the primitive method of selection: some form of election by the people and clergy of Rome was gone through on May 12, and a new Bishop of Rome was presented to the Christian world in the person of Pier di Corbario, an aged Franciscan of high repute for austerity and eloquence. He was Minister of the province of the Abruzzi and papal penitentiary. He had been married, his wife was still living, and he was said to have entered the Order without her consent, which rendered him "irregular" and led to an absurd complication, for the woman, who had never before complained of his leaving her, now came forward and put in her claims to be bought off. He assumed the name of Nicholas V, a college of cardinals was readily created for him, he appointed nuncios and legates and proceeded to degrade the Guelfic bishops and replace them with Ghibellines.

Although the Franciscan prefect of the Roman province assembled a chapter at Anagni which pronounced against Pier di Corbario and ordered him to lay aside his usurped dignity, it was impossible that the Order should escape responsibility for the rebellion, nor is it likely that Michele da Cesena was not privy to the whole proceeding. He had remained quietly at Avignon, and John had manifested no abatement of cordiality until April 9, when, summoning him to an audience, the pope attacked him on the subject of the Chapter of Perugia, which six years before had asserted the poverty of Christ and the apostles. Michele stoutly defended the utterances of the chapter, saying that if they were heretical then Nicholas IV and the other popes who had affirmed the doctrine were heretics. Then the papal wrath exploded. Michele was a headstrong fool and a fautor of heretics; when the stream of invective had exhausted itself he was placed under constructive arrest and ordered not to leave Avignon without permission, under pain of excommunication and forfeiture of office. A few days later, on April 14, in the secrecy of the Franciscan convent, Michele relieved his feelings by executing a solemn notarial protest, in the presence of William of Ockham, Bonagrazia, and other trusty adherents, in which he argued that the pope either was a heretic or no pope, for either his present utterances were erroneous or else Nicholas IV had been a heretic; in the latter case Boniface VIII and Clement V, who had approved the bull *Exiit qui seminat*, were likewise heretics, their nominations of cardinals were void, and the conclave which elected John was illegal. He protested against whatever might be done in derogation of the rights of the Order, that he was in durance and in just fear, and that what he might be forced to do would be null and void.

Michele was detained in Avignon while the General Chapter of the Order was held at Bologna, to which John sent Bertrand, Bishop of Ostia, with instructions to have another general chosen. The Order, however, was stubborn. It sent a somewhat defiant message to the pope and re-elected Michele, requesting him moreover to indicate Paris as the next place of assemblage, to be held, according to rule, in three years, to which he assented. In view of the drama which was developing in Rome he might reasonably fear for liberty or life. Preparations were made for his escape. A galley, furnished, according to John, by the Emperor Louis, but according to other and more trustworthy accounts, by Genoese refugees, was sent to Aigues-mortes. Thither he fled, May 26, accompanied by Ockham and Bonagrazia. He reached Pisa on June

9, and there ensued a war of manifestoes of unconscionable length, in which Michele was pronounced excommunicate and deposed, and John was proved to be a heretic who had rightfully forfeited the papacy. Michele could carry on only a wordy conflict, while John could act. Bertrand de la Tour, Cardinal of San Vitale, was appointed Vicar-General of the Order, another General Chapter was ordered to assemble in Paris, June 1329, and preparations were made for it by removing all provincials favorable to Michele and appointing in their places men who could be relied on. Out of 34 who had met in Bologna only 14 were seen in Paris; Michele was deposed and Gerard Odo was elected in his place; but even under this pressure no declaration condemning the poverty of Christ could be obtained from the chapter. The mass of the Order, reduced to silence, remained faithful to the principles represented by its deposed general, until forced to acquiescence by the arbitrary measures employed by the pope and the examples made of those who dared to express opposition. Still John was not disposed to relax the Franciscan discipline, and when, in 1332, Gerard Odo, in the hope of gaining a cardinal's hat, persuaded fourteen provincial ministers to join him in submitting a gloss which would have virtually annulled the obligation of poverty, his only reward was the ridicule of the pope and sacred college.

The settlement of the question depended upon political much more than upon religious considerations. Louis had abandoned Rome and established himself in Pisa with his pope, his cardinals, and his Franciscans, but the Italians were becoming tired of their kaiser. It mattered little that in January 1329 he indulged in the childish triumph of solemnly burning John XXII in effigy; he was obliged soon after to leave the city, and towards the end of the year he returned to Germany, carrying with him the men who were to defend his cause with all the learning of the schools, and abandoning to their fate those of his partisans who were unable to follow him. The proceedings which ensued at Todi will serve to show how promptly the Inquisition tracked his retreating footsteps, and how useful it was as a political agency in reducing rebellious communities to submission.

The Todini were Ghibelline. In August 1328 they had welcomed Louis as emperor and Pier di Corbario as pope, and had ordered

their notaries to use the regnal years of the latter in their instruments; they had, moreover, attacked and taken the Guelf city of
Orvieto and, like all the cities which adhered to Louis, they had
expelled the Dominicans. In August 1329, abandoned by Louis,
proceedings were commenced against them by the Franciscan, Frà
Bartolino da Perugia, the inquisitor, who announced his intention
of making an inquest of the whole district of Assisi against Patarins
and heretics, against those who assert things not to be sins which
the Church teaches to be sins, against those who understand the
Scriptures in a sense different from what the Holy Spirit demands,
and against those who have detracted from the dignity of the pope
and his constitutions. Under this, searching examinations were
made of the acts of the citizens during the visit of Louis, any sign
of respect paid to him being regarded as a crime, and two sets of
prosecutions were commenced—one against the Ghibellines of the
city and the other against the "rebellious" Franciscans. These latter
were summoned to reply to five articles:

(1) If they believed in, favored, or adhered to the Bavarian and the in-
trusive antipope;
(2) If they had marched with a cross to meet these heretics on their
entrance into Todi;
(3) If they had obeyed or done reverence to the Bavarian as emperor or
to P. di Corbario as pope;
(4) If they had taught or preached that the constitutions of John were
heretical or himself a heretic;
(5) If, after Michele da Cesena was condemned and deposed for heresy,
they had adhered to him and his errors.

The proceedings dragged on, and, July 1, 1330, John condemned the whole community as heretics and fautors of heresy.
July 7 he sent this sentence to the legate, Cardinal Orsini, with
instructions to cite the citizens peremptorily and to try them according to the inquisitorial formula, *"summarie et de plano et
sine strepitu et figura."* Under this the Todini finally made submission, the cardinal sent Frà Bartolino and his colleague thither,
and the city was reconciled, subject to the papal approval. They
had been obliged to make a gift of 10,000 florins to Louis, and
now a fine of equal amount was levied upon them, besides 100 lire

imposed on each of 134 citizens. Apparently the terms exacted were not satisfactory to John, for a papal brief of July 20, 1331, declared the submission of the citizens deceitful, and ordered the interdict renewed. The last document which we have in the case is one of June 1, 1332, in which the legate sends to the Bishop of Todi a list of 197 persons, including Franciscans, parish priests, heads of religious houses, nobles, and citizens, who are ordered to appear before him at Orvieto on June 15, to stand trial on the inquisitions which have been found against them.

As for the unhappy antipope, his fate was even more deplorable. Confided at Pisa by Louis to the care of Count Fazio da Doneratico, the leading noble of the city, he was concealed for a while in a castle in Maremma. June 18, 1329, the Pisans rose and drove out the imperialist garrison, and in the following January they were reconciled to the Church. A part of the bargain was the surrender of Pier di Corbario, to whom John promised to show himself a kind father and benevolent friend, besides enriching Fazio for the betrayal of his trust. After making public abjuration of his heresies in Pisa, Pier was sent to Nice, where he was delivered to the papal agents. In every town on the road to Avignon he was required publicly to repeat his abjuration. August 25, 1330, with a halter around his neck, he was brought before the pope in public consistory. Broken with shame and suffering, he flung himself at his rival's feet and begged for mercy, abjuring and anathematizing his heresies, and especially that of the poverty of Christ. Having thus rendered him an object of contempt and deprived him of all further power of harm, John mercifully spared him bodily torment. He was confined in an apartment in the papal palace, fed from the papal table, and allowed the use of books, but no one was admitted to see him without a special papal order. His wretched life soon came to an end, and when he died, in 1333, he was buried in the Franciscan habit. Considering the ferocity of the age, his treatment is one of the least discreditable acts in the career of John XXII. It was hardly to be expected, after the savage vindictiveness of the curse which he had published, April 20, 1329, on his already fallen rival:

May he in this life feel the wrath of Peter and Paul, whose church he has sought to confound! May his dwelling-place be deserted, and may there be none to live under his roof! May his children be orphans, and his wife a widow! May they be driven forth from their hearth-stones to beggary! May the usurer devour their substance, and strangers seize the work of their hands! May the whole earth fight against him, may the elements be his enemies, may the merits of all the saints at rest confound him and wreak vengeance on him through life!

In Germany the Franciscans for the most part remained faithful to Michele and Louis, and were of the utmost assistance to the latter in the struggle. The test was the observance of the interdict which for so many years suspended divine service throughout the empire, and was a sore trial to the faithful. To a great extent this was disregarded by the Franciscans. It was to little purpose that, in January 1331, John issued a special bull directed against them, deprived of all privileges and immunities those who recognized Louis as emperor and celebrated services in interdicted places, and ordered all prelates and inquisitors to prosecute them. On the other hand, Louis was not behindhand in enforcing obedience by persecution wherever he had the power. An imperial brief of June 1330, addressed to the magistrates of Aix, directs them to assist and protect those teachers of the truth, the Franciscans Sigelbert of Landsberg and John of Royda, and to imprison all their brethren whom they may designate as rebels to the empire and to the Order until the General Michele shall decide what is to be done with them.

All this, however, was but an episode in the political struggle, which was to be decided by the rivalries between the houses of Wittelsbach, Hapsburg, and Luxemburg, and the intrigues of France. Louis gradually succeeded in arousing and centering upon himself the national spirit, aided by the arrogant disdain with which John XXII and his successors received his repeated offers of qualified submission. When in 1330 Louis had temporarily secured the support of John of Luxemburg, King of Bohemia, and the Duke of Austria, and they offered themselves as sureties that he would fulfill what might be required of him, provided the independence of the empire was recognized, John retorted that Louis was a heretic and thus incapacitated; he was a thief and a robber, a wicked man who consorted with Michele, Ockham, Bonagrazia, and Marsiglio; not only had he no title to the empire, but the state of Christendom would be inconceivably deplorable if he were recognized. After the death of John in December 1334, another attempt was made, but it suited the policy of France and of Bohemia to prolong the strife, and Benedict XII was as firm as his predecessor. Louis was ready to sacrifice his Franciscan allies, but the papacy demanded the right practically to dictate who should be emperor, and by a skillful use of appeals to the national pride Louis gradually won the support of an increasing number of states and cities. In 1338 the convention of Rhense and the Reichstag of Frankfort formally proclaimed as a part of the law of the empire that the choice of the electors was final, and that the papacy had no confirmatory power. The interdict was ordered not to be observed, and in all the states adhering to Louis ecclesiastics were given the option of resuming public worship within eight days or of undergoing a ten years' exile.

In the strife between Louis and the papacy the little colony of Franciscan refugees at Munich was of the utmost service to the imperial cause, but their time was drawing to an end. Michele da Cesena died November 29, 1342, his latest work being a long manifesto proving that John had died an unrepentant heretic, and that his successors in defending his errors were likewise heretics. The dithyrambic palinode which passes as his deathbed recantation is clearly a forgery, and there can be no doubt that Michele persisted to the end. When dying he handed the seal of the Order over to William of Ockham, who used it as Vicar-General; he had already, in April 1342, appointed two citizens of Munich, John Schito and Grimold Treslo, as syndics and procurators of the Order, the latter of whom subsequently assumed the generalate. Bonagrazia died in June 1347, declaring with his last breath that the cause of Louis was righteous. The date of William of Ockham's death is uncertain, but it occurred between 1347 and 1350.

Thus dropped off, one by one, the men who had so gallantly defended the doctrine of the poverty of Christ. As regards the political conceptions which were the special province of Marsiglio and Ockham, their work was done, and they could exercise no further influence over the uncontrollable march of events. With the death of Benedict XII in 1342, Louis made renewed efforts for pacification, but John of Bohemia was intriguing to secure the succession for his house, and they were fruitless, except to strengthen Louis by demonstrating the impossibility of securing terms tolerable to the empire. In July 1346, the three ecclesiastical electors, Mainz, Trèves, and Cologne, with Rodolph of Saxony, and John of Bohemia, assembled at Rhense under the impulsion of Clement VI and elected the son of John, Charles Margrave of Moravia, as a rival king of the Romans. The movement, however, had no basis of popular support, and when Louis hastened to the Rhinelands all the cities and nearly all the princes and nobles adhered to him. Had the election been postponed for a few weeks it would never have taken place, for the next month occurred the battle of Crécy, where John of Bohemia died a chivalrous death, Charles, the newly elected king, saved his life by flight, and French influence was temporarily eclipsed. Thus unauspiciously commenced, the reign of Charles IV had little promise of duration, when, in October 1347, Louis, while indulging in his favorite pastime of hunting, was struck with apo- plexy and fell dead from his horse, and Charles had no further organized opposition to dread.

Desirous of obtaining the fullest advantage from this unlooked- for good fortune, Clement VI commissioned the Archbishop of Prague and the Bishop of Bamberg to reconcile all communities and individuals who had incurred excommunication by supporting the Bavarian, with a formula of absolution by which they were obliged to swear that they held it heresy for an emperor to depose a pope, and that they would never obey an emperor until he had been ap- proved by the pope. This excited intense disgust, and in many places it could not be enforced. The teachings of Marsiglio and Ockham had at least borne fruit in so far that the papal preten- sions to virtually controlling the empire were disdainfully rejected. The German spirit thus aroused is well exemplified by what oc- curred at Basle, a city which had observed the interdict and was eager for its removal. When Charles and the Bishop of Bamberg appeared before the gates they were received by the magistrates and a great crowd of citizens. Conrad of Barenfels, the burgo- master, addressed the bishop:

"My Lord of Bamberg, you must know that we do not believe, nor will we confess, that our late lord, the Emperor Louis, ever was a heretic. Whomsoever the electors or a majority of them shall choose as King of the Romans we will hold as such, whether he applies to the pope or not, nor will we do anything else that is contrary to the rights of the empire. But if you have power from the pope and are willing to remit all our sins, so be it."

Then, turning to the people, he called out, "Do you give to me and to Conrad Münch power to ask for the absolution of your sins?" The crowd shouted assent; the two Conrads took an oath in accordance with this; divine services were resumed, and the king and bishop entered the town.

The question as to the poverty of Christ, which had been put forward by John and Louis as the cause of quarrel, sank completely out of sight north of the Alps with the death of Louis and the extinction of the Munich colony of refugees. It was otherwise in the south, and especially in Italy, the native home of Franciscanism and of the peculiar influences which moulded the ascetic development of the Order. There the impulses which had led the earlier Spirituals to endure persecution in vindication of the holiness of absolute poverty were still as strong as ever. Under Boniface and Clement and during the earlier years of John its professors had lain in hiding or had sought the friendly refuge of Sicily. In the confusion of the Franciscan schism they had emerged and multiplied. With the downfall of the antipope and the triumph of John they were once more proscribed. In the quarrel over the poverty of Christ, that tenet had naturally become the distinguishing mark of the sectaries, and its condemnation by John necessarily entailed the consequence of denying the papal authority and asserting the heresy of the Holy See.

In 1335, one of the earliest cares of Benedict XII after his accession was the repression of these *Fratres de paupere Vita*, as they styled themselves. They still in many places publicly displayed their contumacy by wearing the short and narrow gowns of the Spirituals. They still held Michele to be their general, insulted the memory of John XXII, and were earnestly and successfully engaged in proselytism. Moreover, they were openly protected by men of rank and power. All the inquisitors, from Treviso and Lombardy to Sicily, were commanded to free the Church from these impious hypocrites by vigorous action, and directions were sent to the prelates to lend efficient assistance. The whole Order, in fact, was still infected with these dangerous doctrines, and could not be brought to view the dissidents with proper abhorrence. Benedict complained that in the

kingdom of Naples many Franciscan convents gave shelter to these
perverse brethren, and in a bull regulating the Order issued this
same year he alludes to those among them who wear peculiar vestments and, under pretended sanctity, maintain heresies condemned
by the Church of Rome; all such, together with those who protect
them, are to be imprisoned until they submit. It was not always easy
to enforce obedience to these mandates. The Bishop of Camerino
was stubborn, and in 1337 Frà Giovanni di Borgo, the Inquisitor of
the Mark of Ancona, was instructed to proceed severely against him
and other fautors of these heretics.

The test of the heresy, as I have said, was the assertion that Christ
and the apostles held no property. That such continued to be the
customary formula appears from Eymerich, who instructs his inquisitor to make the penitent declare under oath, "I swear that I believe in
my heart and profess that our Lord Jesus Christ and his apostles
while in this mortal life held in common the things which Scripture declares them to have had, and that they had the right of giving,
selling, and alienating."

Camerino continued to be a place of refuge. In 1343 Clement VI
ordered the Bishops of Ancona and Osimo to cite before him within
three months Gentile, Lord of Camerino, for various offenses, among
which was protecting the Fraticelli, impeding the inquisitors in the
prosecution of their duties, and despising for several years the excommunication which they had pronounced against him. In such
districts the Fraticelli showed themselves with little concealment.
It is an interesting proof of the state of public opinion in Italy, that
in spite of the thoroughly organized machinery of persecution, men
who held these doctrines were able to disseminate them almost
publicly and to make numerous proselytes. About the middle of the
century they circulated throughout Italy a document written in the
vernacular, "so that it can be understood by everyone," giving their
reasons for separating themselves from pope and prelate. The argument is drawn strictly from Scripture and from the utterances of
the Church itself, and from even the standpoint of a canonist it is
unanswerable. There are no apocalyptic hysterics, no looking forward to Antichrist or to new ages of the world, no mysticism. There
is not even any reference to St. Francis, nor any claim that his
Rule is inspired and inviolable. Yet none the less the whole body

of the Church is declared to be heretic, and all the faithful are summoned to cut loose from it.

The reasons alleged for this are heresy, simony, and fornication. As to the first, John XXII is proved to be a heretic by the bulls pronouncing heretical the doctrine that Christ and the apostles possessed nothing. This is easily done by reason of the definitions of the previous popes confirmed by the Council of Vienne. The corollary of course follows that all his successors and their cardinals are heretics. As regards simony, the canons of the Decretum and the utterances of the doctors are quoted to show that it is heresy. As regards fornication, it was easy to cite the canons embodying the Hildebrandine doctrine that the sacraments of fornicating priests are not to be received. It is true that there are many priests who are not fornicators, but there are none who are not simonists—who have not given or received money for the sacraments. Even if he could be found who is innocent on all these heads, it would be necessary for him to separate himself from the rest, for, as Raymond of Pennaforte shows in his *Summa*, those are guilty of mortal sin and idolatry who receive the sacraments of heretics. The Fraticelli, therefore, have been obliged to withdraw from a heretical church, and they issue this manifesto to justify their course. If in any way it is erroneous, they ask to have the error pointed out; and if it is correct, the faithful are bound to join them, because, after the facts are known, association with prelates and clergy thus heretical and excommunicate will involve in heresy all who are guilty of it.

All the Fraticelli, however, were not uniformly agreed upon all points. In fact, we find them, in 1362, divided into two branches, one of which recognized as its leader Tommaso, ex-Bishop of Aquino, and held that as John XXII and his successors were heretics, the sacrament of ordination derived from them was void, and reordination was required of all ecclesiastics entering the sect. The other, which took its name from Felipe of Majorca, was regularly organized under a general minister, and, while equally regarding the popes as heretics, recognized the ordinations of the establishment. All branches of the sect, however, drew ample store of reasons from the venality and corruption of the Church. There is extant a letter in the vulgar tongue from a *frate* to two female devotees, arguing, like the more formal manifesto, that they are bound to withdraw from the communion of the heretical church. This is the beast with seven horns: (1) supreme pride; (2) supreme cruelty; (3) supreme folly or wrath; (4) supreme deceit and inimitable falsehood; (5) supreme carnality or lust; (6) supreme cupidity or avarice; (7) supreme hatred of truth, or malice. This letter further indicates the legitimate descent of the Fraticelli from the Spirituals by a quotation from Joachim to show that St. Francis is Noah, and the faithful few of his children are those who are saved with him in the Ark.

Of the final shape which the heresy assumed we have an authoritative account from its ruthless exterminator, the Inquisitor Giacomo della Marca. In his *Dialogue with a Fraticello*, written about 1450, there is no word about the follies of the Spirituals or any extraneous dogmas. The question turns wholly on the poverty of Christ and the heresy of John's definitions of the doctrine. The Fraticelli stigmatize the orthodox as *Joannistæ*, and in turn are called *Michaelistæ*, showing that by this time the extravagances of the Spirituals had been forgotten, and that the heretics were the direct descendants of the schismatic Franciscans who followed Michele da Cesena. Giacomo complains that they abused the minds of the simple by representing the priests as simonists and concubinarians, and that the people, imbued with this poison, lost faith in the clergy, refused to confess to them, to attend their masses, to receive their sacraments, and to pay their tithes.

The Fraticelli thus formed one or more separate organizations, each of which asserted itself to be the only true Church. In the scanty information we possess, it is impossible to trace in detail the history of the fragmentary parts into which they split, and we can only say in general terms that the sect did not consist simply of anchorites and friars, but had its regular clergy and laity, its bishops and their supreme head or pope, known as the Bishop of Philadelphia, that being the name assigned to the community. In 1357 this position was filled by Tommaso of Aquino; chance led to the discovery of such a pope in Perugia in 1374; in 1429 we happen to know that a certain Rainaldo filled the position, and shortly after a *frate* named Gabriel. There is even talk of a chief of the laity who styled himself Emperor of the Christians.

It was in vain that successive popes ordered the Inquisition to take the most active measures for the suppression of the sect, and that occasional holocausts rewarded their exertions, as when under Urban V nine were burned at Viterbo, and in 1389 Frà Michele Berti de Calci suffered the same fate at Florence. This last case reveals in its details the popular sympathy which favored the labors of the Fraticelli. Frà Michele had been sent to Florence as a missionary by a congregation of the sect which met in a cavern in the Mark of Ancona. He preached in Florence and made many converts, and was about to leave the city, April 19, when he was betrayed by five female zealots, who sent for him pretending to seek conversion. His trial was short. A colleague saved his life by recantation, but Michele was firm. When brought up to be degraded from the priesthood he refused to kneel before the bishop, saying that heretics are not to be knelt to. In walking to the place of execution many of the crowd exchanged words of cheer with him, and when he was tied to a stake in a sort of cabin which was to be set on fire, a number put their heads inside to beg him to recant. The place was several times filled with smoke to frighten him, but he was unyielding, and after his incremation there were many people, we are told, who regarded him as a saint.

The two Sicilies continued to be thoroughly interpenetrated with the heresy. Francesco Marchisio, Archdeacon of Salerno, was a Fraticello, in spite of which he was elevated to the see of Trivento in 1362, and occupied it till his death about twenty years later. At Perugia, in 1368, the magistrates were induced to throw many of the Fraticelli into prison, but to so little purpose that the people persisted in regarding them as the true children of St. Francis and in giving them shelter, while the Franciscans were despised on account of the laxity of their observance, the costliness of their vestments, and the profusion of their table. They were ridiculed and insulted in the streets until they scarce dared to venture in public; if one chanced to let the collar of his shirt show above his gown, someone would pull up the linen and ask the jeering crowd if this was the austerity of St. Francis. As a last resort, in 1374, they sent for Paoluccio of Foligno and a public disputation was arranged with the Fraticelli. Paoluccio turned the tide of popular favor by proving that obedience to the pope was of greater moment than obedience to the Rule, and the Fraticelli were driven from the town.

The proselyting efforts of the Fraticelli were by no means con-

fined to Italy. Believing themselves the only true Church, earnest
spirits among them were ready to dare as much as the orthodox
among the infidels and barbarians. Already, in 1344, Clement VI
found himself obliged to address the faithful throughout Armenia,
Persia, and the East, warning them against these emissaries of Satan,
who were seeking to scatter among them the seeds of error and
schism. He had no inquisitors to call upon in those regions, but he
ordered the prelates to punish them, authorizing them to invoke,
if necessary, the aid of the secular arm. The Fraticelli made at least
one convert of importance, for in 1346 Clement felt himself obliged
to cite for appearance within four months no less a personage than
the Archbishop of Seleucia, who, infected with pseudo-minorite
errors, had written in Armenian and was circulating throughout Asia
a postil on St. John in which he asserted the forbidden doctrine of
the poverty of Christ. In 1354 Innocent VI heard of Fraticellian
missionaries laboring among the Chazars of the Crimea, and he
forthwith ordered the Bishop of Caffa to repress them with inquisitorial methods. In 1375 Gregory XI learned that they were active in
Egypt, Syria, and Asia, and he promptly ordered the Franciscan
provincial of those regions to enforce on them the severity of the
laws. One, named Lorenzo Carbonello, had ventured to Tunis,
whereupon Gregory commanded Giacomo Patani and Guillen de
Ripoll, the captains of the Christian troops in the service of the
Bey of Tunis, to seize him and send him in chains to the Archbishop
of Naples or of Pisa.

In Languedoc and Provence the rigorous severity with which the
Spirituals had been exterminated seems to have exercised a wholesome influence in repressing the Fraticelli, but a few cases on record
show the existence of the sect. In 1336 we hear of a number confined in the papal dungeons of Avignon—among them a papal chaplain—and that Guillaume Lombard, the judge of ecclesiastical causes,
was ordered to exert against them the full severity of the laws. In
1354 two Tuscan Fraticelli, Giovanni da Castiglione and Francesco
d' Arquata, were arrested at Montpellier for holding that John XXII
had forfeited his authority by altering the definitions of the bull
Exiit, and that his successors were not the true Church. Innocent
VI caused them to be brought before him, but all efforts to make
them recant were vain; they went tranquilly to the stake, singing

Gloria in excelsis, and were reverenced as martyrs by a large number of their brethren.

In northern France we hear little of the heresy. The only recorded case seems to be that of Denis Soulechat, a professor of the University of Paris, who taught in 1363 that the law of divine love does away with property, and that Christ and the apostles held none. Summoned by the Inquisitor Guillaume Rochin, he abjured before the Faculty and then appealed to the pope. At Avignon, when he endeavored to purge himself before an assembly of theologians, he only added new errors to his old ones, and was sent back to the Cardinal of Beauvais and the Sorbonne with orders to make him recant, and to punish him properly with the advice of the inquisitor. In 1368 he was forced to a public abjuration.

The violent measures of John XXII, followed up by his successors, for a while effectually repressed the spiritual asceticism of the Franciscans. Yet the ardent thirst of poverty and the belief that in it lay the only assured path to salvation were too widely diffused to be permanently repressed. Giovanni Colombini, a rich and ambitious citizen of Siena, had his thoughts accidentally directed to heaven. His career strikingly resembles that of Peter Waldo, save that the Church, grown wiser, utilized his zeal instead of antagonizing him. The Order of Jesuats (Apostolic Clerks of St. Jerome) which he founded was approved by Urban V in 1367. It was an order of lay brethren under the Augustinian Rule, vowed to poverty and devoted to the care of the sick, not unlike that of the Cellites or Alexians of the Rhinelands.

It was inevitable that there should be dissatisfaction among the more ascetic Franciscans, and that the more zealous of these should seek some remedy short of heresy. In 1350 Gentile of Spoleto obtained from Clement VI authorization for some houses of stricter observance. Immediately the wrath of the Conventuals was excited. The innovators were accused of adopting the short and narrow gowns which had been the distinguishing mark of the dreaded Olivists. In the General Chapter of 1353, the General Farignano was urged to exterminate them by the measures which had proved so effective in Languedoc. To this he did not assent, but he set spies to work to obtain evidence against them, and soon was able to accuse them of receiving Fraticelli. They admitted the fact, but argued that this had been in the hope of converting the heretics, and when they proved obstinate they had been expelled—but they had not been reported to the Inquisition as duty required. Armed with this, Farignano represented to Innocent VI the grave dangers of the innovation, and obtained a revocation of the papal authorization. The brethren were dispersed, Gentile and two companions were thrown into prison at Orvieto; his coadjutor, Frà Martino, a most exemplary man, who shone in miracles after death, died the next year, and the rest were reduced to obedience. After prolonged captivity Gentile was released, and died in 1362, worn out with fruitless labors to restore the discipline of the Order.

More fortunate was his disciple, Paoluccio da Trinci, of Foligno, a simple and unlearned friar, who had obtained from his kinsman, Ugolino, Lord of Foligno, a dungeon in which to gratify his thirst for asceticism. Though he had permission for this from his superiors, he suffered from the hostility of the laxer brethren, but his austerities gained him great popular reverence and many disciples. In 1368 the General Farignano chanced to attend a provincial chapter at Foligno, and was persuaded to ask of Ugolino a spot called Brulliano, in the mountains between Foligno and Camerino, as a hermitage for Paoluccio and his followers. After his request was granted he dreaded a schism in the Order and wished to recall it, but Ugolino held him to his purpose. The place was wild, rocky, marshy, unwholesome, infested with serpents, and almost uninhabited. Thither Paoluccio led his brethren, and they were forced to adopt the sabots or wooden shoes which became the distinguishing footgear of their Order. Their reputation spread; converts flocked to them; their buildings required enlargement; associate houses were founded in many places, and thus arose the Observantines, or Franciscans of strict observance —an event in the history of the Church only second in importance to the original foundation of the Mendicant Orders.

When Paoluccio died in 1390, he was already reckoned as a provincial within the Order. In 1405 began the marvellous career of St. Bernardino of Siena, who counts as the formal founder of the Observantines. They had merely been called the Brethren of the Hermitages until the Council of Constance established them as an organization virtually independent of the Conventuals, when they took the name by which they have since been known. New houses arose, or those of the Conventuals were reformed and given over to them. In 1426 they were introduced into the province of Strassburg through the intervention of Matilda of Savoy, wife of the Palsgrave Louis the Bearded. Familar in her youth with their virtues, she took occasion at Heidelberg to point out to her husband the Franciscans in their convent garden below them, amusing themselves with military exercises. It resulted in the reform of all the houses in his dominions and the introduction of the Observantine discipline, not without serious trouble. In 1453 Nicholas of Cusa, as legate, forced all the houses in the diocese of Bamberg to adopt the Observantine discipline, under threat of forfeiting their privileges. In 1431 the holy house on Mount Alverno, the Franciscan Mecca, was made over to them, and in 1434 the guardianship of the Holy Places in Jerusalem. In 1460 we hear of their penetrating to distant Ireland. It is not to be supposed that the Conventuals submitted quietly to the triumphs of the hated ascetics whom for a century and a half they had successfully baffled and persecuted. Quarrels, sharper and bitterer even than those with the Dominicans, were of constant occurrence, and were beyond the power of the popes to allay. A promising effort at reunion attempted by Capistrano in 1430, under the auspices of Martin V, was defeated by the incurable laxity of the Conventuals. In 1435 the strife rose to such a pitch in France that Charles VII was obliged to appeal to the Council of Basle, which responded with a decree in favor of the Observantines. The corruption of the Conventuals was so universally recognized that even Pius II does not hesitate to say that, though they generally excel as theologians, virtue is the last thing about which most of them concern themselves. In contrast with this, the holiness of the new organization won for it the veneration of the people, while the unflagging zeal with which it served the Holy See secured for it the favor of the popes precisely as the Mendicant Orders had done in the thirteenth century.

A religious revival such as this brought into service a class of men who were worthy representatives of the Peter Martyrs and Guillem Arnauds of the early Inquisition. Under their ruthless energy the Fraticelli were doomed to extinction. The troubles of the Great Schism had allowed the heretics to flourish almost unnoticed and unmolested, but after the Church had healed its dissensions at

Constance and had entered upon a new and vigorous life, it set to work in earnest to eradicate them. Hardly had Martin V returned to Italy from Constance when he issued from Mantua, November 14, 1418, a bull in which he deplores the increase of the abominable sect in many parts, and especially in the Roman province. The bishops and inquisitors are instructed to proceed against them vigorously, without regard to limits of jurisdiction, and to prosecute their protectors, even if the latter are of episcopal or regal dignity, which sufficiently indicates that the Fraticelli had found favor with those of highest rank in both Church and State. This accomplished little, for in a subsequent bull of 1421 Martin alludes to the continued increase of the heresy, and tries the expedient of appointing the Cardinals of Albano and Porto as special commissioners for its suppression. The cardinals proved as inefficient as their predecessors. In 1423 the General Council of Siena was greatly scandalized at finding that at Peniscola there was a heretic pope with his college of cardinals, apparently flourishing without an attempt at concealment, and the Gallican nation made several ineffectual efforts to induce the council to take active measures against the secular authorities under whose favor these scandals were allowed to exist. How utterly the machinery of persecution had broken down is illustrated by the case of three Fraticelli who had at this period been detected in Florence—Bartolommeo di Matteo, Giovanni di Marino of Lucca, and Bartolommeo di Pietro of Pisa. Evidently distrusting the Florentine Inquisition, which was Franciscan, Martin V entrusted the matter to his legates then presiding over the Council of Siena. On the sudden dissolution of the council the legates returned to Rome, except the Dominican General Leonardo of Florence, who went to Florence. To him, therefore, Martin wrote, April 24, 1424, empowering him to terminate the case himself, and expressly forbidding the Inquisitor of Florence from taking any part in it. In September of the same year Martin instructed Piero, Abbot of Rosacio, his rector of the Mark of Ancona, to extirpate the Fraticelli existing there, and the difficulty of the undertaking was recognized in the unwonted clemency which authorized Piero to reconcile even those who had been guilty of repeated relapses.

There were laws in abundance for the extermination of heresy, and an elaborate organization for their enforcement, but a paralysis seemed to have fallen upon it, and all the efforts of the Holy See to make it do its duty were in vain. The problem was solved when, in 1426, Martin boldly appointed two Observantines as inquisitors, without limitation of districts and with power to appoint deputies, thus rendering them supreme over the whole of Italy. These were the men whom we have so often met before where heresy was to be combated—San Giovanni da Capistrano, and the blessed Giacomo da Monteprandone, generally known as della Marca—both full of zeal and energy, who richly earned their respective canonization and beatification by services which can scarce be overestimated. It is true that Giacomo was commissioned only as a missionary, to preach to the heretics and reconcile them, but the difference was practically undiscoverable, and when, a quarter of a century later, he fondly looked back over the exploits of his youth, he related with pride how the heretics fled from before his face, abandoned their strongholds, and left their flocks to his mercy. Their headquarters seem to have been in the Mark of Ancona, and chiefly in the dioceses of Fabriano and Jesi. There the new inquisitors boldly attacked them. There was no resistance. Such of the teachers as could do so sought safety in flight, and the fate of the rest may be guessed from the instructions of Martin in 1428 to Astorgio, Bishop of Ancona, his lieutenant in the Mark, with respect to the village of Magnalata. As it had been a receptacle of heretics, it is to be levelled with the earth, never to be rebuilt. Stubborn heretics are to be dealt with according to the law—that is, of course, to be burned, as Giacomo della Marca tells us was the case with many of them. Those who repent may be reconciled, but their leaders are to be imprisoned for life, and are to be tortured, if necessary, to force them to reveal the names of their fellows elsewhere. The simple folk who have been misled are to be scattered around in the vicinage where they can cultivate their lands, and are to be recompensed by dividing among them the property confiscated from the rest. The children of heretic parents are to be taken away and sent to a distance, where they can be brought up in the faith. Heretic books are to be diligently searched for throughout the province; and all magistrates and communities are to be warned that any favor or protection shown to heretics will be visited with forfeiture of municipal rights.

Such measures ought to have been effective, as well as the device

of Capistrano, who, after driving the Fraticelli out of Massacio
and Palestrina, founded Observantine houses there to serve as citadels
of the faith, but the heretics were stubborn and enduring. When
Eugenius IV succeeded to the papacy he renewed Capistrano's commission in 1432 as a general inquisitor against the Fraticelli. Giacomo,
until 1440, was at work among the Cathari of Bosnia and the Hussites
of Hungary. The Fraticelli of Ancona were still troublesome, for,
on his return from Asia in 1441, Giacomo was sent thither as special
inquisitor for their suppression. When, in 1447, Nicholas V ascended
the papal throne, he made haste to renew Capistrano's commission,
and in 1449 a combined attack was made on the heretics of the
Mark, possibly stimulated by the capture in his own court of a
bishop of the Fraticelli named Matteo, disguised in a Franciscan
habit. Nicholas himself went to Fabriano, while Capistrano and
Giacomo scoured the country. Magnalata had been rebuilt in spite
of the prohibition, and it, with Migliorotta, Poggio, and Merulo,
was brought back to the faith, by what means we can well guess.
The unlucky captives were brought before Nicholas at Fabriano
and burned. Giacomo tells us that the stench lasted for three days
and extended as far as the convent in which he was staying.

After this we hear little of the Fraticelli, although the sect still
continued to exist for a while in secret. In 1467 Paul II converted
a number of them who were brought from Poli to Rome. In 1471
Frà Tommaso di Scarlino was sent to Piombino and the maritime
parts of Tuscany to drive out some Fraticelli who had been discovered there. This is the last allusion to them that I have met
with, and thereafter they may be considered as virtually extinct.

The Observantine movement may be credited with the destruction
of the Fraticelli, not so much by furnishing the men and the zeal
required for their violent suppression as by supplying an organization in which ascetic longings could be safely gratified, and by attracting to themselves the popular veneration which had so long
served as a safeguard to the heretics. When we read of Capistrano's
reputation among his countrymen—how in Vicenza, in 1451, the
authorities had to shut the city gates to keep out the influx of
surging crowds, and when he walked the streets he had to be accompanied by a guard of *Frati* to keep off the people seeking to
touch him with sticks or to secure a fragment of his garment as a

relic; how in Florence, in 1456, an armed guard was requisite to prevent his suffocation—we can realize the tremendous influence exercised by him and his fellows in diverting the current of public opinion to the Church which they represented. Like the Mendicants of the thirteenth century, they restored to it much of the reverence which it had forfeited, in spite of the relaxation and self-indulgence to which, if Poggio is to be believed, many of them speedily degenerated.

CHAPTER XX
POLITICAL HERESY UTILIZED BY THE CHURCH

AS HERESY grew more and more threatening, and as the application of the theory of indulgences gave to the Church an armed militia ready for mobilization without cost whenever it chose to proclaim danger to the faith, the temptation to invoke the fanaticism of Christendom, for the defense or extension of its temporal interests inevitably increased. In so far as such a resort can be justified, the Albigensian crusades were justified by a real antagonism of faith which foreboded a division of Christianity, but their success irresistibly led to the application of the same means to cases in which there was not the semblance of a similar excuse. Of these one of the earliest, as well as one of the most typical, was that of the Stedingers.

The Stedingers were a mixed race who had colonized on the lower Weser the lands which their industry won from the overflow of river and sea, their territory extending southward to the neighborhood of Bremen. A rough and semi-barbarous folk, no doubt, they were freemen under the spiritual care of the Archbishop of Bremen, who in return enjoyed their tithes. They were governed by judges of their own choice, administering their own laws, until, about 1187, trouble arose from the attempts of the Counts of Oldenburg to extend their authority over the redeemed marshes and islands by building a castle or two which should keep the population in check. There were few churches, and, as the parishes were large, the matrons were accustomed to carry their daughters to mass in wagons. The garrisons were in the habit of sallying forth and seizing these women to solace their solitude, till the people arose, captured the castles, slew the garrisons, and dug a ditch across a neck of their territory, leaving only one gate for entrance. John Count of Oldenburg recovered his castles, but after his death the Stedingers reasserted their independence. Among their rights they included the nonpayment of tithes, and they treated with contumely the priests sent to compel their obedience. Matters became more embroiled when some monks who ventured to inculcate upon the peasants the duty of tithe paying were martyred. Still worse was it when a priest, irritated at the smallness of an oblation offered at Easter by a woman of condition, in derision slipped into her mouth the coin in place of the Eucharist. Unable to swallow it, and fearing to commit sacrilege, the woman kept it in her mouth till her return home, when she ejected it in some clean linen and discovered the trick. Enraged at this insult, her husband slew the priest, and thus increased the general ferment.

Yet the Stedingers were welcomed as fully orthodox when their aid was wanted in the struggle which raged from 1208 till 1217 between the rival archbishops of Bremen, first between Waldemar and Burchard, and then between Waldemar and Gerhardt. Ranged at first on the side of Waldemar, after the triumph of Frederic II over Otho their defection to Gerhardt was decisive, and in 1217 the latter obtained his archiepiscopal seat, where he held his allies in high favor until his death in 1219. He was succeeded by Gerhardt II, of the House of Lippe, a warlike prelate who endeavored to overthrow the liberties of Bremen, and to levy tolls on all the commerce of the Weser. The Stedinger tithes were not likely to escape his attention. His brother, Hermann Count of Lippe, came to his assistance with other nobles, for the independence of the Weser peasant-folk was of evil import to the neighboring feudal lords. To take advantage of the ice in those watery regions, the expedition set forth in December 1229 under the leadership of the count and the archbishop. The Stedingers resisted valiantly. On Christmas Day a battle was fought in which Count Hermann was slain and the crusaders put to flight. To celebrate the triumph the victors in derision appointed mock officials, styling one emperor, another pope, and others archbishops and bishops, and these issued letters under these titles —a sorry jest, which when duly magnified represented them as rebels against all temporal and spiritual authority.

It was evident that some more potent means must be found to overcome the indomitable peasantry, and the device adopted was suggested by the success in 1230 of the crusade preached by Wilbrand, Bishop of Utrecht, against the free Frisians in revenge for their slaying his predecessor Otho. At a synod held in Bremen in 1230, the Stedingers were put to the ban as the vilest of heretics,

who treated the Eucharist with contempt too horrible for description, who sought responses from wise-women, made waxen images,
and wrought many other works of darkness. Doubtless there were
remnants of pagan superstition in Steding which served as a foundation for these accusations, but that in fact there were no religious
principles involved, and that the questions at issue were purely
political, is indicated by the praise which Frederic II, in an epistle
dated June 14, 1230, bestows on the Stedingers for the aid which
they had rendered to a house of the Teutonic Knights, and his
exhortation that they should continue to protect it.

It was simply an episode in the extension of feudalism and
sacerdotalism. The scattered remains of the old Teutonic tribal independence were to be crushed, and the combined powers of Church
and State were summoned to the task. Yet the preliminaries of a
crusade consumed time, and during 1231 and 1232 Archbishop
Gerhardt had all he could do to withstand the assaults of the victorious peasants, who twice captured and destroyed the castle of
Schlütter, which he had rebuilt to protect his territories from their
incursions; he sought support in Rome, and in October 1232, after
ordering an investigation of the heresy by the Bishops of Lubeck,
Ratzeburg, and Minden, Gregory IX came to his aid with bulls
addressed to the Bishops of Minden, Lubeck, and Verden, ordering
them to preach the cross against the rebels. In these there is nothing
said about tithes, but the Stedingers are described as heretics of the
worst description, who deny God, worship demons, consult seeresses,
abuse the sacrament, and commit the foulest excesses on the clergy.
In January 1233 he wrote to the Bishops of Paderborn, Hildesheim,
Verden, Münster, and Osnabrück, ordering them to assist their
brethren of Ratzeburg, Minden, and Lubeck, whom he had commissioned to preach a crusade, with full pardons, against the heretics
called Stedingers. An army had meanwhile been collected which
accomplished nothing during the winter against the steadfast resolution of the peasants, and dispersed on the expiration of its short term
of service. In a papal epistle of June 17, 1233, to the Bishops of
Minden, Lubeck, and Ratzeburg, this lack of success is represented
as resulting from a mistaken belief on the part of the crusaders that
they were not getting the same indulgences as those granted for the
Holy Land. The bishops are therefore ordered to preach a new

crusade in which there shall be no error as to the pardons to be earned, unless meanwhile the Stedingers shall submit to the archbishop and abandon their heresies. Already, however, another band of crusaders had been organized, which, towards the end of June 1233, penetrated eastern Steding, on the right bank of the Weser. This district had hitherto kept aloof from the strife, and was defenseless. The crusaders devastated the land with fire and sword, slaying without distinction of age or sex, and manifesting their religious zeal by burning all the men who were captured. The crusade came to an inglorious end, however, for, encouraged by its easy success, Count Burchard of Oldenburg, its leader, was emboldened to attack the fortified lands on the west bank, when he and some 200 crusaders were slain and the rest were glad to escape with their lives.

The success of the Stedingers in battling for the maintenance of their independence was awakening an uneasy feeling among the populations, and the feudal nobles were no less interested than the prelates in subduing what might prove to be the nucleus of a dangerous and far-reaching revolt. The third crusade was therefore preached with additional energy over a wider circle than before, and preparations were made for an expedition in 1234 on a scale to crush all resistance. Dominicans spread like a cloud over Holland, Flanders, Brabant, Westphalia, and the Rhinelands, summoning the faithful to defend religion. In Friesland they had little success, for the population sympathized with their kindred and were rather disposed to maltreat the preachers, but elewhere their labors were abundantly rewarded. The heaviest contingent came from the west, under Hendrik, Duke of Brabant, consisting, it is said, of 40,000 men led by the *preux chevalier*, Florent, Count of Holland, together with Thierry, Count of Cleves, Arnoul of Oudenarde, Rasso of Gavres, Thierry of Dixmunde, Gilbert of Zotteghem, and other nobles, eager to earn salvation and preserve their feudal rights. Three hundred ships from Holland gave assurance that the maritime part of the expedition should not be lacking. Gregory at the last moment seems to have felt some misgiving, and in March 1234 sent to Bishop Guglielmo, his legate in North Germany, orders to endeavor by peaceful means to bring about the reconciliation of the peasants, but the effort came too late. In April the hosts were already assembling, and the legate did, and probably could do, nothing to avert the final blow. Overwhelming as was the force of the crusaders, the handful of peasants met it with their wonted resolution. At Altenesch, on May 27, they made their stand and resisted with stubborn valor the onslaught of Hendrik of Brabant and Florent of Holland; but, in the vast disparity of numbers, Thierry of Cleves was able to make a flank attack with fresh troops which broke their ranks, and they were slaughtered unsparingly. Six thousand were left dead upon the field, besides those drowned in the Weser in the vain attempt at flight, and we are asked to believe that the divine favor was manifested in that only 7 of the crusaders perished. The land now lay defenseless before the soldiers of the Lord, who improved their victory by laying it waste with fire and sword. Six centuries later, on May 27, 1834, a monument was solemnly dedicated on the field of Altenesch to the heroes who fell in desperate defense of their land and liberty.

Bald as was the pretense for this frightful tragedy, the Church assumed all the responsibility and kept up the transparent fiction to the last. When the slaughter and devastation were over, came the solemn farce of reconciling the heretics. As the land had been so long under their control, their dead were buried indistinguishably with the remains of the orthodox, so, November 28, 1234, Gregory graciously announced that the necessity of exhumation would be waived in view of the impossibility of separating the one from the other, but that all cemeteries must be consecrated anew to overcome the pollution of the heretic bodies within them. Considerable time must have been consumed in the settlement of all details, for it is not until August 1236 that Gregory writes to the archbishop that, as the Stedingers have abandoned their rebellion and humbly supplicated for reconciliation, he is authorized to reconcile them on receiving proper security that they will be obedient for the future and make proper amends for the past. In this closing act of the bloody drama it is noteworthy that there is no allusion to any of the specific heresies which had been alleged as a reason for the extermination of the heretics.

It is not to be supposed that Gregory neglected to employ in his own interest the moral and material forces which he had thus put at the disposal of Gerhardt of Bremen. In 1241 he formally declared the cause of the Church to be more important than that of Palestine, when, being in want of funds to carry on his contest with Frederic II, he ordered that crusaders be induced to commute their vows for money while still receiving full indulgences, or else be persuaded to turn their arms against Frederic in the crusade which he had caused to be preached against him. Innocent IV pursued the same policy when he had set up a rival emperor in the person of William of Holland, and a crusade was preached in 1248 for a special expedition to Aix-la-Chapelle, of which the capture was necessary for his coronation, and vows for Palestine were redeemed that the money should be handed over to him. After Frederic's death his son Conrad IV was the object of similar measures, and all who bore arms in his favor against William of Holland were the subject of papal anathemas. The disastrous expedition to Aragon which cost Philippe le Hardi his life in 1284 was a crusade preached by order of Martin IV to aid Charles of Anjou, and to punish Pedro III for his conquest of Sicily after the Sicilian Vespers.

With the development of the laws against heresy and the organization of special tribunals for their application, it was soon perceived that an accusation of heresy was a peculiarly efficient method of attacking a political enemy. No charge was easier to bring, none so difficult to disprove—in fact, from what we have seen of the procedure of the Inquisition, there was none in which acquittal was so absolutely impossible where the tribunal was desirous of condemnation. When employed politically the accused had the naked alternative of submission or of armed resistance. Besides, an immense advantage was gained over a political enemy by merely citing him to appear, when he was obliged either to submit himself in advance to any terms that might be dictated to him, or, by refusing to appear, expose himself to condemnation for contumacy with its tremendous temporal consequences.

It mattered little on what grounds a charge of heresy was based. With the organization of the Hildebrandine theocracy the heretical character of simple disobedience came to be distinctly formulated. Thomas Aquinas did not shrink from proving that resistance to the authority of the Roman Church was heretical. By embodying in the canon law the bull *Unam Sanctam* the Church accepted the definition of Boniface VIII that whoever resists the power lodged by God in the Church resists God, unless, like a Manichæan, he believes in two principles, which shows him to be a heretic. "We say, declare, define, and pronounce that it is necessary to salvation that every human creature be subjected to the Roman pontiff." Inquisitors, therefore, were fully justified in laying it down as an accepted principle of law that disobedience to any command of the Holy See was heresy. As a corollary to this was the declaration that inquisitors had power to levy war against heretics and to give it the character of a crusade by granting all the indulgences offered for the succor of the Holy Land. Armed with such powers, it would be difficult to exaggerate the importance of the Inquisition as a political instrument.

The manner in which the Inquisition was used as an instrument by the contending factions in the Church is fairly illustrated by the adventures of John Malkaw, of Prussian Strassburg (Brodnitz). He was a secular priest and master of theology, deeply learned, skillful in debate, and unflinching even to rashness. Espousing the cause of the Roman popes against their Avignonese rivals with all the enthusiasm of his fiery nature, he came to the Rhinelands in 1390, where his sermons proved an effective agency in the strife. After some severe experiences in Mainz at the hands of the opposite faction, he undertook a pilgrimage to Rome, but tarried at Strassburg, where he found a congenial field. The city had adhered to Urban VI and his successors, but the bishop, Frederic of Blankenheim, had alienated a portion of his clergy by his oppressions. In the quarrel he excommunicated them; they appealed to Rome and had the excommunication set aside, whereupon he went over, with his following, to Clement VII, the Avignonese antipope, giving rise to inextricable confusion. The situation was exactly suited to Malkaw's temperament; he threw himself into the turmoil, and his fiery eloquence soon threatened to deprive the antipapalists of their preponderance. According to his own statement he quickly won over some 16,000 schismatics and neutrals, and the nature of his appeals to the passions of the hour may be guessed by his report of a sermon in which he denounced Clement VII as less than a man, as worse than the devil, whose portion was with Antichrist, while his followers were all condemned schismatics and heretics; neutrals, moreover, were the worst of men and were deprived of all sacraments. Besides this he assailed with the same unsparing vehemence the deplorable morals of the Strassburg clergy, and in a few weeks he thus excited the bitterest hostility. A plot was made to denounce him secretly in Rome as a heretic, so that on his arrival there he might be seized by the Inquisition and burned; his wonderful learning, it was said, could only have been acquired by necromancy; he was accused of being a runaway priest, and it was proposed to arrest him as such, but the people regarded him as an inspired prophet, and the project was abandoned. After four weeks of this stormy agitation he resumed his pilgrimage, stopping at Basle and Zurich for missionary work, and finally reached Rome in safety. On his return, in crossing the Pass of St. Bernard, he had the misfortune to lose his papers. News of this reached Basle, and on his arrival there the Mendicants, to whom he was peculiarly obnoxious, demanded of Bishop Imer that he should be arrested as a wanderer without license. The bishop, though belonging to the Roman obedience, yielded, but shortly dismissed him with a friendly caution to return to his home. His dauntless combativeness, however, carried him back to Strassburg, where he again began to preach under the protection of the burgomaster, John Bock. On his previous visit he had been personally threatened by the Dominican Inquisitor Böckeler, and it was now determined to act with vigor. He had preached but three sermons when he was suddenly arrested by the familiars of the inquisitor and thrown in prison, whence he was carried in chains to the episcopal castle of Benfeld and deprived of his books and paper and ink. On March 31, 1391, Böckeler summoned an assembly, consisting principally of Mendicants, where Malkaw was found guilty of a series of charges. His real offense was his attacks on the schismatics and on the corruption of the clergy, but nothing of this appears in the articles. It was assumed that he had left his diocese without the consent of his bishop, and this proved him to be a Lollard; that he discharged priestly functions without a license, showing him to be a Vaudois; because his admirers ate what he had already bitten, he was declared to belong to the Brethren of the Free Spirit; because he forbade discussion whether Christ was alive when pierced with the lance, he was asserted to have taught that doctrine and to be a follower of Jean Pierre Olivi. All this was surely enough to warrant his burning if he should refuse to recant, but apparently it was felt that the magistracy would decline to execute the sentence, and the assembly contented itself with referring the matter to the bishop and asking his banishment from the diocese. Nothing further is known of the trial, but as in 1392 Malkaw is found matriculating himself in the University of Cologne, the bishop probably did as he was asked.

We lose sight of Malkaw until about 1414, when we meet him again in Cologne. He had maintained his loyalty to the Roman obedience, but that obedience had been still further fractioned between Gregory XII and the Pisan antipope John XXIII. Malkaw's support of the former was accompanied with the same unsparing denunciation of John as he had formerly bestowed on the Avignonese antipopes. He was soon recognized as a man whose eloquence was highly dangerous amid an excitable population, and again the Inquisition took hold of him as a heretic. The Inquisitor Jacob of Soest, a Dominican and professor in the University, seems to have treated him with exceptional leniency, for while the investigation was on foot he was allowed to remain in the St. Ursula quarter, on parole. He broke his word and betook himself to Bacharach, where, under the protection of the Archbishop of Trèves and of the Palsgrave Louis III, both Gregorians, he maintained the fight with his customary vehemence, assailing the inquisitor and the Johannites, not only in sermons, but in an incessant stream of pamphlets which kept them in a state of indignant alarm. When Cardinal John of Ragusa, Gregory's legate to the Council of Constance, came to Germany, Malkaw had no difficulty in procuring from him absolution from the inquisitorial excommunication and acquittal of the charge of heresy; and this was confirmed when on healing the Schism the council, in July 1415, declared null and void all prosecutions and sentences arising from it. Still, the wounded pride of the inquisitor and of the University of Cologne refused to be placated, and for a year they continued to seek from the council the condemnation of their enemy. Their deputies, however, warned them that the prosecution would be prolonged, difficult, and costly, and they finally came to the resolution that the action of the Cardinal of Ragusa should be regarded as binding, so long as Malkaw kept away from the territory of Cologne, but should be disregarded if he ventured to return —a very sensible, if somewhat illogical conclusion.

When the Schism was past the Inquisition could still be utilized to quell insubordination. Thomas Connecte, a Carmelite of Britanny, seems to have been a character somewhat akin to John Malkaw. In 1428 we hear of him in Flanders, Artois, Picardy, and the neighboring provinces, preaching to crowds of some 20,000 souls, denouncing the prevalent vices of the time. The *hennins*, or tall head-dresses worn by women of rank, were the object of special vituperation, and he used to give boys certain days of pardon for following ladies thus attired, and crying *"au hennin,"* or even slyly pulling them off. Moved by the eloquence of his sermons, great piles would be made of dice, tables, chessboards, cards, head-dresses, and other matters of vice and luxury, which were duly burned. The chief source, however, of the immense popular favor which he enjoyed was his bitter lashing of the corruption of all ranks of the clergy, particularly their public concubinage. He seems to have reached the conclusion that the only cure for this universal sin was the restoration of clerical marriage. In 1432 he went to Rome in the train of the Venetian ambassadors, to declaim against the vices of the curia. Usually there was a good-natured indifference to these attacks—a toleration born of contempt—but the moment was unpropitious. At that time Eugenius IV was engaged in a losing struggle with the Council of Basle, which was bent on reforming the curia, and Sigismund's envoys were representing to him, with more strength than courtliness, the disastrous results to be expected from his efforts to prorogue the council. Connecte might well be suspected of being an emissary of the fathers of Basle, or, if not, his eloquence at least was a dangerous element in the perturbed state of public opinion. Twice Eugenius sent for him, but he refused to come, pretending to be sick; then the papal treasurer was sent to fetch him, but on his appearing Thomas jumped out of the window and attempted to escape. He was promptly secured and carried before Eugenius, who commissioned the Cardinals of Rouen and Navarre to examine him. These found him suspect of heresy; he was duly tried and condemned as a heretic, and his inconsiderate zeal found a lasting quietus at the stake.

There are certain points of resemblance between Thomas Connecte and Girolamo Savonarola, but the Italian was a man of far rarer intellectual and spiritual gifts than the Breton. With equal moral earnestness, his plans and aspirations were wider and of more dangerous import, and they led him into a sphere of political activity in which his fate was inevitable from the beginning.

In Italy the revival of letters, while elevating the intellectual faculties, had been accompanied with deeper degradation in both the moral and spiritual condition of society. Without removing superstition, it had rendered skepticism fashionable, and it had weakened the sanctions of religion without supplying another basis for morality. Increase of culture and wealth seemed only to afford new attractions and enlarged opportunities for luxury and vice, and from the highest to the lowest there was indulgence of unbridled appetites. To the earnest believer it might well seem that God's wrath could not much longer be restrained. For centuries a succession of prophets—Joachim of Flora, St. Catharine of Siena, St. Birgitta of Sweden, the Friends of God, Tommasino of Foligno, the Monk Telesforo—had arisen with predictions which had been received with reverence, and as time passed on and human wickedness increased, some new messenger of God seemed necessary to recall his erring children to a sense of the retribution in store for them if they should continue deaf to his voice.

That Savonarola honestly believed himself called to such a mission, no one who has impartially studied his strange career can well doubt. His profound conviction that God must interfere to work a change which was beyond human power, his marvellous success in moving his hearers, his frequent ecstasies with their resultant visions might well, in a mind like his, produce such a belief, which, moreover, was one taught by the received traditions of the Church as within the possibilities of the experience of any man.

When, in his thirtieth year, Savonarola came to Florence, in 1481, his soul was already full of his mission as a reformer. Such opportunity as he had of expressing his convictions from the pulpit he used with zeal, but he produced little effect upon a community sunk in debauchery, and in the Lent of 1486 he was sent to Lombardy. For three years he preached in the Lombard cities, gradually acquiring the power of touching the hearts and consciences of men, and when he was recalled to Florence in 1489, at the instance of Lorenzo de' Medici, he was already known as a preacher of rare ability. The effect of his vigorous eloquence was enhanced by his austere and blameless life, and within a year he was made Prior of

San Marco—the convent of the Observantine Dominicans, to which Order he belonged. In 1494 he succeeded in re-establishing the ancient separation of the Dominican province of Tuscany from that of Lombardy, and when he was appointed vicar-general of the former he was rendered independent of all authority save that of the General Giovacchino Torriani, who was well affected towards him.

He claimed to act under the direct inspiration of God, who dictated his words and actions and revealed to him the secrets of the future. Whenever he preached, from 12,000 to 15,000 persons hung upon his lips, and in the great Duomo of Santa Maria del Fiore it was necessary to build scaffolds and benches to accommodate the thronging crowds, multitudes of whom would have cast themselves into fire at a word from him. He paid special attention to children, and we are told they could not be kept in bed on the mornings when he preached, but would hurry to the church in advance of their parents. The boys of Frà Girolamo were regularly organized, with officers who had their several spheres of duty assigned to them, and they became a terror to evil-doers. They entered the taverns and gambling houses and put a stop to revelry and dicing and card playing, and no woman dared to appear upon the streets save in fitting attire and with a modest mien. "Here are the boys of the *Frate*" was a cry which inspired fear in the most reckless, for any resistance to them was at the risk of life. Even the annual horse-races of Santo-Barnabo were suppressed, and it was a sign of Girolamo's waning influence when, in 1497, the Signoria ordered them resumed, saying, "Are we all to become monks?"

In one respect we may regret his puritanism and the zeal of his boys. For the profane mummeries of the carnival in 1498 he substituted a bonfire of objects which he deemed immodest or improper, and the voluntary contributions for this purpose were supplemented by the energy of the boys, who entered houses and palaces and carried off whatever they deemed fit for the holocaust. Precious illuminated MSS., ancient sculptures, rare tapestries, and priceless works of art thus were mingled with the gewgaws and vanities of female attire, the musical instruments, the books of divination, astrology, and magic, which went to make up the total. We can understand the sacrifice of copies of Boccaccio, but Petrarch might have escaped even Savonarola's severity of virtue. In this ruthless *auto de fé,* the value of the objects was such that a Venetian merchant offered the Signoria 20,000 scudi for them, which was answered by taking the would-be chapman's portrait and placing it on top of the pyre. We cannot wonder that the pile had to be surrounded the night before by armed guards to prevent the *tiepidi* from robbing it.

It was Savonarola's misfortune that in a republic such as Florence the temptation to take part in politics was irresistible. We cannot wonder that he eagerly embraced what seemed to be an opportunity of regenerating a powerful state, through which he might not unreasonably hope to influence all Italy, and thus effect a reform in Church and State which would renovate Christendom. Misled by these dazzling daydreams, he had no scruple in making a practical use of the almost boundless influence which he had acquired over the populace of Florence. His teachings led to the revolution which in 1494 expelled the Medici, and he humanely averted the pitiless bloodshed which commonly accompanied such movements in the Italian cities. During the Neapolitan expedition of Charles VIII in 1494, he did much to cement the alliance of the republic with that monarch, whom he regarded as the instrument destined by God to bring about the reform of Italy. In the reconstruction of the republic in the same year he had perhaps more to do than anyone else, both in framing its structure and dictating its laws; and when he induced the people to proclaim Jesus Christ as the King of Florence, he perhaps himself hardly recognized how, as the mouthpiece of God, he was inevitably assuming the position of a dictator. It was not only in the pulpit that he instructed his auditors as to their duties as citizens and gave vent to his inspiration, for the leaders of the popular party were constantly in the habit of seeking his advice and obeying his wishes. Yet, personally, for the most part, he held himself in austere retirement, and left the management of details to two confidential agents selected among the friars of San Marco—Domenico da Pescia, who was somewhat hotheaded and impulsive, and Salvestro Maruffi, who was a dreamer and somnambulist. In thus descending from the position of a prophet of God to that of the head of a faction, popularly known by the contemptuous name of *Piagnoni* or Mourners, he staked his all upon the continued supremacy of that faction, and any failure in his political schemes necessarily was fatal to the larger and nobler plans of which they were the unstable foundation. In addition to this, his resolute adherence to the alliance with Charles VIII finally made his removal necessary to the success of the policy of Alexander VI to unite all the Italian states against the dangers of another French invasion.

As though to render failure certain, under a rule dating from the thirteenth century, the Signoria was changed every two months, and thus reflected every passing gust of popular passion. When the critical time came everything turned against him. The alliance with France, on which he had staked his credit both as a statesman and a prophet, resulted disastrously. Charles VIII was glad at Fornovo to cut his way back to France with shattered forces, and he never returned, in spite of the threats of God's wrath which Savonarola repeatedly transmitted to him. He not only left Florence isolated to face the league of Spain, the papacy, Venice, and Milan, but he disappointed the dearest wish of the Florentines by violating his pledge to restore to them the stronghold of Pisa. When the news of this reached Florence, January 1, 1496, the incensed populace held Savonarola responsible, and a crowd around San Marco at night amused itself with loud threats to burn "the great hog of a *Frate*." Besides this was the severe distress occasioned by the shrinking of trade and commerce in the civic disturbances, by the large subsidies paid to Charles VIII, and by the drain of the Pisan war, leading to insupportable taxation and the destruction of public credit, to all which was added the fearful famine of 1497, followed by pestilence; such a succession of misfortunes naturally made the unthinking masses dissatisfied and ready for a change. The *Arrabbiati*, or faction in opposition, were not slow to take advantage of this revulsion of feeling, and they were supported by the dangerous classes and by all those on whom the puritan reform had pressed heavily. An association was formed, known as the *Compagnacci*, composed of reckless and dissolute young nobles and their retainers, with Doffo Spini at their head and the powerful house of Altoviti behind them, whose primary object was Savonarola's destruction, and who were ready to resort to desperate measures at the first opportunity.

Had Savonarola contented himself with simply denouncing the corruptions of the Church and the curia he would have been allowed to exhale his indignation in safety, but he had made himself a political personage of importance whose influence at Florence was hostile to the policy of the Borgias. Still, Alexander VI treated him with good-natured indifference, which for a while almost savored of contempt. When at last his importance was recognized, an attempt was made to bribe him with the archbishopric of Florence and the cardinalate, but the offer was spurned with prophetic indignation—"I want no hat but that of martyrdom, reddened with my own blood!" It was not till July 21, 1495, after Charles VIII had abandoned Italy and left the Florentines to face single-handed the league of which the papacy was the head, that any antagonism was manifested towards him, and then it assumed the form of a friendly summons to Rome to give an account of the revelations and prophecies which he had from God. To this he replied, July 31, excusing himself on the ground of severe fever and dysentery; the republic, moreover, would not permit him to leave its territories for fear of his enemies, as his life had already been attempted by both poison and steel, and he never quitted his convent without a guard; besides, the unfinished reforms in the city required his presence. As soon as possible, however, he would come to Rome, and meanwhile the pope would find what he wanted in a book now printing, containing his prophecies on the renovation of the Church and the destruction of Italy, a copy of which would be submitted to the holy father as soon as ready.

However lightly Savonarola might treat this missive, it was a warning not to be disregarded, and for a while he ceased preaching. Suddenly, on September 8, Alexander returned to the charge with a bull entrusted to the rival Franciscans of Santa Croce, in which he ordered the reunion of the Tuscan congregation with the Lombard province; Savonarola's case was submitted to the Lombard Vicar-General Sebastiano de Madiis; Domenico da Pescia and Salvestro Maruffi were required within eight days to betake themselves to Bologna, and Savonarola was commanded to cease preaching until he should present himself in Rome. To this Savonarola replied September 29, in a labored justification, objecting to Sebastiano as a prejudiced judge, and winding up with a request that the pope should point out any errors in his teaching, which he would at once revoke and submit whatever he had spoken or written to the judgment of the Holy See. Almost immediately after this the enterprise of Piero de' Medici against Florence rendered it impossible for him to keep silent, and, without awaiting the papal answer, on October 11 he ascended the pulpit and vehemently exhorted the people to unite in resisting the tyrant. In spite of this insubordination Alexander was satisfied with Savonarola's nominal submission, and on October 16 replied, merely ordering him to preach no more until he could conveniently come to Rome, or a fitting person be sent to Florence to decide his case; if he obeyed, then all the papal briefs were suspended. To Alexander the whole affair was simply one of politics. The position of Florence under Savonarola's influence was hostile to his designs, but he did not care to push the matter further, provided he could diminish the *Frate's* power by silencing him.

Savonarola's voice, however, was too potent a factor in Florentine affairs for his friends in power to consent to his silence. Long and earnest efforts were made to obtain permission from the pope for him to resume his exhortations during the coming Lent, and at length the request was granted. The sermons on Amos which he then delivered were not of a character to placate the curia, for, besides lashing its vices with terrible earnestness, he took pains to indicate that there were limits to the obedience which he would render to the papal commands. These sermons produced an immense sensation, not only in Florence, but throughout Italy, and on Easter Sunday, April 3, 1496, Alexander assembled fourteen Dominican masters of theology, to whom he denounced their audacious comrade as heretical, schismatic, disobedient, and superstitious. It was admitted that he was responsible for the misfortunes of Piero de' Medici, and it was resolved, with but one dissentient voice, that means must be found to silence him.

Notwithstanding this, Savonarola continued, without interference, to preach at intervals until November 2. Even then it is a significant tribute to his power that Alexander again had recourse to indirect means to suppress him. On November 7, 1496, a papal brief was issued creating a congregation of Rome and Tuscany and placing it under a vicar-general who was to serve for two years, and be ineligible to reappointment except after an interval. Although the first vicar-general was Giacomo di Sicilia, a friend of Savonarola, the measure was ingeniously framed to deprive him of independence, and he might at any moment be transferred from Florence to another post. To this Savonarola replied with open defiance. In a printed *Apologia della Congregazione di San Marco*, he declared that the 250 friars of his convent would resist to the death, in spite of threats and excommunication, a measure which would result in the perdition of their souls. This was a declaration of open war, and on November 26 he boldly resumed preaching. The series of sermons on Ezekiel, which he then commenced and continued through the Lent of 1497, shows clearly that he had abandoned all hope of reconciliation with the pope. The Church was an abominable monster which must be purified and renovated by the servants of God, and in this work excommunication was to be welcomed. To a great extent, moreover, these sermons were political speeches, and indicate how absolutely Savonarola from the pulpit dictated the municipal affairs of Florence. The city had been reduced almost to despair in the unequal contest with Pisa, Milan, Venice, and the papacy, but the close of the year 1496 had brought some unexpected successes which seemed to justify Savonarola's exhortations to trust in God, and with the reviving hopes of the republic his credit was to some extent restored.

Still Alexander, though his wrath was daily growing, shrank from an open rupture and trial of strength, and an effort was made to utilize against Savonarola the traditional antagonism of the Franciscans. The Observantine convent of San Miniato was made the center of operations, and thither were sent the most renowned preachers of the Order—Domenico da Poza, Michele d' Aquis, Giovanni Tedesco, Giacopo da Brescia, and Francesco della Puglia. It is true that when, January 1, 1497, the *Piagnoni*, strengthened by recent successes in the field, elected Francesco Valori as Gonfaloniero di Giustizia, he endeavored to stop the Franciscans from preaching, prohibited them from begging bread and wine and necessaries, and boasted that he would starve them out, and one of them was absolutely banished from the city, but the others persevered, and Savonarola was freely denounced as an imposter from the pulpit of Santo-Spirito during Lent. Yet this had no effect upon his followers, and his audiences were larger and more enthusiastic than ever.

The famine was now at its height, and pestilence became threatening. The latter gave the Signoria, which was now composed of *Arrabbiati*, an excuse for putting a stop to this pulpit warfare, which doubtless menaced the peace of the city, and on May 3 all preaching after Ascension Day (May 4) was forbidden for the reason that, with the approach of summer, crowds would facilitate the dissemination of the plague. That passions were rising beyond control was shown when, the next day, Savonarola preached his farewell sermon in the Duomo. The doors had been broken open in advance, and the pulpit was smeared with filth. The *Compagnacci* had almost openly made preparations to kill him; they gathered there in force, and interrupted the discourse with a tumult, during which the *Frate's* friends gathered around him with drawn swords and conveyed him away in safety.

The affair made an immense sensation throughout Italy, and the sympathies of the Signoria were shown by the absence of any attempt to punish the rioters. Encouraged by this evidence of the weakness of the *Piagnoni*, on May 13 Alexander sent to the Franciscans a bull ordering them to publish Savonarola as excommunicate and suspect of heresy, and that no one should hold converse with him. This, owing to the fears of the papal commissioner charged with it, was not published till June 18. Before the existence of the bull was known, on May 22, Savonarola had written to Alexander an explanatory letter, in which he offered to submit himself to the judgment of the Church; but two days after the excommunication was published he replied to it with a defense in which he endeavored to prove that the sentence was invalid, and on June 25 he had the audacity to address to Alexander a letter of condolence on the murder of his son, the Duke of Gandia. Fortunately for him another revulsion in municipal politics restored his friends to power on July 1, the elections till the end of the year continued favorable, and he did not cease to receive and administer the sacraments, though, under the previous orders of the Signoria, there was no preaching. How little the *Piagnoni* recked of the excommunication is seen by a petition presented September 17 to the Signoria, by the children of Florence, asking that their beloved *Frate* be allowed to resume preaching, and by a sermon delivered in his defense, October 1, by a Carmelite who declared that in a vision God had

told him that Savonarola was a holy man, and that all his opponents
would have their tongues torn out and be cast to the dogs. This
was flat rebellion against the Holy See, but the only punishment inflicted on the Carmelite by the episcopal officials was a prohibition
of further preaching. Meanwhile the Signoria had made vain attempts to have the excommunication removed, and Savonarola had
indignantly refused an offer of the Cardinal of Siena (afterwards
Pius III) to have it withdrawn on the payment of 5,000 scudi to a
creditor of his. Yet, in spite of this disregard of the papal censures,
Savonarola considered himself still an obedient son of the Church.
He employed the enforced leisure of this summer in writing the
Trionfo della Croce, in which he proved that the papacy is supreme,
and that whoever separates himself from the unity and doctrine of
Rome separates himself from Christ.

January 1498 saw the introduction of a Signoria composed of his
zealous partisans, who were not content that a voice so potent
should be hushed. It was an ancient custom that they should go
in a body and make oblations at the Duomo on Epiphany, which
was the anniversary of the Church, and on that day citizens of all
parties were astounded at seeing the still excommunicated Savonarola
as the celebrant, and the officials humbly kiss his hand. Not content
with this act of rebellion, it was arranged that he should recommence
preaching. A new Signoria was to be elected for March, the people
were becoming divided in their allegiance to him, and his eloquence
was held to be indispensable for his own safety and for the continuance in power of the *Piagnoni.* Accordingly, on February 11 he
again appeared in the Duomo, where the old benches and scaffolds
had been replaced to accommodate the crowd. Yet many of the more
timid *Piagnoni* abstained from listening to an excommunicate:
whether just or unjust, they argued, the sentence of the Church
was to be feared.

In the sermons on Exodus preached during this Lent—the last
which he had the opportunity of uttering—Savonarola was more
violent than ever. His position was such that he could only justify
himself by proving that the papal anathema was worthless, and this
he did in terms which excited the liveliest indignation in Rome. A
brief was dispatched to the Signoria, February 26, commanding them,
under pain of interdict, to send Savonarola as a prisoner to Rome.

This received no attention, but at the same time another letter was sent to the canons of the Duomo ordering them to close their church to him, and March 1 he appeared there to say that he would preach at San Marco, whither the crowded audience followed him. His fate, however, was sealed the same day by the advent to power of a government composed of a majority of *Arrabbiati*, with one of his bitterest enemies, Pier Popoleschi, at its head as Gonfaloniero di Giustizia.

The first act of the new Signoria was an appeal to the pope, March 4, excusing themselves for not obeying his orders and asking for clemency towards Savonarola, whose labors had been so fruitful, and whom the people of Florence believed to be more than man. Alexander's reply shows that he recognized fully the advantage of the situation. Savonarola is "that miserable worm" who in a sermon recently printed had adjured God to deliver him to hell if he should apply for absolution. The pope will waste no more time in letters; he wants no more words from them, but acts. They must either send their monstrous idol to Rome, or segregate him from all human society, if they wish to escape the interdict which will last until they submit. Yet Savonarola is not to be perpetually silenced, but, after due humiliation, his mouth shall be again opened.

This reached Florence March 13 and excited a violent discussion. We have seen that an interdict inflicted by the pope might be not merely a deprivation of spiritual privileges, but might comprehend segregation from the outside world and seizure of person and property wherever found, which was ruin to a commercial community. The merchants and bankers of Florence received from their Roman correspondents the most alarming accounts of the papal wrath and of the intention to expose their property to pillage. Fear took possession of the city, as rumors spread from day to day that the dreaded interdict had been proclaimed. It shows the immense influence still wielded by Savonarola that the Signoria could only bring itself, March 17, to send to him five citizens at night to beg him to suspend preaching for the time. He had promised that, while he would not obey the pope, he would respect the wishes of the civil power, but when this request reached him he replied that he must first seek the will of Him who had ordered him to preach. The next day, from the pulpit of San Marco, he gave his answer—"Listen, for this is what the Lord saith: In asking this *Frate* to give up preaching it is to Me that the request is made, and not to him, for it is I who preach; it is I who grant the request and who do not grant it. The Lord assents as regards the preaching, but not as regards your salvation."

It was impossible to yield more awkardly or in a manner more convincing of self-deception, and Savonarola's enemies grew correspondingly bold. The Franciscans thundered triumphantly from the pulpits at their command; the disorderly elements, wearied with the rule of righteousness, commenced to agitate for the license which they could see was soon to be theirs. Profane scoffers commenced to ridicule the *Frate* openly in the streets, and within a week placards were posted on the walls urging the burning of the palaces of Francesco Valori and Paolo Antonio Soderini, two of his leading supporters.

Just at this juncture there came to light a desperate expedient to which Savonarola had recourse. After giving Alexander fair warning, March 13, to look to his safety, for there could no longer be truce between them, Savonarola appealed to the sovereigns of Christendom, in letters purporting to be written under the direct command of God, calling upon the monarchs to convoke a general council for the reformation of the Church. Alexander VI was not pope and was not eligible to the papacy, not only by reason of the simony through which he had bought the tiara, and the wickedness which, when exposed, would excite universal execration, but also because he was not a Christian, and not even a believer in God. All this Savonarola offered to prove by evidence and by miracles which God would execute to convince the most skeptical. This portentous epistle, with trifling variants, was to be addressed to the Kings of France, Spain, England, and Hungary, and to the emperor. A preliminary missive from Domenico Mazzinghi to Giovanni Guasconi, Florentine Ambassador in France, happened to be intercepted by the Duke of Milan, who was hostile to Savonarola, and who promptly forwarded it to the pope.

Alexander's wrath can easily be conceived. It was not so much the personal accusations, which he was ready to dismiss with cynical indifference, as the effort to bring about the convocation of a council which, since those of Constance and Basle, had ever been the cry of the reformer and the terror of the papacy. Wild as was Savonarola's notion that he could, single-handed, stimulate the princes to such action, it was nevertheless a dart aimed at the mortal spot of the papacy, and the combat thereafter was one in which no quarter could be given.

The end came sooner and more dramatically than the shrewdest observer could have anticipated. It is impossible, amid the conflicting statements of friends and foes, to determine with positiveness the successive steps leading to the strange *Sperimento del Fuoco,* which was the proximate occasion of the catastrophe, but it probably occurred in this wise: Frà Girolamo being silenced, Domenico da Pescia took his place and offered to prove the truth of his master's cause by throwing himself from the roof of the Palazzo de' Signori, by casting himself into the river, or by entering fire. Probably this was only a rhetorical flourish, but the Franciscan Francesco della Puglia, who was preaching with much effect at the church of Santa-Croce, took it up and offered to share the ordeal with Frà Girolamo. The latter, however, refused to undertake it unless a papal legate and ambassadors from all Christian princes could be present, so that it might be made the commencement of a general reform in the Church. Frà Domenico then accepted the challenge, and on March 27 or 28 he caused to be affixed to the portal of Santa-Croce a paper in which he offered to prove, by argument or miracle, these propositions:

(ɪ) The Church of God requires renovation;
(ɪɪ) The Church is to be scourged;
(ɪɪɪ) The Church will be renovated;
(ɪᴠ) After chastisement Florence will be renovated and will prosper;
(ᴠ) The infidel will be converted;
(ᴠɪ) The excommunication of Frà Girolamo is void;
(ᴠɪɪ) There is no sin in not observing the excommunication.

Frà Francesco reasonably enough said that most of these propositions were incapable of argument, but, as a demonstration was desired, he would enter fire with Frà Domenico, although he fully expected to be burned; still, he was willing to make the sacrifice in order to liberate the Florentines from their false idol.

Passions were fierce on both sides, and eager partisans kept the city in an uproar. To prevent an outbreak the Signoria sent for both disputants and caused them to enter into a written agreement, March 30, to undergo this strange trial. Three hundred years earlier it would have seemed reasonable enough, but the Council of Lateran, in 1215, had reprobated ordeals of all kinds, and they had been definitely marked with the ban of the Church. When it came to the point Frà Francesco said that he had no quarrel with Domenico; that if Savonarola would undergo the trial, he was ready to share it, but with anyone else he would only produce a champion—and one was readily found in the person of Frà Giuliano Rondinelli, a noble Florentine of the Order. On the other side, all the friars of San Marco, nearly 300 in number, signed the agreement pledging to submit themselves to the ordeal, and Savonarola declared that in such a cause anyone could do so without risk. So great was the enthusiasm that when, on the day before the trial, he preached on the subject in San Marco, all the audience rose in mass and offered to take Domenico's place in vindicating the truth. The conditions prescribed by the Signoria were that if the Dominican champion perished, whether alone or with his rival, Savonarola should leave the city until officially recalled; if the Franciscan alone succumbed, then Frà Francesco should do likewise; and the same was decreed for either side that should decline the ordeal at the last moment.

The Signoria appointed ten citizens to conduct the trial, and fixed it for April 6, but postponed it for a day in hopes of receiving from the pope a negative answer to an application for permission—a refusal which came, but too late, possibly delayed on purpose. On April 7, accordingly, the preparations were completed. In the Piazza de' Signori a huge pile of dry wood was built the height of a man's eyes, with a central gangway through which the champions were to pass. It was plentifully supplied with gunpowder, oil, sulphur, and spirits, to ensure the rapid spread of the flames, and when lighted at one end the contestants were to enter at the other, which was to be set on fire behind them, so as to cut off all retreat. An immense mass of earnest spectators filled the piazza, and every window and housetop was crowded. These were mostly partisans of Savonarola, and the Franciscans were cowed until cheered by the arrival of the *Compagnacci*, the young nobles fully armed on their war horses, and each accompanied by 8 or 10 retainers— some 500 in all, with Doffo Spini at their head.

First came on the scene the Franciscans, anxious and terrified. Then marched in procession the Dominicans, about 200 in number, chanting psalms. Both parties went before the Signoria, when the Franciscans, professing fear of magic arts, demanded that Domenico should change his garments. Although this was promptly acceded to, and both champions were clothed anew, considerable time was consumed in the details. The Dominicans claimed that Domenico should be allowed to carry a crucifix in his right hand and a consecrated wafer in his left. An objection being made to the crucifix he agreed to abandon it, but was unmoved by the cry of horror with which the proposition as to the host was received. Savonarola was firm. It had been revealed to Frà Salvestro that the sacrament was indispensable, and the matter was hotly disputed until the shades of evening fell, when the Signoria announced that the ordeal was abandoned, and the Franciscans withdrew, followed by the Dominicans. The crowd which had patiently waited through torrents of rain, and a storm in which the air seemed filled with howling demons, were enraged at the loss of the promised spectacle, and a heavy armed escort was necessary to convey the Dominicans in safety back to San Marco. Had the matter been one with which reason had anything to do, we might perhaps wonder that it was regarded as a triumph for the Franciscans; but Savonarola had so confidently promised a miracle, and had been so implicitly believed by his followers, that they accepted the drawn battle as a defeat and as a confession that he could not rely on the interposition of God. Their faith in their prophet was shaken, while the exultant *Compagnacci* lavished abuse on him, and they had not a word to utter in his defense.

His enemies were prompt in following up their advantage. The next day was Palm Sunday. The streets were full of triumphant *Arrabbiati*, and such *Piagnoni* as showed themselves were pursued with jeers and pelted with stones. At vespers, the Dominican Mariano de' Ughi attempted to preach in the Duomo, which was crowded, but the *Compagnacci* were there in force, interrupted the sermon, ordered the audience to disperse, and those who resisted were assailed and wounded. Then arose the cry, "To San Marco!" and the crowd hurried thither. Already the doors of the Dominican church had been surrounded by boys whose cries disturbed the service within, and who, when ordered to be silent, had replied with showers of stones which compelled the entrance to be closed. As the crowd surged around, the worshippers were glad to escape with their lives through the cloisters. Francesco Valori and Paolo Antonio Soderini were there in consultation with Savonarola. Soderini made good his exit from the city; Valori was seized while skirting the walls, and carried in front of his palace, which had already been attacked by the *Compagnacci*. Before his eyes, his wife, who was pleading with the assailants from a window, was slain with a missile, one of his children and a female servant were wounded, and the palace was sacked and burned, after which he was struck from behind and killed. Two other houses of Savonarola's partisans were likewise pillaged and burned.

In the midst of the uproar there came forth successive proclamations from the Signoria ordering Savonarola to quit the Florentine territories within twelve hours, and all laymen to leave the church of San Marco within one hour. The assault on San Marco then became a regular siege. Matters had for some time looked so threatening that during the past fortnight the friars had been secretly providing themselves with arms. These they and their friends used gallantly, even against the express commands of Savonarola, and a melée occurred in which more than a hundred on both sides were killed and wounded. At last the Signoria sent guards to capture Savonarola and his principal aids, Domenico and Salvestro, with a pledge that no harm should be done to them. Resistance ceased; the two former were found in the library, but Salvestro had hidden himself, and was not captured till the next day. The prisoners were ironed hand and foot and carried through the streets, where their guards could not protect them from kicks and buffets by the raging mob.

The next day there was comparative quiet. The *Piagnoni* were thoroughly cowed. To render the triumph permanent, however, it was necessary first to discredit Savonarola with the people and then to dispatch him. No time was lost in preparing to give a judicial appearance to the foregone conclusion. During the day a tribunal of seventeen members selected from among his special enemies, such as Doffo Spini, was nominated, which set promptly to work on April 10, although its formal commission, including power to use torture, was not made out until the 11th. Papal authority to disregard the clerical immunity of the prisoners was applied for, but the proceedings were not delayed by waiting for the answer, which, of course, was favorable, and two papal commissioners were adjoined to the tribunal. Savonarola and his companions, still ironed hand and foot, were carried to the Bargello. The official account states that he was first interrogated kindly, but as he would not confess he was threatened with torture, and this proving ineffectual he was subjected to three and a half *tratti di fune*. This was a customary form of torture, known as the *strappado*, which consisted in tying the prisoner's hands behind his back, then hoisting him by a rope fastened to his wrists, letting him drop from a height and arresting him with a jerk before his feet reached the floor. Officially it is stated that this first application was sufficient to lead him to confess freely, but the general belief at the time was that it was repeated with extreme severity.[1]

Be this as it may, Savonarola entreated to be released from the torture and promised to reveal everything. His examination lasted until April 18, but even in his complying frame of mind the resultant confession required to be manipulated before it could be made public. For this infamous piece of work a fitting instrument was at hand. Ser Ceccone was an old partisan of the Medici, whose life had

---

[1] Violi (Villari, II. App. cxvi.-vii.) says that the torture was repeatedly applied —on one evening no less than fourteen times from the pulley to the floor, and that his arms were so injured that he was unable to feed himself; but this must be exaggerated in view of the pious treatises he wrote while in prison. Burlamacchi says that he was tortured repeatedly both with cord and fire (pp. 566, 568). Burchard, the papal prothonotary, states that he was tortured seven times, and Burchard was likely to know and not likely to exaggerate (Burch. Diar. *ap.* Preuves des Mémoires de Commines, Bruxelles, 1706, p. 424). The expression of Commines, who was well-informed, is *"le gesnèrent à merveilles"* (Mémoires, Lib. VIII. ch. 19). But the most emphatic evidence is that of the Signoria, who, in answer to the reproaches of Alexander at their tardiness, declare that they had to do with a man of great endurance; they had assiduously tortured him for many days with slender results, which they would suppress until they could force him to reveal all his secrets—*"multa et assidua quæstione, multis diebus, per vim vix pauca extorsimus, quæ nunc celare animus erat donec omnia nobis paterent sui animi involucra"* (Villari, II. 197).

been saved by Savonarola's secretly giving him refuge in San
Marco and who now repaid the benefit by sacrificing his benefactor.
As a notary he was familiar with such work, and under his skillful
hands the incoherent answers of Savonarola were moulded into a
narrative which is the most abject of self-accusations and most
compromising to all his friends.

He is made to represent himself as being from the first a conscious impostor, whose sole object was to gain power by deceiving
the people. If this project of convoking a council had resulted in
his being chosen pope he would not have refused the position, but
if not he would at all events have become the foremost man in
the world. For his own purposes he had arrayed the citizens against
each other and caused a rupture between the city and the Holy
See, striving to erect a government on the Venetian model, with
Francesco Valori as perpetual doge. The animus of the trial is
clearly revealed in the scant attention paid to his spiritual aberrations, which were the sole offenses for which he could be convicted,
and the immense detail devoted to his political activity and to his
relations with all obnoxious citizens whom it was desired to involve in his ruin. Had there been any pretence of observing ordinary
judicial forms, the completeness with which he was represented as
abasing himself would have overreached its purpose. In forcing him
to confess that he was no prophet, and that he had always secretly
believed the papal excommunication to be valid, he was relieved
from the charge of persistent heresy, and he could legally be sentenced only to penance; but, as there was no intention of being
restricted to legal rules, the first object was to discredit him with
the people, after which he could be judicially murdered with impunity.

The object was thoroughly attained. On April 19, in the great
hall of the council, the confession was publicly read in the presence of all who might see fit to attend. The effect produced is
described by the honest Luca Landucci, who had been an earnest
and devout, though timid, follower of Frà Girolamo. Deep was his
anguish as he listened to the confession of one "whom we believed
to be a prophet and who now confessed that he was no prophet,
and that what he preached was not revealed to him by God. I was
stupefied and my very soul was filled with grief to see the destruction

of such an edifice, which crumbled because it was founded on a lie. I had expected to see Florence a new Jerusalem, whence should issue the laws and the splendor and the example of the holy life; to see the renovation of the Church, the conversion of the infidel, and the rejoicing of the good. I found the reverse of all this, and I swallowed the dose"—a natural enough metaphor, seeing that Landucci was an apothecary.

Yet even with this the Signoria was not satisfied. On April 21 a new trial was ordered; Savonarola was tortured again, and further avowals of his political action were wrung from him, while a general arrest was made of those who were compromised by his confessions and those of Domenico and Salvestro, creating a terror so widespread that large numbers of his followers fled from the city. On the 27th the prisoners were taken to the Bargello and so tortured that during the whole of the afternoon their shrieks were heard by the passers-by, but nothing was wrung from them to incriminate Savonarola. The officials in power had but a short time for action, as their term of office ended with the month. Their last official act, on the 30th, was the exile of ten of the accused citizens, and the imposition on 23 of various fines, amounting in all to 12,000 florins.

The new government which came in power May 1 at once discharged the imprisoned citizens, but kept Savonarola and his companions. These, as Dominicans, were not justiciable by the civil power, but the Signoria immediately applied to Alexander for authority to condemn and execute them. He refused, and ordered them to be delivered to him for judgment, as he had already done when the news reached him of Savonarola's capture. To this the republic demurred, doubtless for the reason privately alleged to the ambassador, that Savonarola was privy to too many state secrets to be entrusted to the Roman curia; but it suggested that the pope might send commissioners to Florence to conduct the proceedings in his name. To this he assented. In a brief of May 11 the Bishop of Vaison, the suffragan of the Archbishop of Florence, is instructed to degrade the culprits from holy orders, at the requisition of the commissioners who had been empowered to conduct the examination and trial to final sentence. In the selection of these commissioners the Inquisition does not appear. In Tuscany it was Franciscan, and to have given special authority to the existing inquisitor, Frà Francesco da Montalcino, would have been injudicious in view of the part taken by the Franciscans in the downfall of Savonarola. Alexander showed his customary shrewdness in selecting for the miserable work the Dominican General Giovacchino Torriani, who bore the reputation of a kindhearted and humane man. He was but a stalking-horse, however, for the real actor was his associate Francesco Romolino, a clerk of Lerida, whose zeal in the infamous business was rewarded with the cardinalate and archbishopric of Palermo. After all, the matter had been prejudged at Rome, for Romolino openly boasted, "We shall have a fine bonfire, for I bring the sentence with me."

The commissioners reached Florence May 19, and lost no time in accomplishing their object. The only result of the papal intervention was to subject the victims to a surplusage of agony and shame. For form's sake, the papal judges could not accept the proceedings already had, but must inflict on Savonarola a third trial. Brought before Romolino on the 20th, he retracted his confession as extorted by torture, and asserted that he was an envoy of God. Under the inquisitorial formulas this retraction of confession rendered him a relapsed heretic, who could be burned without further ceremony, but his judges wanted to obtain information desired by Alexander, and again the sufferer was repeatedly subjected to the strappado, when he withdrew his retraction. Special inquiries were directed to ascertain whether the Cardinal of Naples had been privy to the design of convoking a general council, and under the stress of reiterated torture Savonarola was brought to admit this on the 21st, but on the 22d he withdrew the assertion, and the whole confession, although manipulated by the skillful hand of Ser Ceccone, was so nearly a repetition of the previous one that it was never given to the public.

From some oversight Domenico da Pescia's name had not been included in the papal commission. He was an individual of no personal importance, but some zealous Florentine warned Romolino that there might be danger in sparing him, when the commissioner carelessly replied "A *frataccio* more or less makes no difference," and his name was added to the sentence. He was an impenitent heretic, for with heroic firmness he had borne the most excruciating torture without retracting his faith in his beloved prophet.

The accused were at least spared the torment of suspense. On the 22d judgment was pronounced. They were condemned as heretics and schismatics, rebels from the Church, and were sentenced to be abandoned to the secular arm. To justify relaxation, it was requisite that the culprit should be a relapsed or a defiant heretic, and Savonarola was not regarded as coming under either category. He had always declared his readiness to retract anything which Rome might define as erroneous. He had confessed all that had been required of him, nor was his retraction when removed from torture treated as a relapse, for he and his companions were admitted to communion before execution, without undergoing the ceremony of abjuration, which shows that they were not considered as heretics, nor cut off from the Church. In fact, as though to complete the irregularity of the whole transaction, Savonarola himself was allowed to act as the celebrant, and to perform the sacred mysteries on the morning of the execution. All this went for nothing, however, when a Borgia was eager for revenge. On the previous evening a great pile had been built in the piazza. The next morning, May 23, the ceremony of degradation from holy orders was performed in public, after which the convicts were handed over to the secular magistrates. Was it hyprocrisy or remorse that led Romolino at this moment to give to his victims, in the name of Alexander, plenary indulgence of their sins, thus restoring them to a state of primal innocence? Irregular as the whole affair had been, it was rendered still more so by the Signoria, which modified the customary penalty to hanging before the burning, and the three martyrs endured their fate in silence.

The utmost care was taken that the bodies should be utterly consumed, after which every fragment of ashes was scrupulously gathered up and thrown into the Arno, in order to prevent the preservation of relics. Yet, at the risk of their lives, some earnest disciples secretly managed to secure a few floating coals, as well as some fragments of garments, which were treasured and venerated even to recent times. Though many of the believers, like honest Landucci, were disillusioned, many were persistent in the faith, and for a long while lived in the daily expectation of Savonarola's advent, like a new Messiah, to work out the renovation of Christianity and the conversion of the infidel. So profound and lasting was the impression made by his terrible fate that for more than two centuries, until 1703, the place of execution was secretly strewed with flowers on the night of the anniversary, May 23.

The papal commissioners reaped a harvest by summoning to Rome the followers of Savonarola, and then speculating on their fears by selling them exemptions. Florence itself was not long in realizing the strength of the reaction against the puritanic methods Savonarola had enforced. The streets again became filled with reckless desperadoes, quarrels and murders were frequent, gambling was unchecked, and license reigned supreme. As Landucci says, it seemed as if hell had broken loose. As though in very wantonness to show the Church what were the allies whom it had sought in the effort to crush unwelcome reform, on the following Christmas Eve a horse was brought into the Duomo and deliberately tortured to death, goats were let loose in San Marco, and in all the churches assafœtida was placed in censers.

Savonarola had built his house upon the sand, and was swept away by the waters. Yet, in spite of his execution as a heretic, the Church has tacitly confessed its own crime by admitting that he was no heretic, but rather a saint, and the most convenient evasion of responsibility was devoutly to refer the whole matter, as Luke Wadding does, to the mysterious judgment of God. Even Torriani and Romolino, after burning him, when they ordered, May 27, under pain of excommunication, all his writings to be delivered up to them for examination, were unable to discover any heretical opinions, and were obliged to return them without erasures. Paul III declared that he would hold as a heretic anyone who should assail the memory of Frà Girolamo; and Paul IV had his works rigorously examined by a special congregation, which declared that they contained no heresy. Fifteen of his sermons, denunciatory of ecclesiastical abuses, and his treatise *De Veritate Prophetica*, were placed upon the index as unfitted for general reading, *donec corrigantur*, but not as heretical. Benedict XIII also examined the case thoroughly, and, dreading a renewal of the old controversy on the justice of Savonarola's sentence, ordered the discussion to cease and the proceedings to continue without reference to it. In S. Maria Novella and S. Marco he is pictured as a saint, and in the frescos of the Vatican Raphael included him among the doctors of the Church.

CHAPTER XXI
POLITICAL HERESY UTILIZED BY THE STATE

IT WAS inevitable that secular potentates should follow the example of the Church in the employment of a weapon so efficient as the charge of heresy, when they chanced to be in the position of controlling the ecclesiastical organization. Early in the fourteenth century the methods of the Inquisition had suggested to Philippe le Bel the great crime of the Middle Ages—the destruction of the Order of the Temple.

When, in 1119, Hugues de Payen and Geoffroi de Saint-Adhémar with seven companions devoted themselves to the pious task of keeping the roads to Jerusalem clear of robbers that pilgrims might traverse them in safety, and when Raymond du Puy about the same time organized the Poor Brethren of the Hospital of St. John, they opened a new career that was irresistibly attractive to the warlike ardor and religious enthusiasm of the age. The combination of monasticism and chivalry corresponded so exactly to the ideal of Christian knighthood that the Military Orders thus founded speedily were reckoned among the leading institutions of Europe. At the Council of Troyes, in 1128, a Rule, drawn up it is said by St. Bernard, was assigned to Hugues and his associates, who were known as the Poor Soldiers of the Temple. They were assigned a white habit, as a symbol of innocence, to which Eugenius III added a red cross, and their standard, *Bauséant*, half black and half white, with its legend, "*Non nobis Domine*," soon became the rallying-point of the Christian chivalry. The Rule, based upon that of the strict Cistercian Order, was exceedingly severe. The members were bound by the three monastic vows of obedience, poverty, and chastity, and these were enforced in the statutes of the Order with the utmost rigor. The applicant for admission was required to ask permission to become the serf and slave of the "House" forever, and was warned that he henceforth surrendered his own will irrevocably. He was promised bread and water and the poor vestments of the House; and if after death gold or silver were found among his effects his body was thrust into unconsecrated ground, or, if buried, it was exhumed. Chastity was prescribed in the same unsparing fashion, and even the kiss of a mother was forbidden.

The fame of the Order quickly filled all Europe; knights of the noblest blood, dukes and princes, renounced the world to serve Christ in its ranks, and soon in its General Chapter 300 knights were gathered, in addition to serving brethren. Towns and villages and churches and manors were bestowed upon them, from which the revenues were sent to the Grand Master, whose official residence was Jerusalem, together with the proceeds of the collections of an organized system of beggary, their agents for which penetrated into every corner of Christendom. Scarce had the Order been organized when, in 1133, Alonso I of Aragon, dying without children, left his whole dominions to the Holy Sepulchre and to the Knights of the Temple and of the Hospital in undivided thirds; and though the will was not executed, the knights were promised and doubtless received compensation from his successor, Ramiro el Monje. More practical was the liberality of Philip Augustus in 1222, when he left the two Orders 2,000 marks apiece absolutely, and the enormous sum of 50,000 marks each on condition of keeping in service for three years 300 knights in the Holy Land. We can understand that this enormous development began to excite apprehension and hostility. In fact, the antagonism which we have already traced in the thirteenth century between the Mendicant Orders and the secular clergy was but the repetition of that which had long existed with respect to the Military Orders. These from the first were the especial favorites of the Holy See, whose policy it was to elevate them into a militia depending solely on Rome, thus rendering them an instrument in extending its influence and breaking down the independence of the local churches. Privileges and immunities were showered upon them; they were exempted from tolls and tithes and taxes of all kinds; their churches and houses were endowed with the right of asylum; their persons enjoyed the inviolability accorded to ecclesiastics; they were released from all feudal obligations and allegiance; bishops were forbidden to excommunicate them, and were even ordered to refer to the Roman curia all the infinite questions which arose in local quarrels. In short, nothing was omitted by the popes that would stimulate their growth and bind them firmly to the chair of St. Peter.

That the antagonism on the part of temporal and spiritual potentates had justification there can be little doubt. Such a body as the Templars, composed of ambitious and warlike knights, could hardly be expected long to retain its pristine ascetic devotion. Already in 1152 the selfish eagerness of the Grand Master, Bernard de Tremelai, to secure the spoils of Ascalon nearly prevented the capture of that city, and the fall of the Kingdom of Jerusalem was hastened when, in 1172, the savage ferocity of Eudes de Saint-Amand, then Grand Master, prevented the conversion of the King of the Assassins and all his people. In 1207 Innocent III took the Order to task in an epistle of violent denunciation. His apostolic ears, he said, were frequently disturbed with complaints of their excesses. Apostatizing from God and scandalizing the Church, their unbridled pride abused the enormous privileges bestowed upon them. Employing doctrines worthy of demons, they give their cross to every tramp who can pay them 2 or 3 pence a year, and then assert that these are entitled to ecclesiastical services, even though laboring under excommunication. A concluding allusion to their lack of respect towards papal legates probably explains the venomous vigor of the papal attack, but the accusations it makes touch points on which there is other conclusive evidence. Although by the statutes of the Order the purchase of admission, directly or indirectly, was simony, there can be no doubt that many doubtful characters thus effected entrance into the Order. The evils thence arising were intensified when the policy was adopted of forming a class of serving brethren, by whom their extensive properties were cultivated and managed without the cost of hired labor. Churls of every degree were admitted into the Order, until they constituted at least nine-tenths of it, and although these were distinguished by a brown mantle in place of the white garment of the knights, and although they complained of the contempt and oppression with which they were treated by their knightly brethren, nevertheless, in their relations with the outside world, they were full members of the Order, shrouded with its inviolability and entitled to all its privileges, which they were not likely by moderation to render less odious to the community.

Thus the knights furnished ample cause for external hostility and internal disquiet, though there is probably no ground for the accusation that in 1229 they betrayed Frederic II to the infidel, and, in 1250, St. Louis to the Soldan of Egypt. Yet Frederic II doubtless had ample reason for dissatisfaction with their conduct during his crusade, which he revenged by expelling them from Sicily in 1229 and confiscating their property; and though he recalled them soon after and assumed to restore their possessions, he retained a large portion. Still, pious liberality continued to increase the wealth of the Order, though as the Christian possessions in the East shrank more and more, people began to attribute the ceaseless misfortunes to the jealousy and animosity existing between the rival Orders of the Temple and the Hospital, which in 1243 had broken out into open war in Palestine, to the great comfort of the infidel. A remedy was naturally sought in a union of the two Orders, together with that of the Teutonic Knights. At the Council of Lyons in 1274, Gregory X vainly endeavored to effect this, but the countervailing influences were too powerful.

Thus the Order was somewhat discredited in popular estimation when in 1297 Jacques de Molay, whose terrible fate has cast a sombre shadow over his name through the centuries, was elected Grand Master, after a vigorous and bitter opposition by the partisans of Hugues de Peraud. In contrast to this the Hospitallers were acquiring fresh renown as the champions of Christ by gallantly conquering, after a four years' struggle, the island of Rhodes, in which they so long maintained the cause of Christianity in the East.

In 1306 Clement V sent for de Molay and Guillaume de Villaret, Grand Master of the Hospitallers, to consult about a new crusade and the often discussed project of the union of the Orders. He told them to come as secretly as possible, but while the Hospitaller, engrossed with preparations for the siege of Rhodes, excused himself, de Molay came in state, with a retinue of 60 knights, and manifested no intention of returning to his station in the East. This well might arouse the question whether the Templars were about to abandon their sphere of duty, and if so, what were the ambitious schemes which might lead them to transfer their headquarters to France. The Teutonic Knights in withdrawing from the East were carving out for themselves a kingdom amid the pagans of northeastern

Europe. Had the Templars any similar aspirations nearer home?[1]
Suspicions of the kind might not unnaturally be excited, and
yet be wholly without foundation. Modern writers have exercised
their ingenuity in conjecturing that there was a plot on hand for
the Templars to seize the south of France and erect it into an
independent kingdom. The Order had early multiplied rapidly
in the provinces from the Garonne to the Rhone; it is assumed
that they were deeply tinctured with Catharism and held relations
with the concealed heretics in those regions. All this is the sheer-
est assumption without the slightest foundation.[2] There was not
a trace of Catharism in the Order, and we have seen how by this
time the Cathari of Languedoc had been virtually exterminated,
and how the land had been Gallicized by the Inquisition. Such
an alliance would have been a source of weakness, not of strength,
for it would have brought upon them all Europe in arms, and had
there been a shred of evidence to that effect, Philippe le Bel would
have made the most of it. Neither can it be assumed that they
were intriguing with the discontented, orthodox population. Bernard Délicieux and the Carcassais would never have turned to the
feeble Ferrand of Majorca if they could have summoned to their
assistance the powerful Order of the Temple. Besides, the Order was
by no means so numerous and wealthy as has been popularly supposed. An anonymous contemporary tells us that the Templars were
so rich and powerful that they could scarce have been suppressed but
for the secret and sudden movement of Philippe le Bel. Villani,
who was also a contemporary, says that their power and wealth
were well-nigh incomputable. The peculiar secrecy in which all the
affairs of the Order were shrouded renders such estimates purely con-

[1] It has rather been the fashion with historians to assume that de Molay transferred the headquarters of the Order from Cyprus to Paris. Yet when the papal
orders for arrest reached Cyprus, on May 27, 1308, the marshal, draper, and treasurer surrendered themselves with others, showing that there had been no thought
of removing the active administration of the Order. Raimbaut de Caron,
Preceptor of Cyprus, apparently had accompanied de Molay, and was arrested
with him in the Temple of Paris, but with this exception all the principal knights
seized were only local dignitaries.
[2] Perhaps the most detailed and authoritative contemporary account of the
downfall of the Templars is that of Bernard Gui. It is impossible to doubt that
had there been anything savoring of Catharism in the Order he would have
scented it out and alluded to it.

jectural. As to numbers, it has been overlooked that the great body of members were serving brethren, not fighting-men, and adding little to their effective force. When they considered it a legitimate boast that in 180 years of their active existence 20,000 of the brethren had perished in Palestine, we can see that at no time could the roll of knights have exceeded a few thousand at most.

Yet the wealth of the Order was more than sufficient to excite the cupidity of royal freebooters, and its power and privileges quite enough to arouse distrust in the mind of a less suspicious despot than Philippe le Bel. Many ingenious theories have been advanced to explain his action, but they are superfluous. In his quarrel with Boniface VIII, though the Templars were accused of secretly sending money to Rome in defiance of his prohibition, they stood by him and signed an act approving and confirming the assembly of the Louvre in June 1303, where Boniface was formally accused of heresy, and an appeal was made to a future council to be assembled on the subject. So cordial, in fact, was the understanding between the king and the Templars that royal letters of July 10, 1303, show that the collection of all the royal revenues throughout France was entrusted to Hugues de Peraud, the Visitor of France. In June 1304, Philippe confirmed all their privileges, and in October he issued an *Ordonnance* granting them additional ones and speaking of their merits in terms of warm appreciation. They lent him, in 1299, the enormous sum of 500,000 livres for the dowry of his sister.[3]

When in his extreme financial straits he debased the coinage until a popular insurrection was excited in Paris, it was in the Temple that he took refuge, and it was the Templars that defended him against the assaults of the mob. But these very obligations were too great to be incurred by a monarch who was striving to render himself absolute, and the recollection of them could hardly fail to suggest that the Order was a dangerous factor in a kingdom where feudal institutions were being converted into a despotism. While it might not have strength to sever a portion of the provinces and erect an

---

[3] Schottmüller (*Der Untergang des Templer-Ordens*, Berlin, 1887, i. 65) conjectures that the loan of 500,000 livres to Philippe is probably a popular error arising from the intervention of the Templars as bankers in the payment of the dowry.

independent principality, it might at any moment become a disagreeable element in a contest with the great feudatories to whom
the knights were bound by common sympathies and interests. They
were not his subjects; they owed him no obedience or allegiance;
he could not summon them to perform military service as he could
his bishops, but they enjoyed the right to declare war and make
peace on their own account without responsibility to anyone. Such
a body of armed warriors was an anomaly in a feudal organization,
and when the Templars seemed to have abandoned their military activity in the East, Philippe may well have regarded them as a possible
obstacle to his schemes of monarchical aggrandizement, to be got
rid of at the first favorable moment. At the commencement of his
reign he had endeavored to put a stop to the perpetual acquisitions
of both the religious Orders and the Templars, through which increasing bodies of land were falling under mainmorte, and the fruitless-
ness of the effort must have strengthened his convictions of its
necessity. If it be asked why he attacked the Templars rather than
the Hospitallers, the answer is probably to be found in the fact that
the Temple was the weaker of the two, while the secrecy shrouding
its ritual rendered it an object of popular suspicion.

For the explanation of Philippe's action, however, we need hardly
look further than to financial considerations. He was in desperate
straits for money to meet the endless drain of the Flemish war.
He had imposed taxes until some of his subjects were in revolt,
and others were on the verge of it. He had debased the currency
until he earned the name of the Counterfeiter, had found himself
utterly unable to redeem his promises, and had discovered by experience that of all financial devices it was the most costly and ruinous.
His resources were exhausted and his scruples were few. The stream
of confiscations from Languedoc was beginning to run dry, while
the sums which it had supplied to the royal treasury for more than
half a century had shown the profit which was derivable from
well-applied persecution of heresy. He had just carried out a
financial expedient of arresting all the Jews of the kingdom simultaneously, stripping them of their property, and banishing them
under pain of death. A memorandum of questions for consideration,
still preserved in the Trésor des Chartres, shows that he expected
to benefit in the same way from the confiscation of the Templar

possessions, while, as we shall see, he overlooked the fact that these, as ecclesiastical property, were subject to the imprescriptible rights of the Church.

The secrecy in which the Templars enveloped their proceedings was a natural stimulus of popular curiosity and suspicion. Alone among religious Orders, the ceremonies of reception were conducted in the strictest privacy; chapters were held at daybreak with doors closely guarded, and no participant was allowed to speak of what was done, even to a fellow-Templar not concerned in the chapter, under the penalty of expulsion. That this should lead to gossip and stories of rites too repulsive to bear the light was inevitable. It was common report that the neophyte was subjected to the humiliation of kissing the posteriors of his preceptor—a report which the Hospitallers took special pleasure in circulating. That unnatural lusts should be attributed to the Order is easily understood, for it was a prevalent vice of the Middle Ages, and one to which monastic communities were especially subject; in 1292 a horrible scandal of this kind had led to the banishment of many professors and theologians of the University of Paris. Darker rumors were not lacking of unchristian practices introduced in the Order by a Grand Master taken prisoner by the Soldan of Babylon, and procuring his release under promise of rendering them obligatory on the members. We have seen how readily such stories obtained credence throughout the Middle Ages, how they grew and became embroidered with the most fantastic details. The public mind was ripe to believe anything of the Templars; a spark only was needed to produce a conflagration.

Philippe's ministers and agents—Guillaume de Nogaret, Guillaume de Plaisian, Renaud de Roye, and Enguerrand de Marigny —were quite fitted to appreciate such an opportunity to relieve the royal exchequer, nor could they be at a loss in finding testimony upon which to frame a formidable list of charges. The stories about Squin de Florian, a renegade Templar, and Noffo Dei, a wicked Florentine, both condemned to death and concocting the accusations to save themselves, are probably but the conception of an imaginative chronicler, handed down from one annalist to another. Expelled members there were in plenty who had been ejected for their misdeeds, and who could lose nothing by gratifying their resentments. Apostates also there were, who had fled from the Order and were liable to imprisonment if caught, besides the crowd of worthless ribalds whom the royal agents could always secure when evidence for any purpose was wanted. These were quietly collected by Guillaume de Nogaret and kept in the greatest secrecy at Corbeil under charge of the Dominican, Humbert. Heresy was, of course, the most available charge to bring. The Inquisition was there as an unfailing instrument to secure conviction. Popular rumor, no matter by whom affirmed, was sufficient to require arrest and trial, and when once on trial there were few indeed from whom the inquisitorial process could not wring conviction. To enable Philippe to enjoy the expected confiscations in his own dominions, confiscation must be general throughout Europe, and for this the co-operation of the Holy See was essential. Clement subsequently declared that Philippe broached the subject to him in all its details before his coronation at Lyons, November 14, 1305, but the papal bulls throughout the whole matter are so infected with mendacity that slender reliance is to be placed on their statements.[4] Doubtless there was some discussion about the current reports defaming the Order, but Clement is probably not subject to the imputation which historians have thrown upon him, that his summons to de Molay and de Villaret in 1306 was purely a decoy. It seems to me reasonable to conclude that he sent for them in good faith, and that de Molay's own imprudence in establishing himself in France, as though for a permanence, excited at once the suspicions and cupidity of the king, and ripened into action what had previously been merely a vague conception.

If such was the case, Philippe was not long in maturing the project, nor were his agents slow in gathering material for the accusation. In his interview with Clement at Poitiers, in the spring of 1307, he vainly demanded the condemnation of the memory of Boniface VIII, and, failing in this, he brought forward the charges against the Templars, but with equal lack of immediate result. Clement sent for de Molay, who came to him with Raimbaud de

---

[4] Bull. *Pastoralis præeminentiæ* (Mag. Bull. Rom. Supplem. IX. 126).—Bull. *Faciens misericordiam* (Ib. p. 136).—The Itineraries of Philippe and the record of pastoral visitations by Bertrand de Goth (Clement V) sufficiently disprove the legendary story, originating with Villani, of the conditions entered into in advance at St. Jean d'Angely between Philippe and Clement. None the less, however, was Clement practically subordinated to Philippe.

Caron, Preceptor of Cyprus, Geoffroi de Gonneville, Preceptor of Aquitaine and Poitou, and Hugues de Peraud, Visitor of France, the principal officers of the Order then in the kingdom. The charges were communicated to them in all their foulness. Clement subsequently had the audacity to declare that de Molay before his arrest confessed their truth in the presence of his subordinates and of ecclesiastics and laymen, but this is a manifest lie. The Templars returned to Paris evidently relieved of all anxiety, thinking that they had justified themselves completely, and de Molay, on October 12, the eve of the arrest, had the honor to be one of the four pall-bearers at the obsequies of Catharine, wife of Charles de Valois, evidently for the purpose of lulling him with a sense of security. Moreover, on August 24, Clement had written to Philippe referring to his charges against the Templars in their conversations at Lyons and Poitiers. The charges, he says, appear to him incredible and impossible, but as de Molay and the chief officers of the Order had complained of the reports as injurious, and had repeatedly asked for an investigation, offering to submit to the severest punishment if found guilty, he proposes in a few days, on his return to Poitiers, to commence an examination into the matter, for which he asks the king to send him the proofs.

No impression had evidently thus far been made upon Clement, and he was endeavoring, in so far as he dared, to shuffle the affair aside. Philippe, however, had under his hands the machinery requisite to attain his ends, and he felt assured that when the Church was once committed to it, Clement would not venture to withdraw. The Inquisitor of France, Guillaume de Paris, was his confessor as well as papal chaplain, and could be relied upon. His awful authority overrode all the special immunities and personal inviolability of the Order. As the Templars were defamed for heresy by credible witnesses, it was strictly according to legal form for Frère Guillaume to summon Philippe to arrest those within his territories and bring them before the Inquisition for trial. As the enterprise was a large one, secrecy and combined operations were requisite for its success, and Philippe, as soon as Clement's letter had shown him that he was not to expect immediate papal co-operation, lost no time. He always asserted that he had acted under requisition from the inquisitor, and excused his haste by declaring that his victims were collecting their treasures and preparing to fly. On September 14 royal letters were sent out to the king's representatives throughout France, ordering the simultaneous arrest, under authority from Frère Guillaume, of all members of the Order on October 13, and the sequestration of all property. Frère Guillaume, on September 20, addressed all inquisitors and all Dominican priors, sub-priors, and lectors, commissioning them to act, and reciting the crimes of the Templars, which he characterized as sufficient to move the earth and disturb the elements. He had, he said, examined the witnesses, he had summoned the king to lend his aid, and he cunningly added that the pope was informed of the charges. The royal instructions were that the Templars when seized were to be strictly guarded in solitary confinement; they were to be brought before the inquisitorial commissioners one by one; the articles of accusation were to be read over to them; they were to be promised pardon if they would confess the truth and return to the Church, and be told that otherwise they were to be put to death, while torture was not to be spared in extracting confession. The depositions so obtained were to be sent to the king as speedily as possible, under the seals of the inquisitors.

Under the able management of Guillaume de Nogaret, to whom the direction of the affair was confided, on October 13 at daybreak the arrests took place throughout the land, but few of the Templars escaping. Nogaret himself took charge of the Paris Temple, where about 140 Templars, with de Molay and his chief officials at their head, were seized, and the vast treasure of the Order fell into the king's hands.

Philippe's first care was to secure the support of public opinion and allay the excitement caused by this unexpected move. The next day, Saturday, the masters of the University and the cathedral canons were assembled in Nôtre Dame, where Guillaume de Nogaret, the Prévôt of Paris, and other royal officials made a statement of the offenses which had been proved against the Templars. The following day, Sunday the 15th, the people were invited to assemble in the garden of the royal palace, where the matter was explained to them by the Dominicans and the royal spokesmen, while similar measures were adopted throughout the kingdom. On Monday, royal letters were addressed to all the princes of Christendom announcing the discovery of the Templar heresy, and urging them to aid the king in the defense of the faith by following his example. At once the Inquisition was set busily at work. From October 19 to November 24 Frère Guillaume and his assistants were employed in recording the confessions of 138 prisoners captured in the Temple, and so efficacious were the means employed that but three refused to admit at least some of the charges. The same scenes were enacting all over France, where the commissioners of Frère Guillaume, and sometimes Frère Guillaume himself, with the assistance of the royal officials, were engaged in the same work. A few of the reports of these examinations have been preserved, from Champagne, Normandy, Querci, Bigorre, Beaucaire, and Languedoc, and in these the occasional allusions to torture show that it was employed whenever necessary. In all cases, of course, it was not required, for the promise of pardon and the threat of burning would frequently suffice, in conjunction with starvation and the harshness of the prison. The rigor of the application of the inquisitorial process is shown by the numerous deaths and the occasional suicides to which the records bear testimony. In Paris alone, according to the testimony of Ponsard de Gisiac, 36 Templars perished under torture; at Sens, Jacques de Saciac said that 25 had died of torment and suffering, and the mortality elsewhere was notorious. De Molay, of course, was not spared. He was speedily brought into a complying state of mind. Although his confession, October 24, is exceedingly brief, and only admits a portion of the errors charged, yet he was induced to sign a letter addressed to the brethren stating that he had confessed and recommending them to do the same, as having been deceived by ancient error. As soon as he and other chiefs of the Order were thus committed, the masters and students of all the faculties of the University were summoned to meet in the Temple; the wretched victims were brought before them and were required to repeat their confessions, which they did, with the addition that these errors had prevailed in the Order for thirty years and more.

The errors charged against them were virtually five:

(1) That when a neophyte was received the preceptor led him behind the altar, or to the sacristy or other secret place, showed him a crucifix and made him thrice renounce the prophet and spit upon the cross.

(II) He was then stripped, and the preceptor kissed him thrice, on the posteriors, the navel, and the mouth.

(III) He was then told that unnatural lust was lawful, and it was commonly indulged in throughout the Order.

(IV) The cord which the Templars wore over the shirt day and night as a symbol of chastity had been consecrated by wrapping it around an idol in the form of a human head with a great beard, and this head was adored in the chapters, though only known to the Grand Master and the elders.

(V) The priests of the Order do not consecrate the host in celebrating mass.

When, in August 1308, Clement sent throughout Europe a series of articles for the interrogation of the accused, drawn up for him by Philippe, and varying according to different recensions from 87 to 127 in number, these charges were elaborated, and varied on the basis of the immense mass of confessions which had meanwhile been obtained. The indecent kisses were represented as mutual between the receptor and the received; disbelief in the sacrament was asserted; a cat was said to appear in the chapters and to be worshipped; all brethren were instructed to acquire property for the Order by fair means or foul. Even this, however, did not satisfy the public imagination, and the most absurd exaggerations found credence, such as we have so frequently seen in the case of other heresies. The Templars were said to have admitted betraying St. Louis and the stronghold of Acre, and that they had such arrangements with the Soldan of Babylon that if a new crusade were undertaken the Christians would all be sold to him. The cord of chastity was magnified into a leather belt, worn next the skin, and the *mahommerie* of this girdle was so powerful that as long as it was worn no Templar could abandon his errors. When a child was born of a virgin to a Templar it was roasted, and of its fat an ointment was made wherewith to anoint the idol worshipped in the chapters, to which, according to other rumors, human sacrifices were offered.

It is, perhaps, necessary at this point to discuss the still mooted question as to the guilt or innocence of the Order. Disputants have from various motives been led to find among the Templars Manichæan, Gnostic, and Cabalistic errors justifying their destruction. Hammer-Purgstall boasted that he had discovered and identified

no less than thirty Templar images, in spite of the fact that at the
time of their sudden arrest the Inquisition, aided by the eager
creatures of Philippe, was unable to lay its hands on a single one.
The only thing approaching it was a metal reliquary in the form
of a female head produced from the Paris Temple, which, on
being opened, was found to contain a small skull preserved as a relic
of the 11,000 virgins.

This fact alone would serve to dispose of the gravest of the
charges, for, if the depositions of some of the accused are to be believed, these idols were kept in every commandery and were employed in every reception of a neophyte. With regard to the other
accusations, not admitting thus of physical proof, it is to be
observed that much has been made by modern theorists of the
fact that the rules and statutes of the Order were reserved exclusively for its chiefs, and it has been assumed that in them were
developed the secret mysteries of the heresy. Yet nothing of the
kind was alleged in the proceedings; the statutes were never
offered in evidence by the prosecution, although many of them
must have been obtained in the sudden seizure, and this for the
best of reasons. Sedulously as they were destroyed, two or three
copies escaped, and these, carefully collated, have been printed.
They breathe nothing but the most ascetic piety and devotion to
the Church, and the numerous illustrative cases cited in them show
that up to a period not long anterior to the destruction of the
Order there were constant efforts made to enforce the rigid Rule
framed by St. Bernard and promulgated by the Council of Troyes
in 1128. Thus there is absolutely no external evidence against the
Order, and the proof rests entirely upon confessions extracted by
the alternative of pardon or burning, by torture, by the threat of
torture, or by the indirect torture of prison and starvation.

No one who had studied the criminal jurisprudence of the later
Middle Ages will attach the slightest weight to confessions obtained
under such conditions. We shall see, when we come to consider
persecution for witchcraft, with what facility the rack and *strappado*
procured from victims of all ranks confessions of participating in the
Sabbat, of holding personal intercourse with demons, and of killing
men and cattle with spells. Riding through the air on a broomstick,
and commerce with incubi and succubi rest upon evidence of pre-

cisely the same character and of much greater weight than that upon which the Templars were convicted, for the witch was sure of burning if she confessed, and had a chance of escaping if she could endure the torture, while the Templar was threatened with death for obstinacy and was promised immunity as a reward for confession. If we accept the evidence against the Templar we cannot reject it in the case of the witch.

As the testimony thus has no intrinsic weight, the only scientific method of analyzing the affair is to sift the whole mass of confessions, and determine their credibility according to the internal evidence they afford of being credible or otherwise. Several hundred depositions have reached us, taken in France, England, and Italy, for the most part naturally those incriminating the Order, for the assertions of innocence were usually suppressed and the most damaging witnesses were made the most of. There is, first, the extreme inherent improbability that a rich, worldly, and ambitious body of men like the Templars should be secretly engaged in the dangerous and visionary task of laying the foundations of a new religion, which would bring them no advantage if they succeeded in supplanting Christianity, and which was certain to lead them to destruction in the infinite chances of detection. To admit this is to ascribe to them a spiritual exaltation and a readiness for martyrdom which we might expect from the asceticism of a Catharan or a Dolcinist, but not from the worldliness which was the real corroding vice of the Order. Second, if the Templars were thus engaged in the desperate enterprise of propagating a new faith under the eyes of the Inquisition, they would exercise extreme caution in the admission of members, and only reveal to them their secrets by degrees, as they found them worthy of confidence and willing to incur the risk of martyrdom. Third, if a new dogma were thus secretly taught as an indispensable portion of the Rule, its doctrines would be rigidly defined and its ritual be closely administered. The witnesses who confessed to initiation would all tell the same story and give the same details.

Thus evidence of the weightiest and most coherent character would be requisite to overcome the inherent improbability that the Templars could be embarked in an enterprise so insane, in place of which we have only confessions extracted by the threat or application of torture, and not a single instance of a persistent heretic maintaining the belief imputed to him. Turning to the testimony to see whether it comports with the conditions we have named, we find that no discrimination whatever was exercised in the admission of neophytes. Not a single witness speaks of any preliminary preparation, though several intimate that they obtained entrance by making over their property to the Order. Indeed, one of the charges was that there was no preliminary probation, and that the neophyte at once became a professed member in full standing, which, as explained by a knight of Mas Deu, was because their services were considered to be at once required against the Saracens. Youths and even children were admitted, although in violation of the statutes of the Order, of ages ranging from 10 or 11 years upward. High-born knights, priding themselves on their honor, priests, laborers, husbandmen, menials of all kinds were brought in, and, if we are to believe their evidence, they were without notice obliged, by threats of death and lifelong imprisonment, to undergo the severest personal humiliation, and to perform the awful task of renouncing their Saviour and spitting on, or even more outrageously defiling, the cross which was the symbol of their faith. Such a method of propagating heresy by force in the Europe of the Inquisition, of trusting such fearful secrets to children and to unwilling men of all conditions, is so absurd that its mere assertion deprives the testimony of all claim to credence.

Equally damaging to the credibility of the evidence is the self-contradictory character of its details. It was obtained by examining the accused on a series of charges elaborately drawn up, and by requiring answers to each article in succession, so that the general features of the so-called confessions were suggested in advance. Had the charges been true there could have been little variation in the answers, but in place of a definite faith or a systematic ritual we find every possible variation that could suggest itself to witnesses striving to invent stories that should satisfy their torturers. Some say that they were taught Deism—that God in heaven alone was to be worshipped. Others, that they were forced to renounce God. The usual formula reported, however, was simply to renounce Christ, while others were called upon to renounce Notre Sire, or la Profeta, or Christ, the Virgin, and the Saints. It was the same with the idol which has so greatly exercised the imagination of commentators. Some witnesses swore that it was produced whenever a neophyte was received, and that its adoration was a part of the ceremony; others that it was only exhibited and worshipped in the secrecy of chapters; by far the greater number, however, had never seen it or heard of it. Of those who professed to have seen it, scarce two described it alike, within the limits suggested by the articles of accusation, which spoke of it as a head. Sometimes it is black, sometimes white, sometimes with black hair, and sometimes white and black mixed, and again with a long white beard. Some witnesses saw its neck and shoulders covered with gold; one declared that it was a demon (*Maufé*) on which no one could look without trembling; another that it had for eyes carbuncles which lighted up the room. Sometimes it is called the Saviour, and sometimes *Bafomet* or *Maguineth*—corruptions of Mahomet—and is worshipped as Allah. Sometimes it is God, creating all things, and then again it is a friend of God who can approach him and intercede for the suppliant. Sometimes it gives responses, and sometimes it is accompanied or replaced by the devil in the form of a black or gray cat or raven, who occasionally answers the questions addressed to him, the performance winding up, like the witches' Sabbat, with the introduction of demons in the form of beautiful women.

Similar contradictions are observable in the evidence as to the ritual of reception. The details laid down in the Rule are accurately and uniformly described, but when the witnesses come to speak of the sacrilegious rites imputed to them, they flounder among almost every variation that could suggest itself to their imaginations. Usually renunciation of God or Christ and spitting on the cross are both required, but in many cases renunciation without spitting suffices, and in as many more spitting without renunciation. In fact, the evidence on the enforcement of the sacrilege is hopelessly contradictory.

The same irreconcilable confusion reigns in the evidence as to the other charges—the cord of chastity, the obscene kiss, the mutilation of the canon of the mass, the power of absolution assigned to the Grand Master, the license for unnatural crime. It might be argued, as these witnesses had been received into the Order at times varying from fifty to sixty years previous to within a few months, and at places so widely apart as Palestine and England, that these variations are explicable by local usages or by a gradually perfected belief and ritual. An investigation of the confessions shows, however, that no such explanation will suffice; there can be no grouping as to the time or place of the ceremony. Yet there can be a grouping which is of supreme significance, a grouping as to the tribunal through which the witness passed. This is often very notable among the 225 who were sent to the papal commission from various parts of France, and examined in 1310 and 1311. As a rule they manifested extreme anxiety that their present depositions should accord with those which they had made when subject to inquisition by the bishops—doubtless they made them as nearly so as their memories would permit—and it is easy to see how greater or less rigor, or how concert between those confined in the same prison, had led to the concoction of stories such as would satisfy their judges. Thus the confessions obtained by the Ordinary of Poitiers have a character distinct from those extorted by the Bishop of Clermont, and we can classify the penitents of the Bishop of Le Mans, the Archbishop of Sens, the Archbishop of Tours, the Bishops of Amiens, Rodez, Macon, in fact of nearly all the prelates who took part in the terrible drama.

Another feature indicating the untrustworthy character of the evidence is that large numbers of the witnesses swore that they had confessed the sacrilege committed to priests and friars of all kinds, to bishops, and even to papal penitentiaries, and had received absolution by the imposition of penance, usually of a trifling character, such as fasting on Fridays for a few months or a year. No ordinary confessor could absolve for heresy; it was a sin reserved for the inquisitor, papal or episcopal. The most that the confessor could have done would have been to send the penitent to someone competent to grant absolution, which would only have been administered under the heaviest penance, including denunciation of the Order. To suppose that thousands of men, during a period of fifty or a hundred years, could have been entrapped into such a heresy without its becoming matter of notoriety, is in itself so violent an assumption as to deprive the whole story of all claims upon belief.

Thus the more closely the enormous aggregate of testimony is examined, the more utterly worthless it appears. Had thousands of men been unwillingly forced to abjure their faith and been terrorized into keeping the dread secret, as soon as the pressure was removed by the seizure there would have been a universal eagerness to unburden the conscience and seek reconciliation with the Church. No torture would have been requisite to obtain all the evidence required. In view, therefore, of the extreme improbability of the charge, of the means employed to obtain proof for its support, and the lack of coherence in the proof so obtained, it appears to me that no judicial mind in possession of the facts can hesitate to pronounce a sentence, not merely of not proven, but of acquittal. The theory that there were inner grades in the Order, by which those alone to be trusted were initiated in its secret doctrines, is perfectly untenable. As there is no evidence of any kind to support it, it is a matter of mere conjecture, which is sufficiently negatived by the fact that with scarce an exception those who confessed, whether plowmen or knights, relate the sacrilege as taking place on their admission.

Yet it is by no means improbable that there may have been some foundation for the popular gossip that the neophyte at his reception was forced to kiss the posteriors of his preceptor. As we have seen, a large majority of the Order consisted of serving brethren on whom the knights looked down with infinite contempt. Some such occasional command on the part of a reckless knight, to enforce the principle of absolute obedience, in admitting a plebeian to nominal fraternity and equality, would not have been foreign to the manners of the age. Who can say, moreover, that men, soured with the disillusion of life within the Order, chafing under the bonds of their irrevocable vow, and perhaps released from all religious convictions amid the license of the East, may not occasionally have tested the obedience of a neophyte by bidding him to spit at the cross on the mantle that had grown hateful to him?[5] No one who recognizes the wayward perversity of human nature, or who is familiar with the

---

[5] This would seem not unlikely if we are to believe the confession of Jean d'Aumônes, a serving brother who stated that at his reception his preceptor turned all the other brethren out of the chapel, and after some difficulty forced him to spit at the cross, after which he said, "Go, fool, and confess." This Jean at once did, to a Franciscan who imposed on him only the penance of three Friday fasts, saying that it was intended as a test of constancy in case of capture by the Saracens (Procès, 1. 588-91).

condition of monasticism at the period, can deny the possibilities
of such occasional performances, whether as brutal jokes or spiteful
assertions of supremacy, but the only rational conclusion from the
whole tremendous tragedy is that the Order was innocent of the
crime for which it was punished.

While Philippe was seizing his prey, Clement, at Poitiers, was
occupied in the equally lucrative work of sending collectors throughout Germany to exact a tithe of all ecclesiastical revenues for the
recovery of the Holy Land. When aroused from this with the news
that Philippe, under the authority of Frère Guillaume the inquisitor,
had thus taken decided and irrevocable action in a matter which was
still before him for consideration, he wrote to Philippe, October
27, 1307, expressing his indignation that the king should have taken
action in a matter which the brief of August 24 showed to be receiving papal consideration. Carefully suppressing the fact of the
intervention of the Inquisition, which legally justified the whole
proceeding, Clement sought a further ground of complaint by reminding the king that Templars were not under royal jurisdiction,
but under that of the Holy See, and he had committed a grave act
of disobedience in seizing their persons and property, both of which
must be forthwith delivered to two cardinals sent for the purpose.
These were Berenger de Frédole, Cardinal of SS. Nereo and Achille,
and Étienne de Suissi of S. Ciriaco, both Frenchmen and creatures
of Philippe, who had procured their elevation to the sacred college.
He seems to have had no trouble in coming to an understanding with
them, for, though the trials and tortures were pushed unremittingly,
another letter of Clement's, December 1, praises the king for putting
the matter in the hands of the Holy See, and one of Philippe's of
December 24 announces that he had no intention of infringing on
the rights of the Church and does not intend to abandon his own;
he has, he says, delivered the Templars to the cardinals, and the
administration of their property shall be kept separate from that of
the crown. Clement's susceptibilities being thus soothed, even before
the trials at Paris were ended he issued, November 22, the bull
Pastoralis præeminentiæ, addressed to all the potentates of Europe,
in which he related what Philippe had done at the requisition of
the Inquisitor of France, in order that the Templars might be pre-

sented to the judgment of the Church; how the chiefs of the Order had confessed the crimes imputed to them; how he himself had examined one of them who was employed about his person and had confirmed the truth of the allegations. Therefore he orders all the sovereigns to do likewise, retaining the prisoners and holding their property in the name of the pope and subject to his order. Should the Order prove innocent the property is to be restored to it, otherwise it is to be employed for the recovery of the Holy Land. This was the irrevocable act which decided the fate of the Templars, as we shall see hereafter when we consider the action of the princes of Europe outside France.

Philippe thus had forced Clement's hand, and Clement was fairly committed to the investigation, which in the hands of the Inquisition could only end in the destruction of the Order. Secure in his position, the king pushed on the examination of the prisoners throughout the kingdom, and the vigilance of his agents is shown in the case of two German Templars returning home, whom they arrested at Chaumont and delivered to the Inquisitor of the Three Bishoprics. One was a priest, the other a serving brother, and the inquisitor in reporting to Philippe says that he had not tortured the latter because he was very sick, but that neither had admitted that there was in the Order aught that was not pure and holy. The examinations went on during the winter of 1308, when Clement unexpectedly put a stop to them. What was his motive we can only conjecture; probably he found that Philippe's promises with regard to the Templar possessions were not likely to be fulfilled, and that an assertion of his control was necessary. Whatever his reasons, he suddenly suspended the power of all the inquisitors and bishops in France and evoked to himself the cognizance of the whole affair, alleging that the suddenness of the seizure without consulting him had excited in him grave suspicions, which had not been allayed by the records of the examinations submitted to him, for these were of a character rather to excite incredulity. It shows how completely the whole judicial proceedings were inquisitional that this brought them to an immediate close, provoking Philippe to uncontrollable wrath. Angrily he wrote to Clement that he had sinned greatly: even popes, he hints, may fall into heresy; he had wronged all the prelates and inquisitors of France; he had inspired the Templars with hopes

and they were retracting their confessions, especially Hugues de
Peraud, who had had the honor of dining with the cardinal-deputies.
Philippe at first was disposed to assert his independence and claim
jurisdiction, and he applied to the University for an opinion to support his claims, but the Faculty of Theology replied, March 25, 1308,
as it could not help doing: the Templars were religious and consequently exempt from secular jurisdiction; the only cognizance a
secular court could have over heresy was at the request of the
Church after it had abandoned the heretic; in case of necessity
the secular power could arrest a heretic, but it could only be for the
purpose of delivering him to the ecclesiastical court; and finally the
Templar property must be held for the purpose for which it was
given tò the Order.

Philippe, thus foiled, proceeded to bring a still stronger pressure
to bear on Clement. He appealed to his subservient bishops and
summoned a national assembly, to meet April 15 in Tours, to deliberate with him on the subject of the Templars. Already, at the
Assembly of Paris in 1302, he had called in the *Tiers-État* and had
learned to value its support in his quarrel with Boniface, and now
he again brought in the communes, thus founding the institution
of the States-General. After some delay the assembly met in May.
In his summons Philippe had detailed the crimes of the Templars
as admitted facts. He desired his subjects to participate in the pious
work, and therefore he ordered the towns to select each two deputies
zealous for the faith. From a gathering collected under such impulsion it was not difficult, in spite of the secret leaning of the nobles
to the proscribed Order, to procure a virtually unanimous expression
of opinion that the Templars deserved death.

.With the prestige of the nation at his back, Philippe went, at
the end of May, to Clement at Poitiers, accompanied by a strong
deputation, including his brothers, his sons, and his councillors. Long
and earnest were the disputations over the affair, Philippe urging,
through his spokesman, Guillaume de Plaisian, that the Templars
had been found guilty and that immediate punishment should
follow; Clement reiterating his grievance that an affair of such
magnitude, exclusively appertaining to the Holy See, should be
carried on without his initiative. A body like the Order of the
Temple had powerful friends all over Europe whose influence with

the curia was great, and the papal perplexities were manifold as one side or the other preponderated; but Clement had irrevocably committed himself in the face of all Europe by his bull of November 22, and it was in reality but a question of the terms on which he would allow the affair to go on in France by removing the suspension of the powers of the Inquisition. The bargaining was sharp, but an agreement was reached. As Clement had reserved the matter for papal judgment, it was necessary that some show of investigation should be had. Seventy-two Templars were drawn from the prisons of Paris to be examined by the pope and sacred college, that they might be able to assert personal knowledge of their guilt. Clement might well shrink from confronting de Molay and the chiefs of the Order whom he was betraying, while at the same time they could not be arbitrarily omitted. They were therefore stopped at Chinon near Tours, under pretext of sickness, while the others were sent forward to Poitiers. From the 28th of June to July 1 they were solemnly examined by five cardinals friendly to Philippe, deputed for the purpose. The official report of the examinations shows the care which had been exercised in the selection of those who were to perform this scene in the drama. A portion of them were spontaneous witnesses who had left, or had tried to leave, the Order. The rest, with the terrible penalty for retraction impending over them, confirmed the confessions made before the Inquisition. On July 2, they were brought before the pope in full consistory. Thus the papal jurisdiction was recognized; Clement in his subsequent bulls could speak of his own knowledge, and could declare that the accused had confessed their errors spontaneously and without coercion, and had humbly begged for absolution and reconciliation.

The agreement duly executed between Clement and Philippe bore that the Templars should be delivered to the pope, but be guarded in his name by the king; that their trials should be proceeded with by the bishops in their several dioceses, to whom, at the special and earnest request of the king, the inquisitors were adjoined—but de Molay and the Preceptors of the East, of Normandy, Poitou, and Provence, were reserved for the papal judgment; the property was to be placed in the hands of commissioners named by the pope and bishops, to whom the king was secretly to add appointees of his own, but he was to pledge himself in writing that it should be employed solely for the Holy Land. Clement assumed that the fate of the Order, as an institution, was too weighty a question to be decided without the intervention of a general council, and it was decided to call one in October 1310. The Cardinal of Palestrina was named as the papal representative in charge of the persons of the Templars—a duty which he speedily fulfilled by transferring them to the king under condition that they should be held at the disposition of the Church. Clement performed his part of the bargain by removing, July 5, the suspension of the inquisitors and bishops, and restoring their jurisdiction in the matter. Directions were sent at the same time to each of the bishops in France to associate with himself two cathedral canons, two Dominicans, and two Franciscans, and proceed with the trials of the individual Templars within his diocese, admitting inquisitors to participate at will, but taking no action against the Order as a whole; all persons were ordered, under pain of excommunication, to arrest Templars and deliver them to the inquisitors or episcopal officials, and Philippe furnished twenty copies of royal letters commanding his subjects to restore to the papal deputies all property, real and personal, of the Order.

The rival powers having thus come to an understanding about their victims, proceedings were resumed with fresh energy. Clement made up for his previous hesitation with ample show of zeal. De Molay and the chief officials with him were detained at Chinon until the middle of August, when the Cardinals of SS. Nereo and Achille, of S. Ciriaco and of S. Angelo, were sent thither to examine them. These reported, August 20, to Philippe, that on the 17th and following days they had interrogated the Grand Master, the Master of Cyprus, the Visitor of France, and the Preceptors of Normandy and Poitou, who had confirmed their previous confessions and had humbly asked for absolution and reconciliation, which had been duly given them, and the king is asked to pardon them. There are two things noteworthy in this which illustrate the duplicity pervading the whole affair. In the papal bulls of August 12, five days before this examination was commenced, its results are fully set forth, with the assertion that the confessions were free and spontaneous. Moreover, when in November 1309 this bull was read over by the papal commission to de Molay, on hearing its recital of what he was said to have confessed he was stupefied, and, crossing himself twice, said he wished to God the custom of the Saracens and Tartars were observed towards persons so perverse, for they beheaded or cut in two those who thus perverted the truth.

On August 12 Clement issued a series of bulls which regulated the methods of procedure in the case and showed that he was prepared fully to perform his part of the agreement with Philippe. The bull *Faciens misericordiam*, addressed to the prelates of Christendom, recited at great length the proceedings thus far taken against the accused and the guilt which they had spontaneously acknowledged; it directed the bishops, in conjunction with inquisitorial commissioners appointed by the pope, to summon all Templars before them and make inquisition concerning them. After this provincial councils were to be summoned, where the guilt or innocence of the individuals was to be determined, and in all the proceedings the local inquisitors had a right to take part. The results of the inquisitions, moreover, were to be promptly transmitted to the pope. The bull *Regnans in cœlis*, addressed to all princes and prelates, repeated the narrative part of the other, and ended by convoking, for October 1, 1310, a General Council at Vienne, to decide the fate of the Order, to consult as to the recovery of the Holy Land, and to take such action as might be required for the reformation of the Church. By another bull, *Faciens misericordiam*, dated August 8, a formal summons was issued to all and singular of the Templars to appear before the council, personally or by procurators, on a certain day, to answer to the charges against the Order, and the Cardinal of Palestrina, who was in charge of them, was ordered to produce de Molay and the Preceptors of France, Normandy, Poitou, Aquitaine, and Provence to receive sentence.

The prosecution of the Templars throughout Europe was thus organized. Even such distant points as Achaia, Corsica, and Sardinia were not neglected. The large number of special inquisitors to be appointed was a work of time, and the correspondence between Philippe and Clement on the subject shows that they virtually were selected by the king. In France the work of prosecution was speedily set on foot, and, after a respite of some six months, the Templars found themselves transferred from the improvised inquisitorial tribunals set on foot by Frère Guillaume to the episcopal courts as

provided by Clement. In every diocese the bishops were soon busily
at work. Clement urged forward the proceedings with little regard
to formality, and authorized the bishops to act outside their respective
dioceses and without respect to the place of origin of the accused.
The sole object evidently was to extract from them satisfactory confessions, as a preparation for the provincial councils which were to
be summoned for their final judgment. Those who had already
confessed were not likely to retract. Before the papal commission in
1310, Jean de Cochiac exhibited a letter from Philippe de Vohet and
Jean de Jamville, the papal and royal custodians of the prisoners,
to those confined at Sens at the time the Bishop of Orleans was
sent there to examine them (the archbishopric of Sens was then
vacant), warning them that those who revoked the confessions
made before *"los quizitor"* would be burned as relapsed. Vohet,
when summoned before the commission, admitted the seal to be
his, but denied authorizing the letter, and the commission prudently
abstained from pushing the investigation further. The nervous
anxiety manifested by most of those brought before the commission
that their statements should accord with what they had said before
the bishops shows that they recognized the danger which they incurred.

The treatment of those who refused to confess varied with the
temper of the bishops and their adjuncts. The records of their
tribunals have mostly disappeared, and we are left to gather what
we can from the utterances of a few witnesses who made to the
commission chance allusions to their former experiences. Yet the
proceedings before the Bishop of Clermont would show that they
were not in all cases treated with undue harshness. He had 69
Templars, of whom 40 confessed, and 29 refused to admit any evil in
the Order. Then he assembled them and divided them into the two
groups. The recusants declared that they adhered to their assertion,
and that if they should subsequently confess through fear of torture,
prison, or other affliction, they protested that they should not be
believed, and that it should not prejudice them, nor does it appear
that any constraint was afterwards put upon them. The others were
asked whether they had any defense to offer, or whether they were
ready for definitive sentence, when they unanimously declared that
they had nothing to offer nor wished to hear their sentence, but

submitted themselves to the mercy of the Church. All bishops were not so mild as he of Clermont, but in the fragmentary recitals before the commission it is not always easy to distinguish the action of the episcopal tribunals from that of Frère Guillaume's inquisitors. A few instances will suffice to show how, between the two, testimony was obtained against the Order.

Jean de Rompreye, a husbandman, declared that he knew nothing but good of the Order, although he had confessed otherwise before the Bishop of Orleans after being thrice tortured. Robert Vigier, a serving brother, likewise denied the accusations, though he had confessed them before the Bishop of Nevers at Paris, on account of the fierceness of the torture, under which he understood that three of his comrades, Gautier, Henri, and Chanteloup, had died. Bernard de Vado, a priest, had been tortured by fire applied to the soles of the feet to such an extent that a few days afterwards the bones of his heels dropped out, in testimony of which he exhibited the bones. Nineteen brethren from Périgord had confessed before the Bishop of Périgord through torture and starvation—one of them had been kept for six months on bread and water, without shoes or upper clothing.

These instances will illustrate the nature of the work in which the whole episcopate of France was engaged during the remainder of the year 1308 and through 1309 and 1310. All this, however, concerned merely the members of the Order as individuals. The fate of the Templar possessions depended upon the judgment to be rendered on the Order as a body corporate, and for this purpose Clement had assigned for it a day on which it was to appear by its syndics and procurators before the Council of Vienne. Seeing that the officers and members were scattered in prison throughout Europe, this was a manifest impossibility, and some method was imperatively required by which they could, at least constructively, be represented, if only to hear their sentence. Among the bulls of August 12, 1308, therefore, there was one creating a commission, with the Archbishop of Narbonne at its head, authorized to summon before it all the Templars of France, to examine them, and to report the result. August 8, 1309, the commission assembled in the abbey of Sainte-Geneviève, and by letters addressed to all the archbishops of the kingdom cited all Templars to appear before them on the first working-day after Martinmas, and the Order itself to appear by its syndics and procurators at the Council of Vienne, to receive such sentence as God should decree. On the appointed day, November 12, the commissioners reassembled, but no Templars appeared. For a week they met daily, and daily the form was gone through of a proclamation by the apparitor that if anyone wished to appear for the Order or its members the commission was ready to listen to him kindly, but without result. On examining the replies of the prelates they were found to have imperfectly fulfilled their duty. Philippe evidently regarded the whole proceeding with distrust, and was not inclined to aid it. A somewhat peremptory communication on November 18 was addressed to the Bishop of Paris, explaining that their proceedings were not against individuals, but against the whole Order; that no one was to be forced to appear, but that all who so chose must be allowed to come. This brought the bishop before them on November 22, with explanations and apologies; and a summons to Philippe de Vohet and Jean de Jamville, the papal and royal custodians of the Templars, brought those officials to promise obedience. Yet the obstacles to the performance of their task did not disappear. On the 22d they were secretly informed that some persons had come to Paris in lay garments to defend the Order, and had been thrown in prison. Thereupon they sent for Jean de Plublaveh, *prévôt* of the Châtelet, who said that by royal order he had arrested seven men said to be Templars in disguise, who had come with money to engage advocates in defense of the Order, but on torturing two of them he had found this not to be the case.

At length the commission succeeded in securing the presence of de Molay, Hugues de Peraud, and some of the brethren confined in Paris. De Molay said he was not wise and learned enough to defend the Order, but he would hold himself vile and miserable if he did not attempt it; he prayed to have aid and counsel, and he would do his best. The commissioners reminded him that trials for heresy were not conducted according to legal forms, that advocates were not admitted, and they cautioned him on the risk he incurred in defending the Order after the confession he had made. Kindly they read over to him the report of the cardinals of his confession at Chinon; and on his manifesting indignation and astonishment, Guillaume de Plaisian, who seems to have been watching the proceedings on the part of the king, gave him friendly caution which closed his lips. He asked for delay, and when he reappeared Guillaume de Nogaret was there to take advantage of any imprudence. From the papal letters which had been read to him he learned that the pope had reserved him and the other chiefs of the Order for special judgment, and he therefore asked to have the opportunity of appearing before the papal tribunal without delay. The shrewdness of this device thus made itself apparent. It separated the leaders from the rest; de Molay, Hugues de Peraud, and Geoffroi de Gonneville were led to hope for special consideration, and selfishly abandoned their followers. As for the brethren, their answers to the commission were substantially that of Géraud de Caux—he was a simple knight, without horse, arms, or land; he knew not how, and could not defend the Order.

By this time Philippe seems to have been satisfied that no harm could come from the operations of the commission. His opposition disappeared, and he graciously lent them his assistance. November 28, a second summons was sent to the bishops threatening them with papal indignation for a continuance of their neglect, and, what was far more efficacious, it was accompanied with orders from Philippe directing his jailers to afford to the episcopal officials access to the imprisoned Templars, while the baillis were instructed to send to Paris, under sure guard, all Templars desiring to defend their Order.

February 3, 1310, was the day named in this new citation. By the 5th Templars began to pour in, nearly all eager to defend their Order. They accumulated until the commission was embarrassed how to deal with them, and finally, on March 28th, 546 who had offered to defend were assembled in the garden of the episcopal palace, where the commissioners explained to them what was proposed, and suggested that they should nominate eight or ten of their number to act as procurators; they would not again have an opportunity of meeting, and the commission would proceed on the 31st, but the procurators should have access to them in their several prisons, and should agree with them what defense should be offered. A promiscuous crowd, whose differences of dialect rendered intercommunication impossible, abandoned by their natural leaders, was not fitted for deliberation on so delicate an emergency. Many hesitated about acting without orders from the Master, for all initiative on the part of subordinates was strictly forbidden by the Rule. The commissioners seem to have been sincerely desirous of getting the matter into some sort of shape, and finally, on the 31st, they ordered their notaries to visit the houses in which the Templars were confined and report their wishes and conclusions. This was a process requiring time, and the reports of the notaries after making their daily rounds are pitiful enough. The wretched prisoners floundered helplessly when called upon to resolve on their action. Most of them declared the Order to be pure and holy, but knew not what to do in the absence of their superiors. There was a general clamor for readmission to the sacraments. Many begged to be assured that when they died they should be buried in consecrated ground; others offered to pay for a chaplain out of the miserable allowance doled to them. They were urgent in the impossible request that they should have learned men to advise with and appear for them; and they further begged that security should be given to witnesses, as all who had confessed were threatened with burning if they should retract. A paper presented April 4 by those confined in the house of the Abbot of Tiron is eloquent in its suggestiveness of their treatment, for the houses in which they were quartered had apparently taken them on speculation. They assert the purity of the Order and their readiness to defend it as well as men can who are fettered in prison. They complain of the insufficiency of their allowance of 12 deniers a day, for they pay 3 deniers each per day for their beds; for hire of kitchen, napery, and cloths, 2 sols 6 deniers per week; 2 sols for taking off and replacing their fetters when they appear before the commission; for washing, 18 deniers a fortnight; wood and candles, 4 deniers a day, and ferriage across from Nôtre Dame, 16 deniers. It is evident that the poor creatures were exploited relentlessly.

The outcome of the matter was that on April 7 nine representatives presented a paper in the name of all, declaring that without authority from the Master and Convent they could not appoint procurators, but they offer themselves one and all in defense of the Order, and ask to be present at the council or wherever it is on trial. They declare the charges to be horrible lies fabricated by apostates and fugitives expelled for crime from the Order, confirmed by torturing those who uphold the truth, and encouraging liars with recompenses and great promises. They pray that when the brethren are examined there may be present no laymen or others whom they may fear, and that security may be assured them, for all who have confessed are daily threatened with burning if they retract. In reply the commissioners disavowed responsibility for their ill-usage and promised to ask that they be humanely treated in accordance with the orders of the Cardinal of Palestrina, to whom they had been committed by the pope. The Grand Master, they added, had been urged to defend the Order, but had declined, and claimed that he was reserved for the pope.

Having thus given the Templars a nominal opportunity for defense, the commissioners proceeded to take testimony, appointing four of the representatives, Renaud de Provins, Preceptor of Orleans, Pierre de Boulogne, procurator of the Order in the papal court, and Geoffroi de Chambonnet and Bertrand de Sartiges, knights, to be present at the swearing of the witnesses, and to do what might be requisite without constituting them formal defenders of the Order. These four on April 13 presented another paper in which, after alluding to the tortures employed to extort confessions, they stated it to be a notorious fact that to obtain testimony from Templars sealed royal letters had been given them promising them liberty and large pensions for life, and telling them that the Order was permanently abolished. This was evidently intended as a protest to pave the way for disabling the adverse witnesses, which, as we have seen, was the only defense in the inquisitorial process, and with the same object they also asked for the names of all witnesses. They did not venture to ask for a copy of the evidence, but they earnestly requested that it should be kept secret, to avert the danger that might otherwise threaten the witnesses. Subject to the interruption of the Easter solemnities, testimony, mostly adverse to the Order, continued to be taken up to May 9. On Sunday, May 10, the commissioners were suddenly called together, at the request of Renaud de Provins and his colleagues, to receive the startling announcement that the provincial Council of Sens, which had been hastily assembled at Paris, proposed to prosecute all the Templars who had offered to defend the Order. Most of these had previously confessed; they had heroically taken their lives in their hands when, by asserting the purity of the Order, they had constructively revoked their confessions. The four Templars therefore appealed to the commissioners for protection, as the action of the council would fatally interfere with the work in hand; they demanded *Apostoli,* and that their persons and rights and the whole Order should be placed under the guardianship of the Holy See, and time and money be allowed to prosecute the appeal. They further asked the commissioners to notify the Archbishop of Sens to take no action while the present examination was in progress, and that they be sent before him with one or two notaries to make a protest, as they can find no one who dares to draw up such an instrument for them. The commissioners debated the matter until evening, when they recalled the Templars to say that while they heartily compassionated them they could do nothing, for the Archbishop of Sens and the council were acting under powers delegated by the pope.

It was no part of Philippe's policy to allow the Order any opportunity to be heard. The sudden rally of nearly 600 members, after their chiefs had been skillfully detached from them, and their preparations for defense at the approaching council promised a struggle which he proceeded to crush at the outset with his customary unscrupulous energy. The opportunity was favorable, for after long effort he had just obtained from Clement the archbishopric of Sens (of which Paris was a suffragan see) for a youthful creature of his own, Philippe de Marigny, brother of his minister Enguerrand, who took possession of the dignity only on April 5. The bull *Faciens misericordiam* had prescribed that, after the bishops had completed their inquests, provincial councils were to be called to sit in judgment on the individual brethren. In pursuance of this, the king through his archbishops was master of the situation. Provincial councils were suddenly called, that for Sens to meet at Paris, for Reims at Senlis, for Normandy at Pont de l'Arche, and for Narbonne at Carcassonne, and a demonstration was organized which should paralyze at once and forever all thought of further opposition to his will. No time was wasted in any pretense of judicial proceedings, for the canon law provided that relapsed heretics were to be condemned without a hearing. On the 11th the Council of Sens was opened at Paris. On the 12th, while the commissioners were engaged in taking testimony, word was brought them that 54 of those who had offered to defend the Order had been condemned as relapsed heretics for retracting their confessions, and were to be burned that day. Hastily they sent to the council Philippe de Vohet, the papal custodian of the Templars, and Amis, Archdeacon of Orleans, to ask for delay. Vohet, they said, and many others asserted that the Templars who died in prison declared on peril of their souls that the crimes alleged were false; Renaud de Provins and his colleagues had appealed before them from the council; if the proposed executions took place the functions of the commission would be impeded, for the witnesses that day and the day before were crazed with terror and wholly unfit to give evidence. The envoys hurried to the council hall, where they were treated with contempt and told that it was impossible that the commission could have sent such a message. The 54 martyrs were piled in wagons and carried to the fields near the convent of S. Antoine, where they were slowly tortured to death with fire, refusing all offers of pardon for confession, and manifesting a constancy which, as a contemporary tells us, placed their souls in great peril of damnation, for it led the people into the error of believing them innocent. The council continued its work, and a few days later burned 4 more Templars, so that if there were any who still proposed to defend the Order they might recognize what would be their fate. It ordered the bones of Jean de Tourne, former treasurer of the Temple, to be exhumed and burned; those who confessed and adhered to their confessions were reconciled to the Church and liberated; those who persisted in refusing to confess were condemned to perpetual prison. This was rather more humane than the regular inquisitorial practice, but it suited the royal policy of the moment. A few weeks later, at Senlis, the Council of Reims burned 9 more; at Pont de l'Arche 3 were burned, and a number at Carcassonne.

This ferocious expedient accomplished its purpose. When, on the day after the executions at Paris, May 13, the commission opened its session, the first witness, Aimery de Villiers, threw himself on his knees, pale and desperately frightened; beating his breast and stretching forth his hands to the altar, he invoked sudden death and perdition to body and soul if he lied. He declared that all the crimes imputed to the Order were false, although he had, under torture, confessed to some of them. When he had yesterday seen his 54 brethren carried in wagons to be burned, he felt that he could not endure it and would confess to the commissioners or to anyone

else whatever might be required of him, even that he had slain the
Lord. In conclusion he adjured the commissioners and the notaries
not to reveal what he had said to his jailers, or to the royal officials,
for he would be burned like the 54. Then a previous witness, Jean
Bertrand, came before the commission to supplicate that his deposition be kept secret on account of the danger impending over him.
Seeing all this, the commission felt that during this general terror it
would be wise to suspend its sittings, and it did so. It met again
on the 18th to reclaim fruitlessly from the Archbishop of Sens,
Renaud de Provins, who had been put on trial before the council.
Pierre de Boulogne was likewise snatched away and could not be
obtained again. Many of the Templars who had offered to defend
the Order made haste to withdraw, and all effort to provide for it
an organized hearing before the Council of Vienne was perforce
abandoned. Whether Clement was privy to this highhanded interruption of the functions of his commission is perhaps doubtful, but
he did nothing to rehabilitate it, and his quiescence rendered him an
accomplice. He had only succeeded in betraying to a fiery death the
luckless wretches whom he had tempted to come forward.

On April 4, by the bull *Alma Mater*, Clement had postponed
the Council of Vienne from October 1310 until October 1311, in
consequence of the inquisition against the Templars requiring more
time than had been expected. There was, therefore, no necessity
for haste on the part of the commission, and it adjourned until
November 3. Its members were long in getting together, and it did
not resume its sessions until December 17. Then Guillaume de
Chambonnet and Bertrand de Sartiges were brought before it, when
they protested that they could not act for the Order without the
aid of Renaud de Provins and Pierre de Boulogne. These, the commission informed them, had solemnly renounced the defense of
the Order, had returned to their first confessions, and had been
condemned to perpetual imprisonment by the Council of Sens, after
which Pierre had broken jail and fled. The two knights were offered
permission to be present at the swearing of the witnesses, with opportunity to file exceptions, but they declared themselves unfitted
for the task, and retired. Thus all pretense of affording the Order a
chance to be heard was abandoned, and the subsequent proceedings
of the commission became merely an *ex parte* accumulation of ad-

verse testimony. It sat until June, industriously hearing the witnesses brought before it; but as those were selected by Philippe de Vohet and Jean de Jamville, care was evidently taken as to the character of the evidence that should reach it. Most of the witnesses, in fact, had been reconciled to the Church through confession, abjuration, and absolution, and no longer belonged to the Order, which they had abandoned to its fate. Among the large number of Templars who had refused to confess, only a few, and these apparently by accident, were allowed to appear before it. There were also a few who dared to retract what they had stated before the bishops, but with these slender exceptions all the evidence was adverse to the Order. In fact, it frequently happened that witnesses were sworn who never reappeared to give their testimony, and that this was not accidental is rendered probable by the fact that Renaud de Provins was one of these. Finally, on June 5, the commission closed its labors and transmitted without comment to Clement its records as part of the material to guide the judgment of the assembled Church at the Council of Vienne.

Before proceeding to the last scene of the drama at Vienne, it is necessary to consider briefly the action taken with the Templars outside France. In England, Edward II, on October 30, 1307, replied to Philippe's announcement of October 16, to the effect that he and his council have given the most earnest attention to the matter; it has caused the greatest astonishment, and, to obtain further information, he had sent for his Seneschal of Agen. So strong were his convictions and so earnest his desire to protect the threatened Order that on December 4 he wrote to the Kings of Portugal, Castile, Aragon, and Naples that the accusations must proceed from cupidity and envy, and begging them to do nothing without deliberation, so that an Order so distinguished for purity and honor should not be molested until legitimately convicted. Not content with this, on the 10th he replied to Clement that the reputation of the Templars in England for purity and faith is such that he cannot, without further proof, believe the terrible rumors about them, and he begs the pope to resist the calumnies of envious and wicked men. In a few days, however, he received Clement's bull of November 22, and could no longer doubt the facts asserted by the head of Christendom. He hastened to obey its commands, and on the 15th elaborate orders were sent out to all the sheriffs in England, with minute instructions to capture all the Templars on January 10, 1308, including directions for the sequestration and disposition of their property, and this was followed on the 20th by similar commands to the English authorities in Ireland, Scotland, and Wales.

The seizure was made accordingly, and the Templars were kept in honorable durance, not in prison, awaiting papal action. The delay was long, for though commissions were issued August 12, 1308, to the papal inquisitors, Sicard de Lavaur and the Abbot of Lagny, they did not start until September 1309, and on the 13th of that month the royal safe-conducts issued for them show their arrival in England. Then instructions were sent out to arrest all Templars not yet seized and gather them together in London, Lincoln, and York, for the examinations to be held, and the bishops of those sees were strictly charged to be present throughout. Similar orders were sent to Ireland and Scotland. It apparently was not easy to get the officials to do their duty, for December 14 instructions were required to all the sheriffs to seize the Templars who were wandering in secular habits throughout the land, and in the following March, the Sheriff of York was scolded for allowing those in his custody to wander abroad.

At length, on October 20, 1309, the papal inquisitors and the Bishop of London sat in the episcopal palace to examine the Templars collected in London. Interrogated singly on all the articles of accusation, they all asserted the innocence of the Order. Outside witnesses were called in who mostly declared their belief to the same effect, though some gave expression to the vague popular rumors and scandalous stories suggested by the secrecy of proceedings within the Order. The inquisitors were nonplussed. They had come to a country whose laws did not recognize the use of torture, and without it they were powerless to accomplish the work for which they had been sent. In their disgust they finally applied to the king, and on December 15 they obtained from him an order to the custodians of the prisoners to permit the inquisitors and episcopal ordinaries to do with the bodies of the Templars what they pleased, "in accordance with ecclesiastical law"—ecclesiastical law, by the hideous perversion of the times, having come to mean the worst of abuses, from which secular law still shrank. Still no evidence worth the trouble was gained, though the examinations were prolonged until May 24, when three captured fugitives were induced by means easily guessed to confess what was wanted, of which use was made to the utmost. At length Clement grew impatient under this lack of result. On August 6 he wrote to Edward that it was reported that he had prohibited the use of torture as contrary to the laws of the kingdom, and that the inquisitors were thus powerless to extract confessions. No law or usage, he said, could be permitted to override the canons provided for such cases, and Edward's counsellors and officials who were guilty of thus impeding the Inquisition were liable to the penalties provided for that serious offense, while the king himself was warned to consider whether his position comported with his honor and safety, and was offered remission of his sins if he would withdraw from it—perhaps the most suggestive sale of an indulgence on record. Under this impulsion Edward, August 26, again ordered that the bishops and inquisitors should be allowed to employ ecclesiastical law, and this was repeated October 6 and 23, November 22, and April 28, 1311—in the last instances the word "torture" being used, and in all of them the king being careful to explain that what he does is through reverence for the Holy See.

Thus for once the papal Inquisition found a foothold in England, but apparently its methods were too repugnant to the spirit of the nation to be rewarded with complete success. In spite of examinations prolonged for more than eighteen months, the Templars could not be convicted. The most that could be accomplished was that, in provincial councils held in London and York in the spring and summer of 1311, they were brought to admit that they were so defamed for heresy that they could not furnish the purgation required by law; they therefore asked for mercy and promised to perform what penance might be enjoined on them. The councils ordered them scattered among different monasteries to perform penance until the Holy See should decide about the future of the Order. This was the final disposition of the Templars in England. In Ireland and Scotland their examinations failed to procure any proof against the Order, save the vague conjectures and stories of outside witnesses industriously gathered together.

In Lorraine, as soon as news came of the seizure in France, the Preceptor of Villencourt ordered the brethren under him to shave and abandon their mantles, which was virtually releasing them from the Order. Duke Thiebault followed the exterminating policy of Philippe with complete success. A large number of the Templars were burned, and he managed to secure most of their property.

In Germany the Templars were by no means so numerous as in France, their fate was not so dramatic, and it attracted comparatively little attention from the chroniclers. One annalist informs us that they were destroyed with the assent of the Emperor Henry on account of their collusion with the Saracens in Palestine and Egypt, and their preparation for establishing a new empire for themselves among the Christians. Burchard III of Magdeburg was the first to act. Obliged to visit the papal court in 1307 to obtain the pallium, he returned in May 1308 with orders to seize all the Templars in his province; and as he was already hostile to them, he obeyed with alacrity. There were but four houses in his territories: on these and their occupants he laid his hands, leading to a long series of obscure quarrels, in which he incurred excommunication from the Bishop of Halberstadt, which Clement hastened to remove; by burning some of the more obstinate brethren, moreover, he involved himself in war with their kindred, in which he fared badly. As late as 1318 the Hospitallers are found complaining to John XXII that Templars were still in possession of the greater portion of their property.

The bull *Faciens misericordiam* of August 1308, sent to the German prelates, reserved, with Clement's usual policy, the Grand Preceptor of Germany for papal judgment. With the exception of Magdeburg, its instructions for active measures received slack obedience. It was not until 1310 that the great archbishops could be got to work, and then the results were disappointing. Trèves and Cologne, in fact, made over to Burchard of Magdeburg, in 1310, their authority as commissioners for the seizure of the Templar lands, and Clement confirmed this with instructions to proceed with vigor. As regards the persons of the Templars, at Trèves an inquest was held in which seventeen witnesses were heard, including three Templars, and resulting in their acquittal. At Mainz the Archbishop Peter, who had incurred Clement's displeasure by transferring to his suffragans his powers as commissioner over the Templar property, was at length forced to call a provincial council, May 11, 1310. Suddenly and unbidden there entered the Wild- and Rheingraf, Hugo of Salm, Commander of Grumbach, with 20 knights fully armed. There were fears of violence, but the archbishop asked Hugo what he had to say: the Templar asserted the innocence of the Order; those who had been burned had steadfastly denied the charges, and their truth had been proved by the crosses on their mantles remaining unburned—a miracle popularly believed, which had much influence on public opinion. He concluded by appealing to the future pope and the whole Church, and the archbishop, to escape a tumult, admitted the protest. Clement, on hearing of these proceedings, ordered the council to be reassembled and to do its work. He was obeyed. The Wildgraf Frederic of Salm, brother of Hugo and Master of the Rhine-province, offered to undergo the red-hot iron ordeal, but it was unnecessary. Forty-nine witnesses, of whom 37 were Templars, were examined, and all swore to the innocence of the Order. The 12 non-Templars, who were personages of distinction, were emphatic in their declarations in its favor. Among others, the Archpriest John testified that in a time of scarcity, when the measure of corn rose from 3 sols to 33, the commandery at Mostaire fed a thousand persons a day. The result was a verdict of acquittal, which was so displeasing to the pope that he ordered Burchard of Magdeburg to take the matter in hand and bring it to a more satisfactory conclusion. Archbishop Peter continued to hope for some adjustment, and when, after the Council of Vienne, he was forced to hand over the Templar property to the Hospitallers, he required the latter to execute an agreement to return the manor of Topfstadt if the pope should restore the Order.

In Italy the Templars were not numerous, and the pope had better control over the machinery for their destruction. In Naples the appeal of Edward II was in vain. The Angevine dynasty was too closely allied to the papacy to hesitate, and when a copy of the bull *Pastoralis præeminentiæ*, of November 22, 1307, was addressed to Robert, Duke of Calabria, son of Charles II, there was no hesitation in obedience. Orders were speedily sent out to all the provinces under the Neapolitan crown to arrest the Templars and sequestrate their property. Philip, Duke of Achaia and Romania, the youngest son of Charles, was commanded to carry out the papal instructions in all the possessions in the Levant. January 3, 1308, the officials in Provence and Forcalquier were instructed to make the seizure January 23. The Order was numerous in those districts, but the members must have mostly fled, for only 48 were arrested, who are said to have been tried and executed. The Templar movables were divided between the pope and king, and the landed possessions were made over to the Hospital. In the kingdom of Naples itself, some fragmentary reports of the papal commission sent in 1310 to obtain evidence against the Order as a whole and against the Grand Preceptor of Apulia, Oddo de Valdric, show that no obstacle was thrown in the way of the inquisitors in obtaining by the customary methods the kind of testimony desired. The same may be said of Sicily, where Frederic of Aragon had admitted the Inquisition in 1304.

In the States of the Church we have somewhat fuller accounts of the later proceedings. When the papal commission was sent to Paris to afford the Order an opportunity to prepare its defense at the Council of Vienne, similar commissions, armed with inquisitorial powers, were dispatched elsewhere, and the report of Giacomo, Bishop of Sutri, and Master Pandolfo di Sabello, who were commissioned in that capacity in the Patrimony of St. Peter, although unfortunately not complete, gives us an insight into the real object which underlay the ostensible purpose of these commissions. In October 1309 the inquisitors commenced at Rome, where no one appeared before them, although they summoned not only members of the Order, but everyone who had anything to say about it. In December they went to Viterbo, where five Templars lay in prison, who declined to appear and defend the Order. In January 1310 they proceeded to Spoleto without finding either Templars or other witnesses. In April, at Aquila, they summoned witnesses to ascertain whether the Templars had any churches in the Abruzzi, but not even the preceptor of the Hospitallers could give them any information. All the Franciscans of the place were then assembled, but they knew nothing to the discredit of the Order. A few days later, at Penna, they adopted a new formula by inviting all Templars and others who desired to defend the Order to appear before them. Here two Templars were found, who were personally summoned repeatedly, but they refused, saying that they would not defend the Order. One of them, Walter of Naples, was excused, owing to doubts as to his being a Templar, but the other, named Cecco, was brought before the inquisitors and told them of an idol kept for worship in the treasure-chamber of a preceptory in Apulia. In May, at Chieti, they succeeded in getting hold of another Templar, who confessed to renouncing Christ, idol-worship, and other of the charges. By May 23 they were back in Rome issuing citations, but again without result. The following week they were back at Viterbo, resolved to procure some evidence from the five captives imprisoned there, but the latter again sent word that none of them wished to appear before the inquisitors or to defend the Order. Four of the prisoners were brought forward and were induced to talk. From the 7th of June to the 19th, the inquisitors were employed in receiving their depositions on renouncing Christ, spitting on the cross, etc., all of which was duly recorded as free and spontaneous. Then at Segni they heard five witnesses without obtaining any evidence. Castel Fajole and Tivoli were equally barren, but on the 27th, at Palombara, Walter of Naples was brought to them from Penna, the doubts as to his membership of the Order having apparently been removed. Their persistence in this case was rewarded with full details of heretical practices. Here the record ends, the industrious search of nine months through these extensive territories having resulted in finding eight Templars, and obtaining seven incriminating depositions.

In the rest of Italy Clement's bull of 1307 seems to have been somewhat slackly obeyed. The earliest action on record is an order, in 1308, of Frà Ottone, Inquisitor of Lombardy, requiring the delivery of three Templars to the Podestà of Casale. Some further impulsion apparently was requisite, and in 1309 Giovanni, Archbishop of Pisa, was appointed Apostolic Nuncio in charge of the affair throughout Tuscany, Lombardy, Dalmatia, and Istria, with a stipend of 8 florins *per diem*, to be assessed on the Templar property. In Ancona the Bishop of Fano examined one Templar who confessed nothing, and nineteen other witnesses who furnished no incriminating evidence, and in Romagnuola, Rainaldo, Archbishop of Ravenna, and the Bishop of Rimini interrogated two Templars at Cesena, both of whom testified to the innocence of the Order. Papal letters were published throughout Italy, empowering the inquisitors to look after the Templar property, of which the Archbishops of Bologna and Pisa were appointed administrators; it was farmed out and the proceeds remitted to Clement. Rainaldo of Ravenna sympathized with the Templars, and no very earnest efforts were to be expected of him. He called a synod at Bologna in 1309, where some show was made of taking up the subject, but no results were reached, and when, in 1310, his vicar, Bonincontro, went to Ravenna with the papal bulls, he made no secret of his favor towards the accused. At length Rainaldo was forced to action, and issued a proclamation, November 25, 1310, reciting the papal commands to hold provincial councils for the examination and judgment of the Templars, in obedience to which he summoned one to assemble at Ravenna in January 1311, calling upon the inquisitors to bring thither the evidence which they had obtained by the use of torture. The council was held and the matter discussed, but no conclusion was reached. Another was summoned to meet at Bologna, but was transferred to Ravenna. To this the bishops were ordered to bring all Templars of their dioceses under strict guard, the result of which was that on June 16 seven knights were produced before the council. They were sworn and interrogated *seriatim* on all the articles furnished by the pope, which they unanimously denied. The question was then put to the council whether they should be tortured, and it was answered in the negative, in spite of the opposition of two Dominican inquisitors present. It was decided that the case should not be referred to the pope, in view of the nearness of the Council of Vienne, but that the accused should be put upon their purgation. The next day, however, when the council met this action was reversed and there was a unanimous decision that the innocent should be acquitted and the guilty punished, reckoning among the innocent those who had confessed through fear of torture and had revoked, or who would have revoked but for fear of repetition of torture. As for the Order as a whole, the council recommended that it should be preserved if a majority of the members were innocent, and if the guilty were subjected to abjuration and punishment within the Order. It was no wonder that Clement was indignant and ordered the burning of those who had thus relapsed—though the command was probably not obeyed, as Bishop Bini assures us that no Templars were burned in Italy.

For Tuscany and Lombardy, Clement appointed as special inquisitors Giovanni, Archbishop of Pisa; Antonio, Bishop of Florence; and Pietro Giudici of Rome, a canon of Verona. These were instructed to hold the inquests, one upon the brethren individually and one upon the Order. They were troubled with no scruples about the use of torture and secured a certain amount of the kind of testimony desired. Venice kindly postponed the inevitable uprooting of the Order, and when it eventually took place there was no unnecessary hardship.

Cyprus was the headquarters of the Order. There resided the marshal, Ayme d'Osiliers, who was its chief in the absence of the Grand Master, and there was the "Convent," or governing body. It was not until May 1308 that the papal bull commanding the arrest reached the island, and there could be no pretense of a secret and sudden seizure, for the Templars were advised of what had occurred in France. They had many enemies, for they had taken an active part in the turbulent politics of the time, and it had been by their aid that the regent, Amauri of Tyre, had been placed in power. Resistance was hopeless, and in a few weeks they submitted; their property was sequestrated and they were kept in honorable confinement, without being deprived of the sacraments. This continued for two years, until in April 1310 the Abbot of Alet and the Archpriest Tommaso of Rieti came as papal inquisitors to inquire against them individually and the Order in general, under the guidance of the Bishops of Limisso and Famagosta. The examination commenced May 1 and continued until June 5, when it came abruptly to an end, in consequence, doubtless, of the excitement caused by the murder of the Regent Amauri. All the Templars on the island, 75 in number, together with 56 other witnesses, were duly interrogated upon the long list of articles of accusation. That the Templars were unanimous in asserting the purity of the Order shows that torture cannot have been employed. More convincing as to their innocence is the evidence of the other witnesses, consisting of ecclesiastics of all ranks, nobles, and burghers, many of them political enemies, who yet rendered testimony emphatically favorable. A few alluded to the popular suspicions aroused by the secrecy observed in the holding of chapters and the admission of neophytes, but the evidence is unquestionable that in Cyprus, where they were best known, among friends and foes, and especially among those who had been in intimate relations with the Templars for long periods, there was general sympathy for the Order, and that there had been no evil attributed to it until the papal bulls had so unqualifiedly asserted its guilt.

In Aragon, Philippe's letter of October 16, 1307, to Jayme II was accompanied with one from the Dominican, Fray Romeo de Bruguera, asserting that he had been present at the confession made by de Molay and others. Notwithstanding this, on November 17 Jayme, like Edward II, responded with warm praises of the Templars of the kingdom, whom he refused to arrest without absolute proof of guilt or orders from the pope. To the latter he wrote two days later for advice and instructions, and when, on December 1, he received Clement's bull of November 22, he could hesitate no longer. Ramon, Bishop of Valencia, and Ximenes de Luna, Bishop of Saragossa, who chanced to be with him, received orders to make in their respective dioceses diligent inquisition against the Templars, and Fray Juan Llotger, Inquisitor-General of Aragon, was instructed to extirpate the heresy. Royal letters were issued December 3 for the immediate arrest of all members of the Order and the sequestration of their property, and the inquisitor published edicts summoning them before him in the Dominican Convent of Valencia, to answer for their faith, and prohibiting all local officials from rendering them assistance. A number of arrests were effected; some of the brethren shaved and threw off their mantles and succeeded in hiding themselves; some endeavored to escape by sea with a quantity of treasure, but adverse storms cast them back upon the coast and they were seized. The great body of the knights, however, threw themselves into their castles. Ramon Sa Guardia, Preceptor of Mas Deu in Roussillon, was acting as lieutenant of the Commander of Aragon, and fortified himself in Miravet, while others occupied the strongholds of Ascon, Montço, Cantavieja, Vilell, Castellot, and Chalamera. On January 20, 1308, they were summoned to appear before the Council of Tarragona, but they refused, and Jayme promised the prelates that he would use the whole forces of the kingdom for their subjugation. This proved no easy task. Many noble youths embraced their cause and joined them in their castles, while the people obeyed slackly the order to take up arms against them. The

knights defended themselves bravely. Castellot surrendered in November; Sa Guardia addressed Clement a manly appeal, pointing
out the services rendered to religion by the Order; that many knights
captured by the Saracens languished in prison for 20 or 30 years,
when by abjuring they could at once regain their liberty and be
richly rewarded—70 of their brethren were at that moment enduring
such a fate. They were ready to appear in judgment before the pope,
or to maintain their faith against all accusers by arms, as was
customary with knights, but they had no prelates or advocates to
defend them, and it was the duty of the pope to do so. A month after
this Miravet was forced to surrender at discretion, and in another
month all the rest, except Montço and Chalamera, which held out
until near July 1309. Clement at once took measures to get possession
of the Templar property, but Jayme refused to deliver it to the papal
commissioners, alleging that most of it had been derived from the
crown; the most that he would promise was that if the council
should abolish the Order he would surrender the property, subject
to the rights and claims of the crown.

In 1310 Clement sent to Aragon, as elsewhere, special papal inquisitors to conduct the trials. They were met by the same difficulties as in England: in Aragon torture was not recognized by the
law. Still, the inquisitors did what they could. At their request the
king, July 5, 1310, ordered his baillis to put the Templars in irons
and to render their prison harsher. Then the Council of Tarragona
interfered and asked that they be kept in safe but not afflictive
custody, seeing that nothing had as yet proved their guilt and their
case was still undecided. In accordance with this, on October 20,
the king ordered that they should be free in the castles where they
were confined, giving their parole not to escape under pain of being
reputed heretics. This was not the way to obtain the desired evidence,
and Clement, March 18, 1311, ordered them to be tortured, and
asked Jayme to lend his aid to it, seeing that the proceedings thus
far had resulted only in "vehement suspicion." By August the papal
representatives were growing impatient, as the time set for the
Council of Vienne was approaching, and the papal demands for
adverse evidence remained unsatisfied. Finally, on the eve of the
assembling of the council, the king yielded. September 29 he issued
an order appointing Umbert de Capdepont, one of the royal judges,

to assist at the judgment, when sentence should be rendered by the Inquisitors Pedro de Montclus and Juan Llotger, along with the Bishops of Lerida and Vich, who had been especially commissioned by the pope. We have no knowledge of the details of the investigation, but there is evidence that torture was unsparingly used, for there is a royal letter of December 3 ordering medicaments to be prepared for those of the Templars who might need them in consequence of sickness or torture. At last, in March 1312, the Archbishop of Tarragona asked to have them brought before his provincial council, then about to assemble, and the king assented, but nothing was done, probably because the Council of Vienne was still in session; but after the dissolution of the Order had been proclaimed by Clement, and the fate of the members was relegated to the local councils, one was held, October 18, 1312, at Tarragona, which decided the question so long pending. The Templars were brought before it and rigorously examined. November 4 the sentence was publicly read, pronouncing an unqualified acquittal from all the errors and crimes with which they were charged; they were declared beyond suspicion, and no one should dare to defame them. In view of the dissolution of the Order the council was somewhat puzzled to know what to do with them, but after prolonged debate it was determined that until the pope should otherwise decree they should reside in the dioceses in which their property lay, receiving proper support from their sequestrated lands. This decree was carried out, and when the property passed into the hands of the Hospitallers it was burdened with these charges. In 1319 a list of pensions thus payable by the Hospitallers would seem to show that the Templars were liberally provided for, and received what was due to them.

Jayme I of Majorca was in no position to resist the pressure brought upon him by Philippe le Bel and Clement. His little kingdom consisted of the Balearic Isles, the counties of Roussillon and Cerdagne, the Seignory of Montpellier, and a few other scattered possessions at the mercy of his powerful neighbor. He promptly therefore obeyed the papal bull of November 22, 1307, and by the end of the month the Templars in his dominions were all arrested. In Roussillon the only preceptory was that of Mas Deu, which was one of the strongholds of the land, and there the Templars were collected and confined to the number of 25, including the Preceptor,

Ramon Sa Guardia, the gallant defender of Miravet, who after his surrender was demanded by the King of Majorca and willingly joined his comrades. We know nothing of what took place on the islands beyond the fact of the arrest, but on the mainland we can follow with some exactness the course of events. Roussillon constituted the diocese of Elne, which was suffragan to the archbishopric of Narbonne. May 5, 1309, the archbishop sent to Ramon Costa, Bishop of Elne, the articles of accusation with the papal bull ordering an inquest. The good bishop seems to have been in no haste to comply, but, pleading illness, postponed the matter until January 1310. Then, in obedience to the instructions, he summoned two Franciscans and two Dominicans, and with two of his cathedral canons he proceeded to interrogate the prisoners. It is evident that no torture was employed, for in their prolonged examinations they substantially agreed in asserting the purity of the Order, and their chaplain offered in evidence their book of ritual for receptions in the vernacular, commencing, "*Quan alcum proom requer la compaya de la Mayso.*" They refused to believe that the Grand Master and chiefs of the Order had confessed to the truth of the charges, but if they had done so they had lied in their throats—or, as one of them phrased it, they were demons in human skin. The voluminous testimony was forwarded, with a simple certificate of its accuracy, by Bishop Ramon, August 31, 1310, which shows that he was in no haste to transmit it.

In Castile no action seems to have been taken until the bull *Faciens misericordiam* of August 1308 was sent to the prelates ordering them to act in conjunction with the Dominican, Eymeric de Navas, as inquisitor. Fernando IV then ordered the Templars arrested, and their lands placed in the hands of the bishops until the fate of the Order should be determined. There was no alacrity, however, in pursuing the affair, and the only judicial action of which we have notice was that of the Council of Salamanca for the province of Compostella, where the Templars were unanimously acquitted, and the orders to torture them issued the next year by Clement seem to have been disregarded.

Portugal belonged ecclesiastically to the province of Compostella, and the Bishop of Lisbon, commissioned to investigate the Order, found no ground for the charges. The fate of the Templars there was exceptionally fortunate, for King Diniz, grateful for their services in his wars with the Saracens, founded a new Order, that of Jesus Christ, or *de Avis*, and procured its approval in 1318 from John XXII. To this safe refuge the Templars and their lands were transferred, the commander and many of the preceptors retaining their rank, and the new Order was thus merely a continuation of the old.

The period finally set for the Council of Vienne was approaching, and thus far Clement had failed to procure any evidence of weight against the Templars beyond the boundaries of France. He may at the first have been Philippe's unwilling accomplice, but if so he had long since gone too far to retract. Whether, as believed by many of his contemporaries, he was sharing the spoils is of little moment. He had committed himself personally to the assertion of the Templars' guilt, with details admitting of no retraction or explanation; he, as well as they, was on trial before Christendom, and their acquittal by the council would be his conviction. As the council drew near he cast around for means to secure the testimony which should justify him by proving the heresy of the Order. We have seen how he urged Edward II to introduce torture into the hitherto unpolluted courts of England, and how he succeeded in having the brethren of Aragon tortured in violation of the liberties of the land. These were but specimens of a series of bulls, perhaps the most disgraceful that ever proceeded from a vicegerent of God. It was not merely that those who had hitherto been spared the rack were now subjected to it, but, in the eagerness to supplement the evidence on hand, those who had already undergone torture were again subjected to it with enhanced severity, in order to obtain from them still more extravagant admissions of guilt. In the Château d'Alais the Bishop of Nîmes held 33 Templars who had already been examined and confessions extorted from some of them, which had mostly been retracted. Under Clement's orders 29 survivors of these (four having meanwhile died in prison) were brought out in August 1311. Some of them had already been tortured three years before, but now all were tortured again, with the result of obtaining the kind of testimony required, including demon-worship.

In spite of all these precautions it required the most arbitrary use of both papal and kingly influence to force from the council a reluctant assent to what was evidently regarded by Christendom as the foulest injustice. The first question to be settled was Clement's demand that the Order should be condemned without a hearing. He had, as we have seen, solemnly summoned it to appear, through its chiefs and procurators, before the council, and had ordered the Cardinal of Palestrina, whom he had appointed their custodian, to present them for that purpose. Now the council had met and the chiefs of the Order were not brought before it. The subject was too delicate a one to be trusted to the body of the council, and a picked convocation was formed of prelates selected from the nations represented—Spain, France, Italy, Germany, Hungary, England, Ireland, and Scotland—to discuss the matter with the pope and cardinals. On a day in November, while this body was listening to the reports sent in by the inquisitors, suddenly there appeared before them seven Templars offering to defend the Order in the name, they said, of 1,500 or 2,000 brethren, refugees who were wandering in the mountains of the Lyonnais. In place of hearing them, Clement promptly cast them into prison, and when, a few days later, two more, undeterred by the fate of their predecessors, made a similar attempt, they were likewise incarcerated. This was not calculated to make the prelates feel less keenly the shame of what they were asked to do, for which the only reason alleged was the injury to the Holy Land arising from the delay to be anticipated from discussion; and when the matter came to a vote only one Italian bishop and three Frenchmen (the Archbishops of Sens, Reims, and Rouen) were found to record themselves in favor of the infamy of condemning the Order unheard.

Clement vainly used every effort to win over the council. The most that he could do was to prolong the discussion until the middle of February 1312, when Philippe, who had called a meeting of the Three Estates at Lyons, came thence with Charles de Valois, his three sons, and a following numerous enough to impress the prelates with his power. Philippe dexterously brought forward again the question of the condemnation of Boniface VIII for heresy, which he had promised, a year previous, to abandon. It was an impossibility to grant this without impugning the legitimacy of Boniface's cardinals and of Clement's election, but it served the purpose of affording an apparent concession. The combined pressure brought to bear upon the council became too strong for further resistance, and the Gordian knot was resolutely severed. In a secret consistory of cardinals and prelates held March 22, Clement presented the bull Vox in excelso, in which he admitted that the evidence did not canonically justify the definitive condemnation of the Order, but he argued that it had been so scandalized that no honorable men hereafter could enter it, that delay would lead to the dilapidation of its possessions with consequent damage to the Holy Land, and that therefore its provisional abolition by the Holy See was expedient. April 3 the second session of the council was held, in which the bull was published, and Clement apologized for it by explaining that it was necessary to propitiate his dear son, the King of France. Thus, after all this cruelty and labor, the Order was abolished without being convicted.

The next point to be determined was the disposition of the Templar property, which gave rise to a long and somewhat bitter debate. Various plans were proposed, but finally Clement succeeded in procuring its transfer to the Hospitallers. It may not be true that they bribed him heavily to accomplish this, but such a belief prevailed extensively at the time. May 2 the bull Ad providam announced that, although in view of the proceedings thus far had the Order could not legally be suppressed, it was irrevocably abolished by apostolic ordinance; it was placed under perpetual inhibition, and anyone presuming to enter it or to assume its habit incurred ipso facto excommunication. All the property of the Order was assumed by the Holy See, and was transferred to the Hospital of St. John of Jerusalem, saving in the kingdoms of Castile, Aragon, Majorca, and Portugal. As early as August 1310, Jayme of Aragon had urged his brother monarchs to unite with him in defending their claims before the papal court; and though he disregarded Clement's invitation to appear in person before the council to state his reasons, the three kings took care to have their views energetically represented. Elsewhere, all who occupied and detained such property, no matter what their rank or station, were required, under pain of excommunication, to hand it over to the Hospitallers within a month after summons.

The question as to the property being thus settled, the less mate-

rial one as to the persons of the Templars was shuffled off by referring them to their provincial councils for judgment, with the exception of the chiefs of the Order still reserved to the Holy See. All
fugitives were cited to appear within a year before their bishops for
examination and sentence; failure to do so incurred *ipso facto* excommunication, which if endured for another year became condemnation for heresy. General instructions were given that the
impenitent and relapsed were to be visited with the utmost penalties
of the law. Interest in the subject, however, passed away with the
alienation of the property, and few provincial councils seem to have
been held save those of Tarragona and Narbonne. Many Templars
rotted to death in their dungeons; some of the so-called "relapsed"
were burned; many wandered over Europe as homeless vagabonds;
others maintained themselves as best they might by manual labor.
In Naples, curiously enough, John XXII in 1318 ordered them to
be supported by the Dominicans and Franciscans. When some attempted to marry, he pronounced that their vows were still binding
and their marriages void, thus admitting that their reception had
been regular and not vitiated. He likewise assumed their orthodoxy
when he permitted them to enter other Orders. A certain number
of them did so, especially in Germany, where their fate was less
bitter than elsewhere, and where the Hospitallers welcomed them
by formal resolution of the Conference of Frankfurt-am-Mayn in
1317.

There remained to be disposed of de Molay and the other chiefs
reserved by Clement for his personal judgment—a reservation which,
as we have seen, by inspiring them with selfish hopes, led them to
abandon their brethren. When this purpose had been accomplished
Clement for a while seemed to forget them. It was not till December 22, 1313, that he appointed a commission of three cardinals,
Arnaud of S. Sabina, Nicholas of S. Eusebio, and Arnaldo of S.
Prisca, to investigate the proceedings against them and to absolve
or condemn, or to inflict penance proportionate to their offenses.
The cardinals dallied with their duty until March 19, 1314, when,
on a scaffold in front of Nôtre Dame, de Molay, Geoffroi de Charney,
Hugues de Peraud, and Geoffroi de Gonneville were brought forth
from the jail in which for nearly seven years they had lain, to receive
the sentence agreed upon by the cardinals, in conjunction with the

Archbishop of Sens and some other prelates whom they had called in. Considering the offenses the culprits had confessed and confirmed, the penance imposed was in accordance with rule—that of perpetual imprisonment. The affair was supposed to be concluded when, to the dismay of the prelates and wonderment of the assembled crowd, de Molay and Geoffroi de Charney arose. They had been guilty, they said, not of the crimes imputed to them, but of basely betraying their Order to save their own lives. It was pure and holy; the charges were fictitious and the confessions false. Hastily the cardinals delivered them to the Prévôt of Paris, and retired to deliberate on this unexpected contingency, but they were saved all trouble. When the news was carried to Philippe he was furious. A short consultation with his council only was required. The canons pronounced that a relapsed heretic was to be burned without a hearing; the facts were notorious and no formal judgment by the papal commission need be waited for. That same day, by sunset, a pile was erected on a small island in the Seine, the Isle des Juifs, near the palace garden. There de Molay and de Charney were slowly burned to death, refusing all offers of pardon for retraction, and bearing their torment with a composure which won for them the reputation of martyrs among the people, who reverently collected their ashes as relics. Hugues de Peraud and the Master of Aquitaine lacked courage to imitate them, accepted their penance, and perished miserably in their dungeons. Raimbaud de Caron, the Preceptor of Cyprus, had doubtless been already released by death.

Philippe thus obtained the object of his desires. After 1307 his financial embarrassments visibly decreased. The Order's vast accumulations of treasure and valuables of all kinds fell into his hands and were never accounted for. He collected all the debts due to it, and his successors were still busy at that work as late as 1322. Despite his pretense of surrendering the landed estates to the pope, he retained possession of them till his death and enjoyed their revenues. Even those in Guyenne, belonging to the English crown, he collected in spite of the protests of Edward, and he claimed the Templar castles in the English territories until Clement prevailed upon him to withdraw. The great Paris Temple, half-palace, half-fortress, one of the architectural wonders of the age, was retained with a grip which nothing but death could loosen.

The fact that in little more than a month Clement died in torment of the loathsome disease known as lupus, and that in eight months Philippe, at the early age of 46, perished while hunting, necessarily gave rise to the legend that de Molay had cited them before the tribunal of God. Even in distant Germany Philippe's death was spoken of as a retribution for his destruction of the Templars, and Clement was described as shedding tears of remorse on his deathbed for three great crimes, the poisoning of Henry VI and the ruin of the Templars and of the Beguines.

Thus disappeared an organization which was regarded as one of the proudest, wealthiest, and most formidable in Europe. It is not too much to say that the very idea of its destruction could not have suggested itself but for the facilities which the inquisitorial process placed in able and unscrupulous hands to accomplish any purpose of violence under the form of law.

Criticism would doubtless before this have demonstrated the meteoric career of Joan of Arc to be a myth, but for the concurrent testimony of friend and foe and the documentary evidence, which enable us with reasonable certainty to separate its marvellous vicissitudes from the legendary details with which they have been obscured. For us her story has a special interest, as affording another illustration of the ease with which the inquisitorial process was employed for political ends.

In 1429 the French monarchy seemed doomed beyond hope of resuscitation. In the fierce dissensions which marked the reign of the insane Charles VI, a generation had grown up in whom adherence to faction had replaced fidelity to the throne or to the nation; the loyalists were known not as partisans of Charles VII, but as Armagnacs, and the Burgundians welcomed the foreign domination of England as preferable to that of their hereditary sovereign. Paris, in spite of the fearful privations and losses entailed by the war, submitted cheerfully to the English through the love it bore to their ally, the Duke of Burgundy. Joan of Arc said that in her native village, Domremy, there was but one Burgundian, and his head she wished were cut off; but Domremy and Vaucouleurs constituted the only Armagnac spot in northeastern France, and its boys used to have frequent fights with the Burgundian boys of

Marey, from which they would be brought home wounded and bleeding.

Even the death of Henry V in 1423 had seemed to check in no degree the progress of the English arms. Under the able regency of his brother, the Duke of Bedford, seconded by such captains as Salisbury, Talbot, Scales, and Fastolf, the infant Henry VI appeared destined to succeed to the throne of his grandfather, Charles VI, as provided in the treaty of Troyes. In 1424 the victory of Verneuil repeated the triumph of Agincourt, and but for the fidelity of the provinces won by the Albigensian crusades, Charles VII would already have been a king without a kingdom. Driven beyond the Loire, he was known by the nickname of the *Roi de Bourges*. Vacillating and irresolute, dominated by unworthy favorites, he hardly knew whether to retreat farther to the south and make a final stand among the mountains of Dauphiné, or to seek a refuge in Spain or Scotland. In 1428 his last line of defense on the Loire was threatened by the leaguer of Orleans. As the spring of 1429 opened, further resistance seemed useless, and for Charles there appeared nothing left but ignominious retreat and eventual exile.

Such was the hopeless condition of the French monarchy when the enthusiasm of Joan of Arc introduced a new factor in the tangled problem, kindling anew the courage which had been extinguished by an unbroken series of defeats, arousing the sense of loyalty which had been lost in faction, bringing religion as a stimulus to patriotism, and replacing despair with confidence and hopefulness.

Born January 6, 1484, in the little hamlet of Domremy, on the border line of Lorraine, Jeanne had but completed her seventeenth year when she confidently assumed the function of the saviour of her native land.[6] Her parents, honest peasants, had given her such training as comported with her station; she could, of course, neither read nor write, but she could recite her *Pater Noster*, *Ave Maria*, and *Credo*; she had herded the kine, and was a notable sempstress— on her trial she boasted that no maid or matron of Rouen could teach her anything with the needle. Thanks to her rustic employ-

[6] Though the name Joan of Arc has been naturalized in English, Jeanne's patronymic was Darc, not D'Arc. So close to the border was her birthplace that a new delimitation of the frontier, made in 1571, transferred to Lorraine the group of houses including the Darc cottage, and left a neighboring group in France.

ment she was tall and strong-limbed, active and enduring. Her resolute self-reliance was shown when she was sought in marriage by an honest citizen of Toul, whose suit her parents favored. Finding her obdurate, he had recourse, it would seem with her parents' consent, to the law, and cited her before the Official of Toul to fulfill the marriage promise which he alleged she had made to him. Notwithstanding her youth, Joan appeared undaunted before the court, swore that she had given no pledges, and was released from the too-ardent suitor. At the age of 13 she commenced to have ecstasies and visions. The Archangel Michael appeared to her first, and he was followed by St. Catharine and St. Margaret, whom God had specially commissioned to watch over and guide her. Even the Archangel Gabriel sometimes came to counsel her, and she felt herself the instrument of the divine will. At length she could summon her heavenly advisers at will and obtain from them instructions in any doubtful emergency. In her trial great stress was laid upon an ancient beech tree, near Domremy, known as the Ladies' Tree, or Fairies' Tree, from near the roots of which gushed forth a spring of miraculous healing virtue. A survival of tree and fountain worship was preserved in the annual dances of the young girls of the village around the tree and the garlands which they hung upon its boughs, but Joan, although she joined her comrades in these observances, usually reserved her garlands to decorate the shrine of the Virgin. Extreme religious sensibility was inseparable from such a character as hers, and almost at the first apparition of her celestial visitants she made a vow of virginity. She believed herself consecrated and set apart for some high and holy purpose, to which all earthly ties must be subordinate. When she related to her judges that her parents were almost crazed at her departure, she added that if she had had a hundred fathers and mothers she would have abandoned them to fulfill her mission.

At first her heavenly guides merely told her to conduct herself well and to frequent the church, but as she grew to understand the desperate condition of the monarchy and to share the fierce passions of the time, it was natural that these purely moral instructions should change into commands to bear from God the message of deliverance to the despairing people. At length her Voices, as she habitually called them, urged her several times a week to hasten to

France and to raise the siege of Orleans. To her parents she feared to reveal her mission; some unguarded revelation they must have had, for, two years before her departure, her father, Jacques Darc, had dreams of her going off with the soldiers, and he told her brothers that if he thought that his dreams would come true he wished they would drown her, or he would do it himself. Thenceforth she was closely watched, but the urgency of her celestial counsellors grew into reproaches for her tardiness, and further delay was unendurable. Obtaining permission to visit her uncle, Denis Laxart, she persuaded him to communicate her secret to Robert de Baudricourt, who held for the king the neighboring castle of Vaucouleurs. The good knight, who at first contemptuously advised her uncle to box her ears, at length was persuaded to ask the king's permission to send the girl to him. On the royal permission being accorded, de Baudricourt gave to her a man's dress and a sword, with a slender escort of a knight and four men, and washed his hands of the affair.

The little party started, February 13, 1429, on their perilous ride of 150 leagues, in the depth of winter, through the enemy's country. That they should accomplish it without misadventure in eleven days was in itself regarded as a miracle, and as manifesting the favor of God. On February 24 they reached Chinon, where Charles held his court. Those who relied on worldly wisdom shook their heads and pronounced her mission an absurdity—in fact, it was charitable to regard her as insane. It shows, indeed, to what depth of despair the royal cause had fallen that her pretensions were regarded as of sufficient importance to warrant investigation. Prelates and doctors of theology, jurists and statesmen examined her for a month, and one by one they were won over by her simple earnestness, her evident conviction, and the intelligence of her replies. This was not enough, however. In Poitiers sat Charles's Parlement and a University composed of such schoolmen as had abandoned the anglicized University of Paris. Thither was Joan sent, and for three weeks more she was tormented with an endless repetition of questioning. Charles was advised to ask of her a sign by which to prove that she came from God, but this she refused, saying that it was the divine command that she should give it before Orleans, and nowhere else. Finally, the official conclusion, cautiously expressed, was that in view of her honest life and conversation, and of her promising a sign before Orleans, the king should not prevent her from going there, but should convey her there in safety; for to reject her without the appearance of evil would be to rebuff the Holy Ghost, and to render himself unworthy the grace and aid of God.

Two months had been wasted in these preliminaries, and it was the end of April before the determination was reached. A convoy was in preparation to throw provisions into the town, and it was resolved that Joan should accompany it. Under instructions from her Voices she had a standard prepared, representing on a white field Christ holding the world, with an angel on each side. She had assigned to her a troop or guard, but does not seem to have been entrusted with any command, yet she assumed that she was taking the field as the representative of God, and must first give the enemy due notice of defiance. Accordingly, on April 18, she addressed four letters, one to Henry VI and the others to the Regent Bedford, the captains before Orleans, and the English soldiers there, in which she demanded the surrender of the keys of all the cities held in France; she announced herself ready to make peace if they will abandon the land and make compensation for the damages inflicted, otherwise she is commissioned by God, and will drive them out with a shock of arms such as had not been seen in France for a thousand years. It is scarce to be wondered that these uncourtly epistles excited no little astonishment in the English camp. Rumors of her coming had spread; she was denounced as a sorceress, and all who placed faith in her as heretics. Talbot declared that he would burn her if she was captured, and the heralds who brought her letters were only saved from a similar fate by a determined threat of reprisals on the part of Dunois, then in command at Orleans.

Some ten days later the convoy started under command of Gilles de Rais and the Maréchal de Saint-Sevère. Joan had promised that it should meet with no opposition, and faith in her was greatly enhanced when her words proved true. Although it passed within one or two bow-shots of the English siege works, and though there was considerable delay in ferrying the cattle and provisions across the Loire into the city, not an attempt at interference was made. The same occurred with a second convoy which reached Orleans May 4, to the surprise of the French and the disgust of the Parisians, who watched the affair from a distance, and were unable to understand the paralysis which seemed to have fallen on the English arms. Joan had impatiently awaited these last reinforcements, and urged immediate offensive measures against the besiegers. Without consulting her, on the same day an assault was made on one of the English works on the other side of the Loire. Her legend relates that she started up from slumber exclaiming that her people were being slaughtered, and, scarcely waiting for her armor to be adjusted, sprang on her horse and galloped to the gate leading to the scene of action. The attack had miscarried, but after her arrival on the scene not an Englishman could wound a Frenchman, and the *bastille* was carried. Hot fighting occurred on the following days. On the 6th she was wounded in the foot by a caltrop, and on the 7th in the shoulder by an arrow, but in spite of desperate resistance all the English works on the farther bank of the Loire were taken, and their garrisons slain or captured. The English loss was estimated at from 6,000 to 8,000 men, while that of the French was not over a hundred. On the 8th the English abandoned the siege, marching off in such haste that they left behind them their sick and wounded, their artillery and magazines. The French, flushed with victory, were eager to attack them, but Joan forbade it—"Let them go; it is not the will of Messire that they should be fought today; you will have them another time" —and by this time her moral ascendancy was such that she was obeyed. Even the unfriendly Monstrelet admits that after the raising of the siege of Orleans there was no captain who so filled the mouths of men as she, though she was accompanied by knights so renowned as Dunois, La Hire, and Pothon de Xaintrailles. The Regent Bedford, in writing to the English council, could only describe it as a terrible blow from the divine hand, especially "caused of unleyefulle doubte that thei hadde of a Desciple and Lyme of the Feende called the Pucelle that used fals Enchauntements and Sorcerie."

In the chronic exhaustion of the royal treasury it was not easy for Charles to take full advantage of this unexpected success, but the spirit of the nation was aroused and a force could be kept spasmodically in the field. D'Alençon was sent with troops to clear the Loire valley of the enemy, and took Joan with him. Suffolk had fortified himself in Jargeau, but the place was carried by assault and he was captured with all his men who were not slain. Then want of money caused a return to Tours, where Joan earnestly urged Charles to go to Reims for his coronation: she had always claimed that her mission was to deliver Orleans and to crown the king; that her time was short and that the counsel of her Voices must not be disregarded, but prudence prevailed, and it was felt that the English power in the central provinces must first be crushed. A second expedition was organized. Beaugency was besieged and taken, and on June 18 the battle of Patay gave some slight amends for Agincourt and Verneuil. After feeble resistance the English fled; 2,500 of them were left upon the field, and large numbers were captured, including Talbot, Scales, and others of note. Thus in little more than six weeks all the leading English captains were slain or in captivity, except Fastolf, whose flight from Patay Bedford avenged by tearing from him the Order of the Garter. It was no wonder that in all this one side recognized the hand of God and the other that of the devil. Even the Norman chronicler, P. Cochon, says that the English would have abandoned France if the regent would have allowed it, and that they were so dispirited that one Frenchman would chase three of them.

A letter written from the court of Charles VII to the Duke of Milan three days after the triumph of Patay, recounting the marvels of the previous weeks, shows how Joan was regarded and how rapidly her legend was growing. At her birth the villagers of Domremy were joyously excited, they knew not why, and the cocks for two hours flapped their wings and uttered a song wholly different from their ordinary crowing. Her visions were described in the most exaggerated terms, as well as her personal prowess and endurance. We are told, moreover, that she was already predicting the deliverance of Charles of Orleans, a prisoner in England for fifteen years, and had sent a notice to the English to surrender him.

It could no longer be doubted that Joan was under the direct inspiration of God, and when at Gien, on June 25, there was a consultation as to the next movement, though Charles's councillors advised him to reduce La Charité and clear the Orleannais and Berri of the enemy, it is no wonder that he yielded to Joan's urgency and gave his assent to a march to Reims. The enterprise seemed a desperate one, for it lay through a hostile country with strong cities along the road, and the royal resources were inadequate to equipping and provisioning an army or providing it with siege-trains. But enthusiasm was rising to fever heat, and human prudence was distrust of God. Volunteers came pouring in as soon as the king's intentions were noised abroad, and gentlemen too poor to arm and mount themselves were content to serve as simple archers and retainers. La Trémouille, the royal favorite, thinking his own position endangered, caused the services of multitudes to be rejected, but for which, it was said, an army sufficient to drive the English from France could readily have been collected. On went the ill-conditioned forces. Auxerre, though not garrisoned, refused to open its gates, but gave some provisions, and in spite of Joan's desire to take it by assault the king went forward, induced, it was said, by La Trémouille, who had received from the town a bribe of 2,000 livres. At Troyes there was a strong English and Burgundian garrison; it could not be left behind, and the army encamped before it for five or six days, with no artillery to breach its walls. There was neither money nor food, and the only subsistence was corn and beans plucked in the fields. The situation was discouraging, and a council of war under the impulse of the Chancellor Renaud de Chartres, Archbishop of Reims, advised retreat. Joan was sent for and declared that within two days the town would surrender. She was given the time she asked, and at once proceeded to gather material to fill the trenches. A panic seized the inhabitants and they demanded to surrender; the garrison was allowed to march out, and the city returned to its allegiance.

When Joan entered the town she was met by a Frère Richard, whom the people had sent to examine her and report what she was. The worthy friar, doubtful whether she was of heaven or hell, approached her cautiously, sprinkling holy water and making the sign of the cross, till she smiled and told him to come boldly on, as she was not going to fly away. Frère Richard was a noted Franciscan preacher, who had recently returned from a pilgrimage to Jerusalem and in April had made the deepest impression on Paris with his eloquence. He had preached daily to audiences of five and six thousand souls, and had excited such a tempest of emotion that on one day a hundred bonfires were built in the streets into which men threw their cards and dice and tables, and women their ornaments and frippery. Over this man Joan obtained so complete a mastery that he devoted himself to her and followed her in her campaigns, using his eloquence to convert the people, not from their sins, but from their disloyalty to Charles.

After this the march to Reims was a triumphant progress. Châlons-sur-Marne sent half a day's journey in advance to submit and took the oath of allegiance. At Septsaux the garrison fled and the people welcomed their king, while the Dukes of Lorraine and Bar came to join him with a heavy force. Reims was held for Burgundy by the Seigneur de Saveuse, one of the doughtiest warriors of the day, but the citizens were so frightened by the coming of the Pucelle that they declared for Charles, and Saveuse was obliged to fly. Charles entered the town on July 16 and was joyfully received. The next day, Sunday, he was crowned King of France. During the ceremony Joan stood by the altar with the standard: her judges at her trial seemed to imagine that she held it there for some occult influence it was supposed to exercise, and inquired curiously about her motive; she answered simply, "It had been in the strife, it had a right to be in the honor."

Joan might well claim that her mission was accomplished. In little more than three months she had made the intending fugitive of Chinon a conquering king, to whom his flatterers gave the title of "The Victorious." A few months more of such success would establish him firmly on the throne of a reunited France, and no one could doubt that success would grow more rapid if only with its own momentum. Negotiations were on foot with the Duke of Burgundy which were expected to result in detaching him from the English cause. Joan had written to him some weeks earlier asking him to be present at the coronation, and on the day of the ceremony she addressed him another letter, entreating him to return to his allegiance. In a few days Beauvais, Senlis, Laon, Soissons, Château-Thierry, Provins, Compiègne, and other places acknowledged Charles as king and received his garrisons. All men admitted that this was Joan's work. Christine de Pisan, in a poem written about this time, compares her to Esther, Judith, Deborah, Gideon, and Joshua, and even Moses is not her superior. That she was regarded as an oracle of God on other subjects is seen in the application to her by the Comte d'Armagnac to tell him which of the three popes to believe in; and her acceptance of the position is shown by her answer, that when she is relieved from the pressure of the war she will resolve his doubts by the counsel of the King of all the world. If on the one hand her dizzy elevation turned her head to the extent of addressing threatening letters to the Hussites, on the other she never lost her sympathy with the poor and humble; she protected them as far as she could from the horrors of war, and their grateful veneration shown in kissing her hands and feet and garments was made a crime to her by her pitiless judges.

With all this it does not seem that Joan had any definite rank or command in the royal armies. Christine de Pisan, it is true, speaks of her as being the recognized chief:

> Et de nos gens preux et habiles
> Est principale chevetaine—

but it does not appear that her position had any other warrant than the moral influence which her prodigious exploits and the belief in her divine mission afforded. Charles's gratitude gave her a handsome establishment. She was magnificently attired, noble damsels were assigned to her service, with a *maître d'hotel*, pages, and valets; and at the time of her capture she had in her hands some 12,000 francs, which, as she told her judges, was little enough to carry on war with. Shortly after his coronation, Charles, at her request, granted to Domremy and Greux the privilege of exemption from all taxes, a favor which was respected until the Revolution; and in December 1429 he spontaneously ennobled her family and all their posterity, giving them as arms on a field azure two *fleurs-de-lis or*, traversed by a sword, and authorizing them to bear the name of Du Lis.

All Europe was aroused with so portentous an apparition. It was not only statesmen and warriors that watched with astonishment the strange vicissitudes of the contest, but learned men and theologians were divided in opinion whether she was under the influence of heavenly or of infernal spirits. In England, of course, there was no dissent from the popular belief which Shakespeare puts in the mouth of Talbot:

> A witch by fear, not force, like Hannibal,
> Drives back our troops and conquers as she lists.

So general, indeed, was the terror that she excited that when, in May 1430, it was proposed to send Henry VI to Paris for coronation, both captains and soldiers in the levies appointed for his escort deserted and lay in hiding; and when in December, after Joan lay a prisoner in Rouen Castle and the voyage was performed, the same trouble was experienced, requiring another proclamation to the sheriffs for the arrest of those who were daily deserting. Elsewhere the matter was not thus taken for granted, and was elaborately argued with all the resources of scholastic logic. Some tracts of this character attributed to Gerson have been preserved and exhibit to us the nature of the doubts which suggested themselves to the learned of the time—whether Joan is a woman or a phantasm; whether her acts are to be considered as divine or pythonic and illusory; whether, if they are the result of supernatural causes, they come from good or evil spirits. To Joan's defenders the main difficulty was her wearing male attire and cutting her hair short. Even her advocates in the schools felt that in this the case was weak. It had to be admitted that the Old Law prohibits a woman from wearing man's garments, but this, it was argued, was purely juridical, and was not binding under the New Law; it had merely a moral object, to prevent indecency, and the circumstances and objects were to be considered, so that the Law could not be held to prohibit manly and military vesture to Joan, who was both manly and military. The cutting of her hair, prohibited by the Apostle, was justified in the same manner.

For a few weeks after the coronation Joan was at the culmination of her career. Possibly she may, as has been represented, have declared that all which God had appointed her to do had been accomplished, and that she desired to return to her parents and herd their cattle, as she had been accustomed of old. In view of what followed, this was the only way to uphold the theory of divine inspiration, and such a statement inevitably formed part of her legend, whether it was true or not. In her subsequent failures, as at Paris and La Charité, Joan naturally persuaded herself that they had been undertaken against the counsel of her Voices, but all the evidence goes to prove that at the time she was as confident of success as ever. A letter written from Reims on the day of coronation, evidently by a well-informed person, states that the army was to start the next day for Paris, and that the Pucelle had no doubts of reducing it to obedience. Nor did she really consider her mission ended, for she had at the commencement proclaimed the liberation of Charles of

Orleans as one of her objects, and on her trial she explained that she proposed either to invade England to set him free or to capture enough prisoners to force an exchange: her Voices had promised it to her, and had she not been captured she would have accomplished it in three years.

Be this as it may, from this time the marvellous fortune which had attended her disappears; alternations of success and defeat show that either the French had lost the first flush of confident enthusiasm, or that the English had recovered from their panic and were doggedly resolved to fight the powers of hell. Bedford managed to put a respectable force in the field, with the assistance of Cardinal Beaufort, who made over to him, it was said for a heavy bribe, 4,000 crusaders whom he was leading from England to the Hussite wars. He barred the way to Paris, and three times the opposing armies, of nearly equal strength, lay face to face, but Bedford always skillfully chose a strong position which Charles dared not atttack, showing that human prudence had replaced the reckless confidence of the march to Reims. Towards the end of August, Bedford, fearing an inroad on Normandy, marched thither, leaving the road to Paris open, and Charles advanced to St. Denis, which he occupied without resistance, August 25. On September 7 an attempt was made to capture Paris by surprise, with the aid of friends within the walls, and this failing, on the 8th, the feast of the Nativity of the Virgin, an assault in force was made at the Porte St. Honoré. The water in the inner moat, however, was too deep and the artillery on the walls too well served: after five or six hours of desperate fighting the assailants were disastrously repulsed with a loss of 500 killed and 1,000 wounded. As usual Joan had been at the front till she fell with an arrow through the leg, and her standard-bearer was slain by her side. Joan subsequently averred that she had had no counsel from her Voices to make this attempt, but had been over-persuaded by the army; but this is contradicted by contemporary evidence, and her letter to d'Armagnac promises him a reply when she shall have leisure in Paris, showing that she fully expected to capture the city.

From this time her checkered career was rather of evil fortune than of good. If at St. Pierre-les-Moustiers the old enthusiasm made the forlorn hope imagine that it ascended the breach as easily as a broad stairway, the seige of La Charité, to which it was a preliminary, proved disastrous, and again Joan averred that she had undertaken this without orders from her Voices. It was freely said that La Trémouille had sent her on the enterprise with insufficient forces and had withheld the requisite succors. During the winter she was at Lagny, where occurred a little incident which was subsequently used to confirm the charge of sorcery. A child was born apparently dead; the parents, dreading to have it buried without baptism, had it carried to the church, where it lay, to all appearance, lifeless for three days; the young girls of the town assembled in the church to pray for it, and Joan joined them. Suddenly the infant gave signs of life, gaped thrice, was hurriedly baptized, died, and was buried in consecrated ground, and Joan had the credit of working a miracle.

As the spring of 1430 opened, the Duke of Burgundy came to the assistance of his English allies by raising a large army for the recovery of Compiègne. The activity of Joan was unabated. During Easter week, we hear of her in the trenches at Melun, where her Voices announced to her that she would be a prisoner before St. John's day, but would give her no further particulars. Before the close of the month she attacked the advancing Burgundians at Pont-l'Évêque, and was worsted. Then she had a desperate fight with a Burgundian partisan, Franquet d'Arras, whom she captured with all his troop; he had been a notorious plunderer, the magistrates of Lagny claimed him for trial, and after an investigation which lasted for fifteen days they executed him as a robber and murderer, for which Joan was held responsible, his death being one of the most serious charges pressed against her. About May 1 Compiègne was invested. Its siege was evidently to be the decisive event of the campaign, and Joan hastened to the rescue. Before daylight on the morning of the 5th she succeeded in entering the town with reinforcements. In the afternoon of the same day a sally was resolved upon, and Joan as usual led it, with Pothon and other captains by her side. She fell upon the camp of a renowned knight of the Golden Fleece named Baudoin de Noyelles, who, though taken by surprise, made a gallant resistance. A force of a thousand Englishmen on their way to Paris had tarried to aid Philip of Burgundy, and these were brought up between the French and the town to take them in the rear. Joan fell back and endeavored to bring her men off in safety, but while covering the retreat she was unable to regain the fortifications, and was taken prisoner by the Bâtard de Vendôme, a follower of Jean de Luxembourg, Comte de Ligny, second in command to the duke. There was naturally talk of treachery, but it would seem without foundation. Pothon was also captured, and it evidently was but the fortune of war.

Great was the joy in the Burgundian camp when the news spread that the dreaded Pucelle was a prisoner. English and Burgundians gave themselves up to rejoicing; they crowded around her quarters at Marigny, and even the Duke of Burgundy paid her a visit and exchanged some words with her. At once the question arose as to her possession. She was a prisoner of war, belonging to Jean de Luxembourg, and, in those days of ransoming, prisoners were valuable property. Under existing customs, Henry VI, as chief of the alliance, had the right to claim the transfer of any captured commanding general or prince on paying the captor 10,000 livres. In the exhausted state of the English exchequer, however, even 10,000 livres was a sum not readily procurable. It was a matter of absolute necessity to the English to have her, not only to prevent her ransom by the French, but to neutralize her sorceries by condemning and executing her under the jurisdiction of the Church. To accomplish this the Inquisition was the most available intrumentality: inside the English lines Joan was publicly reported to be a sorceress, and as such was judiciable by the Inquisition, which therefore had a right to claim her for trial. Accordingly, but a few days had elapsed after her capture when Martin Billon, Vicar of the Inquisitor of France, formally demanded her surrender, and the University of Paris addressed two letters to the Duke of Burgundy urging that she should be promptly tried and punished, lest his enemies should effect her deliverance.

Jean de Luxembourg was by no mean disposed to surrender his valuable prize without consideration. Then another device was adopted. Compiègne, where Joan was captured, was in the diocese of Beauvais. Pierre Cauchon, the Count-bishop of Beauvais, though a Frenchman of the Remois, was a bitter English partisan, whose unscrupulous cruelty at a later period excited the cordial detestation even of his own faction. He had been driven from his see the previous year by the returning loyalty of its people under the impulse given by Joan, and may be assumed to have looked upon her with no loving eye. He was told to claim her for trial under his episcopal jurisdiction, but even he shrank from the odious business, and refused unless it could be proved that it was his duty. July 14, the University addressed letters to Jean de Luxembourg reminding him that his oath of knighthood required him to defend the honor of God and the Catholic faith, and the holy Church. Through Joan, idolatries, errors, false doctrines, and evils innumerable had spread through France, and the matter admitted of no delay. The Inquisition had earnestly demanded her for trial, and Jean was urgently begged to surrender her to the Bishop of Beauvais, who had likewise claimed her.

When furnished with this, Pierre Cauchon lost no time. He left Paris at once with a notary and a representative of the University, and on the 16th presented it to the Duke of Burgundy in the camp before Compiègne, together with a summons of his own addressed to the Duke, Jean de Luxembourg, and the Bâtard de Vendôme, demanding the surrender of Joan for trial before him on charges of sorcery, invocation of the devil, and other matters involving the faith. He further offered a ransom of 6,000 livres and a pension to the Bâtard de Vendôme of 200 livres, and if this was not enough the sum would be increased to 10,000 livres, although Joan was not so great a person as the king would have a right to claim on giving that amount; if required, security would be furnished for the payment. These letters the duke transferred to Jean de Luxembourg, who after some discussion agreed to sell her for the stipulated sum. He would not trust his allies, however, even with security, and refused to deliver his prisoner until the money was paid. Bedford was obliged to convene the states of Normandy and levy a special tax to raise it, and it was not till October 20 that Jean received his price and transferred his captive.

During all this long delay Charles, to his eternal dishonor, made no effort to save the woman to whom he owed his crown. While her prolonged trial was under way he did not even appeal to Eugenius IV or to the Council of Basle to evoke the case to their tribunal, an appeal which would hardly have been rejected in a matter of so much interest. But, the party of peace in his court,

headed by La Trémouille, the favorite, had no desire to see the
heroine at large again, and the weak and self-indulgent monarch
abandoned her to her fate.

Meanwhile Joan had been carried, strictly guarded to prevent
her escape by magic arts, from Marigny to the Castle of Beaulieu,
and thence to the Castle of Beaurevoir. In the latter prison she
excited the interest of the Dame de Beaurevoir, and of the De-
moiselle de Luxembourg, aunt of Jean. The latter earnestly remonstrated with her nephew when she learned that he was treating with the English, and both ladies endeavored to persuade Joan
to adopt female habiliments. They must have impressed her with
their kindness, for she subsequently declared that she would have
made the change for them rather than for any other ladies in
France. Her restless energy chafed at the long captivity, and twice
she made attempts to escape. Once she succeeded in shutting her
guards up in her cell, and would have got off but that her jailer
saw her and secured her. Again, when she heard that she was to be
surrendered to the English, she desparingly threw herself from her
lofty tower into the ditch, careless whether it would kill her or not.
Her Voices had forbidden the attempt, but she said that she had
rather die than fall into English hands—and this was subsequently
charged against her as an attempted suicide and a crime. She was
picked up for dead, but she was reserved for a harsher fate, and
speedily recovered. She might well regret the recovery when she was
carried to Rouen, loaded with chains and confined in a narrow cell
where guards watched her day and night. It is even said that an iron
cage was made, into which she was thrust with fetters on wrist,
waist, and ankles. She had been delivered to the Church, not to the
secular authorities; she was entitled to be kept in an ecclesiastical
prison, but the English had paid for her and would listen to no
reclamations. Warwick had charge of her and would trust her to no
one.

Pierre Cauchon still was in no haste to commence the iniquitous work which he had undertaken. After a month had passed,
Paris grew excited at the delay. The city, so ardently Anglicized,
had a special grudge against Joan, not only on account of believing that she had promised her soldiers to allow them to sack the
city and put the inhabitants to the sword, but because they were

exposed to the greatest privations by the virtual blockade resulting from the extension of the royal domination caused by her successes. This feeling found expression in the University, which from the first pursued her with unrelenting ferocity. Not content with having intervened to procure her surrender to the English, it addressed letters, November 21, to Pierre Cauchon, reproaching him with his tardiness in commencing the process, and to the King of England, asking that the trial be held in Paris, where there are so many learned and excellent doctors. Still Cauchon hesitated. His jurisdiction arose from her capture in his diocese, but he was an exile from it, and was expected to try her not only in another diocese, but in another province. The archbishopric of Rouen was vacant, and he adopted the expedient of requesting of the chapter permission to hold an ecclesiastical court within their jurisdiction. The request was granted, and he selected an assembly of experts to sit with him as assessors. A number came willingly from the University, whose expenses were paid by the English, but it was more difficult to find accomplices among the local prelates and doctors. In one of the early sessions, Nicholas de Houppeland plainly told Cauchon that neither he nor the rest, belonging to the party hostile to Joan, could sit as judges, especially as she had already been examined by the Archbishop of Reims, who was the metropolitan of Beauvais. For this Nicholas was imprisoned in the Castle of Rouen, and was threatened with banishment to England and with drowning, but his friends eventually procured his liberation.

Eventually a respectable body of 50 or 60 theologians and jurists was got together, including such men as the Abbots of Fécamp, Jumièges, Ste. Catharine, Cormeilles, and Préaux, the Prior of Longueville, the archdeacon and treasurer of Rouen, and other men of recognized position. On January 3, 1431, royal letters-patent were issued ordering Joan to be delivered to Pierre Cauchon whenever she was wanted for examination, and all officials to aid him when called upon. As though she were already convicted, the letters recited the heresies and evil deeds of the culprit, and significantly concluded with a clause that if she was acquitted she was not to be liberated, but to be returned to the custody of the king. Yet it was not until the 9th that Cauchon assembled his experts, at that time eight in number, and laid before them what had been already done. They decided that the information was insufficient and that a further inquest was necessary, and they also protested ineffectually against Joan's detention in a state prison. Measures were at once taken to make the investigations required. Nicholas Bailly was dispatched to obtain the details of Joan's childhood, and as he brought back only favorable details Cauchon suppressed his report and refused to reimburse his expenses. The inquisitorial method of making the accused betray herself was adopted. One of the assessors, Nicholas l'Oyseleur, disguised himself as a layman and was introduced into her cell, pretending to be a Lorrainer imprisoned for his loyalty. He gained her confidence, and she grew into the habit of talking to him without reserve. Then Warwick and Cauchon with two notaries ensconced themselves in an adjoining cell of which the partition wall had been pierced, while l'Oyseleur led her on to talk about her visions; but the scheme failed, for one of the notaries, unfamiliar with inquisitorial practice, pronounced the whole proceeding to be unlawful and courageously refused to act.

It was not until February 19 that the articles of accusation were ready for submission to the assessors, and then a new difficulty arose. Thus far the tribunal had contained no representative of the Inquisition, and this was recognized as a fatal defect. Frère Jean Graveran was Inquisitor of France, and had appointed Frère Jean le Maître, in 1424, as his vicar or deputy for Rouen. Le Maître seems to have had no stomach for the work, and to have kept aloof, but he was not to be let off, and at the meeting of February 19 it was resolved to summon him, in the presence of two notaries, to take part in the proceedings and to hear read the accusation and the depositions of witnesses. Another session was held in the afternoon, at which he appeared, and on being summoned to act professed himself willing to do so, if the commission which he held was sufficient authorization. The scruple which he alleged was ingenious. He was Inquisitor of Rouen, but Cauchon was bishop in a different province, and, as he was exercising jurisdiction belonging to Beauvais in the "borrowed territory," le Maître doubted his powers to take part in it. It was not till the 22d that his doubts were overcome, and, while awaiting enlarged powers from Graveran, he consented to assist.

At length, on February 21, Jean Estivet, the prosecutor, demanded that the prisoner be produced and examined. Before she was introduced Cauchon explained that she had earnestly begged the privilege of hearing mass, but, in view of the crimes whereof she was accused and her wearing male attire, he had refused. This prejudgment of the case was acquiesced in, and Joan was brought in with fetters on her legs.

It would be superfluous to follow in detail the examinations to which she was subjected during the next three months, with an intermission from April 18 to May 11 on account of sickness which nearly proved mortal. The untaught peasant girl, enfeebled by the miseries of prison, and subjected day after day to the shrewd and searching cross-questions of the trained and subtle intellects of her carefully selected judges, never lost her presence of mind or clearness of intellect. Questions puzzling to a theologian were showered upon her; half a dozen eager disputants would assail her at once and would interrupt her replies; the disorder at times was so great that the notaries finally declared themselves unable to make an intelligent record. Her responses would be carefully scrutinized, and she would be recalled in the afternoon, the same ground would be gone over in a different manner, and her pursuers would again be foiled. In the whole series of interrogatories she manifested a marvellous combination of frank simplicity, shrewdness, presence of mind, and firmness that would do honor to a veteran diplomat. She utterly refused to take an unconditional oath to answer the questions put to her, saying frankly, "I do not know what you will ask me; perhaps it may be about things which I will not tell you"; she agreed to reply to all questions about her faith and matters bearing upon her trial, but to nothing else. When Cauchon's eagerness overstepped the limit she would turn on him and warn him, "You call yourself my judge: I know not if you are, but take care not to judge wrongfully, for you expose yourself to great danger, and I warn you, so that if our Lord chastises you I shall have done my duty." When asked whether St. Michael was naked when he visited her, she retorted, "Do you think the Lord has not wherewith to clothe his angels?"

She could hardly have known that an attempt to escape from an ecclesiastical court was a sin of the deepest dye, and yet when tested with the cunning question whether she would now escape if opportunity offered, she replied that if the door was opened she would walk out; she would try it only to see if the Lord so willed it. When an insidious offer was made to her to have a great procession to entreat God to bring her to the proper frame of mind, she quietly replied that she wished all good Catholics would pray for her. When threatened with torture, and told that the executioner was at hand to administer it, she simply said, "If you extort avowals from me by pain I will maintain that they are the result of violence." Thus alternating the horrors of her dungeon with the clamors of the examination room, she never faltered through all those weary weeks.

In this she was sustained by the state of habitual spiritual exaltation and the unalterable conviction that she was the chosen of the Lord, under whose inspiration she acted and whose will she was prepared to endure with resignation. Frequently she refused to answer questions until she could consult her Voices and learn whether she was permitted to reveal what was wanted, and then, at a subsequent hearing, she would say that she had received permission. The responses evidently sometimes varied with her moods. She would be told that she would be delivered with triumph, and then again be urged not to mind her martyrdom, for she would reach paradise. When she reported this she was cunningly asked if she felt assured of salvation, and on her saying that she was as certain of heaven as if she was already there, she was led on with a question whether she held that she could not commit mortal sin. Instinctively she drew back from the dangerous ground: "I know nothing about it; I depend on the Lord."

Finally, on one important point her judges succeeded in entrapping her. She was warned that if she had done anything contrary to the faith she must submit herself to the determination of the Church. She offered to submit to God and the saints, but this, she was told, was the Church triumphant in heaven, and she must submit to the Church militant on earth, else she was a heretic, to be inevitably abandoned to the secular arm for burning. Taking advantage of her ignorance, the matter was pressed upon her in the most absolute form. When asked if she would submit to the pope she could only say, "Take me to him and I will answer to him." At last she was brought to admit that she would submit to the Church, provided it did not command what was impossible; but, when asked to define the impossible, it was to abandon doing what the Lord had commanded, and to revoke what she had asserted as to the truth of her visions. This she would submit only to God.

The examinations up to March 27 had been merely preparatory. On that day the formal trial commenced by reading to Joan a long series of articles of accusation based upon the information obtained. A lively debate ensued among the experts, but at last it was decided that she must answer them *seriatim* and on the spot, which she did with her wonted clearness and intrepidity, declining the offer of counsel, which Cauchon proposed to select for her. Sundry further interrogatories followed; then her sickness delayed the proceedings, and on May 12, twelve members of the tribunal assembled in Pierre Cauchon's house to determine whether she should be subjected to torture. Fortunately for the reputation of her judges this infamy was spared her. One of them voted in favor of torture to see whether she could be forced to submit to the Church; another, the spy, Nicholas l'Oyseleur, humanely urged it as a useful medicine for her; nine were of opinion either that it was not yet required, or that the case was clear enough without it; Cauchon himself apparently did not vote. Meanwhile a secret junta, selected by Cauchon, had reduced the articles of accusation to twelve, which, though grossly at variance with the truth, were assumed to have been fully proved or confessed, and these formed the basis of the subsequent deliberations and sentence. Copies of the articles were addressed to fifty-eight learned experts, in addition to the Chapter of Rouen and the University of Paris, and their opinions were requested by a certain day. Of all those appealed to, the University was by far the most important, and a special mission was dispatched to it bearing letters from the royal council and the Bishop of Beauvais. The University went through an elaborate form of deliberation, and caused the Faculties of Theology and Law to draw up its decision, which was adopted May 14 and sent to Rouen.

On May 19 the assessors were assembled to hear the report from the University, after which their opinions were taken. Some were in favor of immediate abandonment to the secular arm, which would have been strictly in accordance with the regular inquisitorial proceedings, but probably the violent assumption that the articles represented truthfully Joan's admissions was too much for some of the assessors, and the milder suggestion prevailed that Joan should have another hearing, in which the articles should be read to her, with the decision of the University, and that the verdict should depend upon what she should then say. Accordingly, on May 23, she was again brought before the tribunal. A brief abstract of the document read to her will show, from the triviality of many of the charges and the guilt ascribed to them, how conviction was predetermined. The University, as usual, had guarded itself by conditioning its decision on the basis of the articles being fully proved, but no notice was taken of this, and Joan was addressed as though she had confessed to the articles and had been solemnly condemned.

I. The visions of angels and saints.—These are pronounced superstitious and proceeding from evil and diabolical spirits.

II. The sign given to Charles of the crown brought to him by St. Michael.—After noting her contradictions, the story is declared a lie, and a presumptuous, seductory, and pernicious thing, derogatory to the dignity of the Church.

III. Recognizing saints and angels by their teaching and the comfort they bring, and believing in them as firmly as in the faith of Christ.—Her reasons have been insufficient, and her belief rash; comparing faith in them to faith in Christ is an error of faith.

IV. Predictions of future events and recognition of persons not seen before through the Voices.—This is superstition and divination, presumptuous assertion, and vain boasting.

V. Wearing men's clothes and short hair, taking the sacrament while in them, and asserting that it is by command of God.—This is blaspheming God, despising his sacraments, transgressing the divine law, holy writ, and canonical ordinances, wherefore, "thou savorest ill in the faith, thou boastest vainly and art suspect of idolatry, and thou condemnest thyself in not being willing to wear thy sex's garments and in following the customs of the heathen and Saracen."

VI. Putting Jesus, Maria, and the sign of the cross on her letters, and threatening that if they were not obeyed she would show in battle who had the best right.—"Thou art murderous and cruel, seeking effusion of human blood, seditious, provoking to tyranny, and blaspheming God, his commandments and revelations."

VII. Rendering her father and mother almost crazy by leaving them;

also promising Charles to restore his kingdom, and all by command of God.—"Thou hast been wicked to thy parents, transgressing the commandment of God to honor them. Thou hast been scandalous, blaspheming God, erring in the faith, and hast made a rash and presumptuous promise to thy king."

VIII. Leaping from the tower of Beaurevoir into the ditch and preferring death to falling into the hands of the English, after the Voices had forbidden it.—This was pusillanimity, tending to desperation and suicide; and in saying that God had forgiven it, "thou savorest ill as to human free-will."

IX. Saying that St. Catharine and St. Margaret had promised her paradise if she preserved her virginity, feeling assured of it, and asserting that if she were in mortal sin they would not visit her.—"Thou savorest ill as to the Christian faith."

X. Saying that St. Catharine and St. Margaret spoke French and not English because they were not of the English faction, and that, after knowing that these Voices were for Charles, she had not loved the Burgundians.—This is a rash blasphemy against those saints and a transgression of the divine command to love thy neighbor.

XI. Reverencing the celestial visitants and believing them to come from God without consulting any churchman; feeling as certain of it as of Christ and the Passion; and refusing to reveal the sign made to Charles without the command of God.—"Thou art an idolater, an invoker of devils, erring in the faith, and hast rashly made an illicit oath."[7]

XII. Refusing to obey the mandate of the Church if contrary to the pretended command of God, and rejecting the judgment of the Church on earth.—"Thou art schismatic, believing wrongly as to the truth and authority of the Church, and up to the present time thou errest perniciously in the faith of God."

Maître Pierre Maurice, who read to her this extraordinary document, proceeded to address her with an odious assumption of kindness as *"Jehanne ma chere amie,"* urging her earnestly to submit herself to the judgment of the Church, without which her soul was sure of damnation, and he had shrewd fears for her body. She

[7] In considering the verdict of the University and the Inquisition it must be borne in mind that visions of the Saviour, the Virgin, and the Saints were almost everyday occurrences and were recognized and respected by the Church. As a technical point of ecclesiastical law, moreover, Joan's visions had already been examined and approved by the prelates and doctors at Chinon and Poitiers, including Pierre Cauchon's metropolitan, Renaud, Archbishop of Reims.

answered firmly that if the fire was lighted and the executioner ready to cast her in the flames she would not vary from what she had already said. Nothing remained but to cite her for the next day to receive her final sentence.

On the 24th preparations for an *auto de fé* were completed in the cemetery of St. Ouen. The pile was ready for lighting, and on two scaffolds were assembled the Cardinal of Beaufort and other dignitaries, while on a third were Pierre Cauchon, Jean le Maître, Joan, and Maître Guillaume Erard, who preached the customary sermon. In his eloquence he exclaimed that Charles VII had been proved a schismatic heretic, when Joan interrupted him, "Speak of me, but not of the king; he is a good Christian!" She maintained her courage until the sentence of relaxation was partly read, when she yielded to the persuasion mingled with threats and promises to which she had been exposed since the previous night, and she signified her readiness to submit. A formula of abjuration was read to her, and after some discussion she allowed her hand to be guided in scratching the sign of the cross, which represented her signature. Then another sentence, prepared in advance, was pronounced, imposing on her, as a matter of course, the customary penance of perpetual imprisonment on bread and water. Vainly she begged for an ecclesiastical prison. Had Cauchon wished it he was powerless, and he ordered the guards to conduct her back whence she came.

The English were naturally furious on finding that they had overreached themselves. They could have tried Joan summarily in a secular court for sorcery and burned her out of hand, but to obtain possession of her they had been obliged to call in the ecclesiatical authorities and the Inquisition, and they were too little familiar with trials for heresy to recognize that inquisitorial proceedings were based on the assumption of seeking the salvation of the soul and not the destruction of the body. When they saw how the affair was going a great commotion arose. Joan's death was a political necessity, and their victim was eluding them though in their grasp. In spite of the servility which the ecclesiastics had shown, they were threatened with drawn swords and were glad to leave the cemetery of St. Ouen in safety.

In the afternoon Jean le Maître and some of the assessors visited her in her cell, representing the mercy of the Church and the gratitude with which she should receive her sentence, and warning her to abandon her revelations and follies, for if she relapsed she could have no hope. She was humbled, and when urged to wear female apparel she assented. It was brought and she put it on; her male garments were placed in a bag and left in her cell.

What followed will never be accurately known. The reports are untrustworthy and contradictory—mere surmises, doubtless— and the secret lies buried in the dungeon of Rouen Castle. The guards, enraged at her escape from the flames, no doubt abused her shamefully; perhaps, as reported, they beat her, dragged her by the hair, and offered violence to her, till at last she felt that her man's dress was her only safety. Perhaps, as other stories go, her Voices reproached her for her weakness, and she deliberately re-sumed it. Perhaps, also, Warwick, resolved to make her commit an act of relapse, had her female garments removed at night, so that she had no choice but to resume her male apparel. The fact that it was left within her reach and not conveyed away shows at least that there was a desire to tempt her to resume it. Be this as it may, after wearing her woman's dress for two or three days word was brought to her judges that she had relapsed and abandoned it. On May 28 they hastened to her prison to verify the fact. The inco-herence of her replies to their examination shows how she was breaking down under the fearful stress to which she had been sub-jected. First she merely said that she had taken the dress; then that it was more suitable since she was to be with men; nobody had compelled her, but she denied that she had sworn not to resume it. Then she said that she had taken it because faith had not been kept with her—she had been promised that she should hear mass and receive the sacrament, and be released from her chains; she would rather die than be kept in fetters—could she hear mass and be re-lieved of her irons she would do all that the Church required. She had heard the Voices since her abjuration and had been told that she had incurred damnation by revoking to save her life, for she had only revoked through dread of the fire. The Voices are of St. Catharine and St. Margaret, and come from God: she had never revoked that, or, if she had, it was contrary to truth. She had rather die than endure the torture of her captivity, but if her judges wish she will resume the woman's dress; as for the rest she knows nothing more.

It was enough for the judges; she was a self-confessed relapsed, with whom the Church could have nothing more to do except to declare her abandoned to the secular arm without further hearing. Accordingly, the next day, May 29, Cauchon assembled such of his assessors as were at hand, reported to them how she had relapsed by resuming male apparel and declaring, through the suggestion of the devil, that her Voices had returned. The only discussion was on the purely formal question, whether her abjuration should be read over to her before her judges abandoned her to the secular arm. A majority of the assessors were in favor of this, but Cauchon and le Maître disregarded the recommendation.

At dawn on the following day, May 30, Frère Martin l'Advenu and some other ecclesiastics were sent to her prison to inform her of her burning that morning. She was overcome with terror, threw herself on the ground, tore her hair and uttered piercing shrieks, declaring, as she grew calmer, that it would not have happened had she been placed in an ecclesiastical prison. She confessed to l'Advenu and asked for the sacrament. He was puzzled and sent for instructions to Cauchon, who gave permission, and it was brought to her with all due solemnity. It has been mistakenly argued that this was an admission of her innocence, but the sacrament was never to be denied to a relapsed who asked for it at the last moment, the mere asking, preceded by confession, being an evidence of contrition and desire for reunion to the Church.

The platform for the sermon and the pile for the execution had been erected in the Viel Marché. Thither she was conveyed amid a surging crowd which blocked the streets. It is related that on the way Nicholas l'Oyseleur, the wretched spy, pierced the crowd and the guards and leaped upon the tumbril to entreat her forgiveness, but before she could grant it the English dragged him off and would have slain him had not Warwick rescued him and sent him out of Rouen to save his life. On the platform Nicholas Midi preached his sermon, the sentence of relaxation was read, and Joan was handed over to the secular authorities. Cauchon, le Maître, and the rest left the platform, and the Bailli of Rouen took her and briefly ordered her to be carried to the place of execution and burned. On her head was placed a high paper crown inscribed "Heretic, Relapsed, Apostate, Idolator," and she was carried to the stake. One account states that her shrieks and lamentations moved the crowd to tears of pity; another that she was resigned and composed, and that her last utterance was a prayer. When her clothes were burned off, the blazing fagots were dragged aside, that the crowd might see, from her blackened corpse, that she really was a woman, and when their curiosity was satisfied the incineration was completed, the ashes being thrown into the Seine.

It only remained for those who had taken part in the tragedy to justify themselves by blackening the character of their victim and circulating false reports of the proceedings. That the judges felt that, in spite of sheltering themselves behind the University of Paris, they had incurred dangerous reponsibility is shown by their obtaining royal letters shielding them from accountability for what they had done, the king pledging himself to constitute himself a party in any prosecution which might be brought against them before a general council or the pope. That the regency felt that justification was needed in the face of Europe is seen in the letters which were sent to the sovereigns and the bishops in the name of Henry VI, explaining how Joan had exercised inhuman cruelties until the divine power had in pity to the suffering people caused her capture; how, though she could have been punished by the secular courts for her crimes, she had been handed to the Church, which had treated her kindly and benignantly, and on her confession had mercifully imposed on her the penance of imprisonment; how her pride had burst forth and she had relapsed into her errors and madness; how she had then been abandoned to the secular arm, and, finding her end approaching, had confessed that the spirits which she invoked were false and lying, and that she was deceived and mocked by them, and how she had finally been burned in sight of the people.

This official lying was outdone by the reports which were industriously circulated about her and her trial. The honest Bourgeois of Paris, in entering her execution in his journal, details the offenses for which she was condemned, mixing up with the real articles others showing the exaggerations which were industriously circulated. According to him she habitually rode armed with a great staff with which she cruelly beat her people when they displeased her, and in many places she pitilessly slew men and women who disobeyed her; once, when violence was offered her, she leaped from the top of a lofty tower without injury, and boasted that, if she chose, she could bring thunder and other marvels. He admits, however, that even in Rouen there were many who held her to be martyred for her lawful lord. It evidently was felt that in her dreadful death she had fitly crowned her career, and that sympathy for her fate was continuing her work by arousing popular sentiment, for, more than a month later, on July 4, an effort was made to counteract it by a sermon preached in Paris by a Dominican inquisitor— probably our friend Jean le Maître himself. At great length he expatiated on her deeds of wickedness and the mercy which had been shown her. She had confessed that from the age of 14 she had dressed like a man, and her parents would have killed her could they have done so without wounding their consciences. She had therefore left them, accompanied by the devil, and had thence- forth lived by the homicide of Christians, full of fire and blood, till she was burned. She recanted and abjured, and would have had as penance four years' prison on bread and water, but she did not suffer this a single day, for she had herself served in prison like a lady. The devil appeared to her with two demons, fearing greatly that he would lose her, and said to her, "Wicked creature, who through fear hast abandoned thy dress, be not afraid, for we will protect thee from all." Then at once she disrobed and dressed herself in her male attire, which she had thrust in the straw of her bed, and she so trusted in Satan that she said she repented of hav- ing abandoned it. Then, seeing that she was obstinate, the masters of the University delivered her to the secular arm to be burned, and when she saw herself in this strait she called on the devils, but after she was judged she could not bring them by any invo- cation. She then thought better of it, but it was too late.

Thus Joan passed away, but the spirit which she had aroused was beyond the reach of bishop or inquisitor. Her judicial murder was a useless crime. The Treaty of Arras, in 1435, withdrew Bur- gundy from the English alliance, and one by one the conquests of Henry V were wrenched from the feeble grasp of his son. When, in 1449, Charles VII obtained possession of Rouen he ordered an inquest on the spot into the circumstances of her trial, for it ill comported with the dignity of a King of France to owe his throne to a witch condemned and burned by the Church. The time had not come, however, when a sentence of the Inquisition could be set aside by secular authority, and the attempt was abandoned. In 1452 another effort was made by Archbishop d'Estouteville of Rouen, but though he was a cardinal and a papal legate, and though he adjoined in the matter of Jean Brehal, Inquisitor of France, he could do nothing beyond taking testimony. The papal intervention was held to be necessary for the revision of a case of heresy decided by the Inquisition, and to obtain this the mother and the two brothers of Joan appealed to Rome as sufferers from the sentence. At length, in 1455, Calixtus III appointed as commissioners to hear and judge their complaints the Archbishop of Rouen, the Bishops of Paris and Coutances, and the Inquisitor Jean Brehal. Isabelle Darc and her sons appeared as plaintiffs against Cauchon and le Maître, and the proceedings were carried on at their expense. Cauchon was dead and le Maître in hiding—concealed probably by his Dominican brethren, for no trace of him could be found. Although the University of Paris does not appear in the case, every precaution was taken to preserve its honor by emphasizing at every stage the fraudulent character of the twelve articles submitted to its decision, and in the final judgment special care was taken to characterize them as false and to order them to be judicially torn to pieces. Finally, on July 7, 1456, judgment was rendered in favor of the complainants, who were declared to have incurred no infamy; the whole process was pronounced to be null and void; the decision was ordered to be published in Rouen and all other cities of the kingdom; solemn processions were to be made to the place of her abjuration and that of her execution, and on the latter a cross was to be erected in perpetual memory of her martyrdom. In its restored form it still remains there as a memorial of the utility of the Inquisition as an instrument of statecraft.

CHAPTER XXII
SORCERY AND OCCULT ARTS

FROM the earliest periods of which records have reached us there have been practitioners of magic who were credited with the ability of controlling the spirit world, of divining the future, and of interfering with the ordinary operations of nature. When this was accomplished by the ritual of an established religion it was praiseworthy, like the augural and oracular divination of classic times, or the exorcism of spirits, the excommunication of caterpillars, and the miraculous cures wrought by relics or pilgrimages to noted shrines. When it worked through the invocation of hostile deities, or of a religion which had been superseded, it was blameworthy and forbidden. To attempt to foretell the future in any way was sorcery, and all sorcery was the work of the devil; and it was the same with the amulets and charms, the observance of lucky and unlucky days, and the innumerable trivial superstititions which amused the popular imagination.

In fact, the Church occupied an inconsistent attitude. Occasionally it took the enlightened view that these beliefs were groundless superstitions. In 1080, Gregory VII, in writing to Harold the Simple of Denmark, strongly reproves the custom of attributing to priests and women all tempests, sickness, and other bodily misfortunes: these are the judgments of God, and to wreak vengeance for them on the innocent is only to provoke still more the divine wrath. More generally, however, the Church admitted their truth and sought, though with little energy, to repress them with spiritual censures. This halting position is well illustrated by the canons of Burchard, Bishop of Worms, in the early part of the eleventh century, where sometimes it is the belief in the existence of sorcery that is penanced, and sometimes it is the practice of the art. If confessors, moreover, followed Burchard's instructions and interrogated their penitents in detail about the various magic processes they might have performed, it could only result in disseminating a knowledge of those wicked arts in a most suggestive way. At the same time Burchard gave an ample store of prohibitory canons drawn from the early councils and the writings of the Fathers, showing that the reality of sorcery was freely admitted as well as the duty of the Church to combat it. So implicit was the belief in magic powers that the Church conceded the dissolution of the indissoluble sacrament of matrimony when the consummation of marriage was prevented by the arts of the sorcerer, and exorcisms and prayers and almsgiving and other ecclesiastical remedies proved powerless for three years to overcome the power of Satan. Guibert of Nogent relates, with pardonable pride, that although this occurred when his father and mother were married, through the malice of a stepmother, yet his mother resisted all persuasion to avail herself of a divorce, although the impediment continued for seven years, and the spell was broken at last, not by priestly ministrations, but by an ancient wise-woman. Even so enlightened a man as John of Salisbury airs his learning in describing all the varieties of magic, and is careful to define that if sorcerers kill men with the violence of their spells it is through the permission of God; while Peter of Blois, if he shows himself superior to the vulgar belief in omens, admits the potency of Satanic suggestiveness in the darker forms of magic.

It is true that Roger Bacon, who was in so many things far in advance of the age, argued that much of magic was simply fraud and delusion; that it is an error to suppose that man can summon and dismiss malignant spirits at will, and that it is much simpler to pray directly to God because demons can influence human affairs only through God's permission. Even Bacon, however, in asserting the uselessness of charms and spells, gives as his reason that their efficacy depended on their being made under certain aspects of the heavens, the determination of which was very difficult and uncertain. Bacon's partial incredulity only indicates the universality of the belief in less scientific minds, and in view of the activity assigned to Satan in seeking human agents and servitors, and the ease with which men could evoke him and bind themselves to him, the supineness of the Church with regard to such offenses is remarkable.

The slight attention paid in the thirteenth century by the Church to a crime so abhorrent as sorcery is proved by the fact that when the Inquisition was organized it was for a considerable time restrained from jurisdiction over this class of offenses. In 1248 the Council of Valence, while prescribing to inquisitors the course to be pursued with heretics, directs sorcerers to be delivered to the bishops, to be imprisoned or otherwise punished. In various councils, moreover, during the next sixty years the matter is alluded to, showing that it was constantly becoming an object of increased solicitude, but the penalty threatened is only excommunication. In that of Trèves, for instance, in 1310, which is very full in its description of the forbidden arts, all parish priests are ordered to prohibit them; but the penalty proposed for disobedience is only withdrawal of the sacraments, to be followed, in case of continued obduracy, by excommunication and other remedies of the law administered by the Ordinaries. That the Church, indeed, was disposed to be more rational than the people is visible in a case occurring in 1279 at Ruffach, in Alsace, when a Dominican nun was accused of having baptized a waxen image after the fashion of those who desired either to destroy an enemy or to win a lover. The peasants carried her to a field and would have burned her, had she not been rescued by the friars.

Yet, as the Inquisition perfected its organization and grew conscious of its strength, it naturally sought to extend its sphere of activity, and in 1257 the question was put to Alexander IV whether it ought not to take cognizance of divination and sorcery. In his bull, *Quod super nonnullis*, which was repeatedly reissued by his successors, Alexander replied that inquisitors are not to be diverted from their duties by other occupations, and are to leave such offenders to their regular judges, unless there is manifest heresy involved, and this rule, at the end of the century, was embodied in the canon law by Boniface VIII. The Inquisition, being thus in possession of a portion of the field, rapidly extended its jurisdiction.

Alexander's definition, it is true, had left open for discussion a tolerably wide and intricate class of questions on the degree of heresy involved in the occult arts, but in time these came all to be decided "in favor of the faith." It was not simply the worship of demons and making pacts with Satan that were recognized as heretical by the subtle casuistry of the inquisitors. Scarce any of the arts of the diviner in forecasting the future or in tracing stolen articles could be exercised without what the inquisitors assumed to be at least a tacit invocation of demons. For this they had the authority of John of Salisbury, who, as early as the twelfth century, argued that all divination is an invocation of demons; for if the operator offers no other sacrifice, he sacrifices his body in performing the operation. In time the ingenious dilemma was invented that a man who invoked a demon, thinking it to be no sin, was a manifest heretic; if he knew it to be a sin he was not a heretic, but was to be classed with heretics, while to expect a demon to tell the truth is the act of a heretic. To ask of a demon, even without adoration, that which depends upon the will of God, or of man, or upon the future, indicated heretical notions of the power of demons. In short, as Sylvester Prierias says, it is not necessary to inquire into the motives of those who invoke demons—they are all heretics, real or presumptive. Love-potions and philtres, by a similar system of exegesis, were heretical, and so were spells and charms to cure disease, and all the other devices which fraud and superstition had imposed on popular credulity. Alchemy was one of the *sept ars demonials,* for the aid of Satan was necessary to the transmutation of metals, and the Philosophers' Stone was only to be obtained by spells and charms; although Roger Bacon, in his zeal for practical science, assumes that both objects could be obtained by purely natural means, and that human life could be prolonged for several centuries. Then there was the Notary Art, communicated by God to Solomon, and transmitted through Apollonius of Tyana, which taught the power of the Names and Words of God, and operated through prayers and formulas consisting of unknown polysyllables, by which all knowledge, memory, eloquence, and virtue can be obtained in the space of a month—a harmless delusion enough, which Roger Bacon pronounces to be one of the figments of the magicians, but Thomas Aquinas and Ciruelo prove that it operates solely through the devil.[1]

The most prominent and most puzzling to the lawgiver of all

---

[1] Bernardo di Como draws the nice distinction that it is not heretical to invoke the devil to obtain the illicit love of a woman, for the function of Satan is that of a tempter.

In 1471 the arts of printing and alchemy were coupled together as reprehensible by the Observantine Franciscans, and their practice was forbidden under pain of disgrace and removal. Friar John Neyseeser, disobeyed this rule, and "apostatized" to the Conventual branch of the Order, which was less rigid.

the occult arts was astrology. This was a purely Eastern science—the product of the Chaldean plains and of the Nile valley, unknown to any of the primitive Aryan races. When the dominion of Rome spread beyond the confines of Italy it was not the least of the Orientalizing influences which so profoundly modified the original Roman character; and after a struggle it established itself so firmly that by the early days of the empire some knowledge of the influences of the stars formed an ordinary portion of liberal education. The same motives which led to the prohibition of haruspicium—that the death of the emperor was the subject most eagerly inquired into —caused the Chaldeans, or astrologers, to be the objects of repeated savage edicts, issued even by monarchs who themselves were addicted to consulting them, but it was in vain. Human credulity was too profitable a field to remain uncultivated, and, as Tacitus says, astrologers would always be prohibited and always retained. Although the complexity of the science was such that it could be grasped in its details only by minds exceptionally constituted, it was brought within the reach of all by restricting it to the observation of the moon, and applying the results by means of the diagram and tables known as the Petosiris, a description of which, attributed to the Venerable Bede, shows how the superstitions of pagandom were transmitted to the Northern races, and were eagerly accepted in spite of the arguments of St. Augustin to prove the nullity of the influence ascribed to the heavenly bodies. So thoroughly accepted were its principles that when, in 1305, the College of Cardinals wrote to Clement V to urge his coming to Rome, they reminded him that every planet is most powerful in its own house. Savanarola assures us that at the end of the fifteenth century those who could afford to keep astrologers regulated every action by their advice: if the question were to mount on horseback or to go on board ship, to lay the foundation of a house or to put on a new garment, the astrologer stood by with his astrolabe in hand to announce the auspicious moment—in fact, he says that the Church itself was governed by astrology, for every prelate had his astrologer, whose advice he dared not disregard.

Astrology does not appear for condemnation in the Articles of the University of Paris in 1398, and the great learning of the irreproachable Cardinal Peter d'Ailly was employed in diffusing belief in its truths. On the other hand, as early as the twelfth century John of Salisbury, while asserting that the power of the stars was grossly exaggerated, declares that astrology was forbidden and punished by the Church, that it deprived man of free will by inculcating fatalism, and that it tended to idolatry by transferring omnipotence from the Creator to his creations. These views became virtually the accepted doctrine of the Church as expounded by Thomas Aquinas in the distinction that when astrology was used to predict natural events, such as drought or rain, it was lawful; when employed to divine the future acts of men dependent on free will, it involved the operation of demons, and was unlawful. Zanghino says that though it is one of the seven liberal arts and not prohibited by law, yet it has a tendency to idolatry, and is condemned by the canonists. There was, in fact, much in both the theories and practice of astrologers which trenched nearly upon heresy, not only through demoniac invocations, but because it was impossible that astrology could be cultivated without denying human free will and tacitly admitting fatalism. The very basis of the so-called science lay in the influence which the signs and planets exercised on the fortunes and characters of men at the hour of birth, and no ingenious dialectics could explain away its practical denial of supervision to God and of responsibility to man. Even Roger Bacon failed in this. He fully accepted the belief that the stars were the cause of human events, that the character of every man was shaped by the aspect of the heavens at his birth, and that the past and future could be read by tables which he repeatedly and vainly sought to construct, yet he was illogical enough to think that he could guard against it by nominally reserving human free will. All astrologers thus practiced their profession under liability of being at any moment called to account by the Inquisition. That this did not occur more often may be attributed to the fact that all classes, in Church and State, from the lowest to the highest, believed in astrology and protected astrologers, and some special inducement or unusual indiscretion was required to set in motion the machinery of prosecution.

We can thus understand the case of the celebrated Peter of Abano or Apono, irrespective of his reputation as the greatest magician of his age, earned for him among the vulgar by his marvellous learning and his unsurpassed skill in medicine. In his *Con-*

ciliator Differentium, written in 1303, he not only proved that astrology was a necessary part of medicine, but his estimate of the power of the stars practically eliminated God from the government of the world. Even worse was his Averrhoistic indifference to religion manifested in the statement that the conjunction of Saturn and Jupiter in the head of Aries, which occurs every 960 years, causes changes in the monarchies and religions of the world, as appears in the advent of Nebuchadnezzar, Moses, Alexander the Great, Christ, and Mahomet—a speculation of which the infidelity is even worse than the chronology. It is not surprising that the Inquisition took hold of one whose great name was popularizing such doctrines in the University of Padua, especially as there was a large fortune to be confiscated. We are told that he at first escaped its clutches, but this probably was only through confession and abjuration, so that when he was prosecuted a second time it was for relapse. That he would have been burned there can be little doubt, had he not evaded the stake by opportunely dying in 1316, before the termination of his trial, for he was posthumously condemned: according to one account his bones were burned; according to another his faithful mistress Marietta conveyed them secretly away, and an effigy was committed to the flames in his place. If Benvenuto da Imola is to be believed, he lost his faith in the stars on his deathbed, for he said to his friends that he had devoted his days to three noble sciences, of which philosophy had made him subtle, medicine had made him rich, and astrology had made him a liar. Padua erected a statue to him as to one of her greatest sons, and Frederic, Duke of Urbino, paid him the same tribute. Like Solomon and Hermes and Ptolemy, so long as magic flourished his name served as an attractive frontispiece to various treatises on incantations and the occult sciences.

Very similar, but even more illustrative, is the case of Cecco d'Ascoli. He early distinguished himself as a student of the liberal arts, and devoted himself to astrology, in which he was reckoned the foremost man of his time. His vanity led him to proclaim himself the profoundest adept since Ptolemy, and his caustic and biting humor made him abundance of enemies. Regarding astrology as a science, he inevitably brought it within Aquinas's definition of heresy. In his conception, the stars ruled everything. A man born under a certain aspect of the heavens was doomed to be rich or poor, lucky or unlucky, virtuous or vicious, unless God should interfere specially to turn aside the course of nature. Cecco became official astrologer to Charles of Calabria, but his confidence in his science and his savage independence unfitted him for a court. On the birth of a princess (presumably the notorious Joanna I), he pronounced that the stars in the ascendant would render her not only inclined, but absolutely constrained, to sell her honor. The unwelcome truth cost him his place, and he betook himself to Bologna, where he publicly taught his science. Unluckily for him, he developed his theories in commentaries on the *Sphœra* of Sacrobosco.[2] To illustrate his views he cast the horoscope of Christ, and showed how Libra, ascending in the tenth degree, rendered his crucifixion inevitable; as Capricorn was at the angle of the earth, he was necessarily born in a stable; as Scorpio was in the second degree, he was poor; while Mercury in his own house in the ninth section of the heavens rendered his wisdom profound. In the same way he proved that Antichrist would come two thousand years after Christ, as a great soldier nobly attended, and not surrounded by cowards as was Christ. This was almost a challenge to the Inquisition, and Frà Lamberto del Cordiglio, the Bolognese inquisitor, was not slow to take it up. Cecco was forced to abjure, December 16, 1324, and was mercifully treated. He was condemned to surrender all his books of astrology and forbidden to teach the science in Bologna; he was deprived of his Master's degree and subjected to certain salutary penances of fasting and prayer, together with a fine of 75 lire, which latter may possibly explain the lightness of the rest of the sentence. The most serious feature of the affair for him was that now he was a penitent heretic who could expect no further mercy; it behooved him to walk warily. Cecco's temperament, however, was not one to brook such constraint. He came to Florence, then under the

[2] The *Sphœra* of Sacrobosco is a remarkably lucid and scientific statement of all that was known, in the thirteenth century, about the earth in its cosmical relations. Although it accepts, of course, the current theory of the nine spheres, it indulges in no astrological reveries as to the influence of the signs and planets on human destiny. It remained for centuries a work of the highest authority, and in 1604, sixty years after the death of Copernicus, and on the eve of the development of the new astronomy by Galileo, it was translated, with a copious commentary, by a professor of mathematics in the University of Siena, Francesco Pifferi, whose astrological credulity offers a curious contrast to the severe simplicity of the original.

rule of Charles of Calabria, and resumed the practice of his art. He circulated copies of his forbidden work, which he claimed had been corrected by the Bolognese inquisitor, but which contained the same erroneous doctrines; he advanced them anew in his philosophical poem *L'Acerba*, and he employed them in the responses given to his numerous clients. In May 1327, when all Italy was excited at the coming of Louis of Bavaria, he predicted that Louis would enter Rome and be crowned, he announced the time and manner of his death, and gave advice, which was followed, not to attack him when he passed by Florence. In July 1327, Frà Accursio, the Inquisitor of Florence, arrested him. There was ample evidence that he had continued to teach and act on the fatalistic theories, but the Inquisition as usual required a confession, and torture was freely used to obtain it. A copy of the sentence and abjuration of 1324 was furnished by the Inquisitor of Bologna, and there was no question as to his relapse. He was abandoned to the secular arm and delivered to Charles's vicar, Jacopo da Brescia. All his books and astrological writings were ordered to be surrendered within twenty-four hours to the bishop or inquisitor. Cecco was forthwith conducted to the place of execution beyond the walls. Tradition relates that he had learned by his art that he should die between Africa and "Campo Fiore," and so sure was he of this that on the way to the stake he mocked and ridiculed his guards; but when the pile was about to be lighted he asked whether there was any place named Africa in the vicinage, and was told that that was the name of a neighboring brook flowing from Fiesole to the Arno. Then he recognized that Florence was the Field of Flowers and that he had been miserably deceived.

Astrology continued to hold its doubtful position with a growing tendency to its condemnation. There were few who could take the common-sense view of Petrarch, that astrologers might be useful if they confined themselves to predicting eclipses and storms, and heat and cold, but that when they talked about the fate of men, known only to God, they simply proved themselves to be liars. The only shade on the luster of Cardinal Peter d'Ailly's reputation was his earnest devotion to the science, and it would have gone hard with him had justice been meted out to him as to Cecco d'Ascoli, for it was impossible for the astrologer to avoid fatalism.

The tolerance which spared Cardinal d'Ailly did not proceed from any change in the theory of the Church on the heresy of interfering with the doctrine of free will. Alonso de Spina points out that the astrological belief that men born under certain stars cannot avoid sinning is manifestly heretical. Sprenger, the highest authority on demonology, held that in astrology there was a tacit pact with the demon. All this shows that in the increasing hostility to occult arts astrology had gradually come under the ban, and the disputed question of its position was finally brought to a decision, at least for France, by the case of Simon Pharees, in 1494. He had been condemned by the archiepiscopal court of Lyons for practicing astrology, and was punished with the light penance of Friday fasting for a year, with the threat of perpetual imprisonment for relapse, and his books and astrolabe had been detained. He had the audacity to appeal to the Parlement, which referred his books to the University. The report of the latter was that his books ought to be burned, even as others had recently been to the value of 50,000 deniers. All astrology pretending to be prophetic, or ascribing supernatural virtue to rings, charms, etc., fabricated under certain constellations, was denounced as false, vain, superstitious, and condemned by both civil and canon law, as well as the use of the astrolabe for finding things lost or divining the future, and the Parlement was urged to check the rapid spread of this art invented by Satan. The Parlement accordingly pronounced a judgment handing over the unlucky Simon to the Bishop and Inquisitor of Paris, to be punished for his relapse. Astrology, which is described as practiced openly everywhere, is condemned. All persons are prohibited from consulting astrologers or diviners about the future, or about things lost or found; all printers are forbidden to print books on the subject, and are ordered to deliver whatever copies they may have to their bishops, and all bishops are instructed to prosecute astrologers.

The question of oneiroscopy, or divination by dreams, was a puzzling one. On the one hand there was the formal prohibition of the Deuteronomist (xviii. 10), which in the Vulgate included the observer of dreams in its denunciations; on the other there were the examples of Joseph and Daniel, and the formal assertion of Job "when deep sleep falleth upon man, in slumberings upon the bed, then he openeth the ears of men and sealeth their instruction" (Job xxxiii. 15, 16). In the twelfth century the expounding of dreams was a recognized profession which does not seem to have been forbidden. John of Salisbury endeavors to prove that no reliance is to be placed on them; Joseph and Daniel were inspired, and short of inspiration no divination from dreams is to be trusted. This, at least, was a more sensible and practical solution than the conclusion reached by Thomas Aquinas, that divination from dreams produced by natural causes or divine revelation is licit, but if the dreams proceed from dæmonic influence it is illicit.

When, towards the close of the thirteenth century, the Inquisition succeeded in including sorcery within its jurisdiction, its organizing faculty speedily laid down rules and formulas for the guidance of its members which aided largely in shaping the uncertain jurisprudence of the period and gave a decided impulse to the persecution of those who practiced the forbidden arts. A manual of practice, written probably about 1280, contains a form for the interrogation of the accused covering all the details of sorcery as known at the time. This served as the foundation on which still more elaborate formulas were constructed by Bernard Gui and others. The earliest draught contains no allusion to the nocturnal excursions of the "good women" whence the Witches' Sabbat was derived, while the later ones introduce an interrogation concerning it, showing that during the interval it was attracting increased attention. It is further noteworthy that none of the formulas embrace questions concerning practices of vulgar witchcraft, which in the fifteenth and succeeding centuries, as we shall see, furnished nearly the whole basis of prosecutions for sorcery.

When sorcery thus came under the jurisdiction of the Inquisition it came simply as heresy, and the whole theory of its treatment was altered. All heresies were equal in guilt, whether they consisted in affirming the poverty of Christ or led to demon-worship, pacts with Satan, and attempts on human life. The sorcerer might, therefore, well prefer to fall into the hands of the Inquisition rather than to be judged by the secular tribunals, for in the former case he had the benefit of the invariable rules observed in dealings with heresy. By confession and abjuration he could always be admitted to penance and escape the stake, which was the customary secular punishment; while, having no convictions such as animated the

Cathari and Waldenses, it cost his conscience nothing to make the necessary recantation. It may perhaps be questioned whether the fiery torture of the stake were not preferable to the inquisitorial mercy which confined its penitents to imprisonment for life in chains and on bread and water; but few men have resolution to prefer a speedy termination to their sufferings, and there was always the hope that exemplary conduct in prison might earn a mitigation of the penalty. It was probably in consequence of this apparent lenity that Philippe le Bel, in 1303, forbade the Inquisition to take cognizance of usury, sorcery, and other offenses of the Jews, but we shall see hereafter that when the Church was forced to summon all its energies in the epidemics of witchcraft, it was obliged to abandon the rule and find excuses for delivering its repentant victims to the stake.

Sorcery was one of the aberrations certain to respond to persecution by more abundant development. So long as its reality was acknowledged and its professors were punished, not as sharpers but as the possessors of evil powers, the more public attention was drawn to it, the more it flourished. As soon as the Inquisition had systematized its suppression, we begin to find it occupying a larger and larger share of public attention. In 1303 one of the charges brought against Boniface VIII, in the Assembly of the Louvre, was that he had a familiar demon who kept him informed of everything, and that he was a sorcerer who consulted diviners and soothsayers.

The growing importance of sorcery in popular belief received a powerful impetus from John XXII, who in so many ways exercised on his age an influence so deplorable. He had full conviction of the reality of all the marvels claimed for magic, and his own experience led him to entertain a lively dread of them. The circumstances of his election were such as to render probable the existence of conspiracies for his removal, and he lent a ready ear to suggestions concerning them. In 1317 we find him issuing a commission to Gaillard, Bishop of Reggio, and several assessors to try a barber-surgeon named Jean d'Amant and sundry clerks of the Sacred Palace on the charge of attempting his life. Under the persuasive influence of torture they confessed that they had at first intended to use poison, but finding no opportunity for this they had recourse to figurines, in the fabrication of which they were skilled. Of course, they were

condemned and executed, and John set to work vigorously to extirpate the abhorred race of sorcerers to which he had so nearly fallen
a victim. We hear of proceedings against Robert, Bishop of Aix,
accused of having practiced magic arts at Bologna; and John, regarding the East as the source whence this execrable science spread over
Christendom, sought to attack it in its home. In 1318 he ordered
the Dominican provincial in the Levant to appoint special inquisitors
for the purpose in all places subject to the Latin rite, and he called
upon the Doge of Venice, the Prince of Achaia, and the Latin barons
to lend their effective aid. He even wrote to the Patriarch of Constantinople and the Oriental archbishops, urging them to assist in
the good work.

The necessary result of all this bustling legislation was to
strengthen the popular confidence in sorcery and to multiply its
practice. In Bernard Gui's *Book of Sentences* rendered in the Inquisition of Toulouse from 1309 to 1323, there are no cases of
sorcery, but we meet with several, tried in 1320 and 1321 in the
episcopal Inquisition of Pamiers, and the fragmentary records of
Carcassonne in 1328 and 1329 show quite a number of convictions.
Inquisitors, moreover, commenced to insert a clause renouncing
sorcery in all abjurations administered to repentant heretics, so that
in case they should become addicted to it they could be promptly
burned for relapse.

The monastic orders evidently contributed their full share to
this class of criminals. We happen to have the sentence, in 1329,
by Henri de Chamay, of a Carmelite named Pierre Recordi, which
illustrates the effectiveness of inquisitorial methods in obtaining
avowals. The trial lasted for several years, and though the accused
tergiversated and retracted repeatedly, his endurance finally gave
way. He adhered at last to the confession that on five occasions,
to obtain possession of women, he had made wax figurines with
invocations of demons, mixing with them the blood of toads and
his own blood and saliva, as a sacrifice to Satan. He would then place
the image under the threshold of the woman, and if she did not
yield to him she would be tormented by a demon. In three cases
this had succeeded; in the other two it would have done so, had he
not been suddenly sent by his superiors to another station. He was
condemned to perpetual imprisonment on bread and water, with

chains on hands and feet, in the Carmelite convent of Toulouse; out of respect to the Order he was not subjected to the ceremony of degradation, and the sentence was rendered privately in the episcopal palace of Pamiers.

Even to distant Ireland the persecution of sorcery was brought in 1325 by that zealous Franciscan, Richard Ledrede, Bishop of Ossory. The Lady Alice Kyteler of Kilkenny had had four husbands, and their testamentary dispositions not suiting her children by the last three, the most efficient means of breaking their wills was to accuse her of having killed them by sorcery, after bewitching them to leave their property to her and to her eldest son, William Outlaw. Bishop Ledrede proceeded vigorously to make inquisition, but Lady Alice and William were allied to the leading officials in Ireland, who threw every difficulty in the way, and, as the canons against heresy were unknown in the island, he had an arduous task, being himself at one time arrested and thrown into prison. A less indomitable spirit would have succumbed, but he triumphed at last, though Lady Alice herself escaped his clutches and was conveyed to England. The trials of her assumed accomplices would seem to have been conducted without much respect to form, but with ample energy. Torture being unknown in English law, the bishop might have failed in eliciting confession had he not found an effective, if illegal, substitute in the whip. Petronilla, for instance, one of Lady Alice's women, after being scourged six times could endure no longer the endless increase of agony, and confessed all that was wanted of her. She admitted that she was a skillful sorceress, but inferior to her mistress, who was equal to any in England, or any in the world. She told how, at Lady Alice's command, she had sacrificed cocks in the crossroads to a demon named Robert Artisson, her mistress's incubus or lover, and how they made from the brains of an unbaptized child, with herbs and worms, in the skull of a robber who had been beheaded, powders and charms to afflict the bodies of the faithful, to excite love and hatred, and to make the faces of certain women appear horned in the eyes of particular individuals. She had been the intermediary between her mistress and the demon; on one occasion he had come to Lady Alice's chamber with two others, black as Ethiopians, when followed love scenes of which the disgusting details may be spared. The case illustrates one of the most important points in the criminal jurisprudence of the succeeding centuries, which explains the unquestioning belief universally entertained as to the marvels of sorcery. Torture administered with unlimited repetition not only brought the patient into a condition in which he would confess whatever was required of him, but the impression produced was such that he would not risk its renewal by retraction even at the last. It was so with this poor creature, who persisted to the end with this tissue of absurdities, and who was burned impenitent. Some others involved in the accusation likewise perished at the stake, while some were permitted to abjure and were punished with crosses—probably the only occasion in which this penance was administered in the British Isles.

While Bishop Ledrede was busy at this good work a trial occurred in England which illustrates the difference in efficiency between the ecclesiastical methods of trial by torture and those of the common law. Twenty-eight persons were accused of employing John of Nottingham and his assistant, Richard Marshall of Leicester, to make wax figures for the destruction of Edward II, the two Despensers, and the Prior of Coventry, with two of his officials who had tyrannized over the people and had been sustained by the royal favorites. Richard Marshall turned accuser, and the evidence was complete. The enormous sums of 20 pounds to Master John and 15 pounds to Richard had been promised, and they had been furnished with seven pounds of wax and two ells of canvas. From September 27, 1324, until June 2, 1325, the two magicians labored at their work. They made seven images, the extra one being experimental, to be tried on Richard de Sowe. On April 27 they commenced operating with this by thrusting a piece of lead into its forehead, when at once Richard de Sowe lost his reason and cried in misery until May 20, when the lead was transferred to his breast, and he died May 23. The accused pleaded not guilty and put themselves on the country. An ordinary jury trial followed, with the result that they were all acquitted.

Although Gregory XI, in 1374, had authorized the Inquisition to prosecute in all cases of sorcery, in France the Parlement included the subject within its policy of encroachment upon the ecclesiastical jurisdiction. In 1390 an occurrence at Laon, where a secular official named Poulaillier arrested a number of sorcerers, gave it occasion to intervene. As Bodin says, at that time Satan managed to have it believed that the stories of sorcery were false, so the Parlement stopped the proceedings, and thus having its attention drawn to the matter, decreed that in future cognizance of such offenses should be confined to the secular tribunals, to the exclusion of the spiritual courts. Secular judges, however, were ready to treat these cases with abundant sharpness. A case occurring at the Paris Châtelet in 1390 has much interest as affording us an insight into the details of procedure, and as illustrating the efficacy of torture in securing conviction. Marion l'Estalée was a young *fille de folle vie*, madly in love with a man named Hainsselin Planiete, who deserted her, and, about July 1, 1390, married a woman named Agnesot. Eager to prevent this, if her confession is to be believed, she had applied to an old procuress, named Margot de la Barre, for a philtre to fix his wandering affection, and when this failed Margot made for her two enchanted chaplets of herbs, which she threw where the bride and groom would tread on them during the festivities of the wedding-day, assured that this would prevent the consummation of the marriage. The plot was unsuccessful, but Hainsselin and Agnesot fell sick, leading to the arrest of the two women.

On July 30 Margot was examined and denied all complicity. She was promptly tortured on *le petit et le grand tresteau*—which I conjecture to mean, the former, pouring water down the throat till the stomach was distended and then forcing it out by paddling the belly; the latter, the rack. This reduplicated torture produced no confession, and she was remanded for further hearing. August 17 Marion was taken in hand, when she denied, and was similarly tortured without result. On the 3d she was again examined and denied, and on being again ordered to the torture, she appealed to the Parlement; the appeal was promptly heard and rejected, and she was tortured as before, then taken to the kitchen and warmed, after which she was tortured a third time, but to no effect. On the 4th she was brought in and refused to confess, but the indefinite repetition of torment without prospect of cessation had produced its effect on body and mind; when she was again bound on the *tresteau*, and the executioner was about to commence his work, she yielded and agreed to confess. On being unbound she detailed the whole story, and in the afternoon, on being brought in again,

she confirmed it *"sans aucune force ou constrainte."* Then Margot
was introduced, and Marion repeated her confession, which Margot
denied and offered the wager of battle, of which no notice was
taken. Margot then asserted her ability to prove an alibi on the day
when she was said to have made the chaplets. The parties whom she
named as witnesses were looked up for her and brought in the next
day, when the evidence proved rather incriminating than otherwise.
Marion was then made to repeat her confession, and not till then was
Margot tortured a second time, but still without result. On the
6th Marion was again made to repeat her confession, after which
Margot was brought in and bound to the *tresteau*. Her resolution
gave way, and before the torture commenced she promised to confess.
Her story agreed with that of Marion, except in some embellishments, which serve to show how thoroughly untrustworthy were all
such confessions. When she enchanted the chaplets she invoked
the demon by thrice repeating *"Ennemi je te conjures au nom du
Père, du Fils et du Saint Esperit que tu viegnes a moy icy"*, then
an *ennemi*, or demon, promptly appeared, like those she had seen in
the Passion-play, and after she had instructed him to enter into
the bodies of Hainsselin and Agnesot he flew out of the window in
a whirlwind, making a great noise and throwing her into mortal
fear. The evidence was thus complete, and there would seem to
be nothing left but prompt sentence, yet the tribunal manifested
commendable desire to avoid precipitate judgment. Assessors and
experts were called in. On August 7, 8, and 9 Marion was thrice
made to repeat her confession, and Margot twice. On the latter day
a consultation was held, and the decision was unanimous against
Margot, who was pilloried and burned the same day; but three of
the experts thought that the pillory and banishment would suffice
for Marion. Her case was postponed till the 23d, when another
consultation was held; opinions remained unaltered, and as the
majority was in favor of condemnation the *prévôt* condemned her,
and she was burned the next day. Both the victims may have
been innocent, and the whole story may have been invented to
avoid the repetition of the intolerable torture; but, inevitable as
was the result under the conditions of the trial, the judges manifested every disposition to deal fairly with the unfortunates in
their hands, and could entertain no possible doubt as to the reality

of the offense and of the apparition of the demon as described by Margot. It is necessary to bear this in mind when estimating the conduct of the judges and inquisitors who sent thousands of unfortunates to the stake in the next two centuries for offenses which to a modern mind are purely chimerical, for, according to the jurisprudence of the age, no evidence could be more absolute than that on which rested the cruelly punished absurdities of witchcraft.

About this period may be dated a fresh impulse given to the belief in sorcery, whose continued growth during the fifteenth and sixteenth centuries was destined to produce results so deplorable, and to present one of the most curious problems in the history of human error. The first indication of this new development is found in the action of the University of Paris. September 19, 1398, the theological faculty held a general congregation in the church of St. Mathurin, and adopted a series of 28 articles which thenceforth became a standard for all demonologists, and were regarded as an unanswerable argument to skeptics who questioned the reality of the wickedness of the arts of magic. The preamble recites that action was necessary in view of the active emergence of ancient errors which threatened to infect society. The University then proceeded to declare that there was an implied contract with Satan in every superstitious observance, of which the expected result was not reasonably to be anticipated from God and from Nature, and it condemned as erroneous the assertion that it was permissible to invoke the aid of demons or to seek their friendship, or to enter into compacts with them, or to imprison them in stones, rings, mirrors, and images, or to use sorcery for good purposes or for the cure of sorcery, or that God could be induced by magic arts to compel demons to obey invocations, or that the celebration of masses or other good works used in some forms of thaumaturgy was permissible, or that the prophets and saints of old performed their miracles by these means which were taught by God, or that by certain magic arts we can attain to the sight of the divine essence. These latter clauses point to a dangerous tendency of coalescence between the arts of the sorcerer and of the theurgist, and indicate that in the higher magic of the day there was a claim to be considered as penetrating to the ineffable mysteries which surrounded the throne of God; in fact, these adepts declared that their arts were lawful, and they sought to prove their origin in God by pointing out that good flowed from them, and that the wishes and prophecies of those using them were fulfilled. All this the University condemned, and while on the one hand it denied that images of lead or gold or wax, when baptized, exorcised, and consecrated on certain days, possessed the powers ascribed to them in the books of magic, on the other hand it was equally emphatic in animadverting on the incredulity of those who denied that sorcery, incantations, and the invocation of demons possessed the powers claimed for them by sorcerers.

Like all other efforts to repress sorcery, this of course only served to give it fresh significance and importance. The declaration that it was erroneous to doubt the reality of sorcery and its effects became a favorite argument of the demonologists. Gerson declared that to call in question the existence of demons was not only impious and heretical, but destructive to all human and political society. Sprenger concludes that the denial of the existence of witchcraft is not in itself heresy, as it may proceed from ignorance, but such ignorance in an ecclesiastic is in itself culpable; such denial is sufficient to justify vehement suspicion of heresy, calling for prosecution, and we have seen what was the significance of "vehement suspicion" in inquisitorial practice.

In England, sorcery had thus far attracted little attention. Even as late as 1372 a man was arrested in Southwark with the head and face of a corpse in his possession, and a book of magic was found in his trunk. Tried before the Inquisition he would infallibly have confessed under torture a series of misdeeds and have ended at the stake; but he was brought before Sir J. Knyvet, in the King's Bench. No indictment even was found against him; he was simply sworn not to practice sorcery and was discharged, but the head and book were burned at Tothill at his expense. To the fair and open character of English law is doubtless to be attributed the comparative exemption of the island from the terror of sorcery, but when at last persecuting excitement arose in the Lollard troubles, the Church used its influence with the new Lancastrian dynasty to suppress the emissaries of Satan. In 1407 Henry IV issued letters to his bishops reciting that sorcerers, magicians, conjurers, necromancers, and diviners abounded in their dioceses, perverting the people and perpetrating things horrible and detestable. The bishops, therefore, were commissioned to imprison all such malefactors, either with or without trial, until they should recant their errors or the king's pleasure could be learned respecting them. The placing of the matter thus in the hands of the Church, and depriving the accused of all legal safeguards, is most significant as a recognition that the ordinary forms of English law were not to be depended upon in such cases.

Perhaps the most remarkable trial for sorcery on record is that of the Maréchal de Rais, in 1440, which has long ranked as a *cause célèbre*. In the France of the fifteenth century there was no career more promising than that of Gilles de Rais. Born in 1404 of the noble stock of Montmorency and Craon, grandson of the renowned knight Brumor de Laval, grandnephew of du Guesclin, of kindred with the Constable Clisson, and allied with all that was illustrious in the west of France, his barony of Rais rendered him the head of the baronage of Britanny. His territorial possessions were ample, and when, while still a youth, he married the great heiress Catharine de Thouars, he might count himself among the wealthiest nobles of France. At 22 he entered the desperate service of Charles VII, with a troop maintained at his own expense, and he distinguished himself in the seemingly hopeless resistance to the English arms. When Joan of Arc appeared he was charged with the special duty of watching over her personal safety, and, from the relief of Orleans to the repulse at the gates of Paris, he was ever at her side. In the coronation ceremonies at Reims he received, though but 25 years old, the high dignity of Marshal of France, and in the September following he was honored with permission to add to his arms a border of the royal fleur-de-lis. There was no dignity beneath the crown to which his ambition might not aspire, for he maintained himself so skillfully between the opposing factions of the constable and of the royal favorite La Trémouille, that when the latter fell, in 1433, his credit at the court was unimpaired.

He was, moreover, a man of unusual culture. His restless curiosity and thirst for knowledge led him to accumulate books at a time when it was rare for knights to be able to sign their names. Chance has preserved to us the titles of St. Augustin's *City of God*, Valerius Maximus, Ovid's *Metamorphoses* and Suetonius, as fragments of his library; and on his trial one of the reasons he gave for liking an Italian necromancer was the choice Latinity of his speech.

He delighted in rich bindings and illuminations. On one occasion he is described, but a few months before his arrest, as engaged in his study in ornamenting with enamels the cover of a book of ceremonies for his chapel. Of music and the drama he was also passionately fond.

Yet the life which promised so much in camp and court was blighted by the fatal errors of his training. The death of his father while he was a child of eleven left him to the care of a weak and indulgent grandfather, Jean de Craon, whose authority he soon shook off. His fiery nature ran riot, and he grew up devoured with the wildest ambition, abandoned to sensual excesses of every kind, and with passions unrestrained and untamable. When on trial he repeatedly urged all parents to train their children rigidly in the ways of virtue, for it was his unbridled youth that had led him to crime and a shameful death.

Although, in the charges preferred against him, his aberrations are said to have commenced in 1426, he himself asserted that the fatal plunge was not made until 1432, after the death of his grandfather. Then commenced a strange and unexampled dual existence. To the outward world he was the magnificent seigneur, intent only on display and frivolity. He affected a state almost royal. A military household of over 200 horsemen accompanied him wherever he went. He founded a chapter of canons, with service and choir fit for a cathedral, and this was his private chapel, likewise attached to his person, costing him immense sums, including portable organs carried on the shoulders of six stout serving-men. Not less extravagant was his passion for theatrical displays. The drama of the age, though rude, was costly, and when he exhibited freely to the multitude spectacular performances, there were immense structures to be built and hundreds of actors to be clad in cloths of gold and silver, silks and velvets, and handsome armor, the whole followed by public banquets to the spectators. These were only items in his expenditure; his purse and table were open to all and his artistic tastes were gratified without regard to cost. This ruinous prodigality was accompanied with the utmost disorder in his affairs. It was beneath the dignity of a great seigneur to attend to business, and all details were abandoned to the crowd of pimps and parasites and flatterers attracted by his lavish recklessness, among whom the principal were Roger de Briqueville and Gilles de Sillé. Gold must be raised at any price; his revenues were farmed out in advance, the produce of field and forest and salt works was disposed of at low prices, and he soon began to sell his estates at less than their value, usually reserving a right of redemption within six years.

In 1435 or 1436, his family became alarmed at his mad career; they appealed to Charles VII, who issued letters, in accordance with a legal custom of time, interdicting him from alienating lands and revenues, and all persons from contracting with him. This was published with sound of trump in Orleans, Angers, Blois, Machecoul, and elsewhere outside Britanny. Within the duchy, Jean V prohibited its publication. Nothwithstanding his surname of le Bon and le Sage, Jean was a greedy and unscrupulous prince, who, as one of the chief purchasers of the marshal's estates, was interested in the ruin of his subject. He continued to secure profitable bargains, subject always to the right of redemption, and manifested for his dupe the greatest friendship, appointing him lieutenant-general of the duchy and entering into a brotherhood of arms with him, while privately mocking and ridiculing him as a fool. As a last resort, Gilles's younger brother, René de la Suze, and his cousin, the Admiral de Loheac, captured and garrisoned the castles of Champtocé and Machecoul, but in 1437 and 1438 Gilles retook them, with the aid of the duke, to whom he had sold the former.

Such was the external life of Gilles de Rais, to all appearance that of a liberal, pious noble, whose worst foible was thoughtless extravagance. Beneath the surface, however, lay an existence of crime more repulsive than anything chronicled by Tacitus or Suetonius. Ordinary indulgence having palled upon the senses of the youthful voluptuary, about the year 1432 he abandoned himself to unnatural lusts, selecting as his victims children, whom he promptly slew to secure their silence. At first their bodies were thrown into *oubliettes* at the bottom of towers in his ordinary places of residence. When Champtocé was about to be surrendered to the duke, the bones of about forty children were hastily gathered together and carried off; when René de la Suze was advancing on Machecoul, the same number were extracted from their hiding-place and burned. Scared by this narrow escape from detection, Gilles subsequently had the bodies burned at once in the fireplace of his chamber and the ashes scattered in the moats. So depraved became his appetites that he found his chief enjoyment in the death agonies of his victims, over whose sufferings he gloated as he skillfully mangled them and protracted their torture. When dead he would criticize their beauties with his confidential servitors, would compare one with another, and would kiss with rapture the heads which pleased him most.

While such were his recreations, his serious pursuit was the search for the philosophers' stone—the Universal Elixir which should place unlimited wealth and power in his hands. To this end his agents were on the watch to bring him skilled professors in the art, and he served as the dupe of a succession of charlatans, whose promises kept him ever in the hope that he was on the point of attaining the fulfillment of his desires. This explains the recklessness of his expenditures and his careless alienations, in which he retained a right of redemption, for any morrow might see him placed beyond the need of reckoning with his creditors. Yet, as already stated, although alchemy assumed to be a science, in practice it was almost universally coupled with necromancy, and few alchemists pretended to be able to achieve results without the assistance of demons. So it was with those employed by Gilles de Rais, and no more instructive chapter in the history of the frauds of magic can be found than in his confession and that of his chief magician, Francesco Prelati. The latter had a familiar demon named Barron, whom he never had any difficulty in evoking when alone, but who would never show himself when Gilles was present, and in the naïve accounts which the pair give of their attempts and failures, one cannot help admiring the quick-witted ingenuity of the Italian and the facile credulity of the baron. On one occasion, in answer to Prelati's earnest prayer for gold, the tantalizing demon spread countless ingots around the room, but forbade his touching them for some days. When this was reported to Gilles he naturally desired to feast his eyes upon the treasure, and Prelati conducted him to the chamber. On opening the door, however, he cried out that he saw a great green serpent as large as a dog coiled up on the floor, and both took to their heels. Then Gilles armed himself with a crucifix containing a particle of the true cross, and insisted on returning, but Prelati warned him that such expedients only increased the danger, and he desisted. Finally the malicious demon changed the gold into tinsel, which, when handled, turned into a tawny dust. It was in vain that Gilles gave to Prelati compacts signed with his blood, pledging himself to obedience in return for the three gifts of knowledge, wealth, and power; Barron would have none of them. The demon was offended with Gilles for not keeping a promise to make some offering to him; if a small request were made it should be a trifle, such as a pullet or a dove; if something greater it must be the member of a child. Children's bodies were not scarce where Gilles resided, and he speedily placed in a glass vessel a child's hand, heart, eyes, and blood, and gave them to Prelati to offer. Still the demon was obdurate, and Prelati, as he said, buried the rejected offering in consecrated ground.

It was impossible that a career such as this could continue for eight years without exciting suspicion. Though for the most part Gilles selected his victims from among the beggars who crowded his castle gates, attracted by his ostentatious charities—children for whom there was no one to make inquiry—yet he had his agents out through the land enticing from parents the offspring whom they would see no more. Two women, Etiennette Blanchu and Perrine Martin, better known as La Meffraye, were the most successful of these purveyors, and it came to be noticed that when he was in Nantes the children who frequented the gates of his Hôtel de la Suze were apt to disappear unaccountably. His confidential servants, Henri Griart, known as Henriet, and Étienne Corillaut, nicknamed Poitou, when they saw a handsome youth would engage him as a page without concealment, ride off with him, and he would be heard of no more. It is curious how tardily suspicion was aroused, for up to within a year or two of the end there were mothers who had no hesitation in confiding their children to the terrible baron. Even as far off as St. Jean-d'Angely, Machecoul had the name of a place where children were eaten, and at Tiffauges they said that for one child that disappeared at Machecoul there were seven at Tiffauges. Yet so far was the truth from being guessed that the story ran among the peasantry that Michel de Sillé, when a prisoner with the English, had been obliged to promise, as part of his ransom, twenty-four boys to serve as pages, and that when the tale was complete the disappearances would cease. Still suspicion grew. One of the marshal's confidants, though not fully initiated in his secrets, a priest named Eustache Blanchet, grew alarmed and ran away from Tiffauges, taking up his residence at Mortagne-sur-Sèvre. Here he learned from Jean Mercier, castellan of La Roche-sur-Yon, that in Nantes and Clisson and elsewhere it was public rumor that Gilles killed numbers of children, in order with their blood to write a necromantic book which, when completed, would enable him to capture any castle and prevent anyone from withstanding him. This grew to be the popular belief, as recorded by Monstrelet, and so impressed was Blanchet's imagination with it that, after his return to Tiffauges, at Easter 1440, just before the catastrophe, when Gilles invited him and another priest into his study to exhibit to them his ornamentation of the binding of the ceremonial book of his chapel, some sheets of paper written in red, lying on the desk, convinced him that the popular report was true.

What was the number of his victims can never be known. With the exaggeration customary in such cases some writers have estimated them at approximately 800. In his confession Gilles said that the number was great, but he kept no count. In the civil process against him it is stated at over 200, but in the articles of accusation in the ecclesiastical court, which were elaborately drawn up after obtaining all possible testimony, the figure is given as 140, more or less, and this is probably a full estimate.

Yet, strange as were the crimes of Gilles de Rais, even stranger was his conviction that he had in no way so incurred the wrath of God that the Church could not readily ensure his salvation at the cost of some of the customary penances. He was solicitous about his soul in a fashion very uncommon with demon-worshippers, and in all his projected and rejected compacts with Satan he was careful to insert a clause that he should not suffer in body or soul. When he founded his chapter of canons and dedicated it to the Holy Innocents, there might seem to be a grim pleasantry in his choice of patron saints, yet there can be no doubt that he felt that he was thus atoning for the massacre of the innocents which he himself was constantly perpetrating. More than once he had a transient emotion of repentance; he took vows to abandon his guilty life, and by a pilgrimage to the Holy Sepulchre to obtain pardon for the evil he had wrought—pardon which he never seems to have doubted could be thus easily won. After making his public confession, when he could have no further hope on earth, he turned to the crowded audience and exhorted them to hold fast to the Church and to pay her the highest honor. He had always, he said, kept his heart and his affections on the Church, but for which, in view of his crimes, he believed that Satan would have strangled him and carried him off, body and soul. This trust in the saving power of the Church gave him the absolute confidence in his salvation, which is not the least noteworthy feature in his strange character. When, after he and Francesco Prelati had corroborated each other's confessions, and they were about to part, he embraced and kissed his necromancer with sobs and tears, saying, "*Adieu, Francoys, mon amy*; we shall see each other no more in this world: I pray God to give you patience and knowledge: be certain that if you have patience and hope in God we shall meet each other in the great joy of paradise. Pray God for me, and I will pray for you."

How long Gilles might have continued his devastating career it would be hard to guess, had it not suited the interest of Duke Jean and of his chancellor, Jean de Malestroit, Bishop of Nantes, to bring him to the stake. Both of them had been purchasers of his squandered estates, and might wish to free themselves from the equity of redemption, and both might hope to gain from the confiscation of what remained to him. To assail so redoubtable a baron was, however, a task not lightly to be undertaken: the Church must be the leader, for the civil power dared not risk arousing the susceptibilities of the whole baronage of the duchy. Gilles's impetuous temper furnished them the excuse.

The marshal had sold the castle and fief of Saint-Étienne de Malemort to Geoffroi le Ferron, treasurer of the duke—possibly a cover for the duke himself—and had delivered seizin to Jean le Ferron, brother of the purchaser, a man who had received the tonsure and wore the habit of a clerk, thus entitling him to clerical immunity, even though he performed no clerical functions. Some cause of quarrel subsequently arose, which Gilles proceeded to settle in the arbitrary fashion customary at the time. On Pentecost, 1440, he led a troop of some 60 horsemen to Saint-Étienne, left them in ambush near the castle, and with a few followers went to the church where Jean was at his devotions. Mass was about concluded when the intruders rushed in with brandished weapons, and Gilles addressed Jean: "Ha, scoundrel, thou hast beaten my men and committed extortions on them; come out or I will kill thee!" The frightened clerk was dragged to the gate of the castle and forced to order its surrender, when Gilles garrisoned it and carried him off, finally imprisoning him in Tiffauges, chained hand and foot.

The offense was one for which the customs of Britanny provided a remedy in the civil courts, but the duke zealously took up the cause of his treasurer and summarily ordered his lieutenant-general to surrender the castle and the prisoners under a penalty of 50,000 crowns. Indignant at this unlooked-for intervention, Gilles maltreated the messengers of the duke, who promptly raised a force and recaptured the place in dispute. Tiffauges, where the prisoners lay, was in Poitou, beyond his jurisdiction, but his brother, the Constable de Richemont, besieged it, and Gilles was forced to liberate them. Having thus submitted, he ventured in July to visit the duke at Josselin: he had some doubts as to his reception, but Prelati consulted his demon and announced that Gilles could go in safety. He was graciously received, and imagined that the storm had blown over. So safe did he feel that while at Josselin he continued his atrocities, putting to death several children and causing Prelati to evoke his demon.

While the powers of the State thus hesitated to attack the criminal, the Church was busily preparing his downfall. He had been guilty of sacrilege in the violence committed in the church of Saint-Étienne, and he had violated its immunities in the person of Jean le Ferron. On July 30 Jean de Malestroit, in whose bishopric of Nantes the barony of Rais was situated, issued privately a declaration reciting that in a recent visitation he and his commissioners had found that Gilles was publicly defamed for murdering many children, after gratifying his lust on them, of invoking the demon with horrid rites, of entering into compacts with him, and of other enormities. Though in a general way synodal witnesses were quoted in substantiation of these charges, only eight witnesses were personally named, seven of them women, all residents of Nantes, whose subsequent testimony shows us that they had lost children, whose disappearance they thought they could connect with Gilles. Evidently the awful secrets of Tiffauges and Machecoul had not leaked out. It was necessary to hazard something, to strike boldly, and when Gilles and his retainers were in the hands of justice its methods could be relied upon to procure from them evidence sufficient for their own conviction.

The blow fell September 13, when the bishop issued a citation summoning Gilles to appear for trial before him on the 19th. This was served upon him personally the next day, and he made no resistance. Some rumor of what was impending must have been in the air, for his two chief instigators and confidants, Gilles de Sillé and Roger de Briqueville, saved themselves by flight. The rest of his nearest servitors and procurers, male and female, were seized, including Prelati, and carried to Nantes. On the 19th he had a private hearing before the bishop. The prosecuting officer, Guillaume Capeillon, cunningly preferred certain charges of heresy against him, when he fell into the trap and boldly offered to purge himself before the bishop or any other ecclesiastical judge. He was taken at his word, and the 28th was fixed for his appearance before the bishop and the Vice-Inquisitor of Nantes, Jean Blouyn.

The records are imperfect, and tell us nothing of what was done with the followers of Gilles, but we may be sure that during this interval the methods of the inquisitorial process were not spared to extract information from them, and that it was spread among the people to create public opinion, for by the 28th some of the sorrowing parents who came forward to confirm their previous complaints assert that since La Meffraye had been in the secular prison they had been told that she said their children had been delivered to Gilles. At this hearing only ten witnesses were heard, with their vague conjectures on the loss of their offspring. Gilles was not present, and apparently the result of the torture of his servants had not yet been satisfactory, for further proceedings were adjourned till October 8.

In the succeeding hearings the rule of secrecy seems to have been abandoned. There evidently was extreme anxiety to create popular opinion against the prisoner, for the courtroom in the Tour Neuve was crowded. On October 8 proceedings opened with the frantic cries of the bereaved parents clamoring for justice against him who had despoiled them and had committed a black catalogue of crimes, which shows that since their last appearance their ignorance had been carefully enlightened. Like the chorus of a Greek tragedy, the same dramatic use was made of them on the 11th, after which, as the object was presumably accomplished, they disappear.

At the hearing of the 8th the articles of accusation were presented orally by the prosecutor. Gilles thereupon appealed from the court, but as his appeal was verbal it was promptly set aside, though no offer was made to him of counsel, or even of a notary to reduce it to writing. He doubtless was guilty, but if he had been innocent the result would have been the same. Yet the trial was not carried on *simpliciter et de plano* according to the forms of the Inquisition. There was a semblance of a *litis contestatio*. The prosecutor took the *juramentum de calumnia*, to tell the truth and avoid deceit, and demanded that Gilles should do the same, as prescribed by legal form, but the latter obstinately refused, though summoned four times and threatened with excommunication. The only notice he would take of the proceedings was to denounce all the charges as false.

It was worse at the hearing of the 13th, when the accusations had been reduced to writing in a formidable series of 49 articles. When the bishop and inquisitor asked him what he had to say in defense, Gilles haughtily retorted that they were not his judges; he had appealed from them and would make no reply to the charges. Then, giving rein to his temper, he stigmatized them as simoniacs and scoundrels, before whom it was degradation for him to appear; he wondered that Pierre de l'Hôpital, president or chief judicial officer of Brittany, who was present, would allow ecclesiastics to meddle with such crimes as were alleged against him. In spite of his reclamations the indictment was read, when he simply denounced it as a pack of lies and refused to answer formally. Then, after repeated warnings, the bishop and inquisitor pronounced him contumacious and excommunicated him. He again appealed, but the appeal was rejected as frivolous, and he was given 48 hours in which to frame a defense.

The charges formed a long and most elaborate paper, showing by its detail of individual cases that by this time Gilles's servitors must have been induced to make full confessions. For the first time there appear in it the sacrilege and violation of clerical immunity committed at Saint-Étienne, and the charge of child-murder only figures as an accessory to the other crimes to which it was connected. Everything, however, that could be alleged against him was gathered together, even to inordinate eating and drinking, which were assumed to have led to his other excesses. His transient fits of repentance and vows of amendment were utilized ingeniously to prove that he was a relapsed heretic and thus deprived of all chance of escape. In the conclusion the prosecutor apportioned the charges between the two jurisdictions. The bishop and inquisitor conjointly were prayed to declare him guilty of heretical apostasy and the invocation of demons, while the bishop alone was to pronounce sentence on his unnatural crimes and sacrilege, the Inquisition having no cognizance of these offenses.

It is not easy to understand what followed. When two days later, on the 15th, Gilles was brought into court he was a changed man. We have no means of knowing what influences had meanwhile been brought to bear upon him, but the only probable explanation would seem to be that he recognized from the details of the charges that his servants had been forced to betray him, that further resistance would only subject him to torture, and, in his earnest care for the salvation of his soul, that submission to the Church and endurance of the inevitable was the only path to heaven. He humbly admitted the bishop and inquisitor to be his judges, and on bended knee, with tears and sighs, craved their pardon for the insults which he had showered upon them, and begged for absolution from the excommunication incurred by contumacy; he took with the prosecutor the *juramentum de calumnia;* and in general terms he acknowledged that he had no objection to make to the charges and confessed the crimes alleged against him, yet when he was required to answer to the articles *seriatim* he at once denied that he had invoked, or caused to be invoked, any malignant spirits; he had, it is true, dabbled in alchemy, but he freely offered himself to be burned if the witnesses to be produced, whose testimony he was willing to accept in advance, should prove that he had invoked demons or entered into pacts with them and offered them sacrifices. All the rest of the charges he specifically denied, but he invited the prosecutor to produce what witnesses he chose, and he (Gilles) would admit their evidence to be conclusive. Although in all this there is a contradiction which casts doubt upon the frankness of the official record, it may perhaps be explained by vacillation not improbable in his terrible position. He did not shrink, however, when his servants and agents, Henriet, Poitou, Prelati, Blanchet, and his two procuresses were brought forward and sworn in his presence; he declined the offer of the bishop and inquisitor to frame the interrogatories for their examination, and he declared that he would stand to their depositions and make no exceptions to them or to their evidence. It was the same when, on the 15th and 19th, additional witnesses were sworn in his presence. The examinations of these witnesses, however, were made by notaries in private. The depositions made by Henriet and Poitou, which have been preserved to us, are hideous catalogues of the foulest crimes, minute in their specifications, though the identity between them in trifles, where omissions or discrepancies would be natural, strongly suggests manipulation either of witnesses or of records. That of Prelati is equally full in its details of necromancy, and raises at once the question, not easily answered, why the necromancer, who had richly earned the stake, seems to have escaped all punishment; and the same may be said as to Blanchet, La Meffraye and her colleague, and some others of those involved. It is worthy of note that in these confessions or depositions the customary formula that they are made without fear, force, or favor is conspicuous by its absence.

At the hearing of October 20 Gilles waived all delay as to the publication of the evidence against him, and when the depositions of his accomplices were read he said he had no exceptions to make to them; in fact, that the publication was unnecessary in view of what he had already said, and what he intended to confess. One would think that this was quite sufficient, for his guilt was thus proved and admitted, but the infernal curiosity of the jurisprudence of the time was never satisfied until it had wrung from the accused a detailed and formal confession. The prosecutor, therefore, earnestly demanded of the bishop and inquisitor that Gilles should be tortured, in order, as he said, to develop the truth more fully. They consulted with the experts and decided that torture should be applied.

October 21, the bishop and inquisitor ordered him to be brought in and tortured. Everything was in readiness for it, when he humbly begged them to defer it until the next day, and that meanwhile he would make up his mind so as to satisfy them and render it unnecessary. He further asked that they should commission the Bishop of Saint-Brieuc and Pierre de l'Hôpital to hear his confession in a place apart from the torture. This last prayer they granted, but they would only give him a respite until two o'clock, with the promise of a further postponement until the next day, in case he confessed meanwhile. When the confession made that afternoon, under these circumstances, is officially declared to have been made "freely and willingly and without coercion of any kind," it affords another example of the value of these customary formulas.

Before the commissioners he made no difficulty of accusing himself of all the crimes wherewith he stood charged. Pierre de l'Hôpital found the recital hard of credence, and pressed him vigorously to disclose the motive which had led to their commission. He was not satisfied with Gilles's declaration that it was simply to gratify his passions, till he exclaimed, "Truly, there was no other cause, object, or intention than I have said. I have told you greater things than that—enough to put ten thousand men to death." The president pressed the matter no further, but sent for Prelati, when the two accomplices freely confirmed each other's statements, and they parted in tears with the affectionate farewell already alluded to.

There was no further talk of torture. Gilles was now fairly embarked in his new course. Apparently resolved to win heaven by contrition and by the assistance of the Church, this extraordinary man presents, during the remainder of the trial, a spectacle which is probably without an example. When, on the next day, October 22, he was brought before his judges, the proud and haughty baron desired that his confession should be read in public, so that his humiliation should aid in winning pardon from God. Not content with this, he supplemented his confession with abundant details of his atrocities, as though seeking to make to God an acceptable oblation of his pride. Finally, after exhorting those present to honor and obey the Church, he begged with abundant tears their prayers, and entreated pardon of the parents whose children he had murdered.

On the 25th he was brought up for sentence. After the bishop and inquisitor had duly consulted their assembly of experts, two sentences were read. The first, in the name of both judges, condemned him as guilty of heretical apostasy and horrid invocation of demons, for which he had incurred excommunication and other penalties of the law. The second sentence, rendered by the bishop alone, in the same form, condemned him for unnatural crime, for sacrilege, and for violating the immunities of the Church. In neither sentence was there any punishment indicated. He was not pronounced relapsed, and therefore could not be abandoned to the secular arm, and it was apparently deemed superfluous to enjoin on him any penance, as a prosecution had been going on *pari passu* in the secular court, of which the result was not in doubt. The ecclesiastical court had dropped the accusation of murder, after it had served its purpose in exciting popular odium, and had left it to the civil authorities to which it belonged. In fact, the whole elaborate proceedings were a nullity, except so far as they served as a shield for the civil process, and as a basis for confiscating his estates.

After the reading of the sentences he was asked if he wished reincorporation in the Church. He replied that he had not known what heresy was, nor that he had lapsed into it, but as the Church had declared him guilty, he begged to be reincorporated. When this ceremony was accomplished he asked for absolution, which was granted. It shows the deceptive nature of the whole proceedings, and how little the bishop and inquisitor thought of anything but the secret object to be attained, that although Gilles was condemned for heresy, he was absolved without subjection to the indispensable ceremony of abjuration, and his request for a confessor was promptly met by the appointment of Jean Juvenal, a Carmelite of Ploermel.

From the Tour Neuve, where the ecclesiastical court held its sittings, Gilles was at once hurried before the secular tribunal in the Bouffay. It had commenced its inquest on September 18, and had been busily employed in collecting evidence concerning the child-murders, besides which, its presiding judge, Pierre de l'Hôpital, had been present at much of the ecclesiastical trial, and had personally received Gilles's confession. It was thus fully prepared to act, and indeed had already condemned Henriet and Poitou to be hanged and burned. When Gilles was brought in and arraigned he immediately confessed. Then the president took the opinions of his assessors, who all voted in favor of death, although there was some difference as to the form. Finally Pierre announced that he had incurred the *peines pecunielles*, which were to be levied on his goods and lands "with moderation of justice." As for his crimes, for these he was to be hanged and burned, and that he might have opportunity to crave mercy of God, the time was fixed for one o'clock the next day. Gilles thanked him for the designation of the hour, adding that as he and his servants, Henriet and Poitou, had committed the crimes together, he asked that they might be executed together, so that he who was the cause of their guilt might admonish them, and show them the example of a good death, and by the grace of our Lord be the cause of their salvation. Not only was this request granted, but he was told that he might select the place of his burial, when he chose the Carmelite church, the sepulchre of the dukes, and of all that was most illustrious in Brittany. As a last prayer, he begged that the bishop and clergy might be requested to walk in procession prior to his execution the next day, to pray God to keep him and his servants in firm belief of salvation. This was granted, and the morning saw the extraordinary spectacle of the clergy, followed by the whole population of Nantes, who had been clamoring for his death, marching through the streets and singing and praying for his salvation.

On the way to execution Gilles devoted himself to comforting the servants whom he had brought to a shameful death, assuring them that as soon as their souls should leave their bodies they would all meet in paradise. They were mounted on stands over piles of wood, with halters around their necks attached to the gallows. The stands were pushed aside, and as they swung the fagots were lighted. Henriet and Poitou were allowed to burn to ashes, but when Gilles's halter was burned through and his body fell, the ladies of his kindred rushed forward and plucked it from the flames. It was honored with a magnificent funeral, and it is said that some of the bones were kept by his family as relics of his repentance.

Under the Breton laws execution for crime entailed confiscation of movables to the seigneur justicier, but not of the landed estates. Condemnation for heresy, as we have seen, everywhere carried with it indiscriminate confiscation and inflicted disabilities for two generations. Gilles was convicted as a heretic, but the secular sentence

is obscure on the subject of confiscation, and in the intricate and
prolonged litigation which arose over his inheritance it is difficult
to determine to what extent confiscation was enforced. Some twenty
years later the *Mémoire des Héritiers* argues that death had expiated
his crimes and removed all cause of confiscation, which would seem
to indicate that it had taken place. Certain it is that, to assist the
Duke of Brittany, René of Anjou in 1450 confiscated Champtocé
and Ingrandes, which were under his jurisdiction, and ceded them to
the duke to confirm his title. Charles VII, on the other side, had
already decreed confiscation in order to help the heirs.

No disabilities were inflicted upon the descendants, and the
house was still regarded as eligible to the noblest alliances. After
a year of widowhood, Catharine de Thouars married Jean de Vendôme, Vidame of Chartres, and in 1442 Gilles's daughter, Marie,
espoused Prégent de Coétivy, Admiral of France and one of the
most powerful men in the royal court. He must have considered
the match desirable, for he submitted to hard conditions in the
marriage contract. He resolutely set to work to recover the alienated
or confiscated lands, and succeeded in gaining possession of some
of the finest estates, including Champtocé and Ingrandes, though
his death at the siege of Cherbourg, in 1450, prevented his enjoying
them. Marie not long after was remarried with André de Laval,
Marshal and Admiral of France, who caused her rights to be respected, but on her death without issue in 1457 the inheritance
passed to Gilles's brother, René de la Suze. The interminable litigation revived and continued until after his death in 1474. He left
but one daughter, who had been married to the Prince de Déols
in 1446; they had but one son, André de Chauvigny, who died without issue in 1502, when the race became extinct. The barony of
Rais lapsed into the house of Tournemine, and at length passed into
that of Gondy, to become celebrated in the seventeenth century
through the Cardinal de Retz.

Admitting as we must the guilt of Gilles de Rais, all this throws
an uncomfortable doubt over the sincerity of his trial and conviction,
and this is not lessened by the fate of his accomplices. Only Henriet
and Poitou appear to have suffered; there is no trace of the death
penalty inflicted on any of the rest, though their criminality was
sufficient for the most condign punishment, and the facility with

which self-incriminating evidence was obtainable by the use of torture rendered unknown the device of purchasing testimony with pardon. Gilles de Sillé, who was regarded as the worst of the marshal's instigators, disappeared and was heard of no more. Next to him ranked Roger de Briqueville. It is somewhat mysterious that the family seem to have regarded this man with favor. Marie de Rais cherished his children with tender care. In 1446 he obtained from Charles VII letters of remission rehabilitating him, which he certainly could not have procured had not Prégent de Coétivy favored him, and the latter, in a letter to his brother Oliver, in 1449, desires to be remembered to Roger.

If the student feels that there is an impenetrable mystery shrouding the truth in this remarkable case, the Breton peasant was troubled with no such doubts. To him Gilles remained the embodiment of cruelty and ferocity. I am not sufficiently versed in folklore to express an opinion whether M. Bossard is correct in maintaining that Gilles is the original of Bluebeard, the monster of the nursery tale rendered universally popular in the version of Charles Perrault. Yet, even without admitting that the story is of Breton origin, there would seem to be no doubt that in Brittany, La Vendée, Anjou, and Poitou, where the terrible baron had his chosen seats of residence, he is known by the name of Bluebeard, and the legend—possibly an older one—of cruelty to seven wives, has been attached to him who had but one, and who left that one a widow. Tradition relates how the demon changed to a brilliant blue the magnificent red beard that was his pride; and everywhere, at Tiffauges, at Champtocé, at Machecoul, for the peasant, Bluebeard is the lord of the castle where Gilles ruled over their forefathers. In one ballad the name of Bluebeard and of the Baron de Rais are interchanged as identical, and Jean de Malestroit, Bishop of Nantes, is the champion who delivers the terrorized people from their oppressor.

CHAPTER XXIII
WITCHCRAFT

THERE is no very precise line of demarcation to be drawn between the more pretentious magic of the occult sciences and the vulgar details of witchcraft; they find their origin in the same beliefs and fade into each other by imperceptible gradations, and yet, historically speaking, the witchcraft with which we now have to deal is a manifestation of which the commencement cannot be distinctly traced backward much beyond the fifteenth century. Its practitioners were not learned clerks or shrewd swindlers, but ignorant peasants, for the most part women, who professed to have skill to help or to ban, or who were credited by their neighbors with such power, and were feared and hated accordingly. With the dawn of modern culture they confront us as a strange phenomenon, of which the proximate cause is exceedingly obscure. Probably it may be traced to the effort of the theologians to prove that all superstitious practices were heretical in implying a tacit pact with Satan, as declared by the University of Paris. Thus the innocent devices of the wise women in culling simples or in muttering charms came to be regarded as implying demon-worship. When this conception once came to be firmly implanted in the minds of judges and inquisitors, it was inevitable that with the rack they should extort from their victims confessions in accordance with their expectations. Every new trial would add fresh embellishments to this, until at last there was built up a stupendous mass of facts which demonologists endeavored to reduce to a science for the guidance of the tribunals.

That such was the origin of the new witchcraft is rendered still more probable by the fact that its distinguishing feature was the worship of Satan in the Sabbat, or assemblage, held mostly at night, to which men and women were transported through the air, either spontaneously or astride a stick or stool, or mounted on a demon in the shape of a goat or some other animal, and where hellish rites were celebrated and indiscriminate license prevailed. Divested of the devil-worship now first introduced, such assemblages have formed part of the belief of all races.

In the Middle Ages the first allusion which we meet concerning it occurs in a fragment, not later than the ninth century, in which it is treated as a diabolical illusion:

Some wicked women, reverting to Satan, and seduced by the illusions and phantasms of demons, believe and profess that they ride at night with Diana on certain beasts, with an innumerable multitude of women, passing over immense distances, obeying her commands as their mistress, and evoked by her on certain nights. It were well if they alone perished in their infidelity and did not draw so many along with them. For innumerable multitudes, deceived by this false opinion, believe all this to be true, and thus relapse into pagan errors. Therefore, priests everywhere should preach that they know this to be false, and that such phantasms are sent by the Evil Spirit, who deludes them in dreams. . . . It is to be taught to all that he who believes such things has lost his faith, and he who has not the true faith is not of God, but of the devil.

In some way this utterance came to be attributed to a Council of Anquira, which could never be identified; it was adopted by the canonists and embodied in the successive collections of Regino, Burchard, Ivo, and Gratian—the latter giving it the stamp of un-questioned authority—and it became known among the doctors as the *Cap. Episcopi.* The selection of Diana as the presiding genius of these illusory assemblages carries the belief back to classical times, when Diana, as the moon, was naturally a night-flyer, and was one of the manifestations of the triform Hecate, the favorite patroness of sorcerers. In some inexplicable way Bishop Burchard, in the eleventh century, when copying the text, came to add to Diana Herodias, who remained in the subsequent recensions, but Burchard in another passage substitutes as the leader Holda, the Teutonic deity of various aspects, sometimes beneficent to housewives and sometimes a member of Wuotan's Furious Host. In the year 1211 Gervais of Tilbury shows the growth of this belief in his account of the *lamiæ* or *mascæ*, who flew by night and entered houses, per-forming mischievous pranks rather than malignant crimes, and he prudently avoids deciding whether this is an illusion or not. He also had personal knowledge of women who flew by night in crowds with

these *lamiæ*, when everyone who incautiously pronounced the name
of Christ was precipitated to the earth. Half a century later Jean
de Meung tells us that those who ride with Dame Habonde claim
that they number a third of the population.

The Church, in its efforts to suppress these relics of pagandom,
preferred to regard the nocturnal assemblages as a fiction, and denounced as heretical the belief in the reality of the delusion. This,
as part of the canon law, remained unalterable, but alongside it
grew up, with the development of heresy, tales of secret conventicles,
somewhat similar in character, in which the sectaries worshipped the
demon in the form of a cat or other beast, and celebrated their
impious and impure rites. How the investigators of heresy came to
look for such assemblages as a matter of course, and led the accused
to embellish them until they assumed nearly the development of
the subsequent Witches' Sabbat, is seen in the confessions of Conrad
of Marburg's Luciferans, and in some of those of the Templars.

Yet the belief in the night-riders with Diana and Herodias continued, until the latter part of the fifteenth century, to be denounced
as a heresy, and anyone who persisted in retaining it after learning
the truth was declared to be an infidel. It was too thoroughly implanted, however, in ancestral popular superstition to be eradicated.
Thus, when the peasant wise women came to be examined about
their dealings with Satan, they could hardly help, under intolerable
torture, from satisfying their examiners with accounts of their
nocturnal flights. Between judge and victim it was easy to build
up a coherent story, combining the ancient popular belief with the
heretical conventicles, and the time soon came when the confession
of a witch was regarded as incomplete without an account of her
attendance at the Sabbat. These stories became so universal and so
complete in all their details that they could not be rejected without
discrediting the whole structure of witchcraft. The theory of illusion
was manifestly untenable, and demonologists and inquisitors were
sadly at a loss to reconcile the incontrovertible facts with the denunciations by the Church of such beliefs as heresy.

In 1458 the Inquisitor Nicholas Jaquerius hit upon the solution
of the difficulty by arguing that the existing sect of witches was
wholly different from the heretics alluded to in the *Cap. Episcopi*,
and adduced in evidence of their bodily presence in the Sabbat

numberless cases which had come before him in his official capacity, including one of a man who, as a child, fifty-five years before, had been carried thither by his mother in company with an infant brother, and presented to Satan wearing the form of a goat, who with his hoofs had imprinted on them an indelible mark—the *stigma diabolicum*. Jacquerius, however, adds, reasonably enough, that even if the affair is an illusion, it is none the less heretical, as the followers of Diana and Herodius are necessarily heretics in their waking hours. These speculations of Jaquerius attracted little attention at the time. Thirty years later, Sprenger, who did so much to formulate belief and organize persecution, found the *Cap. Episcopi* a constant stumbling-block in his path, as skeptics were apt to argue that, if the Sabbat was an illusion, all witchcraft was illusory. He endeavored, therefore, to argue it away, assuming that, while the devil undoubtedly possessed the power of transportation, the presence of the witch frequently was only mental. In such case she lay down on the left side and invoked the devil, when a whitish vapor would issue from her mouth, and she saw all that occurred. If she went personally, and had a husband, an accommodating demon would assume her shape and take her place to conceal her absence. The Inquisitor Bernardo di Como, about 1500, in addition to these arguments, triumphantly adduced the fact that numerous persons had been burned for attending the Sabbat, which could not have been done without the assent of the pope, and this was sufficient proof that the heresy was real, for the Church punishes only manifest crimes.

About this time the learned jurist, Gianfrancesco Ponzinibio, wrote a tract on the subject of witchcraft in which he upheld the doctrine of the *Cap. Episcopi* and boldly applied it to all magic and sorcery, which he treated as delusions. With a vast array of authorities he proved his case; he exposed the baldness of the pretense that existing witches belonged to a different sect; he argued that their confessions are not to be received, as they confess what is illusory and impossible, and that their evidence as to their associates is to be rejected, as they are deluded and can only delude others.

This aroused the learned theologian Silvestro Mozzolino of Prierio, Master of the Sacred Palace and subsequently Dominican General, who, in 1521, responded in a voluminous treatise devoted to the disputed canon. He adopts the same reasoning as Jaquerius, and laboriously argues that the heretics to whom it refers had disappeared, that the existing witches are a new sect, originating in 1404, and that the definitions of the canon are, therefore, obsolete and inapplicable to existing circumstances. To deny the bodily presence of witches at the Sabbat, he says, is to discredit the infinite number of cases tried by the Inquisition, and consequently to discredit the laws themselves. He was followed by his successor in the mastership of the Sacred Palace, Bartolomeo de Spina, who devoted three tracts to the annihilation of Ponzinibio. The latter had suggested, logically though maliciously, that as the *Cap. Episcopi* had defined as a heresy the belief that witches are corporally carried to the Sabbat, inquisitors in administering abjuration to their penitents ought to make them abjure this heresy among others. The absurd position in which this placed the Inquisition aroused Spina's indignation to the utmost. "O wonderful presumptions! O detestable insanity!" he exclaimed. "Only heretics abjure, only heresies are abjured before inquisitors. . . . Must, then, all theologians and judges, the inquisitors themselves, of all Italy, France, Germany, and Spain, holding this opinion abjure before the Inquisition?" —and he concludes by calling upon the Inquisition to proceed against Ponzinibio as vehemently suspect of heresy, as a fautor and defender of heretics, and as an impeder of the Holy Office. The question had passed beyond the range of reason and argument, and everywhere throughout Europe the Witches' Sabbat was accepted as an established fact, which it was dangerous to dispute.

That the details of the Sabbat varied but little throughout Europe is doubtless to be ascribed to the leading questions habitually put by judges, and to the desire of the tortured culprits to satisfy their examiners. The first step of the witch was to secure a consecrated wafer by pretending to receive communion, and carrying the sacrament home. On this was fed a toad, which was then burned, and the ashes were mixed with the blood of an infant, unbaptized if possible, powdered bone of a man who had been hanged, and certain herbs. With this mixture the witch anointed the palms of her hands, or her wrist, and a stick or stool which she placed between her legs, and she was at once transported to the place of meeting. As a variant of this, the ride was sometimes made on a demon in the shape of a horse or goat or dog. The assembly might be held anywhere, but there were certain spots specially resorted to—in Germany the Brocken, in Italy an oak tree near Benevento, and there was, besides, the unknown place beyond the Jordan. At all these they gathered in thousands. Thursday night was the one generally selected. They feasted at tables loaded with meat and wine, which rose from the earth at the command of the presiding demon, and they paid homage to the devil, who was present, usually in the form of a goat, dog, or ape. To him they offered themselves, body and soul, and kissed him under the tail, holding a lighted candle. They trampled and spat upon the cross and turned up their backs to heaven in derision of God. The devil preached to them, sometimes commencing with a parody of the mass; he told them that they had no souls and that there was no future life; they were not to go to church or confession, or to use holy water, or, if they did so to avoid suspicion, they must say "By leave of our Master," and they were to bring him as many converts as they could, and work all possible evil to their neighbors. There was usually a dance, which was unlike any seen at honest gatherings. At Como and Brescia a number of children from eight to twelve years of age, who had frequented the Sabbat, and had been reconverted by the inquisitors, gave exhibitions in which their skill showed that they had not been taught by human art. The woman was held behind her partner and they danced backwards, and when they paid reverence to the presiding demon they bent themselves backwards, lifting a foot in the air forwards. The rites ended with indiscriminate intercourse, obliging demons serving as incubi or succubi as required. The reality of all this did not depend alone upon the confessions of the accused, for there was a well-known case occurring about the year 1450, when the Inquisitor of Como, Bartolomeo de Homate, the Podestà Lorenzo da Concorezzo, and the notary Giovanni da Fossato, either out of curiosity or because they doubted the witches whom they were trying, went to a place of assembly at Mendrisio and witnessed the scene from a hiding-place. The presiding demon pretended not to know their presence, and in due course dismissed the assembly, but suddenly recalled his followers and set them on the officials, who were so beaten that they died within fifteen days.

Sprenger divides witches into three classes, those who can injure and not cure, those who can cure and not injure, and those who can do both, and the worst are those who unite these faculties. They kill and eat children, or devote them to the devil if unbaptized. They cause abortion by merely laying a hand upon a woman, or dry up her milk if she is nursing. By twirling a moistened broom, or casting flints behind them towards the east, they raise tempests and hail-storms which devastate whole regions; they bring the plagues of locusts and caterpillars which devour the harvests; they render men impotent and women barren, and cause horses to become suddenly mad under their riders. They can make hidden things known and predict the future, bring about love or hatred at will, or turn men into beasts. We have the unquestioned authority of Eugenius IV that by a simple word or touch or sign they can bewitch whom they please, cause or cure sickness, and regulate the weather. Sometimes they scattered over the fields powders which destroyed the cattle. They constantly entered houses at night, and, sprinkling a powder on the pillows of the parents which rendered them insensible, would touch the children with fingers smeared with a poisonous unguent causing death in a few days; or they would thrust needles under the nails of an infant and suck the blood, which was partly swallowed and partly spit into a vessel to serve in the confection of their infernal ointments; or the child would be put upon the fire and its fat be collected for the same purpose. Ludicrous as all this may seem, every one of these details has served as the basis of charges under which countless human beings have perished in the flames.[1]

To understand the credulity which accepted these marvels as the most portentous and dreadful of realities, it must be borne in mind that they were not the wild inventions of the demonologists, but were facts substantiated by evidence irrefragable according to the system of jurisprudence. Torture by this time had long been used universally in criminal trials when necessary; no jurist conceived that the truth could be elicited in doubtful cases without it. The criminal whom endless repetition of torment had reduced to

---

[1] It is the universal testimony of the demonologists that vastly more women than men were thus involved in the toils of the Devil. To explain this, Sprenger indulges in a most bitter tirade against women, and piously thanks God for preserving the male sex from such wickedness (*Mall. Malef.* P.I. Q. vii.).

stolid despair naturally sought to make his confession square with the requirements of his judge; the confession once made he was doomed, and knew that retraction, in place of saving him, would only bring a renewal and prolongation of his sufferings. He therefore adhered to his confession, and when it was read to him in public at his condemnation he admitted its truth.[2] In many cases, moreover, torture and prolonged imprisonment in the foulest of dungeons doubtless produced partial derangement, leading to belief that he had committed the acts so persistently imputed to him. In either case, desire to obtain the last sacrament, which was essential to salvation and which was only administered to contrite and repentant sinners, would induce him to maintain to the last the truth of his confession. The malignant powers of the witch were repeatedly set forth in the bulls of successive popes for the implicit credence of the faithful, and the University of Cologne, in 1487, when expressing its approval of the *Malleus Maleficarum* of Sprenger, warned everyone that to argue against the reality of witchcraft was to incur the guilt of impeding the Inquisition.

What rendered the powers of the witch peculiarly dreadful was the deplorable fact that the Church had no remedy for the evils which she so recklessly wrought. It is true that the sign of the cross, and holy water, and blessed oil, and palms, and candles, and wax and salt, and the strict observance of religious rites were in some sense a safeguard and a preventive. A witch confessed that she had been employed to kill a certain man, but when she invoked the devil for the purpose he replied that he could not do it, as the intended victim kept himself protected by the sign of the cross, and that the utmost injury that could be inflicted on him was the destruction of one eleventh of his harvests; and another one stated that on their nocturnal rounds to destroy children they were unable to enter houses in which were kept palms and blessed bread or crosses of palms or olive. But it was acknowledged that, when once the spell had been cast, the victim could find no relief on earth or in heaven. The only cure was from the devil through other

---

[2] In England, where torture was illegal, the growth of witchcraft was much slower. When the craze came an efficient substitute for torture was found in "pricking" or thrusting long needles in every part of the victim's body in search of the insensible spot which was a characteristic of the witch.

witches. Curative sorcery had long been a subject of debate in theologic ethics, but it had been formally condemned as inadmissible. It not only was a pact, tacit or expressed, with Satan, but it was ascertained that one of his leading objects in urging his acolytes to injure their neighbors was to force the sufferer in despair to have recourse to sorcery and thus be drawn into evil ways. This was illustrated by a case, celebrated among demonographers, of a German bishop who, in Rome, fell madly in love with a young girl and induced her to accompany him home. During the journey she undertook to kill him by sorcery, that she might make off with the jewels with which he had loaded her, and he was nightly attacked with a burning pain in his chest which resisted all the resources of his physicians. His life was despaired of, when recourse was had to an old woman who recognized the source of his affection and told him he could only be saved by the same methods, involving the death of the bewitcher. His conscience would not allow him to assent to this without permission; he applied to Pope Nicholas V, who kindly granted him a dispensation, and then he ordered the old woman to do what she proposed. That night he was perfectly well, and word was brought him that his young paramour was dying. He went to console her, but she naturally received him with maledictions, and died devoting her soul to Satan. As Bodin admiringly remarks, the devil was cunning enough to make a pope, a bishop, and a witch all obey him, and all become accomplices in a homicide.

When once the belief was fairly started in the existence of beings possessed of the powers I have described, it was destined to inevitable extension under the stimulus afforded by persecution. Every misfortune that occurred in a hamlet would be attributed to witchcraft. Suspicion would gradually attach to some ill-tempered crone, and she would be seized, for inquisitors held that a single careless threat, such as "You will be sorry for this," if followed by a piece of ill-luck, was sufficient to justify arrest and trial. All the neighbors would flock in as accusers—this one had lost a cow, that one's vintage had been ruined by hail, another had lost a promising child, two lovers had quarrelled, a man had fallen from an apple tree and had broken his neck—and under the persuasive influence of starvation or of the rack the unfortunate woman would invent some story to account for each occurrence, would name her accomplices in each, and tell whom she had met in the Sabbats, which she attended regularly. No one can read the evidence adduced at a witch-trial, or the confessions of the accused, without seeing how every misfortune and every case of sickness or death which had occurred in the vicinage for years was thus explained, and how the circle of suspicion widened so that every conviction brought new victims; burnings multiplied, and the terrified community was ready to believe that half or more of its members were slaves of Satan, and that it would never be free from their vengeance until they should all be exterminated. For more than two centuries this craze was perpetually breaking out in one part of Europe after another, nursed and stimulated by popes and inquisitors like Innocent VIII and Leo X, Sprenger and Institoris, Bernardo di Como and Bishop Binsfeld.

Fortunately there was a limitation upon the otherwise illimitable powers of the witch. The contrast was so absurd between the faculties attributed to her and her utter inability to protect herself against those who tortured and burned her with impunity, that some explanation of the inconsistency was requisite. The demonologists therefore invented the comforting theory that through the goodness of God the witch instantaneously lost her power as soon as the hand of an officer of justice was laid upon her. But for this, indeed, it might have been difficult to find men hardy enough to seize, imprison, try, and execute these delegates of Satan, whose slightest ill-will was so dangerous. It was true that, like all theories framed to meet artificial conditions, this one was not always reconcilable to the facts. The strange fortitude with which the culprits occasionally endured the severest and most prolonged tortures, so far from being a proof of innocence, was regarded as showing that even in the hands of justice the devil was sometimes able to protect his servants by endowing them with what was called the gift of taciturnity, and the ingenuity of the inquisitors was taxed to the utmost to overcome his wiles. When this was once admitted it was difficult to deny that he could assist them in other ways, and it was recommended to the officers charged with the arrest that when they seized a witch they should on no account allow her to enter her chamber, lest she should secure some charm that would enable her to endure the torture. It was on record that in Ratisbon some heretics condemned to be burned remained unhurt in the flames; vainly were they submerged in the river and roasted again. A three days' fast was ordered for the whole city, when it was revealed that they had charms concealed in a certain spot under the skin, and after the removal of these there was no further trouble in reducing them to ashes.

Some inquisitors, to break the spell of taciturnity, were wont to try sacred magic by administering to the prisoner, on an empty stomach, after invoking the Trinity, three drinks of holy water in which blessed wax had been melted. In one case the most excruciating torture, continued through two whole days, failed to elicit confession, but the third day chanced to be the feast of the Virgin, and during the celebration of the holy rites the devil lost the power with which he had thus far sustained the prisoner, who revealed a plot to make way with the implacable judge, Peter of Berne, by means of sorcery. These were simple devices; a more elaborate one was to take a strip of paper of the length of the body of Christ, and write on it the seven words uttered on the cross; on a holy day, at the hour of mass, this was to be bound around the waist of the witch with relics, she was to be made to drink holy water, and be at once placed on the rack. One precaution, held indispensable by some experienced practitioners, was that the witch on arrest was to be placed immediately in a basket and thus be carried to prison, without allowing her feet to touch the earth, for if she were permitted to do so she could slay her captors with lightning and escape.

There was another comfortable theory that those who exercised public functions for the suppression of witchcraft were not subject to the influence of witches or demons. Sprenger tells us that he and his colleagues had been many times assailed by devils in the shape of monkeys, dogs, and goats, but by the aid of God they had always been able to overcome the enemy. Yet there were exceptions to this, and the lenity of some judges was explained by the fact that the witch was sometimes able so to affect their minds that they were unable to convict. This steeled the heart of the conscientious inquisitor, who repressed all sentiments of compassion in the belief that they were prompted by Satan. The witch was especially able to exert this power over her judge when she looked upon him before he saw her, and it was a wise precaution to make her enter the court backwards, so that the judge had the advantage of the first glance. He and his assistants were also advised to be very careful not to let a witch touch them, especially on the wrist or other joint, and to wear around the neck a bag containing salt exorcised on Palm Sunday, with consecrated herbs enclosed in blessed wax. It was doubtless through neglect of these salutary precautions that at a witch-burning in the Black Forest, as the executioner was lifting the convict on the pile she blew in his face, saying, "I will reward you," whereupon a horrible leprosy broke out which spread over his body, and in a few days he was dead.

To combat an evil so widespread required the combined exertions of Church and State. The secular and episcopal courts both had jurisdiction over it; this was settled in 1374, when the Inquisitor of France was proceeding against some sorcerers and his competence was disputed, and Gregory XI, to whom the matter was referred, instructed him to prosecute them with the full severity of the laws. Commissions issued in 1409 and 1418 to Pons Feugeyron, Inquisitor of Provence, enumerate sorcerers, conjurers, and invokers of demons among those whom he is to suppress. As the growth of witchcraft became more alarming, Eugenius IV, in 1437, stimulated the inquisitors everywhere to greater activity against it, and these instructions were repeated in 1445. There was occasional clashing, of course, between the episcopal officials and the inquisitors, but the rule seems to have been generally observed that either could proceed separately, while the Clementine regulation should be observed which prescribed their co-operation in the use of torture and punitive imprisonment and when rendering final sentence.

In France at this period the royal jurisdiction, as embodied in the Parlement, was successfully exerting its superiority over both bishops and inquisitors. A curious case occurring in 1460 illustrates both this and the superstitions current at the time. A priest of the diocese of Soissons named Yves Favins brought a suit for tithes against a husbandman named Jean Rogier, who held of the Hospitallers. These, like the Templars, were exempt from tithes; Yves lost his case, was condemned in the expenses, which were heavy, and was eager for revenge. A poor woman of the village, who had come from Merville in Hainault, had quarrelled with the wife of Rogier over the price of some spinning, and to her Yves had recourse. She gave him a great toad and told him to baptize it and feed it on a consecrated wafer, which he did, giving it the name of John. The woman then killed it and made of it a *sorceron*, which her daughter took to Rogier's house under pretense of demanding the money in dispute, and cast it under the table at which Rogier, his wife, and his son were dining. They all died within three days; suspicion was aroused, and the two women were arrested and confessed. The mother was burned, but the daughter obtained a respite on the plea of pregnancy, escaped from jail and fled to Hainault, but was brought back and was carried on appeal to Paris. Yves was rich and well-connected. He was arrested and confined in the prison of the Bishop of Paris, but he obtained counsel and appealed to the Parlement; the Parlement allowed the appeal, tried him, and acquitted him.

In the ecclesiastical tribunals offenders had not the same chance. We have seen how skillfully the inquisitorial process was framed to secure conviction, and when the Inquisition was aroused to renewed exertion in combating the legions of Satan, it sharpened its weapons to a yet keener edge. The old hesitation about pronouncing a sentence of acquittal was no longer entertained, for though the accused might be dismissed with a verdict of not proven, the inquisitor was formally instructed never to declare him innocent. Yet few there were upon whom even this doubtful clemency was exercised, for all the resources of fraud and force, of guile and torment, were exhausted to secure conviction with even less reserve than of old. Formerly endurance of torture might be regarded as an evidence of innocence, now it was only an additional proof of guilt, for it showed that Satan was endeavoring to save his servitor, and the duty to defeat him was plain, even though, as Sprenger tells us was frequently the case, the witch would allow herself to be torn in pieces before she would confess. Though, as formerly, torture could not be repeated, it could be "continued" indefinitely, with prolonged periods of intervening imprisonment in dungeons of which the squalor was purposely heightened to exhaust the mental and physical forces of the victim. Confession was not absolutely requisite, for when the evidence was sufficient the accused could be convicted without it, but it was held that common justice required that the criminal should avow his guilt, and therefore the use of torture was universal when confession could not be otherwise secured.

Yet in view of the Satanic gift of taciturnity it was desirable to avoid recourse to it, and therefore promises of pardon, not indefinitely veiled under a juggle of words as of old, but positive and specifying a moderate penance or exile, were to be freely made. If the fraud was successful, the inquisitor could let the sentence be pronounced by someone else, or allow a decent interval to elapse before himself sending his deluded victim to the stake.

The most significant change, however, between the old proced-ure and the new regarded the death penalty. We have seen that with the heretic the object was held to be the salvation of his soul, and, except in case of relapse, he could always purchase life by re-cantation, at the expense of lifelong imprisonment, with the pros-pect that in time submission might win him release. At what period the rule changed with respect to witches is uncertain. When convicted by the secular courts they were invariably burned, and the Inquisition came to adopt the same practice. In 1445 the Council of Rouen still treats them with singular mildness. Invokers of demons were to be publicly preached with mitres on their heads, when, if they abjured, the bishop was empowered to release them after performance of appropriate penance; after this, if they relapsed, clerks were to be perpetually imprisoned, and laymen abandoned to the secular arm, while for minor superstitions and incantations a month's prison and fasting were sufficient, with heavier penance for relapse. In 1458 Jaquerius laboriously argues that the witch is not to be treated like other heretics, to be spared if she recants, showing that the change was still a novelty, requiring justification. In 1484 Sprenger says positively that while the recanting heretic is to be imprisoned, the sorcerer, even if penitent, is to be put to death. There was, as usual, a pretense of shifting the responsibility of this upon the secular authorities, for Sprenger adds that the most the ecclesiastical judge can do is to absolve the penitent and converted witch from the *ipso facto* excommunication under which she lies and let her go, to be apprehended by the lay courts and be burned for the evil which she has wrought. Silvester Prierias shows us how transparent was this juggle, when he instructs the inquisitor that if the witch confesses and is penitent she is to be received to mercy and not be delivered to the secular arm: she is to abjure, is absolved and sentenced to perpetual imprisonment in a black dress; the dress is put on her and she is led to the church door—but not to prison. The Inquisition takes no further concern about her; if the secular court is content, well and good—if not, it does as it pleases. What the inquisitors would have said if it pleased the secular authorities to let the witch go free may be judged by the maledictions of Sprenger on the incredulous laity who disbelieved in the reality of witchcraft, and through whose supineness the secular arm had allowed the cursed sect so to increase that its extirpation appeared impossible.

As of old, practically the sole defense of the accused lay in disabling the witnesses for enmity, and judges were reminded that the enmity must be of the most violent nature, for, with the wonted happy facility of assuming guilt in advance, they were told that there was almost always some enmity involved, since witches were odious to everybody. At the same time, all the old methods of reducing this slender chance to a minimum were followed, supplemented with such as additional experience had suggested. The names of the witnesses were generally suppressed, but if they were communicated they were so arranged as to mislead, and in advance effort was made to debar the accused from disabling the most damaging ones by enticing her to deny all knowledge of them or to declare them to be her friends. If she insisted on seeing the evidence, it might be given to her after interpolating in it extraneous matters and accusations to lead her astray.

Appeals were always to be refused if possible. Outside France the only one that could be made was to Rome for refusing counsel, for improper torture, and other unjust proceeding; and then, as we have seen, the inquisitor could either refuse *Apostoli* or grant either reverential or negative ones. If conscious of injustice and aware that an appeal was coming, he could elude it by appointing someone to sit in his place. The danger of appeals was small, however, for if the accused insisted on having counsel she was not allowed to select him. The inquisitor appointed him; he was bound not to assume the defense if he knew it to be unjust; he was not allowed to know the names of the witnesses, and his functions were restricted to advising his client either to confess or to disable the witnesses. If he made difficulties and delays and interjected appeals he was subject to excommunication as a fautor of heresy, and was worse than the witches themselves—of all of which he was to be duly warned when accepting the case.

A typical case, of which we happen to have the details, is that of the "Vaudois,"[3] or witches of Arras, showing how witchcraft panics were developed and what could be accomplished by inquisitorial methods, even under the supreme jurisdiction of the Parlement of Paris. In 1459, while a General Chapter of the Dominican Order was in session at Langres, there chanced to be burned there as a witch a hermit named Robinet da Vaulx. He was forced to name all whom he had seen in the Sabbat, and among them was a young *femme de folle vie* of Douai, named Deniselle, and a resident of Arras, advanced in years, named Jean la Vitte—a painter and poet, who had written many beautiful ballads in honor of the Virgin, and who was a general favorite, though, as he was popularly known as the *Abbé-de-peu-de-sens*, he was probably not a very sedate character. Pierre le Brousart, the Inquisitor of Arras, lost no time in looking after the accused. Deniselle was soon arrested and thrown into the episcopal prison; Jean, Bishop of Arras, was then in Rome; his suffragan was a Dominican, Jean, titular Bishop of Beirut, formerly a papal penitentiary, and his vicars were Pierre du Hamel, Jean Thibault, Jean Pochon, and Mathieu du Hamel. These took up the matter warmly and were earnestly supported by Jacques du Boys, a doctor of laws and dean of the chapter, who thrust himself into the affair and pushed it with relentless vigor. After repeated torture, Deniselle confessed to have attended the Sabbat and named various persons seen there, among them Jean la Vitte. He had already been compromised by Robinet, and had gone into hiding, but the inquisitor hunted him up at Abbeville, arrested him, and brought him to Arras, when he was no sooner in prison than in despair he tried to cut out his tongue with a pocket-knife, so as to prevent himself from confessing. He did not succeed, but though he was long unable to speak, this did not save him from torture, for he could use the pen and was obliged to write out his confession. Forced to name all whom he had seen in the Sabbat, he implicated a large

---

[3] By this time in France, V*audois* and V*audoisie* had become the designation of all deviations from faith, and was especially applied to sorcery. Hence is derived the word Voodooism, descriptive of the Negro sorcery of the French colonies, transmitted to the United States through Louisiana.

number, including nobles, ecclesiastics, and common folk. Six more arrests were made among the latter, including several women of the town; the affair threatened to spread further than had at first been expected; the vicars grew timid and concluded to discharge all the prisoners. Then Jacques du Boys and the Bishop of Beirut constituted themselves formal complainants; the latter, moreover, went to Péronne and brought to Arras the Comte d'Estampes, Captain-General of Picardy for Philippe le Bon of Burgundy, who ordered the vicars to do their duty under threats of prosecuting them.

Four women of the last batch of prisoners confessed under torture and implicated a large number of others. The vicars, uncertain as to their duty, sent the confessions to two notable clerks, Gilles Carlier, dean, and Gregoire Nicolai, official, of Cambrai, who replied that if the accused were not relapsed and if they would recant they were not to be put to death, provided they had not committed murder and abused the Eucharist. Here we recognize a transition period between the old practice with heretics and the new with sorcerers, but du Boys and the Bishop of Beirut were fully imbued with the new notions, and insisted that all should be burned. They declare that whoever disputed this was himself a sorcerer, that anyone who should presume to aid or counsel the prisoners should share their fate. The welfare of Christendom was concerned, a full third of nominal Christians were secretly sorcerers, including many bishops, cardinals, and grand masters, and that if they could assemble under a leader it would be difficult to estimate the destruction which they could inflict on religion and society. It was not only religion, but the whole social order, which was threatened by a few strumpets and the Abbé-de-peu-de-sens.

Like the agent of Conrad Tors in the days of Conrad of Marburg, the Bishop of Beirut boasted that he could recognize a Vaudois or sorcerer at sight. In conjunction with du Boys he procured another arrest, and induced the Comte d'Estampes to order the vicars to hasten their proceedings. Under this pressure, an assembly of all the principal ecclesiastics of Arras, with some jurists, was held on May 9, 1460, to consider the evidence. The deliberation was short, and the accused were condemned. The next day, on a scaffold in front of the episcopal palace, and in presence of a crowd which had gathered from 12 leagues around, the convicts were brought forward, together with the body of one of them, Jean le Febvre, who had been found hanging in his cell. The inquisitor preached the sermon, and read the description of the Sabbat and of their visits to it, and then asked them individually if it was true, to which they all assented. Then he read the sentence abandoning them to the secular arm, their property to be confiscated, the real estate to the seigneur and the movables to the bishop, and they were delivered to their several jurisdictions, Deniselle being handed over to the authorities of Douai who were present to receive her, and the rest to those of Arras. At once they began with shrieks to assert that they had been cruelly deceived—that they had been promised that if they would confess they would be discharged with a pilgrimage of 10 or 12 leagues, and had been threatened with burning for persistence in denial. With one voice they declared that they had never been to the *Vauderie*, that their confessions had been extorted under stress of torture and false promises and blandishments, and until they were silenced by the flames they begged the people to pray for them, and their friends to have masses sung in their behalf. The last words heard from the Abbé-de-peu-de-sens, were *"Jesus autem transiens per medium illorum."* Gilles Flameng, an advocate who had been active in the whole proceeding, was the especial object of their reproaches; they reviled him as a traitor who had been particularly earnest in the false promises which had lured them to destruction.

Appetite grew by what it fed on. This execution was followed immediately by the arrest, on the requisition of the inquisitor, of 13 persons, including 6 public women, who had been implicated by the confessions. The managers of the business, however, seemed to tire of the pursuit of such worthless game, and grew bold enough to strike higher. On June 22 Arras was startled by the arrest of Jean Tacquet, an eschevin and one of the richest citizens; on the next day by that of Pierre des Carieulx, equally wealthy and esteemed the best accountant in Artois; and on the next by that of the Chevalier Payen de Beauffort, a septuagenary and the head of one of the most ancient and richest houses in the province, who had manifested his piety by founding three convents. He had been warned that his name was on the list of accused, but had declared that if he were a thousand leagues away he would return to meet the charge, and in fact he had come to the city for the purpose. In his hôtel of la Chevrette his children and friends had entreated him to depart if he felt himself guilty, when with the most solemn oaths he asserted his innocence. His arrest had not been ventured upon without the consent of Philippe le Bon, secured by Philippe de Saveuse; the Comte d'Estampes had come to Arras to ensure it, and refused to see him when he begged an interview. This was followed, July 7, by an *auto de fé* of 7 of those arrested on May 9; 5 of these were burned, and, like their predecessors, asserted that their confessions had been wrung from them by torture. Two were sentenced to imprisonment for definite terms, the reason alleged being that they had not revoked after their first confession—a highly irregular proceeding of which the object was to facilitate further convictions.

The affair was now beginning to attract general attention and animadversion. Philippe le Bon was disturbed, for he heard that at Paris and elsewhere it was reported that he was seizing the rich men of his dominions to confiscate their property. Accordingly he sent to Arras, as supervisors, his confessor, a Dominican and titular Bishop of Selimbria, together with the Chevalier Baudoin de Noyelles, Governor of Péronne, while the Comte d'Estampes deputed his secretary, Jean Forme, together with Philippe de Saveuse, the Seigneur de Crèvecœur, who was bailly of Amiens, and his lieutenant, Guillaume de Berri. The first effort of these newcomers seems to have been to share in the spoils. On July 16 Baudoin de Noyelles arrested Antoine Sacquespée, an eschevin and one of the richest citizens, who had been urged to fly, but who, like de Beauffort, had declared that he would come a thousand leagues to face the accusation. The next day another eschevin, Jean Josset, was seized, and a sergent-de-ville named Henriet Royville, while three whose arrest was pending fled, two of them being wealthy men, Martin Cornille, and Willaume le Febvre, whom the Comte d'Estampes pursued as far as Paris without success. A panic by this time pervaded the community; no one knew when his turn would come, and men scarce dared to leave the city for fear they would be accused of flying through guilt, while citizens who were absent were unwelcome guests everywhere, and could scarce find lodgings. Similarly, strangers would not venture to visit the city. Arras was a prosperous seat of manufactures, and its industries suffered enormously. Its merchants lost their credit; creditors importunately demanded settlement, for the risk of confiscation hung over every man, and we have seen how the rights of creditors in such cases were extinguished. The vicars endeavored to soothe the general alarm and distress by a proclamation that no one need fear arrest who was innocent, for none were arrested unless eight or ten witnesses swore to seeing them at the Sabbat—though it was afterwards found that many were seized on the evidence of only one or two.

At length, at the expense of the prisoners, the inquisitor, with the vicars and Gilles Flameng, was sent to the Duke of Burgundy at Brussels, to lay before him the evidence of the trials. The duke called a great assembly of clerks, including the doctors of Louvain, who gravely debated the matter. Some held, with the *Cap. Episcopi*, that it was all a delusion, others that it was a reality. No conclusion was reached, and the duke finally sent his herald, Toison d'Or (Lefebvre, Seigneur de Saint-Remy), in whom he had great confidence, back with the vicars, to be present at all examinations. They reached Arras August 14, after which there were no further arrests, although innumerable names were on the lists of accused. The prisoners were less inhumanly treated, and but four of the pending trials were pushed to a conclusion. Reports of these were sent to Brussels for the duke's consideration, and they were brought back, October 12, by the president of the ducal chamber, Adrien Collin, in whose presence the accused were again examined. Finally, on October 22, the customary assembly was held, immediately followed by the *auto de fé*, where the sermon was preached by the Inquisitor of Cambrai, and the sentences were read by the Inquisitor of Arras, and by Michael du Hamel, one of the vicars. The four convicts had different fates.

The Chevalier de Beauffort, it was recited, had confessed that he had thrice been to the Sabbat—twice on foot and once by flying on an anointed staff. He had refused to give his soul to Satan, but had given him four of his hairs. The inquisitor asked him if this was true, and he replied in the affirmative, begging for mercy. The inquisitor then announced that, as he had confessed without torture, and had never retracted, he should not be mitred and burned but be scourged (a penance inflicted by the inquisitor on the spot, but without removing the penitent's clothes), be imprisoned for seven years, and pay a long list of fines for pious purposes, amounting in all to 8,200 livres, including 1,500 to the Inquisition. Besides these fines, thus publicly announced, he was obliged to pay 4,000 to the Duke of Burgundy, 2,000 to the Comte d'Estampes, 1,000 to the Seigneur de Crèvecœur, and 100 to his lieutenant, Guillaume de Berri.

The next was the rich eschevin, Jean Tacquet. He admitted that he had been to the Sabbat ten times or more. He had endeavored to withdraw his allegience from Satan, who had forced him to continue it by beating him cruelly with a bull's pizzle. He was now condemned to scourging, to ten years' prison, and to fines amounting to 1,400 livres, of which 200 went to the Inquisition; but, as in de Beauffort's case, there were secret contributions exacted from him.

The third was Pierre du Carieulx, another rich citizen. His sentence recited that he had been to the Sabbat innumerable times; holding a lighted candle he had kissed, under the tail, the devil in the shape of a monkey; he had given him his soul in a compact written with his own blood; he had thrice given to the Abbé-de-peu-de-sens consecrated wafers received at Easter, out of which with the bones of men hanged, which he had picked up under the gallows, and the blood of young children, of whom he had slain four, he had helped to make the infernal ointment and certain powders, with which they injured men and beasts. When asked to confirm this he denied it, saying that it had been forced from him by torture; and he would have added much more, but he was silenced. Abandoned to secular justice, the eschevins demanded him as their bourgeois, and on their paying his prison expenses he was delivered to them. They allowed him to talk in the town hall, when he disculpated all whom he had accused, of whom he said there were many present, eschevins and others, adding that, under torture, he had accused everyone he knew, and if he had known more he would have included them. He was burned the same day.

The fourth was Huguet Aubry, a man of uncommon force and resolution. In spite of the severest and most prolonged torture, he had confessed nothing. He had been accused by nine witnesses, and he was now asked if he would confess under promise of mercy; but he repeated that he knew nothing of *Vauderie*, and had never been to the Sabbat. Then the inquisitor told him that he had broken jail and been recaptured, which rendered him guilty. He threw himself on his knees and begged for mercy, but was condemned to prison, on bread and water, for twenty years; a most irregular sentence, for his constancy under torture only proved that Satan had endowed him with the gift of taciturnity.

This was the last of the persecution. There had been only 34 arrests and 12 burnings, which, in the flourishing times of witchcraft, would have been a trifle, but the novelty of the occurrence in Picardy, the character of the victims, and the subsequent proceedings in the Parlement attracted to it a disproportionate attention. Whatever the cause, the inquisitor and the vicars now put a stop to the prosecutions, without calling in the Bishop of Beirut, Jacques du Boys, de Saveuse, and others, who urged them to proceed with the good work. In vain the latter talked of the imminent dangers impending over Christendom from the innumerable multitude of sorcerers, many of whom held high station in the Church and in the courts of princes. One by one the accused were discharged, as they were able to raise money to pay the expenses of their prison and of the Inquisition, which was a condition of liberation in all cases except those of utter poverty. Some had to undergo the formality of purging themselves with compurgators. Antoine Sacquespée, for instance, who had been tortured without confession, had to furnish seven, and was not allowed to escape without surrendering a portion of his substance. Others had light penance, like Jennon d'Amiens, a woman who had confessed after being several times tortured, and was now only required to make a five-league pilgrimage to Nôtre Dame d'Esquerchin. This was an admission that the whole affair was a fraud; and even more remarkable was the case of a *fille de joie* named Belotte, who had been repeatedly tortured, and had confessed. She would have been burned with the other women on May 9, but it happened, accidentally or otherwise, that her mitre was not ready, and her execution was postponed, and now she was only banished from the diocese, and ordered to make a pilgrimage to Nôtre Dame de Boulogne. Of the whole number arrested, nine had the constancy to endure torture—in most cases long and severe —without confession. As the terror passed away the feelings of the people expressed themselves in some verses scattered through the streets, lampooning the principal actors in the tragedy. The vicars and their advocates and the assembly of experts are all held guilty, and the verses conclude by threatening them:

> But you shall all be punished in a mass,
>   And we shall learn who caused the wondrous tale
> Of Vaudois in our city of Arras.[4]

The prophecy was not wholly unverified. Fortunately there was in France a Parlement, and the relations between the courts of Paris and Brussels were such as to render it nothing loath to interfere. De Beauffort, before his examination, had made an appeal to this supreme tribunal, which had been disregarded and suppressed, but his son Philippe had carried to Paris the tale of the wrongs committed on his father. The Parlement moved slowly, but on January 16, 1461, Philippe came back with an usher commissioned to bring de Beauffort before it after investigating the case. This official took testimony, and on the 25th, accompanied by de Beauffort's four sons and thirty well-armed men, he presented himself before the vicars. Frightened by this formidable demonstration, they refused to see him; but he went to the episcopal palace, took the keys of the prison by force, and carried de Beauffort to the Conciergerie in Paris, after serving notice on the vicars to answer before the Parlement on February 25. The matter was now fairly in train for a legal investigation in which both sides could be heard. The convicts who had been condemned to imprisonment were set at liberty and carried to Paris, where their evidence confirmed that of de Beauffort. Jacques du Boys, the dean, who had been the prime mover, became insane about the time set for the hearing; and though he recovered his senses, his limbs failed him; and he died in about a year. The Bishop of Beirut

---

[4] The Chronicler of Arras tells us that at this time there was no enforcement of the laws in Arras; everyone did as he pleased, and no one was punished but the friendless. His statement is borne out by the cases of homicide and other crimes which he relates, and of which no notice was taken (Mém. de Jacques du Clercq, Liv. IV. ch. 22, 24, 40, 41). Yet vigorous search was made for the author of this pasquinade, and Jacotin Maupetit was arrested by an usher-at-arms of the duke on the charge of writing it. He adroitly slipped out of his doublet, and sought asylum in three successive churches, finally succeeding in getting to Paris, where he constituted himself a prisoner of the Parlement, and returned to Arras free, to find that, meanwhile, his property had been confiscated and sold.

was thrown in prison, charged with having set the affair on foot, but he managed to escape, by miracle as he asserted; he made a pilgrimage to Compostella, and on his return secured the position of confessor to Queen Marie, dowager of Charles VII, where he was safe. Other conspicuous actors in the tragedy left Arras to escape the hatred of their fellow-citizens. Meanwhile the legal proceedings dragged on with the interminable delays for which the Parlement was notorious, enhanced on this occasion by the political vicissitudes of the period, and the final decision was not rendered until 1491, thirty years after its commencement, when all the sufferers had passed off the scene except the indomitable Huguet Aubry, who was still alive to enjoy a rehabilitation celebrated in a manner as imposing as possible. On July 18 the decree was published from a scaffold erected on the spot where the sentences had been pronounced. The magistrates had been ordered to proclaim a holiday, and to offer prizes for the best *folie moralisée* and *pure folie*, and to send notice to all the neighboring towns, so that a crowd of some 9,000 persons was collected. After a sermon of two hours and a half, preached by the celebrated Geoffroi Broussart, subsequently chancellor of the University, the decree was read, condemning the Duke of Burgundy to pay the costs, and the processes and sentences to be torn and destroyed as unjust and abusive; ordering the accused and condemned to be restored to their good name and fame, all confiscations and payments to be refunded, while the vicars were to pay 1,200 livres each, Gilles Flameng 1,000, de Saveuse 500, and others smaller sums, amounting in all to 6,500; out of which 1,500 were to be applied to founding a daily mass for the souls of those executed, and erecting a cross on the spot where they had been burned. The cruel and unusual tortures made use of in the trials were, moreover, prohibited for the future in all secular and ecclesiastical tribunals. It was probably the only case on record in which an inquisitor stood as a defendant in a lay court to answer for his official action.

Besides the general significance of this transaction in the history of witchcraft and of its persecution, there are several points worthy of attention in their bearing on the practical application of the methods of procedure described above. In the first place, it is evident throughout that no counsel were allowed to the accused. Then, the combined episcopal and inquisitorial court permitted no appeals, even to the Parlement, whose supreme jurisdiction was unquestioned. Not only was the attempt of de Beauffort to interject such an appeal contemptuously suppressed, but when Willaume le Febvre, who had fled to Paris and constituted himself a prisoner there to answer all charges, sent his son Willemet with a notary to serve an appeal, the service was rightly regarded as involving considerable risk. After watching their opportunity, Willemet and the notary served the notice on one of the vicars at church, then leaped on their horses and made all speed for Paris, but the vicars instantly dispatched well-mounted horsemen, who overtook them at Montdidier and brought them back. They were clapped in jail, along with a number of friends and kinsmen who had been privy to their intention without betraying it, and were not released until they agreed to withdraw the appeal. Martin Cornille, the other fugitive, had pursued a different policy. He carried with him an ample store of money, part of which he invested in a bull from Pius II, transferring the whole matter to Gilles Carlier and Grégoire Nicolai of Cambrai, and two of the Arras vicars. This was brought to Arras in August 1460 by the Dean of Soignies, after which we hear nothing more of it, though it may have contributed to cool the ardor of those who were expecting to profit by the prosecutions.

The means employed to obtain confession show that Sprenger only recorded the usage of the period in advising recourse to whatever fraud or force might prove necessary. Promises of immunity or of trifling penance were lavished on those whom it was intended to burn if they yielded to the blandishment, and these were supplemented with threats of burning as the punishment of taciturnity. De Beauffort's confession without torture excited general astonishment until it was known that, on his arrest, after he had sworn to his innocence, Jacques du Boys entreated him to confess, even kneeling before him and praying him to do so, assuring him that if he refused he could not be saved from the stake, and that all his property would be confiscated, to the beggaring of his children, while, if he would confess, he should be released within four days without public humiliation or exposure; and when de Beauffort argued that this would be committing perjury, du Boys told him not to mind that, as he should have absolution. Those whose constancy was proof against such persuasiveness were tortured without stint or mercy. The women were frightfully scourged. Huguet Aubry was kept in prison for eleven months, during which, at intervals, he was tortured fifteen times, and when the ingenuity of the executioners failed in devising more exquisite forms of torment, he was threatened with drowning and thrown into the river, and then with hanging and suspended from a tree with his eyes duly bandaged. Le petit Henriot's resolution was tried with seven months' incarceration, during which he was also tortured fifteen times, fire being applied to the soles of his feet until he was crippled for life.

With regard to the death penalty, it is to be observed that none of these were cases of relapse, and under the old inquisitorial practice they would all have been entitled to the penance of imprisonment. Their burning had not even the pretext of being punishment for injuries inflicted on their neighbors, for, with the exception of Pierre du Carieulx, the only offense assigned to them was attendance at the Sabbat. At the same time, there was no resort to the juggle suggested by later authorities, of assigning penance, and then not inquiring what the secular power might see fit to do. The condemned were formally delivered to the magistrates to be burned, and though at the first *auto* a death sentence was pronounced by the eschevins, at the second even this formality was omitted, and the victims were dragged directly from the place of sentence to that of execution.

One specially notable feature of the whole affair was the utter incredulity everywhere excited. Just as the crimes imputed to the Templars found credence nowhere out of France, so, outside of Arras, we are told not one person in a thousand believed in the truth of the charges. This was fortunate, for the victims naturally included in their lists of associates many residents of other places, and the conflagration might readily have spread over the whole country, had it found agents like Pierre le Brousart, who carried the spark from Langres to Arras. On the strength of revelations in the confessions several persons were arrested in Amiens, but the bishop, who was a learned clerk and had long resided in Rome, promptly released them and declared that he would dismiss all brought before him, for he did not believe in the possibility of such offenses. Martin Cornille was caught in Burgundy and brought before the Archbishop of Besançon, who acquitted him on the strength of informations made in Arras. Willaume le Febvre surrendered himself to the Bishop of Paris; the Inquisitor of Paris came to Arras to get the evidence concerning him, and the vicars furnished the confessions of those who had implicated him. The result was that the tribunal, consisting of the Archbishop of Reims, the Bishop of Paris, the Inquisitor of France, and sundry doctors of theology, not only acquitted him, but authorized him to prosecute the vicars for reparation of his honor, and for expenses and damages.

The development of the witchcraft epidemic had not been rapid. The earliest detailed account which we have of it is that of Nider, in his *Formicarius*, written in 1437. Although Nider himself seems to have sometimes acted as inquisitor, he tells us that his information is principally derived from the experience of Peter of Berne, a secular judge, who had burned large numbers of witches of both sexes, and had driven many more from the Bernese territory, which they had infested for about sixty years. This would place the origin of witchcraft in that region towards the close of the fourteenth century. Bernardo di Como, writing about 1510, assigns to it a somewhat earlier origin, for he says the records of the Inquisition of Como showed that it had existed for 150 years. The great jurist Bartolo, who died in 1357, when acting as judge at Novara, tried and condemned a woman who confessed to having adored the devil, trampled on the cross, and killed children by touching and fascinating them. As early as 1353 an allusion to the witches' dance occurs in a trial at Toulouse. Thus the stories grew, under the skillful handling of such judges as Peter of Berne, until they assumed the detailed and definite shape that we find in Nider. According to Peter of Berne, the evil originated with a certain Scavius, who openly boasted of his powers, and always escaped by transforming himself into a mouse, until he was assassinated through a window near which he incautiously sat. His principal disciple was Poppo, who taught Staedelin; the latter fell into the hands of Peter, and, after four vigorous applications of torture, confessed all the secrets of the diabolical sect. The details given are virtually those described above, showing that the subsequent inquisitors who draw their inspiration from Nider were skilled in their work and knew how to extract confessions in accordance with their preconceived notions. There are a few unimportant variants, of course. Apparently, the theory had not yet established itself that the witch was powerless against officers of public justice, for the latter were held to incur great dangers in the performance of their functions. It was only by the most careful observance of religious duties and the constant use of the sign of the cross that Peter of Berne escaped, and even he once, at the castle of Blankenburg, nearly lost his life when, going up a lofty staircase at night in such haste that he forgot to cross himself, he was precipitated violently to the bottom—manifestly the effect of sorcery, as he subsequently learned by torturing a prisoner.

Although, in 1452, a witch tried at Provins declared that in all France and Burgundy the total number of witches did not exceed 60, no believer contented himself with figures so moderate. In 1453 we hear of an epidemic of witchcraft in Normandy, where the witches were popularly known as Scobaces, from *scoba*, a broom, in allusion to their favorite mode of equitation to the Sabbat. The same year occurred the case of Guillaume Edeline, which excited wide astonishment from the character of the culprit, who was a noted doctor of theology and Prior of St. Germain-en-Laye. Madly in love with a noble lady, he sought the aid of sorcery. He doubtless fell victim to some sharper, for on his person was found a compact with Satan, formally drawn up with reciprocal obligations, one of which was that in his sermons he should assert the falsity of the stories told of sorcerers, and this, we are told, greatly increased their number, for the judges were restrained from prosecuting them. Another condition was that he should present himself before Satan whenever required. The methods of his examination must have been sharp, for he confessed that he performed this obligation by striding a broomstick, when he would be at once transported to the Sabbat. Prosecuted before Guillaume de Floques, Bishop of Evreux, he persuaded the University of Caen to defend him; but the bishop procuring the support of the University of Paris, he was forced to confess and was convicted. It shows the uncertainty of procedure as yet that he was not burned, but was allowed to abjure, and was penanced with perpetual imprisonment on bread and water. At the *auto de fé* the inquisitor dwelt upon his former high position and the edification of his teaching, when the unfortunate man burst into tears and begged mercy of God. He was thrown into a *basse-*

fosse at Evreux, where he lingered for four years, showing every sign of contrition, and at last he was found dead in his cell in the attitude of prayer.

It was probably about this time that the Inquisitors of Toulouse were busy with burning the numerous witches of Dauphiné and Gascony, as related by Alonso de Spina, who admired on the walls of the Toulousan Inquisition pictures painted from their confessions, representing the Sabbat, with the votaries adoring, with lighted candles, Satan in the form of a goat. The allusions of Bernardo di Como show that at the same period persecution was busy in Como. In 1456 we hear of two burned at Cologne. They had caused a frost so intense in the month of May that all vegetation was blasted, without hope of recovery. The steward of the archbishop asked one of them to give him an example of her art, when she took a cup of water, and muttering spells over it for the space of a couple of Paternosters, it froze so solidly that the ice could not be broken with a dagger. In 1459 Pius II called the attention of the Abbot of Tréguier to somewhat similar practices in Britanny, and gave him papal authority for their suppression, showing how vain had been the zeal of Duke Artus III, of whom, at his death in 1457, it was eulogistically declared that he had burned more sorcerers in France, Britanny, and Poitou than any man of his time.

These incidents will show the growth and spread of the belief throughout Europe, and it must be borne in mind that they are but the indications of much that never attracted public attention or came to be recorded in history. The material existed everywhere for development into organized persecution when properly handled by the Inquisition, and the *Flagellum Hæreticorum Fascinariorum* of the Inquisitor Nicholas Jacquerius, in 1458, indicates that the Holy Office was beginning to appreciate the necessity of organizing its efforts for systematic work. Unfortunately the Church, in its alarm at the development of this new heresy, stimulated it to the utmost in the endeavor to repress it. Every inquisitor whom it commissioned to suppress witchcraft was an active missionary who scattered the seeds of the belief ever more widely. When Girolamo Visconti was sent to Como he speedily raised such a storm of witchcraft that in 1485 he burned no less than 41 unfortunates in the little district of

Wormserbad in the Grisons—an exploit repeatedly referred to by Sprenger with honest professional pride.

A special impulse was given to this development when Innocent VIII, December 5, 1484, issued his Bull *Summis desiderantes*, in which he bewailed the deplorable fact that all the Teutonic lands were filled with men and women who exercised upon the faithful all the malignant power which we have seen ascribed to witchcraft, and of which he enumerates the details with awe-inspiring amplification. Henry Institoris and Jacob Sprenger had for some time been performing the office of inquisitors in those regions, but their commissions did not specially mention sorcery, wherefore their efforts were impeded by overwise clerks and laymen who used this as an excuse for protecting the guilty. Innocent therefore gives them full authority and orders the Bishop of Strassburg to coerce all who obstruct or interfere with them, calling in, if necessary, the aid of the secular arm. After this, to question the reality of witchcraft was to question the utterance of the Vicar of Christ, and to aid anyone accused was to impede the Inquisition. Armed with these powers the two inquisitors, full of zeal, traversed the land, leaving behind them a track of blood and fire, and awakening in all hearts the dread inspired by the absolute belief thus inculcated in all the horrors of witchcraft. In the little town of Ravenspurg alone they boast that they burned 48 in five years.

It is true that they were not everywhere so successful. In the Tyrol the Bishop of Brixen published Innocent's bull July 23, 1485, and on September 21 he issued to the Inquisitor Henry Institoris a commission granting him full episcopal jurisdiction, but recommending him to associate with him a secular official of the suzerain, Sigismund of Austria. The latter, however, ordered the bishop to appoint a commissioner, and he named Sigismund Samer, pastor of Axams near Innsbruck. The pair commenced operations October 14, but their career, though vigorous, was short and inglorious. It chanced that some of the archduke's courtiers desired to separate him from his wife, Catharine of Saxony, and spread reports that she had endeavored to poison him; and they followed this up by placing in an oven a worthless woman who personated an imprisoned demon and denounced a number of people. Institoris at once seized the accused and applied torture without stint. Then the bishop interposed, and ordered him to leave the diocese and betake himself to his convent, the sooner the better. He was told that the bishop would attend to all that was necessary through the exercise of the ordinary jurisdiction, and he was warned that if he persisted in remaining he was in danger of assassination from the husbands or kinsmen of the women whom he was persecuting. He finally withdrew to Germany, and from his account of the matter it is easy to see that all the sick and withered of Innsbruck had flocked to him with complaints of their neighbors so detailed that he was justified in regarding the place as thoroughly infected. The next year the Tyrolese Landtag complained to the archduke that recently many persons, on baseless denunciations, had been imprisoned, tortured, and disgracefully treated, and we can readily understand the complaint of the *Malleus Maleficarum* that Innsbruck abounded in witches of the most dangerous character, who could bewitch their judges and could not be forced to confess. Still, the seeds of superstition were scattered to fructify in due time. Although in the Tyrolese criminal ordinance issued by Maximilian I, in 1499, there is no allusion to sorcery and witchcraft, yet in 1506 we find the craze fully developed.

One result of this campaign of Institoris in the Tyrol was that it left Sigismund of Austria in a condition of perplexity about the reality of witchcraft. To satisfy his mind, in 1487, he consulted on the subject two learned doctors of the law, Ulric Molitoris and Conrad Stürtzel, and the result was published at Constance in 1489 by Ulric, in the form of a discussion between the three. Sigismund is represented as urging the natural argument that the results obtained by witchcraft were so woefully inadequate to the powers ascribed to it as to cast doubt upon the reality of those powers— if they were real, a conqueror would only have to put a witch at the head of his army to overcome all opposition. Against this view the customary texts and citations were alleged, and the conclusions reached represent fairly the moderate opinions of the conservatives, who had not as yet yielded fully to the witchcraft craze, but who shrank from a rationalistic denial of that which had been handed down by the wisdom of ages. These are summed up in eight propositions:

(1) Satan cannot himself, or by means of human instruments, disturb the elements, or injure men and animals, or render them impotent, but God sometimes permits him to do so to a certain determinate extent.

(2) He cannot exceed this designated limit.

(3) By permission of God he can sometimes cause illusions by which men appear to be transformed.

(4) The night-riding and assemblages of the Sabbat are illusions.

(5) Incubi and succubi are incapable of procreation.

(6) God alone knows the future and the thoughts of men; the devil can only conjecture and use his knowledge of the stars.

(7) Nevertheless witches, by worshipping and sacrificing to Satan, are real heretics and apostates.

(8) Finally, they should therefore be put to death.

In this cautious endeavor to harmonize the old school and the new, the witch thus gained nothing; everything was conceded that had a practical bearing on the tribunals, and it was a mere matter of speculation whether the Sabbat was a dream or a reality, and whether the evil she wrought was the result of a special or a general concession of power by God to Satan.

The fine-drawn distinctions of such men were quickly brushed aside by the aggressive self-confidence of the inquisitors. Even more potent than the personal activity of Sprenger was the legacy which he left behind him in the work which he proudly entitled the *Malleus Maleficarum*, or Hammer of Witches, the most portentous monument of superstition which the world has produced. All his vast experience and wide erudition are brought to the task of proving the reality of witchcraft and the extent of its evils, and, further, of instructing the inquisitor how to elude the wiles of Satan and to punish his devotees. He was no vulgar witch-finder, but a man trained in all the learning of the schools. He apparently was not inhumane. In many places he manifests a laudable desire to give the accused the benefit of whatever pleas they might rightfully put forward, but he is so fully convinced of the gigantic character of the evils to be combated, he so thoroughly believes that his tribunal is engaged in a contest with Satan for human souls, that he eagerly justifies every artifice and every cruelty that could be suggested to outwit the adversary, on whom fair play would be thrown away. His work is an inexhaustible storehouse of marvels to which successive generations resorted whenever evidence was needed to prove any special manifestation of the power or malignity of the witch. Told as the results of his own experience or that of his colleagues, with the utmost good faith, they carried conviction with them. Statements of disinterested eye-witnesses, complaints of sufferers, confessions of the guilty, even after condemnation and at the stake, when there was no hope save of pardon of their sins by God, are innumerable, and so detailed and connected together that the most fertile imagination would seem inadequate to their invention. Besides, the work is so logical in form and so firmly based on scholastic theology and canon law, that we cannot wonder at the position accorded to it for more than a century of a leading authority on a subject of the highest practical importance. Quoted implicitly by all succeeding writers, it did more than all other agencies, save the papal bulls, to stimulate and perfect the persecution, and consequently the extension of witchcraft.

Cornelius Agrippa, whose learned treatises on the occult sciences trench so nearly on forbidden ground, when he held the position of Town Orator and Advocate of Metz, had the hardihood, in 1519, to save from the clutches of the Inquisitor Nicholas Savin an unfortunate woman accused of witchcraft. The only evidence against her was that her mother had been burned as a witch. Savin quoted the *Malleus Maleficarum* to show that if she were not the offspring of an incubus she must undoubtedly have been devoted to Satan at her birth. In conjunction with the episcopal official, John Leonard, he had her tortured, and she was then exposed to starvation in her prison. When Agrippa offered to defend her he was turned out of court and threatened with prosecution as a fautor of heresy, and her husband was refused access to the place of trial, lest he should interject an appeal. Leonard chanced to fall mortally sick, and, touched with remorse on his deathbed, he executed an instrument declaring his conviction of her innocence and asked the chapter to set her at liberty; but Savin demanded that she should be further tortured and then burned. Agrippa, however, labored so effectually with Leonard's successor that the woman was discharged; but his disinterested zeal cost him his office, and he was obliged to leave Metz. Relieved of his presence, the inquisitor speedily found another witch, whom he burned after forcing her by torture to confess all the horrors of the Sabbat and customary evil deeds wrought through the power of Satan. Encouraged by this, he organized a search for others, and imprisoned a number, while others fled, and there would have been a pitiless massacre had not Roger Brennon, parish priest of St. Cross, openly opposed him and vanquished him in disputation, whereupon the jail doors were thrown open and the fugitives returned.

The most decided rebuff, however, which the Inquisition experienced in its new sphere of activity was administered by Venice. Venice had always been careful to preserve the secular jurisdiction over sorcery. A resolution of the Great Council in 1410 allows the Inquisition to act in such cases when they involve heresy or the abuse of sacraments, but if injury had resulted to individuals the spiritual offense alone was cognizable by the Inquisition, while the resultant crimes were justiciable by the lay court; and when, in 1422, some Franciscans were charged with sacrificing to demons, the Council of Ten committed the affair to a councillor, a *capo*, an inquisitor, and an advocate. Brescia was a spot peculiarly infected with witchcraft. As early as 1455 the Inquisitor, Frà Antonio called upon the Senate for aid to exterminate it, which was presumably afforded, but when a fresh persecution arose in 1486 the *podestà* refused to execute the inquisitorial sentences, and the Signoria supported him, calling forth the vigorous protest of Innocent VIII. Under the stimulus of persecution the evil increased with terrible rapidity. In 1510 we hear of 70 women and 70 men burned at Brescia; in 1514 of 300 at Como. In such an epidemic every victim was a new source of infection, and the land was threatened with depopulation. In the madness of the hour it was currently reported that on the plain of Tonale, near Brescia, the customary gathering at the Sabbat exceeded 25,000 souls; and in 1518 the Senate was officially informed that the inquisitor had burned 70 witches of the Valcamonica, that he had as many in his prisons, and that those suspected or accused amounted to about 5,000 or a fourth of the inhabitants of the valleys. It was time to interfere, and the Signoria interposed effectually, leading to violent remonstrances from Rome. Leo X issued, February 15, 1521, his fiery bull, *Honestis*, ordering the inquisitors to use freely the excommunication and the interdict, if their sen-

tences on the witches were not executed without examination or
revision. On March 21 the imperturbable Council of Ten quietly
responded by laying down regulations for all trials, including the
cases in question, of which the sentences were treated as invalid, and
all bail heretofore taken was to be discharged. The examinations
were to be made, without the use of torture, by one or two bishops,
an inquisitor, and two doctors of Brescia, all selected for probity
and intelligence. The result was to be read in the court of the
podestà, with the participation of the two *rettori*, or governors, and
four more doctors. The accused were to be asked if they ratified
their statements, and were to be liable to torture if they modified
them. When all this was done with due circumspection, judgment
was to be rendered in accordance with the counsel of all the above-
named experts, and under no other circumstances was a sentence
to be executed. In this way the Signoria hoped that the errors said
to have been committed would be avoided for the future. Moreover,
the papal legate was to be admonished to see that the expenses of
the Inquisition were moderate and free from extortion, and was to
find expedients to prevent greed for money from causing the condemnation of the innocent, as was said to have often been the case.
He should also depute proper persons to investigate the extortions
and other evil acts of the inquisitors, which had excited general
complaint, and he should summarily punish the perpetrators to
serve as an example. He was further requested to consider that these
poor people of Valcamonica were simple folk of the densest ignorance, much more in need of good preachers than of persecutors,
especially as they were so numerous.

In an age of superstition this utterance of the Council of Ten
stands forth as a monument of considerate wisdom and calm common sense. Had its enlightened spirit been allowed to guide the
counsels of popes and princes, Europe would have been spared the
most disgraceful page in the annals of civilization. Hideous as are the
details of the persecution of witchcraft which we have been considering up to the fifteenth century, they were but the prelude to the
blind and senseless orgies of destruction which disgraced the next
century and a half. Christendom seemed to have grown delirious,
and Satan might well smile at the tribute to his power seen in the
endless smoke of the holocausts which bore witness to his triumph

over the Almighty. Protestant and Catholic rivalled each other in the madness of the hour. A bishop of Geneva is said to have burned 500 witches within three months, a bishop of Bamburg 600, a bishop of Würzburg 900. The Inquisition evidently had worthy pupils. Paramo boasts that in a century and a half from the commencement of the sect, in 1404, the Holy Office had burned at least 30,000 witches who, if they had been left unpunished, would easily have brought the whole world to destruction.

C HAPTER XXIV
INTELLECT AND FAITH

THE heresies that really troubled the Church were those which obtained currency among the people unassisted by the ingenious quodlibets of dialecticians. Possibly there may be an exception to this in the theories of the Brethren of the Free Spirit, which apparently owed their origin to the speculations of Amauri of Bène and David of Dinant; but, as a whole, the Cathari and the Waldenses, the Spirituals and the Fraticelli, even the Hussites, had little or nothing in common with the fine-spun cobwebs of the schoolmen. The schools, consequently, have little to show us in the shape of contests between free thought and authority pushed to the point of invoking the methods of the Inquisition. Yet the latter, by the system which rendered it practicable of enforcing uniformity of belief, exercised too potent an influence on the mental development of Europe for us to pass over this phase of its activity without some brief review.

There were two tendencies at work to provoke collisions between the schoolmen and the inquisitors. The ardor of persecution, which rendered the purity of the faith the most imperative care of the ruler, secular and spiritual, created an exaggerated standard of orthodoxy, which regarded the minutest point of theology as important as the fundamental doctrines of religion. We have already seen instances of this in the questions on the poverty of Christ, whether he was dead when lanced on the cross, and whether the blood which he shed in the Passion remained on earth or ascended to heaven; and Stephen Palecz, at the Council of Constance, proved dialectically that a doctrine in which one point in a thousand was erroneous was thereby rendered heretical throughout. The Christian must be firm in the faith, and doubt itself was heresy.

The other tendency was the insane thirst which inflamed the minds of the schoolmen for determining and defining, with absolute precision, every detail of the universe and of the invisible world. So far as this gratified itself within the lines of orthodoxy laid down by an infallible Church it resulted in building up the most complex and stupendous body of theology that human wit has ever elaborated. The *Sentences* of Peter Lombard grew into the *Summa* of Thomas Aquinas, an elaborate structure to be grasped and retained only by minds of peculiar powers after severe and special training. When this was once defined and accepted as orthodox, theology and philosophy became the most dangerous of sciences, while the perverse ingenuity of the schoolmen, revelling in the subtleties of dialectics, was perpetually rearguing doubtful points, raising new questions, and introducing new refinements in matters already too subtle for the comprehension of the ordinary intellect. The inquirer who disturbs the dust now happily covering the records of these forgotten wrangles can only feel regret that such wonderful intellectual acuteness should have been so woefully wasted when, if rightly applied, it might have advanced by so many centuries the progress of humanity.

The story of Roger Bacon, the *Doctor Mirabilis*, is fairly illustrative of the tendencies of the time. That gigantic intellect bruised itself perpetually against the narrow bars erected around it by an age presumptuous in its learned ignorance. Once a transient gleam of light broke in upon the darkness, when Gui Foucoix was elevated to the papacy, and, as Clement IV, commanded the Englishman to communicate to him the discoveries of which he had vaguely heard. It is touching to see the eagerness with which the unappreciated scholar labored to make the most of this unexpected opportunity; how he impoverished his friends to raise money to pay the scribes who should set forth in a fair copy the tumultuous train of thought in which he sought to embody the whole store of human knowledge, and how, within little more than a year, he thus accomplished the enormous task of writing the *Opus Majus*, the *Opus Minus*, and the *Opus Tertium*. Unfortunately, Clement was more concerned at the moment with the fortunes of Charles of Anjou than with the passing fancy which had led him to call upon the scholar; in two years he was dead, and it is doubtful whether he even repaid the sums expended in gratifying his wishes.

It was inevitable that Bacon should succumb in the unequal struggle at once with the ignorance and the learning of his age. His labors and his utterances were a protest against the whole existing

system of thought and teaching. The schoolmen evolved the universe from their internal consciousness, and then wrangled incessantly over subtleties suggested by the barbarous jargon of their
dialectics. It was the same with theology, which had usurped the
place of religion. Peter Lombard was greater than all the prophets
and evangelists taken together. As Bacon tells us, the study of
Scripture was neglected for that of the *Sentences*, in which lay the
whole glory of the theologian. He who taught the *Sentences* could
select his own hour for teaching, and had accommodations provided
for him. He who taught the Scriptures had to beg for a time in
which to be heard, and had no assistance. It is impossible, he adds,
that the Word of God can be understood, on account of the abuse
of the *Sentences*; and whoso seeks in Scripture to elucidate questions
is not listened to. Worse than all, the text of the Vulgate is horribly
corrupt, and where not corrupt it is doubtful, owing to the ignorance
of would-be correctors and their presumption, for everyone deemed
himself able to correct the text, though he would not venture to alter
a word in a poet. First of moderns, Bacon discerned the importance
of etymology and of comparative philology. His methods were strictly
scientific. He wanted facts, actual facts, as a basis for all reasoning,
whether on dogma or physical and mental experiences. To him all
study of nature or of man was empirical; to know first, and then to
reason. Mathematics was first in the order of sciences; then metaphysics; and to him metaphysics was not a barren effort to frame a
system on postulates assumed at caprice and built up on dialectical
sophisms, but a solid series of deductions from ascertained observa-
tions, for, according to Avicenna, "the conclusions of other sciences
are the principles of metaphysics."

The vast labors of the earnest life of a great genius were lost to
a world too conceited of its petty vanities to recognize how far he
was in advance of it. It was enamored of words; he dealt in things:
the actual was rejected for the unsubstantial, and an intellectual
revolution of priceless value to mankind was stifled in its inception
How completely Bacon was unappreciated by an age unable to under
stand him and his antagonism towards its methods is evidenced by
the scarcity of manuscripts of his works, the fragmentary condition
of some of them, and the utter disappearance of others. "It is easier,"
says Leland, "to collect the leaves of the Sibyl than the titles of the

works of Roger Bacon." The same evidence is furnished by the absence of detail as to his life no less than by the vulgar stories of his proficiency in magic arts. Even the tragic incident of his imprisonment by his Franciscan superiors and the prohibition to pursue his studies is so obscure that it is told in contradictory fashion, and its truth has been not unreasonably denied. According to one account he was accused of unorthodox speculations, in 1278, to Geronimo d'Ascoli, General of the Order; his opinions were condemned, the brethren were ordered scrupulously to avoid them, and he himself was cast into prison, doubtless because he did not submit as serenely as Olivi to Geronimo's sentence. He must have had followers and sympathizers, for Geronimo is said to have prevented their complaints by promptly applying to Nicholas III for a confirmation of the judgment. How long his imprisonment lasted is not known, though there is a tradition that he perished in jail, either through sickness or the ill-treatment. Another statement attributes his incarceration to the ascetic Raymond Gaufridi, who was General of the Order from 1289 to 1295. In either case it would not be difficult to explain the cause of his disgrace. One who antagonized so completely the prevailing currents of thought, and who exposed so mercilessly the ignorance of the learned, could not fail to excite bitter enmities. The politic Geronimo might readily listen to enemies so numeorous and powerful as those whom Bacon must have provoked. The ascetic Raymond, whose aim was to bring back the Order to its primitive rudeness and simplicity, would regard Bacon's labors with the same aversion as that manifested by the early Spirituals to Crescenzio Grizzi's learning.

While Bacon suffered because he antagonized the thought of his time, there was much of scholastic bitterness which escaped animadversion because it was the development of the tendencies of the age, and the schoolmen were allowed to indulge in endless wrangling for the most part without censure. The great quarrel between the Nominalists and the Realists occupies too large a space in the intellectual history of Europe to be wholly passed over, although its relation to our immediate subject is not intimate enough to justify detailed consideration.

In the developed theory of the Realists, genera and species—the distinctive attributes of individual beings, or the conceptions of those attributes—are real entities, if not the only realities. Individuals are ephemeral existences which pass away; the only things that survive are those which are universal and common to all. In man this is humanity, but humanity again is but a portion of a larger existence, the animate, and the animate is but a transitory form of an Infinite Being, which is All and nothing in particular. This is the sole Immutable. These conceptions took their origin in the *Periphyseos* of John Scot Erigena in the ninth century, whose reaction against the prevailing anthropomorphism led him to sublimated views of the Divine Being, which trenched closely on Pantheism. The heresy latent in his work lay undiscovered until developed by the Amaurians, when the book, after nearly four centuries, was condemned by Honorius III, in 1225.

Nominalism, on the other hand, regarded the individual as the primal substance; universals are only abstractions or mental conceptions of qualities common to individuals, with no more of reality than the sounds which express them. Even as Realism in the hands of daring thinkers led to Pantheism, so, step by step, Nominalism could be brought to recognize the originality of the individual and finally to Atomism.

The two antagonistic schools were first clearly defined in the beginning of the twelfth century, with Roscelin, the teacher of Abelard, as the leader of the Nominalists, and William of Champeaux at the head of the Realists. Discussion continued in the schools with constantly increasing bitterness, though neither side dared to push its own views to their ultimate conclusions. Realism in a modified form achieved a triumph with the immense authority of Albertus Magnus and Thomas Aquinas. Duns Scotus was a Realist, though he differed with Aquinas on the problem of individuation, and the Realists became divided into the opposing factions of Thomists and Scotists. While they were thus weakened, William of Ockham revived Nominalism, and it became bolder than ever. The perennial hostility between the Dominicans and Franciscans tended to range the two Orders under the opposing banners, while Ockham's defense of Louis of Bavaria in his quarrel with the papacy served to impress upon the new school of Nominalists his views upon the relations between Church and State.

Under Peter d'Ailly and John Gerson the University of Paris was

Nominalist. With the English domination the Realists triumphed and expelled their adversaries, who were unable to return until the restoration of the French monarchy. In 1465 there arose in the University of Louvain a strife which lasted for ten years over some propositions of Pierre de la Rive on fate and divine foreknowledge, in which the rival sects took sides. The University of Paris was drawn in; the Nominalists triumphed in condemning de la Rive, and the Realists took their revenge by procuring from Louis XI an edict prohibiting the teaching of Nominalist doctrines in the University and in all the schools of the kingdom; all Nominalist books were boxed up and sealed until 1481, when Louis was persuaded to recall his edict, and the University rejoiced to regain her liberty. One tragic incident in the long quarrel has been already alluded to in the trial of John of Wesel, which led to his death in prison, and it illustrates how readily scholastic ardor assumed that in gratifying its vindictiveness it was vindicating the faith. The contemporary reporter of the trial assumes that the persecution was caused by the antagonism of the Dominican Realists to the Nominalism of the victim, and he deplores the rage which led the Thomists to regard everyone who denied the existence of universals as guilty of the sin against the Holy Ghost, and as a traitor to God, to the Christian religion, to justice, and to the State.

The annals of the schools are full of cases which show how the recklessness of disputatious logic led to subleties most perilous in minute details of theology, and also how sensitive were the conservators of the faith to anything that might be construed by perverse ingenuity as savoring of heresy. Duns Scotus did not escape, nor Thomas Bradwardine; William of Ockham and Buridan were enveloped in a common condemnation by the University of Paris, of which the latter had been rector. The boundaries between philosophy and the theology which sought to define everything in the visible and invisible world were impossible of definition, and it was a standing grievance that the philosophers were perpetually intruding on the domains of the theologians.

The audacity of these rash intruders upon the sacred precincts increased immeasurably with the introduction of the works of Averrhoes in the second quarter of the thirteenth century, constituting a real danger of the perversion of Christian thought. In the hands of the Arab commentators the theism of Aristotle became a transcendental materialism, carried to its furthest expression by the latest of them, Ibn Roschd, or Averrhoes, who died in 1198. In his system matter has existed from the beginning, and the theory of creation is impossible. The universe consists of a hierarchy of principles, eternal, primordial, and autonomous, vaguely connected with a superior unity. One of these is the Active Intellect, manifesting itself incessantly and constituting the permanent consciousness of humanity. This is the only form of immortality. As the soul of man is a fragment of a collective whole, temporarily detached to animate the body, at death it is reabsorbed into the Active Intellect of the universe. Consequently there are no future rewards or punishments, no feelings, memory, love, or hatred. The perishable body has the power of reproducing itself and thus enjoys a material immortality in its descendants, but it is only collective humanity that is immortal. To those whose conceptions of paradise and the resurrection were as material as the Swarga of the Brahman or the Kama Loka heavens of the Buddhist, such collective and insensible immortality was virtually equivalent to annihilation, and the Averrhoists were universally stigmatized as materialists.

Such theories as these necessarily induced the loftiest indifferentism to religious formulas, although a wholesome dread of the rising Moslem fanaticism, from which Averrhoes had not escaped scathless, rendered him cautious about assailing the established faith. "The special religion of philosophers," he says, "is to study what exists, for the most sublime worship of God is the contemplation of his works, which leads us to a knowledge of him in all his reality." At the same time the received religions are an excellent instrument of morality. He who inspires among a people doubts of the national religion is a heretic, to be punished as such by the established penalties. The wise man will utter no word against the national religion, and will especially avoid speaking of God in a manner equivocal to the vulgar. When several religions confront each other, one should select the noblest. All religions are of human origin, and the choice between them is a matter of opinion or policy—but policy, if nothing else, must have prevented Averrhoes from uttering the phrase commonly attributed to him—"The Christian faith is impossible; that of Judaism is a religion of children, that of Islam, a religion of hogs."

Still less credible is the popular assertion which assigns to him the famous speech referring to Moses, Christ, and Mahomet as the three impostors who had deluded the human race. This saying became a convenient formula with which the Church horrified the faithful by attributing it successively to those whom it desired to discredit. Thomas of Cantimpré fathered it upon Simon de Tournay, whose paralytic stroke in 1201 he ascribed to this impiety. Gregory IX, when in 1239 he arraigned Frederic II before the face of Europe, did not hesitate to assert that he was the author of this utterance, which Frederic made haste to deny in the most solemn manner. A certain renegade Dominican named Thomas Scotus, who was condemned and imprisoned in Portugal, was said to have been guilty of this blasphemy among others, and the phrase drifted through the centuries until there was a current belief that an impious book existed under the title *De Tribus Impostoribus*, the authorship of which was attributed variously to Petrus de Vineis, Boccaccio, Poggio, Machiavelli, Erasmus, Servetus, Bernardino Ochino, Rabelais, Pietro Aretino, Étienne Dolet, Francesco Pucci, Muret, Vanini, and Milton. Queen Christina of Sweden vainly caused all the libraries of Europe to be searched for it, but it remained invisible until, in the eighteenth century, various scribblers put forth volumes to gratify the popular curiosity.

Yet to Frederic II may be attributed the introduction of Averrhoism in central Europe. In Spain it was so prevalent that about 1260 Alonso X describes heresies as consisting of two principal divisions, of which the worst was that which denies the immortality of the soul and future rewards and punishments, and 1291 we find the Council of Tarragona ordering the punishment of those who disbelieved in a future existence. It was from Toledo that Michael Scot came with translations of Aristotle and Averrhoes, and was warmly welcomed at the court of Frederic, whose insatiable thirst for knowledge and whose slender reverence for formulas led him to grasp eagerly at these unexpected sources of philosophy. It was probably these translations which formed the body of Aristotelism distributed by him to the universities of Italy. Hermannus Alemannus continued Michael's work at Toledo and brought versions of other books to Manfred, who inherited his father's tastes, so that by the middle of the century the principal labors of Averrhoes were accessible to scholars.

The infection spread with rapidity almost incredible. Already, in 1243, Guillaume d'Auvergne, Bishop of Paris, and the Masters of the University condemned a series of scholastic errors, not indeed distinctively Averrhoist, but manifesting in their bold independence the influence which the Arab philosophy was beginning to exercise. In 1247 the papal legate Otto, Bishop of Frascati, condemned Jean de Brescain for certain heretical speculations concerning light and matter; he was banished from Paris and forbidden to teach, or dispute, or to live where there was a college. For the future, logicians were forbidden to argue theologically and theologians logically, as they were growing accustomed to do. This accomplished little, and as little was effected by Albertus Magnus and Thomas Aquinas, who employed their keenest dialectics to check the spread of these dangerous opinions. In 1270, Étienne Tempier, Bishop of Paris, was called upon to condemn a series of 13 errors, distinctively Averrhoist, which found defenders among the schools, to the effect that the intellect of all men is the same and is one in number; that human will is controlled by necessity; that the world is eternal and there never was a first man; that the soul is corrupted with the corruption of the body; that God does not know individual things, he knows nothing but himself, and cannot give immortality and incorruptibility to that which is mortal and corruptible.

This availed as little as the previous effort. In 1277 it was deemed necessary to invoke the authority of John XXI, under which Bishop Tempier condemned a list of 219 errors, mostly the same as the previous ones, or deductions drawn from them, tending to systematize materialism and fatalism. About the same time Robert Kilwarby, Archbishop of Canterbury, together with the Masters of Oxford, condemned some errors evidently originating from the same source, but not asserting materialism in a manner so absolute, and this condemnation was confirmed in 1284 by Archbishop Peckham. These articles were combined with those of Bishop Tempier, and together the collection had wide currency, as shown by the number of MSS. containing it. That the opinions thus condemned continued to be regarded as a source of real danger to the Church is manifested by the articles being customarily printed during the fifteenth and sixteenth centuries at the end of the fourth book of the *Sentences*, and also in an edition each of Thomas Aquinas, Duns Scotus, and Bonaventura.

Yet after the death of Bishop Tempier these articles aroused considerable complaint as interfering with freedom of discussion, and they became the object of no little debate. In fact, in so long a list of errors, it was almost impossible to avoid trenching upon positions held to be orthodox in a theology of which the complexity had grown beyond the grasp of finite intelligence and finite memory. Considerable trouble was occasioned by the fact that some of the articles assailed positions held by Thomas Aquinas himself; others were attacked by William of Ockham and Jean de Poilly. How perilous, indeed, was the position of the theological expert in the war of dialectics is seen in the case of the *Doctor Fundatissimus*, Egidio Colonna, better known as Egidio da Roma. There was no more earnest and active opponent of Averrhoism, and his list of its errors long continued to be the basis of its condemnation. Yet he translated a commentary on Aristotle, and in 1285 he was accused in Paris of entertaining some of the errors condemned in 1277. After considerable discussion the matter was carried before the Holy See, and Honorius IV referred him back to the University of Paris for sentence. He made his peace so effectually that Philippe le Bel, whose tutor he had been, presented him to the great archbishopric of Bourges.

At the close of the thirteenth and the commencement of the fourteenth century the principal figure in the contest with Averrhoes is Raymond Lully—aptly styled by Renan the hero of the crusade against it—but the career of Lullism was so remarkable that it must be considered independently hereafter. All efforts failed to suppress a philosophy which offered such attractions to the rising energies of the human intellect. An avowed school of Averrhoists arose, whose tenets, introduced in the University of Padua seemingly by Peter of Abano, reigned there supreme until the seventeenth century. The University of Bologna likewise adopted them. Jean de Jandun, the collaborator of Marsilio of Padua, was a modified Averrhoist, as were Walter Burleigh, Buridan, and the Ockhamists. John of Baconthorpe, who died in 1346 as General of the Carmelites, rejoiced in the title of Prince of Averrhoists, and through him the philosophy became traditional in the Order. These men might conceal to themselves the dangerous irreligion which lurked under their cherished theories, but when these spread among the people, divested of the subtle dialectics of the schools, they developed into frank materialism.

Averrhoism had thus fairly conquered a position for itself, and it is one of the inscrutable problems why the Inquisition, so unrelenting in its suppression of minor aberrations, should have conceded impunity to speculations which not only sapped the foundations of Christian faith, but by plain implication denied all the doctrines on which were based the wealth and power of the hierarchy. It was not till 1512 that Averrhoism had its first recorded victim since Peter of Abano, in the person of Hermann of Ryswick, who, in 1499, had been condemned for teaching its materialistic doctrines—that matter is uncreated and has existed with God from the beginning, that the soul dies with the body, and that angels, whether good or bad, are not created by God. He abjured and was sentenced to perpetual imprisonment, but escaped and persisted in propagating his errors. When again apprehended, in 1512, the inquisitor at The Hague had no hesitation in handing him over as a relapsed to the secular arm, and he was duly burned.

In northern Europe, where scholastic theology was engaged in mortal combat with Humanism, rigor like this is to be looked for, but the case was different in Italy. There letters had long before got the better of faith. The infection of culture and philosophy, of elegant paganism, pervaded all the more elevated ranks of society. If Rome was to remain the mistress of the world under the New Learning, she could not afford to be relentless in repressing the aspirations and speculations of scholars and philosophers. The battle was fought and lost over Lorenzo Valla. As he not only swept away the foundations of the temporal power, but argued that the papacy should be deprived of it, the impunity which he enjoyed is a remarkable proof of the freedom of speech permitted at the period. His troubles arose from a different cause, and even these he would probably have escaped but for the quarrelsome humor of the man, and his unsparing ridicule of the horrible jargon of the schools and even of the earlier Humanists. He made enemies enough to conspire for his ruin at the court of Naples, where Alfonso had studied Latin under his teaching, and he soon gave occasion for their attack. Becoming involved in a contest with an ignorant priest who asserted that the Symbol was the production of the apostles, the discussion spread to the authenticity of the communications between Christ and King Abgar of Edessa. Valla posted a list of the propositions assailed, and hired a hall in which to defend them against all comers, when his enemies procured from the king a prohibition of disputation. Valla then posted on the hall-door a triumphant distich:

> Rex pacis miserans sternendas Marte phalanges,
> Victoris cupidum continuit gladium.

Then the Inquisition interposed, but Alfonso exercised the royal Neapolitan prerogative of putting a stop to the prosecution, Valla being only forced to make a general declaration that he believed as Holy Mother Church believed—the sincerity of which appeared when, attacked on a point of dialectics, he defended himself by saying: "In this, too, I believe as Mother Church believes, though Mother Church knows nothing about it." When, in 1443, Alfonso and Eugenius were reconciled, Valla sought to go to Rome, but was unable to do so; but when the monkish Eugenius was succeeded by the humanist Nicholas V, the way was opened. Nicholas not only welcomed him, but gave him a position among the papal secretaries and rewarded his translation of Thucydides with a gift of 500 ducats. Calixtus III provided him with a prebend in the pope's own church of St. John Lateran, and here he was honorably buried.

That it was not, however, always safe to presume on this favor shown to Humanism is evident by the case of Giovanni Pico della Mirandola, the wonder of his age, who in 1487, when but twenty-four years old, published a series of 900 propositions which he offered to defend in Rome against all comers, paying the expenses of scholars who might travel for the purpose from distant lands. The list was virtually *de omni scibili*, comprising everything recognized as knowable in theology, philosophy, and science, even including the mysteries of the East. It was doubtless the pretentiousness of the young scholar which provoked enmity leading to animadversion on his orthodoxy, and it was not difficult in so vast an array of conclusions to find some 13 which savored of heresy. To us it might appear a truism to say that belief is independent of volition; we might hesitate to affirm positively whether Christ descended into hell personally or only effectively; we might even agree with him that mortal sin, limited and finite, is not to be visited with chastisement unlimited and infinite; and we might hesitate to embark with him in investigating too narrowly the mysteries of transubstantiation; but these speculative assumptions of the self-sufficient thinker were condemned as heretical by the theologians appointed for their examination by Innocent VIII, who quietly remarked: "This youth wishes to end badly, and be burned some of these days, and then be infamous forever like many another." Pico was urged to resist and raise a schism, but nothing was further from his thoughts. His few remaining years were passed in the assiduous study of Scripture; he designed, after completing certain works in hand, to wander barefoot over Europe preaching Christ; then, changing his purpose, he intended to enter the Dominican Order, but his projects were cut short, at the age of 32, by the fever which carried him off, gratified in his last hours with a vision of the Virgin. Such a man was an easy victim; the voluminous apology which he wrote to explain his errors availed him nothing, and he was compelled to make a full submission, which earned from Alexander VI, in 1493, not long before Pico's death, a bull declaring his orthodoxy and forbidding the Inquisition to trouble him.

Before leaving this branch of our subject we must recur to the curious episode of the career of Raymond Lully, the *Doctor Illuminatus*, of whom Padre Feyjoo truly says, "Raymond Lully, looked upon from every side, is a very problematical object. Some make him a saint, others a heretic; some a most learned man, others an ignoramus; some regard him as illuminated, others as hallucinated; some attribute to him a knowledge of the transmutation of metals, others deny it; finally, some applaud his *Ars Magna*, others depreciate it."

This enigmatical being was born in Palma, the capital of Majorca, January 25, 1235. Sprung from a noble family, he was bred in the royal court, where he rose to the post of seneschal. He married and had children, but followed a gay and dissolute career until, like

Peter Waldo and Jacopone da Todi, he was suddenly converted by an experience of the nothingness of life. He was madly in love with Leonor del Castello, and his reckless temper manifested itself by pursuing her on horseback into the church of Santa Eulalia during a Sunday service, to the great scandal of priest and congregation. To rid herself of such importunate pursuit, Leonor, with consent of her husband, exhibited to him her bosom, which was ravaged by a foul and mortal cancer. The shock brought to him so profound a recognition of the vanity of earthly things that he renounced the world and distributed his wealth in charity, after making provision for his family; and the same indomitable ardor which had rendered him extravagant in his pleasures sustained him to the end in his new vocation. Thenceforth he devoted his life to the rescue of the Holy Sepulchre, to the conversion of the Jews and Saracens, and to the framing of a system which should demonstrate rationally the truth of the Christian faith, and thus overcome the Averrhoism in which he recognized its most dangerous adversary.

Ten years or more were spent in preparation for this new career. We hear of a pilgrimage to Compostella in 1266, and of his retirement to the Monte de Randa, near Palma, in 1275. He was so ignorant of letters that he was not even acquainted with Latin, the key to all the knowledge of the age. This he studied, and also Arabic, from a Saracen slave purchased for the purpose, and the earnest labors of an indefatigable mind can account for the enormous stores of learning which he subsequently displayed, so wonderful that to his followers they appeared necessarily the result of inspiration. In his retreat on Monte de Randa, where he conceived his *Ars Universalis*, he is said to have had repeated visions of Christ and the Virgin, which illuminated his mind; and the mastic tree under which he habitually wrote bore testimony to the miracle, in its leaves inscribed with Latin, Greek, Chaldee, and Arabic characters. It continued to put forth such leaves. In the seventeenth century Vicente Mut vouches for the fact, and says he has some of them, while Wadding tells us that in his time they were carried to Rome, where they excited much wonder. When his work was completed an angel in the guise of a shepherd appeared, who kissed the book many times, and predicted that it would prove an invincible weapon for the faith.

Emerging from his retreat, for forty years he led a wandering life of incessant activity, now stimulating popes and kings to renewed crusades, or to found colleges of the Oriental tongues to aid in missionary labors, now pouring forth volume after volume with incredible fecundity, now disputing and teaching against Averrhoism at Montpellier, Paris, and elsewhere, and now venturing himself among the infidel to spread among them the light of Christianity. In any one of these fields of action his labors would seem enough to exhaust the energies of an ordinary man. While on his way, in 1311, to the Council of Vienne, with projects for founding schools of Oriental tongues, for uniting in one all the military Orders, for a holy war against the infidel, for suppressing Averrhoism, and for teaching his art in all universities, he summed up his life:

I was married and a father, sufficiently rich, worldly, and licentious. For the honor of God, for the public weal, and for the advancement of the faith I abandoned all. I learned Arabic, and I have been repeatedly among the Saracens to preach to them, where I have been beaten and imprisoned. For forty-five years I have labored to excite the rulers of the Church and the princes of Christendom for the public good. Now I am old, I am poor, and I still have the same purpose, which with the help of God, I will retain till I die.

At Vienne his only success was in obtaining a decree founding schools of Hebrew, Arabic, and Chaldee in the papal court and in the Universities of Paris, Oxford, Bologna, and Salamanca. Thence he went, for the second time, to Algiers, where, at Bugia, he made many converts, until thrown into prison and starved; then he was released and ordered out of the country, but continued proselyting. With wonderful forbearance the Moors contented themselves with placing him on board a ship bound for Genoa, and warning him not to return. Shipwrecked in sight of land, he saved his life by swimming, but lost his books. Determined to win the palm of martydom, in August 1314 he again embarked at Palma for Bugia. Promptly recognized, he was thrown into jail, beaten, and starved; but in prison he continued to preach to his fellow-captives, until the Moors, finding him unconquerable, took him out, June 30, 1315, and stoned him. Some Genoese merchants about to sail carried his yet-breathing body on board their ship and laid their course for

Genoa, but to their surprise found themselves at the entrance of the port of Palma. In vain they endeavored to leave the spot till, recognizing the will of Heaven, they carried the body ashore. Immediately it shone in miracles, and the cult of the martyr began. In 1448 a splendid chapel was erected in his honor in the church of the Franciscans, of which Order he was a Tertiary, and another one was dedicated to him in the beginning of the seventeenth century. In 1487 his bones were deposited in a richly carved alabaster urn, standing in a niche in the church wall over an elaborate sepulchral monument, where they still remain.

The results achieved at the moment by the self-devotion of this noble and indefatigable intellect was slender. Averrhoism continued to gain strength, the Christian princes could not be stimulated to a new crusade, and the conversion of Jew and infidel made no progress. Yet the prodigious literary activity of Lully left behind him a mass of writings destined to exercise no little influence on succeeding generations. He was perhaps the most voluminous author on record. Juan Llobet, who in the middle of the fifteenth century taught the Art of Lully in the University of Palma, had read 500 of his books; some authors assert that their total number reached 1,000, others 3,000. Many have been lost, many spurious ones have been attributed to him, and the bibiliography of his works is hopelessly confused; but Nicolas Antonio, after careful sifting, gives the titles of 321 which may safely be ascribed to him. Of these there are 61 on the art of learning and general subjects, 4 on grammar and rhetoric, 15 on logic, 21 on philosophy, 5 on metaphysics, 13 on various sciences—astrology, geometry, politics, war, the quadrature of the circle, and the art of knowing God through grace—7 on medicine, 4 on law, 62 on spiritual contemplation and other religious subjects, 6 on homiletics, 13 on Antichrist, the acquisition of the Holy Land, and other miscellaneous subjects, 46 controversial works against Saracens, Jews, Greeks, and Averrhoists, and 64 on theology, embracing the most abstruse points, and religious poetry. The great collective edition of his works printed in Mainz from 1721 to 1742 forms ten folios. Like all other great scholars of his day, his name was a convenient one to affix to books on alchemy and magic, but all such are supposititious. His reputation as an alchemist is seen in the tradition that in England he made 6 million gold florins and gave them to the king to stimulate him to a crusade, but his own opinion of alchemy is expressed in a passage of his *Ars Magna:* "Each element has its own peculiarities so that one species cannot be transmuted to another, wherefore the alchemists grieve and have occasion to weep," and in other equally outspoken expressions.

For our purpose we need consider but one phase of his marvellous productiveness. In the solitude of Monte de Randa he conceived the Art which passes by his name—a method in which, by diagrams and symbols, the sublimest truths of theology and philosophy can be deduced and memorized. Of this the *Ars Brevis* is a compend, while the *Ars Magna* describes it in greater detail and proceeds to build upon it a system of the universe, revealing a familiar acquaintance with all the secrets of the material and spiritual worlds, the powers, attributes, motives, and purposes of God and his creatures logically deduced, which the Lullists might well hold to be inspired. This Art he himself taught at Montpellier and Paris, and in 1309 forty members of the latter University joined in a cordial recommendation of it as useful and necessary for the defense of the faith. At home it had great and enduring vogue. Favored by successive monarchs, it was taught in the Universities of Aragon and Valencia. In the middle of the fifteenth century the Estudio Lulliano was founded at Palma, subsequently enlarged into the Universidad Lulliana, where the tradition of his teaching was preserved almost to our own days. Cardinal Ximenes was its great admirer; Angelo Politiano says that to it he owed his ability to dispute on any subject; Jean Lefèvre d'Etaples prized it highly, as likewise did other men of note. On the other hand, it was condemned by Gerson and its use forbidden in the University of Paris; it was ill thought of by Cornelius Agrippa and Jerome Cardan; and Mariana tells us that in his time many considered it harmful, while others praised it as a gift from heaven to remedy ignorance, and in 1586 it use was prohibited in the University of Valencia.

In this and in many of his other works Lully's object was to prove by logical processes of thought the truths of Christianity and the positions of theology. He lost no opportunity of declaring that faith is superior to reason, and that they were mistaken who held that faith proved by reason lost its merit. Devoting his life to combating Averrhoism and converting the infidel, he had felt that

Christianity could only be spread by argument—that to convert men he had to convince them. He urged that the heathen might logically complain of God if it were impossible to convince their reason of the truth.

The result showed the danger which lurked in his singleminded efforts. As his reputation spread and his disciples multiplied, Nicholas Eymerich, the Inquisitor of Aragon, undertook to condemn his memory. Perhaps among the Lullists there were men whose zeal outran their discretion. Eymerich speaks of one, named Pedro Rosell, whose errors are a curious echo of the Joachites and Olivists, for he taught that, as the doctrine of the Old Testament was attributable to the Father and that of the New to the Son, so was that of Lully to the Holy Ghost, and that in the time of Antichrist all theologians would apostatize, when the Lullists would convert the world, and all theology but that of their master would disappear. Perhaps also, Eymerich, as a Dominican, was eager to attack one in whom the Franciscans gloried as one of their greatest sons. Doubtless, too, there is truth in the assertion of the Lullists that their defense of the Immaculate Conception rendered Eymerich desirous of suppressing them. Be this as it may, in a mass of writings embracing every conceivable detail of doctrine and faith, it was not difficult for an expert to find points liable to characterization as errors, and in 1371 Eymerich went to Avignon, where he obtained from Gregory XI an order for the examination of Lully's writings. On his return the king peremptorily forbade the publication of the papal mandate, but the irrepressible inquisitor in 1374 sent 20 of the inculpated books to Gregory, and in 1376 he had the satisfaction of exhibiting a bull reciting that these works had been carefully investigated by the Cardinal of Ostia and 20 theologians, who had found in them 200 (or, according to Eymerich, 500) errors manifestly heretical. As the rest of Lully's writings must presumably be erroneous, the Archbishop of Tarragona was ordered to cause all of them to be surrendered and sent to Rome for examination. Then King Pedro again interposed, and asked the pope to have any further proceedings carried on in Barcelona, as Lully's works were mostly in Catalan, and could best be understood there.

Eymerich triumphed for a time, and in his *Directorium Inquisitorum* he gives full rein to his hatred. Lully, he says, was taught his doctrine by the devil, but, to avoid prolixity, he enumerates only 100 of the 500 errors condemned by Gregory. Some of these trench on mystic Illuminism, others are merely extravagant modes of putting ordinary propositions. For the most part they hinge on the assertion, condemned in the 96th error, "that all points of faith and the sacraments and the power of the pope can be and are proved by reasoning, necessary, demonstrative, and evident"; for they consist of efforts to define logically the mysteries of faith in a manner of which conceptions so subtle are incapable. Two or three, however, are manifestly heretical—that faith can err, but not reason, that it is wrong to slay heretics, and that the mass of mankind will be saved, even Jews and Saracens who are not in mortal sin. Eymerich describes the Lullists as numerous and impudent, and guilty of the error of holding that Gregory erred grossly in condemning their master, whose doctrine had been divinely revealed and excelled all other doctrine, even that of St. Augustin; that modern theologians know nothing of true theology, for, on account of their sins, God has transferred all knowledge to the Lullists, who are to constitute the Church in the times of Antichrist.

There was in all this evidently the material which only needed nursing and provocation to develop into a new and formidable heresy under inquisitorial methods. Fortunately the king and a large part of the population were in sympathy with the Lullists; the Great Schism broke out in 1378, and Don Pedro acknowledged neither Urban VI nor Clement VII. The kingdom was thus virtually independent; the Lullists boldly claimed that the bull of Gregory XI had been forged by Eymerich; in 1385 an investigation was held which resulted in driving him from Aragon, when he was succeeded by his enemy, Bernardo Ermengaudi, who was devoted to the king, and who hastened to make a formal declaration that in Lully's *Philosophia Amoris* there were not to be found the errors attributed to it by Eymerich. The banishment of the latter, however, did not long continue. He returned and resumed his office, which he exercised with unsparing rigor against the Lullists. This excited considerable commotion. In 1391 the city of Valencia sent to the pope Doctor Jayme de Xiva to complain of Eymerich's enormous crimes, and to supplicate his removal. The envoy stopped at Barcelona to solicit the co-operation of that powerful community, and the town council, after listening to him, resolved that if the action of Valencia was general and not special, they would make "one arm and one heart" with their sister city; and, moreover, they begged the pope to command some prelate of the kingdom to examine and declare, under papal authority, whether the articles attributed to Lully had been justly or unjusty condemned by Eymerich.

The popular effervescence grew so strong that in 1393 Eymerich was again banished by Juan I. He ended his life in exile, maintaining to the end the enormity of Lully's heresy and the genuineness of Gregory's bull. Meanwhile, in 1395, the Holy See granted the prayer of the Lullists for an examination, and the Cardinal of San Sesto was sent as special commissioner for the purpose. Gregory's registers for 1376 were carefully examined, and the archivists testified that no record of the bull in question could be found. Still the question would not remain settled, for the honor of the Dominican Order and the Inquisition was at stake, and again, in 1419, another investigation was held. The papal legate, Cardinal Alamanni, deputed Bernardo, Bishop of Città di Castello, to examine the matter definitely. His sentence pronounced the bull to be evidently false, and all action taken under it to be null and void, but expressed no opinion on the writings of Lully, which he reserved for the decision of the Holy See. From that time forth the genuineness of the bull remained a matter hotly contested. Father Bremond prints it as authentic, and declares that after a dispassionate examination he is convinced that it is so; that the original autograph is preserved in the archives at Gerona, and he quotes Bzovius to the effect that the Lullists themselves admit that it is in the archives of Barcelona, Tarragona, and Valencia, whose bishops would not have admitted it if false; but Bzovius was a Dominican whose bitterness on the subject is seen in his stigmatizing Lully as a vagabond swindler. Certain it is that in the prolonged and ardent contest which raged over the question of Lully's orthodoxy in the papal court, the Dominicans, with successive popes on their side, were never able to produce the original nor offer any evidence of its authenticity.

In Aragon the decision of 1419 was regarded as settling the question. Royal letters in favor of Lullism were issued by Alonso V in 1415 and 1449, by Ferdinand the Catholic in 1483 and 1503, by Charles V in 1526, and by Philip II in 1597; Philip, indeed, had

great relish for Lully's writings, some of which he habitually carried
with him on his journeys to read on the way, and in the library of
the Escorial many copies of them were found annotated with his
own hand. This royal favor was needed in the curious controversy
which followed. Lully's name had passed into the received catalogues of heretics, and as late as 1608 it was included in the list
published by the Doctor of Sorbonne, Gabriel du Préau. Paul IV,
in 1559, put it in the first papal *Index Expurgatorius*. When this
came to be published in Spain, Bishop Jayme Cassador and the inquisitors suspended it and referred the matter to the *consejo de la
suprema*, which ordered the entry to be *borrado*, or expunged. At
the Council of Trent, Doctor Juan Villeta, acting for Spain, presented a petition in favor of Lully, which was considered in a special
congregation, September 1, 1563, and a unanimous decision was
reached, confirming all the condemnations passed on Eymerich
for falsehood, and ordering the Index of Paul IV to be expurgated
by striking out all that related to Lully. This was a secret determination of the council, and was not allowed to appear in the published
acts. It settled the matter for a time, but the question was revived in
1578, when Francisco Pegna reprinted Eymerich's book with the
special sanction of Gregory XIII, bringing anew before the world
the bull of Gregory XI and the errors condemned in Lully's writings.
Gregory XIII ordered Pegna to examine the papal registers for the
contested bull. Those in Rome were found imperfect, and the missing
portions were sent for from Avignon, but the most diligent search
failed to find the desired document, though it was alleged that two
volumes of the year 1386 could not be found.

Battle was now fairly joined between the partisans of Eymerich
and those of Lully. In 1583 the Congregation of the Index determined to include Lully among the prohibited writers, but again
Spanish influence was strong enough to prevent it. When the Index
of Clement VIII was in preparation the question was again taken
up, June 3, 1594, and rejected out of respect for Spain. In 1611 Philip
III revived the controversy by applying to Paul V for the canonization of Lully and the expurgation of Eymerich's *Directorium*, a
request which was repeated by Philip IV. After a confused controversy, it was determined that certain articles admittedly extracted
from his books were dangerous, audacious, and savoring of heresy,

and some of them manifestly erroneous and heretical. At a sitting under the presidency of the pope himself, held August 29, 1619, it was resolved to send this censure to the Spanish nuncio, with instructions to inform the king and the inquisitors that Lully's books were forbidden. Then came an appeal from the kingdom of Majorca begging that the books might be corrected, to which Paul replied, August 6, 1620, imposing silence; and on August 30 Cardinal Bellarmine drew up for the Inquisition a final report that Lully's doctrine was forbidden until corrected, adding his belief that correction was impossible, but that the condemnation was thus phrased so as to mitigate its severity. Thus Lully was branded by the Holy See as a heretic, but, out of respect for the Spanish court, the sentence was never published, and the worship of him as a saint continued uninterruptedly. In 1662 a translation of his *Triumph of Love* appeared in Paris, on the title of which he was qualified as "Saint Raymond Lully, Martyr and Hermit."

The Dominican ire was aroused: appeal was made to the Congregation of Rites, which reported that Lully was included in the Franciscan martyrology under March 29, but that he must not be qualified as a saint, and that a careful examination should be made of his works, to prohibit them if necessary—a recommendation which was never carried out. Yet when, in 1688, Doctor Pedro Bennazar issued at Palma a book in praise of Lully, it was condemned by the Inquisition in 1690; and a compendium of his theology, by Sebastian Krenzer in 1755, was put on the Index, although this was not done with the great edition of his works published from 1721 to 1742, in the title of which he was qualified as *Beatus*. Benedict XIV, in his work *De Servorum Dei Beatificatione*, after carefully weighing the authorities on both sides, says that his claims to sanctity are to be suspended until the decision of the Holy See. That decision was postponed for a century. In 1847 Pius IX approved an office of "the holy Raymond Lully" for Majorca, where he had been immemorially worshipped; the office reciting that so fully was he imbued with the divine wisdom that he who had previously been uncultured was enabled to discourse most excellently on divine things. In 1858, moreover, Pius permitted the whole Franciscan Order to celebrate his feast on November 27. Yet the Dominicans had not forgotten their old rancor, for in 1857 there appeared in a

Roman journal, published under the approbation of the Master of the Sacred Palace, an argument to prove that the alleged bull of Gregory XI is still in force, and consequently that Lully's books are forbidden, although they do not appear in the Index.

The example of Raymond Lully illustrates the pitfalls which surrounded the footsteps of all who ventured on the dangerous path of theology. The annals of an intellectual center like the University of Paris are crowded with sentences pronounced against novel points of faith. Occasionally, however, some new dogma would arise, would be vehemently debated, would refuse to be suppressed, and would finally triumph after a more or less prolonged struggle, and would then take its place among the eternal verities which it was heresy to call in question.

An instructive instance of the development of theological doctrine is to be found in the history of the dogma of the Immaculate Conception of the Virgin. Up to the twelfth century it was not questioned that the Virgin was conceived and born in sin, and doctors like St. Anselm found their only difficulty in explaining how Christ could be born sinless from a sinner. With the growth of Mariolatry, however, there came a popular tendency to regard the Virgin as free from all human corruption, and towards the middle of the twelfth century the church of Lyons ventured to place on the calendar a new feast in honor of the Conception of the Virgin, arguing that as the Nativity was feasted as holy, the Conception, which was a condition precedent to the Nativity, was likewise holy and to be celebrated. St. Bernard, the great conservative of his day, at once set himself to suppress the new doctrine. He wrote earnestly to the canons of Lyons, showing them that their argument applied equally to the nativity and conception of all the ancestors of the Virgin by the male and female lines; he argued that the only immaculate conception was that of Christ, who was conceived of the Holy Ghost, and proved that Mary, who was sprung of the union between man and woman, must necessarily have been conceived in original sin. He admitted that she was born sanctified, whence the Church properly celebrated the Nativity, but this sanctification was operated in the womb of St. Anne, even as the Lord had said to Jeremiah, "Before thou camest out of the womb I sanctified thee" (Jer. 1. 5). Peter Lombard, the great Master of Sentences, was not willing to concede even as much as St. Bernard, and quotes John of Damascus to show that the Virgin was not cleansed of original sin until she accepted the duty of bearing Christ. To this view of the question Innocent III lent the authority of his great name by asserting it in the most positive manner.

These irresistible authorities settled the question for a while as one of dogma, but the notion had attractiveness to the people, and in the constant development of Mariolatry anything which tended to strengthen her position as a subordinate deity and intercessor found favor. There is something inexpressibly attractive in the mediæval conception of the Virgin, and the extension of her worship was inevitable. She was the embodiment of unalloyed maternal tenderness, whose sufferings for her divine Son had only rendered her more eagerly beneficent in her desire to aid and save the race for which he had died. She was human, yet divine, and whatever exalted her divinity rendered her more helpful, without withdrawing her from the sympathy of men. "The Virgin," says Peter of Blois, "is the sole mediator between man and Christ. We were sinners and feared to appeal to the Father, for he is terrible, but we have the Virgin, in whom there is nothing terrible, for in her is the plenitude of grace and the purity of human life." In fact, he exclaims, "if Mary were taken from heaven there would be to mankind nothing but the blackness of darkness." God, says St. Bonaventura, could have made a greater earth and a greater heaven, but he exhausted his power in creating Mary. Yet Bonaventura, as a doctor of the Church, was careful to limit her sinlessness to sin arising with herself, and not to include the absence of inherited sin. She was sanctified, not immaculately conceived.

In spite of St. Bernard's remonstrance, the celebration of the Feast of the Conception gradually spread. Thomas Aquinas tells us that it was observed in many churches, and that it was not forbidden, but he warns us against the inference that because a feast is holy therefore the conception of Mary was holy. In fact, he denies the possibility of her immaculate conception, though he admits her sanctification at some period which cannot be defined. This settled the question for the Dominicans, whose reverence for their Angelic Doctor rendered it impossible for them to swerve from his teachings. For a while, strange to say, the Franciscans agreed with their rivals.

But as it was impossible for the Dominicans to change their position, it was inevitable that in time the Franciscans should range themselves under the opposite banner. The clash between them first came in 1387, when the struggle was carried on with all the ferocity of the *odium theologicum*. Juan de Monçon, a Dominican professor in the University of Paris, taught that the Virgin was conceived in sin. This aroused great uproar, and he fled to Avignon from impending condemnation. The University sent to Avignon a deputation headed by Pierre d'Ailly, who claimed that they procured the condemnation of Juan, but he escaped to his native Aragon, while the Dominicans of Paris declared that the papal decision had been in their favor. If the chronicler is to believed, the Dominicans preached on the conception of the Virgin in the grossest terms and indulged in the most bestial descriptions, till the fury of the University knew no bounds. The Dominicans were expelled from all positions in the Sorbonne, and the Avignonese Clement VII was too dependent upon France to refuse a bull proclaiming as heretics Juan and all who held with him. Charles VI was persuaded not only to force the Dominicans of Paris to celebrate every year the Feast of the Conception, but to order the arrest of all within the kingdom who denied the Immaculate Conception, that they might be brought to Paris and obliged to recant before the University. It was not until 1403 that the Dominicans were readmitted to the Sorbonne, to the disgust of the other Mendicants, who had greatly profited by their exile.

The University of Paris was the stronghold of the new doctrine, and as its activity and influence were greatly curtailed by the disturbances which preceded the invasion of Henry V and by the English domination, we hear little of the question until the restoration of the French monarchy. The belief, however, had continued to spread. In 1438 the clergy and magistrates of Madrid, on the occasion of a pestilence, made a vow thereafter to observe the Feast of the Conception. The next year the Council of Basle, which had long been discussing the matter in a desultory fashion, came to a decision in favor of the Immaculate Conception, forbade all assertions to the contrary, and ordered the feast to be celebrated on December 8, with due indulgences for attendance. As the council, however, had previously deposed Eugenius IV, its utterances were not received as the inspiration of the Holy Ghost, and the doctrine, though strengthened, was not accepted by the Church. In fact, the rival Council of Florence, in 1441, although it spoke of Christ assuming his humanity in the immaculate womb of the Virgin, showed that this was but a figure of speech, by declaring as a point of faith that no one born of man and woman has ever escaped the domination of Satan except through the merits of Christ.

A new article could not be introduced without creating a new heresy. Here was one on which the Church was divided, and the adherents on each side denounced the other as heretics and persecuted them as far as they dared. In this the Dominicans were decidedly at a disadvantage, as their antagonists had greatly the preponderance and were daily growing in strength. In 1457 the Council of Avignon, presided over by a papal legate, the Cardinal de Foix, who was a Franciscan, confirmed the decree of Basle, and ordered under pain of excommunication that no one should teach to the contrary. In 1474 Vincenzo Bandello, a Dominican, who was subsequently General of the Order, provoked a fierce discussion on the subject in Lombardy by a book on the Conception. The strife continued for two years with so many scandals that in 1477 Sixtus IV evoked the matter before him, when it was hotly debated by Bandello for the Dominicans, or *Maculistæ*, and Francesco, General of the Franciscans, in defense of the Immaculate Conception. The only result seems to have been that Sixtus issued a bull ordering the Feast of the Conception to be celebrated in all the churches, with the grant of appropriate indulgences. This was a decided defeat for the Dominicans, who found it excessively galling to celebrate the feast, and thus admit before the people that they were wrong. In 1482, at Ferrara, the Franciscans and Dominicans preached so fiercely on the subject, and denounced each other as heretics so bitterly, that Sixtus IV was again obliged to intervene. After listening to both sides he issued another bull, in which he excommunicated all who asserted that the feast was in honor of the Sanctification of the Virgin, and also all who on either side should denounce the other as heretics.

As a means of evading a decision without exasperating either Order this policy was successful, but as a measure of peace it was an utter failure. Renewed disturbances forced Alexander VI to confirm the bull of Sixtus IV, with a clause calling upon the secular arm to keep the peace, if necessary; but in France the University of Paris wholly disregarded the prescriptions of both popes and treated as heretics all who denied the Immaculate Conception. On March 3, 1496, it adopted a statute, signed by 112 doctors in theology, affirming the doctrine and ordering that in future no one should be admitted into its body without taking an oath to maintain it, when if he proved recreant he should be expelled, degraded from all honors, and treated as a heathen and a publican. This example was followed by the Universities of Cologne, Tübingen, Mainz, and other places, arraying nearly all the learned bodies against the Dominicans, and training the vast majority of future theologians in the doctrine. Most of the cardinals and prelates everywhere gave in their adhesion; kings and princes joined them; the Carmelites took the same side, and the Dominicans were left almost alone to fight the unequal battle.

So sensitive did the supporters of the Immaculate Conception become that a Dominican preaching on December 8 had needs be wary in the allusions to the Virgin, which were unavoidable on that day of his humiliation. At Dieppe, on the feast of 1496, Jean de Ver, a Dominican, made use of expressions which were thought to oppose the dogma indirectly; he was at once brought to account and forced to confess publicly, and swear that in future he would uphold it. On the next anniversary Frère Jean Aloutier argued that the Virgin had never sinned even venially, although St. John Chrysostom said that she had done so out of vainglory on her weddingday. This was regarded as a covert attack, and Frère Jean was disciplined, though not publicly. It is only this hyperæsthesia of doctrinal sensibility that will explain the rigorous measures taken with Piero da Lucca, a canon of St. Augustin, who, in 1504, at Mantua, in a sermon, said that Christ was not conceived in the womb of the Virgin, but in her heart, of three drops of her purest blood. At once he was seized by the Inquisition, condemned as a heretic, and came near being burned.

The position of the Dominicans was growing desperate. Only the steady refusal of the papacy to pronounce definitely on the question saved them from the adoption of a new article of faith which Aquinas had proved to be false. It never occurred to them, as to his modern commentators, to prove that he did not mean what he said, and, in default of this, to yield on the point of the Immaculate

Conception was to admit his fallibility. They could only hope to secure the neutrality of the papacy and to prolong the hopeless fight against the growing strength of the new doctrine, which their banded enemies propagated with all the enthusiasm of approaching victory. The perplexity of the position was all the more keenly felt, as they claimed the Virgin as the peculiar patroness of their Order; the devotion of the Rosary, in her special honor, was a purely Dominican institution. They who had always worshipped her with the most extravagant devotion were forced to become her apparent detractors, and were everywhere stigmatized as *maculistæ*.

Suddenly, in 1507, the rumor spread that in Berne the Virgin had interposed to save her servants. In a convent of Observantine Dominicans she had repeatedly appeared to a holy friar and revealed to him her vexation at the guilt of the Franciscans in teaching the Immaculate Conception. After conception she had been three hours in original sin before sanctification; the teaching of St. Thomas was true and divinely inspired; Alexander Hales, Duns Scotus, and many other Franciscans were in purgatory for asserting the contrary. Julius II would settle the question and would institute in honor of the truth a greater feast than that of December 8. To help towards this consummation the Virgin gave the friar a cross tinged with her son's blood, three of the tears which he had shed over Jerusalem, the cloths in which he was wrapped in the flight to Egypt, and a vial of the blood which he had shed for man, together with a letter to Julius II in which he was promised glory equal to that of St. Thomas Aquinas in return for what was expected of him, and this letter, duly authenticated by the seals of the Dominican priors of Berne, Basle, and Nürnberg, was sent to the pope. The reports of these divine appearances produced an immense sensation; countless multitudes assembled in the Dominican Church to look upon the friar thus favored, and he performed feats of fasting, prayer, and scourging, which increased the reputation for sanctity acquired by the visitations. After a trance he appeared with the stigmata of Christ; the church was arranged to enable him in his devotions to represent the various acts of the Passion, and an immense crowds looked on with awestruck admiration. Then an image of the Virgin wept, and it was explained that her grief arose from the disregard of her warnings of what would befall the city unless it ceased to receive a pension from France, unless it expelled the Franciscans, and unless it ceased to believe in the Immaculate Conception.

People flocked from all the region around, and the fame of the miraculous apparitions spread, when the magistrates of Berne were surprised by Lester, the favored recipient of the visitations, taking refuge with them, and begging protection from his superiors, who were torturing and endeavoring to poison him. An investigation developed the whole plot. Wigand Wirt, Master of the Observantine Dominicans and professor of theology, had had, in 1501, a quarrel with a parish priest in Frankfort, in which they abused each other from their respective pulpits. In a sermon the priest thanked God that he did not belong to an Order which had slain the Emperor Henry VII with a poisoned host, and which denied the Immaculate Conception. Wirt, who was present, shouted to him that he was a liar and a heretic. An uproar followed, in which the Order sustained Wirt and appealed to Julius II, who appointed a commission. The result was adverse to Wirt, who left Frankfort filled with wrath, and published a savage attack upon his adversaries, which the Archbishop of Mainz caused to be publicly burned, while all his suffragans prohibited its circulation. Greatly excited, the Dominicans, in a chapter held at Wimpffen, resolved to prove by miracle the falsity of the Immaculate Conception. Frankfort was at first selected as the theatre, but was abandoned through fear of the archbishop; then Nürnberg, but the number of learned men there was an obstacle, and Berne was finally chosen as a city populous and powerful, but simple and unlearned. The officials of the Dominican convent there, John Vetter the prior, Francis Ulchi the sub-prior, Stephen Bolshorst the lector, and Henry Steinecker the procurator, undertook to carry out the design, and selected as an instrument a tailor of Zurzach, John Lester, who had been recently admitted to the Order. To suit the taste of the age, it was proved on the trial that they had commenced by invoking the assistance of the devil and had signed compacts with him in their blood, but their own ingenuity was sufficient for what followed, though we are told that when they produced the stigmata on Lester they first rendered him insensible with a magic potion formed of blood from the navel of a new-born Jew and nineteen hairs from his eyelashes. The victim was carefully prepared by a series of apparitions, commencing with an ordinary ghost and ending with the Virgin. According to his own account he believed in the visions till one day entering Bolshorst's room suddenly he found him in female attire like that of the Virgin, preparing for making an appearance. By threats and promises he had been prevailed upon to continue the imposture, till, fearing for his life, he escaped and told his tale.

Lester was sent to the Bishop of Lausanne, who heard his story and authorized the magistrates of Berne to act. The four Dominicans were confined separately in chains, and envoys were sent to Rome, where, only after the greatest difficulty, they obtained audience of the pope. A papal commission was sent, having at its head Achilles afterwards Cardinal of San Sesto, one of the most learned jurists of the age. Torture was freely used on both Lester and the accused, and full confessions were obtained. These were so damaging that the commissioners desired to keep them secret even from the magistrates, and when the latter were dissatisfied it was determined that they should be shown to a select committee of eight under pledge of secrecy, and that, to satisfy the people, only certain articles sufficient to justify burning should be publicly read. These were four, viz., renouncing God, painting and reddening the host, falsely representing the weeping Virgin, and counterfeiting the stigmata. The four culprits were abandoned to the secular arm, and eight days afterwards they were burned in a meadow beyond the Arar, their ashes being thrown into the river to prevent their being reverenced as relics—not without reason, for the Order promptly pronounced them to be martyrs. It is worthy of note that in the published sentence the Immaculate Conception was kept wholly out of sight.

Wigand Wirt did not wholly escape, though he does not seem to have been directly implicated in the fraud. The Observantine Franciscans prosecuted him before the Holy See for his savage tract against his adversaries. The case was heard by two successive commissions of cardinals, until, October 25, 1512, Wirt abandoned the defense and was sentenced to make the most humiliating of retractions. In public he revoked, abolished, repudiated, and extirpated his book as scandalous, insulting, defamatory, useless, and prejudicial; he confessed that in it he had injured theological doctrine and wounded the fraternal charity of many, including the venerable

Franciscans, and he declared his belief that those who upheld the doctrine of the Immaculate Conception did not err.

Despite the fate of the martyrs of Berne the Dominicans still held out gallantly against the constantly increasing preponderance of their antagonists. The controversy went on, as heated as ever, causing tumults and scandals, which the Church deplored but could not cure. In 1570 Paul IV endeavored to suppress them by suppressing public discussion. He renewed the bull of Sixtus IV, pointed out that the Council of Trent permitted everyone to enjoy his own opinion, and he allowed learned men to debate it in universities and chapters until it should be decided by the Holy See. All public disputation or assertion on either side in sermons or addresses was, however, forbidden under pain of deprivation and perpetual disability. This endeavor to preserve the peace of the Church was as futile as its predecessors. In 1616 Paul V deplored that, in spite of the salutary provisions existing on the subject, quarrels and scandals continued and threatened to grow more dangerous. He therefore added to the existing penalties perpetual disability for preaching or teaching, and ordered the bishops and inquisitors everywhere to punish severely all contraventions of these regulations. Yet the scale continued to incline against the Dominicans. A twelvemonth later, in August 1617, Paul issued another constitution, in which he extended these penalties to all who in public should assert the Virgin to have been conceived in original sin. He did not reprove the opinion, but left it as before, and ordered those who asserted publicly the Immaculate Conception to do so simply, without assailing the other side. In 1622 Gregory XV went a step further in suppressing the perpetual discord by a further extension of the penalties to all who in private asserted the Virgin's conception in sin; but at the same time he forbade the use of the word "immaculate" in the office of the Feast of the Conception. The Dominicans grew restive under this gagging, and in a couple of months procured a relaxation of the prohibition in so far as to allow them privately with each other to maintain and defend their opinion. The Jesuits threw the immense weight of their influence in favor of the Immaculate Conception, and in time it became not uncommon among them, at least in certain places, to take the heretical vow to defend it with life and blood. In 1715 Muratori, under the cautious pseudonym of Lamindus Pritanius, published a book attacking this practice. This drew forth a reply, in 1729, from the Jesuit Francesco Burgi, which Muratori answered under the name of Antonius Lampridius. A lively controversy arose which lasted for a quarter of a century or more, and Muratori's second book was in 1765 placed on the Spanish Index. Benedict XIV, in his great work *De Beatificatione*, says that the Church inclines to the doctrine of the Immaculate Conception, but has not yet made it an article of faith, and he even leaves the question undecided whether one who dies in its defense is to be reckoned as a martyr. Yet when, in 1840, Bishop Peter A. Baines, the Apostolic Vicar in England, spoke inconsiderately on the subject in a pastoral letter, he was sharply reproved and obliged to sign a pledge that on the first fitting occasion he would publicly declare his adhesion to whatever the Holy See might define on the subject. The decision was not long in coming. In 1849 Pius IX consulted all the bishops as to the expediency of proclaiming the Immaculate Conception as a dogma of the Church. Those of Italy, Spain, and Portugal, about 490 in number, were almost unanimously in its favor, while many in other lands hesitated and deprecated such action. The latter were not heeded; December 8, 1854, Pius issued a solemn definition declaring it to be an article of faith, and thus, after a struggle protracted through five centuries with unyielding tenacity, the Dominicans were finally defeated, and could only console themselves with ingenious glosses on Thomas Aquinas to prove that he had never really denied the doctrine.

It is interesting thus to trace the evolution of dogma, even though the result cannot be regarded as a finality. In 1876 a condemnation was pronounced on Joseph de Félicité (Vercruysse?) among whose errors was the assertion that Mary was conceived by the operation of the Holy Ghost, without the intervention of St. Joachim. Yet who can say that in the centuries to come this dogma may not also win its place, and the Virgin thus be elevated to an equality with her Son?

One function of the Inquisition remains to be considered—the censorship of the press—although its full activity in this direction belongs to a period beyond our present limits. We have seen how Bernard Gui burned Talmuds by the wagonload, and the special training of the inquisitors would seem to point them out as the

most available conservators of the faith from the dangerous abuse of
the pen. Yet it was long before any definite system was adopted. The
universities were almost the only centers of intellectual activity,
and they usually exercised a watchful care over the aberrations of their
members. When some work of importance was to be condemned, the
authority of the Holy See was frequently invoked, as in the case of
Erigena's *Periphyseos,* *The Everlasting Gospel,* William of St.
Amour's assault upon the Mendicants, and Masilio of Padua's *Defensor Pacis.* On the other hand, in 1316 the episcopal vicar of
Tarragona had no hesitation in assembling some monks and friars
and condemning a number of Arnaldo de Vilanova's writings, and
about the same time the Inquisitors of Bologna took similar action
with respect to Cecco d'Ascoli's commentary on the *Sphœra* of Sacrobosco. Yet no thought seems to have occurred of using the Inquisition for this purpose as a general agency with power of immediate
decision, before Charles IV endeavored to establish the Holy Office
in Germany. The heresy of the Brethren of the Free Spirit was
largely propagated by means of popular books of devotion; to check
this and the forbidden use by the laity of translations of Scripture
in the vernacular, the emperor, in 1369, empowered the inquisitors
and their successors to seize and burn all such books, and to employ
the customary inquisitorial censures to overcome resistance. In 1376
Gregory XI followed this with a bull in which he deplored the dissemination of heretical books in Germany, and directed the inquisitors to
examine all suspected writings, condemning those found to contain
errors, after which it became an offense punishable by the Inquisition
to copy, possess, buy, or sell them. No trace remains of any results of
these regulations, but they are interesting as the first organized
literary censorship. About the same period Eymerich was engaged
in condemning the works of Raymond Lully, of Raymond of
Tarraga, and others, but he seems always to have referred the matter
to the Holy See and to have acted only under special papal authority.
When Archbishop Zbinco burned Wickliff's writings in Prague, a
papal commission decided that his act was not justified, and their
final condemnation was pronounced by the Council of Rome in 1413.

With the gradual revival of letters books assumed more and more
importance as a means of disseminating thought, and this increased
rapidly after the invention of printing. It became a recognized rule

with the Inquisition that he into whose hands a heretical book might fall and who did not burn it at once or deliver it within eight days to his bishop or inquisitor was held vehemently suspect of heresy. The translation of any part of Scripture into the vernacular was also forbidden. It was not, however, until 1501 that any organized censorship of the press seems to have been thought of, and even then Germany was the only land where the issue of dangerous and heretical books was considered to require it. All printers were ordered in future, under pain of excommuncation and of fines applicable to the apostolic chamber, to present to the archbishop of the province or to his ordinary all books before publication, and only to issue those for which a license should be granted after examination. All existing books in stock, moreover, were to be subject to similar inspection, and of such as should be found to contain errors all copies accessible were to be delivered up for burning.

It shows to what a state of contempt the German Inquisition had fallen that in this comprehensive measure to restrict the license of the press it seems not to have been even thought of as an instrumentality, and that dependence was placed on the episcopal organization alone. The archbishops, however, were as usual too much engrossed in the temporal concerns of their princely provinces to pay attention to such details, and there is apparently no result to be traced from the effort. The evil continued to increase, and in 1515, at the Council of Lateran, Leo X endeavored to check it by general regulations still more rigid in a bull which was unanimously approved, except by Alexis, Bishop of Amalfi, who said that he concurred in it as to new books, but not as to old ones. After an allusion to the benefits conferred by the art of printing, the bull proceeded to recite that numerous complaints reached the Holy See that printers in many places printed and sold books translated from the Greek, Hebrew, Arabic, and Chaldee, as well as in Latin and the vernaculars, containing errors in faith and pernicious dogmas, and also libels on persons of dignity, whence many scandals had arisen and more were threatened. Therefore forever thereafter no one should be allowed to print any book or writing without a previous examination, to be testified by manual subscription, by the papal vicar and master of the sacred palace in Rome, and in other cities and dioceses by the Inquisition, and the bishop or an expert appointed by him.

For neglect of this the punishment was excommunication, the loss of the edition, which was to be burned, a fine of 100 ducats to the fabric of St. Peters, and suspension from business for a year.

The precaution came too late. Except with regard to witches, the machinery of persecution was too thoroughly disorganized to curb the rising tide of human intelligence, which speedily swept away all such flimsy barriers. The printing press multipled indefinitely the satires of Erasmus and Ulric Hutten, and when Luther appeared it scattered far and wide among the people his vigorous attacks on the existing system. It required time and the exigencies of the Counter-Reformation to perfect a plan by which, in the lands of the Roman obedience, the faithful could be preserved from the insidious poison flowing from the fountain of the printing press.

C HAPTER XXV
CONCLUSION

THE review we have made of the follies and crimes of our ancestors has revealed to us a scene of almost unrelieved blackness. Yet such a review, rightly estimated, is full of hope and encouragement. In the unrest of modern society, where immediate relief is sought from the mass of evils oppressing mankind, and impatience is eager to overturn all social organization in the hope of founding a new structure where preventable misery shall be unknown, it is well occasionally to take a backward view, to tear away the veil which conceals the passions and the sufferings of bygone generations, and estimate fairly the progress already effected. Human development is slow and irregular; to the observer at a given point it appears stationary or retrogressive, and it is only by comparing periods removed by a considerable interval of time that the movement can be appreciated. Such a retrospect as we have wearily accomplished has shown us how, but a few centuries since, the infliction of gratuitous evil was deemed the highest duty of man. We have seen how the administration of law, both spiritual and secular, was little other than organized wrong and injustice; we have seen how low were the moral standards, and how debased the mental condition of the populations of Christendom. We have seen that the Ages of Faith, to which romantic dreamers regretfully look back, were ages of force and fraud, where evil seemed to reign almost unchecked, justifying the current opinion, so constantly reappearing, that the reign of Antichrist had already begun. Imperfect as are human institutions today, a comparison with the past shows how marvellous has been the improvement, and the fact that this gain has been made almost wholly within the last two centuries affords to the sociologist the most cheering encouragement. Principles have been established which, if allowed to develop themselves naturally and healthfully, will render the future of mankind very different from aught that the world has yet seen. The greatest danger to modern society lies in the impatient theorists who desire to reform the world at a blow, in place

875

of aiding in the struggle of good with evil under the guidance of
eternal laws. Could they be convinced of the advance so swiftly
made and of its steady development, they might moderate their
ardor and direct their energies to wise construction rather than to
heedless destruction.

A few words will suffice to summarize the career of the mediæval Inquisition. It furnished the Holy See with a powerful weapon
in aid of political aggrandizement, it tempted secular sovereigns
to imitate the example, and it prostituted the name of religion to
the vilest temporal ends. It stimulated the morbid sensitiveness
to doctrinal aberrations until the most trifling dissidence was capable
of arousing insane fury, and of convulsing Europe from end to end.
On the other hand, when atheism became fashionable in high
places, its thunders were mute. Energetic only in evil, when its
powers might have been used on the side of virtue, it held its hand
and gave the people to understand that the only sins demanding
repression were doubt of the accuracy of the Church's knowledge
of the unknown, and attendance on the Sabbat. In its long career
of blood and fire, the only credit it can claim is the suppression of
the pernicious dogmas of the Cathari, and in this its agency may be
regarded as superfluous, for those dogmas carried in themselves the
seeds of self-destruction, and higher wisdom might have trusted to
their self-extinction.

On the Church the processes invented and recommended to respect
by the Inquisition had a most unfortunate effect. The ordinary
episcopal courts employed them in dealing with heretics, and found
their arbitrary violence too efficient not to extend it over other
matters coming within their jurisdiction. Thus the spiritual tribunals
rapidly came to employ inquisitorial methods. Already, in 1317,
Bernard Gui speaks of the use of torture being habitual in them;
and in complaining of the Clementine restrictions, he asks why
the bishops should be limited in applying torture to heretics, while
they could employ it without limit in everything else.

Thus habituated to the harshest measures, the Church grew harder
and crueller and more unchristian. The worst popes of the twelfth
and thirteenth centuries could scarce have dared to shock the world
with such an exhibition as that with which John XXII glutted his
hatred of Hugues Gerold, Bishop of Cahors. No sooner did he

mount the pontifical throne than he lost no time in assailing his enemy. May 4, 1317, the unfortunate prelate was solemnly degraded at Avignon and condemned to perpetual imprisonment. This was not enough. On a charge of conspiring against the life of the pope he was delivered to the secular arm, and in July of the same year he was partially flayed alive and then dragged to the stake and burned. This hardening process went on until the quarrels of the loftiest prelates were conducted with a savage ferocity which would have shamed a band of buccaneers.

On secular jurisprudence the example of the Inquisition worked even more deplorably. It came at a time when the old order of things was giving way to the new—when the ancient customs of the barbarians, the ordeal, the Wager of Law, the Wer-gild, were growing obsolete in the increasing intelligence of the age, when a new system was springing into life under the revived study of the Roman law, and when the administration of justice by the local feudal lord was becoming swallowed up in the widening jurisdiction of the crown. The whole judicial system of the European monarchies was undergoing reconstruction, and the happiness of future generations depended on the character of the new institutions. That in this reorganization the worst features of the imperial jurisprudence—the use of torture and the inquisitorial process —should be eagerly adopted, should be divested of the safeguards which in Rome restricted their abuse, should be exaggerated in all their evil tendencies, and should, for five centuries, become the prominent characteristic of the criminal jurisprudence of Europe, may safely be ascribed to the fact that they received the sanction of the Church. Thus recommended, they penetrated everywhere along with the Inquisition; while most of the nations to whom the Holy Office was unknown maintained their ancestral customs, developing into various forms of criminal practice, harsh enough, indeed, to modern eyes, but wholly divested of the more hideous atrocities which characterized the habitual investigation into crime in other regions.

Of all the curses which the Inquisition brought in its train this, perhaps, was the greatest—that, until the closing years of the eighteenth century, throughout the greater part of Europe, the inquisitorial process, as developed for the destruction of heresy, became the customary method of dealing with all who were under accusation; that the accused was treated as one having no rights, whose guilt was assumed in advance, and from whom confession was to be extorted by guile or force. Even witnesses were treated in the same fashion; and the prisoner who acknowledged guilt under torture was tortured again to obtain information about any other evil-doers of whom he perchance might have knowledge. So, also, the crime of "suspicion" was imported from the Inquisition into ordinary practice, and the accused who could not be convicted of the crime laid to his door could be punished for being suspected of it, not with the penalty legally provided for the offense, but with some other, at the fancy and discretion of the judge. It would be impossible to compute the amount of misery and wrong, inflicted on the defenseless up to the present century, which may be directly traced to the arbitrary and unrestricted methods introduced by the Inquisition and adopted by the jurists who fashioned the criminal jurisprudence of the Continent. It was a system which might well seem the invention of demons, and was fitly characterized by Sir John Fortescue as the Road to Hell.

Under the guidance of a Church such as this, the moral condition of the laity was unutterably depraved. Uniformity of faith had been enforced, and so long as faith was preserved, crime and sin were comparatively unimportant except as a source of revenue to those who sold absolution. Correctness of belief was the sole essential; virtue was a wholly subordinate consideration. How completely under such a system religion and morals came to be dissociated is seen in the remark of Pius II that the Franciscans were excellent theologians, but cared nothing about virtue.

This, in fact, was the direct result of the system of persecution embodied in the Inquisition. Heretics who were admitted to be patterns of virtue were ruthlessly exterminated in the name of Christ, while in the same holy name the orthodox could purchase absolution for the vilest of crimes for a few coins. When the only unpardonable offense was persistence in some error of belief; when men had before them the example of their spiritual guides as leaders in vice and debauchery and contempt of sacred things, all the sanctions of morality were destroyed and the confusion between right and wrong became hopeless. The world has probably never seen a society more vile than that of Europe in the fourteenth and fifteenth centuries. The brilliant pages of Froissart fascinate us with their pictures of the artificial courtesies of chivalry; the mystic reveries of Rysbroek and of Tauler show us that spiritual life survived in some rare souls, but the mass of the population was plunged into the depths of sensuality and the most brutal oblivion of the moral law. The chroniclers do not often pause in their narrations to dwell on the moral aspects of the times, but Meyer, in his annals of Flanders, under date of 1379, tells us that it would be impossible to describe the prevalence everywhere of perjuries, blasphemies, adulteries, brawls, murder, rapine, thievery, robbery, gambling, whoredom, debauchery, avarice, oppression of the poor, rape, drunkenness, and similar vices, and he illustrates his statement with the fact that in the territory of Ghent, within the space of ten months, there occurred no less than 1,400 murders committed in the *bagnios*, brothels, gambling-houses, taverns, and other similar places. When, in 1396, Jean sans Peur led his crusaders to destruction at Nicopolis, their crimes and cynical debauchery scandalized even the Turks, and led to the stern rebuke of Bajazet himself, who, as the monk of Saint-Denis admits, was much better than his Christian foes. The same writer, moralizing over the disaster of Agincourt, attributes it to the general corruption of the nation. Luke Wadding is a witness above suspicion; his conscientious study of original sources entitles his opinions to weight, and we may accept his description of Italy in the early part of the fifteenth century:

At that time Italy was sunk in vice and wickedness. In the Church there was no devotion, in the laity no faith, no piety, no modesty, no discipline or morals. Every man cursed his neighbor; the factions of Guelf and Ghibelline flooded the streets of the towns with fraternal blood, the roads were closed by robbers, the seas infested with pirates. Parents slew with rejoicing their children who chanced to be of the opposite faction. The world was full of sorcery and incantations; the churches deserted, the gambling-houses filled.

To what extent the Church was responsible for this may be judged by the condition of Rome under Innocent VIII as pictured in the diary of Infessura. Outrages of all kinds were committed with impunity so long as the criminal had wherewith to compond with the papal chancery; and when Cardinal Borgia, the vice-chancellor, was reproached with this, he piously replied that God did not desire the death of the sinner, but that he should pay and live. A census of the public women showed them to number 6,800, and when the vicar of the city issued a decree ordering all ecclesiastics to dismiss their concubines, Innocent sent for him and ordered its withdrawal, saying that all priests and members of the curia kept them, and that it was no sin.

This was the outcome of the theocracy whose foundation had been laid by Hildebrand in the belief that it would realize the reign of Christ on earth. Power such as was claimed and exercised by the Church could only be wielded by superhuman wisdom. Human nature was too imperfect not to convert it into an instrumentality for the gratification of worldly passions and ambition, and its inevitable result was to plunge society deeper and deeper into corruption. Thus the divine law on which the Church professed to be founded was superseded by human law administered by those who profited by its abuse. As Cardinal d'Ailly tells us, the doctors of civil law regarded the imperial jurisprudence as more binding than the commands of God, while the professors of canon law taught that papal decretals were of greater weight than Scripture. Such a theocracy, practically deeming itself superior to its God, when it had overcome all dissidence, could have but one result.

When we consider, however, the simple earnestness with which such multitudes of humble heretics endured the extremity of outrage and the most cruel of deaths, in the endeavor to obey the will of God in the fashioning of their lives, we recognize what material existed for the development of true Christianity and for the improvement of the race, far down in the obscurer ranks of society. We can see now how greatly advanced might be the condition of humanity had that leaven been allowed to penetrate the whole mass in place of being burned out with fire. The judgment of impartial history must be that the Inquisition was the monstrous offspring of mistaken zeal, utilized by selfish greed and lust of power to smother the higher aspirations of humanity and stimulate its baser appetites.

INDEX

881